Philosophical Problems

An Annotated Anthology

SECOND EDITION

Laurence BonJour
University of Washington

Ann Baker
University of Washington

New York San Francisco Boston
London Toronto Sydney Tokyo Singapore Madrid
Mexico City Munich Paris Cape Town Hong Kong Montreal

Editor-in-Chief: *Eric Stano*
Executive Marketing Manager: *Ann Stypuloski*
Supplements Editor: *Brian Belardi*
Production Manager: *Denise Phillip*
Project Coordination and Text Design: *Pre-Press PMG*
Electronic Page Makeup: *Integra Software Services*
Senior Cover Design Manager/Cover Designer: *Nancy Danahy*
Cover Images: © *Digital Vision/Getty, Inc. and* © *Photodisc/Getty, Inc.*
Senior Manufacturing Buyer: *Dennis J. Para*
Printer and Binder: *Von Hoffman Corporation*
Cover Printer: *Coral Graphics Services*

For permission to use copyrighted material, grateful acknowledgment is made to the copyright holders on pp. 652–654, which are hereby made part of this copyright page.

Library of Congress Cataloging-in-Publication Data
Philosophical problems: an annotated anthology / [edited by] Laurence BonJour and Ann Baker.—2nd ed.
p. cm.
Includes bibliographical references.
ISBN 0-205-63947-X
1. Philosophy. 2. Readers—Philosophy. 3. Philosophy—Authorship.
I. BonJour, Laurence, 1943- II. Baker, Ann, 1953-
B72.P47 2007
100—dc22

2007023087

Please visit us at www.ablongman.com/philosophycafe

ISBN-13: 978-0-205-63947-2
ISBN-10: 0-205-63947-X

1 2 3 4 5 6 7 8 9 10—VH—10 09 08 07

For Jen and David

Contents

Preface

This book grew out of our dissatisfaction and even occasional frustration with the sorts of books that are typically available for a standard, topically organized introductory course in philosophy. As we will elaborate further below, we think that single-author textbooks give students too little exposure to original philosophical sources and also fail to adequately convey to students the inherently controversial, dialectical character of philosophy; while anthologies, even with the sorts of aids to understanding that are usually provided, are simply too difficult for many students to adequately comprehend. What we offer instead is still an anthology, but one that gives students far more help than traditional anthologies in understanding the reading selections and making sense of the overall structure of the philosophical issues being discussed.

The Main Conception of *Philosophical Problems: An Annotated Anthology*

What introductory students really need, we think, is not more help of the same kinds that have standardly been provided, but rather a fundamentally different kind of help. What they need most is much more detailed and specific assistance with the individual reading selections and especially with their argumentative and dialectical *structure:* a kind of ongoing reader's guide that will help them find their way through a particular selection, understanding better what an author is saying (in perhaps unfamiliar language), seeing how the various points fit together, grasping why a particular objection is appropriate in a particular place, when an author is expounding his own view and when he is replying to an imagined critic, and so on.

We have tried to provide help of this sort. Some of it is to be found in the introductions to the chapters and to the individual readings. But the most crucial part of this help is constituted by the most novel element in the book: the detailed annotations that we have included with each selection (together with the closely related discussion questions that follow). Our main thought in writing these annotations was to ask what sort of help or guidance a typical student would need at that specific point in the text: an explanation of a concept, a reference to an issue discussed elsewhere (in either that selection or another one), a critical question or objection to think about, a further elaboration and clarification of the point in question, or perhaps just a clearer restatement or summary of what the philosopher is doing in the text (and why).

In addition, we have tried to edit the selections so as to bring out the main lines of arguments, excising material that, while interesting in itself, is in one way or another too tangential or remote or inaccessible for introductory students. Unlike some editors, we see no real virtue at the introductory level in presenting students with "complete" philosophical texts, when this means that the parts they can realistically be expected to understand are obscured by others that are, in one way or another, difficult to see the point of—and not really worth explaining in the limited class time available in an introductory course. We have also tried to choose and arrange the readings in a way that reflects as clearly as possible the ways in which the issues develop and the different authors can be seen as speaking to each other. (The most extreme example of this occurs in Chapter 7, where we have chosen to divide the material from Hume's *Dialogues Concerning Natural Religion* into three separate selections that correspond to the three main topics that Hume discusses, placing these in the corresponding subsections with other selections addressing those same topics, rather than relying on the student or the instructor to sort them out.)

Our ultimate goal is to enable students to think along *with* Plato, or Locke, or Searle, or whoever is assigned: engaging their ideas and arguing with them as they read, instead of just trying to passively absorb they know not what. The result, we believe, is an anthology with some of the virtues of a textbook, one that encourages students to grapple with original sources by giving them more specific help in doing so, and by highlighting the distinctively philosophical attitudes and habits of mind that are reflected in the readings and which they need to acquire for themselves. Rather than just presenting students with an outline of the philosophical dialectic in the way that both textbooks and anthology introductions standardly do, we attempt to show them how that dialectic is actually discernible in the readings.

In Chapter 1, the introductory essay entitled "Introduction to Philosophical Thinking" explains the pretty old-fashioned conception of philosophy that is reflected in the rest of the book. This conception is self-consciously critical and analytic, focusing on arguments, objections, distinctions, counter-examples, definitions, and so on. We believe that it is an accurate account of the best philosophical thinking, but also is especially good for an introduction to philosophy. In addition to outlining a way of thinking that makes good sense of the classical philosophical issues and introducing students to the intellectual skills that will help them understand what is going on in the reading selections, it also provides students with some concrete guidelines for their own positive contributions to the work of the course, whether they are thinking *actively* about the issues and ideas, discussing them in or outside of class, responding to exam questions, or writing an essay. The course objective is no longer merely to:

- learn philosophy (whatever *that* is), but instead to:
- learn how to read, write, and discuss philosophical topics by evaluating arguments, responding to objections, and explicating the relations between different views, each of which purport to answer the philosophical question of the day.

Features of the Book

- In Chapter 1 we start with **"Introduction to Philosophical Thinking,"** a general introduction elaborating a very traditional conception of philosophy, one that emphasizes basic strategies of argumentation. This essay introduces the students to the fundamental elements of philosophical thinking that will, if they work at it, become second nature to them and also includes an extended discussion of how to read two sample philosophical passages (drawn from later in the book).
- The **introduction to each chapter** describes the main issue or issues discussed in the chapter and provides an outline of the main dialectical structure reflected in the selections that follow. Since the student is not yet in a position to understand the issues in much detail, we have tried to keep these introductions fairly brief—though how much brevity is possible varies with the length and complexity of the chapter. Our expectation is that students will be able to derive an initial overview from these introductions, but that they will often be able to understand them fully only *after* they have worked through the chapter—at which point they will constitute a useful summary.
- The core of the book is a fairly **standard collection of philosophical readings,** both historical and contemporary. These have been carefully chosen and edited in an attempt to focus on the main issues and lines of argument.
- The **introduction to each selection** briefly describes the author's background and explains what he or she is mainly doing in that selection. These introductions sometimes also try to anticipate particular issues or problems with which students might need advance help.

- The **annotations** that accompany each selection are primarily designed to aid the student in coming to see and appreciate the detailed structure of the reading itself: its arguments, its transitions, its nuances.
- Each selection is followed by a set of **discussion questions,** often very detailed, that are designed to stimulate the student to think further about various issues that grow out of that selection, including those that relate to other selections. (These often develop more fully questions or issues first raised in the annotations.)
- The appendix entitled **"Writing a Philosophical Essay"** is devoted to teaching students how to write very elementary philosophy papers, papers that reflect the habits of mind and the argumentative and dialectical structures they have been learning.
- The **glossary** at the end of the book provides further elaboration concerning terms and concepts explained elsewhere and also provides a useful summary of the main concepts and positions discussed in the book. Boldfacing in the text indicates items that are in the glossary—sometimes in variant grammatical forms. (We have tried to be selective about the use of this boldfacing, applying it only where it is not too repetitive and seems likely to be helpful.)

In addition, an **Instructor's Manual** provides chapter overviews, questions for discussion, and additional resources. The **Companion Website** (http://www.ablongman.com/bonjour) includes additional resources for students using *Philosophical Problems,* with unique philosophy tools, interactive practice test questions, and web links for each chapter.

More About the Motivation for This Conception

As already mentioned, the books that have been available up to now for a topically organized introductory philosophy course fall into two main classes. On the one hand, there are textbooks written by a single author (or, sometimes, by two or more authors working together). These have the virtue of presenting an account of the philosophical issues that is cohesive, deliberately oriented to introductory students, and couched in modern language and terminology. But they also have two glaring defects. First, a course that employs a textbook gives students little experience in working through and coming to grips with original philosophical sources, both historical and contemporary. Some items of this sort may be added as a kind of supplement, perhaps even included in the textbook itself. But the main focus is inevitably on the account of the issues and arguments offered by the author or authors of the textbook itself. Second, and even more importantly, a textbook tends for the most part to describe philosophical positions and arguments from the outside, at second hand, rather than actually participating in the to and fro of philosophical discussion. Thus students get little sense of the distinctive flavor of philosophical controversy or of the ways in which philosophers actually think and argue—little sense of the essentially *dialectical* character of philosophy. And a further consequence is that the students' opportunity to begin to participate in philosophical discussion and to develop philosophical habits of mind for themselves is severely limited because they aren't really exposed to examples of philosophical debate in the flesh: real philosophers actually arguing with and criticizing each other.

The alternative is of course an anthology composed of a smorgasbord of selections from actual philosophical works, both historical and contemporary, together with editorial introductions and perhaps aids such as study questions or a glossary. Here students are exposed to original philosophical sources with a vengeance, and the argumentative, dialectical character of philosophy is plainly represented—for those who are able to discern it. But just there lies the problem. Actual philosophical writing is notoriously very difficult for introductory students. It is aimed at other philosophers rather than at novices, employs technical terminology that can be very thorny, and often comes from earlier periods in which language and style were very different. Thus many or even most of the selections in a standard anthology are pieces that an introductory student simply cannot read in a useful way without very substantial help. Some help is usually provided in the anthology itself, but it is, in our judgment, almost always inadequate for many if not most students. General introductions to philosophical issues and method and also to specific sets of readings are fine as far as they go, but they are not enough, in our experience, to enable typical students to actually read and understand representative pieces of philosophical writing in a way that puts them in a position to think about and evaluate them.

There are two sides to this problem. First, students need more help with the specific details of a selection, most importantly with its structure. They need to be able to see how the specific issues and arguments that the selection discusses connect to each other and to the more general issue that is its ultimate concern. Too often students who at least roughly understand the main point that a selection is supposed to be making are entirely unable to see why *this* specific point is made in *this* specific place or why *this* other specific point immediately follows. The structural signposts that the author provides are often either too subtle or couched in ways that the student is unable to grasp. (A collateral problem is that many philosophical writings, especially those that are largely unedited, include many digressions of various sorts that an introductory student cannot hope to understand, including references to unfamiliar works or authors.) Second, most students need specific help in understanding the *point* of much philosophical discussion. There are certain ways of thinking that philosophers take for granted, habits of mind that are not at all obvious to most first-year students. In particular, the critical stance that most philosophers take even to their own ideas, the constant search for arguments, objections, and responses, is unfamiliar to most students and quite unnatural for many of them.

When these two problems are combined, the result of reading philosophical texts is too often bafflement and frustration, rather than enlightenment. One of the most common complaints we've heard is: "I do all the reading, but I have no idea what I'm looking for." Students can sometimes get intimidated by philosophy, thinking that it is too "deep" or profound, and such fears are confirmed when the readings seem opaque, when the student can't see the intellectual point of what the different authors are saying or how they are engaging each other. Other students become convinced that philosophy is trivial or irrelevant, and such a view often has the same source as the previous view: the initial opacity of the reading, an opacity which is the direct result of the difficulty of the material, together with the student's lack of understanding of argumentative and dialectical structure and inexperience with the habits of mind typical of philosophers. While most students will continue to try to do the assignments, few will continue to read in a serious, reflective, thoughtful way under such conditions; instead the perceived fruitlessness of their efforts will lead to a kind of passive, disengaged approach to the reading that is ultimately futile.

A good instructor can of course help a great deal in solving these problems. But even the best instructor will have difficulty explaining a piece of philosophical writing clearly to students who have been unable to read it well enough on their own to be able to grasp the specific points and issues that the instructor refers to. What is often really needed is something like this: the instructor first carefully introduces a given selection, then has the students read it, then talks about it some more, then has them read it again, and finally discusses it in a way that presupposes that they have understood it relatively fully. But there is simply not enough time in an introductory course, at least not one that covers any reasonable amount of ground, to do something like this very often, even though anything less is unlikely to succeed for many of the students. Moreover, and this is really the main point, the instructor's job should not be this difficult because the anthology itself should give the students more help. This is what we have tried to do.

The Value of Studying Philosophy

Our conviction is that teaching students how to do philosophy in the way encouraged by this book can also help them to develop more general abilities. Even the student who fails to be engaged by the specific content of philosophy should come away with some powerful, extremely valuable skills: broad-gauged capacities for critical, creative, and reflective thinking. These skills will provide an excellent basis from which a student can go on to think critically about any number of topics—including even this approach to philosophy itself.

So our book is based on the assumption that there are basic modes of philosophical thinking, philosophical habits of mind, that these habits can be taught, but, as with all habits, not by just telling the students what they are. These habits of mind need to be exercised on philosophical texts. Our book provides the readings and the accompanying pedagogical tools on which students can exercise and thus acquire these philosophical habits of mind.

When we each started teaching philosophy as enthusiastic graduate students long ago, we were each quite sure that all that had to be done was to find a way to open a student's eyes to philosophy. Once that was done, any student would see that philosophy is deeply fascinating. While we no longer believe that every student will find philosophy fascinating (we have read too many student evaluations to continue to believe that!), we do still believe that any student can reap important benefits from taking an introductory philosophy course. According to reports from many students, studying philosophy has taught them that the most important learning does not consist solely in memorizing lots of facts. They've come to see that the ability to think clearly with an appreciation for subtlety and nuance is central to real intellectual accomplishment, and claim that studying philosophy has given them the skill to navigate intelligently through areas of gray, instead of insisting that all disputes must be categorized in clear black-and-white terms. Because of this, they regard philosophy as one of the most valuable and relevant subjects of their whole college career—for, as they recognize, the very most important decisions one makes in life often require exactly that kind of subtlety of thought.

Acknowledgments

With respect to the conception of the book, we owe the greatest debt of gratitude to our many students over the years: at the University of Texas at Austin, the State University of New York at Stony Brook, Illinois Wesleyan University, and the University of Washington. Without their sometimes eager, often puzzled, but usually conscientious efforts to grapple seriously with the contents of various anthologies, we would never have been motivated to think of this alternative approach. We are grateful to our colleagues in the philosophy department at the University of Washington, especially Ken Clatterbaugh, David Keyt, Charles Marks, Angela Smith, and Bill Talbott, for their support, advice, and feedback during the process of preparing this book (and for earlier input on a distant ancestor of it).

With respect to both the development and refinement of the conception and the actual work of creating the book, we owe a tremendous debt of gratitude to Marion Castellucci, our developmental editor: she courageously and tirelessly read through all the reading selections and their associated annotations and discussion questions—in addition to the introductions, glossary, appendix, and preface—and gave us indispensable feedback on every aspect of the book, together with valuable and much appreciated moral support along the way. Without her input, the book would have been very different, if indeed it would have been completed at all. Priscilla McGeehon, our publisher at Longman, also provided valuable help and encouragement: through her unwavering and enthusiastic confidence in the project, through her firm but flexible handling of deadlines, and by providing material support of many kinds.

In addition, we would like to thank all of those who reviewed the project and the manuscript at various stages and offered many helpful comments and suggestions (not all of which we were able to take advantage of in this edition): David Benfield, Montclair State University; Andrei A. Buckareff, University of Rochester; Todd Buras, Baylor University; Susanne D. Claxton, Oklahoma State University; Matti Eklund, University of Colorado at Boulder; Todd S. Ganson, Oberlin College; Philip Goldstein, University of Delaware; Richard V. Greene, Weber State University; Peter Hutcheson, Texas State

University; Jason Kawall, University of Tennessee at Chattanooga; Glenn Kuehn, Mississippi State University; David Lefkowitz, University of Maryland; Dorothea Lotter, Wake Forest University; Marc Moffett, University of Wyoming; Hilde L. Nelson, Michigan State University; Walter Ott, East Tennessee State University; William Richards, University of Dayton; Teresa J. Robertson, University of Kansas; Peter Ross, California State Polytechnic University–Pomona; Samuel Ruhmkorff, Simon's Rock College; Edward L. Schoen, Western Kentucky University; Renée Smith, Coastal Carolina University; John Uglietta, Grand Valley State University; David Weberman, Georgia State University; Chase B. Wrenn, University of Alabama; David J. Yount, Mesa Community College; and John Zeis, Canisius College.

LAURENCE BONJOUR

ANN BAKER

Preface to the Second Edition

In this edition, we have made a large number of changes aimed at improving the readings and making the book as a whole more "user-friendly" for students. The main ones are these:

First, the line-up of readings is not greatly altered. The chapter order has been changed to one that strikes us as a bit more logical, placing the epistemology chapter (which begins with Descartes) first and then following it with two chapters on metaphysical issues. The personal identity section has been removed from the philosophy of mind chapter and combined into one chapter with the previous free will chapter, thereby making one chapter on metaphysical issues relating to the concept of a person. And the philosophy of religion chapter has been placed more logically, coming just after the chapters on moral and political issues and just before the concluding chapter on the meaning of life. A few new selections have been added and some others have been deleted. The most important changes are in the epistemology chapter, where the too-lengthy sections on induction and on a priori knowledge have been combined into one, with induction as the primary topic but still some attention to the a priori; in the free will section of the personal identity and free will chapter, where selections on two relatively recent and widely discussed views (those of Frankfurt and Kane) have been added and others deleted to make room; and in the morality chapter, where the separate (but too brief) section on moral problems has been removed and replaced by illustrative selections on moral problems in the sections discussing the three main moral views (two of them ones that were already in the book and two of them new). Other additions include a selection on skepticism by Sextus Empiricus and a selection from St. Anselm presenting his version of the ontological argument. In addition, all of the readings have been carefully re-edited, with many of them being significantly shortened as a result, thus making for more manageable reading assignments.

Second, the chapter and selection introductions, the annotations, and the discussion questions have all been thoroughly reconsidered and often substantially revised, with some items in the latter two categories being deleted and some others added. In addition, the annotations have now been classified into several main categories, indicated by icons, in a way that we hope will be helpful and informative to students using them. (See the separate introduction to the annotations.) A further change, about which we are very pleased, is that the annotations now appear in the margins of the text, rather than being placed within the readings in a way that was at least somewhat clumsy. Some small changes and revisions have also been made in the glossary.

Third, the introductory essay "Introduction to Philosophical Thinking" has been revised, mainly by adding a detailed consideration of two actual passages (drawn from two of the readings in the text).

Fourth, a new feature of the book is the "Concluding Dialogues" that appear after all chapters other than Chapter 1—or in the case of Chapters 2 and 4, after the major sections of the chapter. These dialogues have several aims: to offer a review of the material of the chapter; in some cases, to raise issues that seem to us important that were not raised or at least not raised clearly enough in the readings; to offer some tentative evaluation of the various views and suggestions as to the result for the overall issue; and to convey perhaps a little better the essentially dialectical and dialogical character of philosophical inquiry. In these dialogues, we have felt a bit freer about offering our own views—views with which students and instructors are of course strongly encouraged to disagree as they see fit. We would also suggest that the dialogues might provide a good basis for writing assignments in which students could start from some point in a dialogue and then try to present an alternative view of how the discussion might have gone, adding new arguments, new objections, or even additional participants. (The two characters in the dialogues reflect to some degree the views of the two editors, though this is only approximate at most and reflects both simplifications and modifications in the interests of a more accessible and more engaging discussion.)

Further Acknowledgments

In preparing this revision, we have been aided by and are grateful for comments and suggestions from many different people. Among the most helpful have been those from graduate students at Washington who have taught from the first edition: Renee Conroy, Karen Mazner, Jason Benchimol, Joe Ricci, Monica Aufrecht, David Alexander, and Ali Hasan. We also received very helpful comments concerning the Chapter 5 Concluding Dialogue from Angela Smith and Karen Mazner; and Renee Conroy read and commented very extensively on five of the Concluding Dialogues, suggesting very many valuable refinements and improvements. We thank the reviewers of the published first edition whose feedback guided our preparations of the second: Harry Adams, Prairie View A & M University; Bryan Benham, University of Utah; Sara Chant, Florida State University; Evelyn Deluty, Nassau Community College; Craig Duncan, Ithaca College; Joan Esposito, Nassau Community College; Richard Greene, Weber State University; Gary Ostertag, Nassau Community College; Jamie Phillips, Clarion University; Hans von Rautenfeld, University of South Carolina; Harvey Siegel, University of Miami; and John Uglietta, Grand Valley State University. Finally, we are very grateful to Eric Stano, our editor at Longman, for his unfailing enthusiasm about the book, his confidence in our ideas and judgment, and his valuable suggestions on many different points.

For the Student: An Introduction to the Annotations

The aim of the annotations is to help you to better understand what is going on in the sometimes difficult reading selections. Introductions can help, but often there is something that can be usefully said at a particular point in a selection that cannot be made clear before you have read to that point and are trying to understand that particular passage. Our mind-set in writing the annotations was essentially to imagine that we were looking over your shoulder as you read, perhaps with a laser pointer somehow connected to your eyes so that it would track exactly where you are. When there is some sort of help that we would be tempted to whisper to you in this situation, we have inserted a corresponding annotation.

There are a number of different things that occur in the annotations, corresponding to the different sorts of help that we think you may need or at least benefit from. Perhaps most often, the point of the annotation is simply to make a difficult passage clearer by restating or summarizing what is going on, hopefully in a more accessible way. But there are other places where something else is going on. We think it may help you in using the annotations to indicate in a broad way what they are attempting to do, and to this end we have inserted the following icons into the annotations at the relevant points (usually but not always at the beginning of a given annotation):

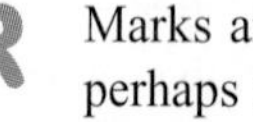

Marks an annotation that either *restates* or *summarizes* the content of the text, perhaps in somewhat different language, but without adding anything that is not already to be found there.

Marks a place where we are urging you to *stop and think*—to pause in your reading to "chew" a little on some question or issue posed in the annotation. It will soon be obvious to you that you need to always be thinking actively and reflectively as you read philosophy. But we have tried to pick out occasions where there is a relatively specific issue that, we believe, you are in a good position to think about right then, on the basis of either what you have read so far or your general background knowledge or both—and where the issue is of some importance in fully understanding and evaluating the selection in question. (We obviously intend the icon to suggest a stop sign.)

 Marks a place where a relatively important term or concept is explained or clarified. (We intend the icon to suggest a philosophical dictionary.)

 Marks a place where something significant is added to what is explicitly present in the selection, but in a way that is still fundamentally in support of or supplementary to the point being made there. (We intend this icon to suggest a helpful instructor, one whose main aim is to clarify what is going on in the text.)

 Marks a place where a criticism or objection is raised that is external and at least somewhat opposed to the point of view of the selection—usually the sort of criticism that another philosopher might make. (We intend this icon to suggest a different sort of helpful instructor, one who is a bit more argumentative. These critical points reflect to some degree the views of the editors. We have tried to be relatively sparing with them, limiting them to places where in our judgment the point in the text cannot be adequately understood without seeing some problem that it faces.)

These last two icons are also employed to represent the two discussants in the Concluding Dialogues. Especially because of their use there, it may be helpful to have names for them, mainly for ease of reference. We will call the character represented by the first of these icons Professor Boulangere; and the one represented by the second icon, Professor Gutentag.

CHAPTER 1

What Is Philosophy?

There are many different views about the nature of philosophy, but probably no very simple definition of the subject. This reflects the fact that—in a way that is true of no other discipline—the nature of philosophy is itself an important subject of philosophical disagreement, one for which there is a long history of competing views. Our view, which many share, is that in the end a person can obtain a really clear idea of what philosophy is only by actually studying the subject in some detail.

Fortunately, however, there are some modest points that are widely enough agreed upon to provide a reasonable starting point. First, the word "philosophy" literally means the love of wisdom, and from the beginning of its long history, philosophers have asked and tried to answer very tough questions about the issues that seemed most important to humankind, thereby searching for wisdom.

Second, since knowledge seems important, even if not sufficient for wisdom, one might ask what kind of *knowledge* the study of philosophy yields. A traditional answer is that philosophers discover the essential nature of various abstract things: truth, knowledge, thought, freedom, duty, justice, beauty, and even reality itself. A more contemporary and perhaps more modest version of this claim is that philosophers discover the content or correct analysis of the *concepts* we use when thinking about truth, knowledge, and the like—or perhaps the meanings of the corresponding words.

Third, everyone agrees that many areas of investigation that started as parts of philosophy have since turned into branches of science. This happens roughly when the issues involved become clearly enough defined to make it possible to investigate them scientifically, through empirical observation and empirically based theorizing. Thus while virtually every sort of knowledge was part of philosophy for the ancient Greek philosopher Aristotle, physics and biology have been distinct from philosophy for a long time, with other areas following along this path more recently. (For example, psychology was still viewed as part of philosophy until the late nineteenth century.) This suggests that philosophy can be identified, though somewhat indirectly, as the home of those issues that people have not yet learned to investigate scientifically. This includes some issues for which it is hard to imagine this ever happening because they are so general, so difficult, and possibly so fundamental.

Fourth, almost all philosophers agree that the *history* of philosophy is important to the very nature of philosophy and to ongoing philosophical investigation in a way that the histories of other disciplines are not equally important to them. This is reflected in the fairly large proportion of historical selections in the present book. But philosophers also disagree about how important the history of philosophy is—and about *why* it is important.

An account of philosophy offered by the twentieth-century American philosopher Wilfrid Sellars may help to summarize some of the foregoing ideas and may also reveal a bit more of the flavor of the subject:

> The aim of philosophy, abstractly formulated, is to understand how things in the broadest possible sense of the term hang together in the broadest possible sense of the term. Under "things in the broadest possible sense" I include such radically different items as not only "cabbages and kings," but numbers and duties, possibilities and finger snaps, aesthetic experience and death. To achieve success in philosophy would be, to use a contemporary turn of phrase, to "know one's way around" with respect to all these things, not in that unreflective way in which the centipede of the story knew its way around before it faced the question, "how do I walk?," but in that reflective way which means that no intellectual holds are barred.[1]

As this suggests, nothing is really beyond the purview of philosophy. Putting the point only slightly differently, philosophy seeks to understand in a fully reflective way how everything relates to and connects with and differs from everything else.

This is a very abstract conception, to say the least, and also a very demanding one. There are people who think that the only way to learn philosophy is just to start reading some philosophical texts, trying to figure out what is going on and what the point is, without any additional help or guidance. This view is reflected in an old instructor's adage: throw them in and see who can swim! On the other hand, some people think that an initial orientation to philosophy, even if necessarily one that is only approximate and partial, can be very helpful. Since we believe the latter view is right, we start this chapter with an essay by Ann Baker about the nature of philosophy and especially about the elements of philosophical thinking.

One of the central philosophical activities, reflected in the endeavor to understand the essential nature of things (or concepts), is *clarification.* Philosophers are constantly asking questions about what various kinds of things really amount to (or what the words in question really mean). Many of Plato's dialogues focus on questions of this sort, especially ones concerned with moral or evaluative notions: "what is courage?," "what is justice?," "what is knowledge?," and so on. In his dialogue *Euthyphro,* Plato asks the question: "what is piety?," which was approximately the same question for the Greeks as "what is moral rightness?" We learn in the *Euthyphro* that Socrates has been charged with corrupting the youth of Athens; and in Plato's *Apology,* we have an account of Socrates's trial, in which he was convicted and condemned to death—thus becoming in effect a martyr for philosophy. In the *Apology,* as Socrates explains why he cannot avoid his punishment by giving up philosophical inquiry, he makes the famous statement that "the unexamined life is not worth living." The outlook and intellectual integrity reflected in this statement have often been regarded as paradigmatic of the true philosopher.

While many people believe that philosophy is obviously important and valuable, there are those who dismiss philosophical thinking as irrelevant, nit-picking, hair-splitting mental play. Bertrand Russell argues that philosophy is valuable even if it turns out to yield little or no secure knowledge. Thus, more than 2000 years after Plato wrote the *Euthyphro* and the *Apology,* Russell defended the study and practice of philosophy as essential to the best sort of life.

Ann Baker

Ann Baker (1953–) is an American philosopher who teaches at the University of Washington in Seattle, and is one of the coeditors of this book. In this essay, she explains what philosophy is, introduces its main branches or subareas, explains the basic elements of philosophical thinking, and discusses how to read a philosophical text.

[1]Wilfrid Sellars, "Philosophy and the Scientific Image of Man," reprinted in his *Science, Perception and Reality* (London: Routledge & Kegan Paul, 1963), p. 1.

Introduction to Philosophical Thinking

So you have decided to study philosophy. You may have a fairly clear idea of what studying philosophy involves, or you may have only a vague idea, or even no idea at all. ❶ Since there are some interestingly different conceptions of philosophy (philosophers philosophize even about philosophy!) and since we need a single conception of philosophy to guide our work, we will begin our study of philosophy by first developing a fairly specific conception of philosophy. While we will rely on this conception of philosophy throughout the book, it is your responsibility (as a budding philosopher) to think carefully about it and have an opinion about its merits by the time you have finished the course. By then you may think that there should be changes or qualifications, small or even large, in the conception of philosophy that we have been using.

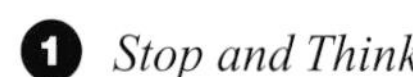

❶ *Stop and Think*

STOP What do you think philosophy is? Have you read anything that you would call philosophical? Have you had any discussions that you would regard as philosophical? Is there anyone in your family who is especially philosophical?

The Content of Philosophy

Let's start building our conception of philosophy by distinguishing between the distinctive content involved in the discipline of philosophy and the distinctive method of philosophical thinking. The content concerns (obviously) what philosophers think about. For example, philosophers typically think about questions like these: What is knowledge? What is truth? What are minds? What is consciousness? Are we genuinely free? Does being morally responsible require being free? Are we, by our very natures, selfish? Is there a genuine difference between right and wrong or good and evil? What is justice? Does God exist? And even, as we have already seen, what is philosophy? In attempting to answer these questions, philosophers think about **claims**—specific, focused assertions that are put forth as being true or false—and also about more comprehensive views or positions (composed of many related claims) that purport to answer questions like the ones listed above.

To generalize from these examples, it would be reasonable to say that the content of philosophy concerns:

1. the fundamental nature of reality—the nature of space and time, of properties and universals, and especially but obviously not exclusively the part of reality that consists of **persons** (the branch of philosophy called **metaphysics**);
2. the fundamental nature of the cognitive relations between persons and other parts of reality—the relations of thinking about, knowing, and so on (the branch of philosophy called **epistemology**); and
3. the fundamental nature of values, especially values pertaining to ethical or social relations between persons and between persons and other parts of reality, such as nonhuman animals, the environment, and so on (the branch of philosophy called **axiology,** which includes the more specific fields of *ethics, political philosophy,* and *aesthetics*). ❷

STOP Place each of the questions in the previous paragraph into one of these three general categories.

The Method of Philosophy

We will forgo for now any further explanation of the *content* of philosophy, since that is the main job of the rest of the book. But there are some implicit assumptions made by philosophers, and the clarification of these will require an explanation of the *method* of philosophical thinking.

The method of philosophical thinking requires a set of skills and some distinctive intellectual habits, what we will call *philosophical habits of mind.* We will explain some of these skills and habits in this introductory essay, but the full appreciation of them requires exercising them on the philosophical views and arguments developed in the rest of the book. Two of the most basic skills involved in philosophical thinking are *clarifying* and *justifying* claims: as philosophers we are in the business of doing two main kinds of things, clarifying and justifying, in relation to a specific kind of object, a claim. What do we mean by *clarifying and justifying claims*? Let's break this phrase down.

First, what is a claim? As we have already seen briefly above, a claim is an assertion, something that is said with the intention of saying something that is either true or false. Here are some examples: there are cherry trees in the quad; Chicago is west of Washington, D.C.; 7 + 5 = 12; grass is red; no dog has ever been lost; politicians are uniformly honest. Notice that claims can be false as well as true. Not everything that you say is a claim, since your intention is not always to state truths. For example, a question is not a claim, nor is an exclamation or a command.

Second, what is meant by *clarification*? When a philosopher *clarifies* a claim, he or she explains or spells out in detail the meaning of the claim. Clarification is often valuable or even urgently required, because the meaning of a claim as it is initially formulated can be seriously unclear in ways that make it difficult to discuss or evaluate. Consider, for example, the claim that God is love. Presumably, the person who says that God is love intends to say something that is true, but some people find that claim very confusing. Does it mean merely that God is a loving person? No—it seems intended to mean something much more significant than that. But what? Since love is a kind of emotion, the literal meaning of the claim doesn't make clear sense (since God is surely not any kind of emotion). So perhaps the claim is metaphorical instead of literal. It is much easier to clarify literal claims than it is to clarify metaphorical claims. But some important clarifying work is done even by saying that the claim is metaphorical.

Obviously, some claims need more clarification than others. Consider the following claims:

a. Money can't buy happiness.
b. God is love.
c. No bachelor is happy.
d. If a person is a mother, then that person is female.
e. Collies are dogs.
f. Studying philosophy is valuable.

These claims are not all equally clear. Which claim most clearly needs clarification? Claims (a) and (b) are both metaphorical, but one can more easily imagine explaining the metaphorical meaning of (a). Of course you cannot literally buy happiness, since it cannot be found in any of the stores you go to (nor can you purchase it on the Internet!). But that is not the real point of the claim. Suppose, for example, that you were advising your younger sister against making what seemed to you to be a very bad marriage: the only good thing you can see about her prospective husband is that he is quite wealthy. It would be natural to say to her that money can't buy happiness, meaning that one can have lots of money and still be very unhappy. (You would, of course, be assuming that she wants to be happy.)

You can clarify a claim without thereby giving any reason to think that the claim is true. Think of how you might clarify claim (c), that no bachelor is happy. This is surely a false claim, but someone might still wonder about what is meant by "happy." Before you think very hard about it, you might think that you surely understand what happiness is. But as soon as you try to clearly define it, all kinds of problems come up (see Chapters 5 and 8). Clarification sometimes requires explaining only one of the terms in the claim (as with (c)), while at other times it requires explaining the meaning of several of the terms (as with (f)). Sometimes a claim just needs to be made more precise. For example, someone might wonder if all collies are dogs, or just most collies are dogs, or only some collies are dogs. How much clarification a claim really needs might depend on the context.

Third, what is meant by **justification**? When philosophers offer justification for a claim, they give reasons to believe the claim, and what better reason is there to believe a claim than a reason to think that it is true? Our conception of philosophy assumes that a reason to think that a claim is true is a good reason to believe it. Moreover, such a reason seems at first glance to be the *only* kind of good reason to believe a claim—since to accept the claim is, after all, to accept it *as true.* In other words, if you don't have a reason to think that a claim is true, then you apparently have no reason at all to believe the claim. (Whether there might be some acceptable basis for believing a claim other than a reason to think that it is true is a question raised explicitly in Chapter 7.)

Let's suppose for the rest of this discussion that a reason for a claim will always be a reason for the truth of the claim. Another supposition that we'll make in explaining what is meant by justification is that the reasons advanced for the truth of a claim will themselves always *be* claims: assertions made in the attempt to say something true. And the assumption made in treating these claims as reasons is that the truth of the reasons provides evidence or warrant of some sort for the truth of the claim in question (the claim that we are trying to justify).

Arguments and Logic

To put forth other claims in support of a claim you are defending is to give an **argument.** Thus, according to our account of justification, when a philosopher justifies a claim, he or she usually gives an argument. In philosophy, an argument is not a disagreement or a fight. According to the standard philosophical definition, an argument is a set of claims, one of which is the **conclusion** and the others of which are **premises** that are offered to support the conclusion: premises that are alleged (by the person putting forth the argument) to make it very likely or perhaps even guarantee that the conclusion is true.

One of the first things you will learn when developing the skills that are important to the philosophical method is to become very sensitive to the difference between the conclusion and the premises of an argument: the claim being asserted by a philosopher (the claim that will be argued *for*) is the conclusion, whereas the claims offered in support of the conclusion are the premises. One of the distinctively philosophical habits of mind is the one that clearly distinguishes between premises and conclusions, between what is being argued for and what is being offered as a reason.

One question that can be asked about the premises of an argument is whether they are true—or at least whether it is reasonable to think that they are true. But while the question of whether the premises are true is crucial to the strength of the argument, that shouldn't be the first question you ask when evaluating an argument. Before you worry about whether the claims offered as reasons are true, you should ask yourself whether, *if true,* they would genuinely support the claim. Reasons can support a claim more or less successfully, and when you ask how good the reasons offered for the claim are (assuming that they are true), you are asking about the *strength* of the relation of support: the evidential relation, between the premises and the conclusion.

So the core idea of a philosophical argument is the idea of giving reasons for a claim: offering premises for the purpose of showing that the conclusion of the argument is true.

Some arguments are valid **deductive arguments:** arguments whose premises, if true, *guarantee* the truth of the conclusion. Consider the following argument for the claim that Mary took the car: either John took the car or Mary took the car, and I know that John didn't take the car, so Mary must have taken it. You can assess the strength of the relation of support of this argument without knowing John or Mary or knowing anything about the car. You simply ask yourself whether the premises, if true, do support the conclusion. They do. If the premises of this argument are true, then the conclusion must be true.

But some arguments that are intended as deductive are **invalid:** it is possible for the premises to be true while the conclusion is false. Consider the following argument for the claim that Mary took the car: if Mary took the car, then John didn't take it; and I know that John didn't take it; so Mary must have taken it. Suppose that all of the premises are true. Does the truth of those premises guarantee (or even support at all) the truth of the conclusion? No, this argument commits the *fallacy of affirming the consequent.* (A fallacy is a mistake in reasoning.) It will be useful to digress just a bit to see clearly what this fallacy is, and why it is a mistake to reason this way.

As you will see, many philosophical arguments include **conditional** statements: statements of the form if *A*, then *B*. For example, if *Mary took the car,* then *John didn't take it.* The first part of the conditional, the *A* part, is called the **antecedent,** and the second part, the *B* part, is called the **consequent.** (A conditional statement can be confusing at first, before one thinks carefully about what exactly it is saying. Consider the claim that if George Washington was an octopus, then George Washington had eight legs. Is that claim true or false? Some students initially say that the claim is false, but once they look again, they see clearly that the claim is true.) The truth of a conditional statement does *not* require the truth of the antecedent (the claim that Mary took the car), because the conditional is claiming only that *if* Mary took the car, then John didn't take it. The *truth* of the conditional requires only that *if* the antecedent is true, then the consequent must be true (cannot be false); in other words, if the consequent is false, then the antecedent must also be false for the whole conditional statement to be true. Whereas if Mary and John both took the car (in which case the antecedent is true and the consequent is false), then the conditional statement (*if* Mary took the car, then John didn't) is itself false. So if a conditional statement is true, and the antecedent is true, then you know that the consequent must also be true; and if a conditional statement is true and the consequent is false, then you know that the antecedent must also be false. But *nothing* follows from the truth of a conditional and the truth of the consequent, and thus arguments that *claim* to draw a conclusion about the truth of the antecedent on the basis of the truth of the conditional and the truth of the consequent are making the mistake in reasoning called the fallacy of affirming the consequent. ❸

STOP There is another, related fallacy called *denying the antecedent*. You should be able to figure out what that mistake is and why it is a mistake, given this explanation of the fallacy of affirming the consequent.

Since the premises in an instance of affirming the consequent don't actually support the conclusion at all, you might be tempted to say that this is no argument at all. But it doesn't seem right to say flatly that this isn't an argument: it seems clearer to say that it is a *bad* argument, and better still to say exactly what is bad about it. (When faced with an invalid argument, you need not worry about whether its premises are true, since even if they are, they don't provide even minimal support for the conclusion.)

There are other kinds of arguments whose premises provide good but not conclusive grounds for the truth of the conclusion: arguments that offer genuine support for their conclusions but where it is still possible, though unlikely, that the conclusion is false even though the premises are true. The arguments most standardly referred to as **inductive arguments** (or, more explicitly, enumerative inductive arguments) are like this, and many scientific arguments are of this kind. When, for example, someone reasons that all swans are white on the basis of many different observations of white swans, he or she is giving a simple example of an inductive argument. You cannot reasonably conclude that all swans are white on the basis of one observation of a white swan, or even two or twenty, but if there are enough observations in sufficiently varied locations and circumstances, then you can reasonably conclude that *all* swans (not just the ones you've observed so far) are white. When you reason that the sun will rise tomorrow on the basis of the claim that it has risen every morning so far for thousands of years, you are giving an inductive argument. Philosophers don't call good inductive arguments ***valid,*** because the definition of validity is that it is impossible for the conclusion to be false while the premises are true. Inductive arguments, by definition, have conclusions which might be false even though the premises are true. But the better the inductive argument, the more unlikely or improbable it is that the conclusion is false while the premises are true. Good inductive arguments, ones where the evidential or support relation between the premises and the conclusion is compelling, are usually described as *strong*. In such an argument, the truth of the premises provides a good reason to think that the conclusion is true.

A different kind of non-deductive argument—one whose premises again provide good but not conclusive reasons for the truth of its conclusion—is what is referred to as an **explanatory argument** (also called an *inference to the best explanation* or an **abductive argument;** and sometimes the term "induction" is used more broadly, so as to also include arguments of this sort). The idea of an explanatory argument is that there is an alleged fact of some sort to be explained, other considerations that are relevant to the explanation of this fact, and some explanation that is claimed to be the best one in light of those considerations. Thus the premises of such an argument include both a statement of the alleged fact to be explained and statements of these other relevant considerations, and the conclusion is a statement of the explanation alleged to be best. And such an argument will be *strong* (never valid) if the explanation offered really is the best one, assuming that the fact in question really is a fact and the other supposedly relevant considerations are also true.

Here is a simple example: Suppose that the police call you at work to tell you that your car has been in an accident, and that the driver of the car left the scene. The question is how to explain the fact that your car has been in an accident (rather than still parked in the driveway where it was when you left to take the bus to work this morning). The following further considerations seem relevant: that only you and your sister Mary ever drive the car, even though she has recently been forbidden by you to drive it because of the many speeding tickets she has received; that there is only one key to this car, kept hanging on a hook by the back door; that Mary is the only person (other than you) with easy access to this key; and that the police found the car with the key still in it. Thus, it might be claimed, the most likely explanation of the fact that your car was in the accident, instead of still sitting in the driveway where you thought it was, is that Mary drove it (in spite of being forbidden to do so). Obviously you will have even better evidence once you talk to her or find out from eyewitness reports what the driver of the car looked like. But don't you, right now, have a pretty good reason for the conclusion that Mary took the car? Your reason is not conclusive—that is, the conclusion is not guaranteed to be true—because there are other possible explanations of the fact that your car is at the scene of an accident that might turn out to be better ones after all. (Maybe someone broke into your house, took the key, and drove the car away.)

We use explanatory arguments of this sort in everyday life, and scientists use explanatory arguments to draw conclusions about laws and theoretical entities. Such arguments also often play an important role in philosophical discussions.

Summing up, according to the standard definition of an argument that we started with, if premises are offered for the purpose of supporting the truth of a conclusion, then the set of claims consisting of those premises and the conclusion constitutes an argument. The argument is **deductive** if the truth of the premises is intended to guarantee the truth of the conclusion; if the truth of the premises is merely intended to make the truth of the conclusion very likely or probable, but not guaranteed, the argument may be **inductive** or **explanatory**—though there are also other possibilities that we have not considered here, such as arguments that appeal to analogies. A deductive argument whose premises are related to its conclusion in the right way to accomplish its purpose is valid, while good inductive or explanatory arguments can only be strong. A further issue about any argument is whether the premises themselves are true.

An Illustration of the Method of Philosophy

We have just thought through an initial explanation of two of the important skills involved in the method of philosophy: clarification and justification. Let's now consider an illustration of those skills by attempting to clarify and justify the claim that studying philosophy is valuable.

Clarification: Defining What We Mean

Let's first clarify the claim that studying philosophy is valuable. You reasonably wonder about the meaning of both parts of the claim: what is meant by "studying philosophy" and what is meant by "valuable"? Suppose that someone read Bertrand Russell's book *The Problems of Philosophy* one night—is that enough to have "studied philosophy"? According to what we mean when we make the claim, it is not. You have to do more than read one philosophy book to have studied philosophy. It takes more than one night to study philosophy. But there is no exact amount of study that can be said to be the precise meaning of "studying philosophy."

Sometimes what is needed to make an issue clear enough to be reasonably discussed is to replace the original claim with one that is clear and more precise, while still saying approximately the same thing. Thus, somewhat arbitrarily, we will understand "studying philosophy" to mean taking and passing at least four philosophy classes or doing something reasonably similar. (You could probably do the equivalent of taking and passing four philosophy courses on your own, if you were sufficiently motivated and had some resources for checking your understanding.)

Now what do we mean by "valuable," in the second part of the claim? All we mean by "valuable" here is that it is good for you, that you will be significantly better off for having done it. You might doubt that our claim is true, but you now have a pretty good sense of what we mean by it. We have clarified (though perhaps not yet enough) our claim that studying philosophy is valuable.

We might make one more clarification. Someone might wonder whether the claim is that studying philosophy is *always* valuable, no matter who does it, or just that it is *usually* valuable. For example, think about the following claims that have the form *doing A is B:*

Running a marathon is demanding.
Giving birth is done by females.
Watching TV is fun.
Regular exercise is important.
Getting a college degree is worthwhile.

The context, together sometimes with the content of the claim, usually determines whether someone who asserts one of these claims means "always" or "most of the time"—though this may sometimes be unclear. Let's assume that what we mean when we say that studying philosophy is valuable is that it is *always* valuable.

So we now have a pretty good restatement of the original claim resulting from this initial effort at clarification: our claim that studying philosophy is valuable means that anyone who does the equivalent of taking and passing at least four philosophy courses will benefit significantly from it. One of the distinctively philosophical habits of mind is that of noticing when claims are more or less clear.

Justification: Giving an Argument

Now let's move from clarification to justification, remembering that philosophical justification typically takes the form of an argument. Here is an argument for the claim we have just clarified:

1. Studying philosophy always makes you think more clearly.
2. Thinking more clearly is always valuable.
3. Therefore, studying philosophy is always valuable.

What makes this an argument? It is a set of claims, one of which is the conclusion and the others of which are premises that are put forward to support the conclusion. (When you give an argument for a claim, the claim is the conclusion of the argument.) So the first two sentences are the premises and the third sentence is the conclusion.

Just pretend for a moment that the premises are true. If they are true, does the conclusion follow? In other words, does the truth of the premises make the conclusion likely or even certain to be true? For this argument, as for many other arguments, you need to *think* about the premises and the conclusion in order to answer that question—the answer to that question is not the result of a clear mechanical test. As you acquire the intellectual habit of assessing arguments, you will get better and better at distinguishing the good ones from the bad ones. What you should do is suppose that the premises are true and then try to imagine whether it would be possible for the conclusion to be false, even given the truth of the premises.

We suggest that the truth of the premises (if they are true) provides a very good reason to think that the conclusion is true. In fact, the argument appears to be valid: it appears to be logically impossible for the premises to be true and the conclusion false. (We will consider later a reason for questioning whether this is really so.) This argument therefore provides a good example of the relationship of *providing a good reason,* which is the core element of an argument.

In the argument above, if the premises are true, then the conclusion is apparently guaranteed to be true. But we obviously can't just assume that the premises are true. And since the conclusion of the argument has been justified only if the premises are true, our job of justifying the original claim is not finished until we have at least defended the premises (given reasons to think that the premises are true). Furthermore, we should also consider and respond to the most obvious objections, if there are any.

Giving Reasons for the Truth of the Premises

Let's begin with the first premise: that studying philosophy always makes you think more clearly. In anticipation, think about what will be involved in studying philosophy: You will read many different philosophical texts from many different periods of history, learning what different philosophers have said about many different topics. Moreover, since the authors are philosophers, they will typically be arguing for their views, so you need to understand and critically evaluate those views and those arguments, in an attempt to figure out what you think about the philosophical topic at issue. In addition, since philosophers have to discuss many other sorts of things in explaining and clarifying their views, presenting arguments, and considering objections to other views (and, as we will see, even to their own), a philosophical work is usually quite complicated, with all of these parts needing to be clearly sorted out. Studying philosophy involves carefully doing all these things.

What then is "thinking clearly"? It obviously involves being able to clarify various ideas and views that you encounter. But it also involves being logical: considering and sometimes discovering reasons for those views, together with being able to successfully evaluate when those reasons are good ones and when they aren't. One clear-thinking skill is the ability to juggle complicated combinations of ideas, while keeping track of the different relationships among them. And like any skill, it takes time and practice to become good at it. You obviously need to think clearly in order even to understand philosophers, and you surely need to be able to think clearly in order to evaluate philosophical views. When you evaluate a view, you decide whether it is a good view (likely to be true) or a bad view (likely to be false), and as a philosopher, you must have reasons for making that evaluation. Therefore, someone who has studied philosophy—given how we have clarified that idea—has either learned to think clearly for the first time or else already knew how to think clearly to some extent but has now had lots of additional practice at it, and so presumably thinks even more clearly. There is a defense of the first premise: a reason to think that the first premise is true.

Now consider a defense for the second premise, that thinking more clearly is always valuable. Surely we can all agree that doing something that helps you get what you want is valuable—that you benefit significantly from doing something that enhances your ability to get what you want (unless, of course, what you want is not good for you). We contend that clear thinking always does that. Suppose, for example, that two people—call them Joe and Doug—each want to finish college as efficiently as possible, and suppose further that Joe thinks much more clearly than Doug. Suppose that Doug never quite thinks hard enough to keep the degree requirements straight or even realize that some of the requirements exist. Suppose that when an advisor suggests to Doug that he take a particular class, Doug never asks why or how that class will fit into his overall program. Doug probably doesn't have a clear plan, but he does have the desire to finish college as efficiently as possible. Suppose that Joe is constantly honing his thinking skills: he always asks the advisor to clarify her advice, always asks why this is a good class to take, and keeps the degree requirements clearly in mind. It is reasonable to assert that because of Joe's ability to think more clearly than Doug, Joe is more likely to realize his goal than Doug is—and this is not even the best example, is it? You do not have to think with exceptional clarity to realize the goal of finishing college as efficiently as possible. Imagine how clearly you have to think to be a responsible citizen or a loving friend or a terrific parent. Being able to distinguish between believing something on the basis of wishful thinking as opposed to believing something on the basis of good evidence might make the difference between doing a good job and doing an inadequate job in many areas of human relations. So thinking clearly is always valuable because it helps you get what you want, whether you want to be a law clerk, a good parent, or a couch potato.

At this point, we have given reasons to think that both premises are true, and it seems initially clear that if the premises are true, then the conclusion must be true. So we have presented and defended an argument, but does that suffice to justify the claim? It surely is a justification, but it is not yet the strongest justification we could give. An even better justification for a claim also includes considering and responding to objections to our own argument.

Objections: Considering Reasons Against the Truth of the Premises

Some students are reluctant to consider **objections** to an argument they are trying to defend, because it seems to them that they are weakening their own position. But an argument that considers and responds to objections is much stronger than an argument that considers no objections at all. Imagine that you are reading two editorials in the newspaper, one of which expresses your own political views, while the other expresses views contrary to yours. Suppose that each piece argues for its position without considering any alternative points of view that might lead to objections. When you read the one you agree with, it is—unfortunately—all too easy just to go along with the argument (you do, after all, already agree with the conclusion). But when you read the one you disagree with, you are probably thinking of objections along the way, and so perhaps you don't feel challenged in your own view because you think that you have good objections to the reasons given for the conclusion you disagree with. But imagine that the editorial you disagree with proceeded to consider objections similar to the ones you are thinking of as you read it, and imagine further that the responses it gives to those objections are pretty compelling.

Wouldn't you feel more uncomfortable shrugging off the view it defends in that case? Wouldn't the challenge to your own view seem more serious? Analogously, wouldn't the piece arguing for the view you agree with be even stronger if it also considered and responded to objections? Any view argued from just one side, without considering alternative perspectives and the resulting objections, is not as compelling as a view that has considered the strongest objections and has also shown how those objections, however strong they seem, can be satisfactorily answered. This is an especially important philosophical habit of mind: see many sides of an issue—don't be satisfied with just one perspective.

We want to consider and respond to objections for the purpose of strengthening our argument, but presumably we find the argument pretty convincing (since we devised it), so how does one go about finding good objections? This is another one of the skills that you'll acquire as you develop philosophical habits of mind: you will need to be able to take up a critical attitude, criticizing the arguments of other philosophers. You can also take that same point of view in relation to your own argument, pretending that you hold the other point of view and looking for weaknesses in your original argument.

You might think at first that the way to object to an argument is to object to its conclusion—to find reasons for thinking that the conclusion is false. But in fact this doesn't really work very well if you are trying to criticize the original argument. For if you offer reasons to think that the conclusion is false, then you have simply produced another argument for the opposite conclusion. You now have two opposed arguments, leading to opposed results, but not really engaging each other in any more substantial way. They can't both be valid arguments with true premises, and it is unlikely—though not impossible—that they are both strong. But the mere conflict between them gives in itself no insight into which one is mistaken or—even more importantly—*how* it is mistaken. Thus what makes more sense, if the goal is to evaluate, criticize, or strengthen the original argument, is to consider objections to its premises or to the reasoning from the premises to the conclusion, rather than reasons to reject the conclusion. If there are good reasons to think that the premises of an argument are false or that the reasoning from the premises to the conclusion is faulty, then the argument fails to support its conclusion; but if those objections can be answered, then the overall case for the conclusion is strengthened.

Let's first consider an objection to each premise of our sample argument. An objection to a premise is a reason to think that the premise is false. Consider the first premise: that studying philosophy makes you think more clearly. Someone might object by saying that studying philosophy is very confusing. To study philosophy, you have to read many different authors on many different questions, and many of the authors lived a long time ago, so their writing style is very different from ours and often hard to understand. Philosophical questions are hard to understand in the first place because they are so abstract and so remote from everyday concerns. Thus many people who study philosophy just end up very confused, and surely someone who is very confused is not someone who thinks clearly. Therefore studying philosophy does not make one think more clearly.

What about the second premise: that thinking more clearly is always valuable? Someone might object to this premise by pointing out that the more clearly one thinks, the more clearly one sees how vulnerable we puny humans are. We have many grand desires, but our ability to "get what we want" is largely dependent upon conditions beyond our control, and thus all our planning and scheming is in the end just pathetic. The more clearly we think, the more clearly we realize this and the more paralyzed we become. We obviously do not benefit from being so paralyzed. On the contrary, ignorance and murky thinking are bliss. Therefore, thinking clearly is not always valuable.

Objections can also be made to the *reasoning* involved in arguing that the conclusion is likely to be true, given the truth of the premises. Consider an objection to the reasoning of the sample argument. Suppose that someone grants the truth of both of the premises but argues that there are other, indeed much easier ways to learn to think more clearly than by studying philosophy. If the conclusion—that studying philosophy is always valuable—means that anyone should, all things considered, study philosophy, then that conclusion might very well be false, in which case the argument isn't really valid after all. Suppose that you are a math major; and suppose also that studying math teaches you to think more clearly; and suppose further that given your talents and interests, taking the time to study philosophy would take time away from other things that you enjoy without adding very much benefit (since you are already learning to think clearly by studying math). So you could argue that even if it is true that studying philosophy would teach you to think more clearly and that thinking more clearly is always valuable, it is false that studying philosophy is valuable for you. It is false that you, given all of what is true about your life, should study philosophy. This objection challenges the reasoning involved in drawing the conclusion from the premises instead of challenging one of the premises.

At this point, we have formulated an objection to each of our premises and an objection to the reasoning of the argument, all with the ultimate goal of strengthening our case for the claim that studying philosophy is valuable by answering these objections. ❹

Can you think of any other objections to this argument?

Responses: Showing Why the Objections Fail

Obviously we need to *respond* to these objections: we need to show why these objections are not strong enough to seriously affect the force of the original argument. In responding to objections, you will sometimes show that the reasoning of the objections is faulty, while at other times you may respond by showing that the original statement of the premise or the reasoning needs to be altered or qualified in order to accommodate the objection (while still being able to make the case for the claim you are defending).

The first objection claims that studying philosophy, rather than leading to clear thinking, is confusing. But while some people do find it confusing at first, that sense of confusion almost always goes away once one works at it a bit harder. It is really not very easy to pass four philosophy classes without acquiring the thinking skills that clear up the confusion. This objection might have had serious weight if we had specified the idea of studying philosophy as meaning passing only one philosophy course, but it has no serious weight against the first premise when studying philosophy is understood as requiring one to have passed four philosophy courses (or done the equivalent).

The second objection claims that we are virtually powerless to get what we want, no matter how carefully we plan and anticipate, so that clear thinking really isn't always valuable. But what evidence can be offered for such a claim? What reason can this objector offer for the view that our planning and careful thinking make no difference (or so little difference as to be irrelevant) to the outcome of our efforts? Suppose that you point out that you know of many examples of people who have often succeeded in getting what they want when they've planned carefully, and of other people who don't plan carefully and fail to get what they want. These examples are **counter-examples** ❺ to the objector's view: examples which give some reason to think that the view is false. Of course no one would claim that careful planning guarantees good results. The defense for the premise under consideration need only claim that careful, clear thinking makes getting what you want more likely—which is enough to make such thinking valuable. So the objector needs to give some reason to think that it is false that careful, clear thinking makes it more likely that you will get what you want.

❺ *Editor Comment*

Another important philosophical skill is giving counter-examples to philosophical claims or theories. To create a counter-example, you need to first figure out just exactly what the claim or view says and then think carefully about how it applies to many situations, looking for examples that show that it is wrong.

The defender of the objection might respond that all of those people who planned carefully were just lucky, and the people who didn't plan well were just unlucky. Suppose that the objector continues to say the same thing (planners are just lucky) no matter how detailed your examples are and no matter how many examples you come up with. There is nothing that anyone can say that would conclusively prove that we have more control than the objection says we do, so the objector's view cannot be shown conclusively to be wrong. Is the objector's insistence on the view thereby legitimate? Is it intellectually respectable to insist on a view despite possible counter-examples, just because the view hasn't been *conclusively* proven to be false? This seems clearly unreasonable.

Our main response to this objection, then, is that the objection relies on a very controversial, ill-defended assumption, one that seems to us to be clearly wrong. Therefore, the objection fails to have any serious force against the premise it is aimed at.

What about the objection to the reasoning of the argument? The main response to that objection is that the objection misunderstood the content of the conclusion. The point of the argument was not to argue that everyone ought to study philosophy, even though it was perhaps not entirely unreasonable for the objector to interpret the conclusion that way. One way to understand the claim that studying philosophy is always valuable is to think that studying philosophy will be valuable for *anyone*. And that strongly suggests that anyone ought to do it. But we could argue that the conclusion of the argument does not mean that anyone, no matter what else is true of him or her, ought to find some time to study philosophy. The conclusion instead just means that *if* you study philosophy, then that study will be valuable for you in the sense that you will benefit from it. This conclusion is completely consistent with the claim that for any particular person, he or she ought not to study philosophy because for that particular person the study of philosophy, in spite of the benefits that it produces, would not be valuable, all things considered, given what would have to be sacrificed to engage in it and given the possibility of acquiring those same or very similar benefits in some other way. (Here you can see how considering objections also can help to clarify a position.)

Summary

We have clarified and justified the claim that studying philosophy is valuable. We have thereby illustrated many of the skills and philosophical habits of mind required by the method of philosophy. Can you see how the claim is clarified further in the process of justification? Can you see how much stronger the justification is because we have considered and responded to objections?

As you can see now, one of the first challenges of doing philosophy is to learn how to tell when a philosopher—whether it is you or someone you are reading or listening to—is arguing for a view, objecting to it, or responding to objections. As you practice thinking philosophically, you will get better at recognizing these different activities, and you will get better at clarifying claims, drawing distinctions, and making arguments, objections, and responses yourself.

Reading Philosophy

With a little work, almost anyone can learn to think philosophically. But you might wonder what you need to do to work effectively at acquiring this ability. The first, most valuable resource on which you should practice thinking philosophically is the set of reading selections in this book (and any other philosophical texts you may read). But we've learned that students often find reading philosophy very difficult at first, and so we've included some advice about reading philosophy, together with some brief illustrations. And while the advice is directed primarily at reading philosophy, the main points also apply to listening to a philosophical lecture or participating in a philosophical discussion.

Philosophical material is primarily argumentative and critical, almost never merely expository. You don't read philosophy in order to gather lots of facts that you will then memorize. You should read philosophy as if you were actively thinking along with the author of the text, as if you were having an intellectual conversation with him or her. Philosophers are arguing for a view or position. You should think of the author (or lecturer or discussant) as saying: "Look—this is *what* I think, and this is *why* I think it. What do you think?" Thus you should always keep four questions in mind while reading (or listening to lectures, or engaging in discussion with another philosopher): first, what view or position is the philosopher advocating? The answer to this question may differ at different places in an article: an article may make more than one point, and you should ask how these points connect with each other. Notice also that what is being advocated at a particular point may be very simple and general (e.g., the claim that God exists) or very complicated and specific (e.g., the claim that a particular objection to a particular argument that God exists is mistaken). The second question to ask is what reasons or arguments are being offered in support of the view being advocated. Try to sketch the answers to these two questions as you read—either in your head or, even better, on paper (perhaps in the margin of the book). You will then be in a good position to ask the next two questions: how *strong* are the reasons offered, and are there objections to them? It is virtually impossible to do this while relaxing in a passive frame of mind. Successfully reading philosophy requires an active, critical, imaginative mindset—one of the distinctively philosophical habits of mind that you need to cultivate in order to learn to think philosophically.

There is one major source of confusion to watch out for. Because philosophy is essentially reflective and critical, a philosopher will typically discuss other positions and arguments besides the one defended in a particular article. These may include any of the following: (1) positions opposed to the one defended; (2) positions similar to, but still significantly different in some respect, from the one defended (where the difference helps to clarify the main view); (3) arguments in favor of positions opposed to the one defended, which will be criticized; (4) objections to the philosopher's own position, which will be responded to; and (5) sometimes even arguments for the view defended that the philosopher does *not* accept and wants to distinguish from ones that he does accept. It is obviously important to distinguish all of these from the philosopher's own positive views and arguments, and this is relatively easy to do if you are alert. (For example, arguments and positions other than his own will often be introduced by noncommittal phrases like "it might be claimed that . . ." or "some writers argue that . . ." or perhaps by a reference to a particular person who holds the view or argument in question.)

It is usually a good idea first to look rather quickly through a reading to get an idea of the general "lay of the land" and then to read it again more carefully and critically. Otherwise it is too easy to lose sight of its main point as one works through the detailed arguments. Remember also that considerable rereading will certainly be necessary, especially but not only when reading a later selection that disagrees with an earlier one. Almost no one (including professional philosophers) is capable of adequately grasping a complicated argument in a single reading. And the most important piece of advice: Don't give up! The more you work at these skills and habits, the better you will become at them, and the more you will also come to see the point of philosophy. In this way, intellectual tenacity is one of the most essential philosophical habits of mind.

Two Sample Passages

Sometimes a general characterization of how to do something, such as how to read philosophy, only goes so far, and what a student really wants and needs is a concrete example: a piece of philosophy with some discussion about how to implement some of that general advice. Here, then, are two sample passages, taken from selections that appear later on in this book: one from J. L. Mackie, on the problem that evil poses to the belief in God's existence; and the other from John Locke, on the problem of justifying our confidence that our senses provide reliable information about the world.

Example 1: A Contemporary Passage

Before we analyze the first passage (given below), we need to say something about its argumentative context. Mackie's own view is that the problem of evil shows that God, conceived as omnipotent and wholly good, does not exist. But he recognizes that some people think that the free will response to the problem of evil undermines his view. According to the free will response to the problem of evil, God gave man free will in spite of the fact that such a gift would result in the occurrence of evil, because, according to Mackie's interpretation of this response: "it is better on the whole that men should act freely, and sometimes err, than that they should be innocent automata, acting rightly in a wholly determined way" (p. 575 in this book).

So in the passage we'll analyze, Mackie is objecting to (giving reasons to reject) the free will response to the problem of evil. Here is the passage:

> . . . if God has made men such that in their free choices they sometimes prefer what is good and sometimes what is evil, why could he not have made men such that they always freely choose the good? If there is no logical impossibility in a man's freely choosing the good on one, or on several occasions, there cannot be a logical impossibility in his freely choosing the good on every occasion. God was not, then, faced with a choice between making innocent automata and making beings who, in acting freely, would sometimes go wrong: there was open to him the obviously better possibility of making beings who would act freely but always go right. Clearly, his failure to avail himself of this possibility is inconsistent with his being both omnipotent and wholly good. (p. 575)

Mackie starts the passage with a question, which is often an effective rhetorical choice to get the reader thinking in the right direction. Notice, however, that he follows it up with a claim, one that is essential to his objection to the free will response:

> If there is no logical impossibility in a man's freely choosing the good on one, or on several occasions, there cannot be a logical impossibility in his freely choosing the good on every occasion.

Immediately after that claim, Mackie draws the conclusion that God could have made free people who (as a result of the way he made them) always freely choose to do the good, but he formulates this in a more complicated and less immediately perspicuous way:

> God was not, then, faced with a choice between making innocent automata and making beings who, in acting freely, would sometimes go wrong: there was open to him the obviously better possibility of making beings who would act freely but always go right.

The last part of this complicated sentence actually formulates the conclusion just stated, while the rest makes clear how it contrasts with the view he is opposing.

What other premises are required to make this argument fully explicit? Obviously Mackie is assuming, without explicitly saying so, that it is logically possible for someone to freely choose the good at least some of the time. It is hard to see how the defender of the free will solution could deny that. So now we have two premises, one explicit and one implicit:

1. If there is no logical impossibility in a man's freely choosing the good on one, or on several occasions, there cannot be a logical impossibility in his freely choosing the good on every occasion.
2. There is no logical impossibility in a man's freely choosing the good on one, or on several occasions.

From these two premises it follows that: there cannot be a logical impossibility in his freely choosing the good on every occasion, and it immediately follows from this intermediate conclusion that it is indeed logically possible that he freely chooses the good on every occasion.

Now what additional assumption is being made before it will follow that God could have made free men who always choose to do the good? There is still one more implicit premise, one that Mackie is quite sure the defenders of the free will solution would agree with.

3. God can make actual whatever is logically possible.

So with just a little thought about logic and what it takes to fill in the argument, we can see what Mackie was up to when he moved from the conditional statement: "if a person can freely choose to do the good at *some* times, then that person can freely choose to do the good at *every* time" to the conclusion: "God could have made people so that (as a result of the way he made them) they freely choose to do the good every time." Here is the whole argument:

1. If there is no logical impossibility in a person's freely choosing the good on one, or on several occasions, there cannot be a logical impossibility in his freely choosing the good on every occasion.
2. There is no logical impossibility in a person's freely choosing the good on one, or on several occasions.

   So, there cannot be a logical impossibility in his freely choosing the good on every occasion.

   So, it is logically possible that he freely chooses the good on every occasion.
3. God can make actual whatever is logically possible.

   So God could have made persons who (as a result of the way he made them) freely choose the good on every occasion.

Notice that you still don't get the conclusion that God could have made people who did no evil, without adding the additional implicit premise that people who freely choose the good on every occasion do no evil. (But how explicit do we really have to be?— that's a matter for you to decide in thinking about the argument.)

Mackie's final sentence in the passage says more than he needs to say to object to the free will solution—do you see that? He is there reiterating his main view that no God who is wholly good and all-powerful could allow this particular possibility: free men who perpetrate evil, when the men could be made just as free and while also being made so as to not perpetrate evil.

Now remember that your task is to read Mackie critically. To do that you must first see clearly what he is saying and why he thinks it is true, which is why we have clearly stated his conclusion as well as his premises. We have clearly laid out his argument, and now we should try to evaluate it: to determine how strong his reasons are. Remember that the first thing to do is to evaluate the form of the argument: is it strong—or perhaps even valid? Is it such that if all the premises are true, then the conclusion is likely (or even guaranteed to be) true? The form of the reasoning seems very strong, doesn't it? (In fact, it is valid.)

Now look to see which, if any, of the premises are most questionable. While there are some philosophers who would accept all of Mackie's premises and thus would accept his argument and his conclusion, there is one premise that many other philosophers, including many or most of those who are sympathetic to the view he is criticizing, would reject. Can you see which premise this is? Which premise would be easiest to object to? (This is not an easy question.)

The premise of this argument that is most likely to be challenged is in fact premise 3. While it sounds initially very reasonable to suppose that an omnipotent God can create anything that is logically possible, there is a subtle way in which this may be wrong. While it is surely possible that a free person might always make the morally best choice ("choose the good"), can God bring it about that a person always chooses in this way without making the person no longer free? The underlying idea here, explored at much greater length in the free will chapter, is that when a person *freely* chooses something, then it is always true that he (or she) could have chosen something else instead. But is this true of someone who makes the morally best choice because God has created him so as to bring about that he will make that very choice?

Now someone might worry that spending this much time on every single paragraph of your philosophy reading would take forever, and the response to that worry is that you obviously don't do this for every paragraph. We've chosen especially important, clearly argumentative passages to use as examples. But you should now be able to see why you are rarely assigned to read as many pages in your philosophy courses as you are for most of your other courses. Reading philosophy takes lots of time and thought and care and imagination. Notice that we could have gone on much longer, since we only began the evaluation phase. How far you go with the evaluation phase depends on your purposes and your level of experience. It is sufficient for just understanding the passage to give fairly brief answers to the questions we framed above, but if you were going to write a paper evaluating Mackie's reasoning, you would have to do more.

Example 2: A Historical Passage

The other passage we will consider was written in a very different time, but it is still distinctively philosophical in that there is a philosophical claim being made and reasons being offered for the truth of that claim. In the *Essay Concerning Human Understanding,* John Locke is defending the very natural view that we have knowledge of the external (material) world and that our sense experience provides us with sufficient justification to ground that knowledge. In the early chapters of the book, Locke focuses on the source and nature of our ideas, because he believes that the reasonable starting point for responding to the skeptic is to show how we can trust that our senses give us the right (that is, largely true) ideas.

In Book IV, Chapter XI, he offers four reasons for the conclusion that our senses "do not err in the information they give us of the existence of things without us." We will focus here on the fourth of those reasons:

> Our senses in many cases bear witness to the truth of each other's report concerning the existence of sensible things without us. He that sees a fire may, if he doubt whether it be anything more than a bare fancy, feel it too and be convinced by putting his hand in it. Which certainly could never be put into such exquisite pain by a bare idea or phantom, unless that the pain be a fancy too: which yet he cannot, when the burn is well, by raising the idea of it, bring upon himself again. (p. 72)

First, what does Locke's conclusion mean? He is talking about ordinary sense perception. By "the existence of things without us" he means the existence of ordinary material objects—trees, buildings, mountains, rivers, and so on—outside of us, outside of both our bodies and our minds. By "the information they [the senses] give us" he just means the beliefs about such objects that we naturally form as a result of sense perception and that seem to reflect the content of perceptual experience. And by saying that our senses "do not err" in this information, he is saying that the beliefs in question are, at least for the most part, true.

So what does his reason for this conclusion amount to? He says: "Our senses in many cases bear witness to the truth of each other's report concerning the existence of sensible things without us." Sensible things are just things that we can (apparently) sense—again, material objects like tables and chairs. But what does he mean by "bear witness"?

Look at the example he gives. (Examples are often crucially important in understanding abstract philosophical claims.) As Locke would put it, your sense of sight reports to you that there is a fire, and then your sense of touch also reports the same thing, because it too will tell you that there is a fire—if you put your hand in (or near to) the place where the fire seems to be. If your visual perception of a fire was a "bare idea or phantom" (that is, was something like a mere mental illusion, not caused by and corresponding to something existing outside of you—something real), then when you tried to feel what you were seeing, you wouldn't get the right feeling (that is, you wouldn't experience pain or heat)—unless, of course, the sensation of pain or of heat was an illusion ("a fancy") too. (But how likely is it that two illusions would fit together in that way?—this is part of Locke's point.) Notice also that when the burn heals, one cannot, through imagination alone, make oneself experience the same pain that one has when one really puts one's hand in a fire—thus showing, Locke thinks, that the pain experienced in the actual case is more than just a bare idea.

So the example suggests that for the different senses to "bear witness to the truth of each other's report" is for one sense to tell us what another sense also tells us. Clearly Locke thinks that this supports the conclusion that our senses "do not err." But we need to say more about how this conclusion is supposed to follow. How can we reason from the premise that our senses agree with each other in this way to the conclusion that what they tell us is true (or at least very likely to be true)? Something seems right about the thought, but just how does the reasoning work?

Locke seems to be thinking that if what our senses tell us was not true, then it would at least be very unlikely that our senses would agree with each other in this way. But why think that is true? One way to make sense of this argument is to see it as an explanatory argument or an inference to the best explanation. What would explain the fact that our senses agree with each other? 6

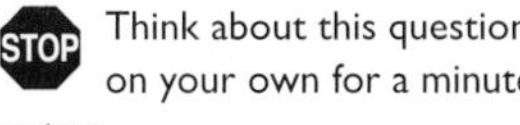

Think about this question on your own for a minute or two.

One possible explanation, the one that Locke seems to have in mind, is this: our perceptual experiences are systematically caused by external objects in a way that makes the perceptual experience accurately reflect the properties of those external objects. This is an explanation of the fact in question: if it were so, then the different senses, being affected by the same external objects (whichever ones are present where our bodies are located), should agree with each other in the way that they do. But is it the best explanation? Or are there other explanations that are at least equally good—equally good from the standpoint from which Locke is making this argument, one in which the accuracy of our perceptions and the very existence of the common-sense material world is in question?

In fact, there are a number of other possible explanations, though a full assessment of them is not possible in this discussion (see Chapter 2 for more on this issue). Perhaps we are dreaming. (Do apparent perceptions agree with each other in dreams?) Perhaps a powerful being of some sort is systematically causing perceptions that do not correspond to any material reality, but which still agree. Perhaps instead your own subconscious mind is doing that. Or what about the possibility that the perceptions in question are systematically caused by external reality (which is why they agree) but in a way that distorts that reality very badly (which is why the resulting beliefs are not in fact true)? Which explanation is best: Locke's or one of these others, and why?

One other thing worth noticing is that we did not set out this argument in numbered steps, in the way that we did with Mackie's argument in the previous passage. This could have been done, but it would not, in our judgment, have been particularly helpful in this case. The structure of this argument is very simple: an alleged fact accompanied by the claim that a certain conclusion is the best explanation of that fact. What is complicated are the reasons for thinking that the alleged fact is a fact and the reasons for thinking that the alleged best explanation really has that status, and neither of these things lends itself very well to the sort of formulation in numbered steps that worked so well with Mackie's argument. The moral here is that formulating an argument in a series of steps—or in any other way—is a *tool* for clarification and should be used where it is helpful and not otherwise.

One challenge to evaluating a philosopher's reasoning, which arises with this passage from Locke and also in many other cases, is that philosophers are often defending views that we already believe to be true. But be careful. Your job as a philosopher is to critically evaluate the cogency of the reasons offered for a claim, whether you independently believe the claim or not. So in order to evaluate this passage, you need to scrutinize the reason Locke actually gives, asking yourself whether it is sufficient to show that the conclusion is true. Answering that question is hard, because evaluating explanatory arguments requires deciding which of many possible explanations is best—an issue for which the relevant standards are not entirely clear. But you can begin to do all of this when reading and trying to understand Locke's view, even if you cannot see through to the end of such a line of reasoning. The harder you push yourself to understand exactly what he is saying and to evaluate how cogent his reasons are, the more skilled you will become at reading philosophy and thinking philosophically.

Discussion Questions

1. Why do we need a single conception of philosophy for the purposes of this course? What if someone said, "We don't need a single conception of philosophy. We can work together, doing philosophy, even if we each have different conceptions of philosophy." Does that sound reasonable? Why or why not?
2. The area of philosophy called *metaphysics* studies the nature of reality. What do you think about reality? Is it clear what things are real and what things are not real? List some things that are real. Then list some other things that are not real. Does science study the nature of reality? What do you think is the difference between science and philosophy?
3. We claim that how much clarification a claim needs varies depending on the context. Consider, for example, the claim that there are trees in the quad. Now imagine the following context where the claim needs no clarification: suppose a landscaping firm has been hired to fertilize all the trees on campus, and they want to know if they need to go to the quad. You tell them that there are trees in the quad, and your claim is sufficiently clear and precise for the purposes at hand. But suppose there is another context: a landscaping firm has been hired to fertilize all the cherry trees on campus, and they want to know if they need to go to the quad. Now the claim that there are trees in the quad needs to be clarified, in this case made more precise: they need to be told whether there are *cherry* trees in the quad. Now you think of an example of a claim and two contexts, one in which the claim needs clarification, and one in which the very same claim needs no clarification.
4. We claim that reasons for believing a claim should be reasons for thinking that the claim is true. Does that sound right? What other kinds of reasons might someone think are good ones for believing a claim? Suppose your best friend says that she believes she has won a $10 million lottery. Should you believe her? Suppose that she offers no real reason for thinking that her claim is true, but wants you to believe her anyway (maybe she wants to celebrate). Is that a good reason to believe a claim: because someone *wants* you to believe it? What about the claim that God exists? On what basis should someone believe that claim? Should you have some reason to think that the claim is true? Suppose that it makes you happy to believe that God exists. Is that a good reason to believe the claim? Think of some examples of claims that you think someone ought not to believe unless there is a good reason to think that they are true, and some examples of claims that you think can *perhaps* be believed on other grounds. You will obviously have to explain the context of the latter examples.
5. Try explaining the argument for the conclusion that studying philosophy is valuable to a friend. What kinds of clarifications did you have to make? Did your friend have any objections? Was your friend convinced?

Plato

Plato (427–347 B.C.) was one of the two major ancient Greek philosophers (the other being Aristotle) and is universally recognized as one of the most important philosophers in the entire history of philosophy. (The twentieth-century British logician and metaphysician Alfred North Whitehead once remarked that the history of Western philosophy "consists of a series of footnotes to Plato"—an exaggeration, but a pardonable one.) Plato's writings consist of dialogues in which the leading figure is his teacher Socrates (469–399 B.C.). It is usually thought that the earlier dialogues, of which the present selection is one, more accurately report the actual views of the historical Socrates, with the later ones developing Plato's own views—views that he perhaps saw as developing out of his teacher's. This dialogue is set on the court steps of Athens, where Socrates stops to talk to Euthyphro about the business that each has with the court. The background of the dialogue is real: Socrates was accused of corrupting the youth of Athens. (The following selection is an account of the trial itself.)

In this dialogue, we see an example of conceptual clarification: Socrates questions Euthyphro in an attempt to clarify the idea of piety. While there are religious connotations to the idea of piety, there is also a broader meaning more appropriate to the arguments in this dialogue: piety is approximately equivalent to moral rightness or correctness. But then the idea of a morally right action itself needs clarification, and that is what the dialogue is really about. Euthyphro is confident that he understands what it is for an action to be pious in this sense and attempts to explain it to Socrates.

Euthyphro

Euthyphro:* What's new, Socrates, to make you leave your usual haunts in the Lyceum and spend your time here by the king-archon's court? Surely you are not prosecuting anyone before the king-archon as I am?

Socrates: The Athenians do not call this a prosecution but an indictment, Euthyphro.

E: What is this you say? Someone must have indicted you, for you are not going to tell me that you have indicted someone else.

S: No indeed.

E: But someone else has indicted you?

S: Quite so.

E: Who is he?

S: I do not really know him myself, Euthyphro. He is apparently young and unknown. They call him Meletus, I believe. He belongs to the Pitthean deme, if you know anyone from that deme called Meletus, with long hair, not much of a beard, and a rather aquiline nose.

E: I don't know him, Socrates. What charge does he bring against you?

S: What charge? A not ignoble one I think, for it is no small thing for a young man to have knowledge of such an important subject. He says he knows how our young men are corrupted and who corrupts them. He is likely to be wise, and when he sees my ignorance corrupting his contemporaries, he proceeds to accuse me to the city as to their mother. I think he is the only one of our public men to start out the right way, for it is right to care first that the young should be as good as possible, just as a good farmer is likely to take care of the young plants first, and of the others later. So, too, Meletus first gets rid of us who corrupt the young shoots, as he says, and then afterwards he will obviously take care of the older ones and become a source of great blessings for the city, as seems likely to happen to one who started out this way.

E: I could wish this were true, Socrates, but I fear the opposite may happen. He seems to me to start out by harming the very heart of the city by attempting to wrong you. Tell me, what does he say you do to corrupt the young?

S: Strange things, to hear him tell it, for he says that I am a maker of gods, and on the ground that I create new gods while not believing in the old gods, he has indicted me for their sake, as he puts it.

E: I understand, Socrates. This is because you say that the divine sign keeps coming to you.  So he has written this indictment against you as one who makes innovations in religious matters, and he comes to court to slander you, knowing that such things are easily misrepresented to the crowd.

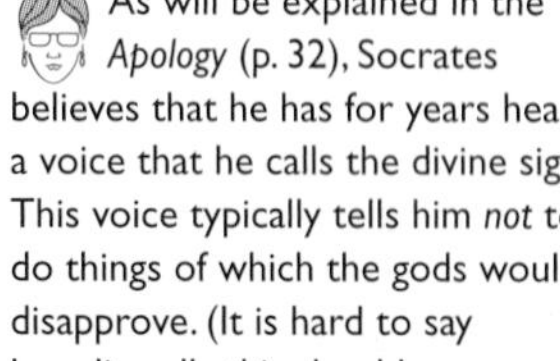

1 As will be explained in the *Apology* (p. 32), Socrates believes that he has for years heard a voice that he calls the divine sign. This voice typically tells him *not* to do things of which the gods would disapprove. (It is hard to say how literally this should be taken.)

From *Five Dialogues,* translated by G. M. A. Grube (Indianapolis: Hackett Publishing Company, 1981).

*We know nothing about Euthyphro except what we can gather from this dialogue. He is obviously a professional priest who considers himself an expert on ritual.

The same is true in my case. Whenever I speak of divine matters in the assembly and foretell the future, they laugh me down as if I were crazy; and yet I have foretold nothing that did not happen. Nevertheless, they envy all of us who do this. One need not worry about them, but meet them head-on.

S: My dear Euthyphro, to be laughed at does not matter perhaps, for the Athenians do not mind anyone they think clever, as long as he does not teach his own wisdom, but if they think that he makes others to be like himself they get angry, whether through envy, as you say, or for some other reason.

E: I have certainly no desire to test their feelings towards me in this matter.

S: Perhaps you seem to make yourself but rarely available, and not to be willing to teach your own wisdom, but I'm afraid that my liking for people makes them think that I pour out to anybody anything I have to say, not only without charging a fee but even glad to reward anyone who is willing to listen. If then they were intending to laugh at me, as you say they laugh at you, there would be nothing unpleasant in their spending their time in court laughing and jesting, but if they are going to be serious, the outcome is not clear except to you prophets.

E: Perhaps it will come to nothing, Socrates, and you will fight your case as you think best, as I think I will mine.

S: What is your case, Euthyphro? Are you the defendant or the prosecutor?

E: The prosecutor.

S: Whom do you prosecute?

E: One whom I am thought crazy to prosecute.

S: Are you pursuing someone who will easily escape you?

E: Far from it, for he is quite old.

S: Who is it?

E: My father.

S: My dear sir! Your own father?

E: Certainly.

S: What is the charge? What is the case about?

E: Murder, Socrates.

S: Good heavens! Certainly, Euthyphro, most men would not know how they could do this and be right. It is not the part of anyone to do this, but of one who is far advanced in wisdom. ❷

E: Yes, by Zeus, Socrates, that is so.

S: Is then the man your father killed one of your relatives? Or is that obvious, for you would not prosecute your father for the murder of a stranger.

E: It is ridiculous, Socrates, for you to think that it makes any difference whether the victim is a stranger or a relative. One should only watch whether the killer acted justly or not; if he acted justly, let him go, but if not, one should prosecute, even if the killer shares your hearth and table. The pollution is the same if you knowingly keep company with such a man and do not cleanse yourself and him by bringing him to justice. The victim was a dependent of mine, and when we were farming in Naxos he was a servant of ours. He killed one of our household slaves in drunken anger, so my father bound him hand and foot and threw him in a ditch, then sent a man here to enquire from the priest what should be done. During that time he gave no thought or care to the bound man, as being a killer, and it was no matter if he died, which he did. Hunger and cold and his bonds caused his death before the messenger came back from the seer. Both my father and my other relatives are angry that I am prosecuting my father for murder on behalf of a murderer when he hadn't even killed him, they say, and even if he had, the dead man does not deserve a thought, since he was a killer. For, they say, it is impious for a son to prosecute his father for murder. But their ideas of the divine attitude to piety and impiety are wrong, Socrates.

S: Whereas, by Zeus, Euthyphro, you think that your knowledge of the divine, and of piety and impiety, is so accurate that, when those things happened as you say, you have no fear of having acted impiously in bringing your father to trial?

E: I should be of no use, Socrates, and Euthyphro would not be superior to the majority of men, if I did not have accurate knowledge of all such things.

S: It is indeed most important, my admirable Euthyphro, that I should become your pupil, and as regards this indictment challenge Meletus about these very things and say to him: that in the past too I considered knowledge about the divine to be most important, and that now that he says that

❷ *Restatement/ Summary*

R Socrates pretends to believe that Euthyphro must be very sure that he knows what is the pious or right thing and what is not, since he is willing to do something as initially questionable as prosecuting his own father.

I am guilty of improvising and innovating about the gods I have become your pupil. I would say to him: "If, Meletus, you agree that Euthyphro is wise in these matters, consider me, too, to have the right beliefs and do not bring me to trial. If you do not think so, then prosecute that teacher of mine, not me, for corrupting the older men, me and his own father, by teaching me and by exhorting and punishing him. If he is not convinced, and does not discharge me or indict you instead of me, I shall repeat the same challenge in court.

E: Yes, by Zeus, Socrates, and, if he should try to indict me, I think I would find his weak spots and the talk in court would be about him rather than about me.

S: It is because I realize this that I am eager to become your pupil, my dear friend. I know that other people as well as this Meletus do not even seem to notice you, whereas he sees me so sharply and clearly that he indicts me for ungodliness. So tell me now, by Zeus, what you just now maintained you clearly knew: what kind of thing do you say that godliness and ungodliness are, both as regards murder and other things; or is the pious not the same and alike in every action, and the impious the opposite of all that is pious and like itself, and everything that is to be impious presents us with one form or appearance in so far as it is impious? ❸

E: Most certainly, Socrates.

S: Tell me then, what is the pious, and what the impious, do you say?

E: I say that the pious is to do what I am doing now, to prosecute the wrongdoer, be it about murder or temple robbery or anything else, whether the wrongdoer is your father or your mother or anyone else; not to prosecute is impious. ❹ And observe, Socrates, that I can quote the law as a great proof that this is so. I have already said to others that such actions are right, not to favour the ungodly, whoever they are. These people themselves believe that Zeus is the best and most just of the gods, yet they agree that he bound his father because he unjustly swallowed his sons, and that he in turn castrated his father for similar reasons. But they are angry with me because I am prosecuting my father for his wrongdoing. They contradict themselves in what they say about the gods and about me. ❺

S: Indeed, Euthyphro, this is the reason why I am a defendant in the case, because I find it hard to accept things like that being said about the gods, and it is likely to be the reason why I shall be told I do wrong. Now, however, if you, who have full knowledge of such things, share their opinions, then we must agree with them too, it would seem. For what are we to say, we who agree that we ourselves have no knowledge of them? Tell me, by the god of friendship, do you really believe these things are true?

E: Yes, Socrates, and so are even more surprising things, of which the majority has no knowledge.

S: And do you believe that there really is war among the gods, and terrible enmities and battles, and other such things as are told by the poets, and other sacred stories such as are embroidered by good writers and by representations of which the robe of the goddess is adorned when it is carried up to the Acropolis? Are we to say these things are true, Euthyphro?

E: Not only these, Socrates, but, as I was saying just now, I will, if you wish, relate many other things about the gods which I know will amaze you.

S: I should not be surprised, but you will tell me these at leisure some other time. For now, try to tell me more clearly what I was asking just now, for, my friend, you did not teach me adequately when I asked you what the pious was, but you told me that what you are doing now, prosecuting your father for murder, is pious.

E: And I told the truth, Socrates.

S: Perhaps. You agree, however, that there are many other pious actions.

E: There are.

S: Bear in mind then that I did not bid you tell me one or two of the many pious actions but that form itself that makes all pious actions pious, for you agreed that all impious actions are impious and all pious actions pious through one form, or don't you remember? ❻

E: I do.

S: Tell me then what this form itself is, so that I may look upon it, and using it as a model,

❸ *Definition*

By asking for the *form* of piety, Socrates is asking for a definition or account of piety itself: of what it is that all pious things or actions have in common by virtue of which they are pious .

❹

Here is Euthyphro's first attempt to respond to Socrates's request for clarification: piety is what Euthyphro is doing now by prosecuting his father. Does this attempt succeed in clarifying the *general form or idea* of piety?

❺

Because Euthyphro is doing something very much like what Zeus did, anyone who says that he is doing something impious must be wrong, since surely Zeus never did anything impious. (Socrates is not impressed by this line of argument.)

❻

Giving an example of something fails to clarify the general idea or form, since you may not know *how* and *why* the thing given as an example is the kind of thing in question, and thus fail to really grasp the general idea. Thus Socrates is looking for a general account—something like a definition—of piety, not just examples of specific things that are pious. (See Discussion Question 1.)

say that any action of yours or another's that is of that kind is pious, and if it is not that it is not.

E: If that is how you want it, Socrates, that is how I will tell you.

S: That is what I want.

E: Well then, what is dear to the gods is pious, what is not is impious.

S: Splendid, Euthyphro! You have now answered in the way I wanted. (7) Whether your answer is true I do not know yet, but you will obviously show me that what you say is true.

(7)

Socrates is approving of the general kind of response that Euthyphro has given, not necessarily of its specific content.

E: Certainly.

S: Come then, let us examine what we mean. An action or a man dear to the gods is pious, but an action or a man hated by the gods is impious. They are not the same, but quite opposite, the pious and the impious. Is that not so? (8)

(8)

Here is Euthyphro's second attempt to respond to Socrates: piety is what is dear to the gods—where it becomes clear in what follows that Socrates takes this to mean dear to *any* of the gods.

E: It is indeed.

S: And that seems to be a good statement?

E: I think so, Socrates.

S: We have also stated that the gods are in a state of discord, that they are at odds with each other, Euthyphro, and that they are at enmity with each other. Has that, too, been said?

E: It has.

S: What are the subjects of difference that cause hatred and anger? Let us look at it this way. If you and I were to differ about numbers as to which is the greater, would this difference make us enemies and angry with each other, or would we proceed to count and soon resolve our difference about this?

E: We would certainly do so.

S: Again, if we differed about the larger and the smaller, we would turn to measurement and soon cease to differ.

E: That is so.

S: And about the heavier and the lighter, we would resort to weighing and be reconciled.

E: Of course.

S: What subject of difference would make us angry and hostile to each other if we were unable to come to a decision? Perhaps you do not have an answer ready, but examine as I tell you whether these subjects are the just and the unjust, the beautiful and the ugly, the good and the bad. Are these not the subjects of difference about which, when we are unable to come to a satisfactory decision, you and I and other men become hostile to each other whenever we do?

E: That is the difference, Socrates, about those subjects.

S: What about the gods, Euthyphro? If indeed they have differences, will it not be about these same subjects?

E: It certainly must be so.

S: Then according to your argument, my good Euthyphro, different gods consider different things to be just, beautiful, ugly, good, and bad, for they would not be at odds with one another unless they differed about these subjects, would they?

E: You are right.

S: And they like what each of them considers beautiful, good, and just, and hate the opposites of these?

E: Certainly.

S: But you say that the same things are considered just by some gods and unjust by others, and as they dispute about these things they are at odds and at war with each other. Is that not so?

E: It is.

S: The same things then are loved by the gods and hated by the gods, and would be both god-loved and god-hated.

E: It seems likely.

S: And the same things would be both pious and impious, according to this argument?

E: I'm afraid so.

S: So you did not answer my question, you surprising man. (9) I did not ask you what same thing is both pious and impious, and it appears that what is loved by the gods is also hated by them. So it is in no way surprising if your present action, namely punishing your father, may be pleasing to Zeus but displeasing to Kronos and Ouranos, pleasing to Hephaestus but displeasing to Hera, and so with any other gods who differ from each other on this subject.

(9)

So Euthyphro's second attempt at a general account of piety is a failure. Think about the problem with it and try to see how this might be fixed.

E: I think, Socrates, that on this subject no gods would differ from one another, that whoever has killed anyone unjustly should pay the penalty.

...

S: Come now, my dear Euthyphro, tell me, too, that I may become wiser, what proof you have that all the gods consider that man to have

10

R Here is Euthyphro's third attempt, a modification or correction of the second, as suggested by Socrates.

Notice how it differs from the second attempt in just the way it needs to in order to avoid the objection that was raised against that attempt.

11

Socrates's objection to Euthyphro's third attempt is more complicated and subtle than any of the others. Think carefully about the question: does the piety of something *explain* why the gods love it—or does the fact that the gods love it *explain* why it is pious? The underlying idea here is that if one thing *A* explains another thing *B*, then *A* is *explanatorily prior* to *B*—and *B* therefore cannot also explain *A*, at least not in the same way.

12

You might have to read this paragraph slowly and more than once. Socrates attempts to make clear what it means for one thing to be explanatorily prior to another by considering some further examples. Which thing *explains* the other thing in each of these examples?

13

So, assuming that love is not just arbitrary, there must be some *other* reason that something is loved by someone: some particular characteristic that made that someone love it. And once it is loved by that someone, it then becomes something being loved. That other characteristic would then be explanatorily prior, both to the person loving and to the thing being loved.

been killed unjustly who became a murderer while in your service, was bound by the master of his victim, and died in his bonds before the one who bound him found out from the seers what was to be done with him, and that it is right for a son to denounce and to prosecute his father on behalf of such a man. Come, try to show me a clear sign that all the gods definitely believe this action to be right. If you can give me adequate proof of this, I shall never cease to extol your wisdom.

E: This is perhaps no light task, Socrates, though I could show you very clearly.

S: I understand that you think me more dull-witted than the jury, as you will obviously show them that these actions were unjust and that all the gods hate such actions.

E: I will show it to them clearly, Socrates, if only they will listen to me.

S: They will listen if they think you show them well. But this thought came to me as you were speaking, and I am examining it, saying to myself: "If Euthyphro shows me conclusively that all the gods consider such a death unjust, to what greater extent have I learned from him the nature of piety and impiety? This action would then, it seems, be hated by the gods, but the pious and the impious were not now defined, for what is hated by the gods has also been shown to be loved by them." So I will not insist on this point; let us assume, if you wish, that all the gods consider this unjust and that they all hate it. However, is this the correction we are making in our discussion, that what all the gods hate is impious, and what they all love is pious, and that what some gods love and others hate is neither or both? Is that how you now wish us to define piety and impiety?

E: What prevents us from doing so, Socrates?

S: For my part nothing, Euthyphro, but you look whether on your part this proposal will enable you to teach me most easily what you promised.

E: I would certainly say that the pious is what all the gods love, and the opposite, what all the gods hate, is the impious. **(10)**

S: Then let us again examine whether that is a sound statement, or do we let it pass, and if one of us, or someone else, merely says that something is so, do we accept that it is so? Or should we examine what the speaker means?

E: We must examine it, but I certainly think that this is now a fine statement.

S: We shall soon know better whether it is. Consider this: Is the pious loved by the gods because it is pious, or is it pious because it is loved by the gods? **(11)**

E: I don't know what you mean, Socrates.

S: I shall try to explain more clearly: we speak of something being carried and something carrying, of something being led and something leading, of something being seen and something seeing, and you understand that these things are all different from one another and how they differ?

E: I think I do.

S: So there is something being loved and something loving, and the loving is a different thing.

E: Of course.

S: Tell me then whether that which is being carried is being carried because someone carries it or for some other reason.

E: No, that is the reason.

S: And that which is being led is so because someone leads it, and that which is being seen because someone sees it?

E: Certainly.

S: It is not seen by someone because it is being seen but on the contrary it is being seen because someone sees it, nor is it because it is being led that someone leads it but because someone leads it that it is being led; nor does someone carry an object because it is being carried, but it is being carried because someone carries it. Is what I want to say clear, Euthyphro? I want to say this, namely, that if anything comes to be, or is affected, it does not come to be because it is coming to be, but it is coming to be because it comes to be; nor is it affected because it is being affected but because something affects it. Or do you not agree? **(12)**

E: I do.

S: What is being loved is either something that comes to be or something that is affected by something?

E: Certainly.

S: So it is in the same case as the things just mentioned; it is not loved by those who love it because it is being loved, but it is being loved because they love it? **(13)**

E: Necessarily.

S: What then do we say about the pious, Euthyphro? Surely that it is loved by all the gods, according to what you say?

E: Yes.

S: Is it loved because it is pious, or for some other reason?

E: For no other reason.

S: It is loved then because it is pious, but it is not pious because it is loved?

E: Apparently.

S: And because it is loved by the gods it is being loved and is dear to the gods?

E: Of course.

S: The god-beloved is then not the same as the pious, Euthyphro, nor the pious the same as the god-beloved, as you say it is, but one differs from the other. (14)

E: How so, Socrates?

S: Because we agree that the pious is beloved for the reason that it is pious, but it is not pious because it is loved. Is that not So?

E: Yes.

S: And that the god-beloved, on the other hand, is so because it is loved by the gods, by the very fact of being loved, but it is not loved because it is god-beloved. (15)

E: True.

S: But if the god-beloved and the pious were the same, my dear Euthyphro, and the pious were loved because it was pious, then the god-beloved would be loved because it was god-beloved, and if the god-beloved was god-beloved because it was loved by the gods, then the pious would also be pious because it was loved by the gods; but now you see that they are in opposite cases as being altogether different from each other: the one is of a nature to be loved because it is loved, the other is loved because it is of a nature to be loved. (16) I'm afraid, Euthyphro, that when you were asked what piety is, you did not wish to make its nature clear to me, but you told me [a feature] or quality of it, that the pious has the quality of being loved by all the gods, but you have not yet told me what the pious is. Now, if you will, do not hide things from me but tell me again from the beginning what piety is, whether loved by the gods or having some other quality—we shall not quarrel about that—but be keen to tell me what the pious and the impious are. (17)

E: But Socrates, I have no way of telling you what I have in mind, for whatever proposition we put forward goes around and refuses to stay put where we establish it.

S: Your statements, Euthyphro, seem to belong to my ancestor, Daedalus. If I were stating them and putting them forward, you would perhaps be making fun of me and say that because of my kinship with him my conclusions in discussion run away and will not stay where one puts them. As these propositions are yours, however, we need some other jest, for they will not stay put for you, as you say yourself.

E: I think the same jest will do for our discussion, Socrates, for I am not the one who makes them go round and not remain in the same place; it is you who are the Daedalus; for as far as I am concerned they would remain as they were.

S: It looks as if I was cleverer than Daedalus in using my skill, my friend, in so far as he could only cause to move the things he made himself, but I can make other people's move as well as my own. And the smartest part of my skill is that I am clever without wanting to be, for I would rather have your statements to me remain unmoved than possess the wealth of Tantalus as well as the cleverness of Daedalus. But enough of this. Since I think you are making unnecessary difficulties, I am as eager as you are to find a way to teach me about piety, and do not give up before you do. See whether you think all that is pious is of necessity just.

E: I think so.

S: And is then all that is just pious? Or is all that is pious just, but not all that is just pious, but some of it is and some is not?

E: I do not follow what you are saying, Socrates.

S: Yet you are younger than I by as much as you are wiser. As I say, you are making difficulties because of your wealth of wisdom. Pull yourself together, my dear sir, what I am saying is not difficult to grasp. I am saying the opposite of what the poet said who wrote:

> You do not wish to name Zeus, who had done it, and who made all things grow, for where there is fear there is also shame.

I disagree with the poet. Shall I tell you why?

14 R If its being pious explains why the gods love something, then piety cannot be *the very same thing* as the gods loving that thing (the same thing as its being "god-beloved").

(As a rough analogy: if a rock striking a window is what *explains* the window breaking, then the rock striking the window cannot be the very same thing as the window breaking.)

15 R On the other hand, being loved by the gods does explain why something is god-beloved, and not the other way around.

16 R So the gods love a thing because it is pious, and it becomes god-beloved because they love it—making it clear that being god-beloved cannot be the same thing as being pious, since they stand in different explanatory relations to the gods actually loving that thing.

(Another way to put the point is to say that piety is in fact *two* explanatory steps prior to being god-beloved, and so obviously cannot be identical to it.)

17 So Euthyphro has failed again: this time because he has merely specified a *quality* that piety has—or more specifically a *result* that it produces (it makes gods love things). But he hasn't yet said what piety *is:* he has yet to clarify the *general form or idea* of piety.

E: Please do.

S: I do not think that "where there is fear there is also shame," for I think that many people who fear disease and poverty and many other such things feel fear, but are not ashamed of the things they fear. Do you not think so?

E: I do indeed.

S: But where there is shame, there is also fear. For is there anyone who, in feeling shame and embarrassment at anything, does not also at the same time fear and dread a reputation for wickedness?

E: He is certainly afraid.

S: It is then not right to say "where there is fear there is also shame," but that where there is shame there is also fear, for fear covers a larger area than shame. Shame is a part of fear just as odd is a part of number, with the result that it is not true that where there is number there is also oddness, but that where there is oddness there is also number. Do you follow me now?

E: Surely.

S: This is the kind of thing I was asking before, whether where there is piety there is also justice, but where there is justice there is not always piety, for the pious is a part of justice. Shall we say that, or do you think otherwise?

E: No, but like that, for what you say appears to be right.

S: See what comes next: if the pious is a part of the just, we must, it seems, find out what part of the just it is. Now if you asked me something of what we mentioned just now, such as what part of number is the even, and what number that is, I would say it is the number that is divisible into two equal, not unequal, parts. Or do you not think so?

18

STOP Here is Euthyphro's final attempt to explain what piety is. Try to figure out what is wrong with it.

E: I do.

S: Try in this way to tell me what part of the just the pious is, in order to tell Meletus not to wrong us any more and not to indict me for ungodliness, since I have learned from you sufficiently what is godly and pious and what is not.

19

One meaning of "care of the gods" is inapplicable, since the gods do not need benefits produced by human beings.

E: I think, Socrates, that the godly and pious is the part of the just that is concerned with the care of the gods, while that concerned with the care of men is the remaining part of justice. 18

S: You seem to me to put that very well, but I still need a bit of information. I do not know yet what you mean by care, for you do not mean the care of the gods in the same sense as the care of other things, as, for example, we say, don't we, that not everyone knows how to care for horses, but the horse breeder does.

E: Yes, I do mean it that way.

S: So horse breeding is the care of horses.

E: Yes.

S: Nor does everyone know how to care for dogs, but the hunter does.

E: That is so.

S: So hunting is the care of dogs.

E: Yes.

S: And cattle raising is the care of cattle.

E: Quite so.

S: While piety and godliness is the care of the gods, Euthyphro. Is that what you mean?

E: It is.

S: Now care in each case has the same effect; it aims at the good and the benefit of the object cared for, as you can see that horses cared for by horse breeders are benefited and become better. Or do you not think so?

E: I do.

S: So dogs are benefited by dog breeding, cattle by cattle raising, and so with all the others. Or do you think that care aims to harm the object of its care?

E: By Zeus, no.

S: It aims to benefit the object of its care?

E: Of course.

S: Is piety then, which is the care of the gods, also to benefit the gods and make them better? Would you agree that when you do something pious you make some one of the gods better?

E: By Zeus, no.

S: Nor do I think that this is what you mean—far from it—but that is why I asked you what you meant by the care of gods, because I did not believe you meant this kind of care. 19

E: Quite right, Socrates, that is not the kind of care I mean.

S: Very well, but what kind of care of the gods would piety be?

E: The kind of care, Socrates, that slaves take of their masters.

S: I understand. It is likely to be a kind of service of the gods.

E: Quite so.

S: Could you tell me to the achievement of what goal service to doctors tends? Is it not, do you think, to achieving health?

E: I think so.

S: What about service to shipbuilders? To what achievement is it directed?

E: Clearly, Socrates, to the building of a ship.

S: And service to housebuilders to the building of a house?

E: Yes.

S: Tell me then, my good sir, to the achievement of what aim does service to the gods tend? You obviously know since you say that you, of all men, have the best knowledge of the divine.

E: And I am telling the truth, Socrates.

S: Tell me then, by Zeus, what is that excellent aim that the gods achieve, using us as their servants?

E: Many fine things, Socrates.

S: So do generals, my friend. Nevertheless you could easily tell me their main concern, which is to achieve victory in war, is it not?

E: Of course.

S: The farmers too, I think, achieve many fine things, but the main point of their efforts is to produce food from the earth.

E: Quite so.

S: Well then, how would you sum up the many fine things that the gods achieve?

E: I told you a short while ago, Socrates, that it is a considerable task to acquire any precise knowledge of these things, but, to put it simply, I say that if a man knows how to say and do what is pleasing to the gods at prayer and sacrifice, those are pious actions such as preserve both private houses and public affairs of state. The opposite of these pleasing actions are impious and overturn and destroy everything.

S: You could tell me in far fewer words, if you were willing, the sum of what I asked, Euthyphro, but you are not keen to teach me, that is clear. You were on the point of doing so, but you turned away. If you had given that answer, I should now have acquired from you sufficient knowledge of the nature of piety. As it is, the lover of inquiry must follow his beloved wherever it may lead him. Once more then, what do you say that piety and the pious are? Are they a knowledge of how to sacrifice and pray?

E: They are.

S: To sacrifice is to make a gift to the gods, whereas to pray is to beg from the gods?

E: Definitely, Socrates.

S: It would follow from this statement that piety would be a knowledge of how to give to, and beg from, the gods.

E: You understood what I said very well, Socrates.

S: That is because I am so desirous of your wisdom, and I concentrate my mind on it, so that no word of yours may fall to the ground. But tell me, what is this service to the gods? You say it is to beg from them and to give to them?

E: I do.

S: And to beg correctly would be to ask from them things that we need?

E: What else?

S: And to give correctly is to give them what they need from us, for it would not be skillful to bring gifts to anyone that are in no way needed.

E: True, Socrates.

S: Piety would then be a sort of trading skill between gods and men?

E: Trading yes, if you prefer to call it that.

S: I prefer nothing, unless it is true. But tell me, what benefit do the gods derive from the gifts they receive from us? What they give us is obvious to all. There is for us no good that we do not receive from them, but how are they benefited by what they receive from us? Or do we have such an advantage over them in the trade that we receive all our blessings from them and they receive nothing from us?

E: Do you suppose, Socrates, that the gods are benefited by what they receive from us?

S: What could those gifts from us to the gods be, Euthyphro?

E: What else, do you think, than honour, reverence, and what I mentioned just now, gratitude?

S: The pious is then, Euthyphro, pleasing to the gods, but not beneficial or dear to them?

E: I think it is of all things most dear to them.

S: So the pious is once again what is dear to the gods.

E: Most certainly.

S: When you say this, will you be surprised if your arguments seem to move about instead of staying put? And will you accuse me of being Daedalus who makes them move, though you are yourself much more skillful than Daedalus and make them go round in a circle? Or do you not realize that our argument has moved around and come again to the same place? You surely remember that earlier the pious and the god-beloved were shown not to be the same but different from each other. Or do you not remember?

E: I do.

S: Do you then not realize now that you are saying that what is dear to the gods is the pious? Is this not the same as the god-beloved? Or is it not?

E: It certainly is.

S: Either we were wrong when we agreed before, or, if we were right then, we are wrong now. 20

R Socrates claims that the alternative account of "care of the gods" is the same as the account already refuted.

E: That seems to be so.

S: So we must investigate again from the beginning what piety is, as I shall not willingly give up before I learn this. Do not think me unworthy, but concentrate your attention and tell the truth. For you know it, if any man does, and I must not let you go, like Proteus, before you tell me. If you had no clear knowledge of piety and impiety you would never have ventured to prosecute your old father for murder on behalf of a servant. For fear of the gods you would have been afraid to take the risk lest you should not be acting rightly, and would have been ashamed before men, but now I know well that you believe you have clear knowledge of piety and impiety. So tell me, my good Euthyphro, and do not hide what you think it is.

E: Some other time, Socrates, for I am in a hurry now, and it is time for me to go.

S: What a thing to do, my friend! By going you have cast me down from a great hope I had, that I would learn from you the nature of the pious and the impious and so escape Meletus's indictment by showing him that I had acquired wisdom in divine matters from Euthyphro, and my ignorance would no longer cause me to be careless and inventive about such things, and that I would be better for the rest of my life.

Discussion Questions

1. Suppose that someone asks you to explain some particular term. Why is giving an example of something an inadequate response? For example, suppose someone asked you to explain reggae music—suppose they said, "What does it mean for a piece of music to be reggae music?" If you gave them *an example* of reggae music, would that explain it to them? What should you do instead? How would you clarify the idea of moral rightness?
2. Many people think that the source of morality derives from God's commands or laws. Some such assumption lies behind Dostoevsky's remark: "If God is dead, then everything is permitted." As natural as that may seem, there is a serious problem with it, one that has come to be called the *Euthyphro problem*. Does God say that something is right or command that we do it because it is right, or does it become right because God says so? There is again an issue of explanatory priority: is God merely a good judge of what is *independently* right (so that its being right explains his command) or does God's command *make* something right (so that his command explains its being right)? What must someone who wants to defend the idea that God is the source of morality say in answer to this question? What is the objection to saying that? (Could God have commanded anything at all—even murder or genocide—and would it then have been right?)

Plato

While this work is still referred to as a dialogue, Plato in fact lets Socrates do almost all of the talking. Socrates is addressing a very large jury, one that will decide whether he is to be convicted of the charge of corrupting the youth of Athens; and if convicted, what his sentence will be. (The procedure after conviction was for both the prosecution and the defense to propose punishments, with the jury then deciding between the two.) Socrates argues that he is innocent of the charge. The outcome of the trial was as Plato reports, though there is no way to be sure how accurate his account of Socrates's speech is. (The title of the dialogue comes from the Greek word for *defense:* Socrates's speech is clearly not an apology in the ordinary sense, but neither is there any irony reflected in the title, as one might be tempted to think.)

Apology

I do not know, men of Athens, how my accusers affected you; as for me, I was almost carried away in spite of myself, so persuasively did they speak. And yet, hardly anything of what they said is true. Of the many lies they told, one in particular surprised me, namely that you should be careful not to be deceived by an accomplished speaker like me. That they were not ashamed to be immediately proved wrong by the facts, when I show myself not to be an accomplished speaker at all, that I thought was most shameless on their part—unless indeed they call an accomplished speaker the man who speaks the truth. If they mean that, I would agree that I am an orator, but not after their manner, for indeed, as I say, practically nothing they said was true. From me you will hear the whole truth, though not, by Zeus, gentlemen, expressed in embroidered and stylized phrases like theirs, but things spoken at random and expressed in the first words that come to mind, for I put my trust in the justice of what I say, and let none of you expect anything else. It would not be fitting at my age, as it might be for a young man, to toy with words when I appear before you.

One thing I do ask and beg of you, gentlemen: if you hear me making my defence in the same kind of language as I am accustomed to use in the market place . . . where many of you have heard me, and elsewhere, do not be surprised or create a disturbance on that account. The position is this: this is my first appearance in a lawcourt, at the age of seventy; I am therefore simply a stranger to the manner of speaking here. Just as if I were really a stranger, you would certainly excuse me if I spoke in that dialect and manner in which I had been brought up, so too my present request seems a just one, for you to pay no attention to my manner of speech—be it better or worse—but to concentrate your attention on whether what I say is just or not, for the excellence of a judge lies in this, as that of a speaker lies in telling the truth.

It is right for me, gentlemen, to defend myself first against the first lying accusations made against me and my first accusers, and then against the later accusations and the later accusers. There have been many who have accused me to you for many years now, and none of their accusations are true. These I fear much more than I fear Anytus and his friends, though they too are formidable. These earlier ones, however, are more so, gentlemen; they got hold of most of you from childhood, persuaded you and accused me quite falsely, saying that there is a man called Socrates, a wise man, a student of all things in the sky and below the earth, who makes the worse argument the stronger. Those who spread that rumour, gentlemen, are my dangerous accusers, for their hearers believe that those who study these things do not even believe in the gods. Moreover, these accusers are numerous, and have been at it a long time; also, they spoke to you at an age when you would most readily believe them, some of you being children and adolescents, and they won their case by default, as there was no defence.

What is most absurd in all this is that one cannot even know or mention their names unless one of them is a writer of comedies.* Those who maliciously and slanderously persuaded you—who also, when persuaded themselves then persuaded others—all those are most difficult to

From *Five Dialogues,* translated by G. M. A. Grube (Indianapolis: Hackett Publishing Company, 1981).

*This refers in particular to Aristophanes, whose comedy, *The Clouds,* produced in 423 B.C., ridiculed the (imaginary) school of Socrates.

deal with: one cannot bring one of them into court or refute him; one must simply fight with shadows, as it were, in making one's defence, and cross-examine when no one answers. . . .

Let us then take up the case from its beginning. What is the accusation from which arose the slander in which Meletus trusted when he wrote out the charge against me? What did they say when they slandered me? I must, as if they were my actual prosecutors, read the affidavit they would have sworn. It goes something like this: Socrates is guilty of wrongdoing in that he busies himself studying things in the sky and below the earth; he makes the worse into the stronger argument, and he teaches these same things to others. You have seen this yourselves in the comedy of Aristophanes, a Socrates swinging about there, saying he was walking on air and talking a lot of other nonsense about things of which I know nothing at all. I do not speak in contempt of such knowledge, if someone is wise in these things—lest Meletus bring more cases against me—but, gentlemen, I have no part in it, and on this point I call upon the majority of you as witnesses. I think it right that all those of you who have heard me conversing, and many of you have, should tell each other if anyone of you has ever heard me discussing such subjects to any extent at all. From this you will learn that the other things said about me by the majority are of the same kind.

Not one of them is true. And if you have heard from anyone that I undertake to teach people and charge a fee for it, that is not true either. Yet I think it a fine thing to be able to teach people as Gorgias of Leontini does, and Prodicus of Ceos, and Hippias of Elis.* Each of these men can go to any city and persuade the young, who can keep company with anyone of their own fellow-citizens they want, without paying, to leave the company of these, to join with themselves, pay them a fee, and be grateful to them besides. . . . Certainly I would pride and preen myself if I had this knowledge, but I do not have it, gentlemen.

One of you might perhaps interrupt me and say: "But Socrates, what is your occupation? From where have these slanders come? For surely if you did not busy yourself with something out of the common, all these rumours and talk would not have arisen unless you did something other than most people. Tell us what it is, that we may not speak inadvisedly about you." Anyone who says that seems to be right, and I will try to show you what has caused this reputation and slander. Listen then. Perhaps some of you will think I am jesting, but be sure that all that I shall say is true. What has caused my reputation is none other than a certain kind of wisdom. What kind of wisdom? Human wisdom, perhaps. It may be that I really possess this, while those whom I mentioned just now are wise with a wisdom more than human; else I cannot explain it, for I certainly do not possess it, and whoever says I do is lying and speaks to slander me. Do not create a disturbance, gentlemen, even if you think I am boasting, for the story I shall tell does not originate with me, but I will refer you to a trustworthy source. I shall call upon the god at Delphi as witness to the existence and nature of my wisdom, if it be such. You know Chairephon. He was my friend from youth, and the friend of most of you, as he shared your exile and your return. You surely know the kind of man he was, how impulsive in any course of action. He went to Delphi at one time and ventured to ask the oracle—as I say, gentlemen, do not create a disturbance—he asked if any man was wiser than I, and the Pythian replied that no one was wiser. (1) Chairephon is dead, but his brother will testify to you about this.

(1) The Greeks believed that ordinary people could communicate with the gods by asking questions of the priests at various temples. One of the most respected of these temples was the temple of Apollo located in a small village named Delphi.

Consider that I tell you this because I would inform you about the origin of the slander. When I heard of this reply I asked myself: "Whatever does the god mean? What is his riddle? I am very conscious that I am not wise at all; what then does he mean by saying that I am the wisest? For surely he does not lie; it is not legitimate for him to do so." For a long time I was at a loss as to his meaning; then I very reluctantly turned to some such investigation as this: I went to one of those reputed wise, thinking that there, if anywhere, I could refute the oracle and say to it: "This man is wiser than I, but you said I was." Then, when I examined this man—there is no need for me to

*These were all well-known Sophists. . . . [The Sophists were itinerant teachers of rhetoric and to some extent of philosophy, who received fees for their services. They are reputed, perhaps not altogether fairly, as being skilled in "making the weaker argument appear the stronger"—hence the derivative term "sophism."]

tell you his name, he was one of our public men—my experience was something like this: I thought that he appeared wise to many people and especially to himself, but he was not. I then tried to show him that he thought himself wise, but that he was not. As a result he came to dislike me, and so did many of the bystanders. So I withdrew and thought to myself: "I am wiser than this man; it is likely that neither of us knows anything worthwhile, but he thinks he knows something when he does not, whereas when I do not know, neither do I think I know; so I am likely to be wiser than he to this small extent, that I do not think I know what I do not know." ❷ After this I approached another man, one of those thought to be wiser than he, and I thought the same thing, and so I came to be disliked both by him and by many others.

After that I proceeded systematically. I realized, to my sorrow and alarm, that I was getting unpopular, but I thought that I must attach the greatest importance to the god's oracle, so I must go to all those who had any reputation for knowledge to examine its meaning. And . . . gentlemen of the jury—for I must tell you the truth—I experienced something like this: in my investigation in the service of the god I found that those who had the highest reputation were nearly the most deficient, while those who were thought to be inferior were more knowledgeable. I must give you an account of my journeyings as if they were labours I had undertaken to prove the oracle irrefutable. After the politicians, I went to the poets, the writers of tragedies and dithyrambs and the others, intending in their case to catch myself being more ignorant then they. So I took up those poems with which they seemed to have taken most trouble and asked them what they meant, in order that I might at the same time learn something from them. I am ashamed to tell you the truth, gentlemen, but I must. Almost all the bystanders might have explained the poems better than their authors could. I soon realized that poets do not compose their poems with knowledge, but by some inborn talent and by inspiration, like seers and prophets who also say many fine things without any understanding of what they say. The poets seemed to me to have had a similar experience. At the same time I saw that, because of their poetry, they thought themselves very wise men in other respects, which they were not. So there again I withdrew, thinking that I had the same advantage over them as I had over the politicians.

Finally I went to the craftsmen, for I was conscious of knowing practically nothing, and I knew that I would find that they had knowledge of many fine things. In this I was not mistaken; they knew things I did not know, and to that extent they were wiser than I. But, gentlemen of the jury, the good craftsmen seemed to me to have the same fault as the poets: each of them, because of his success at his craft, thought himself very wise in other most important pursuits, and this error of theirs overshadowed the wisdom they had, so that I asked myself, on behalf of the oracle, whether I should prefer to be as I am, with neither their wisdom nor their ignorance, or to have both. The answer I gave myself and the oracle was that it was to my advantage to be as I am.

As a result of this investigation, gentlemen of the jury, I acquired much unpopularity, of a kind that is hard to deal with and is a heavy burden; many slanders came from these people and a reputation for wisdom, for in each case the bystanders thought that I myself possessed the wisdom that I proved that my interlocutor did not have. What is probable, gentlemen, is that in fact the god is wise and that his oracular response meant that human wisdom is worth little or nothing, and that when he says this man, Socrates, he is using my name as an example, as if he said: "This man among you, mortals, is wisest who, like Socrates, understands that his wisdom is worthless." So even now I continue this investigation as the god bade me—and I go around seeking out anyone, citizen or stranger, whom I think wise. Then if I do not think he is, I come to the assistance of the god and show him that he is not wise. Because of this occupation, I do not have the leisure to engage in public affairs to any extent, nor indeed to look after my own, but I live in great poverty because of my service to the god.

Furthermore, the young men who follow me around of their own free will, those who have most leisure, the sons of the very rich, take pleasure in hearing people questioned; they themselves often imitate me and try to question others. I think they find an abundance of men who believe they have some knowledge but know little or nothing. The result is that those whom they question are angry, not with

STOP Is someone who knows that he doesn't know something—or indeed that he knows nothing worthwhile—nonetheless wiser than someone who mistakenly thinks that he knows something?

themselves but with me. They say: "That man Socrates is a pestilential fellow who corrupts the young." If one asks them what he does and what he teaches to corrupt them, they are silent, as they do not know, but, so as not to appear at a loss, they mention those accusations that are available against all philosophers, about "things in the sky and things below the earth," about "not believing in the gods" and "making the worse the stronger argument"; they would not want to tell the truth, I'm sure, that they have been proved to lay claim to knowledge when they know nothing. These people are ambitious, violent and numerous; they are continually and convincingly talking about me; they have been filling your ears for a long time with vehement slanders against me. . . . That, gentlemen of the jury, is the truth for you. I have hidden or disguised nothing. I know well enough that this very conduct makes me unpopular, and this is proof that what I say is true, that such is the slander against me, and that such are its causes. If you look into this either now or later, this is what you will find.

Let this suffice as a defence against the charges of my earlier accusers. After this I shall try to defend myself against Meletus, that good and patriotic man, as he says he is, and my later accusers. As these are a different lot of accusers, let us again take up their sworn deposition. It goes something like this: Socrates is guilty of corrupting the young and of not believing in the gods in whom the city believes, but in other new divinities. Such is their charge. Let us examine it point by point.

He says that I am guilty of corrupting the young, but I say that Meletus is guilty of dealing frivolously with serious matters, of irresponsibly bringing people into court, and of professing to be seriously concerned with things about none of which he has ever cared, and I shall try to prove that this is so. Come here and tell me, Meletus. Surely you consider it of the greatest importance that our young men be as good as possible?—Indeed I do.

Come then, tell the jury who improves them. You obviously know, in view of your concern. You say you have discovered the one who corrupts them, namely me, and you bring me here and accuse me to the jury. Come, inform the jury and tell them who it is. You see, Meletus, that you are silent and know not what to say. Does this not seem shameful to you and a sufficient proof of what I say, that you have not been concerned with any of this? Tell me, my good sir, who improves our young men?—The laws.

That is not what I am asking, but what person who has knowledge of the laws to begin with?—These jurymen, Socrates.

How do you mean, Meletus? Are these able to educate the young and improve them?—Certainly.

All of them, or some but not others?—All of them.

Very good, by Hera. You mention a great abundance of benefactors. But what about the audience? Do they improve the young or not?—They do, too.

What about the members of Council?—The Councillors, also.

But, Meletus, what about the assembly? Do members of the assembly corrupt the young, or do they all improve them?—They improve them.

All the Athenians, it seems, make the young into fine good men, except me, and I alone corrupt them. Is that what you mean?—That is most definitely what I mean.

You condemn me to a great misfortune. Tell me: does this also apply to horses do you think? That all men improve them and one individual corrupts them? Or is quite the contrary true, one individual is able to improve them, or very few, namely the horse breeders, whereas the majority, if they have horses and use them, corrupt them? Is that not the case, Meletus, both with horses and all other animals? Of course it is, whether you and Anytus say so or not. It would be a very happy state of affairs if only one person corrupted our youth, while the others improved them.

You have made it sufficiently obvious, Meletus, that you have never had any concern for our youth; you show your indifference clearly; that you have given no thought to the subjects about which you bring me to trial.

And by Zeus, Meletus, tell us also whether it is better for a man to live among good or wicked fellow-citizens. Answer, my good man, for I am not asking a difficult question. Do not the wicked do some harm to those who are ever closest to them, whereas good people benefit them?—Certainly.

And does the man exist who would rather be harmed than benefited by his associates? Answer, my good sir, for the law orders you to answer. Is there any man who wants to be harmed?—Of course not.

Come now, do you accuse me here of corrupting the young and making them worse deliberately or unwillingly?—Deliberately.

What follows, Meletus? Are you so much wiser at your age than I am at mine that you understand that wicked people always do some harm to their closest neighbours while good people do them good, but I have reached such a pitch of ignorance that I do not realize this, namely that if I make one of my associates wicked I run the risk of being harmed by him so that I do such a great evil deliberately, as you say? I do not believe you, Meletus, and I do not think anyone else will. ❸ Either I do not corrupt the young or, if I do, it is unwillingly, and you are lying in either case. Now if I corrupt them unwillingly, the law does not require you to bring people to court for such unwilling wrongdoings, but to get hold of them privately, to instruct them and exhort them; for clearly, if I learn better, I shall cease to do what I am doing unwillingly. You, however, have avoided my company and were unwilling to instruct me, but you bring me here, where the law requires one to bring those who are in need of punishment, not of instruction.

And so, gentlemen of the jury, what I said is clearly true: Meletus has never been at all concerned with these matters. . . .

I do not think, gentlemen of the jury, that it requires a prolonged defence to prove that I am not guilty of the charges in Meletus' deposition, but this is sufficient. On the other hand, you know that what I said earlier is true, that I am very unpopular with many people. This will be my undoing, if I am undone, not Meletus or Anytus but the slanders and envy of many people. This has destroyed many other good men and will, I think, continue to do so. There is no danger that it will stop at me.

Someone might say: "Are you not ashamed, Socrates, to have followed the kind of occupation that has led to your being now in danger of death?" However, I should be right to reply to him: "You are wrong, sir, if you think that a man who is any good at all should take into account the risk of life or death; he should look to this only in his actions, whether what he does is right or wrong, whether he is acting like a good or a bad man." . . .

This is the truth of the matter, gentlemen of the jury: wherever a man has taken a position that he believes to be best, or has been placed by his commander, there he must I think remain and face danger, without a thought for death or anything else, rather than disgrace. It would have been a dreadful way to behave, gentlemen of the jury, if . . . when the god ordered me, as I thought and believed, to live the life of a philosopher, to examine myself and others, I had abandoned my post for fear of death or anything else. That would have been a dreadful thing, and then I might truly have justly been brought here for not believing that there are gods, disobeying the oracle, fearing death, and thinking I was wise when I was not. To fear death, gentlemen, is no other than to think oneself wise when one is not, to think one knows what one does not know. No one knows whether death may not be the greatest of all blessings for a man, yet men fear it as if they knew that it is the greatest of evils. And surely it is the most blameworthy ignorance to believe that one knows what one does not know. It is perhaps on this point and in this respect, gentlemen, that I differ from the majority of men, and if I were to claim that I am wiser than anyone in anything, it would be in this, that, as I have no adequate knowledge of things in the underworld, so I do not think I have. I do know, however, that it is wicked and shameful to do wrong, to disobey one's superior, be he god or man. I shall never fear or avoid things of which I do not know, whether they may not be good rather than things that I know to be bad. Even if you acquitted me now and did not believe Anytus, . . . if you said to me in this regard: "Socrates, we do not believe Anytus now; we acquit you, but only on condition that you spend no more time on this investigation and do not practise philosophy, and if you are caught doing so you will die;" if, as I say, you were to acquit me on those terms, I would say to you: "Gentlemen of the jury, I am grateful and I am your friend, but I will obey the god rather than you, and as long as I draw breath and am able, I shall not cease to practise philosophy, to exhort you and in my usual way to point out to any one of you whom I happen to meet: Good Sir, you are

The underlying assumption is that no one deliberately harms himself.

an Athenian, a citizen of the greatest city with the greatest reputation for both wisdom and power; are you not ashamed of your eagerness to possess as much wealth, reputation and honours as possible, while you do not care for nor give thought to wisdom or truth, or the best possible state of your soul?" Then, if one of you disputes this and says he does care, I shall not let him go at once or leave him, but I shall question him, examine him and test him, and if I do not think he has attained the goodness that he says he has, I shall reproach him because he attaches little importance to the most important things and greater importance to inferior things. ❹ I shall treat in this way anyone I happen to meet, young and old, citizen and stranger, and more so the citizens because you are more kindred to me. Be sure that this is what the god orders me to do, and I think there is no greater blessing for the city than my service to the god. . . .

❹

Here is an account of what Socrates believes his job as a philosopher to be: to examine himself and others about claims to knowledge, to challenge himself and others to attain goodness, and to reproach those who attach importance to the wrong things.

Now if by saying this I corrupt the young, this advice must be harmful, but if anyone says that I give different advice, he is talking nonsense. On this point I would say to you, gentlemen of the jury: "Whether you believe Anytus or not, whether you acquit me or not, do so on the understanding that this is my course of action, even if I am to face death many times." Do not create a disturbance, gentlemen, but abide by my request not to cry out at what I say but to listen, for I think it will be to your advantage to listen, and I am about to say other things at which you will perhaps cry out. By no means do this. Be sure that if you kill the sort of man I say I am, you will not harm me more than yourselves. Neither Meletus nor Anytus can harm me in any way; he could not harm me, for I do not think it is permitted that a better man be harmed by a worse; certainly he might kill me, or perhaps banish or disfranchise me, which he and maybe others think to be great harm, but I do not think so. I think he is doing himself much greater harm doing what he is doing now, attempting to have a man executed unjustly. Indeed, gentlemen of the jury, I am far from making a defence now on my own behalf, as might be thought, but on yours, to prevent you from wrongdoing by mistreating the god's gift to you by condemning me; for if you kill me you will not easily find another like me. I was attached to this city by the god—though it seems a ridiculous thing to say—as upon a great and noble horse which was somewhat sluggish because of its size and needed to be stirred up by a kind of gadfly. ❺ It is to fulfill some such function that I believe the god has placed me in the city. I never cease to rouse each and every one of you, to persuade and reproach you all day long and everywhere I find myself in your company.

❺

A gadfly is a horsefly, the kind of fly that bites and irritates horses and cattle. The metaphorical meaning of a gadfly as a persistent, somewhat irritating critic originates in this dialogue.

Another such man will not easily come to be among you, gentlemen, and if you believe me you will spare me. You might easily be annoyed with me as people are when they are aroused from a doze, and strike out at me; if convinced by Anytus you could easily kill me, and then you could sleep on for the rest of your days, unless the god, in his care for you, sent you someone else. That I am the kind of person to be a gift of the god to the city you might realize from the fact that it does not seem like human nature for me to have neglected all my own affairs and to have tolerated this neglect now for so many years while I was always concerned with you, approaching each one of you like a father or an elder brother to persuade you to care for virtue. Now if I profited from this by charging a fee for my advice, there would be some sense to it, but you can see for yourselves that, for all their shameless accusations, my accusers have not been able in their impudence to bring forward a witness to say that I have ever received a fee or ever asked for one. I, on the other hand, have a convincing witness that I speak the truth, my poverty.

It may seem strange that while I go around and give this advice privately and interfere in private affairs, I do not venture to go to the assembly and there advise the city. You have heard me give the reason for this in many places. I have a divine sign from the god which Meletus has ridiculed in his deposition. This began when I was a child. It is a voice, and whenever it speaks it turns me away from something I am about to do, but it never encourages me to do anything. This is what has prevented me from taking part in public affairs, and I think it was quite right to prevent me. Be sure, gentlemen of the jury, that if I had long ago attempted to take part in politics, I should have died long ago, and benefited neither you nor myself. Do not be angry with me for speaking the truth; no man will survive who genuinely opposes you or any other crowd and prevents the occurrence of many unjust and illegal happenings in the city. A man who really fights for justice must lead a private, not a public, life if he is to survive for even a short time. . . . 6

Do you think I would have survived all these years if I were engaged in public affairs and, acting as a good man must, came to the help of justice and considered this the most important thing? Far from it, gentlemen of the jury, nor would any other man. Throughout my life, in any public activity I may have engaged in, I am the same man as I am in private life. I have never come to an agreement with anyone to act unjustly, neither with anyone else nor with any one of those who they slanderously say are my pupils. I have never been anyone's teacher. If anyone, young or old, desires to listen to me when I am talking and dealing with my own concerns, I have never begrudged this to anyone, but I do not converse when I receive a fee and not when I do not. I am equally ready to question the rich and the poor if anyone is willing to answer my questions and listen to what I say. And I cannot justly be held responsible for the good or bad conduct of these people, as I never promised to teach them anything and have not done so. If anyone says that he has learned anything from me, or that he heard anything privately that the others did not hear, be assured that he is not telling the truth.

Why then do some people enjoy spending considerable time in my company? You have heard why, gentlemen of the jury, I have told you the whole truth. They enjoy hearing those being questioned who think they are wise, but are not. And this is not unpleasant. To do this has, as I say, been enjoined upon me by the god, by means of oracles and dreams, and in every other way that a divine manifestation has ever ordered a man to do anything. This is true, gentlemen, and can easily be established.

If I corrupt some young men and have corrupted others, then surely some of them who have grown older and realized that I gave them bad advice when they were young should now themselves come up here to accuse me and avenge themselves. If they were unwilling to do so themselves, then some of their kindred, their fathers or brothers or other relations should recall it now if their family had been harmed by me. I see many of these present here, first Crito, my contemporary and fellow demesman . . . ; next Lysanias of Sphettus . . . ; also Antiphon the Cephisian . . . ; Nicostratus . . . , brother of Theodotus, and Theodotus has died so he could not influence him; . . . there is Adeimantus . . . , brother of Plato here; Acantidorus, brother of Apollodorus here.

I could mention many others, some one of whom surely Meletus should have brought in as witness in his own speech. If he forgot to do so, then let him do it now; I will yield time if he has anything of the kind to say. You will find quite the contrary, gentlemen. These men are all ready to come to the help of the corruptor, the man who has harmed their kindred, as Meletus and Anytus say. Now those who were corrupted might well have reason to help me, but the uncorrupted, their kindred who are older men, have no reason to help me except the right and proper one, that they know that Meletus is lying and that I am telling the truth.

Very well, gentlemen of the jury. This, and maybe other similar things, is what I have to say in my defence. Perhaps one of you might be angry as he recalls that when he himself stood trial on a less dangerous charge, he begged and implored the jury with many tears, that he brought his children and many of his friends and family into court to arouse as much pity as he could, but that I do none of these things, even though I may seem to be running the ultimate risk. Thinking of this, he might feel resentful toward me and, angry about this, cast his vote in anger. If there is such a one among you—I do not deem there is, but if there is—I think it would be right to say in reply: My good sir, I too have a . . . family, indeed three sons, gentlemen of the jury, of whom one is an adolescent while two are children. Nevertheless, I will not beg you to acquit me by bringing them here. Why do I do none of these things? Not through arrogance, gentlemen, nor through lack of respect for you. Whether I am brave in the face of death is another matter, but with regard to my reputation and yours and that of the whole city, it does not seem right to me to do these things, especially at my age and with my reputation. For it is generally believed, whether it be true or false, that in certain respects Socrates is superior to the majority of men. Now if those of you who are considered superior, be it in wisdom or courage or whatever other virtue makes them so, are seen behaving like that, it would be a

Is Socrates right that a person who really fights for justice cannot survive in public life, in politics?

disgrace. Yet I have often seen them do this sort of thing when standing trial, men who are thought to be somebody, doing amazing things as if they thought it a terrible thing to die, and as if they were to be immortal if you did not execute them. I think these men bring shame upon the city so that a stranger, too, would assume that those who are outstanding in virtue among the Athenians, whom they themselves select from themselves to fill offices of state and receive other honours, are in no way better than women. You should not act like that, gentlemen of the jury, those of you who have any reputation at all, and if we do, you should not allow it. You should make it very clear that you will more readily convict a man who performs these pitiful dramatics in court and so makes the city a laughingstock, than a man who keeps quiet.

Quite apart from the question of reputation, gentlemen, I do not think it right to supplicate the jury and to be acquitted because of this, but to teach and persuade them. It is not the purpose of a juryman's office to give justice as a favour to whoever seems good to him, but to judge according to law, and this he has sworn to do. We should not accustom you to perjure yourselves, nor should you make a habit of it. This is irreverent conduct for either of us.

Do not deem it right for me, gentlemen of the jury, that I should act towards you in a way that I do not consider to be good or just or pious, especially, by Zeus, as I am being prosecuted by Meletus here for impiety; clearly, if I convinced you by my supplication to do violence to your oath of office, I would be teaching you not to believe that there are gods, and my defence would convict me of not believing in them. This is far from being the case, gentlemen, for I do believe in them as none of my accusers do. I leave it to you and the god to judge me in the way that will be best for me and for you.

[The jury now gives its verdict of guilty, and Meletus asks for the penalty of death.]

There are many other reasons for my not being angry with you for convicting me, gentlemen of the jury, and what happened was not unexpected. I am much more surprised at the number of votes cast on each side, for I did not think the decision would be by so few votes but by a great many. As it is, a switch of only thirty votes would have acquitted me. I think myself that I have been cleared on Meletus' charges, and not only this, but it is clear to all that, if Anytus and Lycon had not joined him in accusing me, he would have been fined a thousand drachmas for not receiving a fifth of the votes.

He assesses the penalty at death. So be it. What counter-assessment should I propose to you, gentlemen of the jury? Clearly it should be a penalty I deserve, and what do I deserve to suffer or to pay because I have deliberately not led a quiet life but have neglected what occupies most people: wealth, household affairs, the position of general or public orator or the other offices, the political clubs and factions that exist in the city? I thought myself too honest to survive if I occupied myself with those things. I did not follow that path that would have made me of no use either to you or to myself, but I went to each of you privately and conferred upon him what I say is the greatest benefit, by trying to persuade him not to care for any of his belongings before caring that he himself should be as good and as wise as possible, not to care for the city's possessions more than for the city itself, and to care for other things in the same way. What do I deserve for being such a man? Some good, gentlemen of the jury, if I must truly make an assessment according to my deserts, and something suitable. What is suitable for a poor benefactor who needs leisure to exhort you? Nothing is more suitable, gentlemen, than for such a man to be fed in the Prytaneum,* much more suitable for him than for any one of you who has won a victory at Olympia with a pair or a team of horses. The Olympian victor makes you think yourself happy; I make you be happy. Besides, he does not need food, but I do. So if I must make a just assessment of what I deserve, I assess it at this: free meals in the Prytaneum.

When I say this you may think, as when I spoke of appeals to pity and entreaties, that I speak arrogantly, but that is not the case, gentlemen of the jury; rather it is like this: I am convinced that I never willingly wrong anyone, but I am not convincing you of this, for we have

*The Prytaneum was the magistrates' hall or town hall of Athens in which public entertainments were given, particularly to Olympian victors on their return home.

talked together but a short time. If it were the law with us, as it is elsewhere, that a trial for life should not last one but many days, you would be convinced, but now it is not easy to dispel great slanders in a short time. Since I am convinced that I wrong no one, I am not likely to wrong myself, to say that I deserve some evil and to make some such assessment against myself. What should I fear? That I should suffer the penalty Meletus has assessed against me, of which I say I do not know whether it is good or bad? Am I then to choose in preference to this something that I know very well to be an evil and assess the penalty at that? Imprisonment? Why should I live in prison, always subjected to the ruling magistrates the Eleven? A fine, and imprisonment until I pay it? That would be the same thing for me, as I have no money. Exile? for perhaps you might accept that assessment.

I should have to be inordinately fond of life, gentlemen of the jury, to be so unreasonable as to suppose that other men will easily tolerate my company and conversation when you, my fellow citizens, have been unable to endure them, but found them a burden and resented them so that you are now seeking to get rid of them. Far from it, gentlemen. It would be a fine life at my age to be driven out of one city after another, for I know very well that wherever I go the young men will listen to my talk as they do here. If I drive them away, they will themselves persuade their elders to drive me out; if I do not drive them away, their fathers and relations will drive me out on their behalf.

Perhaps someone might say: But Socrates, if you leave us will you not be able to live quietly, without talking? Now this is the most difficult point on which to convince some of you. If I say that it is impossible for me to keep quiet because that means disobeying the god, you will not believe me and will think I am being ironical. On the other hand, if I say that it is the greatest good for a man to discuss virtue every day and those other things about which you hear me conversing and testing myself and others, for the unexamined life is not worth living for man, you will believe me even less. (7)

What I say is true, gentlemen, but it is not easy to convince you. At the same time, I am not accustomed to think that I deserve any penalty. If I had money, I would assess the penalty at the amount I could pay, for that would not hurt me, but I have none, unless you are willing to set the penalty at the amount I can pay, and perhaps I could pay you one mina of silver.* So that is my assessment.

Plato here, gentlemen of the jury, and Crito and Critoboulus and Apollodorus bid me put the penalty at thirty minae, and they will stand surety for the money. Well then, that is my assessment, and they will be sufficient guarantee of payment.

[The jury now votes again and sentences Socrates to death.]

It is for the sake of a short time, gentlemen of the jury, that you will acquire the reputation and the guilt, in the eyes of those who want to denigrate the city, of having killed Socrates, a wise man, for they who want to revile you will say that I am wise even if I am not. If you had waited but a little while, this would have happened of its own accord. You see my age, that I am already advanced in years and close to death. I am saying this not to all of you but to those who condemned me to death, and to these same jurors I say: Perhaps you think that I was convicted for lack of such words as might have convinced you, if I thought I should say or do all I could to avoid my sentence. Far from it. I was convicted because I lacked not words but boldness and shamelessness and the willingness to say to you what you would most gladly have heard from me, lamentations and tears and my saying and doing many things that I say are unworthy of me but that you are accustomed to hear from others. I did not think then that the danger I ran should make me do anything mean, nor do I now regret the nature of my defence. I would much rather die after this kind of defence than live after making the other kind. Neither I nor any other man should, on trial or in war, contrive to avoid death at any cost. Indeed it is often obvious in battle that one could escape death by throwing away one's weapons and by turning to supplicate one's pursuers, and there are many ways to avoid death in every kind of danger if one will venture to do or say anything

(7)

Here is the famous Socratic saying that the unexamined life is not worth living. It has a rather more literal meaning in this context than it usually does.

*One mina was 100 drachmas, equivalent to, say, twenty-five dollars, though in purchasing power probably five times greater. In any case, a ridiculously small sum under the circumstances.

to avoid it. It is not difficult to avoid death, gentlemen of the jury, it is much more difficult to avoid wickedness, for it runs faster than death. Slow and elderly as I am, I have been caught by the slower pursuer, whereas my accusers, being clever and sharp, have been caught by the quicker, wickedness. I leave you now, condemned to death by you, but they are condemned by truth to wickedness and injustice. So I maintain my assessment, and they maintain theirs. This perhaps had to happen, and I think it is as it should be.

8

STOP How much does Socrates's view of what a philosopher should do when threatened by death depend on the view that death is not an evil? Would a true philosopher be deterred from pursuing truth and justice if death were genuinely the worse of evils?

Now I want to prophesy to those who convicted me, for I am at the point when men prophesy most, when they are about to die. I say gentlemen, to those who voted to kill me, that vengeance will come upon you immediately after my death, a vengeance much harder to bear than that which you took in killing me. You did this in the belief that you would avoid giving an account of your life, but I maintain that quite the opposite will happen to you. There will be more people to test you, whom I now held back, but you did not notice it. They will be more difficult to deal with as they will be younger and you will resent them more. You are wrong if you believe that by killing people you will prevent anyone from reproaching you for not living in the right way. To escape such tests is neither possible nor good, but it is best and easiest not to discredit others but to prepare oneself to be as good as possible. With this prophecy to you who convicted me, I part from you.

I should be glad to discuss what has happened with those who voted for my acquittal during the time that the officers of the court are busy and I do not yet have to depart to my death. So, gentlemen, stay with me awhile, for nothing prevents us from talking to each other while it is allowed. To you, as being my friends, I want to show the meaning of what has occurred. A surprising thing has happened to me, judges—you I would rightly call judges. At all previous times my usual mantic sign frequently opposed me, even in small matters, when I was about to do something wrong, but now that, as you can see for yourselves, I was faced with what one might think, and what is generally thought to be, the worst of evils, my divine sign has not opposed me, either when I left home at dawn, or when I came into court, or at any time that I was about to say something during my speech. Yet in other talks it often held me back in the middle of my speaking, but now it has opposed no word or deed of mine. What do I think is the reason for this? I will tell you. What has happened to me may well be a good thing, and those of us who believe death to be an evil are certainly mistaken. I have convincing proof of this, for it is impossible that my customary sign did not oppose me if I was not about to do what was right. 8

Let us reflect in this way, too, that there is good hope that death is a blessing, for it is one of two things: either the dead are nothing and have no perception of anything, or it is, as we are told, a change and a relocating for the soul from here to another place. If it is complete lack of perception, like a dreamless sleep, then death would be a great advantage. For I think that if one had to pick out that night during which a man slept soundly and did not dream, put beside it the other nights and days of his life, and then see how many days and nights had been better and more pleasant than that night, not only a private person but the great king would find them easy to count compared with the other days and nights. If death is like this I say it is an advantage, for all eternity would then seem to be no more than a single night. If, on the other hand, death is a change from here to another place, and what we are told is true and all who have died are there, what greater blessing could there be, gentlemen of the jury? If anyone arriving in Hades will have escaped from those who call themselves judges here, and will find those true judges who are said to sit in judgement there, Minos and Radamanthus and Aeacus and Triptolemus and the other demi-gods who have been upright in their own life, would that be a poor kind of change? Again, what would one of you give to keep company with Orpheus and Musaeus, Hesiod and Homer? I am willing to die many times if that is true. It would be a wonderful way for me to spend my time whenever I met Palamedes and Ajax, the son of Telamon, and any other of the men of old who died through an unjust conviction, to compare my experience with theirs. I think it would be pleasant. Most important, I could spend my time testing and examining people there, as I do here, as to who among them is wise, and who thinks he is, but is not. 9

9

Socrates pretty obviously ignores the seeming possibility that death is a relocation of the soul to a place of great pain and suffering. Does he have any justification for his view of what a life after death (if there is one) would be like?

What would one not give, gentlemen of the jury, for the opportunity to examine the man who led the great expedition against Troy, or Odysseus, or

Sisyphus, and innumerable other men and women one could mention. It would be an extraordinary happiness to talk with them, to keep company with them and examine them. In any case, they would certainly not put one to death for doing so. They are happier there than we are here in other respects, and for the rest of time they are deathless, if indeed what we are told is true.

You too must be of good hope as regards death, gentlemen of the jury, and keep this one truth in mind, that a good man cannot be harmed either in life or in death, and that his affairs are not neglected by the gods. What has happened to me now has not happened of itself, but it is clear to me that it was better for me to die now and to escape from trouble. That is why my divine sign did not oppose me at any point. So I am certainly not angry with those who convicted me, or with my accusers. Of course that was not their purpose when they accused and convicted me, but they thought they were hurting me, and for this they deserve blame. This much I ask from them: when my sons grow up, avenge yourselves by causing them the same kind of grief that I caused you, if you think they care for money or anything else more than they care for virtue, or if they think they are somebody when they are nobody. Reproach them as I reproach you, that they do not care for the right things and think they are worthy when they are not worthy of anything. If you do this, I shall have been justly treated by you, and my sons also.

Now the hour to part has come. I go to die, you go to live. Which of us goes to the better lot is known to no one, except the god.

Discussion Questions

1. What do you think about the famous Socratic saying that the unexamined life is not worth living? Contrast that with the saying that ignorance is bliss. What assumptions would someone make about the value and importance of human life to defend each one of these very different philosophies of life? Which one strikes you as one you might want to live by? Why? What is wrong with the other one?
2. Do you think that Socrates performed an important function for his society? Do we have any people in our public life who function as gadflies? Do you know anyone personally who functions as a gadfly? Do you think that Socrates should have been put to death? Should someone be punished for being a gadfly?

Bertrand Russell

Bertrand Russell (1872–1970) was a British philosopher who made important contributions to the foundations of mathematics, logic, epistemology, and many other areas of philosophy. Russell was also very active politically. (He spent time in prison because of his antiwar activities.) He won the Nobel Prize for Literature in 1950.

This selection is the last chapter of one of Russell's most famous books, *The Problems of Philosophy*. In this chapter, Russell explains what he thinks is valuable about philosophy, while seeming to admit that there is relatively little genuine philosophical knowledge.

The Value of Philosophy

Having now come to the end of our brief and very incomplete review of the problems of philosophy, it will be well to consider, in conclusion, what is the value of philosophy and why it ought to be studied. It is the more necessary to consider this question, in view of the fact that many men, under the influence of science or of practical affairs, are inclined to doubt whether philosophy is anything better than innocent but useless

From *The Problems of Philosophy* (Oxford University Press, 1959).

trifling, hair-splitting distinctions, and controversies on matters concerning which knowledge is impossible.

This view of philosophy appears to result, partly from a wrong conception of the ends of life, partly from a wrong conception of the kind of goods which philosophy strives to achieve. Physical science, through the medium of inventions, is useful to innumerable people who are wholly ignorant of it; thus the study of physical science is to be recommended, not only, or primarily, because of the effect on the student, but rather because of the effect on mankind in general. Thus utility does not belong to philosophy. If the study of philosophy has any value at all for others than students of philosophy, it must be only indirectly, through its effects upon the lives of those who study it. It is in these effects, therefore, if anywhere, that the value of philosophy must be primarily sought.

But further, if we are not to fail in our endeavour to determine the value of philosophy, we must first free our minds from the prejudices of what are wrongly called 'practical' men. The 'practical' man, as this word is often used, is one who recognizes only material needs, who realizes that men must have food for the body, but is oblivious of the necessity of providing food for the mind. If all men were well off, if poverty and disease had been reduced to their lowest possible point, there would still remain much to be done to produce a valuable society; and even in the existing world the goods of the mind are at least as important as the goods of the body. It is exclusively among the goods of the mind that the value of philosophy is to be found; and only those who are not indifferent to these goods can be persuaded that the study of philosophy is not a waste of time. ❶

Philosophy, like all other studies, aims primarily at knowledge. The knowledge it aims at is the kind of knowledge which gives unity and system to the body of the sciences, and the kind which results from a critical examination of the grounds of our convictions, prejudices, and beliefs. But it cannot be maintained that philosophy has had any very great measure of success in its attempts to provide definite answers to its questions. If you ask a mathematician, a mineralogist, a historian, or any other man of learning, what definite body of truths has been ascertained by his science, his answer will last as long as you are willing to listen. But if you put the same question to a philosopher, he will, if he is candid, have to confess that his study has not achieved positive results such as have been achieved by other sciences. ❷ It is true that this is partly accounted for by the fact that, as soon as definite knowledge concerning any subject becomes possible, this subject ceases to be called philosophy, and becomes a separate science. The whole study of the heavens, which now belongs to astronomy, was once included in philosophy; Newton's great work was called 'the mathematical principles of natural philosophy'. Similarly, the study of the human mind, which was a part of philosophy, has now been separated from philosophy and has become the science of psychology. Thus, to a great extent, the uncertainty of philosophy is more apparent than real: those questions which are already capable of definite answers are placed in the sciences, while those only to which, at present, no definite answer can be given, remain to form the residue which is called philosophy. ❸

This is, however, only a part of the truth concerning the uncertainty of philosophy. There are many questions—and among them those that are of the profoundest interest to our spiritual life—which, so far as we can see, must remain insoluble to the human intellect unless its powers become of quite a different order from what they are now. Has the universe any unity of plan or purpose, or is it a fortuitous concourse of atoms? Is consciousness a permanent part of the universe, giving hope of indefinite growth in wisdom, or is it a transitory accident on a small planet on which life must ultimately become impossible? Are good and evil of importance to the universe or only to man? Such questions are asked by philosophy, and variously answered by various philosophers. But it would seem that, whether answers be otherwise discoverable or not, the answers suggested by philosophy are none of them demonstrably true. Yet, however slight may be the hope of discovering an answer, it is part of the business of philosophy to continue the consideration of such questions, to make us aware of their importance, to examine all the approaches to them, and to keep alive that speculative interest in the universe which is apt to be killed by confining ourselves to definitely ascertainable knowledge. ❹

❶

STOP Think of some examples of things that are "food for the mind" or "goods of the mind." Do you know anyone who is what Russell calls a "practical man" (or woman)?

❷

One could agree with this assessment, while still thinking that philosophy itself has generated *some* body of knowledge that is genuine, even if not to the same extent as the sciences.

❸

This is an important point: when we learn how to investigate a set of issues in a way that yields clear and firmly established results, those issues stop being part of philosophy, and instead become a new area of science (including social science). The questions that we do not yet know how to deal with in this way are the ones that remain in the province of philosophy, including some—as Russell goes on to suggest—that seem unlikely ever to be settled in a scientific way. (Think about why this might be so.)

❹

R If you insisted that you would think about only those questions that had clear, ascertainable black or white answers, then you would have to refuse to think about many of the most important questions concerning the human condition.

Many philosophers, it is true, have held that philosophy could establish the truth of certain answers to such fundamental questions. They have supposed that what is of most importance in religious beliefs could be proved by strict demonstration to be true. In order to judge of such attempts, it is necessary to take a survey of human knowledge, and to form an opinion as to its methods and its limitations. On such a subject it would be unwise to pronounce dogmatically; but if the investigations of our previous chapters have not led us astray, we shall be compelled to renounce the hope of finding philosophical proofs of religious beliefs. We cannot, therefore, include as part of the value of philosophy any definite set of answers to such questions. **5** Hence, once more, the value of philosophy must not depend upon any supposed body of definitely ascertainable knowledge to be acquired by those who study it.

The value of philosophy is, in fact, to be sought largely in its very uncertainty. The man who has no tincture of philosophy goes through life imprisoned in the prejudices derived from common sense, from the habitual beliefs of his age or his nation, and from convictions which have grown up in his mind without the co-operation or consent of his deliberate reason. To such a man the world tends to become definite, finite, obvious; common objects rouse no questions, and unfamiliar possibilities are contemptuously rejected. As soon as we begin to philosophize, on the contrary, we find, as we saw in our opening chapters, that even the most everyday things lead to problems to which only very incomplete answers can be given. Philosophy, though unable to tell us with certainty what is the true answer to the doubts which it raises, is able to suggest many possibilities which enlarge our thoughts and free them from the tyranny of custom. **6** Thus, while diminishing our feeling of certainty as to what things are, it greatly increases our knowledge as to what they may be; it removes the somewhat arrogant dogmatism of those who have never travelled into the region of liberating doubt, and it keeps alive our sense of wonder by showing familiar things in an unfamiliar aspect.

Apart from its utility in showing unsuspected possibilities, philosophy has a value—perhaps its chief value—through the greatness of the objects which it contemplates, and the freedom from narrow and personal aims resulting from this contemplation. The life of the instinctive man is shut up within the circle of his private interests: family and friends may be included, but the outer world is not regarded except as it may help or hinder what comes within the circle of instinctive wishes. In such a life there is something feverish and confined, in comparison with which the philosophic life is calm and free. The private world of instinctive interests is a small one, set in the midst of a great and powerful world which must, sooner or later, lay our private world in ruins. Unless we can so enlarge our interests as to include the whole outer world, we remain like a garrison in a beleagured fortress, knowing that the enemy prevents escape and that ultimate surrender is inevitable. In such a life there is no peace, but a constant strife between the insistence of desire and the powerlessness of will. In one way or another, if our life is to be great and free, we must escape this prison and this strife. **7**

One way of escape is by philosophic contemplation. Philosophic contemplation does not, in its widest survey, divide the universe into two hostile camps—friends and foes, helpful and hostile, good and bad—it views the whole impartially. Philosophic contemplation, when it is unalloyed, does not aim at proving that the rest of the universe is akin to man. All acquisition of knowledge is an enlargement of the Self, but this enlargement is best attained when it is not directly sought. It is obtained when the desire for knowledge is alone operative, by a study which does not wish in advance that its objects should have this or that character, but adapts the Self to the characters which it finds in its objects. **8** This enlargement of Self is not obtained when, taking the Self as it is, we try to show that the world is so similar to this Self that knowledge of it is possible without any admission of what seems alien. The desire to prove this is a form of self-assertion and, like all self-assertion, it is an obstacle to the growth of Self which it desires, and of which the Self knows that it is capable. Self-assertion, in philosophic speculation as elsewhere, views

Some of the authors in Chapter 7 of this book think that one can establish the existence of God through something approaching a demonstrative proof. (But even if Russell is right that such attempts at proofs are very unlikely to succeed, that in itself is something very much worth knowing.)

Russell's point here is at least similar to the one that Socrates made by saying that "the unexamined life is not worth living": a life ruled by custom and common-sense prejudice is not really an examined one.

STOP If Russell is right about the contrast between the philosophic life and the life of "the instinctive man," then the philosophic life seems clearly better. Do you agree with his assessment? (He proceeds to offer further reasons in what follows.)

How is the acquisition of knowledge supposed to result in an "enlargement" of the self? At least part of the idea is that because philosophical contemplation has the goal of understanding something as it is in itself and not merely as it appears to us, philosophical contemplation will rarely just confirm previous prejudices in a way that would promote intellectual stagnation. (In another work, *A History of Western Philosophy*, Russell describes the true philosopher as one who "follows the argument where it leads," meaning that such a person does not shy away from a conclusion just because it does not agree with his own previous views—again we can see here an echo of Socrates.)

The metaphor of the self enlarging, ultimately, to some sort of infinity is hard to make sense of in a clear way. (See Discussion Question 3.) But whatever it means, it will be the result of philosophical contemplation only if there is more to reality than what we, in our practical modes, think there is.

10

R To say that humans are the measure of all things is seemingly to reject the claim that there are aspects of reality that are not created by and do not depend on humans.

Russell has argued in previous chapters of this book for a **realist** view, one which insists that there are aspects of reality that are independent of humans in this way.

11

Some philosophers call this the "God's eye point of view." You will also see it referred to as *sub specie aeternitatis:* from the perspective of eternity. From this perspective, one's own concerns or views are given the proper significance, whereas from the subjective perspective, those same concerns might seem much more important than they really are.

12

It is easy to see how an impartial point of view might lead to the desire for truth and justice, but less easy to see why it should result in universal love (rather than, for example, universal indifference).

13

The questions that do all this must not be thought of as mere questions, involving no development or elaboration. What philosophical study and inquiry yields is rather elaborated **dialectic:** questions together with alternative answers, arguments for those answers, objections to the answers and arguments, replies to those objections, etc. To understand a philosophical issue is to understand this much more complicated picture.

the world as a means to its own ends; thus it makes the world of less account than Self, and the Self sets bounds to the greatness of its goods. In contemplation, on the contrary, we start from the not-Self, and through its greatness the boundaries of Self are enlarged; through the infinity of the universe the mind which contemplates it achieves some share in infinity. (9)

For this reason greatness of soul is not fostered by those philosophies which assimilate the universe to Man. Knowledge is a form of union of Self and not-Self; like all union, it is impaired by dominion, and therefore by any attempt to force the universe into conformity with what we find in ourselves. There is a widespread philosophical tendency towards the view which tells us that Man is the measure of all things, that truth is man-made, that space and time and the world of universals are properties of the mind, and that, if there be anything not created by the mind, it is unknowable and of no account for us. This view, if our previous discussions were correct, is untrue; but in addition to being untrue, it has the effect of robbing philosophic contemplation of all that gives it value, since it fetters contemplation to Self. What it calls knowledge is not a union with the not-Self, but a set of prejudices, habits, and desires, making an impenetrable veil between us and the world beyond. The man who finds pleasure in such a theory of knowledge is like the man who never leaves the domestic circle for fear his word might not be law. (10)

The true philosophic contemplation, on the contrary, finds its satisfaction in every enlargement of the not-Self, in everything that magnifies the objects contemplated, and thereby the subject contemplating. Everything, in contemplation, that is personal or private, everything that depends upon habit, self-interest, or desire, distorts the object, and hence impairs the union which the intellect seeks. By thus making a barrier between subject and object, such personal and private things become a prison to the intellect. The free intellect will see as God might see, without a *here* and *now,* without hopes and fears, without the trammels of customary beliefs and traditional prejudices, calmly, dispassionately, in the sole and exclusive desire of knowledge—knowledge as impersonal, as purely contemplative, as it is possible for man to attain. (11) Hence also the free intellect will value more the abstract and universal knowledge into which the accidents of private history do not enter, than the knowledge brought by the senses, and dependent, as such knowledge must be, upon an exclusive and personal point of view and a body whose sense-organs distort as much as they reveal.

The mind which has become accustomed to the freedom and impartiality of philosophic contemplation will preserve something of the same freedom and impartiality in the world of action and emotion. It will view its purposes and desires as parts of the whole, with the absence of insistence that results from seeing them as infinitesimal fragments in a world of which all the rest is unaffected by any one man's deeds. The impartiality which, in contemplation, is the unalloyed desire for truth, is the very same quality of mind which, in action, is justice, and in emotion is that universal love which can be given to all, and not only to those who are judged useful or admirable. (12) Thus contemplation enlarges not only the objects of our thoughts, but also the objects of our actions and our affections: it makes us citizens of the universe, not only of one walled city at war with all the rest. In this citizenship of the universe consists man's true freedom, and his liberation from the thraldom of narrow hopes and fears.

Thus, to sum up our discussion of the value of philosophy; Philosophy is to be studied, not for the sake of any definite answers to its questions since no definite answers can, as a rule, be known to be true, but rather for the sake of the questions, themselves; because these questions enlarge our conception of what is possible, enrich our intellectual imagination and diminish the dogmatic assurance which closes the mind against speculation; but above all because, through the greatness of the universe which philosophy contemplates, the mind also is rendered great, and becomes capable of that union with the universe which constitutes its highest good. (13)

Discussion Questions

1. A dogmatic belief is a belief firmly held without any basis or reason. Dogmatic beliefs are typically resistant to change. Do you think it is ever appropriate to be dogmatic? Might one argue that there are some arenas in which asking for reasons makes no sense? Think about religion and politics. Some people think that you should never talk about religion or politics with friends or family, because the arguments will just get ugly. How might a philosophically minded person (someone who thinks that you should always look for reasons) respond to such a view?

2. Russell thinks that philosophy can protect you from the "tyranny of custom." Think of some examples of periods of history when the custom dictated that things should be a way that we now disagree with. How could a philosophical attitude protect the people then from the tyranny of custom? What kinds of questions should a philosopher ask now, to be protected from the tyranny of custom?

3. Russell uses the metaphor of a self *enlarging* and achieving some sense of the infinity of the universe by contemplating it philosophically. Suppose that John had never thought about anything philosophical before he went to college in 1969, but 35 years later, he is a very philosophical person, often engaging in philosophical contemplation. What exactly is different about John? One important difference might be that when John thinks now about some important issue, he can conceive of many more possibilities than he could 35 years ago, rather than just being content with the standard answer endorsed by his government or accepted by his peers. He may also ask many more *questions* now than he did then, both of himself, but also of others, asking them to clarify and justify their views. There is a sense in which we might call the younger John "small-minded." Is this what Russell is getting at when he talks about the self enlarging? Is such enlargement valuable for anyone or only for those who are inclined in that direction? Should everyone study philosophy?

2

CHAPTER

Knowledge and Skepticism

The selections in this chapter are concerned with two main issues in the general area of philosophy known as the theory of knowledge or **epistemology,** both having to do with whether and how knowledge of certain specified kinds is possible, and with the possibility and plausibility of **skepticism** with respect to the kinds of knowledge in question. The first and larger section of the chapter focuses on one of the most central issues of modern philosophy: the problem of the external world, which asks whether and how beliefs about material objects outside the mind are justified on the basis of sense perception. A second section deals with the problem of **induction,** which asks whether and why it is justifiable to infer from apparent regularities found in observation to more general conclusions that extend beyond those observations.

Before we discuss these more specific problems, it will be helpful to say something about the concept of knowledge itself. According to a definition often characterized as traditional or standard, knowledge is (1) *belief* that is (2) *true* and (3) adequately *justified.* Problems can be raised about each of these three elements, but it will be adequate for the purposes of this chapter to understand **belief** as the mental acceptance or affirmation of a propositional claim and **truth** as the correspondence or agreement of that claim with whatever it is about. The nature of **justification** in the sense relevant to knowledge has been the subject of widespread debate in recent philosophy, but the authors of all the present selections would have accepted the view that justification is having a good reason or warrant for thinking that the claim in question is true.*

One other preliminary remark is perhaps worth making: the issues discussed in this chapter depend heavily on concepts and terminology that are relatively technical and difficult. You will need to work at mastering these, and you should only expect gradual success, especially at first. This also applies to the material in this introduction: we have kept it short so that you can reread it easily, and if you do so, you will find concepts and issues that were initially puzzling gradually becoming clear.

*It has become clear as a result of relatively recent discussion that the traditional definition of knowledge is inadequate in that there are cases in which the three conditions are satisfied but it is intuitively clear that genuine knowledge is not present. Intuitively, these are cases in which the belief is true in an accidental way that does not connect appropriately with the way in which it is justified. The problem has become known as "the Gettier problem," named after the philosopher who first discovered it, and the interested student can easily find discussions of it in philosophical dictionaries and encyclopedias.

Do We Have Knowledge of the External World?

It seems entirely obvious from the standpoint of both common sense and science, first, that we have a great deal of knowledge of material objects, and of the material world generally; and, second, that the basis of this knowledge is sense experience. The basic issue is how this works, and in particular how sense experience provides us with justification of the sort just explained for the beliefs about material objects that we arrive at on the basis of it. One initial question concerns the nature of sense experience itself: when we have the sense experience of, for example, a table, what is it that we are aware of in the most direct or immediate way—what is it that is "directly before the mind"? Contrary to the apparent view of common sense, *most* of the philosophers in this section would reply that the most *direct* or *immediate* object of awareness in sense experience is *not* the external physical object (the table) whose presence the experience seems in some way to reflect, but rather a subjective mental entity: a perceptual *idea,* in the terminology of John Locke and George Berkeley, or a sense-datum (plural: sense-data), in the terminology of more recent philosophers. Both René Descartes and Locke take such a view more or less for granted, as does Laurence BonJour; Berkeley argues for it at considerable length; and Thomas Reid rejects it. Sextus Empiricus also seems to have something like this view of sense experience in mind.

If this view of the nature of sense experience is accepted, then the question becomes how claims about material objects can be justified on the basis of awareness of sensory ideas or sense-data. One alternative here is **representative realism:** the view that perceptual beliefs about material objects can be justified by an argument or inference starting from an awareness of the ideas or sense-data that lead us to have those beliefs and seem in some way to represent the corresponding objects. Descartes, Locke, and BonJour all defend versions of such a view, while Berkeley and Reid reject the possibility of any cogent inference of this sort.

A second, initially less obvious alternative is to say that material objects, rather than existing outside of and independently of the mind, are in fact themselves nothing more than systematic collections or patterns of sensory ideas or sense-data, including both those that are actually experienced and those that would be experienced under various conditions. All such views are versions of **idealism.** Berkeley defends one specific version of idealism, according to which the ideas that make up "real" material objects are systematically put into our human minds by God (who is thus the ultimate source of their reality). A more recent version of idealism that dispenses with God and takes the availability of orderly patterns of sense-data to be itself the most fundamental, not further explainable fact about reality is called **phenomenalism;** this view is explained and criticized by BonJour. (Views of this sort are likely to seem quite puzzling and hard to take seriously from a common-sense standpoint, and you will have to work to get them clearly in mind.)

A third alternative, seemingly much closer to common sense than either of the others, is to reject the common denominator of these other two views, the idea that the immediate object of awareness in perceptual experience is a sensory idea or sense-datum, and hold instead that we are directly or immediately aware of material objects themselves, with no need for the sort of justifying inference invoked by the representative realists. Once referred to as naïve realism because it was thought to be philosophically untenable in an obvious way, such a view has more recently been referred to simply as **direct realism.** A version of direct realism is defended by Reid, who argues that the acceptability of our sensory beliefs about the material world is a "first principle" of human thought, one that requires no further defense.

A final alternative is **skepticism:** in relation to the problem of knowledge of the external world, the view that we have no such knowledge and that the impression that we do is simply an illusion. One way to argue for skepticism is by appeal to the problems that face the various positive accounts of how such knowledge works, problems that turn out to be very serious. But it is also possible to argue more directly for a skeptical conclusion. The final selection in this part of the chapter is a brief excerpt from perhaps the most famous representative of the ancient skeptical school of philosophy, Sextus Empiricus, who argues that we can have no knowledge of the true nature of external objects.

Is Induction Justified?

The problem of induction concerns the justification for inferring from regularities observed in experience to more general claims. Thus suppose that a large number of cases of some observable property or category A have been observed (by various observers and under widely varied collateral conditions)—for example, a large number of eggs laid by robins have been observed in many different locations with as much variation of other conditions (temperature, time of year, elevation, etc.) as the habits of robins permit. Suppose also that all the observed cases of A have also been cases of some further observable property or category B—all of the observed robin's eggs have been blue-green and speckled. (A more general version of the problem would include the possibility that some definite and stable fraction m/n of A's, rather than all of them, have been B's.) Given an observational premise of this sort, inductive reasoning of the most standard sort leads to the conclusion that *all* cases of A (observed or not, past, present, or future) are also cases of B—that all robin's eggs are blue-green and speckled. (Or in the more general version, the conclusion would be that approximately m/n of all A's are B's.)

It is obvious that reasoning of this sort is generally taken for granted by common sense and very extensively relied upon by science. (Here you should stop to reflect on how very many of the things that we think that we know about the world rely on reasoning of this sort: claims about which foods are safe and nourishing, about the behavior of various sorts of animals, about weather conditions, about human behavior in various sorts of circumstances, about the properties of various sorts of minerals and other substances, etc., etc.) The question is whether such reasoning is rationally justified, and if so, why: that is, why such a conclusion is genuinely likely to be *true* whenever the corresponding premise is true. Hume considers this issue in the more specific context of a causal claim (with A the supposed cause and B the supposed effect, and observed A's all being followed by B's). Having posed the problem, he argues for the skeptical view that there is no rational justification at all for an inductive conclusion because there is no cogent reasoning from the observational premise to the inductive conclusion. (He also offers a psychological account of why we reason in this way.) Wesley Salmon recapitulates Hume's account and then surveys a number of different responses, rejecting most of them but arguing that one response is at least promising. A. C. Ewing (in the course of a more general discussion of a priori knowledge) defends one of the responses that Salmon rejects: a rationalist solution that holds that inductive reasoning is justified a priori.

Appendix: A Priori Justification and Knowledge

A third epistemological issue that is, on some views at least, highly relevant to these other two is the issue of a priori knowledge, knowledge whose justification does not depend on sense experience. Salmon and Ewing differ fundamentally on the nature of such knowledge and, as a result, on whether an a priori justification of induction is possible. And while this is not discussed very explicitly in the readings, the sort of representative realist solution to the problem of the external world that is defended by Descartes, Locke, and BonJour would apparently also have to rely on the sort of a priori knowledge that Ewing accepts and Salmon rejects: a priori knowledge that is not merely definitional (or "tautological") in character. For only knowledge of this sort could apparently justify the inference from claims about sensory experience to claims about external material objects—as BonJour explains (following Hume), such an inference could not be justified by experience since there is no way from a representative realist standpoint to experience a connection or correlation between experience and such objects. What follows is a brief introduction to a priori knowledge and the questions it raises.

The issue of a priori knowledge is structured around three main distinctions, all of them complicated and subtle—and easily confused with one another. First, there is a **metaphysical** distinction between two ways in which a proposition or claim can be true or false. Some propositions, most philosophers agree, are logically or metaphysically **necessary:** true in any world or situation that is logically or metaphysically possible; while others are logically or metaphysically **contingent:** true in some logically or metaphysically possible worlds and not in others. Thus, for example, propositions of logic and mathematics are usually held to be necessary in this sense, while most propositions about things and happenings in the material world are contingent—*contingent truths* if they are in fact true in the actual world. (Some unfortunate propositions are **necessarily false:** false in every logically or metaphysically possible world; the proposition that 2 + 2 = 5 is an example.)

Second, there is the **epistemological** distinction between two different ways in which a proposition can be *justified:* two different sorts of reasons for thinking that it is true (and derivatively, assuming that knowledge requires justification, two different kinds of knowledge). While it seems obvious that much of our knowledge depends for its justification on sense experience and perhaps also other, similar sorts of experience, such as introspective experience (and so is justified **empirically** or *a posteriori*), it has seemed equally obvious to most philosophers that there is knowledge that does not depend on sense experience for its justification, but is instead a priori: justified via pure reason or thought alone. Here the most obvious examples are again the claims of logic and mathematics, but there are many other sorts of claims that have been claimed (rightly or wrongly) to be justified a priori: metaphysical claims (for example, the claim that there must be an explanation for everything that happens or that space has only three dimensions); various claims about common-sense properties and relations (that nothing can be red all over and green all over at the same time or that all cubes have 12 edges); and also some **ethical** claims (such as that causing unnecessary suffering is morally wrong or that racial discrimination is unjust). In cases like these, it is claimed, someone who adequately understands the claim in question can simply "see" on an intuitive basis that it is true, indeed that it *must* be true. The central issues here are: First, how is such a priori knowledge possible, given that it is not justified by sense experience? Where exactly does the justification for such claims come from? If the appeal is to a priori intuition, what does such intuition amount to and how exactly does it work? And, second, what specific sorts of things are knowable on this sort of basis? In particular, does a priori knowledge include only essentially trivial (even though perhaps sometimes complicated) matters of *definition* (such as the claim that all bachelors are unmarried)—claims often referred to as **tautologies** or, more technically, as "analytic"?

Third, there is a logical or structural distinction between two kinds of propositions, analytic and synthetic. The explicit formulation of this distinction derives from the great German philosopher Immanuel Kant. As Kant defines the notion, an **analytic** proposition is one of subject-predicate form whose predicate is included in its subject, either explicitly (for example, the claim that all tall men are tall) or implicitly (for example, the claim that all bachelors are unmarried). The point of the distinction for Kant is that if a proposition is analytic, then it is seemingly quite easy to see how it can be justified and known a priori: simply by understanding the concepts involved and noticing the relation of containment. What is problematic is how any **synthetic** proposition—one that does *not* have this sort of form or logical structure, that is, in which the predicate is *not* contained in the subject—could still be justified and known a priori, though this is something that Kant nonetheless believes to occur. (What makes this distinction especially tricky is that some philosophers, such as Salmon in some places, have retained these terms and the basic idea that a certain sort of logical structure can be used to explain a priori justification, while altering Kant's account of what this structural feature is. This raises the issue, often not addressed very explicitly, of whether the new account of analyticity has the same capacity to explain a priori justification that the old one did, something that cannot be assumed just because the same term "analytic" is used. You should keep this question in mind as you read Salmon.)

The main opposed positions on the issue of the a priori are versions of **empiricism** and **rationalism.** Empiricism is a general view about human cognition that involves two rather different main theses, each of them having to do with the relation between cognition and sense experience, and each of them reflected in Locke's thought, though one much more clearly and unambiguously than the other. The first thesis, most standardly referred to as **concept empiricism** (but it could also, in relation to the terminology used by Locke and others, be called *idea* empiricism), is a claim about where and how the human mind acquires the ideas or concepts that it uses to think about the world or indeed about anything. According to the concept empiricist, all concepts are derived from sense experience (construed broadly so as to also include introspective experience). Here the main opposing view is the claim, held by Descartes and his rationalist successors, that at least some ideas or concepts are innate, "programmed" into the mind at birth (with this "programming" usually attributed to God).

The second main strand of empiricism (the one that is more relevant to the main issue about a priori knowledge) lacks a completely standard label, but will be referred to here as **justificatory empiricism.** This is a view about the *reasons* or *warrant* for thinking that beliefs or propositional claims are true. According to one version of justificatory empiricism, all of the justification for claims that are not mere logical or definitional tautologies (not analytic in Kant's sense or perhaps in some other sense of that term) must derive from sense experience (again construed broadly so as to include introspection). A version of this **moderate empiricist** view is defended by Salmon, in the course of his discussion of induction.* The main alternative to moderate empiricism is the **moderate rationalist** view that a priori justification and a priori knowledge include more than mere definitional tautologies or analytic propositions. Instead, it is claimed, the human mind has the capacity for direct a priori insight into certain necessary features of reality. Here the main examples would be the kinds of claims briefly listed above, none of which are, according to the rationalist, mere matters of definition or analytic in any epistemologically helpful sense. (The moderate rationalist does not claim that all justification and knowledge is a priori—a view that very few philosophers since perhaps Plato have ever held.) Such a view is defended by Ewing.

Do We Have Knowledge of the External World?

René Descartes

René Descartes (1596–1650), a French philosopher and mathematician, was one of the most important and influential philosophers of all time. Descartes is called "the father of modern philosophy" because several of the central problems and themes of modern (post-Renaissance) philosophy first appear in his work: most fundamentally, the insistence on beginning with questions about knowledge (epistemological questions) rather than questions about reality (metaphysical questions). Among the more specific philosophical problems that first appear clearly in Descartes are the problem of the external world (concerning how claims about material objects can be justified on the basis of sense experience) and the mind-body problem (see Chapter 3). The *Meditations* is his most important and influential work.

Descartes's fundamental motivation for asking questions about knowledge is reflected in the very first sentence of the *Meditations:* "Several years have now passed since I first realized how numerous were the false opinions that in my youth I had taken to be true, and thus how doubtful were all those that I had subsequently built upon them." Descartes lived in a time of great intellectual ferment, when medieval views were still being replaced by more modern ones and the scientific revolution was just under way. It was clear to

*There is also a more radical version of empiricism that denies the existence of a priori justification or knowledge of any sort; this view is not represented in the present anthology. The main proponent of this more radical version of empiricism is the American philosopher and logician W. V. O. Quine.

him on the basis of the many conflicting opinions and arguments with which he was confronted, that many of the opinions he had previously accepted from various sources were very likely to be false. The central issue of the *Meditations* is how to correct this situation. In writing the *Meditations,* Descartes is attempting to lay bare his process of thought so that the reader can follow along with him, think with him, and thereby come to the same conclusions he does.

Descartes's solution to the problem of how to eliminate erroneous beliefs is to accept only beliefs that are *indubitable,* in the sense of being incapable of being mistaken and thereby certain. His method for achieving such certainty is to systematically doubt whole categories of belief, withholding assent from them on the basis of the mere *possibility* that they are false. He is thus suggesting that genuine knowledge requires justification that is *conclusive:* reasons that are strong enough to *guarantee* the truth of the claim in question. (Thus understood, Descartes agrees with the traditional conception of knowledge with one addition: knowledge is not merely justified true belief, but rather *conclusively* justified true belief.)

By the end of *Meditation One,* Descartes has suspended belief in every opinion that he has considered, first on the basis of the possibility that he might be dreaming and later on the basis of the much more radical possibility that he might be deceived by an all-powerful "evil genius." But in *Meditation Two,* he finds a belief that cannot be doubted for even the latter of these reasons: the belief that he himself exists as a thinking thing. Later he identifies other beliefs about which he thinks he can be certain on essentially the same basis: beliefs about his various conscious states of mind. And so the project in *Meditations Three* and *Six* is to reclaim as knowledge the previously suspended beliefs (or at least as many of them as possible) on the basis of the indubitable beliefs identified in *Meditation Two.* In the end, you will have to try to judge whether or not Descartes is successful at securing a *foundation* on the basis of which his previously held beliefs can be justified: that is, on the basis of which *conclusive* reasons can be given for thinking that those beliefs are *true.*

From Meditations on First Philosophy

MEDITATION ONE: Concerning Those Things That Can Be Called into Doubt

Several years have now passed since I first realized how numerous were the false opinions that in my youth I had taken to be true, and thus how doubtful were all those that I had subsequently built upon them. ❶ And thus I realized that once in my life I had to raze everything to the ground and begin again from the original foundations, if I wanted to establish anything firm and lasting in the sciences. But the task seemed enormous, and I was waiting until I reached a point in my life that was so timely that no more suitable time for undertaking these plans of action would come to pass. For this reason, I procrastinated for so long that I would henceforth be at fault, were I to waste the time that remains for carrying out the project by brooding over it. Accordingly, I have today suitably freed my mind of all cares, secured for myself a period of leisurely tranquility, and am withdrawing into solitude. At last I will apply myself earnestly and unreservedly to this general demolition of my opinions.

Yet to bring this about I will not need to show that all my opinions are false, which is perhaps something I could never accomplish. But reason now persuades me that I should withhold my assent no less carefully from opinions that are not completely certain and indubitable than I would from those that are patently false. For this reason, it will suffice for the rejection of all of these opinions, if I find in each of them some reason for doubt. ❷ Nor therefore need I survey each opinion individually, a task that would be endless. Rather, because undermining the foundations will cause whatever has been built

From *Meditations on First Philosophy,* 3rd ed., translated by Donald A. Cress (Indianapolis: Hackett, 1993).

❶ *Stop and Think*

Can you think of things that you believed when you were younger but no longer believe are true? Might some (or even many) of the things that you now believe turn out to be false in the same way? (Suppose someone asked you for your reasons for being confident about the truth of various beliefs of which you are confident (think of specific examples): what would your answer be?)

❷ *Definition*

This is Descartes's famous *method of doubt:* doubt anything that can possibly be false, thereby arriving (if anything is left) at certainty. Notice that he is not seeking merely *psychological* certainty. Many people are convinced of various things (perhaps that God exists), even though they can give no reasons for thinking that they are true, but this is not the kind of certainty that will help to avoid error (since something that is psychologically certain can still be false). Instead he is looking for a kind of certainty that guarantees truth: beliefs for which there is a *conclusive* reason.

upon them to crumble of its own accord, I will attack straightaway those principles which supported everything I once believed. ❸

Rather than scrutinizing beliefs individually, Descartes proposes to examine the *foundations* upon which whole categories of beliefs rest; the first such category, discussed in the following paragraphs, is beliefs justified by sense experience. (The idea of a *foundation* for belief or knowledge appeals to an architectural metaphor—think about the analogy between building construction and cognition that it suggests.)

Surely whatever I had admitted until now as most true I received either from the senses or through the senses. However, I have noticed that the senses are sometimes deceptive; and it is a mark of prudence never to place our complete trust in those who have deceived us even once.

But perhaps, even though the senses do sometimes deceive us when it is a question of very small and distant things, still there are many other matters concerning which one simply cannot doubt, even though they are derived from the very same senses: for example, that I am sitting here next to the fire, wearing my winter dressing gown, that I am holding this sheet of paper in my hands, and the like. But on what grounds could one deny that these hands and this entire body are mine? Unless perhaps I were to liken myself to the insane, whose brains are impaired by such an unrelenting vapor of black bile that they steadfastly insist that they are kings when they are utter paupers, or that they are arrayed in purple robes when they are naked, or that they have heads made of clay, or that they are gourds, or that they are made of glass. But such people are mad, and I would appear no less mad, were I to take their behavior as an example for myself.

This would all be well and good, were I not a man who is accustomed to sleeping at night, and to experiencing in my dreams the very same things, or now and then even less plausible ones, as these insane people do when they are awake. How often does my evening slumber persuade me of such ordinary things as these: that I am here, clothed in my dressing gown, seated next to the fireplace—when in fact I am lying undressed in bed! But right now my eyes are certainly wide awake when I gaze upon this sheet of paper. This head which I am shaking is not heavy with sleep. I extend this hand consciously and deliberately, and I feel it. Such things would not be so distinct for someone who is asleep. As if I did not recall having been deceived on other occasions even by similar thoughts in my dreams! As I consider these matters more carefully, I see so plainly that there are no definitive signs by which to distinguish being awake from being asleep. ❹ As a result, I am becoming quite dizzy, and this dizziness nearly convinces me that I am asleep.

❹ *Restatement/Summary*

R This paragraph contains Descartes's reason for doubting this first category of beliefs.

Let us assume then, for the sake of argument, that we are dreaming and that such particulars as these are not true: that we are opening our eyes, moving our head, and extending our hands. Perhaps we do not even have such hands, or any such body at all. Nevertheless, it surely must be admitted that the things seen during slumber are, as it were, like painted images, which could only have been produced in the likeness of true things, and that therefore at least these general things—eyes, head, hands, and the whole body—are not imaginary things, but are true and exist. For indeed when painters themselves wish to represent sirens and satyrs by means of especially bizarre forms, they surely cannot assign to them utterly new natures. Rather, they simply fuse together the members of various animals. Or if perhaps they concoct something so utterly novel that nothing like it has ever been seen before (and thus is something utterly fictitious and false), yet certainly at the very least the colors from which they fashion it ought to be true. And by the same token, although even these general things—eyes, head, hands, and the like—could be imaginary, still one has to admit that at least certain other things that are even more simple and universal are true. It is from these components, as if from true colors, that all those images of things that are in our thought are fashioned, be they true or false. ❺

❺

R The suggestion is that the creativity involved in dreams is limited to the recombination of elements derived in some other way. This means that the dreaming hypothesis does not provide a reason for thinking that everything involved in our experience is mistaken: the basic elements may still be true, even if the ways in which they are combined are mistaken.

This class of things appears to include corporeal nature in general, together with its extension; the shape of extended things; their quantity, that is, their size and number; as well as the place where they exist; the time through which they endure, and the like.

Thus it is not improper to conclude from this that physics, astronomy, medicine, and all the other disciplines that are dependent upon the consideration of composite things are doubtful, and that, on the other hand, arithmetic, geometry, and other such disciplines, which treat of nothing but the simplest and most general things and which are indifferent as to whether these things do or do not in fact exist, contain something certain and indubitable. For whether I am awake or asleep, two plus three make five, and a square does not have more than four sides. It does not seem possible that such obvious truths should be subject to the suspicion of being false. ❻

❻

R Thus while sciences that deal with complex things are called into question by the dreaming hypothesis, those that deal with these simpler elements are not.

The examples Descartes gives at the end of this paragraph suggest that he has in mind at least primarily beliefs justified on a completely different basis than sense experience: **a priori** beliefs justified by reason or rational thought, rather than sense experience (which could be just a dream).

Be that as it may, there is fixed in my mind a certain opinion of long standing, namely that there exists a God who is able to do anything and by whom I, such as I am, have been created. How do I know that he did not bring it about that there is no earth at all, no heavens, no extended thing, no shape, no size, no place, and yet bringing it about that all these things appear to me to exist precisely as they do now? Moreover, since I judge that others sometimes make mistakes in matters that they believe they know most perfectly, may I not, in like fashion, be deceived every time I add two and three or count the sides of a square, or perform an even simpler operation, if that can be imagined? But perhaps God has not willed that I be deceived in this way, for he is said to be supremely good. Nonetheless, if it were repugnant to his goodness to have created me such that I be deceived all the time, it would also seem foreign to that same goodness to permit me to be deceived even occasionally. But we cannot make this last assertion. 7

. . .

Accordingly, I will suppose not a supremely good God, the source of truth, but rather an evil genius, supremely powerful and clever, who has directed his entire effort at deceiving me. I will regard the heavens, the air, the earth, colors, shapes, sounds, and all external things as nothing but the bedeviling hoaxes of my dreams, with which he lays snares for my credulity. I will regard myself as not having hands, or eyes, or flesh, or blood, or any senses, but as nevertheless falsely believing that I possess all these things. I will remain resolute and steadfast in this meditation, and even if it is not within my power to know anything true, it certainly is within my power to take care resolutely to withhold my assent to what is false, lest this deceiver, however powerful, however clever he may be, have any effect on me. 8 But this undertaking is arduous, and a certain laziness brings me back to my customary way of living. I am not unlike a prisoner who enjoyed an imaginary freedom during his sleep, but, when he later begins to suspect that he is dreaming, fears being awakened and nonchalantly conspires with these pleasant illusions. In just the same way, I fall back of my own accord into my old opinions, and dread being awakened, lest the toilsome wakefulness which follows upon a peaceful rest must be spent thenceforward not in the light but among the inextricable shadows of the difficulties now brought forward.

Meditation Two: Concerning the Nature of the Human Mind: That It Is Better Known Than the Body

Yesterday's meditation has thrown me into such doubts that I can no longer ignore them, yet I fail to see how they are to be resolved. It is as if I had suddenly fallen into a deep whirlpool; I am so tossed about that I can neither touch bottom with my foot, nor swim up to the top. Nevertheless I will work my way up and will once again attempt the same path I entered upon yesterday. I will accomplish this by putting aside everything that admits of the least doubt, as if I had discovered it to be completely false. I will stay on this course until I know something certain, or, if nothing else, until I at least know for certain that nothing is certain. Archimedes sought but one firm and immovable point in order to move the entire earth from one place to another. Just so, great things are also to be hoped for if I succeed in finding just one thing, however slight, that is certain and unshaken.

Therefore I suppose that everything I see is false. I believe that none of what my deceitful memory represents ever existed. I have no senses whatever. Body, shape, extension, movement, and place are all chimeras. What then will be true? Perhaps just the single fact that nothing is certain.

But how do I know there is not something else, over and above all those things that I have just reviewed, concerning which there is not even the slightest occasion for doubt? Is there not some God, or by whatever name I might call him, who instills these very thoughts in me? But why would I think that, since I myself could perhaps be the author of these thoughts? Am I not then at least something? But I have already denied that I have any senses and any body. Still I hesitate; for what follows from this? Am I so tied to a body and to the senses that I cannot exist without them? But I have persuaded myself that there is absolutely nothing in the world: no sky, no earth, no minds, no bodies. Is it then the case that I too do not exist? But doubtless I did exist, if I persuaded myself of something. But

7 *Editor Comment*

Here is an issue that will become important later on in *Meditation Six:* God, being perfectly good, would seemingly not have made me so that I fall into error all the time. The problem is that God's goodness seems incompatible with my making any errors at all, which I obviously do. (No resolution of the issue is offered at this point.)

8

R Here is Descartes's second and much more important reason for doubting whole categories of belief, one that is much more powerful than the one that appeals to the possibility of dreaming because it calls many more beliefs into question, including apparently those (like 2 + 3 = 5) that result from a priori reason.

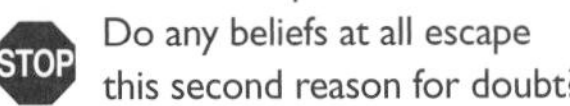

Do any beliefs at all escape this second reason for doubt?

there is some deceiver or other who is supremely powerful and supremely sly and who is always deliberately deceiving me. Then too there is no doubt that I exist, if he is deceiving me. And let him do his best at deception, he will never bring it about that I am nothing so long as I shall think that I am something. Thus, after everything has been most carefully weighed, it must finally be established that this pronouncement "I am, I exist" is necessarily true every time I utter it or conceive it in my mind. 9

9

The insight here is the one that Descartes expresses more succinctly in another work (his *Discourse on Method*) as (in Latin) *"Cogito ergo sum,"* "I think, therefore I am"—often referred to just as the Cogito.

STOP What exactly is the claim that is supposed to be indubitable? Is Descartes right that even the evil genius is unable to deceive him about the truth of that claim: to make him believe that it is true when it is really false?

But I do not yet understand sufficiently what I am—I, who now necessarily exist. And so from this point on, I must be careful lest I unwittingly mistake something else for myself, and thus err in that very item of knowledge that I claim to be the most certain and evident of all. Thus, I will meditate once more on what I once believed myself to be, prior to embarking upon these thoughts. For this reason, then, I will set aside whatever can be weakened even to the slightest degree by the arguments brought forward, so that eventually all that remains is precisely nothing but what is certain and unshaken.

What then did I [formerly] think I was? A man, of course. But what is a man? Might I not say a "rational animal"? No, because then I would have to inquire what "animal" and "rational" mean. And thus from one question I would slide into many more difficult ones. Nor do I now have enough free time that I want to waste it on subtleties of this sort. Instead, permit me to focus here on what came spontaneously and naturally into my thinking whenever I pondered what I was. Now it occurred to me first that I had a face, hands, arms, and this entire mechanism of bodily members: the very same as are discerned in a corpse, and which I referred to by the name "body." It next occurred to me that I took in food, that I walked about, and that I sensed and thought various things; these actions I used to attribute to the soul. But as to what this soul might be, I either did not think about it or else I imagined it a rarified I-know-not-what, like a wind, or a fire, or ether, which had been infused into my coarser parts. But as to the body I was not in any doubt. On the contrary, I was under the impression that I knew its nature distinctly. Were I perhaps tempted to describe this nature such as I conceived it in my mind, I would have described it thus: by "body," I understand all that is capable of being bounded by some shape, of being enclosed in a place, and of filling up a space in such a way as to exclude any other body from it; of being perceived by touch, sight, hearing, taste, or smell; of being moved in several ways, not, of course, by itself, but by whatever else impinges upon it. For it was my view that the power of self-motion, and likewise of sensing or of thinking, in no way belonged to the nature of the body. Indeed I used rather to marvel that such faculties were to be found in certain bodies.

But now what am I, when I suppose that there is some supremely powerful and, if I may be permitted to say so, malicious deceiver who deliberately tries to fool me in any way he can? Can I not affirm that I possess at least a small measure of all those things which I have already said belong to the nature of the body? I focus my attention on them, I think about them, I review them again, but nothing comes to mind. I am tired of repeating this to no purpose. But what about those things I ascribed to the soul? What about being nourished or moving about? Since I now do not have a body, these are surely nothing but fictions. What about sensing? Surely this too does not take place without a body; and I seemed to have sensed in my dreams many things that I later realized I did not sense. What about thinking? Here I make my discovery: thought exists; it alone cannot be separated from me. I am; I exist—this is certain. But for how long? For as long as I am thinking; for perhaps it could also come to pass that if I were to cease all thinking I would then utterly cease to exist. At this time I admit nothing that is not necessarily true. I am therefore precisely nothing but a thinking thing; that is, a mind, or intellect, or understanding, or reason—words of whose meanings I was previously ignorant. Yet I am a true thing and am truly existing; but what kind of thing? I have said it already: a thinking thing.

What else am I? I will set my imagination in motion. I am not that concatenation of members we call the human body. Neither am I even some subtle air infused into these members, nor a wind, nor a fire, nor a vapor, nor a breath, nor anything I devise for myself. For I have supposed these things to be nothing. The assumption still stands; yet nevertheless I am something. But is it perhaps the case that these very things which I take to be nothing, because they are unknown to me, nevertheless are in fact no different from that "me" that I know? This I do not know, and I will not quarrel about it now. I can make a judgment only about things that are known to me. I know that I exist; I ask now who is this "I" whom I know? Most certainly, in the strict sense the knowledge of this "I" does not depend upon things of whose existence I do not yet have knowledge. Therefore it is not dependent upon any of those things that I simulate in my imagination. . . .

But what then am I? A thing that thinks. What is that? A thing that doubts, understands, affirms, denies, wills, refuses, and that also imagines and senses.

Indeed it is no small matter if all of these things belong to me. But why should they not belong to me? Is it not the very same "I" who now doubts almost everything, who nevertheless understands something, who affirms that this one thing is true, who denies other things, who desires to know more, who wishes not to be deceived, who imagines many things even against my will, who also notices many things which appear to come from the senses? What is there in all of this that is not every bit as true as the fact that I exist—even if I am always asleep or even if my creator makes every effort to mislead me? Which of these things is distinct from my thought? Which of them can be said to be separate from myself? For it is so obvious that it is I who doubt, I who understand, and I who will, that there is nothing by which it could be explained more clearly. But indeed it is also the same "I" who imagines; for although perhaps, as I supposed before, absolutely nothing that I imagined is true, still the very power of imagining really does exist, and constitutes a part of my thought. Finally, it is this same "I" who senses or who is cognizant of bodily things as if through the senses. For example, I now see a light, I hear a noise, I feel heat. These things are false, since I am asleep. Yet I certainly do seem to see, hear, and feel warmth. This cannot be false. Properly speaking, this is what in me is called "sensing." But this, precisely so taken, is nothing other than thinking. 10

From these considerations I am beginning to know a little better what I am. But it still seems (and I cannot resist believing) that corporeal things—whose images are formed by thought, and which the senses themselves examine—are much more distinctly known than this mysterious "I" which does not fall within the imagination. And yet it would be strange indeed were I to grasp the very things I consider to be doubtful, unknown, and foreign to me more distinctly than what is true, what is known—than, in short, myself. But I see what is happening: my mind loves to wander and does not yet permit itself to be restricted within the confines of truth. So be it then; let us just this once allow it completely free rein, so that, a little while later, when the time has come to pull in the reins, the mind may more readily permit itself to be controlled.

Let us consider those things which are commonly believed to be the most distinctly grasped of all: namely the bodies we touch and see. Not bodies in general, mind you, for these general perceptions are apt to be somewhat more confused, but one body in particular. Let us take, for instance, this piece of wax. It has been taken quite recently from the honeycomb; it has not yet lost all the honey flavor. It retains some of the scent of the flowers from which it was collected. Its color, shape, and size are manifest. It is hard and cold; it is easy to touch. If you rap on it with your knuckle it will emit a sound. In short, everything is present in it that appears needed to enable a body to be known as distinctly as possible. But notice that, as I am speaking, I am bringing it close to the fire. The remaining traces of the honey flavor are disappearing; the scent is vanishing; the color is changing; the original shape is disappearing. Its size is increasing; it is becoming liquid and hot; you can hardly touch it. And now, when you rap on it, it no longer emits any sound. Does the same wax still remain? I must confess that it does; no one denies it; no one thinks otherwise. So what was there in the wax that was so distinctly grasped? Certainly none of the aspects that I reached by means of the senses. For whatever came under the senses of taste, smell, sight, touch or hearing has now changed; and yet the wax remains.

Perhaps the wax was what I now think it is: namely that the wax itself never really was the sweetness of the honey, nor the fragrance of the flowers, nor the whiteness, nor the shape, nor the sound, but instead was a body that a short time ago manifested itself to me in these ways, and now does so in other ways. But just what precisely is this thing that I thus imagine? Let us focus our attention on this and see what remains

10

Here Descartes is claiming that there are many more things that are beyond doubt in the same way that his own existence is—thus greatly expanding the foundation of (alleged) certainty upon which he will eventually try to rebuild his knowledge. What are these further things, and is he right that they are indubitable in the same way, even given the evil genius possibility? (See Discussion Question 2.)

after we have removed everything that does not belong to the wax: only that it is something extended, flexible, and mutable. But what is it to be flexible and mutable? Is it what my imagination shows it to be: namely, that this piece of wax can change from a round to a square shape, or from the latter to a triangular shape? Not at all; for I grasp that the wax is capable of innumerable changes of this sort, even though I am incapable of running through these innumerable changes by using my imagination. Therefore this insight is not achieved by the faculty of imagination. What is it to be extended? Is this thing's extension also unknown? For it becomes greater in wax that is beginning to melt, greater in boiling wax, and greater still as the heat is increased. And I would not judge correctly what the wax is if I did not believe that it takes on an even greater variety of dimensions than I could ever grasp with the imagination. It remains then for me to concede that I do not grasp what this wax is through the imagination; rather, I perceive it through the mind alone. The point I am making refers to this particular piece of wax, for the case of wax in general is clearer still. But what is this piece of wax which is perceived only by the mind? Surely it is the same piece of wax that I see, touch, and imagine; in short it is the same piece of wax I took it to be from the very beginning. But I need to realize that the perception of the wax is neither a seeing, nor a touching, nor an imagining. Nor has it ever been, even though it previously seemed so; rather it is an inspection on the part of the mind alone. This inspection can be imperfect and confused, as it was before, or clear and distinct, as it is now, depending on how closely I pay attention to the things in which the piece of wax consists.

...

But what am I to say about this mind, that is, about myself? For as yet I admit nothing else to be in me over and above the mind. What, I ask, am I who seem to perceive this wax so distinctly? Do I not know myself not only much more truly and with greater certainty, but also much more distinctly and evidently? For if I judge that the wax exists from the fact that I see it, certainly from this same fact that I see the wax it follows much more evidently that I myself exist. For it could happen that what I see is not truly wax. It could happen that I have no eyes with which to see anything. But it is utterly impossible that, while I see or think I see (I do not now distinguish these two), I who think am not something. Likewise, if I judge that the wax exists from the fact that I touch it, the same outcome will again obtain, namely that I exist. If I judge that the wax exists from the fact that I imagine it, or for any other reason, plainly the same thing follows. But what I note regarding the wax applies to everything else that is external to me. Furthermore, if my perception of the wax seemed more distinct after it became known to me not only on account of sight or touch, but on account of many reasons, one has to admit how much more distinctly I am now known to myself. For there is not a single consideration that can aid in my perception of the wax or of any other body that fails to make even more manifest the nature of my mind. But there are still so many other things in the mind itself on the basis of which my knowledge of it can be rendered more distinct that it hardly seems worth enumerating those things which emanate to it from the body.

But lo and behold, I have returned on my own to where I wanted to be. For since I now know that even bodies are not, properly speaking, perceived by the senses or by the faculty of imagination, but by the intellect alone, (11) and that they are not perceived through their being touched or seen, but only through their being understood, I manifestly know that nothing can be perceived more easily and more evidently than my own mind. But since the tendency to hang on to long-held beliefs cannot be put aside so quickly, I want to stop here, so that by the length of my meditation this new knowledge may be more deeply impressed upon my memory.

(11) R Descartes uses the wax example to argue for this claim (that bodies themselves are not properly perceived by the senses nor by the faculty of imagination, but by the intellect alone).

MEDITATION THREE: Concerning God, That He Exists

I will now shut my eyes, stop up my ears, and withdraw all my senses. I will also blot out from my thoughts all images of corporeal things, or rather, since the latter is hardly possible, I will regard these images as empty, false and worthless. And as I converse with myself alone and look more deeply into myself, I will attempt to render myself gradually better known and more familiar to myself. I am a thing that thinks, that is to say, a thing that doubts, affirms, denies, understands a few things, is ignorant of many things, wills, refrains from willing, and also imagines and senses. For as I observed earlier, even though these things that I sense or imagine may perhaps be nothing at all outside me, nevertheless I am certain that these modes of thinking, which are cases of what I call sensing and imagining, insofar as they are merely modes of thinking, do exist within me.

In these few words, I have reviewed everything I truly know, or at least what so far I have noticed that I know. **12** Now I will ponder more carefully to see whether perhaps there may be other things belonging to me that up until now I have failed to notice. I am certain that I am a thinking thing. But do I not therefore also know what is required for me to be certain of anything? Surely in this first instance of knowledge, there is nothing but a certain clear and distinct perception of what I affirm. Yet this would hardly be enough to render me certain of the truth of a thing, if it could ever happen that something that I perceived so clearly and distinctly were false. And thus I now seem able to posit as a general rule that everything I very clearly and distinctly perceive is true. **13**

Be that as it may, I have previously admitted many things as wholly certain and evident that nevertheless I later discovered to be doubtful. What sort of things were these? Why, the earth, the sky, the stars, and all the other things I perceived by means of the senses. But what was it about these things that I clearly perceived? Surely the fact that the ideas or thoughts of these things were hovering before my mind. But even now I do not deny that these ideas are in me. Yet there was something else I used to affirm,
which, owing t
it, I used to thi
ceived, even th
at all: namely, t
me, things fro
and which tho
But on this poi
judgment was a
the force of my

But what abo
very simple an
or geometry, for example that two plus three make five, and the like? Did I not intuit them at least clearly enough so as to affirm them as true? To be sure, I did decide later on that I must doubt these things, but that was only because it occurred to me that some God could perhaps have given me a nature such that I might be deceived even about matters that seemed most evident. But whenever this preconceived opinion about the supreme power of God occurs to me, I cannot help admitting that, were he to wish it, it would be easy for him to cause me to err even in those matters that I think I intuit as clearly as possible with the eyes of the mind. **14** On the other hand, whenever I turn my attention to those very things that I think I perceive with such great clarity, I am so completely persuaded by them that I spontaneously blurt out these words: "let anyone who can do so deceive me; so long as I think that I am something, he will never bring it about that I am nothing. Nor will he one day make it true that I never existed, for it is true now that I do exist. Nor will he even bring it about that perhaps two plus three might equal more or less than five, or similar items in which I recognize an obvious contradiction." And certainly, because I have no reason for thinking that there is a God who is a deceiver (and of course I do not yet sufficiently know whether there even is a God), the basis for doubting, depending as it does merely on the above hypothesis, is very tenuous and, so to speak, metaphysical. But in order to remove even this basis for doubt, I should at the first opportunity inquire whether there is a God, and, if there is, whether or not he can be a deceiver. For if I am ignorant of this, it appears I am never capable of being completely certain about anything else. **15**

However, at this stage good order seems to demand that I first group all my thoughts into certain classes, and ask in which of them truth or falsity properly resides. Some of these thoughts are like images of things; to these alone does the word "idea" properly apply, as when I think of a man, or a chimera, or the sky, or an angel, or God. Again there are other thoughts that take different forms: for example, when I will, or fear, or affirm, or deny, there is always some thing that I grasp as the subject of my thought, yet I embrace in my thought something more than the likeness of that thing. Some of these thoughts are called volitions or affects, while others are called judgments.

Now as far as ideas are concerned, if they are considered alone and in their own right, without

R Here Descartes summarizes the main result of *Meditation Two:* the tiny amount of knowledge that has (allegedly) escaped the doubt resulting from the evil genius possibility. Stated in the first person (as is obviously appropriate), I can know that I am thinking and also that I am thinking (experiencing, doubting, wondering) about various things, but not that anything beyond myself and my own conscious states exists.

R This is Descartes's suggestion for a general rule or principle that captures the way in which his belief about his own existence escapes the doubt.

But is he right about this? Is "clarity and distinctness" the reason that I can't doubt my own existence? In fact, Descartes himself proceeds to show that it is not, since he goes on to question whether things that are clear and distinct are always true, even though he never questions his own existence.

R Since Descartes has already said that God wouldn't deceive us in this way, it is better to take him to be talking about the evil genius here.

Here Descartes might seem to be questioning even his own existence and states of mind, but the subsequent discussion shows he is not really doing so. (If he did, he would have nothing to start from in attempting to prove God's existence.) Thus the issue seems to be whether he can safely accept things other than his own existence and states of mind that seem "clear and distinct" (things like 2 + 3 = 5). The evil genius could deceive him about such things, so the only way to be sure is to prove the existence of God (and thereby the nonexistence of the evil genius).

being referred to something else, they cannot, properly speaking, be false. For whether it is a she-goat or a chimera that I am imagining, it is no less true that I imagine the one than the other. Moreover, we need not fear that there is falsity in the will itself or in the affects, for although I can choose evil things or even things that are utterly non-existent, I cannot conclude from this that it is untrue that I do choose these things. Thus there remain only judgments in which I must take care not to be mistaken. Now the principal and most frequent error to be found in judgments consists in the fact that I judge that the ideas which are in me are similar to or in conformity with certain things outside me. Obviously, if I were to consider these ideas merely as certain modes of my thought, and were not to refer them to anything else, they could hardly give me any subject matter for error. (16)

Among these ideas, some appear to me to be innate, some adventitious, and some produced by me. For I understand what a thing is, what truth is, what thought is, and I appear to have derived this exclusively from my very own nature. But say I am now hearing a noise, or looking at the sun, or feeling the fire; up until now I judged that these things proceeded from certain things outside me, and finally, that sirens, hippogriffs, and the like are made by me. Or perhaps I can even think of all these ideas as being adventitious, or as being innate, or as fabrications, for I have not yet clearly ascertained their true origin. (17)

But here I must inquire particularly into those ideas that I believe to be derived from things existing outside me. Just what reason do I have for believing that these ideas resemble those things? Well, I do seem to have been so taught by nature. Moreover, I do know from experience that these ideas do not depend upon my will, nor consequently upon myself, for I often notice them even against my will. Now, for example, whether or not I will it, I feel heat. It is for this reason that I believe this feeling or idea of heat comes to me from something other than myself, namely from the heat of the fire by which I am sitting. Nothing is more obvious than the judgment that this thing is sending its likeness rather than something else into me. (18)

I will now see whether these reasons are powerful enough. When I say here "I have been so taught by nature," all I have in mind is that I am driven by a spontaneous impulse to believe this, and not that some light of nature is showing me that it is true. These are two very different things. For whatever is shown me by this light of nature, for example, that from the fact that I doubt, it follows that I am, and the like, cannot in any way be doubtful. This is owing to the fact that there can be no other faculty that I can trust as much as this light and which could teach that these things are not true. (19) But as far as natural impulses are concerned, in the past I have often judged myself to have been driven by them to make the poorer choice when it was a question of choosing a good; and I fail to see why I should place any greater faith in them than in other matters.

Again, although these ideas do not depend upon my will, it does not follow that they necessarily proceed from things existing outside me. For just as these impulses about which I spoke just now seem to be different from my will, even though they are in me, so too perhaps there is also in me some other faculty, one not yet sufficiently known to me, which produces these ideas, just as it has always seemed up to now that ideas are formed in me without any help from external things when I am asleep.

And finally, even if these ideas did proceed from things other than myself, it does not therefore follow that they must resemble those things. Indeed it seems I have frequently noticed a vast difference in many respects. For example, I find within myself two distinct ideas of the sun. One idea is drawn, as it were, from the senses. Now it is this idea which, of all those that I take to be derived from outside me, is most in need of examination. By means of this idea the sun appears to me to be quite small. But there is another idea, one derived from astronomical reasoning, that is, it is elicited from certain notions that are innate in me, or else is fashioned by me in some other way. Through this idea the sun is shown to be several times larger than the earth. Both ideas surely cannot resemble the same sun existing outside me; and reason convinces me that the idea that seems to have emanated from the sun itself from so close is the very one that least resembles the sun.

All these points demonstrate sufficiently that up to this point it was not a well-founded judgment but only a blind impulse that formed the basis of my belief that things existing outside me send ideas or images of themselves to me through the sense organs or by some other means. (20)

16

So Descartes is worried about whether his thoughts *about the world* are accurate, not about whether his thoughts *about his thoughts* are accurate, for (he claims) he could never be in error about those.

An **innate** idea is one that is programmed into a person at birth (by God, in Descartes's view). Ideas produced by me are ones that I make up or that are "fictitious."

STOP What then is an "adventitious" idea? What is the third alternative besides being innate or being "produced by me"?

R Here are two initial reasons for the view that sense experience accurately reflects the nature of external things.

By "the natural light," Descartes seems to mean something like a priori insight into *why* a claim must be true—the sort of insight that is reflected in the claim seeming "clear and distinct." His point is that while I naturally and spontaneously believe what the senses seem to tell me, there is nothing in that case that shows me that the claims in question must be true.

But, as we have seen, the evil genius can apparently deceive me even about things (other than my own existence and states of mind) that seem to be shown by the natural light or that seem clear and distinct (such as 2 + 3 = 5).

R Descartes concludes that the two initial reasons (see Annotation 18) have no real force.

But still another way occurs to me for inquiring whether some of the things of which there are ideas in me do exist outside me: insofar as these ideas are merely modes of thought, I see no inequality among them; they all seem to proceed from me in the same manner. But insofar as one idea represents one thing and another idea another thing, it is obvious that they do differ very greatly from one another. Unquestionably, those ideas that display substances to me are something more and, if I may say so, contain within themselves more objective reality than those which represent only modes or accidents. Again, the idea that enables me to understand a supreme deity, eternal, infinite, omniscient, omnipotent, and creator of all things other than himself, clearly has more objective reality within it than do those ideas through which finite substances are displayed. (21)

Now it is indeed evident by the light of nature that there must be at least as much [reality] in the efficient and total cause as there is in the effect of that same cause. For whence, I ask, could an effect get its reality, if not from its cause? And how could the cause give that reality to the effect, unless it also possessed that reality? Hence it follows that something cannot come into being out of nothing, and also that what is more perfect (that is, what contains in itself more reality) cannot come into being from what is less perfect. But this is manifestly true not merely for those effects whose reality is actual or formal, but also for ideas in which only objective reality is considered. (22) For example, not only can a stone which did not exist previously not now begin to exist unless it is produced by something in which there is, either formally or eminently, everything that is in the stone; nor heat be introduced into a subject which was not already hot unless it is done by something that is of at least as perfect an order as heat—and the same for the rest—but it is also true that there can be in me no idea of heat, or of a stone, unless it is placed in me by some cause that has at least as much reality as I conceive to be in the heat or in the stone. For although this cause conveys none of its actual or formal reality to my idea, it should not be thought for that reason that it must be less real. Rather, the very nature of an idea is such that of itself it needs no formal reality other than what it borrows from my thought, of which it is a mode. But that a particular idea contains this as opposed to that objective reality is surely owing to some cause in which there is at least as much formal reality as there is objective reality contained in the idea. For if we assume that something is found in the idea that was not in its cause, then the idea gets that something from nothing. Yet as imperfect a mode of being as this is by which a thing exists in the intellect objectively through an idea, nevertheless it is plainly not nothing; hence it cannot get its being from nothing.

Moreover, even though the reality that I am considering in my ideas is merely objective reality, I ought not on that account to suspect that there is no need for the same reality to be formally in the causes of these ideas, but that it suffices for it to be in them objectively. For just as the objective mode of being belongs to ideas by their very nature, so the formal mode of being belongs to the causes of ideas, at least to the first and preeminent ones, by their very nature. And although one idea can perhaps issue from another, nevertheless no infinite regress is permitted here; eventually some first idea must be reached whose cause is a sort of archetype that contains formally all the reality that is in the idea merely objectively. (23) Thus it is clear to me by the light of nature that the ideas that are in me are like images that can easily fail to match the perfection of the things from which they have been drawn, but which can contain nothing greater or more perfect.

And the longer and more attentively I examine all these points, the more clearly and distinctly I know they are true. But what am I ultimately to conclude? If the objective reality of any of my ideas is found to be so great that I am certain that the same reality was not in me, either formally or eminently, and that therefore I myself cannot be the cause of the idea, then it necessarily follows that I am not alone in the world, but that something else, which is the cause of this idea, also exists. But if no such idea is found in me, I will have no argument whatsoever to make me certain of the existence of anything other than myself, for I have conscientiously reviewed all these arguments, and so far I have been unable to find any other. (24)

Among my ideas, in addition to the one that displays me to myself (about which there can be no difficulty at this point), are others that represent God, corporeal and inanimate things, angels, animals, and finally other men like myself.

R Another approach is to see whether the claim that some of my ideas correspond to things existing outside my mind can be derived from their *content:* what they seem to represent or depict. Descartes puts this in terms of the obscure (to us, anyway) medieval conception of *objective reality:* reality as an object of thought. (So, for example, Santa Claus would have "objective reality" when anyone has a thought of Santa Claus.) In his view, different ideas contain different degrees of objective reality, corresponding to the degree of *perfection* of the object of the idea. It follows, he thinks, that the idea of God contains more objective reality than any other idea.

Here is the first of two important metaphysical principles involved in Descartes' argument: the principle that any cause must have at least as much reality (must be at least as perfect as) as its effect. He applies this to both formal or actual reality (reality in the ordinary sense) and objective reality. (The labels "formal" and "objective" strike our contemporary ears as terminologically backwards. What we would mean by "objective reality" is what Descartes means by "formal reality".)

Here is the second metaphysical principle involved in Descartes's argument: anything with objective reality must ultimately be caused by something with formal reality. From this, Descartes thinks that it follows, given the previous principle, that something with a specific degree of objective reality must ultimately be caused by something with at least that same degree of formal reality.

STOP Is there any plausibility to this claim? Even more importantly, how does Descartes know that either of these metaphysical principles is true?—look carefully at what he says. Do you see any problem here? See Discussion Question 3.

R Thus the issue becomes whether I have any idea that I myself could not, according to the foregoing principle, be the cause of. If so, I can know on this basis that something outside myself exists.

As to the ideas that display other men, or animals, or angels, I easily understand that they could be fashioned from the ideas that I have of myself, of corporeal things, and of God—even if no men (except myself), no animals, and no angels existed in the world.

As to the ideas of corporeal things, there is nothing in them that is so great that it seems incapable of having originated from me. For if I investigate them thoroughly and examine each one individually in the way I examined the idea of wax yesterday, I notice that there are only a very few things in them that I perceive clearly and distinctly: namely, size, or extension in length, breadth, and depth; shape, which arises from the limits of this extension; position, which various things possessing shape have in relation to one another; and motion, or alteration in position. To these can be added substance, duration, and number. But as for the remaining items, such as light and colors, sounds, odors, tastes, heat and cold and other tactile qualities, I think of these only in a very confused and obscure manner, to the extent that I do not even know whether they are true or false, that is, whether the ideas I have of them are ideas of things or ideas of non-things.

25

Here Descartes has in mind at least approximately the distinction between **primary** and **secondary** qualities (about which Locke will have much more to say).

25 For although a short time ago I noted that falsity properly so called (or "formal" falsity) is to be found only in judgments, nevertheless there is another kind of falsity (called "material" falsity) which is found in ideas whenever they represent a non-thing as if it were a thing. For example, the ideas I have of heat and cold fall so far short of being clear and distinct that I cannot tell from them whether cold is merely the privation of heat or whether heat is the privation of cold, or whether both are real qualities, or whether neither is. And because ideas can only be, as it were, of things, if it is true that cold is merely the absence of heat, then an idea that represents cold to me as something real and positive will not inappropriately be called false. The same holds for other similar ideas.

Assuredly I need not assign to these ideas an author distinct from myself. For if they were false, that is, if they were to represent non-things, I know by the light of nature that they proceed from nothing; that is, they are in me for no other reason than that something is lacking in my nature, and that my nature is not entirely perfect. If, on the other hand, these ideas are true, then because they exhibit so little reality to me that I cannot distinguish it from a non-thing, I see no reason why they cannot get their being from me.

As for what is clear and distinct in the ideas of corporeal things, it appears I could have borrowed some of these from the idea of myself: namely, substance, duration, number, and whatever else there may be of this type. For instance, I think that a stone is a substance, that is to say, a thing that is suitable for existing in itself; and likewise I think that I too am a substance. Despite the fact that I conceive myself to be a thinking thing and not an extended thing, whereas I conceive of a stone as an extended thing and not a thinking thing, and hence there is the greatest diversity between these two concepts, nevertheless they seem to agree with one another when considered under the rubric of substance. Furthermore, I perceive that I now exist and recall that I have previously existed for some time. And I have various thoughts and know how many of them there are. It is in doing these things that I acquire the ideas of duration and number, which I can then apply to other things. However, none of the other components out of which the ideas of corporeal things are fashioned (namely extension, shape, position, and motion) are contained in me formally, since I am merely a thinking thing. But since these are only certain modes of a substance, whereas I am a substance, it seems possible that they are contained in me eminently.

R The crucial idea is, of course, the idea of God.

STOP Can this idea be caused only by me, given the two principles?

Thus there remains only the idea of God. I must consider whether there is anything in this idea that could not have originated from me. 26 I understand by the name "God" a certain substance that is infinite, independent, supremely intelligent and supremely powerful, and that created me along with everything else that exists—if anything else exists. Indeed all these are such that, the more carefully I focus my attention on them, the less possible it seems they could have arisen from myself alone. Thus, from what has been said, I must conclude that God necessarily exists.

For although the idea of substance is in me by virtue of the fact that I am a substance, that fact is not sufficient to explain my having the idea of an infinite substance, since I am finite, unless this idea proceeded from some substance which really was infinite.

Nor should I think that I do not perceive the infinite by means of a true idea, but only through a negation of the finite, just as I perceive rest and darkness by means of a negation of motion and light. On the contrary, I clearly understand that there is more reality in an infinite substance than there is in a finite one. Thus the perception of the infinite is somehow prior in me to the perception of the finite, that is, my perception of God is prior to my perception of myself. For how would I understand that I doubt and that I desire, that is, that I lack something and that I am not wholly perfect, unless there were some idea in me of a more perfect being, by comparison with which I might recognize my defects? [27]

...

But perhaps I am something greater than I myself understand. Perhaps all these perfections that I am attributing to God are somehow in me potentially, although they do not yet assert themselves and are not yet actualized. For I now observe that my knowledge is gradually being increased, and I see nothing standing in the way of its being increased more and more to infinity. Moreover, I see no reason why, with my knowledge thus increased, I could not acquire all the remaining perfections of God. And, finally, if the potential for these perfections is in me already, I see no reason why this potential would not suffice to produce the idea of these perfections.

Yet none of these things can be the case. First, while it is true that my knowledge is gradually being increased and that there are many things in me potentially that are not yet actual, nevertheless, none of these pertains to the idea of God, in which there is nothing whatever that is potential. Indeed this gradual increase is itself a most certain proof of imperfection. Moreover, although my knowledge may always increase more and more, nevertheless I understand that this knowledge will never by this means be actually infinite, because it will never reach a point where it is incapable of greater increase. On the contrary, I judge God to be actually infinite, so that nothing can be added to his perfection. . . .

Nor can one fancy that perhaps several partial causes have concurred in bringing me into being, and that I have taken the ideas of the various perfections I attribute to God from a variety of causes, so that all of these perfections are found somewhere in the universe, but not all joined together in a single being—God. On the contrary, the unity, the simplicity, that is, the inseparability of all those features that are in God is one of the chief perfections that I understand to be in him. Certainly the idea of the unity of all his perfections could not have been placed in me by any cause from which I did not also get the ideas of the other perfections; for neither could some cause have made me understand them joined together and inseparable from one another, unless it also caused me to recognize what they were.

. . . Indeed I have no choice but to conclude that the mere fact of my existing and of there being in me an idea of a most perfect being, that is, God, demonstrates most evidently that God too exists. [28]

All that remains for me is to ask how I received this idea of God. For I did not draw it from the senses; it never came upon me unexpectedly, as is usually the case with the ideas of sensible things when these things present themselves (or seem to present themselves) to the external sense organs. Nor was it made by me, for I plainly can neither subtract anything from it nor add anything to it. Thus the only option remaining is that this idea is innate in me, just as the idea of myself is innate in me. [29]

To be sure, it is not astonishing that in creating me, God should have endowed me with this idea, so that it would be like the mark of the craftsman impressed upon his work, although this mark need not be something distinct from the work itself. But the mere fact that God created me makes it highly plausible that I have somehow been made in his image and likeness, and that I perceive this likeness, in which the idea of God is contained, by means of the same faculty by which I perceive myself. That is, when I turn the mind's eye toward myself, I understand not only that I am something incomplete and dependent upon another, something aspiring indefinitely for greater and greater or better things, but also that the being on whom I depend has in himself all those greater things—not merely indefinitely and potentially, but infinitely and actually, and thus that he is God. The whole force of the argument rests on the fact that I recognize that it would be impossible for me to exist, being of such a nature as I am (namely, having in me the idea of God), unless God did in fact exist. God, I say, that same being the idea of whom is in me: a being

R One reason for thinking that I cannot be the cause of my idea of God is that it involves the property of infinity and I am only finite. Descartes considers the response that the idea of infinity is only the negation of the idea of the finite and claims that, on the contrary, the idea of infinity or of an infinite being comes first.

R The result that is supposed to follow from the ingredients already discussed finally emerges here: only a genuinely existing God could be the cause of Descartes's idea of God. And once Descartes knows that God exists, he can trust that his clear and distinct ideas are true. The rest of *Meditation Three* raises and attempts to answer various objections to his overall argument. But there is a more serious objection that was raised by Descartes's contemporaries: isn't Descartes arguing in a circle by assuming that he can trust the two metaphysical principles before establishing that God exists? (See Discussion Question 3.)

R Here Descartes refers to the three options mentioned at the point in the text where Annotation 17 occurs.

having all those perfections that I cannot comprehend, but can somehow touch with my thought, and a being subject to no defects whatever. From these considerations it is quite obvious that he cannot be a deceiver, for it is manifest by the light of nature that all fraud and deception depend on some defect.

But before examining this idea more closely and at the same time inquiring into other truths that can be gathered from it, at this point I want to spend some time contemplating this God, to ponder his attributes and, so far as the eye of my darkened mind can take me, to gaze upon, to admire, and to adore the beauty of this immense light. For just as we believe by faith that the greatest felicity of the next life consists solely in this contemplation of the divine majesty, so too we now experience that from the same contemplation, although it is much less perfect, the greatest pleasure of which we are capable in this life can be perceived.

...

MEDITATION SIX: Concerning the Existence of Material Things, and the Real Distinction Between Mind and Body

It remains for me to examine whether material things exist. Indeed I now know that they can exist, at least insofar as they are the object of pure mathematics, since I clearly and distinctly perceive them. For no doubt God is capable of bringing about everything that I am capable of perceiving in this way. And I have never judged that God was incapable of something, except when it was incompatible with my perceiving it distinctly. (30) ...

R This amounts to the claim that clear and distinct perception is at least a good criterion for what is *possible*.

But I am in the habit of imagining many other things, over and above that corporeal nature which is the object of pure mathematics, such as colors, sounds, tastes, pain, and the like, though not so distinctly. And I perceive these things better by means of the senses, from which, with the aid of the memory, they seem to have arrived at the imagination. Thus I . . . must see whether I can obtain any reliable argument for the existence of corporeal things from those things that are perceived by the mode of thinking that I call "sense." (31)

R We now come to the main issue: does sense experience yield any good reason for thinking that external material bodies exist?

First of all, to be sure, I will review here all the things I previously believed to be true because I had perceived them by means of the senses and the causes I had for thinking this. Next I will assess the causes why I later called them into doubt. Finally, I will consider what I must now believe about these things.

So first, I sensed that I had a head, hands, feet, and other members that comprised this body which I viewed as part of me, or perhaps even as the whole of me. I sensed that this body was found among many other bodies, by which my body can be affected in various beneficial or harmful ways. I gauged what was opportune by means of a certain sensation of pleasure, and what was inopportune by a sensation of pain. In addition to pain and pleasure, I also sensed within me hunger, thirst, and other such appetites, as well as certain bodily tendencies toward mirth, sadness, anger, and other such affects. And externally, besides the extension, shapes, and motions of bodies, I also sensed their hardness, heat, and other tactile qualities. I also sensed light, colors, odors, tastes, and sounds, on the basis of whose variety I distinguished the sky, the earth, the seas, and the other bodies, one from the other. Now given the ideas of all these qualities that presented themselves to my thought, and which were all that I properly and immediately sensed, still it was surely not without reason that I thought I sensed things that were manifestly different from my thought, namely, the bodies from which these ideas proceeded. For I knew by experience that these ideas came upon me utterly without my consent, to the extent that, wish as I may, I could not sense any object unless it was present to a sense organ. Nor could I fail to sense it when it was present. And since the ideas perceived by sense were much more vivid and explicit and even, in their own way, more distinct than any of those that I deliberately and knowingly formed through meditation or that I found impressed on my memory, it seemed impossible that they came from myself. Thus the remaining alternative was that they came from other things. Since I had no knowledge of such things except from those same ideas themselves, I could not help entertaining the thought that they were similar to those ideas. (32) Moreover, I also recalled that the use of the senses antedated the use of reason. And since I saw that the ideas that I myself fashioned were not as explicit as those that I perceived through the faculty of sense, and were

R This is one of the reasons mentioned earlier at the point in the text where Annotation 20 occurs. It is also one of those that Locke appeals to (in the following selection) in his attempt to argue, without any appeal to God, for the existence of material objects corresponding to sense experience.

for the most part composed of parts of the latter, I easily convinced myself that I had absolutely no idea in the intellect that I did not have beforehand in the sense faculty. Not without reason did I judge that this body, which by a certain special right I called "mine," belongs more to me than did any other. For I could never be separated from it in the same way I could be from other bodies. I sensed all appetites and feelings in and on behalf of it. Finally, I noticed pain and pleasurable excitement in its parts, but not in other bodies external to it. But why should a certain sadness of spirit arise from some sensation or other of pain, and why should a certain elation arise from a sensation of excitement, or why should that peculiar twitching in the stomach, which I call hunger, warn me to have something to eat, or why should dryness in the throat warn me to take something to drink, and so on? I plainly had no explanation other than that I had been taught this way by nature. For there is no affinity whatsoever, at least none I am aware of, between this twitching in the stomach and the will to have something to eat, or between the sensation of something causing pain and the thought of sadness arising from this sensation. But nature also seems to have taught me everything else as well that I judged concerning the objects of the senses, for I had already convinced myself that this was how things were, prior to my assessing any of the arguments that might prove it. 33

Afterwards, however, many experiences gradually weakened any faith that I had in the senses. Towers that had seemed round from afar occasionally appeared square at close quarters. Very large statues mounted on their pedestals did not seem large to someone looking at them from ground level. And in countless other such instances I determined that judgments in matters of the external senses were in error. . . . To these causes for doubt I recently added two quite general ones. The first was that everything I ever thought I sensed while awake I could believe I also sometimes sensed while asleep, and since I do not believe that what I seem to sense in my dreams comes to me from things external to me, I saw no reason why I should hold this belief about those things I seem to be sensing while awake. The second was that, since I was still ignorant of the author of my origin (or at least pretended to be ignorant of it), I saw nothing to prevent my having been so constituted by nature that I should be mistaken even about what seemed to me most true. 34 As to the arguments that used to convince me of the truth of sensible things, I found no difficulty responding to them. For since I seemed driven by nature toward many things about which reason tried to dissuade me, I did not think that what I was taught by nature deserved much credence. And even though the perceptions of the senses did not depend on my will, I did not think that we must therefore conclude that they came from things distinct from me, since perhaps there is some faculty in me, as yet unknown to me, that produces these perceptions.

But now, having begun to have a better knowledge of myself and the author of my origin, I am of the opinion that I must not rashly admit everything that I seem to derive from the senses; but neither, for that matter, should I call everything into doubt.

First, I know that all the things that I clearly and distinctly understand can be made by God such as I understand them. For this reason, my ability clearly and distinctly to understand one thing without another suffices to make me certain that the one thing is different from the other, since they can be separated from each other, at least by God. The question as to the sort of power that might effect such a separation is not relevant to their being thought to be different. For this reason, from the fact that I know that I exist, and that at the same time I judge that obviously nothing else belongs to my nature or essence except that I am a thinking thing, I rightly conclude that my essence consists entirely in my being a thinking thing. And although perhaps (or rather, as I shall soon say, assuredly) I have a body that is very closely joined to me, nevertheless, because on the one hand I have a clear and distinct idea of myself, insofar as I am merely a thinking thing and not an extended thing, and because on the other hand I have a distinct idea of a body, insofar as it is merely an extended thing and not a thinking thing, it is certain that I am really distinct from my body, and can exist without it. 35

Moreover, I find in myself faculties for certain special modes of thinking, namely the faculties of imagining and sensing. I can clearly and distinctly understand myself in my entirety without these faculties, but not vice versa: I cannot understand them clearly and distinctly without me, that is,

R This paragraph describes Descartes's previous *faith* in his senses. He made many assumptions about the existence of bodies and the accuracy of the beliefs based on his sense experiences, but he recognizes that he had no reasons or arguments for the correctness of these assumptions.

STOP Think about this issue: what reason do you have for thinking that the belief you have right now that there is a physical book in front of you (a belief based on your visual sense experience) is true?

R This is an allusion to the evil genius.

R Here is an argument for the conclusion that a person (his or her mind) is distinct from his or her body. (See Discussion Question 4.)

without a substance endowed with understanding in which they inhere, for they include an act of understanding in their formal concept. Thus I perceive them to be distinguished from me as modes from a thing. . . . Now there clearly is in me a passive faculty of sensing, that is, a faculty for receiving and knowing the ideas of sensible things; but I could not use it unless there also existed, either in me or in something else, a certain active faculty of producing or bringing about these ideas. But this faculty surely cannot be in me, since it clearly presupposes no act of understanding, and these ideas are produced without my cooperation and often even against my will. Therefore the only alternative is that it is in some substance different from me, containing either formally or eminently all the reality that exists objectively in the ideas produced by that faculty, as I have just noted above. Hence this substance is either a body, that is, a corporeal nature, which contains formally all that is contained objectively in the ideas, or else it is God, or some other creature more noble than a body, which contains eminently all that is contained objectively in the ideas. But since God is not a deceiver, it is patently obvious that he does not send me these ideas either immediately by himself, or even through the mediation of some creature that contains the objective reality of these ideas not formally but only eminently. For since God has given me no faculty whatsoever for making this determination, but instead has given me a great inclination to believe that these ideas issue from corporeal things, I fail to see how God could be understood not to be a deceiver, if these ideas were to issue from a source other than corporeal things. And consequently corporeal things exist. Nevertheless, perhaps not all bodies exist exactly as I grasp them by sense, since this sensory grasp is in many cases very obscure and confused. But at least they do contain everything I clearly and distinctly understand—that is, everything, considered in a general sense, that is encompassed in the object of pure mathematics. 36

36

R Here finally is Descartes's main reason for thinking that there are external things: My sensory ideas of external things cannot be produced by me, since they are involuntary and the faculty that produces them is not an essential part of my nature as a thinking thing. Therefore they must be produced by something else, and God would be a deceiver if he so arranged things that these ideas were produced by something other than things. But God is not a deceiver (since deception would be an imperfection). Therefore, external things must exist—though not necessarily with all the specific features that I experience. (See Discussion Question 5.)

As far as the remaining matters are concerned, which are either merely particular (for example, that the sun is of such and such a size or shape, and so on) or less clearly understood (for example, light, sound, pain, and the like), even though these matters are very doubtful and uncertain, nevertheless the fact that God is no deceiver (and thus no falsity can be found in my opinions, unless there is also in me a faculty given me by God for the purpose of rectifying this falsity) offers me a definite hope of reaching the truth even in these matters. And surely there is no doubt that all that I am taught by nature has some truth to it; for by "nature," taken generally, I understand nothing other than God himself or the ordered network of created things which was instituted by God. By my own particular nature I understand nothing other than the combination of all the things bestowed upon me by God.

There is nothing that this nature teaches me more explicitly than that I have a body that is ill-disposed when I feel pain, that needs food and drink when I suffer hunger or thirst, and the like. Therefore, I should not doubt that there is some truth in this.

By means of these sensations of pain, hunger, thirst and so on, nature also teaches not merely that I am present to my body in the way a sailor is present in a ship, but that I am most tightly joined and, so to speak, commingled with it, so much so that I and the body constitute one single thing. For if this were not the case, then I, who am only a thinking thing, would not sense pain when the body is injured; rather, I would perceive the wound by means of the pure intellect, just as a sailor perceives by sight whether anything in his ship is broken. And when the body is in need of food or drink, I should understand this explicitly, instead of having confused sensations of hunger and thirst. For clearly these sensations of thirst, hunger, pain, and so on are nothing but certain confused modes of thinking arising from the union and, as it were, the commingling of the mind with the body. 37

R Here is Descartes's account of the relation between his mind and his body: they are two distinct things (**substances**), but still intricately connected with each other.

Moreover, I am also taught by nature that various other bodies exist around my body, some of which are to be pursued, while others are to be avoided. And to be sure, from the fact that I sense a wide variety of colors, sounds, odors, tastes, levels of heat, and grades of roughness, and the like, I rightly conclude that in the bodies from which these different perceptions of the senses proceed there are differences corresponding to the different perceptions—though perhaps the latter do not resemble the former. And from the fact that some of these perceptions are pleasant while others are unpleasant, it is plainly certain that my body, or rather my whole self, insofar as I am comprised of a body and a mind, can be affected by various beneficial and harmful bodies in the vicinity.

Granted, there are many other things that I seem to have been taught by nature; nevertheless it was not really nature that taught them to me but a certain habit of making reckless judgments. And thus it could easily happen that these judgments are false: for example, that any space where there is absolutely nothing happening to move my senses is empty; or that there is something in a hot body that bears an exact likeness to the idea of heat that is in me; or that in a white or green body there is the same whiteness or greenness that I sense; or that in a bitter or sweet body there is the same taste, and so on; or that stars and towers and any other distant bodies have the same size and shape that they present to my senses, and other things of this sort. (38) . . . it is this nature that teaches me to avoid things that produce a sensation of pain and to pursue things that produce a sensation of pleasure, and the like. But it does not appear that nature teaches us to conclude anything, besides these things, from these sense perceptions unless the intellect has first conducted its own inquiry regarding things external to us. For it seems to belong exclusively to the mind, and not to the composite of mind and body, to know the truth in these matters. Thus, although a star affects my eye no more than does the flame from a small torch, still there is no real or positive tendency in my eye toward believing that the star is no larger than the flame. Yet, ever since my youth, I have made this judgment without any reason for doing so. And although I feel heat as I draw closer to the fire, and I also feel pain upon drawing too close to it, there is not a single argument that persuades me that there is something in the fire similar to that heat, any more than to that pain. On the contrary, I am convinced only that there is something in the fire that, regardless of what it finally turns out to be, causes in us those sensations of heat or pain. And although there may be nothing in a given space that moves the senses, it does not therefore follow that there is no body in it. But I see that in these and many other instances I have been in the habit of subverting the order of nature. For admittedly I use the perceptions of the senses (which are properly given by nature only for signifying to the mind what things are useful or harmful to the composite of which it is a part, and to that extent they are clear and distinct enough) as reliable rules for immediately discerning what is the essence of bodies located outside us. Yet they signify nothing about that except quite obscurely and confusedly. (39)

I have already examined in sufficient detail how it could happen that my judgments are false, despite the goodness of God. But a new difficulty now arises regarding those very things that nature shows me are either to be sought out or avoided, as well as the internal sensations where I seem to have detected errors, as for example, when someone is deluded by a food's pleasant taste to eat the poison hidden inside it. In this case, however, he is driven by nature only toward desiring the thing in which the pleasurable taste is found, but not toward the poison, of which he obviously is unaware. I can only conclude that this nature is not omniscient. This is not remarkable, since man is a limited thing, and thus only what is of limited perfection befits him.

But we not infrequently err even in those things to which nature impels us. Take, for example, the case of those who are ill and who desire food or drink that will soon afterwards be injurious to them. . . . It therefore remains to inquire here how the goodness of God does not prevent "nature," thus considered, from being deceptive. (40)

Now my first observation here is that there is a great difference between a mind and a body in that a body, by its very nature, is always divisible. On the other hand, the mind is utterly indivisible. For when I consider the mind, that is, myself insofar as I am only a thinking thing, I cannot distinguish any parts within me; rather, I understand myself to be manifestly one complete thing. Although the entire mind seems to be united to the entire body, nevertheless, were a foot or an arm or any other bodily part to be amputated, I know that nothing has been taken away from the mind on that account. Nor can the faculties of willing, sensing, understanding, and so on be called "parts" of the mind, since it is one and the same mind that wills, senses, and understands. On the other hand, there is no corporeal or extended thing I can think of that I may not in my thought easily divide into parts; and in this way I understand that it is divisible. This consideration alone would suffice to teach me that the mind is wholly diverse from the body, had I not yet known it well enough in any other way. (41)

R Here Descartes lists various sorts of mistaken judgments that his sensory experiences tempt him to make. Locke and Berkeley will have more to say about these matters in the following selections.

R Descartes's view is that the specific perceptions of the senses should not be taken to reveal the actual nature of external objects, but only as a guide to what things are useful or harmful. The sensation of heat does not describe any property that is actually in the fire, but nonetheless warns us not to get too close to it. Thus the fact that people who do not think carefully about such matters are sometimes misled does not show that God is a deceiver.

R There is still a problem, however, since our sense experience sometimes misleads us even concerning which things are helpful or harmful.

(41)

R As a part of his explanation of the fact that our nature is liable to errors of this last sort, Descartes argues again that his mind is distinct from his body, this time appealing to the properties of divisibility and indivisibility. (See Discussion Question 4.)

My second observation is that my mind is not immediately affected by all the parts of the body, but only by the brain, or perhaps even by just one small part of the brain, namely, by that part where the "common" sense is said to reside. Whenever this part of the brain is disposed in the same manner, it presents the same thing to the mind, even if the other parts of the body are able meanwhile to be related in diverse ways. Countless experiments show this, none of which need be reviewed here.

My next observation is that the nature of the body is such that whenever any of its parts can be moved by another part some distance away, it can also be moved in the same manner by any of the parts that lie between them, even if this more distant part is doing nothing. For example, in the cord ABCD, if the final part D is pulled, the first part A would be moved in exactly the same manner as it could be, if one of the intermediate parts B or C were pulled, while the end part D remained immobile. Likewise, when I feel a pain in my foot, physics teaches me that this sensation took place by means of nerves distributed throughout the foot, like stretched cords extending from the foot all the way to the brain. When these nerves are pulled in the foot, they also pull on the inner parts of the brain to which they extend, and produce a certain motion in them. This motion has been constituted by nature so as to affect the mind with a sensation of pain, as if it occurred in the foot. But because these nerves need to pass through the shin, thigh, loins, back, and neck to get from the foot to the brain, it can happen that even if it is not the part in the foot but merely one of the intermediate parts that is being struck, the very same movement will occur in the brain that would occur were the foot badly injured. The inevitable result will be that the mind feels the same pain. The same opinion should hold for any other sensation.

My final observation is that, since any given motion occurring in that part of the brain immediately affecting the mind produces but one sensation in it, I can think of no better arrangement than that it produces the one sensation that, of all the ones it is able to produce, is most especially and most often conducive to the maintenance of a healthy man. Moreover, experience shows that all the sensations bestowed on us by nature are like this. Hence there is absolutely nothing to be found in them that does not bear witness to God's power and goodness. Thus, for example, when the nerves in the foot are agitated in a violent and unusual manner, this motion of theirs extends through the marrow of the spine to the inner reaches of the brain, where it gives the mind the sign to sense something, namely, the pain as if it is occurring in the foot. This provokes the mind to do its utmost to move away from the cause of the pain, since it is seen as harmful to the foot. But the nature of man could have been so constituted by God that this same motion in the brain might have indicated something else to the mind: for example, either the motion itself as it occurs in the brain, or in the foot, or in some place in between, or something else entirely different. But nothing else would have served so well the maintenance of the body. Similarly, when we need something to drink, a certain dryness arises in the throat that moves the nerves in the throat, and, by means of them, the inner parts of the brain. And this motion affects the mind with a sensation of thirst, because in this entire affair nothing is more useful for us to know than that we need something to drink in order to maintain our health; the same holds in the other cases.

From these considerations it is utterly apparent that, notwithstanding the immense goodness of God, the nature of man, insofar as it is composed of mind and body, cannot help being sometimes mistaken. For if some cause, not in the foot but in some other part through which the nerves extend from the foot to the brain, or perhaps even in the brain itself, were to produce the same motion that would normally be produced by a badly injured foot, the pain will be felt as if it were in the foot, and the senses will naturally be deceived. For since an identical motion in the brain can only bring about an identical sensation in the mind, and it is more frequently the case that this motion is wont to arise on account of a cause that harms the foot than on account of some other thing existing elsewhere, it is reasonable that the motion should always show pain to the mind as something belonging to the foot rather than to some other part. And if dryness in the throat does not arise, as is normal, because taking something to drink contributes to bodily health, but from a contrary cause, as happens in the case of someone with dropsy, then it is far better that it should deceive on that occasion than that it should always be deceptive when the body is in good health. The same holds for the other cases. (42)

This consideration is most helpful, not only for my noticing all the errors to which my nature is liable, but also for enabling me to correct or avoid them without difficulty. To be sure, I know that all the senses set forth what is true more frequently than what is false regarding what concerns the welfare of the body. Moreover, I can nearly always make use of several of them in order to examine the same thing. Furthermore, I can use my memory, which connects current happenings with past ones, and my intellect, which now has examined all the causes of error. Hence I should no longer fear that those things that are daily shown me by the senses are false. On the contrary, the hyperbolic doubts of the last few days ought to be rejected as ludicrous. This goes especially for the chief reason for doubting, which dealt with my failure to distinguish being asleep from being awake. For I now notice that there is a considerable difference between these two; dreams are never joined by the memory with all the other actions of life, as is the case with those actions that occur when one is awake. For surely, if, while I am awake, someone were suddenly to appear to me and then immediately disappear, as occurs in dreams, so that I see neither where he came from nor where he went, it is not without reason that I would judge him to be a ghost or a phantom conjured up in my brain, rather than a true man. But when these things happen, and I notice distinctly where they come from, where they are now, and when they come to me, and when I connect my perception of them without interruption with the whole rest of my life, I am clearly certain that these perceptions have happened to me not while I was dreaming but while I was awake. (43) Nor ought I have even the least doubt regarding the truth of these things, if, having mustered all the senses, in addition to my memory and my intellect, in order to examine them, nothing is passed on to me by one of these sources that conflicts with the others. For from the fact that God is no deceiver, it follows that I am in no way mistaken in these matters. But because the need to get things done does not always permit us the leisure for such a careful inquiry, we must confess that the life of man is apt to commit errors regarding particular things, and we must acknowledge the infirmity of our nature.

(42)

R The preceding paragraphs contain Descartes's explanation of why the sorts of mistakes as to what is desirable or harmful that result from various sorts of abnormal conditions do not count against the goodness of God or show that he is a deceiver.

(43)

R And here, finally, is a response to the concern about dreaming.

STOP How does he think that dreams and waking experience can be distinguished? Is he right about this?

Discussion Questions

1. Descartes finally finds something indubitable in *Meditation Two:* his own existence. One question about this is whether Descartes's insight really takes the form of an argument, as the formulation "I think, therefore I am" suggests. On this view, the premise would be the claim (in the first person) "I think," from which the conclusion "I exist" is inferred. There is little doubt about the cogency of this inference, but the obvious question is why the premise is itself justified. Could the evil genius deceive me about the truth of this premise? Why or why not? Or is it perhaps, as some have suggested, a mistake to think of the Cogito as an argument at all, rather than as just one unitary insight? And what exactly would that insight be?
2. In addition to the claim that he cannot be deceived about his own existence, Descartes also claims that he cannot be deceived about the existence and content of his specific conscious states of mind. (See Annotation 10.) This is a crucial step, since very little could be inferred from his existence alone. Is he right that the evil genius could not deceive him about such things? Why or why not? (In thinking about this, it may be helpful to consider carefully just what form such deception would take: what would the evil genius do if he were trying to deceive me into thinking that I had a state of mind—perhaps a certain sensory experience—that I didn't really have?)
3. In *Meditation Three,* Descartes attempts to prove the existence of God in order to establish that he can safely accept claims that seem to him to be clear and distinct—which seems to amount to the same thing as claims revealed by the "light of nature." (See Annotation 19.) But to do this, he has to appeal to two general metaphysical principles (see Annotations 22 and 23). How does Descartes know that these principles are true? (Look carefully at what he says.) Can he safely accept these principles on this basis *before* he has proved the existence of God? What does this show about Descartes's main argument in *Meditation Three:* that God exists and therefore that he can trust his clear and distinct ideas?
4. Descartes offers two arguments for the conclusion that his mind and his body are two distinct entities, one in the passage at Annotation 35 and the second in the passage at Annotation 41. Formulate each of these arguments as carefully as you can and then assess their cogency.

5. How compelling is Descartes's main argument for the existence of external things (see Annotation 36)? One issue is whether this argument really yields the sort of *conclusive* reason for such beliefs that Descartes is seeking. And a second issue is just what specific conclusions about external things can be justified in this way: do we come to know merely that there are things of some sort out there, or can we know more specific facts about the nature and properties of particular things?

John Locke

Like Descartes, the English philosopher John Locke (1632–1704) was one of the most influential philosophers of all time, making major contributions to epistemology, metaphysics, and political philosophy. Locke was the founder of the philosophical movement that has come to be called *British Empiricism* (which also includes George Berkeley, David Hume, and John Stuart Mill, among others). The *Essay Concerning Human Understanding* is his major epistemological and metaphysical work and (like the *Meditations*) one of the most widely read of all philosophical books of all time, having attained the status of both a classic work and a widely used textbook for students almost as soon as it was published. (For more about Locke's rather colorful life, see the introduction to the selection from his *Second Treatise of Government,* in Chapter 6.)

Perhaps the key term of Locke's epistemology is "idea." Ideas are said to be the objects of the understanding when a person thinks, but this must not be taken to mean that we think only *about* ideas and not in some way about various other sorts of things, most of them external to the mind (including material objects). Locke's view is that ideas are the *immediate* objects of consciousness, that which is directly before the mind, but that these ideas *represent* other things and thus allow us to think about them. Thus it might be clearer to describe ideas as the *vehicles* of thinking, the means by which we think about other things. On this view, an idea is essentially the same thing or at least plays the same role as what more recent philosophers refer to with the term "concept": it is something that exists in or is a feature of the mind, and that allows it to think about some specific sort of thing. (But Locke also has at least a tendency to think of ideas as something like mental pictures or images, and it is doubtful that images can do the job of accounting for thought in general. See Discussion Question 1.)

With regard to how the mind acquires ideas, Locke is a thoroughgoing proponent of **concept empiricism** (see the introduction to this chapter). He argues in Book I of the *Essay* (not reproduced here) that there is no reason to hold that any ideas are **innate**, and offers in Book II a detailed account of the derivation of various specific ideas from experience. (The best way to evaluate his general view is to think carefully about these specific examples.)

With regard to **justificatory empiricism**, Locke's stance is more equivocal. Though the main goal of Book IV of the *Essay* is to give an account of the justification of knowledge that relies heavily on sense experience, Locke also holds (though not in the parts of the book excerpted here) that there are claims that are justified a priori rather than empirically and that not all of these are merely trivial matters of definition—"trifling truths," as he calls them. Locke thus holds a view rather similar to that of Descartes, holding much of our knowledge is justified by appeal to experience, but that some substantive, non-trivial claims are justified a priori. (His being standardly labeled an empiricist reflects the fact that the issue about the acquisition of ideas or concepts was formulated both earlier and initially more clearly than the issue about the nature of justification.)

The main focus of Book IV is on the specific issue of the justification of claims about the external material world. It is fair to say that Locke struggles mightily with this question, first giving a definition of knowledge that seems to leave no room for such knowledge and then gradually altering his position as he proceeds. This part of his discussion culminates in Chapter XI of Book IV, where Locke attempts to argue from certain features of our experience to the probable truth of the claims about material objects that we hold on the basis of that experience. This is a **representative realist** view similar to Descartes's attempt in *Meditation Six,* but unlike Descartes, Locke does not invoke God as a basis for his solution.

From *An Essay Concerning Human Understanding*

. . . Were it fit to trouble thee with the history of this *Essay,* I should tell thee that five or six friends, meeting at my chamber and discoursing on a subject very remote from this, found themselves quickly at a stand, by the difficulties that rose on every side. After we had awhile puzzled ourselves, without coming any nearer a resolution of those doubts which perplexed us, it came into my thoughts that we took a wrong course; and that before we set ourselves upon inquiries of that nature, it was necessary to examine our own abilities and see what objects our understandings were, or were not, fitted to deal with. . . .

The commonwealth of learning is not at this time without master-builders, whose mighty designs, in advancing the sciences, will leave lasting monuments to the admiration of posterity; but everyone must not hope to be a *Boyle* or a *Sydenham;* and in an age that produces such masters as the great *Huygenius* and the incomparable Mr. *Newton,* with some others of that strain, it is ambition enough to be employed as an under-labourer in clearing ground a little, and removing some of the rubbish that lies in the way to knowledge. ❶ . . . .

❶

In these two passages, we have a fairly standard conception of **epistemology** and its role: to investigate the nature of human understanding (human cognitive capacities) itself and to remove various sorts of confusions and other mistakes about cognition that impede the quest for more substantive knowledge.

Book II: Of Ideas

Chapter I: Of Ideas in General, and Their Original

1\. Every man being conscious to himself that he thinks, and that which his mind is applied about whilst thinking being the *ideas* that are there, it is past doubt that men have in their minds several *ideas* such as are those expressed by the words *whiteness, hardness, sweetness, thinking, motion, man, elephant, army, drunkenness* and others: it is in the first place then to be inquired, how he comes by them? . . .

2\. Let us then suppose the mind to be, as we say, white paper void of all characters, without any *ideas.* How comes it to be furnished? Whence comes it by that vast store which the busy and boundless fancy of man has painted on it with an almost endless variety? Whence has it all the materials of reason and knowledge? To this I answer, in one word, from *experience;* in that all our knowledge is founded, and from that it ultimately derives itself. Our observation, employed either about *external sensible objects, or about the internal operations of our minds perceived and reflected on by ourselves, is that which supplies our understandings with all the materials of thinking.* These two are the fountains of knowledge, from whence all the *ideas* we have, or can naturally have, do spring. ❷

❷

Here is Locke's initial statement of concept empiricism, which he will elaborate in the rest of Book II. The mind is initially "white paper," in Latin a *tabula rasa,* and it is only through experience that it comes to have the capacity to think about any specific thing.

3\. First, *our senses,* conversant about particular sensible objects, do *convey into the mind* several distinct *perceptions* of things, according to those various ways wherein those objects do affect them. And thus we come by those *ideas* we have of *yellow, white, heat, cold, soft, hard, bitter, sweet,* and all those which we call sensible qualities. . . . This great source of most of the *ideas* we have . . . , I call SENSATION.

4\. Secondly, the other fountain from which experience furnisheth the understanding with *ideas* is the *perception of the operations of our own minds* within us, as it is employed about the *ideas* it has got; which operations, when the soul comes to reflect on and consider, do furnish the understanding with another set of *ideas,* which could not be had from things without. And such are *perception, thinking, doubting, believing,*

From *An Essay Concerning Human Understanding,* 1689.

reasoning, knowing, willing, and all the different actings of our own mind . . . as I call the other *sensation,* so I call this REFLECTION, the *ideas* it affords being such only as the mind gets by reflecting on its own operations within itself. . . .

5. The understanding seems to me not to have the least glimmering of any *ideas* which it doth not receive from one of these two. *External objects furnish the mind with the* ideas *of sensible qualities,* which are all those different perceptions they produce in us; and the *mind furnishes the understanding with* ideas *of its own operations.* (3)

(3) R Try to think of examples of ideas that derive from each of the two main sources Locke mentions, specifying in each case the experience from which Locke would claim that the idea is derived.

These, when we have taken a full survey of them and their several modes, combinations, and relations, we shall find to contain all our whole stock of *ideas,* and that we have nothing in our minds which did not come in one of these two ways. Let anyone examine his own thoughts and thoroughly search into his understanding and then let him tell me whether all the original *ideas* he has there are any other than of the objects of his *senses,* or of the operations of his mind, considered as objects of his *reflection*. . . . (4)

R Here is the basic concept empiricist argument: a challenge to the opponent to identify any idea that cannot be accounted for in the empiricist way.

STOP (You should attempt to do this, in order to see how plausible Locke's claim is.)

Chapter II: Of Simple Ideas

1. The better to understand the nature, manner, and extent of our knowledge, one thing is carefully to be observed concerning the *ideas* we have, and that is that *some* of them are *simple* and *some complex.*

. . . The coldness and hardness which a man feels in a piece of *ice* being as distinct *ideas* in the mind as the smell and whiteness of a lily, or as the taste of sugar, and smell of a rose; and there is nothing can be plainer to a man than the clear and distinct perception he has of those simple *ideas;* which, being each in itself uncompounded, contains in it nothing but *one uniform appearance* or conception in the mind, and is not distinguishable into different *ideas.*

2. These simple *ideas,* the materials of all our knowledge, are suggested and furnished to the mind only by those two ways above mentioned, viz. *sensation* and *reflection.* When the understanding is once stored with these simple *ideas,* it has the power to repeat, compare, and unite them, even to an almost infinite variety, and so can make at pleasure new complex *ideas.* But it is not in the power of the most exalted wit or enlarged understanding, by any quickness or variety of thought, to *invent or frame one new simple* idea in the mind, not taken in by the ways before mentioned . . . .

Chapter III: Of Ideas of One Sense

1. The better to conceive the *ideas* we receive from sensation, it may not be amiss for us to consider them in reference to the different ways whereby they make their approaches to our minds and make themselves perceivable by us.

First, then, There are some which come into our minds *by one sense* only.

Secondly, There are others that convey themselves into the mind *by more senses than one.*

Thirdly, Others that are had from *reflection* only.

Fourthly, There are some that make themselves way and are suggested to the mind *by all the ways of sensation and reflection.*

We shall consider them apart under these several heads.

First, There are *some* ideas *which have admittance only through one sense,* which is peculiarly adapted to receive them. Thus light and colours, as white, red, yellow, blue, with their several degrees or shades and mixtures, as green, scarlet, purple, sea-green, and the rest, come in only by the eyes. All kinds of noises, sounds, and tones, only by the ears. The several tastes and smells, by the nose and palate. . . .

Chapter V: Of Simple Ideas of Divers Senses

The *ideas* we get by more than one sense are of *space* or *extension, figure, rest,* and *motion.* For these make perceivable impressions, both on the eyes and touch; and we can receive and convey into our minds the *ideas* of the extension, figure, motion, and rest of bodies, both by seeing and feeling. . . .

Chapter VI: Of Simple Ideas of Reflection

1. The mind, receiving the *ideas* mentioned in the foregoing chapters from without, when it turns its view inward upon itself and observes its own actions about those *ideas* it has, takes from thence other *ideas,* which are as capable to be the objects of its contemplation as any of those it received from foreign things.

2. The two great and principal actions of the mind, which are most frequently considered, and

which are so frequent that everyone that pleases may take notice of them in himself, are these two:

Perception, or *Thinking;* and
Volition, or *Willing.*

...

Chapter VII: Of Simple Ideas of Both Sensation and Reflection

1. There be other simple *ideas* which convey themselves into the mind by all the ways of sensation and reflection, viz.:

Pleasure or *Delight,* and its opposite.
Pain, or *Uneasiness.*
Power.
Existence.
Unity.

...

7. *Existence* and *unity* are two other *ideas* that are suggested to the understanding by every object without, and every *idea* within. When *ideas* are in our minds, we consider them as being actually there, as well as we consider things to be actually without us; which is, that they exist or have *existence.* And whatever we can consider as one thing, whether a real being or *idea,* suggests to the understanding the *idea* of *unity.*

8. *Power* also is another of those simple *ideas* which we receive from *sensation* and *reflection.* For, observing in ourselves that we can at pleasure move several parts of our bodies which were at rest; the effects, also, that natural bodies are able to produce in one another occurring every moment to our senses, we both these ways get the *idea* of *power.* [5]

...

Chapter VIII: Some Further Considerations Concerning Our Simple Ideas

...

7. To discover the nature of our *ideas* the better, and to discourse of them intelligibly, it will be convenient to distinguish them as they are *ideas* or perceptions in our minds, and as they are modifications of matter in the bodies that cause such perceptions in us: that so we *may not* think (as perhaps usually is done) that they are exactly the images and *resemblances* of something inherent in the subject: most of those of sensation being in the mind no more the likeness of something existing without us, than the names that stand for them are the likeness of our *ideas,* which yet upon hearing they are apt to excite in us.

8. Whatsoever the mind perceives in itself, or is the immediate object of perception, thought, or understanding, that I call *idea;* and the power to produce any *idea* in our mind, I call *quality* of the subject wherein that power is. Thus a snowball having the power to produce in us the *ideas* of *white, cold,* and *round,* the powers to produce those *ideas* in us as they are in the snowball I call *qualities;* and as they are sensations or perceptions in our understandings, I call them *ideas;* which *ideas,* if I speak of sometimes as in the things themselves, I would be understood to mean those qualities in the objects which produce them in us. [6]

9. Qualities thus considered in bodies are:

First, such as are utterly inseparable from the body, in what state soever it be; such as in all the alterations and changes it suffers, all the force can be used upon it, it constantly keeps; and such as sense constantly finds in every particle of matter which has bulk enough to be perceived; and the mind finds inseparable from every particle of matter, though less than to make itself singly be perceived by our senses. V.g., take a grain of wheat, divide it into two parts, each part has still *solidity, extension, figure,* and *mobility;* divide it again, and it retains still the same qualities; and so divide it on, till the parts become insensible: they must retain still each of them all those qualities. For division (which is all that a mill or pestle or any other body does upon another in reducing it to insensible parts) can never take away either solidity, extension, figure, or mobility from any body, but only makes two or more distinct separate masses of matter, of that which was but one before; all which distinct masses, reckoned as so many distinct bodies, after division make a certain number. These I call *original* or *primary qualities* of body; which I think we may observe to produce simple *ideas* in us, viz. solidity, extension, figure, motion or rest, and number.

10. Secondly, such *qualities* which in truth are nothing in the objects themselves but powers to produce various sensations in us by their

5

 The idea of *power* is the general idea of a causal capacity: the capacity of things of various sorts to causally affect other things or be causally affected by them.

6

 An *idea* in the mind is one thing; the corresponding quality in an object is something quite different. (At the beginning of section 7, and elsewhere, Locke seems to say that ideas have two kinds of existence: in minds and in objects. But as he clarifies, by speaking of ideas "as they are modifications of matter in the bodies that cause such perceptions," Locke means to refer to whatever in the body causes that idea—without assuming that it fits the content of the idea very closely.)

primary qualities, i.e. by the bulk, figure, texture, and motion of their insensible parts, as colours, sounds, tastes, etc. These I call *secondary qualities.* [7] To these might be added a third sort, which are allowed to be barely powers, though they are as much real qualities in the subject as those which I, to comply with the common way of speaking, call *qualities,* but for distinction, *secondary qualities.* For the power in fire to produce a new colour, or consistency in wax or clay, by its primary qualities, is as much a quality in fire as the power it has to produce in me a new *idea* or sensation of warmth or burning, which I felt not before, by the same primary qualities, viz. the bulk, texture, and motion of its insensible parts. [8]

. . .

15. . . . the *ideas of primary qualities* of bodies *are resemblances* of them, and their patterns do really exist in the bodies themselves; but the *ideas produced* in us *by* these *secondary qualities have no resemblance* of them at all. There is nothing like our *ideas* existing in the bodies themselves. They are, in the bodies we denominate from them, only a power to produce those sensations in us; and what is sweet, blue, or warm in *idea* is but the certain bulk, figure, and motion of the insensible parts in the bodies themselves, which we call so. [9]

. . .

21. *Ideas* being thus distinguished and understood, we may be able to give an account how the same water, at the same time, may produce the *idea* of cold by one hand and of heat by the other, whereas it is impossible that the same water, if those *ideas* were really in it, should at the same time be both hot and cold. For if we imagine *warmth* as it is *in our hands* to be *nothing but a certain sort and degree of motion in the minute particles of our nerves, or animal spirits,* we may understand how it is possible that the same water may at the same time produce the sensation of heat in one hand and cold in the other; which yet figure never does, that never producing the *idea* of a square by one hand which has produced the *idea* of a globe by another. But if the sensation of heat and cold be nothing but the increase or diminution of the motion of the minute parts of our bodies, caused by the corpuscles of any other body, it is easy to be understood that, if that motion be greater in one hand than in the other, if a body be applied to the two hands, which has in its minute particles a greater motion than in those of one of the hands, and a less than in those of the other, it will increase the motion of the one hand and lessen it in the other, and so cause the different sensations of heat and cold that depend thereon. [10]

. . .

23. The *qualities,* then, that are in *bodies,* rightly considered, are of *three sorts:*

First, The *bulk, figure, number, situation,* and *motion or rest* of their solid parts. Those are in them, whether we perceive them or no; and when they are of that size that we can discover them, we have by these an *idea* of the thing as it is in itself, as is plain in artificial things. These I call *primary qualities.*

Secondly, The *power* that is in any body, by reason of *its* insensible *primary qualities,* to operate after a peculiar manner on any of our senses, and thereby *produce in us* the *different ideas* of several colours, sounds, smells, tastes, etc. These are usually called sensible qualities.

Thirdly, The *power* that is in any body, *by* reason of the particular constitution of *its primary qualities, to* make such a *change* in the *bulk, figure, texture, and motion of another body,* as to make it operate on our senses differently from what it did before. Thus the sun has a power to make wax white, and fire to make lead fluid. These *are* usually called powers.

The first of these, as has been said, I think may be properly called *real, original,* or *primary qualities,* because they are in the things themselves, whether they are perceived or no; and upon their different modifications it is that the secondary qualities depend.

The other two are only powers to act differently upon other things, which powers result from the different modifications of those primary qualities.

. . .

Chapter XI: Of Discerning, and Other Operations of the Mind

. . .

9. The use of words then being to stand as outward marks of our internal *ideas,* and those

Primary qualities are genuinely in bodies *as the ideas in question represent them,* with the main argument being that bodies are inconceivable without such qualities. (Note here that solidity is the only such quality that is not essentially spatial or geometrical in character.) **Secondary qualities** are powers (causal capacities) in bodies to produce ideas in us; these powers result from the "bulk, figure, texture, and motion" of the "insensible parts" of the bodies—that is, from their primary qualities (compare the list of these here with the original one)—but the quality represented by an idea of a secondary quality does not exist, *as thus represented,* in the object.

8

A third sort of quality is a causal capacity in the object that is represented as such. Such qualities are again a result of the primary qualities of the insensible parts of the body.

(Thus what is odd and misleading about secondary qualities is that while they are, in Locke's view, really no more than powers, they are *represented* as though they were qualities on a par with primary qualities.)

9

But a possible source of trouble here is the talk of ideas *resembling* qualities in objects, something Berkeley will strongly object to. Think here of your idea of a certain shape (say, squareness) and an object whose surface has the quality in question. Is *resemblance* the right way to think about the relation between these two?

ideas being taken from particular things, if every particular *idea* that we take in should have a distinct name, names must be endless. To prevent this, the mind makes the particular *ideas* received from particular objects to become general; which is done by considering them as they are in the mind such appearances, separate from all other existences and the circumstances of real existence, as time, place, or any other concomitant *ideas.* This is called ABSTRACTION, whereby *ideas* taken from particular beings become general representatives of all of the same kind; and their names, general names, applicable to whatever exists conformable to such abstract *ideas.* Such precise, naked appearances in the mind, without considering how, whence, or with what others they came there, the understanding lays up (with names commonly annexed to them) as the standards to rank real existences into sorts, as they agree with these patterns, and to *denominate* them accordingly. Thus the same colour being observed to-day in chalk or snow, which the mind yesterday received from milk, it considers that appearance alone, makes it a representative of all of that kind; and having given it the name *whiteness,* it by that sound signifies the same quality wheresoever to be imagined or met with; and thus universals, whether *ideas* or terms, are made. (11)

. . . the *ideas first* in the mind, it is evident, are those of particular things; from whence, by slow degrees, the understanding proceeds to some few general ones; which, being taken from the ordinary and familiar objects of sense, are settled in the minds with general names to them. Thus particular *ideas* are *first* received and distinguished, and so knowledge got about them; and next to them, the less general or specific, which are next to particular. For abstract *ideas* are not so obvious or easy, to children or the yet unexercised mind, as particular ones. If they seem so to grown men, it is only because by constant and familiar use they are made so. For when we nicely reflect upon them, we shall find that general *ideas* are fictions and contrivances of the mind that carry difficulty with them, and do not so easily offer themselves as we are apt to imagine. For example, does it not require some pains and skill to form the *general idea* of a *triangle* (which is yet none of the most abstract, comprehensive, and difficult), for it must be neither oblique nor rectangle, neither equilateral, equicrural, nor scalenon; but all and none of these at once. In effect, it is something imperfect that cannot exist, an *idea* wherein some parts of several different and inconsistent *ideas* are put together. It is true, the mind in this imperfect state has need of such *ideas,* and makes all the haste to them it can, for the conveniency of communication and enlargement of knowledge, to both which it is naturally very much inclined. But yet one has reason to suspect such *ideas* are marks of our imperfection: at least, this is enough to show that the most abstract and general *ideas* are not those that the mind is *first* and most easily acquainted with, nor such as its earliest knowledge is conversant about. (12)

. . .

Chapter XII: Of Complex Ideas

. . .

6. . . . the *ideas* of *substances* are such combinations of simple ideas as are taken to represent distinct particular things subsisting by themselves, in which the supposed or confused *idea* of substance, such as it is, is always the first and chief. Thus if to substance be joined the simple *idea* of a certain dull whitish colour, with certain degrees of weight, hardness, ductility, and fusibility, we have the *idea* of *lead;* and a combination of the *ideas* of a certain sort of figure, with the powers of motion, thought, and reasoning, joined to substance, make the ordinary *idea* of *a man.* (13) . . .

Book IV: Of Knowledge and Opinion

Chapter I: Of Knowledge in General

1. Since *the mind,* in all its thoughts and reasonings, hath no other immediate object but its own *ideas,* which it alone does or can contemplate, it is evident that our knowledge is only conversant about them.

2. *Knowledge* then seems to me to be nothing but *the perception of the connexion and agreement, or disagreement and repugnancy, of any of our ideas.* In this alone it consists.

This example, also used by Berkeley, leads to the **argument from illusion.** To see the point, imagine that one of your hands has previously been in ice water and the other in water as hot as you can stand, while the "same water" in which they are now placed is lukewarm. If the experiences in question were direct apprehensions of actual qualities of the water, the discrepancy between them would be inexplicable. This is taken to show that the directly experienced qualities are only ideas in the mind.

It is the alleged capacity of abstraction that allows the mind to think in general or abstract terms. Locke's account works reasonably well for the example discussed here. In what follows, we insert a later passage (from Book IV, Chapter VII, section 9) in which Locke discusses a different, more difficult, and unfortunately probably more typical example: the abstract idea of a triangle.

This is one of the places where Locke seems to be thinking of ideas as images or mental pictures.

STOP What would an abstract *image* of a triangle (one that represents not one particular sort of triangle but rather triangles in general) be like?

One particularly important class of complex ideas is ideas of *substances:* concrete kinds of stuff or objects, such as lead or a man. By "the supposed or confused idea of substance," Locke means the underlying idea of a *substratum* in which all the various qualities pertaining to a certain kind of thing exist, but which has no qualities in itself. This is a puzzling notion, which Berkeley was quick to attack.

Here is Locke's initial definition of knowledge, which follows very naturally from the account of mental operations in the previous paragraph. If all that is immediately before the mind is ideas, then what can knowledge be but the perception of the ways in which they agree or disagree?

R The immediate problem, however, is how this allows for knowledge of things outside the mind, such as material objects of various sorts. Locke's first attempt to solve this problem is to construe such knowledge as perception of a special sort of agreement of ideas, one of which is the idea of "actual real existence."

But what is it for this idea to agree or disagree with others, and why couldn't it do so even if the thing in question didn't really exist?

Intuitive knowledge is the basis, in Locke's view, for knowledge of simple, self-evident truths like the ones enumerated. Later philosophers will describe these as **a priori.**

A second kind of knowledge is *demonstrative knowledge:* knowledge that results from more extended arguments or proofs, in which the individual steps are known intuitively.

(14) Where this perception is, there is knowledge; and where it is not, there, though we may fancy, guess, or believe, yet we always come short of knowledge. . . .

3. But to understand a little more distinctly wherein this agreement or disagreement consists, I think we may reduce it all to these four sorts:

1. *Identity,* or *diversity.*
2. *Relation.*
3. *Co-existence,* or *necessary connexion.*
4. *Real existence.*

4. *First,* As to the first sort of agreement or disagreement, viz. *identity* or *diversity.* It is the first act of the mind, when it has any sentiments or *ideas* at all, to perceive its *ideas,* and so far as it perceives them, to know each what it is, and thereby also to perceive their difference and that one is not another. . . .

5. *Secondly,* The next sort of agreement or disagreement the mind perceives in any of its *ideas* may, I think, be called *relative,* and is nothing but *the perception of the relation between any two ideas,* of what kind soever, whether substances, modes, or any other. . . .

6. *Thirdly,* The third sort of agreement or disagreement to be found in our *ideas,* which the perception of the mind is employed about, is *co-existence* or *non-co-existence* in the same subject; and this belongs particularly to substances . . . .

7. *Fourthly,* The fourth and last sort is that of *actual real existence* agreeing to any *idea.* (15) Within these four sorts of agreement or disagreement is, I suppose, contained all the knowledge we have or are capable of. . . .

Chapter II: Of the Degrees of Our Knowledge

1. . . . if we will reflect on our own ways of thinking, we shall find that sometimes the mind perceives the agreement or disagreement of two *ideas* immediately by themselves, without the intervention of any other; and this I think we may call *intuitive knowledge.* . . . Thus the mind perceives that *white* is not *black,* that a *circle* is not a *triangle,* that *three* are more than *two* and equal to *one* and *two.* Such kind of truths the mind perceives at the first sight of the *ideas* together, by bare *intuition,* without the intervention of any other *idea;* and this kind of knowledge is the clearest and most certain that human frailty is capable of. (16) . . .

2. The next degree of knowledge is where the mind perceives the agreement or disagreement of any *ideas,* but not immediately. . . . In this case then, when the mind cannot so bring its *ideas* together as by their immediate comparison and as it were juxtaposition or application one to another, to perceive their agreement or disagreement, it is fain, by the intervention of other *ideas* (one or more, as it happens) to discover the agreement or disagreement which it searches; and this is that which we call *reasoning.* Thus the mind, being willing to know the agreement or disagreement in bigness between the three angles of a triangle and two right ones, cannot by an immediate view and comparing them do it, because the three angles of a triangle cannot be brought at once and be compared with any one or two angles; and so of this the mind has no immediate, no intuitive knowledge. In this case the mind is fain to find out some other angles to which the three angles of a triangle have an equality, and finding those equal to two right ones, comes to know their equality to two right ones.

3. Those intervening *ideas* which serve to show the agreement of any two others are called *proofs;* and where the agreement or disagreement is by this means plainly and clearly perceived, it is called *demonstration:* it being *shown* to the understanding, and the mind made see that it is so. (17) . . .

14. These two, viz. intuition and demonstration, are the degrees of our knowledge; whatever comes short of one of these, with what assurance soever embraced, is but faith or opinion, but not knowledge, at least in all general truths. There is, indeed, another *perception* of the mind, employed about *the particular existence of finite beings* without us, which, going beyond bare probability and yet not reaching perfectly to either of the foregoing degrees of certainty, passes under the name of knowledge. There can be nothing more certain than that the *idea* we receive from an external object is in our minds: this is intuitive knowledge. But whether there be anything more than barely that *idea* in our minds, whether we can thence certainly infer the existence of anything without us which corresponds to that *idea* is that whereof some men think there may be a question made: because men may have such *ideas* in their minds,

when no such thing exists, no such object affects their senses. But yet here I think we are provided with an evidence that puts us past doubting: for I ask anyone whether he be not invincibly conscious to himself of a different perception, when he looks on the sun by day and thinks on it by night, when he actually . . . smells a rose or only thinks on that . . . odour? We as plainly find the difference there is between any *idea* revived in our minds by our own memory and actually coming into our minds by our senses, as we do between any two distinct *ideas.* If anyone say a dream may do the same thing, and all these *ideas* may be produced in us without any external objects, he may please to dream that I make him this answer: (1) That it is no great matter whether I remove his scruple or no: where all is but dream, reasoning and arguments are of no use, truth and knowledge nothing. (2) That I believe he will allow a very manifest difference between dreaming of being in the fire and being actually in it. But yet if he be resolved to appear so sceptical as to maintain that what I call being actually in the fire is nothing but a dream, and that we cannot thereby certainly know that any such thing as fire actually exists without us, I answer: that we certainly finding that pleasure or pain follows upon the application of certain objects to us whose existence we perceive or dream that we perceive by our senses, this certainty is as great as our happiness or misery, beyond which we have no concernment to know or to be. So that, I think, we may add to the two former sorts of *knowledge* this also of the existence of particular external objects, by that perception and consciousness we have of the actual entrance of *ideas* from them, and allow these *three degrees of knowledge,* viz. *intuitive, demonstrative, and sensitive,* in each of which there are different degrees and ways of evidence and certainty. [18]

. . .

Chapter IV: Of the Reality of Knowledge

1. I doubt not but my reader, by this time, may be apt to think that I have been all this while only building a castle in the air and be ready to say to me: To what purpose all this stir? Knowledge, say you, is only the perception of the agreement or disagreement of our own *ideas;* but who knows what those *ideas* may be? Is there anything so extravagant as the imaginations of men's brains? Where is the head that has no *chimeras* in it? Or if there be a sober and a wise man, what difference will there be by your rules between his knowledge and that of the most extravagant fancy in the world? . . . If it be true that all knowledge lies only in the perception of the agreement or disagreement of our own *ideas,* the visions of an enthusiast and the reasonings of a sober man will be equally certain. . . .

3. It is evident the mind knows not things immediately, but only by the intervention of the *ideas* it has of them. *Our knowledge,* therefore, is *real* only so far as there is a conformity between our *ideas* and the reality of things. But what shall be here the criterion? How shall the mind, when it perceives nothing but its own *ideas,* know that they agree with things themselves? [19] . . .

Chapter XI: Of Our Knowledge of the Existence of Other Things

1. The knowledge of our own being we have by intuition. The existence of a GOD, reason clearly makes known to us. . . .

The *knowledge of the existence* of any other thing we can have only by *sensation:* for, there being no necessary connexion of *real existence* with any *idea* a man hath in his memory, . . . no particular man can know the *existence* of any other being but only when, by actual operating upon him, it makes itself perceived by him. For the having the *idea* of anything in our mind no more proves the existence of that thing, than the picture of a man evidences his being in the world, or the visions of a dream make thereby a true history.

2. It is therefore the actual receiving of *ideas* from without that gives us notice of the *existence* of other things and makes us know that something doth exist at that time without us which causes that *idea* in us, though perhaps we neither know nor consider how it does it. . . . [20]

3. *The notice we have by our senses of the existing of things without us,* though it be not altogether so certain as our intuitive knowledge or the deductions of our reason employed about the clear abstract *ideas* of our own minds, yet it is an assurance that *deserves the name of knowledge.* If we persuade ourselves that our faculties act and inform us right concerning the existence of those objects that affect them, it cannot pass for an ill-grounded confidence: for I think

Here is Locke's second, and rather different, attempt to account for knowledge of external objects. Rather than an appeal to agreement of an idea of the thing in question with the idea of "actual real existence," Locke now seems to be appealing to the distinctive character of the ideas involved in sense perception, as contrasted with other ideas of the same object that are involved in memory or thought.

But it is far from clear just what this difference amounts to or why it should be taken to indicate actual existence outside the mind. Locke's nervousness about this issue is shown by the way he attempts to ridicule the skeptic—and also by his saying that cognition of the sort in question "passes under the name of knowledge," which surely raises the issue of whether it really *is* knowledge.

R Here the problem is realized and stated more clearly: how can we know, via perception of our ideas, that they accurately depict something existing outside our minds in the world?

R Here is another take on the issue of how external existence is known: not by agreement with the idea of "actual real existence" and not by the character of the ideas, taken in themselves, but by "the actual receiving" of them "from without."

But how, we may ask, is *this* known? What in our ideas reveals whether or not they have been thus "received from without"—that is, caused by external things?

nobody can, in earnest, be so sceptical as to be uncertain of the existence of those things which he sees and feels. At least, he that can doubt so far (whatever he may have with his own thoughts) will never have any controversy with me, since he can never be sure I say anything contrary to his opinion. 21 As to myself, I think GOD has given me assurance enough of the existence of things without me, since, by their different application, I can produce in myself both pleasure and pain, which is one great concernment of my present state. This is certain: the confidence that our faculties do not herein deceive us is the greatest assurance we are capable of concerning the existence of material beings. . . . But besides the assurance we have from our senses themselves, that they do not err in the information they give us of the existence of things without us when they are affected by them, we are further confirmed in this assurance by other concurrent reasons.

21

Again Locke shows his uncertainty about the question (the assurance in question "deserves the name of knowledge") and attempts to refute the skeptic through mockery.

STOP Think about the reasons for trusting our senses that are offered in this paragraph. Do any of them have any serious weight?

4. *First,* It is plain those perceptions are produced in us by exterior causes affecting our senses, because *those that want the organs of any sense never can have the* ideas *belonging to that sense* produced in their minds. This is too evident to be doubted, and therefore we cannot but be assured that they come in by the organs of that sense, and no other way. The organs themselves, it is plain, do not produce them: for then the eyes of a man in the dark would produce colours, and his nose smell roses in the winter; but we see nobody gets the relish of a pineapple till he goes to the *Indies,* where it is, and tastes it.

5. *Secondly,* Because *sometimes I find that I cannot avoid the having those* ideas *produced in my mind.* For though, when my eyes are shut, or windows fast, I can at pleasure recall to my mind the *ideas* of *light,* or the *sun,* which former sensations had lodged in my memory: so I can at pleasure lay by that *idea,* and take into my view that of the *smell* of a rose, or *taste* of sugar. But, if I turn my eyes at noon towards the sun, I cannot avoid the *ideas* which the light or sun then produces in me. So that there is a manifest difference between the *ideas* laid up in my memory (over which, if they were there only, I should have constantly the same power to dispose of them and lay them by at pleasure) and those which force themselves upon me and I cannot avoid having. And therefore it must needs be some exterior cause and the brisk acting of some objects without me, whose efficacy I cannot resist, that produces those *ideas* in my mind, whether I will or no. Besides, there is nobody who doth not perceive the difference in himself between contemplating the sun as he hath the *idea* of it in his memory, and actually looking upon it: of which two, his perception is so distinct that few of his *ideas* are more distinguishable one from another, and therefore he hath certain knowledge that they are not both memory or the actions of his mind and fancies only within him, but that actual seeing hath a cause without.

6. *Thirdly,* Add to this, that *many of those* ideas *are produced in us with pain, which afterwards we remember without the least offence.* Thus, the pain of heat or cold, when the *idea* of it is revived in our minds, gives us no disturbance, which when felt was very troublesome, and is again when actually repeated: which is occasioned by the disorder the external object causes in our bodies when applied to it; and we remember the pain of *hunger, thirst,* or the *headache* without any pain at all: which would either never disturb us, or else constantly do it as often as we thought of it, were there nothing more but *ideas* floating in our minds and appearances entertaining our fancies, without the real existence of things affecting us from abroad. The same may be said of pleasure accompanying several actual sensations. . . .

7. *Fourthly,* Our *senses* in many cases bear *witness* to the truth of each other's report concerning the existence of sensible things without us. He that sees a *fire* may, if he doubt whether it be anything more than a bare fancy, feel it too and be convinced by putting his hand in it. Which certainly could never be put into such exquisite pain by a bare *idea* or phantom, unless that the pain be a fancy too: which yet he cannot, when the burn is well, by raising the *idea* of it, bring upon himself again. 22

22

STOP These four "concurrent" reasons for thinking that our senses "do not err" are the closest that Locke comes to an argument for the truth of perceptual claims about the external world. Think about them carefully. They are of very unequal weight, and each of them can be considered alone or in combination with some or all of the others. Is there a good argument, or at least the beginnings of one, for the thesis that some of our ideas accurately represent external objects that really exist? (See Discussion Question 5.)

. . .

8. But yet, if after all this anyone will be so sceptical as to distrust his senses and to affirm that all we see and hear, feel and taste, think and do during our whole being is but the series and deluding appearances of a long dream, whereof there is no reality, and therefore will question the existence of all things or our knowledge of

anything: I must desire him to consider that, if all be a dream, then he doth but dream that he makes the question, and so it is not much matter that a waking man should answer him. But yet if he pleases he may dream that I make him this answer, that *the certainty of* things existing *in rerum natura,* when we have *the testimony of our senses* for it, is not only *as great* as our frame can attain to, but *as our condition needs.* For our faculties being suited not to the full extent of being, nor to a perfect, clear, comprehensive knowledge of things free from all doubt and scruple, but to the preservation of us in whom they are, and accommodated to the use of life: they serve to our purpose well enough if they will but give us certain notice of those things which are convenient or inconvenient to us. . . . And if our dreamer pleases to try whether the glowing heat of a glass furnace be barely a wandering imagination in a drowsy man's fancy, by putting his hand into it, he may perhaps be wakened into a certainty greater than he could wish that it is something more than bare imagination. 23 So that this evidence is as great as we can desire, being as certain to us as our pleasure or pain, i.e. happiness or misery, beyond which we have no concernment, either of knowing or being. Such an assurance of the existence of things without us is sufficient to direct us in the attaining the good and avoiding the evil which is caused by them, which is the important concernment we have of being made acquainted with them.

9. In fine then, when our senses do actually convey into our understandings any *idea,* we cannot but be satisfied that there doth something at that time really exist without us which doth affect our senses, and by them give notice of itself to our apprehensive faculties, and actually produce that *idea* which we then perceive; and we cannot so far distrust their testimony as to doubt that such collections of simple *ideas,* as we have observed by our senses to be united together, do really exist together. But *this knowledge extends as far as the present testimony of our senses,* employed about particular objects that do then affect them, *and no further.* For if I saw such a collection of simple *ideas* as is wont to be called *man,* existing together one minute since, and am now alone, I cannot be certain that the same man exists now, since there is no necessary connexion of his existence a minute since with his existence now: by a thousand ways he may cease to be since I had the testimony of my senses for his existence. And if I cannot be certain that the man I saw last today is now in being, I can less be certain that he is so who hath been longer removed from my senses and I have not seen since yesterday or since the last year; and much less can I be certain of the existence of men that I never saw. And, therefore, though it be highly probable that millions of men do now exist, yet, whilst I am alone, writing this, I have not that certainty of it which we strictly call knowledge: though the great likelihood of it puts me past doubt, and it be reasonable for me to do several things upon the confidence that there are men (and men also of my acquaintance, with whom I have to do) now in the world; but this is but probability, not knowledge.

23 R Again he resorts to mockery of the skeptic.

10. Whereby yet we may observe how foolish and vain a thing it is for a man of a narrow knowledge who, having reason given him to judge of the different evidence and probability of things and to be swayed accordingly, how *vain,* I say, it is *to expect demonstration* and certainty *in things not capable of it,* and refuse assent to very rational propositions and act contrary to very plain and clear truths because they cannot be made out so evident as to surmount every the least (I will not say reason, but) pretence of doubting. . . .

Discussion Questions

1. Locke often seems to be thinking of ideas as mental images or pictures. This would in effect mean that to think of things is to have a sequence of such images pass through our minds. Is this an adequate view of the general nature of thought? One specific problem is whether images as such, without anything accompanying them in the way that a caption accompanies a picture in the newspaper, really make claims that could be true or false.

2. How plausible is Locke's account in Book II of how we acquire our various concepts? Think of a range of examples, ask what Locke would say about them, and then evaluate whether his view seems correct. Remember that the issue is not whether you can find an experience to which the idea applies in some way or that provides an instance of the idea, but rather whether all the content of that idea can be found in explicit form in that

experience, whether the experience in itself is rich enough to supply all of that content. (Here are some cases to think about: the idea of the taste of lemon, the idea of a dog (not some particular dog or breed of dog, just dog in general), the idea of reflection (to which Locke appeals), the idea of trump (as it figures in various card games), the idea of a politician, and the idea of an electron.)

3. The distinction between primary and secondary qualities (in Book II, Chapter VIII) is one that Locke inherits from earlier thinkers, including Descartes, and he thinks it is obvious enough not to need argument. Does Locke's thesis here seem plausible to you: for example, do shapes really exist in material objects, while colors as we experience them exist only in our minds, with only the power to produce such an experience being in the object? Can you see any way to argue for this thesis? (Hint: think of what would be required to *explain* our having the experiences of these two qualities.)
4. Do we have *abstract* ideas? There are certainly abstract *terms* in our language, and on Locke's theory of meaning (expounded in Book III of the *Essay*—not included in the selections here), this would require that there are corresponding abstract ideas that provide the meanings of such terms. But do such ideas actually exist? Think first of the construal of them as images, considering various cases. Does this work? If not, can you think of any alternative to the image view that would still account for abstract thought?
5. Reconsider Locke's four reasons for thinking that our senses "do not err" in Chapter XI of Book IV. One of these is thoroughly question-begging (that is, it assumes the very sort of knowledge that Locke is trying to account for). Another, while perhaps correct, doesn't seem to point to the desired conclusion in any very clear way. The other two, while more suggestive, don't seem to work when taken individually, but may do better when taken together. With these hints, try to sort out these reasons and figure out which two of them, when taken together, do yield an argument for something like the conclusion Locke is aiming at. How strong is this argument? Can you think of any answer to it?

George Berkeley

George Berkeley (1685–1753) was an Irish philosopher who was also an Anglican bishop. Berkeley is another of the British Empiricists, and was greatly influenced by Locke. He is, however, most famous for his criticisms of Locke and his radically different view of both the objects and nature of human knowledge, especially perceptual knowledge. While both Locke and Berkeley believe that the direct or immediate objects of our experience, including perceptual experience, are ideas in our minds, Locke nonetheless believes in a commonsensical world of mind-independent material objects and thinks that we can have knowledge of such objects through inference from our sense experience, thus holding a **realist** view of the material world. Berkeley, in contrast, thinks that no such inference can be justified, and for this and other reasons holds the **idealist** view that ordinary objects (trees, tables, buildings, and so on) are nothing more than collections of ideas that are caused by God to occur in our minds. (Paradoxical though this may seem, Berkeley thought that in advocating this view, he was *defending* common sense against the threat of skepticism.)

Berkeley first defended idealism in his *Principles of Human Knowledge* (1710). When this book was poorly received, he attempted to restate its arguments in a more popularly accessible form in the *Three Dialogues Between Hylas and Philonous,* including also an extended defense of the thesis that the direct or immediate object of perceptual experience is always an idea in the mind—something that is not defended very explicitly in either Locke's *Essay* or Berkeley's own *Principles.* The two characters in the dialogue are Hylas (the name comes from the Greek word for matter) and Philonous (again from the Greek, meaning lover of mind), with the latter being the spokesman for Berkeley's own views. Hylas begins by defending a commonsensical view, gets driven into a roughly Lockean view, and eventually is forced to accept idealism. (The *Three Dialogues* are usually regarded as one of the most successful philosophical uses of dialogue form, ranking with Plato's dialogues and Hume's *Dialogues Concerning Natural Religion*—see Chapter 7.)

To help you discern the structure of the argument, we have inserted Roman numerals in brackets to mark the main divisions.

From *Three Dialogues Between Hylas and Philonous*

The First Dialogue

[I]

Philonous: Good morrow, Hylas: I did not expect to find you abroad so early.

Hylas: It is indeed something unusual; but my thoughts were so taken up with a subject I was discoursing of last night, that finding I could not sleep, I resolved to rise and take a turn in the garden.

Phil.: It happened well, to let you see what innocent and agreeable pleasures you lose every morning. Can there be a pleasanter time of the day, or a more delightful season of the year? That purple sky, these wild but sweet notes of birds, the fragrant bloom upon the trees and flowers, the gentle influence of the rising sun, these and a thousand nameless beauties of nature inspire the soul with secret transports; its faculties too being at this time fresh and lively, are fit for those meditations, which the solitude of a garden and tranquility of the morning naturally dispose us to. (1) But I am afraid I interrupt your thoughts: for you seemed very intent on something.

...

Hyl.: I was considering the odd fate of those men who have in all ages, through an affectation of being distinguished from the vulgar, or some unaccountable turn of thought, pretended either to believe nothing at all, or to believe the most extravagant things in the world. This however might be borne, if their paradoxes and scepticism did not draw after them some consequences of general disadvantage to mankind. But the mischief lies here; that when men of less leisure see them who are supposed to have spent their whole time in the pursuits of knowledge, professing an entire ignorance of all things, or advancing such notions as are repugnant to plain and commonly received principles, they will be tempted to entertain suspicions concerning the most important truths, which they had hitherto held sacred and unquestionable.

Phil.: I entirely agree with you, as to the ill tendency of the affected doubts of some Philosophers, and fantastical conceits of others . . . .

Hyl.: I am glad to find there was nothing in the accounts I heard of you.

Phil.: Pray, what were those?

Hyl.: You were represented in last night's conversation, as one who maintained the most extravagant opinion that ever entered into the mind of man, to wit, that there is no such thing as *material substance* in the world. (2)

Phil.: That there is no such thing as what Philosophers call *material substance,* I am seriously persuaded: but if I were made to see anything absurd or sceptical in this, I should then have the same reason to renounce this, that I imagine I have now to reject the contrary opinion.

Hyl.: What! Can anything be more fantastical, more repugnant to common sense, or a more manifest piece of scepticism, than to believe there is no such thing as *matter*?

Phil.: Softly, good Hylas. What if it should prove, that you, who hold there is, are by virtue of that opinion a greater *sceptic,* and maintain more paradoxes and repugnancies to common sense, than I who believe no such thing? . . . Pray, Hylas, what do you mean by a *sceptic*?

Hyl.: I mean what all men mean, one that doubts of everything.

Phil.: He then who entertains no doubt concerning some particular point, with regard to that point cannot be thought a *sceptic.*

Hyl.: I agree with you.

Phil.: . . . does doubting consist in embracing the affirmative or negative side of a question?

Hyl.: In neither; for whoever understands English, cannot but know that *doubting* signifies a suspense between both.

...

Phil.: How comes it then, Hylas, that you pronounce me a *sceptic,* because I deny what you affirm, to wit, the existence of matter?

From *Three Dialogues Between Hylas and Philonous,* 1713.

(1) This opening speech is intended to make clear at the outset that Philonous is not denying the existence of ordinary objects, such as those found in nature. Instead, as we will see further, he is offering an *interpretation* of what that existence amounts to, one that Berkeley at least believes to be in accord with common sense.

(2) The doctrine of material substance is Berkeley's interpretation of Locke's view of material objects, according to which an object consists of a **substance** (an independently existing thing) that has various qualities (for Locke, only primary qualities). Thus material substance is the sort of substance that exists outside the mind.

Since, for aught you can tell, I am as peremptory in my denial, as you in your affirmation.

Hyl.: Hold, Philonous, I have been a little out in my definition; but every false step a man makes in discourse is not to be insisted on. I said indeed, that a *sceptic* was one who doubted of everything; but I should have added, or who denies the reality and truth of things.

. . . What think you of distrusting the senses, of denying the real existence of sensible things, or pretending to know nothing of them. Is not this sufficient to denominate a man a *sceptic?*

Phil.: Shall we therefore examine which of us it is that denies the reality of sensible things, or professes the greatest ignorance of them since, if I take you rightly, he is to be esteemed the greatest *sceptic*?

Hyl.: That is what I desire.

[II]

Phil.: What mean you by sensible things?

Hyl.: Those things which are perceived by the senses. Can you imagine that I mean anything else?

Phil.: Pardon me, Hylas, if I am desirous clearly to apprehend your notions, since this may much shorten our inquiry. Suffer me then to ask you this further question. Are those things only perceived by the senses which are perceived immediately? Or, may those things properly be said to be *sensible,* which are perceived mediately, or not without the intervention of others?

Hyl.: I do not sufficiently understand you.

Phil.: In reading a book, what I immediately perceive are the letters, but mediately, or by means of these, are suggested to my mind the notions of God, virtue, truth, &c. Now, that the letters are truly sensible things, or perceived by sense, there is no doubt: but I would know whether you take the things suggested by them to be so too.

Hyl.: No certainly, it were absurd to think *God* or *virtue* sensible things, though they may be signified and suggested to the mind by sensible marks, with which they have an arbitrary connection.

Phil.: It seems then, that by *sensible things* you mean those only which can be perceived immediately by sense.

. . .

Hyl.: . . . I tell you once for all, that by *sensible things* I mean those only which are perceived by sense, and that in truth the senses perceive nothing which they do not perceive immediately: for they make no inferences. The deducing therefore of causes or occasions from effects and appearances, which alone are perceived by sense, entirely relates to reason. 3

3

Most of the First Dialogue is concerned with the question of just what it is that is *directly* or *immediately* perceived, directly before the mind, in sense perception—rather than being in some way inferred or perhaps arrived at via some other sort of transition.

STOP Before reading further, ask yourself what the answer is to this question.

Phil.: This point then is agreed between us, that *sensible things are those only which are immediately perceived by sense.* You will farther inform me, whether we immediately perceive by sight anything beside light, and colors, and figures: or by hearing anything but sounds: by the palate, anything beside tastes: by the smell, beside odors: or by the touch, more than tangible qualities.

Hyl.: We do not.

Phil.: It seems therefore, that if you take away all sensible qualities, there remains nothing sensible.

Hyl.: I grant it.

Phil.: Sensible things therefore are nothing else but so many sensible qualities, or combinations of sensible qualities.

Hyl.: Nothing else. 4

4

R The initial suggestion is that it is sensible qualities, qualities like color or shape or sound or taste or odor, that are immediately perceived, and that *sensible things* (things immediately perceived) consist only of these qualities. The next issue is then the nature or status of such qualities, in particular whether they are inside or outside of the mind, and the argument proceeds by considering separately various specific kinds of sensible qualities.

[III]

Phil.: Heat then is a sensible thing.

Hyl.: Certainly.

Phil.: Does the reality of sensible things consist in being perceived? Or, is it something distinct from their being perceived, and that bears no relation to the mind?

Hyl.: To *exist* is one thing, and to be *perceived* is another.

Phil.: I speak with regard to sensible things only: and of these I ask, whether by their real existence you mean a subsistence exterior to the mind, and distinct from their being perceived?

Hyl.: I mean a real absolute being, distinct from, and without any relation to, their being perceived.

Phil.: Heat therefore, if it be allowed a real being, must exist without the mind. 5

5

Berkeley's eventual thesis is that such qualities are only ideas in the mind and exist only by being perceived. Hylas attempts to attribute an independent existence to them, starting with the first example of heat (and cold).

Hyl.: It must.

Phil.: Tell me, Hylas, is this real existence equally compatible to all degrees of heat, which we perceive: or is there any reason why we should attribute it to some, and deny it to others? And if there be, pray let me know that reason.

Hyl.: Whatever degree of heat we perceive by sense, we may be sure the same exists in the object that occasions it.

Phil.: What, the greatest as well as the least?

Hyl.: I tell you, the reason is plainly the same in respect of both: they are both perceived by sense; nay, the greater degree of heat is more sensibly perceived; and consequently, if there is any difference, we are more certain of its real existence than we can be of the reality of a lesser degree.

Phil.: But is not the most vehement and intense degree of heat a very great pain?

Hyl.: No one can deny it.

Phil.: And is any unperceiving thing capable of pain or pleasure?

Hyl.: No, certainly.

Phil.: Is your material substance a senseless being, or a being endowed with sense and perception?

Hyl.: It is senseless, without doubt.

Phil.: It cannot therefore be the subject of pain.

Hyl.: By no means.

Phil.: Nor consequently of the greatest heat perceived by sense, since you acknowledge this to be no small pain.

Hyl.: I grant it.

Phil.: What shall we say then of your external object; is it a material substance, or no?

Hyl.: It is a material substance with the sensible qualities inhering in it. 6

Phil.: How then can a great heat exist in it, since you own it cannot in a material substance? I desire you would [clarify] this point.

Hyl.: Hold, Philonous, I fear I was out in yielding intense heat to be a pain. It should seem rather, that pain is something distinct from heat, and the consequence or effect of it.

Phil.: Upon putting your hand near the fire, do you perceive one simple uniform sensation, or two distinct sensations?

Hyl.: But one simple sensation.

Phil.: Is not the heat immediately perceived?

Hyl.: It is.

Phil.: And the pain?

Hyl.: True.

Phil.: Seeing therefore they are both immediately perceived at the same time, and the fire affects you only with one simple, or uncompounded idea, it follows that this same simple idea is both the intense heat immediately perceived, and the pain; and consequently, that the intense heat immediately perceived, is nothing distinct from a particular sort of pain. 7

Hyl.: It seems so.

Phil.: Again, try in your thoughts, Hylas, if you can conceive a vehement sensation to be without pain, or pleasure.

Hyl.: I cannot.

Phil.: Or can you frame to yourself an idea of sensible pain or pleasure in general, abstracted from every particular idea of heat, cold, tastes, smells? &c.

Hyl.: —I do not find that I can.

Phil.: Does it not therefore follow, that sensible pain is nothing distinct from those sensations or ideas, in an intense degree?

Hyl.: It is undeniable; and to speak the truth, I begin to suspect a very great heat cannot exist but in a mind perceiving it.

Phil.: What! Are you then in that *sceptical* state of suspense, between affirming and denying?

Hyl.: I think I may be positive in the point. A very violent and painful heat cannot exist without the mind. 8

Phil.: It has not therefore, according to you, any real being.

Hyl.: I own it.

Phil.: Is it therefore certain, that there is no body in nature really hot?

Hyl.: I have not denied there is any real heat in bodies. I only say, there is no such thing as an intense real heat.

Phil.: But did you not say before, that all degrees of heat were equally real: or if there was any difference, that the greater were more undoubtedly real than the lesser?

Hyl.: True: but it was, because I did not then consider the ground there is for distinguishing between them, which I now plainly see. And it is this: because intense heat is nothing else but a particular kind of painful sensation; and pain cannot exist but in a perceiving being; it follows that no intense heat can really exist in an unperceiving corporeal substance. But this is no reason why we should deny heat in an inferior degree to exist in such a substance.

If the quality of heat exists outside the mind, it must exist in a material **substance.** Being a quality or property, it couldn't simply exist on its own. This is a rather deep and subtle metaphysical point, which you will have to think carefully about. ("Inhere" is a metaphysical term for the relation between qualities and the substance they belong to—for example, the qualities of redness, approximate sphericality, juiciness, etc., *inhere* in a ripe apple.)

STOP Is this claim correct? Is an intense sensation of heat the very same quality as the corresponding sensation of pain, so that there is only one idea and not two?

R Having said "yes" to the question in the previous annotation, Hylas is forced to admit that heat of this degree cannot exist outside the mind.

Phil.: But how shall we be able to discern those degrees of heat which exist only in the mind, from those which exist without it?

Hyl.: That is no difficult matter. You know, the least pain cannot exist unperceived; whatever, therefore, degree of heat is a pain, exists only in the mind. But as for all other degrees of heat, nothing obliges us to think the same of them.

Phil.: I think you granted before, that no unperceiving being was capable of pleasure, any more than of pain.

Hyl.: I did.

Phil.: And is not warmth, or a more gentle degree of heat than what causes uneasiness, a pleasure?

Hyl.: What then?

Phil.: Consequently it cannot exist without the mind in any unperceiving substance, or body.

Hyl.: So it seems.

Phil.: Since therefore, as well those degrees of heat that are not painful, as those that are, can exist only in a thinking substance; may we not conclude that external bodies are absolutely incapable of any degree of heat whatsoever?

Hyl.: On second thoughts, I do not think it so evident that warmth is a pleasure, as that a great degree of heat is a pain.

Phil.: I do not pretend that warmth is as great a pleasure as heat is a pain. But if you grant it to be even a small pleasure, it serves to make good my conclusion.

Hyl.: I could rather call it an *indolence*. It seems to be nothing more than a privation of both pain and pleasure. And that such a quality or state as this may agree to an unthinking substance, I hope you will not deny.

Phil.: If you are resolved to maintain that warmth, or a gentle degree of heat, is no pleasure, I know not how to convince you otherwise than by appealing to your own sense. But what think you of cold?

Hyl.: The same that I do of heat. An intense degree of cold is a pain; for to feel a very great cold, is to perceive a great uneasiness: it cannot therefore exist without the mind; but a lesser degree of cold may, as well as a lesser degree of heat.

Phil.: Those bodies, therefore, upon whose application to our own, we perceive a moderate degree of heat, must be concluded to have a moderate degree of heat or warmth in them: and those, upon whose application we feel a like degree of cold, must be thought to have cold in them.

Hyl.: They must. 9

> **9** R Hylas resists saying that all degrees of heat and cold exist only in the mind, conceding this only for degrees of heat and cold extreme enough to involve pain. STOP (How plausible is the resulting view?)

Phil.: Can any doctrine be true that necessarily leads a man into an absurdity?

Hyl.: Without doubt it cannot.

Phil.: Is it not an absurdity to think that the same thing should be at the same time both cold and warm?

Hyl.: It is.

Phil.: Suppose now one of your hands hot, and the other cold and that they are both at once put into the same vessel of water, in an intermediate state; will not the water seem cold to one hand, and warm to the other?

Hyl.: It will.

Phil.: Ought we not therefore by your principles to conclude, it is really both cold and warm at the same time, that is, according to your own concession, to believe an absurdity?

Hyl.: I confess it seems so. 10

> **10** Here is quite a different argument, one usually regarded as substantially more compelling: the argument from illusion (or from perceptual relativity). STOP Try to formulate this argument more explicitly. Philonous argues that it is absurd to say that *both* of the experienced qualities are in the water, but does it follow (as is eventually concluded) that *neither* of them is? How might Philonous argue more explicitly for this further claim?

Phil.: Consequently, the principles themselves are false, since you have granted that no true principle leads to an absurdity.

Hyl.: But after all, can anything be more absurd than to say, *there is no heat in the fire*?

Phil.: To make the point still clearer; tell me, whether in two cases exactly alike, we ought not to make the same judgment?

Hyl.: We ought.

Phil.: When a pin pricks your finger, does it not rend and divide the fibres of your flesh?

Hyl.: It does.

Phil.: And when a coal burns your finger, does it any more?

Hyl.: It does not.

Phil.: Since therefore you neither judge the sensation itself occasioned by the pin, nor anything like it to be in the pin; you should not, conformably to what you have now granted, judge the sensation occasioned by the fire, or anything like it, to be in the fire.

Hyl.: Well, since it must be so, I am content to yield this point, and acknowledge, that heat and cold are only sensations existing in our minds: but there still remain qualities enough to secure the reality of external things.

[IV]

Phil.: But what will you say, Hylas, if it shall appear that the case is the same with regard to all other sensible qualities, and that they can no more be supposed to exist without the mind, than heat and cold?

Hyl.: Then indeed you will have done something to the purpose; but that is what I despair of seeing proved. (11)

Phil.: Let us examine them in order. What think you of tastes, do they exist without the mind, or no?

Hyl.: Can any man in his senses doubt whether sugar is sweet, or wormwood bitter?

Phil.: Inform me, Hylas. Is a sweet taste a particular kind of pleasure or pleasant sensation, or is it not?

Hyl.: It is.

Phil.: And is not bitterness some kind of uneasiness or pain?

Hyl.: I grant it.

Phil.: If therefore sugar and wormwood are unthinking corporeal substances existing without the mind, how can sweetness and bitterness, that is, pleasure and pain, agree to them?

Hyl.: Hold, Philonous, I now see what it was deluded me all this time. You asked whether heat and cold, sweetness and bitterness, were not particular sorts of pleasure and pain; to which I answered simply, that they were. Whereas I should have thus distinguished: those qualities, as perceived by us, are pleasures or pains, but not as existing in the external objects. We must not therefore conclude absolutely, that there is no heat in the fire, or sweetness in the sugar, but only that heat or sweetness, as perceived by us, are not in the fire or sugar. What say you to this?

Phil.: I say it is nothing to the purpose. Our discourse proceeded altogether concerning sensible things, which you defined to be the things we *immediately perceived by our senses*. Whatever other qualities therefore you speak of, as distinct from these, I know nothing of them, neither do they at all belong to the point in dispute. You may indeed pretend to have discovered certain qualities which you do not perceive, and assert those insensible qualities exist in fire and sugar. But what use can be made of this to your present purpose, I am at a loss to conceive. Tell me then once more, do you acknowledge that heat and cold, sweetness and bitterness, (meaning those qualities which are perceived by the senses) do not exist without the mind?

Hyl.: I see it is to no purpose to hold out, so I give up the cause as to those mentioned qualities. Though I profess it sound oddly, to say that sugar is not sweet.

Phil.: But for your farther satisfaction, take this along with you: that which at other times seems sweet, shall to a distempered palate appear bitter. And nothing can be plainer, than that divers persons perceive different tastes in the same food, since that which one man delights in, another abhors. And how could this be, if the taste was something really inherent in the food?

Hyl.: I acknowledge I know not how. (12)

Phil.: In the next place, odors are to be considered. And, with regard to these, I would fain know whether what has been said of tastes does not exactly agree to them? Are they not so many pleasing or displeasing sensations?

Hyl.: They are.

Phil.: Can you then conceive it possible that they should exist in an unperceiving thing?

Hyl.: I cannot.

Phil.: Or can you imagine, that filth and ordure affect those brute animals that feed on them out of choice, with the same smells which we perceive in them?

Hyl.: By no means.

Phil.: May we not therefore conclude of smells, as of the other forementioned qualities, that they cannot exist in any but a perceiving substance or mind?

Hyl.: I think so. (13)

Phil.: Then as to sounds, what must we think of them: are they accidents really inherent in external bodies, or not?

Hyl.: That they inhere not in the sonorous bodies, is plain from hence; because a bell struck in the exhausted receiver of an air-pump, sends forth no sound. The air therefore must be thought the subject of sound.

Phil.: What reason is there for that, Hylas?

Hyl.: Because when any motion is raised in the air, we perceive a sound greater or lesser, to the air's motion; but without some motion in the air, we never hear any sound at all.

(11)

R Can the conclusion regarding heat be extended to all other sensible qualities as well? This is the issue in the next several sections.

(12)

R Here is a brief reprisal of the argument from illusion, in application to taste.

STOP Think again of how the argument could be spelled out more explicitly.

(13)

The pain/pleasure argument is applied to odor, raising the same issue as before. No version of the argument from illusion is offered for qualities of smell, but you should be able to construct one.

Phil.: And granting that we never hear a sound but when some motion is produced in the air, yet I do not see how you can infer from thence, that the sound itself is in the air.

Hyl.: It is this very motion in the external air, that produces in the mind the sensation of *sound.* For, striking on the drum of the ear, it causes a vibration, which by the auditory nerves being communicated to the brain, the soul is thereupon affected with the sensation called *sound.*

Phil.: What! Is sound then a sensation?

Hyl.: I tell you, as perceived by us, it is a particular sensation in the mind.

Phil.: And can any sensation exist without the mind?

Hyl.: No certainly.

Phil.: How then can sound, being a sensation, exist in the air, if by the *air* you mean a senseless substance existing without the mind?

Hyl.: You must distinguish, Philonous, between sound as it is perceived by us, and as it is in itself; or (which is the same thing) between the sound we immediately perceive and that which exists without us. The former indeed is a particular kind of sensation, but the latter is merely a vibrative or undulatory motion in the air. [14]

[14] R Hylas does not question that sound *as heard* is a sensation in the mind, but attempts to argue that sound in a different sense exists as a vibration in the air. In the immediately following passage, Philonous insists again that it is only immediately perceived qualities with which the argument is concerned.

Phil. I thought I had already obviated that distinction by the answer I gave when you were applying it in a like case before. But to say no more of that; are you sure then that sound is really nothing but motion?

Hyl.: I am.

Phil.: Whatever therefore agrees to real sound, may with truth be attributed to motion.

Hyl.: It may.

Phil.: It is then good sense to speak of *motion,* as of a thing that is *loud, sweet, acute,* or *grave.*

Hyl.: I see you are resolved not to understand me. Is it not evident, those accidents or modes belong only to sensible sound, or *sound* in the common acceptation of the word, but not to *sound* in the real and Philosophic sense, which, as I just now told you, is nothing but a certain motion of the air?

Phil.: It seems then there are two sorts of sound, the one vulgar, or that which is heard, the other Philosophical and real.

Hyl.: Even so.

Phil.: And the latter consists in motion.

Hyl.: I told you so before.

Phil.: Tell me, Hylas, to which of the senses, think you, the idea of motion belongs: to the hearing?

Hyl.: No certainly, but to the sight and touch.

Phil.: It should follow then, that according to you, real sounds may possibly be *seen* or *felt,* but never *heard.*

Hyl.: Look you, Philonous, you may if you please make a jest of my opinion, but that will not alter the truth of things. I own indeed, the inferences you draw me into, sound something oddly; but common language, you know, is framed by, and for the use of, the vulgar: we must not therefore wonder, if expressions adapted to exact Philosophic notions, seem uncouth and out of the way.

Phil.: Is it come to that? I assure you, I imagine myself to have gained no small point, since you make so light of departing from common phrases and opinions; it being a main part of our inquiry, to examine whose notions are widest of the common road, and most repugnant to the general sense of the world. But can you think it no more than a Philosophical paradox, to say that *real sounds are never heard,* and that the idea of them is obtained by some other sense. And is there nothing in this contrary to nature and the truth of things?

Hyl.: To deal ingenuously, I do not like it. And after the concessions already made, I had as well grant that sounds too have no real being without the mind. [15]

[15] R The further argument is offered that sound as a motion is not the sort of thing that could be heard. How compelling is this?

(Note that the issue doesn't really matter very much, since the sensible qualities that are immediately perceived have already been conceded to exist only in the mind. Think how Berkeley might have argued further for such a claim about sound *as heard* by using arguments of the same sorts as were applied to heat and tastes.)

[V]

Phil.: And I hope you will make no difficulty to acknowledge the same of colors.

Hyl.: Pardon me: the case of colors is very different. Can anything be plainer, than that we see them on the objects?

Phil.: The objects you speak of are, I suppose, corporeal substances existing without the mind.

Hyl.: They are.

Phil.: And have true and real colors inhering in them?

Hyl.: Each visible object has that color which we see in it. [16]

[16]  The claim that corporeal objects have the color we see in them is at least roughly the common-sense view of color.

Phil.: How! Is there anything visible but what we perceive by sight.

Hyl.: There is not.

Phil.: And do we perceive anything by sense, which we do not perceive immediately?

Hyl.: How often must I be obliged to repeat the same thing? I tell you, we do not.

Phil.: Have patience, good Hylas; and tell me once more, whether there is anything immediately perceived by the senses, except sensible qualities. I know you asserted there was not: but I would now be informed, whether you still persist in the same opinion.

Hyl.: I do.

Phil.: Pray, is your corporeal substance either a sensible quality, or made up of sensible qualities?

Hyl.: What a question that is! Who ever thought it was?

Phil.: My reason for asking was, because in saying, *Each visible object has that color which we see in it,* you make visible objects to be corporeal substances; which implies either that corporeal substances are sensible qualities, or else that there is something beside sensible qualities perceived by sight: but as this point was formerly agreed between us, and is still maintained by you, it is a clear consequence, that your corporeal substance is nothing distinct from sensible qualities. 17

Hyl.: You may draw as many absurd consequences as you please, and endeavor to perplex the plainest things; but you shall never persuade me out of my senses. I clearly understand my own meaning.

Phil.: I wish you would make me understand it too. But since you are unwilling to have your notion of corporeal substance examined, I shall urge that point no farther. Only be pleased to let me know, whether the same colors which we see, exist in external bodies, or some other.

Hyl.: The very same.

Phil.: What! Are then the beautiful red and purple we see on yonder clouds, really in them? Or do you imagine they have in themselves any other form, than that of a dark mist or vapor?

Hyl.: I must own, Philonous, those colors are not really in the clouds as they seem to be at this distance. They are only apparent colors.

Phil.: *Apparent* call you them? How shall we distinguish these apparent colors from real?

Hyl.: Very easily. Those are to be thought apparent, which appearing only at a distance, vanish upon a nearer approach.

Phil.: And those I suppose are to be thought real, which are discovered by the most near and exact survey.

Hyl.: Right.

Phil.: Is the nearest and exactest survey made by the help of a microscope, or by the naked eye?

Hyl.: By a microscope, doubtless.

Phil.: But a microscope often discovers colors in an object different from those perceived by the unassisted sight. And in case we had microscopes magnifying to any assigned degree; it is certain, that no object whatsoever, viewed through them, would appear in the same color which it exhibits to the naked eye.

Hyl.: And what will you conclude from all this? You cannot argue that there are really and naturally no colors on objects: because by artificial managements they may be altered, or made to vanish.

Phil.: I think it may evidently be concluded from your own concessions, that all the colors we see with our naked eyes, are only apparent as those on the clouds, since they vanish upon a more close and accurate inspection, which is afforded us by a microscope. Then as to what you say by way of prevention: I ask you, whether the real and natural state of an object is better discovered by a very sharp and piercing sight, or by one which is less sharp?

Hyl.: By the former without doubt.

Phil.: Is it not plain . . . that microscopes make the sight more penetrating, and represent objects as they would appear to the eye in case it were naturally endowed with a most exquisite sharpness?

Hyl.: It is.

Phil.: Consequently the microscopical representation is to be thought that which best sets forth the real nature of the thing, or what it is in itself. The colors, therefore, by it perceived, are more genuine and real, than those perceived otherwise.

Hyl.: I confess there is something in what you say.

. . .

Phil.: The point will be past all doubt, if you consider, that in case colors were real properties or affections inherent in external

17

R This is an argument against Locke's conception of substance (see Annotation 13 to the Locke selection): a material or corporeal substance is supposed to be something that *has* sensible qualities like color, but is itself distinct from them; but all we perceive is sensible qualities, so such a substance must be nothing more than sensible qualities—or else something that we do not perceive at all and so arguably have no idea at all of.

bodies, they could admit of no alteration, without some change wrought in the very bodies themselves: but is it not evident from what has been said, that upon the use of microscopes, upon a change happening in the humors of the eye, or a variation of distance, without any manner of real alteration in the thing itself, the colors of any object are either changed, or totally disappear? Nay, all other circumstances remaining the same, change but the situation of some objects, and they shall present different colors to the eye. The same thing happens upon viewing an object in various degrees of light. And what is more known, than that the same-bodies appear differently colored by candle-light from what they do in the open day? Add to these the experiment of a prism, which separating the heterogeneous rays of light, alters the color of any object; and will cause the whitest to appear of a deep blue or red to the naked eye. And now tell me, whether you are still of opinion that every body has its true real color inhering in it: and if you think it has, I would fain know farther from you, what certain distance and position of the object, what peculiar texture and formation of the eye, what degree or kind of light is necessary for ascertaining that true color, and distinguishing it from apparent ones. 18

Hyl.: I own myself entirely satisfied, that they are all equally apparent; and that there is no such thing as color really inhering in external bodies, but that it is altogether in the light. And what confirms me in this opinion is, that in proportion to the light, colors are still more or less vivid; and if there be no light, then are there no colors perceived. Besides, allowing there are colors on external objects, yet how is it possible for us to perceive them? For no external body affects the mind, unless it act first on our organs of sense. But the only action of bodies is motion; and motion cannot be communicated otherwise than by impulse. A distant object therefore cannot act on the eye, nor consequently make itself or its properties perceivable to the soul. Whence it plainly follows, that it is immediately some contiguous substance, which operating on the eye occasions a perception of colors: and such is light.

Phil.: How! Is light then a substance?

Hyl.: I tell you, Philonous, external light is nothing but a thin fluid substance, whose minute particles being agitated with a brisk motion, and in various manners reflected from the different surfaces of outward objects to the eyes, communicate different motions to the optic nerves; which, being propagated to the brain, cause therein various impressions: and these are attended with the sensations of red, blue, yellow, &c.

Phil.: It seems then, the light does no more than shake the optic nerves.

Hyl.: Nothing else.

Phil.: And consequent to each particular motion of the nerves, the mind is affected with a sensation, which is some particular color.

Hyl.: Right.

Phil.: And these sensations have no existence without the mind.

Hyl.: They have not.

Phil.: How then do you affirm that colors are in the light, since by *light* you understand a corporeal substance external to the mind?

Hyl.: Light and colors, as immediately perceived by us, I grant cannot exist without the mind. But in themselves they are only the motions and configurations of certain insensible particles of matter.

Phil.: Colors then, in the vulgar sense, or taken for the immediate objects of sight, cannot agree to any but a perceiving substance.

Hyl.: That is what I say.

Phil.: Well then, since you give up the point as to those sensible qualities, which are alone thought colors by all mankind beside, you may hold what you please with regard to those invisible ones of the Philosophers. 19 It is not my business to dispute about them; only I would advise you to bethink yourself, whether considering the inquiry we are upon, it be prudent for you to affirm, *The red and blue which we see are not real colors, but certain unknown motions and figures which no man ever did or can see are truly so.* Are not these shocking notions and are not they subject to as many ridiculous inferences, as those you were obliged to renounce before in the case of sounds?

18

Here is another version of the argument from illusion, this time applied to colors. This version is more complicated, because the different color qualities are not experienced at the same moment. The additional premise needed is that the changes that yield different color experiences involve no change in the object itself. (Philonous's remark at the end of this last paragraph may suggest a way of dealing with the issue, raised in Annotation 10, of why the conclusion should be that *none* of the experienced qualities are external to the mind, rather than merely that not all of them are.)

19

R Hylas accepts the result that color is not in bodies, but suggests that it is in light instead (which would still be something external to the mind). But in trying to explain how color is in light, he is forced to admit that the color sensations we directly experience are in the mind, even if their cause is external.

[VI]

Hyl.: I frankly own, Philonous, that it is in vain to stand out any longer. Colors, sounds, tastes, in a word, all those termed *secondary qualities,* have certainly no existence without the mind. But by this acknowledgment I must not be supposed to derogate anything from the reality of matter or external objects, seeing it is no more than several Philosophers maintain, who nevertheless are the farthest imaginable from denying matter. For the clearer understanding of this, you must know sensible qualities are by Philosophers divided into *primary* and *secondary.* The former are extension, figure, solidity, gravity, motion, and rest. And these they hold exist really in bodies. The latter are those above enumerated; or briefly, all sensible qualities beside the primary, which they assert are only so many sensations or ideas existing nowhere but in the mind. But all this, I doubt not, you are already apprised of. For my part, I have been a long time sensible there was such an opinion current among Philosophers, but was never thoroughly convinced of its truth till now. [20]

Phil.: You are still then of opinion that extension and figures are inherent in external unthinking substances.

Hyl.: I am.

Phil.: But what if the same arguments which are brought against secondary qualities, will hold good against these also?

Hyl.: Why then I shall be obliged to think, they too exist only in the mind.

Phil.: Is it your opinion, the very figure and extension which you perceive by sense, exist in the outward object or material substance?

Hyl.: It is.

. . .

Phil.: . . . have you not acknowledged that no real inherent property of any object can be changed, without some change in the thing itself?

Hyl.: I have.

Phil.: But as we approach to or recede from an object, the visible extension varies, being at one distance ten or a hundred times greater than at another. Does it not therefore follow from hence likewise, that it is not really inherent in the object?

Hyl.: I own I am at a loss what to think.

Phil.: Your judgment will soon be determined, if you will venture to think as freely concerning this quality, as you have done concerning the rest. Was it not admitted as a good argument, that neither heat nor cold was in the water, because it seemed warm to one hand, and cold to the other?

Hyl.: It was.

Phil.: Is it not the very same reasoning to conclude, there is no extension or figure in an object, because to one eye it shall seem little, smooth, and round, when at the same time it appears to the other, great, uneven, and angular?

Hyl.: The very same. But does this latter fact ever happen?

Phil.: You may at any time make the experiment, by looking with one eye bare, and with the other through a microscope.

Hyl.: I know not how to maintain it, and yet I am loath to give up *extension,* I see so many odd consequences following upon such a concession. [21]

Phil.: Odd, say you? After the concessions already made, I hope you will stick at nothing for its oddness. . . .

Hyl.: I give up the point for the present, reserving still a right to retract my opinion, in case I shall hereafter discover any false step in my progress to it.

[20] R Hylas retreats to the Lockean distinction between primary and secondary qualities, agreeing that secondary qualities exist only in the mind, but claiming that primary qualities exist in external objects. (See Annotation 7 to the Locke selection and the associated text.)

R Philonous proceeds to apply the argument from illusion to figure (shape) and extension (size).

[VII]

Phil.: That is a right you cannot be denied. Figures and extension being dispatched, we proceed next to *motion.* Can a real motion in any external body be at the same time both very swift and very slow?

Hyl.: It cannot.

Phil.: Is not the motion of a body swift in a reciprocal proportion to the time it takes up in describing any given space? Thus a body that describes a mile in an hour, moves three times faster than it would in case it described only a mile in three hours.

Hyl.: I agree with you.

Phil.: And is not time measured by the succession of ideas in our minds?

Hyl.: It is.

Phil.: And is it not possible ideas should succeed one another twice as fast in your mind, as they do in mine, or in that of some spirit of another kind.

Hyl.: I own it.

Phil.: Consequently the same body may to another seem to perform its motion over any space in half the time that it does to you. And the same reasoning will hold as to any other proportion: that is to say, according to your principles (since the motions perceived are both really in the object) it is possible one and the same body shall be really moved the same way at once, both very swift and very slow. How is this consistent either with common sense, or with what you just now granted?

Hyl.: I have nothing to say to it. 22

22

Here it is important to realize that what the argument is concerned with is motion as directly experienced, not motion as measured (for example, by a speedometer). The claim that time is measured by the speed with which ideas succeed each other in the mind is not particularly plausible. Can you think of a better argument here? (See Discussion Question 4.)

Phil.: Then as for *solidity;* either you do not mean any sensible quality by that word, and so it is beside our inquiry: or if you do, it must be either hardness or resistance. But both the one and the other are plainly relative to our senses: it being evident, that what seems hard to one animal, may appear soft to another, who hath greater force and firmness of limbs. Nor is it less plain, that the resistance I feel is not in the body.

Hyl.: I own the very sensation of resistance, which is all you immediately perceive, is not in the *body;* but the cause of that sensation is.

Phil.: But the causes of our sensations are not things immediately perceived, and therefore not sensible. This point I thought had been already determined.

Hyl.: I own it was; but you will pardon me if I seem a little embarrassed: I know not how to quit my old notions. 23

23

Here is a quick gesture at the argument from illusion in application to solidity—you should try to spell it out more fully. In the following paragraph, Philonous argues further that other primary qualities presuppose extension and so cannot be outside the mind if it is not.

Phil.: To help you out, do but consider that if extension be once acknowledged to have no existence without the mind, the same must necessarily be granted of motion, solidity, and gravity, since they all evidently suppose extension. It is therefore superfluous to inquire particularly concerning each of them. In denying extension, you have denied them all to have any real existence.

. . .

Phil.: Can you even separate the ideas of extension and motion, from the ideas of all those qualities which they who make the distinction, term *secondary*?

Hyl.: What! Is it not an easy matter, to consider extension and motion by themselves, abstracted from all other sensible qualities? Pray how do the mathematicians treat of them?

Phil.: I acknowledge, Hylas, it is not difficult to form general propositions and reasonings about those qualities, without mentioning any other; and in this sense to consider or treat of them abstractedly. But how does it follow that because I can pronounce the word *motion* by itself, I can form the idea of it in my mind exclusive of body? Or because theorems may be made of extension and figures, without any mention of *great* or *small,* or any other sensible mode or quality; that therefore it is possible such an abstract idea of extension, without any particular size or figure, or sensible quality, should be distinctly formed, and apprehended by the mind? . . .

Hyl.: But what say you to *pure intellect*? May not abstracted ideas be framed by that faculty?

Phil.: Since I cannot frame abstract ideas at all, it is plain, I cannot frame them by the help of *pure intellect,* whatsoever faculty you understand by those words. Besides, . . . thus much seems manifest, that sensible things are only to be perceived by sense, or represented by the imagination. Figures, therefore, and extension, being originally perceived by sense, do not belong to pure intellect. But for your farther satisfaction, try if you can frame the idea of any figure, abstracted from all particularities of size, or even from other sensible qualities.

Hyl.: Let me think a little—I do not find that I can.

Phil.: And can you think it possible, that should really exist in nature, which implies a repugnancy in its conception?

Hyl.: By no means.

Phil.: Since therefore it is impossible even for the mind to disunite the ideas of extension and motion from all other sensible qualities, does it not follow, that where the one exist, there necessarily the other exist likewise?

Hyl.: It should seem so.

Phil.: Consequently the very same arguments which you admitted, as conclusive against the secondary qualities, are, without any farther application of force, against the primary too. Besides, if you will trust your senses, is it not plain, all sensible qualities coexist, or, to them, appear as being in the same place? Do they ever represent a motion, or figure, as being divested of all other visible and tangible qualities?

Hyl.: You need say no more on this head. I am free to own, if there be no secret error or oversight in our proceedings hitherto, that all sensible qualities are alike to be denied existence without the mind. But my fear is, that I have been too liberal in my former concessions, or overlooked some fallacy or other. In short, I did not take time to think. 24

...

[VIII]

Hyl.: I acknowledge, Philonous, that upon a fair observation of what passes in my mind, I can discover nothing else, but that I am a thinking being, affected with variety of sensations; neither is it possible to conceive how a sensation should exist in an unperceiving substance. But then on the other hand, when I look on sensible things in a different view, considering them as so many modes and qualities, I find it necessary to suppose a material *substratum,* without which they cannot be conceived to exist.

Phil.: *Material substratum* call you it? Pray, by which of your senses came you acquainted with that being?

Hyl.: It is not itself sensible; its modes and qualities only being perceived by the senses.

Phil.: I presume then it was by reflection and reason you obtained the idea of it.

Hyl.: I do not pretend to any proper positive idea of it. However I conclude it exists, because qualities cannot be conceived to exist without a support. 25

Phil.: It seems then you have only a relative notion of it, or that you conceive it not otherwise than by conceiving the relation it bears to sensible qualities.

Hyl.: Right.

Phil.: Be pleased therefore to let me know wherein that relation consists.

Hyl.: Is it not sufficiently expressed in the term *substratum,* or *substance*?

Phil.: If so, the word *substratum* should import, that it is spread under the sensible qualities or accidents.

Hyl.: True.

Phil.: And consequently under extension.

Hyl.: I own it.

Phil.: It is therefore somewhat in its own nature entirely distinct from extension.

Hyl.: I tell you, extension is only a mode, and matter is something that supports modes. And is it not evident the thing supported is different from the thing supporting?

Phil.: So that something distinct from, and exclusive of, extension, is supposed to be the *substratum* of extension.

Hyl.: Just so.

Phil.: Answer me, Hylas. Can a thing be spread without extension? Or is not the idea of extension necessarily included in *spreading*?

Hyl.: It is.

Phil.: Whatsoever therefore you suppose spread under anything, must have in itself an extension distinct from the extension of that thing under which it is spread.

Hyl.: It must.

Phil.: Consequently every corporeal substance, being the *substratum* of extension, must have in itself another extension by which it is qualified to be a *substratum:* and so on to infinity. And I ask whether this be not absurd in itself, and repugnant to what you granted just now, to wit, that the *substratum* was something distinct from, and exclusive of, extension.

Hyl.: Aye but, Philonous, you take me wrong. I do not mean that matter is *spread* in a gross literal sense under extension. The word *substratum* is used only to express in general the same thing with *substance.*

Phil.: Well then, let us examine the relation implied in the term *substance.* Is it not that it stands under accidents?

Hyl.: The very same.

Phil.: But that one thing may stand under or support another, must it not be extended?

Hyl.: It must.

Phil.: Is not therefore this supposition liable to the same absurdity with the former?

Hyl.: You still take things in a strict literal sense: that is not fair, Philonous.

Phil.: I am not for imposing any sense on your words: you are at liberty to explain them as

R A further argument against the separate existence of primary qualities is that we have no ideas of them in isolation from secondary qualities. At this point, Hylas surrenders and concedes that all sensible qualities exist only in the mind.

Here, as elsewhere, ideas seem to be regarded as *images,* with the point being that any image of, for example, a particular shape must also involve other qualities like color that delineate the shape.

Here is another attack on the Lockean idea of substance, spelling out the argument that was only hinted at in the text corresponding to Annotation 17. Hylas uses the variant term *substratum* for substance, with the idea being that material substance *underlies* or *supports* the qualities that inhere in it. But since all our ideas are of qualities, he is forced to admit that he has no real idea of material substance itself.

you please. Only I beseech you, make me understand something by them. You tell me, matter supports or stands under accidents. How! Is it as your legs support your body?

Hyl.: No; that is the literal sense.

Phil.: Pray let me know any sense, literal or not literal, that you understand it in.—How long must I wait for an answer, Hylas?

Hyl.: I declare I know not what to say. I once thought I understood well enough what was meant by matter's supporting accidents. But now the more I think on it, the less can I comprehend it; in short, I find that I know nothing of it.

Phil.: It seems then you have no idea at all, neither relative nor positive of matter; you know neither what it is in itself, nor what relation it bears to accidents.

Hyl.: I acknowledge it. 26

26

R Philonous ruthlessly drives home the point that Hylas has no intelligible idea of either substance itself or its relation to qualities.

Phil.: And yet you asserted, that you could not conceive how qualities or accidents should really exist, without conceiving at the same time a material support of them.

Hyl.: I did.

Phil.: That is to say, when you conceive the real existence of qualities, you do withal conceive something which you cannot conceive.

[IX]

Hyl.: It was wrong I own. But still I fear there is some fallacy or other. Pray what think you of this? It is just come into my head, that the ground of all our mistake lies in your treating of each quality by itself. Now, I grant that each quality cannot singly subsist without the mind. Color cannot without extension, neither can figure without some other sensible quality. But as the several qualities united or blended together form entire sensible things, nothing hinders why such things may not be supposed to exist without the mind.

Phil.: Either, Hylas, you are jesting, or have a very bad memory. Though indeed we went through all the qualities by name one after another; yet my arguments, or rather your concessions, nowhere tended to prove, that the secondary qualities did not subsist each alone by itself; but that they were not *at all* without the mind. Indeed in treating of figure and motion, we concluded they could not exist without the mind, because it was impossible even in thought to separate them from all secondary qualities, so as to conceive them existing by themselves. . . . But (to pass by all that hath been hitherto said, and reckon it for nothing, if you will have it so) I am content to put the whole upon this issue. If you can conceive it possible for any mixture or combination of qualities, or any sensible object whatever, to exist without the mind, then I will grant it actually to be so.

Hyl.: If it comes to that, the point will soon be decided. What more easy than to conceive a tree or house existing by itself, independent of, and unperceived by, any mind whatsoever? I do at this present time conceive them existing after that manner.

Phil.: How say you, Hylas, can you see a thing which is at the same time unseen?

Hyl.: No, that were a contradiction.

Phil.: Is it not as great a contradiction to talk of *conceiving* a thing which is *unconceived*?

Hyl.: It is.

Phil.: The tree or house therefore which you think of, is conceived by you.

Hyl.: How should it be otherwise?

Phil.: And what is conceived is surely in the mind.

Hyl.: Without question, that which is conceived is in the mind.

Phil.: How then came you to say, you conceived a house or tree existing independent and out of all minds whatsoever?

Hyl.: That was I own an oversight; but stay, let me consider what led me into it.—It is a pleasant mistake enough. As I was thinking of a tree in a solitary place, where no one was present to see it, methought that was to conceive a tree as existing unperceived or unthought of, not considering that I myself conceived it all the while. But now I plainly see, that all I can do is to frame ideas in my own mind. I may indeed conceive in my own thoughts the idea of a tree, or a house, or a mountain, but that is all. And this is far from proving, that I can conceive them *existing out of the minds of all spirits.*

Phil.: You acknowledge then that you cannot possibly conceive, how any one corporeal sensible thing should exist otherwise than in a mind.

Hyl.: I do. 27

Phil.: And yet you will earnestly contend for the truth of that which you cannot so much as conceive.

Hyl.: I profess I know not what to think. . . .

[X]

Hyl.: . . . but inform me, Philonous, can we perceive or know nothing beside our ideas?

Phil.: As for the rational deducing of causes from effects, that is beside our inquiry. And by the senses you can best tell, whether you perceive anything which is not immediately perceived. And I ask you whether the things immediately perceived, are other than your own sensations or ideas? Your have indeed more than once, in the course of this conversation, declared yourself on those points; but you seem by this last question to have departed from what you then thought.

Hyl.: To speak the truth, Philonous, I think there are two kinds of objects, the one perceived immediately, which are likewise called *ideas;* the other are real things or external objects perceived by the mediation of ideas, which are their images and representations. Now I own, ideas do not exist without the mind; but the latter sort of objects do. I am sorry I did not think of this distinction sooner; it would probably have cut short your discourse.

Phil.: Are those external objects perceived by sense, or by some other faculty?

Hyl.: They are perceived by sense.

Phil.: How! Is there anything perceived by sense, which is not immediately perceived?

Hyl.: Yes, Philonous, in some sort there is. For example, when I look on a picture or statue of Julius Caesar, I may be said after a manner to perceive him (though not immediately) by my senses.

Phil.: It seems then, you will have our ideas, which alone are immediately perceived, to be pictures of external things; and that these also are perceived by sense, inasmuch as they have a conformity or resemblance to our ideas. 28

Hyl.: That is my meaning.

Phil.: And in the same way that Julius Caesar, in himself invisible, is nevertheless perceived by sight; real things, in themselves imperceptible, are perceived by sense.

Hyl.: In the very same.

. . .

Phil.: . . . I grant we may in one acceptation be said to perceive sensible things mediately by sense: that is, when from a frequently perceived connection, the immediate perception of ideas by one sense suggests to the mind others, perhaps belonging to another sense, which are wont to be connected with them. For instance, when I hear a coach drive along the streets, immediately I perceive only the sound; but from the experience I have had that such a sound is connected with a coach, I am said to hear the coach. It is nevertheless evident, that in truth and strictness, nothing can be *heard* but *sound:* and the coach is not then properly perceived by sense, but suggested from experience. So likewise when we are said to see a red-hot bar of iron; the solidity and heat of the iron are not the objects of sight, but suggested to the imagination by the color and figure, which are properly perceived by that sense. In short, those things alone are actually and strictly perceived by any sense, which would have been perceived, in case that same sense had then been first conferred on us. As for other things, it in plain they are only suggested to the mind by experience grounded on former perceptions. But to return to your comparison of Caesar's picture, it is plain, if you keep to that, you must hold the real things, or archetypes of our ideas, are not perceived by sense, but by some internal faculty of the soul, as reason or memory. I would therefore fair know, what arguments you can draw from reason for the existence of what you call *real things* or *material objects.* Or whether you remember to have seen them formerly as they are in themselves? Or if you have heard or read of any one that did.

Hyl.: I see, Philonous, you are disposed to raillery; but that will never convince me.

Phil.: My aim is only to learn from you, the way to come at the knowledge of *material beings.* Whatever we perceive, is perceived immediately or mediately: by sense, or by reason

27

R According to the **realist** view that objects exist outside the mind, it would be possible for such an object to exist even though conceived by no one. But if one attempts to conceive of such a situation, it seems to follow that the object is both allegedly unconceived but also conceived, which is seemingly a contradiction. Thus both the possibility in question and the view that leads to it appear to be inconceivable, and so apparently impossible.

STOP This is one of Berkeley's favorite arguments, one that is unique to him and also very tricky. Can you see any way to reply to it?

28

At this point, Hylas has finally arrived at Locke's main view: we are immediately or directly aware of ideas in the mind, but these represent objects outside the mind in virtue of the "conformity or resemblance" between the two.

and reflection. But as you have excluded sense, pray show me what reason you have to believe their existence; or what *medium* you can possibly make use of, to prove it either to mine or your own understanding.

Hyl.: To deal ingenuously, Philonous, now I consider the point, I do not find I can give you any good reason for it. 29 . . .

29

Philonous raises the same issue that Locke was grappling with in Book IV, chapter XI of the *Essay* (pp. 71–73): what reason is there to believe in the existence of external objects that are never directly perceived or experienced? In the case of the coach and the bar of iron, the claim is that some immediately perceived ideas suggest others previously perceived along with them—but this account will not work for something that is *never* immediately perceived. Hylas has no reply.

Phil.: . . . if I understand you rightly, you say our ideas do not exist without the mind; but that they are copies, images, or representations of certain originals that do.

Hyl.: You take me right.

Phil.: They are then like external things.

Hyl.: They are.

. . .

Phil.: Which are material objects in themselves, perceptible or imperceptible?

Hyl.: Properly and immediately nothing can be perceived but ideas. All material things therefore are in themselves insensible, and to be perceived only by their ideas.

Phil.: Ideas then are sensible, and their archetypes or originals insensible.

Hyl.: Right.

Phil.: But how can that which is sensible be like that which is insensible? Can a real thing in itself *invisible* be like a *color;* or a real thing which is not *audible,* be like a *sound*? In a word, can anything be like a sensation or idea, but another sensation or idea?

. . .

Hyl.: Upon inquiry, I find it is impossible for me to conceive or understand how anything but an idea can be like an idea. And it is most evident, that *no idea can exist without the mind.* 30

30

R Philonous now challenges the claim that ideas *resemble* external objects. It is hard to see how an insensible, unperceiving thing can literally *resemble* a bit of experience like an idea or sensation—how could two things as different as that be literally alike? Hylas concedes that he can make no sense of this.

Phil.: You are therefore by your principles forced to deny the reality of sensible things, since you made it to consist in an absolute existence exterior to the mind. That is to say, you are a downright *sceptic.* So I have gained my point, which was to show your principles led to scepticism.

Hyl.: For the present I am, if not entirely convinced, at least silenced.

Phil.: I would fain know what more you would require in order to a perfect conviction. Have you not had the liberty of explaining yourself all manner of ways? Were any little slips in discourse laid hold and insisted on? Or were you not allowed to retract or reinforce anything you had offered, as best served your purpose? Has not everything you could say been heard and examined with all the fairness imaginable? In a word, have you not in every point been convinced out of your own mouth? And if you can at present discover any flaw in any of your former concessions, or think of any remaining subterfuge, any new distinction, color, or comment whatsoever, why do you not produce it?

Hyl.: A little patience, Philonous. I am at present so amazed to see myself ensnared, and as it were imprisoned in the labyrinths you have drawn me into, that on the sudden it cannot be expected I should find my way out. You must give me time to look about me, and recollect myself.

Phil.: Hark; is not this the college bell?

Hyl.: It rings for prayers.

Phil.: We will go in then if you please, and meet here again tomorrow morning. In the meantime you may employ your thoughts on this morning's discourse, and try if you can find any fallacy in it, or invent any new means to extricate yourself.

Hyl.: Agreed.

The Second Dialogue

[XI]

Hyl.: I beg your pardon, Philonous, for not meeting you sooner. All this morning my head was so filled with our late conversation, that I had not leisure to think of the time of the day, or indeed of anything else.

Phil.: I am glad you were so intent upon it, in hopes if there were any mistakes in your concessions, or fallacies in my reasonings from them, you will now discover them to me.

Hyl.: I assure you, I have done nothing ever since I saw you, but search after mistakes and fallacies, and with that view have minutely examined the whole series of yesterday's discourse: but all in vain, for the notions it led me into, upon review, appear still more clear and evident; and the more I consider them, the more irresistibly do they force my assent.

Phil.: And is not this, think you, a sign that they are genuine, that they proceed from nature, and are conformable to right reason? Truth and beauty are in this alike, that the strictest survey sets them both off to advantage. While the false lustre of error and disguise cannot endure being reviewed, or too nearly inspected.

Hyl.: I own there is a great deal in what you say. Nor can any one be more entirely satisfied of the truth of those odd consequences, so long as I have in view the reasonings that lead to them. . . .

Phil.: Well then, are you at length satisfied that no sensible things have a real existence; and that you are in truth an arrant *sceptic*?

Hyl.: It is too plain to be denied.

Phil.: Look! Are not the fields covered with a delightful verdure? Is there not something in the woods and groves, in the rivers and clear springs, that soothes, that delights, that transports the soul? At the prospect of the wide and deep ocean, or some huge mountain whose top is lost in the clouds, or of an old gloomy forest, are not our minds filled with a pleasing horror? Even in rocks and deserts, is there not an agreeable wildness? How sincere a pleasure is it to behold the natural beauties of the earth! . . . Is not the whole system immense, beautiful, glorious beyond expression and beyond thought! What treatment then do those Philosophers deserve, who would deprive these noble and delightful scenes of all reality? How should those principles be entertained, that lead us to think all the visible beauty of the creation a false imaginary glare? To be plain, can you expect this scepticism of yours will not be thought extravagantly absurd by all men of sense? [31]

Hyl.: Other men may think as they please: but for your part you have nothing to reproach me with. My comfort is, you are as much a *sceptic* as I am.

Phil.: There, Hylas, I must beg leave to differ from you.

Hyl.: What! Have you all along agreed to the premises, and do you now deny the conclusion, and leave me to maintain those paradoxes by myself which you led me into? This surely is not fair.

Phil.: I deny that I agreed with you in those notions that led to scepticism. You indeed said, the reality of sensible things consisted in an *absolute existence* out of the minds of spirits, or distinct from their being perceived. And pursuant to this notion of reality, you are obliged to deny sensible things any real existence: that is, according to your own definition, you profess yourself a *sceptic*. But I neither said nor thought the reality of sensible things was to be defined after that manner. To me it is evident, for the reasons you allow of, that sensible things cannot exist otherwise than in a mind or spirit. Whence I conclude, not that they have no real existence, but that seeing they depend not on my thought, and have an existence distinct from being perceived by me, *there must be some other mind wherein they exist*. As sure therefore as the sensible world really exists, so sure is there any infinite omnipresent spirit who contains and supports it. [32]

. . . Sensible things do really exist: and if they really exist, they are necessarily perceived by an infinite mind: therefore there is an infinite mind, or God. This furnishes you with a direct and immediate demonstration, from a most evident principle, of the being of a God. [33] . . .

Take here in brief my meaning. It is evident that the things I perceive are my own ideas, and that no idea can exist unless it be in a mind. Nor is it less plain that these ideas or things by me perceived, either themselves or their archetypes, exist independently of my mind, since I know myself not to be their author, it being out of my power to determine at pleasure, what particular ideas I shall be affected with upon opening my eyes or ears. [34] They must therefore exist in some other mind, whose will it is they should be exhibited to me. The things, I say, immediately perceived, are ideas or sensations, call them which you will. But how can any idea or sensation exist in, or be produced by, anything but a mind or spirit? This indeed is inconceivable; and to assert that which is inconceivable, is to talk nonsense: is it not?

Hyl.: Without doubt.

Phil.: But on the other hand, it is very conceivable that they should exist in, and be produced by, a spirit; since this is no more than I daily experience in myself,

R Having driven Hylas into what *Hylas* regards as skepticism about the world of ordinary objects, Philonous launches into another oration on the glories of nature, again suggesting that he is not denying the existence of such things.

R Philonous denies that he is a skeptic. Instead, he views himself as merely offering a different and more correct account of what the reality of objects like those in nature (whose existence he does not deny) amounts to: such things exist only as ideas in the mind, and if they have an existence that is independent of his mind (and those of others like him), this must be because there is some other mind (God's mind) in which they exist.

R Here is an outline of one of Berkeley's arguments for the existence of God, the details of which are elaborated in the following passages.

Here is a reason for thinking that sensible things exist independently of Philonous's mind (or of any human mind): the ideas that make them up are not within his (or any other human's) voluntary control. How compelling a reason is this? (Compare this with the second of Locke's "four concurrent reasons" in chapter XI of Book IV of the *Essay*.)

R Berkeley's view is that the ideas corresponding to real objects (as opposed, for example, to merely imaginary ones) are produced in us by God. He suggests that this can be understood by analogy with our own weaker power to deliberately imagine or think of various things.

This is an appeal to something like the argument from design (see Chapter 7).

R Hylas can give no account of *how* matter would cause ideas, and hence has to admit that he could just as well have the same ideas if there were no matter, in which case there is no reason to believe in it.

(The underlying concern here is how minds and bodies can causally interact—see the discussion in Chapter 3.)

inasmuch as I perceive numberless ideas; and by an act of my will can form a great variety of them, and raise them up in my imagination: [35] though it must be confessed, these creatures of the fancy are not altogether so distinct, so strong, vivid, and permanent, as those perceived by my senses, which latter are called *real things.* From all which I conclude, *there is a mind which affects me every moment with all the sensible impressions I perceive.* And from the variety, order, and manner of these, I conclude the author of them to be *wise, powerful, and good, beyond comprehension.* [36] . . . the things by me perceived are known by the understanding, and produced by the will, of an infinite spirit. And is not all this most plain and evident? Is there any more in it, than what a little observation of our own minds, and that which passes in them not only enables us to conceive, but also obliges us to acknowledge?

[XII]

Hyl.: I think I understand you very clearly; and own the proof you give of a deity seems no less evident, than it is surprising. But allowing that God is the supreme and universal cause of all things, yet may not there be still a third nature besides spirits and ideas? May we not admit a subordinate and limited cause of our ideas? In a word, may there not for all that be *matter*?

. . . I would by no means be thought to deny that God or an infinite spirit is the supreme cause of all things. All I contend for, is, that subordinate to the supreme agent there is a cause of a limited and inferior nature, which concurs in the production of our ideas, not by any act of will or spiritual efficiency, but by that kind of action which belongs to matter, *viz. motion.*

Phil.: . . . you are loath to part with your old prejudice. But to make you quit it more easily, I desire that, beside what has been hitherto suggested, you will farther consider whether, upon supposition that matter exists, you can possibly conceive how you should be affected by it? Or supposing it did not exist, whether it be not evident you might for all that be affected with the same ideas you now are, and consequently have the very same reasons to believe its existence that you now can have.

Hyl.: I acknowledge it is possible we might perceive all things just as we do now, though there was no matter in the world; neither can I conceive, if there be matter, how it should produce any idea in our minds. [37] . . .

I acknowledge you have proved that matter is impossible; nor do I see what more can be said in defense of it. But at the same time that I give up this, I suspect all my other notions. For surely none could be more seemingly evident than this once was: and yet it now seems as false and absurd as ever it did true before. But I think we have discussed the point sufficiently for the present. The remaining part of the day I would willingly spend, in running over in my thoughts the several heads of this morning's conversation, and tomorrow shall be glad to meet you here again about the same time.

Phil.: I will not fail to attend you.

The Third Dialogue

[XIII]

Philonous: Tell me, Hylas, what are the fruits of yesterday's meditation? Has it confirmed you in the same mind you were in at parting? Or have you since seen cause to change your opinion?

Hylas:: Truly my opinion is, that all our opinions are alike vain and uncertain. What we approve to-day, we condemn tomorrow. We keep a stir about knowledge, and spend our lives in the pursuit of it, when, alas! we know nothing all the while: nor do I think it possible for us ever to know anything in this life. Our faculties are too narrow and too few. Nature certainly never intended us for speculation.

Phil.: What! Say you we can know nothing, Hylas?

Hyl.: There is not that single thing in the world, whereof we can know the real nature, or what it is in itself.

Phil.: Will you tell me I do not really know what fire or water is?

Hyl.: You may indeed know that fire appears hot, and water fluid: but this is no more than knowing what sensations are produced in your own mind, upon the application of fire and water to your organs of sense. Their internal constitution, their true and real nature, you are utterly in the dark as to *that.*

Phil.: Do I not know this to be a real stone that I stand on, and that which I see before my eyes to be a real tree?

Hyl.: *Know?* No, it is impossible you or any man alive should know it. All you know, is, that you have such a certain idea or appearance in your own mind. But what is this to the real tree or stone? I tell you, that color, figure, and hardness, which you perceive, are not the real natures of those things, or in the least like them. The same may be said of all other real things or corporeal substances which compose the world. They have none of them anything in themselves, like those sensible qualities by us perceived. We should not therefore pretend to affirm or know anything of them, as they are in their own nature.

...

Phil.: . . . And so you are plunged into the deepest and most deplorable *scepticism* that ever man was. Tell me, Hylas, is it not as I say?

[XIV]

Hyl.: I agree with you. *Material substance* was no more than an hypothesis, and a false and groundless one too. I will no longer spend my breath in defence of it. But whatever hypothesis you advance, or whatsoever scheme of things you introduce in its stead, I doubt not it will appear every whit as false: let me but be allowed to question you upon it. That is, suffer me to serve you in your own kind, and I warrant it shall conduct you through as many perplexities and contradictions, to the very same state of scepticism that I myself am in at present.

Phil.: I assure you, Hylas, I do not pretend to frame any hypothesis at all. I am of a vulgar cast, simple enough to believe my senses, and leave things as I find them. To be plain, it is my opinion, that the real things are those very things I see and feel, and perceive by my senses. These I know, and finding they answer all the necessities and purposes of life, have no reason to be solicitous about any other unknown beings. A piece of sensible bread, for instance, would stay my stomach better than ten thousand times as much of that insensible, unintelligible, real bread you speak of. It is likewise my opinion, that colors and other sensible qualities are on the objects. I cannot for my life help thinking that snow is white, and fire hot. You indeed, who by *snow* and *fire* mean certain external, unperceived, unperceiving substances, are in the right to deny whiteness or heat to be affections inherent in them. But I, who understand by those words the things I see and feel, am obliged to think like other folks. And as I am no sceptic with regard to the nature of things, so neither am I as to their existence. That a thing should be really perceived by my senses, and at the same time not really exist, is to me a plain contradiction; since I cannot prescind or abstract, even in thought, the existence of a sensible thing from its being perceived. Wood, stones, fire, water, flesh, iron, and the like things, which I name and discourse of, are things that I know; . . . And I should not have known them, but that I perceived them by my senses; and things perceived by the senses are immediately perceived; and things immediately perceived are ideas; and ideas cannot exist without the mind; their existence therefore consists in being perceived; when therefore they are actually perceived, there can be no doubt of their existence. Away then with all that scepticism, all those ridiculous Philosophical doubts. (38) What a jest is it for a Philosopher to question the existence of sensible things, till he has it proved to him from the veracity of God: or to pretend our knowledge in this point falls short of intuition or demonstration? I might as well doubt of my own being, as of the being of those things I actually see and feel.

R Philonous's contrary view is that for a thing to exist is just for the relevant ideas to exist, and that to know those ideas is to know all there is to know about the nature of such a thing.

(The immediately following passage is aimed at Descartes and Locke.)

Hyl.: Not so fast, Philonous: you say you cannot conceive how sensible things should exist without the mind. Do you not?

Phil.: I do.

Hyl.: Supposing you were annihilated, cannot you conceive it possible, that things perceivable by sense may still exist?

Phil.: I can; but then it must be in another mind. When I deny sensible things an existence out of the mind, I do not mean my mind in particular, but all minds. Now it is plain they have an existence exterior to my mind, since I find them by experience to be independent of it. There is therefore some other mind wherein they exist, during the intervals between the times of my perceiving them: as likewise they did before my birth, and would do after my supposed annihilation. And as the same is true, with regard to all other finite created spirits; it necessarily follows, there is an *omnipresent eternal mind,* which knows and comprehends all things, and exhibits them to our view in such a manner, and according to such rules as he himself has ordained, and are by us termed the *laws of nature.*

. . .

[XV]

Hyl.: But according to your notions, what difference is there between real things, and chimeras formed by the imagination, or the visions of a dream, since they are all equally in the mind?

Phil.: The ideas formed by the imagination are faint and indistinct; they have, besides, an entire dependence on the will. But the ideas perceived by sense, that is, real things, are more vivid and clear, and being imprinted on the mind by a spirit distinct from us, have not a like dependence on our will. There is therefore no danger of confounding these with the foregoing: and there is as little of confounding them with the visions of a dream, which are dim, irregular, and confused. And though they should happen to be never so lively and natural, yet by their not being connected, and of a piece with the preceding and subsequent transactions of our lives, they might easily be distinguished from realities. In short, by whatever method you distinguish *things* from *chimeras* on your own scheme, the same, it is evident, will hold also upon mine. For it must be, I presume, by some perceived difference, and I am not for depriving you of any one thing that you perceive. (39)

. . .

Hyl.: What say you to this? Since, according to you, men judge of the reality of things by their senses, how can a man be mistaken in thinking the moon a plain lucid surface, about a foot in diameter; or a square tower, seen at a distance, round; or an oar, with one end in the water, crooked?

Phil.: He is not mistaken with regard to the ideas he actually perceives; but in the inferences he makes from his present perceptions. Thus in the case of the oar, what he immediately perceives by sight is certainly crooked; and so far he is in the right. But if he thence conclude, that upon taking the oar out of the water he shall perceive the same crookedness; or that it would affect his touch, as crooked things are wont to do: in that he is mistaken. In like manner, if he shall conclude from what he perceives in one station, that in case he advances toward the moon or tower, he should still be affected with the like ideas, he is mistaken. But his mistake lies not in what he perceives immediately and at present, (it being a manifest contradiction to suppose he should err in respect of that) but in the wrong judgment he makes concerning the ideas he apprehends to be connected with those immediately perceived: or concerning the ideas that, from what he perceives at present, he imagines would be perceived in other circumstances. (40) . . .

Hyl.: I have been a long time distrusting my senses; methought I saw things by a dim light, and through false glasses. Now the glasses are removed, and a new light breaks in upon my understanding. I am clearly convinced that I see things in their native forms; and am no longer in pain about their unknown natures or absolute existence. This is the state I find myself in at present: though indeed the course that brought me to it, I do not yet thoroughly comprehend. You set out upon the same principles that Academics, Cartesians, and the like sects, usually do; and for a long time it looked as if you were advancing their Philosophical *scepticism;* but in the end your conclusions are directly opposite to theirs.

Phil.: You see, Hylas, the water of yonder fountain, how it is forced upwards, in a round column, to a certain height; at which it breaks and falls back into the basin from

(39)

R If the reality of things consists only of ideas in minds, how can we tell the difference between *real things* (those that exist in God's mind and are caused by God to exist in our minds) and various sorts of illusion? Philonous's response is that any criterion for this distinction that appeals to experience, that is to ideas of perception, will be equally available to him.

(40)

R Here is Berkeley's account of perceptual error: the ideas in question are not mistaken in themselves; rather, the mistake lies in the inferences we draw from them as to other ideas that are or could be perceived.

whence it rose: its ascent as well as descent, proceeding from the same uniform law or principle of *gravitation.* Just so, the same principles which at first view lead to *scepticism,* pursued to a certain point, bring men back to common sense.

Discussion Questions

1. Some of Berkeley's arguments rely on the claim that certain of our sensory ideas are indistinguishable from ideas of pleasure or pain. Is he right about this claim?
2. Spell out the argument from illusion for the case of the two buckets of water and then for the case of colors seen with the naked eye and through a microscope. (Assuming that you cannot look at something simultaneously in both ways, the second argument will have to be more complicated, involving the claim that the object does not change when you shift from one view to the other). In each case, start with an argument for the conclusion that at least one of the perceived qualities is not in the object, and then argue for the claim that none of them is. (See Annotation 18 for a suggestion about this.) How compelling are these arguments? Can you think of an answer to them?
3. Locke invoked the idea of substance because it seemed to him impossible that qualities could simply exist on their own, even in groups, without being qualities of anything. Consider Berkeley's criticisms of this view, centering around the claim that we have no intelligible idea of such an underlying thing. Do these objections also apply to Berkeley's idea of a mind that perceives ideas? Why or why not? If material objects do after all exist outside the mind, must there also be material substance?
4. It is a fairly common experience for a given speed, for example while riding in a car, to seem faster or slower depending on how fast one was traveling just before: 30 mph seems slow after going 60, but fast after sitting still. Construct on this basis an argument that is parallel to the other versions of the argument from illusion that Berkeley formulates and that leads to the conclusion that *apparent speed* (speed as directly perceived or experienced) exists only in the mind.
5. Both Locke and Berkeley tend to think of ideas as mental images and of representation of things by ideas as depending on resemblance between the two. Are all ideas images? (See Discussion Question 1 for the Locke selection.) Do we have images of our own minds or selves? If a person does have a mental image, is it automatically a representation of any object that the image resembles (assuming that such resemblance makes sense)?
6. Locke and Berkeley both appeal to roughly the same features of our perceptual ideas: their involuntary character and their systematic regularity and order. Locke can be viewed as arguing that these features are best explained by supposing that ideas are systematically caused by a world of external objects; while Berkeley argues that they are best explained by supposing that the ideas are caused in us by an infinite mind or spirit. Whose explanation do you think is better? How would you argue for one as against the other?

Thomas Reid

The Scottish philosopher Thomas Reid (1710–1796) was one of the founders of what became known as the "common sense" school of philosophy. He is best known for his contributions to epistemology, which are mainly focused on defending the common-sense view of our knowledge of the material world against what he sees as the skeptical tendencies to be found in his British predecessors, Locke, Berkeley, and Hume, as well as in Descartes and others.

In the following selection, Reid attacks the Lockean view that we perceive external material objects by perceiving in a more immediate way ideas that represent them. His alternative is an early version of direct realism, according to which material objects are themselves the most direct objects of our perceptions. As Reid recognizes, the view that perception is in this way direct does not in itself answer the question of what reason or ground we have for thinking that our direct perceptual judgments are true. Thus he also argues that the claim that the "evidence of the senses" is good evidence for the claims we accept on that basis has the status of an axiom or "first principle": something that is immediately known without any need for further justification.

Direct Realism, from *Essays on the Intellectual Powers of Man*

Of Perception

...

If . . . we attend to that act of our mind which we call the perception of an external object of sense, we shall find in it these three things. *First,* Some conception or notion of the object perceived. *Secondly,* A strong and irresistible conviction and belief of its present existence. And, *thirdly,* That this conviction and belief are immediate, and not the effect of reasoning. (1)

1 This is Reid's basic account of what happens when a person perceives an external material object. Notice, however, that it so far says nothing at all about whether and how the resulting belief is *justified,* that is, whether and how the person has a ground or reason for thinking that it is true.

1st, It is impossible to perceive an object without having some notion or conception of that which we perceive. We may indeed conceive an object which we do not perceive; but when we perceive the object, we must have some conception of it at the same time; and we have commonly a more clear and steady notion of the object while we perceive it, than we have from memory or imagination when it is not perceived. . . .

2dly, In perception we not only have a notion more or less distinct of the object perceived, but also an irresistible conviction and belief of its existence. This is always the case when we are certain that we perceive it. There may be a perception so faint and indistinct, as to leave us in doubt whether we perceive the object or not. Thus, when a star begins to twinkle as the light of the sun withdraws, one may, for a short time, think he sees it, without being certain, until the perception acquires some strength and steadiness. When a ship just begins to appear in the utmost verge of the horizon, we may at first be dubious whether we perceive it or not: but when the perception is in any degree clear and steady, there remains no doubt of its reality; and when the reality of the perception is ascertained, the existence of the object perceived can no longer be doubted.

...

Can any stronger proof be given, that it is the universal judgment of mankind that the evidence of sense is a kind of evidence which we may securely rest upon in the most momentous concerns of mankind; that it is a kind of evidence against which we ought not to admit any reasoning; and therefore, that to reason either for or against it, is an insult to common sense? (2)

2 There are two importantly different claims being made here: first, that skeptical doubts about perceptual knowledge should not be taken seriously because they go against "the universal judgment of mankind"; and, second, that this universal judgment shows that "the evidence of sense" does not depend on or require any sort of reasoning in its support.

The whole conduct of mankind, in the daily occurrences of life, as well as the solemn procedure of judicatories in the trial of causes, civil and criminal, demonstrates this. I know only of two exceptions that may be offered against this being the universal belief of mankind.

The first exception is that of some lunatics, who have been persuaded of things that seem to contradict the clear testimony of their senses. It is said there have been lunatics and hypochondriacal persons, who seriously believed themselves to be made of glass; and, in consequence of this, lived in continual terror of having their brittle frame shivered into pieces.

...

The other exception that may be made to the principle we have laid down, is that of some philosophers who have maintained, that the testimony of sense is fallacious, and therefore ought never to be trusted. Perhaps it might be a sufficient answer to this to say, that there is nothing so absurd which some philosophers have not maintained. It is one thing to profess a doctrine of this kind, another seriously to believe it, and to be governed by it in the conduct of life. It is evident, that a man who did not believe his senses, could not keep out of harm's way an hour of his life; yet, in all the history of philosophy, we never read of any skeptic that ever stepped into fire or water because he did not believe his senses, or that showed, in the conduct of life, less trust in his senses than other men have. This gives us just ground to apprehend, that philosophy was never able to conquer that natural belief which men have in their senses; and that all their subtile reasonings against this belief were never able to persuade themselves.

It appears, therefore, that the clear and distinct testimony of our senses carries irresistible

From *Essays on the Intellectual Powers of Man* (Cambridge, Mass.: MIT Press, 1969).

conviction along with it, to every man in his right judgment.

I observed, 3dly, That this conviction is not only irresistible, but it is immediate; that is, it is not by a train of reasoning and argumentation that we come to be convinced of the existence of what we perceive; we ask no argument for the existence of the object, but that we perceive it; perception commands our belief upon its own authority, and disdains to rest its authority upon any reasoning whatsoever. 3

The conviction of a truth may be irresistible, and yet not immediate. Thus, my conviction that the three angles of every plain triangle, are equal to two right angles, is irresistible, but it is not immediate: I am convinced of it by demonstrative reasoning. There are other truths in mathematics of which we have not only an irresistible, but an immediate conviction. Such are the axioms. Our belief of the axioms in mathematics is not grounded upon argument. Arguments are grounded upon them, but their evidence is discerned immediately by the human understanding.

It is, no doubt, one thing to have an immediate conviction of a self evident axiom; it is another thing to have an immediate conviction of the existence of what we see: but the conviction is equally immediate and equally irresistible in both cases. No man thinks of seeking a reason to believe what he sees; and, before we are capable of reasoning, we put no less confidence in our senses than after. The rudest savage is as fully convinced of what he sees, and hears, and feels, as the most expert logician. . . .

Of the Sentiments of Mr. Locke

[Locke] sets out in his Essay with a full conviction, common to him with other philosophers, that ideas in the mind are the objects of all our thoughts in every operation of the understanding. This leads him to use the word *idea* so very frequently, beyond what was usual in the English language, that he thought it necessary in his introduction to make [an] apology. . . .

Speaking of the reality of our knowledge, he says, "It is evident the mind knows not things immediately, but only by the intervention of the ideas it has of them. Our knowledge therefore is real, only so far as there is a conformity between our ideas and the reality of things. But what shall be here the criterion? How shall the mind, when it perceives nothing but its own ideas, know that they agree with things themselves? . . ."

We see that Mr. Locke was aware no less than Des Cartes, that the doctrine of ideas made it necessary, and at the same time difficult, to prove the existence of a material world without us; because the mind, according to that doctrine, perceives nothing but a world of ideas in itself. Not only Des Cartes, but Malebranche, Arnauld, and Norris, had perceived this difficulty, and attempted to remove it with little success. Mr. Locke attempts the same thing; but his arguments are feeble. He even seems to be conscious of this: for he concludes his reasoning with this observation, "That we have evidence sufficient to direct us in attaining the good and avoiding the evil, caused by external objects, and that this is the important concern we have in being made acquainted with them." This indeed is saying no more than will be granted by those who deny the existence of a material world.

As there is no material difference between Locke and Des Cartes with regard to the perception of objects by the senses, there is the less occasion, in this place, to take notice of all their differences in other points. . . .

Although no author has more merit than Mr. Locke in pointing out the ambiguity of words, and resolving by that means many knotty questions, which had tortured the wits of the schoolmen; yet, I apprehend he has been sometimes misled by the ambiguity of the word *idea,* which he uses so often almost in every page of his Essay.

In the explication given of this word, we took notice of two meanings given to it; a popular and a philosophical. In the popular meaning, to have an idea of any thing, signifies nothing more than to think of it.

. . . When the word *idea* is taken in this popular sense, there can be no doubt of our having ideas in our minds. To think without ideas would be to think without thought, which is a manifest contradiction. 4

But there is another meaning of the word *idea* peculiar to philosophers, and grounded upon a philosophical theory, which the vulgar never think of. Philosophers, ancient and modern, have maintained, that the operations of the mind, like the tools of an artificer, can only be employed upon objects that are present in the mind, or in the brain, where the mind is

3

Reid is clearly right that perceptual judgments are not ordinarily arrived at through an explicit process of reasoning. Does it follow that no reasoning is involved, even implicitly, or that no reasoning is required to show that the resulting belief is indeed likely to be true?

4

Thus in one sense, to have an idea of something is just to think of it, without any implication that the idea is a distinct entity that has to be perceived on its own.

supposed to reside. Therefore, objects that are distant, in time or place, must have a representative in the mind, or in the brain; some image or picture of them, which is the object that the mind contemplates. 5 . . . Since the time of Des Cartes, [this representative image] has . . . been called an *idea;* and every thought is conceived to have an idea for its object. As this has been a common opinion among philosophers, as far back as we can trace philosophy, it is the less to be wondered at, that they should be apt to confound the operation of the mind in thinking, with the idea or object of thought, which is supposed to be its inseparable concomitant.

5

R In contrast to the view in the previous paragraph, the Lockean view treats ideas as mental entities that are perceived on their own and are (somehow) the basis for the perception of things outside the mind.

. . .

From this, I think it is evident, that if the word *idea* in a work where it occurs in every paragraph, be used without any intimation of the ambiguity of the word, sometimes to signify thought, or the operation of the mind in thinking, sometimes to signify those internal objects of thought which philosophers suppose, this must occasion confusion in the thoughts both of the author and of the readers. I take this to be the greatest blemish in the Essay on Human Understanding, I apprehend this is the true source of several paradoxical opinions in that excellent work, which I shall have occasion to take notice of.

Here it is very natural to ask, Whether it was Mr. Locke's opinion, that ideas are the only objects of thought? or, Whether it is not possible for men to think of things which are not ideas in the mind?

To this question it is not easy to give a direct answer. On the one hand, he says often, in distinct and studied expressions, that the term *idea* stands for whatever is the object of the understanding when a man thinks, or whatever it is which the mind can be employed about in thinking: that the mind perceives nothing but its own ideas: that all knowledge consists in the perception of the agreement or disagreement of our ideas: that we can have no knowledge further than we have ideas. These, and many other expressions of the like import, evidently imply, that every object of thought must be an idea, and can be nothing else.

On the other hand, I am persuaded that Mr. Locke would have acknowledged, that we may think of Alexander the Great, or of the planet Jupiter, and of numberless things, which he would have owned are not ideas in the mind, but objects which exist independent of the mind that thinks of them.

How shall we reconcile the two parts of this apparent contradiction? All I am able to say upon Mr. Locke's principles to reconcile them, is this, That we cannot think of Alexander, or of the planet Jupiter, unless we have in our minds an idea, that is, an image or picture of those objects. The idea of Alexander is an image, or picture, or representation of that hero in my mind; and this idea is the immediate object of my thought when I think of Alexander. That this was Locke's opinion, and that it has been generally the opinion of philosophers, there can be no doubt. 6

6

Notice that Locke is thereby attempting to offer an account of *how* the mind perceives something outside of it. Reid, in contrast, makes no attempt to offer any such account.

But, instead of giving light to the question proposed, it seems to involve it in greater darkness.

When I think of Alexander, I am told there is an image or idea of Alexander in my mind, which is the immediate object of this thought. The necessary consequence of this seems to be, that there are two objects of this thought; the idea, which is in the mind, and the person represented by that idea; the first, the immediate object of the thought, the last, the object of the same thought, but not the immediate object. This is a hard saying; for it makes every thought of things external to have a double object. Every man is conscious of his thoughts, and yet, upon attentive reflection, he perceives no such duplicity in the object he thinks about. Sometimes men see objects double, but they always know when they do so: and I know of no philosopher who has expressly owned this duplicity in the object of thought, though it follows necessarily from maintaining, that, in the same thought, there is one object that is immediate and in the mind itself; and another object, which is not immediate, and which is not in the mind. 7

7

This suggests at least that the two objects are not perceived in the same way—that in ordinary cases the focus of awareness is on the external object, with the idea (if there is one) serving as the way in which the mind is able to access that external object.

. . .

I apprehend, therefore, that if philosophers will maintain, that ideas in the mind are the only immediate objects of thought, they will be forced to grant that they are the sole objects of thought, and that it is impossible for men to think of any thing else. Yet, surely Mr. Locke believed that we can think of many things that are not ideas in the mind; but he seems not to have perceived, that the maintaining that ideas in the mind are the only immediate objects of thought, must necessarily draw this consequence along with it.

The consequence, however, was seen by bishop Berkeley and Mr. Hume, who rather chose to admit the consequence than to give up the principle from which it follows. 8

...

Reflections on the Common Theory of Ideas

After so long a detail of the sentiments of philosophers, ancient and modern, concerning ideas, it may seem presumptuous to call in question their existence. But no philosophical opinion, however ancient, however generally received, ought to rest upon authority. There is no presumption in requiring evidence for it, or in regulating our belief by the evidence we can find.

To prevent mistakes, the reader must again be reminded, that if by *ideas* are meant only the acts or operations of our minds in perceiving, remembering, or imagining objects, I am far from calling in question the existence of those acts; we are conscious of them every day, and every hour of life; and I believe no man of a sound mind ever doubted of the real existence of the operations of mind, of which he is conscious. Nor is it to be doubted, that by the faculties which God has given us, we can conceive things that are absent, as well as perceive those that are within the reach of our senses; and that such conceptions may be more or less distinct, and more or less lively and strong. . . . The ideas, of whose existence I require the proof, are not the operations of any mind, but supposed objects of those operations. They are not perception, remembrance, or conception, but things that are said to be perceived, or remembered, or imagined.

Nor do I dispute the existence of what the vulgar call the objects of perception. These, by all who acknowledge their existence, are called *real things*, not *ideas*. But philosophers maintain, that, besides these, there are immediate objects of perception in the mind itself: that, for instance, we do not see the sun immediately, but an idea. . . . This idea is said to be the image, the resemblance, the representative of the sun, if there be a sun. 9 It is from the existence of the idea that we must infer the existence of the sun. But the idea being immediately perceived, there can be no doubt, as philosophers think, of its existence.

...

The *first* reflection I would make on this philosophical opinion is, that it is directly contrary to the universal sense of men who have not been instructed in philosophy. When we see the sun or moon, we have no doubt that the very objects which we immediately see, are very far distant from us, and from one another. We have not the least doubt, that this is the sun and moon which God created some thousands of years ago, and which have continued to perform their revolutions in the heavens ever since. But how are we astonished when the philosopher informs us, that we are mistaken in all this; that the sun and moon which we see, are not, as we imagine, many miles distant from us, and from each other, but that they are in our own mind; that they had no existence before we saw them, and will have none when we cease to perceive and to think of them; because the objects we perceive are only ideas in our own minds, which can have no existence a moment longer than we think of them. 10

If a plain man, uninstructed in philosophy, has faith to receive these mysteries, how great must be his astonishment. He is brought into a new world, where every thing he sees, tastes, or touches, is an idea; a fleeting kind of being which he can conjure into existence, or can annihilate in the twinkling of an eye.

After his mind is somewhat composed, it will be natural for him to ask his philosophical instructor, pray, sir, are there then no substantial and permanent beings called the sun and moon, which continue to exist whether we think of them or not?

Here the philosophers differ. Mr. Locke, and those that were before him, will answer to this question, that it is very true, there are substantial and permanent beings called the sun and moon; but they never appear to us in their own person, but by their representatives, the ideas in our own minds, and we know nothing of them but what we can gather from those ideas. 11

Bishop Berkeley and Mr. Hume, would give a different answer to the question proposed. They would assure the querist, that it is a vulgar error,

Berkeley's view was, of course, idealism. (Hume holds a somewhat similar view.)

The most crucial claim here is that ideas *represent* external objects. That they do it by *resembling* them or that they are mental *images* are further claims made in an effort to explain how the relation of representation works. (Thus it would be at least possible to reject these latter claims and the account of representation they embody, while still holding onto the claim of representation itself—though then some other account of representation would be needed.)

Here Reid seriously misrepresents the view he is criticizing. Locke does not say that the sun and moon are in our minds or cease to exist when we are not thinking of them. And while Berkeley says the first of these things, he would not agree to the second (think about why).

This is a more accurate statement of Locke's view. What is Reid's alternative? Do the sun and moon "appear to us in their own person," and if so, how do they do this—given that Reid too holds that they exist outside the mind? Can the mind think about something outside it without there being some internal feature—whether or not it is an entity like an idea—that represents the thing in question?

a mere prejudice of the ignorant and unlearned, to think that there are any permanent and substantial beings called the sun and moon; that the heavenly bodies, our own bodies, and all bodies whatsoever, are nothing but ideas in our minds; and that there can be nothing like the ideas of one mind, but the ideas of another mind. There is nothing in nature but minds and ideas, says the bishop. . . .

In this representation of the theory of ideas, there is nothing exaggerated or misrepresented, as far as I am able to judge; and surely nothing further is necessary to show, that, to the uninstructed in philosophy, it must appear extravagant and visionary, and most contrary to the dictates of common understanding.

. . .

A *second* reflection upon this subject is, that the authors who have treated of ideas, have generally taken their existence for granted, as a thing that could not be called in question; and such arguments as they have mentioned incidentally, in order to prove it, seem too weak to support the conclusion.

Mr. Locke, in the introduction to his Essay, tells us, that he uses the word *idea* to signify whatever is the immediate object of thought; and then adds, "I presume it will be easily granted me that there are such ideas in men's minds; every one is conscious of them in himself, and men's words and actions will satisfy him that they are in others." I am indeed conscious of perceiving, remembering, imagining; but that the objects of these operations are images in my mind I am not conscious. I am satisfied by men's words and actions, that they often perceive the same objects which I perceive, which could not be, if those objects were ideas in their own minds. (12)

12 Locke would not, of course, deny that different people can perceive the same external object, though he would insist that they do so by each of them having their own separate ideas of it. (Again, what is Reid's alternative? *How* do different people perceive the same object?)

. . .

There remains only one other argument that I have been able to find urged against our perceiving external objects immediately. It is proposed by Mr. Hume, who, in the Essay already quoted, after acknowledging that it is an universal and primary opinion of all men, that we perceive external objects immediately, subjoins what follows:

"But this universal and primary opinion of all men is soon destroyed by the slightest philosophy, which teaches us, that nothing can ever be present to the mind but an image or perception; and that the senses are only the inlets through which these images are received, without being ever able to produce any immediate intercourse between the mind and the object. The table, which we see, seems to diminish as we remove further from it; but the real table, which exists independent of us, suffers no alteration. It was therefore nothing but its image which was present to the mind. These are the obvious dictates of reason. . . ." (13)

13  Though Reid is focusing on Hume, this is the same basic line of argument, the argument from illusion (or perceptual relativity), that appears many times in Berkeley's *Three Dialogues*.

. . .

The passage now quoted is all I have found in Mr. Hume's writings upon this point; and indeed there is more reasoning in it than I have found in any other author; I shall therefore examine it minutely. . . .

To judge of the strength of this argument, it is necessary to attend to . . . the distinction between real and apparent magnitude. The real magnitude of a line is measured by some known measure of length, as inches, feet, or miles. . . . .

Apparent magnitude is measured by the angle which an object subtends at the eye. . . .

From what has been said, it is evident that the real magnitude of a body must continue unchanged, while the body is unchanged. This we grant. But is it likewise evident, that the apparent magnitude must continue the same while the body is unchanged? So far otherwise, that every man who knows any thing of mathematics can easily demonstrate, that the same individual object, remaining in the same place, and unchanged, must necessarily vary in its apparent magnitude, according as the point from which it is seen is more or less distant; and that its apparent length or breadth will be nearly in a reciprocal proportion to the distance of the spectator. This is as certain as the principles of geometry.

. . .

If these things be considered, it will appear, that Mr. Hume's argument has no force to support his conclusion, nay, that it leads to a contrary conclusion. The argument is this. The table we see, seems to diminish as we remove further from it; that is, its apparent magnitude is diminished; but the real table suffers no alteration, to wit, in its real magnitude; therefore it is not the real table we see. I admit both the premises in this syllogism, but I deny the conclusion. . . .

Let us suppose, for a moment, that it is the real table we see. Must not this real table seem to diminish as we remove further from it? It is demonstrable that it must. How then can this apparent diminution be an argument that it is not the real table? When that which must happen to the real table, as we remove further from it, does actually happen to the table we see, it is absurd to conclude from this, that it is not the real table we see. It is evident, therefore, that this ingenious author has imposed upon himself, by confounding real magnitude with apparent magnitude, and that his argument is a mere sophism. 14

. . .

The *last* reflection I shall make upon this theory is, that the natural and necessary consequences of it furnish a just prejudice against it to every man who pays a due regard to the common sense of mankind.

. . .

It was this theory or means that led Des Cartes, and those that followed him, to think it necessary to prove, by philosophical arguments, the existence of material objects. And who does not see that philosophy must make a very ridiculous figure in the eyes of sensible men, while it is employed in mustering up metaphysical arguments, to prove that there is a sun and a moon, an earth and a sea? Yet we find these truly great men, Des Cartes, Malebranche, Arnauld, and Locke, seriously employing themselves in this argument.

Surely their principles led them to think, that all men, from the beginning of the world, believed the existence of these things upon insufficient grounds, and to think that they would be able to place upon a more rational foundation this universal belief of mankind. But the misfortune is, that all the laboured arguments they have advanced, to prove the existence of those things we see and feel, are mere sophisms. Not one of them will bear examination.

. . .

However, all these consequences of the doctrine of ideas were tolerable, compared with those which came afterward to be discovered by Berkeley and Hume: That there is no material world: No abstract ideas or notions: That the mind is only a train of related impressions and ideas, without any subject on which they may be impressed: That there is neither space nor time, body nor mind, but impressions and ideas only: And, to sum up all, That there is no probability, even in demonstration itself, nor any one proposition more probable than its contrary.

These are the noble fruits which have grown upon this theory of ideas, since it began to be cultivated by skilful hands. It is no wonder that sensible men should be disgusted at philosophy, when such wild and shocking paradoxes pass under its name. However, as these paradoxes have, with great acuteness and ingenuity, been deduced by just reasoning from the theory of ideas, they must at last bring this advantage, that positions so shocking to the common sense of mankind, and so contrary to the decisions of all our intellectual powers, will open men's eyes, and break the force of the prejudice which has held them entangled in that theory. 15

. . .

Of the Evidence of Sense, and of Belief in General

The intention of nature in the powers which we call the external senses, is evident. They are intended to give us that information of external objects which the Supreme Being saw to be proper for us in our present state; and they give to all mankind the information necessary for life, without reasoning, without any art or investigation on our part.

The most uninstructed peasant has as distinct a conception, and as firm a belief of the immediate objects of his senses, as the greatest philosopher; and with this he rests satisfied, giving himself no concern how he came by this conception and belief. But the philosopher is impatient to know how his conception of external objects, and his belief of their existence, is produced. This, I am afraid, is hid in impenetrable darkness. But where there is no knowledge, there is the more room for conjecture: and of this philosophers have always been very liberal.

. . .

We give the name of evidence to whatever is a ground of belief. To believe without evidence is

14

But is this an adequate response to the argument? What is it for a person to be aware of the apparent magnitude of the table and for that to diminish while the table does not change? Berkeley (and Hume) would say that our awareness of this apparent magnitude involves having something like a mental image that changes (in the sense that the table occupies a smaller part of it) even while the table undergoes no change, so that it is this image (and idea) that we are most immediately aware of. Does Reid offer any clear alternative to this view?

15

Is Reid right that the view that the existence of the material world needs to be proved and the skepticism that results from failed attempts to do so results only from the theory of ideas? Does rejecting that theory preclude raising essentially the same problem—and if so, why?

a weakness which every man is concerned to avoid, and which every man wishes to avoid. Nor is it in a man's power to believe any thing longer than he thinks he has evidence. (16)

...

The common occasions of life lead us to distinguish evidence into different kinds, to which we give names that are well understood; such as the evidence of sense, the evidence of memory, the evidence of consciousness, the evidence of testimony, the evidence of axioms, the evidence of reasoning. . . .

I confess that, although I have, as I think, a distinct notion of the different kinds of evidence above mentioned, and perhaps of some others, which it is unnecessary here to enumerate, yet I am not able to find any common nature to which they may all be reduced. They seem to me to agree only in this, that they are all fitted by nature to produce belief in the human mind; some of them in the highest degree, which we call certainty, others in various degrees according to circumstances.

I shall take it for granted, that the evidence of sense, when the proper circumstances concur, is good evidence, and a just ground of belief. (17) My intention in this place is only to compare it with the other kinds that have been mentioned, that we may judge whether it be reducible to any of them, or of a nature peculiar to itself.

1st, It seems to be quite different from the evidence of reasoning. All good evidence is commonly called reasonable evidence, and very justly, because it ought to govern our belief as reasonable creatures. And, according to this meaning, I think the evidence of sense no less reasonable than that of demonstration. . . .

But when we speak of the evidence of reasoning as a particular kind of evidence, it means the evidence of propositions that are inferred by reasoning, from propositions already known and believed. . . .

That the evidence of sense is of a different kind, needs little proof. No man seeks a reason for believing what he sees or feels; and if he did, it would be difficult to find one. But though he can give no reason for believing his senses, his belief remains as firm as if it were grounded on demonstration.

Many eminent philosophers, thinking it unreasonable to believe, when they could not show a reason, have laboured to furnish us with reasons for believing our senses; but their reasons are very insufficient, and will not bear examination. (18) Other philosophers have shown very clearly the fallacy of these reasons, and have, as they imagine, discovered invincible reasons against this belief; but they have never been able either to shake it in themselves, or to convince others . . . a man may as soon, by reasoning, pull the moon out of her orbit, as destroy the belief of the objects of sense.

. . . when I . . . see an object before my eyes, this commands my belief no less than an axiom. But when, as a philosopher, I reflect upon this belief, and want to trace it to its origin, I am not able to resolve it into necessary and self-evident axioms, or conclusions that are necessarily consequent upon them. I seem to want that evidence which I can best comprehend, and which gives perfect satisfaction to an inquisitive mind; yet it is ridiculous to doubt, and I find it is not in my power. An attempt to throw off this belief, is like an attempt to fly, equally ridiculous and impracticable. (19)

To a philosopher, who has been accustomed to think that the treasure of his knowledge is the acquisition of that reasoning power of which he boasts, it is no doubt humiliating to find, that his reason can lay no claim to the greater part of it.

By his reason, he can discover certain abstract and necessary relations of things; but his knowledge of what really exists, or did exist, comes by another channel, which is open to those who cannot reason. He is led to it in the dark, and knows not how he came by it.

It is no wonder that the pride of philosophy should lead some to invent vain theories, in order to account for this knowledge; and others who see this to be impracticable, to spurn at a knowledge they cannot account for, and vainly attempt to throw it off, as a reproach to their understanding. But the wise and the humble will receive it as the gift of Heaven, and endeavour to make the best use of it.

...

Of First Principles in General

. . . there are . . . propositions which are no sooner understood than they are believed. The judgment follows the apprehension of them necessarily, and both are equally the work of

(16) This last part is highly questionable. But the main problem here is that what is *thought* to be good evidence need not actually *be* good evidence.

(17)  This is in keeping with Reid's common-sense outlook.  But even if it is acceptable to take this for granted, it can still be asked *why* and *how* this is so.

(18)  Here Reid has Descartes and Locke mainly in mind.

(19)  But doubt isn't really the issue. Even if Reid is right that doubt is "ridiculous," a philosopher can (and seemingly should) ask what makes beliefs of this sort acceptable.

nature, and the result of our original powers. There is no searching for evidence; no weighing of arguments; the proposition is not deduced or inferred from another; it has the light of truth in itself, and has no occasion to borrow it from another.[20]

Propositions of the last kind . . . are called *first principles, principles of common sense, common notions, self-evident truths. . . .*

I take it for granted, that there are self-evident principles. Nobody, I think, denies it. And if any man were so skeptical as to deny that there is any proposition that is self-evident, I see not how it would be possible to convince him by reasoning.

But yet there seems to be great difference of opinions among philosophers about first principles. What one takes to be self-evident, another labours to prove by arguments, and a third denies altogether.

Thus, before the time of Des Cartes, it was taken for a first principle, that there is a sun and a moon, an earth and sea, which really exist, whether we think of them or not. Des Cartes thought that the existence of those things ought to be proved by argument; and in this he has been followed by Malebranche, Arnauld, and Locke. They have all laboured to prove, by very weak reasoning, the existence of external objects of sense; and Berkeley, and Hume, sensible of the weakness of their arguments, have been led to deny their existence altogether.

. . .

The First Principles of Contingent Truths

. . .

As the minds of men are occupied much more about truths that are contingent than about those that are necessary, I shall first endeavour to point out the principles of the former kind.

1st. *First,* Then, I hold, as a first principle, the existence of every thing of which I am conscious.

. . .

When a man is conscious of pain, he is certain of its existence; when he is conscious that he doubts, or believes, he is certain of the existence of those operations.

But the irresistible conviction he has of the reality of those operations is not the effect of reasoning; it is immediate and intuitive. The existence therefore of those passions and operations of our minds, of which we are conscious, is a first principle, which nature requires us to believe upon her authority.

If I am asked to prove that I cannot be deceived by consciousness, to prove that it is not a fallacious sense; I can find no proof. I cannot find any antecedent truth from which it is deduced, or upon which its evidence depends. It seems to disdain any such derived authority, and to claim my assent in its own right.

If any man could be found so frantic as to deny that he thinks, while he is conscious of it; I may wonder, I may laugh, or I may pity him, but I cannot reason the matter with him. We have no common principles from which we may reason, and therefore can never join issue in an argument.[21]

. . .

3dly, Another first principle I take to be, That those things did really happen which I distinctly remember.

This has one of the surest marks of a first principle; for no man ever pretended to prove it, and yet no man in his wits calls it in question; the testimony of memory, like that of consciousness, is immediate; it claims our assent upon its own authority.

. . .

Indeed the theory concerning ideas, so generally received by philosophers, destroys all the authority of memory, as well as the authority of the senses. Des Cartes, Malebranche, and Locke, were aware that this theory made it necessary for them to find out arguments to prove the existence of external objects, which the vulgar believe upon the bare authority of their senses; but those philosophers were not aware, that this theory made it equally necessary for them to find arguments to prove the existence of things past, which we remember, and to support the authority of memory.

All the arguments they advanced to support the authority of our senses, were easily refuted by bishop Berkeley and Mr. Hume, being indeed very weak and inconclusive. And it would have been as easy to answer every argument they could have brought, consistent with their theory, to support the authority of memory.[22]

There are two different features indicated here, which should not be run together (as Reid at least sometimes seems to do): first, that the proposition is accepted as soon as it is understood, without any searching for evidence or weighing of arguments; and, second, that there is some sort of ground or basis for thinking that it is true (it has the "light of truth in itself").

Here Reid has in mind consciousness of mental entities and processes, not consciousness of external objects. Is he right that there is no reason or argument that supports the truth of claims resulting from such consciousness?

Here is Reid's response to another very difficult epistemological issue, one that there is no further consideration of in this book. Reid is suggesting in part that the problem of memory and the problem of perception are parallel, and that the futility of trying to defend perceptual beliefs via argument can be made even more obvious by reflecting on this parallel case. (See Discussion Question 3.)

. . .

5thly, Another first principle is, That those things do really exist which we distinctly perceive by our senses, and are what we perceive them to be. (23)

(23) This is Reid's basic response to the issue of how perceptual beliefs are justified: that the things we perceive (probably?) exist and are as we perceive them to be is a first principle. Is this an adequate solution to the problem? (See Discussion Question 2.)

It is too evident to need proof, that all men are by nature led to give implicit faith to the distinct testimony of their senses, long before they are capable of any bias from prejudices of education or of philosophy.

. . .

We have before examined the reasons given by philosophers, to prove that ideas, and not external objects, are the immediate objects of perception, and the instances given to prove the senses fallacious. Without repeating what has before been said upon those points, we shall only here observe, that if external objects be perceived immediately, we have the same reason to believe their existence as philosophers have to believe the existence of ideas, while they hold them to be the immediate objects of perception. (24)

(24) R Reid offers a further argument: once it is granted that external objects are perceived immediately, we have as good a reason to accept the perceptual beliefs that result as we would have for beliefs about ideas (if they existed)—or, presumably, as we do in the case of beliefs about states of mind such as sensations. (See Discussion Question 1.)

. . .

7thly, Another first principle is, that the natural faculties, by which we distinguish truth from error, are not fallacious. If any man should demand a proof of this, it is impossible to satisfy him. For suppose it should be mathematically demonstrated, this would signify nothing in this case; because, to judge of a demonstration, a man must trust his faculties, and take for granted the very thing in question.

If a man's honesty were called in question, it would be ridiculous to refer it to the man's own word, whether he be honest or not. The same absurdity there is in attempting to prove, by any kind of reasoning, probable or demonstrative, that our reason is not fallacious, since the very point in question is, whether reasoning may be trusted.

If a skeptic should build his skepticism upon this foundation, that all our reasoning, and judging powers are fallacious in their nature, or should resolve at least to withhold assent until it be proved that they are not; it would be impossible by argument to beat him out of this strong hold, and he must even be left to enjoy his skepticism.

Des Cartes certainly made a false step in this matter; for having suggested this doubt among others, that whatever evidence he might have from his consciousness, his senses, his memory, or his reason; yet possibly some malignant being had given him those faculties on purpose to impose upon him; and therefore, that they are not to be trusted without a proper voucher: to remove this doubt, he endeavours to prove the being of a Deity who is no deceiver; whence he concludes, that the faculties he had given him are true and worthy to be trusted.

It is strange that so acute a reasoner did not perceive, that in this reasoning there is evidently a begging of the question. (25)

(25) R Here Reid has in mind the power of reasoning and rational thought. He points out, correctly, that there is no way to prove the reliability of this basic capacity, since any proof would rely on the very capacity in question and so would beg the question.

. . .

Discussion Questions

1. Consider an introspective belief about one of your own conscious states of mind: the belief that you are experiencing a pain in your wrist, perhaps, or the belief that you are thinking about Reid. What sort of reason or basis do you have for thinking that such beliefs are true? Is this just something that has to be accepted as a "first principle," or is there something more to be said? (If there is a reason of this sort, then the next question is whether anything parallel can be said about perceptual beliefs concerning external objects.)
2. Even if external objects are perceived directly in the sense that there is no intermediate entity that is perceived more immediately, it can still apparently be asked whether the specific belief or conviction that is the content of a perceptual judgment is true (or likely to be true). Is it enough of a response to this question to say, as Reid does, that it is simply a first principle that beliefs of this sort are true—especially if it is admitted, as he does, that such a claim is not self-evident or necessary? Bertrand Russell remarks that the method of postulation "has all the advantages of theft over honest toil," by which he means that simply postulating that something is so is too easy to be satisfying. Does this same objection pertain to Reid's first principles (and if not, why not)?
3. Think about the somewhat analogous problem of how, if at all, memory beliefs can be justified (where we are using the term "memory belief" to refer to beliefs that seem to be memories, whether they are actually so or not). Reid is right

that philosophers who discuss perception at great length often say very little about memory, even though very similar issues seem to arise there. Think of how solutions parallel to Locke's and to Berkeley's would apply to the case of memory, and consider the problems that arise in each case. Can memory beliefs be justified in either of these two ways? If not, is a Reidian solution the only one available? And if this is so, does it, by analogy, support Reid's account of perception?

Laurence BonJour

Laurence BonJour (1943–) is an American philosopher who teaches at the University of Washington. He has written or co-written several books in epistemology and is also the coeditor of this volume. In this selection, BonJour recapitulates the problem of the external world, as it grows out of the work of Descartes, Locke, and Berkeley; then explains and criticizes the phenomenalist response to this problem, growing out of Berkeley's view (and Hume's); and finally offers a tentative solution along very roughly Lockean lines. At the end, he also has a bit to say about direct realist views like the one offered by Reid.

Knowledge of the External World, from *Epistemology: Classic Problems and Contemporary Responses*

We have so far tentatively accepted the conclusion that the *immediate* object of awareness in perceptual experience is never an external material object, but is instead something of a quite different sort: . . . a sense-datum. . . . (1) It will be useful to have a brief label for this disjunctive result, and I will refer to it here as *perceptual subjectivism* . . . .

We have now to consider the implications of perceptual subjectivism for the epistemological issue upon which it bears most directly, which is also arguably the most central issue of the modern period of epistemology, which began with Descartes: the issue of whether and, if so, how beliefs concerning the external material world and the objects that it allegedly contains can be justified on the basis of our immediate sensory experience, thus understood . . . we will first look at the views of Descartes's immediate successors, the so-called British Empiricists Locke, Berkeley, and Hume, whose arguments played a major role in shaping the subsequent discussion. We will then examine the two main alternative accounts of "knowledge of the external world" (on the assumption that perceptual subjectivism or something like it is indeed true) that have subsequently emerged, mainly in the forms that they have taken in the twentieth century: *phenomenalism* and *representationalism.* Difficulties with these views will then prompt, in the last part of the chapter, a reconsideration of whether rejecting perceptual subjectivism might make available a further, more promising alternative.

(1)  Sense-data (singular: sense-datum) are roughly the same things that Locke and Berkeley have in mind when they speak of perceptual ideas: entities that have the qualities that are directly or immediately experienced and that exist in the mind.

Locke, Berkeley, and Hume on Perception and the External World

As noted earlier, Locke and Berkeley speak not of sense-data . . . but of "ideas" or "ideas of sense"—with the former term being applied also to contents of thought and indeed apparently to conscious contents of any kind. The way that they use these rather slippery terms suggests in many places something like a sense-datum theory of the immediate objects of sensory experience. For our purposes, however, it will suffice to take the term "idea" merely to refer to conscious contents of any sort, and "ideas of sense" to the distinctive contents of sensory experience, without supposing these terms to indicate any definite metaphysical picture of the nature of such contents.

From *Epistemology: Classic Problems and Contemporary Responses* (Lanham, Md.: Rowman & Littlefield, 2002). Some footnotes have been deleted.

Locke's view is clearly that our beliefs or opinions about material objects existing outside of our minds are justified by our ideas of sense.* But his discussion of this point is both rather uncertain and quite guarded. He says that our assurance on this basis concerning material objects "deserves the name of knowledge" [p. 71], thus seeming to suggest that it is not knowledge simply and with no qualification. He also questions whether anyone can be genuinely skeptical about the existence of the things that he sees and feels, and speaks rather vaguely of "the assurance we have from our senses themselves, that they do not err in the information they give us" [p. 72].

But the closest that Locke comes to explaining *how* such beliefs are justified by sensory experience is his citing of four "concurrent reasons" that are supposed to further confirm the assurance derived from the senses: First, we can know that sensory ideas are "produced in us by exterior causes" by observing that those lacking a particular sense organ can never have the corresponding sensory ideas [p. 72]. (Thus, for example, a blind man can never have immediate sensory experiences of visual qualities such as color.) Second, another reason for thinking that our sensory ideas result from external causes is their *involuntary* character, as contrasted with imagination and, to a lesser extent, memory [p. 72]. (Thus if I have my eyes open and am facing in a particular direction, I have no choice as to what apparent objects or properties I will experience, that is, in Locke's view, what ideas of vision I will experience—as I look out my study window, I cannot help being aware of a mass of variegated green and brown that I take to be a perception of trees, branches, and leaves.) Third, another difference between our immediate sensory experiences and other sorts of ideas, such as those of imagination and memory, is that sensory ideas of certain kinds are accompanied by *pain,* whereas the corresponding ideas of imagination and memory are not [p. 72]. (For example, if I have the immediate sensory experience of apparently hitting my hand with a hammer while attempting to drive a nail, I will usually experience pain along with it; but if I merely imagine or remember such an experience, there is no pain.†) Fourth, "our senses, in many cases, bear witness to the truth of each other's report, concerning the existence of sensible things without us" [p. 72]. (For example, my visual experience of the appearance of a fire close to my body is normally accompanied by tactile experiences of heat, apparent smells of burning, the apparent hearing of cracklings or other distinctive firelike sounds, etc.—think here of other examples of your own.) But Locke has little to say as to just *how* these "concurrent reasons" are supposed to show that our beliefs concerning material objects that are arrived on the basis of our immediate sensory experiences are justified by those experiences. Does such a conclusion really follow, and, if so, how and why? . . .

In fact, Locke's supposed reasons are of very unequal weight. The first one is totally worthless, because it begs the very question at issue and also would require a prior solution of another, related epistemological problem. Until the problem of justifying belief in external objects on the basis of his sensory experience has been solved, Locke is obviously not in a position to appeal to supposed facts about other people's sense organs, since sense organs are physical structures and so beliefs about them would have to be justified in just the way that is in question. Moreover, to invoke this first reason, he would also have to have justified beliefs about the mental states of other people, specifically concerning whether they do or do not have sensory ideas of the relevant sort. How this latter sort of knowledge is possible is a serious problem in itself (the "problem of other minds" . . .) But it is pretty clear on reflection . . . that knowledge of other people's mental states normally depends on *prior* knowledge of the behavior and condition of their physical bodies, thus again presupposing the very knowledge of the material world that has not yet been accounted for. 2 . . .

Locke's second reason is at least a bit better. The involuntary or spontaneous character of my sensory experience does at least distinguish it

2

STOP How do you know of the existence and specific character of other people's mental states? What reason do you have for thinking that they are not, for example, just cleverly designed robots that have no conscious mental states at all? (See Discussion Question 1.)

*Locke, *Essay Concerning Human Understanding,* Book IV, ch. XI. Subsequent page references in the text are to the selection in the present book.

†There may of course be *imagined* or *remembered* pain, but that is obviously not the same thing as really experienced pain.

from other sorts of mental states and experience (albeit perhaps not in a completely sharp way—aren't many memories and even some imaginings similarly involuntary?). But this fact does not by itself seem to establish that immediate sensory experiences are, as he claims, caused by something external to the person who has them. Why couldn't my involuntary sensory experiences result instead from some subconscious or unconscious faculty of my own mind that is outside my voluntary control? And, even more obviously, that the ideas are involuntary tells us nothing at all about whether the external cause, if there is one, has the specific properties that my sensory experience seems to portray (whether it "resembles my ideas," as Locke would put it). Why couldn't the external cause of my idea of a green tree, again if there is one, neither be green nor have the other properties of a tree? Indeed, why couldn't it, as Berkeley will suggest, be something utterly different from a material object? And the third reason, while again perhaps showing that sensory experiences are importantly different from many other mental phenomena, also does not support in any clear way a conclusion about what is responsible for this difference.

What about the fourth reason? Surely it is a striking fact that my various sensory experiences fit together in an extremely orderly and coherent fashion to depict an ongoing world that is both extremely complicated and highly regular or law-governed. The information or apparent information derived at a given time from one sense agrees to a very great degree with both that derived at that time from other senses and also with that derived from both the same sense and others at other times—allowing, of course, for the ongoing change and development of the world, which is also something that is reflected in regularities within our sensory experience. Thus if I seem to see a chair, I can normally also have the experience of touching it, given that I also have the experience of moving my body in the right direction and far enough. And the experiences that I have of the furniture and contents of my office before leaving for a class agree very well with the similar experiences that I have after I have apparently returned—allowing, in some cases, for the actions of the janitor or my dog (who is sometimes left there) or my wife (who has a key). ❸ . . .

But how exactly is this admittedly striking fact supposed to support Locke's intended conclusion, namely that there is good reason or justification for thinking that the beliefs about the material world that we arrive at on the basis of our immediate sensory experience are likely to be true? On this obviously crucial question, Locke has very little to say. . . .

In fact, if you think carefully about it, the order of my immediate sensory experience and the seeming agreement between experiences apparently produced by different senses would not be striking, or at least not nearly so striking, if those ideas were under my voluntary control—for then I could deliberately imagine an orderly world, in something like the way in which this is done by an artist or novelist. What makes the order so noteworthy is precisely that it is not voluntarily created, but just occurs spontaneously and, in many of its details, unexpectedly. Thus we see that Locke's fourth "concurrent reason" needs to be supplemented by his second, and that it is these two *together* that might provide at least the beginnings of a real argument. Experience that was involuntary but chaotic would show very little, and neither would experience that was orderly but voluntarily controlled. It is experience that is *both* involuntary and highly orderly that seems to demand some sort of further *explanation:* what is it that produces and sustains the order? Thus it is natural to interpret Locke as arguing, admittedly without formulating the point very clearly or explicitly, that the *best explanation* of his involuntary but orderly experience is that it is systematically caused by a world of independent material objects which it depicts with at least approximate accuracy. (The main way in which the depiction is only approximately accurate is that, according to Locke, material objects have only *primary qualities* like size, shape, and motion, but not *secondary qualities* like color, smell, taste, and temperature (as felt).)

Does this argument really show that our beliefs about the material world that are arrived at on the basis of our involuntary sensory experience are likely to be true and hence justified? It seems reasonable to think that there must be *some* explanation for these features of our sensory ideas, which is just to say that the sort of order that they exhibit is extremely unlikely to

STOP Think of some further examples of order and agreement between the perceptions of different senses or between the perceptions of one sense at different times, trying to specify them in detail.

result from mere chance. But is Locke's proposed explanation the right one?

Berkeley, while appealing to essentially the same features of our sensory ideas (their being independent of our will and their being orderly and coherent), offers a quite different and in his view superior explanation: that our sensory ideas are produced in our minds by God, who determines and controls their orderly character, so that there is thus no need or justification for supposing that the independent material realm advocated by Locke really exists. Berkeley's God obviously bears a striking resemblance to Descartes's evil genius, with the crucial difference that whereas Descartes assumes that the evil genius would be *deceiving* us, Berkeley's view is in effect that having sensory ideas systematically produced in us by God (presumably reflecting God's ideally complete picture of the world thus depicted) is *just what it is* for a world of ordinary objects to exist. Thus we have at least two competing explanations for the same facts concerning our sensory experience, and the question is how we should decide between such explanations. ❹

❹

Can you think of any way to rationally choose between these two explanations? Can you think of any other possible explanations?

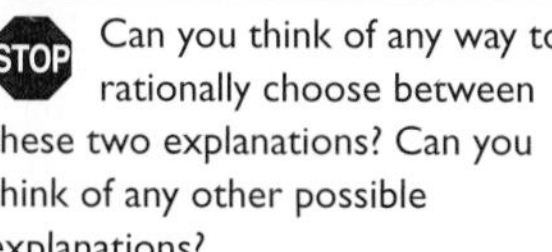

Assuming, that is, that we can rationally decide at all. Hume's response to the problem is to deny that *any* such attempt to explain our experience by appeal to objects or entities existing outside of that experience could ever be justified. An essential ingredient of both Locke's and Berkeley's proposed explanations is the claim that our immediately experienced sensory ideas (or "impressions," as Hume calls them, in order to distinguish them from other kinds of ideas) are *caused* by the external entities that those explanations invoke—by material objects, according to Locke's explanation, and by God, according to Berkeley's. Moreover, it seems obvious that any similar attempt to explain experience by appeal to something existing outside experience (even the person's own unconscious mind) will require a similar causal claim (for how else would the explanation work?). But, argues Hume, causal relations can be known only by *experiencing* the regular sequence of cause and effect, something that is impossible in the case of an alleged causal relation between something outside immediate experience and that experience itself. ❺ In relation to Locke's explanation specifically, the point is that I cannot immediately experience material bodies causing my sensory ideas because I have no immediate experience of such bodies at all; and the claim that I *indirectly* perceive material bodies presupposes for its justification an explanation relying on the very causal relation in question and so cannot be used to establish that such a causal relation exists.

❺

For Hume's discussion of this, see the selection in the induction section.

Is Hume right that causal relations are always known by repeated experiences of the sequence of cause and effect? Think here of various examples of causal relations that seem to be known. Can you think of any plausible causal claims that don't seem to be known in this way?

Hume's further discussion of the issue of the external world is characteristically muddled by his general tendency to conflate and confuse issues concerning justification with issues having to do with the psychological causation or genesis of the beliefs in question. . . . But it is nonetheless easy to see how Hume who was clearer about the distinction between psychological explanation and epistemic justification might have argued that the content of our claims about material objects, to the extent that this is justified, must have to do *solely* with features and patterns of our sensory experience, rather than with genuinely mind-transcendent objects. . . .

Thus we have initial adumbrations of the two main views that we will now proceed to discuss more systematically. Locke's view, according to which our subjective sensory experience and the beliefs that we adopt on the basis of it constitute a *representation* of the external material world, one that is caused by that world and that we are justified in thinking to be at least approximately accurate, is a version of the more general position known as *representationalism* or *representative realism.* (So also is Descartes's view.) The second main view, which Hume's discussion suggests but never quite arrives at, is that (i) we can have no knowledge (or perhaps even no intelligible conception) of a realm of external causes of our experience, but also (ii) that our beliefs about the material world can still be in general justified and true because their content in fact has to do only with the features and order of our subjective experience. This is the view that has come to be known as *phenomenalism,* a version of idealism. ❻ . . . Yet a third possibility would be the essentially skeptical view that we can know that our experiences are externally caused in *some* way, but can know nothing further about the nature of those causes. Such a skeptical view would, of course, not be a *solution* to the problem of the external world, but rather a confession that there is no

❻

The phenomenalist view is at least similar to Berkeley's view of material objects, though without the reference to God: for both views, material objects exist only as patterns of ideas or experiences or sense-data in minds, and have no existence outside of all minds (that would be "mind-transcendent" existence).

solution; it is thus a view to be adopted only after the other two possibilities have clearly failed.

Historically, the objections to the representationalism of Descartes and Locke, especially the Humean one discussed above, were widely taken to be decisive, with positions in the direction of phenomenalism being viewed as the main nonskeptical alternative, especially in the first two-thirds or so of the twentieth century. Thus we will begin our more systematic discussion with a consideration of phenomenalism, and then return later to the consideration of representationalism that was begun in the discussion of Locke.

Phenomenalism

As just briefly formulated, the phenomenalist view is that the content of propositions about material objects and the material world is *entirely* concerned with features and relations of the immediate objects of our perceptual experience, that is, the features and relations of our sense-data. According to the phenomenalist, to believe that a physical or material object of a certain sort exists just *is* to believe that sense-data of various sorts have been experienced, are being experienced, will be experienced, and/or would be experienced under certain specifiable conditions. Thus, for example, to believe that there is a large brown table in a certain room in the University of Washington Library is to believe, roughly, (i) that the sorts of sense-data that seem from a common-sense standpoint to reflect the presence of such a table either have been, are presently, or will in the future be experienced in the context of other sense-data, themselves experienced concurrently or immediately before or after, that reflect the location as the room in question; and in addition—or instead, if the table has never in fact been perceived and never in fact will be perceived—(ii) that such sense-data *would* be experienced *if* other sense-data that reflect the perceiver's going to the library and to that room were experienced. (This is quite a complicated specification, and you will have to think very carefully about what it is saying.) 7

In a fairly standard formula, to believe that such a material object exists is, according to the phenomenalist, to believe nothing more than that sense-data of the appropriate sort are actual (in the past, present, or future) and/or possible—where to say that certain sense-data are *possible* is to say, not just that it is logically possible for them to be experienced (which would apparently always be so as long as the description of them is not contradictory), but that they *would* in fact actually be experienced under certain specifiable circumstances (specifiable in sense-datum terms); thus it would be somewhat clearer to speak of actual and *obtainable* sense-data. The British philosopher John Stuart Mill put this point by saying that material objects are nothing but "permanent possibilities of sensation," that is, of sense-data—where, of course, the possibilities in question are only *relatively* permanent, since objects can change or be destroyed. The crucial thing to see is that what Mill and the other phenomenalists are saying is that there are no independently existing objects that are responsible for the possibilities of sensation or the obtainability of sense-data; the actuality and obtainability of sense-data are *all there is* to the physical or material world.

Phenomenalism is in fact one of those occasional (some would say more than occasional) philosophical views that is *so* monumentally bizarre and implausible, at least from anything close to a common-sense standpoint, as to perhaps make it difficult . . . to believe that it really says what it does—and even more difficult to believe that such a view has in fact sometimes been widely advocated and (apparently) believed, indeed that it was arguably the dominant view concerning the problem of the external world for a good portion of the twentieth century. The first and most important thing to say about this situation is that you must not, as sometimes happens, allow it to cause you to fail to understand what the view is saying by trying to make it more reasonable than it is. The phenomenalist really is saying that there is *nothing more* to the material world (including, of course, our own physical bodies! . . .) than our subjective sensory experiences and the possibility, in the sense explained, of further such experiences (though there is, as we will eventually see, a serious problem about the "our").

But why should such an obviously implausible view be taken seriously, even for a moment? We have already in fact encountered the essential ingredients of the main argument for phenomenalism, but it will be helpful to reiterate them in a somewhat more

STOP Try to spell out the details of this example more fully, and think of some others of your own.

explicit fashion. One main premise of the argument is the Humean thesis that causal relations can be known only via experience of the causal sequence, so that, as already explained, there is no way in which a causal relation between the immediate content of experience and something outside that immediate content could be known, and hence no way to justifiably invoke such external causes as explanations of that experience. This thesis has a good deal of initial plausibility, and can be rebutted only by offering some other account of how causal relations can be known. The other main premise is simply the common-sense conviction that skepticism is false, that we do *obviously* have justified beliefs and knowledge concerning ordinary objects like trees and rocks and buildings and about the material world in which they exist. And the argument is then just that the only way that such justified beliefs and knowledge are possible, given that no causal or explanatory inference from immediate experience to material objects that are genuinely external to that experience could ever even in principle be justified, is if the content of our beliefs about the material world does not really have to do with objects existing outside our immediate experience, but instead pertains just to the objects of that experience and the order that they manifest. (8) Most phenomenalists will admit that this seems initially very implausible, but will try to argue that this apparent implausibility is in some way an illusion, one that can be explained away once the phenomenalist view and the considerations in favor of it have been fully understood.

An underlying additional premise is the thesis of perceptual subjectivity. This argument is similar to Berkeley's argument, except that Berkeley claims only that causal relations between experience and external material objects are unknowable.

STOP Does Berkeley have any good reasons for thinking that causation of experience by God is more knowable?

Objections to Phenomenalism

The foregoing argument, like most arguments for implausible philosophical views that are nonetheless widely held, is a serious argument, one not easily dismissed. Neither premise is easy to rebut, and the conclusion does seem to follow from these premises. But it is, of course, still abundantly obvious that this conclusion cannot be correct, and so that something must have gone wrong. For it is obvious upon even the slightest unbiased reflection that the content of propositions about physical or material objects does pertain, whether justifiably or not, to a realm of entities that, if genuine, exist outside of our minds and experiences in an independent physical realm.

This basic insight seems in fact to constitute by itself a more than adequate reason to reject phenomenalism. But since it nevertheless amounts to little more than a direct, unargued denial of the view, it will be useful to see if we can find further objections and problems of a more articulated sort pertaining to phenomenalism. (Considering such objections and the responses available to the phenomenalist will also help you to better understand the view.) In fact, there are many such objections and problems that have been advanced. Here we will be content with a few of the most interesting ones.

Consider, first, what is perhaps the most obvious question about the phenomenalist view: *Why,* according to the phenomenalist, are the orderly sense-data in question obtainable or "permanently possible"? What is the *explanation* for the pattern of actual and obtainable sense experiences that allegedly constitutes the existence of a material object or of the material world as a whole, if this is not to be explained by appeal to genuinely external objects? The only possible phenomenalist response to this question is to say that the fact that sensory experience reflects this sort of order is simply the most fundamental fact about reality, not further explainable in terms of anything else. For *any* attempted further explanation, since it would obviously have to appeal to something outside of that experience, would be (for the reasons already discussed) unjustified and unknowable. The phenomenalist will add that it is obvious anyway that not everything can be explained, since each explanation just introduces some further fact for which an explanation might be demanded.

But while this last point seems correct (doesn't it?), it seems quite implausible to suppose that something as large and complicated as the total order of our immediate experience has no explanation at all—and also very obvious that common sense (at least if it accepted perceptual subjectivism) would regard claims about material objects as providing such an explanation, rather than as just a redescription of the experiential order itself (as the phenomenalist claims them to be).

Perhaps, for all we have seen so far, the phenomenalist is right that we cannot ever know that any such explanation is correct, but this, if so, is an argument for *skepticism* about the material world, not a justification for perversely reinterpreting the meaning or content of claims about material objects. (Here it is important to be very clear that phenomenalism is *not* supposed to be a skeptical view, but rather an account of how beliefs about material objects are indeed justified and do constitute knowledge—given the phenomenalist account of the content of such beliefs.) 9

A second problem (or rather a set of related problems) has to do with the specification of the *conditions* under which the various sense-data that (according to phenomenalism) are what a material-object proposition is about either are or would be experienced. It is clear that such conditions must be specified to have even a hope of capturing the content of at least most such propositions in sense-datum terms. To recur to our earlier example, to say merely that the sense-data that are characteristic of a brown table are actual or obtainable in some circumstances or other may perhaps capture the content of the claim that the world contains at least one brown table (though even that is doubtful), but surely not of any more specific claim, such as the one about such a table being in a particular room in the University of Washington Library. For that, as we saw briefly, conditions must be specified that say, as it were, that it is in relation to that particular room that the sense-data are or would be experienced. (But remember here that for the phenomenalist, the room does not exist as a mind-external place; talk of a room or of any physical location is to be understood merely as a way of indicating one aspect of the order of immediate experience, namely that the various sense-data that reflect the various features ascribed to the room tend to be experienced together or in close succession, with this whole "cluster" of sense-data standing in similar relations to the further sense-data that pertain to the surrounding area.)

What makes this problem extremely difficult at best is that for phenomenalism to be a viable position, the conditions under which sense-data are experienced or obtainable must themselves (as just in effect indicated) be specifiable in terms of *other sense-data,* not in terms of material objects and structures such as the library or room in question. For the essential claim of phenomenalism is that the content of propositions about material objects can be *entirely* given in terms of sense-data. If in specifying the conditions under which the actual and obtainable sense-data relevant to one material-object proposition would occur, it were necessary to make reference to other material objects, then the account of the content of the first proposition would not yet be completely in sense-datum terms. And if in specifying the conditions relevant to claims about those other material objects, still other material objects would have to be mentioned, and so on, then the phenomenalist account would never be complete. If the content of propositions about material objects cannot be given *entirely* in terms of sense-data, if that content involves essential and ineliminable reference to further such objects, then phenomenalism fails.

There are in fact many problems here, but we may continue to focus on the one suggested by the example of the table in the library room. How can the idea that sense-data are or would be observed in a certain location be adequately captured in purely sense-datum terms? The natural response, which was in effect invoked when the example was originally discussed, is to appeal to the idea of a *sensory route:* a series of juxtaposed and often overlapping sense-data that would be experienced in what we think of intuitively as moving to the location in question. (But, to reiterate, there is not supposed to be any real mind-external location or bodily movement; according to the phenomenalist, claims about this sort of experienced movement have to do *only* with sequences of sense-data that are experienced or could be experienced—including those that we think of intuitively as the feelings associated with bodily movements like walking.)

There are at least two serious problems pertaining to this answer, however. One is that there are normally many *different* sensory routes to a given location, depending on where one starts and how one approaches it; and if the starting location is itself determined by a previous sensory route, then a regress threatens, in which the sensory conditions must go further and further back in time without ever reaching a place from which they can begin. A second

9

R The phenomenalist, like Berkeley, means to be giving an account of what the existence of ordinary objects amounts to, *not* to be denying their existence.

problem is that it seems clear that we can often understand the claim that a certain material object or set of objects exists at a certain physical location without having any clear idea of the relevant sensory route: for example, I understand the claim that there are penguins at the South Pole, but have no clear idea of the sensory route that I would have to follow to guarantee or even make it likely that I have reached the South Pole. (Note that it is a *guarantee* that is actually required, for otherwise the content of the claim in question as not been fully captured.)

...

And there is also the related, but still much more difficult problem of what the phenomenalist can say about the content of propositions about material objects and events in the *past,* perhaps the very distant past. Consider this one carefully on your own, focusing on the most difficult case: past events that were not observed by anyone at the time in question. Under what sensory conditions would sense-data of a tree have to have been obtainable to make it true that there was a pine tree in the place now occupied by my house in 1000 B.C.? It is thus very doubtful that the sort of specification of conditions that the phenomenalist needs is possible in general.

...

A . . . final objection to phenomenalism, one that is, thankfully, much simpler and more straightforward, concerns what the phenomenalist must apparently say about the knowledge of the mental states of people other than myself (or other than whoever is thinking about the issue—for reasons that will become clear, each of you will have to formulate this issue for yourselves). The whole thrust of the phenomenalist position, as we have seen, is that *any* inference beyond immediate experience is impossible, that claims that might seem to be about things outside of experience must, if they are to be justified and knowable, be understood as pertaining only to features and orderly patterns of that experience. But the mental states of *other* people, their experiences and feelings and conscious thoughts, are surely outside of *my* immediate experience. Indeed, to reach justified conclusions about what people distinct from me are genuinely thinking and experiencing would apparently require *two* inferences: first, an inference from my immediate experience of sense-data pertaining to their physical bodies to conclusions about those bodies; and then, second, an inference from the facts about those bodies thus arrived at to further conclusions about the minds and mental states of the people in question. *Both* of these inferences depend on causal relations that are, according to the phenomenalist, unknowable, because we cannot experience both sides, or in the second case even one side, of the relation; and thus neither inference, construed in that way, is justified according to the basic phenomenalist outlook.

What phenomenalism must apparently say here, in order to be consistent, is (i) that the content of propositions about the conditions and behavior of other people's bodies (like that of all other material object propositions) pertains only to facts about *my* immediate experience; and (ii) that the content of further claims about the mental states associated with those bodies is only a further, more complicated and less direct description of, once again, *my* experience. Though the phenomenalist would perhaps resist putting it this way, the upshot is that *my* mind and mental states, including my immediate experience, is the only mind and the only collection of mental states that genuinely exist, with claims that are apparently about other minds amounting only to further descriptions of this one mind and its experiences. This is the view known as *solipsism*—which each of you must obviously formulate for yourselves (assuming that any of you are really out there!). It seems clearly to be an absurd consequence, thus yielding a really decisive objection, if one were still needed, to phenomenalism.*

Back to Representationalism

If phenomenalism is indeed untenable, and assuming that we continue to accept perceptual subjectivism, then the only nonskeptical alternative apparently left is *representationalism:* the view, restating it a bit, that our immediately experienced sense-data, together with the further beliefs that we arrive at on the basis of them,

*A woman once allegedly wrote to Bertrand Russell that she found solipsism to be so obviously a correct view that she couldn't understand why it wasn't more widely accepted. (Think about it!)

constitute a *representation* or depiction of an independent realm of material objects—one that we are in general, according to the representationalist, justified in believing to be true.

Defenses of representationalism have taken a variety of forms, but I will assume here that the best sort of defense for such a view is one along the general lines that we found to be suggested, albeit not very explicitly, in Locke (and indeed also, though even less explicitly, in Descartes). The central idea is, first, that (contrary to the claim of the phenomenalist) some *explanation* is needed for the complicated and intricate order that we find in our involuntarily experienced sense-data . . . ; and, second, that the *best* explanation, that is, the one most likely to be correct, is that those experiences are caused by and, with certain qualifications, systematically reflect the character of a world of genuinely independent material objects, which we accordingly have good reasons for believing to exist.

I have already remarked that representationalism was widely repudiated as untenable during most of the period between Locke and recent times, with the main argument being the one that we found in Hume about the unknowability of any causal relation between something outside experience and experience itself. We will begin by looking further at that argument and considering in a general way how it might be answered. Having argued that representationalism cannot be simply ruled out as impossible in the way that Hume tries to do, we will then consider the further issue of whether and how the specific explanation of experience that the representationalist proposes can be defended against other alternatives, such as Berkeley's. Finally, we will look at the significant qualification, already briefly mentioned, advocated by Descartes, Locke, and many others with regard to the accuracy with which our experience represents the true character of material objects: the one having to do with the distinction between *primary* and *secondary* qualities.

A Response to Hume's Argument: Theoretical or Explanatory Inference

To recall, Hume's objection to representationalism rests on the premise that causal relations can be known only by experiencing the regular sequence between cause and effect, which requires experiencing both sides of the causal relation. This, he argues, is impossible for an alleged causal relation between something outside of direct experience and the experience itself, so that the claim that such a causal relation exists can never be justified or known. And therefore, he concludes, neither can the representationalist's proposed explanation of the order of our experience, since that depends essentially on such an unknowable and unjustifiable causal claim.

If Hume's initial premise is accepted, then the rest of his argument seems to follow. But should that premise be accepted? One way to approach this issue is to consider examples where we seem to reason in ways that conflict with that premise but which still seem intuitively cogent. Here I will consider [one example] of this kind, . . . having to do with knowledge concerning unobservable entities and events, such as electrons or quarks or radioactivity, in theoretical physics. In [this case], we seem intuitively to have justified belief and knowledge pertaining to causal relations that could not be arrived at in the way that Hume's premise, if correct, would require. (In considering [this example], we adopt the standpoint of common sense, thus assuming that the problem of the external world has—somehow—been solved.)

. . .

[In the] case of unobservable scientific entities and events[,] . . . we seem to have justified belief and knowledge concerning causal relations among such entities and events and between them and various sorts of observable results, even though the entities and events themselves cannot be experienced in even the indirect sense: knowledge, for example, that radioactivity results from the splitting or decay of various sorts of atoms and that it produces a crackling sound in a Geiger counter. Obviously beliefs concerning relations of these kinds cannot be justified by experiencing both sides of the causal relation in the way that Hume's premise would require.

Notice carefully that the claim so far is *not* that these alleged cases of causal knowledge are genuine, so that Hume's premise would have to be mistaken. It is possible for a proponent of Hume's view to respond by claiming either that

This is a *counter-example* to Hume's general claim about knowledge of causality: a case where the sort of knowledge that he rejects as impossible seems nonetheless to exist. How clear is it that such knowledge is genuine (and hence that fictionalism is mistaken)?

Deductive reasoning is reasoning that is logically conclusive and entirely a priori. Inductive reasoning, as BonJour is using the term, is reasoning that involves simple generalization from observed patterns in experience: from the observation of many ravens that are black (and none that are any other color) to the conclusion that all ravens are black. Theoretical reasoning also depends on observations, but concludes to an explanation in other terms rather than just a generalization. (Sometimes the term "induction" is used for both of these last sorts of reasoning, but they are nonetheless importantly different.)

Theoretical or explanatory reasoning is in fact quite common. Try to think of other examples, drawn from outside of science.

we do not really have the causal knowledge in question. . . . Thus defenders of Hume's view have often also been advocates . . . of *fictionalism* (the view that seemingly unobservable scientific entities do not really exist, but only reflect ways of talking that help to systematically describe observations). But [this view seems] desperately implausible, so that if a reasonably plausible general account can be given of how such causal knowledge can be justifiably arrived at, this would be enough to warrant the rejection of Hume's premise and the argument that results from it. [10]

The account that has been offered . . . holds that knowledge of the sort in question depends on a fundamental and sometimes unrecognized mode of reasoning, one that is quite distinct from both deductive reasoning and . . . inductive reasoning [:] . . . *theoretical* or *explanatory* reasoning. In reasoning of this sort, a hypothesis is advanced to explain some relevant set of data and is justified simply on the basis of being the *best explanation* of the data in question.* [11] Exactly what makes an explanation the *best* is a difficult and complicated issue, as we will see to some extent below, but the point for the moment is that *if* such an assessment can be defended, then it allegedly becomes justifiable to accept the entire explanatory hypothesis, *including any causal claims that it may involve,* on that basis—without any requirement that there be experiential evidence of the sort that Hume's premise would require for those causal claims by themselves. Thus for example when the entire physical theory of radioactive isotopes and their decay into other kinds of atoms is justified as the best explanation of a variety of observed phenomena, including the fogging of photographic film, changes in the composition of samples, tracks in cloud chambers, etc., the causal relations between the various kinds of atoms and particles and also between these unobservable entities and processes and their observable manifestations are justified as part of the total package, with accordingly no need for them to be justified separately.

A full defense of the idea of theoretical or explanatory reasoning is obviously not possible [here]. The suggestion for the moment is only that the idea is plausible enough, especially in light of examples like those given, to make it reasonable to reject Hume's thesis about knowledge of causal relations, at least tentatively, thus opening the door to the possibility that the representationalist position on the problem of the external world might be defensible after all. [12]

The Representationalist Explanation

But this only opens the door. We still need to worry about whether the representationalist's proposed explanation of our experience is really the *best* one. And before we can do that, we need to consider in substantially more detail what the rationale for that explanation might be and how it is supposed to work.

The place to start is to ask what it is about the character of our immediate sensory experience that points to or perhaps even seems to demand such an explanation. As we saw earlier, Locke points to two features of our experience in this connection: its involuntary character and its systematic order. But while these features may indeed demand *some* sort of explanation, they do not, at least when described at that level of abstraction, seem to point at all clearly at the specific one that the representationalist favors (which is why the door is seemingly open to Berkeley's alternative). If anything about experience does this, it will thus have to be, I would suggest, more specific features than any that Locke explicitly mentions.

Here is a question for you to think hard about, preferably before reading beyond this paragraph—one that is both historically and substantively as fundamental as any in the whole field of epistemology. Think as carefully as you can about your immediate sensory experience: your experience of qualities like colors and shapes and apparent spatial relations and apparent sounds and tactile qualities and so on. You are presently experiencing patterns of black and white marks that according to the representationalist are caused by and represent the pages of this book, along with other colors reflecting the immediate surrounding environment; your auditory sensations might be those allegedly reflecting the steps of people in the library or the

*Thus the sort of reasoning in question is also sometimes referred to as "inference to the best explanation."

music that you listen to while you read; you have tactile sensations allegedly reflecting things like the book in your hand, the chair or couch you are sitting on, and so on; perhaps there is an odd smell of some sort as well. What, if anything, about those experienced qualities *taken in themselves* suggests that their source or cause is an independent realm of material objects of the sort that the representationalist advocates? Why, apart from mere familiarity, does such an explanation of experience seem so natural and compelling?

My suggestion is that the answer to this question has two main parts. The first points to the presence in immediate experience of repeatable *sequences* of experienced qualities, qualities that overlap and often shade gradually into one another. Here I have in mind something like the "sensory routes" that are, as discussed earlier, invoked by the phenomenalist. While these "sensory routes" cannot ultimately do the job that the phenomenalist needs them to do, for the reasons given there, they are nonetheless very real and pervasive. Think of the ways in which such "sensory routes" can be experienced in opposite orders (imagine here what common sense would regard as walking from one place to another and then returning to the first place by the same route—perhaps even walking backwards, so as to make the two sequences as similar as possible). Think of the ways in which such "sensory routes" intersect with each other, thus, for example, allowing one to get from one end to the other without going through the "route" itself, thereby delineating a sensory loop. Think of the resulting structure of a whole set of overlapping and intersecting "sensory routes."

Here it may be helpful, as a kind of analogy, to think from a common-sense standpoint of how you would go about programming a computer game to simulate a "space" containing "objects" through which the computer character can move. You would program successive "screens" of visually observable colors and shapes in such a way as to mimic the appearance of objects that are gradually approached and passed, perhaps with concomitant sound qualities that get louder and then softer and imaginably even other systematically varying qualities like smells or temperatures. (Perhaps the game is played in an enclosed booth that can be heated or cooled.) You would also include some controllable way in which the character can be made to face in different directions, move at different rates, and stand still. In these terms, my suggestion is that our actual immediate experience has more or less exactly the features that an ideal program of this sort would create. (Again, you will have to ponder this point, "chew on" it, in relation to a range of your own examples, in order to fully understand it.)

The idea is then that at least the most obvious and natural explanation of these features of our experience is that we are located in a spatial realm of objects through which we move and of which we can perceive at any given moment only the limited portion that is close enough to be accessible to our various senses (what this requires differs from sense to sense)—a kind of experiential "tunnel." Our experience reflects both the qualities of these objects and the different perspectives from which they are perceived as we gradually approach them from different directions, at different speeds, under different conditions of perception, etc. Thus the relatively permanent structure of this spatial array of objects is partially reflected in the much more temporary and variable, but broadly repeatable features of our immediate experience. . . . 13

STOP Think carefully about patterns of experience of the sort indicated, making them as detailed as possible. Think about why the hypothesis that the experiences are caused by a stable world of external objects seems to explain those experiences quite well. Can you think of any alternative explanation that doesn't invoke a being like Berkeley's God or a Cartesian evil genius?

The second part of the answer to the question of what it is about the character of immediate experience that points to the representationalist explanation cites the fact, already noticed in our discussion of phenomenalism, that the experiential order just described, though undeniably impressive, is in fact *incomplete* or *fragmentary* in a number of related ways. The easiest way to indicate these is by reference to the sorts of situations that, from a common-sense standpoint, produce and explain them (though the representationalist cannot, of course, assume at this stage, without begging the question, that these things are what is actually going on). Imagine then traversing a "sensory route" of the sort just indicated, but doing so (i) with one's eyes closed (or one's ears plugged, etc.) during some of the time required, or perhaps while asleep during part of the time (traveling in a car or train); or (ii) while the conditions of perception, including those pertaining to the functioning of your sense-organs and to your mental "processing," are changing or being varied (involving such things as changing lighting, including complete darkness; jaundice and similar diseases that affect perception; objects and conditions that temporarily block or interfere with perception; even something as simple as turning one's head in a different direction, blinking, or wiping one's eyes). If you think about it carefully, you will see that interfering factors of these various kinds make the sensory sequences that define the various "routes" far less regular and dependable than they might at first seem. . . . 14

14

STOP Try to think of specific examples of fragmentary or interrupted order. How common are they?

Thus the basic claim is that the realm of immediate sensory experience, of sense-data . . . , is both *too orderly* not to demand an explanation and *not orderly enough* for that explanation to be that the sense-data have an intrinsic order of their own. What this strongly suggests, the representationalist will argue, is an independent realm of objects outside our experience, one that has its own patterns of (mainly spatial) order, with the partial and fragmentary order of our experience resulting from our partial and intermittent perceptual contact with that larger and more stable realm.

The discussion so far provides only an initial and highly schematic picture of the representationalist's proposed explanation. It would have to be filled out in a number of ways in order to be even approximately complete. Here I will be content with three further points. First, the main focus of the discussion so far has been on *spatial* properties of material objects and the features of immediate experience that seem to suggest them. Thus the result to this point is at best only a kind of skeletal picture of the material world, one that would have to be "fleshed out" in various ways in order to even approximate the common-sense picture of the world. In fact, it is useful to think of the representationalist explanation as starting with spatial properties as a first and most fundamental stage and then adding further refinements to that starting point.

Second, the main addition to this initial spatial picture of the world would be various sorts of *causal* relations among material objects and between such objects and perceivers, together with the causal and dispositional properties of objects (flammability, solubility, malleability, brittleness, toxicity, etc.) that underlie such relations. These are, from the representationalist standpoint, basically added in order to explain apparent changes in material objects that are reflected in relatively permanent changes in the otherwise stable "sensory routes." . . .

Third, there is the issue of primary and secondary qualities. As already noted, Locke's view is that material objects have *primary* qualities like size, shape, and motion through space, but not *secondary* qualities like color, smell, taste, and felt temperature, a view with which most other representationalists have tended to agree. Here it will suffice to focus on color, surely the most apparently pervasive and interesting of the secondary qualities. Clearly to deny that material objects are genuinely colored complicates the representationalist's proposed explanation by making the relation between material objects and our immediate experiences much less straightforward than it would otherwise be: according to such a view, whereas our immediate experiences of spatial properties are caused more or less directly by closely related spatial properties of objects (allowing, importantly, for perspective), our immediate experiences of color properties are caused by utterly different properties of material objects, primarily by how their surfaces differentially reflect wavelengths of light.

Locke offers little real argument for this view, but the argument he seems to have in mind is that as the causal account of the material world develops, it turns out that ascribing a property like color (construed as the "sensuous" property that is present in immediate visual experience) to material objects is in fact quite useless for explaining our experiences of colors. What colors we experience depends on the properties of the light that strikes our eyes and this in turn, in the most standard cases, depends on how material objects reflect and absorb light, which yet in turn depends on the structure of their surfaces as constituted by primary and causal properties . . . *if* [this] is correct, then the denial that material objects are really colored simply follows from the basic logic of the representationalist position: according to representationalism, the only justification for ascribing *any* property to the material world is that it best explains some aspect of our immediate experience, so that the ascription of properties that do not figure in such explanations is automatically unjustified. 15

15

Is this a good reason for thinking that color is not a genuine feature of external material objects? (See Discussion Question 2.)

Alternatives to the Representationalist Explanation

The discussion so far has perhaps made a reasonable case, though of course nothing like a conclusive one, first, that the representationalist's proposed explanation of the order of our immediate experience cannot be ruled out on Humean grounds; and, second, that this explanation has a good deal of plausibility in relation to that experience. But this is still not enough to show that it is the *best* explanation and hence the one, even assuming the general acceptability of theoretical reasoning, whose acceptance is thereby justified. Here we are essentially back to the question posed very early on in this chapter: why, if at all, should the explanation of our experience that invokes external, mind-independent material objects be preferred to other possible explanations such as Berkeley's (or the very similar if not identical one that appeals to Descartes's evil genius)?

It should be obvious that Berkeley's explanatory hypothesis is capable of explaining the very same features of immediate experience that the representationalist appeals to. All that is needed, as suggested earlier, is for God to have an ideally complete conception or picture of the representationalist's material world and then to systematically cause experiences in perceivers that reflect their apparent location in and movement through such a world. (This assumes that God can recognize intentions to "move" in various directions and adjust the person's perceptions accordingly; of course, no genuine movement really takes place, nor does the perceiver really have a physical location.)* A different, but essentially parallel explanatory hypothesis, is provided by a science fiction scenario: the perceiver is a disembodied brain floating in a vat of brain nutrients and receiving electrical impulses from a computer that again contains an ideally complete model or representation of a material world and generates the impulses accordingly, taking account of motor impulses received from the brain that reflect the person's intended movements. And further explanatory hypotheses can be generated according to the same basic formula: there must be some sort of a representation or model of a material world together with some sort of mechanism (which need not be mechanical in the ordinary sense) that systematically produces experience in perceivers, allowing for their subjectively intended movements. *Any* pattern of immediate experience that can be explained by the representationalist's explanatory hypothesis can thus automatically be also explained by explanatory hypotheses of this latter sort, probably indefinitely many of them, with no possible experiential basis for deciding between them or between any one of them and the representationalist hypothesis.

If there is to be a reason for favoring the representationalist hypothesis, therefore, it will have to be *a priori* in character, 16 and it is more than a little difficult to see what it might be. Here I will limit myself to one fairly tentative suggestion. . . .

16 Because all of the explanations are equally compatible with the relevant experience.

One striking contrast between the representationalist's explanatory hypothesis and the others we have looked at is that under the representationalist view there is a clear intuitive sense in which the qualities of the objects that explain our immediate experience are directly reflected in the character of that experience itself, so that the latter can be said to be, allowing for perspective and perhaps other sorts of distortion, experiences of the former, albeit indirect ones. Once again this applies most straightforwardly to spatial properties: thus, for example, the rectangular or trapezoidal shape that is immediately experienced can be said to be an indirect perception of a rectangular face of the material object that causes that experience. In contrast, the features of the elements in the other explanatory hypotheses that are responsible for the various features of our experience are not directly reflected in that experience. For example, what is responsible in these other hypotheses for the rectangular or trapezoidal shape in my immediate experience is one aspect of God's total picture or conception of a material world, or perhaps one aspect of a representation of such a world stored in a computer. This aspect has in itself no shape of any sort (or at least, in the case of the computer, none that is at all relevant to the shape that I experience); it is merely a *representation* of a related shape, according to some system of representation or coding. Thus its relation to the character of the experience that it is supposed to explain is inherently less direct, more

*Here again a computer game provides a helpful analogy. In playing many such games, you control the "movement" of a computer character through the "world," often in a fairly realistic way, even though there is really no movement of that sort nor any world of that sort in which it might take place. In Berkeley's explanatory hypothesis, God plays the role of the computer.

convoluted than in the case of the representationalist's explanation.

My suggestion is that the inherently less direct, more convoluted character of the way that these competing explanatory hypotheses account for the features of our immediate experience may yield a reason for preferring the more direct and thus in a sense simpler representationalist explanatory hypothesis, for regarding it as more likely to be true. But how, exactly? The idea is that an explanatory hypothesis like Berkeley's, at least as we have construed it, depends for its explanatory success on the truth of two equally essential claims: first, the claim that a material world of the sort postulated by the representationalist *could* account for the features of our experience, for it is precisely by emulating or mimicking the action of such a world that God (or the computer) decides just what experiences to produce in us; and, second, that God (or the computer) can indeed successfully produce the required emulation. But the representationalist view requires only the truth of the first of these two claims. It is thus, I suggest, inherently less vulnerable to problems and challenges and so more likely to be true. And this is an apparent reason for regarding the representationalist's explanatory hypothesis as providing the best of these competing explanations. . . . 17

STOP Is this a good reason for favoring the representationalist's explanation over Berkeley's? Can you think of any reason for preferring Berkeley's explanation to the representationalist's?

Is this a successful argument for representationalism? There are at least two questions about it that need to be considered. First, the argument assumes that the competitors to representationalism are all parasitic upon the representationalist explanatory hypothesis in the way indicated, and it is worth asking whether this is really so. Is there an explanation of our immediate experience that does not in this way rely on an emulation of the way in which a material world would produce that experience? It will not do to say simply that God causes our experience without saying how and why he produces the specific results that he does, for that is not really to give a complete explanation. But is there some other way of filling out Berkeley's explanatory hypothesis or one of the parallel ones that does not invoke a conception or model of a material world? Second, even if the argument succeeds to a degree, *how* probable or likely does it make the material world hypothesis in comparison to these others? Is the resulting degree of probability or likelihood high enough to agree approximately with our common-sense convictions in this regard (or to yield knowledge . . .)? I will leave these further difficult questions for you to think about.

Is There a Better Alternative?: Direct Realism

The upshot of our discussion so far is that phenomenalism appears entirely untenable, and that at least a better defense than many have supposed possible can be offered for representationalism. Many recent philosophers, however, have thought that there is a *third* alternative that is superior to either of these: one usually referred to as *direct realism.* The central idea of direct realism is that the view we have called perceptual subjectivism is false, that is, that instead of immediately experiencing . . . sense-data . . . , we instead *directly* experience external material objects, without the mediation of these other sorts of entities or states. And the suggestion often seems to be, though this is usually not explained very fully, that such a view can simply bypass the representationalist's problem of justifying an inference from immediate experience to the material world and do so without having to advocate anything as outlandish as phenomenalism.

For anyone who has struggled with the idea of sense-data . . . and with the difficulties and complexities of representationalism and phenomenalism, the apparent simplicity of direct realism, the way in which it seems to make extremely difficult or even intractable problems simply vanish, may be difficult to resist. We must be cautious, however. What does such a view amount to, and can it really deliver the results that it promises?

We may begin with a point that is often advanced in arguments for direct realism, one that, while correct as far as it goes, turns out in fact to be of much less help than has sometimes been thought in either defending or even explaining the view. Think about an ordinary example of perceptual experience: standing in my back yard, I watch my dogs chasing each other in a large circle around some bushes, weaving in and out of the sunshine and shadows, as a car drives by on the street. The direct realist's claim is that in such a case (assuming that I am in a normal, nonphilosophical frame of mind), the picture that it is easy to find in or read into some representationalists, according to which I *first* have thoughts or occurrent beliefs about the character of my experience (. . . in sense-datum . . . terms) and *then* infer explicitly from these to thoughts or beliefs about material objects is simply and flatly wrong as a description of my actual conscious state. In fact, the only things that I think about at all *directly* and explicitly in such a case are things like dogs and bushes and cars and sunlight, not anything as subtle and abstruse as sense-data. . . . The direct realist need not deny (though some have seemed to) that my sensory experience somehow involves the various qualities, such as complicated patterns of shape and color, that these other views have spoken of, or even that I am in *some* way aware or conscious of these. His point is that whatever may be said about these other matters, from an intuitive standpoint it is material objects and nothing else that are "directly before my mind"—and that any view that denies this obvious truth is simply mistaken about the facts.

I have already said that I think that the direct realist is at least mostly right about this. What happens most centrally in perceptual experience is that we have explicit thoughts or "perceptual judgments" about what we are perceiving; and in normal cases (apart from very special artistic or perhaps philosophical contexts), these perceptual judgments are directly and entirely about things (and processes and qualities) in the external material world. Philosophers speak of that which a propositional state of mind is directly about as its *intentional object,* and we can accordingly say that the intentional objects of our basic perceptual judgments are normally alleged or apparent material objects. In this way, the relation of such judgments to material objects is, it might be said, *intentionally* direct. [18]

But what bearing, if any, does this intentional directness have on the central epistemological question of what reason or justification we have for thinking that such perceptual judgments about the material world are *true*? Perhaps the sort of direct presence to the mind that is involved in the idea of immediate experience . . . yields the result that one's beliefs or awarenesses concerning the objects of such experience are automatically justified, simply because there is no room for error to creep in. [19] But is there any way in which it follows from the mere fact that perceptual judgments about material objects are *intentionally* direct that they are also *justified*? It still seems obvious that both a perceptual judgment and the total state of mind of which it is a part are quite distinct from the material object, if any, that is its intentionally direct object. This is shown by the fact that in cases like hallucination, the object in question need not exist at all, but it would be clear enough even without such cases—phenomenalist views having been rejected, the material object does not somehow literally enter the mind. Thus even though perceptual judgments are directly about such objects in the intentional sense, the question of whether they represent them *correctly* still arises in exactly the same way that it does for the representationalist. And this question must apparently still be answered, if at all, by appeal to the immediately experienced features involved in the perceiver's state of mind, with the specific character of the sensory experience being the only obvious thing to invoke.

Thus while the idea of intentional directness can be used to present a somewhat more accurate picture of a normal perceiver's state of mind, the view that results is still fundamentally a version of representationalism in that it faces the same essential problem of justifying the transition (whether it is an explicit inference or not) from the character of the person's experience to beliefs or judgments about the material world. If this is all that direct realism amounts to, then it is not a genuinely distinct third alternative with regard to the basic issue of how perceptual beliefs or judgments are justified. [20]

. . .

My tentative conclusion . . . is that the idea that direct realism represents a further alternative on the present issue is a chimera. Thus, once phenomenalism is rejected as hopeless, the only alternatives with regard to knowledge of the external world appear to be skepticism and some version of representationalism, perhaps one that recognizes and incorporates the view that perceptual judgments about the material world are intentionally direct.

This does not mean that ideas or sense-data play no role, but only that they are not the object of the perceptual judgment that results. Instead, they might be essential vehicles for our perceptual consciousness, essential to explaining how we are able to think "directly" of objects outside the mind. (See the introduction to the Locke selection.)

The suggestion is that only ideas or sense-data and other states of mind are immediately experienced in this sense.

The claim is that the way in which we are directly aware of external objects (the fact that such objects and not our experiences or ideas or sense-data are what we are thinking about in such experience) really does nothing at all to explain why our perceptual claims are justified, why we have good reasons to think that they are true. Our state of mind is still distinct from the object, and so the issue of whether it represents such an object correctly can still be raised—in exactly the same way that it arises for Locke.

Discussion Questions

1. Can you think of a good argument for the existence of mental states other than your own in what appear to be other people? The obvious starting point is the behavior of other bodies. Try to construct such an argument, and evaluate its strength.

2. Think of how a scientific explanation of color experience might go. Are Locke and BonJour right that color as a feature of material objects plays no role in such an explanation? If so, does it follow that we have no reason to believe that such objects are really colored, or is there some other reason (besides a role in explanation) for thinking they are colored?

3. Whose explanation of the patterns of experience is better: the representationalist's or Berkeley's? Why? Can you think of other explanations that are significantly different from either of these? What general standards are the right ones for choosing among such explanations, and why?

4. BonJour offers what is admittedly only a sketch of an argument for the existence of material objects. How hard would it be to fill this out into a complete argument (where a large part of the job would be giving a much fuller description of the relevant features of experience)? Is it plausible to suppose that ordinary people who have beliefs about material objects have this argument or anything like it in mind? If not, does this mean that they have no good reasons to think that their beliefs are true? How implausible is such a result?

Sextus Empiricus

Sextus Empiricus (third century A.D.) was a Greek philosopher who seems to have served as a kind of historian of the Skeptical school of philosophy. Very little is known about his life, though he was apparently a medical doctor who taught in a Skeptical academy, perhaps in Alexandria. The following selection comes from his explanation of the Ten Modes of argument, via which skeptics can reach suspension of belief—viewed by them as an intrinsically desirable state in which one is cured of dogmatism.

From Outlines of Pyrrhonism

The Fourth Mode

But we can also reach suspension by basing our argument on each sense separately, or even by disregarding the senses. To this end we employ the fourth mode of suspension, which we call the mode based on the circumstances. We understand by "circumstances" the states in which we are. This mode, we say, is seen in cases of natural or unnatural states, in states of waking or sleeping, in cases where age, motion or rest . . . are involved; or where the determining factor is a state of want or satiety. . . . For example, things appear dissimilar according to whether we are in a natural or unnatural state; delirious people, and those who are possessed by a god, think that they hear divine voices, while we do not. Often they claim that they perceive, among a number of other things, the odor of . . . frankincense, or something of that sort, where we perceive nothing. And the same water that seems hot to a person when poured on inflamed parts seems lukewarm to us. The coat which appears yellowish-orange to men with bloodshot eyes does not appear so to me, yet it is the same coat. And the same honey that appears sweet to me appears bitter to those suffering from jaundice. (1)

Now, one might object that in those whose condition is unnatural it is the intermingling of certain humors that causes them to get unnatural impressions from the external objects. Our reply to this would be that it is possible that the external objects actually are in reality such as they appear to those who are said to be in an unnatural state; and that since persons in a state of good health also have mixed humors, it may be that it is these humors that make the

(1) Examples of these kinds and the ones that follow are also the basis for the **argument from illusion,** as formulated repeatedly by Berkeley in the earlier selection. Sextus is probably assuming something like Berkeley's conclusion that what we are most immediately aware of is an idea (he uses the term "sense-impression") in the mind. But he is also aiming at a different, more clearly skeptical conclusion as well.

From *Selections from the Major Writings on Skepticism, Man, and God,* translated by Sanford G. Etheridge (Indianapolis: Hackett, 1985).

objects appear different to them. For it would be a fabrication to attribute to the humors of sick people a power to change external objects, and to deny this power to the humors of the healthy. After all, it is natural for the healthy to be in a healthy state, and unnatural for them to be in a sick state. By the same token it is unnatural for the sick to be in a healthy state, but natural for them to be in a sick state. Consequently, the sick warrant credence also, since they too are in some respect in a natural state. Whether one is in a sleeping or a waking state also makes a difference in the sense-impressions, since our manner of perception while awake differs from the perception we have in sleep; and our manner of perception in sleep is not like our waking perception. As a result, the existence or non-existence of our sense-impressions is not absolute but relative, since they bear a relation to our sleeping or waking state. It is probable, therefore, that although our dream-images are unreal in our waking state, they are nevertheless not absolutely unreal, for they do exist in our dreams. In the same manner the realities of the waking state, even if they do not exist in dreams, nevertheless exist. Age also makes a difference. Old men, for example, may think the air is cold, but the same air seems mild to those who are in the prime of life. The same color appears dim to older persons but full to those in their prime. And a sound, likewise the same, seems faint to the former but quite audible to the latter. . . . From this it follows that differences of age also can cause the sense-impressions to be different where the external objects are the same. Motion or rest may also be the determining factor when objects appear different. For instance, things which we see to be motionless when we are stationary seem to be moving when we are sailing past, them. . . . Hunger or satiety may also be the cause, as the same food can seem very tasty to the hungry and yet disagreeable to those who have had their fill. . . . Predispositions are another cause, since the same wine seems to be sour if you have eaten dates or dried figs beforehand, and sweet if you have eaten nuts or chick-peas. Also, the vestibule of the bath-house is warming to those who come in from the outside, but chills those who are coming out, if they tarry in it. . . .

Now, considering the fact that so much discrepancy is due to the states we are in, and that men are in different states at different times, it is easy, perhaps, to state the nature of each object as it appears to this or that person, but difficult to say further what its real nature is. This is because the discrepancy does not lend itself to judgment. **2** In fact, whoever attempts to resolve this discrepancy will find himself either in one or the other of the aforesaid states or else in no state at all. But now to say that he is in no state at all, that he is neither healthy nor sick, neither in motion nor at rest, that he is not of any particular age, and that he is free from the other states, is perfectly absurd. On the other hand, the fact of his being in some state or other while attempting to pass judgment will make him a party to the controversy. And moreover, he will be confused by the states in which he finds himself, and this will prevent him from being an absolute judge in the matter. A person, therefore, who is in the waking state cannot compare the impressions of a sleeping person with those of waking persons, and a healthy person cannot compare the impressions of sick people with those of the healthy. We do, after all, tend to give our assent to those things which are present and have a present influence over us rather than to things which are not present. **3**

The discrepancy between such impressions is irresolvable on other grounds also, for if a person prefers one sense-impression to another, and one circumstance to another, he does so either without judging and without proof or by judging and offering proof. But he cannot do so without judgment and proof, for then he will be discredited. Nor can he do so even with judgment and proof, for if he judges the impressions, he must at all events use a criterion in judging them. And this criterion he will declare to be either true or false. If false, he will not be worthy of belief; but if he claims it is true, then his statement that the criterion is true will be offered either without proof or with proof. If without proof, again he will not be worthy of belief; but if he offers proof for his statement, the proof must in any case be a true one, otherwise he will not be worthy of belief. Now, if he says that the proof employed for the confirmation of his criterion is true, will he say this after having passed judgment on the proof, or without having judged it? If he has not judged it, he will not be worthy of belief, but if

2

Given that what we assume (on what basis?) to be the same object or situation gives rise to different sense-impressions, depending on the "circumstances" that the perceiver is in, the issue arises of how to decide which such sense-impressions (if any) reveal the true nature of that object.

3

Sextus argues that there is no reason to view the sense-impressions of the healthy as more accurate than those of the sick and points out that neither a healthy nor a sick person is in a position to make such an assessment in an unbiased way. And he would say the same thing about the other differences in "circumstances."

he has, obviously he will say he has used a criterion in his judgment. We shall ask for a proof for this criterion, and for this proof another criterion. For the proof always needs a criterion to confirm it, and the criterion needs a proof to show that it is true. A proof cannot be sound without the preexistence of a true criterion, and a criterion cannot be true either without prior confirmation of the proof. And so both the criterion and the proof fall into circular argument, in which both are found to be untrustworthy. The fact that each expects confirmation from the other makes both of them equally untrustworthy. It is impossible, then, for a person to give the preference to one sense-impression over another. This being so, such differences in sense-impressions as arise from a disparity of states will be irresolvable. As a result, this mode also serves to introduce suspension of judgment with regard to the nature of external objects. 4

Here we have a version of a famous skeptical argument, one whose implications extend far beyond the specific issue that Sextus is discussing. The underlying issue is how any criterion or standard of rational acceptability can be established as correct: if by a proof, then what criterion or standard can be used to show that the proof is itself cogent? (Sextus says here that the upshot is circularity, in which the very criterion whose correctness is at issue is used to validate the proof; but there is another possibility, discussed in the next section, that is equally unacceptable.)

The Fifth Mode

The fifth argument is the one based on positions, distances, and places. Each of these can cause the same objects to appear different. Take a portico for example. When seen from either end, it appears tapered, yet the same portico viewed from the middle appears symmetrical on all sides. Also, the same boat appears small and stationary from a distance, and large and moving from close by. And the same tower appears round from afar but square from near by.

These differences are the result of the distances involved. Then there are differences due to the places involved. For example, the light of a lamp appears dim in sunlight but bright in the dark, the same oar appears broken in the water but straight when out of the water. . . .

Position also may be the cause of different appearances. The same picture appears smooth when inclined backwards, but seems to have hollows and prominences when inclined forward to a certain angle. Also, the necks of pigeons appear different in color according to differences in inclination. 5

Here we have a somewhat different set of examples, based on the general phenomenon of *perceptual relativity:* the way in which the sense-impressions a person receives from an object depend on the perspective from which it is perceived. Again the issue arises of how to decide which of the various, seemingly conflicting sense-impressions reveal the true nature of the object.

Thus all objects appearing to us are seen as being in some place or other, at a certain distance, and in a certain position, and each of these factors makes a great difference in the sense-impressions, as we have mentioned. Hence, by this mode also we shall be compelled to have recourse to suspension of judgment. In point of fact, anyone who wishes to give any of these sense-impressions the preference over the others will be undertaking an impossible task. For if he makes his judgment simply and without proof, he will be discredited; and if he wishes to employ a proof, then says his proof is false, he will be refuting himself; if he says the proof is true, he will be asked for a proof of its truth, and another proof for that one, and so on ad infinitum. But it is impossible to present an infinite series of proofs; therefore he will not be able, even by the use of proofs, to prefer one sense-impression to another. And if a person is unable to pass judgment on the above-mentioned impressions either without proof or with proof, then the necessary result is suspension of judgment. Thus, while we are perhaps able to state of what nature each object appears to be in one particular position, at one particular distance, and in one location, it is not in our power, for the reasons just given, to declare what its true nature is. 6

R And again the argument is that there is no basis available for choosing one sense-impression over another as revealing the object's true nature because there is no criterion for such a choice that can be established as the right one to appeal to.

(Notice that the objection at the end of the Fourth Mode was that the appeal to such a criterion leads to *circularity,* while here the objection is that it leads to an *infinite regress* of further criteria and further proofs. Obviously either result is possible. Thus the clearest version of the argument would say that it must lead to one or the other of these two equally unacceptable results.)

Discussion Questions

1. Imagine a detailed example in which a particular object seems to different people to have different and conflicting qualities, depending on their "circumstances"—expanding the category of "circumstances" to include also the differences of position discussed in the Fifth Mode. Try to formulate a criterion or standard for judging that some of the sense-impressions in question reveal the true nature of the object and others do not. Then try to give a justification or proof for this criterion and ask what established this justification or proof as itself correct. Is there any way to avoid falling into either circularity or an infinite regress?
2. One possible way to respond to Sextus is to say that a correct account of the nature of such an object must be able to *explain* all of the different appearances or sense-impressions, rather than just selecting among them. (See BonJour's account of how a representative realist might appeal to explanatory inference.) In relation to a suitable example, try to decide whether this approach helps to any significant degree in solving the problem raised by Sextus.

Concluding Dialogue on the Problem of the External World

As I think you realize, this issue is sometimes hard to get people to take seriously. That we have lots of knowledge about material objects—trees and buildings and cars and mountains—just seems so utterly obvious and undeniable that philosophers who raise doubts about it look like they need some sort of therapy—or maybe just need to be locked up so they won't hurt themselves!

I agree that the existence of the material world *seems* utterly obvious. But the philosophical problem is to say—in a sufficiently clear and perspicuous way—just why and how it really is obvious. If no one, after many, many tries, is able to do this, then it's hard to dismiss the possibility that it isn't really so obvious after all—that perhaps common sense is ignoring or failing to notice problems that are perfectly genuine.

If we take the problem seriously, many recent epistemologists seem to think, following Reid, that the right response is direct realism: we apprehend material objects directly or immediately, and so the issue of trying to justify beliefs about the material world on the basis of subjective ideas or sense experience, in the way that Descartes or Locke or BonJour try to do, just doesn't arise. We don't have to somehow *reason* our way to the existence of the external world because that's where we start.

Direct realism, like almost any view that makes an otherwise very difficult problem just go away, is initially very appealing. But does it really deal adequately with the underlying issue?

Well, even BonJour concedes that the direct realist is right about at least one thing: that we rarely if ever think very explicitly about our experiences, but instead just leap directly to beliefs or judgments about material objects. Surely even Descartes or Locke wouldn't seriously disagree about that?

I think that's right, though one could wish that they were clearer about this issue. But the problem is that this point doesn't really speak in any clear way to the issue of *justification*. Even if we don't think explicitly about our experience, it still seems hard to deny that material objects and the conscious experiences on the basis of which we seem somehow to know them are, from a metaphysical standpoint, quite distinct from each other: the occurrence of an experience (over here, in me) is one state of affairs and the existence of the object it seems to depict (over there, outside of me) is a separate, quite different state of affairs. Our mind doesn't somehow literally reach out to grasp the world, nor do material objects somehow literally enter the mind. But then it still seems possible to ask whether those experiences provide good reasons or evidence for our claims about those external objects, and there is apparently nothing but facts about those experiences and our other mental states to appeal to in trying to answer this question.

So you're saying that a successful answer to this question would still amount to some sort of a representative realist view. Maybe we don't have to first think about our experience and then explicitly infer to the world. But features of that experience or at least of our conscious states of mind generally are the only place to look for good reasons for our beliefs about material objects—so we still seem to need the sort of inference that Descartes and Locke and BonJour try to give an account of.

Yes. And if that is right, then direct realism really doesn't speak to the main issue in any very helpful way.

But the representative realist project seems so desperately difficult! It's very hard to give a clear and detailed description of the specific features of experience that might seem to be relevant and even harder to say *why* they are relevant in the right way—why those features really do yield *good* reasons for thinking that a world containing just such-and-such sorts of material objects exists.

I agree that it's difficult and that no one has done either of those things in a detailed and convincing way—at least not so far. But it's a peculiar fact about the history of this issue that relatively little philosophical effort has been put into this project, with the vast majority of philosophers either adopting some sort of idealism or else embracing skepticism. (Until recently they wouldn't have been tempted by direct realism—what they would have called "naïve realism.")

I guess I've always had a soft spot in my heart for Berkeley's view—or maybe for phenomenalism. If all that we have direct knowledge of is our experiences, why suppose that there is anything more? Why not just view ordinary objects as just patterns of experience of the right sort? What more do we really need?

Are you entirely sure that soft spot isn't in your head?? In any case, it's really important to distinguish phenomenalism from Berkeley's view, even though the two are often treated as pretty much the same thing. People who do that aren't taking Berkeley's appeal to God seriously, but Berkeley surely took it *very* seriously.

I suppose I see what you mean. While the phenomenalist says that there is no further explanation for our experience and its patterns (or at least none that is knowable), Berkeley is proposing a quite definite further explanation—one that is completely different from Locke's, but still an explanation—and one that appeals to something that is also outside of experience!

Exactly. And, strange as it may seem at first, this makes Berkeley in effect an odd sort of representative realist—only what our sensory ideas represent or at least correspond to isn't independent material objects of the sort Locke advocates, but rather something about God: the specific picture of the world that he has in mind and conveys to us. But Berkeley still faces a quite parallel problem of justifying an inference from our experience to something outside of our experience—the sort of inference that Hume (as BonJour reports) thinks can never be justified.

So, as BonJour more or less suggests, the central issue between Berkeley and Locke is whose explanation is better, with both of them agreeing in opposition to the phenomenalist that some explanation is needed. They surely seem right on this last point: it would be better to say that our experience must have an explanation, even if we don't or even can't know what it is, than to say that all of that order and complexity is merely a brute fact that has no explanation at all. And, as BonJour points out, phenomenalism faces lots of other problems that no one has ever come close to solving.

Thus the crucial issue is whether there is any way to argue that one of these explanations—or maybe yet some further explanation—is clearly better than any other in a way that makes it more likely to be true. BonJour's tentative suggestion is that the Lockean material object explanation is to be preferred because it faces less risk of failure than the others by appealing directly to the causation of experience by a material world rather than to some further being or mechanism that emulates such causation.

But that assumes that all of the other explanations must take that form. That isn't clearly wrong. At the very least, it isn't easy to think of an explanation not fitting this pattern that really explains why we have just the specific experiences that we do. But maybe (always a problem with inferences to the best explanation!) there is some possibility that we haven't thought of.

That concern can, of course, be raised about almost any scientific explanation, so BonJour's argument would be in good company if that were the worst problem. But such an argument also needs a lot of detailed elaboration, both with respect to the patterns of experience in question and with regard to the details of the explanation, elaboration that won't be easy to provide—if it can be done at all.

So maybe the lesson to be learned from all this is that we should lower our expectations. Though it isn't in the readings, one important view about lowered expectations is the one that Immanuel Kant defends in his famous book *Critique of Pure Reason*. Without going into the pretty convoluted details of Kant's actual position, what he says is essentially that while we can't know what the external world that causes our experience is really like "in itself," we *can* know that it will regularly and reliably cause various sorts of experiential appearances. Why isn't that good enough? Why aren't those regular and reliable appearances, whatever their ultimate source may be, an adequate basis for choices and actions and human life generally?

But the problem is that "regular and reliable" part. If we could know about the external cause or source of our experience in the way that a successful Lockean or even Berkeleyan view would make possible, then perhaps we could know not just that experience has been "regular and reliable" *so far*, but also that this will continue to be so. But if all we can know is that the appearances have been generally regular and reliable up to now, it's hard to see what good reason there is for thinking that this regularity and reliability will persist. Why couldn't the familiar patterns of experience suddenly change, in ways that would make our normal choices and actions no longer yield satisfactory results? (Here we are pretty close to the issue of induction, but we'll talk about that in a separate discussion.)

So the point is that if, for example, our experience is really being produced by something-we-know-not-what—rather than by a knowable material world or even by a Berkeleyan God who is somehow known to be reliable—then we have no reason for thinking that such a cause won't suddenly and arbitrarily produce entirely different patterns of experiences. Maybe the experience of a solid-looking floor, instead of being followed by the experience of being supported as we try to walk on it, will instead be followed by experiences of falling through, being injured, and so on.

Right! And if we can't find any good reason why such an alteration isn't just as likely as continued "regularity and reliability," then merely knowing appearances (so far) in the way that Kant suggests isn't very satisfactory from even a practical standpoint.

I guess you've convinced me, if I needed convincing, that this problem has to be taken seriously—and also that there isn't any easy solution. It does seem as though there really isn't any very good alternative to the representative realist's attempt to find a justification for the claim that the best explanation of our experience is some definite sort of independent reality. But I don't think we should assume too quickly that the best such explanation will appeal to material objects—especially material objects as conceived by common sense.

I think that's right. The issue of secondary qualities already seems to show that the best explanation is likely to depart from common sense in important ways: common sense seems to attribute qualities like the colors we experience to material objects, but it's pretty hard to see how such properties will have any serious explanatory role—and therefore hard to justify this part of the common-sense view via an explanatory argument. What will explain our color experience is much more likely to be properties that are not at all like the ones that we seem to experience—structural properties of the surfaces of objects in virtue of which they reflect one sort of light rather than another.

But I had a more radical departure from common sense in mind. Maybe something like Berkeley's God is still in the running, after all?

There you go again.

Is Induction Justified?

David Hume

David Hume (1711–1776), a Scottish philosopher and historian, is usually regarded as one of the most important and influential philosophers of all time. He did very influential work in epistemology, metaphysics, ethics, and the philosophy of religion, producing a comprehensive philosophical position that is most distinctive for its skeptical tendencies—tendencies that are reflected in the present selection.

In the first section (Section IV) included in this selection, Hume presents what is perhaps the first reasonably clear formulation of the problem of induction. His initial concern is with knowledge of causal relations, which he claims to be the only basis for knowledge of matters of fact that go beyond direct experience and memory. His view is that causal relations can themselves be known only through repeated experience of the causal sequence. But this raises in turn the more general problem of how repeated experience of thing or property A always being followed by thing or property B can justify the conclusion that A will probably always be followed by B (which is at least part of the meaning of the claim that A causes B, in the sense of being a causally **sufficient condition** for B). Hume's skeptical thesis is that there is no cogent reasoning that leads from such an experiential premise to this conclusion, so that inductive reasoning of this sort is in fact *not* justified. (It is important to realize that he is not claiming merely that inductive conclusions cannot be known with certainty: his stronger and much more startling claim is that there is no good reason at all to accept them even as probable.)

In the second of the two sections (Section V—only briefly excerpted here), Hume offers a fundamentally psychological account of how and why we reason inductively, according to which such inferences rely on custom or habit (rather than on reason).

1

This distinction is the main basis for the subsequent argument and needs to be considered carefully. "Relations of ideas" suggests the idea of **analyticity** (see the Appendix to the chapter introduction), but Hume is also claiming that anything knowable a priori has this status—and also, in the next paragraph, that all such claims are necessary, since nothing contingent has this status. Thus Hume is assuming in effect that the three main distinctions pertaining to a priori knowledge (see again the Appendix to the chapter introduction) coincide (in which case, among other things, there would be no synthetic a priori truths).

2

The primary meaning of "matters of fact" seems to be claims that can be denied without contradiction and so are contingent rather than necessary. But Hume is also saying that these are not knowable a priori, and also not relations of ideas and so not analytic, but rather synthetic. The overall implication is again that all three distinctions (a priori/*a posteriori,* necessary/contingent, analytic/synthetic) coincide, though Hume gives no real argument for this claim (a version of moderate empiricism).

3

Thus the claim is that any contingent fact that goes beyond direct sense perception or the memory of such perception can be known only through causal reasoning.

From *An Enquiry Concerning Human Understanding*

Section IV: Skeptical Doubts Concerning the Operations of the Understanding

Part I

All the objects of human reason or inquiry may naturally be divided into two kinds, to wit, *relations of ideas,* and *matters of fact.* Of the first kind are the sciences of geometry, algebra, and arithmetic; and in short, every affirmation which is either intuitively or demonstratively certain. *That the square of the hypotenuse is equal to the squares of the two sides,* is a proposition which expresses a relation between these figures. *That three times five is equal to the half of thirty,* expresses a relation between these numbers. Propositions of this kind are discoverable by the mere operation of thought, without dependence on what is anywhere existent in the universe. Though there never was a circle or triangle in nature, the truths demonstrated by Euclid would for ever retain their certainty and evidence. (1)

Matters of fact, which are the second objects of human reason, are not ascertained in the same manner; nor is our evidence of their truth, however great, of a like nature with the foregoing. The contrary of every matter of fact is still possible; because it can never imply a contradiction, and is conceived by the mind with the same facility and distinctness, as if ever so conformable to reality. *That the sun will not rise tomorrow* is no less intelligible a proposition, and implies no more contradiction than the affirmation, *that it will rise.* We should in vain, therefore, attempt to demonstrate its falsehood. Were it demonstratively false, it would imply a contradiction, and could never be distinctly conceived by the mind. (2)

It may, therefore, be a subject worthy of curiosity, to inquire what is the nature of that evidence which assures us of any real existence and matter of fact, beyond the present testimony of our senses, or the records of our memory. . . .

All reasonings concerning matter of fact seem to be founded on the relation of *cause and effect.* By means of that relation alone we can go beyond the evidence of our memory and senses. (3) If you were to ask a man, why he believes any matter of fact, which is absent; for instance, that his friend is in the country, or in France; he would give you a reason; and this reason would be some other fact; as a letter received from him, or the knowledge of his former resolutions and promises. A man finding a watch or any other machine in a desert island, would conclude that there had once been men in that island. All our reasonings concerning fact are of the same nature. And here it is constantly supposed that there is a connection between the present fact and that which is inferred from it. Were there nothing to bind them together, the inference would be entirely precarious. The hearing of an articulate voice and rational discourse in the dark assures us of the presence of some person: Why? because these are the effects of the human make and fabric, and closely connected with it. If we anatomize all the other reasonings of this

From *An Enquiry Concerning Human Understanding,* 1748.

nature, we shall find that they are founded on the relation of cause and effect, and that this relation is either near or remote, direct or collateral. Heat and light are collateral effects of fire, and the one effect may justly be inferred from the other.

If we would satisfy ourselves, therefore, concerning the nature of that evidence, which assures us of matters of fact, we must inquire how we arrive at the knowledge of cause and effect.

I shall venture to affirm, as a general proposition, which admits of no exception, that the knowledge of this relation is not, in any instance, attained by reasonings a priori; but arises entirely from experience, when we find that any particular objects are constantly conjoined with each other. (4) Let an object be presented to a man of ever so strong natural reason and abilities; if that object be entirely new to him, he will not be able, by the most accurate examination of its sensible qualities, to discover any of its causes or effects. Adam, though his rational faculties be supposed, at the very first, entirely perfect, could not have inferred from the fluidity and transparency of water that it would suffocate him, or from the light and warmth of fire that it would consume him. No object ever discovers, by the qualities which appear to the senses, either the causes which produced it, or the effects which will arise from it; nor can our reason, unassisted by experience, ever draw any inference concerning real existence and matter of fact.

This proposition, *that causes and effects are discoverable, not by reason but by experience,* will readily be admitted with regard to such objects, as we remember to have once been altogether unknown to us; since we must be conscious of the utter inability, which we then lay under, of foretelling what would arise from them. Present two smooth pieces of marble to a man who has no tincture of natural philosophy; he will never discover that they will adhere together in such a manner as to require great force to separate them in a direct line, while they make so small a resistance to a lateral pressure. Such events, as bear little analogy to the common course of nature, are also readily confessed to be known only by experience; nor does any man imagine that the explosion of gunpowder, or the attraction of a loadstone, could ever be discovered by arguments a priori. In like manner, when an effect is supposed to depend upon an intricate machinery or secret structure of parts, we make no difficulty in attributing all our knowledge of it to experience. Who will assert that he can give the ultimate reason, why milk or bread is proper nourishment for a man, not for a lion or a tiger?

But the same truth may not appear, at first sight, to have the same evidence with regard to events, which have become familiar to us from our first appearance in the world, which bear a close analogy to the whole course of nature, and which are supposed to depend on the simple qualities of objects, without any secret structure of parts. We are apt to imagine that we could discover these effects by the mere operation of our reason, without experience. We fancy, that were we brought on a sudden into this world, we could at first have inferred that one billiard ball would communicate motion to another upon impulse; and that we needed not to have waited for the event, in order to pronounce with certainty concerning it. Such is the influence of custom, that, where it is strongest, it not only covers our natural ignorance, but even conceals itself, and seems not to take place, merely because it is found in the highest degree. (5)

But to convince us that all the laws of nature, and all the operations of bodies without exception, are known only by experience, the following reflections may, perhaps, suffice. Were any object presented to us, and were we required to pronounce concerning the effect, which will result from it, without consulting past observation; after what manner, I beseech you, must the mind proceed in this operation? It must invent or imagine some event, which it ascribes to the object as its effect; and it is plain that this invention must be entirely arbitrary. The mind can never possibly find the effect in the supposed cause, by the most accurate scrutiny and examination. For the effect is totally different from the cause, and consequently can never be discovered in it. Motion in the second billiard ball is a quite distinct event from motion in the first: nor is there anything in the one to suggest the smallest hint of the other. A stone or piece of metal raised into the air, and left without any support, immediately falls: but to consider the matter a priori, is there anything we discover in this situation which can beget the idea of a downward, rather than an upward, or any other motion, in the stone or metal?

R Thus A can be known to be the cause of B only by finding in experience that the two are constantly conjoined (in the right order), that is that A is always followed by B.

R In the case of events that are similar enough to those with which we are familiar, we may seem to ourselves to have direct insights into what will cause what that do not depend on experience. Hume is saying that this is an illusion.

And as the first imagination or invention of a particular effect, in all natural operations, is arbitrary, where we consult not experience; so must we also esteem the supposed tie or connection between the cause and effect, which binds them together, and renders it impossible that any other effect could result from the operation of that cause. When I see, for instance, a billiard ball moving in a straight line towards another; even suppose motion in the second ball should by accident be suggested to me, as the result of their contact or impulse; may I not conceive, that a hundred different events might as well follow from that cause? May not both these balls remain at absolute rest? May not the first ball return in a straight line, or leap off from the second in any line or direction? All these suppositions are consistent and conceivable. Why then should we give the preference to one, which is no more consistent or conceivable than the rest? All our reasonings a priori will never be able to show us any foundation for this preference.

In a word, then, every effect is a distinct event from its cause. It could not, therefore, be discovered in the cause, and the first invention or conception of it, a priori, must be entirely arbitrary. And even after it is suggested, the conjunction of it with the cause must appear equally arbitrary; since there are always many other effects, which, to reason, must seem fully as consistent and natural. In vain, therefore, should we pretend to determine any single event, or infer any cause or effect, without the assistance of observation and experience. 6 . . .

6

One important sort of causal relation that this does not seem to account for is that which involves unobservable entities, as in theoretical science. See the BonJour selection (in the external world section of this chapter) for a discussion of how such causal relations might be known.

Part II

But we have not yet attained any tolerable satisfaction with regard to the question first proposed. Each solution still gives rise to a new question as difficult as the foregoing, and leads us on to farther inquiries. When it is asked, *What is the nature of all our reasonings concerning matter of fact?* the proper answer seems to be, that they are founded on the relation of cause and effect. When again it is asked, *What is the foundation of all our reasonings and conclusions concerning that relation?* it may be replied in one word, *experience.* But if we still carry on our sifting humor, and ask, *What is the foundation of all conclusions from experience?* this implies a new question, which may be of more difficult solution and explication. . . .

I shall content myself, in this section, with an easy task, and shall pretend only to give a negative answer to the question here proposed. I say then, that, even after we have experience of the operations of cause and effect, our conclusions from that experience are *not* founded on reasoning, or any process of the understanding. This answer we must endeavor both to explain and to defend.

It must certainly be allowed, that nature has kept us at a great distance from all her secrets, and has afforded us only the knowledge of a few superficial qualities of objects; while she conceals from us those powers and principles on which the influence of those objects entirely depends. Our senses inform us of the color, weight, and consistence of bread; but neither sense nor reason can ever inform us of those qualities which fit it for the nourishment and support of a human body. Sight or feeling conveys an idea of the actual motion of bodies; but as to that wonderful force or power, which would carry on a moving body for ever in a continued change of place, and which bodies never lose but by communicating it to others; of this we cannot form the most distant conception. But notwithstanding this ignorance of natural powers and principles, we always presume, when we see like sensible qualities, that they have like secret powers, and expect that effects, similar to those which we have experienced, will follow from them. If a body of like color and consistence with that bread, which we have formerly eat, be presented to us, we make no scruple of repeating the experiment, and foresee, with certainty, like nourishment and support. Now this is a process of the mind or thought, of which I would willingly know the foundation. It is allowed on all hands that there is no known connection between the sensible qualities and the secret powers; and consequently, that the mind is not led to form such a conclusion concerning their constant and regular conjunction, by anything which it knows of their nature. 7 As to past *experience,* it can be allowed to give *direct* and *certain* information of those precise objects only, and that precise period of time, which fell under its cognizance: but why this experience should be extended to future times, and to other objects, which, for aught we know, may be only in appearance similar; this is the main question on which I would insist. The bread, which I formerly eat, nourished me; that is,

7

Hume might seem here to be suggesting that causal knowledge would be easier to obtain if it were somehow possible to directly observe these "secret powers." But this is misleading. Even if we could somehow observe the inner nature of things (by which Hume seems to have in mind something like their molecular or atomic structure) and not merely their "superficial qualities," the causal relations between those qualities and any further effects would still have to be established through experience in essentially the same way.

a body of such sensible qualities was, at that time, endued with such secret powers: but does it follow, that other bread must also nourish me at another time, and that like sensible qualities must always be attended with like secret powers? The consequence seems no wise necessary. At least, it must be acknowledged that there is here a consequence drawn by the mind; that there is a certain step taken; a process of thought, and an inference, which wants to be explained. These two propositions are far from being the same, *I have found that such an object has always been attended with such an effect,* and *I foresee, that other objects, which are, in appearance, similar, will be attended with similar effects.* I shall allow, if you please, that the one proposition may justly be inferred from the other; I know, in fact, that it always is inferred. But if you insist that the inference is made by a chain of reasoning, I desire you to produce that reasoning. The connection between these propositions is not intuitive. There is required a medium, which may enable the mind to draw such an inference, if indeed it be drawn by reasoning and argument. What that medium is, I must confess, passes my comprehension; and it is incumbent on those to produce it, who assert that it really exists, and is the origin of all our conclusions concerning matter of fact. (8)

This negative argument must certainly, in process of time, become altogether convincing, if many penetrating and able philosophers shall turn their inquiries this way and no one be ever able to discover any connecting proposition or intermediate step, which supports the understanding in this conclusion. But as the question is yet new, every reader may not trust so far to his own penetration, as to conclude, because an argument escapes his inquiry, that therefore it does not really exist. For this reason it may be requisite to venture upon a more difficult task: and enumerating all the branches of human knowledge, endeavor to show that none of them can afford such an argument.

All reasonings may be divided into two kinds, namely demonstrative reasoning, or that concerning relations of ideas, and moral reasoning, or that concerning matter of fact and existence. (9) That there are no demonstrative arguments in the case seems evident; since it implies no contradiction that the course of nature may change, and that an object, seemingly like those which we have experienced, may be attended with different or contrary effects. May I not clearly and distinctly conceive that a body, falling from the clouds, and which, in all other respects, resembles snow, has yet the taste of salt or feeling of fire? Is there any more intelligible proposition than to affirm, that all the trees will flourish in December and January, and decay in May and June? Now whatever is intelligible, and can be distinctly conceived, implies no contradiction, and can never be proved false by any demonstrative argument or abstract reasoning a priori. (10)

If we be, therefore, engaged by arguments to put trust in past experience, and make it the standard of our future judgment, these arguments must be probable only, or such as regard matter of fact and real existence, according to the division above mentioned. But that there is no argument of this kind, must appear, if our explication of that species of reasoning be admitted as solid and satisfactory. We have said that all arguments concerning existence are founded on the relation of cause and effect; that our knowledge of that relation is derived entirely from experience; and that all our experimental conclusions proceed upon the supposition that the future will be conformable to the past. To endeavor, therefore, the proof of this last supposition by probable arguments, or arguments regarding existence, must be evidently going in a circle, and taking that for granted, which is the very point in question. (11)

In reality, all arguments from experience are founded on the similarity which we discover among natural objects, and by which we are induced to expect effects similar to those which we have found to follow from such objects. And though none but a fool or madman will ever pretend to dispute the authority of experience, or to reject that great guide of human life, it may surely be allowed a philosopher to have so much curiosity at least as to examine the principle of human nature, which gives this mighty authority to experience, and makes us draw advantage from that similarity which nature has placed among different objects. From causes which appear *similar* we expect similar effects. This is the sum of all our experimental conclusions. Now it seems evident that, if this conclusion were formed by reason, it would be as perfect at first, and upon one instance, as after ever so long a course of experience. But the case is far otherwise. . . . It is only after a long course of uniform experiments in any kind, that we attain

R Hume is claiming that there is no cogent reasoning of any sort from the observational premise that constant conjunction has been observed to the conclusion that the same sequence will occur in other cases. His first reason for this is a challenge to his opponent to produce such reasoning, to spell out in detail how an argument from that sort of premise to that sort of conclusion would go—something Hume is confident cannot be done.

R His second and more important argument takes the form of a dilemma, relying on the distinction explained at the beginning of the selection. According to this distinction, there are only two possible sorts of reasoning: a priori reasoning and reasoning that appeals to experience. (Hume's use of the term "moral" to refer to the latter is an archaic usage that has nothing to do with the modern use of the term to refer to matters having to do with ethics.)

R A priori reasoning will not work because such reasoning depends in Hume's view on the avoidance of contradiction, and there is no contradiction in supposing that "the course of nature may change" in such a way that a sequence that has been experienced so far may cease to hold.

R And reasoning that appeals to experience will not work, since the only way that experience can support a general conclusion of the sort in question is by generalizing from repeated sequences in exactly the way that is at issue. Thus to appeal to any such reasoning (such as by arguing that inductive reasoning has been observed in the past to yield true conclusions and so is likely to do so in the future as well) would thus **beg the question.**

a firm reliance and security with regard to a particular event. Now where is that process of reasoning which, from one instance, draws a conclusion, so different from that which it infers from a hundred instances that are nowise different from that single one? This question I propose as much for the sake of information, as with an intention of raising difficulties. I cannot find, I cannot imagine any such reasoning. But I keep my mind still open to instruction, if anyone will vouchsafe to bestow it on me.

Should it be said that, from a number of uniform experiments, we *infer* a connection between the sensible qualities and the secret powers; this, I must confess, seems the same difficulty, couched in different terms. The question still recurs, on what process of argument this *inference* is founded? Where is the medium, the interposing ideas, which join propositions so very wide of each other? It is confessed that the color, consistence, and other sensible qualities of bread appear not, of themselves, to have any connection with the secret powers of nourishment and support. For otherwise we could infer these secret powers from the first appearance of these sensible qualities, without the aid of experience; contrary to the sentiment of all philosophers, and contrary to plain matter of fact. Here, then, is our natural state of ignorance with regard to the powers and influence of all objects. How is this remedied by experience? It only shows us a number of uniform effects, resulting from certain objects, and teaches us that those particular objects, at that particular time, were endowed with such powers and forces. When a new object, endowed with similar sensible qualities, is produced, we expect similar powers and forces, and look for a like effect. From a body of like color and consistence with bread we expect like nourishment and support. But this surely is a step or progress of the mind, which wants to be explained. When a man says, *I have found, in all past instances, such sensible qualities conjoined with such secret powers:* And when he says, *Similar sensible qualities will always be conjoined with similar secret powers,* he is not guilty of a tautology, nor are these propositions in any respect the same. You say that the one proposition is an inference from the other. But you must confess that the inference is not intuitive; neither is it demonstrative: 12 Of what nature is it, then? To say it is experimental, is begging the question. For all inferences from experience suppose, as their foundation, that the future will resemble the past, and that similar powers will be conjoined with similar sensible qualities. If there be any suspicion that the course of nature may change, and that the past may be no rule for the future, all experience becomes useless, and can give rise to no inference or conclusion. It is impossible, therefore, that any arguments from experience can prove this resemblance of the past to the future; since all these arguments are founded on the supposition of that resemblance. Let the course of things be allowed hitherto ever so regular; that alone, without some new argument or inference, proves not that, for the future, it will continue so. In vain do you pretend to have learned the nature of bodies from your past experience. Their secret nature, and consequently all their effects and influence, may change, without any change in their sensible qualities. This happens sometimes, and with regard to some objects: Why may it not happen always, and with regard to all objects? What logic, what process of argument secures you against this supposition? My practice, you say, refutes my doubts. But you mistake the purport of my question. As an agent, I am quite satisfied in the point; but as a philosopher, who has some share of curiosity, I will not say scepticism, I want to learn the foundation of this inference. No reading, no inquiry has yet been able to remove my difficulty, or give me satisfaction in a matter of such importance. Can I do better than propose the difficulty to the public, even though, perhaps, I have small hopes of obtaining a solution? We shall, at least, by this means, be sensible of our ignorance, if we do not augment our knowledge.

I must confess that a man is guilty of unpardonable arrogance who concludes, because an argument has escaped his own investigation, that therefore it does not really exist. I must also confess that, though all the learned, for several ages, should have employed themselves in fruitless search upon any subject, it may still, perhaps, be rash to conclude positively that the subject must, therefore, pass all human comprehension. Even though we examine all the sources of our knowledge, and conclude them unfit for such a subject, there may still remain a suspicion, that the enumeration is not complete, or the examination not accurate. But with regard to the present subject, there are some considerations which seem to

To say that the inference is "intuitive" would be to say we have a direct a priori insight that the conclusion follows; to say it is "demonstrative" would be to say there is a more extended a priori argument involving intermediate steps. But both of these ways of justifying the inference depend, Hume thinks, on it being contradictory to accept the experiential premise and reject the conclusion—which, he has argued, is not the case here.

remove all this accusation of arrogance or suspicion of mistake.

It is certain that the most ignorant and stupid peasants—nay infants, nay even brute beasts—improve by experience, and learn the qualities of natural objects, by observing the effects which result from them. When a child has felt the sensation of pain from touching the flame of a candle, he will be careful not to put his hand near any candle; but will expect a similar effect from a cause which is similar in its sensible qualities and appearance. If you assert, therefore, that the understanding of the child is led into this conclusion by any process of argument or ratiocination, I may justly require you to produce that argument; nor have you any pretense to refuse so equitable a demand. You cannot say that the argument is abstruse, and may possibly escape your inquiry; since you confess that it is obvious to the capacity of a mere infant. If you hesitate, therefore, a moment, or if, after reflection, you produce any intricate or profound argument, you, in a manner, give up the question, and confess that it is not reasoning which engages us to suppose the past resembling the future, and to expect similar effects from causes which are, to appearance, similar. This is the proposition which I intended to enforce in the present section. If I be right, I pretend not to have made any mighty discovery. And if I be wrong, I must acknowledge myself to be indeed a very backward scholar; since I cannot now discover an argument which, it seems, was perfectly familiar to me long before I was out of my cradle. [13]

Section V: Skeptical Solution of These Doubts

. . . Though we should conclude, for instance, as in the foregoing section, that, in all reasonings from experience, there is a step taken by the mind which is not supported by any argument or process of the understanding; there is no danger that these reasonings, on which almost all knowledge depends, will ever be affected by such a discovery. If the mind be not engaged by argument to make this step, it must be induced by some other principle of equal weight and authority; and that principle will preserve its influence as long as human nature remains the same. What that principle is may well be worth the pains of inquiry.

Suppose a person, though endowed with the strongest faculties of reason and reflection, to be brought on a sudden into this world; he would, indeed, immediately observe a continual succession of objects, and one event following another; but he would not be able to discover anything farther. He would not, at first, by any reasoning, be able to reach the idea of cause and effect; since the particular powers, by which all natural operations are performed, never appear to the senses; nor is it reasonable to conclude, merely because one event, in one instance, precedes another, that the one is the cause, the other the effect. Their connection may be arbitrary and casual. There may be no reason to infer the existence of one from the appearance of the other. And in a word, such a person, without more experience, could never employ his conjecture or reasoning concerning any matter of fact, or be assured of anything beyond what was immediately present to his senses.

Suppose again, that he has acquired more experience and has lived so long in the world as to have observed familiar objects or events to be constantly conjoined together; what is the consequence of this experience? He immediately infers the existence of one object from the appearance of the other. Yet he has not, by all his experience, acquired any idea or knowledge of the secret power by which the one object produces the other [14] ; nor is it, by any process of reasoning, he is engaged to draw this inference. But still he finds himself determined to draw it: And though he should be convinced that his understanding has no part in the operation, he would nevertheless continue in the same course of thinking. There is some other principle which determines him to form such a conclusion.

This principle is *custom* or *habit*. For wherever the repetition of any particular act or operation produces a propensity to renew the same act or operation, without being impelled by any reasoning or process of the understanding, we always say, that this propensity is the effect of *custom*. By employing that word, we pretend not to have given the ultimate reason of such a propensity. We only point out a principle of human nature, which is universally acknowledged, and which is well known by its effects. Perhaps we can push our inquiries no farther, or pretend to give the cause of this cause; but must rest contented with it as the ultimate principle which we can assign, of all our

R Hume reinforces the challenge to his opponent by claiming that the reasoning in question, if it existed, could not be very difficult to specify, since it would have to be familiar even to young children (who obviously draw such conclusions).

As already noted (see Annotation 7), the reference to "secret powers" is highly misleading, in that there is no reason to think that we would not face the same essential problem no matter how much knowledge of such powers we might have.

Here Hume seems to be assuming that the fact that there are many repeated instances (and no conflicting ones) is itself *rationally* irrelevant, that only the character of the individual instances makes any difference to reason, which is why the same conclusion would follow from one instance as from many. But might not the fact of repetition support a general conclusion even if individual instances do not?

But that we have *knowledge* rather than ignorance on this basis seems to depend on there being some reason for thinking that the results arrived at in this way are at least likely to be true. According to Hume, there is no such reason.

This is a very puzzling passage. Hume seems to be assuming that the general conclusions arrived at through the operation of custom will in fact be in accordance with "the other works of nature"—that is, that they will be true. (This is the "pre-established harmony," though it is not "pre-established" in any very clear way.) But by his own earlier argument, he has no good reason to think that this will be so in general or even some of the time.

Here the unjustified assumption that customary or habitual inductive reasoning will nonetheless lead to the truth is even clearer. Such reasoning may be "infallible" in the sense that it never fails to function, but if Hume's earlier argument was correct, there is no reason to think that its results will be infallible in the sense of producing true conclusions.

conclusions from experience. It is sufficient satisfaction, that we can go so far, without repining at the narrowness of our faculties because they will carry us no farther. And it is certain we here advance a very intelligible proposition at least, if not a true one, when we assert that, after the constant conjunction of two objects—heat and flame, for instance, weight and solidity—we are determined by custom alone to expect the one from the appearance of the other. This hypothesis seems even the one which explains the difficulty, why we draw from a thousand instances, an inference that we are not able to draw from one instance, that is, in no respect, different from them. Reason is incapable of any such variation. The conclusions that it draws from considering one circle are the same which it would form surveying all the circles in the universe. But no man, having seen only one body move after being impelled by another, could infer that every other body will move after a like impulse. All inferences from experience, therefore, are effects of custom, not of reasoning. [15]

Custom, then, is the great guide of human life. It is that principle alone which renders our experience useful to us, and makes us expect, for the future, a similar train of events with those which have appeared in the past. Without the influence of custom, we should be entirely ignorant of every matter of fact beyond what is immediately present to the memory and senses. We should never know how to adjust means to ends, or to employ our natural powers in the production of any effect. [16] There would be an end at once of all action, as well as of the chief part of speculation.

. . .

What, then, is the conclusion of the whole matter? A simple one; though, it must be confessed, pretty remote from the common theories of philosophy. All belief of matter of fact or real existence is derived merely from some object, present to the memory or senses, and a customary conjunction between that and some other object. Or in other words; having found, in many instances, that any two kinds of objects—flame and heat, snow and cold—have always been conjoined together; if flame or snow be presented anew to the senses, the mind is carried by custom to expect heat or cold, and to believe that such a quality does exist, and will discover itself on a nearer approach. This belief is the necessary result of placing the mind in such circumstances. . . . All these operations are a species of natural instincts, which no reasoning or process of the thought and understanding is able either to produce or to prevent.

. . .

Here, then, is a kind of pre-established harmony between the course of nature and the succession of our ideas; and though the powers and forces, by which the former is governed, be wholly unknown to us; yet our thoughts and conceptions have still, we find, gone on in the same train with the other works of nature. Custom is that principle, by which this correspondence has been effected; so necessary to the subsistence of our species, and the regulation of our conduct, in every circumstance and occurrence of human life. Had not the presence of an object, instantly excited the idea of those objects, commonly conjoined with it, all our knowledge must have been limited to the narrow sphere of our memory and senses; and we should never have been able to adjust means to ends, or employ our natural powers, either to the producing of good, or avoiding of evil. Those who delight in the discovery and contemplation of final causes, have here ample subject to employ their wonder and admiration. [17]

I shall add, for a further confirmation of the foregoing theory, that, as this operation of the mind, by which we infer like effects from like causes, and *vice versa,* is so essential to the subsistence of all human creatures, it is not probable, that it could be trusted to the fallacious deductions of our reason, which is slow in its operations; appears not, in any degree, during the first years of infancy; and at best is, in every age and period of human life, extremely liable to error and mistake. It is more conformable to the ordinary wisdom of nature to secure so necessary an act of the mind, by some instinct or mechanical tendency, which may be infallible in its operations, may discover itself at the first appearance of life and thought, and may be independent of all the labored deductions of the understanding. As nature as taught us the use of our limbs, without giving us the knowledge of the muscles and nerves, by which they are actuated; so has she implanted in us an instinct, which carries forward the thought in a correspondent course to that which she has established among external objects; though we are ignorant of those powers and forces, on which this regular course and succession of objects totally depends. [18]

Discussion Questions

1. Attempts are sometimes made to justify inductive reasoning by adding a further premise or principle to the argument: the premise that the future will probably resemble the past, or perhaps that unobserved cases will probably resemble observed cases. What would be Hume's likely response to such an attempt?
2. Hume seems to assume that any case in which one sort of event A was always followed (in the future as well) by another sort of event B would be a case of causation, but this is too simple a picture. Can you think of one or more common-sense examples in which it is plausible (apart from worries about induction) to suppose that A is always followed by B, but in which A is not the cause or even part of the cause of B? (Hint: think of cases where both A and B are caused by some third sort of event C.)
3. Look back at the discussion of theoretical or explanatory reasoning in the BonJour selection (in the external world section of this chapter). Could the acceptance of an inductive conclusion be justified by this sort of reasoning on the grounds that the existence of an objective regularity in nature is the best explanation of the observed regular sequence? What other explanations are possible for such an observed sequence? Does such an argument show that the inductive conclusion is probably true, given the truth of the premise? What do you think Hume would say about this sort of defense of induction? Is he perhaps even tacitly assuming something like this at the end of his discussion? (This question is much harder and more complicated than most of the discussion questions.)

Wesley Salmon

Wesley Salmon (1925–2001) was an American philosopher who taught at Indiana University, the University of Arizona, and the University of Pittsburgh. Salmon wrote widely in the philosophy of science, with his work on explanation and the related topic of causality being especially influential. In the following selection, Salmon restates the problem of induction as it grows out of Hume's discussion and then considers and evaluates a variety of possible solutions (some of which have been omitted here). In the process of doing this, he also offers a version of the moderate empiricist view of a priori knowledge (see the chapter introduction). This is relevant because Salmon wants to argue against the possibility of an a priori justification of induction. (See the following selection from Ewing for a contrasting view.) This is one of the more challenging selections in this book, and you will have to work hard to try to understand it.

The Problem of Induction, from *The Foundations of Scientific Inference*

We all believe that we have knowledge of facts extending far beyond those we directly perceive. The scope of our senses is severely limited in space and time; our immediate perceptual knowledge does not reach to events that happened before we were born, to events that are happening now in certain other places, or to any future events. We believe, nevertheless, that we have some kind of indirect knowledge of such facts. We know that a glacier once covered a large part of North America, that the sun continues to exist at night, and that the tides will rise and fall tomorrow. Science and common sense have at least this one thing in common: Each embodies knowledge of matters of fact that are not open to our direct inspection. Indeed, science purports to establish general laws or theories that apply to all parts of space and time without restriction. A "science" that consisted of no more than a mere summary of the results of direct observation would not deserve the name.

From *The Foundations of Scientific Inference* (Pittsburgh: University of Pittsburgh Press, 1967).

Hume's profound critique of induction begins with a simple and apparently innocent question: How do we acquire knowledge of the unobserved?* This question, as posed, may seem to call for an empirical answer. We observe that human beings utilize what may be roughly characterized as inductive or scientific methods of extending knowledge from the observed to the unobserved. The sciences, in fact, embody the most powerful and highly developed methods known, and we may make an empirical investigation of scientific methods much as we might for any other sort of human behavior. We may consider the historical development of science. We may study the psychological, sociological, and political factors relevant to the pursuit of science. We may try to give an exact characterization of the behavior of scientists. In doing all these things, however, important and interesting as they are, we will have ignored the *philosophical* aspect of the problem Hume raised. Putting the matter very simply, these empirical investigations may enable us to describe the ways in which people arrive at *beliefs* about unobserved facts, but they leave open the question of whether beliefs arrived at in this way actually constitute *knowledge*. It is one thing to describe how people go about seeking to extend their knowledge; it is quite another to claim that the methods employed actually do yield knowledge.

One of the basic differences between knowledge and belief is that knowledge must be founded upon evidence—i.e., it must be belief founded upon some rational justification. To say that certain methods yield knowledge of the unobserved is to make a cognitive claim for them. Hume called into question the justification of such cognitive claims. The answer cannot be found entirely within an empirical study of human behavior, for a *logical* problem has been raised. It is the problem of understanding the logical relationship between evidence and conclusion in logically correct inferences. It is the problem of determining whether the inferences by which we attempt to make the transition from knowledge of the observed to knowledge of the unobserved are logically correct. The fact that people do or do not use a certain type of inference is irrelevant to its justifiability. Whether people have confidence in the correctness of a certain type of inference has nothing to do with whether such confidence is justified. If we should adopt a logically incorrect method for inferring one fact from others, these facts would not actually constitute evidence for the conclusion we have drawn. The problem of induction is the problem of explicating the very concept of *inductive evidence*. (1)

1 It would be somewhat more perspicuous to say that the problem is explaining why inductive evidence, as standardly understood (see the chapter introduction), is good evidence—why it genuinely supports the sort of conclusion that is standardly drawn from it.

. . .

Consider a simple and highly artificial situation. Suppose a number of balls have been drawn from an urn, and that all of the black ones that have been drawn are licorice-flavored. . . . The problem—Hume's basic *philosophical* problem—is this: Given that all of the observed black balls have been licorice-flavored, and given that somehow the conclusion has been entertained that the unobserved black balls in the urn are also licorice-flavored, do the observed facts constitute sound *evidence* for that conclusion? Would we be *justified* in accepting that conclusion on the basis of the facts alleged to be evidence for it? (2)

2 This is not the best example. There is no reason to think that drawing from an urn reflects any real regularity in nature, which is what the problem of induction is mainly concerned with.

As a first answer to this question we may point out that the inference does conform to an accepted inductive principle, a principle saying roughly that observed instances conforming to a generalization constitute evidence for it. (3) It is, however, a very small step to the next question: What grounds have we for accepting this or any other inductive principle? Is there any reason or justification for placing confidence in the conclusions of inferences of this type? Given that the premises of this inference are true, and given that the inference conforms to a certain rule, can we provide any rational justification for accepting its conclusion rather than, for instance, the conclusion that black balls yet to be drawn will taste like quinine?

3  That is, that observations of cases of A's that are also B's constitute evidence for the generalization that all A's are B's.

It is well known that Hume's answer to this problem was essentially skeptical. It was his great merit to have shown that a justification of induction, if possible at all, is by no means easy to provide. In order to appreciate the force of his

*David Hume, *Enquiry Concerning Human Understanding*.

argument it is first necessary to clarify some terminological points. This is particularly important because the word *induction* has been used in a wide variety of ways.

For purposes of systematic discussion one distinction is fundamental, namely, the distinction between demonstrative and nondemonstrative inference. A *demonstrative* inference is one whose premises necessitate its conclusion; the conclusion cannot be false if the premises are true. All valid deductions are demonstrative inferences. A *nondemonstrative* inference is simply one that fails to be demonstrative. Its conclusion is not necessitated by its premises; the conclusion could be false even if the premises are true. A demonstrative inference is *necessarily truth-preserving;* a nondemonstrative inference is not. (4)

The category of nondemonstrative inferences, as I have characterized it, contains, among other things perhaps, all kinds of fallacious inferences. If, however, there is any kind of inference whose premises, although not necessitating the conclusion, do lend it weight, support it, or make it probable, then such inferences possess a certain kind of logical rectitude. It is not deductive validity, but it is important anyway. Inferences possessing it are *correct inductive inferences.*

Since demonstrative inferences have been characterized in terms of their basic property of necessary truth preservation, it is natural to ask how they achieve this very desirable trait. For a large group of demonstrative inferences, including those discussed under "valid deduction" in most logic texts, the answer is rather easy. Inferences of this type purchase necessary truth preservation by sacrificing any extension of content. The conclusion of such an inference says no more than do the premises—often less. The conclusion cannot be false if the premises are true *because* the conclusion says nothing that was not already stated in the premises. The conclusion is a mere reformulation of all or part of the content of the premises. In some cases the reformulation is unanticipated and therefore psychologically surprising, but the conclusion cannot augment the content of the premises. Such inferences are *nonampliative;* an ampliative inference, then, has a conclusion with content not present either explicitly or implicitly in the premises. (5)

While it is easy to understand why nonampliative inferences are necessarily truth-preserving, the further question arises whether there are any necessarily truth-preserving inferences that are also ampliative. Is there any type of inference whose conclusion must, of necessity, be true if the premises are true, but whose conclusion says something not stated by the premises? Hume believed that the answer is negative and so do I, but it is not easy to produce an adequate defense of this answer. Let us see, however, what an affirmative answer would amount to.

Suppose there were an ampliative inference that is also necessarily truth-preserving. Consider the implication from its premises, $P_1, \ldots, P_k$, to its conclusion C. If the inference were an ordinary nonampliative deduction, this implication would be analytic and empty; but since the argument is supposed to be ampliative, the implication must be synthetic. At the same time, because the argument is supposed to be necessarily truth-preserving, this implication must be not only true but necessarily true. Thus, to maintain that there are inferences that are both ampliative and necessarily truth-preserving is tantamount to asserting that there are synthetic a priori truths. (6) . . .

If we agree that there are no synthetic a priori truths, then we must identify necessarily truth-preserving inference with nonampliative inference. All ampliative inference is nondemonstrative. This leads to an exhaustive trichotomy of inferences: valid deductive inference, correct inductive inference, and assorted fallacies. The first question is, however, whether the second category is empty or whether there are such things as correct inductive inferences. This is Hume's problem of induction. Can we show that any particular type of ampliative inference can be justified in any way? If so, it will qualify as correct induction.

Consider, then, any ampliative inference whatever. The example of the licorice-flavored black balls illustrates the point. We cannot show *deductively* that this inference will have a true conclusion given true premises. If we could, we would have proved that the conclusion must be true if the premises are. That would make it necessarily truth-preserving, hence, demonstrative. This, in turn, would mean that it was nonampliative, contrary to our hypothesis. Thus, if an ampliative inference could be justified deductively it would not be ampliative. It follows that ampliative inference cannot be justified deductively.

It is also important to be clear that a demonstrative argument guarantees only that the conclusion will be true *if* the premises are true.

Notice that this so far says nothing about *why* particular arguments have the feature of being necessarily truth-preserving.

R Salmon's view is that all logically valid arguments are "nonampliative" because the content of the conclusion is present, at least "implicitly," in the content of the premises—where this is supposed to explain why the conclusion must be true if the premises are true. (See the following selection by Ewing for more discussion of this issue.)

R The statement that all cases where the premises are true are cases where the conclusion is true would be a necessary truth (and, Salmon is assuming, thereby knowable a priori), but would be synthetic (in Kant's sense) because the predicate is not included in the subject. (See the discussion of a priori knowledge in the Appendix to the chapter introduction.)

At the same time, we cannot justify any sort of ampliative inference *inductively*. To do so would require the use of some sort of nondemonstrative inference. But the question at issue is the justification of nondemonstrative inference, so the procedure would be question begging. Before we can properly employ a nondemonstrative inference in a justifying argument, we must already have justified that nondemonstrative inference. 7

7

This paragraph and the preceding one contain Salmon's version of Hume's dilemma argument.

Hume's position can be summarized succinctly: We cannot justify any kind of ampliative inference. If it could be justified deductively it would not be ampliative. It cannot be justified nondemonstratively because that would be viciously circular. It seems, then, that there is no way in which we can extend our knowledge to the unobserved. We have, to be sure, many beliefs about the unobserved, and in some of them we place great confidence. Nevertheless, they are without rational justification of any kind!

This is a harsh conclusion, yet it seems to be supported by impeccable arguments. It might be called "Hume's paradox," for the conclusion, although ingeniously argued, is utterly repugnant to common sense and our deepest convictions. We *know* ("in our hearts") that we have knowledge of unobserved fact. The challenge is to show how this is possible. 8

8

STOP To see just how "harsh" or "repugnant" this conclusion is, ask yourself how much of our knowledge would be undermined if induction were rejected, and how much would be left. (See Discussion Question 1.)

II. Attempted Solutions

It hardly needs remarking that philosophers have attempted to meet Hume's intriguing challenge in a wide variety of ways. . . . In this section I shall survey what seem to me to be the most important efforts to deal with the problem.

1. Inductive Justification. If Hume's arguments had never been propounded and we were asked why we accept the methods of science, the most natural answer would be, I think, that these methods have proved themselves by their results. We can point to astonishing technological advances, to vastly increased comprehension, and to impressive predictions. Science has provided us with foresight, control, and understanding. No other method can claim a comparable record of successful accomplishment. If methods are to be judged by their fruits, there is no doubt that the scientific method will come out on top.

Unfortunately, Hume examined this argument and showed that it is viciously circular. It is an example of an attempt to justify inductive methods inductively. From the premise that science has had considerable predictive success in the past, we conclude that it will continue to have substantial predictive success in the future. Observed cases of the application of scientific method have yielded successful prediction; therefore, as yet unobserved cases of the application of scientific method will yield successful predictions. This argument has the same structure as our black-balls-in-the-urn example; it is precisely the sort of ampliative inference from the observed to the unobserved whose justifiability is in question.

Consider the parallel case for a radically different sort of method. A crystal gazer claims that his method is the appropriate method for making predictions. When we question his claim he says, "Wait a moment; I will find out whether the method of crystal gazing is the best method for making predictions." He looks into his crystal ball and announces that future cases of crystal gazing will yield predictive success. If we should protest that his method has not been especially successful in the past, he might well make certain remarks about parity of reasoning. "Since you have used your method to justify your method, why shouldn't I use my method to justify my method? If you insist upon judging my method by using your method, why shouldn't I use my method to evaluate your method? By the way, I note by gazing into my crystal ball that the scientific method is now in for a very bad run of luck." 9

9

Not all "methods" will automatically be self-justifying in this way: if crystal balls do sometimes give clear and definite answers to questions, then some of them might say that crystal balls are *not* reliable or might give no definite answer either way to this particular question.

But while a method that undermined itself in this way would be even less defensible, this does nothing to show that self-justification is enough for genuine justification.

The trouble with circular arguments is obvious: with an appropriate circular argument you can prove anything. . . .

4. Synthetic a priori Principles. A long philosophical tradition, dating back to antiquity, denies the empiricist claim that knowledge of the world rests solely upon observational evidence—that factual knowledge is limited to what we can observe and what we can infer therefrom. In the modern period, this rationalistic tradition is represented by men like Descartes and Leibniz who took their inspiration from the abstract aspect of modern physics. After Hume's devastating criticism of induction, Kant provided a more precise formulation, a fuller elaboration, and a more subtle defense of rationalism than any that had been given earlier (or, quite possibly, subsequently). As Kant himself testified, it was Hume who awakened him from his "dogmatic slumbers" and thereupon stimulated the *Critique of Pure Reason.*

The doctrine that there are synthetic a priori truths is, as I explained above, tantamount to the view that there are necessarily truth-preserving ampliative inferences. If we could find a *bona fide* demonstrative ampliative inference we would have a solution to Hume's problem of the ground of inference from the observed to the unobserved. This solution could be presented in either of two ways. First, one could assert that there are factual propositions that can be established by pure reason—without the aid of empirical evidence—and that these synthetic a priori propositions, in conjunction with premises established by observation, make it possible to deduce (nonampliatively) conclusions pertaining to unobserved matters of fact. Second, one could claim that these synthetic a priori propositions, although not added as premises to ampliative inferences to render them nonampliative, do instead provide a warrant for genuinely ampliative inferences from the observed to the unobserved. (10) . . .

In order to appreciate the philosophical issues involved in the attempt to justify induction by means of a synthetic a priori principle, we must introduce some reasonably precise definitions of key terms. Two pairs of concepts are involved: first, the distinction between *analytic* and *synthetic* statements, and second, the distinction between *a priori* and *a posteriori* statements. . . .

Although it is reasonable to maintain, I think, that all logical truths are analytic, there seem to be analytic statements that are not logical truths. (11)

For instance,

All bachelors are unmarried

is not [a logical truth]. However, given the definition,

Bachelor = unmarried adult male,

the foregoing statement can be transformed into a logical truth, for the definition gives license to substitute the *definiens,* "unmarried adult male," for the *definiendum* "bachelor." This substitution yields,

All unmarried adult males are unmarried,

which is a logical truth. To incorporate cases of this sort, we may define an *analytic statement* as one that is a logical truth or can be transformed into a logical truth by definitional substitution of *definiens* for *definiendum.* (12) The negation of an analytic truth is a *self-contradiction.* Any statement that is neither analytic nor self-contradictory is *synthetic.* . . .

. . .

Analytic statements are often said . . . to be devoid of any factual content. Although there are difficulties in giving an adequate account of the concept of factual content, enough can be said to illuminate its relation to analytic statements. The basic feature seems to be that factual content of a statement is a measure of the capacity of that statement to *rule out* possibilities. In this respect, it is a negative concept. In a state of total ignorance all possible states of affairs are live possibilities; any possible state of affairs might, for all we know, be the actual state of things. As knowledge accumulates, we realize that some of the possibilities are not actualized. The statements expressing our knowledge are incompatible with descriptions of various possible worlds, so we know that these possibilities are ruled out—our actual world does not coincide with any of these possibilities that are incompatible with what we know. Generally speaking, moreover, the greater our knowledge—the greater the factual content of the statements we know—the more possibilities are disqualified from being actual. Imagine, for instance, the inhabitants of Plato's famous cave, who are totally ignorant of the nature of the external world. They can imagine birds of all sorts, including ravens of various colors. When the emissary to the outer world returns and reports that all ravens are black, those who remained in the cave can rule out all possibilities that had room for ravens of other colors. The statement, "All ravens are black," has factual content because of the descriptions of possible worlds with which it is incompatible. If, however, the emissary should return and remark that every raven is either black or nonblack, his statement would be totally lacking in content, and the permanent inhabitants of the cave—anxious for knowledge of the external world—would be justly furious with him for his empty report. His statement would lack content because it is com-

(10)

The first of these alternatives has no plausibility at all. No one has ever claimed that the conclusion of an inductive argument is guaranteed to be true, since it is beyond question that such conclusions are occasionally false—for example, when the observed regularity was just an accident. The second alternative can avoid this problem because the principle in question might say only that the conclusion of an inductive argument is *probably* true when the observational premises are true.

(11)

A *logical truth* is one that is guaranteed to be true by virtue of its *form.* (We have omitted Salmon's more technical account, which amounts to the same thing.)

(12)

This is Salmon's main definition of "analytic." You should compare it to Kant's, as discussed in the Appendix to the chapter introduction. ("All unmarried adult males are unmarried" is a logical truth because it is of the form "All FGH are F," and any claim of that form is necessarily true.) (See Discussion Question 2.)

patible with every possibility. It is . . . a logical truth. . . . Since it is true under any possible circumstances and is not incompatible with any description of a possible world, its content is zero. Any analytic statement will, as we have seen above, share this characteristic. We are, therefore, entitled to assert that analytic statements have no factual content. 13 . . .

13

STOP Does the fact that a claim has no factual content in this sense help to explain how it can be justified or known a priori (as Salmon seems to be suggesting)? How would such an explanation go?

Let us now turn to the other distinction required for our discussion. A statement is a priori if its truth or falsity can be established without recourse to observational evidence; it is a posteriori if observational evidence is needed to establish its truth or falsity. The distinction between a priori and a posteriori statements refers exclusively to the justification of statements and has nothing to do with discovery. The statements of arithmetic, for example, are regarded by most philosophers as a priori; the fact that children may learn arithmetic by counting physical objects (e.g., fingers) has nothing to do with the issue. Arithmetic statements can be established . . . without the aid of empirical observation or experiment, and this qualifies them as a priori. It is evident, moreover, that analytic statements, as they have been described above, are a priori. Since their truth follows from logical truths and definitions alone—that is, from syntactical and semantical considerations alone—observation and experiment are not required for their proof.

Most philosophers would acknowledge that many synthetic statements are a posteriori. It would seem that no amount of pure ratiocination would reveal whether I had eggs for breakfast this morning or whether there is a typewriter on the desk in the next office. Some sort of observation would seem to be indispensable. However, it is not nearly as evident that *all* synthetic statements are a posteriori. The doctrine that there are synthetic a priori statements is, I take it, the thesis of rationalism. It was maintained by Kant, as well as by many other philosophers both before and after him. The doctrine that all a priori statements are either analytic or self-contradictory is the thesis of empiricism as I understand it. 14

14

That is, moderate empiricism.

15

Salmon is right that this is what Descartes's claim amounts to. Think back to Descartes and try to see clearly why this is so.

STOP (Would there be any plausibility to the claim that Descartes's principle is *analytic* under either Kant's or Salmon's definition?)

I know of no easy way to argue the question of whether there are any synthetic a priori statements. The history of human thought has provided many attempts to establish synthetic a priori truths, with a notable lack of success in my opinion. . . .

Descartes provides an especially clear example of the use of synthetic a priori principles to justify ampliative inference. Starting from his famous *cogito,* he set out to deduce a complete account of the real world. He never supposed that nonampliative deduction would be equal to the task; instead, he appealed to principles he considered evident to the natural light of reason: "Now it is manifest by the natural light that there must at least be as much reality in the efficient and total cause as in its effect. For, pray, whence can the effect derive its reality, if not from its cause?"* The man who thought he could not be certain that 2 + 2 = 4 or that he had hands unless he could prove that God is not a deceiver found the foregoing principle so clear and distinct that it is impossible to conceive its falsity! 15

. . .

Kant's approach to the question of synthetic a priori principles is profoundly instructive. So convinced was he that geometry provided examples of synthetic a priori propositions that he did not need to tarry long over the question of whether there are any such things. Instead, he moved on the question of how they are possible. Synthetic a priori knowledge (if there is such) does exhibit a genuine epistemological mystery. After some exposure to formal logic one can see without much difficulty how linguistic stipulations can yield analytic statements that hold in any possible world. It is easy to see that "Snow is white or snow is not white" is true simply because of the meanings we attach to "or" and "not." Analytic a priori statements are no great mystery. Likewise, it is not too difficult to see how our senses can provide clues to the nature of physical reality, helping us to establish propositions that are true in some but not all possible worlds. . . . But how could we conceivably establish by pure thought that some logically consistent picture of the real world is false? How could we, without any aid of experience whatever, find out anything about our world in contradistinction to other possible worlds? Given a logically

*René Descartes, "Of God: That He Exists," *Meditations,* III [p. 160]; the translation in this book varies slightly.

contingent formula—one that admits of true as well as false interpretations—how could we hope to decide on a completely a priori basis which of its interpretations are true and which false? [16] The empiricist says it is impossible to do so, and in this I think he is correct. Nevertheless, it is tempting to endow various principles with the status of synthetic a priori truths. It was to Kant's great credit that he saw the urgency of the question: *How is this possible?*

Various causal principles, as we have seen, have been accorded the status of synthetic a priori truths—for example, the traditional *exnihilo* principle, the principle of sufficient reason, and Descartes' principle that the cause must be as great as the effect. [17] Kant also, in addition to claiming that the propositions of arithmetic and geometry are synthetic a priori, maintained that the principle of universal causation—everything that happens presupposes something from which it follows according to a rule—is synthetic a priori. It is by means of this principle that he hoped to dispose of the problem of induction. However, Kant's attempt to explain the possibility of synthetic a priori propositions is unsatisfactory. The propositions of Euclidean geometry do not enjoy epistemological primacy; the propositions of arithmetic lack synthetic content, [18] and the physical world can be made intelligible in nondeterministic terms. Human powers of conception and visualization far exceed the limits Kant saw as necessary constraints upon the human intellect and as the source of synthetic a priori truths.

It is unfortunate that subsequent philosophers have paid little attention to Kant's central question: How are synthetic a priori propositions possible? Instead, the category of synthetic a priori propositions has too often become a convenient wastebasket for statements not readily classifiable as analytic or a posteriori. . . . It seems to me that all such statements can be shown, on careful examination, to be analytic or a posteriori, and that no convincing example of a synthetic a priori proposition has yet been produced. Even if this is so, of course, it does not prove that there are no synthetic a priori statements. It should, however, give us pause, and it does relieve us of any obligation to accept the positive rationalistic thesis that there are synthetic a priori propositions. It does place the burden of proof upon those who hope to escape Hume's problem of induction by way of a synthetic a priori principle. Moreover, even if a recalcitrant example were given—one that seemed to defy all analysis as either analytic or a posteriori—it might still be reasonable to suppose that we had not exercised sufficient penetration in dealing with it. If we are left with a total epistemological mystery on the question of how synthetic a priori propositions are possible, it might be wise to suppose it more likely that our analytic acumen is deficient than that an epistemological miracle has occurred. [19]

5. The Principle of Uniformity of Nature. A substantial part of Hume's critique of induction rested upon his attack on the principle of the uniformity of nature. He argued definitively that the customary forms of inductive inference cannot be expected to yield correct predictions if nature fails to be uniform—if the future is not like the past—if like sensible qualities are not accompanied by like results.

> All inferences from experience suppose, as their foundation, that the future will resemble the past, and that similar powers will be conjoined with similar sensible qualities. If there be any suspicion that the course of nature may change, and that the past may be no rule for the future, all experience becomes useless, and can give rise to no inference or conclusion.*

He argued, moreover, that there is no logical contradiction in the supposition that nature is not uniform—that the regularities we have observed up to the present will fail in wholesale fashion in the future. . . . He argues, in addition, that the principle of uniformity of nature cannot be established by an inference from experience: "It is impossible, therefore, that any arguments from experience can prove this resemblance of the past to the future; since all these arguments are founded on the supposition of that resemblance."‡ [20] Throughout Hume's discussion there is, however, a strong suggestion that we might have full confidence in the customary inductive methods if nature were known to be uniform.

*David Hume, *Human Understanding* [p. 290].

‡Ibid. [p. 290].

Here Salmon does not get the issue quite right: A rationalist proponent of synthetic a priori knowledge does think that some *logically* contingent or consistent claims—that is claims that are not necessary solely by virtue of their form—can be known to be true a priori. But he does not think that such claims are really contingent or consistent, but instead that they are necessary, even if not *formally* necessary. (See the Ewing selection, especially Annotation 1 and the corresponding text.) Thus a synthetic a priori claim is supposed to be true in every possible world and so would not tell us something "about our world in contradistinction to other possible worlds."

The "*ex nihilo* principle" is the principle that something cannot come from nothing, and the principle of sufficient reason is the claim that everything that exists must have a cause or explanation. Both of these "principles" are often appealed to in discussions of the cosmological argument (see Chapter 7).

See Ewing for a discussion of the issue of whether arithmetical propositions such as 5 + 7 = 12 are analytic or synthetic.

This is probably Salmon's strongest argument against the existence of synthetic a priori claims. But it depends on the claim that the idea of analyticity can explain all *clear* cases of a priori justification and knowledge with no such mystery. (See Discussion Questions 2 and 3.)

To be plausible, as we have already seen, the claim would have to be that the future resembles the past to a substantial degree, not that it does so perfectly in the sense that all observed regularities also obtain in the future—since we know that this isn't true.

Kant attempted to deal with the problem of induction in just this way, by establishing a principle of uniformity of nature, in the form of the principle of universal causation, as a synthetic a priori truth. Kant claimed, in other words, that every occurrence is governed by causal regularities, and this general characteristic of the universe can be established by pure reason, without the aid of any empirical evidence. He did not try to show that the principle of universal causation is a principle of logic, for to do so would have been to show that it was analytic—not synthetic—and thus lacking in factual content. He did not reject Hume's claim that there is no logical contradiction in the statement that nature is not uniform; he did not try to prove his principle of universal causation by deducing a contradiction from its denial. He did believe, however, that this principle, while not a proposition of pure logic, is necessarily true nevertheless. (21) Hume, of course, argued against this alternative as well. He maintained not only that the uniformity of nature is not a logical or analytic truth, but also that it cannot be any other kind of a priori truth either. Even before Kant had enunciated the doctrine of synthetic a priori principles, Hume had offered strong arguments against them:

21

Kant's claim is roughly that the mind orders experience so as to make the causal principle true within the realm of experience, though not necessarily true of things as they exist in themselves outside of experience.

> I shall venture to affirm, as a general proposition, which admits of no exception, that the knowledge of this relation [of cause and effect] is not, in any instance, attained by reasonings a priori.*
>
> Adam, though his rational faculties be supposed, at the very first, entirely perfect, could not have inferred from the fluidity and transparency of water that it would suffocate him, or from the light and warmth of fire that it would consume him.†
>
> . . .
>
> Now whatever is intelligible, and can be distinctly conceived . . . can never be proved false by any . . . abstract reasoning a priori.§

Hume argues, by persuasive example and general principle, that nothing about the causal structure of reality can be established by pure reason. He poses an incisive challenge to those who would claim the ability to establish a priori knowledge of a particular causal relation or of the principle of universal causation. In the foregoing discussion of synthetic a priori statements, I have given reasons for believing that Kant failed to overcome Hume's previous objections.

. . .

7. A Probabilistic Approach. It may seem strange in the extreme that this discussion of the problem of induction has proceeded at such great length without seriously bringing in the concept of probability. It is very tempting to react immediately to Hume's argument with the admission that we do not have *knowledge* of the unobserved. Scientific results are not established with absolute certainty. At best we can make probabilistic statements about unobserved matters of fact, and at best we can claim that scientific generalizations and theories are highly confirmed. We who live in an age of scientific empiricism can accept with perfect equanimity the fact that the quest for certainty is futile; indeed, our thanks go to Hume for helping to destroy false hopes for certainty in science.

Hume's search for a justification of induction, it might be continued, was fundamentally misconceived. He tried to find a way of proving that inductive inferences with true premises would have *true* conclusions. He properly failed to find any such justification precisely because it is the function of *deduction* to prove the truth of conclusions, given true premises. Induction has a different function. An inductive inference with true premises establishes its conclusions as *probable.* No wonder Hume failed to find a justification of induction. He was trying to make induction into deduction, and he succeeded only in proving the platitude that induction is not deduction. If we want to justify induction, we must show that inductive inferences establish their conclusions as probable, not as true.

The foregoing sort of criticism of Hume's arguments is extremely appealing, and it has given rise to the most popular sort of attempt, currently, to deal with the problem. In order to examine this approach, we must consider, at

*Ibid. [p. 286].
†Ibid. [p. 286].
§Ibid. [pp. 288–89].

least superficially, the meaning of the concept of probability. Two basic meanings must be taken into account at present.

One leading probability concept identifies probability with frequency—roughly, the probable is that which happens often, and the improbable is that which happens seldom. Let us see what becomes of Hume's argument under this interpretation of probability. If we were to claim that inductive conclusions are probable in this sense, we would be claiming that inductive inferences with true premises often have true conclusions, although not always. Hume's argument shows, unhappily, that this claim cannot be substantiated. It was recognized long before Hume that inductive inferences cannot be expected always to lead to the truth. Hume's argument shows, not only that we cannot justify the claim that *every* inductive inference with true premises will have a true conclusion, but also, that we cannot justify the claim that *any* inductive inference with true premises will have a true conclusion. Hume's argument shows that, for all we can know, every inductive inference made from now on might have a false conclusion despite true premises. Thus, Hume has proved, we can show neither that inductive inferences establish their conclusions as true nor that they establish their conclusions as probable in the frequency sense. [22] The introduction of the frequency concept of probability gives no help whatever in circumventing the problem of induction, but this is no surprise, for we should not have expected it to be suitable for this purpose.

A more promising probability concept identifies probability with degree of rational belief. To say that a statement is probable in this sense means that one would be rationally justified in believing it; the degree of probability is the degree of assent a person would be rationally justified in giving. We are not, of course, referring to the degree to which anyone *actually* believes in the statement, but rather to the degree to which one could *rationally* believe it. . . . To say that a statement is probable in this sense means that it is supported by evidence. But, so the argument goes, if a statement is the conclusion of an inductive inference with true premises, it is supported by evidence—by inductive evidence—this is part of what it *means* to be supported by evidence. The very concept of evidence depends upon the nature of induction, and it becomes incoherent if we try to divorce the two. Trivially, then, the conclusion of an inductive inference is probable under this concept of probability. To ask, with Hume, if we should accept inductive conclusions is tantamount to asking if we should fashion our beliefs in terms of the evidence, and this, in turn, is tantamount to asking whether we should be rational. In this way we arrive at an "ordinary language dissolution" of the problem of induction. Once we understand clearly the meanings of such key terms as "rational," "probable," and "evidence," we see that the problem arose out of linguistic confusion and evaporates into the question of whether it is rational to be rational. Such tautological questions, if meaningful at all, demand affirmative answers. [23]

Unfortunately, the dissolution is not satisfactory. . . . The fundamental difficulty arises from the fact that the very notion of inductive evidence is determined by the rules of inductive inference. If a conclusion is to be supported by inductive evidence, it must be the conclusion of a correct inductive inference with true premises. Whether the inductive inference is correct depends upon whether the rule governing that inference is correct. . . . In order to be able to say whether a given statement is supported by inductive evidence we must be able to say which inductive rules are correct.

For example, suppose that a die has been thrown a large number of times, and we have observed that the side two came up in one sixth of the tosses. This is our "evidence" e. Let h be the conclusion that, "in the long run," side two will come up one sixth of the times. Consider the following three rules:

1. (Induction by enumeration) Given m/n of observed A are B, to infer that the "long run" relative frequency of B among A is m/n.
2. (A priori rule) Regardless of observed frequencies, to infer that the "long run" relative frequency of B among A is $1/k$, where k is the number of possible outcomes—six in the case of the die.
3. (Counterinductive rule) Given m/n of observed A are B, to infer that the "long run" relative frequency of B among A is $(n - m)/n$. [24]

The proof is just the dilemma argument (see Annotations 9, 10, and 11 to the Hume selection and the corresponding text). Think carefully about how that argument would apply to the probabilistic claim.

R The claim is that reasoning inductively is just what we mean by "rational" in this sort of case, so that inductive reasoning is guaranteed to be rational.

Here the first rule is just the standard conception of inductive reasoning, generalized slightly to cover also cases where some fraction of observed A's are B's (in the case where all observed A's are B's, *m* and *n* are the same number). The second rule is the so-called "principle of indifference"—which might be badly wrong if the dice are "loaded." The third rule is the intuitively bizarre rule which says that the truth is just the opposite of what the evidence so far seems to show.

R Thus if reasoning inductively just means whatever way of reasoning is rational in this sort of case, it will not be automatically true that this is following the first rule rather than one of the others or some further rule—so some further defense will be needed, which is just the problem of induction all over again. Whereas if reasoning inductively means following the first rule, then it cannot just be assumed that this is the rational way to proceed (where "rational" means roughly that a method will probably lead to true or reliable results).

. . . In order to say which conclusions are supported by what evidence, it is necessary to arrive at a decision as to what inductive rules are acceptable. If Rule 1 is correct, the evidence *e* supports the conclusion *h*. If Rule 2 is correct, we are justified in drawing the conclusion *h,* but this is entirely independent of the observational evidence *e;* the same conclusions would have been sanctioned by Rule 2 regardless of observational evidence. If Rule 3 is correct, we are not only prohibited from drawing the conclusion *h,* but also we are permitted to draw a conclusion *h*9 which is logically incompatible with *h.* Whether a given conclusion is *supported* by *evidence*—whether it would be *rational to believe* it on the basis of given evidence—whether it is *made probable* by virtue of its relation to given evidence—depends upon selection of the correct rule or rules from among the infinitely many rules we might conceivably adopt.

The problem of induction can now be reformulated as a problem about evidence. What rules ought we to adopt to determine the nature of inductive evidence? . . . If we take the customary inductive rules to define the concept of inductive evidence, have we adopted a proper concept of evidence? Would the adoption of some alternative inductive rules provide a more suitable concept of evidence? These are genuine questions which need to be answered.

We find, moreover, that what appeared earlier as a pointless question now becomes significant and difficult. If we take the customary rules of inductive inference to provide a suitable definition of the relation of inductive evidential support, it makes considerable sense to ask whether it is rational to believe on the basis of evidence as thus defined rather than to believe on the basis of evidence as defined according to other rules. . . .

There is danger of being taken in by an easy equivocation. One meaning we may assign to the concept of inductive evidence is, roughly, the basis on which we ought to fashion our beliefs. Another meaning results from the relation of evidential support determined by whatever rule of inductive inference we adopt. It is only by supposing that these two concepts are the same that we suppose the problem of induction to have vanished. The problem of induction is still there; it is the problem of providing adequate grounds for the selection of inductive rules. We want the relation of evidential support determined by these rules to yield a concept of inductive evidence which is, in fact, the basis on which we ought to fashion our beliefs. 25

. . .

8. Pragmatic Justification. Of all the solutions and dissolutions proposed to deal with Hume's problem of induction, Hans Reichenbach's attempt to provide a pragmatic justification seems to me the most fruitful and promising.* This approach accepts Hume's arguments up to the point of agreeing that it is impossible to establish, either deductively or inductively, that any inductive inferences will ever again have true conclusions. Nevertheless, Reichenbach claims, the standard method of inductive generalization can be justified. Although its *success* as a method of prediction cannot be established in advance, it can be shown to be superior to any alternative method of prediction.

The argument can be put rather simply. Nature may be sufficiently uniform in suitable respects for us to make successful inductive inferences from the observed to the unobserved. On the other hand, for all we know, she may not. Hume has shown that we cannot prove in advance which case holds. All we can say is that nature may or may not be uniform—if she is, induction works; if she is not, induction fails. Even in the face of our ignorance about the uniformity of nature, we can ask what would happen if we adopted some radically different method of inference. Consider, for instance, the method of the crystal gazer. Since we do not know whether nature is uniform or not, we must consider both possibilities. If nature is uniform, the method of crystal gazing might work successfully, or it might fail. We cannot prove a priori that it will not work. At the same time, we cannot prove a priori that it will work, even if nature exhibits a high degree of uniformity. Thus, in case nature is reasonably

*Hans Reichenbach, *Experience and Prediction* (Chicago: U. of Chicago Press, 1938), Chap. 5, and *The Theory of Probability* (Berkeley: U. of California Press, 1949), Chap. 11.

uniform, the standard inductive method *must* work while the alternative method of crystal gazing *may or may not* work. In this case, the superiority of the standard inductive method is evident. Now, suppose nature lacks uniformity to such a degree that the standard inductive method is a complete failure. In this case, Reichenbach argues, the alternative method must likewise fail. Suppose it did not fail—suppose, for instance, that the method of crystal gazing worked consistently. This would constitute an important relevant uniformity that could be exploited inductively. If a crystal gazer had consistently predicted future occurrences, we could infer inductively that he has a method of prediction that will enjoy continued success. The inductive method would, in this way, share the success of the method of crystal gazing, and would therefore be, contrary to hypothesis, successful. Hence, Reichenbach concludes, the standard inductive method will be successful *if any other method could succeed.* As a result, we have everything to gain and nothing to lose by adopting the inductive method. If any method works, induction works. If we adopt the inductive method and it fails, we have lost nothing, for any other method we might have adopted would likewise have failed. Reichenbach does not claim to prove that nature is uniform, or that the standard inductive method will be successful. He does not postulate the uniformity of nature. He tries to show that the inductive method is the best method for ampliative inference, whether it turns out to be successful or not. [26]

This ingenious argument, although extremely suggestive, is ultimately unsatisfactory. As I have just presented it, it is impossibly vague. I have not specified the nature of the standard inductive method. I have not stated with any exactness what constitutes success for the inductive method or any other. Moreover, the uniformity of nature is not an all-or-none affair. Nature appears to be uniform to some extent and also to be lacking in uniformity to some degree. . . . The vagueness of the foregoing argument is not, however, its fundamental drawback. It can be made precise. . . . When it is made precise, as we shall see, it suffers the serious defect of equally justifying too wide a variety of rules for ampliative inference. [27]

I have presented Reichenbach's argument rather loosely in order to make intuitively clear its basic strategy. The sense in which it is a pragmatic justification should be clear. Unlike many authors who have sought a justification of induction, Reichenbach does not try to prove the truth of any synthetic proposition. He recognizes that the problem concerns the justification of a rule, and rules are neither true nor false. Hence, he tries to show that the adoption of a standard inductive rule is practically useful in the attempt to learn about and deal with the unobserved. He maintains that this can be shown even though we cannot prove the truth of the assertion that inductive methods will lead to predictive success. This pragmatic aspect is, it seems to me, the source of the fertility of Reichenbach's approach. Even though his argument does not constitute an adequate justification of induction, it seems to me to provide a valid core from which we may attempt to develop a more satisfactory justification.

. . .

R Reichenbach's claim is not that reasoning inductively will even *probably* lead to true conclusions, but only that it will do so if any method can succeed in this way.

This is some justification, but is it enough to really solve the problem? (See Discussion Question 1.)

Reichenbach's basic claim is that the method of generalizing from experience ("positing" that the proportion of all A's that are B's is the same as the currently observed proportion and then correcting that posit as new observations come in) is guaranteed to succeed in the long run if success is possible, that is, if there is an objective regularity to be found. The problem Salmon is indicating is that there are many other methods that can be justified in the same way. (See Discussion Question 3.)

Discussion Questions

1. If Hume's skepticism about induction is correct, then we have no reason at all to think that any conclusion that depends on inductive reasoning is true. How implausible a result is this from the standpoint of common sense? Notice in thinking about this that at least most of the results of theoretical science are arrived at as the best explanations of inductively established observational regularities. Notice also that evidence for historical claims also depends on inductively established regularities pertaining to various sorts of evidence. (How much would it help to be told that although we have no good reason for thinking that inductive conclusions are true, the inductive method is still guaranteed to succeed in finding the truth if success is possible, which is what Reichenbach's pragmatic justification—see Discussion Question 3—amounts to?)

2. Are all plausible a priori justifiable claims analytic in Salmon's sense? Consider, for example, the claim that nothing can be red all over and green all over at the same time. Is this something that can be justified a priori? It is not a logical truth as it stands (since many claims of the form "nothing can be F all over and G all over at the same time" are false—think about this). Can it be made into a logical truth by giving definitions of one or more of its terms, presumably "red" and/or "green"? (Remember that to be acceptable, a definition must actually capture the meaning of the term.)

3. Think about the rationale for Reichenbach's pragmatic justification of induction. Can you see why the method described in Annotation 27 is guaranteed to eventually find an objective regularity in nature if one actually exists? Why is such success only guaranteed in the long run? Can you think of another method that is equally guaranteed to succeed in the long run, but that gives a significantly different answer in the short run (think here of cases where the observed proportion of A's that are B's is some fraction rather than all—see Annotation 24 and the associated text). Hint: what you want is a rule that deviates from the observed proportion but where the deviation gets smaller and smaller as the number of cases gets larger, so that in the long run—but not in the short run, which is where the method is always actually applied—the result arrived at will be the same as that of the inductive method. A further issue: how long a run is necessary for the inductive method to be guaranteed to succeed if success is possible?

A. C. Ewing

Alfred Cyril Ewing (1899–1973) was a British philosopher who taught at Cambridge University and made important contributions to ethics and metaphysics. In this selection, he defends a rationalist view of a priori justification, according to which the human mind has a fundamental capacity for insight into necessary truths. Along the way, he replies to many popular arguments for moderate empiricism and also suggests an a priori solution to the problem of induction, though without really developing this idea very far.

The "A Priori" and the Empirical, from *The Fundamental Questions of Philosophy*

Meaning of the Distinction; "A Priori" Character of Mathematics

In the theory of knowledge, the first point that confronts us is the sharp distinction between two kinds of knowledge which have been called respectively a priori and empirical. Most of our knowledge we obtain by observation of the external world (sense-perception) and of ourselves (introspection). This is called empirical knowledge. But some knowledge we can obtain by simply thinking. That kind of knowledge is called a priori. Its chief exemplifications are to be found in logic and mathematics. In order to see that 5 + 7 = 12 we do not need to take five things and seven things, put them together, and then count the total number. We can know what the total number will be simply by thinking.

Another important difference between a priori and empirical knowledge is that in the case of the former we do not see merely that something, S, is in fact P, but that it must be P and why it is P. (1) I can discover that a flower is yellow (or at least produces sensations of yellow) by looking at it, but I cannot thereby see why it is yellow or that it must be yellow. For anything I can tell it might equally well have been a red flower. But with a truth such as that 5 + 7 = 12 I do not see merely that it is a fact but that it must be a fact. It would be quite absurd to suppose that 5 + 7 might have been equal to 11 and just happened to be equal to 12, and I can see that the nature of 5 and 7 constitutes a fully adequate and intelligible reason why their sum should be 12 and not some other number. It is indeed conceivable that some of the things which make the two groups of 5 and 7 might, when they were put together,

(1) R This is an important claim about the apparent character of a priori insight: it seems to reveal not only that the claim in question is true, but also that the claim is *necessary* (in the logical or metaphysical sense) and *why* the claim is true.

From *The Fundamental Questions of Philosophy* (New York: Collier, 1962). Some footnotes have been omitted.

fuse like drops of water, or even vanish, so that there were no longer 12 things; but what is inconceivable is that there could *at the same time* be 5 + 7 things of a certain kind at once in a certain place and yet less than 12 things of that kind in that place. Before some of the things fused or vanished they would be 5 + 7 in number and also 12 in number, and after the fusion or disappearance they would be neither 5 + 7 nor 12. When I say in this connection that something is inconceivable, I do not mean merely or primarily that we cannot conceive it—this is not a case of a mere psychological inability like the inability to understand higher mathematics. It is a positive insight: we definitely see it to be impossible that certain things could happen. This we do not see in the case of empirical propositions which are false: they are not true but might for anything we know have been true. It is even conceivable, so far as we can see, that the fundamental laws of motion might have been quite different from what they are, but we can see that there could not have been a world which contradicted the laws of arithmetic. This is expressed by saying that empirical propositions are *contingent,* but true a priori propositions *necessary.* 2 . . .

We must not be misled here by the fact that in order to come to understand arithmetic we originally required examples. Once we have learnt the beginnings of arithmetic in the kindergarten with the help of examples, we do not need examples any more to grasp it, and we can see the truth of many arithmetical propositions, e.g. that 3112 + 2467 = 5579, of which we have never had examples. We have probably never taken 3112 things and 2467 things, put them together and counted the resulting set, but we still know that this is what the result of the counting would be. If it were empirical knowledge, we could not know it without counting. The examples are needed, not to prove anything, but only in order to enable us to come to understand in the first instance what is meant by number.

. . .

The "A Priori" in Logic

Another important field for a priori knowledge is logic. The laws of logic must be known a priori or not at all. They certainly are not a matter for empirical observation, and the function of logical argument is just to give us conclusions which we have not discovered by observation. The argument would be superfluous if we had observed them already. We are able to make inferences because there is sometimes a logical connection between one or more propositions (the premise or premises) and another proposition, the conclusion, such that the latter must be true if the former is. Then, if we know the former, we can assert the latter on the strength of it, thus anticipating any experience. To take an example, there is a story that Mr. X., a man of high reputation and great social standing, had been asked to preside at a big social function. He was late in coming, and so a Roman Catholic priest was asked to make a speech to pass the time till his arrival. The priest told various anecdotes, including one which recorded his embarrassment when as confessor he had to deal with his first penitent and the latter confessed to a particularly atrocious murder. Shortly afterwards Mr. X. arrived, and in his own speech he said: "I see Father _____ is here. Now, though he may not recognize me, he is an old friend of mine, in fact I was his first penitent." It is plain that such an episode would enable one to infer that Mr. X. had committed a murder without having observed the crime. 3 . . .

Other Cases of the "A Priori"

A priori knowledge, while most prominent in mathematics and logic, is not limited to these subjects. For instance, we can see a priori that the same surface cannot have two different colours all over at the same time, or that a thought cannot have a shape. Philosophers have been divided into rationalists and empiricists according to whether they stressed the a priori or the empirical element more. The possibility of metaphysics depends on a priori knowledge, for our experience is quite inadequate to enable us to make on merely empirical grounds any sweeping generalizations of the kind the metaphysician desires. The term a priori covers both self-evident propositions, i.e. those which are seen to be true in their own right, and those which are derived by inference from propositions themselves self-evident.

2

Could a *contingent* claim, one that is false in some possible worlds, ever be known a priori to be true in the actual world? Ewing is denying that this could happen, but some recent philosophers have questioned this. The standard example (due to Saul Kripke) is "the standard meter stick (the platinum-iridium bar in Paris) is one meter long." Is this a counterexample to Ewing's claim?

3

The claim that Mr. X is a murderer *follows logically* from the two premises indicated. Is it *contained* in them in any sense that would help to explain *why* it follows logically? (In Salmon's terms, is this an ampliative or a non-ampliative inference?)

The Linguistic Theory of the "A Priori" and the Denial That "A Priori" Propositions or Inferences Can Give New Knowledge

At the present time even empiricist philosophers recognize the impossibility of explaining away a priori propositions as merely empirical generalizations, but they are inclined to the view that a priori propositions and a priori reasoning are merely concerned with language, and so cannot tell us anything new about the real world. Thus it is said that, when we make an inference, the conclusion is just part of the premises expressed in different language. (4) If so, inference would be of use merely for clarifying our language and would involve no real advance in knowledge. Some inferences are of this type, e.g. A is a father, therefore A is male. But are they all? That would be hard indeed to square with the *prima facie* novelty of many conclusions. Take, for instance, the proposition that the square on the hypotenuse of a right-angled triangle is equal to the sum of the squares on the other two sides. Such a proposition can be inferred from the axioms and postulates of Euclid, but it certainly does not seem to be included in their meaning. Otherwise we should know it as soon as we understood the axioms and postulates. The example I gave of the murder discovered by a logical argument seems to be another case of a fact not known at all beforehand by the reasoner which is discovered by his reasoning. Extreme empiricist philosophers contend that this appearance of novelty is really illusory, and that in some sense we knew the conclusion all along; but they have never succeeded in making clear in what sense we did so. It is not enough to say that the conclusion is implicit in the premises. "Implicit" means "implied by," and of course a conclusion is implied by its premises, if the inference is correct at all. But this admission leaves quite open the question whether or not a proposition can follow from a different one which does not contain it as part of itself; and since we obviously can by deductive inference come to know things which we did not know before in any ordinary sense of "know," we must treat the empiricist's claim as unjustified till he has produced a clearly defined sense of "implicit in" or "contained in" which leaves room for that novelty in inference which we all cannot help really admitting. In any ordinary sense of "know" the conclusion is not in the cases I have mentioned known prior to the inference, and since the premises are and indeed must be known before we know the conclusion, it is therefore in no ordinary sense of "part" part of the premises. (5)

That is, as Salmon puts it, all such inferences are non-ampliative.

R If the claim of containment just means that the conclusion follows from the premises, then it cannot explain why this is so (or how we are able to see that it is).

...

Nevertheless, the view that inference cannot yield new conclusions dies hard, and so it will not be superfluous to bring further arguments. (1) "This has shape" admittedly follows logically from "this has size" and vice versa. If the view I am criticizing were true, "this has size" would, therefore, have to include in its meaning "this has shape," and "this has shape" would also have to include in its meaning "this has size." But this would only be possible if the two sentences meant exactly the same thing, which they obviously do not. (6) (2) Take an argument such as—Montreal is to the north of New York, New York is to the north of Washington, therefore Montreal is to the north of Washington. If the view I am discussing is true, the conclusion is part of the premises. But it is not part of either premise by itself, otherwise both premises would not be needed. So the only way in which it could be part of both together would be if it were divisible into two propositions one of which was part of the first and the other part of the second. I defy anybody to divide it in this way. (3) The proposition "Socrates was a philosopher" certainly entails the proposition "if Socrates had measles some philosophers have had measles," but it cannot be that the second proposition is included in the first. For the first proposition certainly does not include the notion of measles.

An analogy: if the membership of group A is contained in that of group B, and vice versa, then the two groups must have exactly the same membership. Thus if all the elements included in the meaning of one claim are included in that of the other and vice versa, the total set of elements must be exactly the same.

What is really the same view is often expressed by saying that all a priori propositions are "analytic." A distinction has commonly been drawn between *analytic* propositions, in which the predicate is in the notion of the subject already formed before the proposition is asserted, so that the proposition gives no new information, and *synthetic* propositions in which the predicate is not so contained and which are thus capable of giving new information. Analytic propositions are essentially verbal, being all true by definition, e.g. all fathers are male. As an example of a synthetic proposition we could take any proposition established by experience such as "I am cold" or

"It is snowing," but empiricists often assert that there are no synthetic a priori propositions. That this view cannot be justified may be shown at once. The proposition that there are no synthetic a priori propositions, since it cannot be established by empirical observations, would be, if justified, itself a synthetic a priori proposition, and we cannot affirm it as a synthetic a priori proposition that there are no synthetic a priori propositions. [7] We may therefore dismiss offhand any arguments for the theory. Such arguments, whatever they were, would have to involve synthetic a priori propositions. . . .

The analytic view seems plausible when we are concerned with the simplest propositions of logic and arithmetic, but we must not assume that a proposition is analytic because it is obvious. Though it may be very difficult to determine precisely where analytic propositions end and synthetic propositions begin, we cannot use this as a ground for denying the latter. It is very difficult to say precisely where blue ends and green begins, since the different shades run into each other imperceptibly, but we cannot therefore argue that all blue is really green. Taking arithmetic, even if there is a good deal of plausibility in saying that 2 + 2 is included in the meaning of "4," there is none in saying 95 – 91 or > 216 > ÷ 2 – (> 287 + 25) > ÷ 3 are so included. [8] Yet, if the analytic view were true, all the infinite numerical combinations which could be seen a priori to be equal to 4 would have to be included in the meaning of "4."

. . .

People have been inclined to deny synthetic a priori propositions because they could not see how one characteristic could necessarily involve another, but that this could not happen would be itself a synthetic a priori metaphysical proposition. People have also thought that it was necessary to give some sort of explanation of a priori knowledge, and could not see how this could be done except in terms of language. To this I should reply that there is no reason to suppose that a priori knowledge requires some special explanation any more than does our ability to attain knowledge empirically by observation. Why not take it as an ultimate fact? Human beings certainly cannot explain everything, whether there is ultimately an explanation for it or not.

. . .

Induction

The chief use of a priori knowledge is to enable us to make inferences. Whenever we can make an inference from p to q, we must know, or at least be justified in believing, the hypothetical "if p, then q." For q to follow necessarily from p that hypothetical proposition must be a priori; necessary connection is not a matter of empirical observation. An important distinction is, however, drawn between deduction and induction. . . . Induction in all its more characteristic forms is a matter of empirical generalization, i.e. we argue that, because something has proved true in a number of observed cases, it will be likely to prove true in similar cases that have not yet been observed. The conclusion is not (except in very special cases) certain, but it may be highly probable, and all our rational predictions about the future depend on an inference of this kind. Induction has presented very serious problems to logicians and philosophers generally. The inference in induction is certainly not a merely empirical matter: we use it to enable us to forecast the future, but we have not observed the future empirically. The whole use of induction is indeed to enable us to infer what we have never observed. Therefore some a priori principle about the world is required if induction is to be justified. [9] The principle must be of such a nature as to justify us in supposing that what has happened in observed cases is likely to recur in unobserved ones; but logicians have certainly not hit upon a principle which is both self-evident and adequate to justify inductive inference. The one which has been most commonly put forward as supplying what is needed is the principle that every change has a cause, but it would be much disputed nowadays whether this was either necessary or sufficient to justify induction. The meaning of "cause" itself is also very much a subject on which there are varying views. So the justification of induction is one of the worst problems of logic. The fact that we must use induction if we are to have any science at all is a proof that science cannot be merely empirical (even where it does not use mathematics), but we cannot say that the conclusion of an inductive inference follows from its premises with the same necessity as does the conclusion of a deductive one.

This is a tricky point. To think about it clearly, you need to restate the claim in question to make it explicitly of subject-predicate form. (See Discussion Question 1.)

Notice also that it would also have to be claimed that the meaning of each of these more complicated expressions is included in that of the other—and hence that they also have the same meaning.

There is an implicit argument here: if an inductive argument provides a good reason or justification for thinking that its conclusion is true, then, since the transition from the inductive evidence to the conclusion cannot be justified on empirical or experiential grounds (since we have not observed the future), this justification must be a priori. Salmon would deny this conclusion, but can he do so without conceding that the conclusion of an inductive argument isn't really justified after all?

Most of the propositions we call empirical are not justified by mere observation but by that together with induction. This applies to all conclusions of science, for these are never statements of single observed facts but generalizations about what usually happens or inferences from such generalizations. It applies also to all our ordinary judgments about physical objects, for we always read in more than is actually observed and the only justification for what we read in must be found in induction (i.e. we assume that objects will have besides the characteristics we actually observe at the time those characteristics which we observed in the past in similar objects, e.g. that the ice we see is cold though we are not feeling the cold). This does not mean that, whenever we observe, we are consciously making inferences. But we can speak of "implicit inferences," meaning that without making conscious inferences we hold beliefs on the strength of experiences which could be used as premises to justify the beliefs by explicit inferences.

Intuition

A necessary, though not always recognized, presupposition of inference is intuition. To argue validly—A ∴ B ∴ C—we must see a connection between A and B and a connection between B and C.(10) But how do we know that that connection itself holds? We may be able to interpolate further terms, D and E, and say A, ∴ D, ∴ B, ∴ E, ∴ C; but we obviously cannot go on in this way *ad infinitum.* Sooner or later we must come to a point where we just see immediately that there is a connection, but cannot *prove* this to be so. When we see immediately something to be true otherwise than by observing it empirically, we are said to have an *intuition.*(11) No doubt apparent intuitions are often to be explained as really implicit or suppressed inferences, but the argument I have just given shows that this cannot be so with all cases of intuition. Even when we have made explicit all the omitted steps, the logical point remains that for it to be possible to infer any one proposition from any other we must see the connection between them, and this connection cannot always be proved by interpolating fresh propositions, yet it must be known somehow. The connection may be said to be derived from the

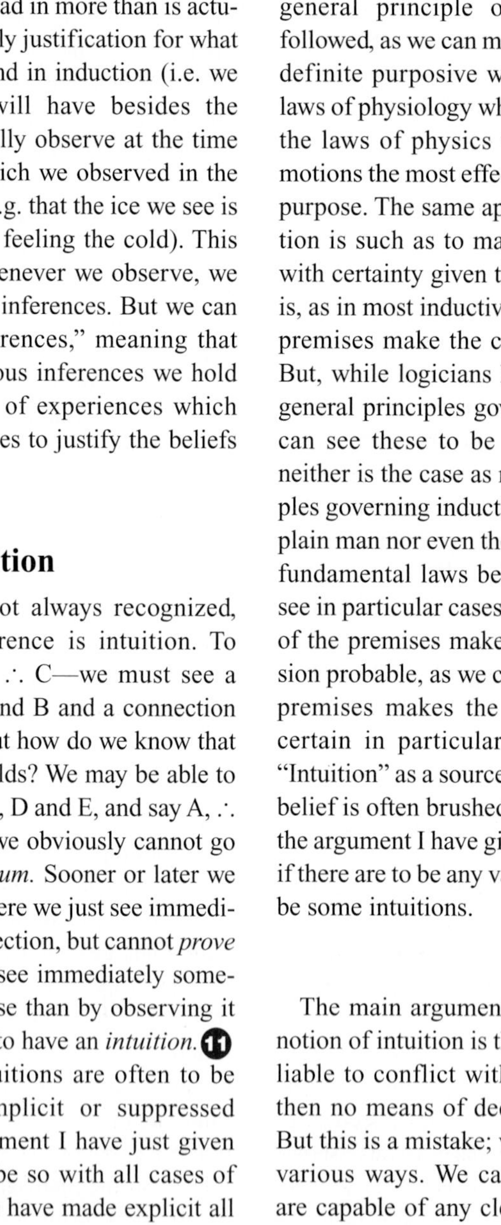

fundamental laws of logic, but the laws themselves are known intuitively. Further, before we can see their validity in the abstract, we must have seen their validity in particular cases. All of us have used syllogisms long before we knew anything about the rules of syllogistic inference. That was because we could see that a conclusion followed from its premises without knowing the general principle on account of which it followed, as we can move our arms effectively in definite purposive ways without knowing the laws of physiology which govern our motions or the laws of physics which make the selected motions the most effective ones for our practical purpose. The same applies whether the connection is such as to make the conclusion follow with certainty given the premises, or whether it is, as in most inductive arguments, such that the premises make the conclusion only probable. But, while logicians have easily agreed on the general principles governing deduction and we can see these to be completely self-evident, neither is the case as regards the general principles governing induction. Yet though neither the plain man nor even the logician is clear as to the fundamental laws behind the process, we can see in particular cases of induction that the truth of the premises makes the truth of the conclusion probable, as we can see that the truth of the premises makes the truth of the conclusion certain in particular cases of deduction.(12) "Intuition" as a source of knowledge or justified belief is often brushed aside with contempt, but the argument I have given at any rate shows that, if there are to be any valid inferences, there must be some intuitions.

...

The main argument of those who attack the notion of intuition is that apparent intuitions are liable to conflict with each other and there is then no means of deciding which is right.(13) But this is a mistake; we can in fact test them in various ways. We can consider whether they are capable of any clear and internally consistent statement. We can ask whether they fit into a coherent system with the rest of our well-established beliefs. We can also ask whether intuitions of the same kind have been confirmed in the past. We can ask whether an intuition stands or falls by itself or is a presupposition of a whole number of other beliefs which we

The symbol ∴ means "therefore."

What Ewing is describing here is a priori intuition, sometimes referred to as a priori insight. (This is not intuition in the sense of a hunch or premonition.) Empiricists typically deny that there is any such thing.

Ewing is saying that particular inductive arguments can be seen a priori to be rationally cogent, even if we cannot state a general principle in relation to which they are so. (See Discussion Question 3.)

This is one standard objection to a priori intuition.

cannot help holding, as some (though confused) intuition of the occurrence of causation or the uniformity of nature seems a necessary presupposition of all inductive beliefs. We can consider the plausibility of giving an alternative explanation of the intuitive belief. The result may then be negative or positive. It may be that our apparent intuition will evaporate when we think of the explanation, and then the latter is probably a correct one at least as to why *we* held the belief. Or it may be that the intuition will persist unshaken, in which case the explanation is probably at least inadequate. We can again consider whether the intuition repeats itself when considered in different contexts and different moods or with different examples.

So when two people have conflicting intuitions we need not suppose that there is just an irreducible difference of intuitive faculty between them and that there is nothing more to be done about it. Arguments may well be available which without strictly proving either side to be wrong put a disputant into a position in which he can see better for himself whether he is right or wrong or at least partially confirm or cast doubt on the truth of his view. In general, the clearer we have made ourselves about a subject by inferential thought, by analysing the different factors involved and by clearing up our terminology, the more likely are we to have correct intuitions on the matter if such are available at all. Again, intellectual confusions may be revealed which were responsible for the truth of the belief in question. Thus a person who really sees that A is B may confuse B with C and will then think he sees intuitively that A is C. Some such conflicts may be caused simply or mainly by ambiguities of terminology or the attaching of different meanings to some word. And of course we need not deny that differences of intuition may sometimes be due on one side or even on both to "wishful thinking" or to the kind of cause which it is the business of the psycho-analyst (or of a patient and tactful friend) to remove. . . . We cannot of course settle all disputes in these ways, but neither can we in practice settle all disputes in science. The most we can say is that they are soluble in principle, though we may not have the ability to hit on the right way of solving a particular dispute. Similarly, there is no reason to believe that conflicts between rival intuitions would not all be capable of a solution if these methods were applied aright and with good will on both sides, though in fact we cannot so apply them. (14)* . . .

R Ewing's response is that there are many ways to attempt to resolve the dispute between opposed intuitions, even though none of these is guaranteed to succeed. (Try to think how these would work in particular cases.)

Discussion Questions

1. How might the claim that there are no synthetic a priori truths—that is, that no synthetic proposition is capable of being justified a priori—be restated in the form "all A's are B's"? One attempt, albeit a bit clumsy, would be "all synthetic propositions are propositions incapable of being justified a priori." Is the predicate of this claim included in its subject in any clear or obvious way? Is there any way that its truth can be seen to follow from the definitions of the terms involved? Assume that "synthetic" is defined as "nonanalytic."
2. Is 5 + 7 = 12 knowable a priori? If so, is it analytic or synthetic (as Kant defines these concepts—see the Appendix to the introduction to this chapter)? Here it is important to get the issue into very clear focus: The issue is not merely whether the claim is one such that anyone who understands it can see it to be true. It is rather whether the *way* it is seen to be true is by analyzing the concept of 7 + 5 and finding 12 to be *contained* in it, in the way in which *unmarried* is contained in *bachelor*. Another way to put this question: is the denial of 7 + 5 = 12 a contradiction in the way that the claim that some bachelors are married is? It is false and indeed necessarily false, but is it contradictory in itself—without bringing in other mathematical principles or axioms? (This is a hard question.)
3. Is 18,697 + 23,849 = 42,546 analytic or synthetic? Clearly most people can understand the concept of *the sum of 18,697 and 23,849* without thereby knowing that it has the property of *being equal to 42,546*, in a way that they could not understand the concept of *bachelor* without thereby knowing that the property of *unmarried* is contained in it. Does this show that the claim is synthetic? Why or why not?
4. Consider the claim that nothing can be red all over and green all over at the same time. Is this claim knowable a priori? Is it analytic or synthetic? This claim is not clearly of subject-predicate form

*Similarly, the phrase "is contained in" is sometimes used just to mean "follows from" or "is implied by" and need not connote that the conclusion is actually part of the premises, as would be the case on the literal meaning of "contained."

as it stands, but here is a somewhat convoluted rewording that is of subject-predicate form and is parallel to "all bachelors are unmarried": all things that are red all over at a given time have the property of not being green all over at that same time. Is the predicate of this claim included in its subject—which amounts to asking whether not being green is included in red? (One relevant question here: could one understand the concept of red without yet having learned the concept of green?)

5. Think of an actual instance of inductive reasoning: a case in which there have been many observations of A's that are B's under varied conditions and circumstances and no observations of A's that are not B's, and in which it is inferred that all A's are B's. How plausible is it that we have an a priori intuition (or at least "ostensible intuition") that the conclusion of the argument is probably true—that the premises of the argument support the conclusion in a way analogous to that which occurs in a deductive argument?

Concluding Dialogue on the Problem of Induction

Here again we have a problem that many people have trouble taking very seriously—perhaps that's a feature of most epistemological issues. It again just seems so *obvious* that inductive reasoning is justified, that it does make its conclusions likely to be true, even if not guaranteed. Even Hume, who challenged whether that is really so, admitted that he couldn't help believing it as soon as he left his study and went out into the world.

But again, as you know, the problem is to explain *how* and *why* inductive reasoning is justified—why inductive arguments are genuinely cogent. I doubt whether anyone, in their heart of hearts, really doubts that they are. But that fact still doesn't constitute a solution to the philosophical problem.

So what are the possibilities here? Salmon favors Reichenbach's "pragmatic" solution (his number 8), while admitting that there are still serious problems about it that have yet to be solved. Ewing favors an a priori solution (Salmon's number 4)—but I can't help pointing out that a lot of people regard that as hopeless, a non-starter (which is pretty clearly Salmon's view). And then there is the "ordinary language" solution that Salmon explains and argues against (his number 7). These really seem to me to be the only significant candidates. Appeals to a Principle of Uniformity only make sense as versions of an a priori solution, which is the way that Salmon views them (his number 5).

I think that you're basically right about those being the main alternatives. But I suppose that we should at least mention the so-called "inductive justification of induction" (Salmon's number 1). This seems, as he argues, obviously circular or question begging, because it uses the very sort of argument whose justification is in question to try to show that arguments of that sort are justified. But people have now and then been tempted by this idea. I think that's because inductive reasoning really does seem intuitively cogent so that *any* argument that employs it seems cogent too—even the inductive defense of induction. But the thing to say, I think, is that even if such an argument really is in fact cogent—so that it really does in a way give a good reason for thinking that the conclusions of inductive arguments are likely to be true—offering this argument does nothing to *explain* why any inductive argument—*including that one*—is cogent. Thus it doesn't really speak to the main issue.

Right. What we want is a perspicuous account of why inductive reasoning is justified, not just an argument that presupposes—even if correctly—that it is. So what about Reichenbach's view? Salmon points to one problem: that the same sort of defense will work for lots of other rules for inferring from observed instances to general conclusions. This, as I understand it, is a fairly tricky technical point. The other rules in question are all pretty contrived ones that will yield a result very close to that yielded by the inductive rule in the long run—as the number of observed cases becomes very large (that's why they will also succeed if success is possible). But they can support results that will deviate quite widely from the standard inductive conclusion in the short run—with a smaller number of cases.

Yes, that's the basic idea. You just need a rule that "corrects" or "adjusts" the inductive conclusion in a way that will diminish to zero as the number of cases becomes very large, in the long run, but where the "correction" can still be very substantial in the short run. And the reason that this problem is really serious is that any actual use of induction will always be in the short run in relation to at least some of these rules, so that some alternative rule that is *equally* justified on Reichenbachian grounds could yield more or less any other conclusion you like about the proportion of A's that are B's.

That's pretty bad! But Reichenbach can still say—can't he?—that if we reason inductively we are following a rule that is guaranteed to succeed eventually in finding the true regularity in nature, if there is one to be found, even if only in the infinitely long run. Why isn't that still at least *some* justification for reasoning in that way, even if we don't quite know what to say about these other contrived rules (ones that no one really takes seriously anyway)?

Unfortunately, there is another problem lurking here that seems to me even more serious. Reichenbach says that induction will succeed in finding a regularity in nature *if* there is one there to be found. But he is in effect *admitting* that inductive evidence in any particular case, no matter how much of it there may be or how completely without exceptions it may be, still gives us no reason at all for thinking that there is in fact a regularity in nature. And this amounts to admitting that such evidence gives us *no reason at all* for thinking that the conclusion of the corresponding inductive argument, which of course asserts that there is such a regularity, is true. His view may still yield some sort of justification—induction is better than guessing at random, which isn't likely to succeed even if there is a regularity—but not the sort of justification that is needed for *knowledge:* a reason for thinking that the claim or belief in question is *true*.

It's really hard to believe that inductive conclusions, and all of the further scientific and technological claims that ultimately depend on them, have no more justification than that. What about the "ordinary language" justification? Is it maybe better than Salmon thinks?

Unfortunately, Salmon seems to be right about that one. It may be true that in ordinary contexts what we have mainly in mind—and in that sense intend to convey—by speaking of "good evidence" is inductive evidence. Certainly that's a plausible interpretation of what someone might intend by asking whether there is good evidence for, say, the view that taking vitamin C will prevent colds or similar sorts of claims. But what we really *ultimately* mean, in the strictest sense, by "good evidence" is precisely evidence that *genuinely* shows that the claim in question is likely to be true, and the fact that we ordinarily believe and even take for granted that inductive evidence does this doesn't establish that it really does.

I see. If "good evidence" is just whatever common sense regards as good, then inductive evidence surely qualifies. But if we take "good evidence" to mean evidence that really *is* good in the sense of genuinely showing that the conclusions it is taken to support are true, then what common sense thinks is irrelevant—or at least there is just the same problem all over again of trying to say why common sense is correct in thinking what it thinks.

Yes. The "ordinary language" solution is really just a disguised appeal to common sense, and thus (like all such appeals) fails to really address the underlying *philosophical* issue. Here, as elsewhere, common sense may of course be right, but we want to understand *why* it's right—and, of course, the answer can't be that it is right because it agrees with common sense, that is, with itself.

So if all of this so far is correct, we seem to be left with only the a priori solution as a possibility. I know that you are sympathetic with that view, but I need a better explanation of how and why it is supposed to work. Certainly Ewing's discussion of it doesn't get us very far. If we can't articulate any sort of general principle, then just saying that inductive inferences are justified according to a priori "intuition" seems like nothing more than saying that we are sure that they are *somehow* justified and that we don't see how the justification can be anything but a priori, but that we really have no idea of how it actually goes. Surely that doesn't help very much with the problem!

I have to agree that Ewing's account of the a priori solution isn't very illuminating in that regard. But I think that he is still making a very important point. Suppose that we agree (as we must) that the empirical evidence collected in the inductive premise doesn't in and of itself contain the more general conclusion—that is, that the conclusion genuinely goes beyond the evidence (so that the inference is, as Salmon says, "ampliative"). Suppose also that we think that inductive inferences really do establish that their conclusions are likely to be true—and we do all think that, after all. Then the *hypothetical* claim that says that *if* the premise of such an argument is true, *then* the conclusion is likely to be true must itself be justified somehow. And to say that it isn't justified empirically (because the empirical evidence establishes only the "if" part) seems to leave *only* a priori justification as a possibility. That is a significant result because so many (like Salmon) have wanted to reject it, while still seeming to say that induction is nonetheless justified. If Ewing is right, that simply isn't a tenable position.

But even if you and Ewing are right about that (and I admit that I can't see any way around it), it still doesn't take us very far. Aren't a priori truths supposed to be rationally self-evident or something like that? And if there is a general self-evident truth here, shouldn't we be able to say what it is? Ewing's appeal to the intuitive cogency of individual arguments just isn't satisfactory—he can't be saying that they are each justified a priori in a way that is independent of all the others, which would be the only way to avoid the demand for a general principle or at least some sort of general rationale.

I agree that if the a priori solution is right, then there must be a general principle or rationale to be found. The place to look, I think (though we can't go very far into this here), is the *repeated* regularity that is involved in inductive evidence—something that Hume at one point claims to have no rational relevance at all. The question to ask, and I think it's an obvious one, is *why* this general pattern of evidence persists: what the best *explanation* for this persistence is. The underlying rationale for inductive reasoning might be then that, in general and in the absence of specific reasons to the contrary, the best explanation of such a pattern of evidence is that it corresponds to and is produced by an objective regularity in nature—which would then mean that the inductive conclusion is true.

That's a little too fast. I can agree that if the pattern of evidence is quite extensive, then it is very unlikely to be due to chance—which is to say that *some* explanation is needed. But why should we think that the objective regularity explanation is the best one, where that means the one that is most likely to be true?

I agree that a lot more elaboration is needed. That would be a long story, and we really don't have time for it here. But the way to think about it is to try to think of *other* possible explanations for a persisting pattern of evidence of this sort and then try to find reasons why they are less likely—or maybe more likely—than the objective regularity explanation. Have a good time with that!

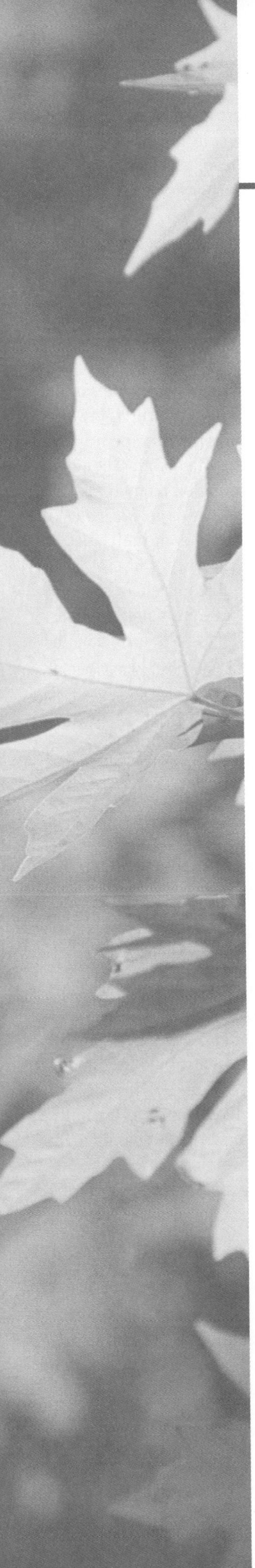

CHAPTER 3

Minds and Bodies

The reading selections in this chapter fall into the general area of philosophy known as the philosophy of mind, focusing on the central problem in that area: the mind-body problem—an issue that the German philosopher Arthur Schopenhauer described, because of its combination of centrality and difficulty, as "the world knot." Philosophers attempt to untie this knot by making clear the nature of mind and the relation between *minds* and mental (or spiritual) states and events, on the one hand, and physical *bodies* and their physical or material states, on the other.

Are Minds and Mental States Distinct from Bodies and Material States?

It is abundantly obvious that people have conscious mental states, including such things as sensations and feelings of various kinds, but also conscious beliefs, desires, emotions, and so on; and if the mind is what these various states are states *of,* then it is also obvious that people have minds. At the same time, it is equally obvious that people have physical bodies, including in particular physical brains, involving various sorts of physical states and processes. The fundamental issue that the reading selections in this chapter are concerned with is the relation between these two aspects of persons: Are minds and mental states distinct from bodies and physical or bodily states (as **dualism** claims), so that human beings are made up of two fundamentally different kinds of ingredients? Or are minds and mental states somehow nothing more than, **reducible** to, bodies and material states (as **materialism** claims)? In spite of a tendency in recent times to assume that the brain is central to mental activity and even perhaps in some way to be identified with the mind, in fact the connection between these two basic aspects of human persons is far from obvious.

In thinking about these views, it will help to have available a simple example involving both mental and material states. Suppose that I walk out my front door and stop halfway to my car, noticing that it is cold and damp, that there are dark clouds, and that the wind seems to be increasing; I decide that it is probably going to be rainy and cold, so I walk back to the house to get my coat and an umbrella; and having done this, I start out again for the car. Here we have various mental states: *sensations* of cold, dampness, darkness, and windiness; perceptual *beliefs* about these matters and the further belief that it is going to be rainy and cold; and presumably a *desire* not to be wet and cold. And there are also various physical or material states: in addition to the physical condition of my environment, there is the physical *behavior* of my body in walking, stopping, turning my head, and walking again, together with the physical condition of my body and my various sensory organs: the coldness and dampness of my skin, the light waves striking my eyes, and so on.

Dualism

According to a dualist view, the mental states involved in this example are quite distinct from the physical or material states. The initial motivation for dualism is the realization, which only one group of philosophers (the logical behaviorists—discussed later) have ever denied, that conscious mental states do not *seem,* as we are aware of them, to be states of the brain or indeed physical states of any kind. Think here of my sensation of cold or of my conscious belief that it is going to be rainy and cold: if these mental states are in some way just states of the brain (as J. J. C. Smart and Jerry Fodor, among others, both claim—though in importantly different ways), this is surely not obvious just by reflecting on them. (One way to see this is to realize that they certainly do not present themselves as any *specific* states of the brain: not even proponents of materialism would claim that one could tell, just by reflecting on the conscious appearance of such a state, which specific neurophysiological state or process it is.) This fact by itself creates a prima facie case in favor of dualism—one that, paradoxically enough, is based not on any real understanding of non-material, dualist states or of what the appearance of such a state would be like, but rather on a fairly detailed knowledge of *material* states and, as a result, of what *their* appearances should seemingly be like. Moreover, as we will see, philosophers have often claimed that there are more specific arguments seemingly showing that mental states could not be identical to physical states of any kind, thus further supporting a dualist account of minds and mental states.

Dualism comes in a number of importantly different versions. On the most straightforward and historically prominent version, the mental states are states of one thing or entity or **substance,** the mind; and the physical or material states are states of a separate thing or entity or substance, the body. And a human being is thus in effect a kind of team composed of these two separate elements, operating (or at least seeming to operate) in tandem. This was the view of René Descartes (see the selection from his *Meditations* in Chapter 2, especially pp. 59, 61), and it also seems to be the version of dualism that John Foster has mainly in mind in the immediately following selection. But many of the more recent proponents of dualism, such as Frank Jackson and David Chalmers, have opted instead for an **attribute** or property version of dualism (the main reason being doubts as to whether there is any clear conception of what a mental or spiritual *substance,* as distinct from its states and properties, would amount to). Attribute dualism is the view that there are two fundamentally different kinds of attributes or properties or features, mental or spiritual attributes and material or physical attributes, but that all of these are attributes of the same underlying thing or substance. This substance is what we refer to as the body (or more likely a part of the body, namely the brain), but on this view, this substance is neither purely material nor purely mental in nature, since it has both kinds of properties. (The most obvious importance of the difference between substance and attribute dualism is that the survival of a person after the death of his body seems at least possible under substance dualism, but not under attribute dualism.)

A second issue that divides different versions of dualism concerns the *causal* relations (if any) that exist between the mind and the body. Here the common-sense view is **interactionism:** the view that mental states causally influence physical states and that physical states causally influence mental states. Think about our example again, and in particular about the natural explanation of my behavior. Here we *seem* to have both causation of mental states by material states and causation of material states by mental states: The material states of cold, cloudiness, and windiness causally affect my bodily sense organs which in turn produce sensations reflecting these conditions and then the beliefs that they obtain. These beliefs, together with my standing desire not to be cold and wet, produce the further mental state of deciding to go back for my coat and umbrella. And this decision (or perhaps an intention—a further mental state—that results from it) in turn causes my material body to make the specific movements that it makes while walking back into the house and then out again to the car. There are innumerable other, similar examples that would also illustrate our common assumption that our minds affect our bodies and that our bodies affect our minds.

Some dualists accept at face value the view that mind and body causally interact in these ways. Foster defends such a view, and thus must explain how immaterial and material things can causally interact. But other dualists, along with most materialists (see the discussion in the Fodor selection), question whether causal relations between such fundamentally different kinds of things are possible or even intelligible. Some dualists think that the view that mental states causally influence the material world—thus making it impossible in principle to adequately explain all material events in terms of other material events alone—is especially implausible, leading them to adopt the view that the causal relations between body and mind are one-way only: while bodily states can causally affect or even completely produce mental states, mental states cannot causally affect physical states. This view, called **epiphenomenalism,** cannot accept the common-sense explanation of my behavior in the example, since that explanation depends on causal relations in both directions. Surprisingly enough, epiphenomenalism, despite its disagreement with a fundamental aspect of the common-sense picture, is probably the most popular version of dualism in recent times; Foster, however, argues against it.

A third kind of dualism, once popular but now rarely if ever held, is **parallelism:** the view that there are no causal relations *either* way—that the mental realm is causally isolated from the physical realm. A parallelist obviously has to find some explanation for the *appearance* of causal interaction (as in the foregoing example), and historically the defenders of this view have appealed to God for this purpose: either God creates the mental and material realms in such a way that they run in parallel like two clocks, always in agreement with each other *(preestablished harmony)* or God constantly intervenes to keep the two in synch with each other *(occasionalism)*. You are not alone if you find parallelism difficult to take seriously.*

The distinction between interactionism and epiphenomenalism is independent of and cuts across that between substance and attribute dualism, so that there are really four main dualist views (in addition to two versions of parallelism, which can safely be set aside): substance and attribute versions of each of the two main alternatives with respect to causal relations. And since the issue between substance and attribute versions receives substantially less discussion and is perhaps not even very well understood, the main issue dividing versions of dualism is that between interactionism and epiphenomenalism.

Materialism

While some philosophers still defend dualism, by far the most widely accepted general position in recent times has been materialism (or **physicalism**): the view that there is no separate dualist mind or separate dualist attributes, so that the mind and its mental states are in some way entirely **reducible** to bodies and material states.† Here again, there are several different views.

One materialist position that was once widely held (roughly in the middle of the twentieth century) but is now held by virtually no one is **logical behaviorism:** the extremely implausible view that mental states are nothing more than bodily behavior and dispositions

*There is a fourth view that is at least logically possible: that the mind causally influences the body, but the body does not causally influence the mind. But this last possibility has never been advocated by anyone. See if you can figure out why.

†If, that is, minds and mental states exist at all. There is one radical version of materialism, not represented in the selections in this volume, that denies the very existence of minds and mental states, holding that they are merely things advocated by a bad common-sense theory of human behavior (in roughly the same way that phlogiston was once advocated by a mistaken physical theory of how combustion works). This view is called *eliminative materialism.*

to such behavior (so that to be in pain is just to wince and moan and ask for help, or to be disposed to do these things; and to believe that it will rain is just to do or be disposed to do things like carrying an umbrella, deliberately not watering the lawn, and so on). According to the logical behaviorist, this identity between mental states, on the one hand, and behavior and dispositions to behave, on the other, is simply a matter of *definition:* what various mental state concepts *mean* is just behavior and dispositions to behave. Philosophical arguments against logical behaviorism have pointed out the logical possibility of people: (a) who mimic behavior perfectly but still are not really in the corresponding mental state ("perfect pretenders"); or (b) who experience states like pain but are so stoic and have so much control over their reactions that they are not even disposed to exhibit characteristic pain behavior ("super-Spartans"). But the main problem is that the logical behaviorist is in effect denying that there are really conscious mental states at all—and also, perhaps even more implausibly, that such states ever cause or explain behavior in the way that seems to be reflected in our example. Both of these claims are extremely implausible (though remember that the epiphenomenalist version of dualism also accepts the second one). Fodor briefly discusses logical behaviorism (along with another version of behaviorism that simply denies the need to appeal to mental states in giving explanations of behavior, without explicitly denying the existence of such states in themselves).

A second, more recent version of materialism, though one that is also no longer widely held, is the **identity theory** (of mind and body), also known as *central state materialism.* According to this view, mental states and processes are nothing more than neurophysiological states and processes of the brain. But, in contrast to logical behaviorism, this is not supposed to be true by definition or simply by virtue of the common-sense meaning or content of mental-state concepts, nor is it reflected in our introspective experience of such states. It is obvious that the common-sense *concepts* of the various sorts of mental states can be understood perfectly well without having any idea that the states involved are in the brain or indeed have anything to do with the brain;* and also, as mentioned above, that mental states do not present themselves introspectively as specific brain states. Instead, according to the identity theory, the identity between these two sorts of states is an *empirical* discovery, analogous to the empirical discovery that lightning (the visible flash in the sky) is identical to a certain sort of electrical discharge (again, not a matter of meaning or definition and also not something obvious just from the experience of lightning, but a discovery that required rather complicated empirical investigation—involving, among other things, people like Benjamin Franklin doing things like flying kites in thunderstorms).

But if the content of mental state concepts does not explicitly involve brain processes, then in order for the identity theory to be correct, there must be some other account of the content of such concepts: one that is *neutral* between materialism and dualism in that it does not *require* but still *allows* the identity that is claimed by the identity theory to hold. (Compare again the lightning case: if there had not been an *independent* concept of what lightning is—one that made no reference to electricity— there would have been no idea of a kind of thing or process that could be subsequently *discovered* to be in fact a kind of electrical discharge.) Smart defends the identity theory, focusing mainly on conscious sensations, and tries to offer such a neutral account of mental properties (his "topic-neutral" account). Fodor also discusses the identity theory and suggests some problems with it, problems that in his view point toward yet a further materialist view.

This third materialist view, currently by far the most popular, is called **functionalism**—though the label is far from perspicuous, and you will have to work hard to understand the position to which it refers. Like the identity theory, functionalism does not hold that mental states are material states simply as a matter of the meaning or content

*Think about this point: one useful way to elaborate it is to point out that one who knew nothing at all about the brain—or even that people have organs of that sort—could still have the same understanding of the concepts of various kinds of sensations, thoughts, and so on as anyone else; such a person, if a materialist view like the identity theory is correct, would be ignorant of an important fact about mental states, but might still grasp the concepts of such states as well as anyone else.

of mental concepts, nor in a way that is obvious in our mental experience. Instead, like the identity theorist, the functionalist offers an account of mental concepts—or equivalently of the essential nature of mental states—that is in itself neutral between materialism and dualism, but then adds that it is in fact certain material states, specifically states of the brain and central nervous system, that in fact satisfy or realize this essential nature (at least in human beings).

The functionalist account of mental states grows out of Smart's "topic-neutral" account of the meaning of mentalistic concepts and also reflects certain aspects of the logical behaviorist view. According to this account, mental states are *functional* states, defined in terms of their *causal role* (also called "functional role"). What characterizes a particular mental state is (a) the particular ways in which it is caused by external (mainly perceptual) *inputs,* (b) the particular ways in which it relates causally to other specific mental states (through inference, psychological association, and the like), and (c) the specific ways in which it causally produces behavioral *outputs*—with the scope and importance of these three aspects varying from state to state. Thus, for example, the belief that it is going to rain is a state that is (a) caused by certain distinctive sorts of perceptual experiences (such as the experience of seeing dark clouds, feeling wind, and hearing thunder in the distance) and ultimately by the physical stimuli that lead to such experiences, (b) causally interacts with other mental states (such as the desire to stay dry or the belief that the lawn needs water), and (c) tends to lead (indirectly in this case, via its relations to other mental states, such as the desire to stay dry) to actions such as carrying an umbrella or wearing a raincoat. According to the functionalist, to have the belief that it is going to rain just *is* to be in a state that realizes this causal, functional role (of which nothing like a complete characterization has been given here)—and any state that realizes this role, whether a brain state, a state of a dualist immaterial mind, or a state of some still further kind, *is* a belief that it is going to rain. And the same is true, with appropriate modifications of the causal role, for all other mental states—though some of these three main aspects of causal role will be more important for some specific kinds of mental states than for others.* The selection by Fodor offers an explanation and defense of functionalism.

Summing up this so far rather complicated discussion, while there are many more positions that are theoretically possible (some of which were seriously held in earlier times), recent discussion in the philosophy of mind has tended to focus on a very small set of alternatives: interactionist and epiphenomenalist version of dualism, on the one hand (with the substance-attribute distinction lurking in the background), and the functionalist version of materialism, on the other.

Since it is clear that materialism in general and functionalism in particular are to be preferred on grounds of economy or simplicity if everything else is equal, the main resulting issue is whether the functionalist view can adequately account for the features that mental states seem to have, especially conscious features—thereby explaining why states that are in fact neurophysiological states would present the conscious appearance that they do. As Fodor emphasizes, there are two main features of mental states that are relevant here: *intentional* content and *qualitative* content (though he lists them in the opposite order). A mental state is **intentional** insofar as it is *about* or *represents* something else: my belief that it is going to rain is a mental state that is *about* the weather and *represents* it as having a certain specific character. The problem is to understand how such representation works: how my mind is able to reach out and grasp the world in this way. In contrast, my mental state of being in pain as a result of, for example, a sprained

*Smart's "topic-neutral account" can be seen as in effect a limited version of the functionalist account that is focused on the sorts of states—mainly sensations—where component (a) of the causal role is so important that the other two components matter very little. To expand Smart's view so as to account for states where components (b) and (c) are more important—states such as beliefs and desires—would be to turn his view into essentially a full-fledged version of functionalism. In this way, the identity theory can be seen as a kind of early and incomplete version of functionalism, which is why it is no longer regarded as an important independent alternative.

ankle does not represent anything (even though it is *caused* by the sprained ankle), but it does have a distinctive qualitative character or feel, an aspect of mental states that philosophers call a *quale* (plural **qualia**)—where part of this character is the very feature of being *conscious* at all. It is at least unclear how a merely material state can have this sort of distinctive experiential character. The other two sections of the chapter focus on the two resulting issues: whether functionalism (or any materialist view) can satisfactorily account for (1) intentional content and (2) conscious qualia.

Are Intentional Mental States Analogous to the States of a Computer?

Since, as Fodor discusses, the program states of a computer are also functional states, another way to put the functionalist view is to say that mental states are analogous to computer states—thereby raising the possibility that a computer of the right sort might also be capable of intentional thought. The selection by Alan Turing presents a widely discussed way of formulating this issue.

While Turing is very optimistic about the possibility of machines thinking, John Searle, writing 30 years later, is quite convinced that machines like computers whose essential nature is to manipulate symbols not only cannot now think, but in principle never will—and hence that a functionalist view, which characterizes mental states in terms of computer-like states, cannot successfully account for the intentionality of mental states. Searle rests his case on his famous Chinese Room thought experiment, an experiment designed to emphasize the difference between the intrinsically meaningful elements of human thought and the intrinsically meaningless symbols that computers manipulate. Searle insists that genuine thought and intentionality require *intrinsic* meaning, something that neither a computer program nor, more generally, any state characterized merely in terms of functional role can ever yield. In a further selection, Fodor, still confident that functionalism can solve the intentionality problem, objects to Searle's Chinese Room thought experiment, arguing that a particular kind of program with particular kinds of inputs and outputs will indeed have contentful thoughts. In a further selection, Searle responds to Fodor's objections.

Can Materialism Account for Qualitative Consciousness?

The selections in the final section of the chapter are concerned with the other main problem faced by functionalism (and indeed, like the problem of intentionality, by any materialist view): can such a view account for the particular qualitative character of mental states—or indeed for consciousness itself (which is really just a central aspect of any sort of qualitative character)? The selection by Thomas Nagel, which has become widely recognized as presenting one fundamental challenge to materialism, raises the issue, among some others, of whether the qualitative character of experience—specifically the experience of a non-human creature, a bat—could be known on the basis of a knowledge of its material makeup (including a functional description of its states). This is something that seemingly should be possible if the material story is, as the materialist claims, the complete story about the nature of such beings. Both Frank Jackson and Laurence BonJour elaborate this point, developing it into what has become known as "the knowledge argument" against materialism or physicalism.

One response to the seeming cogency of the knowledge argument, advocated in the selection by David Lewis, is to retain the claim that mental states are entirely material or physical in character, that the physical account leaves nothing out, by denying the very existence of qualitative content or qualia (which Lewis refers to as phenomenal qualities). Another, quite different response would be to reevaluate dualism and try to solve some of its problems. David Chalmers suggests and tentatively defends this second sort of response, arguing that philosophers should be trying to find the **psychophysical laws** that will explain the relationship between minds and bodies.

Are Minds and Mental States Distinct from Bodies and Material States?

John Foster

John Foster (1941–) teaches at Oxford University. He has written widely in metaphysics and epistemology, as well as in the philosophy of religion and philosophy of mind. In this selection, Foster defends an **interactionist** version of dualism by replying to a range of objections, all of which criticize the view that there could be causal relations between a physical body and a nonphysical mind. He also seems to have **substance** dualism at least primarily in mind. (In speaking of *psychophysical causation,* Foster is referring to causal relations between mental (psychological) states and physical states.)

As we have seen (in the chapter introduction), the fact that mental states, as they are consciously experienced, do not seem to be material states creates a prima facie argument for dualism. This is why a defense of dualism can plausibly rely merely on replying to objections.

A Defense of Dualism

By "dualism" I mean the thesis that the mind and its contents are radically nonphysical, that is, that they are neither themselves physical, nor the logical product of anything physical, nor, except causally or nomologically, dependent on anything physical. (1)

It is nowadays generally assumed that dualism has been discredited. Even those who see problems for the alternatives usually are unwilling to countenance dualism as a possible solution. I believe that dualism is correct. . . . I shall consider some of the main objections to dualism and try to show why they are ineffective.

. . .

Of course, I do not have space to consider all the objections. Some are nothing more than rhetoric (I would put into this category such objections as "nonphysical entities are queer" and "postulating nonphysical entities is ontologically extravagant" . . .

. . . the . . . objections I consider all concern, in one way or another, the dualist's account of psychophysical causation—his account of the causal relations between body and mind. Dualism itself, of course, does not entail that there are such relations. There is no contradiction in maintaining that the mind, as well as being nonphysical, is causally isolated from the physical world; and with the help of a suitable theism, it may even be possible to explain why things are empirically organized as if there were psychophysical causation, when there is not. But since I do not want my defense of dualism to force me into such an eccentric position, I shall work on the assumption that parallelism, in this extreme form, is untenable and that mind and body are indeed causally related. (2) This still leaves the dualist with a choice between interactionism, which takes the causal relations to run in both directions, and epiphenomenalism, which takes them to run only from body to mind. Here my sympathies, again in line with common sense, are with the interactionist. And consequently, I would feel at least very uncomfortable if there were something which obliged me to choose between abandoning dualism altogether and adopting its epiphenomenalist version. That I do face such a choice is the substance of the [final] objection.

The Traditional Objection. Perhaps the oldest objection to dualism is that if the mind is nonphysical, the very idea of psychophysical causation—of the body causally affecting the mind or the mind causally affecting the body—is deeply puzzling, if not incoherent. How can

From *The Case for Dualism,* edited by John R. Smythies and John Beloff (Charlottesville: University Press of Virginia, 1989).

(1) *Definition*

To say that mental states are "the logical product" of something physical (presumably brain states) is to say that talk about mental states is in some way just a redescription of those physical states. (Functionalism, discussed in the chapter introduction and many of the later selections, would be an example of such a view.) If that were so, then mental states would *not* have an existence independent of the relevant physical states—and so could not cause them. "Nomological" means having to do with laws of nature, so Foster is allowing that there may be laws (presumably causal laws) that describe the relations between mind and body or between mental states and bodily states.

(2)

If one sphere of existence is *causally isolated* from another sphere, then no thing in either sphere can causally affect any other thing in the other sphere. Parallelism (see the chapter introduction) is the view that the mental sphere of existence is in this way causally isolated from the physical sphere. (By "a suitable theism," Foster means theories about how God makes it look as though there are psychophysical causal relations even though there really aren't—again, see the chapter introduction.)

such different kinds of thing—the physical and the nonphysical—come into causal contact? How can the material body gain purchase on the immaterial mind, or vice versa? However, put like this, I cannot see what the problem is supposed to be. Obviously, dualistic causation does not operate through physical contact, as when one billiard ball displaces another. But why should it not just be in the nature of things that in certain psychophysical conditions, certain types of neural event cause certain types of mental event, or vice versa? According to Thomas Nagel, we cannot understand how such causation would work. Nagel assumes, I think correctly, though contrary to Hume's account, that causation involves some kind of objective necessitation. ❸ He then argues, in effect, that so long as we think of mental and physical events as radically different in their intrinsic nature, such necessitation is incomprehensible: "what we cannot understand is *how* . . . the brain process necessitates the sensation." But what I cannot understand is how this "how"-question arises . . . since the causation is direct (the brain event directly causing the mental event, or vice versa), there is no question of an intervening mechanism. Perhaps it is this very directness which Nagel finds puzzling. For in the physical world causal processes are, in general, spatiotemporally continuous, thus providing an intervening mechanism between a cause and any subsequent effect. ❹ But there is surely nothing incoherent or problematic about the notion of direct causation. And where causation is direct, I do not see in what sense there could be a question of how it operates, except as a request to specify the causally relevant properties and . . . laws.

The Problem of Causal Pairings. While the traditional objection to dualistic psychophysical causation is totally misconceived, there is a related objection which is more troublesome and for which, ironically, I have to take the credit. It is normally assumed that where two events are causally related, they are so wholly by virtue of the way in which, via their noncausal properties and relations, they fall under some natural law. Thus if, on a particular occasion, my heating of a lump of metal caused it to melt, it is assumed that what makes this true is that the metal was of a certain type and reached a certain temperature and that it is a law of nature (or a consequence of a law of nature) that whenever a lump of metal of that type reaches that temperature, it melts. However, when we apply this model to the case of psychophysical causation, dualistically conceived, we encounter a problem. Suppose that *B* is the event of Smith's brain being in state ϕ at time *t* and that *E* is a mental event of type ψ which occurs in Smith's mind a tenth of a second after *t* and as the direct causal result of *B*. ❺ What psychophysical law could we postulate to account for this causal episode? We might begin by postulating the law (L_1) that whenever a brain is in a state ϕ a mental event of type ψ occurs a tenth of a second later. But this would be inadequate. For suppose that Jones's brain is also in state ϕ at *t*, giving us the event *B* which is a simultaneous duplicate of B', and that this causes in Jones's mind, a tenth of a second later, an event E' of type ψ which is a simultaneous duplicate of *E*. *Ex hypothesi, B* is the cause of *E* and B' is the cause of E'. But the law L_1 does not account for these causal pairings. Because it only specifies the temporal relation between cause and effect, it is neutral between these pairings and the alternative, but false, hypothesis that *B* is the cause of E' and B' is the cause of *E*. ❻ The obvious remedy is to replace L_1 by the stronger law (L_2) that whenever a brain *x* is in state ϕ a mental event of type ψ occurs a tenth of a second later in that mind which *x*, or the *x*-containing organism, embodies—in other words, in the mind of that subject whose brain *x* is. L_2 would then yield the unique causal pairings of *B* with *E* and of B' with E'. But the problem with this is that, for a dualist, the relation of embodiment itself must be analyzed, wholly or partly, in causal terms: at least part of what makes a particular brain *x* the brain of a particular subject *y* is that things are psychophysically arranged in a way which gives *x* (and *x* alone) the capacity to have a direct causal influence on *y* (and *y* alone) and, for the interactionist, vice versa. It would be circular to account for this arrangement by laws like L_2 and, because of the original problem, impossible to account for it by laws like L_1. ❼ In view of this, it might seem that the right solution is to abandon dualism. For if we identified mental events with neural

"Objective necessitation" means that there is a stronger kind of connection between a cause and its effect than merely regular sequence or constant conjunction—that the causal event *makes* the effect happen in some stronger way. (This is surely the common-sense view.) But if that were right, then there might be some specific limitations as to what kind of cause could do this in relation to any particular effect. Whereas if Hume's regularity theory is right, then there are no general restrictions on what kind of thing can be a cause for any particular effect. (See Discussion Question 1.)

Foster is suggesting that purely physical causal relations are never direct because any such process is spatio-temporally continuous. Think of a continuous line: between any two points there is another point. Foster is saying that between any physical cause and any physical effect (no matter how close the two are spatio-temporally), there will always be intermediate causal steps. But this is not so for the supposedly direct causal relation between a mental event and a physical event, or vice versa.

❺ *Restatement/Summary*

Here *B* and *E* are specific events in Smith's brain and mind, while ϕ is the general type of which *B* is an instance and ψ is the general type of which *E* is an instance.

L_1, since it refers only to *types* of events, cannot distinguish between a brain state in Smith causing a mental state of a certain type in Smith, and a brain state in Smith causing a mental state of that same type in Jones. Thus L_1 does not adequately capture the actual causal relation.

events, we could envisage laws that guaranteed unique causal pairings by specifying the precise spatiotemporal relation between cause and effect. Indeed, we could hope to account for psychophysical causation wholly in terms of the ordinary laws of physics and chemistry.

When I first wrote about this problem . . . I argued that the right response, for the dualist, was to postulate psychophysical laws restricted to particular pairs of brains and minds (or brains and subjects). Thus in the case of Smith and Jones, we can secure the correct causal pairings by postulating a separate law for each person—the law (relevant to Smith) that whenever brain x_1 is in state ϕ, a ψ event occurs a tenth of a second later in mind M_1 (or to subject *S*) and the law (relevant to Jones) that whenever brain x_2 is in state ϕ, a ψ event occurs a tenth of a second later in mind M_2 (or to subject *J*), where x_1 and M_1 are the brain and mind of Smith and x_2 and M_2 are the brain and mind of Jones. (8) More recently, I have tried to meet the problem in a quite different way. I have argued that even in the physical realm we can envisage cases in which the fundamental laws do not account for the causal pairings. Thus suppose that, for a certain kind *K* of metal, it is a law that when any spherical *K* lump reaches a specified temperature, a flash occurs a tenth of a second later somewhere (unspecified) in the region of points no farther from the center of the sphere than twice its diameter. Suppose further that there is no stronger law which fixes the position of the flash more precisely. Now imagine the case in which two adjacent *K* spheres simultaneously reach the critical temperature and, a tenth of a second later, two flashes occur, both within the specified region for each sphere. (9) It is coherent and indeed plausible to suppose that each flash is the effect of just one of the sphere-temperatures and that each sphere-temperature is the cause of just one of the flashes. But the causal pairings are not determined by the law and the noncausal conditions, since each flash falls within the specified region for each sphere. From this I concluded that we should abandon the assumption that causal relations can be wholly accounted for in terms of noncausal properties and laws. And once this assumption is abandoned, the problem of psychophysical causal pairings no longer arises; it no longer matters if the pairing of *B* with *E* and *B′* and *E′* is not determined by the noncausal conditions and the covering law. (10)

Reviewing these alternative responses, I now think that in a sense, both were correct. On the one hand, the hypothetical case of the *K* spheres does indeed show that causal pairings can be law-transcendent; (11) and, in that respect, the original objection to the dualist's position fails. On the other hand, it does seem quite plausible to envisage laws of the restricted kind as underlying the relation of embodiment. As we have said, at least part of what makes a particular brain *x* the brain of a particular mental subject *y* is that things are psychophysically arranged in a way which gives *x* (and *x* alone) the capacity to have a direct causal influence on *y* (and *y* alone)—and, for the interactionist, vice versa. It is hard to see in what this arrangement could consist except in certain psychophysical laws which specifically link *x* and *y,* and such laws would guarantee unique causal pairings. (12) At all events, it is clear that the dualist has sufficient resources to meet the objection.

...

An Objection to Dualistic Interactionism. Some dualists, while accepting that there are psychophysical causal relations, hold that they only run in one direction—from body to mind. They accept, for example, that if I am stung by a wasp, the subsequent pain is caused by the neural response which the sting induces, but they deny that if I decide to smoke my pipe, the subsequent bodily movements involving pipe and matches are caused by my decision. And, quite generally, they accept that a person's mental states are causally affected by the states of his body but deny that his mental states have any causal influence on the states of his body or on anything else in the physical world. This version of dualism is known as "epiphenomenalism," and the version it contrasts with, which accepts psychophysical causation in both directions, is known as "interactionism." I should add that most epiphenomenalists, as well as denying that the mind has any causal influence on the body, also deny that it has a causal influence on anything at all. In particular, they deny that

R To say that "the relation of embodiment must be analyzed . . . in causal terms" is to say that the account of which mind goes with which body will appeal to causal relations between them: what makes Smith's mind and body constitute one person (Smith) is that they causally influence each other directly (and neither has any direct causal influence on other minds or bodies). But then the laws describing these causal relations cannot presuppose these connections between specific bodies and specific minds, since that is part of what they are supposed to explain.

R On this view, there will be a separate psychophysical law (or set of laws) for each person.

STOP How plausible (or implausible) is such a view?

R The idea is that the spheres are close enough to each other that the specified regions for each sphere overlap, making it possible for both flashes to occur in the area of overlap. In this case, the law will not determine which flash is caused by which spherical lump of K.

R Thus, according to Foster, we should abandon the general view that correct causal laws must always be able to determine which effect goes with which cause—in which case, the failure of the causal laws in the mind-body case to do this would no longer constitute an objection to dualistic psychophysical causation.

"Law-transcendent" just means that the relevant laws do not determine which pairings are correct.

R Since such a restricted law applies only to states of a single individual, the causes and effects are always events within the same individual, and thus no pairings of a cause in one person and an effect in another person would fall under the law.

13

R Foster offers three reasons to reject epiphenomenalism before going on to discuss the objection to interactionism mentioned at the beginning of the previous paragraph. The first objection is that on an epiphenomenalist view, bodily actions (like picking up his pipe) are never caused by mental states (like intending to smoke). But this means that human behavior is *never* genuinely intentional—which surely conflicts with our "common-sense." (See Discussion Question 2.)

14

R A corollary of the previous objection is that if epiphenomenalism is true, then our current psychological explanations of human behavior which seem to be highly successful, must be mistaken.

15 *Editor Comment*

Oral speech and writing are *physical* events (involving vibrating vocal cords or ink marks on paper). According to epiphenomenalism, a person's mental states of introspective knowledge cannot cause that person to say or write certain things, and so neither speech nor writing could in any way reflect or express such knowledge. And, even worse, it seems impossible for language to even refer to or describe mental events if it is entirely causally isolated from them.

16

An "identity thesis" is any view according to which mental states are identical to brain states. This includes both the view (defended by Smart in the next selection) that all mental states of a given *type* are identical with brain states of a specific type (type-type identity) and the view that each individual mental state is identical with some individual brain state but not necessarily the same kind of brain state for each instance of the same kind of mental state (the "token-token" view, where a "token" is an individual instance of a type).

mental states can cause, or contribute to the causation of, other mental states.

Like most other current philosophers, I regard epiphenomenalism as unnatural and implausible. In the first place, it is in radical conflict with our conception of ourselves as agents. If mental states have no causal influence on behavior, then behavior cannot be thought of as intentional in any decent sense, even if the subject happens to have certain intentions which it fulfills. And if behavior is not intentional, it does not qualify as action in a sense which distinguishes it from mere bodily movement. The epiphenomenalist might reply that the general conformity of our behavior to our intentions is not merely accidental; it is ensured by the very structure of our brains and their muscular extensions in the framework of physical and psychophysical law. But even so, the behavior would not be intentional in the requisite sense, since the intentions and the psychophysical laws that control their occurrence would be irrelevant to its production. **13** Second, human behavior exhibits certain complex regularities that call for explanation and that, at present, we explain (at least partly) in psychological terms. These psychological explanations . . . attribute a causal efficacy to the mental; they represent behavior as falling under the control of the subject's beliefs and desires, or under the control of the subject's decisions, which are responsive to (if not determined by) his beliefs and desires. And these explanations gain credence from the fact that, as well as being, in their own terms, successful, they cannot, at present, be replaced by non-psychological explanations that cover the same ground. **14** Third, it is difficult to see how, if epiphenomenalism were true, the mind could form a subject matter for overt discussion. Certainly, if mental states have no causal access to our speech centers, the notion of an introspective report collapses: even if the subject retains an introspective knowledge of his mental states, his utterances would not count as expressing that knowledge if it contributes nothing to their production. But it is not even clear how, on the epiphenomenalistic view, our language, as a medium for our utterances, makes semantic contact with the mind at all. In what sense, for example, could the word "pain," as overtly used, be said to signify a certain type of sensation, if neither the occurrence of the sensations nor our introspective conception of their type affects the overt use . . . ? **15**

None of these points shows that epiphenomenalism is logically untenable, in the sense of being incoherent or self-contradictory . . . . Nonetheless, we have, I think, very strong, and perhaps even conclusive, reasons for rejecting it. And, because of this, I should not want my defense of dualism to involve my acceptance of anything but an interactionist position.

It is at this point that the [final] objection arises. For there is an argument which purports to show that dualism of any but an epiphenomenalistic kind is scientifically unacceptable. The argument runs like this:

1. The body is a physical system.
2. As such, the body must be subject to ordinary physical laws.
3. Our theories as to what physical laws obtain are subject to revision. But our current scientific evidence strongly supports the view that at any level of description relevant to a theory of human behavior, these laws are, for all practical purposes, deterministic.
4. So we can reasonably conclude that any bodily event, of a sort which might be cited in a description or explanation of behavior, is causally determined by prior physical events and conditions.
5. But such a conclusion leaves no room for a nonphysical mind to have any causal influence on behavior.
6. Hence, on our present scientific evidence, we face a choice between epiphenomenalism and some kind of identity thesis (if only of the token-token variety). **16**

If it is correct, this argument constitutes an objection to dualistic interactionism. It also, on the face of it, constitutes an objection to dualism as such, if epiphenomenalism is, as I would concede, unacceptable. And, nowadays, it is normally as an objection to dualism, and in support of the identity thesis, that the argument is offered. But here we must be careful. It is true that epiphenomenalism is very implausible and, overtly expressed, may even be self-refuting. And this means that, other things being equal, we should reject it. But it does not mean that we should reject it at all costs. If the only alternative were the identity thesis, then, in my view, epiphenomenalism, despite its implausibility, would be the preferable option. . . . The choice between epiphenomenalism and the identity thesis only counts against dualism on the assumption, which I hold to be false, that epiphenomenalism is not only very implausible but less plausible than its rival. [17] . . .

However, whether it is an objection to dualism as such or only to interactionism, I have to find some answer to the argument; for I am not willing to concede that epiphenomenalism and the identity thesis are the only empirically acceptable options. In fact, the error in the argument is not hard to identify. We must begin by distinguishing two ways in which science might provide evidence that the functioning of the body is wholly explicable in terms of deterministic physical law. The first way would be by direct research on the body itself—in particular, on the brain, since it is on brain activity, if on anything, that we might expect the mind to exert a direct causal influence. Thus, by monitoring neural activity in various parts of the brain (without disturbing normal functioning), scientists might build up a strong inductive case for the conclusion that the electrochemical state of any neuron at any time is determined by its immediately prior electrochemical state and the states of other neurons directly connected to it. [18] The second way would be by discovering, without reference to the functioning of the human body, that the rest of the physical world seems to be subject to certain physical laws of a sort which, if they applied universally, would make the body a deterministic system. This is the evidence provided by the investigations of physics and chemistry into the properties of matter and energy in general. Now it is predominantly evidence of the second kind to which the argument appeals. The claim is not that a thorough sampling of brain activity reveals a wholly deterministic system, for no such sampling has been conducted. Rather, the claim is that the human body, including the brain, must be physically deterministic if it is to conform to those theories which apply to physical systems in general. But this evidence, just because it bears on the question of the human system only indirectly, is not decisive. It has to be weighed against what we know or have reason to believe, independently, about the relation between body and mind. . . . [19] When everything is taken into account, the most reasonable conclusion to draw is, surely, that through its attachment to a nonphysical mind, the brain is subject to certain influences which do not affect the other physical systems that science investigates and on whose behavior its nomological theories are based. It is conceivable that this conclusion will be called into question by future brain research (if it were, I should have to reconsider my rejection of epiphenomenalism). But as things stand, we are entitled to assume that it will not.

. . .

Foster's claim here is that any identity thesis is so implausible that epiphenomenalism looks good in comparison—in spite of the objections to epiphenomenalism that he has just given. (Foster's own objections to identity views have been omitted here, but similar objections are discussed in later selections.)

"Determined by" here means something much stronger than "influenced by": it means that the cause in question completely accounts for the result, leaving no room for any other influence.

Evidence of the second kind (that the *rest* of the physical world is deterministic), therefore, doesn't help establish the crucial claim without evidence of the first kind (that any particular brain state is completely determined by some prior physical state). And it is clear that we don't yet have evidence of the first kind.

Discussion Questions

1. Is causality merely regular sequence or constant conjunction of events, as Hume's regularity theory claims, or does genuine causation require some stronger relation between cause and effect (what Nagel—cited by Foster on p. 158—refers to as "objective necessitation")? What might this stronger connection amount to, and how would we tell whether it was present? Can you think of a plausible example of regular succession where there nonetheless seems to be no causal relation between the two events in question themselves? Is it possible to have a causal relation between two specific events *without* there being any relation of regular succession between the corresponding kinds of events?
2. Foster's first objection to epiphenomenalism (p. 160) is that if epiphenomenalism is true, then we aren't genuine agents (since being a genuine agent requires that our intentions are genuinely effective in causing our behavior)—which conflicts strongly with common sense. He considers the following response from an epiphenomenalist: our

intentions *seem* from the standpoint of common sense to cause our behavior because the real cause of some particular bit of behavior (a brain state) is *also* the cause of the mental intention to behave in that way. Because we are not consciously aware of the brain state, we think that the intention is the cause of the behavior, but it is really just another effect of one cause (with the other effect being the behavior). Consider Foster's example of deciding to smoke his pipe. According to the interactionist dualist, his conscious decision to smoke caused his bodily movements to get his pipe. According to this epiphenomenalist response, a single brain state is responsible for *both* his bodily movements to get his pipe and his conscious decision to smoke, and thus his conscious decision to smoke is *not* the cause of his bodily movements to get his pipe. How plausible or implausible is this epiphenomenalist response, and why? Might the appearance that intentions cause actions be in this way only an illusion?

3. Do we have good reason to think that the material or physical world is *causally closed:* not causally influenced by anything that is not physical? Many philosophers of mind regard this thesis as obviously correct and so any view (such as interactionism) that conflicts with it as obviously mistaken. Foster tries to show that we have no good reason for thinking that the thesis of causal closure is true. Which view is right here?

J. J. C. Smart

J. J. C. Smart (1920–) is an Australian philosopher whose work has been very influential in the philosophy of mind, the philosophy of science, and ethics. He collaborated with Bernard Williams to write a well-respected book about utilitarianism (see Chapter 5).

This selection explains and defends what many philosophers have come to call the central state identity theory (or just the identity theory), the materialist or physicalist view that mental states are *strictly identical* to brain states or processes. This is *not* merely the view that mental states are caused by or correlated with brain states, since most dualist views accept and even insist on that. A proponent of the identity theory, on the other hand, says that a mental state *just is* a brain state, that there is only one state and not two, a single state that can be referred to with either a mental state description or a brain state description. (Smart, like most materialists, takes the results of science very seriously and is very suspicious of anything outside the boundaries of scientific inquiry.)

The views described would be versions of **logical behaviorism:** the once widely accepted (but still extremely implausible) thesis that mental states are nothing more than overt behavior or dispositions to such behavior (see the chapter introduction). Smart eventually rejects this view.

To say that the experience, whether of pain or the afterimage, is something "irreducibly psychical" is at least mainly to say that it is something more than physical, something that cannot be reduced to the physical.

By citing **"Occam's razor,"** Smart appeals to a principle of *parsimony,* a principle that recommends *simplicity* in theory construction: don't multiply entities beyond necessity.

Sensations and Brain Processes

. . . Suppose that I report that I have at this moment a roundish, blurry-edged after-image which is yellowish towards its edge and is orange towards its center. What is it that I am reporting? One answer to this question might be that I am not reporting anything, that when I say that it looks to me as though there is a roundish yellowy-orange patch of light on the wall I am expressing some sort of *temptation,* the temptation to say that there *is* a roundish yellowy-orange patch on the wall (though I may know that there is not such a patch on the wall). . . . Similarly, when I "report" a pain, I am not really reporting anything (or, if you like, I am reporting in a queer sense of "reporting"), but am doing a sophisticated sort of wince. (1) . . . The suggestion I wish if possible to avoid is . . . that "I am in pain" is a genuine report, and that what it reports is an irreducibly psychical something. And similarly the suggestion I wish to resist is also that to say "I have a yellowish-range after-image" is to report something irreducibly psychical. (2)

Why do I wish to resist this suggestion? Mainly because of Occam's razor. (3) It seems to me that science is increasingly giving us a

From *The Philosophy of Mind,* edited by V. C. Chappell (Englewood Cliffs, N.J.: Prentice-Hall, 1962).

viewpoint whereby organisms are able to be seen as physicochemical mechanisms: it seems that even the behavior of man himself will one day be explicable in mechanistic terms. There does seem to be, so far as science is concerned, nothing in the world but increasingly complex arrangements of physical constituents. All except for one place: in consciousness. That is, for a full description of what is going on in a man you would have to mention not only the physical processes in his tissues, glands, nervous system, and so forth, but also his states of consciousness: his visual, auditory, and tactual sensations, his aches and pains. That these should be *correlated* with brain processes does not help, for to say that they are *correlated* is to say that they are something "over and above." (4) You cannot correlate something with itself. You correlate footprints with burglars, but not Bill Sikes the burglar with Bill Sikes the burglar. So sensations, states of consciousness, do seem to be the one sort of thing left outside the physicalist picture, and for various reasons I just cannot believe that this can be so. That everything should be explicable in terms of physics (together of course with descriptions of the ways in which the parts are put together . . .) except the occurrence of sensations seems to me to be frankly unbelievable. Such sensations would be "nomological danglers," to use Feigl's expression. (5) It is not often realized how odd would be the laws whereby these nomological danglers would dangle. It is sometimes asked, "Why can't there by psychophysical laws which are of a novel sort, just as the laws of electricity and magnetism were novelties from the standpoint of Newtonian mechanics?" Certainly we are pretty sure in the future to come across new ultimate laws of a novel type, but I expect them to relate simple constituents: for example, whatever ultimate particles are then in vogue. I cannot believe that ultimate laws of nature could relate simple constituents to configurations consisting of perhaps billions of neurons (and goodness knows how many billion billions of ultimate particles) all put together for all the world as though their main purpose in life was to be a negative feedback mechanism of a complicated sort. Such ultimate laws would be like nothing so far known in science. They have a queer "smell" to them. I am just unable to believe in the nomological danglers themselves, or in the laws whereby they would dangle. If any philosophical arguments seemed to compel us to believe in such things, I would suspect a catch in the argument. (6) In any case it is the object of this paper to show that there are no philosophical arguments which compel us to be dualists.

The above is largely a confession of faith, but it explains why I find [the logical behaviorist view] so congenial. For on this view there are, in a sense, no sensations. A man is a vast arrangement of physical particles, but there are not, over and above this, sensations or states of consciousness. There are just behavioral facts about this vast mechanism, such as that it expresses a temptation (behavior disposition) to say "there is a yellowish-red patch on the wall" or that it goes through a sophisticated sort of wince, that is, says "I am in pain."

Though for the reasons given above, I am very receptive to the above "expressive" account of sensation statements, I do not feel that it will quite do the trick. Maybe this is because I have not thought it out sufficiently, but it does seem to me as though, when a person says "I have an after-image," he *is* making a genuine report, and that when he says "I have a pain," he *is* doing more than "replace pain-behavior," and that "this more" is not just to say that he is in distress. I am not so sure, however, that to admit this is to admit that there are nonphysical correlates of brain processes. Why should not sensations just be brain processes of a certain sort? There are, of course, well-known (as well as lesser-known) philosophical objections to the view that reports of sensations are reports of brain-processes, but I shall try to argue that these arguments are by no means as cogent as is commonly thought to be the case.

Let me first try to state more accurately the thesis that sensations are brain-processes. It is not the thesis that, for example, "after-image" or "ache" means the same as "brain process of sort X" (where "X" is replaced by a description of a certain sort of brain process). (7) It is that, in so far as "afterimage" or "ache" is a report of a process, it is a report of a process that *happens to be* a brain process. It follows that the thesis does not claim that sensation statements can be *translated* into statements

R A materialist or physicalist isn't satisfied with the claim that mental states are merely *correlated* with brain states. A dualist could agree with this claim, since it is consistent with the view that mental states are still something metaphysically distinct from brain states.

"Nomological" just means having to do with or in accordance with laws of nature. By saying that sensations are "nomological danglers," Smart means that they are caused by physical states according to laws but cannot cause physical states—and thus "dangle" in relation to the physical world. Smart is assuming that the only dualist view that is even worth taking seriously is **epiphenomenalism.**

As Smart admits in the next paragraph, he has given no very specific argument against dualism here, merely reported that he just can't believe it is true.

When someone says "A is B," the claim is sometimes based on an identity of meaning and sometimes not. For example, the claim that bachelors are unmarried adult males depends on and can be taken as a way of saying that "bachelor" *means the same as* "unmarried adult male." In contrast, the claim that the president of the United States in 2003 was George W. Bush is not based on an identity of meaning: a person could fully understand the meaning of both of these two expressions and not thereby know that they refer to the same entity.

8

R There is one smallest prime number greater than 5, is namely 7. You can refer to *that thing* either with the label "7" or with the label "the smallest prime number greater than 5." Smart's claim is that there are not two things, a sensation and a brain process, but just one thing, which you can refer to with the label "sensation" or with the label "brain process."

9

The objection assumes that if there are two different terms or labels for the same thing, then someone who understands one of them would understand the other and also know that they refer to the same thing. (See Discussion Question 1.)

10

R There are not two things here but just one thing, described in two different ways.

(The lightning example is an excellent analogy for understanding Smart's view about the relation between the common-sense idea of a sensation and the account in terms of brain processes.)

11

A **contingent** statement is one that is not made true simply by the meaning of its terms.

12

R The descriptions "the Morning Star" and "the Evening Star" both in fact refer to the planet Venus. But that the astronomical object often visible early in the morning is the very same one that is often visible early in the evening does not follow from the meanings of these expressions and had to be empirically discovered.

13

Smart refers here to the view called property or attribute dualism (see the chapter introduction).

about brain processes. Nor does it claim that the logic of a sensation statement is the same as that of a brain-process statement. All it claims is that in so far as a sensation statement is a report of something, that something is in fact a brain process. Sensations are nothing over and above brain processes. Nations are nothing "over and above" citizens, but this does not prevent the logic of nation statements being very different from the logic of citizen statements, nor does it insure the translatability of nation statements into citizen statements. (I do not, however, wish to assert that the relation of sensation statements to brain-process statements is very like that of nation statements to citizen statements. Nations do not just *happen to be* nothing over and above citizens, for example. I bring in the "nations" example merely to make a negative point: that the fact that the logic of A-statements is different from that of B-statements does not insure that A's are anything over and above B's.)

Remarks on Identity. When I say that a sensation is a brain process or that lightning is an electric discharge, I am using "is" in the sense of *strict identity*. (Just as in the—in this case necessary—proposition "7 is identical with the smallest prime number greater than 5.") [8] When I say that a sensation is a brain process or that lightning is an electric discharge I do not mean just that the sensation is somehow spatially or temporally continuous with the brain process or that the lightning is just spatially or temporally continuous with the discharge. . . .

I shall now discuss various possible objections to the view that the processes reported in sensation statements are in fact processes in the brain. Most of us have met some of these objections in our first year as philosophy students. All the more reason to take a good look at them. Others of the objections will be more recondite and subtle.

Objection 1. Any illiterate peasant can talk perfectly well about his after-images, or how things look or feel to him, or about his aches and pains, and yet he may know nothing whatever about neurophysiology. A man may, like Aristotle, believe that the brain is an organ for cooling the body without any impairment of his ability to make true statements about his sensations. Hence the things we are talking about when we describe our sensations cannot be processes in the brain. [9]

Reply. . . . Consider lightning. Modern physical science tells us that lightning is a certain kind of electrical discharge due to ionization of clouds of water vapor in the atmosphere. This, it is now believed, is what the true nature of lightning is. Note that there are not two things: a flash of lightning and an electrical discharge. There is one thing, a flash of lightning, which is described scientifically as an electrical discharge to the earth from a cloud of ionized water molecules. [10] . . . We say that what lightning really is, what its true nature as revealed by science is, is an electrical discharge. . . .

...

In short, the reply to Objection 1 is that there can be contingent statements of the form "A is identical with B," and a person may well know that something is an A without knowing that it is a B. [11] An illiterate peasant might well be able to talk about his sensations without knowing about his brain processes, just as he can talk about lightning though he knows nothing of electricity.

. . . Again, "I see the Evening Star" does not *mean* the same as "I see the Morning Star," and yet "The Evening Star and the Morning Star are one and the same thing" is a contingent proposition . . . . [12]

Objection 3. Even if Objection 1 [does] . . . not prove that sensations are something over and above brain-processes, [it does] prove that the qualities of sensations are something over and above the qualities of brain-processes. That is, it may be possible to get out of asserting the existence of irreducibly psychic processes, but not out of asserting the existence of irreducibly psychic *properties*. . . . [13]

Indeed, it might be thought that the objection succeeds at one jump. For consider the property of "being a yellow flash." It might seem that this property lies inevitably outside the physicalist framework within which I am trying to work . . . I must therefore digress for a moment and indicate how I deal with secondary qualities. [14] I shall concentrate on color.

First of all, let me introduce the concept of a normal percipient. One person is more a normal percipient than another if he can make color discriminations that the other cannot. For example, if A can pick a lettuce leaf out of a heap of cabbage leaves, whereas B cannot though he can pick a lettuce leaf out of a heap of beetroot leaves, then A is more normal than B. (I am assuming that A and B are not given time to distinguish the leaves by their slight difference in shape, and so forth.) From the concept of "more normal than" it is easy to see how we can introduce the concept of "normal." . . . I say that "This is red" means something roughly like "A normal percipient would not easily pick this out of a clump of geranium petals though he would pick it out of a clump of lettuce leaves." (15) Of course it does not exactly mean this: a person might know the meaning of "red" without knowing anything about geraniums, or even about normal percipients. But the point is that a person can be *trained* to say "This is red" of objects which would not easily be picked out of geranium petals by a normal percipient, and so on. (Note that even a color-blind person can reasonably assert that something is red, though of course he needs to use another human being, not just himself, as his "color meter.") This account of secondary qualities explains their unimportance in physics. For obviously the discriminations and lack of discriminations made by a very complex neurophysiological mechanism are hardly likely to correspond to simple and nonarbitrary distinctions in nature.

I therefore elucidate colors as powers, in Locke's sense, to evoke certain sorts of discriminatory responses in human beings. They are also, of course, powers to cause sensations in human beings (an account still nearer Locke's). But these sensations, I am arguing, are identifiable with brain processes. (16)

Now how do I get over the objection that a sensation can be identified with a brain process only if it has some phenomenal property, not possessed by brain processes, whereby one-half of the identification may be, so to speak, pinned down? (17)

Reply. My suggestion is as follows. When a person says, "I see a yellowish-orange after-image," he is saying something like this: "*There is something going on which is like what is going on when* I have my eyes open, am awake, and there is an orange illuminated in good light in front of me, that is, when I really see an orange." . . . Notice that the italicized words, namely "there is something going on which is like what is going on when," are all quasilogical or topic-neutral words. (18) This explains why the ancient Greek peasant's reports about his sensations can be neutral between dualistic metaphysics or my materialistic metaphysics. It explains how sensations can be brain-processes and yet how a man who reports them need know nothing about brain-processes. For he reports them only very abstractly as "something going on which is like what is going on when . . . ." Similarly, a person may say "someone is in the room," thus reporting truly that the doctor is in the room, even though he has never heard of doctors. (There are not two people in the room: "someone" *and* the doctor.) This account of sensation statements also explains the singular elusiveness of "raw feels" (19) —why no one seems to be able to pin any properties on them. Raw feels, in my view, are colorless for the very same reason that *something* is colorless. This does not mean that sensations do not have plenty of properties, for if they are brain-processes they certainly have lots of neurological properties. It only means that in speaking of them as being like or unlike one another we need not know or mention these properties.

This, then, is how I would reply to Objection 3. The strength of my reply depends on the possibility of our being able to report that one thing is like another without being able to state the respect in which it is like. I do not see why this should not be so. If we think cybernetically about the nervous system we can envisage it as able to respond to certain likenesses of its internal processes without being able to do more. (20) It would be easier to build a machine which would tell us, say on a punched tape, whether or not two objects were similar, than it would be to build a machine which would report wherein the similarities consisted.

Objection 4. The after-image is not in physical space. The brain-process is. So the after-image is not a brain-process.

John Locke (see Chapter 2), said that primary qualities (shape, size, motion) really exist in objects, but that secondary qualities (color, taste, odor) are mere powers in objects to cause us to have certain experiences—so that such objects do not really have any quality like the one we experience.

Pretend here that geranium petals are always red and lettuce leaves never red.

A discriminatory response is a kind of behavior and thus publicly observable; while a sensation is a mental event, not publicly observable.

Phenomenal properties (also referred to as *qualia*) are the distinctive properties allegedly found in subjective experience, such as color as directly experienced.

The objection is that sensations must be picked out via such properties and that brain processes do not have such properties, so sensations cannot after all be identical to brain processes.

By "quasilogical or topic-neutral," Smart means that these reports are highly abstract, saying only that two situations are similar in some unspecified way.

"Raw feel" is a way of referring to the qualities of immediately experienced sensations. Smart is suggesting that we are not really aware of the specific character of such qualities.

STOP The raw feel of sucking on a lemon is very different from the raw feel of sucking on a sugar cube. Are we aware of the specific qualities involved, or only of an otherwise unspecified similarity between two cases of sucking on a lemon or two of sucking on a sugar cube?

Reply. This is an *ignoratio elenchi.* [21] I am not arguing that the after-image is a brain-process, but that the experience of having an after-image is a brain-process. It is the *experience* which is reported in the introspective report. Similarly, if it is objected that the after-image is yellowy-orange, my reply is that it is the experience of seeing yellowy-orange that is being described, and this experience is not a yellowy-orange something. So to say that a brain-process cannot be yellowy-orange is not to say that a brain-process cannot in fact be the experience of having a yellowy-orange after-image. There is, in a sense, no such thing as an after-image . . . , though there is such a thing as the experience of having an image, and this experience is described indirectly in material object language, not in phenomenal language, for there is no such thing. [22] We describe the experience by saying, in effect, that it is like the experience we have when, for example, we really see a yellowy-orange patch on the wall. Trees and wallpaper can be green, but not the experience of seeing or imagining a tree or wallpaper. (Or if they are described as green or yellow this can only be in a derived sense.)

Objection 5. It would make sense to say of a molecular movement in the brain that it is swift or slow, straight or circular, but it makes no sense to say this of the experience of seeing something yellow.

Reply. So far we have not given sense to talk of experiences as swift or slow, straight or circular. But I am not claiming that "experience" and "brain-process" mean the same or even that they have the same logic. "Somebody" and "the doctor" do not have the same logic, but this does not lead us to suppose that talking about somebody telephoning is talking about someone over and above, say, the doctor. The ordinary man when he reports an experience is reporting that something is going on, but he leaves it open as to what sort of thing is going on, whether in a material solid medium or perhaps in some sort of gaseous medium, or even perhaps in some sort of nonspatial medium (if this makes sense). All that I am saying is that "experience" and "brain-process" may in fact refer to the same thing, and if so we may easily adopt a convention (which is not a change in our present rules for the use of experience words but an addition to them) whereby it would make sense to talk of an experience in terms appropriate to physical processes. [23]

Objection 6. Sensations are private, brain processes are *public.* If I sincerely say, "I see a yellowish-orange after-image," and I am not making a verbal mistake, then I cannot be wrong. But I can be wrong about a brain-process. . . . Moreover, it makes sense to say that two or more people are observing the same brain-process but not that two or more people are reporting the same inner experience.

Reply. This shows that the language of introspective reports has a different logic from the language of material processes. It is obvious that until the brain-process theory is much improved and widely accepted there will be no *criteria* for saying "Smith has an experience of such-and-such a sort" *except* Smith's introspective reports. [24] So we have adopted a rule of language that (normally) what Smith says goes.

...

If it is asked what is the difference between those brain processes which, in my view, are experiences and those brain processes which are not, I can only reply that it is at present unknown. . . . [25] But at the very least, we can classify the brain processes which are experiences as those brain processes which are, or might have been, causal conditions of those pieces of verbal behavior which we call reports of immediate experience.

I have now considered a number of objections to the brain-process thesis. I wish now to conclude with some remarks on the logical status of the thesis itself. U. T. Place seems to hold that it is a straight-out scientific hypothesis. If so, he is partly right and partly wrong. If the issue is between (say) a brain-process thesis and a heart thesis, or a liver thesis, or a kidney thesis, then the issue is a purely empirical one, and the verdict is overwhelmingly in favor of the brain. The right sorts of things don't go on in the heart, liver, or kidney, nor do these organs possess the right sort of complexity of structure. On the other hand, if the issue is between a brain-or-liver-or-kidney thesis

Smart is saying, not just that we don't have terms for phenomenal properties, but we are not aware of any specific properties at all, only of unspecified similarities between situations. Is his claim plausible? (See Discussion Question 2.)

An ***ignoratio elenchi*** is the mistake one makes when one argues for or objects to an irrelevant claim, as opposed to the one that is at issue.

Phenomenal language would directly describe phenomenal properties. Since Smart denies the existence of phenomenal properties, he also holds that there is no such thing as phenomenal language.

Smart's claim is that after it is discovered that sensations are brain processes, the claims that they have properties like speed or direction could come to be meaningful even if they aren't at present. The underlying suggestion is that before this change occurs, such claims may be empty or unintelligible, but not absurd or nonsensical.

The suggestion here is that after we come to realize that the identity theory is true, we could in principle tell when Smith is having a particular experience just by examining his brain. (This idea will be important later on in the chapter.)

This amounts to a further expression of faith on Smart's part: there must be some sort of difference between a brain process that is an experience (or is conscious) and one that is not. And, if Smart is right that an experience is just a brain process and nothing more, whatever that difference turns out to be, it will be a purely physical difference.

(that is, some form of materialism) on the one hand and epiphenomenalism on the other hand, then the issue is not an empirical one. For there is no conceivable experiment which could decide between materialism and epiphenomenalism. 26 This latter issue is not like the average straight-out empirical issue in science, but like the issue between the nineteenth-century English naturalist Philip Gosse and the orthodox geologists and paleontologists of his day. According to Gosse, the earth was created about 4000 B.C. exactly as described in *Genesis,* with twisted rock strata, "evidence" of erosion, and so forth, and all sorts of fossils, all in their appropriate strata, just as if the usual evolutionist story had been true. Clearly this theory is in a sense irrefutable: no evidence can possibly tell against it. Let us ignore the theological setting in which Philip Gosse's hypothesis had been placed, thus ruling out objections of a theological kind, such as "what a queer God who would go to such elaborate lengths to deceive us." Let us suppose that it is held that the universe just *began* in 4004 B.C. with the initial conditions just everywhere as they were in 4004 B.C., and in particular that our own planet began with sediment in the rivers, eroded cliffs, fossils in the rocks, and so on. No scientist would ever entertain this as a serious hypothesis, consistent though it is with all possible evidence. The hypothesis offends against the principles of parsimony and simplicity. There would be far too many brute and inexplicable facts. Why are pterodactyl bones just as they are? No explanation in terms of the evolution of pterodactyls from earlier forms of life would any longer be possible. We would have millions of facts about the world as it was in 4004 B.C. that just have to be *accepted.*

The issue between the brain-process theory and epiphenomenalism seems to be of the above sort. . . . If it be agreed that there are no cogent philosophical arguments which force us into accepting dualism, and if the brain process theory and dualism are equally consistent with the facts, then the principles of parsimony and simplicity seem to me to decide overwhelmingly in favor of the brain-process theory. 27 As I pointed out earlier, dualism involves a large number of irreducible psychophysical laws (whereby the "nomological danglers" dangle) of a queer sort, that just have to be taken on trust, and are just as difficult to swallow as the irreducible facts about the paleontology of the earth with which we are faced on Philip Gosse's theory.

26 *Stop and Think*

Think carefully about this claim and about the difference between the identity theory and epiphenomenalism. Is Smart right that there is no *empirical* way to decide between the two views? (See Discussion Question 3.)

27

The appeal to simplicity is relevant *only* if everything else is equal, if there are no other considerations either way. Contrary to Smart's claim here, some philosophers think that there are serious objections to physicalism (for example, the so-called *knowledge argument* discussed later in the chapter). If so, these would override the appeal to simplicity.

Discussion Questions

1. It is common to have more than one way of referring to or describing the same thing: "George Washington" and "the first president of the United States" refer to the same thing (a person), but not in the same way. Make a list of examples of this sort of situation, trying to think of cases that are as different from each other as possible. If your list is comprehensive enough, there will be cases where someone could not understand either of two ways of referring to or describing the same thing without both understanding the other one and realizing that they are references to or descriptions of the same thing. But how often is this the case? How common are cases where one way of referring or describing could be understood without understanding the other? How common are cases where both could be understood without realizing that they refer to or describe the same thing?

2. Suppose that you are much better than one of your friends at identifying musical instruments simply by hearing the sound they produce: you can distinguish the sound of a viola from the sound of a cello or the sound of a guitar from the sound of a lute, but your friend cannot. It seems plausible to say that you are able to do this because either (a) your sensations are more differentiated than your friend's (a cello and a viola playing a given note produce qualitatively different sensations in you but the same ones in your friend) or (b) you are more sensitive to the differences between different sensations than your friend (though the cello and viola produce different sensations in each of you, you can recognize the difference but your friend cannot). Someone who accepts the existence of phenomenal properties will say that in case (a) your sensations have different phenomenal properties, while your friend's do not; and that in case (b),

you are able to recognize a difference between two different phenomenal properties, but your friend is not. What will Smart have to say about these cases, since he denies the very existence of phenomenal properties? How plausible is his view? Are you in fact aware of phenomenal properties when you make such discriminations?

3. Suppose that for each kind of sensation, there is a kind of brain process that is at least *correlated* with it in the sense that they always occur at the same times in the same persons. According to the identity theory, the sensation and the brain process are the very same entity; while according to epiphenomenalism, the brain process causes the sensation according to a law of nature (but the sensation itself has no further effect on anything physical). These seem to be *very* different views. Is Smart right that there is no way to decide empirically which is true: no observation or experiment of any sort that would provide evidence one way or the other?

Jerry Fodor

Jerry Fodor (1935–) is an American philosopher who teaches at Rutgers University and has been one of the main contributors to the debates in the philosophy of mind (and allied fields, such as philosophy of language and cognitive science) in the last several decades. He argues that functionalism, the view that mental states are functional states defined in terms of causal role, is preferable to either dualism or various earlier versions of materialism. His argument for that claim proceeds by considering the other views in roughly their order of historical development and arguing that each is fatally flawed. Fodor's suggestion is that functionalism in effect combines the best features of previous theories into one view. The guiding constraint in his discussion is to find a theory that will justify and make sense of the practice and theorizing of working psychologists, people who explain our behavior by appealing to our mental states (think of the umbrella example in the chapter introduction).

Largely because functionalism is initially a difficult view to grasp, this is a quite difficult article, and our annotations are therefore themselves longer and more complicated (and sometimes more critical, in the aim of clarity) than is the case with most other articles in this book. Be patient and try to work yourself gradually into an understanding of functionalism and of the issues that it raises.

Mind-Body Problem

. . . It is only rather recently that philosophers have become seriously interested in the methodological tenets of psychology. Psychological explanations of behavior refer liberally to the mind and to states, operations and processes of the mind. The philosophical difficulty comes in stating in unambiguous language what such references imply.

Traditional philosophies of mind can be divided into two broad categories: dualist theories and materialist theories. In the dualist approach the mind is a nonphysical substance. In materialist theories the mental is not distinct from the physical; indeed, all mental states, properties, processes and operations are in principle identical with physical states, properties, processes and operations. Some materialists, known as behaviorists, maintain that all talk of mental causes can be eliminated from the language of psychology in favor of talk of environmental stimuli and behavioral responses. Other materialists, the identity theorists, contend that there are mental causes and that they are identical with neurophysiological events in the brain.

In the past 15 years a philosophy of mind called functionalism that is neither dualist nor materialist has emerged from philosophical reflection on developments in artificial intelligence,

From *Scientific American,* Vol. 262 (January 1990).

computational theory, linguistics, cybernetics, and psychology. [1] All these fields, which are collectively known as the cognitive sciences, have in common a certain level of abstraction and a concern with systems that process information. Functionalism, which seeks to provide a philosophical account of this level of abstraction, recognizes the possibility that systems as diverse as human beings, calculating machines and disembodied spirits could all have mental states. In the functionalist view the psychology of a system depends not on the stuff it is made of (living cells, metal or spiritual energy) but on how the stuff is put together. Functionalism is a difficult concept, and one way of coming to grips with it is to review the deficiencies of the dualist and materialist philosophies of mind it aims to displace.

The chief drawback of dualism is its failure to account adequately for mental causation. If the mind is nonphysical, it has no position in physical space. How, then, can a mental cause give rise to a behavioral effect that has a position in space? To put it another way, how can the nonphysical give rise to the physical without violating the laws of the conservation of mass, of energy and of momentum? [2]

The dualist might respond that the problems of how an immaterial substance can cause physical events is not much obscurer than the problem of how one physical event can cause another. Yet there is an important difference: there are many clear cases of physical causation but not one clear case of nonphysical causation. Physical interaction is something philosophers, like all other people, have to live with. Nonphysical interaction, however, may be no more than an artifact of the immaterialist construal of the mental. Most philosophers now agree that no argument has successfully demonstrated why mind-body causation should not be regarded as a species of physical causation. [3]

Dualism is also incompatible with the practices of working psychologists. The psychologist frequently applies the experimental methods of the physical sciences to the study of the mind. If mental processes were different in kind from physical processes, there would be no reason to expect these methods to work in the realm of the mental. In order to justify their experimental methods many psychologists urgently sought an alternative to dualism. [4]

In the 1920s John B. Watson of Johns Hopkins University made the radical suggestion that behavior does not have mental causes. He regarded the behavior of an organism as its observable responses to stimuli, which he took to be the causes of its behavior. Over the next 30 years psychologists such as B. F. Skinner of Harvard University developed Watson's ideas into an elaborate world view in which the role of psychology was to catalogue the laws that determine causal relations between stimuli and responses. In this "radical behaviorist" view the problem of explaining the nature of the mind-body interaction vanishes; there is no such interaction. [5]

Radical behaviorism has always worn an air of paradox. For better or worse, the idea of mental causation is deeply ingrained in our everyday language and in our ways of understanding our fellow men and ourselves. For example, people commonly attribute behavior to beliefs, to knowledge, and to expectations. Brown puts gas in his tank because he believes the car will not run without it. Jones writes not "acheive" but "achieve" because he knows the rule about putting *i* before *e*. Even when a behavioral response is closely tied to an environmental stimulus, mental processes often intervene. Smith carries an umbrella because the sky is cloudy, but the weather is only part of the story. There are apparently also mental links in the causal chain: observation and expectation. The clouds affect Smith's behavior only because he observes them and because they induce in him an expectation of rain. [6] Thus the radical behaviorist must reject an enormous number of common-sense explanations of behavior as mistaken. Is it plausible to any serious degree that we are all as mistaken as that? (Notice that a radical behaviorist cannot consistently say that he advocates radical behaviorism because he *believes* it to be true.)

The radical behaviorist is unmoved by appeals to such cases. He is prepared to dismiss references to mental causes, however plausible they may seem, as the residue of outworn creeds. The radical behaviorist predicts that as psychologists come to understand more about the relations between stimuli and responses they will find it increasingly possible to explain behavior without postulating mental causes.

It is somewhat misleading to describe functionalism as "neither dualist nor materialist." While the functionalist account of mental states is neutral between the two views, virtually all functionalists believe that it is material states that satisfy that account and actually constitute mental states—and much of the point of functionalism is to find a defensible materialist view.

Fodor actually raises two different objections here, one concerning spatial position and the other invoking conservation laws. Neither is developed very fully. (See Discussion Question 1.)

If some materialist account is true, then obviously there will be no reason to regard mind-body causation as something other than physical causation. The arguments to the contrary are just the objections to materialist accounts—which Fodor discusses later.

This objection assumes that the general rationale for the experimental methods of science applies only to investigations of physical things and processes, rather than to any sort of empirical inquiry.

What Fodor calls "radical behaviorism" is different from logical behaviorism (discussed later): it simply denies that mental states are in any way relevant to behavior, without saying anything more about their nature or existence. (But such a denial makes it quite tempting to deny their very existence.)

R Thus the radical behaviorist must reject an enormous number of common-sense explanations of behavior as mistaken.

The strongest argument against behaviorism is that psychology has not turned out this way; the opposite has happened. As psychology has matured, the framework of mental states and processes that is apparently needed to account for experimental observations has grown all the more elaborate. Particularly in the case of human behavior psychological theories satisfying the methodological tenets of radical behaviorism have proved largely sterile, as would be expected if the postulated mental processes are real and causally effective.

Nevertheless, many philosophers were initially drawn to radical behaviorism because, paradoxes and all, it seemed better than dualism. Since a psychology committed to immaterial substances was unacceptable, philosophers turned to radical behaviorism because it seemed to be the only alternative materialist philosophy of mind. The choice as they saw it, was between radical behaviorism and ghosts. (7)

7

Fodor's talk of "ghosts" is a way of mocking dualism.

STOP Think about the claim that radical behaviorism is at least better than dualism. Are the objections to mind-body causation really so strong as to make it better to deny that mental states causally affect behavior at all?

By the early 1960s philosophers began to have doubts that dualism and radical behaviorism exhausted the possible approaches to the philosophy of mind. Since the two theories seemed unattractive, the right strategy might be to develop a materialist philosophy of mind that nonetheless allowed for mental causes. Two such philosophies emerged, one called logical behaviorism and the other called the central-state identity theory.

Logical behaviorism is a semantic theory about what mental terms mean. (8) The basic idea is that attributing a mental state (say thirst) to an organism is the same as saying that the organism is disposed to behave in a particular way (for example to drink if there is water available). On this view every mental ascription is equivalent in meaning to an if-then statement (called a behavioral hypothetical) that expresses a behavioral disposition. For example, "Smith is thirsty" might be taken to be equivalent to the dispositional statement "If there were water available, then Smith would drink some." By definition a behavioral hypothetical includes no mental terms. The if-clause of the hypothetical speaks only of stimuli and the then-clause speaks only of behavioral responses. Since stimuli and responses are physical events, logical behaviorism is a species of materialism.

8

It would be clearer to say that logical behaviorism is a theory about the nature of mental states that relies on and advocates such a semantic theory. Notice in the following discussion that thirst (as opposed to a *sensation* of thirst) is a somewhat odd example—perhaps not really a *mental* state at all (as opposed to a physiological state).

The strength of logical behaviorism is that by translating mental language into the language of stimuli and responses it provides an interpretation of psychological explanations in which behavioral effects are attributed to mental causes. Mental causation is simply the manifestation of a behavioral disposition. More precisely, mental causation is what happens when an organism has a behavioral disposition and the if-clause of the behavioral hypothetical expressing the disposition happens to be true. For example, the causal statement "Smith drank some water because he was thirsty" might be taken to mean "If there were water available, then Smith would drink some, and there was water available."

I have somewhat oversimplified logical behaviorism by assuming that each mental ascription can be translated by a unique behavioral hypothetical. Actually the logical behaviorist often maintains that it takes an open-ended set (perhaps an infinite set) of behavioral hypotheticals to spell out the behavioral disposition expressed by a mental term. The mental ascription "Smith is thirsty" might also be satisfied by a hypothetical "If there were orange juice available, then Smith would drink some" and by a host of other hypotheticals. In any event, the logical behaviorist does not usually maintain he can actually enumerate all the hypotheticals that correspond to a behavioral disposition expressing a given mental term. He only insists that in principle the meaning of any mental term can be conveyed by behavioral hypotheticals. (9)

9

Logical behaviorism claims that *all* there is to any mental state is the truth of a large set of hypothetical statements of this sort. On this view, there is no conscious inner experience involved at all.

The way the logical behaviorist has interpreted a mental term such as thirsty is modeled after the way many philosophers have interpreted a physical disposition such as fragility. The physical disposition "The glass is fragile" is often taken to mean something like "If the glass were struck, then it would break." By the same token the logical behaviorist's analysis of mental causation is similar to the received analysis of one kind of physical causation. The causal statement "The glass broke because it was fragile" is taken to mean something like "If the glass were struck, then it would break, and the glass was struck." (10)

10

This appeal to dispositions raises more problems than the discussion here suggests. What exactly is being claimed about the metaphysical nature of the glass itself when we say, for example, that it is fragile? (See Discussion Question 2.)

By equating mental terms with behavioral dispositions the logical behaviorist has put mental terms on a par with the non-behavioral dispositions of the physical sciences. That is a promising move, because the analysis of non-behavioral dispositions is on relatively solid philosophical ground. An explanation attributing the breaking of a glass to its fragility is surely something even the staunchest materialist can accept. By arguing that mental terms are synonymous with dispositional terms, the logical behaviorist has provided something the radical behaviorist could not: a materialist account of mental causation. [11]

As we will see shortly, Fodor doesn't really agree with this claim.

Nevertheless, the analogy between mental causation as construed by the logical behaviorist and physical causation goes only so far. The logical behaviorist treats the manifestation of a disposition as the sole form of mental causation, whereas the physical sciences recognize additional kinds of causation. There is the kind of causation where one physical event causes another, as when the breaking of a glass is attributed to its having been struck. In fact, explanations that involve event-event causation are presumably more basic than dispositional explanations, because the manifestation of a disposition (the breaking of a fragile glass) always involves event-event causation and not vice versa. . . .

Event-event causation actually seems to be quite common in the realm of the mental. Mental causes typically give rise to behavioral effects by virtue of their interaction with other mental causes. For example, having a headache causes a disposition to take aspirin only if one also has the desire to get rid of the headache, the belief that aspirin exists, the belief that taking aspirin reduces headaches and so on. Since mental states interact in generating behavior, it will be necessary to find a construal of psychological explanations that posits mental processes: causal sequences of mental events. It is this construal that logical behaviorism fails to provide.

Such considerations bring out a fundamental way in which logical behaviorism is quite similar to radical behaviorism. It is true that the logical behaviorist, unlike the radical behaviorist, acknowledges the existence of mental states. Yet since the underlying tenet of logical behaviorism is that references to mental states can be translated out of psychological explanations by employing behavioral hypotheticals, all talk of mental states and processes is in a sense heuristic. The only facts to which the behaviorist is actually committed are facts about relations between stimuli and responses. In this respect logical behaviorism is just radical behaviorism in a semantic form. Although the former theory offers a construal of mental causation, the construal is Pickwickian. What does not really exist cannot cause anything, and the logical behaviorist, like the radical behaviorist, believes deep down that mental causes do not exist. [12]

Now it has become clear that logical behaviorism cannot account for genuine mental causation, since it really denies that mental causes even exist (and so doesn't really "acknowledge the existence of mental states," as was claimed earlier in this rather confusing paragraph).

An alternative materialist theory of the mind to logical behaviorism is the central-state identity theory. According to this theory, mental events, states and processes are identical with neurophysiological events in the brain, and the property of being in a certain mental state (such as having a headache or believing it will rain) is identical with the property of being in a certain neurophysiological state. On this basis it is easy to make sense of the idea that a behavioral effect might sometimes have a chain of mental causes; that will be the case whenever a behavioral effect is contingent on the appropriate sequence of neurophysiological events.

The central-state identity theory acknowledges that it is possible for mental causes to interact causally without ever giving rise to any behavioral effect, as when a person thinks for a while about what he ought to do and then decides to do nothing. If mental processes are neurophysiological, they must have the causal properties of neurophysiological processes. Since neurophysiological processes are presumably physical processes, the central-state identity theory ensures that the concept of mental causation is as rich as the concept of physical causation. [13]

The "richness" of each concept of causation really isn't the main point—instead just that the identity theory allows mental states to genuinely cause behavior and logical behaviorism does not.

The central-state identity theory provides a satisfactory account of what the mental terms in psychological explanations refer to, and so it is favored by psychologists who are dissatisfied with behaviorism. The behaviorist maintains that mental terms refer to nothing or that they refer to the parameters of stimulus-response relations. Either way the existence of mental entities is only illusory. The identity theorist, on the other hand, argues that mental terms refer to neurophysiological states. Thus he can take seriously the project of explaining behavior by appealing to its mental causes.

The chief advantage of the identity theory is that it takes the explanatory constructs of psychology at face value, which is surely something a philosophy of mind ought to do if it can. [14] The identity theory shows how the mentalistic explanations of psychology could be not mere

R According to the central-state identity theory (as contrasted with logical behaviorism), the kinds of states involved in psychological explanations (things like beliefs and desires and reasoning of various sorts—these are the "explanatory constructs") have genuine existence and can therefore function as genuine causes.

See the previous selection by Smart for more on this point.

Both views agree that a specific mental state (for example, John's current headache) is identical to a certain specific neurophysiological state. The issue between them is whether all headaches of that same kind are identical to neurophysiological states of that same kind—so that only a being with a brain exactly like John's could have such a headache.

The underlying issue is *why* that specific neurophysiological state is a headache of that specific sort: is it because of its specific physical properties, or because of something more abstract, like a causal role, that might be also realized by other sorts of "brains"?

That it is logically possible for machines to have mental properties is not as obvious as Fodor makes it sound. The Martian example is better: if they are sentient creatures like ourselves, then it is plausible to suppose that they can have beliefs and desires and also experience pain, even if their brains are very different from ours. That this is a matter of "programming" is essentially the functionalist claim, which Fodor will eventually defend, but hasn't yet.

(To say that two properties are "coextensive" is to say that they apply to exactly the same things; this does not necessarily mean that they are really the same property, since the coextensiveness could be a coincidence.)

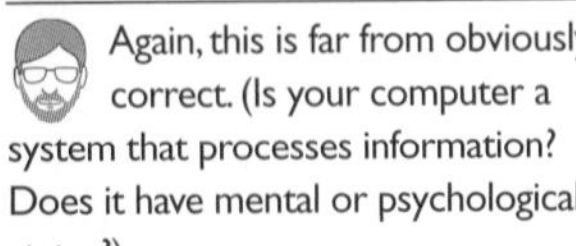
Again, this is far from obviously correct. (Is your computer a system that processes information? Does it have mental or psychological states?)

It is unclear whether or not Fodor is endorsing this suggestion. The problem with it is that it at least seems to leave out the most obvious and important aspect of a headache: the conscious experience, the way it *feels*.

heuristics but literal accounts of the causal history of behavior. Moreover, since the identity theory is not a semantic thesis, it is immune to many arguments that cast in doubt logical behaviorism. A drawback of logical behaviorism is that the observation "John has a headache" does not seem to mean the same thing as a statement of the form "John is disposed to behave in such and such a way." The identity theorist, however, can live with the fact that "John has a headache" and "John is in such and such a brain state" are not synonymous. The assertion of the identity theorist is not that these sentences mean the same thing but only that they are rendered true (or false) by the same neurophysiological phenomena. (15)

The identity theory can be held either as a doctrine about mental particulars (John's current pain or Bill's fear of animals) or as a doctrine about mental universals, or properties (having a pain or being afraid of animals). The two doctrines, called respectively token physicalism and type physicalism, differ in strength and plausibility. Token physicalism maintains only that all the mental particulars that happen to exist are neurophysiological, whereas type physicalism makes the more sweeping assertion that all the mental particulars there could possibly be are neurophysiological. Token physicalism does not rule out the logical possibility of machines and disembodied spirits having mental properties. Type physicalism dismisses this possibility because neither machines nor disembodied spirits have neurons. (16)

Type physicalism is not a plausible doctrine about mental properties even if token physicalism is right about mental particulars. The problem with type physicalism is that the psychological constitution of a system seems to depend not on its hardware, or physical composition, but on its software, or program. Why should the philosopher dismiss the possibility that silicon-based Martians have pains, assuming that the silicon is properly organized? And why should the philosopher rule out the possibility of machines having beliefs, assuming that machines are correctly programmed? If it is logically possible that Martians and machines could have mental properties, then mental properties and neurophysiological processes cannot be identical, however much they may prove to be coextensive. (17)

What it all comes down to is that there seems to be a level of abstraction at which the generalizations of psychology are most naturally pitched. This level of abstraction cuts across differences in the physical composition of the systems to which psychological generalizations apply. In the cognitive sciences, at least, the natural domain for psychological theorizing seems to be all systems that process information. (18) The problem with type physicalism is that there are possible information-processing systems with the same psychological constitution as human beings but not the same physical organization. In principle all kinds of physically different things could have human software.

This situation calls for a relational account of mental properties that abstracts them from the physical structure of their bearers. In spite of the objections to logical behaviorism that I presented above, logical behaviorism was at least on the right track in offering a relational interpretation of mental properties: to have a headache is to be disposed to exhibit a certain pattern of relations between the stimuli one encounters and the responses one exhibits. If that is what having a headache is, however, there is no reason in principle why only heads that are physically similar to ours can ache. Indeed, according to logical behaviorism, it is a necessary truth that any system that has our stimulus-response contingencies also has our headaches. (19)

All of this emerged 10 to 15 years ago as a nasty dilemma for the materialist program in the philosophy of mind. On the one hand the identity theorist (and not the logical behaviorist) had got right the causal character of the interactions of mind and body. On the other the logical behaviorist (and not the identity theorist) had got right the relational character of mental properties. Functionalism has apparently been able to resolve the dilemma. By stressing the distinction computer science draws between hardware and software the functionalist can make sense of both the causal and the relational character of the mental.

The intuition underlying functionalism is that what determines the psychological type to which a mental particular belongs is the causal role of the particular in the mental life of the organism. Functional individuation is differentiation with respect to causal role. A headache, for example, is identified with the type of mental state that among other things causes a disposition for taking aspirin in people who believe aspirin relieves a headache, causes a desire to rid oneself of the pain one is feeling, often causes someone who speaks English to say such things as "I have a headache" and is brought on by overwork, eyestrain, and tension. This list is presumably not complete. More will be known about the nature of a headache as psychological and physiological research discovers more about its causal role.

Functionalism construes the concept of causal role in such a way that a mental state can be defined by its causal relations to other mental states. In this respect functionalism is completely different from logical behaviorism. Another major difference is that functionalism is not a reductionist thesis. It does not foresee, even in principle, the elimination of mentalistic concepts from the explanatory apparatus of psychological theories.

The difference between functionalism and logical behaviorism is brought out by the fact that functionalism is fully compatible with token physicalism. The functionalist would not be disturbed if brain events turn out to be the only things with the functional properties that define mental states. Indeed, most functionalists fully expect it will turn out that way. [20]

Since functionalism recognizes that mental particulars may be physical, it is compatible with the idea that mental causation is a species of physical causation. In other words, functionalism tolerates the materialist solution to the mind-body problem provided by the central-state identity theory. It is possible for the functionalist to assert both that mental properties are typically defined in terms of their relations and that interactions of mind and body are typically causal in however robust a notion of causality is required by psychological explanations. The logical behaviorist can endorse only the first assertion and the type physicalist only the second. As a result functionalism seems to capture the best features of the materialist alternatives to dualism. [21] It is no wonder that functionalism has become increasingly popular.

Machines provide good examples of two concepts that are central to functionalism: the concept that mental states are interdefined and the concept that they can be realized by many systems. [This can be illustrated by contrasting] a behavioristic Coke machine with a mentalistic one. Both machines dispense a Coke for 10 cents. (The price has not been affected by inflation.) The states of the machines are defined by reference to their causal roles, but only [one] machine would satisfy the behaviorist. Its single state (*S0*) is completely specified in terms of stimuli and responses. *S0* is the state a machine is in if, and only if, given a dime as the input, it dispenses a Coke as the output. [22]

The [second] machine has interdefined states (*S1* and *S2*), which are characteristic of functionalism. *S1* is the state a machine is in if, and only if, (1) given a nickel, it dispenses nothing and proceeds to *S2,* and (2) given a dime, it dispenses a Coke and stays in *S1*. *S2* is the state a machine is in if, and only if, (1) given a nickel, it dispenses a Coke and proceeds to *S1,* and (2) given a dime, it dispenses a Coke and a nickel and proceeds to *S1*. What *S1* and *S2* jointly amount to is the machine's dispensing a Coke if it is given a dime, dispensing a Coke and a nickel if it is given a dime and a nickel and waiting to be given a second nickel if it has been given a first one. [23]

Since *S1* and *S2* are each defined by hypothetical statements, they can be viewed as dispositions. Nevertheless, they are not behavioral dispositions because the consequences an input has for a machine in *S1* or *S2* are not specified solely in terms of the output of the machine. Rather, the consequences also involve the machine's internal states.

Nothing about the way I have described the behavioristic and mentalistic Coke machines puts constraints on what they could be made of. Any system whose states bore the proper relations to inputs, outputs and other states could be one of these machines. No doubt it is reasonable to expect such a system to be constructed out of such things as wheels, levers and diodes (token physicalism for Coke machines). Similarly, it is reasonable to expect that our minds may prove to be neurophysiological (token physicalism for human beings).

Nevertheless, the software description of a Coke machine does not logically require wheels, levers and diodes for its concrete realization. By the same token, the software description of the mind does not logically require neurons. As far as functionalism is concerned a Coke machine

The point here is that the description of causal role says nothing about the intrinsic character of the state—about what it is made of, for example—thus leaving open the possibility that it is a brain state, though not requiring that this be so. (But notice that it also seems to say nothing at all about what it is like to consciously experience such a state—or indeed that there is any conscious experience involved at all.)

That is, mental particulars are both defined in terms of relations and capable of genuinely causing other states.

S0 isn't really an internal state of the machine in any interesting sense at all, nor does it involve much in the way of programming or information processing. It could involve just a small lever that is tripped by the dime as it falls into a bin and that then releases a Coke.

S1 and *S2,* on the other hand, do involve information (about whether a nickel has been received since the last Coke was dispensed) and do play different roles in something at least roughly like a program.

with states *S1* and *S2* could be made of ectoplasm, if there is such stuff and if its states have the right causal properties. Functionalism allows for the possibility of disembodied Coke machines in exactly the same way and to the same extent that it allows for the possibility of disembodied minds. [24]

To say that *S1* and *S2* are interdefined and realizable by different kinds of hardware is not, of course, to say that a Coke machine has a mind. Although interdefinitions and functional specification are typical features of mental states, they are clearly not sufficient for mentality. What more is required is a question to which I shall return below.

Some philosophers are suspicious of functionalism because it seems too easy. Since functionalism licenses the individuation of states by reference to their causal role, it appears to allow a trivial explanation of any observed event *E*, that is, it appears to postulate an *E*-causer. For example, what makes the valves in a machine open? Why, the operation of anything that has the functionally defined property causing valves to open.

In psychology this kind of question-begging often takes the form of theories that in effect postulate homunculi with the selfsame intellectual capacities the theorist sets out to explain. [25] Such is the case when visual perception is explained by simply postulating psychological mechanisms that process visual information. The behaviorist has often charged the mentalist, sometimes justifiably, of mongering this kind of question-begging pseudo explanation. The charge will have to be met if functionally defined mental states are to have a serious role in psychological theories.

The burden of the accusation is not untruth but triviality. There can be no doubt that it is a valve opener that opens valves, and it is likely that visual perception is mediated by the processing of visual information. The charge is that such putative functional explanations are mere platitudes. The functionalist can meet this objection by allowing functionally defined theoretical constructs only where mechanisms exist that can carry out the function and only where he has some notion of what such mechanisms might be like. [26] One way of imposing this requirement is to identify the mental processes that psychology postulates with the operations of the restricted class of possible computers called Turing machines.

A Turing machine can be informally characterized as a mechanism with a finite number of program states. The inputs and outputs of the machine are written on a tape that is divided into squares each of which includes a symbol from a finite alphabet. The machine scans the tape one square at a time. It can erase the symbol on a scanned square and print a new one in its place. The machine can execute only the elementary mechanical operations of scanning, erasing, printing, moving the tape and changing state. [27]

The program states of the Turing machine are defined solely in terms of input symbols on the tape, the output symbols on the tape, the elementary operations and the other states of the program. Each program state is therefore functionally defined by the part it plays in the overall operation of the machine. Since the functional role of a state depends on the relation of the state to other states as well as to inputs and outputs, the relational character of the mental is captured by the Turing-machine version of functionalism. Since the definition of a program state never refers to the physical structure of the system running the program, the Turing-machine version of functionalism also captures the idea that the character of a mental state is independent of its physical realization. A human being, a roomful of people, a computer and a disembodied spirit would all be a Turing machine if they operated according to a Turing-machine program. [28]

The proposal is to restrict the functional definition of psychological states to those that can be expressed in terms of the program states of Turing machines. If this restriction can be enforced, it provides a guarantee that psychological theories will be compatible with the demands of mechanisms. Since Turing machines are very simple devices, they are in principle quite easy to build. Consequently by formulating a psychological explanation as a Turing-machine program the psychologist ensures that the explanation is mechanistic, even though the hardware realizing the mechanism is left open.

There are many kinds of computational mechanisms other than Turing machines, and so the formulation of a functionalist psychological

"Ectoplasm" is a term once used to refer to spiritual stuff. Any material complex enough to allow for different states standing in the indicated relations could serve as the "inner states of the Coke machine." (Of course, whatever holds and dispenses the Cokes, together with the Cokes themselves, would still have to be material.)

A "homunculus" ("homunculi" is the plural) is just a little human or human-like being inside the person or the mind or the brain, who is introduced to perform some mysterious process. The point is that postulating a homunculus that, for example, computes sums obviously does nothing really to explain psychologically how people compute sums, because the inner action of the homunculus is just as mysterious as the overt one for which the explanation was originally sought.

To speak of a "mechanism" does not necessarily mean a physical mechanism. The idea is rather that it is a process that is fully understood, for which no further issue of explanation arises. If we can describe a mechanism that processes visual information, then there is no further explanatory issue about how this is done.

Anything that operates in an analogous way counts as a Turing machine—it needn't take this explicit form.

STOP Is the second Coke machine described above a Turing machine? That is, can you see how the operations of the machine could be carried out by a device of the sort described earlier? (See Discussion Question 3.)

theory in Turing-machine notation provides only a sufficient condition for the theory's being mechanically realizable. What makes the condition interesting, however, is that the simple Turing machine can perform many complex tasks. Although the elementary operations of the Turing machine are restricted, iterations of the operations enable the machine to carry out any well-defined computation on discrete symbols.

An important tendency in the cognitive sciences is to treat the mind chiefly as a device that manipulates symbols. [29] If a mental process can be functionally defined as an operation on symbols, there is a Turing machine capable of carrying out the computation and a variety of mechanisms for realizing the Turing machine. Where the manipulation of symbols is important, the Turing machine provides a connection between functional explanation and mechanistic explanation.

The reduction of psychological theory to a program for a Turing machine is a way of exorcising the homunculi. [30] The reduction ensures that no operations have been postulated except those that could be performed by a familiar mechanism. Of course, the working psychologist usually cannot specify the reduction for each functionally individuated process in every theory he is prepared to take seriously. In practice the argument usually goes in the opposite direction; if the postulation of a mental operation is essential to some cherished psychological explanation, the theorist tends to assume that there must be a program for a Turing machine that will carry out that operation.

...

Such is the origin, the provenance and the promise of contemporary functionalism. How much has it actually paid off? This question is not easy to answer because much of what is now happening in the philosophy of mind and the cognitive sciences is directed at exploring the scope and limits of the functionalist explanation of behavior. I shall, however, give a brief overview.

An obvious objection to functionalism as a theory of the mind is that the functionalist definition is not limited to mental states and processes. Catalysts, Coke machines, valve openers, pencil sharpeners, mousetraps and ministers of finance are all in one way or another concepts that are functionally defined, but none is a mental concept such as pain, belief and desire. What, then, characterizes the mental? And can it be captured in a functionalist framework?

The traditional view in the philosophy of mind has it that mental states are distinguished by their having what are called either qualitative content or intentional content. I shall discuss qualitative content first.

It is not easy to say what qualitative content is; indeed, according to some theories, it is not even possible to say what it is because it can be known not by description but only by direct experience. I shall nonetheless attempt to describe it. Try to imagine looking at a blank wall through a red filter. Now change the filter to a green one and leave everything else exactly the way it was. Something about the character of your experience changes when the filter does, and it is this kind of thing that philosophers call qualitative content. I am not entirely comfortable about introducing qualitative content in this way, but it is a subject with which many philosophers are not comfortable. [31]

The reason qualitative content is a problem for functionalism is straightforward. Functionalism is committed to defining mental states in terms of their causes and effects. It seems, however, as if two mental states could have all the same causal relations and yet could differ in their qualitative content. Let me illustrate this with the classic puzzle of the inverted spectrum.

It seems possible to imagine two observers who are alike in all relevant psychological respects except that experiences having the qualitative content of red for one observer would have the qualitative content of green for the other. Nothing about their behavior need reveal the difference because both of them see ripe tomatoes and flaming sunsets as being similar in color and both of them call that color "red." [32] Moreover, the causal connection between their (qualitatively distinct) experiences and their other mental states could also be identical. Perhaps they both think of Little Red Riding Hood when they see ripe tomatoes, feel depressed when they see the color green and so on. It seems as if anything that could be packed into the notion of the causal role of their experiences could be shared by them, and yet the qualitative content of the experiences could be as different as you like. If this is possible, then the

29

This suggestion is in fact fairly pervasive in recent philosophy of mind. How plausible is it? Could manipulation of symbols really be the main thing that the mind does? (See Discussion Question 4.)

30

R If every process and operation is performed by a mechanism (see Annotation 25), then there is no mystery left and thus no need for homunculi.

31

The idea of qualitative content is essentially the same as that of **phenomenal properties** or qualia. (See Annotation 17 to the Smart selection.)

32

At first you might think that if the same object looked differently colored to different people, then the difference would quickly be discovered. But if color words are learned by pointing at objects, then whatever differences there are in color experience will correlate systematically with differences in the way each person understands those words: two such people will agree in calling ripe tomatoes "red" even if they have totally different color experiences when they look at a ripe tomato. And hence their verbal descriptions will not reveal the difference. (Is there any other way in which it might be revealed?)

functionalist account does not work for mental states that have qualitative content. If one person is having a green experience while another person is having a red one, then surely they must be in different mental states. (33)

(33) If two people are in this situation with respect to their experiences of ripe tomatoes, then the qualitative content of their experiential states may be totally different even though the causal role of each of those states is exactly the same: they are caused by ripe tomatoes (and other things such as fire engines, fresh raw beef, etc.) and cause each of them to say "red" when asked what color is being experienced (and to do various other things depending on what else is going on). But then the functionalist account of such experiential states in terms of causal role is mistaken because it leaves out the central feature of such a state.

The example of the inverted spectrum is more than a verbal puzzle. Having qualitative content is supposed to be a chief factor in what makes a mental state conscious. Many psychologists who are inclined to accept the functionalist framework are nonetheless worried about the failure of functionalism to reveal much about the nature of consciousness. Functionalists have made a few ingenious attempts to talk themselves and their colleagues out of this worry, but they have not, in my view, done so with much success. (For example, perhaps one is wrong in thinking one can imagine what an inverted spectrum would be like.) As matters stand, the problem of qualitative content poses a serious threat to the assertion that functionalism can provide a general theory of the mental.

Functionalism has fared much better with the intentional content of mental states. Indeed, it is here that the major achievements of recent cognitive sciences are found. To say that a mental state has intentional content is to say that it has certain semantic properties. For example, for Enrico to believe Galileo was Italian apparently involves a three-way relation between Enrico, a belief and a proposition that is the content of the belief (namely the proposition that Galileo was Italian). In particular it is an essential property of Enrico's belief that it is about Galileo (and not about, say, Newton) and that it is true if, and only if, Galileo was indeed Italian. Philosophers are divided on how these considerations fit together, but it is widely agreed that beliefs involve semantic properties such as expressing a proposition, being true or false and being about one thing rather than another.

...

The current idea is that the semantic properties of a mental representation are determined by aspects of its functional role. In other words, a sufficient condition for having semantic properties can be specified in causal terms. . . .

No philosopher is now prepared to say exactly how the functional role of a mental representation determines its semantic properties. Nevertheless, the functionalist recognizes three types of causal relation among psychological states involving mental representations, and they might serve to fit the semantic properties of mental representations. The three types are causal relations among mental states and stimuli, mental states and responses and some mental states and other ones.

Consider the belief that John is tall. Presumably the following facts, which correspond respectively to the three types of causal relation, are relevant to determining the semantic properties of the mental representation involved in the belief. First, the belief is a normal effect of certain stimulations, such as seeing John in circumstances that reveal his height. Second, the belief is the normal cause of certain behavioral effects, such as uttering "John is tall." Third, the belief is a normal cause of certain other beliefs and a normal effect of certain other beliefs. For example, anyone who believes John is tall is very likely also to believe someone is tall. Having the first belief is normally causally sufficient for having the second belief. And anyone who believes everyone in the room is tall and also believes John is in the room will very likely believe John is tall. The third belief is a normal effect of the first two. In short, the functionalist maintains that the proposition expressed by a given mental representation depends on the causal properties of the mental states in which that mental representation figures. (34)

(34)

All these things seem to be true of the belief that John is tall. The question is whether they are *sufficient* to characterize that mental state: whether *any* state that has this causal role will automatically be such a belief. (The other beliefs involved must also be identified only by causal role.) How plausible is this? (See Discussion Question 5.)

The concept that the semantic properties of mental representations are determined by aspects of their functional role is at the center of current work in the cognitive sciences. Nevertheless, the concept may not be true. Many philosophers who are unsympathetic to the cognitive turn in modern psychology doubt its truth, and many psychologists would probably reject it in the bald and unelaborated way that I have sketched it. Yet even in its sketched form, there is this much to be said in its favor: It legitimizes the notion of mental representation, which has become increasingly important to theorizing in every branch of the cognitive sciences. Recent advances in formulating and testing hypotheses about the character of mental representation in fields ranging from phonetics to computer vision suggest that the concept of mental representation is fundamental to empirical theories of the mind. 35

The behaviorist has rejected the appeal to mental representation because it runs counter to his view of the explanatory mechanisms that can figure in psychological theories. Nevertheless, the science of mental representation is now flourishing. The history of science reveals that when a successful theory comes into conflict with a methodological scruple, it is generally the scruple that gives way. Accordingly, the functionalist has released the behaviorist constraints on psychological explanations. There is probably no better way to decide what is methodologically permissible in science than by investigating what successful science requires.

A mental representation is a mental state that has a content that describes or says something about some thing or situation. To think that baseball is an exciting sport is to have a mental representation whose content makes a specific claim about that specific game.

Discussion Questions

1. On page 169, Fodor raises two objections to dualist accounts of mental causation.

   a. One of these has to do with spatial location: why does a mental state, which according to the dualist does not have a spatial position, produce an effect at one spatial location rather than another—that is, affect one body rather than another? The selection from Foster contains one possible response to this objection (in his discussion of "the problem of causal pairings"). How plausible is this response? Can you think of any other response on behalf of the dualist?

   b. Fodor's second objection appeals to various conservation laws: consider, for example, the law of conservation of energy. Fodor's idea here may be that causal transactions involve energy, so that if there were causal relations between mental states and physical states, energy would be either entering (if the mental state causally affects the physical state) or leaving (if the physical state causally affects the mental state) the physical realm, in either case violating the principle of conservation of energy—assuming that this applies to the physical realm taken by itself. Can you think of a way of understanding the law that would not be violated by such cases? How sure and on what basis are we that the law, understood in the way that Fodor has in mind, is true? (You may have to do a little research about the law of conservation of energy to answer this question.)

2. Think carefully about what it means for something to be *fragile*. Suppose that you've always been told to be very careful with your mother's favorite vase because it is fragile. At one level, you know what that means: this vase will break more easily than most, given similar treatment. But what must be true of the vase itself for this to be so? A dispositional property like fragility describes how an object will behave under certain circumstances, but many philosophers think that such a description is only the first stage of an explanation of the behavior. One might also ask *why* the object behaves in that way in those circumstances, and the answer to this question will usually appeal to some more fundamental, nondispositional property—in the case of the vase, something about its molecular structure. Now think about the analogous question for the behaviorist's dispositions. One answer would be that such a disposition is a result of an underlying mental state, in which case the behaviorist hasn't accounted for mental states after all. Is there some other plausible answer that the behaviorist can give?

3. Try to figure out how a Turing machine would have to be programmed in order to serve as the inner processor of the Coke machine. The machine starts by scanning a blank square of the tape. There is a device of some sort that causes a specific symbol to be printed on the tape when a nickel is inserted and a different symbol for a dime (perhaps just the numerals "5" and "10"); and some further symbols (perhaps a Coke logo and a "minus 5") that cause another device to dispense a Coke or a nickel when they appear on the tape. (These additional devices are not part of the Turing machine, but rather represent its "input" and "output.") Your task is to describe a set of Turing machine states (*S0, S1, S2,* etc.—contrary to what Fodor's discussion suggests, you will need more than two), where *S0* is the starting state as it scans the blank tape before any money has been inserted. For each state, you need to say what the machine does when it is in that state and is looking at each of the five possible states of the tape (including a blank): it can erase the symbol that is there, write a new symbol (but only if the tape is previously blank), or leave that symbol unchanged; and it can move left or right along the tape or stay in the same place (but only one printing or erasing action and one movement per combination of state and symbol). You need to arrange the states so that the machine "knows" how much money has been inserted, prints the Coke symbol when it

has received 10 cents, prints the "minus 5" symbol when change is due, and finishes the process by erasing all of the symbols so that the tape is blank again for the next time. Assume that the "input" device prints the relevant symbol on the square that the machine is scanning if that square is blank and otherwise on the first blank square to the right. Assume also that the people attempting to buy Cokes never put more than 15 cents into the machine and put in more than 10 only if it is a nickel followed by a dime.

4. Fodor suggests (along with many others) that the operations of the mind may be manipulations of symbols. Here a symbol is something analogous to a word in language: something that stands for something, but not in virtue of its intrinsic character. Thus the word "bird" stands for birds, but not because of its intrinsic shape; that shape could just as well have stood for something entirely different or might just have been a meaningless squiggle. (In contrast, a drawing of a bird would stand for a bird because of its specific shape, and so would not in this sense be a symbol.) Fodor's suggestion is essentially that people think about and reason about things by virtue of having symbols in their minds or brains: not symbols of a "natural language" like English, but rather symbols in a "language of thought" that is perhaps innate. To think about birds is to be in a state analogous to having the word "bird" written on a mental blackboard; and to infer from the fact that something is a bird to the conclusion that it is warm-blooded is something like having an occurrence of the mental word "bird" cause an occurrence of the mental word "warm-blooded." One problem with this sort of view is whether and how the person in question *understands* the meanings of the symbols. Think of your computer: it contains symbols of an analogous sort (digital strings of 0 and 1), but does it understand what any of them mean? Is merely processing symbols enough for meaningful mental activity (such as thinking, reasoning, wondering, fearing, etc.)? (The first selection by Searle has more to say about this issue.)
5. Suppose that there is a mental state having the causal role that Fodor describes in the passage corresponding to Annotation 34—or perhaps some more elaborate causal role, with further causal relations added. Will the fact that it satisfies any such set of causal relations be enough to guarantee that it is the *conscious* thought that John is tall? Is there any clear reason why a state could not satisfy any causal role of this sort, however elaborate, and involve no consciousness at all?
6. Foster (p. 160) raises the objection that on a functionalist ("token-token identity") view, only the *physical* features of the brain state that satisfies the functional role required to be a particular mental state will causally affect other physical states, with the mentalistic description of the state being causally irrelevant. If this is so, then functionalism seems objectionable from the standpoint of common sense in the same way that epiphenomenalism was, since it also implies that people's mental states do not causally affect their behavior. Is this a serious problem for functionalism? Would it make sense for a functionalist to attribute causal significance to the fact that a brain state satisfies a certain functional or causal role? If not, does this mean that the mental state is causally irrelevant, even though the brain state is not? Or is it enough that the brain state (which is the mental state) is causally relevant, even though its character as a mental state is not? (This is a *very* hard question, one that functionalists have trouble answering—but still very much worth considering.)

Are Intentional Mental States Analogous to the States of a Computer?

A. M. Turing

Alan Turing (1912–1954) was a British mathematician who is sometimes described as the father of computer science. Turing worked for the British government during World War II and played a vital role in the decoding of German radio communications.

In this article, Turing considers the question "Can computers think?"—a question that is indirectly important for assessing the functionalist view of mental states. Turing argues that the best way to approach this question is to reformulate it in terms of a distinctive game that he describes ("the imitation game")—and one important question about the article is whether this reformulation really captures the original question in an adequate way.

Computing Machinery and Intelligence

I propose to consider the question "Can machines think?" This should begin with definitions of the meaning of the terms "machine" and "think." The definitions might be framed so as to reflect so far as possible the normal use of the words, but this attitude is dangerous. If the meaning of the words "machine" and "think" are to be found by examining how they are commonly used it is difficult to escape the conclusion that the meaning and the answer to the question, "Can machines think?" is to be sought in a statistical survey such as a Gallup poll. But this is absurd. Instead of attempting such a definition I shall replace the question by another, which is closely related to it and is expressed in relatively unambiguous words.

The new form of the problem can be described in terms of a game which we call the "imitation game." It is played with three people, a man (A), a woman (B), and an interrogator (C) who may be of either sex. The interrogator stays in a room apart from the other two. The object of the game for the interrogator is to determine which of the other two is the man and which is the woman. He knows them by labels X and Y, and at the end of the game he says either "X is A and Y is B" or "X is B and Y is A." The interrogator is allowed to put questions to A and B thus:

> C: Will X please tell me the length of his or her hair?

Now suppose X is actually A, then A must answer. It is A's object in the game to try to cause C to make the wrong identification. His answer might therefore be

> "My hair is shingled, and the longest strands are about nine inches long."

In order that tones of voice may not help the interrogator the answers should be written, or better still, typewritten. The ideal arrangement is to have a teleprinter communicating between the two rooms. Alternatively the question and answers can be repeated by an intermediary. The object of the game for the third player (B) is to help the interrogator. The best strategy for her is probably to give truthful answers. She can add such things as "I am the woman, don't listen to him!" to her answers, but it will avail nothing as the man can make similar remarks.

We now ask the question, "What will happen when a machine takes the part of A in this game?" Will the interrogator decide wrongly as often when the game is played like this as he does when the game is played between a man and a woman? These questions replace our original, "Can machines think?" (1)

(1)

Turing's account here of the modification of the game for the computer case is not very clear. As emerges from the following discussion, he has in mind a game in which the interrogator is trying to decide which of the other two players (one a human of either gender and the other a computer) is the computer and which is the human. The human is trying to help him and so will answer truthfully, while the computer is programmed so as to attempt to fool him.

2. Critique of the New Problem

...

The new problem has the advantage of drawing a fairly sharp line between the physical and the intellectual capacities of a man. No engineer or chemist claims to be able to produce a material which is indistinguishable from the human skin. It is possible that at some time this might be done, but even supposing this invention available we should feel there was little point in trying to make a "thinking machine" more human by dressing it up in such artificial flesh. The form in which we have set the problem reflects this fact in the condition which prevents the interrogator from seeing or touching the other competitors, or hearing their voices. (2)

(2)

Since what is at issue is whether the computer can *think*, other features like what it looks like are irrelevant. Communicating via a teleprinter (or the more modern alternative of something like e-mail) is a way of setting aside these irrelevant matters.

The game may perhaps be criticized on the ground that the odds are weighted too heavily against the machine. If the man were to try and pretend to be the machine he would clearly make a very poor showing. He would be given away at once by slowness and inaccuracy in arithmetic. May not machines carry out something which ought to be described as thinking but which is very different from what a man does? This objection is a very strong one, but at least we can say that if, nevertheless, a machine can be constructed to play the imitation game satisfactorily, we need not be troubled by this objection. (3)

(3)

So Turing is saying that being able to fool the interrogator often enough is a **sufficient condition** for deciding (reasonably) that the computer can think, even though perhaps not a **necessary condition:** there might be computers that do not succeed in the game but are still thinking in some other way. This has come to be referred to as "the Turing Test" (see, for example, the Searle selection later in this section).

...

6. Contrary Views on the Main Question

We may now consider the ground to have been cleared and we are ready to proceed to the debate on our question, "Can machines think?" . . .

From *Mind,* Vol. LIX, No. 236 (1950).

It will simplify matters for the reader if I explain . . . my own beliefs in the matter. Consider first the more accurate form of the question. I believe that in about fifty years' time [that is, in about 2000] it will be possible to program computers, with a storage capacity of about 10^9, to make them play the imitation game so well that an average interrogator will not have more than 70 per cent chance of making the right identification after five minutes of questioning. The original question, "Can machines think?" I believe to be too meaningless to deserve discussion. Nevertheless I believe that at the end of the century the use of words and general educated opinion will have altered so much that one will be able to speak of machines thinking without expecting to be contradicted. . . .

Discussion Questions

1. Do you think that your computer (or the one you use in the library or a computer lab) actually thinks in the same sense that you do? When, for example, you play a game on it (perhaps with the computer as your opponent), is it in any way aware of what is going on? Or is it just a calculating machine? Suppose that the program for a computer game includes (as some do) instructions that generate statements from the computer about how much it hates losing or gloating when it defeats you—does that give you any more reason to suppose that it is genuinely thinking? Perhaps most importantly, is there any good reason to think that computers are *conscious*?
2. Does the ability to simulate an apparently intelligent pattern of answers in response to questions provide a good reason for believing that a computer understands the questions and answers and so is thinking? Suppose that an encyclopedia program is able to answer questions and even to answer follow-up questions. Would that show that it is thinking, or might it be just a matter of mechanical information retrieval with no thought or understanding on the part of the computer? Is there some level of performance on such tasks that would make it much more reasonable to suppose that the computer is thinking than that it is merely operating mechanically, and if so, how might that level be specified?
3. Chess-playing programs have achieved a very high level of sophistication: they can easily defeat the average human player and can do very well even against the best human chess players in the world. Is this a good reason for thinking that a computer running such a program is thinking? One thing that seems to be true is that the computer program determines its moves in a very different way from human players, namely by calculating the results of very long strings of alternative moves in a way that no human is capable of. Suppose that in a given chess position, a human and a computer come up with the same excellent move. The human does so by thinking about the position, thinking ahead for several moves but also employing general strategic ideas. The computer merely calculates all the possibilities for many more moves ahead than the human is capable of. Does the fact that it achieves the same result that the human achieves by thinking, but in this very different way, yield any strong reason for believing that the computer is thinking too? Why or why not?
4. Think about contemporary movies in which the issue of whether computers can think is either addressed or assumed. For example, in a movie called *Blade Runner,* there is a robot who acts as if "she" is a human. The film portrays her as "believing" that she is a human; she has been programmed with "memories" of a childhood and has pictures that purport to show her playing when she was a child. But she was never a child, since she was built as a full-grown "woman." She has "skin," and "bleeds" when cut, but her "skin" and "blood" are presumably not chemically the same as human skin and blood. She can move and talk, however, and would clearly pass the Turing Test. She initially fools everyone in the movie—the character played by Harrison Ford even falls in love with her! Assuming that such a case is really possible, what has to be true of this being in order for it to be true that she really thinks? Must there be real consciousness involved, or is the mere behavior enough?—which is essentially Turing's claim.

John R. Searle

John Searle (1932–) is an American philosopher who teaches at the University of California at Berkeley. Most of his work has focused on questions in the philosophy of mind, but he has also made important contributions to the philosophy of language and the philosophy of the social sciences.

Searle is perhaps most famous for his provocative thought experiment called "the Chinese Room." In this article, he uses the Chinese Room thought experiment to argue against a view that he calls Strong AI **(artificial intelligence).** While he never mentions functionalism explicitly, functionalism is in fact the philosophy of mind that underlies and supports strong AI. (There has continued to be a lively debate about this thought experiment ever since Searle first published it in 1980.) In this article, Searle also presents a positive alternative to functionalism: a view, still a version of materialism, according to which mental states are biological or neurobiological in character.

Is the Brain's Mind a Computer Program?

Can a machine think? Can a machine have conscious thoughts in exactly the same sense that you and I have? If by "machine" one means a physical system capable of performing certain functions (and what else can one mean?), then humans are machines of a special biological kind, and humans can think, and so of course machines can think. ❶ And, for all we know, it might be possible to produce a thinking machine out of different materials altogether—say, out of silicon chips or vacuum tubes. Maybe it will turn out to be impossible, but we certainly do not know that yet.

In recent decades, however, the question of whether a machine can think has been given a different interpretation entirely. The question that has been posed in its place is, Could a machine think just by virtue of implementing a computer program? Is the program by itself constitutive of thinking? ❷ This is a completely different question because it is not about the physical, causal properties of actual or possible physical systems but rather about the abstract, computational properties of formal computer programs that can be implemented in any sort of substance at all provided only that the substance is able to carry the program.

A fair number of researchers in artificial intelligence (AI) believe the answer to the second question is yes; that is, they believe that by designing the right programs with the right inputs and outputs, they are literally creating minds. They believe furthermore that they have a scientific test for determining success or failure: the Turing test devised by Alan M. Turing, the founding father of artificial intelligence. The Turing test, as currently understood, is simply this: If a computer can perform in such a way that an expert cannot distinguish its performance from that of a human who has a certain cognitive ability—say, the ability to do addition or to understand Chinese—then the computer also has that ability. ❸ So the goal is to design programs that will simulate human cognition in such a way as to pass the Turing test. What is more, such a program would not merely be a model of the mind: it would literally be a mind, in the same sense that a human mind is a mind.

By no means does every worker in artificial intelligence accept so extreme a view. A more cautious approach is to think of computer models as being useful in studying the mind in the same way that they are useful in studying the weather, economics or molecular biology. To distinguish these two approaches, I call the first strong AI and the second weak AI. It is important to see just how bold an approach strong AI is. Strong AI claims that thinking is merely the manipulation of formal symbols and that is exactly what the computer does: manipulate formal symbols. This view is often summarized by saying, "The mind is to the brain as the program is to the hardware." ❹

Strong AI is unusual among theories of the mind in at least two respects: it can be stated clearly, and it admits of a simple and decisive refutation. The refutation is one that any person can try for himself or herself. Here is how it goes. Consider a language you don't understand. In my case, I do not understand Chinese. To me Chinese writing looks like so many meaningless squiggles. Now suppose I am placed in a room containing baskets full of Chinese symbols. Suppose also that I am given a rule book in English for matching Chinese symbols with other Chinese symbols. The rules identify the symbols entirely by their shapes and do not require that I understand any of them. ❺ The rules might say such things as, "Take a squiggle-squiggle sign from basket number one and put it next to a squoggle-squoggle sign from basket number two."

From *Scientific American*, Vol. 262, (January 1990).

This is of course not the ordinary notion of a "machine" and not the one that Searle is mainly interested in. Note also that he rejects dualism from the outset, though he offers no real argument against it here.

If the program were *constitutive* of thinking, then simply running that program would, by itself, be logically sufficient for thinking (in the same way that being an unmarried adult male is logically sufficient for being a bachelor).

According to this version of the Turing Test, a computer has a certain ability just in case an expert cannot tell on the basis of its responses to inputs that it is *not* a human exercising that very ability.

(Clearly this would not be a good test if the time period involved were very short—say the 5 minutes originally specified by Turing. To make the resulting claim plausible, the requirement seemingly has to be that the difference between a human and the computer cannot be discerned even in an unlimited amount of time.)

As Searle will make clear later, he means by "formal symbols" symbols with no *meaning* that plays any role in the computer's manipulation of them. (The earlier selection from Fodor expresses a view very similar to the one ascribed here to strong AI.)

If the rules identify the symbols by their shape (and order), then obviously the person in the room need not understand the meanings of the symbols in order to follow the rules.

Imagine that people outside the room who understand Chinese hand in small bunches of symbols and that in response I manipulate the symbols according to the rule book and hand back more small bunches of symbols. Now, the rule book is the "computer program." The people who wrote it are "programmers," and I am the "computer." The baskets full of symbols are the "data base," the small bunches that are handed in to me are "questions" and the bunches I then hand out are "answers."

Now suppose that the rule book is written in such a way that my "answers" to the "questions" are indistinguishable from those of a native Chinese speaker. For example, the people outside might hand me some symbols that unknown to me mean, "What's your favorite color?" and I might after going through the rules give back symbols that, also unknown to me, mean, "My favorite is blue, but I also like green a lot." I satisfy the Turing test for understanding Chinese. (6) All the same, I am totally ignorant of Chinese. And there is no way I could come to understand Chinese in the system as described, since there is no way that I can learn the meanings of any of the symbols. Like a computer, I manipulate symbols, but I attach no meaning to the symbols.

6

In order to satisfy the requirements of strong AI for understanding Chinese, the person following these rules would have to be able to produce answers indiscernible from those of a native speaker of Chinese for an essentially unlimited group of questions of this sort. Obviously if this is so, then he will satisfy the Turing Test. (But a relatively short version of the Turing Test might be passed by a person running a program that isn't fully adequate in this way: one that satisfactorily answers the questions that are in fact asked, but would not do so for other questions that don't happen to be asked in the time in question. See Discussion Question 1.)

The point of the thought experiment is this: If I do not understand Chinese solely on the basis of running a computer program for understanding Chinese, then neither does any other digital computer solely on that basis. Digital computers merely manipulate formal symbols according to rules in the program.

What goes for Chinese goes for other forms of cognition as well. (7) Just manipulating the symbols is not by itself enough to guarantee cognition, perception, understanding, thinking and so forth. And since computers, qua computers, are symbol-manipulating devices, merely running the computer program is not enough to guarantee cognition.

7

By "cognition," Searle means thinking of any sort.

This simple argument is decisive against the claims of strong AI. The first premise of the argument simply states the formal character of a computer program. Programs are defined in terms of symbol manipulations, and the symbols are purely formal, or "syntactic." The formal character of the program, by the way, is what makes computers so powerful. The same program can be run on an indefinite variety of hardwares, and one hardware system can run an indefinite range of computer programs. Let me abbreviate this "axiom" as:

> Axiom 1. Computer programs are formal (syntactic).

This point is so crucial that it is worth explaining in more detail. A digital computer processes information by first encoding it in the symbolism that the computer uses and then manipulating the symbols through a set of precisely stated rules. These rules constitute the program. For example, in Turing's early theory of computers, the symbols were simply 0's and 1's, and the rules of the program said such things as. "Print a 0 on the tape, move one square to the left and erase a 1." The astonishing thing about computers is that any information that can be stated in a language can be encoded in such a system and any information-processing task that can be solved by explicit rules can be programmed. (8)

8

See Fodor's discussion of a Turing machine in the earlier selection. It can be proved rigorously that anything that any computer can do can be done by a Turing machine with a sufficiently complicated program.

Two further points are important. First, symbols and programs are purely abstract notions: they have no essential physical properties to define them and can be implemented in any physical medium whatsoever. The 0's and 1's, qua symbols, have no essential physical properties and a fortiori have no physical, causal properties. I emphasize this point because it is tempting to identify computers with some specific technology—say, silicon chips—and to think that the issues are about the physics of silicon chips or to think that syntax identifies some physical phenomenon that might have as yet unknown causal powers, in the way that actual physical phenomena such as electromagnetic radiation or hydrogen atoms have physical, causal properties. The second point is that symbols are manipulated without reference to any meanings. The symbols of the program can stand for anything the programmer or user wants. In this sense the program has syntax but no semantics. (9)

9

The sense in which a program has syntax but no semantics is just that (as we have seen) the rules of the program make no reference to the *meanings* of the symbols (whether or not they have any), but only to their syntactical features: shape, order, and the like.

The next axiom is just a reminder of the obvious fact that thoughts, perceptions, understandings and so forth have a mental content. By virtue of their content they can be about objects and states of affairs in the world. If the content involves language, there will be syntax in addition to semantics, but linguistic understanding requires at least a semantic framework.

If, for example, I am thinking about the last presidential election, certain words will go through my mind but the words are about the election only because I attach specific meanings to these words, in accordance with my knowledge of English. In this respect they are unlike Chinese symbols for me. [10] Let me abbreviate this axiom as:

Axiom 2. Human minds have mental contents (semantics).

Now let me add the point that the Chinese room demonstrated. Having the symbols by themselves—just having the syntax—is not sufficient for having the semantics. Merely manipulating symbols is not enough to guarantee knowledge of what they mean. I shall abbreviate this as:

Axiom 3. Syntax by itself is neither constitutive of nor sufficient for semantics.

At one level this principle is true by definition. One might, of course, define the terms syntax and semantics differently. The point is that there is a distinction between formal elements, which have no intrinsic meaning or content, and those phenomena that have intrinsic content. [11] From these premises it follows that:

Conclusion 1. Programs are neither constitutive of nor sufficient for minds.

And that is just another way of saying that strong AI is false.

It is important to see what is proved and not proved by this argument.

First, I have not tried to prove that "a computer cannot think," since anything that can be simulated computationally can be described as a computer, and since our brains can at some levels be simulated, it follows trivially that our brains are computers and they can certainly think. [12] But from the fact that a system can be simulated by symbol manipulation and the fact that it is thinking, it does not follow that thinking is equivalent to formal symbol manipulation.

Second, I have not tried to show that only biologically based systems like our brains can think. Right now those are the only systems we know for a fact can think, but we might find other systems in the universe that can produce conscious thoughts, and we might even come to be able to create thinking systems artificially. [13] I regard this issue as up for grabs.

Third, strong AI's thesis is not that, for all we know, computers with the right programs might be thinking, that they might have some as yet undetected psychological properties; rather it is that they must be thinking because that is all there is to thinking.

Fourth, I have tried to refute strong AI so defined. I have tried to demonstrate that the program by itself is not constitutive of thinking because the program is purely a matter of formal symbol manipulation—and we know independently that symbol manipulations by themselves are not sufficient to guarantee the presence of meanings. [14] That is the principle on which the Chinese room argument works.

...

. . . the Chinese room argument also refutes any strong AI claims made for the new parallel technologies that are inspired by and modeled on neural networks. Unlike the traditional von Neumann computer, which proceeds in a step-by-step fashion, these systems have many computational elements that operate in parallel and interact with one another according to rules inspired by neurobiology. Although the results are still modest, these "parallel distributed processing," or "connectionist" models raise useful questions about how complex, parallel network systems like those in brains might actually function in the production of intelligent behavior.

The parallel "brainlike" character of the processing, however, is irrelevant to the purely computational aspects of the process. [15] Any function that can be computed on a parallel machine can also be computed on a serial machine. Indeed, because parallel machines are still rare, connectionist programs are usually run on traditional serial machines. Parallel processing, then, does not afford a way around the Chinese room argument.

What is more, the connectionist system is subject even on its own terms to a variant of the objection presented by the original Chinese room argument. Imagine that instead of a Chinese room, I have a Chinese gym: a hall containing many monolingual English-speaking men. These men would carry out the same operations as the nodes and synapses in a connectionist

The process of thinking seems at least to fundamentally depend on the *meanings* or *contents* of our thoughts. We seem to understand what we are thinking about and to reason accordingly, rather than just manipulating symbols with no reference to their meanings. (See Discussion Question 2.)

Something has *intrinsic* content if it has that content entirely because of its internal features and not because of any external relations to other things. Searle thinks that thoughts have intrinsic content in this way. (Fodor would deny this.) But the essential point is that the syntactical features that a computer program relies on are independent of any sort of content. (See Discussion Question 3.)

Contrary to what Searle says here, it isn't at all obvious that anything that can be simulated computationally can be correctly described as a computer. (He later suggests that a stomach digesting pizza can be thus simulated, but it would be extremely odd to say that such a stomach is a computer.)

Searle hasn't mentioned *consciousness* explicitly so far. But in fact the reason that it seems so obvious that the person in the Chinese room doesn't understand Chinese is that there seems to be no consciousness of the meanings of the Chinese characters present.

And, as we have already seen, meaning (or content) appears to be essential to thinking as we ordinarily understand it.

Parallel processing still relies on manipulating formal symbols according to syntactical rules, and therefore does not rely on meaning. The rules are more complex, but they are still merely syntactical.

architecture . . . , and the outcome would be the same as having one man manipulate symbols according to a rule book. No one in the gym speaks a word of Chinese, and there is no way for the system as a whole to learn the meanings of any Chinese words. Yet with appropriate adjustments, the system could give the correct answers to Chinese questions. [16]

There are, as I suggested earlier, interesting properties of connectionist nets that enable them to simulate brain processes more accurately than traditional serial architecture does. But the advantages of parallel architecture for weak AI are quite irrelevant to the issues between the Chinese room argument and strong AI.

...

Many people who are impressed by this argument are nonetheless puzzled about the differences between people and computers. If humans are, at least in a trivial sense, computers, and if humans have a semantics, then why couldn't we give semantics to other computers? Why couldn't we program a Vax or a Cray so that it too would have thoughts and feelings? Or why couldn't some new computer technology overcome the gulf between form and content, between syntax and semantics? What, in fact, are the differences between animal brains and computer systems that enable the Chinese room argument to work against computers but not against brains? [17]

The most obvious difference is that the processes that define something as a computer—computational processes—are completely independent of any reference to a specific type of hardware implementation. One could in principle make a computer out of old beer cans strung together with wires and powered by windmills.

But when it comes to brains, although science is largely ignorant of how brains function to produce mental states, one is struck by the extreme specificity of the anatomy and the physiology. Where some understanding exists of how brain processes produce mental phenomena—for example, pain, thirst, vision, smell—it is clear that specific neurobiological processes are involved. Thirst, at least of certain kinds, is caused by certain types of neuron firings in the hypothalamus, which in turn are caused by the action of a specific peptide, angiotensin II. The causation is from the "bottom up" in the sense that lower-level neuronal processes cause higher-level mental phenomena. Indeed, as far as we know, every "mental" event, ranging from feelings of thirst to thoughts of mathematical theorems and memories of childhood, is caused by specific neurons firing in specific neural architectures. [18]

But why should this specificity matter? After all, neuron firings could be simulated on computers that had a completely different physics and chemistry from that of the brain. The answer is that the brain does not merely instantiate a formal pattern or program (it does that, too), but it also *causes* mental events by virtue of specific neurobiological processes. Brains are specific biological organs, and their specific biochemical properties enable them to cause consciousness and other sorts of mental phenomena. Computer simulations of brain processes provide models of the formal aspects of these processes. But the simulation should not be confused with duplication. The computational model of mental processes is no more real than the computational model of any other natural phenomenon.

One can imagine a computer simulation of the action of peptides in the hypothalamus that is accurate down to the last synapse. But equally one can imagine a computer simulation of the oxidation of hydrocarbons in a car engine or the action of digestive processes in a stomach when it is digesting pizza. And the simulation is no more the real thing in the case of the brain than it is in the case of the car or the stomach. Barring miracles, you could not run your car by doing a computer simulation of the oxidation of gasoline, and you could not digest pizza by running the program that simulates such digestion. It seems obvious that a simulation of cognition will similarly not produce the effects of the neurobiology of cognition. [19]

All mental phenomena, then, are caused by neurophysiological processes in the brain. Hence,

Axiom 4. *Brains cause minds.* 

In conjunction with my earlier derivation, I immediately derive, trivially,

Conclusion 2. Any other system capable of causing minds would have to have causal power (at least) equivalent to those of brains.

R The idea is that each person in the gym receives input symbols, both from outside and from other people in the gym, and then proceeds to follow his own set of rules about what symbols to supply as output, again both to the outside and to others in the gym. (One could just as well have many Chinese rooms with appropriate connections between them along which symbols can pass.)

Here Searle assumes that it is the brain that thinks (and hence once again that dualism is false). Given this assumption, the question is then how and why the brain is able to do this, while computers relying on formal manipulation of symbols are not.

Searle's view is that mental states are "higher-level" properties of the brain that are produced by "lower-level" properties like neuron firings. Elsewhere he offers as an analogy the liquidity of a substance (such as water): just as liquidity is a higher-order property that is caused by the properties of the molecules that make up the substance, so also mental properties are higher-level properties that are caused by the lower-level, "neurobiological" properties of the brain.

R As these examples make clear, the simulation of a certain sort of process is not to be identified with the process itself.

The statement that brains cause minds is highly misleading, since it makes it sound as though the mind is a separate entity from the brain, and this is not Searle's view. Rather, as we have seen, the idea is that specific neurobiological processes in the brain cause particular mental events. But Searle has really offered no clear reason for this view. How plausible is it? (See Discussion Question 4.)

This is like saying that if an electrical engine is to be able to run a car as fast as a gas engine, it must have (at least) an equivalent power output. This conclusion says nothing about the mechanisms. As a matter of fact cognition is a biological phenomenon: mental states and processes are caused by brain processes. This does not imply that only a biological system could think but it does imply that any alternative system, whether made of silicon, beer cans or whatever, would have to have the relevant causal capacities equivalent to those of brains. So now I can derive:

> Conclusion 3. Any artifact that produced mental phenomena, any artificial brain, would have to be able to duplicate the specific causal powers of brains, and it could not do that just by running a formal program. [21]

Furthermore. I can derive an important conclusion about human brains:

> Conclusion 4. The way that human brains actually produce mental phenomena cannot be solely by virtue of running a computer program.

I first presented the Chinese room parable in the pages of *Behavioral and Brain Sciences* in 1980, where it appeared, as is the practice of the journal along with peer commentary, in this case, 26 commentaries. Frankly, I think the point it makes is rather obvious, but to my surprise the publication was followed by a further flood of objections that—more surprisingly—continues to the present day. The Chinese room argument clearly touched some sensitive nerve.

The thesis of strong AI is that any system whatsoever—whether it is made of beer cans, silicon chips or toilet paper—not only might have thoughts and feelings but *must* have thoughts and feelings, provided only that it implements the right program, with the right inputs and outputs. Now, that is a profoundly antibiological view, and one would think that people in AI would be glad to abandon it. Many of them, especially the younger generation, agree with me, but I am amazed at the number and vehemence of the defenders. Here are some of the common objections. [22]

a. In the Chinese room you really do understand Chinese, even though you don't know it. It is, after all, possible to understand something without knowing that one understands it.

b. You don't understand Chinese, but there is an (unconscious) subsystem in you that does. It is, after all, possible to have unconscious mental states, and there is no reason why your understanding of Chinese should not be wholly unconscious.

c. You don't understand Chinese, but the whole room does. You are like a single neuron in the brain, and just as such a single neuron by itself cannot understand but only contributes to the understanding of the whole system you don't understand, but the whole system does.

d. Semantics doesn't exist anyway; there is only syntax. It is a kind of prescientific illusion to suppose that there exist in the brain some mysterious "mental contents," "thought processes" or "semantics." All that exists in the brain is the same sort of syntactic symbol manipulation that goes on in computers. Nothing more.

e. You are not really running the computer program—you only think you are. Once you have a conscious agent going through the steps of the program, it ceases to be a case of implementing a program at all.

f. Computers would have semantics and not just syntax if their inputs and outputs were put in appropriate causal relation to the rest of the world. Imagine that we put the computer into a robot, attached television cameras to the robot's head, installed transducers connecting the television messages to the computer and had the computer output operate the robot's arms and legs. Then the whole system would have a semantics. [23]

g. If the program simulated the operation of the brain of a Chinese speaker, then it would understand Chinese. Suppose that we simulated the brain of a Chinese person at the level of neurons. Then surely such a system would understand Chinese as well as any Chinese person's brain.

And so on.

All of these arguments share a common feature: they are all inadequate because they fail to come to grips with the actual Chinese room argument. That argument rests on the distinction between the formal symbol manipulation that is done by the computer and the mental contents

21

If Searle is right that mental states are biological phenomena, produced by specific properties of the brain, then he is right that only something with those same causal powers could produce such states. And if this is right, then the functionalist view that being a mental state involves only running the right program (having the right software) and not any specific hardware is mistaken.

22

Think carefully about these objections. Many of them may seem sufficiently implausible as to not require much of an answer, but still try to spell out what the answer would be for a, b, d, and e, since those are not discussed further in this selection or the ones that follow. (See Discussion Question 5.) Objection g, as Searle says later, has already been answered, but be sure you see clearly what his answer to it is.

23

The suggestion here is that a mental symbol comes to be meaningful or have a specific content by standing in a causal relation of the right sort to something, normally something outside the person. Thus for example, a mental symbol would come to mean *dog* (or have the content *dog*) by standing in the right sort of causal relation to dogs. Fodor elaborates this objection in the next selection.

biologically produced by the brain, a distinction I have abbreviated—I hope not misleadingly—as the distinction between syntax and semantics. I will not repeat my answers to all of these objections, but it will help to clarify the issues if I explain the weaknesses of the most widely held objection, argument c—what I call the systems reply. (The brain simulator reply, argument g, is another popular one, but I have already addressed that one in the previous section.)

The systems reply asserts that of course *you* don't understand Chinese but the whole system—you, the room, the rule book, the bushel baskets full of symbols—does. When I first heard this explanation, I asked one of its proponents, "Do you mean the room understands Chinese?" His answer was yes. It is a daring move, but aside from its implausibility, it will not work on purely logical grounds. The point of the original argument was that symbol shuffling by itself does not give any access to the meanings of the symbols. But this is as much true of the whole room as it is of the person inside. One can see this point by extending the thought experiment. Imagine that I memorize the contents of the baskets and the rule book, and I do all the calculations in my head. You can even imagine that I work out in the open. There is nothing in the "system" that is not in me, and since I don't understand Chinese, neither does the system. [24]

...

Because the points I have been making are rather obvious—syntax is not the same as semantics, brain processes cause mental phenomena—the question arises, How did we get into this mess? How could anyone have supposed that a computer simulation of a mental process must be the real thing? After all, the whole point of models is that they contain only certain features of the modeled domain and leave out the rest. No one expects to get wet in a pool filled with ping-pong-ball models of water molecules. So why would anyone think a computer model of thought processes would actually think?

Part of the answer is that people have inherited a residue of behaviorist psychological theories of the past generation. The Turing test enshrines the temptation to think that if something behaves as if it had certain mental processes, then it must actually have those mental processes. And this is part of the behaviorists' mistaken assumption that in order to be scientific, psychology must confine its study to externally observable behavior. Paradoxically, this residual behaviorism is tied to a residual dualism. Nobody thinks that a computer simulation of digestion would actually digest anything, but where cognition is concerned, people are willing to believe in such a miracle because they fail to recognize that the mind is just as much a biological phenomenon as digestion. The mind, they suppose, is something formal and abstract, not part of the wet and slimy stuff in our heads. The polemical literature in AI usually contains attacks on something the authors call dualism, but what they fail to see is that they themselves display dualism in a strong form, for unless one accepts the idea that the mind is completely independent of the brain or of any other physically specific system, one could not possibly hope to create minds just by designing programs. [25]

Historically, scientific developments in the West that have treated humans as just a part of the ordinary physical, biological order have often been opposed by various rear-guard actions—Copernicus and Galileo were opposed because they denied that the earth was the center of the universe; Darwin was opposed because he claimed that humans had descended from the lower animals. It is best to see strong AI as one of the last gasps of this antiscientific tradition, for it denies that there is anything essentially physical and biological about the human mind. The mind according to strong AI is independent of the brain. It is a computer program and as such has no essential connection to any specific hardware.

Many people who have doubts about the psychological significance of AI think that computers might be able to understand Chinese and think about numbers but cannot do the crucially human things, namely—and then follows their favorite human specialty—falling in love, having a sense of humor, feeling the angst of postindustrial society under late capitalism, or whatever. But workers in AI complain—correctly—that this is a case of moving the goal posts. As soon as an AI simulation succeeds, it ceases to be of psychological importance. In this debate, both sides fail to see the distinction between simulation and

[24]

 Another way to put the point is to say that understanding Chinese involves being *conscious* of the appropriate meanings, and there is no reason at all for thinking that such a consciousness somehow exists in the room, apart from the consciousness of the symbol manipulator.

[25]

 This is a quite different use of the term "dualism" from the one discussed in the chapter introduction and that applies to Foster's view. Functionalists and proponents of strong AI do not think that thinking occurs in a substance distinct from the brain, nor do they think that there are mental properties that are distinct from physical properties. What is true is that the functionalist account of what it is to be a mental state is not one that could be satisfied only by a physical brain, even though all actual functionalists believe that it is brains that actually run the relevant program. Thus functionalism allows the bare possibility of immaterial minds in a way that Searle's view does not.

duplication. As far as simulation is concerned, there is no difficulty in programming my computer so that it prints out. "I love you, Suzy"; "Ha ha"; or "I am suffering the angst of post-industrial society under late capitalism." The important point is that simulation is not the same as duplication, and that fact holds as much import for thinking about arithmetic as it does for feeling angst. The point is not that the computer gets only to the 40-yard line and not all the way to the goal line. The computer doesn't even get started. It is not playing that game.

Discussion Questions

1. Think carefully about the Turing Test for thinking. What (if anything) seems right about it? What (if anything) seems wrong about it? On what do you base your judgment that any one of your friends or family is thinking, either in general or about some specific thing? What if you met an alien from another planet? How would you judge whether it could think? On what basis do you believe that your pet can or cannot think? (Should we perhaps be more tentative in our judgments about each other than we ordinarily are?) How important is *consciousness* to thinking? Can something think if it is not conscious? On what basis do you judge that someone or something is conscious?
2. Is it true, as Searle claims, that normal thinking essentially involves and depends on meaning or content? Think again about the umbrella example in the chapter introduction: I understand what rain is and also what an umbrella is, and it is because of this understanding that I am led to conclude that I should go back and get the umbrella to guard against the rain. Is there any way to understand examples of this kind that appeal only to formal manipulation of symbols?
3. Many philosophers have claimed that thoughts have *intrinsic* meaning or content, that any particular thought means what it does because of properties of the thought itself and not because of any external connections or relations it has to anything else. While that claim is controversial for thought, it is clearly false for the symbols of any ordinary language (such as English or French or Chinese). The English word "dog" and the French word "chien" have the same meaning, but there is nothing about the letters themselves or the way the letters are put together that requires those combinations of letters to have the meaning that they have or indeed to have any meaning at all. Their meaning is purely conventional, and thus results in some way from external facts about how they are used. Thus the word "dog" could have had the meaning that the word "alligator" has, and vice versa. Is there a difference between the way your thoughts are meaningful and the way language is meaningful? Could your *thought* of dogs have been instead a *thought* about alligators (which would seem to be possible if it, as Fodor believes, is or involves just a mental symbol)?
4. Searle's view that mental states like thinking are caused by and essentially depend on the specific neurobiological properties of the brain has sometimes been characterized as the "meatist" theory of the mind—because according to it, thought depends on the distinctive sort of "meat" that the brain is made up of, rather than on merely formal structure as the functionalist claims. How plausible is this view (which does not follow in any direct way from Searle's arguments against functionalism and strong AI)? Can you see any reason for thinking that it is the specific "neurobiological" character of the brain that accounts for conscious thought—or any glimmer of an idea of how this might work?
5. Consider again objections a, b, d, and e to the Chinese Room thought experiment. Can any of these objections be spelled out and defended in a way that makes it a cogent objection? If so, how? If not, why not?

Jerry Fodor

This selection is taken from Fodor's reply to Searle's original presentation of the Chinese Room argument (in 1980)—which did not differ in any essential way from the later version contained in the previous selection. Fodor is specifically criticizing Searle's reply to the objection that was referred to in the earlier version as the "robot reply" and that appears as objection f in the list in the previous selection. This objection insists that while the Chinese Room argument may successfully show that merely running the supposedly right program is not sufficient for having genuine mental states and processes, it fails to show that running the right program together with the satisfaction of certain further conditions may not be sufficient. Consider a system in which the program operates a robot having perceptual and motor systems: systems for taking in information (for example, a video camera and microphone) and the capability for movement (so that it could, for example, walk around or make things). The program running in such a robot would be the "brain" that coordinates the inputs (analogous to our sensory inputs) and the outputs (analogous to our actions). In this sort of case, there will be what Fodor refers to as "causal linkages" between the symbols involved in the formal manipulations that constitute the running of the program and the things in the outside world with which the robot interacts—thereby, Fodor claims, giving those symbols the semantic content or meaning that Searle claims is lacking.

Searle's response to the "robot reply" in the original article was to imagine that the system running the program inside the robot is replaced with a person who manipulates symbols in the same formal way as in the original Chinese Room. His claim is that there is still no genuine meaning or content to be found in the system. Fodor insists that there wouldn't be the *right kind* of causal linkages if a person was inside the robot manipulating symbols in this way, but that there might be the right kind of causal linkages if an internal computer was running the program.

Searle on What Only Brains Can Do

1. Searle is certainly right that instantiating the same program that the brain does is not, in and of itself, a sufficient condition for having those propositional attitudes characteristic of the organism that has the brain. If some people in AI think that it is, they're wrong. As for the Turing test, it has all the usual difficulties with predictions of "no difference"; you can't distinguish the truth of the prediction from the insensitivity of the test instrument.*

2. However, Searle's treatment of the "robot reply" is quite unconvincing. Given that there are the right kinds of causal linkages between the symbols that the device manipulates and things in the world—including the afferent and efferent transducers of the device—it is quite unclear that intuition rejects ascribing propositional attitudes to it. All that Searle's example shows is that the kind of causal linkage he imagines—one that is, in effect, mediated by a man sitting in the head of a robot—is, unsurprisingly, not the right kind.

From *Behavioral and Brain Sciences,* Vol. 3 (September 1980).

3. We don't know how to say what the right kinds of causal linkage are. This, also, is unsurprising since we don't know how to answer the closely related question as to what kinds of connection between a formula and the world determine the interpretation under which the formula is employed. We don't have an answer to this question for *any* symbolic system; a fortiori, not for mental representations. These questions are closely related because, given the mental representation view, it is natural to assume that what makes mental states intentional is primarily that they involve relations to semantically interpreted mental objects; again, relations of the right kind.

4. It seems to me that Searle has misunderstood the main point about the treatment of intentionality in representational theories of the mind; this is not surprising since proponents of the theory—especially in AI—have been notably unlucid in expounding it. For the record, then, the main point is this: intentional properties of propositional attitudes are viewed as inherited from semantic properties of mental representations (and not from the functional

*I assume, for simplicity, that there is only one program that the brain instantiates (which, of course, there isn't). Notice, by the way, that even passing the Turing test requires doing more than *just* manipulating symbols. A device that can't run a typewriter can't play the game.

"Propositional attitudes" is a standard label for mental states like belief and desire that involve an "attitude" toward a proposition (such as the proposition that it will rain tomorrow): accepting it (in the case of belief) or wanting it to be true (in the case of desire). Fodor here is agreeing with Searle that merely running the program in some way is not enough to yield genuine beliefs and desires. (Fodor also agrees that satisfying the Turing Test is not enough to show that whatever satisfies it is thinking, basically because the standards for the test might not be demanding enough.)

Fodor is claiming that a device running such a program inside a robot might genuinely have beliefs and desires *if* there are the *right kinds* of *causal* connections between the symbols manipulated by the device and things in the world. Saying that "intuition" does not clearly reject the ascription of propositional attitudes to such a device is just saying that it does not seem clearly mistaken in the case where the program is *not* being run by a man inside the robot's head. (Thus Fodor rejects Searle's reply as irrelevant to the most important case.)

There is a subtle argument lurking here. It is obvious that some symbolic formulas have meanings ("interpretations"), namely those that are employed in ordinary languages like English. Fodor admits that we don't understand how this works, but is suggesting that however it works for those languages, it can work in the same way for the "language of thought"—and that mental states are meaningful because they involve meaningful symbols in the "language of thought." (But the question still remains whether causal relations of the sort that might be involved in the robot case are enough to account for meaning or content in *any* case—whether that of a language of thought or that of more ordinary sorts of languages. See Discussion Question 1.)

role of mental representations, unless "functional role" is construed broadly enough to include symbol-world relations). (4) In effect, what is proposed is a reduction of the problem *what makes mental states intentional* to the problem *what bestows semantic properties on (fixes the interpretation of) a symbol.* This reduction looks promising because we're going to have to answer the latter question anyhow (for example, in constructing theories of natural languages); and we need the notion of mental representation anyhow (for example, to provide appropriate domains for mental processes).

It may be worth adding that there is nothing new about this strategy. Locke, for example, thought (a) that the intentional properties of mental states are inherited from the semantic (referential) properties of mental representations; (b) that mental processes are formal (associative); and (c) that the objects from which mental states inherit their intentionality are the same ones over which mental processes are defined: namely ideas. (5) It's my view that no serious alternative to this treatment of propositional attitudes has ever been proposed.

5. To say that a computer (or a brain) performs formal operations on symbols is not the same thing as saying that it performs operations on formal (in the sense of "uninterpreted") symbols. This equivocation occurs repeatedly in Searle's paper, and causes considerable confusion. If there are mental representations they must, of course, be interpreted objects; it is because they are interpreted objects that mental states are intentional. But the brain might be a computer for all that. (6)

6. This situation—needing a notion of causal connection, but not knowing which notion of causal connection is the right one—is entirely familiar in philosophy. It is, for example, extremely plausible that "a perceives b" can be true only where there is the right kind of causal connection between a and b. And we don't know what the right kind of causal connection is here either.

Demonstrating that some kinds of causal connection are the *wrong* kinds would not, of course, prejudice the claim. For example, suppose we interpolated a little man between a and b, whose function it is to report to a on the presence of b. We would then have (inter alia) a sort of causal link from a to b, but we wouldn't have the sort of causal link that is required for a to perceive b. (7) It would, of course, be a fallacy to argue from the fact that this causal linkage fails to reconstruct perception to the conclusion that *no* causal linkage would succeed. Searle's argument against the "robot reply" is a fallacy of precisely that sort.

7. It is entirely reasonable (indeed it must be true) that the right kind of causal relation is the kind that holds between our brains and our transducer mechanisms (on the one hand) and between our brains and distal objects (on the other). (8) It would not begin to follow that *only* our brains can bear such relations to transducers and distal objects; and it would also not follow that being the same sort of thing our brain is (in any biochemical sense of "same sort") is a necessary condition for being in that relation; and it would also not follow that formal manipulations of symbols are not among the links in such causal chains. And, even if our brains *are* the only sorts of things that can be in that relation, the fact that they are might quite possibly be of no particular interest; that would depend on *why* it's true.

Searle gives no clue as to why he thinks the bio-chemistry is important for intentionality and, prima facie, the idea that what counts is how the organism is connected to the world seems far more plausible. After all, it's easy enough to imagine, in a rough and ready sort of way, how the fact that my thought is causally connected to a tree might bear on its being a thought about a tree. But it's hard to imagine how the fact that (to put it crudely) my thought is made out of hydrocarbons could matter, except on the unlikely hypothesis that only hydrocarbons can be causally connected to trees in the way that brains are. (9)

...

10. *Talking* involves performing certain formal operations on symbols: stringing words together. Yet, not everything that can string words together can talk. It does not follow from these banal observations that what we utter are uninterpreted sounds, or that we don't understand what we say, or that whoever talks talks nonsense, or that only hydrocarbons can assert—similarly, mutatis mutandis, if you substitute "thinking" for "talking."

R Fodor's claim is that the best version of functionalism does not claim that meaning or content arises from formal manipulations of symbols alone, but rather from semantic properties of symbols that depend in part on the external causal relations.

Locke's "ideas" seem, however, to be *intrinsically* meaningful states or entities, rather than mere symbols that acquire a meaning through external causal relations.

R Fodor's point here is that while computer operations do not rely on the meanings of the symbols, this does not mean that those symbols have no meanings. Fodor agrees that they must have meanings if contentful mental states are to result, but, to repeat, thinks those meanings derive from external causal relations rather than from the formal manipulations.

As an analogy, imagine a blind woman who has a little man (with normal vision) who sits on her shoulder constantly telling her what is going on around her. This may lead to her having lots of correct beliefs about what is going on in her environment. In such a case, there would be a kind of causal connection between the blind person's beliefs and the things in the environment, but it wouldn't be the "right kind" of causal connection for it to be true that she visually perceives those things.

This "must be true" only on the assumption that our brains involve symbols of the sort in question rather than (as Searle thinks) intrinsically contentful states.

That is, Searle has really given no reason for the "meatist" theory other than the objections to functionalism.

Discussion Questions

1. How plausible (or implausible) is Fodor's view that the semantic properties (meanings) of mental symbols in the "language of thought" result from external causal relations of the sort that exist in the case of the robot? Suppose that there is a symbol involved in your mental operations—we may suppose that it is something analogous to the English word "dog" written on something analogous to a mental blackboard. By virtue of external perceptual and motor relations (and also the internal, purely formal processing), this symbol comes to stand in some complicated network of causal relations to real dogs in the world: perhaps it tends to be produced (written in a specific place on the "blackboard") when your sense organs are stimulated in the right ways by passing dogs and tends to produce bodily movements that depend also on states that according to Fodor are desires for or aversions to animals (though these will also depend essentially on symbols whose meaningfulness raises the same problem). Let us suppose that the resulting network of causal relations is of the "right kind," whatever that may be, to result in this symbol meaning or standing for dogs. If you have no independent knowledge of these external causal relations (which you ordinarily wouldn't) but are only, as it were, aware of the symbol on the "blackboard," is there any way that you would be able to become aware of the meaning of the symbol in a way that could enable you to thereby have *conscious* thoughts about dogs? (This is a difficult question, but one very much worth thinking about.)
2. Fodor claims that the causal relations that occur in the version of the robot case where there is a person in the head of the robot running the program are not the "right kind" to yield meaning for the symbols involved, but that those that result when there is a computer running the program might be. The reason for thinking that the causal relations are not the right kind in the former version of the case is that the person has no awareness of the resulting meaning or content, whereas this reason does not apply in the version where there is no such person. But is there any plausible reason for thinking that whatever *causal* relations are involved in the computer case might not be duplicated in the person case (so that the causal role of the internal states might be exactly the same, from a functionalist standpoint)?

John R. Searle

Searle first published the Chinese Room argument in *Behavioral and Brain Sciences* along with 27 commentaries and his response to those commentaries. The following selection consists of Searle's response to Fodor, together with a bit of material that comes earlier in his reply, further elaborating his biological (or "meatist") view of mental states.

Author's Response

Strong AI. One of the virtues of the commentaries is that they make clear the extreme character of the strong AI thesis. The thesis implies that of all known types of specifically biological processes, from mitosis and meiosis to photosynthesis, digestion, lactation, and the secretion of auxin, one and only one type is completely independent of the biochemistry of its origins, and that one is cognition. The reason it is independent is that cognition consists entirely of computational processes, and since those processes are purely formal, any substance whatever that is capable of instantiating the formalism is capable of cognition. (1) Brains just happen to be one of the indefinite number of different types of computers capable of cognition, but computers made of water pipes, toilet paper and stones, electric wires—anything solid and enduring enough to carry the right program—will necessarily have thoughts, feelings, and the rest of the forms of intentionality, because that is all that intentionality consists in: instantiating the right programs. The point of strong AI is . . . that there isn't anything to intentionality other than instantiating the right program.

Now I find the thesis of strong AI incredible in every sense of the word. But it is not enough to find a thesis incredible, one has to have an

(1) Searle is right that functionalism and strong AI make mental states independent of any specific facts about biochemistry. States of any kind, no matter what their composition or makeup might be, could play the role of symbols in formal manipulations (and also, in Fodor's version, stand in external causal relations as a result of input and output connections). But this is an "extreme" or surprising view only if one assumes that "cognition" is a biological process at least roughly on a par with things like digestion and photosynthesis—something that is by no means obviously the case.

From *Behavioral and Brain Sciences,* Vol. 3 (September 1980).

argument, and I offer an argument that is very simple: instantiating a program could not be constitutive of intentionality, because it would be possible for an agent to instantiate the program and still not have the right kind of intentionality. [2] That is the point of the Chinese room example. Much of what follows will concern the force of that argument.

* * * * *

Fodor agrees with my central thesis that instantiating a program is not a sufficient condition of intentionality. He thinks, however, that if we got the right causal links between the formal symbols and things in the world that would be sufficient. Now there is an obvious objection to this variant of the robot reply that I have made several times: the same thought experiment as before applies to this case. That is, no matter what outside causal impacts there are on the formal tokens, these are not by themselves sufficient to give the tokens any intentional content. No matter what caused the tokens, the agent still doesn't understand Chinese. Let the egg foo yung symbol be causally connected to egg foo yung in any way you like, that connection by itself will never enable the agent to interpret the symbol as meaning egg foo yung. [3] To do that he would have to have, for example, some *awareness* of the causal relation between the symbol and the referent; but now we are no longer explaining intentionality in terms of symbols and causes but in terms of symbols, causes, and intentionality, and we have abandoned both strong AI and the robot reply. Fodor's only answer to this is to say that it shows we haven't yet got the right kind of causal linkage. But what is the right kind, since the above argument applies to any kind? He says he can't tell us, but it is there all the same. Well I can tell him what it is: it is any form of causation sufficient to produce intentional content in the agent, sufficient to produce, for example, a visual experience, or a memory, or a belief, or a semantic interpretation of some word. [4]

Fodor's variant of the robot reply is therefore confronted with a dilemma. If the causal linkages are just matters of fact about the relations between the symbols and the outside world, they will never by themselves give any interpretation to the symbols; they will carry by themselves no intentional content. [5] If, on the other hand, the causal impact is sufficient to produce intentionality in the agent, it can only be because there is something more to the system than the *fact* of the causal impact and the *symbol,* namely the intentional content that the impact produces in the agent. Either the man in the room doesn't learn the meaning of the symbol from the causal impact, in which case the causal impact adds nothing to the interpretation, or the causal impact teaches him the meaning of the word, in which case the cause is relevant only because it produces a form of intentionality that is something in addition to itself and the symbol. [6] In neither case is symbol, or cause and symbol, constitutive of intentionality.

...

In what is perhaps his crucial point, Fodor suggests that we should think of the brain or the computer as performing formal operations only on *interpreted* and not just on *formal* symbols. But who does the interpreting? And what is an interpretation? If he is saying that for intentionality there must be intentional content in addition to the formal symbols, then I of course agree. Indeed, two of the main points of my argument are that in our own case we have the "interpretation," that is, we have intrinsic intentionality, and that the computer program could never by itself be sufficient for that . . . . [7]

Discussion Questions

1. Dilemmas usually start by stating a *disjunction,* an either-or statement, each side of which leads to a result that the view being criticized cannot accept. What is the disjunction that Searle has in mind when he says that Fodor's reply is confronted with a dilemma? Why is each side of the dilemma supposed to create a problem for Fodor's position?
2. Searle and Fodor agree that mental states have meaning or content, with the main issue between them being where that meaning or content comes from. Searle's "meatist" view holds that the content resides in intrinsically meaningful or contentful states, which are in turn a result of lower-level neurobiological or ultimately biochemical causes. Fodor's view is that content depends on mental symbols that become meaningful by being connected with external things of various kinds through causal linkages of the right kind. Both of these views seem to face problems.

Recall here Fodor's response to this way of putting the objection.

Searle is saying that external causal connections, no matter of what sort, will never allow the person in the room (or in the robot's head) to attach any meaning to the characters he is manipulating. Fodor's response will be that the causal relations will never be of the right kind as long as such an agent is involved, but does he have any good reason for this claim?

This doesn't do much to say what the right kind of causal linkage actually is. The important claim is the one made earlier: that causal relations cannot yield meaning unless the person is aware of them (in which case intentionality is being presupposed, and the causal relations alone are not doing the main job).

This reiterates the point that the external causal relations can yield meaning in a way that is accessible to the agent on the inside only if the agent has an independent awareness of them.

The other alternative making up the alleged dilemma is the possibility that the causal relations help to cause (rather than constituting) an *independently* meaningful intentional state (Searle means one that is intrinsically meaningful, more than just a symbol.) In this case, the meaningful intentional state must be something more than just the symbol and the external causal relations.

Thus the crucial issue between Searle and Fodor is not whether mental states have meaning or content, but where that meaning or content comes from. (See Discussion Question 2.)

Can Searle explain *how* the underlying causes produce meaningful or contentful states and in particular what determines the specific meaning or content of such a state? Can Fodor explain how the meaning that allegedly results from external causal relations becomes accessible to the person in a way that allows it to play a role in conscious, meaningful thoughts of the sort we seem to have? Which of these views seems to you more promising—or is there any real hope for either of them? What would be the right response to a dualist who suggests that these problems simply show that materialist views cannot adequately account for conscious, meaningful mental content—and hence that some version of dualism must be true after all?

Can Materialism Account for Qualitative Consciousness?

Thomas Nagel

Thomas Nagel (1937–) is an American philosopher who currently teaches at New York University. He is very well known for his work in philosophy of mind and ethics. The article from which the present selection is drawn has been extremely influential and the ideas in it continue to be widely discussed and debated in contemporary philosophy of mind.

It is notoriously difficult to define, explain, or give an account of consciousness. Nagel, using the conscious experiences of bats as an example, argues that conscious experiences are essentially tied to a subjective, first-person point of view. Since physical brain states are essentially objective, and thus accessible from many points of view, this creates a problem for any view that claims that mental states are identical to or realized by brain states.

What Is It Like to Be a Bat?

Consciousness is what makes the mind-body problem really intractable. Perhaps that is why current discussions of the problem give it little attention or get it obviously wrong. The recent wave of reductionist euphoria has produced several analyses of mental phenomena and mental concepts designed to explain the possibility of some variety of materialism, psychophysical identification, or reduction. (1) But the problems dealt with are those common to this type of reduction and other types, and what makes the mind-body problem unique, and unlike the water-H_2O problem or the Turing machine-IBM machine problem or the lightning-electrical discharge, problem . . . , is ignored.

Every reductionist has his favorite analogy from modern science. It is most unlikely that any of these unrelated examples of successful reduction will shed light on the relation of mind to brain. But philosophers share the general human weakness for explanations of what is incomprehensible in terms suited for what is familiar and well understood, though entirely different. This has led to the acceptance of implausible accounts of the mental largely because they would permit familiar kinds of reduction. (2) I shall try to explain why the usual examples do not help us to understand the relation between mind and body—why, indeed, we have at present no conception of what an explanation of the physical nature of a mental phenomenon would be. Without consciousness the mind-body problem would be much less interesting. With consciousness it seems hopeless. The most important and characteristic feature of conscious mental phenomena is very poorly understood. Most reductionist theories do not even try to explain it. And careful examination will show that no currently available concept of reduction is applicable to it. Perhaps a new theoretical form can be devised for the purpose, but such a solution, if it exists, lies in the distant intellectual future.

(1) As reflected in the earlier selections by Smart and Fodor, many philosophers are tempted by the view that psychological states can be identified with or somehow reduced to physical brain states, with functionalism currently being the most widely accepted version of such a view.

(2)  There is no real objection to attempting to explain what is presently incomprehensible in terms of what is familiar and well understood. Nagel's point is that such attempts are unlikely to succeed if the things we are trying to understand are radically different in nature from the familiar and well understood ones—which he will argue to be so for conscious mental states.

From *Mortal Questions* (Cambridge: Cambridge University Press, 1979).

Conscious experience is a widespread phenomenon. It occurs at many levels of animal life, though we cannot be sure of its presence in the simpler organisms, and it is very difficult to say in general what provides evidence of it. (Some extremists have been prepared to deny it even of mammals other than man.) No doubt it occurs in countless forms totally unimaginable to us, on other planets in other solar systems throughout the universe. But no matter how the form may vary, the fact that an organism has conscious experience *at all* means, basically, that there is something it is like to *be* that organism. There may be further implications about the form of the experience; there may even (though I doubt it) be implications about the behavior of the organism. But fundamentally an organism has conscious mental states if and only if there is something that it is like to be that organism—something it is like *for* the organism. (3)

We may call this the subjective character of experience. It is not captured by any of the familiar, recently devised reductive analyses of the mental, for all of them are logically compatible with its absence. It is not analyzable in terms of any explanatory system of functional states, or intentional states, since these could be ascribed to robots or automata that behaved like people though they experienced nothing. It is not analyzable in terms of the causal role of experiences in relation to typical human behavior—for similar reasons. I do not deny that conscious mental states and events cause behavior, nor that they may be given functional characterizations. I deny only that this kind of thing exhausts their analysis. Any reductionist program has to be based on an analysis of what is to be reduced. If the analysis leaves something out, the problem will be falsely posed. (4) It is useless to base the defense of materialism on any analysis of mental phenomena that fails to deal explicitly with their subjective character. For there is no reason to suppose that a reduction which seems plausible when no attempt is made to account for consciousness can be extended to include consciousness. Without some idea, therefore, of what the subjective character of experience is, we cannot know what is required of physicalist theory.

While an account of the physical basis of mind must explain many things, this appears to be the most difficult. It is impossible to exclude the phenomenological features of experience from a reduction in the same way that one excludes the phenomenal features of an ordinary substance from a physical or chemical reduction of it—namely, by explaining them as effects on the minds of human observers. (5) If physicalism is to be defended, the phenomenological features must themselves be given a physical account. But when we examine their subjective character it seems that such a result is impossible. The reason is that every subjective phenomenon is essentially connected with a single point of view, and it seems inevitable that an objective, physical theory will abandon that point of view.

Let me first try to state the issue somewhat more fully than by referring to the relation between the subjective and the objective. . . . This is far from easy. Facts about what it is like to be an X are very peculiar, so peculiar that some may be inclined to doubt their reality, or the significance of claims about them. To illustrate the connection between subjectivity and a point of view, and to make evident the importance of subjective features, it will help to explore the matter in relation to an example that brings out clearly the divergence between the two types of conception, subjective and objective.

I assume we all believe that bats have experience. After all, they are mammals, and there is no more doubt that they have experience than that mice or pigeons or whales have experience. I have chosen bats instead of wasps or flounders because if one travels too far down the phylogenetic tree, people gradually shed their faith that there is experience there at all. (6) Bats, although more closely related to us than those other species, nevertheless present a range of activity and a sensory apparatus so different from ours that the problem I want to pose is exceptionally vivid (though it certainly could be raised with other species). Even without the benefit of philosophical reflection, anyone who has spent some time in an enclosed space with an excited bat knows what it is to encounter a fundamentally *alien* form of life.

I have said that the essence of the belief that bats have experience is that there is something that it is like to be a bat. Now we know that most bats (the microchiroptera, to be precise)

Nagel is pointing here to what he takes to be the essential feature of consciousness. If, for example, frogs have conscious experience, then there must be something that it is like *for the frog* to be a frog.

Nagel's claim is that reductive accounts such as functionalism do not capture this essential subjective character of conscious experience: describing the causal role of a state does not tell us what it is like to be in that state, or indeed that there is anything it is like—that the state is conscious at all. (An *analysis* of something, as Nagel is using the term, is an allegedly complete and detailed account of what it involves.)

This is a crucial point: a reductive physical or chemical analysis of an ordinary substance like coffee need not include its taste (a phenomenal feature) because *the taste* of coffee can plausibly be regarded as just the subjective response of a person who drinks the coffee and not an intrinsic feature of the coffee itself. Nagel's point is that while physical reductions of many things can ignore phenomenological (experiential) features by treating them in this way as features of the person experiencing the item being reduced rather than features of that item itself, the reduction of mental states cannot ignore such features, since mental states are essentially experiential (and there is no independent observer involved).

The use of the bat example is not really essential to the argument—indeed, as Nagel suggests later, the same problem arises in relation to other people with different sensory capacities. But it is surely quite plausible that bats do have conscious experience, so that there is something that it is like to be a bat.

perceive the external world primarily by sonar, or echolocation, detecting the reflections, from objects within range, of their own rapid, subtly modulated, high-frequency shrieks. Their brains are designed to correlate the outgoing impulses with the subsequent echoes, and the information thus acquired enables bats to make precise discriminations of distance, size, shape, motion, and texture comparable to those we make by vision. But bat sonar, though clearly a form of perception, is not similar in its operation to any sense that we possess, and there is no reason to suppose that it is subjectively like anything we can experience or imagine. ❼ This appears to create difficulties for the notion of what it is like to be a bat. We must consider whether any method will permit us to extrapolate to the inner life of the bat from our own case,* and if not, what alternative methods there may be for understanding the notion.

❼

One might be tempted to imagine the bat experiencing something like a visual image, perhaps a very schematic one like the picture on a radar screen. But there is no reason at all to think that this is a correct view of bat experience—or that it isn't. The point is that we just can't tell.

Our own experience provides the basic material for our imagination, whose range is therefore limited. It will not help to try to imagine that one has webbing on one's arms, which enables one to fly around at dusk and dawn catching insects in one's mouth; that one has very poor vision, and perceives the surrounding world by a system of reflected high-frequency sound signals; and that one spends the day hanging upside down by one's feet in an attic. Insofar as I can imagine this (which is not very far), it tells me only what it would be like for *me* to behave as a bat behaves. But that is not the question. I want to know what it is like for a *bat* to be a bat. Yet if I try to imagine this, I am restricted to the resources of my own mind, and those resources are inadequate to the task. I cannot perform it either by imagining additions to my present experience, or by imagining segments gradually subtracted from it, or by imagining some combination of additions, subtractions, and modifications.

...

So if extrapolation from our own case is involved in the idea of what it is like to be a bat, the extrapolation must be incompletable. We cannot form more than a schematic conception of what it *is* like. For example, we may ascribe general *types* of experience on the basis of the animal's structure and behavior. Thus we describe bat sonar as a form of three-dimensional forward perception; we believe that bats feel some versions of pain, fear, hunger, and lust, and that they have other, more familiar types of perception besides sonar. But we believe that these experiences also have in each case a specific subjective character, which it is beyond our ability to conceive. And if there is conscious life elsewhere in the universe, it is likely that some of it will not be describable even in the most general experiential terms available to us. (The problem is not confined to exotic cases, however, for it exists between one person and another. The subjective character of the experience of a person deaf and blind from birth is not accessible to me, for example, nor presumably is mine to him. This does not prevent us each from believing that the other's experience has such a subjective character.) ❽

❽

STOP Imagine trying to describe the pain involved in a toothache or a broken arm to someone who has never had the experience in question or anything very similar. What would you say?

If anyone is inclined to deny that we can believe in the existence of facts like this whose exact nature we cannot possibly conceive, he should reflect that in contemplating the bats we are in much the same position that intelligent bats or Martians would occupy if they tried to form a conception of what it was like to be us. The structure of their own minds might make it impossible for them to succeed, but we know they would be wrong to conclude that there is not anything precise that it is like to be us: that only certain general types of mental state could be ascribed to us (perhaps perception and appetite would be concepts common to us both; perhaps not). We know they would be wrong to draw such a skeptical conclusion because we know what it is like to be us. And we know that while it includes an enormous amount of variation and complexity, and while we do not possess the vocabulary to describe it adequately, its subjective character is highly specific, and in some respects describable in terms that can be understood only by creatures like us. The fact that we cannot expect ever to accommodate in our language a detailed description of Martian or bat phenomenology should not lead us to dismiss as meaningless the claim that bats and Martians have experiences fully comparable in richness of detail to our own. ❾ . . .

❾

The claim here is that our total inability to conceive of the nature of a fact is not itself a reason to conclude that there is no such fact.

*By 'our own case' I do not mean just 'my own case', but rather the mentalistic ideas that we apply unproblematically to ourselves and other human beings.

I am not adverting here to the alleged privacy of experience to its possessor. The point of view in question is not one accessible only to a single individual. Rather it is a *type.* It is often possible to take up a point of view other than one's own, so the comprehension of such facts is not limited to one's own case. There is a sense in which phenomenological facts are perfectly objective: one person can know or say of another what the quality of the other's experience is. They are subjective, however, in the sense that even this objective ascription of experience is possible only for someone sufficiently similar to the object of ascription to be able to adopt his point of view—to understand the ascription in the first person as well as in the third, so to speak. (10) The more different from oneself the other experiencer is, the less success one can expect with this enterprise. In our own case we occupy the relevant point of view, but we will have as much difficulty understanding our own experience properly if we approach it from another point of view as we would if we tried to understand the experience of another species without taking up *its* point of view.*

This bears directly on the mind-body problem. For if the facts of experience—facts about what it is like for the experiencing organism—are accessible only from one point of view, then it is a mystery how the true character of experiences could be revealed in the physical operation of that organism. The latter is a domain of objective facts *par excellence*—the kind that can be observed and understood from many points of view and by individuals with differing perceptual systems. There are no comparable imaginative obstacles to the acquisition of knowledge about bat neurophysiology by human scientists, and intelligent bats or Martians might learn more about the human brain than we ever will. (11)

In the case of experience, on the other hand, the connection with a particular point of view seems much closer. It is difficult to understand what could be meant by the *objective* character of an experience, apart from the particular point of view from which its subject apprehends it. After all, what would be left of what it was like to be a bat if one removed the viewpoint of the bat? But if experience does not have, in addition to its subjective character, an objective nature that can be apprehended from many different points of view, then how can it be supposed that a Martian investigating my brain might be observing physical processes which were my mental processes (as he might observe physical processes which were bolts of lightning), only from a different point of view? How, for that matter, could a human physiologist observe them from another point of view?†

We appear to be faced with a general difficulty about psychophysical reduction. In other areas the process of reduction is a move in the direction of greater objectivity, toward a more accurate view of the real nature of things. This is accomplished by reducing our dependence on individual or species-specific points of view toward the object of investigation. We describe it not in terms of the impressions it makes on our senses, but in terms of its more general effects and of properties detectable by means other than the human senses. The less it depends on a specifically human viewpoint, the more objective is our description. It is possible to follow this path because although the concepts and ideas we employ in thinking about the external world are initially applied from a point of view that involves our perceptual apparatus, they are used by us to refer to things beyond themselves—toward which we *have* the phenomenal point of view. Therefore we can abandon it in favor of another, and still be thinking about the same things. (12)

...

R I can say objectively that you are in pain, but what I *mean* when I say that depends on my understanding of what pain is, given my first-person perspective. My own point of view thus makes an essential contribution to the meaning of my claim about your pain, and that is the way in which the claim is, in a sense, subjective.

R Physical facts, by virtue of being accessible from many different points of view, are clearly objective, in Nagel's sense of objectivity. And if he is right that experiential facts are essentially subjective, in the sense of being accessible from only one point of view, then there is an obvious difficulty in identifying an experiential fact with a physical fact.

For example, our initial investigations of heat were tied to our experiential access to the property because our very conception of heat was largely defined in terms of our experience of heat (only largely, because other effects of heat were obvious from the beginning). But the more we studied the phenomenon, the more we were able to focus on heat in objects as the cause of our sensation of heat, leading gradually to our current conception of heat as mean kinetic energy—a conception that is very far removed from our experience of heat. We have progressed from the *subjective appearance* of heat to the *objective reality* of heat (*if* we are right now about what heat is).

*It may be easier than I suppose to transcend inter-species barriers with the aid of the imagination. For example, blind people are able to detect objects near them by a form of sonar, using vocal clicks or taps of a cane. Perhaps if one knew what that was like, one could by extension imagine roughly what it was like to possess the much more refined sonar of a bat. The distance between oneself and other persons and other species can fall anywhere on a continuum. . . .

†The problem is not just that when I look at the *Mona Lisa,* my visual experience has a certain quality, no trace of which is to be found by someone looking into my brain. For even if he did observe there a tiny image of the *Mona Lisa,* he would have no reason to identify it with the experience.

Experience itself, however, does not seem to fit the pattern. The idea of moving from appearance to reality seems to make no sense here. What is the analogue in this case to pursuing a more objective understanding of the same phenomena by abandoning the initial subjective viewpoint toward them in favor of another that is more objective but concerns the same thing? Certainly it *appears* unlikely that we will get closer to the real nature of human experience by leaving behind the particularity of our human point of view and striving for a description in terms accessible to beings that could not imagine what it was like to be us. If the subjective character of experience is fully comprehensible only from one point of view, then any shift to greater objectivity—that is, less attachment to a specific viewpoint—does not take us nearer to the real nature of the phenomenon: it takes us farther away from it. (13)

In a sense, the seeds of this objection to the reducibility of experience are already detectable in successful cases of reduction; for in discovering sound to be, in reality, a wave phenomenon in air or other media, we leave behind one viewpoint to take up another, and the auditory, human or animal viewpoint that we leave behind remains unreduced. Members of radically different species may both understand the same physical events in objective terms, and this does not require that they understand the phenomenal forms in which those events appear to the senses of members of the other species. Thus it is a condition of their referring to a common reality that their more particular viewpoints are not part of the common reality that they both apprehend. The reduction can succeed only if the species-specific viewpoint is omitted from what is to be reduced. (14)

But while we are right to leave this point of view aside in seeking a fuller understanding of the external world, we cannot ignore it permanently, since it is the essence of the internal world, and not merely a point of view on it. Most of the neobehaviorism of recent philosophical psychology results from the effort to substitute an objective concept of mind for the real thing, in order to have nothing left over which cannot be reduced. (15) If we acknowledge that a physical theory of mind must account for the subjective character of experience, we must admit that no presently available conception gives us a clue how this could be done. The problem is unique. If mental processes are indeed physical processes, then there is something it is like, intrinsically, to undergo certain physical processes. What it is for such a thing to be the case remains a mystery. (16)

What moral should be drawn from these reflections, and what should be done next? It would be a mistake to conclude that physicalism must be false. Nothing is proved by the inadequacy of physicalist hypotheses that assume a faulty objective analysis of mind. It would be truer to say that physicalism is a position we cannot understand because we do not at present have any conception of how it might be true. (17) Perhaps it will be thought unreasonable to require such a conception as a condition of understanding. After all, it might be said, the meaning of physicalism is clear enough: mental states are states of the body; mental events are physical events. We do not know *which* physical states and events they are, but that should not prevent us from understanding the hypothesis. What could be clearer than the words 'is' and 'are'?

But I believe it is precisely this apparent clarity of the word 'is' that is deceptive. Usually, when we are told that X is Y we know *how* it is supposed to be true, but that depends on a conceptual or theoretical background and is not conveyed by the 'is' alone. We know how both 'X' and 'Y' refer, and the kinds of things to which they refer, and we have a rough idea how the two referential paths might converge on a single thing, be it an object, a person, a process, an event or whatever. But when the two terms of the identification are very disparate it may not be so clear how it could be true. We may not have even a rough idea of how the two referential paths could converge, or what kind of things they might converge on, and a theoretical framework may have to be supplied to enable us to understand this. Without the framework, an air of mysticism surrounds the identification. (18)

This explains the magical flavor of popular presentations of fundamental scientific discoveries, given out as propositions to which one must subscribe without really understanding them. For

Experiences do not have the kind of gap between appearance and reality that properties and objects in the world have. The appearance of an experience just *is* its reality, so that leaving out the appearance loses the reality.

Imagine here two people investigating the same physical objects, one by sight only and one by touch only. It seems plausible that they could agree on an objective description of the objects and their relations to each other, one that they could both understand without understanding the way that the objects were experienced by the other person.

Functionalism is the clearest example of such a "neobehaviorist" view.

What physical property could account for the distinctively experiential aspect of our mental life? Why do some brain processes have such an experiential dimension, while others do not?

As you will see in the next two selections, others have used Nagel's ideas to argue that physicalism is false. Nagel's own conclusion is that we are unable to understand how physicalism could be true—even though it still might be true.

To understand the claim that two "referential paths" converge on the same object, the way that the two paths work must be such as to make clear what it would be for them to converge. Nagel's claim is that we do not (yet?) have a clear understanding of how this could happen in the experience-brain process case. (See Discussion Question 2.)

example, people are now told at an early age that all matter is really energy. But despite the fact that they know what 'is' means, most of them never form a conception of what makes this claim true, because they lack the theoretical background. (19)

At the present time the status of physicalism is similar to that which the hypothesis that matter is energy would have had if uttered by a pre-Socratic philosopher. We do not have the beginnings of a conception of how it might be true. In order to understand the hypothesis that a mental event is a physical event, we require more than an understanding of the word 'is'. The idea of how a mental and a physical term might refer to the same thing is lacking, and the usual analogies with theoretical identification in other fields fail to supply it. They fail because if we construe the reference of mental terms to physical events on the usual model, we either get a reappearance of separate subjective events as the effects through which mental reference to physical events is secured, or else we get a false account of how mental terms refer (for example, a causal behaviorist one). (20)

Strangely enough, we may have evidence for the truth of something we cannot really understand. Suppose a caterpillar is locked in a sterile safe by someone unfamiliar with insect metamorphosis, and weeks later the safe is reopened, revealing a butterfly. If the person knows that the safe has been shut the whole time, he has reason to believe that the butterfly is or was once the caterpillar, without having any idea in what sense this might be so. (One possibility is that the caterpillar contained a tiny winged parasite that devoured it and grew into the butterfly.) (21)

...

(19)

STOP Think about this example, focusing on specific kinds of energy (heat, electricity, the kinetic energy of a moving object, the potential energy of an object suspended above the Earth, etc.) and various sorts of matter (wood, water, metal, etc.). Is it clear to you what it means for matter to just *be* energy (not just to be convertible into energy)?

(20)

How is the brain event that is to be identified with a mental event to be picked out? Either as the one that is experienced in a certain way (in which case the experiential dimension has not been accounted for), or else by something like causal or functional role (in which case the experiential dimension that is essential to a mental state has simply been ignored).

(21)

STOP Do we have any analogous evidence that our mental states just are physical brain states even though we don't understand how that could be true? (See Discussion Question 3.)

Discussion Questions

1. Suppose you are familiar with what you think of as two "stars": one that you call "the morning star" because you see it in the morning, and another that you call "the evening star" because you see it in the evening. You assume that these two names refer to different things (that there are two "referential paths" leading to two distinct objects). But as you investigate further, you discover that both the morning star and the evening star are the planet Venus, which sometimes appears in the morning and sometimes in the evening. You would have discovered that two referential paths converge onto one object. Think about how you might do this. One way might be by plotting the position of one "star" in relation to other celestial objects, independently of the Earth's movement and rotation, and then discovering that the position of the second "star" is the same. Another might be to travel to the first "star" in a rocket ship and keep track of it long enough to see that it appears later as the second "star." These possibilities make sense because the "referential path" for each object fundamentally involves spatial location. Now think of the case of an experience and a brain process. The "referential path" for the experience does not involve spatial location (think about this), so the same sort of approach will not work. How then can we understand what it would be for the two "referential paths" to converge? What might a functionalist like Fodor say about this issue?
2. Philosophers vary widely in their attitude toward the claim that mental states are really physical states of some sort. Some think that we have very strong reasons to think that this is true—even if, as Nagel suggests, we are not yet in a position to understand how it is true, and possibly never will be. A philosopher of this sort will regard the various objections to materialism as problems to be solved, but not as serious reasons to think that some version of dualism might be true after all. Other philosophers view the issue as much more open, with dualism being a serious possibility, one that should perhaps be accepted if the objections to materialist views cannot be adequately met. Who is right here? Is there any strong reason for thinking that materialism is true that is prior to and independent of the success of particular materialist views? (Some of the earlier selections contain suggestions about this.)
3. Is Nagel right that there is no way to know "what it is like to be a bat" merely by knowing about bat physiology and neurophysiology (including the causal roles of bat brain states)? Imagine that you have the relevant physical knowledge. Can you think of any way to infer or even to guess or conjecture on that basis what bat experience is like? Consider, for example, the speculation mentioned in Annotation 7: is there any way on the basis of physical knowledge of bats to decide, even fairly tentatively, whether that conjecture is true or false?

Frank Jackson

Frank Jackson (1943–) is an Australian philosopher best known for his work in philosophy of mind and metaphysics. He teaches at the Australian National University.

In this reading, Jackson returns to a thought experiment he had developed in an earlier paper in order to respond to objections made in the intervening years. This paper develops one of the clearest versions of what philosophers have come to call the *knowledge argument* against materialism. Jackson's main claim is that this argument provides a compelling reason to reject the claim that mental states are nothing more than physical states. (Interestingly enough, Jackson has since changed his mind about this.)

What Mary Didn't Know

Mary is confined to a black-and-white room, is educated through black-and-white books and through lectures relayed on black-and-white television. In this way she learns everything there is to know about the physical nature of the world. (1) She knows all the physical facts about us and our environment, in a wide sense of 'physical' which includes everything in *completed* physics, chemistry, and neurophysiology, and all there is to know about the causal and relational facts consequent upon all this, including of course functional roles. (2) If physicalism is true, she knows all there is to know. For to suppose otherwise is to suppose that there is more to know than every physical fact, and that is just what physicalism denies.

Physicalism is not the noncontroversial thesis that the actual world is largely physical, but the challenging thesis that it is entirely physical. (3) This is why physicalists must hold that complete physical knowledge is complete knowledge simpliciter. . . .

It seems, however, that Mary does not know all there is to know. For when she is let out of the black-and-white room or given a color television, she will learn what it is like to see something red, say. (4) This is rightly described as *learning*—she will not say "ho, hum." Hence, physicalism is false. This is the knowledge argument against physicalism in one of its manifestations. This note is a reply to three objections to it mounted by Paul M. Churchland.

From *The Journal of Philosophy,* Vol. LXXXIII, No. 5 (May 1986).

I . . . . Clarifications

The knowledge argument does not rest on the dubious claim that logically you cannot imagine what sensing red is like unless you have sensed red. Powers of imagination are not to the point. The contention about Mary is not that, despite her fantastic grasp of neurophysiology and everything else physical, she *could not imagine* what it is like to sense red; it is that, as a matter of fact, she *would not know.* But if physicalism is true, she would know; and no great powers of imagination would be called for. Imagination is a faculty that those who *lack* knowledge need to fall back on. (5)

. . . the knowledge Mary lacked which is of particular point for the knowledge argument against physicalism is *knowledge about the experiences of others,* not about her own. When she is let out, she has new experiences, color experiences she has never had before. It is not, therefore, an objection to physicalism that she learns *something* on being let out. Before she was let out, she could not have known facts about her experience of red, for there were no such facts to know. That physicalist and nonphysicalist alike can agree on. After she is let out, things change; and physicalism can happily admit that she learns this; after all, some physical things will change, for instance, her brain states and their functional roles. The trouble for physicalism is that, after Mary sees her first ripe tomato, she will realize how impoverished her conception of the mental life of *others* has been *all along.* She will realize that there was, all the time she was carrying out her laborious investigations into

(1) Mary is assumed to have no color experiences at all, only black-and-white visual experiences. We thus have to suppose that she never cuts herself (and sees red blood) or looks in the mirror or at her own body (and sees pinkish skin). (It might be easier to imagine that Mary starts out entirely color-blind and then later has an operation that gives her normal color vision.)

(2) Mary is also assumed to know *all* the physical facts about human beings. Obviously no one now has a complete knowledge of this sort, but this is a philosophical thought experiment: we are trying to determine what would follow if these assumptions were true.

(3) R If physicalism is true, then there are no real things or states or events that are anything but entirely physical—no nonphysical parts or aspects of things or states or events. Thus if Mary knows all the physical facts about human beings, she knows all the facts there are.

(4) She will have an experience of red, and thus she will know something that she didn't know before: what specific sort of experience results from perceptual processes that she knew about earlier under physical descriptions. But what she has now learned cannot be a physical fact, since, by hypothesis, she already knew all the physical facts.

(5) According to Jackson, what Mary (or the investigator of bats) might or might not be able to *imagine* is strictly irrelevant. Even if Mary somehow managed to imagine color experience perfectly, she would still have no way before she is let out of the room to *know* that her imaginative conception was correct.

the neurophysiologies of others and into the functional roles of their internal states, something about these people she was quite unaware of. All along their experiences (or many of them, those got from tomatoes, the sky, . . .) had a feature conspicuous to them but until now hidden from her. . . . (6) But she knew all the physical facts about them all along; hence, what she did not know until her release is not a physical fact about their experiences. But it is a fact about them. That is the trouble for physicalism.

II. Churchland's Three Objections

(i) Churchland's first objection is that the knowledge argument contains a defect that "is simplicity itself." The argument equivocates on the sense of 'knows about'. How so? Churchland suggests that the following is "a conveniently tightened version" of the knowledge argument:

1. Mary knows everything there is to know about brain states and their properties.
2. It is not the case that Mary knows everything there is to know about sensations and their properties.

Therefore, by Leibniz's law,

1. Sensations and their properties $\neq$ brain states and their properties. (7)

Churchland observes, plausibly enough, that the type or kind of knowledge involved in premise 1 is distinct from the kind of knowledge involved in premise 2. We might follow his lead and tag the first 'knowledge by description', and the second 'knowledge by acquaintance' (8) but, whatever the tags, he is right that the displayed argument involves a highly dubious use of Leibniz's law.

My reply is that the displayed argument may be convenient, but it is not accurate. It is not the knowledge argument. Take, for instance, premise 1. The whole thrust of the knowledge argument is that Mary (before her release) does *not* know everything there is to know about brain states and their properties, because she does not know about certain qualia associated with them. What is complete, according to the argument, is her knowledge of matters physical. A convenient and accurate way of displaying the argument is:

1. Mary (before her release) knows everything physical there is to know about other people.
2. Mary (before her release) does not know everything there is to know about other people (because she *learns* something about them on her release).

Therefore,

1. There are truths about other people (and herself) which escape the physicalist story.

What is immediately to the point is not the kind, manner, or type of knowledge Mary has, but *what* she knows. What she knows beforehand is ex hypothesi everything physical there is to know, but is it everything there is to know? That is the crucial question. (9)

There is, though, a relevant challenge involving questions about kinds of knowledge. It concerns the *support* for premise 2. The case for premise 2 is that Mary learns something on her release, she acquires knowledge, and that entails that her knowledge beforehand (*what* she knew, never mind whether by description, acquaintance, or whatever) was incomplete. The challenge, mounted by David Lewis and Laurence Nemirow, is that on her release Mary does *not* learn something or acquire knowledge in the relevant sense. What Mary acquires when she is released is a certain representational or imaginative ability; it is knowledge how rather than knowledge that. Hence, a physicalist can admit that Mary acquires something very significant of a knowledge kind—which can hardly be denied—without admitting that this shows that her earlier factual knowledge is defective. She knew all *that* there was to know about the experiences of others beforehand, but lacked an ability until after her release. (10)

Now it is certainly true that Mary will acquire abilities of various kinds after her release. She will, for instance, be able to imagine what seeing red is like, be able to remember what it is like, and be able to understand why her friends regarded her as so deprived (something which, until her release, had always mystified her). But is it plausible that that is *all* she will acquire? Suppose she received a lecture on skepticism about other minds while she was incarcerated. On her

Her knowledge of other people's mental states included a knowledge of all the physical facts about someone's brain when, for example, he or she experiences a ripe tomato (including whatever brain states a materialist would claim to be identical with those experiences). She also knew, since she knew all physical facts, that a particular person's experience of a ripe tomato is caused by the light bouncing off the tomato and entering his or her eyes, and also the wavelength of the light, and so on. What she allegedly did not know and learns when she is let out is what these experiences were like for those who had them.

According to Leibniz's law, if any two items are identical, then anything that is true of one must be true of the other. The claim of this argument is that since there is something true of sensations that is not true of brain states, sensations cannot be the same thing as brain states.

"Knowledge by acquaintance" requires direct experience of something, whereas "knowledge by description" does not. Churchland claims that Mary's complete knowledge of brain states is knowledge by description, whereas the knowledge that she at first lacks and then comes to have of sensations is knowledge by acquaintance. If this "conveniently tightened" version is an accurate interpretation of Jackson's original argument, then Churchland has a good objection, since the premises support the conclusion only if "know" means the same thing in both premises.

"Ex hypothesi" means according to the hypothesis being considered.

R Lewis and Nemirow are claiming that what Mary acquires is the ability to imagine red or perhaps to represent it in one particular way, but that she does not learn any new *facts*.

What Mary is supposed to be worrying about here is whether she is justified in ascribing the new feature she has seemingly learned about through her own experiences to the experiences of other people as well.

R Mary decides that this skeptical worry is mistaken. But Jackson's point is that there was a factual claim about the experiences of others about whose correctness she was uncertain, in which case the view that she had acquired *only* a new imaginative or representational ability is wrong. (See Discussion Question 1.)

Didn't Mary in any case learn a new fact about *herself*: that when she has certain physical states, she also has a specific sort of experience?

R The objection is that if Mary does learn something new, it would still be something new for her even if she had also learned everything about dualist mental states in the same way that she learned everything about physical things, again through black-and-white books and television. Therefore, Churchland is suggesting, the Mary example counts just as much against dualism as against materialism.

15

R Jackson's response is that while we have every reason to think that Mary's black-and-white educational process is adequate for her to acquire a complete account of the physical world, there is no reason to think that the same thing is true for nonphysical facts of the sort advocated by dualism. (See Discussion Question 2.) (*Attribute dualism* is the version of dualism that holds that there are both physical and nonphysical *properties*, but not necessarily two different sorts of things or substances.)

release she sees a ripe tomato in normal conditions, and so has a sensation of red. Her first reaction is to say that she now knows more about the kind of experiences others have when looking at ripe tomatoes. She then remembers the lecture and starts to worry. Does she really know more about what their experiences are like, or is she indulging in a wild generalization from one case? (11) In the end she decides she does know, and that skepticism is mistaken (even if, like so many of us, she is not sure how to demonstrate its errors). What was she to-ing and fro-ing about—her abilities? Surely not; her representational abilities were a known constant throughout. What else then was she agonizing about than whether or not she had gained factual knowledge of others? There would be nothing to agonize about if ability was *all* she acquired on her release. (12)

I grant that I have no *proof* that Mary acquires on her release, as well as abilities, factual knowledge about the experiences of others—and not just because I have no disproof of skepticism. (13) My claim is that the knowledge argument is a valid argument from highly plausible, though admittedly not demonstrable, premises to the conclusion that physicalism is false. And that, after all, is about as good an objection as one could expect in this area of philosophy.

(ii) Churchland's second objection . . . is that there must be something wrong with the argument, for it proves too much. Suppose Mary received a special series of lectures over her black-and-white television from a full-blown dualist, explaining the "laws" governing the behavior of "ectoplasm" and telling her about qualia. This would not affect the plausibility of the claim that on her release she learns something. So if the argument works against physicalism, it works against dualism too. (14)

My reply is that lectures about qualia over black-and-white television do not tell Mary all there is to know about qualia. They may tell her some things about qualia, for instance, that they do not appear in the physicalist's story, and that the quale we use 'yellow' for is nearly as different from the one we use 'blue' for as is white from black. But why should it be supposed that they tell her everything about qualia? On the other hand, it is plausible that lectures over black-and-white television might in principle tell Mary everything in the physicalist's story. You do not need color television to learn physics or functionalist psychology. To obtain a good argument against dualism (attribute dualism; ectoplasm is a bit of fun), the premise in the knowledge argument that Mary has the full story according to physicalism before her release, has to be replaced by a premise that she has the full story according to dualism. The former is plausible; the latter is not. Hence, there is no "parity of reasons" trouble for dualists who use the knowledge argument. (15)

(iii) Churchland's third objection is that the knowledge argument claims "that Mary could not even *imagine* what the relevant experience would be like, despite her exhaustive neuroscientific knowledge, and hence must still be missing certain crucial information" . . . , a claim he goes on to argue against.

But, as we emphasized earlier, the knowledge argument claims that Mary would not know what the relevant experience is like. What she could imagine is another matter. If her knowledge is defective, despite being all there is to know according to physicalism, then physicalism is false, whatever her powers of imagination.

Discussion Questions

1. It is hard to deny that Mary learns or acquires *something* new when she leaves the black-and-white room and experiences colors. But is it new *facts* that she learns? Or is it, as Lewis and Nemirow suggest, new *abilities* to imagine or represent? Or is it something still different? One way to think about this issue is to try to say what the new facts are, if indeed there are any. Can these new facts be linguistically formulated, and if so, how? If not, what does that show?

2. Jackson claims that while it is very plausible to suppose that Mary can learn everything about the physical description of the world in a black-and-white way, this is much less obviously plausible for a dualist account of mental states. How plausible is this claim? Does Jackson offer any real argument for it? Can you think of an argument? (One approach might be to appeal to Nagel's distinction between objective and subjective facts.)

Laurence BonJour

Laurence BonJour (1943–) is an American philosopher who teaches at the University of Washington in Seattle and is best known for his work in epistemology. He is a coeditor of this book.

BonJour claims that there is a compelling argument against physicalism or materialism, one that grows out of the main insights of the Nagel and Jackson selections. (This paper is not published anywhere else, but a more complete version can be found at http://faculty.washington.edu/bonjour.)

What Is It Like to Be a Human (Instead of a Bat)?

My purpose in this paper is to discuss and defend an objection to physicalist or materialist accounts of the mind—one that I believe to be essentially conclusive. (1) The argument in question is not new. A version of it seems to be lurking, along with much else, in Thomas Nagel's famous paper "What Is It Like to Be a Bat?";* and a somewhat more explicit version is to be found in a well-known paper by Frank Jackson.† Despite the efforts of Nagel and Jackson (and some others), however, I believe that the most compelling version of the argument has not emerged clearly, with the result that materialist replies that in fact fail to speak to its central point are often taken to be adequate. Thus the purpose of the present paper is to offer what I regard as a more perspicuous restatement of the Nagel-Jackson argument, one which shows clearly why the replies in question do not work.

I

What is needed, in my judgment, is a version of the argument that makes it clear that there are *facts* or *truths* about human mental states that someone in Mary's position does not and cannot know on the basis of purely physical knowledge, however complete that may be. And one way to do this, I suggest, is in effect to invert Nagel's original example, in a way that he himself suggests in passing but does not develop: instead of imagining ourselves trying to know or comprehend the experiences of an alien form of life, we need instead to imagine an alien form of life trying to know or comprehend our experiences.

Suppose then that a brilliant Martian scientist comes to Earth to investigate, with our full cooperation, the nature and makeup of human beings. Being a Martian, he has, we may suppose, a quite different sensory apparatus from ours, but one which is still quite adequate, given his complete mastery of scientific reasoning, to arrive at a complete knowledge of any purely physical phenomenon. Thus, in time, the Martian arrives at an ideally complete knowledge of the physical facts concerning human beings, including those pertaining to causally defined functional roles. Does he thereby come to know all of the facts about human mental states such as experiences of color?

Suppose that I am one of the subjects studied by the Martian. On a particular occasion, I look at a newly mowed, well-watered, and healthy lawn and thereby have an experience of a certain specific phenomenal or sensuous property, one which is somewhere toward the middle of the range of such properties that I am accustomed to call "green." Shortly thereafter, I look at a newly painted fire engine and thereby have an experience of a second specific phenomenal or sensuous property, one which is somewhere toward the middle of the range of properties that I am accustomed to call "red." That on the first occasion I experience the first property and on the second occasion the second property, rather than the other way around, are simply facts about me in the most straightforward possible sense. Suppose that the Martian is present on both occasions and is carefully monitoring my physical and brain states with an elaborate set of instruments that he has devised for this purpose. He thereby, we may suppose, comes to know *everything* about those physical

(1)

When BonJour refers to physicalist or materialist accounts of the mind, he has in mind not just what Fodor calls central state materialism, but also functionalist theories. Since most functionalists are what Fodor calls token physicalists, their claim is that each mental state is some brain state or other, that, in other words, there is nothing more to a mental state than the particular brain state that it is (including its physically specified causal role).

*Reprinted in this book, pages 192–197.

†Frank Jackson, "What Mary Didn't Know," reprinted in this book, pages 198–200.

states, including their causal relations to other states, to as fine a level of detail as could possibly be relevant. Is he thereby able to know that I am experiencing the first sensuous property on the first occasion and the second sensuous property on the second occasion? ❷

I have stipulated that the Martian does not possess senses like ours. In particular, he does not possess eyes and a faculty of vision like ours. Thus one thing that he cannot do is determine what property I am experiencing by looking at the relevant objects himself. Nor should he need to do this, since facts about his own experiences are of course no part of his supposedly complete physical account of humans in general and of me in particular. ❸ (The same thing is in fact true of Mary: Though she happens to be a member of the species that she is investigating, her introspective awareness of her own experiences is still not a part of the ideally complete physical account of humans at which she arrives by the methods of physical science. This is why speculations about her imaginative extrapolations are simply irrelevant to the issue.)

The Martian does not experience colors in the way and in the contexts that we do. But it is still possible that he is familiar in some other way with the specific phenomenal or sensuous properties in question, and it will help to focus the essential point if we suppose that this is so. Thus suppose that he does experience those very properties, albeit in some quite different causal context. Perhaps he experiences colors when he hears or otherwise senses vibrations in the air corresponding to music. Or perhaps he does have something like eyes and vision, but in relation to a quite different range of electromagnetic radiation, and thereby experiences all of the colors that we experience (and perhaps others?), but in relation to different objects and situations than those that cause our specific experiences. Thus, we may suppose, he has a perfectly good grasp of the *concepts* of having an experience of each of the two properties in question, and the issue is only whether he can apply those concepts correctly to me.

We may even concede to the Martian one more quite useful piece of information, albeit one that he almost certainly could not in fact arrive at on his own. Let us stipulate not only that he is familiar with color properties and possesses the concepts of having such experiences, but even that he somehow knows—perhaps God whispers it in his ear or appropriate alternative sense organ—that two specific color properties out of the ones with which he is familiar are in fact the two that I am experiencing on the two occasions in question (but not of course which is which). In addition, we may suppose that the Martian has solved the difficult problem of isolating the specific features of my neurophysiology that are relevant to the issue we are concerned with, so that he is able to focus on two relatively restricted brain states (perhaps characterized in functional terms) that are, supposing that physicalism is true, identical to my experiencing of the two colors. Thus he is able to formulate to himself two pairs of propositions, one pair identifying the first of these restricted states with an experiencing of the first of the two properties and the second restricted state with an experiencing of the second of the two properties, and the other pair reversing these ascriptions. ❹ He thus knows, we are supposing, that the propositions in one of these pairs are true and those in the other pair false, but not which is which. Can he tell, solely on the basis of his complete physical knowledge, which is the correct pair? ❺

In thinking about this question, it is important to be quite clear about the exact shape of the issue. If physicalism is true, I submit, then the Martian should not have to extrapolate or surmise or guess, in however educated a fashion, in order to determine which pair of propositions is the correct one. If the ideal physical account is indeed a *complete* account of all the facts concerning humans and their mental states, and if one of the two pairs of propositions is true and the other false in relation to that subject-matter, then it seems to follow that the propositions of the true pair must be already *included* in some way in that account, and that the propositions in the other pair must be in some way *incompatible* with that account. And this would apparently mean in turn that the ideas or concepts of the two phenomenal or sensuous properties in question would have to be either already present in the physical account or somehow strictly definable on the basis of the physical ideas or concepts pertaining to the relevant physical states. ❻ The former of these alternatives seems clearly mistaken, which is just to say that neither the physical description

R If physicalism is true, then BonJour's experience of green is identical to some particular brain state—perhaps described in terms of its causal role, but the Martian will also know that.

Even if he did have eyes and could look at the lawn, he wouldn't know that we experience it in the same way he does.

The Martian then knows what the two experiences of (what we call) red and (what we call) green are like, though not which is which. And he also knows which are the relevant brain states, though again not which is which. He can thus formulate and understand the question that asks which brain state is the experience of red and which one is the experience of green.

If we name the first brain state A and the second brain state B, and we name the experience of red R and the experience of green G then one pair of propositions is A is R and B is G, and the other pair of propositions is A is G and B is R. If physicalism is true, BonJour is claiming, the Martian should be able to tell, which pair of propositions is true.

This claim is crucial to BonJour's argument that the Martian scientist is unable to know which of the two pairs of propositions is the right one: color concepts have to either be part of the physical theory or be definable in terms of physical concepts. (It is important to emphasize here that BonJour is concerned with the qualitative *experience* of color, not with such things as the corresponding wavelength of light, which the Martian can of course know.)

of the brain nor that of the human organism as a whole explicitly invokes the idea of sensuous or phenomenal color. And the latter alternative is equally implausible. One way to argue this point is to appeal to the familiar view that color concepts are essentially indefinable, a view that I believe to be correct. But even apart from this sort of appeal, the idea that the concepts of the various sensuous or phenomenal colors are strictly definable on the basis of physical concepts pertaining to brain states and other strictly physical states has, if anything, even less plausibility than the old phenomenalist idea that concepts pertaining to physical object are definable in purely sensory terms. I do not know how to strictly prove that no such definition is possible, but I know of no one who has ever seriously defended such a view, nor of any way to make it even minimally plausible.

Thus it seems utterly plain that the answer to our original question is "no." All that the Martian's physical knowledge can give him is increasingly complicated accounts of the structure of the two restricted brain states and of their structural and causal relations to each other and to other states and processes of the same kind. But all of this knowledge, however detailed and elaborate we may suppose it to be, would still be entirely compatible with the truth of either of the two pairs of propositions concerning the relations of brain states to my color experiences. Thus although the Martian scientist knows all the *physical* facts there are, he does not know all the *facts* there are, and it follows that physicalism is false.

III

I want to consider one more application of our general line of argument, in some ways the most fundamental of all, but one that is fortunately capable of being dealt with very briefly. It is obvious that on any plausible version of physicalism, only some of our brain states will be identified with conscious mental states. There is no consciousness associated with those states, for example, that control breathing and heartbeat. But this suggests the issue of whether our Martian scientist, on the basis of his complete physical knowledge, can tell which brain states are conscious and which are not. 7 My suggestion, once again, is that there is no way that he can do this in the logically tight way that is required.

STOP This is an issue that was originally raised by Smart. This line of argument about consciousness could be more fully developed in ways very similar to the original argument about color. Think about how it would go.

We may suppose, reasonably enough, that there is some structural difference between states that are conscious and states that are not, and hence that the Martian can divide our states into two groups, corresponding to this difference. But even if he can get this far, how can he possibly determine, as opposed to merely surmise or conjecture, that the states in one group involve consciousness and that those in the other do not? It is, if anything, even more obvious that consciousness is not explicitly mentioned as such in his complete physical account, nor definable in terms of things that are mentioned. And again, as with the case of phenomenal properties, I know of no one who has ever seriously suggested otherwise.

My conclusion is that the Martian scientist, in spite of possessing complete physical knowledge of me, could not know many important facts about my conscious mental life, nor indeed even that I have a conscious mental life at all. This means that the physical account is radically incomplete as an account of my complete personal makeup and hence that physicalism or materialism, as an account of human beings, is surely and irredeemably false.

Discussion Questions

1. Is BonJour right that the Martian scientist would be unable to tell which of BonJour's brain states is a sensation of one color and which is an experience of the other (both as experienced by the Martian)? Think about this question by listing all of the things that the Martian would plausibly be able to know (which external things cause the brain state in question, which frequencies of light are involved in each case, what BonJour calls the two experiences, which one BonJour likes better, etc.). Can you see any way, on the basis of physical knowledge of the brain states together with any of this other knowledge (all pertaining to causal role), to tell which experience is which?
2. Think about the application of the Martian scientist thought experiment to the problem of intentional content. Suppose that BonJour is thinking about various kinds of things, and that the Martian scientist has a complete knowledge of each of the relevant brain states. Can he determine on this

basis the specific content of BonJour's thoughts? Consider a range of examples—and remember that if physicalism is true, the Martian seemingly should be able to know the exact content of BonJour's thoughts: not just what things he is thinking about, but how exactly he conceives them.

3. Suppose that the result of the Martian scientist thought experiment is that the Martian scientist cannot know at least some facts about BonJour's mental life on the basis of a complete physical knowledge. Is there any plausible way for a materialist to argue that this result is compatible with his view?

David Lewis

David Lewis (1941–2001) was a major American philosopher who taught at Princeton University. He is best known for his work in metaphysics, but also made important contributions to many other areas.

When J. J. C. Smart considered the problem of phenomenal properties 20 years earlier, before the knowledge argument was proposed, he was very confident that science would discover the physical facts that in some way constituted these phenomenal properties. Lewis, writing 20 years later, says that the physicalist ultimately must deny the very existence of phenomenal properties in order to respond to the knowledge argument.

Knowing What It's Like

The most formidable challenge to any sort of materialism and functionalism comes from the friend of phenomenal qualia. He says we leave out the phenomenal aspect of mental life (1): we forget that pain is a feeling, that there is something it is like to hold one's hand in a flame, that we are aware of something when we suffer pain, that we can recognize that something when it comes again. . . . So far, our proper reply is the one sketched in [Lewis's article "Mad Pain and Martian Pain"]: we deny none of that! We say to the friend of qualia that, beneath his tendentious jargon, he is just talking about pain and various aspects of its functional role. We have already said what we take pain to be; and we do not doubt that part of its causal role is to give rise to judgments that one is in pain, and part is to enable one to recognize pain (the same realizer of the same role) when it comes again. (2)

So far, so good. But if he persists, the friend of qualia can succeed in escaping our unwelcome agreement; and when he does, we must reverse our strategy. Suppose he makes his case as follows.* You have not tasted Vegemite (a celebrated yeast-based condiment). So you do not know what it is like to taste Vegemite. And you never will, unless you taste Vegemite. (Or unless the same experience, or counterfeit traces of it, are somehow produced in you by artificial means.) No amount of the information whereof materialists and functionalists speak will help you at all. But if you taste Vegemite, *then* you will know what it is like. So you will have gained a sort of information that the materialists and functionalists overlook entirely. Call this *phenomenal information*. By qualia I mean the special subject matter of this phenomenal information.

Now we must turn eliminative. (3) We dare not grant that there is a sort of information we overlook; or, in other words, that there are possibilities exactly alike in the respects we know of, yet different in some other way. That would be defeat. Neither can we credibly claim that lessons in physics, physiology, . . . could teach the inexperienced what it is like to taste Vegemite. Our proper answer, I think, is that knowing what it's like is not the possession of information at all. It isn't the elimination of any hitherto open possibilities. Rather, knowing what it's like is the possession of abilities: abilities to recognize, abilities to imagine, abilities to predict one's behavior by means of imaginative experiments. (Someone who

1 — Lewis himself advocates a functionalist version of materialism about the mind, which is why he uses "we" to refer to the proponents of the view being challenged.

2 — These are some of the things that a functionalist might say when trying to account for pain, or any other experiential state.

3 — That is, the functionalist must, according to Lewis, deny the very existence of the sort of phenomenal information to which Jackson's argument appeals. Pay close attention to exactly what is going to be eliminated.

From *Philosophical Papers*, Vol. 1 (New York: Oxford University Press, 1983).

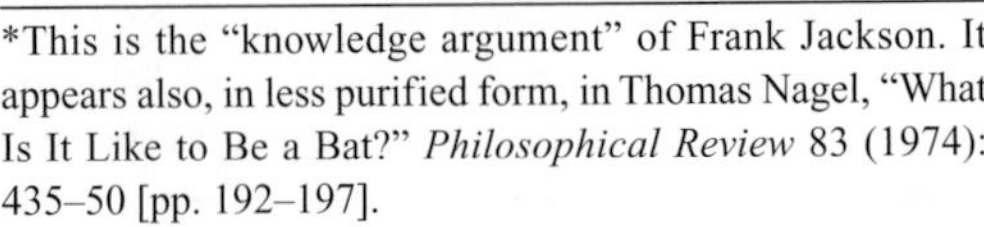

*This is the "knowledge argument" of Frank Jackson. It appears also, in less purified form, in Thomas Nagel, "What Is It Like to Be a Bat?" *Philosophical Review* 83 (1974): 435–50 [pp. 192–197].

knows what it's like to taste Vegemite can easily and reliably predict whether he would eat a second helping of Vegemite ice cream.) Lessons cannot impart these abilities—who would have thought they could? There is a state of knowing what it's like, sure enough. And Vegemite has a special power to produce that state. But phenomenal information and its special subject matter do not exist. (4)

...

STOP On this view, knowing what it's like does not involve having any special sort of information, knowing any *facts*, but rather being able to *do* something: recognize, discriminate, predict. It is still perhaps a kind of knowing, but not a kind that involves information. How plausible is the view that these things are *all* that is involved in coming to know how something tastes? (See Discussion Question 1.)

Discussion Questions

1. Lewis denies that "knowing what it is like" to have a certain experience involves coming to have any sort of new information. But then it seems that he must also deny that such experience involves becoming aware of distinctive phenomenal properties, for if it did, there would seemingly be information involved: that the experience involved one such phenomenal property rather than another. (See BonJour's version of the knowledge argument.) How plausible is it to deny the very existence of such properties? Try to think of other specific examples—maybe you could even try tasting some actual thing that you haven't ever tasted before and see if you encounter a new phenomenal property.
2. Lewis says that one of the abilities that one might acquire by tasting Vegemite is the ability to predict whether he would eat another serving of Vegemite ice cream—or presumably whether he would even eat a first serving. One way to understand this predictive ability is that it depends on becoming familiar with a specific phenomenal property and either liking or disliking it—but then phenomenal properties would have to exist. Can you think of any other accounts of how the ability in question might work, ones that do not involve any appeal to phenomenal properties?

David J. Chalmers

David Chalmers (1966–) is an Australian philosopher who has taught in the United States, but currently teaches at the Australian National University. He is best known for his work in the philosophy of mind, particularly on the topic of consciousness

In this selection, Chalmers distinguishes between the *hard problem* and the *easy problems* of consciousness. The easy problems ultimately have to do with how the brain does the various things it does, while the hard problem concerns how the brain gives rise to conscious experience. He argues that the results of neuroscience are insufficient to solve the hard problem of consciousness because of what he calls "the explanatory gap." Chalmers does not develop a dualist view in any detail, but he seems to have in mind a version of **epiphenomenalism**, according to which conscious states or properties do not have any effect on the physical world.

The Puzzle of Conscious Experience

Conscious experience is at once the most familiar thing in the world and the most mysterious. There is nothing we know about more directly than consciousness, but it is extraordinarily hard to reconcile it with everything else we know. Why does it exist? What does it do? How could it possibly arise from neural processes in the brain? These questions are among the most intriguing in all of science.

From *Scientific American* (December 1995).

From an objective viewpoint, the brain is relatively comprehensible. When you look at this page, there is a whir of processing: photons stirring your retina, electrical signals are passed up your optic nerve and between different areas of your brain, and eventually you might respond with a smile, a perplexed frown or a remark. But there is also a subjective aspect. When you look at the page, you are conscious of it, directly experiencing the images and words as part of your private,

While you have no vivid impressions of flowers and sky when looking at *this* page, you would have such impressions if you were looking at flowers and sky outside or at a picture of flowers and sky. Chalmers is pointing here to the same thing that Nagel was talking about when he said that there is "something that it is like" to, for example, see flowers and sky.

A reductionist theory of consciousness reduces consciousness to something more familiar: for example, the central state identity theory reduces mental states to brain states, since mental states *just are* brain states. Some philosophers (usually materialists) think that all dualists are "mysterians."

These are the kinds of questions that the scientist in Nagel's example could answer about bats and that BonJour's Martian scientist could answer about humans.

The real mystery, according to Chalmers, is how something physical like the brain can "give rise to" or cause experiences like these.

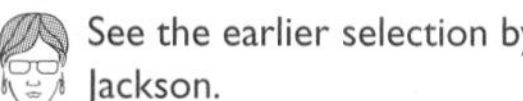

See the earlier selection by Jackson.

mental life. You have vivid impressions of colored flowers and vibrant sky. (1) At the same time, you may be feeling some emotions and forming some thoughts. Together such experiences make up consciousness: the subjective, inner life of the mind.

For many years, consciousness was shunned by researchers studying the brain and the mind. The prevailing view was that science, which depends on objectivity, could not accommodate something as subjective as consciousness. The behaviorist movement in psychology, dominant earlier in this century, concentrated on external behavior and disallowed any talk of internal mental processes. Later, the rise of cognitive science focused attention on processes inside the head. Still, consciousness remained off-limits, fit only for late-night discussion over drinks.

Over the past several years, however, an increasing number of neuroscientists, psychologists and philosophers have been rejecting the idea that consciousness cannot be studied and are attempting to delve into its secrets. As might be expected of a field so new, there is a tangle of diverse and conflicting theories, often using basic concepts in incompatible ways. To help unsnarl the tangle, philosophical reasoning is vital.

The myriad views within the field range from reductionist theories, according to which consciousness can be explained by the standard methods of neuroscience and psychology, to the position of the so-called mysterians, who say we will never understand consciousness at all. (2) I believe that on close analysis both of these views can be seen to be mistaken and that the truth lies somewhere in the middle.

Against reductionism I will argue that the tools of neuroscience cannot provide a full account of conscious experience, although they have much to offer. Against mysterianism I will hold that consciousness might be explained by a new kind of theory. The full details of such a theory are still out of reach, but careful reasoning and some educated inferences can reveal something of its general nature. For example, it will probably involve new fundamental laws, and the concept of information may play a central role. These faint glimmerings suggest that a theory of consciousness may have startling consequences for our view of the universe and of ourselves.

The Hard Problem

Researchers use the word "consciousness" in many different ways. To clarify the issues, we first have to separate the problems that are often clustered together under the name. For this purpose, I find it useful to distinguish between the "easy problems" and the "hard problem" of consciousness. The easy problems are by no means trivial—they are actually as challenging as most in psychology and biology—but it is with the hard problem that the central mystery lies.

The easy problems of consciousness include the following: How can a human subject discriminate sensory stimuli and react to them appropriately? How does the brain integrate information from many different sources and use this information to control behavior? How is it that subjects can verbalize their internal states? Although all these questions are associated with consciousness, they all concern the objective mechanisms of the cognitive system. Consequently, we have every reason to expect that continued work in cognitive psychology and neuroscience will answer them. (3)

The hard problem, in contrast, is the question of how physical processes in the brain give rise to subjective experience. This puzzle involves the inner aspect of thought and perception: the way things feel for the subject. When we see, for example, we experience visual sensations, such as that of vivid blue. Or think of the ineffable sound of a distant oboe, the agony of an intense pain, the sparkle of happiness or the meditative quality of a moment lost in thought. All are part of what I am calling consciousness. It is these phenomena that pose the real mystery of the mind. (4)

To illustrate the distinction, consider a thought experiment devised by the Australian philosopher Frank Jackson. (5) Suppose that Mary, a neuroscientist in the 23rd century, is the world's leading expert on the brain processes responsible for color vision. But Mary has lived her whole life in a black-and-white room and has never seen any other colors. She knows everything there is to know about physical processes in the brain—its biology, structure and function. This understanding enables her to grasp everything there is to know about the easy problems: how the brain discriminates stimuli, integrates information and produces verbal reports. From her knowledge of color vision, she knows the way color names correspond with wavelengths on the light spectrum. But there is still something crucial about color vision that Mary does not know: what it is like to experience a color such as red. It follows that there are facts about conscious experience that cannot be deduced from physical facts about the functioning of the brain. [6]

Indeed, nobody knows why these physical processes are accompanied by conscious experience at all. Why is it that when our brains process light of a certain wavelength, we have an experience of deep purple? Why do we have an experience at all? Could not an unconscious automaton have performed the same tasks just as well? These are questions that we would like a theory of consciousness to answer.

I am not denying that consciousness arises from the brain. [7] We know, for example, that the subjective experience of vision is closely linked to processes in the visual cortex. It is the link itself that perplexes, however. Remarkably, subjective experience seems to emerge from a physical process. But we have no idea how or why this is.

Is Neuroscience Enough?

Given the flurry of recent work on consciousness in neuroscience and psychology, one might think this mystery is starting to be cleared up. On closer examination, however, it turns out that almost all the current work addresses only the easy problems of consciousness. The confidence of the reductionist view comes from the progress on the easy problems, but none of this makes any difference where the hard problem is concerned.

Consider the hypothesis put forward by neurobiologist Francis Crick of the Salk Institute for Biological Studies in San Diego and Christof Koch of the California Institute of Technology. They suggest that consciousness may arise from certain oscillations in the cerebral cortex, which become synchronized as neurons fire 40 times per second. Crick and Koch believe the phenomenon might explain how different attributes of a single perceived object (its color and shape, for example), which are processed in different parts of the brain, are merged into a coherent whole. In this theory, two pieces of information become bound together precisely when they are represented by synchronized neural firings.

The hypothesis could conceivably elucidate one of the easy problems about how information is integrated in the brain. But why should synchronized oscillations give rise to a visual experience, no matter how much integration is taking place? [8] This question involves the hard problem, about which the theory has nothing to offer. Indeed, Crick and Koch are agnostic about whether the hard problem can be solved by science at all.

. . .

The critical common trait among these easy problems is that they all concern how a cognitive or behavioral function is performed. All are ultimately questions about how the brain carries out some task—how it discriminates stimuli, integrates information, produces reports and so on. Once neurobiology specifies appropriate neural mechanisms, showing how the functions are performed, the easy problems are solved. The hard problem of consciousness, in contrast, goes beyond problems about how functions are performed. Even if every behavioral and cognitive function related to consciousness were explained, there would still remain a further mystery: Why is the performance of these functions accompanied by conscious experience? [9] It is this additional conundrum that makes the hard problem hard.

The Explanatory Gap

Some have suggested that to solve the hard problem, we need to bring in new tools of physical explanation: nonlinear dynamics, say, or new discoveries in neuroscience, or quantum mechanics. But these ideas suffer from exactly the same difficulty. . . .

The trouble is that physical theories are best suited to explaining why systems have a certain physical structure and how they perform various functions. Most problems in science have this form; to explain life, for example, we need to describe how a physical system can reproduce, adapt and metabolize. But consciousness is a different sort of problem entirely, as it goes beyond the explanation of structure and function.

Of course, neuroscience is not irrelevant to the study of consciousness. For one, it may be able to reveal the nature of the neural correlate of consciousness—the brain processes most directly associated with conscious experience.

Chalmers is assuming, with Jackson (and BonJour), that Mary's experience of red involves a phenomenal feature that Mary would have known about previously only if she could have *deduced* an adequate description of it from physical facts about the brain. (Notice the similarity between this argument and BonJour's Martian scientist argument.)

In saying that consciousness *arises* from the brain, Chalmers is not saying, as the materialist does, that conscious states just are brain states. Instead, he is saying that conscious states are entirely caused by brain states (something that some versions of dualism would accept, but others would deny).

The emphasis here is on *experience*. How can these oscillations be responsible for the distinctively subjective experience: the way it is for someone to, for example, *see* the color and shape of a perceived object?

What is it about the performance of these functions, or any functions, that results in conscious experience, instead of no experience at all? (A closely related problem is why, in a particular case, there is one distinctive sort of experience rather than another.)

This is the sort of thing that Mary and the Martian scientist are depicted as knowing. But even if we knew exactly which brain state was correlated with some particular experiential state, without understanding *why* that particular brain state gives rise to any experiential state and indeed to that particular experiential state, we have still not solved the hard problem of consciousness.

11

R Psychophysical laws will provide the bridge over the explanatory gap, relating the psychological (experiential) states to the physical (brain) states. But if these laws do not "interfere" with those of the physical world, so that physical laws form a "closed system," then conscious states do not influence the physical world—which amounts to epiphenomenalism.

The reason that the sorts of theories that Chalmers has in mind will not be "conclusively testable" is that the experiences of other people are not directly accessible and any single person's first-person experiences do not provide enough evidence for "conclusive" testing. (This is more or less the same reason that motivated behavioral psychologists to attempt to explain behavior without appealing to consciousness—see the discussion of "radical behaviorism" in the first Fodor selection.)

It may even give a detailed correspondence between specific processes in the brain and related components of experience. 10 But until we know why these processes give rise to conscious experience at all, we will not have crossed what philosopher Joseph Levine has called the explanatory gap between physical processes and consciousness. Making that leap will demand a new kind of theory.

A True Theory of Everything

In searching for an alternative, a key observation is that not all entities in science are explained in terms of more basic entities. In physics, for example, space-time, mass and charge (among other things) are regarded as fundamental features of the world, as they are not reducible to anything simpler. Despite this irreducibility, detailed and useful theories relate these entities to one another in terms of fundamental laws. Together these features and laws explain a great variety of complex and subtle phenomena.

It is widely believed that physics provides a complete catalogue of the universe's fundamental features and laws. As physicist Steven Weinberg puts it in his 1992 book *Dreams of a Final Theory,* the goal of physics is a "theory of everything" from which all there is to know about the universe can be derived. But Weinberg concedes that there is a problem with consciousness. Despite the power of physical theory, the existence of consciousness does not seem to be derivable from physical laws. He defends physics by arguing that it might eventually explain what he calls the objective correlates of consciousness (that is, the neural correlates), but of course to do this is not to explain consciousness itself. If the existence of consciousness cannot be derived from physical laws, a theory of physics is not a true theory of everything. So a final theory must contain an additional fundamental component.

Toward this end, I propose that conscious experience can be considered a fundamental feature, irreducible to anything more basic. The idea may seem strange at first, but consistency seems to demand it. In the 19th century it turned out that electromagnetic phenomena could not be explained in terms of previously known principles. As a consequence, scientists introduced electromagnetic charge as a new fundamental entity and studied the associated fundamental laws. Similar reasoning should apply to consciousness. If existing fundamental theories cannot encompass it, then something new is required.

When there is a fundamental property, there are fundamental laws. In this case, the laws must relate experience to elements of physical theory. These laws will almost certainly not interfere with those of the physical world; it seems that the latter form a closed system in their own right. Rather the laws will serve as a bridge, specifying how experience depends on underlying physical processes. It is this bridge that will cross the explanatory gap.

Thus, a complete theory will have two components: physical laws, telling us about the behavior of physical systems from the infinitesimal to the cosmological, and what we might call psycho-physical laws, telling us how some of those systems are associated with conscious experience. These two components will constitute a true theory of everything. 11

Searching for a Theory

Supposing for the moment that they exist, how might we uncover such psychophysical laws? The greatest hindrance in this pursuit will be a lack of data. As I have described it, consciousness is subjective, so there is no direct way to monitor it in others. But this difficulty is an obstacle, not a dead end. For a start, each one of us has access to our own experiences, a rich trove that can be used to formulate theories. We can also plausibly rely on indirect information, such as subjects' descriptions of their experiences. Philosophical arguments and thought experiments also have a role to play. Such methods have limitations, but they give us more than enough to get started.

These theories will not be conclusively testable, so they will inevitably be more speculative than those of more conventional scientific disciplines. Nevertheless, there is no reason they should not be strongly constrained to account accurately for our own first-person experiences, as well as the evidence from subjects' reports. If we find a theory that fits the data better than any other theory of equal simplicity, we will have good reason to accept it. Right now we do not have even a single theory that fits the data, so worries about testability are premature. 12

We might start by looking for high-level bridging laws, connecting physical processes to experience at an everyday level. The basic contour of such a law might be gleaned from the observation that when we are conscious of something, we are generally able to act on it and speak about it—which are objective, physical functions. Conversely, when some information is directly available for action and speech, it is generally conscious. Thus, consciousness correlates well with what we might call "awareness": the process by which information in the brain is made globally available to motor processes such as speech and bodily action. 13

The notion may seem trivial. But as defined here, awareness is objective and physical, whereas consciousness is not. Some refinements to the definition of awareness are needed, in order to extend the concept to animals and infants, which cannot speak. But at least in familiar cases, it is possible to see the rough outlines of a psychophysical law: where there is awareness, there is consciousness, and vice versa.

To take this line of reasoning a step further, consider the structure present in the conscious experience. The experience of a field of vision, for example, is a constantly changing mosaic of colors, shapes and patterns and as such has a detailed geometric structure. The fact that we can describe this structure, reach out in the direction of many of its components and perform other actions that depend on it suggests that the structure corresponds directly to that of the information made available in the brain through the neural processes of awareness. 14

Similarly, our experiences of color have an intrinsic three-dimensional structure that is mirrored in the structure of information processes in the brain's visual cortex. This structure is illustrated in the color wheels and charts used by artists. Colors are arranged in a systematic pattern—red to green on one axis, blue to yellow on another, and black to white on a third. Colors that are close to one another on a color wheel are experienced as similar. It is extremely likely that they also correspond to similar perceptual representations in the brain, as part of a system of complex three-dimensional coding among neurons that is not yet fully understood. We can recast the underlying concept as a principle of structural coherence: the structure of conscious experience is mirrored by the structure of information in awareness, and vice versa. 15

. . .

Information: Physical and Experiential

The ultimate goal of a theory of consciousness is a simple and elegant set of fundamental laws, analogous to the fundamental laws of physics. The principles described above are unlikely to be fundamental, however. Rather they seem to be high-level psychophysical laws, analogous to macroscopic principles in physics such as those of thermodynamics or kinematics. What might the underlying fundamental laws be? No one knows, but I don't mind speculating.

I suggest that the primary psychophysical laws may centrally involve the concept of information. The abstract notion of information . . . is that of a set of separate states with a basic structure of similarities and differences between them. We can think of a 10-bit binary code as an information state, for example. Such information states can be embodied in the physical world. This happens whenever they correspond to physical states (voltages, say); the differences between them can be transmitted along some pathway, such as a telephone line.

We can also find information embodied in conscious experience. The pattern of color patches in a visual field, for example, can be seen as analogous to that of the pixels covering a display screen. Intriguingly, it turns out that we find the same information states embedded in conscious experience and in underlying physical processes in the brain. The three-dimensional encoding of color spaces, for example, suggests that the information state in a color experience corresponds directly to an information state in the brain. We might even regard the two states as distinct aspects of a single information state, which is simultaneously embodied in both physical processing and conscious experience.

According to Chalmers's use of the term, "awareness" is a physical process that does not in itself involve consciousness. (This is not the ordinary meaning of the term.)

The hypothesis that there is a correlation between our experience of colored shapes and the information processed by the brain is supported by our ability to perform physical actions that relate directly to the details of such experience—including giving a verbal description of it.

(But on an epiphenomenalist view, paradoxically enough, such a description cannot be caused by the experience itself, because that would be a case of consciousness causally affecting the physical world. See Discussion Question 3.)

Here is an initial candidate for a very rough and approximate psycho-physical law: one connecting the structure of conscious experience with the physical states involved in the neural process of "awareness"—remember that "awareness" is not a conscious state for Chalmers.

STOP The claim that *any* informational state has a conscious aspect would apparently mean that even the sorts of informational states that are involved in monitoring things like breathing and heartbeat in human beings have such aspects, even though we do not seem to be consciously aware of them. Chalmers doesn't commit himself to such a view, but he considers the possibility. Does it seem plausible?

To "bite the bullet" is to affirm a seemingly counterintuitive or seemingly implausible implication of a view—the more implausible, the bigger the "bullet." It does seem extremely odd to say that a thermostat has experiences, and so affirming this consequence of the view that all physical states are informational, and all informational states have an experiential aspect, would be "biting the bullet."

A natural hypothesis ensues. Perhaps information, or at least some information, has two basic aspects: a physical one and an experiential one. This hypothesis has the status of a fundamental principle that might underlie the relation between physical processes and experience. Wherever we find conscious experience, it exists as one aspect of an information state, the other aspect of which is embedded in a physical process in the brain. (16) This proposal needs to be fleshed out to make a satisfying theory. But it fits nicely with the principles mentioned earlier—systems with the same organization will embody the same information, for example—and it could explain numerous features of our conscious experience.

...

A potential problem is posed by the ubiquity of information. Even a thermostat embodies some information, for example, but is it conscious? There are at least two possible responses. First, we could constrain the fundamental laws so that only some information has an experiential aspect, perhaps depending on how it is physically processed. Second, we might bite the bullet and allow that all information has an experiential aspect—where there is complex information processing, there is complex experience, and where there is simple information processing, there is simple experience. (17) If this is so, then even a thermostat might have experiences, although they would be much simpler than even a basic color experience, and there would certainly be no accompanying emotions or thoughts. This seems odd at first, but if experience is truly fundamental, we might expect it to be widespread. In any case, the choice between these alternatives should depend on which can be integrated into the most powerful theory.

Of course, such ideas may be all wrong. On the other hand, they might evolve into a more powerful proposal that predicts the precise structure of our conscious experience from physical processes in our brains. If this project succeeds, we will have good reason to accept the theory. If it fails, other avenues will be pursued, and alternative fundamental theories may be developed. In this way, we may one day resolve the greatest mystery of the mind.

Discussion Questions

1. Suppose that the claim that every informational state has a conscious aspect is true. Consider the informational states of a thermometer. That thermometer would have states with at least some minimal conscious aspect. Does it follow from this supposition that "there is something it is like" to be a thermometer? Thomas Nagel has flirted with a view called "panpsychism" (the view that mind or consciousness is a fundamental feature of all of reality). To some, the view seems just crazy, while to others, it seems at least somewhat plausible. How would you argue for or against this view?
2. Can you think of other times in the history of science when there was an explanatory gap between two domains that seemed to be related? Think about the relation between biological descriptions of an organism (you, for example) and a description in terms of physics (maybe even quantum mechanics). Another example, made famous by Sir Arthur Eddington, involves two descriptions of a table: on the one hand you can describe the table in common-sense terms that will include its color and solidity and shape, and so on; while on the other hand, someone could give a description of the table in terms of the most advanced physics as a cloud of particles with large gaps between them and no properties like color. But the two descriptions are presumably of the same table. Is the common-sense description simply false? What is the relation between the two descriptions?
3. Chalmers seems to accept an epiphenomenalist version of dualism, probably of attribute dualism. Think carefully about the implications of this view, including the one mentioned in Annotation 14. How implausible is such a view? Does it seem obvious that your conscious states do influence the physical world through your physical reactions to them, including both deliberate actions and things like wincing from pain? How might an epiphenomenalist respond to this objection? Are there, as Chalmers thinks, strong reasons to think that consciousness has no effect on the physical world, and if so, what are they?

Concluding Dialogue on the Mind-Body Problem

So after all this, what should someone conclude about the mind-body problem? Are we merely material creatures, or are our minds or mental states something over and above the material? Most of the discussion in this chapter has been about problems with materialist views, mainly problems with functionalism. These problems, especially the one about qualitative experiential content, seem serious, so why do most philosophers still seem to end up endorsing materialism in general and functionalism in particular?

It's easy, after all, to see why it can seem so obvious that *some* version of materialism must be true. The underlying reason is what sometimes gets called *naturalism:* the view that human beings are just another species of animal, emerging and evolving through basically material or more specifically biochemical processes—so that *everything* about them must be capable of being understood in material terms.

Right. That seems like nothing more than scientific good sense. So why isn't it enough to settle the issue?

You know perfectly well why. Because it doesn't by itself really speak to the distinctively philosophical issue at all. It's not enough to be confident that materialism must be true. The philosophical problem is really to explain *how* it can be true: how mental states as we know them—and especially as we each experience them in our own individual cases—can be just material states.

Some materialists end up just denying that conscious mental states exist at all. That's what logical behaviorism really amounts to. And there are also a few philosophers, the so-called *eliminative materialists,* who reject the existence of conscious mental states more openly and explicitly—though their views didn't make it into this chapter!

That's because eliminativism is *so* hard to take seriously. I once ran into an eliminativist about beliefs and other propositional attitudes at a convention. I told him teasingly that I didn't *believe* that his view was correct. He proceeded to try to argue with me, but what he really should have said was that *of course* I didn't believe it and he didn't either—since there are no beliefs. But then what would his advocacy of the view amount to?

I agree that eliminativism seems pretty desperate: denying something that seems just too obvious to be reasonably denied. But there are of course more moderate materialist views—such as functionalism.

You say "such as functionalism." What people don't always realize is that once logical behaviorism and eliminativism are set aside as too implausible to be taken seriously and once it is realized that the identity theory is only an initial stab in the direction of functionalism, there really is *only* functionalism left as a serious possibility for a materialist view. Which may be why functionalism is still by far the most widely held view, in spite of serious problems that everybody recognizes.

That's a little too fast for me. Why can't there be other materialist views as well, ones that are different from any of those?

Well, in principle there could be, I suppose. But the only idea that anyone has ever had about what is really the overwhelmingly central issue—*how* what we experience and conceive as a mental state could really just be some sort of material state, presumably a brain state—is the one reflected in Smart's idea of a "topic-neutral" description of an experiential state and developed more fully and broadly in the functionalist idea that the "mental" description of such a state is really just a description of it in terms of its causal role. If it were plausible that descriptions in "topic neutral" or causal role terms could capture *everything* that seems undeniably true about the various sorts of mental states, then those states—the ones that fill those causal roles—could turn out to be brain states, and the mind-body problem would be solved.

I see. So what makes the problem persist is that even if such a causal role description perhaps captures *part* of what is true of a particular mental state, it seems—at least in the case of qualitative states like experiences of color—to leave something out. Indeed, not just something but the most important something, the feature that is really essential to that mental state. My experience of red may fill a certain causal role, but what is it like *experientially*? What is the specific quality of which I am aware in such an experience, and what does my conscious awareness of that quality really amount to?

Yes. That's why the reversed spectrum problem is such a bugaboo for functionalists. There seems to be no reason at all why the state that satisfies a certain causal role in me couldn't be experientially quite different from the one that satisfies the same causal role in you—why my sensation of red couldn't be *experientially* the same as your sensation of what you call green and vice-versa. But if the causal role account doesn't capture this crucial experiential dimension, then it also doesn't really explain how a brain state could just be that experiential state.

So that's really the key point. And it also explains why we don't seem to be able to know "what it's like to be a bat" on the basis of a physical and causal-role account of bat physiology—and why Mary or the Martian Scientist can't know about the distinctive nature of color experiences merely by knowing about brain physiology and causal roles.

Right. But then the materialist seems to be left with no viable account of how these experiential states could just be brain states—or how they could be any other sort of material state either. Maybe what Nagel suggests is right: we have good reasons for thinking that materialism is true, even though we don't understand at all *how* it could be true. But why isn't the fact that we don't understand how something could be true a good philosophical reason for thinking that it probably isn't true? If we can't see how material states can have the features that we *know* that mental states have, why isn't that a good reason—maybe not conclusive, but pretty strong—for thinking that materialism is false?

In fact, many materialists seem to agree that qualitative experiential properties—so-called "qualia"—are a difficult and so far unsolved problem for their view. But what about mental states like beliefs and other propositional attitudes? My conscious thought that there are pine trees on the University of Washington campus doesn't seem to have any distinctive qualitative content or features—nothing that the reversed spectrum thought experiment could apply to. And many, many people think that functionalism does much better in giving an account of them—and that propositional attitudes are so much more important for psychological explanation that if a materialist view can handle them, then materialism is still in pretty good shape.

Maybe it would be. But I'm not convinced that functionalism really does any better with propositional attitudes. It's true that states of this sort don't have distinctive qualitative content in the way that states like color experiences do. But a conscious belief or thought still involves an awareness of a particular content. If you are thinking consciously that there are many pine trees on the University of Washington campus, then you are consciously aware of a specific content, one that involves the idea of a pine tree and the idea of a campus and the idea of a certain geographical location. Do we really understand how a brain state could essentially involve the *awareness* of such ideas or contents?

And that's what Searle is worried about, I suppose. According to functionalists like Fodor, the state in question is supposed to involve a mental *symbol,* one that is meaningful or contentful merely by virtue of being causally connected to other symbols and to external inputs and outputs. And Searle's point is that the guy in the Chinese room could realize all the right causal connections for the thought that there are many pine trees on the UW campus and still have no realization at all that this specific content or anything like it is involved.

Exactly. So it really is sort of like a reversed spectrum case for mental content. A person who satisfies the causal role in question might have some quite different conscious content in mind, if indeed he has any conscious content in mind at all. Thus the functionalist hasn't explained how a conscious awareness of that content could be a brain state either.

So another way to put the point would be to say that the Martian Scientist wouldn't be able, merely by determining the causal or functional role of the state I am in when I am thinking about the pine trees, to know what conscious content—if any—it is a thought of.

Fodor responds to Searle by appealing to external causal relations "of the right kinds." The idea is that what makes a particular brain state the thought that there are many pine trees on the UW campus is that this particular brain state is related in the right, very complicated

causal ways to real pine trees and real campuses and the state of Washington. But the problem is that all this is still just a part of the causal role and doesn't seem to explain how and why the person having such a state will be *consciously aware* of any of these things—or indeed of anything at all. I'm not entirely sure that this is exactly what Searle is getting at, but I still think it's the main problem. As Nagel and Chalmers both say, it's consciousness that makes the mind-body problem so hard!

So, since you think that what is really the only serious candidate for a materialist view doesn't work, I suppose you must think that dualism is the right answer?

Not really—at least not with very much confidence. The problem with materialism is that it doesn't seem to have a good explanation of how a conscious mental state could be a brain state. The problem with dualism is that it doesn't really have much of an account at all of the *non-material* states it appeals to. Almost everything that dualists say about these states is negative rather than positive—mainly just that they aren't material states—and that isn't enough to constitute very much of a solution to the problem.

It seems worse to me than that. It's not just that dualists don't say very much, but also that there are further materialist objections to dualism, some of which seem to me pretty strong. One main materialist objection is that an immaterial state, and especially one that isn't in space, can't causally interact with a material state, even though mental states seem clearly to causally interact with non-mental bodily states. Even if you are willing to be an epiphenomenalist, a dualist view would have to involve at least causation from the material world to the mind, in order to account for perceptual experience. (I'm assuming that parallelism is too implausible to take seriously.)

I have to admit that I've never been very worried about this particular objection, even though lots of materialists (such as Fodor) seem to regard it as more or less decisive. I agree that we don't have anything approaching a detailed account of how such causation would work, but that is very far from having a knockdown argument that it can't work. If we had a detailed account of the nature of mind or mental states as understood by dualism, maybe a problem of this sort would emerge. But not with the account—or really the non-account!—that we presently have. Why (as Foster suggests) couldn't there just be *direct* causation between mental states and certain material states, with no sort of intervening mechanism?

I still don't see how things as different as dualist minds and material bodies are supposed to be can have any sort of causal impact, direct or not, on each other. But there are also other issues about dualism that lead to further problems. If you were to finally opt for dualism, which kind would you pick? Interactionism or epiphenomenalism? Substance dualism or attribute dualism?

On the first issue, surely interactionism. A lot of recent dualists (like Chalmers) seem to opt for epiphenomenalism, but I find that extremely hard to understand. At least this much is true: if epiphenomenalism were true, then no one would ever be able to *say* anything about mental states—not even that epiphenomenalism is true! Saying something about anything surely has to involve some sort of causal relation between the thing in question (various mental states, in this case) and the physical verbal statements, and epiphenomenalism would rule that out. If the existence and specific character of a mental state (such as an experience of red) has no causal impact at all on which words are uttered (such as my saying "I am having an experience of red")—so that the state could have been completely different (such as an experience of green) and the words still exactly the same—what would make it true that those words are really about that state at all?

There's a real paradox! No one who seems to advocate epiphenomenalism about mental states can really be doing so if what they seem to be saying is right. So either that isn't what they are saying (but then what are they saying?), or else they're wrong!

Right. The main motivation for epiphenomenalism is the idea that the material world is causally autonomous, so that physical science can be predictively and explanatorily complete, even though it doesn't mention mental states. But I've never been able to see that this amounts to much of an argument against interactionism. The argument seems to just *assume* that there is no mental-physical causal influence or to point out that scientists

assume this or to point out that there are no cases *not* involving mental states where we have any reason to think that the material world isn't "causally closed." Those just aren't very strong reasons. The problem with the last one is that conscious mental states seem to be so different from everything else that generalizing from cases that don't involve them to those that do seems very questionable.

So what then about the substance or attribute issue?

I'm not very sure I have a good grip on that—and, like most philosophers, if I don't think I understand an issue, that leads me to think that maybe there isn't a clear issue to be understood! But I suppose I would opt for attribute dualism if I had to make a choice. The nature of mental *substances* is very obscure, and it is after all mental *properties*—being an experience of a particular color or an awareness of a particular propositional content—that seem most obviously undeniable.

You don't sound very confident.

I'm not—about this or about anything concerning dualism. The state of the issue seems to me to be that the only materialist view in town fails utterly to account for one main feature of conscious mental states (qualitative content) and probably for the other one as well (thought content)—but that the dualist alternative isn't well enough developed to yield much confidence that it can do any better. Maybe more work on dualism will make it a more substantial view—there really hasn't been very much, even though the view has been around for a long time. Or maybe there is some other materialist alternative that no one has yet thought of. But right now Schopenhauer's "world knot" seems still to be quite firmly tied.

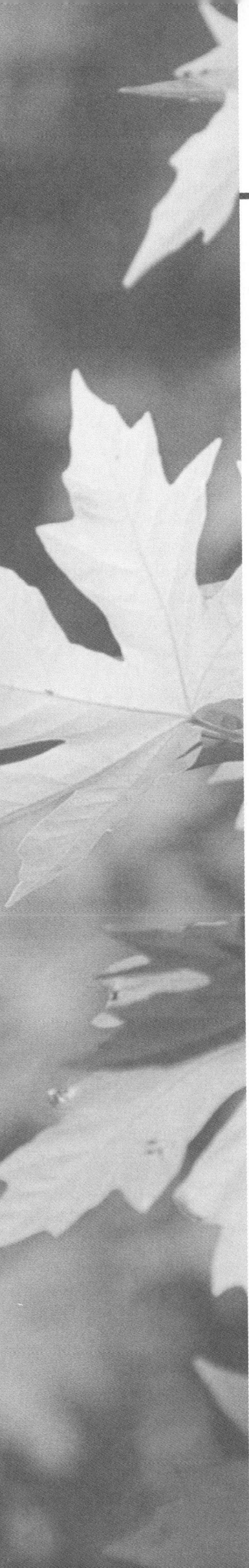

CHAPTER 4

Personal Identity and Free Will

The selections in this chapter are concerned with two metaphysical issues about persons (in addition to the mind-body problem considered in the previous chapter). By a **person,** we will understand any being with the moral status and moral characteristics that we ascribe to normal human beings, leaving open at least the possibility that members of species other than ours (such as, perhaps, dolphins or extraterrestrials) might count as persons. Each of the two issues to be considered is importantly relevant, though in very different ways, to the ascription of *moral responsibility* to a person.

In order to be morally responsible for an action or its results at another time, it seems initially obvious that the later person to whom responsibility is ascribed must be *identical* to, the very same person as, the earlier person who performed that action. And in addition to its bearing on the issue of moral responsibility, personal identity is also even more central to the issue of *survival:* for a person to survive, that is, to continue to exist in the future (something that most people desire very strongly) seems obviously to require that the future person be *identical* to the one who exists at an earlier time. Thus any discussion of either responsibility or survival must confront the difficult question of what conditions must be satisfied for such a relation of identity over time to hold in the case of a person.

In addition, it is standardly assumed that to correctly be held responsible, a person must have performed the action in question *freely.* Thus a second issue (or set of related issues) is whether people are ever genuinely free—and, even more fundamentally, of what freedom in the relevant sense really amounts to.

Each of these issues turns out to be extremely difficult, though in somewhat different ways. Under the pressure of various problematic examples, the concept of personal identity and the closely related concept of personal survival over time threaten to dissolve, leaving it seriously unclear what these things that we in some moods care about so much really amount to. In the case of free will, on the other hand, the main worry is that the sort of freedom that we think we care about (which seems initially at least very clear) may turn out not to exist or indeed not even to be possible.

What Is Required for Personal Identity?

The selections in the first (and shorter) main section of the chapter are concerned with the problem of personal identity. The first thing to say is that this is primarily a **metaphysical** issue and not an **epistemological** one: the main question is what it is for such a relation of identity to obtain, not how we can know or justifiably believe that it does.

Two aspects of this issue require some initial clarification. First, the main issue is the identity of *persons* and not the identity of *humans.* A human is a certain kind of biological organism, a member of a certain animal species. Because life involves taking in and expelling material parts of various kinds, there is a question about what it is for a biological organism existing at one time to be identical to one existing at another time. But to resolve this question would not automatically settle the question of personal identity, since it is far from clear that a person, roughly the sort of being that has responsibilities and rights and cares about its own survival, is to be simply identified with a biological organism.

Second, what is at issue is *numerical identity* (being the very same individual entity), as opposed to what is sometimes called *qualitative identity* (being exactly similar in qualities and features). Another car that is the same make, model, and color as my car, with the same kinds of accessories, the very same kinds of scratches in the paint, and so forth, might perhaps be qualitatively identical to my car, but would still obviously be numerically distinct. And, on the other hand, my car is normally taken to be the numerically same individual entity at different times even though its qualities change as it ages, becomes dirty or is washed, acquires scratches and dents, and so forth.*

In addition to its theoretical interest, the issue of personal identity is practically important in two quite distinct ways. First, as we have seen, there is the issue of moral responsibility—or, more specifically, of the justifiability of such things as blame, praise, punishment, reward, and so on. For a person to be justifiably blamed, praised, punished, or rewarded for some earlier action seems to require that he or she be numerically the very same person as the one who actually performed that action, again making it important to figure out what such identity requires. (For example, is a person who has suffered total amnesia still the same person as the one who existed before the amnesia and perhaps performed some action worthy of praise or blame?) Second, there is the issue of individual *survival.* Most people hope to survive into the future, and many are concerned with the possibility of survival after death. But for a person to survive seems, at first glance at least, to require that some later person be *identical* to the earlier one who survives, making it important for those concerned with survival to discover what such identity requires. (To take one familiar example, could a person who is resurrected in the sense advocated in Christianity be genuinely numerically the same person as one who died earlier, and if so, what specifically would this require?)

One thing that makes the problem of personal identity so difficult is that it seemingly cannot be solved without deciding just what sort of entity a person really is. Here there are a variety of possible answers, none of them free of problems. Is a person

---

*The car example raises an issue that is related to though still distinct from the problem of personal identity: what is it for a material object to be the numerically identical or the same from one time to another, as its qualities change in various ways and as material parts get added or subtracted? No one would say that my car today is not the same car as my car yesterday just because it has received a new scratch or dent in the meantime—even though this presumably means that it is not the very same collection of atoms and molecules in the same arrangement (since some molecules have been scratched off and others rearranged). But suppose that many parts of the original car have been replaced: the tires, the muffler, one or more of the windows, some or even all of the engine or even the whole engine, some or all of the seats, and so on. At what point (if any) is the resulting car no longer numerically identical to the original car? And does the shift from identity to nonidentity happen gradually or all at once? There is also a closely analogous though still somewhat different problem for living things of various kinds, including human bodies (and the bodies of other sorts of persons, if there are any). What makes the issue of personal identity importantly different from either of these is that on most views a person is not just a material object or even a living body. It has also often been assumed (though Parfit challenges this) that personal identity, unlike the identity of material objects or living things, could not in principle be a matter of degree.

just an animal of a certain distinctive sort—or perhaps such an animal over part of its history (excluding very early and perhaps also very late stages)? Is a person perhaps just a functioning brain of a certain sort—or perhaps even just one half of such a brain? Is a person a Cartesian mind or soul of the sort advocated by a dualist view on the mind-body problem? Is a person a composite entity consisting of such a mind or soul together with a material component (which might be any of the possibilities already listed)? Or is a person perhaps something like an abstract program or collection of information, something that could be stored in various forms? (Some of these possibilities are elaborated in the selections that follow.)

What then does personal identity require? The predominant tendency in recent discussions, growing out of Locke, is to appeal to *psychological* conditions of some sort: things like memories or apparent memories of earlier actions or experiences. Locke's own view, as defended in the first of the following selections, is that personal identity requires that the later person have the "same consciousness" as the earlier person with which he or she is identical: where this means at least roughly that the later person has an apparent memory of the earlier person's actions and experiences (perhaps this memory also has to be caused in the right way). Thomas Reid offers a number of objections to Locke's view. Bernard Williams then considers the issue of whether, as Locke suggests, a person inhabiting one human body could be identical to a later person inhabiting a different body—whether two people could "exchange bodies," arguing that the answer to this question is seriously uncertain. Finally, Derek Parfit argues that there are describable cases in which the issue of whether one person is identical with an earlier one has no clear and determinate answer, but also that the issue of identity is less important than it has usually been taken to be—and in particular that, contrary to what has almost always been assumed, the *survival* of a person does *not* require that there be a later person to whom the previously existing person is identical.

Are Human Actions Genuinely Free?

The main question in the second (and longer) section of the chapter is whether human actions are normally—or even ever—the result of genuinely *free* choices in the sense—whatever exactly that is—that seems to be required for moral responsibility. The primary reason, after all, that we are reluctant to punish someone who is thought to be insane, even for a crime that is very serious, is that we don't think that an insane person is really responsible in a moral sense for what he does. And the most obvious reason for this is that we think that a truly insane person is incapable of making a genuinely free choice to act in a certain way. But are ordinary people really any freer than insane persons, however much they may differ from them in other ways? And even more fundamentally, what does it mean for an action to be genuinely free: what does free will really amount to?

Hard Determinism

The initial reason (though, as we will see, not in the end the most important one) for doubting that freedom genuinely exists is the thesis of **causal determinism:** the thesis that everything that happens, including every human action, is rigidly determined by antecedent causes operating in accordance with laws of nature. If this is so, then any human action could in principle have been predicted thousands or millions of years before it occurred, given enough knowledge of the conditions at that earlier time and of the relevant laws of nature. This seems to show that the person who performed the action could not in fact have performed some other action instead: *could not have done otherwise*. And this in turn seems to many to show that the action was not free in the sense that moral responsibility requires. How, it is asked, can a person be morally blamed for doing something that was inevitable long before his birth? The view that accepts the thesis of causal determinism and argues in this way for the nonexistence of genuine freedom and genuine moral responsibility is one version of **hard determinism.**

But is the thesis of causal determinism actually true? Arguments for determinism that appeal to scientific success in explanation and prediction are less than conclusive, since there are still many, many things that cannot so far be explained and predicted in full detail. Moreover, recent scientific developments in the field of quantum theory seem to offer very strong reasons for thinking that causal determinism is in fact false. On the standard interpretation of quantum theory, there are certain very small-scale physical events that are inherently random or chance in character, events for which there are no deterministic causes. An example here is radioactive decay: on the standard theory it is impossible in principle to predict when a particular radioactive atom will decay into another (by emitting either an alpha or beta particle, depending on which specific kind of radioactive atom it is) because this is a genuinely random occurrence that involves no underlying deterministic mechanism. (All that can be predicted is that out of a given collection of atoms of that kind, half will decay within a certain specifiable interval—the so-called "half life" for that isotope.)

Contrary to what might initially be supposed, however, the rejection of causal determinism really does very little to make the existence of free choices more likely. It raises at least the possibility that some human actions (or perhaps their immediate causes) might be *random* events, events that happen for no cause or reason at all, but unfortunately a random or randomly produced event is no more plausibly viewed as an instance of free action than one that is causally determined—indeed, perhaps even less so. If an action takes place at random, then something else could equally have happened at random, but it is still not the case that the person could have *done* otherwise in the sense that what he did was within his voluntary *control*. If, for example, your body suddenly starts doing things at random—perhaps running pointlessly around a tree or attacking other people or doing other silly or outrageous things—you seem to be no more responsible and as much a helpless victim as anyone else, indeed really more so. Thus a hard determinist whose main claim is that genuine freedom does not exist can in fact accept the existence of random events and the denial of causal determinism, while still insisting that this result does nothing at all to establish the existence of freedom. It is fairly standard, albeit a bit misleading, to continue to refer to such a modified position with the label "hard determinism," even though it no longer accepts the general thesis of causal determinism, and we will follow that usage here. (In the final selection in the free will part of the chapter, Galen Strawson refers to this same view, more perspicuously but less standardly, as the "no-freedom theory" or as "pessimism about free will.")

Thus the most important argument for the denial of freedom does not in fact depend at all on whether causal determinism is true or not. Once it is realized that randomness is also incompatible with freedom, the defender of freedom is faced with a serious dilemma. It is at least plausible to assume that any event, including any human action, must be either causally determined or else random, that these are the only alternatives. But according to the argument so far, *neither* of these alternatives is compatible with freedom, thus seemingly leading to the conclusion that freedom is not only nonexistent, but in fact entirely impossible. (Having an action be partly determined and then random within the bounds imposed by determinism also doesn't seem to help, since neither the determined aspect nor the random aspect would be free.)

This, however, is a very difficult conclusion to swallow. Is it really believable from an intuitive standpoint that the very idea of freedom is somehow contradictory or unintelligible? Surely our overriding common-sense conviction that we at least sometimes act freely, especially as it arises in situations of difficult choice, could not be as totally mistaken as that. Or could it?

Hard determinists also often appeal more specifically to *heredity* and *environment* as the deterministic causes of human actions. A view of this sort is developed in the initial selection by Robert Blatchford. (Two of the selections later on, those by Paul Edwards and Galen Strawson, also defend versions of hard determinism, in response to the other positions to be considered.)

Compatibilism (or "Soft Determinism")

Despite the initial cogency of the argument for hard determinism, very few philosophers have been convinced by it. One possible response is to concede that events that are not determined must occur at random and so cannot be free actions, but to question whether *any* sort of causal determinism is incompatible with freedom in the way that the hard determinist argument claims. This sort of response leads to the second main position on the free will problem: **compatibilism** (also called **"soft determinism"**—a fairly standard but somewhat misleading label, since it is not the determinism as such but rather the conclusion about freedom drawn from it that is "soft").

Appealing to our common-sense judgments about which actions are in fact free, the compatibilist rejects the claim that freedom and causal determinism are incompatible (while agreeing with the hard determinist that freedom is incompatible with randomness and so, he argues, with indeterminism). His view is that rather than being incompatible with any sort of causal determination, freedom in fact is just a special sort of causal determination: in first approximation, determination by the agent's own will or desires or psychological states, rather than by something external to the agent. A person whose action is determined in this way *could have done otherwise* in the specific sense that *if* his desires had been different or if he had reasoned in a different way, he would have done something else. And this can be true even if both his action and the desires and other psychological states and processes of reasoning that led to it were in fact entirely causally determined. Thus freedom is compatible with determinism, and the free will problem seems to disappear.

A slightly more refined version of compatibilism may add that freedom also requires the absence of external *constraints* (such as threats) and may even extend this to the absence of psychological *compulsions* of various sorts (such as the compulsion to incessantly wash one's hands). But even with this modification, there can be little doubt that on the compatibilist view freedom genuinely exists in a wide range of cases. (Compatibilists standardly accept the possibility of random events on the scientific grounds already discussed, but insist that this possibility is irrelevant to the issue of freedom since random actions clearly aren't free.) David Hume and W. T. Stace present versions of this fairly standard form of compatibilism.

But is compatibilism of the Hume-Stace variety really a satisfactory resolution of the problem? Paul Edwards raises doubts about the compatibilist account of "could have done otherwise" and about whether the sort of freedom advocated by compatibilists is really enough for moral responsibility. Harry Frankfurt then presents a recent refinement of the compatibilist view: *hierarchical compatibilism,* as it has come to be called, a view that can be viewed as a response to some of the problems suggested by Edwards. According to hierarchical compatibilism, freedom of the will requires not just that a person be able to act according to his desires, but also that the desires from which he acts are determined by his "second-order desires"—his desires about his own desires. This more complicated requirement for freedom is still compatible with determinism, since the second-order desires may themselves still be determined. Frankfurt also denies that being able to do otherwise is a requirement for either freedom or moral responsibility.

Libertarianism

Doubts of the sorts raised by Edwards may lead back to hard determinism (this is Edwards's conclusion), or they may lead instead to the third main position, namely **libertarianism:** the view that freedom is incompatible with causal determinism but nonetheless still genuinely exists. Since most libertarians also agree, for the reasons already discussed, that merely random actions are not free, a libertarian is apparently forced to find some third alternative to causal determination and randomness by arguing that an event that is not causally determined need not be (though it may be) random. The view will then be that freedom is a species of *indeterminism,* but one that is different from randomness. And the central problem for the libertarian is thus to explain how there can be occurrences that are not causally determined but also not random—how there can be a third alternative to causal determinism and randomness.

One possibility here is what has become known as "agent causation": the view that a free action is one that is caused, not by earlier *events,* but rather by the *agent* or the *self,* in a way that is not caused by his antecedent character or makeup (or by anything else)—and thus is not causally determined. C. A. Campbell offers one version of such a view, according to which free choices always occur in situations where the self must decide whether or not to exert the effort required to overcome its own strongest desire and do the morally right thing. The main problem for any view of this sort is to explain why such an instance of "agent causation," since it is claimed to not to be a result of the agent's previously formed character or anything else previously true of him, isn't after all a random occurrence—in which case the problem hasn't really been solved.

Robert Nozick offers a somewhat similar view, though he does not appeal explicitly to the idea of agent causation. According to Nozick's view, a free action involves the agent *assigning* weights to the relevant reasons for and against that action, weights that are not determined by his or her previously formed character. And again, the main difficulty is to understand why this assigning of weights, since it is uncaused, is not merely random.

Robert Kane offers a third version of libertarianism, one that does not appeal to the metaphysically difficult idea that an agent or self can be a cause (or can assign weights to reasons in an uncaused way). Kane's aim is a version of libertarianism that is compatible with modern scientific views of human beings. On his view, the fundamental situation of free choice is one in which a person is faced with competing motives for two different actions, neither of them strong enough to determine the outcome. In such a fundamentally indeterministic situation, he argues, the person can *choose* which motivation wins out, thereby shaping the kind of person he or she will be in a way that is undetermined but, he claims, still rational and voluntary. It is in such "self-forming actions," Kane argues, that free will primarily resides. But here again the main problem will be to understand why such a choice, being undetermined by anything about the previous self, isn't in fact random.

Back to Hard Determinism?

The final selection in the free will part of the chapter, by Galen Strawson, returns to the issue of moral responsibility. Strawson criticizes both compatibilist and libertarian views. He questions whether either of these views really allow for people to be morally responsible in the deep or ultimate way that libertarians especially are seeking and whether such ultimate responsibility is really possible. The "pessimism" about free will that he tentatively defends is thus a version of hard determinism.

Personal Identity

John Locke

The English philosopher John Locke (1632–1704) was one of the most influential philosophers of all time, making major contributions to epistemology, metaphysics, and political philosophy. (For more about Locke's rather colorful life, see the introduction to the selection from his *Second Treatise of Government,* in Chapter 6.)

In this selection from his *Essay Concerning Human Understanding,* Locke offers a very influential account of the nature of personal identity. Since Locke was, like Descartes, a substance dualist (holding that a human being consists of a material body together with an immaterial mind or soul), it would have been natural for him to hold that personal identity is just identity of body or identity of mind or perhaps identity of both. He rejects all of these possibilities, however, and claims instead that what makes a later person B identical with an earlier person A is the continuity of *consciousness* whereby B is conscious of (that is, presumably, has an apparent memory of) the various conscious states of A—or at least some of them. This requirement could, Locke thinks, be satisfied even if neither the material body nor the immaterial mind of B were identical to those of A.

Personal Identity

. . . 8. An animal is a living organized body; and consequently the same animal, as we have observed, is the same continued life communicated to different particles of matter as they happen successively to be united to that organized living body. (1) And whatever is talked of other definitions, ingenuous observation puts it past doubt that the *idea* in our minds of which the sound *man* in our mouths is the sign, is nothing else but of an animal of such a certain form: since I think I may be confident that whoever should see a creature of his own shape and make, though it had no more reason all its life than a *cat* or a *parrot,* would call him still a *man;* or whoever should hear a *cat* or a *parrot* discourse, reason, and philosophize would call or think it nothing but a *cat* or a *parrot* and say the one was a dull irrational *man,* and the other a very intelligent rational *parrot.* . . .

it is not the *idea* of a thinking or rational being alone that makes the *idea* of a *man* in most people's sense, but of a body so and so shaped, joined to it; and if that be the *idea* of a *man,* the same successive body not shifted all at once must, as well as the same immaterial spirit, go to the making of the same *man.* (2)

9. This being premised, to find wherein *personal identity* consists, we must consider what *person* stands for; which, I think, is a thinking intelligent being that has reason and reflection and can consider itself as itself, the same thinking thing in different times and places; which it does only by that consciousness which is inseparable from thinking and, as it seems to me, essential to it. . . . For since consciousness always accompanies thinking, and it is that that makes everyone to be what he calls *self,* and thereby distinguishes himself from all other thinking things: in this alone consists *personal identity,* i.e. the sameness of a rational being. And as far as this consciousness can be extended backwards to any past action or thought, so far reaches the identity of that *person:* it is the same *self* now it was then, and it is by the same *self* with this present one that now reflects on it, that that action was done. (3)

10. But it is further inquired whether it be the same identical substance? This, few would think they had reason to doubt of, if these perceptions, with their consciousness, always remained present in the mind whereby the same thinking thing would be always consciously present and, as would be thought, evidently the same to itself. But that which seems to make the difficulty is this: that this consciousness being interrupted always by forgetfulness, there being no moment of our lives wherein we have the whole train of all our past actions before our eyes in one view, but even the best memories losing the sight of one part whilst they are viewing another; and we sometimes, and that the greatest part of our lives, not reflecting on our past selves, being intent on our present thoughts, and in sound sleep having no thoughts at all, or at least none with that consciousness which remarks our waking thoughts; I say, in all these cases, our consciousness being interrupted, and we losing the sight of our past *selves,* doubts are raised whether we are the same thinking thing, i.e. the same substance, or no. (4) Which, however reasonable or unreasonable, concerns not *personal identity* at all: the question being what makes the same *person,* and not whether it be the same identical substance, which always thinks in the same person; which, in

From *An Essay Concerning Human Understanding,* 1694.

Restatement/

(1) *Summary*

R Locke's view is that for an animal (that is, an animal body) at one time to be identical to an animal at an earlier time is not for all of their material parts to be identical (which is never true for very long), but only for the matter at each stage to be so organized as to be part of the same "continued life."

(2)

R What makes something a *man* (that is, a human) is its having a living animal body of a certain distinctive sort, not anything specific about its mental or intellectual capabilities (though it must also have a mind or soul of some sort). Thus for a particular human at one time to be identical to one at an earlier time is, Locke claims, for both the body and the soul to be identical. (Souls, unlike bodies, do not in his view have parts that could be replaced, so identity of soul means that the soul at one stage is the very same particular entity as the soul at a later stage.)

(3) *Definition*

A *person,* as opposed to a human, is a conscious rational being that is aware of its own continued existence. And it is this awareness of being at one time the same conscious being that existed at an earlier time that, according to Locke, makes the later person identical with the earlier one. Thus the identity of a person reaches only as far into the past as its consciousness of its earlier self, including only those previous conscious states and actions that the later person is conscious of—that is, remembers or at least seems to remember.

(4)

R Is the mental substance (the mind or soul) at one stage of a person's life identical to that at a later stage of the same person's life? Locke suggests that partial failures of memory, times when one is attending only to what is going on in the present, and the complete absence of consciousness in sleep raise doubts about this.

R But whether or not the mental substance is identical makes no difference, on Locke's view, to personal identity. As long as the later person has the "same consciousness" of the thoughts and actions of the earlier person, the two are identical, even if this later consciousness exists in a different mental substance or soul than the one at the earlier stage.

(What does it mean for the consciousness to be "the same"? See Discussion Questions 1 and 2.)

R Pursuing the issue further, Locke asks whether there can be (a) different thinking substances in the same person or (b) the same thinking substance in different people.

7

R His first response is that the answer to (a) is obviously "yes" for nondualists for whom the thinking entity is just the animal body (which can remain the same entity even if its material constituents change).

R For a dualist, the answer to (a) will depend on whether it is possible for the consciousness of past actions (and states of mind) to be transferred from the mind or soul that actually did or experienced them to one that did not. Locke argues that there is no clear reason for thinking that this is not possible.

R With regard to part (b) of the question, the issue is whether a mind or soul could have the consciousness of its actions and states of mind entirely removed and then begin a new and different conscious life.

(Locke would probably say, as with part (a), that there is no clear reason to the contrary.)

this case, matters not at all: different substances, by the same consciousness (where they do partake in it) being united into one person, as well as different bodies by the same life are united into one animal, whose *identity* is preserved in that change of substances by the unity of one continued life. For, it being the same consciousness that makes a man be himself to himself, *personal identity* depends on that only, whether it be annexed only to one individual substance, or can be continued in a succession of several substances. For as far as any intelligent being can repeat the *idea* of any past action with the same consciousness it had of it at first, and with the same consciousness it has of any present action, so far it is the same *personal self.* For it is by the consciousness it has of its present thoughts and actions that it is *self* to *itself* now, and so will be the same *self* as far as the same consciousness can extend to actions past or to come . . . : the same consciousness uniting those distant actions into the same *person,* whatever substances contributed to their production. 5

. . .

12. But the question is whether, if the same substance, which thinks, be changed, it can be the same person, or, remaining the same, it can be different persons. 6

And to this I answer, first, this can be no question at all to those who place thought in a purely material animal constitution, void of an immaterial substance. For, whether their supposition be true or no, it is plain they conceive personal identity preserved in something else than identity of substance, as animal identity is preserved in identity of life and not of substance. . . . 7

13. But next, as to the first part of the question, whether, if the same thinking substance (supposing immaterial substances only to think) be changed, it can be the same person, I answer: That cannot be resolved but by those who know what kind of substances they are that do think, and whether the consciousness of past actions can be transferred from one thinking substance to another. I grant, were the same consciousness the same individual action, it could not. . . . But that which we call the *same consciousness* not being the same individual act, why one intellectual substance may not have represented to it, as done by itself, what it never did, and was perhaps done by some other agent . . . will be difficult to conclude from the nature of things. . . . But yet . . . it must be allowed that, if the same consciousness . . . can be transferred from one thinking substance to another, it will be possible that two thinking substances may make but one person. For the same consciousness being preserved, whether in the same or different substances, the personal identity is preserved. 8

14. As to the second part of the question, whether, the same immaterial substance remaining, there may be two distinct persons, which question seems to me to be built on this: whether the same immaterial being, being conscious of the actions of its past duration, may be wholly stripped of all the consciousness of its past existence and lose it beyond the power of ever retrieving again and so, as it were beginning a new account from a new period, have a consciousness that cannot reach beyond this new state. . . . 9 Let anyone reflect upon himself and conclude that he has in himself an immaterial spirit, which is that which thinks in him and in the constant change of his body keeps him the same and is that which he calls himself; let him also suppose it to be the same soul that was in *Nestor* or *Thersites* at the siege of *Troy* (for souls being, as far as we know anything of them, in their nature indifferent to any parcel of matter, the supposition has no apparent absurdity in it), which it may have been, as well as it is now the soul of any other man; but he now having no consciousness of any of the actions either of *Nestor* or *Thersites,* does or can he conceive himself the same person with either of them? Can he be concerned in either of their actions, attribute them to himself, or think them his own, more than the actions of any other men that ever existed? So that, this consciousness not reaching to any of the actions of either of those men, he is no more one *self* with either of them than if the soul or immaterial spirit that now informs him had been created and began to exist, when it began to inform his present body. . . . But let him once find himself conscious of any of the actions of *Nestor,* he then finds himself the same person with *Nestor.* 10

15. And thus we may be able, without any difficulty, to conceive the same person at the resurrection, though in a body not exactly in

make or parts the same which he had here, the same consciousness going along with the soul that inhabits it. But yet the soul alone, in the change of bodies, would scarce, to anyone but to him that makes the soul the *man,* be enough to make the same *man.* For should the soul of a prince, carrying with it the consciousness of the prince's past life, enter and inform the body of a cobbler as soon as deserted by his own soul, everyone sees he would be the same person with the prince, accountable only for the prince's actions; but who would say it was the same man? The body too goes to the making the man and would, I guess, to everybody, determine the man in this case, wherein the soul, with all its princely thoughts about it, would not make another man: but he would be the same cobbler to everyone besides himself. . . . (11)

16. But though the same immaterial substance or soul does not alone, wherever it be, and in whatsoever state, make the same man: yet, it is plain, consciousness, as far as ever it can be extended, should it be to ages past, unites existences and actions very remote in time into the same person, as well as it does the existence and actions of the immediately preceding moment, so that whatever has the consciousness of present and past actions is the same person to whom they both belong. Had I the same consciousness that I saw the ark and *Noah's* flood as that I saw an overflowing of the *Thames* last winter, or as that I write now, I could no more doubt that I that write this now, that saw the *Thames* overflowed last winter, and that viewed the flood at the general deluge, was the same *self,* place that *self* in what substance you please, than I that write this am the same *myself* now whilst I write (whether I consist of all the same substance, material or immaterial, or no) that I was yesterday. For as to this point of being the same *self,* it matters not whether this present *self* be made up of the same or other substances, I being as much concerned and as justly accountable for any action that was done a thousand years since, appropriated to me now by this self-consciousness, as I am for what I did the last moment.

17. *Self* is that conscious thinking thing (whatever substance made up of, whether spiritual or material, simple or compounded, it matters not) which is sensible or conscious of pleasure and pain, capable of happiness or misery, and so is concerned for *itself,* as far as that consciousness extends. Thus everyone finds that, whilst comprehended under that consciousness, the little finger is as much a part of *itself* as what is most so. Upon separation of this little finger, should this consciousness go along with the little finger and leave the rest of the body, it is evident the little finger would be the *person,* the *same person;* and self then would have nothing to do with the rest of the body. As in this case it is the consciousness that goes along with the substance, when one part is separate from another, which makes the same *person* and constitutes this inseparable *self:* so it is in reference to substance remote in time. That with which the *consciousness* of this present thinking thing can join itself makes the same *person* and is one *self* with it, and with nothing else, and so attributes to *itself* and owns all the actions of that thing as its own, as far as that consciousness reaches, and no further; as everyone who reflects will perceive. (12)

18. In this *personal identity* is founded all the right and justice of reward and punishment: happiness and misery being that for which everyone is concerned for *himself,* not mattering what becomes of any substance not joined to or affected with that consciousness. For, as it is evident in the instance I gave but now, if the consciousness went along with the little finger when it was cut off, that would be the same *self* which was concerned for the whole body yesterday, as making part of *itself,* whose actions then it cannot but admit as its own now. Though, if the same body should still live and immediately from the separation of the little finger have its own peculiar consciousness, whereof the little finger knew nothing, it would not at all be concerned for it as a part of *itself,* or could own any of its actions, or have any of them imputed to him. (13)

19. This may show us wherein *personal identity* consists: not in the identity of substance but, as I have said, in the identity of *consciousness,* wherein, if *Socrates* and the present mayor of *Queenborough* agree, they are the same person; if the same *Socrates* waking and sleeping do not partake of the same *consciousness, Socrates* waking and sleeping is not the same person. And to punish *Socrates* waking for what sleeping *Socrates* thought, and waking *Socrates* was never conscious of, would be no more of right than to punish one twin for what his brother-twin did,

R If such a total removal of consciousness followed by a new and different consciousness is possible, then there is, Locke argues, no reason to say that the person in whom that soul resided before the removal and the one in whom it resides after the new consciousness has emerged are the same person.

R This makes it possible for a person to be resurrected with a different body, as long as the soul involved has a consciousness of the original person's actions and states of mind. But while having the same consciousness is enough to make an individual human the same *person,* it is not enough to make it the same *man* (since being the same man requires having the same animal body). Thus the cobbler with the prince's soul and consciousness is the same *person* as the prince, but the same *man* as the cobbler—the requirements for identity depend on what sort of thing is in question.

R Locke reiterates his view: a *person* at one time is the same person as any earlier person, no matter how remote, of whose actions (and states of mind) it is conscious (that is, remembers or seems to remember) along with its own. It does not matter whether the substance or substances involved are the same. If consciousness of the right sort can reside in a little finger, then that little finger is a person.

R The justifiability of reward and punishment depends on personal identity, thus understood, not on sameness of substance. Thus if the consciousness of having committed some crime remains with the little finger and not the rest of the body, it is only the little finger that can justifiably be punished.

whereof he knew nothing, because their outsides were so like that they could not be distinguished; for such twins have been seen. (14)

20. But yet possibly it will still be objected, suppose I wholly lose the memory of some parts of my life beyond a possibility of retrieving them, so that perhaps I shall never be conscious of them again: yet am I not the same person that did those actions, had those thoughts that I once was conscious of, though I have now forgot them? To which I answer that we must here take notice what the word *I* is applied to, which, in this case, is the man only. And the same man being presumed to be the same person, *I* is easily here supposed to stand also for the same person. But if it be possible for the same man to have distinct incommunicable consciousness at different times, it is past doubt the same man would at different times make different persons; which, we see, is the sense of mankind in the solemnest declaration of their opinions, human laws not punishing the *mad man* for the *sober man's* actions, nor the *sober man* for what the *mad man* did, thereby making them two persons: which is somewhat explained by our way of speaking in *English* when we say such an one *is not himself,* or is *beside himself;* in which phrases it is insinuated, as if those who now, or at least first used them, thought that *self* was changed, the *self*-same person was no longer in that man. (15)

...

22. But is not a man drunk and sober the same person, why else is he punished for the act he commits when drunk, though he be never afterwards conscious of it? Just as much the same person as a man that walks and does other things in his sleep is the same person and is answerable for any mischief he shall do in it. Human laws punish both, with a justice suitable to their way of knowledge; because, in these cases, they cannot distinguish certainly what is real, what counterfeit; and so the ignorance in drunkenness or sleep is not admitted as a plea. For, though punishment be annexed to personality, and personality to consciousness, and the drunkard perhaps be not conscious of what he did, yet human judicatures justly punish him, because the fact is proved against him, but want of consciousness cannot be proved for him. But in the Great Day, wherein the secrets of all hearts shall be laid open, it may be reasonable to think no one shall be made to answer for what he knows nothing of, but shall receive his doom, his conscience accusing or excusing him. (16)

...

24. Indeed [the self] may conceive the substance whereof it is now made up to have existed formerly, united in the same conscious being; but consciousness removed, that substance is no more *itself* or makes no more a part of it than any other substance, as is evident in the instance we have already given of a limb cut off, of whose heat or cold or other affections having no longer any consciousness, it is no more of a man's self than any other matter of the universe. In like manner it will be in reference to any immaterial substance which is void of that consciousness whereby I am my *self* to *myself.* If there be any part of its existence which I cannot upon recollection join with that present consciousness whereby I am now my *self,* it is in that part of its existence no more my *self* than any other immaterial being. For whatsoever any substance has thought or done, which I cannot recollect and by my consciousness make my own thought and action, it will no more belong to me, whether a part of me thought or did it, than if it had been thought or done by any other immaterial being anywhere existing.

25. I agree the more probable opinion is that this consciousness is annexed to and the affection of one individual immaterial substance.

But let men, according to their divers hypotheses, resolve of that as they please. This every intelligent being, sensible of happiness or misery, must grant: that there is something that is *himself* that he is concerned for and would have happy; that this *self* has existed in a continued duration more than one instant, and therefore it is possible may exist, as it has done, months and years to come, without any certain bounds to be set to its duration; and may be the same *self* by the same consciousness, continued on for the future. And thus, by this consciousness, he finds himself to be the *same self* which did such or such an action some years since, by which he comes to be happy or miserable now. In all which account of *self,* the same numerical substance is not considered as making the same

(14) R If Socrates waking and Socrates sleeping have two different consciousnesses, neither including the actions and events included in the other, then there are in effect two persons in the same body.

(This resembles cases of multiple personality, with which Locke was presumably not familiar. See Discussion Question 4.)

(15) R Someone who totally and irretrievably forgets some of his earlier actions is, in Locke's view, no longer the same *person* who did them—though he may still be the same *man* (human).

(16) R Human laws punish people for things that they can no longer remember, but this is unjust and is done only because it is too hard to determine whether a person can actually remember or not. (By "the Great Day," Locke means Judgment Day, as conceived in Christianity.)

self, but the same continued consciousness, in which several substances may have been united and again separated from it, which, whilst they continued in a vital union with that wherein this consciousness then resided, made a part of that same *self.* Thus any part of our bodies, vitally united to that which is conscious in us, makes a part of our *selves;* but upon separation from the vital union, by which that consciousness is communicated, that which a moment since was part of our *selves* is now no more so than a part of another man's *self* is a part of me; and it is not impossible but in a little time may become a real part of another person. And so we have the same numerical substance become a part of two different persons, and the same person preserved under the change of various substances. . . .

26. *Person,* as I take it, is the name for this *self.* Wherever a man finds what he calls *himself,* there, I think, another may say is the *same person.* It is a forensic term, appropriating actions and their merit, and so belongs only to intelligent agents, capable of a law, and happiness and misery.  This personality extends *itself* beyond present existence to what is past, only by consciousness; whereby it becomes concerned and accountable, owns and imputes to *itself* past actions, just upon the same ground and for the same reason that it does the present. All which is founded in a concern for happiness, the unavoidable concomitant of consciousness: that which is conscious of pleasure and pain desiring that that self that is conscious should be happy. And therefore whatever past actions it cannot reconcile or appropriate to that present *self* by consciousness, it can be no more concerned in than if they had never been done; and to receive pleasure or pain, i.e. reward or punishment, on the account of any such action, is all one as to be made happy or miserable in its first being, without any demerit at all. For supposing a man punished now for what he had done in another life, whereof he could be made to have no consciousness at all, what difference is there between that punishment and being created miserable? . . .

17 By saying that "person" is a *forensic* term, Locke is saying that it has to do with law, justice, and rights, not primarily with the metaphysical nature of the entities in question.

Discussion Questions

1. Locke speaks of a later individual having the "same consciousness" as an earlier one and so being the same person, but he does not explain very clearly what is required for the consciousness in question to be the *same* in the relevant sense—though he does make it clear that the mind or soul in which the consciousness resides (assuming, as he mainly does, a dualist view) need not be the one that actually performed a certain action or experienced a certain state of mind in order for it to have the "same consciousness" of those things. Suppose that, over a period of time, person A has various experiences and performs various actions. Discuss whether in the following cases person B has the "same consciousness" in the sense required for person A and person B to be (according to Locke) the same person:

a. At a later period of time, person B, entirely by coincidence (perhaps as a result of a brain tumor) comes to have apparent memories of having done or experienced some or all of the things that A did (and is conscious of these along with its own actions and experiences).

b. At a later period of time, person B is hypnotized by a third person who is intimately familiar with A's life and experiences, and who brings it about by post-hypnotic suggestion that B has apparent memories of some or all of A's actions and experiences (and is conscious of these along with its own actions and experiences).

c. As a result of brain trauma, person A entirely forgets its actions and experiences. At a later time, person B (whose body is the same living human body that was involved in person A and whose immaterial mind or soul is also the same as that of person A, but whose memory at first goes back only to the time of the trauma) has a second episode of brain trauma that produces, entirely by coincidence, apparent memories of having done and experienced some or all of the same things that A did or experienced (and is conscious of these along with its own actions and experiences).

d. Person A comes to have no conscious memory of its earlier history, though memory traces of its actions and experiences remain stored in its brain or immaterial mind. After a lengthy period, these memory traces are reactivated and the person at that time (person B), who has the same human body and the same immaterial mind, comes to have conscious apparent memories of some or all of A's actions and experiences (and is conscious of these along with its own actions and experiences).

e. Person A dies and its consciousness of its actions and experiences thereby ceases. But via a brain scan, a record of those actions and experiences is kept in storage in a computer. At a later time, that record is used to create new apparent memories of some or all of A's actions and experiences in person B, and person B is conscious of these along with its own actions and experiences. (Person B does not have the same human body as person A. Does it matter whether or not person B's immaterial mind or soul—if there is one—is the same?)

f. At the end of the initial period, person A enters a Star Trek–style "transporter." The transporter scans both his body and his mind, making a complete and accurate record of both, and then destroys that body (and also A's immaterial mind, if there is one). The information about A is sent to a second transporter, which then creates a new body (and immaterial soul, if A had one), each qualitatively similar in every respect to A's, and programs it (or them) with A's memories, character traits, and so on. The result of this process, person B, then exits the second transporter. It has conscious apparent memories of some or all of A's actions and experiences (and is conscious of these along with its own actions and experiences).

2. On the basis of your responses to the foregoing cases, try to formulate an explicit account of what is required for the consciousness of two persons to be *the same* in the sense required by Locke for them to be the same person.

3. On Locke's view, for a person at a later time to be identical to one at an earlier time requires that the later person be conscious of, that is, remember (or at least seem to remember), the experiences and actions of the earlier person. As he understands it, this seems to mean that a person who has committed some serious crime can at a later time escape all responsibility for it simply by having his or her memory of the experiences and actions involved in the crime erased—something that might well come to be technologically feasible. Is this a reasonable result? Would it be reasonable (or even more reasonable) if all earlier memories of specific experiences and actions were thus erased?

4. Suppose that one body is seemingly inhabited by two or more very different personalities, having different character traits, behavior patterns, knowledge, or even different degrees of intelligence. (There are many alleged cases of this sort, which you may want to look up.) Supposing that none of these personalities is conscious of the others' actions (except indirectly, by being informed by others), is this a case of one body inhabited by multiple *persons*? Suppose that one of the personalities commits a serious crime, of which the other personalities are ignorant (and about which they express shock and horror when informed). Can the body in question be justly imprisoned for the crime?

Thomas Reid

Thomas Reid (1710–1796), a Scottish philosopher, was one of the founders of what became known as the "common sense" school of philosophy. He is best known for his contributions to epistemology, which are mainly focused on defending the common-sense view of our knowledge of the material world against what he sees as the skeptical tendencies to be found in his British predecessors, Locke, Berkeley, and Hume, as well as Descartes and others.

In this selection, Reid discusses and criticizes Locke's account of personal identity. Reid's own view, which does not emerge clearly here, is that personal identity is unanalyzable or indefinable, so that no account of the sort that Locke attempts to give is possible.

Of Mr. Locke's Account of Personal Identity

In a long chapter upon identity and diversity, Mr. Locke has made many ingenious and just observations, and some which, I think, cannot be defended. I shall only take notice of the account he gives of our own personal identity. . . .

From *Essays on the Intellectual Powers of Man* (Cambridge, Mass.: MIT Press, 1969).

Identity . . . supposes the continued existence of the being of which it is affirmed, and therefore can be applied only to things which have a continued existence. While any being continues to exist, it is the same being; but two beings which have a different beginning or a different ending of their existence, cannot possibly be the same. To this I think Mr. Locke agrees.

He observes very justly, that to know what is meant by the same person, we must consider what the word *person* stands for; and he defines a person to be an intelligent being, endowed with reason and with consciousness, which last he thinks inseparable from thought.

From this definition of a person, it must necessarily follow, that while the intelligent being continues to exist and to be intelligent, it must be the same person. To say that the intelligent being is the person, and yet that the person ceases to exist, while the intelligent being continues, or that the person continues while the intelligent being ceases to exist, is, to my apprehension, a manifest contradiction.

One would think that the definition of a person should perfectly ascertain the nature of personal identity, or wherein it consists, though it might still be a question how we come to know and be assured of our personal identity. (1)

Mr. Locke tells us, however, "that personal identity, that is, the sameness of a rational being, consists in consciousness alone; and, as far as this consciousness can be extended backward to any past action or thought, so far reaches the identity or that person. So that whatever has the consciousness of present and past actions, is the same person to whom they belong."

This doctrine has some strange consequences, which the author was aware of. Such as, that if the same consciousness can be transferred from one intelligent being to another, which he thinks we cannot show to be impossible, then two or twenty intelligent beings may be the same person. And if the intelligent being may lose the consciousness of the actions done by him, which surely is possible, then he is not the person that did those actions; so that one intelligent being may be two or twenty different persons, if he shall so often lose the consciousness of his former actions. (2)

There is another consequence of this doctrine, which follows no less necessarily, though Mr. Locke probably did not see it. It is, that a man may be, and at the same time not be, the person that did a particular action.

Suppose a brave officer to have been flogged when a boy at school, for robbing an orchard, to have taken a standard from the enemy in his first campaign, and to have been made a general in advanced life. Suppose also, which must be admitted to be possible, that when he took the standard, he was conscious of his having been flogged at school; and that when made a general, he was conscious of his taking the standard, but had absolutely lost the consciousness of his flogging.

These things being supposed, it follows, from Mr. Locke's doctrine, that he who was flogged at school is the same person who took the standard; and that he who took the standard is the same person who was made a general. Whence it follows, if there be any truth in logic, that the general is the same person with him who was flogged at school. But the general's consciousness does not reach so far back as his flogging, therefore, according to Mr. Locke's doctrine, he is not the person who was flogged. Therefore the general is, and at the same time is not, the same person with him who was flogged at school. (3)

Leaving the consequences of this doctrine to those who have leisure to trace them, we may observe, with regard to the doctrine itself;

1st, That Mr. Locke attributes to consciousness the conviction we have of our past actions, as if a man may now be conscious of what he did twenty years ago. It is impossible to understand the meaning of this, unless by consciousness he meant memory, the only faculty by which we have an immediate knowledge of our past actions.

Sometimes, in popular discourse, a man says he is conscious that he did such a thing, meaning that he distinctly remembers that he did it. It is unnecessary, in common discourse, to fix accurately the limits between consciousness and memory. . . .

But this ought to be avoided in philosophy, otherwise we confound the different powers of the mind, and ascribe to one what really belongs to another. If a man can be conscious of what he did twenty years, or twenty minutes ago, there is no use for memory, nor ought we to allow that there is any such faculty. The faculties of consciousness and memory are chiefly distinguished by this, that the first is an immediate knowledge of the present, the second an immediate knowledge of the past.

When, therefore, Mr. Locke's notion of personal identity is properly expressed, it is, that personal identity consists in distinct remembrance: for, even in the popular sense, to say that I am conscious of a past action, means nothing else than that I distinctly remember that I did it. (4)

2dly, It may be observed, that in this doctrine, not only is consciousness confounded with memory, but which is still more strange, personal identity is confounded with the evidence which we have of our personal identity.

1 *Editor Comment*

That is, a "definition" of what sort of thing a person is should settle the *metaphysical* issue of *what it is* for a person at one time to be identical to one at another time, even if not the *epistemological* issue of how we can *tell* when this relation of identity actually holds. (See the chapter introduction.)

2 *Stop and Think*

STOP Reid points out some of the consequences of Locke's view that Locke himself endorses. How strange (and thus implausible) are these?

Reid's strongest objection to Locke is this counter-example, one which most have found quite decisive. The underlying principle of logic is that identity (of any sort) is *transitive:* if A is identical to B, and B is identical to C, then A is identical to C. So the general must be identical to the schoolboy who was flogged, even though Locke's account says otherwise. (Is there a way to amend Locke's view so as to avoid this problem? See Discussion Question 1.)

Remember correctly or incorrectly—that is, *seem* to remember. To appeal to genuine memory would presuppose identity rather than explain it, since I can't genuinely remember doing or experiencing something unless I am in fact the same person who did or experienced it.

5

Reid's view is that seeming to remember that I did something (or had a certain experience) is *evidence* that I am identical to the earlier person (supposing that there is one) who did (or experienced) the thing in question. But if it is evidence for identity, then, he seems to be suggesting, it can't also be what identity consists in (since then it would be evidence for itself, which makes no sense).

6

How good is this analogy? It seems to show quite convincingly that evidence for something is sometimes or even usually quite distinct from that for which it is evidence. But is this true in every case? Or might there be a case where for something to be true simply amounts to the obtaining of the best evidence for it?

7

This is a looser and less obviously compelling objection, though one that is made more serious by Locke's failure to explain what having the "same consciousness" amounts to. Is there any clear way in which the fact that consciousness itself is "transient and momentary" prevent persons at different times from having the *same* consciousness in the sense that Locke intends?

It is very true, that my remembrance that I did such a thing is the evidence I have that I am the identical person who did it. And this, I am apt to think, Mr. Locke meant: but to say that my remembrance that I did such a thing, or my consciousness, makes me the person who did it, is, in my apprehension, an absurdity too gross to be entertained by any man who attends to the meaning of it: for it is to attribute to memory or consciousness, a strange magical power of producing its object, though that object must have existed before the memory or consciousness which produced it.

Consciousness is the testimony of one faculty; memory is the testimony of another faculty: and to say that the testimony is the cause of the thing testified, this surely is absurd, if any thing be, and could not have been said by Mr. Locke, if he had not confounded the testimony with the thing testified. 5

When a horse that was stolen is found and claimed by the owner, the only evidence he can have, or that a judge or witnesses can have, that this is the very identical horse which was his property, is similitude.

But would it not be ridiculous from this to infer that the identity of a horse consists in similitude only? The only evidence I have that I am the identical person who did such actions, is, that I remember distinctly I did them; or, as Mr. Locke expresses it, I am conscious I did them. To infer from this, that personal identity consists in consciousness, is an argument, which, if it had any force, would prove the identity of a stolen horse to consist solely in similitude. 6

3dly, Is it not strange that the sameness or identity of a person should consist in a thing which is continually changing, and is not any two minutes the same?

Our consciousness, our memory, and every operation of the mind, are still flowing like the water of a river, or like time itself. The consciousness I have this moment can no more be the same consciousness I had last moment, than this moment can be the last moment. Identity can only be affirmed of things which have a continued existence. Consciousness, and every kind of thought, is transient and momentary, and has no continued existence; and therefore, if personal identity consisted in consciousness, it would certainly follow, that no man is the same person any two moments of his life; and as the right and justice of reward and punishment is founded on personal identity, no man could be responsible for his actions. 7

...

Discussion Questions

1. Consider again the sort of situation involved in Reid's case of the general, and suppose that the same sort of situation is repeated through the general's whole life: though there are many earlier actions and states of mind that the person at a given stage cannot remember, each such person can remember actions and states of mind back to some earlier stage, and the person at that stage can remember actions and states of mind back to some still earlier stage, and so on, so that starting from the general and appealing to intermediate stages, one can trace back to the very beginning of the general's life (or nearly so) via links of memory. This is roughly what is sometimes referred to as *psychological continuity*. Is psychological continuity a sufficient condition for personal identity, in which case the general at the end of his human life would still be the same person as the young child at the beginning of that life? Is it a necessary condition? Why or why not?
2. One of Reid's objections to Locke's view of personal identity is that Locke is confusing the *evidence* for personal identity with what such identity actually amounts to or consists in. Is this always a mistake (consider a range of cases), and do you think Locke is doing this?

Bernard Williams

Bernard Williams (1929–2003) was a British philosopher who taught mainly at Cambridge University. He made major contributions to many areas of philosophy, most importantly to ethics and to discussions of personal identity.

In this selection, Williams approaches the issue of personal identity by asking whether or not it is possible for two persons to "exchange" their material bodies by having the memories, character traits, and so on of one erased from his brain and transferred into the brain of the other, and vice versa. Thus after the exchange, the person inhabiting one of the bodies will seemingly satisfy the correct psychological requirement for personal identity (*if* there is one): it will stand in the same psychological relations to the previous actions, experiences, and character traits of the person that originally inhabited the other body that persons normally stand in to their own previous actions, experiences, and character traits; and again, vice versa. (This allows for a psychological criterion that is broader than Locke's, in that it appeals to more than memory.) But does this mean that the bodies have genuinely been "exchanged," so that each of the persons now inhabits a new body? Williams gives one account of such a case that seems to support this conclusion. He then contrasts it with a second account that agrees on the basic facts of the case, but portrays them in a quite different way—one that seems to support the conclusion that the bodies have not been "exchanged," but that instead each of the persons, still inhabiting the same bodies that they originally did, have suffered a combination of amnesia and artificially induced memories and character traits. Williams very tentatively opts for the latter account of the case, while admitting that it is very hard to be sure which one is correct.

The Self and the Future

The Self and the Future

Suppose that there were some process to which two persons, *A* and *B*, could be subjected as a result of which they might be said—question-beggingly—to have *exchanged bodies*. That is to say—less question-beggingly—there is a certain human body which is such that when previously we were confronted with it, we were confronted with person *A*, certain utterances coming from it were expressive of memories of the past experiences of *A*, certain movements of it partly constituted the actions of *A* and were taken as expressive of the character of *A*, and so forth; but now, after the process is completed, utterances coming from this body are expressive of what seem to be just those memories which previously we identified as memories of the past experiences of *B*, its movements partly constitute actions expressive of the character of *B*, and so forth; and conversely with the other body. (1)

There are certain important philosophical limitations on how such imaginary cases are to be constructed, and how they are to be taken when constructed in various ways. I shall mention two principal limitations, not in order to pursue them further here, but precisely in order to get them out of the way.

From *Problems of the Self* (Cambridge: Cambridge University Press, 1973).

There are certain limitations, particularly with regard to character and mannerisms, to our ability to imagine such cases even in the most restricted sense of our being disposed to take the later performances of that body which was previously *A*'s as expressive of *B*'s character; if the previous *A* and *B* were extremely unlike one another both physically and psychologically, and if, say, in addition, they were of different sex, there might be grave difficulties in reading *B*'s dispositions in any possible performances of *A*'s body. Let us forget this, and for the present purpose just take *A* and *B* as being sufficiently alike (however alike that has to be) for the difficulty not to arise; after the experiment, persons familiar with *A* and *B* are just *overwhelmingly struck* by the *B*-ish character of the doings associated with what was previously *A*'s body, and conversely. Thus the feat of imagining an exchange of bodies is supposed possible in the most restricted sense. But now there is a further limitation which has to be overcome if the feat is to be not merely possible in the most restricted sense but also is to have an outcome which, on serious reflection, we are prepared to describe as *A* and *B* having changed bodies—that is, an outcome where, confronted with what was previously *A*'s body, we are prepared seriously to say that we are now confronted with *B*.

It would seem a necessary condition of so doing that the utterances coming from that

R If the utterances and behavior are taken at face value, the person now in the body that was previously inhabited by person *A* has the same sort of memory of the previous actions and experiences of person *B* that person *B* would have had of them if the "exchange" had not taken place. The person in the body previously inhabited by person *A* also apparently has all the character traits of person *B*.

There are at least two different requirements suggested here for genuine memory: First, the present beliefs and images must be *caused* by the earlier experiences (rather than just happening by coincidence to fit those earlier experiences). Second, as it is often put, the causal relation must be "of the right sort": if, for example, the person's present knowledge of his or her earlier experiences depends on being told about them by a second person (who was previously told about them by the original person), then this is not a case of memory.

In the case described, the information is removed, stored externally, and then replaced. The later knowledge is thus not caused in the same way as ordinary memory knowledge (since the causal process involves external storage—and so runs outside the person's body); but it also does not involve another person who remembers and then relates the information (this would be one example of "learning again"). By saying that it would "seem exaggerated" to say that the result in this case is not genuine memory, Williams is suggesting, rather tentatively, that this *is* a case of genuine memory—so that it is not a general requirement for memory that the causal process does not run outside the person's body. (See Discussion Question 1.)

So the A-body-person now *apparently* has the memories and character traits of person *B;* and the B-body-person now apparently has the memories and character traits of person *A*.

Since the choice is to be made on *selfish* grounds, each person apparently believes (rightly or wrongly) that after the process occurs he will be the person in the other body (so that the bodies will indeed have been exchanged). But whether they are right about this is a further issue.

body be taken as genuinely expressive of memories of *B*'s past. But memory is a causal notion; and as we actually use it, it seems a necessary condition of *x*'s present knowledge of *x*'s earlier experiences constituting memory of those experiences that the causal chain linking the experiences and the knowledge should not run outside *x*'s body. **2** Hence if utterances coming from a given body are to be taken as expressive of memories of the experiences of *B,* there should be some suitable causal link between the appropriate state of that body and the original happening of those experiences to *B*. One radical way of securing that condition in the imagined exchange case is to suppose . . . that the brains of *A* and of *B* are transposed. We may not need so radical a condition. Thus suppose it were possible to extract information from a man's brain and store it in a device while his brain was repaired, or even renewed, the information then being replaced: it would seem exaggerated to insist that the resultant man could not possibly have the memories he had before the operation. With regard to our knowledge of our own past, we draw distinctions between merely recalling, being reminded, and learning again, and those distinctions correspond (roughly) to distinctions between no new input, partial new input, and total new input with regard to the information in question; and it seems clear that the information-parking case just imagined would not count as new input in the sense necessary and sufficient for 'learning again'. Hence we can imagine the case we are concerned with in terms of information extracted into such devices from *A*'s and *B*'s brains and replaced in the other brain; this is the sort of model which, I think not unfairly for the present argument, I shall have in mind. **3**

We imagine the following. The process considered above exists; two persons can enter some machine, let us say, and emerge changed in the appropriate ways. If *A* and *B* are the persons who enter, let us call the persons who emerge the *A-body-person* and the *B-body-person:* the *A*-body-person is that person (whoever it is) with whom I am confronted when, after the experiment, I am confronted with that body which previously was *A*'s body. . . . A non-question-begging description of the experiment will leave it open which (if either) of the persons *A* and *B* the *A*-body-person is; the description of the experiment as 'persons changing bodies' of course implies that the *A*-body-person is actually *B*. **4**

We take two persons *A* and *B* who are going to have the process carried out on them. (We can suppose . . . that they are willing for this to happen. . . .) We further announce that one of the two resultant persons, the *A*-body-person and the *B*-body-person, is going after the experiment to be given $100,000, while the other is going to be tortured. We then ask each of *A* and *B* to choose which treatment should be dealt out to which of the persons who will emerge from the experiment, the choice to be made (if it can be) on selfish grounds.

Suppose that *A* chooses that the *B*-body-person should get the pleasant treatment and the *A*-body-person the unpleasant treatment; and *B* chooses conversely (this might indicate that they thought that 'changing bodies' was indeed a good description of the outcome). The experimenter cannot act in accordance with both these sets of preferences, those expressed by *A* and those expressed by *B*. Hence there is one clear sense in which *A* and *B* cannot both get what they want: namely, that if the experimenter, before the experiment, announces to *A* and *B* that he intends to carry out the alternative (for example), of treating the *B*-body-person unpleasantly and the *A*-body-person pleasantly—then *A* can say rightly, 'That's not the outcome I chose to happen', and *B* can say rightly, 'That's just the outcome I chose to happen'. **5** . . . But is it also true that when the experimenter proceeds after the experiment to act in accordance with one of the preferences and not the other, *then* one of *A* and *B* will have got what he wanted, and the other not?

There seems very good ground for saying so. For suppose the experimenter, having elicited *A*'s and *B*'s preference, says nothing to *A* and *B* about what he will do; conducts the experiment; and then, for example, gives the unpleasant treatment to the *B*-body-person and the pleasant treatment to the *A*-body-person. Then the *B*-body-person will not only complain of the unpleasant treatment as such, but will complain (since he has *A*'s memories) that that was not the outcome he chose, since he chose that the *B*-body-person should be well treated; and since *A* made his choice in selfish spirit, he may add that he precisely chose in that way because he did not want the unpleasant things to happen to *him.* The *A*-body-person meanwhile will express satisfaction both at the receipt of the $100,000, and also at the fact that the experimenter has chosen to act in the way that he, *B,* so wisely chose. These facts make a strong case for saying that the experimenter has brought it about that *B* did in the outcome get what he wanted and *A* did not. It is therefore a strong case for saying that the *B*-body-person really is *A,* and the *A*-body-person really is *B;* and therefore for saying that the process of the experiment really is that of changing bodies. **6** For the same reasons it would seem that *A* and *B* in our example really did choose wisely, and that it was *A*'s bad luck that the choice he correctly made was not carried out, *B*'s good luck that the choice he correctly made was carried out. This seems to show that to care about what happens to me in the future is not necessarily to care about what happens to *this* body (the one I now have). . . .

These suggestions seem to be reinforced if we consider the cases where *A* and *B* make other choices with regard to the experiment. Suppose that *A* chooses that the *A*-body-person should get the money, and the *B*-body-person get the pain, and *B* chooses conversely. Here again there can be no outcome which matches the expressed preferences of both of them: they cannot both get what they want. The experimenter announces, before the experiment, that the *A*-body-person will in fact get the money, and the *B*-body-person will get the pain. So *A* at this stage gets what he wants (the announced outcome matches his expressed preference). After the experiment, the distribution is carried out as announced. Both the *A*-body-person and the *B*-body-person will have to agree that what is happening is in accordance with the preference that *A* originally expressed. The *B*-body-person will naturally express this acknowledgement (since he has *A*'s memories) by saying that this is the distribution he chose; he will recall, among other things, the experimenter announcing this outcome, his approving it as what he chose, and so forth. However, he (the *B*-body-person) certainly does not like what is now happening to him, and would much prefer to be receiving what the *A*-body-person is receiving—namely, $100,000. The *A*-body-person will on the other hand recall choosing an outcome other than this one, but will reckon it good luck that the experimenter did not do what he recalls choosing. It looks, then, as though the *A*-body-person has got what he wanted, but not what he chose, while the *B*-body-person has got what he chose, but not what he wanted. So once more it looks as though they are, respectively, *B* and *A;* and that in this case the original choices of both *A* and *B* were unwise. **7**

Suppose, lastly, that in the original choice *A* takes the line of the first case and *B* of the second: that is, *A* chooses that the *B*-body-person should get the money and the *A*-body-person the pain, and *B* chooses exactly the same thing. In this case, the experimenter would seem to be in the happy situation of giving both persons what they want. . . . In this case, the *B*-body-person likes what he is receiving, recalls choosing it, and congratulates himself on the wisdom of (as he puts it) his choice; while the *A*-body-person does not like what he is receiving, recalls choosing it, and is forced to acknowledge that (as he puts it) his choice was unwise. So once more we seem to get results to support the suggestions drawn from the first case. **8**

...

Let us now consider something apparently different. Someone in whose power I am tells me that I am going to be tortured tomorrow. I am frightened, and look forward to tomorrow in great apprehension. He adds that when the time comes, I shall not remember being told that this was going to happen to me, since shortly before the torture something else will be done to me which will make me forget the announcement. This certainly will not cheer me up, since I know perfectly well that I can forget things, and that there is such a thing as indeed being tortured unexpectedly because I had forgotten or been made to forget a prediction of the torture: that will still be a torture which, so long as I do know about the prediction, I look forward to in fear. He then adds that my forgetting the announcement will be only part of a larger process: when the moment of torture comes, I shall not remember any of the things I am now in a position to remember. This does not cheer me up, either, since I can readily conceive of being involved in an accident, for instance, as a result of which I wake up in a completely amnesiac state and also in great pain; that could certainly happen to me,

6

The *A*-body-person, having *B*'s memories and character traits, will seem to himself to be *B*, and in particular will remember having opted for the result where the *A*-body-person receives the money rather than being tortured. Thus it will *seem* to that person that he received the result that he asked for (and to the other person that he did not). But it is again not yet decided whether each of them is correct in their assessments.

7

Now each person apparently believes that the bodies will not be "exchanged" and so opts, in light of his selfish preferences, to have the person in his previous body treated well and the other person treated badly. After the process is complete, it *seems* to each that he made the wrong choice, because it *seems* to him (because of the memories he has) that he is now in the other body.

8

Now *A* apparently thinks that the "exchange" will occur and *B* thinks that it will not occur, so each opts that the *B*-body-person after the process be treated well and the other person treated badly. When this is done, the *B*-body-person likes the result (and *seems* to himself to be *A* and to have made a wise choice), while the *A*-body-person does not like the result (and *seems* to himself to be *B* and to have made an unwise choice).

I should not like it to happen to me, nor to know that it was going to happen to me. He now further adds that at the moment of torture I shall not only not remember the things I am now in a position to remember, but will have a different set of impressions of my past, quite different from the memories I now have. I do not think that this would cheer me up, either. For I can at least conceive the possibility, if not the concrete reality, of going completely mad, and thinking perhaps that I am George IV or somebody; and being told that something like that was going to happen to me would have no tendency to reduce the terror of being told authoritatively that I was going to be tortured, but would merely compound the horror. Nor do I see why I should be put into any better frame of mind by the person in charge adding lastly that the impressions of my past with which I shall be equipped on the eve of torture will exactly fit the past of another person now living, and that indeed I shall acquire these impressions by (for instance) information now in his brain being copied into mine. Fear, surely, would still be the proper reaction: and not because one did not know what was going to happen, but because in one vital respect at least one did know what was going to happen—torture, which one can indeed expect to happen to oneself, and to be preceded by certain mental derangements as well.

If this is right, the whole question seems now to be totally mysterious. For what we have just been through is of course merely one side, differently represented, of the transaction which we considered before; and it represents it as a perfectly hateful prospect, while the previous considerations represented it as something one should rationally, perhaps even cheerfully, choose out of the options there presented. It is differently presented, of course, and in two notable respects; but when we look at these two differences of presentation, can we really convince ourselves that the second presentation is wrong or misleading, thus leaving the road open to the first version which at the time seemed so convincing? Surely not. **9**

9

STOP Think carefully about this account in relation to the earlier one. Apart from the issue of voluntary preference, it seems to fit the situation of *B* in the original example—except that here it is assumed that there is no "exchange" of bodies, so that the *B*-body-person who is tortured is the original person *B* (albeit with very different memories and character traits). Is the second account that assumes that the bodies have not been "exchanged" in any clear way wrong or objectionable? How should one decide between these two accounts of what is in many ways the same set of facts?

The first difference is that in the second version the torture is throughout represented as going to happen to *me:* 'you', the man in charge persistently says. Thus he is not very neutral. But should he have been neutral? Or, to put it another way, does his use of the second person have a merely emotional and rhetorical effect on me, making me afraid when further reflection would have shown that I had no reason to be? It is certainly not obviously so. The problem just is that through every step of his predictions I seem to be able to follow him successfully. And if I reflect on whether what he has said gives me grounds for fearing that I shall be tortured, I could consider that behind my fears lies some principle such as this: that my undergoing physical pain in the future is not excluded by any psychological state I may be in at the time, with the platitudinous exception of those psychological states which in themselves exclude experiencing pain, notably (if it is a psychological state) unconsciousness. In particular, what impressions I have about the past will not have any effect on whether I undergo the pain or not. This principle seems sound enough. **10**

10

The point of the principle described is to say that no differences in a person's psychological states that are compatible with the occurrence of pain itself—even complete alterations of memory and character—rule out the possibility that it is still that very same person who suffers the future pain. (See Discussion Question 2.)

It is an important fact that not everything I would, as things are, regard as an evil would be something that I should rationally fear as an evil if it were predicted that it would happen to me in the future and also predicted that I should undergo significant psychological changes in the meantime. For the fact that I regard that happening, things being as they are, as an evil can be dependent on factors of belief or character which might themselves be modified by the psychological changes in question. Thus if I am appallingly subject to acrophobia, and am told that I shall find myself on top of a steep mountain in the near future, I shall to that extent be afraid; but if I am told that I shall be psychologically changed in the meantime in such a way as to rid me of my acrophobia (and as with the other prediction, I believe it), then I have no reason to be afraid of the predicted happening, or at least not the same reason. . . .

Physical pain, however, the example which for simplicity (and not for any obsessional reason) I have taken, is absolutely minimally dependent on character or belief. No amount of change in my character or my beliefs would seem to affect substantially the nastiness of tortures applied to me; correspondingly, no degree of predicted change in my character and beliefs can unseat the fear of torture which, together with those changes, is predicted for me. **11**

11

R Thus no description of such changes, Williams is claiming, can make it unreasonable for someone to fear the future pain.

. . .

I said that there were two notable differences between the second presentation of our situation and the first. The first difference, which we have just said something about, was that the man predicted the torture for *me,* a psychologically very changed 'me'. We have yet to find a reason for saying that he should not have done this, or that I really should be unable to follow him if he does; I seem to be able to follow him only too well. The second difference is that in this presentation he does not mention the other man, except in the somewhat incidental role of being the provenance of the impressions of the past I end up with. He does not mention him at all as someone who will end up with impressions of the past derived from me (and, incidentally, with $100,000 as well—a consideration which, in the frame of mind appropriate to this version, will merely make me jealous).

But why *should* he mention this man and what is going to happen to him? My selfish concern is to be told what is going to happen to me, and now I know: torture, preceded by changes of character, brain operations, changes in impressions of the past. The knowledge that one other person, or none, or many will be similarly mistreated may affect me in other ways, of sympathy, greater horror at the power of this tyrant, and so forth; but surely it cannot affect my expectations of torture? But—someone will say—this is to leave out exactly the feature which, as the first presentation of the case showed, makes all the difference: for it is to leave out the person who, as the first presentation showed, will be you. It is to leave out not merely a feature which should fundamentally affect your fears, it is to leave out the very person for whom you are fearful. So of course, the objector will say, this makes all the difference. 12

But can it? Consider the following series of cases. In each case we are to suppose that after what is described, *A* is, as before, to be tortured; we are also to suppose the person *A* is informed beforehand that just these things followed by the torture will happen to him:

i. *A* is subjected to an operation which produces total amnesia;

ii. amnesia is produced in *A,* and other interference leads to certain changes in his character;

iii. changes in his character are produced, and at the same time certain illusory 'memory' beliefs are induced in him: these are of a quite fictitious kind and do not fit the life of any actual person;

iv. the same as (iii), except that both the character traits and the 'memory' impressions are designed to be appropriate to another actual person, *B;*

v. the same as (iv), except that the result is produced by putting the information into *A* from the brain of *B,* by a method which leaves *B* the same as he was before;

vi. the same happens to *A* as in (v), but *B* is not left the same, since a similar operation is conducted in the reverse direction.

I take it that no-one is going to dispute that A has reasons, and fairly straightforward reasons, for fear of pain when the prospect is that of situation (i); there seems no conceivable reason why this should not extend to situation (ii), and the situation (iii) can surely introduce no difference of principle—it just seems a situation which for more than one reason we should have grounds for fearing, as suggested above. Situation (iv) at least introduces the person *B,* who was the focus of the objection we are now discussing. But it does not seem to introduce him in any way which makes a material difference; if I can expect pain through a transformation which involves new 'memory'-impressions, it would seem a purely external fact, relative to that, that the 'memory'-impressions had a model. Nor, in (iv), do we satisfy a causal condition which I mentioned at the beginning for the 'memories' actually being memories; though notice that if the job were done thoroughly, I might well be able to elicit from the *A*-body-person the kinds of remarks about his previous expectations of the experiment—remarks appropriate to the original *B*—which so impressed us in the first version of the story. I shall have a similar assurance of this being so in situation (v), where, moreover, a plausible application of the causal condition is available. 13

But two things are to be noticed about this situation. First, if we concentrate on *A* and the *A*-body-person, we do not seem to have added anything which from the point of view of his fears makes any material difference; just as, in the move from (iii) to (iv), it made no relevant difference that the new 'memory'-impressions which precede the pain had, as it happened, a model, so in the move from (iv) to (v) all we have added is that they have a model which is also their cause: and it is still difficult to see why that,

R The objection claims that the inclusion of the other person existing after the "exchange"—the person who in the description of the original case started in *A*'s body and after the process *seems* to be *B*—should remove *B*'s fear of the future torture by making it clear that it is *A* and not *B* who will in fact be tortured.

In the original case, it was the *B*-body-person who was tortured, but this change makes no real difference to the main issues. Cases (i)–(iv) here correspond to the successive steps in the original account of the non-exchange case (pp. 230–231), while cases (v) and (vi) also include a similar non-exchange version of the second person's situation.

to him looking forward, could possibly make the difference between expecting pain and not expecting pain. To illustrate that point from the case of character: if *A* is capable of expecting pain, he is capable of expecting pain preceded by a change in his dispositions—and to that expectation it can make no difference, whether that change in his dispositions is modeled on, or indeed indirectly caused by; the dispositions of some other person. If his fears can, as it were, reach through the change, it seems a mere trimming how the change is in fact induced. The second point about situation (v) is that if the crucial question for *A*'s fears with regard to what befalls the *A*-body-person is whether the *A*-body-person is or is not the person *B*, then that condition has not yet been satisfied in situation (v): for there we have an undisputed *B* in addition to the *A*-body-person, and certainly those two are not the same person. [14]

But in situation (vi), we seemed to think, that is finally what he is. But if *A*'s original fears could reach through the expected changes in (v), as they did in (iv) and (iii), then certainly they can reach through in (vi). Indeed, from the point of view of *A*'s expectations and fears, there is less difference between (vi) and (v) than there is between (v) and (iv) or between (iv) and (iii). In those transitions, there were at least differences—though we could not see that they were really relevant differences—in the content or cause of what happened to him; in the present case there is absolutely no difference at all in what happens to him, the only difference being in what happens to someone else. If he can fear pain when (v) is predicted, why should he cease to when (vi) is? [15]

I can see only one way of relevantly laying great weight on the transition from (v) to (vi); and this involves a considerable difficulty. This is to deny that, as I put it, the transition from (v) to (vi) involves merely the addition of something happening to *somebody else;* what rather it does, it will be said, is to involve the reintroduction of *A* himself, as the *B*-body-person; since he has reappeared in this form, it is for this person, and not for the unfortunate *A*-body-person, that *A* will have his expectations. This is to reassert, in effect, the viewpoint emphasised in our first presentation of the experiment. But this surely has the consequence that *A* should not have fears for the *A*-body-person who appeared in situation (v). For by the present argument, the *A*-body-person in (vi) is not *A;* the *B*-body-person is. But the *A*-body-person in (v) is, in character, history, everything, exactly the same as the *A*-body-person in (vi); so if the latter is not *A,* then neither is the former. [16] (It is this point, no doubt, that encourages one to speak of the difference that goes with (vi) as being, on the present view, the *reintroduction* of *A*.) But no-one else in (v) has any better claim to be *A*. So in (v), it seems, *A* just does not exist. This would certainly explain why *A* should have no fears for the state of things in (v)—though he might well have fears for the path to it. But it rather looked earlier as though he could well have fears for the state of things in (v). Let us grant, however, that that was an illusion, and that *A* really does not exist in (v); then does he exist in (iv), (iii), (ii), or (i)? It seems very difficult to deny it for (i) and (ii); are we perhaps to draw the line between (iii) and (iv)? [17]

Here someone will say: you must not insist on drawing a line—borderline cases are borderline cases, and you must not push our concepts beyond their limits. But this well-known piece of advice, sensible as it is in many cases, seems in the present case to involve an extraordinary difficulty. It may intellectually comfort observers of *A*'s situation; but what is *A* supposed to make of it? To be told that a future situation is a borderline one for its being myself that is hurt, that it is conceptually undecidable whether it will be me or not, is something which, it seems, I can do nothing with; because, in particular, it seems to have no comprehensible representation in my expectations and the emotions that go with them. [18]

If I expect that a certain situation, *S,* will come about in the future, there is of course a wide range of emotions and concerns, directed on *S,* which I may experience now in relation to my expectation. Unless I am exceptionally egoistic, it is not a condition on my being concerned in relation to this expectation, that I myself will be involved in *S*—where my being 'involved' in *S* means that I figure in *S* as someone doing something at that time or having something done to me, or, again, that *S* will have consequences affecting me at that or some subsequent time. There are some emotions, however, which I will feel only if I will be involved in *S,* and fear is an obvious example.

Now the description of *S* under which it figures in my expectations will necessarily be, in various ways, indeterminate; and one way in

14

The issue is whether the addition of the elements of cases (v) and (vi) makes any difference to whether the person (*A*, as the case is described) whose body will eventually be tortured is unreasonable or mistaken in some way in expecting and fearing that *he* will be tortured. The additions in case (v) by themselves clearly make no difference: *B* still exists in the *B*-body, so that it cannot be that *A* is now in the *B*-body.

15

But if *A* is reasonably fearful of being tortured in cases (i)–(v), how can the additional ingredients in case (vi) make any difference? If the person in the *A*-body is still *A* in case (v), how can doing something to the other person and nothing at all further to *A* somehow bring it about in case (vi) that *A* is now in the *B*-body (and so should not fear the torture that will happen to the *A*-body)?

The underlying principle being assumed here is that the identity of the person in the *A*-body cannot be affected by the existence or situation of another person in a different body.

16

To insist that the *B*-body-person in case (vi) is the original person *A* requires one to also say, Williams is arguing, that the *A*-body-person in case (v) was also not *A*—presumably because that person then had *B*'s memories and character traits. But of course the *A*-body-person was also not *B*, since *B* still exists in the *B*-body in cases (i)–(v). So who is the person in the *A*-body, according to this view—which Williams does not accept? (See Discussion Question 3.)

17

STOP If *A* does not exist in case (v)—since he is neither the person in the *B*-body nor the person in the *A*-body, according to the view being considered—when in the sequence of cases does he cease to exist? (What might Locke say about this?)

which it may be indeterminate is that it leaves open whether I shall be involved in *S* or not. Thus I may have good reason to expect that one of us five is going to get hurt, but no reason to expect it to be me rather than one of the others. My present emotions will be correspondingly affected by this indeterminacy. Thus, sticking to the egoistic concern involved in fear, I shall presumably be somewhat more cheerful than if I knew it was going to be me, somewhat less cheerful than if I had been left out altogether. Fear will be mixed with, and qualified by, apprehension; and so forth. These emotions revolve around the thought of the eventual determination of the indeterminacy; moments of straight fear focus on its really turning out to be me, of hope on its turning out not to be me. All the emotions are related to the coming about of what I expect: and what I expect in such a case just cannot come about save by coming about in one of the ways or another.

There are other ways in which indeterminate expectations can be related to fear. Thus I may expect (perhaps neurotically) that something nasty is going to happen to me, indeed expect that when it happens it will take some determinate form, but have no range, or no closed range, of candidates for the determinate form to rehearse in my present thought. Different from this would be the fear of something radically indeterminate—the fear (one might say) of a nameless horror. If somebody had such a fear, one could even say that he had, in a sense, a perfectly determinate expectation: if what he expects indeed comes about, there will be nothing more determinate to be said about it after the event than was said in the expectation. Both these cases of course are cases of *fear* because one thing that is fixed amid the indeterminacy is the belief that it is me to whom the things will happen. (19)

...

Suppose now that there is an *S* with regard to which it is for conceptual reasons undecidable whether it involves me or not, as is proposed for the experimental situation by the line we are discussing. It is important that the expectation of *S* is not *indeterminate* in any of the ways we have just been considering. It is not like the nameless horror, since the fixed point of that case was that it was going to happen to the subject, and that made his state unequivocally fear. Nor is it like the expectation of the man who expects one of the five to be hurt; his fear was indeed equivocal, but its focus, and that of the expectation, was that when *S* came about, it would certainly come about in one way or the other. In the present case, fear (of the torture, that is to say, not of the initial experiment) seems neither appropriate, nor inappropriate, nor appropriately equivocal. Relatedly, the subject has an incurable difficulty about how he may think about *S*. If he engages in projective imaginative thinking (about how it will be for him), he implicitly answers the necessarily unanswerable question; if he thinks that he cannot engage in such thinking, it looks very much as if he also answers it, though in the opposite direction. Perhaps he must just refrain from such thinking; but is he just refraining from it, if it is incurably undecidable whether he can or cannot engage in it? (20)

It may be said that all that these considerations can show is that fear, at any rate, does not get its proper footing in this case; but that there could be some other, more ambivalent, form of concern which would indeed be appropriate to this particular expectation, the expectation of the conceptually undecidable situation. There are, perhaps, analogous feelings that actually occur in actual situations. Thus material objects do occasionally undergo puzzling transformations which leave a conceptual shadow over their identity. Suppose I were sentimentally attached to an object to which this sort of thing then happened; it might be that I could neither feel about it quite as I did originally, nor be totally indifferent to it, but would have some other and rather ambivalent feeling towards it. (21) Similarly, it may be said, toward the prospective sufferer of pain, my identity relations with whom are conceptually shadowed, I can feel neither as I would if he were certainly me, nor as I would if he were certainly not, but rather some such ambivalent concern.

But this analogy does little to remove the most baffling aspect of the present case—an aspect which has already turned up in what was said about the subject's difficulty in thinking either projectively or non-projectively about the situation. For to regard the prospective pain-sufferer *just* like the transmogrified object of sentiment, and to conceive of my ambivalent distress about

R The suggestion is that while person *A* does not exist in case (v) and clearly exists (in the *A*-body) before any of the changes involved in the sequence of cases have taken place, there is no clear line at which he ceases to exist. Some at least of the intervening cases are *borderline* cases where it is simply unclear whether *A* exists or not—and presumably would remain unclear no matter how much additional detail of the general sort given so far were added.

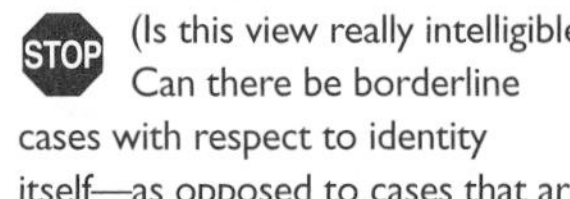

(Is this view really intelligible? Can there be borderline cases with respect to identity itself—as opposed to cases that are borderline merely with respect to our *knowledge* of identity?)

R I can be afraid in varying degrees because it is indeterminate what will happen to me in a future situation, as long as it is clear that it is indeed me to whom the indeterminate things will happen.

R But in the case where it is indeterminate whether I will be involved at all, I simply do not know, according to Williams, what to think—whether to be fearful to any degree or not. Notice that this is not merely a case of ignorance, not one in which I am in fact definitely there or definitely not there, but just do not know which.

Suppose, for example, that a car which I have a long history with and am very fond of is heavily damaged in an accident and is very substantially rebuilt, with many new parts, a new engine, and so on.

his future pain as just like ambivalent distress about some future damage to such an object, is of course to leave him and me clearly distinct from one another, and thus to displace the conceptual shadow from its proper place. (22) I have to get nearer to him than that. But is there any nearer that I can get to him without expecting his pain? If there is, the analogy has not shown us it. We can certainly not get nearer by expecting, as it were, *ambivalent* pain; there is no place at all for that. There seems to be an obstinate bafflement to mirroring in my expectations a situation in which it is conceptually undecidable whether I occur. (23)

The bafflement seems, moreover, to turn to plain absurdity if we move from conceptual undecidability to its close friend and neighbour, conventionalist decision. This comes out if we consider another description, overtly conventionalist, of the series of cases which occasioned the present discussion. This description would reject a point I relied on in an earlier argument—namely, that if we deny that the *A*-body-person in (vi) is *A* (because the *B*-body-person is), then we must deny that the *A*-body-person in (v) is *A*, since they are exactly similar. 'No', it may be said, 'this is just to assume that we say the same in different sorts of situation. No doubt when we have the very good candidate for being *A*—namely, the *B*-body-person—we call him *A;* but this does not mean that we should not call the *A*-body-person *A* in that other situation when we have no better candidate around. Different situations call for different descriptions.' This line of talk is the sort of thing indeed appropriate to lawyers deciding the ownership of some property which has undergone some bewildering set of transformations; they just have to decide, and in each situation, let us suppose, it has got to go to somebody, on as reasonable grounds as the facts and the law admit. But as a line to deal with a person's fears or expectations about his own future, it seems to have no sense at all. If *A*'s fears can extend to what will happen to the *A*-body-person in (v), I do not see how they can be rationally diverted from the fate of the exactly similar person in (vi) by his being told that someone would have a reason in the latter situation which he would not have in the former for deciding to call another person *A*. (24)

Thus, to sum up, it looks as though there are two presentations of the imagined experiment and the choice associated with it, each of which carries conviction, and which lead to contrary conclusions. The idea, moreover, that the situation after the experiment is conceptually undecidable in the relevant respect seems not to assist, but rather to increase, the puzzlement; while the idea (so often appealed to in these matters) that it is conventionally decidable is even worse. Following from all that, I am not in the least clear which option it would be wise to take if one were presented with them before the experiment. I find that rather disturbing.

. . .

I will end by suggesting one rather shaky way in which one might approach a resolution of the problem, using only the limited materials already available.

The apparently decisive arguments of the first presentation, which suggested that *A* should identify himself with the *B*-body-person, turned on the extreme neatness of the situation in satisfying, if any could, the description of 'changing bodies'. But this neatness is basically artificial; it is the product of the will of the experimenter to produce a situation which would naturally elicit, with minimum hesitation, that description. By the sorts of methods he employed, he could easily have left off earlier or gone on further. He could have stopped at situation (v), leaving *B* as he was; or he could have gone on and produced two persons each with *A*-like character and memories, as well as one or two with *B*-like characteristics. (25) If he had done either of those, we should have been in yet greater difficulty about what to say; he just chose to make it as easy as possible for us to find something to say. Now if we had some model of ghostly persons in bodies, which were in some sense actually moved around by certain procedures, we could regard the neat experiment just as the *effective* experiment: the one method that really did result in the ghostly persons' changing places without being destroyed, dispersed, or whatever. But we cannot seriously use such a model. The experimenter has not in the sense of that model *induced* a change of bodies; he has rather produced the one situation out of a range of equally possible situations which we should

If the case were like the car case (try to imagine how this could be—if it is even possible), then it would be clear that I am not fully and unequivocally identical to the resulting person—so that the sort of fear I would have in the case where the person to be tortured is clearly me would be inappropriate. Williams's point is that this is *not* the way the situation seems to be—instead it is uncertain on conceptual grounds whether it is me and so uncertain what I should feel.

We might, Williams is suggesting in part, know how to think about the situation in which identity is indeterminate from a third-person perspective, but not from a first-person perspective.

R And the view that it is a matter of *convention*, something that we are free to decide either way, whether *A* still exists in case (v) is, Williams suggests, absurd. When *A* worries about whether to be fearful about this situation, what he is worrying about is not something that can be settled in this essentially arbitrary way.

It seems clear that if there were two or more persons having *A*'s memories and character after the process is complete, they could not both be identical with the original *A*. (See Discussion Question 4.)

be most disposed to call a change of bodies. As against this, the principle that one's fears can extend to future pain whatever psychological changes precede it seems positively straightforward. Perhaps, indeed, it is not; but we need to be shown what is wrong with it. Until we are shown what is wrong with it, we should perhaps decide that if we were the person *A* then, if we were to decide selfishly, we should pass the pain to the *B*-body-person. It would be risky: that there is room for the notion of a *risk* here is itself a major feature of the problem.

Discussion Questions

1. When the person in the *A*-body seems (after the process is complete) to remember *B*'s experiences, is this genuine memory? Obviously the process that produces such apparent memories is different from the normal case, but is it still similar enough (as Williams suggests) to make the results still count as genuine memories—which is apparently required if the resulting person is to be *B*?
2. Obviously there are many sorts of psychological changes that are compatible with the continued existence of the same person, but is this true for any sort of psychological change (as the second way of describing the case claims)? Is a person who has suffered severe and irreversible amnesia still identical to the person who existed before this happens? Is a person who after amnesia has new experiences and forms totally new character traits still identical with the earlier person? Or is there some degree or kind of change that rules out continuing identity? What is the bearing of such changes on the issues of moral responsibility and the justification for reward and punishment?
3. In the second version of the case, the person in the *A*-body in case (v) is not yet *B* (because *B* still exists) but also arguably no longer *A* (since all the changes to him that will lead to his being *B* in case (vi) have already taken place). What should we say about the identity of this person? If *A* and *B* before the process in case (v) were each worried about whether they would survive it, should either of them be reassured by knowing that the person in the *A*-body will exist after the process is completed? If so, which one (and why)?
4. Suppose that *A*'s memories and character traits are transferred into *two* or more other bodies (and that the original *A*-body is either destroyed or has the memories and character of someone else transferred into it). On the approach that interprets Williams's original case as involving exchange of bodies, what should we say about the persons having *A*'s memories and character in this new case? Is one of them identical to person *A*, and if so, how could we determine *which* one? If neither of them is identical to *A*, does this mean that *A* does not survive in this new case? If *A* were able before the process occurs to take steps that might harm or hurt these later persons, what should his attitude toward them be (and why)?
5. Would you be willing to undergo the process described by Williams in the original case if *both* of the resulting people received sufficiently large amounts of money? (Assume that there is no doubt that the process will succeed as described.) If, as in the original case, only one person will receive money and the other will be tortured (and you cannot escape the process occurring), who would you want to receive the money: the person (whoever it is) that ends up in your original body or the person (having your memories and character traits) in the new (to you) body? Would the fact that your present body has terminal cancer and the other body is perfectly healthy change your attitude toward undergoing the process (assuming that you can be guaranteed that the healthy body that ends up with your memories and character traits will not be tortured)? Try to give reasons for each of your answers.

Derek Parfit

Derek Parfit (1942–) is a British philosopher who has made major contributions to both metaphysics and ethics. He teaches at Oxford University.

In this selection, Parfit argues for two main theses: First, there are describable cases, some of which may be scientifically possible, in which there is no clearly right yes-or-no answer to the question of whether a future person is numerically identical to some previously existing person. Second, the issue of personal identity is much less important than it has usually seemed to be: in particular, the issue of whether a previously existing person has *survived* in some future situation does not depend on the question of identity in the way that has standardly been thought. This is a view that some philosophers have found extremely paradoxical, and you should carefully consider his reasons for it.

Toward the end of section IV of the selection, Parfit draws a distinction between psychological *continuity* and psychological *connectedness*. Of these, psychological continuity is the weaker and less demanding relation. It holds between a series of persons (or "person-stages") existing at different times as long as there are *direct* psychological relations (one remembering the experiences of another, one intending an action that another does, and so forth) between them that overlap in such a way that any two successive persons or stages are connected by some of them. (How many such direct relations hold between the various stages is a matter of degree, as thus is psychological continuity itself.) Thus in Reid's example (p. 227), the direct relation of remembering an earlier experience holds between the general and the young officer who captured the standard and also between the young officer and the schoolboy. Since there are direct relations between any two of these stages, the whole series satisfies the requirement of psychological continuity to at least this degree. But psychological connectedness (also a matter of degree) requires direct relations between *all* the members of the series, not just between successive members. Thus the series consisting of the schoolboy, the young officer, and the general does not, as Reid describes it, possess psychological connectedness to any degree, since there are no direct psychological relations between the general and the schoolboy. (This assumes that the general does not remember any of the experiences of the schoolboy, does not act so as to fulfill any of the schoolboy's intentions, and so on.)

Personal Identity

We can, I think, describe cases in which, though we know the answer to every other question, we have no idea how to answer a question about personal identity. These cases are not covered by the criteria of personal identity that we actually use.

Do they present a problem?

It might be thought that they do not, because they could never occur. I suspect that some of them could. (Some, for instance, might become scientifically possible.) But I shall claim that even if they did they would present no problem.

My targets are two beliefs: one about the nature of personal identity, the other about its importance.

The first is that in these cases the question about identity must have an answer.

No one thinks this about, say, nations or machines. Our criteria for the identity of these do not cover certain cases. No one thinks that in these cases the questions "Is it the same nation?" or "Is it the same machine?" must have answers.

Some people believe that in this respect they are different. They agree that our criteria of personal identity do not cover certain cases, but they believe that the nature of their own identity through time is, somehow, such as to guarantee that in these cases questions about their identity must have answers. This belief might be expressed as follows: "Whatever happens between now and any future time, either I shall still exist, or I shall not. Any future experience will either be *my* experience, or it will not." ❶

❶ R The belief in question is that there must always be a correct yes-or-no answer to the question of whether a person existing at one time still exists at some later time (and if the answer is "yes," it is also assumed, a definite answer as to *which* person at the later time is identical with that earlier existing person).

...

I cannot see how to disprove this first belief. I shall describe a problem case. But this can only make it seem implausible.

Another approach might be this. We might suggest that one cause of the belief is the projection of our emotions. When we imagine ourselves in a problem case, we do feel that the question "Would it be me?" must have an answer. But what we take to be a bafflement about a further fact may be only the bafflement of our concern. ❷

❷  Parfit is suggesting that what might seem to be factual uncertainty about whether or not I would exist in some possible situation (and if I do exist, which person I would be) may instead be a more general uncertainty about whether and how my normal concern for my own well-being applies to the case in question, if at all.

I shall not pursue this suggestion here. But one cause of our concern is the belief which is my second target. This is that unless the question about identity has an answer, we cannot answer certain important questions (questions about such matters as survival, memory, and responsibility).

From *Philosophical Review,* Vol. 80, No.1 (January 1971).

Against this second belief my claim will be this. Certain important questions do presuppose a question about personal identity. But they can be freed of this presupposition. And when they are, the question about identity has no importance.

I

We can start by considering the much discussed case of the man who, like an amoeba, divides.

Wiggins has recently dramatized this case.* He first referred to the operation imagined by Shoemaker.† We suppose that my brain is transplanted into someone else's (brainless) body, and that the resulting person has my character and apparent memories of my life. Most of us would agree, after thought, that the resulting person is me. I shall here assume such agreement.

Wiggins then imagined his own operation. My brain is divided, and each half is housed in a new body. Both resulting people have my character and apparent memories of my life.

What happens to me? There seem only three possibilities: (1) I do not survive; (2) I survive as one of the two people; (3) I survive as both. [3]

The trouble with (1) is this. We agreed that I could survive if my brain were successfully transplanted. And people have in fact survived with half their brains destroyed. It seems to follow that I could survive if half my brain were successfully transplanted and the other half were destroyed. But if this is so, how could I *not* survive if the other half were also successfully transplanted? How could a double success be a failure? [4]

We can move to the second description. Perhaps one success is the maximum score. Perhaps I shall be one of the resulting people.

The trouble here is that in Wiggins' case each half of my brain is exactly similar, and so, to start with, is each resulting person. So how can I survive as only one of the two people? What can make me one of them rather than the other? [5]

It seems clear that both of these descriptions—that I do not survive, and that I survive as one of the people—are highly implausible. Those who have accepted them must have assumed that they were the only possible descriptions.

What about our third description: that I survive as both people?

It might be said, "If 'survive' implies identity, this description makes no sense—you cannot be two people. If it does not, the description is irrelevant to a problem about identity."

I shall later deny the second of these remarks. But there are ways of denying the first. We might say, "What we have called 'the two resulting people' are not two people. They are one person. I do survive Wiggins' operation. Its effect is to give me two bodies and a divided mind." [6]

It would shorten my argument if this were absurd. But I do not think it is. It is worth showing why.

We can, I suggest, imagine a divided mind. We can imagine a man having two simultaneous experiences, in having each of which he is unaware of having the other.

We may not even need to imagine this. Certain actual cases, to which Wiggins referred, seem to be best described in these terms. These involve the cutting of the bridge between the hemispheres of the brain. The aim was to cure epilepsy. But the result appears to be, in the surgeon's words, the creation of "two separate spheres of consciousness,"‡ each of which controls one half of the patient's body. What is experienced in each is, presumably, experienced by the patient. [7]

There are certain complications in these actual cases. So let us imagine a simpler case.

Suppose that the bridge between my hemispheres is brought under my voluntary control. This would enable me to disconnect my hemispheres as easily as if I were blinking. By doing this I would divide my mind. And we can suppose that when my mind is divided I can, in each half, bring about reunion.

This ability would have obvious uses. To give an example: I am near the end of a maths exam, and see two ways of tackling the last problem. I decide to divide my mind, to work, with each half, at one of two calculations, and then to reunite my mind and write a fair copy of the best result.

What shall I experience?

When I disconnect my hemispheres, my consciousness divides into two streams. But this

Think about this case before reading further: If this happened to you, would one of the resulting people be you (and if so, which one)? Does it make sense to say that *both* of them are you? Or have you ceased to exist—and if so, did you *die* (or if not, what happened to you)?

Do you agree that you would continue to exist (survive) if *half* your brain were successfully transplanted and the other half destroyed? (Notice that this assumes that the rest of your body does not matter for your survival as a person—and thus that you are not just a human animal.)

Remember that the question is not how someone else could *tell* which one is me (an epistemological question), but rather why it would be *true* that one is and one is not me. (Can you think of an answer that a mind-body dualist might give to this question? See Discussion Question 1.)

The result of the operation is two functioning bodies, each with its own separate functioning brain (though each is only half of the original brain) and separate resulting stream of conscious experience. Can any sense be made of the claim there is still only one person and not two?

The evidence for two separate spheres of consciousness involves experiments in which each eye (each one being connected to only one hemisphere of the brain) is shown only part of a phrase like "key ring." When this is done, the parts of the body under the control of the separate hemispheres respond in a way appropriate to the part of the phrase that the corresponding eye saw, but not to both parts together (thus selecting from a set of options a key or a wedding ring, but not a key ring). This at least suggests separate awarenesses in those two parts.

---

*David Wiggins, *Identity and Spatio-Temporal Continuity* (Oxford, 1967), p. 50.

†Sydney S. Shoemaker, *Self-Knowledge and Self-Identity* (Ithaca, N. Y., 1963), p. 22.

‡R. W. Sperry, in *Brain and Conscious Experience,* ed. J. C. Eccles (New York, 1966), p. 299.

division is not something that I experience. Each of my two streams of consciousness seems to have been straightforwardly continuous with my one stream of consciousness up to the moment of division. The only changes in each stream are the disappearance of half my visual field and the loss of sensation in, and control over, half my body. (8)

As a matter of fact, the right hemisphere controls the left side of the body, and the left hemisphere controls the right side of the body. A complication that Parfit does not mention but which is still worth thinking about is that speech and language use are normally controlled only by the left hemisphere—so that the right hemisphere and the left hand might not be able to do math problems, though this could perhaps be overcome through training.

Consider my experiences in what we can call my "right-handed" stream. I remember that I assigned my right hand to the longer calculation. This I now begin. In working at this calculation I can see, from the movements of my left hand, that I am also working at the other. But I am not aware of working at the other. So I might, in my right-handed stream, wonder how, in my left-handed stream, I am getting on.

My work is now over. I am about to reunite my mind. What should I, in each stream, expect? Simply that I shall suddenly seem to remember just having thought out two calculations, in thinking out each of which I was not aware of thinking out the other. This, I submit, we can imagine. And if my mind was divided, these memories are correct. (9)

STOP Try to imagine what this would be like. (See Discussion Question 2.)

In describing this episode, I assumed that there were two series of thoughts, and that they were both mine. If my two hands visibly wrote out two calculations, and if I claimed to remember two corresponding series of thoughts, this is surely what we should want to say.

If it is, then a person's mental history need not be like a canal, with only one channel. It could be like a river, with islands, and with separate streams.

To apply this to Wiggins' operation: we mentioned the view that it gives me two bodies and a divided mind. We cannot now call this absurd. But it is, I think, unsatisfactory.

There were two features of the case of the exam that made us want to say that only one person was involved. The mind was soon reunited, and there was only one body. If a mind was permanently divided and its halves developed in different ways, the point of speaking of one person would start to disappear. Wiggins' case, where there are also two bodies, seems to be over the borderline. After I have had his operation, the two "products" each have all the attributes of a person. They could live at opposite ends of the earth. (If they later met, they might even fail to recognize each other.) It would become intolerable to deny that they were different people.

Suppose we admit that they are different people. Could we still claim that I survived as both, using "survive" to imply identity?

We could. For we might suggest that two people could compose a third. We might say, "I do survive Wiggins' operation as two people. They can be different people, and yet be me. . . ."

This is a possible way of giving sense to the claim that I survive as two different people, using "survive" to imply identity. But it keeps the language of identity only by changing the concept of a person. And there are obvious objections to this change.* (10)

(10)

R Everything about the subsequent lives of each of the two could be as different from the other as for any two ordinary people—in particular one may be happy at a time when the other is sad, asleep when the other is awake, and so on. This is why it is "intolerable" to deny that they are separate people—and also why it seems absurd to say that the original person is somehow identical to both of them.

The alternative, for which I shall argue, is to give up the language of identity. We can suggest that I survive as two different people without implying that I am these people.

When I first mentioned this alternative, I mentioned this objection: "If your new way of talking does not imply identity, it cannot solve our problem. For that is about identity. The problem is that all the possible answers to the question about identity are highly implausible."

We can now answer this objection.

We can start by reminding ourselves that this is an objection only if we have one or both of the beliefs which I mentioned at the start of this paper.

The first was the belief that to any question about personal identity, in any describable case, there must be a true answer. For those with this belief, Wiggins' case is doubly perplexing. If all the possible answers are implausible, it is hard to decide which of them is true, and hard even to keep the belief that one of them must be true. If we give up this belief, as I think we should, these problems disappear. We shall then regard the case as like many others in which, for quite unpuzzling reasons, there *is* no answer to a question about identity. (Consider "Was England the same nation after 1066?") (11)

(11)

There are many sorts of things for which it is clear that the question of whether such a thing at one time is identical with one at a later time need have no correct yes-or-no answer: nations after changes of government, or major territorial additions or subtractions, or large-scale population changes; physical objects (a car, a house, a ship) after major additions or subtractions or alterations of parts; and even living things (a divided plant, a cloned animal). The issue is whether *personal* identity can be uncertain in the same way.

*Suppose the resulting people fight a duel. Are there three people fighting, one on each side, and one on both? And suppose one of the bullets kills. Are there two acts, one murder and one suicide? How many people are left alive? One? Two? (We could hardly say, "One and a half.") We could talk in this way. But instead of saying that the resulting people are the original person—so that the pair is a trio—it would be far simpler to treat them as a pair, and describe their relation to the original person in some new way. (I owe this suggested way of talking, and the objections to it, to Michael Woods.)

Wiggins' case makes the first belief implausible. It also makes it trivial. For it undermines the second belief. This was the belief that important questions turn upon the question about identity. . . .

Against this second belief my claim is this. Certain questions do presuppose a question about personal identity. And because these questions *are* important, Wiggins' case does present a problem. But we cannot solve this problem by answering the question about identity. We can solve this problem only by taking these important questions and prizing them apart from the question about identity. After we have done this, the question about identity (though we might for the sake of neatness decide it) has no further interest. (12)

Because there are several questions which presuppose identity, this claim will take some time to fill out.

We can first return to the question of survival. This is a special case, for survival does not so much presuppose the retaining of identity as seem equivalent to it. It is thus the general relation which we need to prize apart from identity. We can then consider particular relations, such as those involved in memory and intention.

"Will I survive?" seems, I said, equivalent to "Will there be some person alive who is the same person as me?"

If we treat these questions as equivalent, then the least unsatisfactory description of Wiggins' case is, I think, that I survive with two bodies and a divided mind.

Several writers have chosen to say that I am neither of the resulting people. Given our equivalence, this implies that I do not survive, and hence, presumably, that even if Wiggins' operation is not literally death, I ought, since I will not survive it, to regard it *as* death. But this seemed absurd.

It is worth repeating why. An emotion or attitude can be criticized for resting on a false belief, or for being inconsistent. A man who regarded Wiggins' operation as death must, I suggest, be open to one of these criticisms.

He might believe that his relation to each of the resulting people fails to contain some element which is contained in survival. But how can this be true? We agreed that he *would* survive if he stood in this very same relation to only *one* of the resulting people. So it cannot be the nature of this relation which makes it fail, in Wiggins' case, to be survival. (13) It can only be its duplication.

Suppose that our man accepts this, but still regards division as death. His reaction would now seem wildly inconsistent. He would be like a man who, when told of a drug that could double his years of life, regarded the taking of this drug as death. The only difference in the case of division is that the extra years are to run concurrently. This is an interesting difference. But it cannot mean that there are *no* years to run. (14)

...

My first conclusion, then, is this. The relation of the original person to each of the resulting people contains all that interests us—all that matters—in any ordinary case of survival. This is why we need a sense in which one person can survive as two.

One of my aims in the rest of this paper will be to suggest such a sense. But we can first make some general remarks.

II

Identity is a one-one relation. Wiggins' case serves to show that what matters in survival need not be one-one. (15)

Wiggins' case is of course unlikely to occur. The relations which matter are, in fact, one-one. It is because they are that we can imply the holding of these relations by using the language of identity.

This use of language is convenient. But it can lead us astray. We may assume that what matters *is* identity and, hence, has the properties of identity.

In the case of the property of being one-one, this mistake is not serious. For what matters is in fact one-one. But in the case of another property, the mistake *is* serious. Identity is all-or-nothing. Most of the relations which matter in survival are, in fact, relations of degree. If we ignore this, we shall be led into quite ill-grounded attitudes and beliefs. (16)

The claim that I have just made—that most of what matters are relations of degree—I have yet to support. Wiggins' case shows only that these relations need not be one-one. The merit of the case is not that it shows this in particular, but that it makes the first break between what

The suggestion is that answering the question of identity is not genuinely essential to answering these other questions, thus making it possible to formulate them in a way that is independent of it.

Whatever is true about the relations between the original person and one of the resulting people, considered only by themselves, is not affected by the presence or absence of the second resulting person.

(But think again about what a dualist says about this case. See Discussion Question 1.)

This analogy doesn't seem very close. But it does seem paradoxical to say that the presence of the second person means that the original person does not survive, when otherwise he would have. Should he try to ensure his survival by taking steps in advance to make sure that one of the hemisphere transplants fails? (See Discussion Question 3.)

A *one-one* relation is a relation that a thing of the relevant kind can have only to exactly one second thing. (The relation between numbers of *x* being half as large as *y* is one-one; while the relation of *x* being smaller than *y* is *one-many,* since a given number *x* is smaller than very many other numbers.)

Parfit's point is that although in normal cases (not including hemisphere transplants and the like) the relation of identity and "the relations that matter in survival" (not yet specified) are alike in being one-one, they differ in that the relation of identity is all or nothing, while the "relations that matter" are (according to him) matters of degree.

matters and identity. The belief that identity *is* what matters is hard to overcome. This is shown in most discussions of the problem cases which actually occur: cases, say, of amnesia or of brain damage. Once Wiggins' case has made one breach in this belief, the rest should be easier to remove.*

To turn to a recent debate: most of the relations which matter can be provisionally referred to under the heading "psychological continuity" (which includes causal continuity). My claim is thus that we use the language of personal identity in order to imply such continuity. This is close to the view that psychological continuity provides a criterion of identity.

Williams has attacked this view with the following argument. Identity is a one-one relation. So any criterion of identity must appeal to a relation which is logically one-one. Psychological continuity is not logically one-one. So it cannot provide a criterion. 17 †

Some writers have replied that it is enough if the relation appealed to is always in fact one-one.

I suggest a slightly different reply. Psychological continuity is a ground for speaking of identity when it is one-one.

If psychological continuity took a one-many or branching form, we should need, I have argued, to abandon the language of identity. So this possibility would not count against this view.

We can make a stronger claim. This possibility would count in its favor.

The view might be defended as follows. Judgments of personal identity have great importance. What gives them their importance is the fact that they imply psychological continuity. This is why, whenever there is such continuity, we ought, if we can, to imply it by making a judgment of identity.

If psychological continuity took a branching form, no coherent set of judgments of identity could correspond to, and thus be used to imply, the branching form of this relation. But what we ought to do, in such a case, is take the importance which would attach to a judgment of identity and attach this importance directly to each limb of the branching relation. So this case helps to show that judgments of personal identity do derive their importance from the fact that they imply psychological continuity. It helps to show that when we can, usefully, speak of identity, this relation is our ground. 18

...

To sum up these remarks: even if psychological continuity is neither logically, nor always in fact, one-one, it can provide a criterion of identity. For this can appeal to the relation of *non-branching* psychological continuity, which is logically one-one.

The criterion might be sketched as follows. "*X* and *Y* are the same person if they are psychologically continuous and there is no person who is contemporary with either and psychologically continuous with the other." We should need to explain what we mean by "psychologically continuous" and say how much continuity the criterion requires. We should then, I think, have described a sufficient condition for speaking of identity.‡

We need to say something more. If we admit that psychological continuity might not be one-one, we need to say what we ought to do if it were not one-one. Otherwise our account would be open to the objections that it is incomplete and arbitrary.

I have suggested that if psychological continuity took a branching form, we ought to speak in a new way, regarding what we describe as having the same significance as identity. This answers these objections.

We can now return to our discussion. We have three remaining aims. One is to suggest a sense of "survive" which does not imply identity. Another is to show that most of what matters in survival are relations of degree. A third is to show that none of these relations needs to be described in a way that presupposes identity.

We can take these aims in the reverse order.

17

 *Psychological continuity* is similar to but more general than the relation of memory suggested by Locke. It is, roughly, a relation in which the psychological states (apparent memories and others) at one stage are caused by and grow out of those at earlier stages in a way that is mostly gradual and continuous, rather than involving jumps or gaps. (See the introduction to this selection.)

18

R It is possible, Parfit is suggesting, for the psychological states of more than one person at a given time to be psychologically continuous with the states of one and the same person at an earlier time (as in the hemisphere transplant case). Thus while identity requires and so implies psychological continuity, psychological continuity can exist without identity. And it is psychological continuity—with or without identity—that is, according to Parfit, what really matters for issues like survival (and also moral responsibility).

---

*Bernard Williams' "The Self and the Future," *Philosophical Review,* 79 (1970), 161–180 [pp. 228–237], is relevant here. He asks the question "Shall I survive?" in a range of problem cases, and he shows how natural it is to believe (1) that this question must have an answer, (2) that the answer must be all-or-nothing, and (3) that there is a "risk" of our reaching the wrong answer. . . .

†"Personal Identity and Individuation," *Proceedings of the Aristotelian Society,* 57 (1956–1957), 229–253; also *Analysis,* 21 (1960–1961), 43–48.

‡But not a necessary condition, for in the absence of psychological continuity bodily identity might be sufficient.

III

The most important particular relation is that involved in memory. This is because it is so easy to believe that its description must refer to identity. . . .

It may be a logical truth that we can only remember our own experiences. But we can frame a new concept for which this is not a logical truth. Let us call this "*q*-memory."

To sketch a definition I am *q*-remembering an experience if (1) I have a belief about a past experience which seems in itself like a memory belief, (2) someone did have such an experience, and (3) my belief is dependent upon this experience in the same way (whatever that is) in which a memory of an experience is dependent upon it.

According to (1) *q*-memories seem like memories. So I *q*-remember *having* experiences. **19**

This may seem to make *q*-memory presuppose identity. One might say, "My apparent memory of *having* an experience is an apparent memory of *my* having an experience. So how could I *q*-remember my having other people's experiences?"

This objection rests on a mistake. When I seem to remember an experience, I do indeed seem to remember *having* it. But it cannot be a part of what I seem to remember about this experience that I, the person who now seems to remember it, am the person who had this experience. **20** That I am is something that I automatically assume. (My apparent memories sometimes come to me simply as the belief that *I* had a certain experience.) But it is something that I am justified in assuming only because I do not in fact have *q*-memories of other people's experiences.

Suppose that I did start to have such *q*-memories. If I did, I should cease to assume that my apparent memories must be about my own experiences. **21** I should come to assess an apparent memory by asking two questions: (1) Does it tell me about a past experience? (2) If so, whose?

Moreover (and this is a crucial point) my apparent memories would now come to me *as* *q*-memories. Consider those of my apparent memories which do come to me simply as beliefs about my past: for example, "I did that." If I knew that I could *q*-remember other people's experiences, these beliefs would come to me in a more guarded form: for example, "Someone—probably I—did that." I might have to work out who it was.

I have suggested that the concept of *q*-memory is coherent. Wiggins' case provides an illustration. The resulting people, in his case, both have apparent memories of living the life of the original person. If they agree that they are not this person, they will have to regard these as only *q*-memories. And when they are asked a question like "Have you heard this music before?" they might have to answer "I am sure that I *q*-remember hearing it. But I am not sure whether I remember hearing it. I am not sure whether it was I who heard it, or the original person."

We can next point out that on our definition every memory is also a *q*-memory. Memories are, simply, *q*-memories of one's own experiences. Since this is so, we could afford now to drop the concept of memory and use in its place the wider concept *q*-memory. . . . **22**

But we must move on. We can next take the relation between an intention and a later action. It may be a logical truth that we can intend to perform only our own actions. But intentions can be redescribed as *q*-intentions. And one person could *q*-intend to perform another person's actions.

Wiggins' case again provides the illustration. We are supposing that neither of the resulting people is the original person. If so, we shall have to agree that the original person can, before the operation, *q*-intend to perform their actions. He might, for example, *q*-intend, as one of them, to continue his present career, and, as the other, to try something new. (I say "*q*-intend *as* one of them" because the phrase "*q*-intend that one of them" would not convey the directness of the relation which is involved. If I intend that someone else should do something, I cannot get him to do it simply by forming this intention. But if I am the original person, and he is one of the resulting people, I can.)

The phrase "*q*-intend *as* one of them" reminds us that we need a sense in which one person can survive as two. But we can first point out that the concepts of *q*-memory and *q*-intention give us our model for the others that we need: thus, a man who can *q*-remember could *q*-recognize, and be a *q*-witness of, what he has never seen; and a man who can *q*-intend could have *q*-ambitions, make *q*-promises, and be *q*-responsible for.

19

Others have used the term "quasi-memory." Condition 3 is vague and would need to be spelled out more fully in a complete account. But each of the persons whose states are psychologically continuous with those of an earlier person (as in the brain transplant case) would have *q*-memories of his experiences—though not memories if there is more than one such person and if memory requires identity.

20

Actual identity is not the sort of thing that could be part of the content of the memory.

21

This assumes that I am somehow able to tell that at least some of my *q*-memories are about other people's experiences (and so aren't simply memories of the normal sort).

22

All actual memories are also *q*-memories, but not all *q*-memories are actual memories.

To put this claim in general terms: many different relations are included within, or are a consequence of, psychological continuity. We describe these relations in ways which presuppose the continued existence of one person. But we could describe them in new ways which do not. [23]

. . . What I shall try to describe is a way of thinking of our own identity through time which is more flexible, and less misleading, than the way in which we now think.

This way of thinking will allow for a sense in which one person can survive as two. A more important feature is that it treats survival as a matter of degree.

IV

We must first show the need for this second feature. I shall use two imaginary examples.

The first is the converse of Wiggins' case: fusion. Just as division serves to show that what matters in survival need not be one-one, so fusion serves to show that it can be a question of degree.

Physically, fusion is easy to describe. Two people come together. While they are unconscious, their two bodies grow into one. One person then wakes up.

The psychology of fusion is more complex. One detail we have already dealt with in the case of the exam. When my mind was reunited, I remembered just having thought out two calculations. The one person who results from a fusion can, similarly, *q*-remember living the lives of the two original people. None of their *q*-memories need be lost. [24]

But some things must be lost. For any two people who fuse together will have different characteristics, different desires, and different intentions. How can these be combined?

We might suggest the following. Some of these will be compatible. These can coexist in the one resulting person. Some will be incompatible. These, if of equal strength, can cancel out, and if of different strengths, the stronger can be made weaker. And all these effects might be predictable.

To give examples—first, of compatibility: I like Palladio and intend to visit Venice. I am about to fuse with a person who likes Giotto and intends to visit Padua. I can know that the one person we shall become will have both tastes and both intentions. Second, of incompatibility: I hate red hair, and always vote Labour. The other person loves red hair, and always votes Conservative. I can know that the one person we shall become will be indifferent to red hair, and a floating voter. [25]

If we were about to undergo a fusion of this kind, would we regard it as death?

Some of us might. This is less absurd than regarding division as death. For after my division the two resulting people will be in every way like me, while after my fusion the one resulting person will not be wholly similar. This makes it easier to say, when faced with fusion, "I shall not survive," thus continuing to regard survival as a matter of all-or-nothing.

This reaction is less absurd. But here are two analogies which tell against it.

First, fusion would involve the changing of some of our characteristics and some of our desires. But only the very self-satisfied would think of this as death. Many people welcome treatments with these effects. [26]

Second, someone who is about to fuse can have, beforehand, just as much "intentional control" over the actions of the resulting individual as someone who is about to marry can have, beforehand, over the actions of the resulting couple. And the choice of a partner for fusion can be just as well considered as the choice of a marriage partner. The two original people can make sure (perhaps by "trial fusion") that they do have compatible characters, desires, and intentions. [27]

I have suggested that fusion, while not clearly survival, is not clearly failure to survive, and hence that what matters in survival can have degrees.

To reinforce this claim we can now turn to a second example. This is provided by certain imaginary beings. These beings are just like ourselves except that they reproduce by a process of natural division.

We can illustrate the histories of these imagined beings with the aid of a diagram. The lines on the diagram represent the spatiotemporal paths which would be traced out by the bodies of these beings. We can call each single line (like the double line) a "branch"; and we can call the whole structure a "tree." And let us suppose that each "branch" corresponds to what is thought of as the life of one individual. These individuals are referred to as "A," "B + 1," and so forth.

In order to have future-oriented *q*-states (such as intending that one of the persons who results from the transplants of the hemispheres of my brain goes on with my career and the other tries something new), I seemingly must have some way now of specifying each of the relevant future persons that those later persons will be able to recognize and apply to themselves when the time comes, or else the intention will be ineffective. Each of the future persons must be able to tell which specific things he or she is supposed to do according to the original intention. It isn't very clear how this would work.

This is a little tricky. The fused person can remember each of the previous people doing whatever they did. But can he remember doing those things *himself*—even though this would require him to have been in two different places and to have had seemingly incompatible experiences at the very same time?

STOP Think carefully about these examples, inventing some more of your own. How clear is it what states the fused person would have?

Would anyone welcome a treatment that changed his characteristics by melding them with those of an arbitrarily chosen other person in the way indicated?

STOP How good an analogy is this? You at least have to imagine a marriage in which every choice and decision is made jointly.

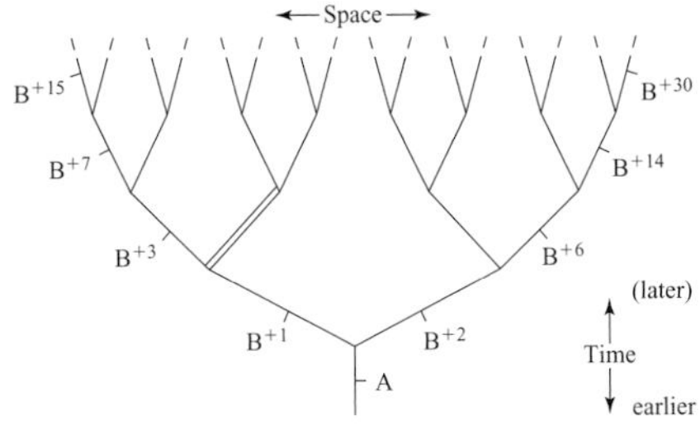

Now, each single division is an instance of Wiggins' case. So A's relation to both B + 1 and B + 2 is just as good as survival. But what of A's relation to B + 30?

I said earlier that what matters in survival could be provisionally referred to as "psychological continuity." I must now distinguish this relation from another, which I shall call "psychological connectedness."

Let us say that the relation between a *q*-memory and the experience *q*-remembered is a "direct" relation. Another "direct" relation is that which holds between a *q*-intention and the *q*-intended action. A third is that which holds between different expressions of some lasting *q*-characteristic.

"Psychological connectedness," as I define it, requires the holding of these direct psychological relations. "Connectedness" is not transitive, since these relations are not transitive. Thus, if *X q*-remembers most of *Y*'s life, and *Y q*-remembers most of *Z*'s life, it does not follow that *X q*-remembers most of *Z*'s life. And if *X* carries out the *q*-intentions of *Y,* and *Y* carries out the *q*-intentions of *Z,* it does not follow that *X* carries out the *q*-intentions of *Z.*

"Psychological continuity," in contrast, only requires overlapping chains of direct psychological relations. So "continuity" is transitive. (28)

To return to our diagram. A is psychologically continuous with B + 30. There are between the two continuous chains of overlapping relations. Thus, A has *q*-intentional control over B + 2, B + 2 has *q*-intentional control over B + 6, and so on up to B + 30. Or B + 30 can *q*-remember the life of B + 14, B + 14 can *q*-remember the life of B + 6, and so on back to A.*

A, however, need *not* be psychologically connected to B + 30. Connectedness requires direct relations. And if these beings are like us, A cannot stand in such relations to every individual in his indefinitely long "tree." *Q*-memories will weaken with the passage of time, and then fade away. *Q*-ambitions, once fulfilled, will be replaced by others. *Q*-characteristics will gradually change. In general, A stands in fewer and fewer direct psychological relations to an individual in his "tree" the more remote that individual is. And if the individual is (like B + 30) sufficiently remote, there may be between the two *no* direct psychological relations.

Now that we have distinguished the general relations of psychological continuity and psychological connectedness, I suggest that connectedness is a more important element in survival. As a claim about our own survival, this would need more arguments than I have space to give. But it seems clearly true for my imagined beings. A is as close psychologically to B + 1 as I today am to myself tomorrow. A is as distant from B + 30 as I am from my great-great-grandson. (29)

Even if connectedness is not more important than continuity, the fact that one of these is a relation of degree is enough to show that what matters in survival can have degrees. And in any case the two relations are quite different. So our imagined beings would need a way of thinking in which this difference is recognized.

V

What I propose is this.

First, A can think of any individual, anywhere in his "tree," as "a descendant self." This phrase implies psychological continuity. Similarly, any later individual can think of any earlier individual on the single path which connects him to A as "an ancestral self."

Since psychological continuity is transitive, "being an ancestral self of" and "being a descendant self of" are also transitive.

To imply psychological connectedness I suggest the phrases "one of my future selves" and "one of my past selves." (30)

These are the phrases with which we can describe Wiggins' case. For having past and future selves is, what we needed, a way of continuing to exist which does not imply identity through time. The original person does, in this sense, survive Wiggins' operation: the two resulting people are his later selves. And they can each refer to him as

*The chain of continuity must run in one direction of time. B + 2 is not, in the sense I intend, psychologically continuous with B + 1.

(28)

A *transitive* relation is one such that if A has it to B and B has it to C, then A has it to C. Thus the relation of being a biological ancestor is transitive, while the relation of being someone's mother is not: if A is the mother of B and B is the mother of C, then A is *not* the mother of C. (See the introduction to this selection for more about the difference between psychological continuity and psychological connectedness.)

(29)

Not perhaps the best comparison, since there is of course no psychological continuity between a person and his children, grandchildren, and so on.

(30)

So being one of my *future* selves requires more than just being one of my *descendant* selves, as Parfit explains these concepts: all future selves are descendant selves, but not all descendant selves are future selves. The relation of being a descendant self is transitive: if B is a descendant self of A and C is a descendant self of B, then C is a descendant self of A. But the relation of being a future self is not transitive: B may be a future self of A and C a future self of B, without C being a future self of A (if both the relation between B and A and that between C and B are psychologically direct enough, but that between C and A is too indirect with few if any direct psychological relations).

"my past self." (They can share a past self without being the same self as each other.)

Since psychological connectedness is not transitive, and is a matter of degree, the relations "being a past self of" and "being a future self of" should themselves be treated as relations of degree. We allow for this series of descriptions: "my most recent self," "one of my earlier selves," "one of my distant selves," "hardly one of *my* past selves (I can only *q*-remember a few of his experiences)," and, finally, "not in any way one of *my* past selves—just an ancestral self."

This way of thinking would clearly suit our first imagined beings. But let us now turn to a second kind of being. These reproduce by fusion as well as by division. And let us suppose that they fuse every autumn and divide every spring. This yields the following diagram:

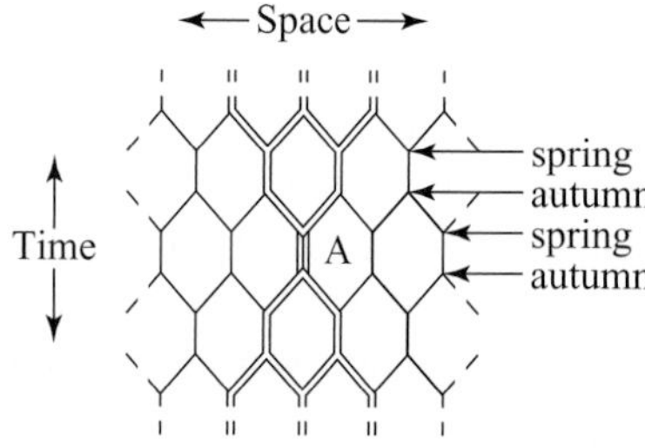

If A is the individual whose life is represented by the three-lined "branch," the two-lined "tree" represents those lives which are psychologically continuous with A's life. (It can be seen that each individual has his own "tree," which overlaps with many others.)

For the imagined beings in this second world, the phrases "an ancestral self" and "a descendant self" would cover too much to be of much use. (There may well be pairs of dates such that every individual who ever lived before the first date was an ancestral self of every individual who ever will live after the second date.) Conversely, since the lives of each individual last for only half a year, the word "I" would cover too little to do all of the work which it does for us. So part of this work would have to be done, for these second beings, by talk about past and future selves. (31)

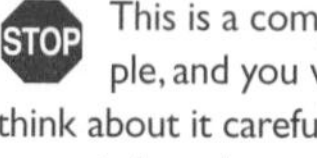

This is a complicated example, and you will need to think about it carefully. If A is concerned about his own survival, what exactly is he concerned about (that is, what would it take to satisfy this concern)?

...

But let us look, finally, at a third kind of being. In this world there is neither division nor union. There are a number of everlasting bodies, which gradually change in appearance. And direct psychological relations, as before, hold only over limited periods of time. This can be illustrated with a third diagram. . . . In this diagram the two shadings represent the degrees of psychological connectedness to their two central points.

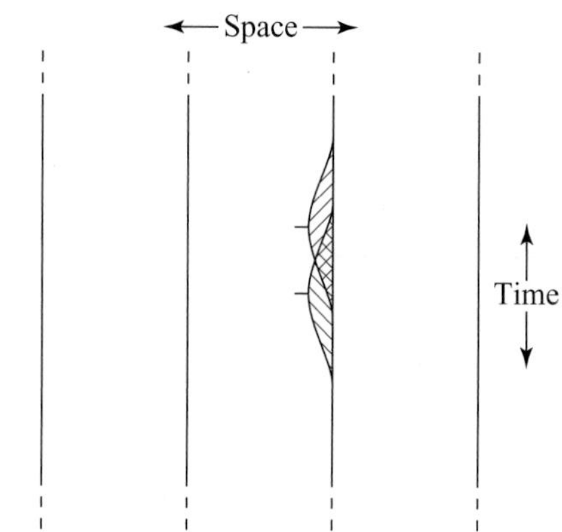

These beings could not use the way of thinking that we have proposed. Since there is no branching of psychological continuity, they would have to regard themselves as immortal. It might be said that this is what they are. But there is, I suggest, a better description.

Our beings would have one reason for thinking of themselves as immortal. The parts of each "line" are all psychologically continuous. But the parts of each "line" are not all psychologically connected. Direct psychological relations hold only between those parts which are close to each other in time. This gives our beings a reason for *not* thinking of each "line" as corresponding to one single life. For if they did, they would have no way of implying these direct relations. When a speaker says, for example, "I spent a period doing such and such," his hearers would not be entitled to assume that the speaker has any memories of this period, that his character then and now are in any way similar, that he is now carrying out any of the plans or intentions which he then had, and so forth. Because the word "I" would carry none of these implications, it would not have for these "immortal" beings the usefulness which it has for us. (32)

That is, "I" (and "me" and "myself"), if used in the way indicated, would not capture for these beings the important part of what is captured by our use of these terms. I care about *my* past and *my* future (picked out as cases in which these terms, as ordinarily used, would correctly apply). But, Parfit is suggesting, the beings in question would not care (or at least would have no reason to care) about their distant pasts and futures where all relations of psychological connectedness to their present selves are gone.

To gain a better way of thinking, we must revise the way of thinking that we proposed above. The revision is this. The distinction between successive selves can be made by reference, not to the branching of psychological continuity, but to the degrees of psychological connectedness. Since this connectedness is a matter of degree, the drawing of these distinctions can be left to the choice of the speaker and be allowed to vary from context to context.

On this way of thinking, the word "I" can be used to imply the greatest degree of psychological connectedness. When the connections are reduced, when there has been any marked change of character or style of life, or any marked loss of memory, our imagined beings would say, "It was not I who did that, but an earlier self." They could then describe in what ways, and to what degree, they are related to this earlier self. 33

This revised way of thinking would suit not only our "immortal" beings. It is also the way in which we ourselves could think about our lives. And it is, I suggest, surprisingly natural.

One of its features, the distinction between successive selves, has already been used by several writers. To give an example, from Proust: "we are incapable, while we are in love, of acting as fit predecessors of the next persons who, when we are in love no longer, we shall presently have become. . . ."*

Although Proust distinguished between successive selves, he still thought of one person as being these different selves. This we would not do on the way of thinking that I propose. If I say, "It will not be me, but one of my future selves," I do not imply that I will be that future self. He is one of my later selves, and I am one of his earlier selves. There is no underlying person who we both are.

To point out another feature of this way of thinking. When I say, "There is no person who we both are," I am only giving my decision. Another person could say, "It will be you," thus deciding differently. There is no question of either of these decisions being a mistake. Whether to say "I," or "one of my future selves," or "a descendant self" is entirely a matter of choice. The matter of fact, which must be agreed, is only whether the disjunction applies. (The question "Are X and Y the same person?" thus becomes "Is X *at least* an ancestral [or descendant] self of Y?") 34

VI

I have tried to show that what matters in the continued existence of a person are, for the most part, relations of degree. And I have proposed a way of thinking in which this would be recognized.

I shall end by suggesting two consequences and asking one question.

It is sometimes thought to be especially rational to act in our own best interests. But I suggest that the principle of self-interest has no force. There are only two genuine competitors in this particular field. One is the principle of biased rationality: do what will best achieve what you actually want. The other is the principle of impartiality: do what is in the best interests of everyone concerned. 35

The apparent force of the principle of self-interest derives, I think, from these two other principles.

The principle of self-interest is normally supported by the principle of biased rationality. This is because most people care about their own future interests.

Suppose that this prop is lacking. Suppose that a man does not care what happens to him in, say, the more distant future. To such a man, the principle of self-interest can only be propped up by an appeal to the principle of impartiality. We must say, "Even if you don't care, you ought to take what happens to you then equally into account." But for this, as a special claim, there seem to me no good arguments. It can only be supported as part of the general claim, "You ought to take what happens to everyone equally into account."

The special claim tells a man to grant an *equal* weight to all the parts of his future. The argument for this can only be that all the parts of his future are *equally* parts of *his* future. This is true. But it is a truth too superficial to bear the weight of the argument. (To give an analogy: The unity of a nation is, in its nature, a matter of degree. It is therefore only a superficial truth that all of a man's compatriots are *equally* his compatriots. This truth cannot support a good argument for nationalism.)† 36

I have suggested that the principle of self-interest has no strength of its own. If this is so, there is no special problem in the fact that what we ought to do can be against our interests. There is only the general problem that it may not be what we want to do.

The second consequence which I shall mention is implied in the first. Egoism, the fear not

33

Notice that this is a stronger requirement than we impose on the use of "I" (and related terms) even in our own situation: we often still use "I" to refer to a being with a seriously different character or lifestyle or even the one who exists or will exist after a serious loss of memory.

34

How plausible is this suggestion? Is it really just a matter of *choice* whether a future person with the same living body that you have but with a very different character or lifestyle is still you, is a future self, or is merely a descendant self—as opposed to saying that it is just a fact that the future person is still identical with you despite the various changes?

35

The difference between the first principle and the principle of self-interest is that "what you actually want" will normally include things that are in the interests of others and will not necessarily include things pertaining to your very remote future or descendant selves.

36

Parfit is saying that the fact that your distant future selves are still your selves gives you no good reasons to care about them as much as you do in fact care about your closer selves—or even, in the extreme case, to care about them at all. (See Discussion Question 4.)

* *Within a Budding Grove* (London, 1949), I, 226 (my own translation).

†The unity of a nation we seldom take for more than what it is. This is partly because we often think of nations, not as units, but in a more complex way. If we thought of ourselves in the way that I proposed, we might be less likely to take our own identity for more than what it is. We are, for example, sometimes told, "It is irrational to act against your own interests. After all, it will be you who will regret it." To this we could reply, "No, not me. Not even one of my future selves. Just a descendant self."

of near but of distant death, the regret that so much of one's *only* life should have gone by—these are not, I think, wholly natural or instinctive. They are all strengthened by the beliefs about personal identity which I have been attacking. If we give up these beliefs, they should be weakened. 37

...

37 The suggestion is that the concern about whether you will survive in the future should diminish as your future selves become psychologically more and more remote from your present self, perhaps eventually disappearing altogether. (See Discussion Question 4.)

Discussion Questions

1. Suppose that your brain is divided, and half of it is transplanted into another body, while the remaining half is left in your present body, so that there are two persons after the operation. Does the person whose body is your original body have a stronger claim to be identical to you than the other person, and if so, why? Suppose instead that both halves are transplanted into new bodies. If consciousness involves a separate immaterial mind or soul, either (a) it somehow divides too, (b) it goes with one of the two halves and a new mind or soul somehow emerges for the other, or (c) it is destroyed, and both of the resulting persons have new minds or souls. Here the interesting case is (b): Does the (supposed) fact that one person has your original soul and the other does not give the one who does a stronger claim to be identical with you? Why or why not?
2. How would it seem from the standpoint of each of the separate streams of consciousness when the two streams that have been voluntarily divided in order to do two math problems are reunited (or are there such standpoints)? Would I still remember the two separate streams of consciousness *as separate*? Do you ever think about two things at the same time (perhaps a present conversation and a problem you are mulling in the background)? Might the combined memory of this be something like the memory in Parfit's case?
3. Do you survive if both parts of your brain are successfully transplanted into two new bodies? If you knew that the two parts of your brain were going to be transplanted, would it be reasonable for you to pay someone to destroy one of them or otherwise prevent the success of the operation, in order to bring it about that you survive? If you think that you survive when both are transplanted, would it be rational for you to pay to have such a transplant done in order to increase your overall chances of survival (assuming that the risks involved are negligible)?
4. Suppose that you have good reason to believe that you will be alive 20 years into the future, and that you are in a position to take steps to make your future self happier, safer, and so forth. Should your degree of concern for that future self depend on how closely connected its psychological states will be to yours: how much of your experience it will remember, how similar its character traits and values will be, and so forth? Why or why not? Is there a point in the future (defined in terms of psychological connectedness and continuity, not time) when it is no longer reasonable for you to care *at all* about the well-being of your future self?
5. Though Parfit mentions responsibility in a couple of places, he says very little about it. What are the implications of his view for the question of when people can be justly held morally responsible (and accordingly rewarded or punished) for the actions of earlier people? Consider here the original transplant case, together with the cases depicted in the three diagrams. Could responsibility be a matter of degree in the same way that, on Parfit's view, survival is?

Concluding Dialogue on Personal Identity

Well this is a very puzzling issue! As you know, I care a lot about survival, maybe even more than most people. I often say, at least half seriously, that I would like to live—that is, survive—forever, if that were possible. But now I'm not sure just what specifically it is that I want. What would have to be true of some future person for him (could it be her?) to be identical to me? And, even more fundamentally, what sort of an entity am I anyway?

Maybe we can start with the one view in the reading that clearly can't be right—namely Locke's view that a later person is identical with an earlier person if and only if the later person has memories of events in the life of the earlier person. As almost everyone agrees, Reid is right that Locke's view is unacceptable on sheerly logical grounds. It would have the absurd consequence that the old general is identical to the young officer who captured the standard and the young officer is identical to the boy who was flogged, but the general isn't identical to the boy. Genuine identity just can't work like that!

I'm not going to try to defend Locke's main account, at least not without a lot of revision. But there are other things he says that seem to me to be right. One is that a *person* is not the same thing as a certain kind of *animal,* such as a certain member of the species *homo sapiens*. From one standpoint, I am such an animal—or at least am intimately connected with one. And if you told me that this specific animal would be alive at some time in the future, that would surely make me more optimistic about whether I will in fact still survive at that time. But it nonetheless wouldn't be a *guarantee* that I would survive. The animal might survive in what people call "a permanent vegetative state." I also think that Locke is right that it might be associated (if that is the right word) with a person whose memories, desires, intentions, character traits, habits, and so on are entirely different from mine. And in either of these cases, it doesn't seem to me that *I* would in fact have survived.

If you're not just an animal, maybe you're an animal with an immaterial soul or mind. But while I know you have at least some sympathy with mind-body dualism, that won't help here either, if Locke is right. He argues that your immaterial Cartesian soul or mind, if you have one, could also continue to exist, but contain memories (and also other kinds of psychological states) that would make it be—or be the host of or whatever the exact relation is—a different person.

We might have a solution if we could believe both that persons really do have a soul or mind, and also that the consciousness associated with it can't change so much as to become that of an entirely different person. But I have to admit that there is no real argument for especially the second of those things.

All these problems seem to point to a view at least in the direction of Locke's *psychological* account of personal identity. According to such a view, what makes two individuals the same person is something about the relations between their psychological states. This is in fact by far the most popular general sort of account. To get the best version of it, we need to change Locke's account in at least two ways. First, we need to add psychological ingredients over and above memories, adding further elements like the ones you just mentioned: desires, intentions, character traits, habits, and the like. Just memories aren't enough, since these other things are obviously also relevant to identity. And second, we need a more complicated relation among these—something like what Parfit refers to as *psychological continuity*—in which there are overlapping elements of all these kinds that connect together the various stages of a person's life. This at least helps with the case of the boy-soldier-general, since it is reasonable to suppose that the boy and the general will be connected by a series of stages involving overlapping elements of these kinds.

A relation of continuity like this could be stronger or weaker, depending on how many elements are involved and how long they individually persist and how much they overlap, and it isn't clear how strong it needs to be for personal identity. Merely a weak relation of continuity, one with only a very few overlapping psychological states, doesn't seem good enough. It also seems very plausible that some aspects of the stronger relation that Parfit called *psychological connectedness* are also required: at least *some* psychological elements (maybe basic character traits) that are the same all the way through the sequence of stages seem to be needed. We could pursue that further, but let's not: let's just stipulate that there is some relation of continuity and connectedness of this general sort—we can refer to it as *adequate psychological continuity*—that is strong enough for personal identity *if* (and it's a big if) this general sort of view is going to work at all.

OK. So the main question then is this: is what it is for a future person to be (numerically) identical with me just the same thing as that person being "adequately psychologically continuous" with me? And furthermore—what we've been assuming so far to be the same question—is what we *care* about when we care about *surviving* into the future fully captured by the idea of there being a future person to which we stand in this relation of "adequate psychological continuity"? Here I think we should add explicitly what most later philosophers tend to take for granted: that this relation has to be *causally grounded* in a way that makes it more than a mere accident or coincidence that it holds. (But just what specific sort of causal connection is required—what it is for the causal relation to be "of the right kind," as people say—is something we'll have to talk about more later.)

That last point is certainly right. It surely isn't enough for identity—or survival—if some later person happens by a sheer fluke to have a set of states that are psychologically continuous with or even identical to mine. A good way to pursue this issue is to look at the cases that

Williams describes. We can assume that in the case he begins with, the relation between the original person A and what Williams calls the B-body person is strong enough to constitute what we're calling "adequate psychological continuity," and similarly for other cases that work in the same way. Indeed Williams seems to suppose that the two persons in question are exactly the same psychologically at the last moment for the original A and the first moment after the procedure for the so-called B-body person.

So the question raised by that case is whether there being a later person related to you in that specific way would be enough to constitute identity and survival—whether in the first of his cases the B-body person is identical to the original A, so that A has survived. Williams is of two minds about this, but seems to lean to the view that is reflected in his second account of the case: that the A-body person is still A and the B-body person is still B, despite the total psychological change in each of them.

I can see why Williams might be a bit unsure, since the case strains our intuitions so much. But if the psychological change in the A-body person is supposed to be as total as that—so that nothing of A's original psychology survives (unless A and B just happen by chance to be the same in some respects)—I don't think that I would have survived in a meaningful way if the same thing happened to me. Just the fact that my previous *body* is still alive afterwards isn't enough. If, in the original Williams case, the B-body dies for some reason as a result of the procedure, but the A-body lives, I don't think that the original A has survived.

I agree, and so I think would most recent philosophers who have dealt with this issue. But we should note that there are some who think that a person is after all nothing but an animal of a certain sort. For them, if the animal has survived, then the person has survived. I don't have any real inclination to defend that view, however. I think what Locke says about it is right.

I agree. But the problem is that if I am the original A (before the procedure), then the existence of the B-body person (after the procedure) also doesn't seem to me to be enough for my survival, at least not clearly so. One way to see this is to notice that there is nothing about the described procedure that would rule out producing even more people that are adequately psychologically continuous to the very same degree with the original A: a C-body person, a D-body person, and so on, all produced in essentially the same way as the B-body person. These can't *all* be identical to the original A, since they obviously aren't identical to each other. But then there is no reason to think that *any* of them are, since they are all related to the original A in exactly the same way. But an even stronger reason for thinking that the original A isn't identical to the B-body person after the procedure is that there seems to be no reason why we couldn't produce beings like the B-body person (and also the C-body person, and so on), while still leaving the original A psychologically unaltered: we copy the psychological information and put it into the other bodies, but don't erase it in A. And then, surely, it is the subsequent A-body person who is identical with the original A, and the others are just *duplicates*.

Of course, someone who agrees with the general psychological approach to identity could accept everything you just said by insisting that the causal relation in the other cases isn't "of the right kind" to preserve the right kind of psychological continuity—maybe, as Williams suggests, because the causal chain is partly outside the bodies of the individuals in question. But there might also be some diehard defenders of the view that *only* the psychological relations matter. They would say that the subsequent, unaltered A-body person has no more claim to be the original A than do any of the others, that the exact nature of the causal relation doesn't really matter. Such a person might want to regard this version of the example as a case of *fission,* like those discussed by Parfit.

I don't see how that can be right. The one thing that seems clear is that if we have the same body, the same soul or mind (if there is one), and adequate psychological continuity, then we have identity and genuine survival. That means that in the case where A is unaltered, it is the subsequent A-body person who is identical to the original A and not the others. And this seems to me to suggest strongly that if the A-body dies during the procedure and the others survive, then person A has in fact died and doesn't survive. I don't see how any of the others can be identical to A in that case when this wouldn't have been so if A had survived. (Though I know there are some who would say this, at least in the case where there is only one other such person—advocates of the so-called "best candidate" view.)

Having raised the issue of fission, we should look at Parfit's cases, starting with the one that might someday turn out to be a real-life case: the one that involves transplanting hemispheres of the brain. The initial question to ask, I think, is what to say about the case where half of your brain is transplanted to a new body and the other half, along with your original body, is destroyed. Are you identical with the resulting person, so that you have survived? Parfit seems to think that the answer to this question is clearly "yes."

I know he says this, but I don't think that answer is as obviously right as he does. It all seems to me to depend on exactly what the relation is between the two halves of the brain and the person's consciousness. We really don't know very much about that. But suppose it were like this: suppose that my consciousness is directly associated with (or lodged in or however exactly we should put it) only one half of my brain, with the other serving normally as something like backup storage. Then if one half is transplanted and the other destroyed, it seems to me to matter for the issues of identity and survival which one is which. If it's the "backup" half that is transplanted, then even if it is now able to take over the primary brain functions, I'm not at all sure that *I* have survived and am identical with the result. Maybe this is just a way of transferring information, as in the Williams cases, and the result is a new person. If I have an immaterial soul or mind, maybe it dies with the previously primary half of my brain. Maybe a *new* soul or mind is created or comes to be connected with the old backup, which is now functioning in quite a different way than it did before. And then the resulting person again seems to me to be a duplicate and not me. I'm not saying that this is the way things actually work, only that it might be, so that we can't really be sure what to say about the case you describe.

Wow, you really are a closet dualist! So in Parfit's main case, in which *both* halves are transplanted, you would say that it *might* be that one of the resulting persons (the one who gets the "primary" hemisphere) is you, and the other one (the one who gets the "backup" hemisphere) isn't. But of course your speculation might be wrong: it might be that in the normal, pre-transplant case, the two hemispheres function together, with neither being primary, even though each half is still capable of doing the job alone if they are separated. If it works like that—and if we don't worry about the very real possibility that some functions (such as speech) and perhaps also some other psychological information are found in only one hemisphere and not the other—then we have the case that Parfit wants, in which it seems to him that each of the resulting persons has the same claim to be identical to the original you. What do you say about *that* case?

Even then it isn't clear to me that Parfit's view is the right one. It all depends on how my mind or my stream of consciousness comes into the picture. If I have an immaterial soul or mind, does it also somehow split into two or does it perhaps stay with one of the hemispheres? If the second of these possibilities is the right one, then the person who gets my original soul or mind has, I think, a stronger claim to be me. But even if nothing like a separate mind or soul is involved, I still think it is worth asking what it would be like, subjectively or phenomenologically, to have this operation done, assuming—which may be practically unlikely but surely not impossible—that consciousness continues through the whole procedure.

We know what Parfit would say about what it would be like. It would be like his case where the connection between the two hemispheres can be voluntarily broken and then restored, allowing the two halves to work on two separate tasks for a while—except that the separation would be permanent.

But again that is not the only possible picture. Here's a different version of the voluntary separation case. When the two hemispheres are separated, my original stream of consciousness goes on as if nothing has happened, presumably in one of the hemispheres. But also, presumably in the other hemisphere, a *new* stream of consciousness starts up. It has lots of the same apparent memories and other information, reflects the same character traits, and so on, but it is as though it had been asleep and had just awakened at that moment. It would remember that various things had been going on in the main stream of consciousness just before, but it wouldn't remember actually *experiencing* those things in a way that flows into its own consciousness. And then when the reconnection takes place, this new stream of consciousness would just stop, as though the person had gone to sleep, and the original stream of consciousness would be suddenly flooded with new information together with memories of conscious processes that would seem as though they were those of another person because they didn't occur in that stream of consciousness.

That's pretty creative! But, OK, *maybe* it could be like that. And if so, I can see why you would want to say that in the double transplant case, the one who is identical with you is the one with the continued stream of consciousness (or the one whose consciousness *would* have been the continued one if consciousness had continued throughout the procedure—assuming that this is a meaningful thing to say!). And the one whose consciousness begins fresh at that point isn't you. This resembles your "primary"-"backup" view of the two hemispheres, though it doesn't really require that things work that way. But couldn't it also work the way Parfit thinks it does, with the two streams of consciousness just continuing smoothly from the original one—and also rejoining, though not quite so smoothly (that part is really pretty hard to imagine) in the voluntary disconnection version?

I guess I'm not convinced that Parfit's version really *is* possible. But suppose that it is. Then I think we really do get the result he is after. In the case where the hemispheres are separately transplanted, *neither* of the two resulting persons is identical to me (since they obviously aren't identical to each other). And yet their existence seems to give me all I could want for survival (assuming again that no important information or abilities are located in only one hemisphere and so are lost to the other person). So the basic point that *survival* in the relevant sense doesn't necessarily require a subsequent person with whom I am *identical* still seems correct, given all that. And something of the same sort could be said about the more complicated fission case and about the fusion case, assuming again (which I guess I doubt) that these are really possible: in these cases too, I might have all that I could want for survival without identity.

Of course Parfit is not really claiming, at least not in any very strong way, that the cases beyond the dual brain transplant case really are possible. He's just using these alleged possibilities to suggest a different way of thinking about survival and about self-interest—about a person's concern for his own future self. Thus the example that really matters is the last one: the one with the immortal bodies whose minds involve degrees of psychological connectedness that diminish to zero over time. And his point is that such a being might not care very much (if at all) about stages of his continued existence that are very distant in the future and with which he has no psychological connectedness at all. He might view those stages as involving entirely distinct "descendant selves"—and might even extend this way of thinking to intermediate "future selves," who have only relatively weak degrees of psychological connectedness with his present self. And while he might care more about these future selves than about the descendant ones, that concern still might not be as great as that which he has for his present and near-future self.

All that is a little hard to imagine, at least for me. But the main point, I think, is that we are not at all like that. Though it can vary from case to case, normal people have a reasonably high degree of psychological connectedness, not just continuity, throughout their lives. They aren't like these imaginary beings and, at least when other psychological properties are brought in, they aren't like the case of the boy-officer-general either. Where that is so and where the body or at least the brain is the same, we have the sort of survival and ongoing identity that most people want—certainly it's what I want. Anything less than that isn't good enough.

But I don't think you are saying—are you?—that nothing less than that would suffice for personal identity? What you are really saying is that it's survival in that robust sense and not mere identity that matters to you. You could still agree with Parfit that there could be cases of survival without identity—and perhaps also of identity without survival, since there is nothing that precludes saying that the eternal beings with diminishing psychological connectedness are nonetheless identical as persons throughout their history.

I suppose. One way to put Parfit's point, I guess, is to say that if we don't view the eternal beings with diminishing psychological connectedness as being the same persons throughout their histories, then it will be at least somewhat arbitrary where to draw the lines between different persons within the history of one such being. So the most reasonable view will be that each of those beings is after all the same person throughout its history. In that case, personal identity as such might not be very important in relation to the kind of survival we care about. But, contrary to what he seems to suggest, nothing about *that* result shows that there is anything irrational about wanting to survive in a stronger way or about my caring very strongly about the future persons whose existence would constitute such strong survival in my own case. What I really want, I think, is to be one of Parfit's eternal beings, but with adequate psychological continuity (including a reasonably high degree of connectedness) throughout!

Are Human Actions Genuinely Free?

Hard Determinism

Robert Blatchford

Robert Blatchford (1851–1943) was an English journalist and politician who helped found the British Labor Party and was a strong advocate of socialism. In this selection, he defends hard determinism on what he regards as essentially common-sense grounds, arguing that everything that a person does is determined by the combination of heredity and environment, and hence that no one is ever free to do other than he or she does, or morally responsible, or deserving of either blame or praise. His argument is not dependent in any important way on the general thesis of causal determinism.

Blatchford's motive for advocating this conclusion is intensely practical: he wants to convince us that even the "bottom dogs" in society, people who may seem utterly beyond redemption and entirely unworthy of sympathy or concern, are not responsible for the way they are and so do not deserve the punishments and other negative treatment they receive. His argument is perhaps best understood as a pair of challenges to other views: what alternative is there to an action being rigidly determined by heredity and environment, and how can an action that is determined in this way be free (in the sense required for moral responsibility)?

A Defense of Hard Determinism, from *Not Guilty: A Defense of the Bottom Dog*

The Author's Apology

. . . I claim that men should not be classified as good and bad, but as fortunate and unfortunate; that they should be pitied, and not blamed; helped instead of being punished.

I claim that since we do not hold a man worthy of praise for being born beautiful, nor of blame for being born ugly, neither should we hold him worthy of praise for being born virtuous, nor of blame for being born vicious.

I base this claim upon the self-evident and undeniable fact that man has no part in the creation of his own nature.

I shall be told this means that no man is answerable for his own acts.

That is exactly what it does mean.

But, it will be urged, every man has a free will to act as he chooses; and to deny that is to imperil all law and order, all morality and discipline.

I deny both these inferences, and I ask the reader to hear my case patiently, and to judge it on its merits.

. . .

From *Not Guilty: A Defense of the Bottom Dog* (New York: Boni and Liveright, 1918).

Where Do Our Natures Come From?

. . . I deal with heredity before environment, because it is needful to take them one at a time, and heredity comes first; as birth before schooling.

But we must not fall into the bad habit of thinking of heredity and environment apart from each other, for it is *both,* and not either of them that make man's character.

It is often said that neither heredity nor environment accounts for a man's conduct. And that is true. But it is true, also, that heredity *and* environment account for every quality in the human "make-up." . . .

Now, what do we mean by "heredity"?

Heredity is "descent," or "breed." Heredity, as the word is here used, means those qualities which are handed down from one generation to the next. It means those qualities which a new generation inherits from the generation from whom it descends. It means all that "is bred in the bone." If a man inherits a Grecian nose, a violent temper, well-knit muscles, a love of excitement, or a good ear for music, from his father or mother, that quality or feature is part of his heredity. It is "bred in him."

Every quality a child possesses at the moment of birth, *every* quality of body or of mind, is inherited from his parents and their ancestors. And the whole of those qualities—which *are* the child—are what we call "heredity."

No child brings into the world one single quality of body or mind that has not been handed down to it by its ancestors.

. . .

Now, since a child inherits some qualities from its father and some from its mother, it follows that if the father and mother are different from each other, the child must differ from both, and yet resemble both. For he will inherit from the father qualities which the mother has not inherited from her ancestors, and he will inherit from the mother qualities which the father did not inherit from his ancestors. So the child will resemble both parents, without being an exact copy of either. It "varies" from both parents by inheriting from each.

. . .

Environment

What is environment?

When we speak of a man's environment we mean his surroundings, his experiences; all that he sees, hears, feels, and learns, from the instant that the lamp of life is kindled to the instant when the light goes out.

By environment we mean everything that develops or modifies the child or the man for good or for ill.

We mean his mother's milk; the home, and the state of life into which he was born. We mean the nurse who suckles him, the children he plays with, the school he learns in, the air he breathes, the water he drinks, the food he eats. We mean the games he plays, the work he does, the sights he sees, the sounds he hears. We mean the girls he loves, the woman he marries, the children he rears, the wages he earns. We mean the sickness that tries him, the griefs that sear him, the friends who aid and the enemies who wound him. We mean all his hopes and fears, his victories and defeats; his faiths and his disillusionments. We mean all the harm he does, and all the help he gives; all the ideals that beckon him, all the temptations that lure him; all his weepings and laughter, his kissings and cursings, his lucky hits and unlucky blunders: everything he does and suffers under the sun.

I go into all this detail because we must remember that everything that happens to a man, everything that influences him, is a part of his environment.

It is a common mistake to think of environment in a narrow sense, as though environment implied no more than poverty or riches. Everything outside our skin belongs to our environment.

Let us think of it again. Education is environment; religion is environment; business and politics are environment; all the ideals, conventions, and prejudices of race and class are environment; literature, science, and the Press are environment; music, history, and sport are environment; beauty and ugliness are environment; example and precept are environment; war and travel and commerce are environment; sunshine and ozone, honour and dishonour, failure and success, are environment; love is environment.

I stress and multiply examples because the power of environment is so tremendous that we can hardly over-rate its importance.

A child is not born with a conscience; but with the rudiments of a conscience: the materials from which a conscience may or may not be developed—by environment.

A child is not born with capacities, but only with potentialities, or possibilities, for good or evil, which may or may not be developed—by environment.

A child is born absolutely without knowledge. Every atom of knowledge he gets must be got from his environment.

...

How Heredity and Environment Work

There are many who have some understanding of heredity and of environment when taken separately who fail to realise their effects upon each other.

The common cause of the stumbling is easy to remove.

It is often said that two men are differently affected by the same environment, or what seems to be the same environment, and that therefore there must be some power in men to "overcome" their environment.

. . . the contest between a man and his environment is really a contest between heredity and environment. . . .

A given environment will affect two different men differently, because their heredity is different.

...

Let us take the case of two children. One has bad and one good heredity. One is a healthy baby, born of moral stock. The other is a degenerate, born of immoral stock. We will call the healthy baby Dick, and the degenerate baby Harry. (1)

They are taken at birth into an environment of theft, drunkenness, and vice. They are taught to lie, to steal, and to drink. They never hear any good, never see a good example.

Harry, the degenerate, will take to evil as a duck to water. Of that, I think, there is no question. But what of Dick, the healthy baby?

Dick is born without knowledge. He is also born with undeveloped propensities. He will learn evil. His propensities will be trained to evil. How is he to "overcome his environment and become good"? He *cannot*. What will happen in Dick's case is that he will become a different kind of criminal—a stronger and cleverer criminal than Harry.

But, I hear some one say, "we know that children, born of thieves and sots, and reared in bad surroundings, have turned out honest and sober men." And the inference is that they rose superior to their environment.

But that inference is erroneous. The *fact* is that these children were saved by some *good* environment, acting against the bad.

...

Two children may be born of the same parents, reared in the same hovel, in the same slum, taught the same evil lesson. But they will meet different companions, and will have different experiences.

...

And we shall always find that the man who rises above his environment has really been helped by good environment to overcome the bad environment. He has learnt some *good*. And that learning is part of his environment. He must have been *taught* some good if he knows any, for he was born destitute of knowledge.

...

It is a mistake to think of heredity as all good, or all bad. It is mixed. We inherit, *all* of us, good and bad qualities.

It is a mistake to think of environment as all good or all bad. It is mixed. There are always good and bad influences around every one of us.

It is a mistake to think that any two men ever did or can have exactly the same environment.

It is as impossible for the environment of any two men to be identical, as for their heredity to be identical. As there are no two men exactly alike, so there are no two men whose experiences are exactly alike. (2)

...

Free Will

The free will delusion has been a stumbling block in the way of human thought for thousands of years. Let us try whether common sense and common knowledge cannot remove it.

...

(1) That there are hereditary inclinations to immorality in the way suggested here is something many people would nowadays reject. But it is enough for Blatchford's purposes that some people are hereditarily more susceptible to environmental influences in the direction of immorality. And if even that isn't true, then the role of environment just becomes larger, which would not affect Blatchford's main conclusions.

(2) But how can Blatchford (or anyone else) justify the claim that two people with exactly the same heredity and environment will behave in exactly the same ways in the same circumstances? Even identical twins raised in the same house do not have exactly the same environment. How then can this claim be established if such cases never occur?

When a man says his will is free, he means that it is free of all control or interference: that it can over-rule heredity and environment. ❸

This is an overstatement. "Overruling" heredity and environment would suggest that they have no influence at all. But it would be enough for at least some degree of freedom if these things *influenced* but did not completely *determine* a person's actions—that is, if there were at least two significantly different alternatives open to him.

We reply that the will is ruled by heredity and environment.

...

To begin with, the average man will be against me. He knows that he chooses between two courses every hour, and often every minute, and he thinks his choice is free. But that is a delusion: his choice is not free. He can choose, and does choose. But he can only choose as his heredity and his environment cause him to choose. He never did choose and never will choose except as his heredity and his environment—his temperament and his training—cause him to choose. And his heredity and his environment have fixed his choice before he makes it.

The average man says "I know that I can act as I wish to act." But what causes him to wish?

The free will party say, "We know that a man can and does choose between two acts." But what settles the choice?

There is a cause for every wish, a cause for every choice; and every cause of every wish and choice arises from heredity, or from environment.

For a man acts always from temperament, which is heredity, or from training, which is environment.

And in cases where a man hesitates in his choice between two acts, the hesitation is due to a conflict between his temperament and his training, or, as some would express it, "between his desire and his conscience."

...

Let us suppose a case. A young woman gets two letters by the same post; one is an invitation to go with her lover to a concert, the other is a request that she will visit a sick child in the slums. The girl is very fond of music, and is rather afraid of the slums. She wishes to go to the concert, and to be with her lover; she dreads the foul street and the dirty home, and shrinks from the risk of measles or fever. But she goes to the sick child, and she foregoes the concert. Why?

Because her sense of duty is stronger than her self-love.

Now, her sense of duty is partly due to her nature—that is, to her heredity—but it is chiefly due to environment. Like all of us, this girl was born without any kind of knowledge, and with only the rudiments of a conscience. But she has been well taught, and the teaching is part of her environment.

We may say that the girl is free to act as she chooses, but she *does* act as she has been *taught* that she *ought* to act. This teaching, which is part of her environment, controls her will.

We may say that a man is free to act as he chooses. He is free to act as *he* chooses, but *he* will choose as heredity and environment cause *him* to choose. For heredity and environment have made him that which he is.

...

Macbeth was ambitious; but he had a conscience. He wanted Duncan's crown; but he shrank from treason and ingratitude. Ambition pulled him one way, honour pulled him the other way. The opposing forces were so evenly balanced that he seemed unable to decide. Was Macbeth free to choose? To what extent was he free? He was so free that he could arrive at no decision, and it was the influence of his wife that turned the scale to crime.

Was Lady Macbeth free to choose? She did not hesitate. Because her ambition was so much stronger than her conscience that she never was in doubt. She chose as her overpowering ambition compelled her to choose.

And most of us in our decisions resemble either Macbeth or his wife. Either our nature is so much stronger than our training, or our training is so much stronger than our nature, that we decide for good or evil as promptly as a stream decides to run down hill; or our nature and our training are so nearly balanced that we can hardly decide at all.

In Macbeth's case the contest is quite clear and easy to follow. He was ambitious, and his environment had taught him to regard the crown as a glorious and desirable possession. But environment had also taught him that murder, and treason, and ingratitude were wicked and disgraceful.

Had he never been taught these lessons, or had he been taught that gratitude was folly, that honour was weakness, and murder excusable when it led to power, he would not have hesitated at all. It was his environment that hampered his will.

...

We say that a drunkard and a lifelong abstainer are free to drink or to refuse a glass of whisky. But we know that in both cases the action of the free will is a foregone conclusion.

In all cases the action of the will depends upon the relative strength of two or more motives. The stronger motive decides the will; just as the heavier weight decides the balance of a pair of scales.

In Macbeth's case the balance seemed almost even: Lady Macbeth's persuasion brought down the scale on the wrong side.

If the will were free, it would be independent of the temperament and training, and so would act as freely in one case as in another. So that it would be as easy for the drunkard as for the lifelong abstainer to refuse to drink; as easy for the thief as for the Cardinal to be honest; as easy for Macbeth as for Lady Macbeth to seal the fate of Duncan.

But we all know that it is harder for one man than for another to be sober, or honest, or virtuous; and we all know that the sobriety, or honesty, or virtue of any man depends upon his temperament and training; that is to say, upon his heredity and his environment. 4

How, then, can we believe that free will is outside and superior to heredity and environment?

...

The apostles of free will believe that all men's wills are free. But a man can only will that which he is able to will. And one man is able to will that which another man is unable to will. To deny this is to deny the commonest and most obvious facts of life. 5

...

We all know that we can foretell the action of certain men in certain cases, because we know the men.

We know that under the same conditions Jack Sheppard would steal and Cardinal Manning would not steal. We know that under the same conditions the sailor would flirt with the waitress, and the priest would not; that the drunkard would get drunk, and the abstainer would remain sober. We know that Wellington would refuse a bribe, that Nelson would not run away, that Buonaparte would grasp at power, that Abraham Lincoln would be loyal to his country, that Torquemada would not spare a heretic. Why? If the will is free, how can we be sure, before a test arises, how the will must act? 6

...

Guilty or Not Guilty?

We are to ask whether it is true that everything a man does is the only thing he could do, at the instant of his doing it.

This is a very important question, because if the answer is yes, all praise and all blame are undeserved.

All praise and *all* blame.

Let us take some revolting action as a test.

A tramp has murdered a child on the highway, has robbed her of a few coppers, and has thrown her body into a ditch.

"Do you mean to say that tramp could not help doing that? Do you mean to say he is not to blame? Do you mean to say he is not to be punished?"

Yes. I say all those things; and if all those things are not true this book is not worth the paper it is printed on.

Prove it? I have proved it. But I have only instanced venial acts, and now we are confronted with murder. And the horror of murder drives men almost to frenzy, so that they cease to think: they can only feel.

Murder. Yes, a brutal murder. It comes upon us with a sickening shock. . . . I have to plead for the *bottom* dog: the lowest, the most detested, the worst.

...

The tramp has committed a murder. It was a cowardly and cruel murder, and the motive was robbery.

But I have proved that all motives and all powers; all knowledge and capacity, all acts and all words, are caused by heredity and environment.

I have proved that a man can only be good or bad as heredity and environment cause him to be good or bad; and I have proved these things because I have to claim that all punishments and rewards, all praise and blame, are undeserved.

...

4

That it is *harder* for one person to be sober than it is for another (which again seems obvious) doesn't yet show that what each person does is *entirely* determined by heredity and environment.

5

But the fact that one person can will things that a second person cannot will does not show that *everything* they will is determined—that there are *no* significant alternatives open to them.

6

Does the fact that people's behavior is mostly *predictable* show that it is entirely *determined*? If it were completely predictable, so that we could be "sure" what each person will do in every situation, would this establish determinism? (And is it plausible that people's behavior is in fact *completely* predictable? Think of some examples here.)

Discussion Questions

1. Blatchford gives reasons for thinking that heredity and especially environment influence people's choices, make it more difficult for them to do some things than others, and perhaps even rule out some choices entirely. Do any of these reasons, or any other reasons that he gives, make a strong case for the claim that what a person does is *entirely determined* by heredity and environment, so that no other alternative than what he did was genuinely possible for him?
2. Suppose that Blatchford is wrong in claiming that a person's actions are entirely determined by his heredity and environment. One possibility is that there is a degree of randomness in human action: that there is more than one possible choice for a person with a specified heredity and environment in a particular situation and that it is a matter of chance which of the possible choices he or she will make. What would Blatchford probably say about a choice that is to this degree random, and do you think he would be right? Is there any further alternative besides complete determination by heredity and environment or partial determination plus a degree of randomness?
3. If Blatchford's deterministic view is correct, does it follow that it is pointless to punish (or praise) people for what they do? Can you think of any justification for punishment that is compatible with hard determinism?

Compatibilism

David Hume

David Hume (1711–1776), a Scottish philosopher and historian, is usually regarded as one of the most important and influential philosophers of all time. He did very important work in epistemology, metaphysics, ethics, and the philosophy of religion, producing a comprehensive philosophical position that is most distinctive for its skeptical tendencies.

In this selection, Hume defends compatibilism (or "soft determinism"), arguing that normal human actions are characterized by both necessity (causal determinism) and liberty (freedom). He attempts to show that the view that necessity and liberty are incompatible results from misunderstandings of these concepts.

Of Liberty and Necessity, from *An Enquiry Concerning Human Understanding*

Of Liberty and Necessity

Part I

It might reasonably be expected in questions which have been canvassed and disputed with great eagerness, since the first origin of science and philosophy, that the meaning of all the terms, at least, should have been agreed upon among the disputants; and our inquiries, in the course of two thousand years, been able to pass from words to the true and real subject of the controversy. For how easy may it seem to give exact definitions of the terms employed in reasoning, and make these definitions, not the mere sound of words, the object of future scrutiny and examination? But if we consider the matter more narrowly, we shall be apt to draw a quite opposite conclusion. From this circumstance alone, that a controversy has been long kept on foot, and remains still undecided, we may presume that there is some ambiguity in the expression, and that the disputants affix different ideas to the terms employed in the controversy. For as the faculties of the mind are supposed to be naturally alike in every individual; otherwise nothing could be more fruitless

From *An Enquiry Concerning Human Understanding* (1748).

than to reason or dispute together; it were impossible, if men affix the same ideas to their terms, that they could so long form different opinions of the same subject; especially when they communicate their views, and each party turn themselves on all sides, in search of arguments which may give them the victory over their antagonists. . . . ❶

This has been the case in the long disputed question concerning liberty and necessity; and to so remarkable a degree that, if I be not much mistaken, we shall find, that all mankind, both learned and ignorant, have always been of the same opinion with regard to this subject, and that a few intelligible definitions would immediately have put an end to the whole controversy. . . .

I hope, therefore, to make it appear that all men have ever agreed in the doctrine both of necessity and of liberty, according to any reasonable sense, which can be put on these terms; and that the whole controversy has hitherto turned merely upon words. We shall begin with examining the doctrine of necessity.

It is universally allowed that matter, in all its operations, is actuated by a necessary force, and that every natural effect is so precisely determined by the energy of its cause that no other effect, in such particular circumstances, could possibly have resulted from it. The degree and direction of every motion is, by the laws of nature, prescribed with such exactness that a living creature may as soon arise from the shock of two bodies as motion in any other degree or direction than what is actually produced by it. Would we, therefore, form a just and precise idea of *necessity,* we must consider whence that idea arises when we apply it to the operation of bodies. ❷

It seems evident that, if all the scenes of nature were continually shifted in such a manner that no two events bore any resemblance to each other, but every object was entirely new, without any similitude to whatever had been seen before, we should never, in that case, have attained the least idea of necessity, or of a connection among these objects. We might say, upon such a supposition, that one object or event has followed another; not that one was produced by the other. The relation of cause and effect must be utterly unknown to mankind. . . . Our idea, therefore, of necessity and causation arises entirely from the uniformity observable in the operations of nature, where similar objects are constantly conjoined together, and the mind is determined by custom to infer the one from the appearance of the other. These two circumstances form the whole of that necessity, which we ascribe to matter. Beyond the constant *conjunction* of similar objects, and the consequent *inference* from one to the other, we have no notion of any necessity or connection. ❸

If it appear, therefore, that all mankind have ever allowed, without any doubt or hesitation, that these two circumstances take place in the voluntary actions of men, and in the operations of mind; it must follow, that all mankind have ever agreed in the doctrine of necessity, and that they have hitherto disputed, merely for not understanding each other.

As to the first circumstance, the constant and regular conjunction of similar events, we may possibly satisfy ourselves by the following considerations. It is universally acknowledged that there is a great uniformity among the actions of men, in all nations and ages, and that human nature remains still the same, in its principles and operations. The same motives always produce the same actions; the same events follow from the same causes. Ambition, avarice, self-love, vanity, friendship, generosity, public spirit: these passions, mixed in various degrees, and distributed through society, have been, from the beginning of the world, and still are, the source of all the actions and enterprises, which have ever been observed among mankind. Would you know the sentiments, inclinations, and course of life of the Greeks and Romans? Study well the temper and actions of the French and English: you cannot be much mistaken in transferring to the former *most* of the observations which you have made with regard to the latter. Mankind are so much the same, in all times and places, that history informs us of nothing new or strange in this particular. Its chief use is only to discover the constant and universal principles of human nature, by showing men in all varieties of circumstances and situations, and furnishing us with materials from which we may form our observations and become acquainted with the regular springs of human action and behavior. These records of wars, intrigues, factions, and revolutions, are so many collections of experiments, by which the politician or moral philosopher fixes the principles of his science, in the same manner as the physician or natural philosopher becomes acquainted with the nature of plants, minerals,

The idea that philosophical disputes result from confusions about the meanings of terms and can be resolved if these are clarified is one of the central doctrines of what has come to be known as the *analytic* school of philosophy. In this respect (and some others), Hume is plausibly viewed as one of the main historical sources of the analytic view.

R Hume takes it to be beyond question that necessity (causal determinism) applies to the realm of material bodies. Thus he proposes to determine what necessity is by investigating what it amounts to in that realm.

R Hume's suggestion is that necessity as it applies to the realm of material bodies amounts to nothing more than (a) *constant conjunction* (events or objects of a specific kind being regularly followed by events or objects of another specific kind) together with (b) the consequent tendency of the mind to *infer* from the occurrence of one of these kinds of events or objects to the other. (See chapter 5 of the Hume selection in the induction section of Chapter 2.)

and other external objects, by the experiments which he forms concerning them. Nor are the earth, water, and other elements, examined by Aristotle, and Hippocrates, more like to those which at present lie under our observation than the men described by Polybius and Tacitus are to those who now govern the world.

Should a traveler, returning from a far country, bring us an account of men, wholly different from any with whom we were ever acquainted; men, who were entirely divested of avarice, ambition, or revenge; who knew no pleasure but friendship, generosity, and public spirit; we should immediately, from these circumstances, detect the falsehood, and prove him a liar, with the same certainty as if he had stuffed his narration with stories of centaurs and dragons, miracles and prodigies. And if we would explode any forgery in history, we cannot make use of a more convincing argument, than to prove, that the actions ascribed to any person are directly contrary to the course of nature, and that no human motives, in such circumstances, could ever induce him to such a conduct. (4) . . . So readily and universally do we acknowledge a uniformity in human motives and actions as well as in the operations of body.

(4)

R The issue is then whether the two ingredients of necessity are also to be found in the realm of human actions. Hume's claim is that the first one is—and moreover, that no one really disputes this. Human actions occur in regular ways, and we would be suspicious of reports to the contrary.

. . .

We must not, however, expect that this uniformity of human actions should be carried to such a length as that all men, in the same circumstances, will always act precisely in the same manner, without making any allowance for the diversity of characters, prejudices, and opinions. Such a uniformity in every particular, is found in no part of nature. On the contrary, from observing the variety of conduct in different men, we are enabled to form a greater variety of maxims, which still suppose a degree of uniformity and regularity.

Are the manners of men different in different ages and countries? We learn thence the great force of custom and education, which mold the human mind from its infancy and form it into a fixed and established character. Is the behavior and conduct of the one sex very unlike that of the other? Is it thence we become acquainted with the different characters which nature has impressed upon the sexes, and which she preserves with constancy and regularity? Are the actions of the same person much diversified in the different periods of his life, from infancy to old age? This affords room for many general observations concerning the gradual change of our sentiments and inclinations, and the different maxims which prevail in the different ages of human creatures. Even the characters, which are peculiar to each individual, have a uniformity in their influence; otherwise our acquaintance with the persons and our observation of their conduct could never teach us their dispositions, or serve to direct our behavior with regard to them. (5)

R People do not always act the same way in the same external circumstances. But this just shows that custom, education, and character are also causally relevant.

I grant it possible to find some actions, which seem to have no regular connection with any known motives, and are exceptions to all the measures of conduct which have ever been established for the government of men. But if we would willingly know what judgment should be formed of such irregular and extraordinary actions, we may consider the sentiments commonly entertained with regard to those irregular events which appear in the course of nature, and the operations of external objects. . . .

The vulgar, who take things according to their first appearance, attribute the uncertainty of events to such an uncertainty in the causes as makes the latter often fail of their usual influence; though they meet with no impediment in their operation. But philosophers, observing that, almost in every part of nature, there is contained a vast variety of springs and principles, which are hid, by reason of their minuteness or remoteness, find, that it is at least possible the contrariety of events may not proceed from any contingency in the cause, but from the secret operation of contrary causes. This possibility is converted into certainty by further observation, when they remark that, upon an exact scrutiny, a contrariety of effects always betrays a contrariety of causes, and proceeds from their mutual opposition. A peasant can give no better reason for the stopping of any clock or watch than to say that it does not commonly go right: but an artist easily perceives that the same force in the spring or pendulum has always the same influence on the wheels; but fails of its usual effect, perhaps by reason of a grain of dust, which puts a stop to the whole movement. From the observation of several parallel instances, philosophers form a maxim that the connection between all causes and effects is equally necessary, and that its seeming uncertainty in some instances proceeds from the secret opposition of contrary causes.

...

The philosopher, if he be consistent, must apply the same reasoning to the actions and volitions of intelligent agents. The most irregular and unexpected resolutions of men may frequently be accounted for by those who know every particular circumstance of their character and situation. A person of an obliging disposition gives a peevish answer; but he has the toothache, or has not dined. A stupid fellow discovers an uncommon alacrity in his carriage; but he has met with a sudden piece of good fortune. Or even when an action, as something happens, cannot be particularly accounted for, either by the person himself or by others; we know, in general, that the characters of men are, to a certain degree, inconstant and irregular. This is, in a manner, the constant character of human nature; though it be applicable, in a more particular manner, to some persons who have no fixed rule for their conduct, but proceed in a continued course of caprice and inconstancy. The internal principles and motives may operate in a uniform manner, notwithstanding these seeming irregularities; in the same manner as the winds, rain, clouds, and other variations of the weather are supposed to be governed by steady principles; though not easily discoverable by human sagacity and inquiry. 6

Thus it appears, not only that the conjunction between motives and voluntary actions is as regular and uniform as that between the cause and effect in any part of nature; but also that this regular conjunction has been universally acknowledged among mankind, and has never been the subject of dispute, either in philosophy or common life. Now, as it is from past experience that we draw all inferences concerning the future, and as we conclude that objects will always be conjoined together which we find to have always been conjoined; it may seem superfluous to prove that this experienced uniformity in human actions is a source whence we draw *inferences* concerning them. But in order to throw the argument into a greater variety of lights we shall also insist, though briefly, on this latter topic.

The mutual dependence of men is so great in all societies that scarce any human action is entirely complete in itself, or is performed without some reference to the actions of others, which are requisite to make it answer fully the intention of the agent. The poorest artificer, who labors alone, expects at least the protection of the magistrate, to ensure him the enjoyment of the fruits of his labor. He also expects that, when he carries his goods to market, and offers them at a reasonable price, he shall find purchasers, and shall be able, by the money he acquires, to engage others to supply him with those commodities which are requisite for his subsistence. In proportion as men extend their dealings, and render their intercourse with others more complicated, they always comprehend, in their schemes of life, a greater variety of voluntary actions, which they expect, from the proper motives, to cooperate with their own. In all these conclusions they take their measures from past experience, in the same manner as in their reasonings concerning external objects; and firmly believe that men, as well as all the elements, are to continue, in their operations, the same that they have ever found them. A manufacturer reckons upon the labor of his servants for the execution of any work as much as upon the tools which he employs, and would be equally surprised were his expectations disappointed. In short, this experimental inference and reasoning concerning the actions of others enters so much into human life, that no man, while awake, is ever a moment without employing it. Have we not reason, therefore, to affirm that all mankind have always agreed in the doctrine of necessity according to the foregoing definition and explication of it?

Nor have philosophers ever entertained a different opinion from the people in this particular. For, not to mention that almost every action of their life supposes that opinion, there are even few of the speculative parts of learning to which it is not essential. What would become of *history*, had we not a dependence on the veracity of the historian according to the experience which we have had of mankind? How could *politics* be a science, if laws and forms of government had not a uniform influence upon society? Where would be the foundation of *morals*, if particular characters had no certain or determinate power to produce particular sentiments, and if these sentiments had no constant operation on actions? And with what pretense could we employ our *criticism* upon any poet or polite author, if we could not pronounce the conduct and sentiments of his actors either natural or

R In both realms (material bodies and human actions), there are exceptions to the general regularities of succession. Hume takes this to show, in both cases, only that there are further causes at work that have not yet been discovered.

unnatural to such characters, and in such circumstances? It seems almost impossible, therefore, to engage either in science or action of any kind without acknowledging the doctrine of necessity, and this *inference* from motive to voluntary actions, from characters to conduct. 7

7

R Moreover, there is no doubt that in the realm of human actions, just as in the realm of material bodies, we rely on the patterns of uniformity to infer what people will do in various circumstances, given specified motives. Both ordinary actions in the world and the scholarly study of human actions depend essentially on these inferences.

And indeed, when we consider how aptly *natural* and *moral* evidence link together, and form only one chain of argument, we shall make no scruple to allow that they are of the same nature, and derived from the same principles. A prisoner who has neither money nor interest, discovers the impossibility of his escape, as well when he considers the obstinacy of the [jailer], as the walls and bars with which he is surrounded; and, in all attempts for his freedom, chooses rather to work upon the stone and iron of the one, than upon the inflexible nature of the other. The same prisoner, when conducted to the scaffold, foresees his death as certainly from the constancy and fidelity of his guards, as from the operation of the axe or wheel. His mind runs along a certain train of ideas: the refusal of the soldiers to consent to his escape; the action of the executioner; the separation of the head and body; bleeding, convulsive motions, and death. Here is a connected chain of natural causes and voluntary actions; but the mind feels no difference between them in passing from one link to another. Nor is less certain of the future event than if it were connected with the objects present to the memory or senses, by a train of causes, cemented together by what we are pleased to call a *physical* necessity. The same experienced union has the same effect on the mind, whether the united objects be motives, volition, and actions; or figure and motion. We may change the name of things; but their nature and their operation on the understanding never change.

Were a man, whom I know to be honest and opulent, and with whom I live in intimate friendship, to come into my house, where I am surrounded with my servants, I rest assured that he is not to stab me before he leaves it in order to rob me of my silver standish; and I no more suspect this event than the falling of the house itself, which is new, and solidly built and founded.—*But he may have been seized with a sudden and unknown frenzy.*—So may a sudden earthquake arise, and shake and tumble my house about my ears. I shall therefore change the suppositions. I shall say that I know with certainty that he is not to put his hand into the fire and hold it there till it be consumed: and this event, I think I can foretell with the same assurance, as that, if he throw himself out at the window, and meet with no obstruction, he will not remain a moment suspended in the air. No suspicion of an unknown frenzy can give the least possibility to the former event, which is so contrary to all the known principles of human nature. A man who at noon leaves his purse full of gold on the pavement at Charing Cross, may as well expect that it will fly away like a feather, as that he will find it untouched an hour after. Above one half of human reasonings contain inferences of a similar nature, attended with more or less degrees of certainty proportioned to our experience of the usual conduct of mankind in such particular situations. 8

R Indeed, we often reason in a way that integrates regularities pertaining to material bodies with those pertaining to human actions, with no more uncertainty about the latter than about the former.

I have frequently considered, what could possibly be the reason why all mankind, though they have ever, without hesitation, acknowledged the doctrine of necessity in their whole practice and reasoning, have yet discovered such a reluctance to acknowledge it in words, and have rather shown a propensity, in all ages, to profess the contrary opinion. The matter, I think, may be accounted for after the following manner. If we examine the operations of body, and the production of effects from their causes, we shall find that all our faculties can never carry us farther in our knowledge of this relation than barely to observe that particular objects are *constantly conjoined* together, and that the mind is carried, by a *customary transition,* from the appearance of one to the belief of the other. But though this conclusion concerning human ignorance be the result of the strictest scrutiny of this subject, men still entertain a strong propensity to believe that they penetrate farther into the powers of nature, and perceive something like a necessary connection between the cause and the effect. When again they turn their reflections towards the operations of their own minds, and *feel* no such connection of the motive and the action; they are thence apt to suppose, that there is a difference between the effects which result from material force, and those which arise from thought and intelligence. But being once convinced that we know nothing farther of causation of any kind than merely the *constant conjunction* of objects, and the consequent *inference* of the mind from one to another, and finding that these two circumstances are universally allowed to have place in voluntary actions; we may be more easily led to own the same necessity common to all causes. And though this reasoning may contradict the systems of many philosophers, in ascribing necessity to the determinations of the will, we shall find, upon reflection, that they dissent from it in words only, not in their real sentiment. Necessity, according to the sense in which it is here taken, has never yet been rejected, nor can ever, I think, be rejected by any philosopher. . . . 9

It would seem, indeed, that men begin at the wrong end of this question concerning liberty and necessity, when they enter upon it by examining the faculties of the soul, the influence of the understanding, and the operations of the will. Let them first discuss a more simple question, namely, the operations of body and of brute unintelligent matter; and try whether they can there form any idea of causation and necessity, except that of a constant conjunction of objects, and subsequent inference of the mind from one to another. If these circumstances form, in reality, the whole of that necessity, which we conceive in matter, and if these circumstances be also universally acknowledged to take place in the operations of the mind, the dispute is at an end; at least, must be owned to be thenceforth merely verbal. But as long as we will rashly suppose, that we have some farther idea of necessity and causation in the operations of external objects; at the same time, that we can find nothing farther in the voluntary actions of the mind; there is no possibility of bringing the question to any determinate issue, while we proceed upon so erroneous a supposition. The only method of undeceiving us is to mount up higher; to examine the narrow extent of science when applied to material causes; and to convince ourselves that all we know of them is the constant conjunction and inference above mentioned. We may, perhaps, find that it is with difficulty we are induced to fix such narrow limits to human understanding: but we can afterwards find no difficulty when we come to apply this doctrine to the actions of the will. For as it is evident that these have a regular conjunction with motives and circumstances and characters, and as we always draw inferences from one to the other, we must be obliged to acknowledge in words that necessity, which we have already avowed, in every deliberation of our lives, and in every step of our conduct and behavior.*

But to proceed in this reconciling project with regard to the question of liberty and necessity; the most contentious question of metaphysics, the most contentious science; it will not require many words to prove, that all mankind have ever agreed in the doctrine of liberty as well as in that of necessity, and that the whole dispute, in this respect also, has been hitherto merely verbal. For what is meant by liberty, when applied to voluntary actions? We cannot surely mean that actions have so little

R One way in which people are led astray in these matters, Hume suggests, is by thinking that necessary connection of a sort that goes beyond the two elements he has indicated is perceivable in nature, but not in the actions of their own minds—that we can somehow perceive the causal connection itself, and not just the regularity that results from it. Hume denies that this is the case.

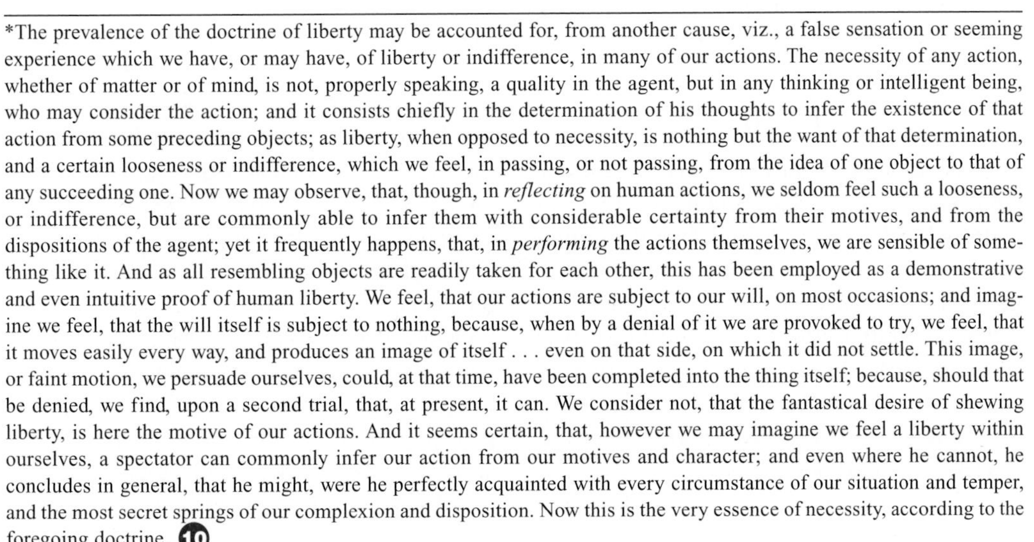

*The prevalence of the doctrine of liberty may be accounted for, from another cause, viz., a false sensation or seeming experience which we have, or may have, of liberty or indifference, in many of our actions. The necessity of any action, whether of matter or of mind, is not, properly speaking, a quality in the agent, but in any thinking or intelligent being, who may consider the action; and it consists chiefly in the determination of his thoughts to infer the existence of that action from some preceding objects; as liberty, when opposed to necessity, is nothing but the want of that determination, and a certain looseness or indifference, which we feel, in passing, or not passing, from the idea of one object to that of any succeeding one. Now we may observe, that, though, in *reflecting* on human actions, we seldom feel such a looseness, or indifference, but are commonly able to infer them with considerable certainty from their motives, and from the dispositions of the agent; yet it frequently happens, that, in *performing* the actions themselves, we are sensible of something like it. And as all resembling objects are readily taken for each other, this has been employed as a demonstrative and even intuitive proof of human liberty. We feel, that our actions are subject to our will, on most occasions; and imagine we feel, that the will itself is subject to nothing, because, when by a denial of it we are provoked to try, we feel, that it moves easily every way, and produces an image of itself . . . even on that side, on which it did not settle. This image, or faint motion, we persuade ourselves, could, at that time, have been completed into the thing itself; because, should that be denied, we find, upon a second trial, that, at present, it can. We consider not, that the fantastical desire of shewing liberty, is here the motive of our actions. And it seems certain, that, however we may imagine we feel a liberty within ourselves, a spectator can commonly infer our action from our motives and character; and even where he cannot, he concludes in general, that he might, were he perfectly acquainted with every circumstance of our situation and temper, and the most secret springs of our complexion and disposition. Now this is the very essence of necessity, according to the foregoing doctrine. 10

R By the "doctrine of liberty," Hume means here the mistaken (according to him) idea that there is a kind of liberty pertaining to human actions that is distinct from and incompatible with causal necessity. His suggestion is that the plausibility of this idea results from its seeming, in a situation where a person is actually performing an action, that more than one alternative is possible, that even though he does one thing, he could just as well have done something else. Hume regards this as a kind of illusion, as shown by the fact that an external observer (or even the same person reflecting later) will find the action as regular and predictable as anything else.

R What then does liberty amount to, if not a denial of the regularity and inferability that everyone admits? Hume suggests that liberty means only acting (or not acting) according to the determinations of the will, that is, as one chooses. Since this is entirely compatible with the action and choice being causally determined, Hume thus claims to *reconcile* liberty (freedom) with necessity (causal determinism).

A liberty that was incompatible with necessity would amount to chance or randomness. Hume's claim, much more plausible then than now, is that genuine chance does not exist.

connection with motives, inclinations, and circumstances, that one does not follow with a certain degree of uniformity from the other, and that one affords no inference by which we can conclude the existence of the other. For these are plain and acknowledged matters of fact. By liberty, then, we can only mean *a power of acting or not acting, according to the determinations of the will;* that is, if we choose to remain at rest, we may; if we choose to move, we also may. Now this hypothetical liberty is universally allowed to belong to everyone who is not a prisoner and in chains. Here, then, is no subject of dispute. [11]

Whatever definition we may give of liberty, we should be careful to observe two requisite circumstances; *first,* that it be consistent with plain matter of fact; *secondly,* that it be consistent with itself. If we observe these circumstances, and render our definition intelligible, I am persuaded that all mankind will be found of one opinion with regard to it.

. . .

Had not objects a regular conjunction with each other, we should never have entertained any notion of cause and effect; and this regular conjunction produces that inference of the understanding, which is the only connection, that we can have any comprehension of. Whoever attempts a definition of cause, exclusive of these circumstances, will be obliged either to employ unintelligible terms or such as are synonymous to the term which he endeavors to define. And if the definition above mentioned be admitted; liberty, when opposed to necessity, not to constraint, is the same thing with chance; which is universally allowed to have no existence. [12]

Part II

There is no method of reasoning more common, and yet none more blamable, than, in philosophical disputes, to endeavor the refutation of any hypothesis, by a pretense of its dangerous consequences to religion and morality. When any opinion leads to absurdities, it is certainly false; but it is not certain that an opinion is false, because it is of dangerous consequence. Such topics, therefore, ought entirely to be forborne; as serving nothing to the discovery of truth, but only to make the person of an antagonist odious. This I observe in general, without pretending to draw any advantage from it. I frankly submit to an examination of this kind, and shall venture to affirm that the doctrines, both of necessity and of liberty, as above explained, are not only consistent with morality, but are absolutely essential to its support.

Necessity may be defined two ways, conformably to the two definitions of *cause,* of which it makes an essential part. It consists either in the constant conjunction of like objects, or in the inference of the understanding from one object to another. Now necessity, in both these senses (which, indeed, are at bottom the same), has universally, though tacitly, in the schools, in the pulpit, and in common life, been allowed to belong to the will of man; and no one has ever pretended to deny that we can draw inferences concerning human actions, and that those inferences are founded on the experienced union of like actions, with like motives, inclinations, and circumstances. The only particular in which anyone can differ, is, that either, perhaps, he will refuse to give the name of necessity to this property of human actions: but as long as the meaning is understood, I hope the word can do no harm; or that he will maintain it possible to discover something farther in the operations of matter. But this, it must be acknowledged, can be of no consequence to morality or religion, whatever it may be to natural philosophy or metaphysics. We may here be mistaken in asserting that there is no idea of any other necessity or connection in the actions of body; but surely we ascribe nothing to the actions of the mind, but what everyone does, and must readily allow of. We change no circumstance in the received orthodox system with regard to the will, but only in that with regard to material objects and causes. Nothing, therefore, can be more innocent, at least, than this doctrine.

All laws being founded on rewards and punishments, it is supposed as a fundamental principle, that these motives have a regular and uniform influence on the mind, and both produce the good and prevent the evil actions. We may give to this influence what name we please; but, as it is usually conjoined with the action, it must be esteemed a *cause,* and be looked upon as an instance of that necessity, which we would here establish. 13

The only proper object of hatred or vengeance is a person or creature, endowed with thought and consciousness; and when any criminal or injurious actions excite that passion, it is only by their relation to the person, or connection with him. Actions are, by their very nature, temporary and perishing; and where they proceed not from some *cause* in the character and disposition of the person who performed them, they can neither redound to his honor, if good; nor infamy, if evil. The actions themselves may be blamable; they may be contrary to all the rules of morality and religion. But the person is not answerable for them; and as they proceeded from nothing in him that is durable and constant, and leave nothing of that nature behind them, it is impossible he can, upon their account, become the object of punishment or vengeance. According to the principle, therefore, which denies necessity, and consequently causes, a man is as pure and untainted, after having committed the most horrid crime, as at the first moment of his birth, nor is his character anywise concerned in his actions, since they are not derived from it, and the wickedness of the one can never be used as a proof of the depravity of the other.

Men are not blamed for such actions as they perform ignorantly and casually, whatever may be the consequences. Why? but because the principles of these actions are only momentary, and terminate in them alone. Men are less blamed for such actions as they perform hastily and unpremeditatedly than for such as proceed from deliberation. For what reason? but because a hasty temper, though a constant cause or principle in the mind, operates only by intervals, and infects not the whole character. Again, repentance wipes off every crime, if attended with a reformation of life and manners. How is this to be accounted for? but by asserting that actions render a person criminal merely as they are proofs of criminal principles in the mind; and when, by an alteration of these principles, they cease to be just proofs, they likewise cease to be criminal. But, except upon the doctrine of necessity, they never were just proofs, and consequently never were criminal. 14

It will be equally easy to prove, and from the same arguments, that *liberty,* according to that definition above mentioned, in which all men agree, is also essential to morality, and that no human actions, where it is wanting, are susceptible of any moral qualities, or can be the objects either of approbation or dislike. For as actions are objects of our moral sentiment, so far only as they are indications of the internal character, passions, and affections; it is impossible that they can give rise either to praise or blame, where they proceed not from these principles, but are derived altogether from external violence. 15

. . .

R Necessity is also required to make sense of the practice of rewarding or punishing people, which assumes that such things will influence (that is, causally affect) their behavior (and that of others) in a regular way.

R And blaming or punishing someone for an action makes sense only if the action flows in a regular way from the person's character, thus again presupposing causal necessity.

R Thus liberty in the compatibilist sense is essential to any sort of moral assessment of human actions.

Discussion Questions

1. Hume's view is that causal necessity, to the extent that we have any knowledge of it, amounts only to (a) regular succession together with (b) the tendency of the mind to infer from one of the regularly conjoined things to the other. He denies that any stronger sort of connection between cause and effect is knowable. Does this seem right? Or does causality seem essentially to involve the idea that one event *makes* the other happen? Assess Hume's view on this point by thinking about a range of examples.
2. In the long footnote on page 263, Hume recognizes that in an actual situation of action, one's choice does not *seem* to be determined, but instead that two or more options *seem* to be genuinely open. This sort of experience provides the basic argument for the existence of freedom in the libertarian sense that is incompatible with determinism. Is Hume right to reject it as an illusion? How can we decide this difficult issue? Think about this issue by considering some actual examples of significant choice.
3. Hume denies that chance or randomness genuinely exists. Suppose that he is mistaken about this (as the results of quantum theory seem to show). Would it then be plausible to identify a free action with one that results from chance? Does Hume's discussion suggest any further objections to such a view?

W. T. Stace

Walter Terence Stace (1886–1967) was an English philosopher who served in the British Civil Service in Ceylon and later taught at Princeton. Stace was both an **empiricist** (see Chapter 2) and a **utilitarian** (see Chapter 5), but he also tried to make room in his philosophy for religious experience. In this selection, he defends a compatibilist (soft determinist) position, according to which freedom is not incompatible with causal determinism, but instead requires that an action be determined *in the right way:* by the person's own psychological states, rather than by something outside the person. His view is in many respects quite close to Hume's, though with many more examples and some further arguments.

A Compatibilist Account of Free Will, from *Religion and the Modern Mind*

. . . I shall first discuss the problem of free will, for it is certain that if there is no free will there can be no morality. Morality is concerned with what men ought and ought not to do. But if a man has no freedom to choose what he will do, if whatever he does is done under compulsion, then it does not make sense to tell him that he ought not to have done what he did and that he ought to do something different. All moral precepts would in such case be meaningless. Also if he acts always under compulsion, how can he be held morally responsible for his actions? How can he, for example, be punished for what he could not help doing?

It is to be observed that those learned professors of philosophy or psychology who deny the existence of free will do so only in their professional moments and in their studies and lecture rooms. For when it comes to doing anything practical, even of the most trivial kind, they invariably behave as if they and others were free. They inquire from you at dinner whether you will choose this dish or that dish. They will ask a child why he told a lie, and will punish him for not having chosen the way of truthfulness. All of which is inconsistent with a disbelief in free will. This should cause us to suspect that the problem is not a real one; and this, I believe, is the case. The dispute is merely verbal, and is due to nothing but a confusion about the meanings of words. It is what is now fashionably called a semantic problem. ❶

❶ R Like Hume, Stace regards the free will problem as fundamentally arising from semantic confusion.

From *Religion and the Modern Mind* (Philadelphia: Lippincott, 1952).

How does a verbal dispute arise? Let us consider a case which, although it is absurd in the sense that no one would ever make the mistake which is involved in it, yet illustrates the principle which we shall have to use in the solution of the problem. Suppose that someone believed that the word "man" means a certain sort of five-legged animal; in short that "five-legged animal" is the correct *definition* of man. He might then look around the world, and rightly observing that there are no five-legged animals in it, he might proceed to deny the existence of men. This preposterous conclusion would have been reached because he was using an incorrect definition of "man." All you would have to do to show him his mistake would be to give him the correct definition; or at least to show him that his definition was wrong. Both the problem and its solution would, of course, be entirely verbal. The problem of free will, and its solution, I shall maintain, is verbal in exactly the same way. The problem has been created by the fact that learned men, especially philosophers, have assumed an incorrect definition of free will, and then finding that there is nothing in the world which answers to their definition, have denied its existence. As far as logic is concerned, their conclusion is just as absurd as that of the man who denies the existence of men. The only difference is that the mistake in the latter case is obvious and crude, while the mistake which the deniers of free will have made is rather subtle and difficult to detect.

Throughout the modern period, until quite recently, it was assumed, both by the philosophers who denied free will and by those who defended it, that *determinism is inconsistent with free will.* If a man's actions were wholly determined by chains of causes stretching back into the remote past, so that they could be predicted beforehand by a mind which knew all the causes, it was assumed that they could not in that case be free. ❷ This implies that a certain definition of actions done from free will was assumed, namely that they are actions *not* wholly determined by causes or predictable beforehand. Let us shorten this by saying that free will was defined as meaning indeterminism. ❸ This is the incorrect definition which has led to the denial of free will. As soon as we see what the true definition is we shall find that the question whether the world is deterministic, as Newtonian science implied, or in a measure indeterministic, as current physics teaches, is wholly irrelevant to the problem. ❹

Of course there is a sense in which one can define a word arbitrarily in any way one pleases. But a definition may nevertheless be called correct or incorrect. It is correct if it accords with a *common usage* of the word defined. It is incorrect if it does not. And if you give an incorrect definition, absurd and untrue results are likely to follow. For instance, there is nothing to prevent you from arbitrarily defining a man as a five-legged animal, but this is incorrect in the sense that it does not accord with the ordinary meaning of the word. Also it has the absurd result of leading to a denial of the existence of men. This shows that *common usage is the criterion for deciding whether a definition is correct or not.* And this is the principle which I shall apply to free will. I shall show that indeterminism is not what is meant by the phrase "free will" *as it is commonly used.* And I shall attempt to discover the correct definition by inquiring how the phrase is used in ordinary conversation.

Here are a few samples of how the phrase might be used in ordinary conversation. It will be noticed that they include cases in which the question whether a man acted with free will is asked in order to determine whether he was morally and legally responsible for his acts.

Jones: I once went without food for a week.
Smith: Did you do that of your own free will?
Jones: No. I did it because I was lost in a desert and could find no food.

But suppose that the man who had fasted was Mahatma Gandhi. The conversation might then have gone

Gandhi: I once fasted for a week.
Smith: Did you do that of your own free will?
Gandhi: Yes. I did it because I wanted to compel the British Government to give India its independence.

Take another case. Suppose that I had stolen some bread, but that I was as truthful as George Washington. Then, if I were charged with the crime in court, some exchange of the following sort might take place:

Judge: Did you steal the bread of your own free will?
Stace: Yes. I stole it because I was hungry.

Or in different circumstances the conversation might run:

Judge: Did you steal of your own free will?
Stace: No. I stole because my employer threatened to beat me if I did not.

At a recent murder trial in Trenton some of the accused had signed confessions, but afterwards asserted that they had done so under police duress. The following exchange might have occurred:

Judge: Did you sign this confession of your own free will?
Prisoner: No. I signed it because the police beat me up.

Now suppose that a Philosopher had been a member of the jury. We could imagine this conversation taking place in the jury room.

Foreman of the Jury: The Prisoner says he signed the confession because he was beaten, and not of his own free will.
Philosopher: This is quite irrelevant to the case. There is no such thing as free will.
Foreman: Do you mean to say that it makes no difference whether he signed because his conscience made him want to tell the truth or because he was beaten?
Philosopher: None at all. Whether he was caused to sign by a beating or by some desire of his own—the desire to tell the truth, for example—in either case his signing was causally determined, and therefore in neither case did he act of his own free will. Since there is no such thing as free will, the question whether he signed of his own free will ought not to be discussed by us. ❺

Here is the most fundamental reason why causal determinism seems to rule out free will: because it means that a person's actions are determined (and thus compelled) by causal antecedents (presumably heredity and environment, and ultimately by whatever caused those) in a way that leaves him no real choice. Stace will reject this view.

This is too fast: to say that freedom is incompatible with determinism does not require saying that freedom just means indeterminism. Just as the compatibilist will say that freedom is *one sort* of determinism (an action being determined in one way rather than others), so a *libertarian* (who claims that freedom and determinism are incompatible and that freedom exists) can say that freedom is *one* sort of indeterminism.

A compatibilist need not insist that everything is determined and so need not deny that there are purely random events. (He will, however, deny that free actions are random events.)

Someone like "Philosopher," who denies the existence of freedom, could still admit that the absence of freedom is clearer and more obvious in a case of external compulsion, like the one where the prisoner is forced to sign the confession by being beaten until he does.

The Foreman and the rest of the jury would rightly conclude that the Philosopher must be making some mistake. What sort of a mistake could it be? There is only one possible answer. The Philosopher must be using the phrase "free will" in some peculiar way of his own which is not the way in which men usually use it when they wish to determine a question of moral responsibility. That is, he must be using an incorrect definition of it as implying action not determined by causes. [6]

"Philosopher" would of course deny that he was using an incorrect definition and would probably claim instead that people who say the uncoerced signing is free simply do not realize that it too was entirely determined by antecedent causes.

Suppose a man left his office at noon, and were questioned about it. Then we might hear this:

Jones: Did you go out of your own free will?
Smith: Yes. I went out to get my lunch.

But we might hear:

Jones: Did you leave your office of your own free will?
Smith: No. I was forcibly removed by the police.

We have now collected a number of cases of actions which, in the ordinary usage of the English language, would be called cases in which people have acted of their own free will. We should also say in all these cases that they *chose* to act as they did. We should also say that they could have acted otherwise, if they had chosen. For instance, Mahatma Gandhi was not compelled to fast; he chose to do so. He could have eaten if he had wanted to. When Smith went out to get his lunch, he chose to do so. He could have stayed and done some more work, if he had wanted to. [7] We have also collected a number of cases of the opposite kind. They are cases in which men were not able to exercise their free will. They had no choice. They were compelled to do as they did. The man in the desert did not fast of his own free will. He had no choice in the matter. He was compelled to fast because there was nothing for him to eat. And so with the other cases. It ought to be quite easy, by an inspection of these cases, to tell what we ordinarily mean when we say that a man did or did not exercise free will. We ought therefore to be able to extract from them the proper definition of the term. Let us put the cases in a table:

The compatibilist will say that a person whose action is caused by his own psychological states (which are in turn determined by antecedent causes stretching back into the past) still *could have done otherwise* in the sense that *if* the person had wanted to do something else (that is, if his psychological states had been different—which they could not have been, given the antecedent causes), he would have done that something else.

Free Acts	**Unfree Acts**
Gandhi fasting because he wanted to free India.	The man fasting in the desert because there was no food.
Stealing bread because one is hungry.	Stealing because one's employer threatened to beat one.
Signing a confession because one wanted to tell the truth.	Signing because the police beat one.
Leaving the office because one wanted one's lunch.	Leaving because forcibly removed.

It is obvious that to find the correct definition of free acts we must discover what characteristic is common to all the acts in the left-hand column, and is, at the same time, absent from all the acts in the right-hand column. This characteristic which all free acts have, and which no unfree acts have, will be the defining characteristic of free will.

Is being uncaused, or not being determined by causes, the characteristic of which we are in search? It cannot be, because although it is true that all the acts in the right-hand column have causes, such as the beating by the police or the absence of food in the desert, so also do the acts in the left-hand column. Mr. Gandhi's fasting was caused by his desire to free India, the man leaving his office by his hunger, and so on. Moreover there is no reason to doubt that these causes of the free acts were in turn caused by prior conditions, and that these were again the results of causes, and so on back indefinitely into the past. [8] Any physiologist can tell us the causes of hunger. What caused Mr. Gandhi's tremendously powerful desire to free India is no doubt more difficult to discover. But it must have had causes. Some of them may have lain in peculiarities of his glands or brain, others in his past experiences, others in his heredity, others in his education. [9] Defenders of free will have usually tended to deny such facts. But to do so is plainly a case of special pleading, which is unsupported by any scrap of evidence. The only reasonable view is that all human actions, both those which are freely done and those which are not, are either wholly determined by causes, or at least as much determined as other events in nature. It may be true, as the physicists tell us, that nature is not as deterministic as was once thought. But whatever degree of determinism prevails in the world, human actions appear to be as much

R Stace's claim here is that it is obvious that the actions we regard as free are just as causally determined as the ones we regard as unfree, so that determinism or lack of determinism does not mark the difference between them.

That Gandhi's actions were at least *influenced* by prior causes seems extremely plausible. But is it as obvious as Stace thinks that they were *entirely* determined by such causes?

determined as anything else. And if this is so, it cannot be the case that what distinguishes actions freely chosen from those which are not free is that the latter are determined by causes while the former are not. Therefore, being uncaused or being undetermined by causes, must be an incorrect definition of free will.

What, then, is the difference between acts which are freely done and those which are not? What is the characteristic which is present to all the acts in the left-hand column and absent from all those in the right-hand column? Is it not obvious that, although both sets of actions have causes, the causes of those in the left-hand column are *of a different kind* from the causes of those in the right-hand column? The free acts are all caused by desires, or motives, or by some sort of internal psychological states of the agent's mind. The unfree acts, on the other hand, are all caused by physical forces or physical conditions, outside the agent. Police arrest means physical force exerted from the outside; the absence of food in the desert is a physical condition of the outside world. We may therefore frame the following rough definitions. *Acts freely done are those whose immediate causes are psychological states in the agent. Acts not freely done are those whose immediate causes are states of affairs external to the agent.* (10)

It is plain that if we define free will in this way, then free will certainly exists, and the philosopher's denial of its existence is seen to be what it is—nonsense. For it is obvious that all those actions of men which we should ordinarily attribute to the exercise of their free will, or of which we should say that they freely chose to do them, are in fact actions which have been caused by their own desires, wishes, thoughts, emotions, impulses, or other psychological states.

In applying our definition we shall find that it usually works well, but that there are some puzzling cases which it does not seem exactly to fit. These puzzles can always be solved by paying careful attention to the ways in which words are used, and remembering that they are not always used consistently. I have space for only one example. Suppose that a thug threatens to shoot you unless you give him your wallet, and suppose that you do so. Do you, in giving him your wallet, do so of your own free will or not? If we apply our definition, we find that you acted freely, since the immediate cause of the action was not an actual outside force but the fear of death, which is a psychological cause. Most people, however, would say that you did not act of your own free will but under compulsion. Does this show that our definition is wrong? I do not think so. Aristotle, who gave a solution of the problem of free will substantially the same as ours (though he did not use the term "free will") admitted that there are what he called "mixed" or borderline cases in which it is difficult to know whether we ought to call the acts free or compelled. In the case under discussion, though no actual force was used, the gun at your forehead so nearly approximated to actual force that we tend to say the case was one of compulsion. It is a borderline case. (11)

Here is what may seem like another kind of puzzle. According to our view an action may be free though it could have been predicted beforehand with certainty. But suppose you told a lie, and it was certain beforehand that you would tell it. How could one then say, "You could have told the truth"? The answer is that it is perfectly true that you could have told the truth *if* you had wanted to. In fact you would have done so, for in that case the causes producing your action, namely your desires, would have been different, and would therefore have produced different effects. It is a delusion that predictability and free will are incompatible. This agrees with common sense. For if, knowing your character, I predict that you will act honorably, no one would say when you do act honorably, that this shows you did not do so of your own free will. (12)

Since free will is a condition of moral responsibility, we must be sure that our theory of free will gives a sufficient basis for it. To be held morally responsible for one's actions means that one may be justly punished or rewarded, blamed or praised, for them. But it is not just to punish a man for what he cannot help doing. . . . We have not attempted to decide whether, as a matter of fact, all events, including human actions, are completely determined. For that question is irrelevant to the problem of free will. But if we assume for the purposes of argument that complete determinism is true, but that we are nevertheless free, it may then be asked whether such a deterministic free will is compatible with moral responsibility. For it may seem unjust to punish a man for an action which it could have been predicted with certainty beforehand that he would do.

(10)

Here is an explicit formulation of Stace's version of compatibilism. Some compatibilists would add a second requirement for freedom: that the acts not be externally *constrained* by something like a threat (which would be compatible with Stace's first requirement, since a threat operates by affecting the psychological states of the agent). In fact, two of Stace's own examples of unfree actions (the ones involving a beating or a threat of a beating) are in fact free if judged by his account, since the agent's psychological states are the *immediate* cause of what he does.

(11)

Most compatibilists would say that such an action is clearly not free to any meaningful extent because it is externally *constrained*. (But notice that the person does still have some small latitude within which his choice determines the result: he can hand over the wallet or he can refuse—and be shot if the robber is serious. And something analogous is true in the case where one is threatened with a beating by one's employer or is beaten by the police.)

(12)

R Stace reiterates the sense in which the person could have done otherwise, and makes the point that this sort of predictability is not ordinarily taken to rule out freedom.

(Does it matter how *surely* and *exactly* predictable the action is?)

13

This is a **utilitarian** justification for punishment: punishment is justified because it leads to better overall consequences than any of the alternatives. Whether the person is *responsible* or *deserves* to be punished is irrelevant—unless responsibility or desert are interpreted as meaning just that punishment will lead to better consequences.

14

STOP Think carefully about this comparison: does treating *people* in a certain way require only the sort of justification that is required for doing various things to plants or machines?

15

Stace is assuming that the only alternative to a determinist account of free human actions is one according to which such actions are random in character.

But that determinism is incompatible with moral responsibility is as much a delusion as that it is incompatible with free will. You do not excuse a man for doing a wrong act because, knowing his character, you felt certain beforehand that he would do it. Nor do you deprive a man of a reward or prize because, knowing his goodness or his capabilities, you felt certain beforehand that he would win it.

Volumes have been written on the justification of punishment. But so far as it affects the question of free will, the essential principles involved are quite simple. The punishment of a man for doing a wrong act is justified, either on the ground that it will correct his own character, or that it will deter other people from doing similar acts. 13 The instrument of punishment has been in the past, and no doubt still is, often unwisely used; so that it may often have done more harm than good. But that is not relevant to our present problem. Punishment, if and when it is justified, is justified only on one or both of the grounds just mentioned, The question then is how, if we assume determinism, punishment can correct character or deter people from evil actions.

Suppose that your child develops a habit of telling lies. You give him a mild beating. Why? Because you believe that his personality is such that the usual motives for telling the truth do not cause him to do so. You therefore supply the missing cause, or motive, in the shape of pain and the fear of future pain if he repeats his untruthful behavior. And you hope that a few treatments of this kind will condition him to the habit of truthtelling, so that he will come to tell the truth without the infliction of pain. You assume that his actions are determined by causes, but that the usual causes of truth-telling do not in him produce their usual effects. You therefore supply him with an artificially injected motive, pain and fear, which you think will in the future cause him to speak truthfully.

The principle is exactly the same where you hope, by punishing one man, to deter others from wrong actions. You believe that the fear of punishment will cause those who might otherwise do evil to do well.

We act on the same principle with non-human, and even with inanimate, things, if they do not behave in the way we think they ought to behave. The rose bushes in the garden produce only small and poor blooms, whereas we want large and rich ones. We supply a cause which will produce large blooms, namely fertilizer. Our automobile does not go properly. We supply a cause which will make it go better, namely oil in the works. The punishment for the man, the fertilizer for the plant, and the oil for the car, are all justified by the same principle and in the same way. The only difference is that different kinds of things require different kinds of causes to make them do what they should. Pain may be the appropriate remedy to apply, in certain cases, to human beings, and oil to the machine. It is, of course, of no use to inject motor oil into the boy or to beat the machine. 14

Thus we see that moral responsibility is not only consistent with determinism, but requires it. The assumption on which punishment is based is that human behavior is causally determined. If pain could not be a cause of truth-telling there would be no justification at all for punishing lies. If human actions and volitions were uncaused, it would be useless either to punish or reward, or indeed to do anything else to correct people's bad behavior. For nothing that you could do would in any way influence them. Thus moral responsibility would entirely disappear. If there were no determinism of human beings at all, their actions would be completely unpredictable and capricious, and therefore irresponsible. And this is in itself a strong argument against the common view of philosophers that free will means being undetermined by causes. 15

...

Discussion Questions

1. Think carefully about the compatibilist account of the sense in which a person "could have done otherwise," applying it to some examples, and getting as clear as you can about how it is compatible with causal determinism. Is being able to do otherwise in this sense enough for freedom in the sense required for moral responsibility?

2. Is the person who hands over his wallet because another person has a gun to his head free in a meaningful sense? Could he have done otherwise? Should a compatibilist add the requirement that an action not be externally constrained? What should be said about different degrees of constraint?

3. Think about some of Blatchford's examples. What would Stace say about such cases? Do you think he is right?
4. Compare Stace's overall position with Blatchford's. They actually agree on quite a lot. What do they agree about? Where exactly are their points of disagreement, and who is right?
5. How successful is Stace's argument that his conception of free will makes sense of the assumption that free will is a condition of moral responsibility? His argument depends on showing that his view of free will can justify punishment. Is Stace's utilitarian justification for punishment enough to show that punishment is *morally* (as opposed to practically) justified?

Paul Edwards

Paul Edwards (1923–2004) was an Austrian-born philosopher who was educated in Australia, but did most of his teaching in the United States, mainly at Columbia. Though perhaps best known as the editor-in-chief of the Macmillan *Encyclopedia of Philosophy* (1967), Edwards also wrote widely on topics in the philosophy of religion, metaphysics, and ethics. In the following selection, he criticizes soft determinist or compatibilist views on the grounds that their account of freedom evades the deepest problems about free will and does not provide an acceptable basis for moral responsibility. His conclusion is that hard determinism is the correct position.

Hard and Soft Determinism

In his essay "The Dilemma of Determinism," William James makes a distinction that will serve as a point of departure for my remarks. He there distinguishes between the philosophers he calls "hard" determinists and those he labels "soft" determinists. The former, the hard determinists, James tells us, "did not shrink from such words as fatality, bondage of the will, necessitation and the like." He quotes a famous stanza from Omar Khayyám as representing this kind of determinism:

> With earth's first clay they did the last man knead,
> And there of the last harvest sowed the seed.
> And the first morning of creation wrote
> What the last dawn of reckoning shall read.

Another of Omar's verses expresses perhaps even better the kind of theory that James has here in mind:

> Tis all a checker-board of nights and days,
> Where destiny with men for pieces plays;
> Thither and thither moves, and metes, and slays,
> And one by one back to the closet lays.

James mentioned no names other than Omar Khayyám. But there is little doubt that among the hard determinists he would have included Jonathan Edwards, Anthony Collins, Holbach, Priestley, Robert Owen, Schopenhauer, Freud, and also, if he had come a little earlier, Clarence Darrow. 

James of course rejected both hard and soft determinism, but for hard determinism he had a certain respect: the kind of respect one sometimes has for an honest, straightforward adversary. For soft determinism, on the other-hand, he had nothing but contempt, calling it a "quagmire of evasion." "Nowadays," he writes, "we have a *soft* determinism which abhors harsh words, and repudiating fatality, necessity, and even predetermination, says that its real name is 'freedom.'...

The theory James calls soft determinism, especially the Hume-Mill-Schlick variety of it, has been extremely fashionable during the last twenty-five years, while hardly anybody can be found today who has anything good to say for hard determinism. 2 In opposition to this contemporary trend, I should like to strike a blow on behalf of hard determinism in my talk today. I shall also try to bring out exactly what is really at issue between hard and soft determinism. I think the nature of this dispute has frequently been misconceived chiefly because many writers, including James, have a very inaccurate notion

1

And Robert Blatchford.

2

Soft determinism is also, of course, the view advocated by Stace—and, in an importantly different form, by Frankfurt, in the following selection.

From *Determinism and Freedom,* edited by Sidney Hook (New York: Collier Books, 1961).

of what is maintained by actual hard determinists, as distinct from the bogey men they set up in order to score an easy victory.

To begin with, it is necessary to spell more fully the main contentions of the soft determinists. Since it is the dominant form of soft determinism at the present time, I shall confine myself to the Hume-Mill-Schlick theory. According to this theory there is in the first place no contradiction whatsoever between determinism and the proposition that human beings are sometimes free agents. When we call an action "free" we never in any ordinary situation mean that it was uncaused; and this emphatically includes the kind of action about which we pass moral judgments. By calling an action "free" we mean that the agent was not compelled or constrained to perform it. Sometimes people act in a certain way because of threats or because they have been drugged or because of a posthypnotic suggestion or because of an irrational overpowering urge such as the one that makes a kleptomaniac steal something he does not really need. On such occasions human beings are not free agents. (3) But on other occasions they act in certain ways because of their own rational desires, because of their own unimpeded efforts, because they have chosen to act in these ways. On these occasions they are free agents although their actions are just as much caused as actions that are not deemed free. In distinguishing between free and unfree actions we do not try to mark the presence and absence of causes but attempt to indicate the *kind* of causes that are present.

(3) Edwards is here reporting the most widely held version of the soft determinist view. But it is fairly clear that according to both Hume and Stace, the kleptomaniac acts freely (because his action is determined by his own psychological states or by his will). What would these two soft determinists say about these other cases?

Secondly there is no antithesis between determinism and moral responsibility. When we judge a person morally responsible for a certain action, we do indeed presuppose that he was a free agent at the time of the action. But the freedom presupposed is not the contra-causal freedom about which indeterminists go into such ecstatic raptures. (4) It is nothing more than the freedom already mentioned—the ability to act according to one's choices or desires. Since determinism is compatible with freedom in this sense, it is also compatible with moral responsibility. In other words, the world is after all wonderful: we can be determinists and yet go on punishing our enemies and our children, and we can go on blaming ourselves, all without a bad intellectual conscience.

(4)  That is, it is neither randomness nor some third alternative to determinism and randomness of the sort advocated by libertarians.

Mill, who was probably the greatest moralizer among the soft determinists, recognized with particular satisfaction the influence or alleged influence of one class of human desires. Not only, for example, does such lowly desire as my desire to get a new car influence my conduct. It is equally true, or so at least Mill believed, that my desire to become a more virtuous person does on occasion influence my actions. (5) By suitable training and efforts my desire to change my character may in fact bring about the desired changes. If Mill were alive today he might point to contemporary psychiatry as an illustration of his point. Let us suppose that I have an intense desire to become famous, but that I also have an intense desire to become a happier and more lovable person who, among other things, does not greatly care about fame. Let us suppose, furthermore, that I know of a therapy that can transform fame-seeking and unlovable into lovable and fame-indifferent character structures. If, now, I have enough money, energy, and courage, and if a few other conditions are fulfilled, my desire may actually lead to a major change in my character. (6) Since we can, therefore, at least to some extent, form our own character, determinism according to Mill is compatible not only with judgments of moral responsibility about this or that particular *action* flowing from an unimpeded desire, but also, within limits, with moral judgments about the *character* of human beings.

(5)  Mill's view here is a partial anticipation of Frankfurt's view (in the following selection).

(6)  But of course whether or not I have the desire in question and satisfy the conditions for being able to do this is itself determined, according to Mill's view.

I think that several of Mill's observations were well worth making and that James's verdict on his theory as a "quagmire of evasion" is far too derogatory. I think hard determinists have occasionally written in such a way as to suggest that they deny the causal efficacy of human desires and efforts. Thus Holbach wrote:

> You will say that I feel free. This is an illusion, which may be compared to that of the fly in the fable, who, lighting upon the pole of a heavy carriage, applauded himself for directing its course. Man, who thinks himself free, is a fly who imagines he has power to move the universe, while he is himself unknowingly carried along by it.

There is also the following passage in Schopenhauer:

> Every man, being what he is and placed in the circumstances which for the moment obtain, but which on their part also arise by strict necessity, can absolutely never do anything else than just

> what at that moment he does do. Accordingly, the whole course of a man's life, in all its incidents great and small, is as necessarily predetermined as the course of a clock. 7

...

Furthermore there can be little doubt that Hume and Mill and Schlick were a great deal clearer about the relation between motives and actions than the hard determinists. . . .

But when all is said and done, there remains a good deal of truth in James's charge that soft determinism is an evasion. For a careful reading of their works shows that none of the hard determinists really denied that human desires, efforts, and choices make a difference in the course of events. Any remarks to the contrary are at most temporary lapses. This, then, is hardly the point at issue. If it is not the point at issue, what is? Let me at this stage imagine a hard determinist replying to a champion of the Hume-Mill theory: "You are right," he would say, "in maintaining that some of our actions are caused by our desires and choices. But you do not pursue the subject far enough. You arbitrarily stop at the desires and volitions. We must not stop there. We must go on to ask where *they* come from; and if determinism is true there can be no doubt about the answer to this question. Ultimately our desires and our whole character are derived from our inherited equipment and the environmental influences to which we were subjected at the beginning of our lives. It is clear that we had no hand in shaping either of these." 8 A hard determinist could quote a number of eminent supporters. "Our volitions and our desires," wrote Holbach in his little book *Good Sense,* "are never in our power. You think yourself free, because you do what you will; but are you free to will or not to will; to desire or not to desire?" And Schopenhauer expressed the same thought in the following epigram: "A man can surely do what he wills to do, but he cannot determine what he wills."

Let me turn once more to the topic of character transformation by means of psychiatry to bring out this point with full force. Let us suppose that both *A* and *B* are compulsive and suffer intensely from their neuroses. Let us assume that there is a therapy that could help them, which could materially change their character structure, but that it takes a great deal of energy and courage to undertake the treatment. Let us suppose that *A* has the necessary energy and courage while *B* lacks it. *A* undergoes the therapy and changes in the desired way. *B* just gets more and more compulsive and more and more miserable. Now, it is true that *A* helped form his own later character. But his starting point, his desire to change, his energy and courage, were already there. They may or may not have been the result of previous efforts on his own part. But there must have been a first effort, and the effort at that time was the result of factors that were not of his making.

The fact that a person's character is ultimately the product of factors over which he had no control is not denied by the soft determinists, though many of them don't like to be reminded of it when they are in a moralizing mood. Since the hard determinists admit that our desires and choices do on occasion influence the course of our lives, there is thus no disagreement between the soft and the hard determinists about the empirical facts. 9 However, some hard determinists infer from some of these facts that human beings are never morally responsible for their actions. The soft determinists, as already stated, do not draw any such inference. In the remainder of my paper I shall try to show just what it is that hard determinists are inferring and why, in my opinion, they are justified in their conclusion.

I shall begin by adopting for my purposes a distinction introduced by C. A. Campbell in his extremely valuable article "Is Free Will a Pseudo-Problem?"* in which he distinguishes between two conceptions of moral responsibility. Different persons, he says, require different conditions to be fulfilled before holding human beings morally responsible for what they do. First, there is what Campbell calls the ordinary unreflective person, who is rather ignorant and who is not greatly concerned with the theories of science, philosophy, and religion. If the unreflective person is sure that the agent to be judged was acting under coercion or constraint, he will not hold him responsible. If, however, he is sure that the action was performed in accordance with the agent's unimpeded rational desire, if he

Read these passages carefully. Is it clear that either Holbach or especially Schopenhauer is denying the "causal efficacy of human desires and efforts"—as opposed to just saying that these too are determined?

This is what Blatchford would say.

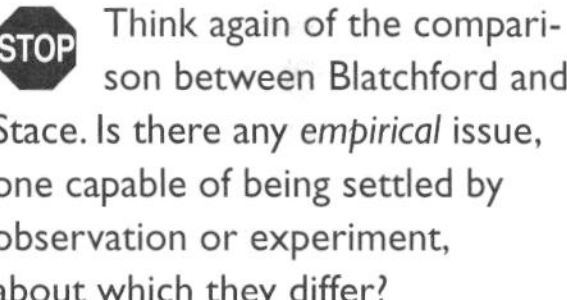

Think again of the comparison between Blatchford and Stace. Is there any *empirical* issue, one capable of being settled by observation or experiment, about which they differ?

**Mind,* 1951.

is sure that the action would not have taken place but for the agent's decision, then the unreflective person will consider ascription of moral responsibility justified. The fact that the agent did not ultimately make his own character will either not occur to him, or else it will not be considered a sufficient ground for withholding a judgment of moral responsibility.

In addition to such unreflective persons, continues Campbell, there are others who have reached "a tolerably advanced level or reflection."

> Such a person will doubtless be acquainted with the claims advanced in some quarters that causal law operates universally; or/and with the theories of some philosophies that the universe is throughout the expression of a single supreme principle; or/and with the doctrines of some theologians that the world is created, sustained and governed by an Omniscient and Omnipotent Being.

Such a person will tend to require the fulfillment of a further condition before holding anybody morally responsible. He will require not only that the agent was not coerced or constrained but also—and this is taken to be an additional condition—that he "could have chosen otherwise than he actually did." 10 I should prefer to put this somewhat differently, but it will not affect the main conclusion drawn by Campbell, with which I agree. The reflective person, I should prefer to express it, requires not only that the agent was not coerced; he also requires that the agent *originally chose his own character*—the character that now displays itself in his choices and desires and efforts. 11 Campbell concludes that determinism is indeed compatible with judgments of moral responsibility in the unreflective sense, but that it is incompatible with judgments of moral responsibility in the reflective sense.

10

Soft determinists like Hume and Stace, of course, accept the verbal formulation of this requirement—see Stace, p. 268. The issue between them and libertarians like Campbell (and Nozick and Kane) is what is required for the quoted phrase to correctly apply to an action.

11

STOP Think carefully about this very demanding condition. What would it mean to choose your own character? On what basis would you make such a choice?

Although I do not follow Campbell in rejecting determinism, I agree basically with his analysis, with one other qualification. I do not think it is a question of the different senses in which the term is used by ignorant and unreflective people, on the one hand, and by those who are interested in science, religion, and philosophy, on the other. The very same persons, whether educated or uneducated, use it in certain contexts in the one sense and in other contexts in the other. Practically all human beings, no matter how much interested they are in science, religion, and philosophy, employ what Campbell calls the unreflective conception when they are dominated by violent emotions like anger, indignation, or hate, and especially when the conduct they are judging has been personally injurious to them. On the other hand, a great many people, whether they are educated or not, will employ what Campbell calls the reflective conception when they are not consumed with hate or anger—when they are judging a situation calmly and reflectively and when the fact that the agent did not ultimately shape his own character has been vividly brought to their attention. Clarence Darrow in his celebrated pleas repeatedly appealed to the jury on precisely this ground. If any of you, he would say, had been reared in an environment like that of the accused or had to suffer from his defective heredity, *you* would now be standing in the dock. . . . Darrow nearly always convinced the jury that the accused could not be held morally responsible for his acts; and certainly the majority of the jurors were relatively uneducated.

I have so far merely distinguished between two concepts of moral responsibility. I now wish to go a step farther and claim that only one of them can be considered, properly speaking, a moral concept. This is not an easy point to make clear, but I can at least indicate what I mean. We do not normally consider just any positive or negative feeling a "moral" emotion. Nor do we consider just any sentence containing the words "good" or "bad" expressions of "moral" judgment. . . . A feeling or judgment must in a certain sense be "impersonal" before we consider it moral. To this I would add that it must also be independent of violent emotions. Confining myself to judgments, I would say that a judgment was "moral" only if it was formulated in a calm and reflective mood, or at least if it is supported in a calm and reflective state of mind. If this is so, it follows that what Campbell calls the reflective sense of "moral responsibility" is the only one that qualifies as a properly moral use of the term. 12

12

Edwards is saying that anyone who approaches the issue in a "calm and reflective state of mind" will agree that the soft determinist's account of moral responsibility is inadequate. (Do you think he is right about this?)

Before I conclude I wish to avoid a certain misunderstanding of my remarks. From the fact that human beings do not ultimately shape their own character, I said, it *follows* that they are never morally responsible. I do not mean that by reminding people of the ultimate causes of their character one makes them more charitable and less vengeful. Maybe one does, but that is not what I mean. I mean "follow" or "imply" in the same sense as, or in a sense closely akin to, that in which the conclusion of a valid syllogism follows from the premises. The effectiveness of Darrow's pleas does not merely show, I am arguing, how powerfully he could sway the emotions of the jurors. His pleas also brought into the open one of the conditions the jurors, like others, consider necessary on reflection before they hold an agent morally responsible. . . .

Discussion Questions

1. Assuming that freedom and moral responsibility do require that a person "could have done otherwise," is the compatibilist (or soft determinist) account of what this amounts to the right one? Think of examples like those listed by Edwards on page 272 (before Annotation 3). Could the people in question have done otherwise in the compatibilist sense? If so, does this show that they are free and morally responsible, or does it show that the compatibilist account of "could have done otherwise" is not the right one for genuine freedom?
2. Consider now Edwards's alternative account of "could have done otherwise" (p. 274). If this is the right account, is anyone ever free and responsible? Can you even imagine how this requirement (which others have suggested too) could be satisfied? What would it be like to choose your own character—and on what basis would you make the choice? Can you think of any case where it seems plausible that you choose at least some significant part of your own character? Did the choice in question derive from other parts or aspects of your character?

Harry Frankfurt

Harry Frankfurt is an American philosopher who has taught at a number of different universities, including Yale and most recently Princeton (where he is now Professor Emeritus). He is widely known for work on Descartes, moral psychology, and the free will problem. In this selection, Frankfurt presents and defends a version of compatibilism that is more complicated and sophisticated than that of Hume and Stace.

In Frankfurt's view, genuine free will requires more than just having your actions be determined by your wants or desires. It also requires that your ordinary desires be themselves determined by "second-order desires": desires about your own desires. Thus a person who has free will according to Frankfurt's account must have a kind of control over his own desires that is not required by Hume and Stace. (The account of human psychology that Frankfurt is offering is complicated and subtle; you will understand him better if you try to think of plausible examples in your own life of the various kinds of desires he discusses.)

Freedom of the Will and the Concept of a Person

...

There is a sense in which the word 'person' is merely the singular form of 'people' and in which both terms connote no more than membership in a certain biological species. In those senses of the word which are of greater philosophical interest, however, the criteria for being a person do not serve primarily to distinguish the members of our own species from the members of other species. Rather they are designed to capture those attributes which are the subject of our most humane concern and the source of what we regard as most important and most problematical in our lives. Now these attributes would be of equal significance to us even if they were not in fact peculiar and common to the members of our own species.

From *Journal of Philosophy,* Vol. 68 (1971).

A **person** is, roughly, a being that has those attributes that, we believe, give human beings a special status in the world (where this means at least mainly a special *moral* status). Frankfurt doesn't say here just what those attributes are, though he will give an account of what he claims to be one central one later on.

Frankfurt's suggestion is that the features that make human beings special in this way do *not* logically require being a member of the human biological species, so that members of other species could possibly have them. But he also insists that there is a presumption (which he will rely on later) that only humans in fact have these features.

STOP You almost certainly have some second-order desires: think of some examples. Does it seem right that animals of other kinds do not have such second-order desires?

STOP You should easily be able to think of cases where you do not act upon one (or more) of your wants or desires because, as it is sometimes put, that desire is "overridden" by another, stronger desire. Can you think of some genuine wants or desires of yours that it is plausible to think will *always* be overridden in this way, so that they will never in fact be acted on—will never be "effective" or identical, in Frankfurt's usage, with your *will*? (This is a bit harder, but should still be fairly easy to do.)

What interests us most in the human condition would not interest us less if it were also a feature of the condition of other creatures as well. ❶

Our concept of ourselves as persons is not to be understood, therefore, as a concept of attributes that are necessarily species-specific. It is conceptually possible that members of novel or even of familiar nonhuman species should be persons; and it is also conceptually possible that some members of the human species are not persons. We do in fact assume, on the other hand, that no member of another species is a person. Accordingly, there is a presumption that what is essential to persons is a set of characteristics that we generally suppose—whether rightly or wrongly, to be uniquely human. ❷

It is my view that one essential difference between persons and other creatures is to be found in the structure of a person's will. Human beings are not alone in having desires and motives, or in making choices. They share these things with the members of certain other species, some of whom even appear to engage in deliberation and to make decisions based upon prior thought. It seems to be peculiarly characteristic of humans, however, that they are able to form what I shall call "second-order desires" or "desires of the second order."

Besides wanting and choosing and being moved *to do* this or that, men may also want to have (or not to have) certain desires and motives. They are capable of wanting to be different, in their preferences and purposes, from what they are. Many animals appear to have the capacity for what I shall call "first-order desires" or "desires of the first order," which are simply desires to do or not to do one thing or another. No animal other than man, however, appears to have the capacity for reflective self-evaluation that is manifested in the formation of second-order desires. ❸

I

. . .

Consider . . . those statements of the form "A wants to X" which identify first-order desires—that is, statements in which the term 'to X' refers to an action. A statement of this kind does not, by itself, indicate the relative strength of A's desire to X. It does not make it clear whether this desire is at all likely to play a decisive role in what A actually does or tries to do. For it may correctly be said that A wants to X even when his desire to X is only one among his desires and when it is far from being paramount among them. Thus, it may be true that A wants to X when he strongly prefers to do something else instead; and it may be true that he wants to X despite the fact that, when he acts, it is not the desire to X that motivates him to do what he does. On the other hand, someone who states that A wants to X may mean to convey that it is this desire that is motivating or moving A to do what he is actually doing or that A will in fact be moved by this desire (unless he changes his mind) when he acts.

It is only when it is used in the second of these ways that, given the special usage of 'will' that I propose to adopt, the statement identifies A's will. To identify an agent's will is either to identify the desire (or desires) by which he is motivated in some action he performs or to identify the desire (or desires) by which he will or would be motivated when or if he acts. An agent's will, then, is identical with one or more of his first-order desires. But the notion of the will, as I am employing it, is not coextensive with the notion of first-order desires. It is not the notion of something that merely inclines an agent in some degree to act in a certain way. Rather, it is the notion of an *effective* desire"—one that moves (or will or would move) a person all the way to action. . . . ❹

Now consider those statements of the form "A wants to X" which identify second-order desires"—that is, statements in which the term 'to X' refers to a desire of the first order. There are also two kinds of situation in which it may be true that A wants to want to X. In the first place, it might be true of A that he wants to have a desire to X despite the fact that he has a univocal desire, altogether free of conflict and ambivalence, to refrain from X-ing. Someone might want to have a certain desire, in other words, but univocally want that desire to be unsatisfied.

Suppose that a physician engaged in psychotherapy with narcotics addicts believes that his ability to help his patients would be enhanced if he understood better what it is like for them to desire the drug to which they are addicted. Suppose that he is led in this way to want to have a desire for the drug. If it is a genuine desire that he wants, then what he wants is not merely to feel the sensations that addicts characteristically feel when they are gripped by their desires for the drug. What the physician wants, insofar as he wants to have a desire, is to be inclined or moved to some extent to take the drug.

It is entirely possible, however, that, although he wants to be moved by a desire to take the drug, he does not want this desire to be effective. He may not want it to move him all the way to action. He need not be interested in finding out what it is like to take the drug. And insofar as he now wants only to *want* to take it, and not to *take* it, there is nothing in what he now wants that would be satisfied by the drug itself. He may now have, in fact, an altogether univocal desire *not* to take the drug; and he may prudently arrange to make it impossible for him to satisfy the desire he would have if his desire to want the drug should in time be satisfied. [5]

It would thus be incorrect to infer, from the fact that the physician now wants to desire to take the drug, that he already does desire to take it. His second-order desire to be moved to take the drug does not entail that he has a first-order desire to take it. If the drug were now to be administered to him, this might satisfy no desire that is implicit in his desire to want to take it. While he wants to want to take the drug, he may have *no* desire to take it; it may be that *all* he wants is to taste the desire for it. That is, his desire to have a certain desire that he does not have may not be a desire that his will should be at all different than it is. [6]

Someone who wants only in this truncated way to want to X stands at the margin of preciosity, and the fact that he wants to want to X is not pertinent to the identification of his will. There is, however, a second kind of situation that may be described by 'A wants to want to X'; and when the statement is used to describe a situation of this second kind, then it does pertain to what A wants his will to be. In such cases the statement means that A wants the desire to X to be the desire that moves him effectively to act. It is not merely that he wants the desire to X to be among the desires by which, to one degree or another, he is moved or inclined to act. He wants this desire to be effective"—that is, to provide the motive in what he actually does. Now when the statement that A wants to want to X is used in this way, it does entail that A already has a desire to X. It could not be true both that A wants the desire to X to move him into action and that he does not want to X. It is only if he does want to X that he can coherently want the desire to X not merely to be one of his desires but, more decisively, to be his will. [7]

Suppose a man wants to be motivated in what he does by the desire to concentrate on his work. It is necessarily true, if this supposition is correct, that he already wants to concentrate on his work. This desire is now among his desires. But the question of whether or not his second-order desire is fulfilled does not turn merely on whether the desire he wants is one of his desires. It turns on whether this desire is, as he wants it to be, his effective desire or will. If, when the chips are down, it is his desire to concentrate on his work that moves him to do what he does, then what he wants at that time is indeed (in the relevant sense) what he wants to want. If it is some other desire that actually moves him when he acts, on the other hand, then what he wants at that time is not (in the relevant sense) what he wants to want. This will be so despite the fact that the desire to concentrate on his work continues to be among his desires. [8]

II

Someone has a desire of the second order either when he wants simply to have a certain desire or when he wants a certain desire to be his will. In situations of the latter kind, I shall call his second-order desires "second-order volitions" or "volitions of the second order." [9] Now it is having second-order volitions, and not having second-order desires generally, that I regard as essential to being a person. It is logically possible, however unlikely, that there should be an agent with second-order desires but with no volitions of the second order. Such a creature, in my view, would not be a person. I shall use the term 'wanton' to refer to agents who have first-order desires but who are not persons because, whether or not they have desires of the second order, they have no second-order volitions.*

*Creatures with second-order desires but no second-order volitions differ significantly from brute animals, and, for some purposes, it would be desirable to regard them as persons. My usage, which withholds the designation 'person' from them, is thus somewhat arbitrary. I adopt it largely because it facilitates the formulation of some of the points I wish to make. Hereafter, whenever I consider statements of the form "A wants to want to X," I shall have in mind statements identifying second-order volitions and not statements identifying second-order desires that are not second-order volitions.

R So he does not want to take the drug but does want to want to take it—that is, wants to experience such a desire.

R That is, he may want to have a desire for the drug (so he can tell what it feels like), but not actually have any such desire.

Is Frankfurt right about this? Why couldn't someone want to have a desire that he doesn't in fact have and also want that desire to be effective—to be his will? This would admittedly be an odd thing to want, but why couldn't the "physician engaged in psychotherapy with narcotics addicts" want this if (as might be the case) he thinks that he can understand his patients adequately only by experiencing what it is like for the desire to take drugs to be effective, to be a person's will, rather than being merely a weaker desire that is overridden? (Of course, if he now has some way of bringing this situation about in the future, he may now also want to make arrangements for someone else to intervene and prevent him from actually taking the drug.)

It might be that the man in question does in fact concentrate on his work, but that his motivation for so doing is that he does not want to face some personal problem and is using his work as a distraction. He might still have a weaker desire to concentrate on his work, but this would not be his effective desire—his will.

So a "second-order volition" is a desire to have an effective first-order desire of some specific sort.

The essential characteristic of a wanton is that he does not care about his will. His desires move him to do certain things, without its being true of him either that he wants to be moved by those desires or that he prefers to be moved by other desires. The class of wantons includes all nonhuman animals that have desires and all very young children. Perhaps it also includes some adult human beings as well. In any case, adult humans may be more or less wanton; they may act wantonly, in response to first-order desires concerning which they have no volitions of the second order, more or less frequently. 10

STOP Unless you are *very* unusual, you often act wantonly in this sense. Think of some examples.

The fact that a wanton has no second-order volitions does not mean that each of his first-order desires is translated heedlessly and at once into action. He may have no opportunity to act in accordance with some of his desires. Moreover, the translation of his desires into action may be delayed or precluded either by conflicting desires of the first order or by the intervention of deliberation. For a wanton may possess and employ rational faculties of a high order. Nothing in the concept of a wanton implies that he cannot reason or that he cannot deliberate concerning how to do what he wants to do. What distinguishes the rational wanton from other rational agents is that he is not concerned with the desirability of his desires themselves. He ignores the question of what his will is to be. Not only does he pursue whatever course of action he is most strongly inclined to pursue, but he does not care which of his inclinations is the strongest.

Thus a rational creature, who reflects upon the suitability to his desires of one course of action or another, may nonetheless be a wanton. In maintaining that the essence of being a person lies not in reason but in will, I am far from suggesting that a creature without reason may be a person. For it is only in virtue of his rational capacities that a person is capable of becoming critically aware of his own will and of forming volitions of the second order. The structure of a person's will presupposes, accordingly, that he is a rational being.

The distinction between a person and a wanton may be illustrated by the difference between two narcotics addicts. Let us suppose that the physiological condition accounting for the addiction is the same in both men, and that both succumb inevitably to their periodic desires for the drug to which they are addicted. One of the addicts hates his addiction and always struggles desperately, although to no avail, against its thrust. He tries everything that he thinks might enable him to overcome his desires for the drug. But these desires are too powerful for him to withstand, and invariably, in the end, they conquer him. He is an unwilling addict, helplessly violated by his own desires.

The unwilling addict has conflicting first-order desires: he wants to take the drug, and he also wants to refrain from taking it. In addition to these first-order desires, however, he has a volition of the second order. He is not a neutral with regard to the conflict between his desire to take the drug and his desire to refrain from taking it. It is the latter desire, and not the former, that he wants to constitute his will; it is the latter desire, rather than the former, that he wants to be effective and to provide the purpose that he will seek to realize in what he actually does. 11

STOP Again, you should find it fairly easy to think of examples in your own case that have the same structure as the case of the unwilling addict: two competing desires and a second-order volition that one of them be effective, but where it is in fact the other one that is effective.

The other addict is a wanton. His actions reflect the economy of his first-order desires, without his being concerned whether the desires that move him to act are desires by which he wants to be moved to act. If he encounters problems in obtaining the drug or in administering it to himself, his responses to his urges to take it may involve deliberation. But it never occurs to him to consider whether he wants the relations among his desires to result in his having the will he has. The wanton addict may be an animal, and thus incapable of being concerned about his will. In any event he is, in respect of his wanton lack of concern, no different from an animal.

The second of these addicts may suffer a first-order conflict similar to the first-order conflict suffered by the first. Whether he is human or not, the wanton may (perhaps due to conditioning) both want to take the drug and want to refrain from taking it. Unlike the unwilling addict, however, he does not prefer that one of his conflicting desires should be paramount over the other; he does not prefer that one first-order desire rather than the other should constitute his will. It would be misleading to say that he is neutral as to the conflict between his desires, since this would suggest that he regards them as equally acceptable. Since he has no identity apart from his first-order desires, it is true neither that he prefers one to the other nor that he prefers not to take sides.

It makes a difference to the unwilling addict, who is a person, which of his conflicting first-order desires wins out. Both desires are his, to be sure; and whether he finally takes the drug or finally succeeds in refraining from taking it, he acts to satisfy what is in a literal sense his own desire. In either case he does something he himself wants to do, and he does it not because of some external influence whose aim happens to coincide with his own but because of his desire to do it. The unwilling addict identifies himself, however, through the formation of a second-order volition, with one rather than with the other of his conflicting first-order desires. He makes one of them more truly his own and, in so doing, he withdraws himself from the other. It is in virtue of this identification and withdrawal, accomplished through the formation of a second-order volition, that the unwilling addict may meaningfully make the analytically puzzling statements that the force moving him to take the drug is a force other than his own, and that it is not of his own free will but rather against his will that this force moves him to take it. [12]

"Analytically puzzling" because the external or alien force in question is, after all, one of his own desires.

The wanton addict cannot or does not care which of his conflicting first-order desires wins out. His lack of concern is not due to his inability to find a convincing basis for preference. It is due either to his lack of the capacity for reflection or to his mindless indifference to the enterprise of evaluating his own desires and motives.* There is only one issue in the struggle to which his first-order conflict may lead: whether the one or the other of his conflicting desires is the stronger. Since he is moved by both desires, he will not be altogether satisfied by what he does no matter which of them is effective. But it makes no difference *to him* whether his craving or his aversion gets the upper hand. He has no stake in the conflict between them and so, unlike the unwilling addict, he can neither win nor lose the struggle in which he is engaged. When a *person* acts, the desire by which he is moved is either the will he wants or a will he wants to be without. When a *wanton* acts, it is neither.

III

There is a very close relationship between the capacity for forming second-order volitions and another capacity that is essential to persons—one that has often been considered a distinguishing mark of the human condition. It is only because a person has volitions of the second order that he is capable both of enjoying and of lacking freedom of the will. The concept of a person is not only, then, the concept of a type of entity that has both first-order desires and volitions of the second order. It can also be construed as the concept of a type of entity for whom the freedom of its will may be a problem. This concept excludes all wantons, both infrahuman and human, since they fail to satisfy an essential condition for the enjoyment of freedom of the will. And it excludes those suprahuman beings, if any, whose wills are necessarily free.

Just what kind of freedom is the freedom of the will? This question calls for an identification of the special area of human experience to which the concept of freedom of the will, as distinct from the concepts of other sorts of freedom, is particularly germane. In dealing with it, my aim will be primarily to locate the problem with which a person is most immediately concerned when he is concerned with the freedom of his will.

According to one familiar philosophical tradition, being free is fundamentally a matter of doing what one wants to do. [13] . . . I believe that this notion does capture at least part of what is implicit in the idea of an agent who *acts* freely. It misses entirely, however, the peculiar content of the quite different idea of an agent whose *will* is free. [14]

This is the standard compatibilist (or "soft determinist") view, as found in Hume and Stace, among many others.

We do not suppose that animals enjoy freedom of the will, although we recognize that an animal may be free to run in whatever direction it wants. Thus, having the freedom to do what one wants to do is not a sufficient condition of having a free will. It is not a necessary condition either. For to deprive someone of his freedom of action is not necessarily to undermine the freedom of his will.

R So *acting freely* is not sufficient, according to Frankfurt, for *freedom of the will*.

*In speaking of the evaluation of his own desires and motives as being characteristic of a person, I do not mean to suggest that a person's second-order volitions necessarily manifest a *moral* stance on his part toward his first-order desires. It may not be from the point of view of morality that the person evaluates his first-order desires. Moreover, a person may be capricious and irresponsible in forming his second-order volitions and give no serious consideration to what is at stake. Second-order volitions express evaluations only in the sense that they are preferences. There is no essential restriction on the kind of basis, if any, upon which they are formed.

Imagine a person sitting in a room whose door is locked from the outside, though he believes it to be unlocked. Such a person might have a desire to leave and go to a movie, a competing desire to stay in that room (and work on some project), and a second-order volition that the desire to stay there be the one that is effective—that this latter desire be his will. If he is able (through "willpower") to bring it about that the desire to stay is effective, and he therefore remains in the room, then (Frankfurt would say) he has both acted freely and exercised freedom of the will, even though he was not in fact free to act in accordance with the competing desire—he could not have done otherwise.

And whether it is the way it is as a result of his wanting it to be that way.

According to this account, a person can have free will only with regard to those cases where he has second-order volitions. Since these are, for most people at least, fairly rare, so also will be cases of free will. A different and perhaps more plausible view, though still in the same general direction, would be that a person has free will just in case his will is controlled by any second-order volitions he may have, thus allowing an action in relation to which there are no second-order volitions to still count as an exercise of free will.

Try to think of examples, perhaps from movies or fiction, that fit this description.

Think carefully about what exactly a third-order desire or volition would amount to. Do you have any third-order desires or volitions?

When an agent is aware that there are certain things he is not free to do, this doubtless affects his desires and limits the range of choices he can make. But suppose that someone, without being aware of it, has in fact lost or been deprived of his freedom of action. Even though he is no longer free to do what he wants to do, his will may remain as free as it was before. Despite the fact that he is not free to translate his desires into actions or to act according to the determinations of his will, he may still form those desires and make those determinations as freely as if his freedom of action had not been impaired. [15]

When we ask whether a person's will is free we are not asking whether he is in a position to translate his first-order desires into actions. That is the question of whether he is free to do as he pleases. The question of the freedom of his will does not concern the relation between what he does and what he wants to do. Rather, it concerns his desires themselves. But what question about them is it?

It seems to me both natural and useful to construe the question of whether a person's will is free in close analogy to the question of whether an agent enjoys freedom of action. Now freedom of action is (roughly, at least) the freedom to do what one wants to do. Analogously, then, the statement that a person enjoys freedom of the will means (also roughly) that he is free to want what he wants to want. More precisely, it means that he is free to will what he wants to will, or to have the will he wants. Just as the question about the freedom of an agent's action has to do with whether it is the action he wants to perform, so the question about the freedom of his will has to do with whether it is the will he wants to have. [16]

It is in securing the conformity of his will to his second-order volitions, then, that a person exercises freedom of the will. And it is in the discrepancy between his will and his second-order volitions, or in his awareness that their coincidence is not his own doing but only a happy chance, that a person who does not have this freedom feels its lack. The unwilling addict's will is not free. This is shown by the fact that it is not the will he wants. It is also true, though in a different way, that the will of the wanton addict is not free. The wanton addict neither has the will he wants nor has a will that differs from the will he wants. Since he has no volitions of the second order, the freedom of his will cannot be a problem for him. He lacks it, so to speak, by default. [17]

People are generally far more complicated than my sketchy account of the structure of a person's will may suggest. There is as much opportunity for ambivalence, conflict, and self-deception with regard to desires of the second order, for example, as there is with regard to first-order desires. If there is an unresolved conflict among someone's second-order desires, then he is in danger of having no second-order volition; for unless this conflict is resolved, he has no preference concerning which of his first-order desires is to be his will. This condition, if it is so severe that it prevents him from identifying himself in a sufficiently decisive way with *any* of his conflicting first-order desires, destroys him as a person. For it either tends to paralyze his will and to keep him from acting at all, or it tends to remove him from his will so that his will operates without his participation. In both cases he becomes, like the unwilling addict though in a different way, a helpless bystander to the forces that move him. [18]

Another complexity is that a person may have, especially if his second-order desires are in conflict, desires and volitions of a higher order than the second. There is no theoretical limit to the length of the series of desires of higher and higher orders; nothing except common sense and, perhaps, a saving fatigue prevents an individual from obsessively refusing to identify himself with any of his desires until he forms a desire of the next higher order. The tendency to generate such a series of acts of forming desires, which would be a case of humanization run wild, also leads toward the destruction of a person. [19]

It is possible, however, to terminate such a series of acts without cutting it off arbitrarily. When a person identifies himself *decisively* with one of his first-order desires, this commitment "resounds" throughout the potentially endless array of higher orders. Consider a person who, without reservation or conflict, wants to be motivated by the desire to concentrate on his work. The fact that his second-order volition to be moved by this desire is a decisive one means that there is no room for questions concerning the pertinence of desires or volitions of higher orders. Suppose the person is asked whether he wants to want to want to concentrate on his work. He can properly insist that this question concerning a third-order desire does not arise. It would be a mistake to claim that, because he has not considered whether he wants the second-order volition he has formed, he is indifferent to the question of whether it is with this volition or with some other that he wants his will to accord. The decisiveness of the commitment he has made means that he has decided that no further question about his second-order volition, at any higher order, remains to be asked. It is relatively unimportant whether we explain this by saying that this commitment implicitly generates an endless series of confirming desires of higher orders, or by saying that the commitment is tantamount to a dissolution of the pointedness of all questions concerning higher orders of desire. [20]

Examples such as the one concerning the unwilling addict may suggest that volitions of the second order, or of higher orders, must be formed deliberately and that a person characteristically struggles to ensure that they are satisfied. But the conformity of a person's will to his higher-order volitions may be far more thoughtless and spontaneous than this. Some people are naturally moved by kindness when they want to be kind, and by nastiness when they want to be nasty, without any explicit forethought and without any need for energetic self-control. Others are moved by nastiness when they want to be kind and by kindness when they intend to be nasty, equally without forethought and without active resistance to these violations of their higher-order desires. The enjoyment of freedom comes easily to some. Others must struggle to achieve it.

IV

My theory concerning the freedom of the will accounts easily for our disinclination to allow that this freedom is enjoyed by the members of any species inferior to our own. It also satisfies another condition that must be met by any such theory, by making it apparent why the freedom of the will should be regarded as desirable. The enjoyment of a free will means the satisfaction of certain desires—desires of the second or of higher orders—whereas its absence means their frustration. The satisfactions at stake are those which accrue to a person of whom it may be said that his will is his own. The corresponding frustrations are those suffered by a person of whom it may be said that he is estranged from himself, or that he finds himself a helpless or a passive bystander to the forces that move him.

A person who is free to do what he wants to do may yet not be in a position to have the will he wants. Suppose, however, that he enjoys both freedom of action and freedom of the will. Then he is not only free to do what he wants to do; he is also free to want what he wants to want. It seems to me that he has, in that case, all the freedom it is possible to desire or to conceive. There are other good things in life, and he may not possess some of them. But there is nothing in the way of freedom that he lacks. [21]

It is far from clear that certain other theories of the freedom of the will meet these elementary but essential conditions: that it be understandable why we desire this freedom and why we refuse to ascribe it to animals. Consider, for example, Roderick Chisholm's quaint version of the doctrine that human freedom entails an absence of causal determination.* Whenever a person performs a free action, according to Chisholm, it's a miracle. The motion of a person's hand, when the person moves it, is the outcome of a series of physical causes; but some event in this series, "and presumably one of those that took place within the brain, was caused by the agent and not by any other events" (18). A free agent has, therefore, "a prerogative which some would attribute only to God: each of us, when we act, is a prime mover unmoved" (23). [22]

This account fails to provide any basis for doubting that animals of subhuman species enjoy the freedom it defines. Chisholm says nothing that makes it seem less likely that a rabbit performs a miracle when it moves its leg than that a man does so when he moves his hand. But why, in any case, should anyone care whether he can interrupt the natural order of causes in the way Chisholm describes? Chisholm offers no reason for believing that there is a discernible difference between the experience of a man who miraculously initiates a series of causes when he moves his hand and a

*"Freedom and Action," in K. Lehrer, ed., *Freedom and Determinism* (New York: Random House, 1966), pp. 11–44.

STOP Can you think of examples, from your own life or elsewhere, of such "decisive identification" with a first-order desire?

This could be true even if the person's first-order desires, his second-order desires and volitions, and his success in bringing it about that his effective first-order desires—his will—conform to his second-order volitions are all entirely causally determined. This is why Frankfurt's view is still a version of compatibilism.

Chisholm's view is a libertarian view, roughly similar to the one advocated (in later selections) by Campbell and (though a bit less clearly) by Nozick.

man who moves his hand without any such breach of the normal causal sequence. There appears to be no concrete basis for preferring to be involved in the one state of affairs rather than in the other.[23]

Chisholm's view (and that of Campbell and Nozick) is that a person or agent who directly causes an action genuinely *controls* the result and could genuinely have done otherwise in a sense that does not hold for the person whose action is causally determined, even via second-order volitions. Their view is that this sort of control is required for genuine moral responsibility.

It is generally supposed that, in addition to satisfying the two conditions I have mentioned, a satisfactory theory of the freedom of the will necessarily provides an analysis of one of the conditions of moral responsibility. The most common recent approach to the problem of understanding the freedom of the will has been, indeed, to inquire what is entailed by the assumption that someone is morally responsible for what he has done. In my view, however, the relation between moral responsibility and the freedom of the will has been very widely misunderstood. It is not true that a person is morally responsible for what he has done only if his will was free when he did it. He may be morally responsible for having done it even though his will was not free at all.

A person's will is free only if he is free to have the will he wants. This means that, with regard to any of his first-order desires, he is free either to make that desire his will or to make some other first-order desire his will instead. Whatever his will, then, the will of the person whose will is free could have been otherwise; he could have done otherwise than to constitute his will as he did.[24] It is a vexed question just how 'he could have done otherwise' is to be understood in contexts such as this one. But although this question is important to the theory of freedom, it has no bearing on the theory of moral responsibility. For the assumption that a person is morally responsible for what he has done does not entail that the person was in a position to have whatever will he wanted.

If his second-order volition had been different. But if everything about him is causally determined, then that second-order volition could not have been different.

This assumption *does* entail that the person did what he did freely, or that he did it of his own free will. It is a mistake, however, to believe that someone acts freely only when he is free to do whatever he wants or that he acts of his own free will only if his will is free. Suppose that a person has done what he wanted to do, that he did it because he wanted to do it, and that the will by which he was moved when he did it was his will because it was the will he wanted. Then he did it freely and of his own free will. Even supposing that he could have done otherwise, he would not have done otherwise; and even supposing that he could have had a different will, he would not have wanted his will to differ from what it was. Moreover, since the will that moved him when he acted was his will because he wanted it to be, he cannot claim that his will was forced upon him or that he was a passive bystander to its constitution. Under these conditions, it is quite irrelevant to the evaluation of his moral responsibility to inquire whether the alternatives that he opted against were actually available to him.[25]

Think here of the example described in Annotation 15. (Frankfurt offers a more complicated example of the same general kind in his paper "Alternate Possibilities and Moral Responsibility," *Journal of Philosophy*, Vol. 66 (1969).)

In illustration, consider a third kind of addict. Suppose that his addiction has the same physiological basis and the same irresistible thrust as the addictions of the unwilling and wanton addicts, but that he is altogether delighted with his condition. He is a willing addict, who would not have things any other way. If the grip of his addiction should somehow weaken, he would do whatever he could to reinstate it; if his desire for the drug should begin to fade, he would take steps to renew its intensity.

The willing addict's will is not free, for his desire to take the drug will be effective regardless of whether or not he wants this desire to constitute his will. But when he takes the drug, he takes it freely and of his own free will. I am inclined to understand his situation as involving the overdetermination of his first-order desire to take the drug. This desire is his effective desire because he is physiologically addicted. But it is his effective desire also because he wants it to be. His will is outside his control, but, by his second-order desire that his desire for the drug should be effective, he has made this will his own. Given that it is therefore not only because of his addiction that his desire for the drug is effective, he may be morally responsible for taking the drug.[26]

Frankfurt's description of this case is puzzling. If this third addict's desire to take the drug will be effective no matter what his second-order volition is, why is this a case of "overdetermination" (determination of a result by more than one sufficient cause), rather than just determination by the addiction? And why is it "not only because of his addiction that his desire for the drug is effective," since the second-order volition makes no real difference? How does the fact that he endorses what he does (even though he would be unable to control it in any case) make him morally responsible for it?

My conception of the freedom of the will appears to be neutral with regard to the problem of determinism. It seems conceivable that it should be causally determined that a person is free to want what he wants to want. If this is conceivable, then it might be causally determined that a person enjoys a free will. There is no more than an innocuous appearance of paradox in the proposition that it is determined, ineluctably and by forces beyond their control, that certain people have free wills and that others do not. There is no incoherence in the proposition that some agency other than a person's own is responsible (even *morally* responsible) for the fact that he enjoys or fails to enjoy freedom of the will. It is possible that a person should be morally responsible for what he does of his own free will and that some other person should also be morally responsible for his having done it. (27)

On the other hand, it seems conceivable that it should come about by chance that a person is free to have the will he wants. If this is conceivable, then it might be a matter of chance that certain people enjoy freedom of the will and that certain others do not. Perhaps it is also conceivable, as a number of philosophers believe, for states of affairs to come about in a way other than by chance or as the outcome of a sequence of natural causes. If it is indeed conceivable for the relevant states of affairs to come about in some third way, then it is also possible that a person should in that third way come to enjoy the freedom of the will. (28)

Philosophers have sometimes imagined cases where a person's desires are controlled from the outside by someone else (via hypnosis, remotely controlled implants, or whatever). Frankfurt seems to be saying that such a person might still have free will and be morally responsible, as long as the outside controller determines which of the person's first-order desires (produced by the controller) are effective by producing effective second-order volitions, rather than in some other way.

What would have to come about in these other ways is the fact that the relevant second-order volition is effective, not the choice or the effectiveness of the first-order desires themselves.

Discussion Questions

1. Consider again the example suggested in Annotation 15. The person described chooses to stay in the room and does so. Is such a person acting freely and exercising free will in so doing? Could the person have done otherwise in the sense relevant to free will?
2. Consider the three drug addicts described by Frankfurt: (1) the unwilling addict, (2) the wanton addict, and (3) the willing addict. Frankfurt's view is that none of them have genuine free will (though the last two act freely); but that the last two addicts are nonetheless morally responsible for taking the drug, though the first addict is not. Assuming that the situation of all three is causally determined, is this the right result? What would Hume and Stace say? What would a libertarian say? What do you say?
3. Consider the example suggested in Annotation 27. Is Frankfurt right that a person can still act freely and have free will even when all of his desires (including second-order desires and volitions) are deliberately controlled by another person from the outside? Would a person controlled in this way still be (as Frankfurt seems to claim) morally responsible for what he does?
4. Edwards's objection to the Hume-Stace version of compatibilism is that while (even if determinism is true) a person may be able to do what he wants or desires, he does not choose and has no control over those desires and the character from which they flow. On Frankfurt's "hierarchical compatibilist" view, a person who has free will does choose and thus have control over which of his first-order desires are effective. But if determinism is true, he does not choose and has no control over the second-order volitions that determine which first-order desires are effective (or the character from which those second-order volitions result)—unless he also has higher-order volitions, but then the same thing will ultimately be true for them. Is this enough to meet Edwards's objection and allow for genuine free will (and moral responsibility)?

Libertarianism

C. A. Campbell

Charles Arthur Campbell (1897–1974) was a Scottish philosopher who taught at the University of Glasgow and the University of North Wales. He is best known for his work on the free will problem, but he also made important contributions to ethics and the philosophy of religion. In the following selection, he attempts to elaborate and defend a libertarian view of free will.

Campbell's view is a version of the doctrine of agent causation. The central idea is that a free choice (in his case the choice of whether or not to exert the effort required to overcome the balance of one's desires and do what one perceives to be the morally right thing) is caused by the agent or self, but not by some specific event (or set of events) occurring within the agent—because otherwise one could ask for the cause of that event, and so on, leading either to causal determinism or to one or more random events. Thus the cause of the choice is a thing or substance, not an event.

In Defence of Free Will

. . . Let us begin by noting that the problem of free will gets its urgency for the ordinary educated man by reason of its close connection with the conception of moral responsibility. When we regard a man as morally responsible for an act, we regard him as a legitimate object of moral praise or blame in respect of it. But it seems plain that a man cannot be a legitimate object of moral praise or blame for an act unless in willing the act he is in some important sense a 'free' agent. Evidently free will in some sense, therefore, is a pre-condition of moral responsibility. . . .

We raise the question at once, therefore, what are the conditions, in respect of freedom, which must attach to an act in order to make it a morally responsible act? It seems to me that the fundamental conditions are two. I shall state them with all possible brevity, for we have a long road to travel.

The first condition is the universally recognised one that the act must be *self*-caused, *self*-determined. But it is important to accept this condition in its full rigour. The agent must be not merely *a* cause but the *sole* cause of that for which he is deemed morally responsible. If entities other than the self have also a causal influence upon an act, then that act is not one for which we can say without qualification that the *self* is morally responsible. If in respect of it we hold the self responsible at all, it can only be for some feature of the act—assuming the possibility of disengaging such a feature—of which the self *is* the sole cause. I do not see how this conclusion can be evaded. But it has awkward implications which have led not a few people to abandon the notion of individual moral responsibility altogether. [1]

This first condition, however, is quite clearly not sufficient. It is possible to conceive an act of which the agent is the sole cause, but which is at the same time an act *necessitated* by the agent's nature. . . . In the case of such an act, where the agent could not do otherwise than he did, we must all agree, I think, that it would be inept to say that he *ought* to have done otherwise and is thus morally blameworthy, or *ought not* to have done otherwise and is thus morally praiseworthy. It is perfectly true that we do sometimes hold a person morally responsible for an act, even when we believe that he, being what he now is, virtually could not do otherwise. But underlying that judgment is always the assumption that the person has *come* to be what he now is in virtue of past acts of will in which he *was* confronted by real alternatives, by genuinely open possibilities: and, strictly speaking, it is in respect of these *past* acts of his that we praise or blame the agent *now.* [2] For ultimate analysis, the agent's power of alternative action would seem to be an inexpugnable condition of his liability to moral praise or blame, i.e. of his moral responsibility.

We may lay down, therefore, that an act is a 'free' act in the sense required for moral responsibility only if the agent (*a*) is the sole cause of the act; and (*b*) could exert his causality in alternative ways. . . .

And now, the conditions of free will being defined in these general terms, we have to ask whether human beings are in fact capable of performing free acts; and if so, where precisely such acts are to be found. In order to prepare the way for an answer, it is desirable, I think, that we should get clear at once about the significance of a certain very familiar, but none the less formidable, criticism of free will which . . . the Libertarian has to meet. This is the criticism which bases itself upon the facts of heredity on the one hand and of environment on the other. I may briefly summarize the criticism as follows.

Every historic self has an hereditary nature consisting of a group of inborn propensities, in range more or less common to the race, but specific to the individual in their respective strengths. With this equipment the self just *happens* to be born. Strictly speaking, it antedates the existence of the self proper, i.e. the existence of the self-conscious subject, and it is itself the effect of a series of causes leading back to indefinitely remote antiquity. It follows, therefore, that any of the self's choices that manifests the influence of his hereditary nature is not a choice of which *he,* the actual historic self, is the sole cause. The choice is determined, at least in part, by factors external to the self. The

From *In Defence of Free Will* (London: George Allen & Unwin LTD, 1967).

1

This is a very strong requirement. Can you think of an example of an action that it is plausible to think is caused *solely* by your self, with no causal influence by anything else? Indeed, does it even make sense to think of a *self*—as opposed to one or more of its states, such as desires or motives—as a cause?

Campbell adds the requirement that the person could have done otherwise, which means on his view that the nature of the self or agent did not necessitate the action in question—or else that the nature that does necessitate the action was itself a result of one or more earlier choices, in which the self or agent could have done otherwise.

same thing holds good of 'environment'. Every self is born and bred in a particular physical and social environment, not of his own choosing, which plays upon him in innumerable ways, encouraging this propensity, discouraging that, and so on. Clearly any of the self's choices that manifests the influence of environmental factors is likewise a choice which is determined, at least in part, by factors external to the self. But if we thus grant, as seems inevitable, that heredity and environment are external influences, where shall we find a choice in the whole history of a self that is not subject to external influence? Surely we must admit that every particular act of choice bears the marks of the agent's hereditary nature and environmental nurture; in which case a free act, in the sense of an act determined solely by the self, must be dismissed as a mere chimaera. ❸

...

The externality of these influences is taken for granted in our reflective practical judgments upon persons. On those occasions when we are in real earnest about giving a critical and considered estimate of a man's moral calibre—as, e.g., in any serious biographical study—we impose upon ourselves as a matter of course the duty of enquiring with scrupulous care into his hereditary propensities and environmental circumstances, with a view to discovering how far his conduct is influenced by these factors. And having traced these influences, we certainly do not regard the result as having no bearing on the question of the man's moral responsibility for his conduct. On the contrary, the very purpose of the enquiry is to enable us, by due appreciation of the *external* influences that affect his conduct, to gain as accurate a view as possible of that which can justly be attributed to the man's own *self*-determination. The allowances that we all of us do in practice make for hereditary and environmental influences in passing judgment on our fellows would be meaningless if we did not suppose these influences to be in a real sense 'external' to the self.

Now the recognition of this externality is, of course, a [serious] matter for the Libertarian. For the Libertarian, as we saw, accepts condition (*a*) . . . i.e. that an act is free only if it is determined by the self and nothing but the self. . . . We know now that condition (*a*) is not fulfilled by any act in respect of which inheritance or environment exerts a causal influence. For that type of influence has been shown to be in a real sense external to the self. The free act of which we are in search has therefore got to be one into which influences of this kind do not enter at all. ❹

Moreover, one encouraging portent has emerged in the course of our brief discussion. For we noticed that our reflective practical judgments on persons, while fully recognizing the externality of the influence of heredity and environment, do nevertheless presuppose throughout that there *is something* in conduct which is genuinely self-determined; something which the agent contributes solely on his own initiative, unaffected by external influences; something for which, accordingly, he may justly be held morally responsible. That conviction may, of course, be a false one. But the fact of its widespread existence can hardly be without significance for our problem. ❺

Let us proceed, then, by following up this clue. Let us ask, why do human beings so obstinately persist in believing that there is an indissoluble core of purely *self*-originated activity which even heredity and environment are powerless to affect? There can be little doubt, I think, of the answer in general terms. They do so, at bottom, because they feel certain of the existence of such activity from their immediate practical experience of themselves. ❻ Nor can there be in the end much doubt, I think, in what function of the self that activity is to be located. There seems to me to be one, and only one, function of the self with respect to which the agent can even pretend to have an assurance of that absolute self-origination which is here at issue. But to render precise the nature of that function is obviously of quite paramount importance: and we can do so, I think, only by way of a somewhat thorough analysis—which I now propose to attempt—of the experiential situation in which it occurs, viz., the situation of 'moral temptation'.

It is characteristic of that situation that in it I am aware of an end A which I believe to be morally right, and also of an end B, incompatible with A, towards which, in virtue of that system of conative dispositions which constitutes my 'character' as so far formed, I entertain a strong desire. There may be, and perhaps must be, desiring elements in my nature which are

❸

This sounds most like Blatchford. But all the other authors so far in this chapter would agree pretty closely that freedom in the sense that Campbell describes is impossible.

❹

Again, this is a *very* strong requirement—one that may seem quite impossible to satisfy.

❺

Of course, none of the compatibilists would agree that moral responsibility requires this self-determining sort of freedom.

❻

Campbell is referring to the actual experience of choice, especially in a situation in which one is pulled in more than one way.

directed to A also. But what gives to the situation its specific character as one of moral temptation is that the urge of our desiring nature towards the right end, A, is felt to be *relatively* weak. We are sure that if our desiring nature is permitted to issue directly in action, it is end B that we shall choose. That is what is meant by saying, as William James does, that end B is 'in the line of least resistance' relatively to our conative dispositions. The expression is, of course, a metaphorical one, but it serves to describe, graphically enough, a situation of which we all have frequent experience, viz., where we recognize a specific end as that towards which the 'set' of our desiring nature most strongly inclines us, and which we shall indubitably choose if no inhibiting factor intervenes. [7]

But inhibiting factors, we should most of us say, *may* intervene: and that in two totally different ways which it is vital to distinguish clearly. The inhibiting factor may be of the nature of another desire (or aversion), which operates by changing the balance of the desiring situation. Though at one stage I desire B, which I believe to be wrong, more strongly than I desire A, which I believe to be right, it may happen that before action is taken I become aware of certain hitherto undiscerned consequences of A which I strongly desire, and the result may be that now not *B* but *A* presents itself to me as the end in the line of least resistance. Moral temptation is here overcome by the simple process of ceasing to be a moral temptation. [8]

That is one way, and probably by far the commoner way, in which an inhibiting factor intervenes. But it is certainly not regarded by the self who is confronted by moral temptation as the *only* way. In such situations we all believe, rightly or wrongly, that even although B *continues* to be in the line of least resistance, even although, in other words, the situation remains one with the characteristic marks of moral temptation, we *can* nevertheless align ourselves with A. We can do so, we believe, because we have the power to introduce a new energy, to make what we call an 'effort of will', whereby we are able to act contrary to the felt balance of mere desire, and to achieve the higher end despite the fact that it continues to be in the line of greater resistance relatively to our desiring nature. The self in practice believes that it has this power; and believes, moreover, that the decision rests solely with its self, here and now, whether this power be exerted or not. [9]

Now the objective validity or otherwise of this belief is not at the moment in question. I am here merely pointing to its existence as a psychological fact. No amount of introspective analysis, so far as I can see, even tends to disprove that we do as a matter of fact believe, in situations of moral temptation, that it rests with our self absolutely to decide whether we exert the effort of will which will enable us to rise to duty, or whether we shall allow our desiring nature to take its course.

I have now to point out, further, how this act of moral decision, at least in the significance which it has for the agent himself, fulfils in full the two conditions which we found it necessary to lay down at the beginning for the kind of 'free' act which moral responsibility presupposes.

For obviously it is, in the first place, an act which the agent believes he could perform in alternative ways. He believes that it is genuinely open to him to put forth effort—in varying degrees, if the situation admits of that—or withhold it altogether. And when he *has* decided—in whatever way—he remains convinced that these alternative courses were really open to him.

It is perhaps a little less obvious, but, I think, equally certain, that the agent believes the second condition to be fulfilled likewise, i.e. that the act of decision is determined *solely* by his self. It appears less obvious, because we all realize that formed character has a great deal to do with the choices that we make; and formed character is, without a doubt, partly dependent on the external factors of heredity and environment. But it is crucial here that we should not misunderstand the precise nature of the influence which formed character brings to bear upon the choices that constitute conduct. No one denies that it determines, at least largely, what things we desire, and again how greatly we desire them. It may thus fairly be said to determine the felt balance of desires in the situation of moral temptation. But all that that amounts to is that formed character prescribes the nature of the situation *within* which the act of moral decision takes place. It does not in the least follow that it has any influence whatsoever in determining the act of decision itself—the decision as to whether we shall exert effort or take the easy course of

7

The morally wrong action, B, is supposed to be the one that your "desiring nature" would choose and thus the one that you want most, all things considered—the one that accords with the overall balance of your desires. You may have some desire to do the morally right thing, A, but not enough, by itself, to overcome the stronger desire for B. Everyone has experienced situations that at least *seem* to fit this specification, and you should think of an example of your own.

8

R New information or just a change of mind may alter the balance of desire in favor of A. Acting in accord with the new balance of desire would be simply doing what follows most naturally from one's "desiring nature" and would not, in Campbell's view, be a genuine example of free choice.

9

Note carefully that Campbell is here describing only what he thinks we all *believe* to be true in a situation of this sort: that it is within one's power to exert the effort to overcome the overall balance of desire in favor of B and do A instead.

STOP (Is he right that this is what everyone believes about such a situation? Do you believe it? Think about this question in relation to some examples.)

following the bent of our desiring nature: take, that is to say, the course which, in virtue of the determining influence of our character as so far formed, we feel to be in the line of least resistance. (10)

When one appreciates this, one is perhaps better prepared to recognize the fact that the agent himself in the situation of moral temptation does not, and indeed could not, regard his formed character as having any influence whatever upon his act of decision as such. For the very nature of that decision, as it presents itself to him, is as to whether he will or will not permit his formed character to dictate his action. In other words, the agent distinguishes sharply between the self which makes the decision, and the self which, as formed character, determines not the decision but the situation within which the decision takes place. Rightly or wrongly, the agent believes that through his act of decision he can oppose and transcend his own formed character in the interest of duty. We are therefore obliged to say, I think, that the agent *cannot* regard his formed character as in any sense a determinant of the act of decision as such. The act is felt to be a genuinely creative act, originated by the self *ad hoc,* and by the self alone. (11)

Here then, if my analysis is correct, in the function of moral decision in situations of moral temptation, we have an act of the self which at least *appears to the agent* to satisfy both of the conditions of freedom which we laid down at the beginning. The vital question now is, is this 'appearance' true or false? Is the act of decision really what it appears to the agent to be, determined solely by the self, and capable of alternative forms of expression? If it is, then we have here a free act which serves as an adequate basis for moral responsibility. We shall be entitled to regard the agent as morally praiseworthy or morally blameworthy according as he decides to put forth effort or to let his desiring nature have its way. We shall be entitled, in short, to judge the agent as he most certainly judges himself in the situation of moral temptation. If, on the other hand, there is good reason to believe that the agent is the victim of illusion in supposing his act of decision to bear this character, then in my opinion the whole conception of moral responsibility must be jettisoned altogether. For it seems to me certain that there is no other function of the self that even looks as though it satisfied the required conditions of the free act.

Now in considering the claim to truth of this belief of our practical consciousness, we should begin by noting that the onus of proof rests upon the critic who rejects this belief. Until cogent evidence to the contrary is adduced, we are entitled to put our trust in a belief which is so deeply embedded in our experience as practical beings as to be, I venture to say, ineradicable from it. Anyone who doubts whether it is ineradicable may be invited to think himself imaginatively into a situation of moral temptation as we have above described it, and then to ask himself whether in that situation he finds it possible to *disbelieve* that his act of decision has the characteristics in question. I have no misgivings about the answer. It is possible to disbelieve only when we are thinking abstractly about the situation; not when we are living through it, either actually or in imagination. This fact certainly establishes a strong prima facie presumption in favour of the Libertarian position. (12) Nevertheless I agree that we shall have to weigh carefully several criticisms of high authority before we can feel justified in asserting free will as an ultimate and unqualified truth.

Fortunately for our purpose, however, there are some lines of criticism which, although extremely influential in the recent past, may at the present time be legitimately ignored. . . .

Libertarianism is certainly inconsistent with a rigidly determinist theory of the physical world. It is idle to pretend that there can be open possibilities for psychical decision, while at the same time holding that the physical events in which such decisions manifest themselves are determined in accordance with irrevocable law. But whereas until a few years ago the weight of scientific authority was thrown overwhelmingly on the side of a universal determinism of physical phenomena, the situation has, as everybody knows, profoundly altered during the present century more especially since the advent of Planck's Quantum Theory and Heisenberg's Principle of Uncertainty. Very few scientists today would seek to impugn free will on the ground of any supposed implications of the aims or achievements of physical science. . . .

I may turn at once, therefore, to lines of argument which do still enjoy a wide currency among anti-Libertarians. And I shall begin with

If a person really does have the ability to put forth this special sort of effort (and also, of course, not to do it), then whether or not he does so seems to be controlled by him alone and not to any degree determined by other causes (since all other causes merely contribute to constituting the situation in relation to which this effort is or is not exerted).

While formed character determines the balance of one's desires, the choice as to whether to exert the effort to overcome that balance of desires or not cannot be due to formed character—*if* such a thing really occurs.

R Campbell claims, first, that a person cannot help believing in such a situation that he does have the ability in question, that whether he chooses to exert the effort or not is not determined by his formed character. Second, he claims that this is enough to create "a strong prima facie presumption" in favor of libertarianism, thereby putting the burden of proof strongly on the opposing position.

STOP (Is he right about this second claim, even if the first is granted? Is the fact that in such a situation of choice we cannot help believing that we have this sort of freedom a reason for thinking that the libertarian claim that we do have it is *true*?)

Here is an obvious objection to libertarianism, one that is raised by both Blatchford and Hume.

14

R Freedom, according to Campbell, involves a choice between one's overall balance of desires and the demands of morality. Since both one's desires and one's conception of morality are a part of the formed character that is a result of heredity and environment, there will still be a basis for many approximate predictions: predictions that a person will not do a wide range of things that are favored by neither desire nor morality and that his action will fall within a certain range (one that includes both the desired option and the one favored by morality).

Thus, if situations of choice between desire and morality are fairly rare, most actions will be predictable on the basis for formed character. This apparently means that we are free and morally responsible on only these fairly rare occasions.

But if it is very hard to overcome the balance of desire that results from formed character, is a person who fails to do so still fully free and fully morally responsible? Isn't his action very largely determined by formed character, which is in turn determined by environment and heredity, leaving very little room for freedom?

one which, though it is a simple matter to show its irrelevance to the Libertarian doctrine as I have stated it, is so extremely popular that it cannot safely be ignored.

The charge made is that the Libertarian view is incompatible with the *predictability* of human conduct. For we do make rough predictions of people's conduct, on the basis of what we know of their character, every day of our lives, and there can be no doubt that the practice, within certain limits, is amply justified by results. Indeed if it were not so, social life would be reduced to sheer chaos. The close relationship between character and conduct which prediction postulates really seems to be about as certain as anything can be. But the Libertarian view, it is urged, by ascribing to the self a mysterious power of decision uncontrolled by character, and capable of issuing in acts inconsistent with character, denies that continuity between character and conduct upon which prediction depends. If Libertarianism is true, prediction is impossible. But prediction *is* possible, therefore Libertarianism is untrue. 13

My answer is that the Libertarian view is perfectly compatible with prediction within certain limits, and that there is no empirical evidence at all that prediction is in fact possible beyond these limits. The following considerations will, I think, make the point abundantly clear.

(1) There is no question, on our view, of a free will that can will just anything at all. The range of possible choices is limited by the agent's character in every case; for nothing can be an object of possible choice which is not suggested by either the agent's desires or his moral ideals, and these depend on 'character' for us just as much as for our opponents. We have, indeed explicitly recognized at an earlier stage that character determines the situation within which the act of moral decision takes place, although not the act of moral decision itself. This consideration obviously furnishes a broad basis for at least approximate predictions. 14

(2) There is *one* experiential situation, and *one only,* on our view, in which there is any possibility of the act of will not being in accordance with character; viz. the situation in which the course which formed character prescribes is a course in conflict with the agent's moral ideal: in other words, the situation of moral temptation. Now this is a situation of comparative rarity. Yet with respect to all other situations in life we are in full agreement with those who hold that conduct is the response of the agent's formed character to the given situation. Why should it not be so? There could be no reason, on our view any more than on another, for the agent even to consider deviating from the course which his formed character prescribes and he most strongly desires, *unless* that course is believed by him to be incompatible with what is right. 15

(3) Even within that one situation which is relevant to free will, our view can still recognize a certain basis for prediction. In that situation our character as so far formed prescribes a course opposed to duty, and an effort of will is required if we are to deviate from that course. But of course we are all aware that a greater effort of will is required in proportion to the degree in which we have to transcend our formed character in order to will the right. Such action is, as we say, 'harder'. But if action is 'harder' in proportion as it involves deviation from formed character, it seems reasonable to suppose that, on the whole, action will be of rarer occurrence in that same proportion: though perhaps we may not say that at any level of deviation it becomes flatly impossible. It follows that even with respect to situations of moral temptation we may usefully employ our knowledge of the agent's character as a clue to prediction. It will be a clue of limited, but of by no means negligible, value. It will warrant us in predicting, e.g., of a person who has become enslaved to alcohol, that he is unlikely, even if fully aware of the moral evil of such slavery, to be successful immediately and completely in throwing off its shackles. Predictions of this kind we all make often enough in practice. And there seems no reason at all why a Libertarian doctrine should wish to question their validity. 16

Now when these three considerations are borne in mind, it becomes quite clear that the doctrine we are defending is compatible with a very substantial measure of predictability indeed. And I submit that there is not a jot of empirical evidence that any larger measure than this obtains in fact.

Let us pass on then to consider a much more interesting and, I think, more plausible criticism. It is constantly objected against the Libertarian doctrine that it is fundamentally *unintelligible.* Libertarianism holds that the act of moral decision is the *self's* act, and yet insists at the same time that it is not influenced by any of those determinate features in the self's nature which go to constitute its 'character'. But, it is asked, do not these two propositions contradict one another? Surely a *self*-determination which is determination by something other than the self's *character* is a contradiction in terms? What meaning is there in the conception of a 'self' in abstraction from its 'character'? If you really wish to maintain, it is urged, that the act of decision is not determined by the self's character, you ought to admit frankly that it is not determined by the *self* at all. But in that case, of course, you will not be advocating a freedom which lends any kind of support to moral responsibility; indeed very much the reverse. 17

Now this criticism, and all of its kind, seem to me to be the product of a simple, but extraordinarily pervasive, error: the error of confining one's self to the categories of the external observer in dealing with the actions of human agents. Let me explain.

It is perfectly true that the standpoint of the external observer, which we are obliged to adopt in dealing with physical processes, does not furnish us with even a glimmering of a notion of what can be meant by an entity which acts causally and yet not through any of the determinate features of its character. So far as we confine ourselves to external observation, I agree that this notion must seem to us pure nonsense. But then we are *not* obliged to confine ourselves to external observation in dealing with the human agent. Here, though here alone, we have the inestimable advantage of being able to apprehend operations from the *inside,* from the standpoint of *living experience.* But if we do adopt this internal standpoint—surely a proper standpoint, and one which we should be only too glad to adopt if we could in the case of other entities—the situation is entirely changed. We find that we not merely can, but constantly do, attach meaning to a causation which is the self's causation but is yet not exercised by the self's character. We have seen as much already in our analysis of the situation of moral temptation. When confronted by such a situation, we saw, we are certain that it lies with our *self* to decide whether we shall let our character as so far formed dictate our action or whether we shall by effort oppose its dictates and rise to duty. We are certain, in other words, that the act is *not* determined by our *character,* while we remain equally certain that the act *is* determined by our *self.*

Or look, for a further illustration (since the point we have to make here is of the very first importance for the whole free will controversy), to the experience of effortful willing itself, where the act of decision has found expression in the will to rise to duty. In such an experience we are certain that it is our self which makes the effort. But we are equally certain that the effort does not flow from that system of conative dispositions which we call our formed character; for the very function that the effort has for us is to enable us to act against the 'line of least resistance', i.e. to act in a way *contrary* to that to which our formed character inclines us. 18

I conclude, therefore, that those who find the Libertarian doctrine of the self's causality in moral decision inherently unintelligible find it so simply because they restrict themselves, quite arbitrarily, to an inadequate standpoint: a standpoint from which, indeed, a genuinely creative activity, if it existed, never *could* be apprehended.

...

What is required of the critic, of course, if he is to make good his case, is a reasoned justification of his cavalier attitude towards the testimony of practical self-consciousness. That is the primary desideratum. And the lack of it in the bulk of Determinist literature is in my opinion something of a scandal. Without it, the criticism we have just been examining is sheer dogmatism. It is, indeed, dogmatism of a peculiarly perverse kind. For the situation is, in effect, as follows. From our practical self-consciousness we gain a notion of a genuinely creative act—which might be defined as an act which nothing determines save the agent's doing of it. Of such a character is the act of moral decision as we experience it. But the critic says 'No! This sort of thing cannot be. A person cannot without affront to reason be conceived to be the author of an act which bears, *ex hypothesi,* no intelligible relation to his character. A mere intuition of practical self-consciousness is the solitary prop of this fantastic notion, and surely that is quite incapable of bearing the weight that you would thrust upon it.' Now observe the perversity! The critic says, excluding the evidence of practical self-consciousness, the notion makes nonsense. In other words, excluding the only evidence there ever *could* be for such a notion,

17

There is one obvious way in which a choice that does not accord with the agent's character seems to be possible: if the choice is simply random. But a random choice would not be the act of the self in any sense relevant to moral responsibility. Thus another way to put the problem is to say that it is hard to understand how a choice can be *neither* the result of formed character nor random. If it is neither of these, where does it come from?

18

Campbell appeals to our *experience* of actually making choices in this way. But even if he is right (is he?) that our experience *seems* to support the view that such choices actually occur, this isn't enough to *explain* what is going on: what determination by the self but not by the formed character or nature of the self really amounts to. Or how such a thing is possible.

Again the real problem is not so much whether there is a kind of evidence for the existence of such choices as whether we can understand what such a choice would amount to and how it would be arrived at.

the notion makes nonsense! For, of course, if there should be such a thing as creative activity, there is absolutely no other way save an intuition of practical self-consciousness in which we could become aware of it. Only from the inside, from the standpoint of the agent's living experience, can 'activity' possibly be apprehended. So that what the critic is really doing is to condemn a notion as nonsensical on the ground that the only evidence for it is the only evidence there ever could be for it. (19)

...

Discussion Questions

1. Clearly, on Campbell's view, a person who exerts the effort needed to overcome the balance of his desires has acted freely. Is the action of a person who chooses *not* to exert this effort and so does what he most desires to do also a free action (so that people would not be morally responsible only when they do the right thing)? Why or why not? What if the desires opposed to morality are very strong (see Annotation 16 and the associated text)?
2. Does the idea of agent causation, in general and in Campbell's specific version, really make sense? How is the choice fixed or arrived at if it is not a result of formed character (and also not random)?
3. On Campbell's view, a person is free and morally responsible only in situations where there is a conflict between desire and morality (and perhaps only when he follows morality and not desire). Is this a plausible view of freedom? Is there any way to expand Campbell's view so as to allow a wider range of free choices?

Robert Nozick

Robert Nozick (1938–2002) taught philosophy for many years at Harvard and was a major figure in twentieth-century philosophy. He made important contributions to many areas, but was perhaps best known for his book *Anarchy, State, and Utopia* (from which two of the selections in Chapter 6 are excerpted).

In the following selection, Nozick defends a version of libertarianism. In his view, free actions occur as a result of an agent *assigning* weights to reasons favoring various alternatives (rather than simply acting in accord with the antecedently most weighty reasons). This could be viewed as a version of agent causation, since the assignment of weight is brought about by the agent, but is not determined by any specific features of the agent (including his own formed character). But Nozick makes no explicit appeal to the idea of agent causation and attempts to explain in other ways why such an assignment of weights is not merely random.

Choice and Indeterminism, from *Philosophical Explanations*

Weigh(t)ing Reasons

Making some choices feels like this. There are various reasons for and against doing each of the alternative actions or courses of action one is considering, and it seems and feels as if one could do any one of them. In considering the reasons, mulling them over, one arrives at a view of which reasons are more important, which ones have more weight. One decides which reasons to act on; or one may decide to act on none of them but to seek instead a new alternative since none previously considered was satisfactory.

After the choice, however, others will say we were caused to act by the considerations which were (or turned out to be) more weighty. And it is not just others. We too, in looking back at our past actions, will see which reasons swayed us and will view (accepting) those considerations

From *Philosophical Explanations* (Cambridge, Mass.: Harvard University Press, 1981).

as having caused us to act as we did. Had we done the other act, though, acting on the opposing considerations, we (along with the others) would have described those considerations as causing us to do that other act. Whichever act we do, the (different) background considerations exist which can be raised to causal status. Which considerations will be so raised depends upon which act we do. Does the act merely show which of the considerations was the weightier cause, or does the decision make one of them weightier?

The reasons do not come with previously given precisely specified weights; the decision process is not one of discovering such precise weights but of assigning them. The process not only weighs reasons, it (also) weights them. At least, so it sometimes feels. This process of weighting may focus narrowly, or involve considering or deciding what sort of person one wishes to be, what sort of life one wishes to lead. [1]

What picture of choice emerges if we take seriously the feeling that the (precise) weights to be assigned to reasons is "up to us"? It is causally undetermined (by prior factors) which of the acts we will decide to do. It may be causally determined that certain reasons are reasons (in the one direction or the other), but there is no prior causal determination of the precise weight each reason will have in competition with others. [2] . . . Psychology, sociobiology, and the various social sciences, on this view, will offer causal explanations of why something is or is not a reason for a person (in a situation). They will not always be able to explain why the reasons get the precise weights they do. . . .

It is neither necessary nor appropriate, on this view, to say the person's action is uncaused. As the person is deciding, mulling over reasons R_A which are reasons for doing act A and over R_B which are reasons for doing act B, it is undetermined which act he will do. In that very situation, he could do A and he could do B. [3] He decides, let us suppose, to do act A. It then will be true that he was caused to do act A by (accepting) R_A. However, had he decided to do act B, it then would have been R_B that caused him to do B. Whichever he decides upon, A or B, there will be a cause of his doing it, namely R_A or R_B. His action is not (causally) determined, for in that very situation he could have decided differently; if the history of the world had been replayed up until that point, it could have continued with a different action. With regard to his action the person has what has been termed contra-causal freedom—we might better term it contra-deterministic. [4]

Thus, we draw a distinction between an action's being caused, and its being causally determined. Some philosophers would deny this distinction, maintaining that whenever one event causes another, there holds a general law in accordance with which it does so: some specification of the first event (along with other conditions which hold) always is and would be followed by an event of the same type as the second. It is a metaphysical thesis that the root notion of causality, producing or making something happen, can operate only through such lawlike universality. [5] If this were correct, . . . then causality necessarily would involve causal determination: under exactly the same conditions repeated, exactly the same thing would have (again) to happen. According to the view that distinguishes causality from causal determination, an act can be done because of something and have a cause even though in exactly the same conditions another act could have been done. It is common, in retrospect, to see what caused us to act as we did. Although we can retrospectively identify a cause, this does not mean our action was causally determined; had we acted differently in that situation (as we could have) we retrospectively would have identified a different cause— R_B instead of R_A. [6]

The weights of reasons are inchoate until the decision. The decision need not bestow exact quantities, though, only make some reasons come to outweigh others. A decision establishes inequalities in weight, even if not precise weights.

These bestowed weights (or comparative weightings of reasons) are not so evanescent as to disappear immediately after the very decision that bestows them. They set up a framework within which we make future decisions, not eternal but one we tentatively are committed to. The process of decision fixes the weights reasons are to have. The situation resembles that of precedents within a legal system; an earlier decision is not simply ignored though it may be overturned for reason, the decision represents a tentative commitment to make future decisions in accordance with the weights it establishes, and so on. [7]

Sometimes it is uncertain how much *weight* the various reasons for different alternatives should have. Nozick's suggestion is that sometimes there are no antecedent weights to be discovered, so that they have to be *assigned*.

R It is only the *weights* of the reasons that are claimed, in a case of genuinely free choice, not to be causally determined.

Thus whatever act he ultimately does, he *could have done otherwise*—not just in the compatibilist sense that he would have done otherwise *if* his desires or character had been different, but in the stronger sense that the other act could have occurred with no change in his desires or character prior to his decision.

R Nozick's view is that the action is still *caused* by the reason to which the agent assigns the greater weight, even though not causally *determined* (since it was not determined that this reason would be assigned greater weight).

R Nozick does not accept this metaphysical thesis.

But the cause of the action isn't really R_A by itself, but rather R_A with an assigned weight that exceeds that of R_B. And there is a general law that a more weighty reason will triumph over a less weighty one. It is the assigning of weights that is the ultimate cause of the action, and that assigning seems to be *neither* determined nor caused on Nozick's view.

In this way, Nozick is suggesting, such a choice can shape a person's subsequent desires and character in roughly the way that Edwards thinks is required for genuine freedom (but also thinks to be impossible).

Blatchford, among others, claims that a person always acts from his antecedently strongest motive. Nozick questions how this motive is to be identified (since to say that it is just whatever motive he ends up acting on makes the claim trivial). Thus some other way of identifying the antecedently strongest motive is needed.

One solution to this problem is to identify the pre-existing strongest motive by what the person says or does on some other occasion. Nozick responds that this procedure cannot distinguish between a motive that was antecedently the strongest motive and one that becomes the strongest as a result of an assignment of strength by the agent (on the occasion of the question or previous action)—and thus cannot support Blatchford's claim.

STOP (Is there any other way to identify an *antecedently* strongest motive, one that distinguishes it from a motive that *becomes* strongest only by being at some point *assigned* greater weight?)

Here is one important way in which Nozick's view differs from Campbell's.

Nozick does not really explain how this can be done.

Thus the idea of assigning weights to reasons cannot by itself solve the central problem for libertarianism: that of finding a third alternative to determinism and randomness.

The idea is that the limitations on the reasons and the interval would themselves be causally determined.

The claim that we always do what we most prefer or always act from the strongest motive is sometimes said to be empty of content, since the preference or the strength of motive is identified by what the person does. If the claim is to have empirical content, it must sometimes be possible to discover what a person's preference or strongest motive is via some other situation, to independently identify it in order then to check in this situation whether the person is doing what he most prefers or has the strongest motive to do. (8) Defenders of the claim do point out other situations (of choice or answering questions) where the relevant preference or motive can be identified; so the truth of the claim in this decision situation is testable, given the assumption that the preference or motive is stable from the one situation to the other. However, if our conception of the bestowal of weights (with a commitment that lingers) holds true, then these independent "tests" are to be interpreted differently. We do not always act on what was a preexistingly strongest preference or motive; it can become strongest in the process of making the decision, thereafter having greater weight (in other future decisions) than the reasons it vanquished. The prior independent test of a preference therefore need not discover one that existed; it may establish a preference which then consistently carries over into a new decision situation. The testing procedure cannot show that we always act on a preexistingly strongest preference or motive. (9)

Only when there are opposed reasons for different actions is it necessary to arrive at a weighting; otherwise, one can just do what all the reasons favor. However, neither group of these opposed reasons need be moral; decisions that involve a conflict of duty or other moral motives with (nonmoral) desires are only a subclass of the free decisions. (10) Shall we say, though, that every free decision involves a conflict of some sort, with reasons pulling in different directions? The reasons in conflict need not then have indeterminate weight, for a free decision may "act out" an earlier weighting decision as precedent. (But is there always present a reason of indeterminate weight to reexamine and overturn an earlier precedent, which reason itself must be given a determinate lesser weight in the decision to follow the precedent?) Even though it will include no interesting cases we especially want to judge, still, we may formulate the theory to avoid the uncomfortable consequence that actions in the face of no contrary reasons are not free ones. (11)

...

Nonrandom Weighting

Granting the coherence of the conception wherein the process of decision bestows weights, still, is that free will? An action's being non-determined . . . is not sufficient for it to be free—it might just be a random act. If we acted in the way uranium 238 emits alpha particles, determinism would be false but (unless we are greatly mistaken about uranium 238) we would not thereby have free will. What makes the bestowal of weights on reasons any different? If that too is a random act, then is acting on those weights in that very decision other than random? Acting on those same weights later will not be random, but is it better than any other determined act if it traces its history back not to causes before birth but to a recent random weighting of reasons? (12)

How can the giving of weights be other than random? Since (by hypothesis) there is no cause for giving or bestowing these particular weights on reasons rather than other weights, must it be merely a random act when these are bestowed? . . . If the absence of causation entailed randomness, then the denial of (contra-causal) free will would follow immediately. However, 'uncaused' does not entail 'random'. To be sure, the theorist of free will still has to explain wherein the act not causally determined is nonrandom, but at least there is room for this task.

In what way is the bestowal of weights not simply random? There may be causes limiting the reasons on which (nonzero) weight can be bestowed, and the interval within which these weights fall may similarly be limited. However, although it is not a random matter that the weights bestowed fall within this range, neither is that decided by the person. (13) The question remains: how is her decision among the alternatives causally open to her (the alternatives it is not causally determined she won't choose) not simply a random matter?

First, the decision may be self-subsuming; the weights it bestows may fix general principles that mandate not only the relevant act but also the bestowing of those (or similar) weights. The bestowal of weights yields both the action and (as a subsumption, not a repetition) that very bestowal. For example, consider the policy of choosing so as to track bestness: if the act weren't best you wouldn't do it, while if it were best you would. The decision to follow this policy may itself be an instance of it, subsumed under it. [14]

...

Consider a self-subsuming decision that bestows weights to reasons on the basis of a then chosen conception of oneself and one's appropriate life, a conception that includes bestowing those weights and choosing that conception (where the weights also yield choosing that self-conception). Such a self-subsuming decision will not be a random brute fact; it will be explained as an instance of the very conception and weights chosen. (I do not say that all of one's choices or all that bestow weights are self-subsuming in this way; however, the other ones that are based on weights previously given in such decisions, revokable weights, will inherit autonomy.) It will no more be a random brute fact than is the holding of a fundamental deep explanatory law that subsumes and thereby explains itself. . . . A self-subsuming decision does not happen inexplicably, it is not random in the sense of being connected to no weighted reasons (including the self-subsuming ones then chosen). But although it doesn't happen just randomly, still, there are different and conflicting self-subsuming decisions that could be made; just as there are different fundamental, self-subsuming laws that could hold true, could have held true. Is it not arbitrary then that one self-subsuming decision is made rather than another? Won't it be left inexplicable why this one was made (rather than another one)? [15]

Understanding and Explaining Free Choices

...

In what . . . way . . . can we understand the process of making free choices? By making them, perhaps. [16] We might interpret those theorists who pointed to our choices not as trying to prove that we made free choices but as ostensively explaining the notion, showing its intelligibility. Were they saying that we understand free choice and agency by virtue of making free choices as agents? . . . Our problem is that we are puzzled about the nature of free choices, so any inside knowledge we may have of such choices due to and in making them obviously hasn't served to clear up our puzzles about their nature. It is tempting to say our puzzlement stems from supposing we must be able discursively to say or describe what a free choice is like, yet the fact that we cannot, when we are directly acquainted with them, doesn't interfere with understanding them. But too many ineffabilities spoil the philosophical broth. Since I do not myself have even the feeling of understanding, I will continue the (discursive) attempts at explanation. [17]

. . . We have said already that the decision process (sometimes) bestows weights on the reasons for and against the various alternatives, and that this bestowal of weights is self-subsuming and so to that extent not random. Still, there can be different self-subsuming bestowals of weight. Although after one occurs we will be able retrospectively to give a reason as the cause (though without causal determination), can anything be said about why that one self-subsuming decision is made rather than another? No, the weights are bestowed in virtue of weights that come into effect in the very act of bestowal. This is the translation into this context of the notion of reflexivity: the phenomenon, such as reference or a law's holding, has an "inside" character when it holds or occurs in virtue of a feature bestowed by its holding or occurring.

The free decision is reflexive; it holds in virtue of weights bestowed by its holding. An explanation of why the act was chosen will have to refer to its being chosen. However, not every act you do is a minor miracle of reflexive self-subsumption, only the ones involving choice of fundamental principles and self-conception. (Yet since such a choice is revokable, do later choices reaffirm it, and so also involve reflexive self-subsumption?) [18]

Suppose a process of decision can have these features, bestowing weights in a self-subsuming fashion which is reflexive. The decision then does not simply dangle there at random—we can see the many ties and connections it has (including internal ones); the particular decision is not inexplicable—we see it as something that could arise from a process of this sort.

14

A random occurrence is sometimes thought of as one that happens for no reason. Nozick is suggesting that there might, in a way, be a reason for the assigning of weights. It might operate via a general principle that is *self-subsuming:* that is, whose adoption is an instance of itself. Nozick's example is the general policy or principle of choosing in such a way as to "track bestness," that is, do whatever is morally best. Adopting that principle is *itself* arguably an instance of doing what is morally best, so that the principle is self-subsuming. (Another way to put this is to say that the principle adopted may provide a reason for the adoption of that very principle.)

15

Such a self-subsuming decision may be as general as a choice of an overall kind of life: live the morally best life, where adopting that principle is part of living the morally best life.

But while there is in this odd way a reason for the adoption of such a principle or conception of one's life, in the most important cases there will be alternative choices that would have similarly been self-subsuming. So why isn't the choice between these still arbitrary—that is, random?

16

This is essentially Campbell's suggestion.

17

Experiencing such a choice doesn't really explain how it works and in particular how it can be neither determined nor random. Nozick concedes (and it is a very large concession) that he doesn't really even *seem* to himself to understand this.

18

To say that the assignment of weights is *reflexive* is to say that it is adopted by virtue of itself: it explains its own adoption. (But does it really?)

To say that this picture seems "phenomenologically accurate" is to say that it seems to accurately reflect what goes on in an actual *experience* of free choice.

If the assignment of weights is a part of creating or constituting the sort of self that one chooses to be, then there will be another (related) way that it is non-random: it reflects the very nature of the *resulting* self.

(But there would still be alternative choices that would reflect the nature of alternative resulting selves, still making it unclear why the choice among these different selves isn't random.)

Nozick is saying that the choice of self was something the person *did,* not something that merely happened to him (as a result of either causal determination or randomness). Thus the person could have done otherwise in the sense that he could have chosen a different self with a correspondingly different assignment of weights.

(But this still doesn't explain why the choice between the different weights and the different selves isn't random.)

More might be demanded, however; it might be demanded that the theorist of free will show how the decision is causally determined. Otherwise, it will be said, the character and nature of the decision will remain mysterious. But clearing up any mystery in that way would come at the cost of the act's contra-causal freedom. No adequate condition on explanation or understanding necessitates . . . causal explanation. . . . Free will is to be explained differently, by delineating a decision process that can give rise to various acts in a nonrandom nonarbitrary way; whichever it gives rise to—and it could give rise to any one of several—will happen nonarbitrarily. These remarks are independent of the particular process we have delineated here, involving the bestowal of weights, reflexive self-subsumption, and so on. What is inappropriate is to demand that a free choice be explained in a way that shows it is unfree.

The theme of the bestowal of weights to reasons, in a situation of no preexistingly determinate weights, seems to me phenomenologically accurate and proper to emphasize. [19] I have more worries about terming this bestowal nonarbitrary and nonrandom because it is self-subsuming and reflexive. This position has too much the flavor of applying shiny new tools and ideas everywhere, as a magic key—except that some of the applications depend, perhaps, upon these ideas being not so well understood, not so shiny. So we should be somewhat wary of this use of the themes of self-subsumption and reflexiveness to delineate the nonarbitrary nature of a free choice. They do have the right flavor, though. . . .

Could One Have Bestowed Otherwise?

. . . Another way in which bestowal of weight upon reasons can be nonarbitrary is that the self can synthesize itself around this bestowing: "I value things in this way." If in that reflexive self-reference, the I synthesizes itself (in part) around the act of bestowing weight on reasons, then it will not be arbitrary or random that *that* self bestowed those weights. [20]

The process of decision can yield the intentional doing of different actions, and it would have if different weights had been assigned, which could have happened. But does it follow that the person could have done otherwise, that it was within the person's power to bestow different weights, as opposed to that merely happening? In what way could the person have *done* otherwise, not merely been the arena in which otherwise happened?

It would be fruitless to embark upon the theoretical regress wherein a different intentional action of bestowing weights occurs with its own separate weights which have to be bestowed by a still separate act. And why is it asked only if another bestowal could have been done; why is it not similarly asked whether the bestowal that did occur was a doing or merely a happening? Maybe it is possible for weights somehow to just happen to get bestowed on reasons; however, when the bestowal is anchored and tied in the way we have described, to a formed self-conception (even if formed just then), if it is self-subsuming and reflexive, leading to later (revokable) commitment, then it is a doing, not a happening merely. If all that context and stage setting . . . does not make it an action, what alternative conception of action is being presupposed? The actual bestowal of weights on reasons is a doing and not merely a happening; another and alternative bestowal of weights on reasons could have occurred instead—this one wasn't causally determined, and others aren't causally excluded—with all of the accompanying context and stage setting appropriate to it, so that alternative bestowal too would have been a doing and not merely a happening. The person could have bestowed differently. . . . [21]

Discussion Questions

1. Is Nozick right that his view seems "phenomenologically accurate"? Think of a realistic example or two and try to spell out just how Nozick's view of such a case differs from that of either the hard determinist or the two sorts of compatibilists. (The comparison with Frankfurt is especially interesting.)
2. Does the idea of *self-subsumption* solve the problem of why the assigning of weights isn't random? Does it even contribute to a solution of this problem? Why or why not?
3. Nozick concedes that he does not "have even the feeling of understanding" with regard to the question of how a free choice really works, how it is

different from either determinism or randomness. Assuming that no one is in any better position in this respect, how serious a problem is this for libertarianism? Is it possible that we have good reasons for thinking that there are such choices and perhaps even that we can tell which ones they are, even if we don't really understand their nature?

Robert Kane

Robert Kane (1938–) is an American philosopher who has taught mainly at the University of Texas. He is best known for his work on the free will problem, but has also made contributions to many other areas. In the following selection, Kane defends a libertarian view that does not appeal to causation by agents (as opposed to events) or to anything else that is outside the purview of modern science. His view is that freedom depends on *self-forming actions:* actions that occur in situations in which a person is strongly pulled in conflicting directions by strong reasons and chooses among them in a way that is not determined, but is still (he claims) rational and voluntary.

Free Will and Modern Science

1. Introduction

Can we make sense of a free will that requires Ultimate Responsibility . . . ? **1** Many philosophers think not. They argue . . . that being the *ultimate* source of one's will and actions is an incoherent and impossible ideal, since it would require us to be "prime movers unmoved" or "uncaused causes of ourselves"—"the best self-contradiction that has been conceived so far," as Nietzsche put it. Ultimate Responsibility, or UR, requires that there be some acts in our lifetimes that do not have sufficient causes or motives. But how could acts having neither sufficient causes nor motives be free and responsible actions?

In [an earlier] chapter, I noted that traditional libertarian theories of free will have usually appealed to "extra factors" in response to these problems. Realizing that free will cannot merely be indeterminism or chance, libertarians have introduced additional and often mysterious forms of agency or causation to make up the difference, such as immaterial minds, noumenal selves outside space and time or non-event agent-causes. **2** The idea behind such extra-factor strategies is easy enough to understand: since indeterminism leaves it open which way an agent will chose or act, some "extra" kind of causation or agency must be posited over and above the natural flow of events to account for the agent's going one way or the other—something else must tip the balance. This is a tempting way to think. But introducing extra forms of causation or agency beyond the natural flow of events has invited charges that libertarian theories of free will are obscure and mysterious and cannot be reconciled with modern scientific views about human beings.

Libertarians in general have not done a good job explaining how their view of free will can be reconciled with modern scientific views about human beings and the cosmos. This is the challenge I want to take up in the present chapter. Can a libertarian view of free will requiring Ultimate Responsibility be made intelligible without appealing to obscure or mysterious forms of agency or causation? Can such a free will be reconciled with what we know about human beings in the modern physical, biological, and human sciences? To answer these questions, I believe we have to rethink issues about freedom, responsibility, and indeterminism from the ground up, without relying on appeals to extra factors unless absolutely necessary. What follows is my own attempt to do this. Consider it a proposal meant to stimulate thinking about how free will might exist in the natural world where we humans exist and must exercise our freedom.

2. Physics, Chaos, and Complexity

We must grant, first of all, that if any libertarian theory of free will is to succeed there must be some genuine indeterminism in nature to make

From *A Contemporary Introduction to Free Will* (New York: Oxford University Press, 2005).

1

In an earlier chapter of the book from which this selection is drawn, Kane says that "to be *ultimately responsible* for an action, an agent must be responsible for anything that is a sufficient reason, cause, or motive for the action's occurring."

Clearly this requirement is not satisfied for an action that is causally determined by conditions that existed before the agent was born. Nor does it seem to be satisfied for an action that results from a random or chance occurrence. (Is it satisfied by actions that occur in the ways described by Campbell and Nozick?)

2

Campbell's account is a clear example of a libertarian view that appeals to an additional form of causation or agency. Whether Nozick means to appeal to something like this is less clear, though he says nothing that would rule it out.

room for it. As the ancient Epicurean philosophers said, the atoms must sometimes "swerve" in undetermined ways if there is to be room in nature for free will. Moreover, it would be no use if the atoms swerved in outer space somewhere far from human affairs. They must swerve where it would matter for human choice and action, for example, in the brain. This is true even if one postulates special kinds of agent-causes or a nonmaterial self to intervene in the brain. If these special forms of agency are to have any room to operate, the indeterminism must be there to begin with.

This is the point, as we have seen, where some scientists want to bring modern quantum physics into the picture to help account for free will. Suppose there were quantum jumps or other undetermined quantum events occurring in the brain. We know that information processing in the brain takes place through the firing of individual neurons or nerve cells in complex patterns. Individual firings of neurons in turn involve the transmission of chemical ions across neuronal cell walls, stimulated by various chemicals, called neurotransmitters, and by electrical stimuli coming from other neurons. Some neuroscientists have suggested that quantum indeterminacies in the transmission of these chemical ions across the cell walls of neurons might make the exact timing of the firings of individual neurons uncertain, thus introducing indeterminism into the activity of the brain and making "room" for free will.

Such suggestions are speculative. But even if they were correct, how would they help with free will? It was noted earlier that if choices were to occur as the result of quantum jumps or other undetermined events in the brain, the choices would not be under the control of the agents and would scarcely count as free and responsible actions. A similar criticism was made of the ancient Epicurean view. How could the chance swerve of atoms help to give us free will? Another problem about using quantum indeterminacy to defend free will was also mentioned in [an earlier] chapter. . . . Determinists . . . point out that quantum indeterminacy is usually insignificant in the behavior of larger physical systems like the human brain and body. When large numbers of particles are involved, as in the transmission of chemical ions across cell walls, any quantum indeterminacies would most likely be "damped" out and would have negligible effects on the larger activity of the brain and body.

Maybe so. But there is another possibility suggested by some scientists. Quantum theory alone will not account for free will, they concede. But perhaps quantum physics could be combined with the new sciences of "chaos" and "complexity" to help make sense of free will. In "chaotic" physical systems, very small changes in initial conditions lead to large and unpredictable changes in the system's subsequent behavior. You may have heard the narrative in which the fluttering of a butterfly's wings in South America initiates a chain of events that affects weather patterns in North America. Perhaps that famous example is something of an exaggeration. But chaotic phenomena, in which small changes lead to large effects, are now known to be far more common in nature than previously believed, and they are particularly common in living things. There is growing evidence that chaos may play a role in the information processing of the brain, providing some of the flexibility that the nervous system needs to adapt creatively—rather than in predictable or rigid ways—to an ever-changing environment.

Determinists, to be sure, are quick to point out that chaotic behavior in physical systems, though unpredictable, is usually deterministic and does not itself imply genuine indeterminism in nature. But some scientists have suggested that a combination of chaos and quantum physics might provide the genuine indeterminism one needs. If the processing of the brain does "make chaos in order to make sense of the world" (as one recent research paper puts it), then the resulting chaos might magnify quantum indeterminacies in the firings of individual neurons. These chaotically magnified indeterminacies in the firings of neurons would have large-scale indeterministic effects on the activity of neural networks in the brain as a whole. The indeterminacy at the neuron level would no longer be "damped out," but would have significant effects on cognitive processing and deliberation.

But once again we might ask how even this would help with free will. If indeterminacy in our neurons were amplified to have significant effects on our mental processing and deliberation, would that give us any greater control and freedom? More likely it would give us less control and freedom. Wouldn't deliberation become something like spinning a roulette wheel in one's mind to make a choice? [3] Maybe. But before we jump to conclusions, we need to look more deeply into the situation. If there were some significant indeterminism available in the brain, could we make more sense of it than simply spinning roulette wheels? Let us see. What is required to answer these questions, as I suggested, is a thorough rethinking of issues about freedom, responsibility, and indeterminism.

3. Conflicts in the Will

The first step in this rethinking is to note that indeterminism does not have to be involved in *all* acts done "of our own free wills" for which we are ultimately responsible. . . . Not all acts done of our own free wills have to be undetermined, only those acts by which we made ourselves into the kinds of persons we are—namely, the "will-setting" or "self-forming actions" (SFAs) that are required for ultimate responsibility. [4]

Now I believe that these undetermined self-forming actions, or SFAs, occur at those difficult times of life when we are torn between competing visions of what we should do or become. Perhaps we are torn between doing the moral thing or acting from ambition, or between powerful present desires and long-term goals; or we may be faced with difficult tasks for which we have aversions. In all such cases of difficult self-forming choices in our lives, we are faced with competing motivations and have to make an effort to overcome the temptation to do something else we also strongly want. There is tension and uncertainty in our minds about what to do at such times, let us suppose, that is reflected in appropriate regions of our brains by movement away from thermodynamic equilibrium—in short, a kind of "stirring up of chaos" in the brain that makes it sensitive to micro-indeterminacies at the neuronal level. The uncertainty and inner tension we feel at such soul-searching moments of self-formation would thus be reflected in the indeterminacy of our neural processes themselves. What we experience internally as uncertainty about what to do on such occasions would correspond physically to the opening of a window of opportunity that temporarily screens off complete determination by influences of the past. [5]

When we do decide under such conditions of uncertainty the outcome is not determined, thanks to the indeterminacy that preceded it. Yet the outcome can be willed either way we choose, rationally and voluntarily, because in such self-formation, the agents' prior wills are divided by conflicting motives. Consider a businesswoman who faces a conflict of this kind. She is on her way to an important meeting when she observes an assault taking place in an alley. An inner struggle arises between her conscience on the one hand (to stop and call for help for the assault victim) and her career ambitions, on the other hand, which tell her she cannot miss this important business meeting. She has to make an effort of will to overcome the temptation to do the selfish thing and go on to the meeting. If she overcomes this temptation, it will be the result of her effort to do the moral thing; but if she fails, it will be because she did not *allow* her effort to succeed. For while she willed to overcome temptation, she also willed to fail. That is to say, she had strong reasons to will the moral thing, but she also had strong reasons, ambitious reasons, to make the selfish choice that were different from, and incommensurable with, her moral reasons. When we, like the woman, decide in such circumstances, and the indeterminate efforts we are making become determinate choices, we *make* one set of competing reasons or motives prevail over the others then and there *by deciding*. Thus the choice we eventually make, though undetermined, can still be rational (made for reasons) and voluntary (made in accordance with our wills), whichever way we choose. [6]

Now let us add a further piece to the puzzle. Just as indeterminism need not undermine the rationality and voluntariness of choices, so indeterminism in and of itself need not undermine control and responsibility. Suppose you are trying to think through a tough math problem. Say there is an indeterminacy in your neural processes complicating the task. This indeterminacy would make your task more difficult, in much the same way that low background noise would be slightly distracting if you were trying to solve a tough math problem. Whether you are going to succeed in solving the problem is uncertain and undetermined because of the distracting neural noise. Yet, if

3

That is, wouldn't such amplified indeterminacy, along with anything that results from it, be merely a random or chance occurrence?

4

A *self-forming action* is one that (a) is not determined by prior, already fixed desires, motives, or character, and (b) that helps to form the agent's subsequent desires, motives, or character. (An action that results directly from the undetermined assigning of weights to reasons described by Nozick would be self-forming in this sense; so also, presumably, would be the sort of free choice described by Campbell.)

5

It is important to be clear that this is a merely speculative suggestion on Kane's part, one that results from the attempt to explain how a genuinely free choice for which a person is ultimately responsible might possibly occur.

6

Kane is right that such a choice can be seen as *rational*, at least to some degree—there were reasons for it, (though there were also reasons for the alternative choice that was not made). But was it *voluntary* in the sense of being within the businesswoman's *control*? Did she (as Kane says) *make* one set of reasons prevail over the other? Or is the fact that one choice rather than the other occurred just something that happened willy-nilly to her, in a way over which she had no real control—and thus a random or chance occurrence, if it was genuinely not determined by anything else?

you manage to concentrate and solve the problem nonetheless, we have reason to say you did it and are responsible for it—even though it was undetermined whether you would succeed. The indeterministic noise would have been an obstacle that you overcame by your effort.

There are many examples supporting this idea of indeterminism functioning as an obstacle to success without precluding responsibility. Included among these examples are the Austin-style examples discussed in [an earlier] chapter. . . . Recall the assassin, who was trying to shoot the prime minister but might miss because undetermined events in his nervous system might lead to a jerking or wavering of his arm. If the assassin did succeed in hitting his target, despite the indeterminism, can he be held responsible? The answer is clearly yes because he intentionally and voluntarily succeeded in doing what he was *trying* to do—kill the prime minister. Yet his action, killing the prime minister, was undetermined. The indeterminism here functioned as an obstacle to his success but did not rule out his responsibility *if* he succeeded.

Here is another example. A husband, beside himself with rage while arguing with his wife, swings his arm down on her favorite glass-top table, intending to break it. Again, we suppose that some indeterminism in his outgoing neural pathways makes the momentum of his arm indeterminate, so that it is undetermined whether the table will break right up to the moment it is struck. Whether the husband breaks the table is undetermined, and yet he is clearly responsible if he does break it. (It would be a poor excuse to offer his wife if he claimed, "Chance did it, not me." Though indeterminism was involved, chance didn't do it, he did.) In this example as in the preceding one, the agent can be held responsible for an action even though the action is undetermined. [7]

Kane seems right that these examples show that a person can correctly be said to have done something and to be responsible for it even where the connection between what he most directly does (try hard to think through the math problem, aim as carefully as he can at the prime minister, swing as hard as he can at the table) and the eventual result involves a degree of indeterminism. They do not show, however, that a person can be responsible in a case (like the businesswoman case) where the "action" most directly performed is indeterministic.

Now these examples—of the math problem, the assassin, and the husband—are not all we want for free will. They do not amount to genuine exercises of self-forming actions (SFAs) like the businesswoman whose will is divided between conflicting motives. The businesswoman wants to help the assault victim, but she also wants to go on to her meeting. By contrast, the assassin's will is not equally divided. He wants to kill the prime minister, but he does *not* also want to fail. (If he fails therefore, it will be *merely* by chance.) So while the examples of the assassin, the husband, and the like do not tell us all we need to know about free will, they do provide some clues to what free will requires. To go further, we have to appeal to some additional ideas.

4. Parallel Processing

Imagine in cases of conflict characteristic of self-forming actions or SFAs, like the businesswoman's that the indeterministic noise, which is providing an obstacle to her overcoming temptation, is coming not from an external source but from her own will, since she also deeply desires to do the opposite. Imagine that two crossing recurrent neural networks are involved, each influencing the other, and representing the woman's conflicting motivations. (These neural networks are complex networks of interconnected neurons in the brain, circulating impulses in feedback loops that are generally involved in higher-level cognitive processing.) The input of one of these neural networks consists of the woman's reasons for acting morally and stopping to help the victim; the input of the other network comprises her ambitious motives for going on to the meeting. The two neural networks are connected, so that the indeterministic noise, which is an obstacle to the woman's making one of her choices, is coming from her own desire to make the opposite choice. In these circumstances, when either of the pathways "wins" (i.e., reaches an activation threshold, which amounts to choice), the woman will be making her choice in spite of the indeterministic noise she had to overcome. Her choosing in spite of the noise obstacle will be like your solving the tough math problem in spite of distracting background noise. And just as we can say, when you solved the math problem by overcoming the distracting noise, that you did it and are responsible for it, so we can say this as well, I would argue, in the woman's case, *whichever way she chooses*. The pathway through which the woman succeeds in reaching a choice threshold will have overcome the obstacle in the form of indeterministic noise generated by the other pathway.

Note that under such conditions of indeterminism arising from conflicting alternatives, choices going either way will not be "inadvertent," "accidental," "capricious," or "merely random" (as critics of indeterminism say). On the contrary, the choices will be *willed* by the agents either way when they are made, and done for reasons either way—reasons that the agents then and there *endorse*. But these are the conditions usually required to say that something is done "on purpose" rather than accidentally, capriciously, or merely by chance. Moreover, these conditions for saying the actions were done on purpose, taken together, I would argue, rule out each of the reasons we have for saying that agents act but do not have *control* over their actions. The agents need not have been acting under compulsion, coercion, constraint, inadvertence, accident, control by others, and so on. To be sure, we must grant that when choices are undetermined SFAs, agents do not control or determine which choice-outcome will occur *before* it occurs. But it does not follow that, because one does not control or determine which of a set of outcomes is going to occur before it occurs, one does not control or determine which of them occurs, *when* it occurs. 8

When the preceding conditions for SFAs are satisfied, and the agents exercise control over their future lives *then and there* by deciding, they have what I call *plural voluntary control* over the options in the following sense: the agents are able to bring about *whichever* of the options they will, *when* they will to do so, *for* the reasons they will to do so, *on* purpose, rather than accidentally or by mistake, *without* being coerced or compelled in doing so or in willing to do so, or otherwise controlled in doing or in willing to do so by any other agents or mechanisms. Each of these conditions can be satisfied for SFAs, like the businesswoman's, as I have described them. The conditions can be summed up by saying that the agents can choose either way *at will*. In other words, the choices are "will-setting": we set our wills one way or the other in the *act* of deciding, and not before. 9

Note also that this account of self-forming choices amounts to a kind of "doubling" of the difficulty seen in the math problem example, where the agent had to make an effort to overcome indeterministic background noise. It is as if an agent faced with a self-forming choice is *trying* or making an effort to solve two cognitive problems at once, or to complete *two* competing (deliberative) tasks at once. In our example the businesswoman is trying to make a moral choice and to make a conflicting self-interested choice. The two competing choices correspond to two competing neural networks in her brain. Each task is being thwarted by the indeterminism coming from the other, so it might fail. But if it succeeds, then the agents can be held responsible because, as in the case of solving the math problem, the agents will have succeeded in doing what they were knowingly and willingly trying to do. Recall the assassin and the husband. Owing to indeterminacies in their neural pathways, the assassin might miss his target or the husband might fail to break the table. But if these two agents *succeed,* despite the probability of failure, they are responsible, since they will have succeeded in doing what they were trying to do. And so it is, I suggest, with self-forming choices like the businesswoman's. The agents will be responsible *whichever way they choose* because whichever way they choose they will have succeeded in doing what they were trying to do. Their failure to do one thing is not a mere failure, but a voluntary success in doing the other. 10

Does it make sense to talk about an agent's trying to do two competing things at once in this way, or to solve two cognitive problems at once? Well, we now know that the brain is a "parallel processor"; it can simultaneously process different kinds of information relevant to tasks such as perception or recognition through different neural pathways. Such a capacity, I believe, is essential to the exercise of free will. In cases of self-formation (SFAs), agents are simultaneously trying to resolve plural and competing cognitive tasks. They are, as we say, of two minds. Yet they are not two separate persons. They are not dissociated from either task. The businesswoman who wants to do something to help the victim is the same ambitious woman who wants to go to her meeting and make a sale. She is torn inside by different visions of who she is and what she wants to be, as we all are from time to time. But this is the kind of complexity needed for genuine self-formation and free will. And when she succeeds in doing one of the things she is trying to do, she will endorse that outcome as *her* resolution of the conflict in her will, voluntarily and intentionally, not by accident or mistake. 11

The central question is whether the woman has any control over *which* of the competing neural networks or pathways wins out. She has reasons for each of the competing choices; and when one network wins out, this may count as her willing that choice and perhaps also as her endorsing the result. But each of these things would have been true of the other choice if that network had won out instead, making it unclear why they have any tendency to show that the woman controlled the result.

Part of this is clearly correct: such agents are not coerced or compelled; they do have reasons that lead to their choices; and the choices are not merely accidental or made by mistake. But is it really true that they are able to "bring about *whichever* of the options they will" or that they can "choose either way *at will*"? The other choice could indeed have occurred (in the same way), but is there any clear way in which they could have deliberately brought it about instead?

10

Such an agent may perhaps be said to succeed in doing one thing and to fail in doing the other. But does he have any real *control* over which is which? Or is this merely a random or chance result? (And, if it is, how can the person be correctly held responsible for doing one thing rather than the other?)

She may endorse it retrospectively, but did she really control the result at the time when it happened?

5. Challenges to This View: Responsibility, Luck, and Chance

Obviously, many questions arise about the preceding view and a number of objections may be made to it. We cannot address all these questions and objections here, but let us consider some of the more important ones. Some people have objected that if choices like the businesswoman's really are undetermined, they *must* happen merely by chance—and so must be "random," "capricious," "uncontrolled," "irrational," and all the other things usually charged. The first step in responding to this objection is to question the assumption that if indeterminism is involved in an occurrence, that occurrence must happen *merely* as a matter of chance or luck. "Chance" and "luck" are terms of ordinary language that carry the meaning of "its being out of my control." So using them already begs certain questions. "Indeterminism," by contrast, is a technical term that merely rules out *deterministic* causation, but not causation altogether. Indeterminism is consistent with nondeterministic or probabilistic causation, where the outcome is not inevitable. It is therefore a mistake (in fact, one of the most common mistakes in debates about free will) to assume that "undetermined" means "uncaused" or "*merely* a matter of chance."

12 It isn't clear why the randomness objection must say that there is some point in the process where the woman's efforts (both of them, in competing directions) stop and chance takes over. The question is whether there is any way in which she determines *which* effort eventually succeeds, or whether this is just a matter of chance.

A second objection is related to the first. One might argue that in the case of the businesswoman, since the outcome of her effort (the choice) is undetermined up to the last minute, she must have first made the effort to overcome the temptation to go on to her meeting and then at the last instant "chance takes over" and decides the issue for her. But this is a mistaken image. On the view just presented, one cannot separate the indeterminism from the effort of will, so that *first* the woman's effort occurs, to be *followed* by chance or luck. One must think of the effort and the indeterminism as fused; the effort is indeterminate and the indeterminism is a property of the effort, not something separate that occurs after or before the effort. The fact that the effort has this property of being indeterminate does not make it any less the woman's *effort*. The complex recurrent neural network that realizes the effort in the brain is circulating impulses in feedback loops, and there is some indeterminacy in these circulating impulses. But the whole process is the woman's effort of will, and it persists right up to the moment when the choice is made. There is no point at which the effort stops and chance "takes over." The woman chooses as a result of the effort, even though she might have failed. 12 Similarly, the husband breaks the table as a result of his effort, even though he might have failed because of the indeterminacy. (That is why his excuse, "Chance broke the table, not me," is so lame.)

A third objection has to do with the notion of luck. If the businesswoman's efforts were undetermined, so that either effort might have failed, some critics argue, then it was just a matter of luck which effort succeeded. To address this by-now familiar objection, we need to look more closely at the issue of luck. Recall that one might say of the assassin and the husband that "they got lucky" in killing the prime minister and breaking the table, because their actions were undetermined and might have failed. Yet the surprising thing is that we still say the assassin and the husband were *responsible* if they succeeded in killing the prime minister or breaking the table. So we should ask ourselves the following question: why is it wrong to say "He got lucky, *so he was not responsible*" in the cases of the husband and the assassin? For it *is* wrong to say this, since they did get lucky and yet they were *still* responsible. (Imagine the assassin's lawyer arguing in the courtroom that his client is not guilty because his killing the prime minister was undetermined and might therefore have failed by chance. Would such a defense succeed?)

The first part of an answer to why the assassin and the husband are still responsible has to do with the point made earlier about "luck" and "chance." These two words have question-begging implications in ordinary language that are not necessarily implications of "indeterminism" (for indeterminism implies only the absence of deterministic causation). The core meaning of "he got lucky" in the assassin and husband cases is "he succeeded *despite the probability or chance of failure*"; and this core meaning does not imply lack of responsibility *if he succeeds*. If "he got lucky" had other meanings in these cases, meanings that are often associated in ordinary usage with "luck" and "chance," the inference that a person "got lucky so he was not responsible" would not fail, as it clearly does. For example, if "luck" in these cases meant that the outcome was not his doing, or had occurred by mere chance, or that he was not responsible, then the inference "he got lucky so he was not responsible" would hold for the husband and assassin. But the point is that these further meanings of "luck" and "chance" do not follow *from the mere presence of indeterminism.*

The second reason why the inference "he got lucky, so he was not responsible" does not work in the cases of the assassin and the husband is that *what* they succeeded in doing was what they were *trying* and wanting to do all along (kill the minister and break the table, respectively). The third reason is that *when* they succeeded, their reaction was not "Oh dear, that was a mistake, an accident—something that *happened* to me, not something I *did*." Rather they *endorsed* the outcomes as something they were trying and wanting to do all along, knowingly and purposefully, not by mistake or accident.

But these conditions are satisfied in the businesswoman's case as well, *either way* she chooses. If she succeeds in choosing to return to help the victim (or in choosing to go on to her meeting), then (1) she will have "succeeded *despite the probability or chance of failure,*" (2) she will have succeeded in doing what she was *trying* and *wanting* to do all along (she wanted both outcomes very much, but for different reasons, and was trying to make those reasons prevail in both cases), and (3) when she succeeded (in choosing to return to help) her reaction was not "Oh dear, I did that by mistake, it was an accident; it was something that happened to me, not something I did." Rather she *endorsed* the outcome as something she was trying and wanting to do all along; she recognized the choice as her resolution of the conflict in her will. And if she had chosen to go on to her meeting, she would have endorsed that outcome, recognizing it as her resolution of the conflict in her will. 13

6. Choice and Agency

Here is a fourth objection that may have occurred to you. Perhaps we are begging the question by assuming that the outcomes of the woman's efforts are *choices* to begin with. If indeterminism is involved in a process (such as the woman's deliberation) so that its outcome is undetermined, one might argue that the outcome must merely *happen* and therefore cannot be somebody's *choice*. But there is no reason to assume that such a claim is true. A choice is the formation of an intention or purpose to do something. It resolves uncertainty and indecision in the mind about what to do. Nothing in such a description implies that there could not be some indeterminism in the deliberation and neural processes of an agent's preceding choice corresponding to the agent's prior uncertainty about what to do. Recall from our earlier arguments that the presence of indeterminism does not mean the outcome happened *merely* by chance and not by the agent's effort. Self-forming choices are undetermined but not uncaused. They are caused by the agent's efforts.

Well, say some critics, perhaps indeterminism does not undermine the idea that something is a *choice,* but rather that it is *the agent's* choice. This objection raises some important questions about agency. What makes the woman's choice her own on the foregoing account is that it results from her efforts and deliberation, which in turn are causally influenced by her reasons and her intentions (e.g., her intention to resolve indecision in one way or another). And what makes these efforts, deliberations, reasons, and intentions *hers* is that they are embedded in a larger motivational system realized in her brain in terms of which she defines herself as a practical reasoner and actor. A choice is the agent's when it is produced intentionally by efforts, by deliberations, and by reasons that are part of this self-defining motivational system and when, in addition, the agent *endorses* the new intention or purpose, created by the choice, into that motivational system, making it a further purpose that will guide *future* practical reasoning and action. 14

Well then, say other critics, perhaps the issue is not whether an undetermined SFA, such as the businesswoman's, is a *choice,* or even whether it is the *agent's* choice, but rather how much *control* she has over it. For while it may be true, as argued earlier (in the discussion of plural voluntary control), that the presence of indeterminism need not eliminate control altogether, wouldn't it be the case that the presence of indeterminism at least *diminishes* the control persons have over their choices and actions? Is it not the case that the assassin's control over whether the prime minister is killed (his ability to carry out his purposes and do what he is trying to do) is

13

Do points (1) and (2) of Kane's response to the luck objection (which is very similar to the randomness objection) work for the businesswoman case? Or does the fact that she was *equally* wanting and trying to do two competing things make the one that results no longer her doing, no longer something for which she is responsible? (And does point (3)—the fact that she *retrospectively* endorses the result—make any difference?)

14

Once again, all of these things would have apparently been true of the alternative choice, had it been made instead. Is there anything that makes the choice she made, as opposed to the other one, *her* choice—beyond the fact that it, rather than the other one, occurred (which would also be true of a random choice)?

15

And here again, the main problem isn't the hindrance that results from the competing desires, motives, or purposes. The real issue is whether the businesswoman herself in any clear way decides or has control over which of the opposing motivations wins out—whether she genuinely "overcomes" one of the opposing hindrances—or whether (assuming that they are equal in strength—see Discussion Question 4) the result is merely a matter of chance.

lessened by the undetermined impulses in his arm? This criticism is related to a problem about libertarian freedom. . . . The problem is that indeterminism, wherever it occurs, seems to be a *hindrance* or *obstacle* to our realizing our purposes and hence is an obstacle to our freedom rather than an *enhancement* of it.

There is some truth to this objection. But I think what is true in it may reveal something important about free will. Perhaps we should concede that indeterminism, wherever it occurs, *does* diminish control over what we are trying to do and *is* a hindrance or obstacle to the realization of our purposes. But recall that in the case of the businesswoman (and SFAs generally), the indeterminism that is admittedly diminishing the agent's control over one thing she is trying to do *is coming from her own will*—from her desire and effort to do a different thing that she also wants to do. And the indeterminism that is diminishing her control over that different thing (in this case the selfish thing) is coming from her desire and effort to do its opposite (to be a moral person who acts on moral reasons). So, in each case, the indeterminism *is* in fact functioning as a hindrance or obstacle to her realizing one of her purposes—a hindrance or obstacle in the form of resistance within her will which has to be overcome by effort.

If there were no such hindrance—if there were no resistance in her will—the woman would indeed in a sense have "complete control" over one of her options. There would no competing motives to stand in the way of her choosing it. But then also she would not be free to rationally and voluntarily choose the other option because she would have no good competing reasons to do so. Thus, by *being* a hindrance to the realization of some of our purposes, indeterminism paradoxically opens up the genuine possibility of pursuing other purposes—of choosing or doing *otherwise* in accordance with, rather than against, our wills (voluntarily) and reasons (rationally). To be genuinely self-forming agents (creators of ourselves)—to have free will—there must at times in life be obstacles and hindrances in our wills of this sort for us to overcome. 15

Another objection to the preceding theory is that we are not consciously aware of making two competing efforts when we engage in self-forming choices. But the theory does not require that we be consciously aware of these competing efforts. The idea was to compare exercises of free will to other cases of parallel processing in the brain, such as vision. Neuroscientists tell us that when we see a visual object, such as a red barn, the brain actually processes different properties of the object (like shape and color) separately, through parallel pathways whose results are eventually brought together in the visual image. We are not introspectively aware of processing the redness of the barn and its shape separately and in parallel. In fact, this information about parallel processing in the brain comes as a surprise to us. But if these neurological theories are correct, that is what we are doing.

The preceding account of free will is suggesting that something similar may be going on when we make self-forming choices. We are not introspectively aware that our efforts (our efforts to make one or another of our competing choices succeed) are being processed on separate, though interacting, pathways in the brain; but that process may in fact be what is going on. If we actually introspected all that was going on when we made free choices, free will would be less mysterious and the problem of free will would be a lot easier to solve than it is. To solve it, we have to consider what may be going on behind the scenes when we are conscious of trying to decide about which of two options to choose and either choice is a difficult one because there are resistant motives pulling us in different directions.*

Let us conclude with one final objection to the account of free will presented in this chapter.

*Is it irrational to make efforts to do incompatible things? In most ordinary situations it is. But I believe that in certain special circumstances it is not irrational to make competing efforts: (i) when we are deliberating between competing options (such as a moral choice and an ambitious choice); (ii) when we intend to choose one or the other but cannot choose both; (iii) when we have powerful motives for wanting to choose each of the options for different and incommensurable reasons, so that we are deeply conflicted; (iv) when there is thus resistance in our will to either choice so that (v) if either choice is to have a chance of being made, effort will be needed to overcome the temptation to make the other choice; and (vi) we want to give each choice a fighting chance of being made because the motives for each choice are important to us. The motives for each choice define in part what sort of person we are; and we would be taking them lightly if we did not make an effort in their behalf. These conditions are, of course, the conditions of SFAs.

This objection is perhaps the most telling and has not yet been discussed. It goes like this: even if one grants that persons, such as the businesswoman, could make genuine self-forming choices that were undetermined, isn't there something to the charge that such choices would be *arbitrary*? A residual arbitrariness seems to remain in all self-forming choices, since the agents cannot in principle have sufficient or conclusive *prior* reasons for making one option and one set of reasons prevail over the other.

There is considerable truth to this objection as well, but again I think it may be a truth that tells us something important about free will. It tells us that every undetermined self-forming free choice is the initiation of what might be called a *value experiment* whose justification lies in the future and is not fully explained by past reasons. In making such a choice we say, in effect, "Let's try this. It is not required by my past, but it is consistent with my past and is one branching pathway in the garden of forking paths my life can now meaningfully take. Whether it is the right choice, only time will tell. Meanwhile, I am willing to take responsibility for it one way or the other."

It is worth noting that the term "arbitrary" comes from the Latin *arbitrium,* which means "judgment". . . . Imagine a writer in the middle of a novel. The novel's heroine faces a crisis and the writer has not yet developed her character in sufficient detail to say exactly how she will act. The author makes a "judgment" about this that is not determined by the heroine's already formed past which does not give unique direction. In this sense, the judgment (*arbitrium*) of how she will react is "arbitrary," but not entirely so. It had input from the heroine's fictional past and in turn gave input to her projected future. In a similar way, agents who exercise free will are both authors of and characters in their own stories all at once. By virtue of "self-forming" judgments of the will . . . (SFAs), they are "arbiters" of their own lives, "making themselves" out of a past that, if they are truly free, does not limit their future pathways to one.

Suppose we were to say to such persons, "But look, you didn't have sufficient or *conclusive* prior reasons for choosing as you did since you also had viable reasons for choosing the other way." They might reply, "True enough. But I did have *good* reasons for choosing as I did, which I'm willing to stand by *and take responsibility for*. If these reasons were not sufficient or conclusive reasons, that's because, like the heroine of the novel, I was not a fully formed person before I chose (and still am not, for that matter). Like the author of the novel, I am in the process of writing an unfinished story and forming an unfinished character who, in my case, is myself."

To sum up, in this chapter I have suggested how a libertarian free will requiring ultimate responsibility and indeterminism might be reconciled with current scientific knowledge. There is much to debate about the theory of this chapter and many objections can and have been made to it. I have tried to answer some of these objections here; but many other objections that also deserve answers have not been addressed. (Those who wish to pursue the issues further can look at the suggested readings that follow.) Many persons believe libertarian free will can never be reconciled with science and cannot exist in the natural order. Perhaps they will turn out to be right. But we should not conclude too hastily that free will of the deeper kind that libertarians believe in cannot be reconciled with science without first trying our best to see how it might be done.

Discussion Questions

1. One of Kane's explicit goals is an account of free will that is compatible with "modern scientific theories about human beings." How important is this goal as a criterion for an acceptable view? Are there strong reasons for thinking that everything that might be relevant to human actions and choices is already known (and well understood) by science—so that a view that cannot be "reconciled" with *current* science must be mistaken?

2. Consider again the example of the businesswoman, as described by Kane in terms of two neural nets or pathways attempting to complete two competing tasks. Is the fact that the eventual choice constitutes success for one (but not the other) of these two competing efforts enough to make it the case that the woman is in control and is responsible for the result? Does the fact that she *endorses* the result make a difference with respect to this issue?

3. Is it *possible* that in a case like that of the businesswoman, the fact that one of the competing neural nets (and systems of reasons and motivation) wins out is just a random occurrence, not selected or controlled by the businesswoman or anyone else? If not, why not? But if this is possible, then how, if at all, are things supposed to be different in Kane's actual case, in which the businesswoman decides, is in control, and is responsible?
4. Kane seems (?) to assume that the strengths of the competing motivations and resulting efforts in the businesswoman case are equal. Suppose they aren't equal: that one is somewhat stronger than the other, but not enough to simply determine the choice. (Perhaps this requires that if the same choice occurs repeatedly, the stronger motivation must win out in a correspondingly higher percentage of the cases.) Does this modification make any difference in relation to Kane's account of how free choice is possible—and if so, how? Does it make a genuinely free choice more or less likely?

Back to Hard Determinism?

Galen Strawson

Galen Strawson (1952–) teaches philosophy at the University of Reading (in England) and the City University of New York. He has done important and influential work on a variety of philosophical topics, especially the philosophy of mind, issues concerning causation, and the free will problem. (He is also the son of the perhaps even better known British philosopher P. F. Strawson.)

In the following selection, Strawson, in addition to offering a useful summary of the main positions on the free will problem, argues that moral responsibility (and freedom) in the most ultimate sense would require a kind of control over one's own nature or character that it is impossible to have. His view is thus a version of what we have called *hard determinism*—one that is not committed to the thesis of causal determinism itself, but simply argues that whether or not causal determinism is true there is no logical room for freedom.

Free Will

'Free will' is the conventional name of a topic that is best discussed without reference to the will. Its central questions are 'What is it to act (or choose) freely?', and 'What is it to be morally responsible for one's actions (or choices)?' These two questions are closely connected, for freedom of action is necessary for moral responsibility, even if it is not sufficient.

Philosophers give very different answers to these questions, hence also to two more specific questions about ourselves: (1) Are we free agents? and (2) Can we be morally responsible for what we do? Answers to (1) and (2) range from 'Yes, Yes' to 'No, No'—via 'Yes, No' and various degrees of 'Perhaps', 'Possibly', and 'In a sense'. (The fourth pair of outright answers, 'No, Yes', is rare, but appears to be accepted by some Protestants.) (1) Prominent among the 'Yes, Yes' sayers are the *compatibilists*, who hold that free will is compatible with *determinism*. Briefly, determinism is the view that everything that happens is necessitated by what has already gone before, in such a way that nothing can happen otherwise than it does. According to compatibilists, freedom is compatible with determinism because freedom is essentially just a matter of not being constrained or hindered in certain ways when one acts or chooses. Thus normal adult human beings in normal circumstances are able to act and choose freely. No one is holding a gun to their heads. They are not drugged, or in chains, or subject to a psychological compulsion. They are therefore wholly free to choose and act even if their whole physical and psychological make-up is entirely determined by things for which they are in no way ultimately responsible—starting with their genetic inheritance and early upbringing.

(1)

You should be able to figure out roughly what views these answers reflect. The "Yes, No" answer might be given by someone who accepts the compatibilist account of freedom as the only intelligible one, but thinks that it is still inadequate for genuine moral responsibility. The Protestant view in question is the idea that everything a person does is predestined by God, but that people are still responsible at least in the sense that they can be appropriately rewarded or punished.

From *Routledge Encyclopedia of Philosophy,* edited by Edward Craig (New York: Routledge, Ltd., 1998).

Incompatibilists hold that freedom is not compatible with determinism. They point out that if determinism is true, then every one of one's actions was determined to happen as it did before one was born. They hold that one cannot be held to be truly free and finally morally responsible for one's actions in this case. They think compatibilism is a 'wretched subterfuge . . . a petty word-jugglery', as Kant put it. It entirely fails to satisfy our natural convictions about the nature of moral responsibility.

The incompatibilists have a good point, and may be divided into two groups. *Libertarians* answer 'Yes, Yes' to questions (1) and (2). They hold that we are indeed free and fully morally responsible agents, and that determinism must therefore be false. Their great difficulty is to explain why the falsity of determinism is any better than the truth of determinism when it comes to establishing our free agency and moral responsibility. For suppose that not every event is determined, and that some events occur randomly, or as a matter of chance. How can our claim to moral responsibility be improved by the supposition that it is partly a matter of chance or random outcome that we and our actions are as they are? [2]

The second group of incompatibilists is less sanguine. They answer 'No, No' to questions (1) and (2). They agree with the libertarians that the truth of determinism rules out genuine moral responsibility, but argue that the falsity of determinism cannot help. Accordingly, they conclude that we are not genuinely free agents or genuinely morally responsible, whether determinism is true or false. One of their arguments can be summarized as follows. When one acts, one acts in the way one does because of the way one is. So to be truly morally responsible for one's actions, one would have to be truly responsible for the way one is: one would have to be *causa sui,* or the cause of oneself, at least in certain crucial mental respects. But nothing can be *causa sui*—nothing can be the ultimate cause of itself in any respect. So nothing can be truly morally responsible. [3]

Suitably developed, this argument against moral responsibility seems very strong. But in many human beings, the experience of choice gives rise to a conviction of absolute responsibility that is untouched by philosophical arguments. This conviction is the deep and inexhaustible source of the free will problem; powerful arguments that seem to show that we cannot be morally responsible in the ultimate way that we suppose keep coming up against equally powerful psychological reasons why we continue to believe that we are ultimately morally responsible. [4]

1. Compatibilism

Do we have free will? It depends what you mean by the word 'free'. More than two hundred senses of the word have been distinguished: the history of the discussion of free will is rich and remarkable. David Hume called the problem of free will 'the most contentious question of metaphysics, the most contentious science'.

According to *compatibilists,* we do have free will. They propound a sense of the word 'free' according to which free will is compatible with *determinism,* even though determinism is the view that the history of the universe is fixed in such a way that nothing can happen otherwise than it does because everything that happens is necessitated by what has already gone before.

Suppose tomorrow is a national holiday. You are considering what to do. You can climb a mountain or read Lao Tse. You can mend your bicycle or go to the zoo. At this moment you are reading . . . philosophy. You are free to go on reading or stop now. You have started on this sentence, but you don't have to . . . finish it.

In this situation, as so often in life, you have a number of options. Nothing forces your hand. It seems natural to say that you are *entirely* free to choose what to do. And, given that nothing hinders you, it seems natural to say that you act entirely freely when you actually do (or try to do) what you have decided to do.

Compatibilists claim that this is the right thing to say. They believe that to have free will, to be a free agent, to be free in choice and action, is simply to be free from *constraints* of certain sorts. Freedom is a matter of not being physically or psychologically forced or compelled to do what one does. Your character, personality, preferences, and general motivational set may be entirely determined by events for which you are in no way responsible (by your genetic inheritance, upbringing, subsequent experience, and so on). But you do not have to be in control of any of these things in order to

2

Thus the libertarian, as we have seen earlier in this chapter, must seemingly find a third alternative to determinism and randomness—a version of indeterminism that is somehow not mere randomness.

3

This is essentially the view of Blatchford and, even more clearly, of Edwards—and also in the end of Strawson himself.

4

As we have seen, this psychological conviction, especially as it arises in situations of actual choice, is among the most basic reasons for believing in free will.

have compatibilist freedom. They do not constrain or compel you, because compatibilist freedom is just a matter of being able to choose and act in the way one prefers or thinks best *given how one is.* As its name declares, it is compatible with determinism. It is compatible with determinism even though it follows from determinism that every aspect of your character, and everything you will ever do, was already inevitable before you were born.

If determinism does not count as a constraint or compulsion, what does? Compatibilists standardly take it that freedom can be limited by such things as imprisonment, by a gun at one's head, or a threat to the life of one's children, or a psychological obsession and so on.

It is arguable, however, that compatibilist freedom is something one continues to possess undiminished so long as one can choose or act in any way at all. One continues to possess it in any situation in which one is not actually panicked, or literally compelled to do what one does, in such a way that it is not clear that one can still be said to choose or act at all (as when one presses a button, because one's finger is actually forced down on the button).

Consider pilots of hijacked aeroplanes. They usually stay calm. They *choose* to comply with the hijackers' demands. They act responsibly, as we naturally say. They are able to do other than they do, but they choose not to. They do what they most want to do, all things considered, in the circumstances in which they find themselves.

All circumstances limit one's options in some way. It is true that some circumstances limit one's options much more drastically than others; but it does not follow that one is not free to choose in those circumstances. Only literal compulsion, panic, or uncontrollable impulse really removes one's freedom to choose, and to (try to) do what one most wants to do given one's character or personality. Even when one's finger is being forced down on the button, one can still act freely in resisting the pressure, and in many other ways. 5

5

Strawson is saying here that the central compatibilist view that we found in Hume and Stace (that a free action is one that results from one's own will or psychological processes) does not really justify excluding cases of constraint or compulsion from the class of free actions. (This was acknowledged to some extent by Stace when he described such cases as "borderline cases": they involve some degree of freedom in that one still has options, even though very limited ones.)

Most of us are free to choose throughout our waking lives, according to the compatibilist conception of freedom. We are free to choose between the options that we perceive to be open to us. (Sometimes we would rather not face options, but are unable to avoid awareness of the fact that we do face them.) One has options even when one is in chains, or falling through space. Even if one is completely paralysed, one is still free in so far as one is free to choose to think about one thing rather than another. Sartre observed that there is a sense in which we are 'condemned' to freedom, not free not to be free.

Of course one may well not be able to do everything one wants—one may want to fly unassisted, vapourize every gun in the United States by an act of thought, or house all those who sleep on the streets of Calcutta by the end of the month. But few have supposed that free will, or free agency, is a matter of being able to do everything one wants. That is one possible view of what it is to be free; but according to the compatibilists, free will is simply a matter of having genuine options and opportunities for action, and being able to choose between them according to what one wants or thinks best.

It may be said that dogs and other animals can be free agents, according to this basic account of compatibilism. Compatibilists may reply that dogs can indeed be free agents. And yet we do not think that dogs can be free or morally responsible in the way we can be. So compatibilists need to say what the relevant difference is between dogs and ourselves.

Many suppose that it is our capacity for self-conscious thought that makes the crucial difference, because it makes it possible for us to be explicitly aware of ourselves as facing choices and engaging in processes of reasoning about what to do. This is *not* because being self-conscious can somehow liberate one from the facts of determinism; if determinism is true, one is determined to have whatever self-conscious thoughts one has, whatever their complexity. Nevertheless, many are inclined to think that a creature's explicit self-conscious awareness of itself as chooser and agent can constitute it as a free agent in a fundamental way that is unavailable to any unself-conscious agent. 6

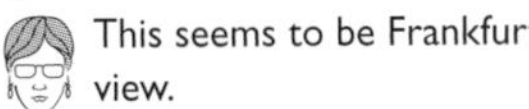

This seems to be Frankfurt's view.

Compatibilists can agree with this. They can acknowledge and incorporate the view that self-conscious awareness of oneself as facing choices can give rise to a kind of freedom that is unavailable to unself-conscious agents. They may add that human beings are sharply marked off from dogs by their capacity to act for reasons that they explicitly take to be moral reasons. In general, compatibilism has many variants. According to Harry Frankfurt's version, for example, one has free will if one wants to be moved to action by the motives that do in fact move one to action. On this view, freedom is a matter of having a personality that is harmonious in a certain way. Freedom in this sense is clearly compatible with determinism.

Compatibilism has been refined in many ways, but this gives an idea of its basis. 'What more could free agency possibly be?', compatibilists like to ask. And this is a very powerful question.

2. Incompatibilism

Those who want to secure the conclusion that we are free agents do well to adopt a compatibilist theory of freedom, for determinism is unfalsifiable, and may be true. [7] . . . Many, however, think that the compatibilist account of things does not even touch the real problem of free will. They believe that all compatibilist theories of freedom are patently inadequate.

What is it, they say, to define freedom in such a way that it is compatible with determinism? It is to define it in such a way that a creature can be a free agent even if all its actions throughout its life are determined to happen as they do by events that have taken place before it is born; so that there is a clear sense in which it could not at any point in its life have done otherwise than it did. This, they say, is certainly not free will. More importantly, it is not a sufficient basis for true moral responsibility. One cannot possibly be truly or ultimately morally responsible for what one does if everything one does is ultimately a deterministic outcome of events that took place before one was born; or (more generally) a deterministic outcome of events for whose occurrence one is in no way ultimately responsible.

These anti-compatibilists or *incompatibilists* divide into two groups: the *libertarians* and the *no-freedom theorists* or *pessimists* about free will and moral responsibility. [8] The libertarians think that the compatibilist account of freedom can be improved on. They hold (1) that we do have free will, (2) that free will is not compatible with determinism, and (3) that determinism is therefore false. But they face an extremely difficult task: they have to show how *indeterminism* (the falsity of determinism) can help with free will and, in particular, with moral responsibility.

The pessimists or no-freedom theorists do not think that this can be shown. They agree with the libertarians that the compatibilist account of free will is inadequate, but they do not think it can be improved on. They agree that free will is not compatible with determinism, but deny that indeterminism can help to make us (or anyone else) free. They believe that free will, of the sort that is necessary for genuine moral responsibility, is probably impossible.

The pessimists about free will grant what everyone must: that there is a clear and important compatibilist sense in which we can be free agents (we can be free, when unconstrained, to choose and to do what we want or think best, given how we are). But they insist that this compatibilist sense of freedom is not enough: it does not give us what we want, in the way of free will; nor does it give us what we believe we have. And it is not as if the compatibilists have missed something. The truth is that nothing can give us what we (think we) want, or what we ordinarily think we have. All attempts to furnish a stronger notion of free will fail. We cannot be morally responsible, in the absolute, buck-stopping way in which we often unreflectively think we are. We cannot have 'strong' free will of the kind that we would need to have, in order to be morally responsible in this way. [9]

The fundamental motor of the free will debate is the worry about moral responsibility. If no one had this worry, it is doubtful whether the problem of free will would be a famous philosophical problem. The rest of this discussion will therefore be organized around the question of moral responsibility.

First, though, it is worth remarking that the worry about free will does not have to be expressed as a worry about the grounds of moral responsibility. A commitment to belief in free will may be integral to feelings that are extremely important to us independently of the issue of moral responsibility: feelings of gratitude, for example, and perhaps of love. One's belief in strong free will may also be driven simply by the conviction that one is or can be *radically self-determining* in one's actions (in a way that is incompatible with determinism) and this conviction need not involve giving much—or any—thought to the issue of moral responsibility. It seems that a creature could conceive of itself as radically self-determining

Strawson means here that the failure to find causes doesn't establish that there aren't any, so that determinism could never be conclusively refuted. Even in the case of quantum theory, some still think that underlying deterministic causes (so-called hidden variables) will eventually be found.

"No-freedom theorists" or "pessimists about free will" are hard determinists, as that term has been used here.

This "absolute, buckstopping" kind of freedom is the one that yields what Kane describes as "ultimate responsibility." It is also the kind of freedom being advocated by Campbell and Nozick: one in which a person is responsible for free choices, but without those choices depending on his formed character or nature (which would make them instead dependent on heredity and environment). The "pessimists" deny that this sort of freedom is possible.

without having any conception of moral right or wrong at all—and so without being any sort of moral agent.

3. Pessimism

One way of setting out the no-freedom theorists' argument is as follows.

1. When you act, you do what you do, in the situation in which you find yourself, because of the way you are. (10)

(10) Think very carefully about the content of this premise. It is not supposed to assert that causal determinism is true. Nor is it supposed to rule out external influences or randomness—it merely asserts that anything you *do* (as opposed to something that merely happens to you) derives in some way from your nature and not from external influences or randomness.

It seems to follow that

2. To be truly or ultimately morally responsible for what you *do,* you must be truly or ultimately responsible for the way you *are,* at least in certain crucial mental respects. (Obviously you don't have to be responsible for the way you are in all respects. You don't have to be responsible for your height, age, sex, and so on. But it does seem that you have to be responsible for the way you are at least in certain mental respects. After all, it is your overall mental make-up that leads you to do what you do when you act.)

But

3. You cannot be ultimately responsible for the way you are in any respect at all, so you cannot be ultimately morally responsible for what you do.

Why is that you cannot be ultimately responsible for the way you are? Because

4. To be ultimately responsible for the way you are you would have to have intentionally brought it about that you are the way you are, in a way that is impossible.

The impossibility is shown as follows. Suppose that

5. You have somehow intentionally brought it about that you are the way you now are, in certain mental respects: suppose that you have intentionally brought it about that you have a certain mental nature N, and that you have brought this about in such a way that you can now be said to be ultimately responsible for having nature N. (The limiting case of this would be the case in which you had simply endorsed your existing mental nature N from a position of power to change it.) (11)

(11) Notice that this would be possible even under Frankfurt's view.

For this to be true

6. You must already have had a certain mental nature N_{-1}, in the light of which you intentionally brought it about that you now have nature N. (If you did not already have a certain mental nature, then you cannot have had any intentions or preferences, and even if you did change in some way, you cannot be held to be responsible for the way you now are.) (12)

(12) Step (6) is the crucial step in the argument. It claims that a choice of one's own nature (perhaps via a choice to overcome one's strongest desire and do the right thing, as discussed by Campbell; or via the adoption of a principle for assigning weights to reasons, as discussed by Nozick; or via a "self-forming action," as discussed by Kane) *must* be based on intentions or preferences that derive from one's previous nature. The implicit idea is that otherwise it would be merely random and so not anything for which the person would be responsible.

But then

7. For it to be true that you and you alone are truly responsible for how you now are, you must be truly responsible for having had the nature N_{-1} in the light of which you intentionally brought it about that you now have nature N.

So

8. You must have intentionally brought it about that you had that nature N_{-1}. But in that case, you must have existed already with a prior nature. N_{-2}, in the light of which you intentionally brought it about that you had the nature N_{-1}.

And so on. Here one is setting off on a potentially infinite regress. In order for one to be truly or ultimately responsible for *how one is,* in such a way that one can be truly morally responsible for *what one does,* something impossible has to be true: there has to be, and cannot be, a starting point in the series of acts of bringing it about that one has a certain nature—a starting point that constitutes an act of ultimate self-origination. (13)

(13) Since an infinite regress of natures is impossible, there must be a starting point in which one constitutes one's own nature for the first time, on the basis of no previous nature. Strawson claims that this is impossible. In the following paragraph, this claim is elaborated by appeal to the allegedly impossible idea of causing oneself.

There is a more concise way of putting the point: in order to be truly morally responsible for what one does, it seems that one would have to be the ultimate cause or origin of oneself, or at least of some crucial part of one's mental nature. One would have to be *causa sui,* in the old terminology. But nothing can be truly or ultimately *causa sui* in any respect at all. Even if the property of being *causa sui* is allowed to belong (unintelligibly) to God, it cannot plausibly be supposed to be possessed by ordinary finite human beings. . . .

In fact, nearly all of those who believe in strong free will do so without any conscious thought that it requires ultimate self-origination.

Nevertheless, this is the only thing that could actually ground the kind of strong free will that is regularly believed in, and it does seem that one way in which the belief in strong free will manifests itself is in the very vague and (necessarily) unexamined belief that many have that they are somehow or other radically responsible for their general mental nature, or at least for certain crucial aspects of it.

The pessimists' argument may seem contrived, but essentially the same argument can be given in a more natural form as follows. (i) It is undeniable that one is the way one is, initially, as a result of heredity and early experience. (ii) It is undeniable that these are things for which one cannot be held to be in any way responsible (this might not be true if there were reincarnation, but reincarnation would just shift the problem backwards). (iii) One cannot at any later stage of one's life hope to accede to true or ultimate responsibility for the way one is by trying to change the way one already is as a result of one's heredity and previous experience. For one may well try to change oneself, but (iv) both the particular way in which one is moved to try to change oneself, and the degree of success in one's attempt at change, will be determined by how one already is as a result of heredity and previous experience. And (v) any further changes that one can bring about only after one has brought about certain initial changes will in turn be determined, via the initial changes, by heredity and previous experience. (vi) This may not be the whole story, for it may be that some changes in the way one is are traceable to the influence of indeterministic or random factors. But (vii) it is foolish to suppose that indeterministic or random factors, for which one is *ex hypothesi* in no way responsible, can in themselves contribute to one's being truly or ultimately responsible for how one is. [14]

The claim, then, is not that people cannot change the way they are. They can, in certain respects (which tend to be exaggerated by North Americans and underestimated, perhaps, by members of many other cultures). The claim is only that people cannot be supposed to change themselves in such a way as to be or become truly or ultimately responsible for the way they are, and hence for their actions. One can put the point by saying that the way you are is, ultimately, in every last detail, a matter of luck—good or bad.

4. Moral Responsibility

Two main questions are raised by the pessimists' arguments. First, is it really true that one needs to be self-creating or *causa sui* in some way, in order to be truly or ultimately responsible for what one does, as step (2) of the pessimists' argument asserts? Addressing this question will be delayed until §6, because a more basic question arises: What notion of responsibility is being appealed to in this argument? What exactly is this 'ultimate' responsibility that we are held to believe in . . . ? And if we do believe in it, what makes us believe in it?

One dramatic way to characterize the notion of ultimate responsibility is by reference to the story of heaven and hell: 'ultimate' moral responsibility is responsibility of such a kind that, if we have it, it *makes sense* to propose that it could be just to punish some of us with torment in hell and reward others with bliss in heaven. It makes sense because what we do is absolutely up to us. The words 'makes sense' are stressed because one certainly does not have to believe in the story of heaven and hell in order to understand the notion of ultimate responsibility that it is used to illustrate. Nor does one have to believe in the story of heaven and hell in order to believe in ultimate responsibility (many atheists have believed in it). One does not have to have heard of it. [15]

The story is useful because it illustrates the *kind* of absolute or ultimate responsibility that many have supposed—and do suppose—themselves to have. It becomes particularly vivid when one is specifically concerned with moral responsibility, and with questions of desert: but it serves equally well to illustrate the sense of radical freedom and responsibility that may be had by a self-conscious agent that has no concept of morality. And one does not have to refer to the story of heaven and hell in order to describe the sorts of everyday situation that seem to be primarily influential in giving rise to our belief in ultimate responsibility. Suppose you set off for a shop on the eve of a national holiday, intending to buy a cake with your last ten pound note. Everything is closing down. There is one cake left: it costs ten pounds. On the steps of the shop someone is shaking an Oxfam tin. [16] You stop, and it seems completely clear to you that it is entirely up to you

14

Here is a simpler version of the argument, one that Blatchford and Edwards would endorse. Nozick (and presumably Campbell) would reject step (iv), claiming that one can sometimes change one's self in ways not determined by one's previously formed character. (Frankfurt is not explicitly committed to the acceptance of step (iv), but it is compatible with his view.) Kane's view is less clear: would he reject step (iv) or step (vii)?

15

The last point here is worth underlining: Strawson is using the idea of heaven and hell to illustrate what "ultimate moral responsibility" is supposed to be like. But he is *not* saying that the existence of heaven and hell—or God—is required for ultimate moral responsibility to exist or for the idea of it to be intelligible.

16

Oxfam is an international charitable and emergency relief organization.

what you do next. That is, it seems clear to you that you are truly, radically free to choose, in such a way that you will be ultimately responsible for whatever you do choose. You can put the money in the tin, or go in and buy the cake, or just walk away. (You are not only completely free to choose. You are not free not to choose.)

Standing there, you may believe that determinism is true. You may believe that in five minutes' time you will be able to look back on the situation and say, of what you will by then have done, 'It was determined that I should do that'. But even if you do believe this, it does not seem to undermine your current sense of the absoluteness of your freedom, and of your moral responsibility for your choice.

One diagnosis of this phenomenon is that one cannot really believe that determinism is true, in such situations of choice, and cannot help thinking that the falsity of determinism might make freedom possible. But the feeling of ultimate responsibility seems to remain inescapable even if one does not think this, and even if one has been convinced by the entirely general argument against ultimate responsibility given in section 3. Suppose one accepts that no one can be in any way *causa sui,* and yet that one would have to be *causa sui* (in certain crucial mental respects) in order to be ultimately responsible for one's actions. This does not seem to have any impact on one's sense of one's radical freedom and responsibility, as one stands there, wondering what to do. One's radical responsibility seems to stem simply from the fact that one is fully conscious of one's situation, and knows that one can choose, and believes that one action is morally better than the other. This seems to be immediately enough to confer full and ultimate responsibility. And yet it cannot really do so, according to the pessimists. For whatever one actually does, one will do what one does because of the way one is, and the way one is is something for which one neither is nor can be responsible, however self-consciously aware of one's situation one is.

The example of the cake may be artificial, but similar situations of choice occur regularly in human life. They are the experiential rock on which the belief in ultimate responsibility is founded. The belief often takes the form of belief in specifically moral, desert-implying responsibility. But, as noted, an agent could have a sense of ultimate responsibility without possessing any conception of morality. . . .

5. Metaphysics and Moral Psychology

We now have the main elements of the problem of free will. It is natural to start with the compatibilist position; but this has only to be stated to trigger the objection that compatibilism cannot possibly satisfy our intuitions about moral responsibility. According to this objection, an incompatibilist notion of free will is essential in order to make sense of the idea that we are genuinely morally responsible. But this view, too, has only to be stated to trigger the pessimists' objection that indeterministic occurrences cannot possibly contribute to moral responsibility: one can hardly be supposed to be more truly morally responsible for one's choices and actions or character if indeterministic occurrences have played a part in their causation than if they have not played such a part. Indeterminism gives rise to unpredictability, not responsibility. It cannot help in any way at all.

The pessimists therefore conclude that strong free will is not possible, and that ultimate responsibility is not possible either. So no punishment or reward is ever truly just or fair, when it comes to moral matters.

...

Now the argument may cycle back to compatibilism. Pointing out that 'ultimate' moral responsibility is obviously impossible, compatibilists may claim that we should rest content with the compatibilist account of things—since it is the best we can do. But this claim reactivates the incompatibilist objection, and the cycle continues.

There is an alternative strategy at this point; quit the traditional metaphysical circle for the domain of *moral psychology.* The principal positions in the traditional metaphysical debate are clear. No radically new option is likely to emerge after millennia of debate. The interesting questions that remain are primarily psychological: Why do we believe we have strong free will and ultimate responsibility? . . . What is it like to live with this belief? What are its varieties? How might we be changed by dwelling intensely on the view that ultimate responsibility is impossible?

A full answer to these questions is beyond the scope of this [article] but one fundamental cause of our belief in ultimate responsibility has been mentioned. It lies in the experience of choice that we have as self-conscious agents who are able to be fully conscious of what they are doing when they deliberate about what to do and make choices. (We choose between the Oxfam box and the cake; or we make a difficult, morally neutral choice about which of two paintings to buy.) This raises an interesting question: Is it true that any possible self-conscious creature that faces choices and is fully aware of the fact that it does so must experience itself as having strong free will, or as being radically self-determining, simply in virtue of the fact that it is a self-conscious agent (and whether or not it has a conception of moral responsibility)? It seems that we cannot live or experience our choices as determined, even if determinism is true. But perhaps this is a human peculiarity, not an inescapable feature of any possible self-conscious agent. And perhaps it is not even universal among human beings. (17)

...

6. Challenges to Pessimism

The preceding discussion attempts to illustrate the internal dynamic of the free will debate, and to explain why the debate is likely to continue for as long as human beings can think. The basic point is this: powerful logical or metaphysical reasons for supposing that we cannot have strong free will keep coming up against equally powerful psychological reasons why we cannot help believing that we do have it. The pessimists' or no-freedom theorists' conclusions may seem irresistible during philosophical discussion, but they are likely to lose their force, and seem obviously irrelevant to life, when one stops philosophizing.

Various challenges to the pessimists' argument have been proposed, some of which appear to be supported by the experience or 'phenomenology' of choice. One challenge grants that one cannot be ultimately responsible for one's mental nature—one's character, personality, or motivational structure—but denies that it follows that one cannot be truly morally responsible for what one does (it therefore challenges step (2) of the argument set out in section 3).

This challenge has at least two versions. One has already been noted: we are attracted by the idea that our capacity for fully explicit self-conscious deliberation, in a situation of choice, suffices by itself to constitute us as truly morally responsible agents in the strongest possible sense. The idea is that such full self-conscious awareness somehow renders irrelevant the fact that one neither is nor can be ultimately responsible for any aspect of one's mental nature. On this view, the mere fact of one's self-conscious presence in the situation of choice can confer true moral responsibility; it may be undeniable that one is, in the final analysis, wholly constituted as the sort of person one is by factors for which one cannot be in any way ultimately responsible; but the threat that this fact appears to pose to one's claim to true moral responsibility is simply obliterated by one's self-conscious awareness of one's situation. (18)

The pessimists reply: This may correctly describe a strong source of *belief* in ultimate (moral) responsibility, but it is not an account of something that could *constitute* ultimate (moral) responsibility. When one acts after explicit self-conscious deliberation, one acts for certain reasons. But which reasons finally weigh with one is a matter of one's mental nature, which is something for which one cannot be in any way ultimately responsible. (19) One can certainly be a morally responsible agent in the sense of being aware of distinctively moral considerations when one acts. But one cannot be morally responsible in such a way that one is ultimately deserving of punishment or reward for what one does.

The conviction that fully explicit self-conscious awareness of one's situation can be a sufficient foundation of strong free will is extremely powerful. The no-freedom theorists' argument seems to show that it is wrong, but it is a conviction that runs deeper than rational argument, and it survives untouched, in the everyday conduct of life, even after the validity of the no-freedom theorists' argument has been admitted. (20)

Another version of the challenge runs as follows. The reason why one can be truly or ultimately (morally) responsible for what one does is that one's *self*—what one might call the 'agent self'—is, in some crucial sense, independent of one's general *mental nature* (one's character, personality, motivational structure, and so on). One's

(17)

What would it be like to have the opposite experience: to *experience* one's choices as determined? Do people ever have such an experience?

This is Frankfurt's view.

This is essentially the reply that Blatchford and Edwards would give to Frankfurt.

Is this conviction really as strong as Strawson claims? Is there any clear rationale for why "fully explicit self-conscious awareness" is enough for "strong free will" (and ultimate responsibility)? Note that Frankfurt himself does not seem to make such a claim.

mental nature *inclines* one to do one thing rather than another, but it does not thereby *necessitate* one to do one thing rather than the other. . . . As an agent-self, one incorporates a power of free decision that is independent of all the particularities of one's mental nature in such a way that one can, after all, count as truly and ultimately morally responsible in one's decisions and actions even though one is not ultimately responsible for any aspect of one's mental nature. 21

21

This is Campbell's view, and presumably also Nozick's (for where else would the assigning of weights to reasons come from?). Strawson's reply is given in the following paragraph.

The pessimists reply: Even if one grants the validity of this conception of the agent-self for the sake of argument, it cannot help to establish ultimate moral responsibility. According to the conception, the agent-self decides in the light of the agent's mental nature but is not determined by the agent's mental nature. The following question immediately arises: *Why* does the agent-self decide as it does? The general answer is clear. Whatever the agent-self decides, it decides as it does because of the overall way it is; and this necessary truth returns us to where we started. For once again, it seems that the agent-self must be responsible for being the way it is, in order to be a source of true or ultimate responsibility. But this is impossible, for the reasons given in section 3; nothing can be *causa sui* in the required way. Whatever the nature of the agent-self, it is ultimately a matter of luck (or, for those who believe in God, a matter of grace). It may be proposed that the agent-self decides as it does partly or wholly because of the presence of indeterministic occurrences in the decision process. But it is clear that indeterministic occurrences can never be a source of true (moral) responsibility. 22

22

The underlying idea here is that any aspect of an action that does not derive in some way from the "agent-self" being the way that it is must be merely random (since it is not controlled by anything about the agent). This is also what Strawson would say about Kane's view.

Some believe that free will and moral responsibility are above all a matter of being governed in one's choices and actions by reason—or by Reason with a capital 'R'. But possession of the property of being governed by Reason cannot be a ground of radical moral responsibility as ordinarily understood. It cannot be a property that makes punishment (for example) ultimately just or fair for those who possess it, and unfair for those who do not possess it. 23 Why not? Because to be morally responsible, on this view, is simply to possess one sort of motivational set among others. It is to value or respond naturally to rational considerations—which are often thought to include moral considerations by those who propound this view. It is to have a general motivational set that may be attractive, and that may be more socially beneficial than many others. But there is no escape from the fact that someone who does possess such a motivational set is simply lucky to possess it—if it is indeed a good thing—while someone who lacks it is unlucky.

23

This would be a version of compatibilism, but importantly different from the ones discussed so far, in the emphasis on reason. Strawson's response is essentially the same one that he gives to other versions of compatibilism.

This may be denied. It may be said that some people struggle to become more morally responsible, and make an enormous effort. Their moral responsibility is then not a matter of luck; it is their own hard-won achievement.

The pessimists' reply is immediate. Suppose you are someone who struggles to be morally responsible, and make an enormous effort. Well, that, too, is a matter of luck. You are lucky to be someone who has a character of a sort that disposes you to make that sort of effort. Someone who lacks a character of that sort is merely unlucky. . . .

In the end, luck swallows everything. This is one way of putting the point that there can be no ultimate responsibility, given the natural, strong conception of responsibility that was characterized at the beginning of section 4. Relative to that conception, no punishment or reward is ever ultimately just or fair, however natural or useful or otherwise humanly appropriate it may be or seem.

The facts are clear, and they have been known for a long time. When it comes to the metaphysics of free will. André Gide's remark is apt: 'Everything has been said before, but since nobody listens we have to keep going back and beginning all over again.' It seems that the only freedom that we can have is compatibilist freedom. If—since—that is not enough for ultimate responsibility, we cannot have ultimate responsibility. The only alternative to this conclusion is to appeal to God and mystery—this in order to back up the claim that something that appears to be provably impossible is not only possible but actual.

The debate continues; some have thought that philosophy ought to move on. There is little reason to expect that it will do so, as each new generation arises bearing philosophers gripped by the conviction that they can have ultimate responsibility. Would it be a good thing if philosophy did move on, or if we became more clear-headed about the topic of free will than we are? It is hard to say.

Discussion Questions

1. Think carefully through the two related arguments for hard determinism that Strawson gives on pages 308–309. How would a compatibilist of the Hume-Stace variety reply? How would Frankfurt reply? How would Campbell, Nozick, and Kane reply? (Don't assume that their replies would be the same.) Which view do you find most plausible, and why?
2. Strawson says in several places that an agent causation view is impossible. Does he have any clear argument for this claim—over and above the challenge (already seen earlier) to explain how free choices of the sort they attempt to describe can fail to be determined by the antecedent nature of the self without being random?
3. How intuitively implausible is the rejection of "strong free will" and "ultimate responsibility"? Imagine yourself in the process of making a very difficult moral decision. Can you bring yourself to believe that whatever you eventually do is entirely determined by conditions that existed before you were born or that it is even partly a random event? How would you approach such a choice if you believed either of these things?

Concluding Dialogue on Free Will

Though all of the major philosophical issues are very difficult—that's what makes them major issues, after all!—the free will problem has always seemed to me probably the most difficult of all. More clearly than with any of the other issues, the main alternatives seem to capture all the real possibilities. One can say that there is no genuine free will (because it is incompatible with both determinism and randomness, and there's no third alternative). One can say that free will exists and involves some kind of determinism. Or one can say that free will exists and involves some kind of indeterminism. It seems awfully clear that one of these three views *must* be correct, and yet there are also extremely compelling reasons—admittedly reasons of very different sorts in each case—for thinking that each of them is wrong. Does the issue seem as intractable to you as it does to me?

I might not say intractable, but definitely very difficult. So let's think about it, starting with compatibilism. In a way, this would be the easiest solution. A compatibilist doesn't have to reject the seemingly obvious fact that free will exists, and he also doesn't have to explain how an occurrence can be undetermined and at the same time not merely random. This is probably what makes the compatibilist position so attractive to so many philosophers—it's probably held by many more of those who have a position on this issue than the two other views put together.

Well, maybe it is initially attractive—most views that allow you to have your cake and eat it too are—but the problems are also pretty obvious. One important problem for the more traditional compatibilist view (that of Hume and Stace and lots of others) is exactly where to draw the line between free and unfree actions. Hume says that freedom is just being able to do what you choose, and Stace says that freedom is having an action be immediately caused by your own psychological states. These seem to me to amount to pretty much the same thing. But Edwards points to some cases that raise serious problems for this view—cases where an action that is immediately caused by a person's psychological states still doesn't seem genuinely free.

Right. Something you do because someone threatens to harm you if you don't is still, after all, *immediately* caused by your own psychological states and your own choice. So such an action ought to count as free, according to Stace's account, but that seems wrong. (In fact, this is one of Stace's own examples of an *unfree* action!) The circumstances obviously limit your choices in that case (assuming that the other person is able and willing to carry out the threat), but *all* choices are constrained to some extent by circumstances, so this doesn't make for a very clear line. Post-hypnotic suggestion is another case where the immediate cause of an action is the agent's own psychological states, but where it is doubtful that the person is really free.

But those aren't the worst cases. The most difficult ones are various kinds of psychological *compulsion:* kleptomania, compulsive hand-washing, and so on. Again, the immediate cause of the behavior—even to call it an action seems a little strained—is the agent's own psychological states, which in these cases are not externally influenced or controlled in any way. But at least in the more extreme cases, compulsive behavior of this sort doesn't look very much like real freedom.

One response a compatibilist could make to such cases, one that Edwards seems perhaps to have in mind, is to appeal to *rationality:* to say that the psychological processes that lead to an action must be rational if the action is to be free—which doesn't seem to be true in the compulsive cases. But while this has some plausibility, it would make the line between free and unfree actions awfully fuzzy and debatable, since people surely can and do disagree about what is rational and what isn't.

Frankfurt, on the other hand, offers a quite different sort of response to such cases, leading to a significantly different compatibilist view. His unwilling addict doesn't have free will because he acts on a desire to take drugs that is in conflict with a *second-order volition* not to act on that desire. So if the kleptomaniac (or the compulsive hand-washer) has a second-order volition that the compulsive desires not be the ones on which he acts, then he won't count as having free will either, according to Frankfurt.

That seems like the right result for those specific cases. But I am bothered by Frankfurt's claim that someone who simply fails to have a relevant second-order volition thereby isn't free. This in fact seems to be the situation that most people are in most of the time—second-order volitions seem to me too sophisticated to be very common. So the range of free will under Frankfurt's view will be pretty limited, not enough to satisfy the common-sense intuition that people are free most of the time.

Be careful. Frankfurt's view is a bit tricky here. He says that people who have no relevant second-order volitions don't have *free will*, but still may *act freely*. If the common-sense intuition is that people act freely most of the time, then Frankfurt can still agree. And of course his view of what moral responsibility requires is also a lot more complicated, as we'll discuss a bit later on.

I doubt that common sense really recognizes a distinction between free action and free will. But the real problem for him, it seems to me, is the one that grows out of the case of the *willing* addict: the one who has a second-order volition that the desire to take the drugs be effective. (There could, as far as I can see, be willing kleptomaniacs or willing compulsive hand-washers too.) In Frankfurt's version, the following three things are true of the willing addict. First, he acts freely (because his desire to take the drug causes his action). Second, he is morally responsible (because he endorses that desire). And third, he still doesn't have free will (because the first-order desire would be effective even if it conflicted with his second-order volition—though Frankfurt also says, puzzlingly, that he takes the drug "of his own free will"). I'm not sure that the second claim is right. But in any case, why couldn't there be a second-order volition in such a case that really does control whether the first-order desire is effective, but is *itself* compulsive in character?

That would depend, I suppose, on what makes a desire (or volition) count as compulsive. Frankfurt might say that compulsion necessarily involves a higher-order desire that is ineffective. But whether or not a compatibilist can resolve these issues of where to draw the line between free and unfree actions, I still think that there is a much more serious problem with compatibilism. Does compatibilism of any sort really do justice to the compelling intuition that we do have genuine free will? Hume and Stace seem to be right that the compatibilist draws the line between actions that are free and actions that aren't free in at least approximately the place that common sense would draw it (though we've seen some problems with that supposition). But *maybe* this is only because common sense—especially as reflected in the thinking of people actually making important choices—just doesn't regard determinism as a serious possibility, or randomness either. It just seems so obvious in normal cases that when a person does one thing, he or she could also have freely chosen to do something else: that both possibilities (and usually many more than

two) are genuinely open and really could have occurred. But this is just what the compatibilist in effect denies. For a compatibilist, there is really only one possibility for a free choice that is genuinely open, given antecedent conditions and natural laws (and setting aside randomness as irrelevant to freedom). And that is both very hard to swallow and seems intuitively incompatible with genuine free will—since the person really couldn't have done otherwise.

I think you're right about that. I guess I have to admit having been at one time seriously tempted by compatibilism. There is something so satisfying about a view that can apparently make a seemingly intractable problem just go away, and there is a mind-set that a lot of so-called "analytic" philosophers have that says in effect that any philosophical (as opposed to scientific) problem that appears to be *that* difficult has to somehow be based on some mistake or confusion—as Hume and Stace suggest. But solutions like that almost never seem to stand up under further scrutiny, and I agree that this one doesn't, mainly for the reason you give.

That's the way it seems to me. It just isn't clear that the sense in which a person could have done otherwise under a compatibilist view is strong enough for genuine freedom and moral responsibility. And this is just as much a problem for Frankfurt as for the more standard compatibilist. And this is the basic reason that compatibilism doesn't seem to me to work.

Of course, we're assuming in all this that the sort of freedom required for moral responsibility requires genuinely being able to do otherwise. Remember that Frankfurt (in another paper) denies that moral responsibility requires being able to do otherwise. His famous example is a case where one person (the controller) is in a position to control the actions of another (the victim), through radio-activated implants or whatever. The controller wants the controlled person to do a certain thing and is ready to control him to that end if necessary. But the victim chooses on his own to do the very thing the controller wants, so that the controller never actually needs to intervene. So the person couldn't really have done otherwise (because the controller would have intervened to make him do the thing in question), but still seems (unless there is some other problem) to be morally responsible. Indeed, even if some libertarian account of freedom is right, the actual (uncontrolled) choice in this case might still be free—might involve agent causation or assigning weights to reasons or whatever.

The example is very clever, but it doesn't seem to me ultimately convincing. *Maybe* it shows that there are some special cases in which a person can still be morally responsible and even free, even though he couldn't—for this fairly unusual sort of reason—have done otherwise. But this isn't enough to show that if people can't do otherwise simply because their actual choices are determined by conditions that existed hundreds or millions of years before they were born, they can still be free or responsible in any meaningful sense—which is what the compatibilist claims.

As I've already said, I agree with this fundamental point. Surely genuine freedom and genuine moral responsibility require that I myself could have actually chosen something other than what I did (and also, as Frankfurt's case points out, that this choice would have actually led to the corresponding action). Compatibilists say in effect that I could have chosen and could have done otherwise only in the sense that if there had been someone similar to me in a different possible world with different antecedent causes that led to a different desire in the case in question, *that* person would have done something else. But that doesn't seem good enough, since that other person just isn't me.

Yes. And this, of course, is the fundamental insight that makes libertarianism so appealing from a sheerly intuitive standpoint. Only a libertarian view makes it really possible that the very person who does one thing—not some other-world doppelganger—could genuinely have done something else instead.

But you know the problem with that: once we realize that really being able to *do* otherwise has to mean more than just that something different could have *happened* at random in a way that wasn't within my control, it becomes very hard to be sure that the libertarian view even makes sense. How can there be an action that is not determined by any antecedent conditions, including all of the ones that pertain to my character and personal makeup and antecedent desires and antecedent thought processes, but is also not merely a random or chance occurrence? Libertarians, including the three in the readings, struggle awfully hard with this problem, but it's not clear to me that any of them really succeed.

Well, let's talk about them. Campbell says that a free action is caused by the agent, but not by his formed character—which really has to mean not by anything having to do with his antecedent psychological states. He thinks that this takes place in situations of moral choice, when one exerts the effort to overcome one's strongest desire and do the morally right thing. One problem with this is that it seems again to constrain free will too narrowly to satisfy the common-sense intuition that is the main motivation for the view. From an intuitive standpoint, I seem to be free in lots of cases where no moral issue is involved—and also in cases where my strongest desire is to behave morally. Another problem is that the appeal to morality might seem to be just an appeal to a different aspect of a person's character or makeup, one that is sometimes strong enough to override more selfish motives.

But the main problem is still surely the worry about randomness. On Campbell's view, it appears as though *everything* about the person—heredity, environment, resulting character traits, thought processes, and so on—could have been exactly the same right up to the magical point where the free choice occurs and a different choice has been made instead. But then how did the person *control* which of the two (or more) possible choices was made? Why wasn't it just random in relation to everything about him?

And I suppose you think that the same issue arises for Nozick. In his view, free choices occur when an agent assigns *weights* to his various reasons for different actions in a particular situation. The agent could have done otherwise because he could have assigned different weights. But once again, if the weights assigned were not determined by anything about his previous makeup or history, then it becomes unclear why we should say that he *assigned* them, rather than simply that they just were somehow set at random in a way over which he had no real control.

Right. Nozick tries to say how the assignment of weights could be non-random by appealing to the idea of "reflexive self-subsumption." The idea is that a general principle for assigning weights might include, as a particular case, the assignment of weights that leads to the adoption of that very principle. This is very tricky and clever, but it doesn't really seem to help. One problem is that it again seems to restrict freedom too narrowly: from a common-sense standpoint, I am free to do lots of things that seemingly can't be captured by such general self-subsuming principles—free to be quite capricious and erratic. But the main problem is again the worry about randomness. Assuming that there are alternative self-subsuming principles, why isn't it still random which one the agent actually adopts?

I guess I agree that Nozick's view is more clever than really helpful. But what about Kane? Though one could worry again that he restricts free choice to too narrow a range of cases, the ones that he focuses on seem intuitively the most important ones, and what he says about them seems to make a lot of sense on a sheerly intuitive level. And remember that at this point we are just trying to determine whether a libertarian can make sense of the idea of a genuinely free action, not whether the particular view draws exactly the right line between actions that are free and those that are unfree. His example of the businesswoman is helpful: she is pulled in both directions, has desires and motives that compete with each other, and struggles with the decision. Ultimately, she doesn't resolve the issue through some mysterious sort of agent causation and she doesn't have to come up with a self-subsuming principle. (What would *that* be, in this sort of case?) She just *decides* in the end to do one thing rather than another, thereby allowing one set of desires and motives to win out over the other. And that seems intuitively to be just what happens in at least the most important examples of free choice.

I agree that Kane has the intuitive phenomenology at least approximately right, but does he really explain adequately how such a "decision" works? What makes it true that the

businesswoman *decides* and is in *control,* instead of one choice rather than the other just *happening* by chance (assuming that the whole situation is, as Kane insists, indeterministic in character)? Indeed, I'm not at all sure that this isn't exactly Kane's view: the choice occurs at random, but it's still one of the ones for which she has strong reasons (that part is determined), and she also endorses it retrospectively (though she would equally have endorsed the opposite choice, if it had occurred instead). This makes Kane's view sound rather like Frankfurt's discussion of the willing addict: in both cases, the choice isn't really controlled by the agent, but retrospective endorsement is supposed to make it still compatible with moral responsibility and, at least for Kane, with freedom. And the problem is that retrospective endorsement just isn't relevant to whether the person could really have done otherwise in the sense that the result was genuinely within her control.

I see what you're worried about. If what you're suggesting is right, Kane really just gives us randomness with some window dressing, just as Frankfurt just gives us determinism with some window dressing. And it may well be that Nozick is really no different than Kane: that his version of free choice too makes it fundamentally random, albeit with a different sort of window dressing. And agent causation, as in Campbell, also doesn't really help because it isn't clear how it excludes randomness. But I worry that these arguments against the various libertarian views beg the question in a subtle way. You asked earlier how there can be an action that is not determined by anything about the agent (or by anything outside of him either), but is still also not random. And you still seem to me too quick to draw the conclusion that the only possibility, once we've eliminated determinism, is randomness.

Wait a minute. I would *love* to find a way in which libertarianism could work. I have most certainly not embraced the claim that anything undetermined is automatically random, but I do need to be able to see clearly just *how* and *why* something undetermined can still also not be random. When Kane, for example, says that we *decide,* I have to ask myself what that really means. Consistent with everything that has happened so far, including everything I have previously thought and desired, I could do either A or B. And when I've done A, for example, instead of B, there is not a single thing prior to the decision itself that can explain *why* I did A instead of B. Don't get me wrong—there are lots of reasons for both A and B, but there is *nothing* that determines that I do one instead of the other.

Yes, exactly. Don't you hear yourself? There is nothing that *determines* it, only things that incline or influence or tempt or something less strong than determine. So, you're saying, if that is all that can be pointed to before the decision itself (or whatever effort of will is being appealed to), then the ultimate result must be random. You're just *assuming* that anything that isn't determined is random!

No—not only not exactly, but not even close! Let me say it again without using that inflammatory word "determine." If all of the same things are true before the decision—whether I choose A or whether I choose B—then *none* of those things can be what brings it about that I choose one instead of the other. If those are all the things there are, then nothing about me or what I think *picks out* or *selects* A instead of B (or vice versa). I could *just as easily* have done B instead of A, given *everything* prior to the decision. And what else is randomness except something occurring without any explanation or anything that in any way brings about one alternative rather than the other?

I have to admit, even though very reluctantly, that I don't see any clear answer to that. And I also agree that the libertarian needs one. So the prospects for genuine free will are starting to look pretty bleak.

And that is Strawson's basic point and the strength of what we've been calling hard determinism (though "hard incompatibilism" might be a better label, since Strawson doesn't need to accept causal determinism). The hard determinist doesn't have to do tricky metaphysics or fancy footwork to avoid or soft-pedal randomness, and he doesn't have to convince us that we can be free and responsible even though we really couldn't have chosen anything else. He only has to say that the common-sense intuition of genuine freedom is really just

an illusion. Maybe our actions are determined and maybe they are to some degree random (though surely not entirely random), but either way there's simply no logical room for freedom. I don't like that result—and I'm not sure that anyone can really believe it while actually engaged in choosing and acting. But none of that shows in any strong way that it couldn't still be true.

But the intuition of freedom is still *awfully* powerful, and not just in morally difficult cases like the ones that libertarians focus on. Think of something as simple as whether, beginning with my arm stretched out to the side, I lift it up or lower it down. *Surely* I really can do either of these things in a way that means that no one could have rigorously predicted 10,000 years ago which I would do and also that which (if either) I do doesn't just happen at random, but rather is under my control. This seems to me just too obvious to be reasonably denied, which is why it still seems to me that some version of libertarianism must be right, even if no one has been able to figure out how it should go.

I guess I basically agree, even though I may be a little less confident than you are. Sometimes I wonder, however, whether the whole problem isn't misconceived. Maybe it's just a mistake to put as many different kinds of cases as we do under the general label "causation" and then define causal determinism on that basis. Maybe the way in which a decision is produced in a rational, reflective agent is so different from merely mechanical occurrences that it's just a mistake to view them as two versions of essentially the same general sort of process. I guess I do think that if the problem is as difficult as it seems, there must be *something* that we are misunderstanding or confused about, even if not something as simple and easy as what Hume and Stace point to.

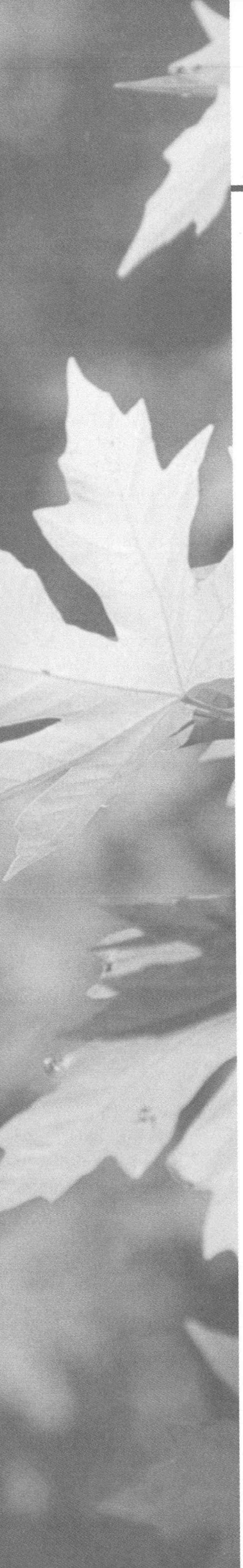

CHAPTER 5

Morality and Moral Problems

The selections in this chapter are concerned with issues pertaining to ethics or moral philosophy: the philosophical study of what makes actions morally right or morally wrong (and also of other kinds of moral value pertaining to such things as ends or character). The first and larger main section of the chapter is concerned with competing accounts of the principles or standards that determine the moral acceptability, the rightness or wrongness, of actions. The second and smaller main section is concerned with views that in different ways challenge the very existence of the objectively or universally correct interpersonal moral standards that all of the views in the first section assume to exist.

What Is the Best Theory of Morality: Utilitarianism, Deontological Views, or Virtue Ethics?

The selections in this section explain and discuss three competing accounts of the content of morality: one that appeals to the *consequences* of an action; one that appeals to the *intrinsic nature* of an action (in a way that makes no mention of consequences) and also to moral *rights;* and one that appeals to whether or not an action would be performed by a person possessing moral *virtue*. Since seeing how a moral view applies to concrete issues is helpful in understanding and evaluating it, each of the three subsections also includes one or more examples of such an application for the view in question. (To make comparisons among the views a little easier, we have focused here on only two moral issues, famine relief and abortion, with two contrasting selections discussing each of them.)

Utilitarianism: Morality Depends on Consequences

The first and initially most obvious of these views is **utilitarianism:** the view that the moral acceptability of an action depends on the *utility* (value or goodness in relation to human desires or preferences) that it produces as compared with other alternatives. (Utilitarianism is the main version of **consequentialism:** the view that the moral correctness or acceptability of an action is determined by its consequences; other consequentialist views appeal to values that include more than just utility.) The most straightforward version of utilitarianism is **act utilitarianism:** the view that the morally correct action in any situation of choice is the one out of the available alternatives that produces the greatest overall utility (for all who are affected by it, in the indefinitely long run). Jeremy Bentham presents a straightforward version of **hedonistic** act utilitarianism, the historically most prominent version of utilitarianism, according to which the utility that makes actions good (or bad) is simply the *pleasure* or *happiness* (as contrasted with the *pain* or *unhappiness*) they lead to. John Stuart Mill then offers a revised and more subtle version of hedonistic act utilitarianism, one that, among other things, recognizes different *qualities* (as opposed to quantities) of pleasure or happiness.

Act utilitarianism is thought by many to face serious counter-examples: cases where conforming to the act utilitarian principle would lead to actions that seem unacceptable from an intuitive standpoint, with the most important such examples being apparent violations of justice. This problem has motivated some utilitarians to opt for a different version of utilitarianism: **rule utilitarianism,** according to which (a) the morally correct action in a given situation is determined by a set of general rules, and (b) the correct set of rules is the one whose *general* observance leads to the greatest utility. Thus the idea is that everyone following a rule like "never tell lies" might produce more utility *overall* even if conforming to this rule produced less utility in some specific cases. J. J. C. Smart discusses the issue between these two versions of utilitarianism, arguing that there is no good rationale for rule utilitarianism from a utilitarian standpoint. Bernard Williams offers some further influential criticisms of utilitarianism. Finally, Peter Singer applies what amounts to a version of utilitarianism to the issue of moral obligations with respect to famine relief.

It should also be mentioned that while hedonistic versions of utilitarianism are the most prominent historically, there are two other accounts of utility that are accepted by some versions of utilitarianism: according to what is sometimes called **ideal utilitarianism,** there are many different sorts of **intrinsic good,** things that are good in themselves or for their own sake as opposed to being merely good as a means to something else (**instrumental good**), with pleasure or happiness being only one—or perhaps two—of these (knowledge, on some views, is another). The fundamental moral principle of ideal utilitarianism is that the sum of *all* these different goods should be maximized, either by each action (the act version) or by the set of rules (the rule version). A third, much more recently developed account of utility defines it in terms of the satisfaction of people's *preferences,* with the morally correct action or set of rules being the one that maximizes the satisfaction of such preferences (allowing also for the importance or weight that they have for those who have them). When we use the term "utilitarianism" in this book (without the qualification "hedonistic"), we will mean the general view of which hedonistic utilitarianism, ideal utilitarianism, and preference utilitarianism are specific versions. (Some recent philosophers instead use the term "consequentialism" to refer to this general view.)

Deontological Views: Morality Depends on Duties and Rights

The second main sort of view is a **deontological** moral theory, according to which the rightness or wrongness of an action is determined, not by its consequences, but just by the kind of action it is—with the crucial claim being that some sorts of actions are morally unacceptable no matter what results they may lead to in terms of utility. Here the most influential view by far is that of Immanuel Kant, so much so indeed that the main alternative to utilitarianism is often referred to as a Kantian moral theory. The selection from Kant offers an account of this sort of position, centering around several supposedly equivalent versions of what Kant regards as the fundamental principle of morality: the **categorical imperative.** Onora O'Neill then discusses the contrast between utilitarian and Kantian views in relation to a specific moral issue: again the issue of famine relief.

One deontological idea that plays a relatively minor explicit role in Kant's view but that has come to be very prominent in recent moral discussions is the idea of moral **rights.** What makes this a deontological moral concept is that rights are normally taken to override considerations of utility in the sense that it is morally wrong to violate a person's right to something even if doing so produces better overall results. The idea of people having rights also seems to reflects Kant's view that people must be treated as ends in themselves. David T. Ozar explains and develops the idea of moral rights, while Judith Jarvis Thomson discusses the morality of abortion from a perspective that emphasizes rights.

Virtue Ethics: Morality Depends on Character Traits

A third sort of moral view has very ancient roots but has been revived as a main view only fairly recently (and is, far more than the other two views, still in the process of elaboration and development). This view centers around the idea of **moral virtues:** morally valuable or admirable traits of individual character, such as courage, temperance, charity, and so on. There are two importantly different versions of virtue ethics, one of them making a substantially stronger and more controversial claim than the other. The weaker view presents itself less as a rival than as a supplement to utilitarian and Kantian views: it insists that there are important moral questions that go beyond that of the morally right or acceptable choice of action. One of these questions is what sort of person one should be, with the idea of moral virtue playing a major role in the answer. In contrast, a second, much more ambitious version of virtue ethics attempts to provide an alternative account of the standard for a morally correct or acceptable action: a morally correct action is one that would be performed (in the situation in question) by an ideally virtuous person. A selection from Aristotle offers the historically most influential account of the nature of moral virtue. Rosalind Hursthouse defends a version of the second, more ambitious version of virtue ethics, contrasting it with utilitarian and Kantian views. A second selection from Hursthouse then discusses how virtue ethics would deal with the issue of abortion.

Moral Investigation: The Method of Reflective Equilibrium

There is one other topic that needs to be discussed here, one that is especially relevant to the discussion of specific, concrete moral issues. There is a general method of thinking about moral questions that has come in recent times to be very widely accepted among philosophers, at least in its general outlines. This method is motivated by two general facts that are also widely acknowledged: first, that moral claims are rarely if ever so obviously and straightforwardly true that they can simply be accepted on that basis; and, second, that while non-moral facts can be relevant in various ways to moral issues, the truth of moral claims is always logically independent of such non-moral facts and incapable of being settled by appeal to them.

How then can the truth or correctness of moral claims be assessed on a rational basis? The starting point here is the realization that while, as already noted, such claims are rarely just obviously or self-evidently true, we very frequently have opinions of varying degrees of strength about their truth, opinions that are not inferred from other moral opinions but are instead direct or immediate. Thus, for example, upon observing a simple case of theft (or, importantly, having such a case described in some detail), most people will judge immediately and non-inferentially that the thief's action was wrong. (They may *also* infer this result from more general principles, but this will not normally be the sole or even the main basis for the resulting belief.) Such immediate, non-inferential moral opinions have come to be referred to as *moral intuitions*.

The starting point for the method of reflective equilibrium is moral intuitions pertaining both to specific cases, whether actual or invented, and to issues at higher levels of generality. There is no doubt that we do have such intuitions and also that many of them are matters of substantial agreement among different persons. But there is also no doubt that the intuitions of different people about the same issue can conflict with each other—and also, even more interestingly, that the intuitions of a single person about different issues and at different levels can conflict among themselves. Thus even if it is assumed that people have *some* capacity for insight into moral truth and thus that their carefully considered moral intuitions have *some* claim to be correct, it is obvious that not all such intuitions are correct. The hope, however, is that by reflectively weighing such intuitions against each other, discarding those that seem to be in conflict with many others, and perhaps refining or adjusting others to avoid such conflicts, an overall coherent package of claims at varying degrees of generality can be arrived at. The claim is then that the overall view of this sort that best preserves the clearest and strongest moral intuitions (and also explains away many of the intuitions that it has to reject as mistaken or in some way confused) has the strongest claim to be correct. The situation in which such a result has been achieved is referred to as *reflective equilibrium:* "equilibrium" because the sorts of conflicts that make one's moral views unstable and subject to change have, for the moment anyway, been eliminated. The suggestion is that a philosopher's main goal in thinking about moral issues is to seek and (it is hoped) achieve such reflective equilibrium.

Perhaps no one can seriously claim to have achieved such a result in a fully satisfactory way. But implicit appeals to this method pervade the readings that follow, with intuitions about various sorts of cases and examples being cited as reasons for or against particular moral views.

Challenges to Morality: Relativism and Egoism

As briefly noted above, all three of the views of morality discussed so far share the assumption that there are moral truths that are objective and universally applicable, in relation to which the actions of persons in different societies and periods of history can correctly be evaluated. Implicit in this discussion is also the idea that, of course, a person acting in his or her own self-interest may be doing something morally wrong, and that the claims of morality often override self-interest. The readings in the final section of the chapter discuss views that challenge these two assumptions.

Relativism

Many people, especially but not only students, are highly suspicious of **moral objectivism:** the idea that there are objective or universal moral truths. For many of them, the preferred alternative is some form of **moral relativism.** This is the view (a) that there are indeed moral truths of some sort, but also (b) that moral truth is *relative* to something, in the most familiar version to a person's culture, rather than being objective or universal.

Here part (a) is crucial, for there is a third alternative to moral objectivism and moral relativism that very few people find palatable: **moral nihilism,** the view that there are no moral truths of any sort, that morality is just a mistake or illusion. The moral nihilist does not, of course, deny the obvious fact that people have moral *opinions;* his claim is just that none of these opinions are ever true or correct in any way, so that there is no good reason why anyone's choices should be guided or restricted by them. Thus one requirement for a significant version of moral relativism is that it not turn out to really amount to moral nihilism. This requires moral relativism to offer some account of how and why its relative moral truths are still genuinely binding on those to whom they are alleged to apply—and to do this without appealing to any objective, universal truth of the sort that the view repudiates. (Thus, for example, the cultural relativist must explain why people are genuinely obligated to conform to the moral principles advocated by their cultures, and do this without adopting an objective principle that any person should conform to the morality of his or her culture.)

It is a striking fact about the current state of moral discussion that despite the popularity of relativist views among non-philosophers, very few philosophers find them plausible. Whether or not you ultimately agree, you should try to understand the reasons for this widespread philosophical rejection of relativism. Many of the most important of these are presented in the selection by James Rachels, which focuses on cultural relativism.

Egoism

A different sort of challenge to the idea of objective or universal moral truths is posed by ethical egoism. Here there are two distinct, but related views. First, there is **psychological egoism,** the view that as a matter of psychological fact, no one is *capable* of pursuing anything but his own selfish interests. Second, there is **ethical egoism,** the view that no one is ever morally obligated to act in any way that is contrary to his own interests (with the rationale being a person cannot be *morally obligated* to do anything that is psychologically impossible)—and perhaps, even less plausibly, that people are morally obligated to pursue their own best interests. Ethical egoism, in either of these versions, would, if correct, amount in a way to an objective moral truth, but it would mean that there are no objective moral truths of the more familiar sort that restrain people's selfish behavior by appeal to the interests and rights of others. The selection by Joel Feinberg offers a detailed critique of psychological egoism, which Feinberg claims to appear plausible only as a result of confusions of various sorts. (If psychological egoism is rejected, then there is no clear rationale of any sort for ethical egoism.)

The final selection, from Plato's most famous dialogue *Republic,* raises an issue that is distinct from but related to ethical egoism: whether or not it is in a person's self-interest to behave in a way that conforms to morality. The claim of psychological egoism was in effect that moral behavior is impossible if the demands of morality conflict with those of self-interest. Plato's striking thesis is that such a conflict does not arise, not because ethical egoism is true, but rather because conforming to the demands of a non-egoistic morality (like the views discussed in the first section) is in fact best for the individual person—or, more specifically, for the health of his or her soul.

What Is the Best Theory of Morality?

Utilitarianism: Morality Depends on Consequences

Jeremy Bentham

Jeremy Bentham (1748–1832) was an English moral, political, and legal philosopher, and the main founder of the utilitarian approach to ethics. Bentham's main concern was with practical legal and social reform along utilitarian lines, and he became the leader of an important group of reformers (the "Philosophical Radicals"), whose influence led to significant changes in British law, particularly in the area of criminal law. In the following selection from his most important work, Bentham presents, explains, and defends a hedonistic version of act utilitarianism based on the *principle of utility,* which he regards as the only reasonable basis for moral judgments.

From *An Introduction to the Principles of Morals and Legislation*

Of the Principle of Utility

I. Nature has placed mankind under the governance of two sovereign masters, *pain* and *pleasure.* It is for them alone to point out what we ought to do, as well as to determine what we shall do. On the one hand the standard of right and wrong, on the other the chain of causes and effects, are fastened to their throne. They govern us in all we do, in all we say, in all we think: every effort we can make to throw off our subjection, will serve but to demonstrate and

From *An Introduction to the Principles of Morals and Legislation* (1823).

1 *Editor Comment*

As will become clear later, the party in question is the entire community.

2 *Stop and Think*

Bentham clearly assumes that all varieties of pleasure and happiness amount to essentially the same thing; and similarly for pain and unhappiness. How plausible is this?

3

What Bentham presumably means here (as suggested by the previous footnote) is that the morally right action is the one whose tendency in favor of happiness as opposed to unhappiness is the *greatest* of the available alternatives: the action that *maximizes* the net balance of pleasure or happiness over pain or unhappiness. (Notice that in a sufficiently unfortunate situation, this net balance might still be negative—that is, all the alternatives might produce more unhappiness than happiness.)

4

Why does Bentham say that an action that conforms to his principle might *merely* be "not one that ought not to be done"? He seems to be allowing here for the possibility that there might be two or more actions that are *equally* good from the standpoint of utility, in which case each of them would be permitted (it would be "not one that ought not to be done"), but no particular one of them would be required ("one that ought to be done").

confirm it. In words a man may pretend to abjure their empire: but in reality he will remain subject to it all the while. The *principle of utility** recognises this subjection, and assumes it for the foundation of that system, the object of which is to rear the fabric of felicity by the hands of reason and of law. Systems which attempt to question it, deal in sounds instead of sense, in caprice instead of reason, in darkness instead of light.

But enough of metaphor and declamation: it is not by such means that moral science is to be improved.

II. The principle of utility is the foundation of the present work: it will be proper therefore at the outset to give an explicit and determinate account of what is meant by it. By the principle of utility is meant that principle which approves or disapproves of every action whatsoever, according to the tendency which it appears to have to augment or diminish the happiness of the party whose interest is in question: or, what is the same thing in other words, to promote or to oppose that happiness. **1** I say of every action whatsoever; and therefore not only of every action of a private individual, but of every measure of government.

III. By utility is meant that property in any object, whereby it tends to produce benefit, advantage, pleasure, good, or happiness, (all this in the present case comes to the same thing) or (what comes again to the same thing) to prevent the happening of mischief, pain, evil, or unhappiness to the party whose interest is considered: if that party be the community in general, then the happiness of the community: if a particular individual, then the happiness of that individual. **2**

IV. The interest of the community is one of the most general expressions that can occur in the phraseology of morals: no wonder that the meaning of it is often lost. When it has a meaning, it is this. The community is a fictitious *body*, composed of the individual persons who are considered as constituting as it were its *members*. The interest of the community then is, what?—the sum of the interests of the several members who compose it.

V. It is in vain to talk of the interest of the community, without understanding what is the interest of the individual. A thing is said to promote the interest, or to be *for* the interest, of an individual, when it tends to add to the sum total of his pleasures: or, what comes to the same thing, to diminish the sum total of his pains.

VI. An action then may be said to be conformable to the principle of utility, or, for shortness sake, to utility, (meaning with respect to the community at large) when the tendency it has to augment the happiness of the community is greater than any it has to diminish it. **3**

VII. A measure of government (which is but a particular kind of action, performed by a particular person or persons) may be said to be conformable to or dictated by the principle of utility, when in like manner the tendency which it has to augment the happiness of the community is greater than any which it has to diminish it.

...

X. Of an action that is conformable to the principle of utility one may always say either that it is one that ought to be done, or at least that it is not one that ought not to be done. One may say also, that it is right it should be done; at least that it is not wrong it should be done: that it is a right action; at least that it is not a wrong action. **4** When thus interpreted, the words *ought*, and *right* and *wrong*, and others of that stamp, have a meaning: when otherwise, they have none.

XI. Has the rectitude of this principle been ever formally contested? It should seem that it had, by those who have not known what they have been meaning. Is it susceptible of any direct proof? it should seem not: for that which is used to prove every thing else, cannot itself be proved: a chain of proofs must have their commencement somewhere. To

*Note by the Author, July 1822.
To this denomination has of late been added, or substituted, the *greatest happiness* . . . principle: . . . *that principle* which states the greatest happiness of all those whose interest is in question, as being the right and proper, and only right and proper and universally desirable, end of human action: of human action in every situation, and in particular in that of a functionary or set of functionaries exercising the powers of Government. . . .

give such proof is as impossible as it is needless. (5)

XII. Not that there is or ever has been that human creature breathing, however stupid or perverse, who has not on many, perhaps on most occasions of his life, deferred to it. By the natural constitution of the human frame, on most occasions of their lives men in general embrace this principle, without thinking of it: if not for the ordering of their own actions, yet for the trying of their own actions, as well as of those of other men. There have been, at the same time, not many, perhaps, even of the most intelligent, who have been disposed to embrace it purely and without reserve. There are even few who have not taken some occasion or other to quarrel with it, either on account of their not understanding always how to apply it, or on account of some prejudice or other which they were afraid to examine into, or could not bear to part with. For such is the stuff that man is made of: in principle and in practice, in a right track and in a wrong one, the rarest of all human qualities is consistency.

XIII. When a man attempts to combat the principle of utility, it is with reasons drawn, without his being aware of it, from that very principle itself.* His arguments, if they prove any thing, prove not that the principle is *wrong,* but that, according to the applications he supposes to be made of it, it is *misapplied.* Is it possible for a man to move the earth? Yes; but he must first find out another earth to stand upon.

. . .

Chapter II

Of Principles Adverse to That of Utility

I. If the principle of utility be a right principle to be governed by, and that in all cases, it follows from what has been just observed, that whatever principle differs from it in any case must necessarily be a wrong one. To prove any other principle, therefore, to be a wrong one, there needs no more than just to show it to be what it is, a principle of which the dictates are in some point or other different from those of the principle of utility: to state it is to confute it. (6)

. . .

XI. Among principles adverse to that of utility, that which at this day seems to have most influence in matters of government, is what may be called the principle of sympathy and antipathy. By the principle of sympathy and antipathy, I mean that principle which approves or disapproves of certain actions, not on account of their tending to augment the happiness, nor yet on account of their tending to diminish the happiness of the party whose interest is in question, but merely because a man finds himself disposed to approve or disapprove of them: holding up that approbation or disapprobation as a sufficient reason for itself, and disclaiming the necessity of looking out for any extrinsic ground. . . . (7)

. . .

XIII. In looking over the catalogue of human actions (says a partizan of this principle) in order to determine which of them are to be marked with the seal of disapprobation, you need but to take counsel of your own feelings: whatever you find in yourself a propensity to condemn, is wrong for that very reason. For the same reason it is also meet for punishment: in what proportion it is adverse to utility, or whether it be adverse to utility at all, is a matter that makes no difference. In that same *proportion* also is it meet for punishment: if you hate much, punish much: if you hate little, punish little: punish as you hate. If you hate not at all, punish not at all: the fine feelings of the soul are not to be overborne and tyrannized by the harsh and rugged dictates of political utility.

XIV. The various systems that have been formed concerning the standard of right and wrong, may all be reduced to the principle of sympathy and antipathy. One account may serve for all of them. They consist all of them in so many contrivances for avoiding the obligation of appealing to any external standard, and for prevailing upon the reader to accept of

What Bentham seems to be saying here is that the principle of utility is **self-evident,** that one can see that it is true just by understanding the content of the principle.

Again the assumption seems to be (?) that the principle of utility is self-evidently true, so that Bentham can appeal to it in refuting opposing views.

The principle of sympathy and antipathy is Bentham's label for the moral view that assesses the rightness or wrongness of actions simply by appeal to one's immediate inclination to approve or disapprove of them—what is sometimes referred to as moral intuition. As we have already seen, his view is that there is no rational basis apart from utility for such inclinations.

*'The principle of utility, (I have heard it said) is a dangerous principle: it is dangerous on certain occasions to consult it.' This is as much as to say, what? that it is not consonant to utility, to consult utility: in short, that it is *not* consulting it, to consult it.

the author's sentiment or opinion as a reason for itself. The phrases different, but the principle the same.* 8

Restatement/
8 *Summary*

R This important footnote lists a variety of ways of formulating what Bentham regards as essentially the same appeal to unargued and fundamentally irrational moral inclinations or intuitions.

 (Is he right that these all amount to the same thing?)

. . .

XVI. The principle of sympathy and antipathy is most apt to err on the side of severity. It is for applying punishment in many cases which deserve none: in many cases which deserve some, it is for applying more than they deserve. There is no incident imaginable, be it ever so trivial, and so remote from mischief, from which this principle may not extract a ground of punishment. Any difference in taste: any difference in opinion: upon one subject as well as upon another. No disagreement so trifling which perseverance and altercation will not render serious. Each becomes in the other's eyes an enemy, and, if laws permit, a criminal. This is one of the circumstances by which the human race is distinguished (not much indeed to its advantage) from the brute creation.

XVII. It is not, however, by any means unexampled for this principle to err on the side of lenity. A near and perceptible mischief moves antipathy. A remote and imperceptible mischief, though not less real, has no effect. . . .

. . .

Chapter IV

Value of a Lot of Pleasure or Pain, How to Be Measured

I. Pleasures then, and the avoidance of pains, are the *ends* which the legislator has in view: it behooves him therefore to understand their *value*. Pleasures and pains are the *instruments* he has to work with: it behooves him therefore to understand their force, which is again, in other words, their value.

II. To a person considered *by himself,* the value of a pleasure or pain considered *by itself,* will be greater or less, according to the four following circumstances:

1. Its *intensity.*
2. Its *duration.*
3. Its *certainty* or *uncertainty.*
4. Its *propinquity* or *remoteness.* 

The first two of these are the most obvious features bearing on the utility or disutility of pleasures and pains: how intense they are and how long they last. "Certainty or uncertainty" really pertains to our knowledge that the pleasure or pain will result from the action in question, not to the pain or pleasure itself; Bentham is pointing out the obvious fact that we can base a decision only on what we *believe* will result. "Propinquity or remoteness" has to do with how close the result in question is in time; Bentham seems to be suggesting that a temporally distant pleasure or pain should count for less than one that will occur sooner.

III. These are the circumstances which are to be considered in estimating a pleasure or a pain considered each of them by itself. But when the value of any pleasure or pain is considered for the purpose of estimating the tendency of any *act* by which it is produced, there are two other circumstances to be taken into the account; these are,

1. Its *fecundity,* or the chance it has of being followed by sensations of the *same* kind: that is, pleasures, if it be a pleasure: pains, if it be a pain.
2. Its *purity,* or the chance it has of *not* being followed by sensations of the *opposite* kind: that is, pains, if it be a pleasure: pleasures, if it be a pain. 10

As Bentham proceeds to say, "fecundity" and "purity" are not really qualities of the pleasures or pains themselves. It would be clearer to put his point here by saying that all of the consequences of an action in terms of pleasure and pain must be counted in assessing it, including of course pleasures and pains that are caused by earlier pleasures and pains.

These two last, however, are in strictness scarcely to be deemed properties of the pleasure or the pain itself; they are not, therefore, in strictness to be taken into the account of the value of that pleasure or that pain. They are in strictness to be deemed properties only of the act, or other event, by which such pleasure or pain has been produced; and accordingly are only to be taken into the account of the tendency of such act or such event.

IV. To a *number* of persons, with reference to each of whom the value of a pleasure or a pain is considered, it will be greater or less, according to seven circumstances: to wit, the six preceding ones; *viz.*

1. Its *intensity.*
2. Its *duration.*
3. Its *certainty* or *uncertainty.*
4. Its *propinquity* or *remoteness.*
5. Its *fecundity.*
6. Its *purity.*

And one other; to wit:

7. Its *extent;* that is, the number of persons to whom it *extends;* or (in other words) who are affected by it.

V. To take an exact account then of the general tendency of any act, by which the interests of a community are affected, proceed as follows.

*It is curious enough to observe the variety of inventions men have hit upon, and the variety of phrases they have brought forward, in order to conceal from the world, and, if possible, from themselves, this very general and therefore very pardonable self-sufficiency.

Begin with any one person of those whose interests seem most immediately to be affected by it: and take an account,

1. Of the value of each distinguishable *pleasure* which appears to be produced by it in the *first* instance.
2. Of the value of each *pain* which appears to be produced by it in the *first* instance.
3. Of the value of each pleasure which appears to be produced by it *after* the first. This constitutes the *fecundity* of the first *pleasure* and the *impurity* of the first *pain.*
4. Of the value of each *pain* which appears to be produced by it after the first. This constitutes the *fecundity* of the first *pain,* and the *impurity* of the first pleasure.
5. Sum up all the values of all the *pleasures* on the one side, and those of all the pains on the other. The balance, if it be on the side of pleasure, will give the *good* tendency of the act upon the whole, with respect to the interests of that *individual* person; if on the side of pain, the *bad* tendency of it upon the whole. [11]
6. Take an account of the *number* of persons whose interests appear to be concerned; and repeat the above process with respect to each. *Sum up* the numbers expressive of the degrees of *good* tendency, which the act has, with respect to each individual, in regard to whom the tendency of it is *good* upon the whole: do this again with respect to each individual, in regard to whom the tendency of it is *bad* upon the whole. Take the *balance;* which, if on the side of *pleasure,* will give the general *good tendency* of the act, with respect to the total number or community of individuals concerned; if on the side of pain, the general *evil tendency,* with respect to the same community. [12]

VI. It is not to be expected that this process should be strictly pursued previously to every moral judgment, or to every legislative or judicial operation. It may, however, be always kept in view: and as near as the process actually pursued on these occasions approaches to it, so near will such process approach to the character of an exact one. [13]

VII. The same process is alike applicable to pleasure and pain, in whatever shape they appear: and by whatever denomination they are distinguished: to pleasure, whether it be called *good* (which is properly the cause or instrument of pleasure) or *profit* (which is distant pleasure, or the cause or instrument of distant pleasure,) or *convenience,* or *advantage, benefit, emolument, happiness,* and so forth: to pain, whether it be called *evil,* (which corresponds to *good*) or *mischief,* or *inconvenience,* or *disadvantage,* or *loss,* or *unhappiness,* and so forth.

VIII. Nor is this a novel and unwarranted, any more than it is a useless theory. In all this there is nothing but what the practice of mankind, wheresoever they have a clear view of their own interest, is perfectly conformable to. An article of property, an estate in land, for instance, is valuable, on what account? On account of the pleasures of all kinds which it enables a man to produce, and what comes to the same thing the pains of all kinds which it enables him to avert. But the value of such an article of property is universally understood to rise or fall according to the length or shortness of the time which a man has in it: the certainty or uncertainty of its coming into possession; and the nearness or remoteness of the time at which, if at all, it is to come into possession. As to the *intensity* of the pleasures which a man may derive from it, this is never thought of, because it depends upon the use which each particular person may come to make of it; which cannot be estimated till the particular pleasures he may come to derive from it, or the particular pains he may come to exclude by means of it, are brought to view. For the same reason, neither does he think of the *fecundity* or *purity* of those pleasures.

...

1. One man says, he has a thing made on purpose to tell him what is right and what is wrong; and that it is called a *moral sense:* and then he goes to work at his ease, and says, such a thing is right, and such a thing is wrong—why? 'because my moral sense tells me it is.'
2. Another man comes and alters the phrase: leaving out *moral,* and putting in *common,* in the room of it. He then tells you, that his common sense teaches him what is right and wrong, as surely as the other's moral sense

Thus Bentham assumes that all pleasures and pains for a given individual are *commensurable:* that the positive and negative values they represent can be combined in one total. It is suggested here and made clear in the following paragraph that these values are to be thought of in numerical terms.

He also assumes, even more controversially, that positive and negative values pertaining to different people can be combined into one numerically expressed total.

R Strictly carrying out this process in a real-life case would require enormous expenditures of time and effort (if it could be done at all—see Discussion Question 2). This would be wasteful and inefficient, and so mistaken *according to the principle of utility itself,* since the resources involved would produce more pleasure or avoidance of pain if used in other ways than is gained by figuring out the best action with complete precision.

did: meaning by common sense, a sense of some kind or other, which, he says, is possessed by all mankind: the sense of those, whose sense is not the same as the author's, being struck out of the account as not worth taking. This contrivance does better than the other; for a moral sense, being a new thing, a man may feel about him a good while without being able to find it out: but common sense is as old as the creation; and there is no man but would be ashamed to be thought not to have as much of it as his neighbours. . . .

3. Another man comes, and says, that as to a moral sense indeed, he cannot find that he has any such thing: that however he has an *understanding,* which will do quite as well. This understanding, he says, is the standard of right and wrong: it tells him so and so. All good and wise men understand as he does: if other men's understandings differ in any point from his, so much the worse for them: it is a sure sign they are either defective or corrupt.

4. Another man says, that there is an eternal and immutable Rule of Right: that that rule of right dictates so and so: and then he begins giving you his sentiments upon any thing that comes uppermost: and these sentiments (you are to take for granted) are so many branches of the eternal rule of right.

5. Another man, or perhaps the same man (it's no matter) says, that there are certain practices conformable, and others repugnant, to the Fitness of Things; and then he tells you, at his leisure, what practices are conformable and what repugnant: just as he happens to like a practice or dislike it.

6. A great multitude of people are continually talking of the Law of Nature; and then they go on giving you their sentiments about what is right and what is wrong: and these sentiments, you are to understand, are so many chapters and sections of the Law of Nature.

7. Instead of the phrase, Law of Nature, you have sometimes, Law of Reason, Right Reason, Natural Justice, Natural Equity, Good Order. Any of them will do equally well. This latter is most used in politics. The three last are much more tolerable than the others, because they do not very explicitly claim to be any thing more than phrases: they insist but feebly upon the being looked upon as so many positive standards of themselves, and seem content to be taken, upon occasion, for phrases expressive of the conformity of the thing in question to the proper standard, whatever that may be. . . .

It is upon the principle of antipathy that such and such acts are often reprobated on the score of their being *unnatural:* the practice of exposing children, established among the Greeks and Romans, was an unnatural practice. Unnatural, when it means any thing, means unfrequent: and there it means something; although nothing to the present purpose. But here it means no such thing: for the frequency of such acts is perhaps the great complaint. It therefore means nothing; nothing, I mean, which there is in the act itself. All it can serve to express is, the disposition of the person who is talking of it: the disposition he is in to be angry at the thoughts of it. Does it merit his anger? Very likely it may: but whether it does or no is a question, which, to be answered rightly, can only be answered upon the principle of utility.

. . .

Discussion Questions

1. Bentham seems to regard the principle of utility as self-evidently correct. Does this amount to any more than saying that he (and many others) have a strong inclination or intuition in favor of this principle? If so, Bentham seems to be appealing to the very principle of sympathy or antipathy that he wants to reject. Is there any way of assessing moral claims that does not appeal, directly or indirectly, to such moral inclinations or intuitions? (See the discussion of the method of reflective equilibrium in the introduction to this chapter.)
2. Consider a choice between two actions, A and B, assuming that only your own utility is in question. Action A involves going out with friends, having pizza and beer, and going to a concert; but it also involves considerable expense, driving in heavy traffic, and so on. Action B involves staying home with your significant other, eating food you prepare yourself, drinking lemonade, watching a movie on

cable, and relaxing, with little effort or expense. (You may need to adjust the examples to make them better fit your particular desires and tastes.) How plausible is it that the various pleasures and pains (including various sorts of discomfort) involved in each of these cases can be combined into two total net values that are reasonably precise and can be numerically compared with each other?

3. How feasible is the larger utilitarian calculation Bentham describes? Suppose you are considering a choice between two different actions, each of which will cause a variety of pleasures and pains (or states of happiness and unhappiness) for many different individuals. (Try to think of a specific, fairly detailed example of your own here.) Is there any way to arrive at a total net value of each action for all the different individuals involved by combining all of their different sorts of pleasure and pain (or happiness and unhappiness) into one total—especially if consequences indefinitely into the future are considered?
4. Here is a slightly more specific problem for such calculations: suppose that one alternative action leads to the *death* of one or more people, while the other does not. How should death be figured into the calculation? How much pleasure or happiness does it take to offset someone's death (or how much pain of other sorts is it equivalent to)? Is there any answer to this question that is both clear and defensible?
5. One moral value that is often regarded as very important is justice (or fairness). What role, if any, does justice play in a utilitarian evaluation of alternative actions? Suppose one action produces a certain amount of positive utility (pleasure or happiness) that is divided fairly evenly among the members of the relevant community, while a second action produces an amount of utility that is slightly greater, but most of which is enjoyed by a small group of people, with most of the members of the community receiving very little. Which action will apparently be preferred according to the principle of utility? Does this seem like the right result? (This is an appeal to moral intuition.) Can you think of any response to this objection on behalf of utilitarianism?

John Stuart Mill

John Stuart Mill (1806–1873) was a British philosopher who made important contributions to many areas of philosophy, including logic, ethics, political philosophy, and epistemology. His father, James Mill, was a close follower of Bentham, and John Stuart was essentially raised as a utilitarian. In the following selection, Mill defends a version of hedonistic utilitarianism, but one that departs from Bentham by bringing the quality of pleasures, as well as their quantity, into the utilitarian assessment. Mill's discussion also contains some passages that seem to move in the direction of **rule utilitarianism.** Mill also offers a controversial "proof" of the principle of utility.

From *Utilitarianism*

Chapter I
General Remarks

There are few circumstances among those which make up the present condition of human knowledge more unlike what might have been expected, or more significant of the backward state in which speculation on the most important subjects still lingers, than the little progress which has been made in the decision of the controversy respecting the criterion of right and wrong. From the dawn of philosophy, the question concerning the *summum bonum,* or, what is the same thing, concerning the foundation of morality, has been accounted the main problem in speculative thought, has occupied the most gifted intellects and divided them into sects and schools carrying on a vigorous warfare against one another. And after more than two thousand years the same discussions continue, philosophers are still ranged under the same contending banners, and neither thinkers nor mankind at large seem nearer to

From *Utilitarianism* (published 1861).

being unanimous on the subject than when the youth Socrates listened to the old Protagoras and asserted (if Plato's dialogue be grounded on a real conversation) the theory of utilitarianism against the popular morality of the so-called sophist. 1

1 The reference is to Plato's dialogue *Protagoras*.

. . .

To inquire how far the bad effects of this deficiency have been mitigated in practice, or to what extent the moral beliefs of mankind have been vitiated or made uncertain by the absence of any distinct recognition of an ultimate standard, would imply a complete survey and criticism of past and present ethical doctrine. It would, however, be easy to show that whatever steadiness or consistency these moral beliefs have attained has been mainly due to the tacit influence of a standard not recognized. Although the nonexistence of an acknowledged first principle has made ethics not so much a guide as a consecration of men's actual sentiments, still, as men's sentiments, both of favor and of aversion, are greatly influenced by what they suppose to be the effects of things upon their happiness, the principle of utility, or, as Bentham latterly called it, the greatest happiness principle, has had a large share in forming the moral doctrines even of those who most scornfully reject its authority. . . .

On the present occasion, I shall, without further discussion of the other theories, attempt to contribute something toward the understanding and appreciation of the "utilitarian" or "happiness" theory, and toward such proof as it is susceptible of. It is evident that this cannot be proof in the ordinary and popular meaning of the term. Questions of ultimate ends are not amenable to direct proof. Whatever can be proved to be good must be so by being shown to be a means to something admitted to be good without proof. . . .

Before . . . I attempt to enter into the philosophical grounds which can be given for assenting to the utilitarian standard, I shall offer some illustrations of the doctrine itself, with the view of showing more clearly what it is, distinguishing it from what it is not, and disposing of such of the practical objections to it as either originate in, or are closely connected with, mistaken interpretations of its meaning. . . .

Chapter II

What Utilitarianism Is

. . .

The creed which accepts as the foundation of morals "utility" or the "greatest happiness principle" holds that actions are right in proportion as they tend to promote happiness; wrong as they tend to produce the reverse of happiness. By happiness is intended pleasure and the absence of pain; by unhappiness, pain and the privation of pleasure. To give a clear view of the moral standard set up by the theory, much more requires to be said; in particular, what things it includes in the ideas of pain and pleasure, and to what extent this is left an open question. But these supplementary explanations do not affect the theory of life on which this theory of morality is grounded—namely, that pleasure and freedom from pain are the only things desirable as ends; and that all desirable things (which are as numerous in the utilitarian as in any other scheme) are desirable either for pleasure inherent in themselves or as means to the promotion of pleasure and the prevention of pain. 2

2 Pleasure (understood as including the avoidance of pain) is thus, for Mill, the only **intrinsic good,** with other things being valuable either for the pleasure they involve or for their **instrumental** value in leading to pleasure (or the avoidance of pain).

Now such a theory of life excites in many minds, and among them in some of the most estimable in feeling and purpose, inveterate dislike. To suppose that life has (as they express it) no higher end than pleasure—no better and nobler object of desire and pursuit—they designate as utterly mean and groveling, as a doctrine worthy only of swine, to whom the followers of Epicurus were, at a very early period, contemptuously likened; and modern holders of the doctrine are occasionally made the subject of equally polite comparisons by its German, French, and English assailants.

When thus attacked, the Epicureans have always answered that it is not they, but their accusers, who represent human nature in a degrading light, since the accusation supposes human beings to be capable of no pleasures except those of which swine are capable. If this supposition were true, the charge could not be gainsaid, but would then be no longer an imputation; for if the sources of pleasure were precisely the same to human beings and to swine, the rule of life which is good enough for the one would be good enough for the other. The comparison of the Epicurean life to that of beasts is felt as degrading, precisely because a beast's pleasures do not satisfy a human being's conceptions of happiness. Human beings have faculties more elevated than the animal appetites and, when once made conscious of them, do not regard anything as happiness which does not include their gratification. **3** . . . It must be admitted, however, that utilitarian writers in general have placed the superiority of mental over bodily pleasures chiefly in the greater permanency, safety, uncostliness, etc., of the former—that is, in their circumstantial advantages rather than in their intrinsic nature. **4** And on all these points utilitarians have fully proved their case; but they might have taken the other and, as it may be called, higher ground with entire consistency. It is quite compatible with the principle of utility to recognize the fact that some kinds of pleasure are more desirable and more valuable than others. It would be absurd that, while in estimating all other things quality is considered as well as quantity, the estimation of pleasure should be supposed to depend on quantity alone. **5**

If I am asked what I mean by difference of quality in pleasures, or what makes one pleasure more valuable than another, merely as a pleasure, except its being greater in amount, there is but one possible answer. Of two pleasures, if there be one to which all or almost all who have experience of both give a decided preference, irrespective of any feeling of moral obligation to prefer it, that is the more desirable pleasure. If one of the two is, by those who are competently acquainted with both, placed so far above the other that they prefer it, even though knowing it to be attended with a greater amount of discontent, and would not resign it for any quantity of the other pleasure which their nature is capable of, we are justified in ascribing to the preferred enjoyment a superiority in quality so far outweighing quantity as to render it, in comparison, of small account. **6**

Now it is an unquestionable fact that those who are equally acquainted with and equally capable of appreciating and enjoying both do give a most marked preference to the manner of existence which employs their higher faculties. Few human creatures would consent to be changed into any of the lower animals for a promise of the fullest allowance of a beast's pleasures; no intelligent human being would consent to be a fool, no instructed person would be an ignoramus, no person of feeling and conscience would be selfish and base, even though they should be persuaded that the fool, the dunce, or the rascal is better satisfied with his lot than they are with theirs. They would not resign what they possess more than he for the most complete satisfaction of all the desires which they have in common with him. . . . Whoever supposes that this preference takes place at a sacrifice of happiness—that the superior being, in anything like equal circumstances, is not happier than the inferior—confounds the two very different ideas of happiness and content. It is indisputable that the being whose capacities of enjoyment are low has the greatest chance of having them fully satisfied; and a highly endowed being will always feel that any happiness which he can look for, as the world is constituted, is imperfect. But he can learn to bear its imperfections, if they are at all bearable; and they will not make him envy the being who is indeed unconscious of the imperfections, but only because he feels not at all the good which those imperfections qualify. It is better to be a human being dissatisfied than a pig satisfied; better to be Socrates dissatisfied than a fool satisfied. And if the fool, or the pig, are of a different opinion, it is because they only know their own side of the question. The other party to the comparison knows both sides. **7**

. . .

According to the greatest happiness principle, as above explained, the ultimate end, with reference to and for the sake of which all other things are desirable—whether we are considering our own good or that of other people—is an existence exempt as far as possible from pain, and as rich as possible in enjoyments, both in point of quantity and quality; the test of quality and the rule for measuring it against quantity being the preference felt by those who, in their opportunities of experience, to which must be added their habits of self-consciousness and self-observation, are best furnished with the means of comparison. This, being according to the utilitarian opinion the end of human action, is necessarily also the standard of morality, which may accordingly be defined "the rules and precepts for human conduct," by the observance of which an existence such as has been

3

R Mill suggests not only that human beings are capable of experiencing kinds of pleasure that animals are not (which is obvious), but also that nothing will count as human happiness that does not include these "higher" pleasures.

4

R Here is one rationale for the claim that "higher" pleasures are more valuable: they are *instrumentally* superior to bodily pleasures, in that they last longer, involve less risk (of unpleasant experiences), and are less costly (again in terms of unpleasant experiences, not just money).

5

While not rejecting the previous point, Mill suggests a different reason for preferring "higher" to "lower" pleasures: "higher" pleasures are superior in *quality* to "lower" pleasures, where this means that a given quantity of a higher pleasure is preferable *in terms of its intrinsic pleasureableness alone* to the same or even a greater quantity (how much greater?) of a "lower" pleasure.

6

Mill seems to present the appeal to what has been described as "a jury of pleasure testers" as giving the very *meaning* of the claim that one pleasure is of a better quality than another, but it is perhaps better to regard this as simply a practical *test* or *criterion*. Can the "competence" of such jurors can be decided in a way that does not beg the question at issue? (See Discussion Question 1.)

7

The issue is not just whether it is "better to be a human being dissatisfied than a pig satisfied" (that is, that anyone familiar with both sorts of lives would choose the former), but whether this is so because the human life is superior *in terms of pleasure or happiness*. Mill cannot simply assume that pleasure or happiness is the only basis for this choice.

8

There are at least three different issues raised by this passage: (1) Is it true that happiness and enjoyment are the ultimate ends of human life in the sense that they capture everything that people actually aim at? (See the selection from Nozick in Chapter 8 for more on this issue.) (2) Even if this were true, does it follow that happiness is thereby the standard of morality—that people *ought* to be guided only by the pursuit of happiness (their own and that of others)? (3) If circumstances do not allow all of mankind and even "the whole sentient creation" to be maximally happy, does utilitarianism have anything to say about how the choice of who is to be happy (and to what degree), and who is not, is to be made?

9

Since all that matters is achieving the greatest total, utilitarianism does not allow a person to give *any* preference to his own happiness or well-being (or that of his family and friends)—nor to be any more concerned about his own projects and commitments than about those of anyone else.

STOP How reasonable a requirement is this? (See the selection from Williams later in this chapter.)

10

R One objection to act utilitarianism is that it would sanction violating various common-sense moral rules (rules that seem to be supported by our intuitive moral convictions, such as the rules not to lie, not to break promises, etc.) whenever even a very small gain in utility would result. A response to this objection is that when the damaging effects of such actions on valuable social institutions and practices are added in, such violations will be justified only in very unusual cases, where it is no longer clear that they are objectionable. (Does this work? See Discussion Question 3.)

described might be, to the greatest extent possible, secured to all mankind; and not to them only, but, so far as the nature of things admits, to the whole sentient creation. 8

. . .

I must again repeat what the assailants of utilitarianism seldom have the justice to acknowledge, that the happiness which forms the utilitarian standard of what is right in conduct is not the agent's own happiness but that of all concerned. As between his own happiness and that of others, utilitarianism requires him to be as strictly impartial as a disinterested and benevolent spectator. In the golden rule of Jesus of Nazareth, we read the complete spirit of the ethics of utility. "To do as you would be done by," and "to love your neighbor as yourself," constitute the ideal perfection of utilitarian morality. . . . 9

It may not be superfluous to notice a few more of the common misapprehensions of utilitarian ethics, even those which are so obvious and gross that it might appear impossible for any person of candor and intelligence to fall into them; since persons, even of considerable mental endowment, often give themselves so little trouble to understand the bearings of any opinion against which they entertain a prejudice, and men are in general so little conscious of this voluntary ignorance as a defect that the vulgarest misunderstandings of ethical doctrines are continually met with in the deliberate writings of persons of the greatest pretensions both to high principle and to philosophy. . . .

. . . utility is often summarily stigmatized as an immoral doctrine by giving it the name of "expediency," and taking advantage of the popular use of that term to contrast it with principle. But the expedient, in the sense in which it is opposed to the right, generally means that which is expedient for the particular interest of the agent himself. . . . When it means anything better than this, it means that which is expedient for some immediate object, some temporary purpose, but which violates a rule whose observance is expedient in a much higher degree. The expedient, in this sense, instead of being the same thing with the useful, is a branch of the hurtful. Thus it would often be expedient, for the purpose of getting over some momentary embarrassment, or attaining some object immediately useful to ourselves or others, to tell a lie. But inasmuch as the cultivation in ourselves of a sensitive feeling on the subject of veracity is one of the most useful, and the enfeeblement of that feeling one of the most hurtful, things to which our conduct can be instrumental; and inasmuch as any, even unintentional, deviation from truth does that much toward weakening the trustworthiness of human assertion, which is not only the principal support of all present social well-being, but the insufficiency of which does more than any one thing that can be named to keep back civilization, virtue, everything on which human happiness on the largest scale depends—we feel that the violation, for a present advantage, of a rule of such transcendent expediency is not expedient, and that he who, for the sake of convenience to himself or to some other individual, does what depends on him to deprive mankind of the good, and inflict upon them the evil, involved in the greater or less reliance which they can place in each other's word, acts the part of one of their worst enemies. Yet that even this rule, sacred as it is, admits of possible exceptions is acknowledged by all moralists; the chief of which is when the withholding of some fact (as of information from a malefactor, or of bad news from a person dangerously ill) would save an individual (especially an individual other than oneself) from great and unmerited evil, and when the withholding can only be effected by denial. But in order that the exception may not extend itself beyond the need, and may have the least possible effect in weakening reliance on veracity, it ought to be recognized and, if possible, its limits defined; and, if the principle of utility is good for anything, it must be good for weighing these conflicting utilities against one another and marking out the region within which one or the other preponderates. 10

Again, defenders of utility often find themselves called upon to reply to such objections as this—that there is not time, previous to action, for calculating and weighing the effects of any line of conduct on the general happiness. . . . The answer to the objection is that there has been ample time, namely, the whole past duration of the human species. During all that time mankind have been learning by experience the tendencies of actions; on which experience all the prudence as well as all the morality of life are dependent. People talk as if the commencement of this course of experience had hitherto been put off, and as if, at the moment when some man feels tempted to meddle with the property or life of another, he had to begin considering for the first time whether murder and theft are injurious to human happiness. . . . There is no difficulty in proving any ethical standard whatever to work ill if we suppose universal idiocy to be conjoined with it; but on any hypothesis short of that, mankind must by this time have acquired positive beliefs as to the effects of some actions on their happiness; and the beliefs which have thus come down are the rules of morality for the multitude, and for the philosopher until he has succeeded in finding better. That philosophers might easily do this, even now, on many subjects; that the received code of ethics is by no means of divine right; and that mankind have still much to learn as to the effects of actions on the general happiness, I admit or rather earnestly maintain. The corollaries from the principle of utility, like the precepts of every practical art, admit of indefinite improvement, and, in a progressive state of the human mind, their improvement is perpetually going on. But to consider the rules of morality as improvable is one thing; to pass over the intermediate generalization entirely and endeavor to test each individual action directly by the first principle is another. It is a strange notion that the acknowledgment of a first principle is inconsistent with the admission of secondary ones. To inform a traveler respecting the place of his ultimate destination is not to forbid the use of landmarks and direction-posts on the way. The proposition that happiness is the end and aim of morality does not mean that no road ought to be laid down to that goal, or that persons going thither should not be advised to take one direction rather than another. Men really ought to leave off talking a kind of nonsense on this subject, which they would neither talk nor listen to on other matters of practical concernment. Nobody argues that the art of navigation is not founded on astronomy because sailors cannot wait to calculate the Nautical Almanac. Being rational creatures, they go to sea with it ready calculated; and all rational creatures go out upon the sea of life with their minds made up on the common questions of right and wrong, as well as on many of the far more difficult questions of wise and foolish. And this, as long as foresight is a human quality, it is to be presumed they will continue to do. Whatever we adopt as the fundamental principle of morality, we require subordinate principles to apply it by; the impossibility of doing without them, being common to all systems, can afford no argument against any one in particular; but gravely to argue as if no such secondary principles could be had, and as if mankind had remained till now, and always must remain, without drawing any general conclusions from the experience of human life is as high a pitch, I think, as absurdity has ever reached in philosophical controversy. (11)

. . . It is not the fault of any creed, but of the complicated nature of human affairs, that rules of conduct cannot be so framed as to require no exceptions, and that hardly any kind of action can safely be laid down as either always obligatory or always condemnable. . . . There exists no moral system under which there do not arise unequivocal cases of conflicting obligation. These are the real difficulties, the knotty points both in the theory of ethics and in the conscientious guidance of personal conduct. . . . If utility is the ultimate source of moral obligations, utility may be invoked to decide between them when their demands are incompatible. Though the application of the standard may be difficult, it is better than none at all; while in other systems, the moral laws all claiming independent authority, there is no common umpire entitled to interfere between them; their claims to precedence one over another rest on little better than sophistry, and, unless determined, as they generally are, by the unacknowledged influence of consideration of utility, afford a free scope for the action of personal desires and partialities. We must remember that only in these cases of conflict between secondary principles is it requisite that first principles should be appealed to. There is no case of moral obligation in which some secondary principle is not involved; and if only one, there can seldom be any real doubt which one it is, in the mind of any person by whom the principle itself is recognized. (12)

. . .

(11)

Even act utilitarianism can sanction the use of general rules of morality in cases where it is too difficult or costly or time-consuming to do a full utilitarian calculation (a point also made by Bentham). The issue between act and rule utilitarianism is whether one should follow such rules even when it is *clear* that doing so will not produce the greatest utility in the situation in question. (See the following selection from Smart for more on this.)

(12)

Here Mill may be saying that a utilitarian calculation should be made only where the "secondary rules" conflict. This would mean that in the absence of conflict, the relevant secondary rule should *always* be followed—even in cases where it clearly does not lead to the greatest utility. This would be a rule utilitarian view (see the chapter introduction and the following selection by Smart). But he may only be saying that an appeal to a utilitarian calculation is not required ("requisite") where there is no conflict but is still permitted and perhaps even desirable where feasible—which would still be an act utilitarian view.

Chapter IV

Of What Sort of Proof the Principle of Utility Is Susceptible

It has already been remarked that questions of ultimate ends do not admit of proof, in the ordinary acceptation of the term. To be incapable of proof by reasoning is common to all first principles, to the first premises of our knowledge, as well as to those of our conduct. But the former, being matters of fact, may be the subject of a direct appeal to the faculties which judge of fact—namely, our senses and our internal consciousness. Can an appeal be made to the same faculties on questions of practical ends? *Or by what other faculty is cognizance taken of them?*

Questions about ends are, in other words, questions what things are desirable. The utilitarian doctrine is that happiness is desirable, and the only thing desirable, as an end; all other things beings only desirable as means to that end. What ought to be required of this doctrine, what conditions is it requisite that the doctrine should fulfill—to make good its claim to be believed?

The only proof capable of being given that an object is visible is that people actually see it. The only proof that a sound is audible is that people hear it; and so of the other sources of our experience. In like manner, I apprehend, the sole evidence it is possible to produce that anything is desirable is that people do actually desire it. [13] If the end which the utilitarian doctrine proposes to itself were not, in theory and in practice, acknowledged to be an end, nothing could ever convince any person that it was so. No reason can be given why the general happiness is desirable, except that each person, so far as he believes it to be attainable, desires his own happiness. This, however, being a fact, we have not only all the proof which the case admits of, but all which it is possible to require, that happiness is a good, that each person's happiness is a good to that person, and the general happiness, therefore, a good to the aggregate of all persons. Happiness has made out its title as *one* of the ends of conduct and, consequently, one of the criteria of morality. [14]

But it has not, by this alone, proved itself to be the sole criterion. To do that, it would seem, by the same rule, necessary to show, not only that people desire happiness, but that they never desire anything else. Now it is palpable that they do desire things which, in common language, are decidedly distinguished from happiness. They desire, for example, virtue and the absence of vice no less really than pleasure and the absence of pain. The desire of virtue is not as universal, but it is as authentic a fact as the desire of happiness. And hence the opponents of the utilitarian standard deem that they have a right to infer that there are other ends of human action besides happiness, and that happiness is not the standard of approbation and disapprobation.

But does the utilitarian doctrine deny that people desire virtue, or maintain that virtue is not a thing to be desired? The very reverse. It maintains not only that virtue is to be desired, but that it is to be desired disinterestedly, for itself. Whatever may be the opinion of utilitarian moralists as to the original conditions by which virtue is made virtue, however they may believe (as they do) that actions and dispositions are only virtuous because they promote another end than virtue, yet this being granted, and it having been decided, from considerations of this description, what *is* virtuous, they not only place virtue at the very head of the things which are good as means to the ultimate end, but they also recognize as a psychological fact the possibility of its being, to the individual, a good in itself, without looking to any end beyond it; and hold that the mind is not in a right state, not in a state conformable to utility, not in the state most conducive to the general happiness, unless it does love virtue in this manner—as a thing desirable in itself, even although, in the individual instance, it should not produce those other desirable consequences which it tends to produce, and on account of which it is held to be virtue. [15] This opinion is not, in the smallest degree, a departure from the happiness principle. The ingredients of happiness are very various, and each of them is desirable in itself, and not merely when considered as swelling an aggregate. The principle of utility does not mean that any given pleasure, as music, for instance, or any given exemption from pain, as for example health, is to be looked upon as means to a collective something termed happiness, and to be desired on that account. They are desired and desirable in and for themselves; besides being means, they are a part of the end. Virtue, according to the utilitarian

This is the first stage of Mill's "proof," purporting to establish that happiness is *desirable* in the sense of being an intrinsic good for all people (given the further premise that all people in fact desire their own happiness).

How good is the analog between visibility or audibility and the relevant sense of "desirability"? (See Discussion Question 4.)

Here is the second stage of the argument: if the happiness of each person is an intrinsic good for that person (supposedly established in the first stage), then "the general happiness" of all people is an intrinsic good for "the aggregate of all people."

Does this, as Mill is claiming, establish that individual people should aim at "the general happiness" (as utilitarianism claims)? (See Discussion Question 4.)

It is clearly compatible with utilitarianism that something other than happiness (such as virtue) be desired as an *instrumental* means to the end of happiness. Somewhat more surprisingly, it is also compatible with utilitarianism to hold that more utility will be produced if virtue is desired as an end in itself, as intrinsically valuable, rather than being *explicitly* sought only as a means to happiness.

(But this might just mean that it is instrumentally valuable for people to believe *falsely* that virtue is an intrinsic good.)

doctrine, is not naturally and originally part of the end, but it is capable of becoming so; and in those who live it disinterestedly it has become so, and is desired and cherished, not as a means to happiness, but as a part of their happiness.

. . . Life would be a poor thing, very ill provided with sources of happiness, if there were not this provision of nature by which things originally indifferent, but conducive to, or otherwise associated with, the satisfaction of our primitive desires, become in themselves sources of pleasure more valuable than the primitive pleasures, both in permanency, in the space of human existence that they are capable of covering, and even in intensity.

Virtue, according to the utilitarian conception, is a good of this description. There was no original desire of it, or motive to it, save its conduciveness to pleasure, and especially to protection from pain. But through the association thus formed it may be felt a good in itself, and desired as such with as great intensity as any other good. . . .

It results from the preceding considerations that there is in reality nothing desired except happiness. Whatever is desired otherwise than as a means to some end beyond itself, and ultimately to happiness, is desired as itself a part of happiness, and is not desired for itself until it has become so. . . .

We have now, then, an answer to the question, of what sort of proof the principle of utility is susceptible. If the opinion which I have now stated is psychologically true—if human nature is so constituted as to desire nothing which is not either a part of happiness or a means of happiness—we can have no other proof, and we require no other, that these are the only things desirable. If so, happiness is the sole end of human action, and the promotion of it the test by which to judge of all human conduct; from whence it necessarily follows that it must be the criterion of morality, since a part is included in the whole.

And now to decide whether this is really so, whether mankind do desire nothing for itself but that which is a pleasure to them, or of which the absence is a pain, we have evidently arrived at a question of fact and experience, dependent, like all similar questions, upon evidence. It can only be determined by practiced self-consciousness and self-observation, assisted by observation of others. I believe that these sources of evidence, impartially consulted, will declare that desiring a thing and finding it pleasant, aversion to it and thinking of it as painful, are phenomena entirely inseparable or, rather, two parts of the same phenomenon—in strictness of language, two different modes of naming the same psychological fact; that to think of an object as desirable (unless for the sake of its consequences) and to think of it as pleasant are one and the same thing; and that to desire anything except in proportion as the idea of it is pleasant is a physical and metaphysical impossibility. 16

. . .

16

Here is the third and final stage of the argument: Mill argues, that if virtue (or anything else) is desired as an end in itself, then realizing that end becomes in itself a source of pleasure or happiness, so that it becomes "part of happiness," in which case it is still only pleasure or happiness that is desired.

Here he seems to be making a mistake (one that is discussed in the later selection by Feinberg): the pleasure or happiness that results when a desire for something is satisfied cannot be the main end of that desire, for it is only because there is an *independent* desire for that thing that pleasure results when the desire is satisfied.

Discussion Questions

1. Suppose you are attempting to assess the relative quality of two pleasures: the pleasure of attending an opera and the pleasure of eating pizza. Mill says this question should be decided by appealing to a jury composed of people who have experienced both pleasures or, he says a bit later, are "competently acquainted with both." How is it to be decided which people qualify to be members of this jury? Clearly merely having some brief exposure to both pizza and opera is not enough, especially for opera, which seems to be an "acquired taste." But then how much exposure is required to produce "competent acquaintance" with something like opera (or other "higher" pleasures)? Clearly we cannot say that a person is not "competently acquainted" with a "higher" pleasure unless he or she prefers it (in general) to "lower" pleasures, since that would load the dice in favor of the "higher" pleasures.
2. Even if the utilitarian calculation were possible under Bentham's view (see Discussion Questions 2 and 3 to the Bentham selection), is it still possible given Mill's recognition of qualities as well as quantities of pleasure? How are qualities to be figured into the calculation? Can pleasures of different quality be combined into one total, and if so, how? (Remember how differences of quality are supposed to be determined: does this plausibly yield a numerical value for the quality of a pleasure that could perhaps be multiplied with the numerical measure of quantity?) If not, how is a definite result as to which action leads to the most pleasure (and least pain) supposed to be arrived at?

3. One objection to act utilitarianism is that it would allow or indeed require actions such as telling lies or breaking promises whenever even a slight gain in utility results from doing so. Suppose, for example, that you have promised a friend that you will go to a movie with him, but that you are invited at the last minute to go to a concert with a different friend instead. Suppose also that it is clear to you that you will enjoy the concert enough more than the movie that the total utility (allowing for both the disappointment and unhappiness experienced by the first friend and the increased happiness experienced by the second friend) will be greater if you break the promise and go to the concert. (Assume there is no way to reschedule the movie in a satisfactory way with the first friend.) Act utilitarianism seems to say that you should go to the concert, but this is the wrong choice according to at least most people's considered moral convictions. Mill suggests (see the passage at Annotation 10) that your calculation should also include the negative value resulting from the effect of your action on the valuable *practice* of relying on other people's promises: this practice allows people to coordinate their actions in ways that lead to a great deal of pleasure and happiness, and the breaking of promises tends to undermine the practice by making people less willing to rely on it. There is no doubt that this additional consideration might be enough to alter the result of the utilitarian calculation if the original difference in utility was small enough. But how plausible is it that it will make enough difference in most or all cases to avoid a serious conflict between act utilitarianism and our considered moral convictions?

4. How compelling are the three stages of Mill's "proof" of the principle of utility (see Annotations 13, 14, and 15)? A further hint for the first stage: "visible" means "able to be seen," but does "desirable" (in the sense relevant to intrinsic value) mean "able to be desired"? And for the second stage, does it follow from the fact that something is a good for "the aggregate of persons" that it is a good for each individual member of that aggregate (something that such an individual should aim at, rather than aiming at his or her own individual good)? Indeed, what is it for something to be a good for "the aggregate of persons" when only individual people and not aggregates ever make choices or act? For the third stage, see the point raised in Annotation 15.

J. J. C. Smart

John Jamieson Carswell Smart (1920–) is a British-born philosopher who has done virtually all his professional work and teaching in Australia. Smart has made major contributions to the philosophy of mind (see the selection in Chapter 3), the philosophy of science, and ethics, and is one of the main recent advocates of act utilitarianism. In the following selection, Smart discusses the issues that divide act utilitarianism (which he refers to as "extreme utilitarianism") and rule utilitarianism (which he refers to as "restricted utilitarianism"). He argues that an act utilitarian can still appeal to moral "rules of thumb," and that once this is realized, there is no justification (from a utilitarian standpoint) for giving rules the more fundamental status that is advocated by rule utilitarianism.

Extreme and Restricted Utilitarianism

I

Utilitarianism is the doctrine that the rightness of actions is to be judged by their consequences. What do we mean by 'actions' here? Do we mean particular actions or do we mean classes of actions? According to which way we interpret the word 'actions' we get two different theories, both of which merit the appellation 'utilitarian.'

1. If by 'actions' we mean particular individual actions we get the sort of doctrine held by Bentham, Sidgwick, and Moore. According to this doctrine we test individual actions by their consequences, and general rules, like 'keep promises,' are mere rules of thumb which we use only to avoid the necessity of estimating the probable consequences of our actions at every

From *Philosophical Quarterly,* 6 (1956).

step. The rightness or wrongness of keeping a promise on a particular occasion depends only on the goodness or badness of the consequences of keeping or of breaking the promise on that particular occasion. Of course part of the consequences of breaking the promise, and a part to which we will normally ascribe decisive importance, will be the weakening of faith in the institution of promising. However, if the goodness of the consequences of breaking the rule is *in toto* greater than the goodness of the consequences of keeping it, then we must break the rule, irrespective of whether the goodness of the consequences of *everybody's* obeying the rule is or is not greater than the consequences of *everybody's* breaking it. To put it shortly, rules do not matter, save *per accidens* as rules of thumb and as *de facto* social institutions with which the utilitarian has to reckon when estimating consequences. I shall call this doctrine 'extreme utilitarianism.' [1]

2. A more modest form of utilitarianism has recently become fashionable. The doctrine is to be found in Toulmin's book *The Place of Reason in Ethics,* in Nowell-Smith's *Ethics* (though I think Nowell-Smith has qualms), in John Austin's *Lectures on Jurisprudence* (Lecture II), and even in J. S. Mill, if Urmson's interpretation of him is correct. . . . Part of its charm is that it appears to resolve the dispute in moral philosophy between intuitionists and utilitarians in a way which is very neat. The above philosophers hold, or seem to hold, that moral rules are more than rules of thumb. In general the rightness of an action is *not* to be tested by evaluating its consequences but only by considering whether or not it falls under a certain rule. Whether the rule is to be considered an acceptable moral rule, is, however, to be decided by considering the consequences of adopting the rule. Broadly, then, actions are to be tested by rules and rules by consequences. The only cases in which we must test an individual action directly by its consequences are (*a*) when the action comes under two different rules, one of which enjoins it and one of which forbids it, and (*b*) when there is no rule whatever that governs the given case. I shall call this doctrine 'restricted utilitarianism.' [2]

. . .

The issue between extreme and restricted utilitarianism can be illustrated by considering the remark 'But suppose everyone did the same.' . . . To say that you ought not to do an action A because it would have bad results if everyone (or many people) did action A may be merely to point out that while the action A would otherwise be the optimific one, nevertheless when you take into account that doing A will probably cause other people to do A too, you can see that A is not, on a broad view, really optimific. If this causal influence could be avoided (as may happen in the case of a secret desert island promise) then we would disregard the universalisation principle. This is the causal form of the principle. [3] A person who accepted the universalisation principle in its hypothetical form would be one who was concerned only with what would happen *if* everyone did the action A: he would be totally unconcerned with the question of whether in fact everyone would do the action A. That is, he might say that it would be wrong not to vote because it would have bad results if everyone took this attitude, and he would be totally unmoved by arguments purporting to show that my refusing to vote has no effect whatever on other people's propensity to vote. Making use of [this] distinction, we can say that an extreme utilitarian would apply the universalisation principle in the causal form, while a restricted utilitarian would apply it in the hypothetical form. [4]

. . .

II

For an extreme utilitarian moral rules are rules of thumb. In practice the extreme utilitarian will mostly guide his conduct by appealing to the rules ('do not lie,' 'do not break promises,' etc.) of common sense morality. This is not because there is anything sacrosanct in the rules themselves but because he can argue that probably he will most often act in an extreme utilitarian way if he does not think as a utilitarian. For one thing, actions have frequently to be done in a hurry. Imagine a man seeing a person drowning. He jumps in and rescues him. There is no time to reason the matter out, but usually this will be the course of action which an extreme utilitarian would recommend if he did reason the matter out. If, however, the man drowning had been drowning in a river near Berchtesgaden in 1938, and if he had had the well known black forelock

As already noted, this is Smart's term for what is more standardly referred to as "act utilitarianism."

And this is his term for what is more standardly referred to as "rule utilitarianism."

3

R For an act utilitarian, the utility that would result if other people acted in the same way as the action being evaluated is relevant only to the extent that the action in question will tend to lead to others acting in the same way (so that the results of those other, similar actions will then be part of the results of the original action).

(Rarely if ever would one action result in everyone acting in that way or anything very close to that, making it at least misleading to speak of "the causal form" of "the universalization principle.")

4

For a rule utilitarian, in contrast to an act utilitarian, the assessment of the action depends essentially on the assessment of the results of *everyone* acting that way, that is, of everyone following a rule requiring such an action—independently of any question of whether one action of that sort would tend to causally produce others.

(Since the results of everyone acting in the way in question would depend on what *other* rules people also follow, it is better, as discussed in the introduction to this chapter, to think in terms of the consequences of everyone following a comprehensive set of rules. An action is then morally correct if it is sanctioned by a rule in the set of rules that leads to the maximum of utility.)

5

As noted by both Bentham and Mill, maximal utility is very unlikely to be achieved by doing a full utilitarian calculation for every action. One reason is that there is often not enough time (or enough information). Thus adopting and generally following "rules of thumb" (those such that following them will produce more utility than other rules or sets of rules of the same kind) is *itself* a choice that will be sanctioned by the act utilitarian principle—even though it is bound to lead to less than optimal results or even very bad results in some cases.

Praising an action is *itself* an action and therefore should also be assessed on utilitarian grounds. Thus we should praise (or blame), not the actions that are in themselves right (or wrong) in terms of utility, but rather those actions the praising (or blaming) of which will produce the most utility—which will normally be those that follow the rules of thumb that are most conductive to utility.

R Another reason for relying on rules of thumb is that personal bias is likely to lead to an incorrect utilitarian calculation.

(Notice that Smart is assuming that the rules of "common sense morality" are in fact those that will tend to produce the greatest utility if used in this way—something that is not clearly or obviously correct.)

Should the act utilitarian try to convince people that act utilitarianism is correct—that is, try to convince them to believe what he thinks is true? Since this is just another action to be assessed, according to act utilitarianism, in the same way, the act utilitarian should do this only if it produces the best results in terms of utility—which might very well not be the case if people are not very good at the relevant sorts of calculations.

and moustache of Adolf Hitler, an extreme utilitarian would, if he had time, work out the probability of the man's being the villainous dictator, and if the probability were high enough he would, on extreme utilitarian grounds, leave him to drown. The rescuer, however, has not time. He trusts to his instincts and dives in and rescues the man. And this trusting to instincts and to moral rules can be justified on extreme utilitarian grounds. (5) Furthermore, an extreme utilitarian who knew that the drowning man was Hitler would nevertheless praise the rescuer, not condemn him. For by praising the man he is strengthening a courageous and benevolent disposition of mind, and in general this disposition has great positive utility. (Next time, perhaps, it will be Winston Churchill that the man saves!) We must never forget that an extreme utilitarian may praise actions which he knows to be wrong. Saving Hitler was wrong, but it was a member of a class of actions which are generally right, and the motive to do actions of this class is in general an optimific one. In considering questions of praise and blame it is not the expediency of the praised or blamed action that is at issue, but the expediency of the praise. It can be expedient to praise an inexpedient action and inexpedient to praise an expedient one. (6)

Lack of time is not the only reason why an extreme utilitarian may, on extreme utilitarian principles, trust to rules of common sense morality. He knows that in particular cases where his own interests are involved his calculations are likely to be biased in his own favour. Suppose that he is unhappily married and is deciding whether to get divorced. He will in all probability greatly exaggerate his own unhappiness (and possibly his wife's) and greatly underestimate the harm done to his children by the break up of the family. He will probably also underestimate the likely harm done by the weakening of the general faith in marriage vows. So probably he will come to the correct extreme utilitarian conclusion if he does not in this instance think as an extreme utilitarian but trusts to common sense morality. (7)

There are many more and subtle points that could be made in connection with the relation between extreme utilitarianism and the morality of common sense. . . . One further point raised by Sidgwick in this connection is whether an (extreme) utilitarian ought on (extreme) utilitarian principles to propagate (extreme) utilitarianism among the public. As most people are not very philosophical and not good at empirical calculations, it is probable that they will most often act in an extreme utilitarian way if they do not try to think as extreme utilitarians. (8) We have seen how easy it would be to misapply the extreme utilitarian criterion in the case of divorce. Sidgwick seems to think it quite probable that an extreme utilitarian should not propagate his doctrine too widely. However, the great danger to humanity comes nowadays on the plane of public morality—not private morality. There is a greater danger to humanity from the hydrogen bomb than from an increase of the divorce rate, regrettable though that might be, and there seems no doubt that extreme utilitarianism makes for good sense in international relations. . . . I myself have no hesitation in saying that on extreme utilitarian principles we ought to propagate extreme utilitarianism as widely as possible. But Sidgwick had respectable reasons for suspecting the opposite.

The extreme utilitarian, then, regards moral rules as rules of thumb and as sociological facts that have to be taken into account when deciding what to do, just as facts of any other sort have to be taken into account. But in themselves they do not justify any action.

III

The restricted utilitarian regards moral rules as more than rules of thumb for short-circuiting calculations of consequences. Generally, he argues, consequences are not relevant at all when we are deciding what to do in a particular case. In general, they are relevant only to deciding what rules are good reasons for acting in a certain way in particular cases. This doctrine is possibly a good account of how the modern unreflective twentieth century Englishman often thinks about morality, but surely it is monstrous as an account of how it is most rational to think about morality. Suppose that there is a rule *R* and that in 99% of cases the best possible results are obtained by acting in accordance with *R*. Then clearly *R* is a useful rule of thumb; if we have not time or are not impartial enough to assess the consequences of an action it is an extremely good bet that the thing to do is to act in accordance with *R*. But is it not monstrous to suppose that if we *have* worked out the consequences and if we have perfect faith in the impartiality of our calculations, and if we *know* that in this instance to break *R* will have better results than to keep it, we should nevertheless obey the rule? Is it not to erect *R* into a sort of idol if we keep it when breaking it will prevent, say, some avoidable misery? Is not this a form of superstitious rule-worship (easily explicable psychologically) and not the rational thought of a philosopher? 9

The point may be made more clearly if we consider Mill's comparison of moral rules to the tables in the nautical almanack. . . . This comparison of Mill's is adduced by Urmson as evidence that Mill was a restricted utilitarian, but I do not think that it will bear this interpretation at all. (Though I quite agree with Urmson that many other things said by Mill are in harmony with restricted rather than extreme utilitarianism. Probably Mill had never thought very much about the distinction and was arguing for utilitarianism, restricted or extreme, against other and quite non-utilitarian forms of moral argument.) Mill says: 'Nobody argues that the art of navigation is not founded on astronomy, because sailors cannot wait to calculate the Nautical Almanack. Being rational creatures, they go out upon the sea of life with their minds made up on the common questions of right and wrong, as well as on many of the far more difficult questions of wise and foolish. . . . Whatever we adopt as the fundamental principle of morality, we require subordinate principles to apply it by.' Notice that this is, as it stands, only an argument for subordinate principles as rules of thumb. The example of the nautical almanack is misleading because the information given in the almanack is in all cases the same as the information one would get if one made a long and laborious calculation from the original astronomical data on which the almanack is founded. Suppose, however, that astronomy were different. Suppose that the behaviour of the sun, moon and planets was very nearly as it is now, but that on rare occasions there were peculiar irregularities and discontinuities, so that the almanack gave us rules of the form 'in 99% of cases where the observations are such and such you can deduce that your position is so and so.' Furthermore, let us suppose that there were methods which enabled us, by direct and laborious calculation from the original astronomical data, not using the rough and ready tables of the almanack, to get our correct position in 100% of cases. Seafarers might use the almanack because they never had time for the long calculations and they were content with a 99% chance of success in calculating their positions. Would it not be absurd, however, if they *did* make the direct calculation, and finding that it disagreed with the almanack calculation, nevertheless they ignored it and stuck to the almanack conclusion? Of course the case would be altered if there were a high enough probability of making slips in the direct calculation: then we might stick to the almanack result, liable to error though we knew it to be, simply because the direct calculation would be open to error for a different reason, the fallibility of the computer. This would be analogous to the case of the extreme utilitarian who abides by the conventional rule against the dictates of his utilitarian calculations simply because he thinks that his calculations are probably affected by personal bias. But if the navigator were sure of his direct calculations would he not be foolish to abide by his almanack? I conclude, then, that if we change our suppositions about astronomy and the almanack (to which there are no exceptions) to bring the case into line with that of morality (to whose rules there are exceptions), Mill's example loses its appearance of supporting the restricted form of utilitarianism. Let me say once more that I am not here concerned with how ordinary men think about morality but with how they ought to think. We could quite well imagine a race of sailors who acquired a superstitious reverence for their almanack, even though it was only right in 99% of cases, and who indignantly threw overboard any man who mentioned the possibility of a direct calculation. But would this behaviour of the sailors be rational?

Let us consider a much discussed sort of case in which the extreme utilitarian might go against the conventional moral rule. I have promised to a friend, dying on a desert island from which I am subsequently rescued, that I will see that his fortune (over which I have control) is given to a jockey club. However,

R Here is the fundamental problem for rule utilitarianism: *Why*, from a utilitarian standpoint, should a given rule be followed even when the person is completely sure that doing something else will lead to greater utility? That rule is, we are assuming, one that produces maximal results in terms of utility when generally followed (or a member of a comprehensive set of rules that has this feature), but why does that matter if following it will not produce the best results in the case actually in question? (As Smart proceeds to argue, Mill's navigational example does not support such a result.)

10

R Here are two further, closely related things that the act utilitarian can appeal to in trying to show that his view does not conflict with our considered moral convictions in cases like this one: first, the effects of breaking the promise on the agent's moral character (because it will, as a matter of psychological fact, make it easier for him to break promises in other cases, even where such an action does not produce greater utility); and, second, the disutility resulting from the psychological conflict and discomfort experienced by the agent.

11

Smart seems to suggest that the right action in the case as described is to break the promise. But it does not follow (see Annotation 6 and the corresponding passage) that the person should not be condemned (or even punished) if he is caught doing this—once again the choice of whether to praise or condemn or neither (as well as the choice whether to reward or punish or neither) are separate choices, themselves to be assessed in the same utilitarian way.

(Note that this means that whether a person should be punished no longer depends on whether he has done something wrong and so *deserves* to be punished.)

12

That is, for an act utilitarian, the case could go either way, depending on the details with regard to these matters. Whereas for a rule utilitarian, there may be no uncertainty at all (if the optimal rule or set of rules says to always follow such edicts). Smart is suggesting that the right result does in fact depend on these uncertain details, so that the rule utilitarian view on which the issue is completely clear is itself mistaken.

when I am rescued I decide that it would be better to give the money to a hospital, which can do more good with it. It may be argued that I am wrong to give the money to the hospital. But why? (*a*) The hospital can do more good with the money than the jockey club can. (*b*) The present case is unlike most cases of promising in that no one except me knows about the promise. In breaking the promise I am doing so with complete secrecy and am doing nothing to weaken the general faith in promises. That is, a factor, which would normally keep the extreme utilitarian from promise breaking even in otherwise unoptimific cases, does not at present operate. (*c*) There is no doubt a slight weakening in my own character as an habitual promise keeper, and moreover psychological tensions will be set up in me every time I am asked what the man made me promise him to do. For clearly I shall have to say that he made me promise to give the money to the hospital, and, since I am an habitual truth teller, this will go very much against the grain with me. **10** Indeed I am pretty sure that in practice I myself would keep the promise. But we are not discussing what my moral habits would probably make me do; we are discussing what I ought to do. Moreover, we must not forget that even if it would be most rational of me to give the money to the hospital it would also be most rational of you to punish or condemn me if you did, most improbably, find out the truth (e.g. by finding a note washed ashore in a bottle). Furthermore, I would agree that though it was most rational of me to give the money to the hospital it would be most rational of you to condemn me for it. We revert again to Sidgwick's distinction between the utility of the action and the utility of the praise of it. **11**

. . . It will be useful . . . to consider one other example. . . . Suppose that during hot weather there is an edict that no water must be used for watering gardens. I have a garden and I reason that most people are sure to obey the edict, and that as the amount of water that I use will be by itself negligible no harm will be done if I use the water secretly. So I do use the water, thus producing some lovely flowers which give happiness to various people. Still, you may say, though the action was perhaps optimific, it was unfair and wrong.

There are several matters to consider. Certainly my action should be condemned. We revert once more to Sidgwick's distinction. A right action may be rationally condemned. Furthermore, this sort of offence is normally found out. If I have a wonderful garden when everybody else's is dry and brown there is only one explanation. So if I water my garden I am weakening my respect for law and order, and as this leads to bad results an extreme utilitarian would agree that I was wrong to water the garden. Suppose now that the case is altered and that I can keep the thing secret: there is a secluded part of the garden where I grow flowers which I give away anonymously to a home for old ladies. Are you still so sure that I did the wrong thing by watering my garden? However, this is still a weaker case than that of the hospital and the jockey club. There will be tensions set up within myself: my secret knowledge that I have broken the rule will make it hard for me to exhort others to keep the rule. These psychological ill effects in myself may be not inconsiderable: directly and indirectly they may lead to harm which is at least of the same order as the happiness that the old ladies get from the flowers. You can see that on an extreme utilitarian view there are two sides to the question. **12**

. . .

I conclude that in every case if there is a rule *R* the keeping of which is in general optimific, but such that in a special sort of circumstances the optimific behaviour is to break *R*, then in these circumstances we should break *R*. Of course we must consider all the less obvious effects of breaking *R*, such as reducing people's faith in the moral order, before coming to the conclusion that to break *R* is right: in fact we shall rarely come to such a conclusion. Moral rules, on the extreme utilitarian view, are rules of thumb only, but they are not bad rules of thumb. But if we *do* come to the conclusion that we should break the rule and if we have weighed in the balance our own fallibility and liability to personal bias, what good reason remains for keeping the rule? I can understand 'it is optimific' as a reason for action, but why should 'it is a member of a class of actions which are usually optimific' or 'it is a member of a class of actions which as a class are more optimific than any alternative general class' be a good reason? . . .

Discussion Questions

1. Consider again the case of the broken promise formulated by Smart at Annotation 9. (a) According to your considered moral convictions, what is the right choice to make in this case? (b) What does the act utilitarian view say is the right result? This will require assessing all the relevant results in terms of utility, including those mentioned in Annotation 11. Does this case constitute a serious objection to act utilitarianism? Does it constitute a good argument for rule utilitarianism?

2. Here is another fairly standard sort of problem case for act utilitarianism: Suppose that a series of horrible, apparently racially motivated murders of members of a minority group have been committed in some city, and the police are unable to catch the person or persons responsible. Tensions are rising, and there is a serious threat of riots and open conflict between the minority group and the larger majority group. You are the detective in charge of the case, and are in a position to successfully frame an innocent member of the majority group for some of the murders. Moreover, this person has no family, no regular job, and contributes little to the community. Should you frame this person, bringing about the conviction and eventual execution for the crimes in question, thereby relieving much of the tension and also perhaps deterring people on both sides who might otherwise be motivated to commit further murders or engage in other sorts of violence?

a. What would an act utilitarian like Smart say about such a case, considering all of the relevant factors, and remembering that framing the innocent person is an action to be assessed entirely in terms of its consequences, according to act utilitarianism? (Fill in further details of the case or consider different alternatives if you need to.)

b. What might a rule utilitarian say about this case?

3. One problem with rule utilitarianism, not mentioned by Smart, is the possibility of more complicated rules, specifying exceptions to the main rule where they lead to increased utility. Thus one might have a rule that says to keep promises unless breaking them can be done in secret and with increased utility; or a rule that says that innocent people should not be punished unless they can be successfully framed (so that everyone thinks they are guilty), and increased utility again results. If such rules are allowable, then rule utilitarianism does not really succeed in avoiding these standard problems for utilitarianism, since the best set of rules will still lead to the seemingly unacceptable actions in question. Is there any reason a rule utilitarian can give for excluding rules of this sort? Indeed, is there any reason for excluding the principle of utility itself as the relevant rule (understanding that this will lead to frequent reliance on rules of thumb in the way that Smart discusses)? (If the principle of utility is an acceptable rule, then there seems to be no real difference at all between act and rule utilitarianism.)

Bernard Williams

Bernard Williams (1929–2003) was a British philosopher who taught mainly at Cambridge University. Williams made important contributions to many areas of philosophy, most importantly to ethics, where his subtle criticisms of both utilitarianism and Kantianism reflect a distinctively skeptical temperament. In the following selection, taken from his most influential discussion of utilitarianism, Williams poses two widely discussed problem cases and argues, among other things, that utilitarianism fails to give adequate weight to a person's own individual projects and commitments.

A Critique of Utilitarianism

Negative Responsibility: And Two Examples

. . . Consequentialism is basically indifferent to whether a state of affairs consists in what I do, or is produced by what I do, where that notion is itself wide enough to include, for instance, situations in which other people do things which I have made them do, or allowed them to do, or encouraged them to do, or given them a chance to do. All that consequentialism is interested in is the idea of these doings being *consequences* of what I do, and that is a relation broad enough to include the relations just mentioned, and many others. (1)

From *Utilitarianism: For and Against,* by J. J. C. Smart and Bernard Williams (Cambridge: Cambridge University Press, 1973).

(1) *Definition*

Consequentialism is the more general view of which utilitarianism is the most important species: the view that the morally best action is the one that produces the best total consequences.

. . . There are certain situations in which the causation of the situation, the relation it has to what I do, is in no way remote or problematic in itself, and entirely justifies the claim that the situation is a consequence of what I do: for instance, it is quite clear, or reasonably clear, that if I do a certain thing, this situation will come about, and if I do not, it will not. So from a consequentialist point of view it goes into the calculation of consequences along with any other state of affairs accessible to me. Yet from some, at least, non-consequentialist points of view, there is a vital difference between some such situations and others: namely, that in some a vital link in the production of the eventual outcome is provided by *someone else's* doing something. But for consequentialism, all causal connexions are on the same level, and it makes no difference, so far as that goes, whether the causation of a given state of affairs lies through another agent, or not. (2)

(2) Thus, for example, if someone else deliberately harms another person in a way that I could have prevented, then the resulting harm is just as much a consequence of my action (or inaction) as harm that I deliberately produce myself.

. . . It is because consequentialism attaches value ultimately to states of affairs, and its concern is with what states of affairs the world contains, that it essentially involves the notion of *negative responsibility:* that if I am ever responsible for anything, then I must be just as much responsible for things that I allow or fail to prevent, as I am for things that I myself, in the more everyday restricted sense, bring about. Those things also must enter my deliberations, as a responsible moral agent, on the same footing. What matters is what states of affairs the world contains, and so what matters with respect to a given action is what comes about if it is done, and what comes about if it is not done, and those are questions not intrinsically affected by the nature of the causal linkage, in particular by whether the outcome is partly produced by other agents.

The strong doctrine of negative responsibility flows directly from consequentialism's assignment of ultimate value to states of affairs. Looked at from another point of view, it can be seen also as a special application of something that is favoured in many moral outlooks not themselves consequentialist—something which, indeed, some thinkers have been disposed to regard as the essence of morality itself: a principle of impartiality. Such a principle will claim that there can be no relevant difference from a moral point of view which consists just in the fact, not further explicable in general terms, that benefits or harms accrue to one person rather than to another—'it's me' can never in itself be a morally comprehensible reason. This principle, familiar with regard to the reception of harms and benefits, we can see consequentialism as extending to their production: from the moral point of view, there is no comprehensible difference which consists just in my bringing about a certain outcome rather than someone else's producing it. . . .

. . . Now, . . . let us look more concretely at two examples, to see what utilitarianism might say about them, what we might say about utilitarianism and, most importantly of all, what would be implied by certain ways of thinking about the situations. . . .

(1) George, who has just taken his Ph.D. in chemistry, finds it extremely difficult to get a job. He is not very robust in health, which cuts down the number of jobs he might be able to do satisfactorily. His wife has to go out to work to keep them, which itself causes a great deal of strain, since they have small children and there are severe problems about looking after them. The results of all this, especially on the children, are damaging. An older chemist, who knows about this situation, says that he can get George a decently paid job in a certain laboratory, which pursues research into chemical and biological warfare. George says that he cannot accept this, since he is opposed to chemical and biological warfare. The older man replies that he is not too keen on it himself, come to that, but after all George's refusal is not going to make the job or the laboratory go away; what is more, he happens to know that if George refuses the job, it will certainly go to a contemporary of George's who is not inhibited by any such scruples and is likely if appointed to push along the research with greater zeal than George would. Indeed, it is not merely concern for George and his family, but (to speak frankly and in confidence) some alarm about this other man's excess of zeal, which has led the older man to offer to use his influence to get George the job . . . George's wife, to whom he is deeply attached, has views (the details of which need not concern us) from which it follows that at least there is nothing particularly wrong with research into CBW. What should he do?

(2) Jim finds himself in the central square of a small South American town. Tied up against

the wall are a row of twenty Indians, most terrified, a few defiant, in front of them several armed men in uniform. A heavy man in a sweat-stained khaki shirt turns out to be the captain in charge and, after a good deal of questioning of Jim which establishes that he got there by accident while on a botanical expedition, explains that the Indians are a random group of the inhabitants who, after recent acts of protest against the government, are just about to be killed to remind other possible protestors of the advantages of not protesting. However, since Jim is an honoured visitor from another land, the captain is happy to offer him a guest's privilege of killing one of the Indians himself. If Jim accepts, then as a special mark of the occasion, the other Indians will be let off. Of course, if Jim refuses, then there is no special occasion, and Pedro here will do what he was about to do when Jim arrived, and kill them all. Jim, with some desperate recollection of schoolboy fiction, wonders whether if he got hold of a gun, he could hold the captain, Pedro and the rest of the soldiers to threat [that is, threaten them and thereby prevent the killing], but it is quite clear from the set-up that nothing of that kind is going to work: any attempt at that sort of thing will mean that all the Indians will be killed, and himself. The men against the wall, and the other villagers, understand the situation, and are obviously begging him to accept. What should he do? (3)

To these dilemmas, it seems to me that utilitarianism replies, in the first case, that George should accept the job, and in the second, that Jim should kill the Indian. Not only does utilitarianism give these answers but, if the situations are essentially as described and there are no further special factors, it regards them, it seems to me, as *obviously* the right answers. (4) But many of us would certainly wonder whether, in (1), that could possibly be the right answer at all; and in the case of (2), even one who came to think that perhaps that was the answer, might well wonder whether it was obviously the answer. Nor is it just a question of the rightness or obviousness of these answers. It is also a question of what sort of considerations come into finding the answer. A feature of utilitarianism is that it cuts out a kind of consideration which for some others makes a difference to what they feel about such cases: a consideration involving the idea, as we might first and very simply put it, that each of us is specially responsible for what *he* does, rather than for what other people do. (5) This is an idea closely connected with the value of integrity. It is often suspected that utilitarianism, at least in its direct forms, makes integrity as a value more or less unintelligible. I shall try to show that this suspicion is correct. Of course, even if that is correct, it would not necessarily follow that we should reject utilitarianism; perhaps, as utilitarians sometimes suggest, we should just forget about integrity, in favour of such things as a concern for the general good. However, if I am right, we cannot merely do that, since the reason why utilitarianism cannot understand integrity is that it cannot coherently describe the relations between a man's projects and his actions.

Two Kinds of Remoter Effect

A lot of what we have to say about this question will be about the relations between my projects and other people's projects. (6) But before we get on to that, we should first ask whether we are assuming too hastily what the utilitarian answers to the dilemmas will be. In terms of more direct effects of the possible decisions, there does not indeed seem much doubt about the answer in either case; but it might be said that in terms of more remote or less evident effects counterweights might be found to enter the utilitarian scales. Thus the effect on George of a decision to take the job might be invoked, or its effect on others who might know of his decision. The possibility of there being more beneficent labours in the future from which he might be barred or disqualified, might be mentioned; and so forth. Such effects—in particular, possible effects on the agent's character, and effects on the public at large—are often invoked by utilitarian writers dealing with problems about lying or promise-breaking, and some similar considerations might be invoked here.

There is one very general remark that is worth making about arguments of this sort. The certainty that attaches to these hypotheses about possible effects is usually pretty low; in some cases, indeed, the hypothesis invoked is so implausible that it would scarcely pass if it were not being used to deliver the respectable moral answer, as in the standard fantasy that one of the

STOP Williams's whole discussion focuses on these two examples. You should try to decide, before reading further, (a) what the right action is in each case, and (b) what you think a utilitarian would say about them. (Williams has mainly act utilitarianism in mind, but you can also think about whether some version of rule utilitarianism might yield a different result.)

Be sure you understand clearly why this is so.

Here is a basic anti-consequentialist and anti-utilitarian idea: that the morality of a person's action depends primarily on what he or she actually does—the specific kind of action performed (and the consequences that result directly from that without any intervention from other persons)—and much less on other consequences that the action leads to as a result of the actions of others. (See the following selection by Kant for a version of such a view.)

By "projects," Williams means a person's ends or goals or purposes, especially those to which more importance is attached, that are broader in scope, and that persist over a long period of time.

effects of one's telling a particular lie is to weaken the disposition of the world at large to tell the truth. The demands on the certainty or probability of these beliefs as beliefs about particular actions are much milder than they would be on beliefs favouring the unconventional course. (7) . . .

(7)

R The point is that the likelihood of these further sorts of remote consequences is rarely great enough to make it plausible that taking note of them will genuinely alter the overall utilitarian assessment.

Leaving aside that very general point, I want to consider now two types of effect that are often invoked by utilitarians, and which might be invoked in connexion with these imaginary cases. . . .

First, there is the psychological effect on the agent. Our descriptions of these situations have not so far taken account of how George or Jim will be after they have taken the one course or the other; and it might be said that if they take the course which seemed at first the utilitarian one, the effects on them will be in fact bad enough and extensive enough to cancel out the initial utilitarian advantages of that course. Now there is one version of this effect in which, for a utilitarian, some confusion must be involved, namely that in which the agent feels bad, his subsequent conduct and relations are crippled and so on, *because he thinks that he has done the wrong thing*—for if the balance of outcomes was as it appeared to be *before* invoking this effect, then he has not (from the utilitarian point of view) done the wrong thing. So that version of the effect, for a rational and utilitarian agent, could not possibly make any difference to the assessment of right and wrong. (8) However, perhaps he is not a thoroughly rational agent, and is disposed to have bad feelings, whichever he decided to do. Now such feelings, which are from a strictly utilitarian point of view irrational—nothing, a utilitarian can point out, is advanced by having them—cannot, consistently, have any great weight in a utilitarian calculation. I shall consider in a moment an argument to suggest that they should have no weight at all in it. But short of that, the utilitarian could reasonably say that such feelings should not be encouraged, even if we accept their existence, and that to give them a lot of weight is to encourage them. Or, at the very best, even if they are straightforwardly and without any discount to be put into the calculation, their weight must be small: they are after all (and at best) one man's feelings.

(8)

R There is no good reason for the person to be distressed if he has indeed, as utilitarianism claims, done the right thing. (And also, it might be added, no reason for his moral character to be affected in undesirable ways.)

That consideration might seem to have particular force in Jim's case. In George's case, his feelings represent a larger proportion of what is to be weighed, and are more commensurate in character with other items in the calculation. In Jim's case, however, his feelings might seem to be of very little weight compared with other things that are at stake. . . .

If, then, one is really going to regard one's feelings from a strictly utilitarian point of view, Jim should give very little weight at all to his; it seems almost indecent, in fact, once one has taken that point of view, to suppose that he should give any at all. . . .

The psychological effect on the agent was the first of two general effects considered by utilitarians, which had to be discussed. The second is in general a more substantial item, but it need not take so long, since it is both clearer and has little application to the present cases. This is the *precedent effect.* As Burke rightly emphasized, this effect can be important: that one morally *can* do what someone has actually done, is a psychologically effective principle, if not a deontically valid one. For the effect to operate, obviously some conditions must hold on the publicity of the act and on such things as the status of the agent . . . ; what these may be will vary evidently with circumstances. (9)

(9)

By "the status of the agent," Williams just means things such as whether the person in question is especially prominent or respected, since an action by a person who is especially conspicuous in these ways will be more likely to influence others. (To say that the principle "that one *can* do what someone has actually done" is not "deontically" valid is just to say that it does not reflect good moral reasoning: what another person has done can still be morally unacceptable, for him and for you.)

In order for the precedent effect to make a difference to a utilitarian calculation, it must be based upon a confusion. For suppose that there is an act which would be the best in the circumstances, except that doing it will encourage by precedent other people to do things which will not be the best things to do. Then the situation of those other people must be relevantly different from that of the original agent; if it were not, then in doing the same as what would be the best course for the original agent, they would necessarily do the best thing themselves. But if the situations are in this way relevantly different, it must be a confused perception which takes the first situation, and the agent's course in it, as an adequate precedent for the second.

However, the fact that the precedent effect, if it really makes a difference, is in this sense based on a confusion, does not mean that it is not perfectly real, nor that it is to be discounted: social effects are by their nature confused in this sort of way. What it does emphasize is that calculations of the precedent effect have got to be realistic, involving considerations of how people are actually likely to be influenced. In the present examples, however, it is very implausible to think that the precedent effect could be invoked to make any difference to the calculation. Jim's case is extraordinary enough, and it is hard to imagine who the recipients of the effect might be supposed to be; while George is not in a sufficiently public situation or role for the question to arise in that form, and in any case one might suppose that the motivations of others on such an issue were quite likely to be fixed one way or another already.

No appeal, then, to these other effects is going to make a difference to what the utilitarian will decide about our examples. Let us now look more closely at the structure of those decisions.

Integrity

The situations have in common that if the agent does not do a certain disagreeable thing, someone else will, and in Jim's situation at least the result, the state of affairs after the other man has acted, if he does, will be worse than after Jim has acted, if Jim does. The same, on a smaller scale, is true of George's case. I have already suggested that it is inherent in consequentialism that it offers a strong doctrine of negative responsibility: if I know that if I do *X*, O_1 will eventuate, and if I refrain from doing *X*, O_2 will, and that O_2 is worse than O_1, then I am responsible for O_2 if I refrain voluntarily from doing *X*. 'You could have prevented it', as will be said, and truly, to Jim, if he refuses, by the relatives of the other Indians. . . .

That may be enough for us to speak, in some sense, of Jim's responsibility for that outcome, if it occurs; but it is certainly not enough, it is worth noticing, for us to speak of Jim's *making* those things happen. For granted this way of their coming about, he could have made them happen only by making Pedro shoot, and there is no acceptable sense in which his refusal makes Pedro shoot. If the captain had said on Jim's refusal, 'you leave me with no alternative', he would have been lying, like most who use that phrase. While the deaths, and the killing, may be the outcome of Jim's refusal, it is misleading to think, in such a case, of Jim having an *effect* on the world through the medium (as it happens) of Pedro's acts; for this is to leave Pedro out of the picture in his essential role of one who has intentions and projects, projects for realizing which Jim's refusal would leave an opportunity. (10) Instead of thinking in terms of supposed effects of Jim's projects on Pedro, it is more revealing to think in terms of the effects of Pedro's projects on Jim's decision. This is the direction from which I want to criticize the notion of negative responsibility.

It is Pedro, not Jim, who will have an effect on the world if he kills the prisoners.

. . .

What projects does a utilitarian agent have? As a utilitarian, he has the general project of bringing about maximally desirable outcomes; how he is to do this at any given moment is a question of what causal levers, so to speak, are at that moment within reach. The desirable outcomes, however, do not just consist of agents carrying out *that* project; there must be other more basic or lower-order projects which he and other agents have, and the desirable outcomes are going to consist, in part, of the maximally harmonious realization of those projects ('in part', because one component of a utilitarianly desirable outcome may be the occurrence of agreeable experiences which are not the satisfaction of anybody's projects). Unless there were first-order projects, the general utilitarian project would have nothing to work on, and would be vacuous. (11) What do the more basic or lower-order projects comprise? Many will be the obvious kinds of desires for things for oneself, one's family, one's friends, including basic necessities of life, and in more relaxed circumstances, objects of taste. Or there may be pursuits and interests of an intellectual, cultural or creative character. . . .

Happiness in any meaningful sense seems to presuppose the existence of other sorts of desires and commitments besides just seeking happiness—what Williams refers to as *projects*. A particular agent might aim only at the maximal satisfaction of other people's projects, but that could not be everyone's only aim, for then there would be no more specific projects to be realized. (This point is closely related to Feinberg's distinction between two senses of pleasure [see pp. 432–33].)

Beyond these, someone may have projects connected with his support of some cause: Zionism, for instance, or the abolition of chemical and biological warfare. Or there may be projects which flow from some more general disposition towards human conduct and character, such as a hatred of injustice, or of cruelty, or of killing.

. . . Utilitarianism would do well then to acknowledge the evident fact that among the things that make people happy is not only making other people happy, but being taken up or involved in any of a vast range of projects, or—if we waive the evangelical and moralizing associations of the word—commitments. One can be committed to such things as a person, a cause, an institution, a career, one's own genius, or the pursuit of danger.

Now none of these is itself the *pursuit of happiness:* by an exceedingly ancient platitude, it is not at all clear that there could be anything which was just that, or at least anything that had the slightest chance of being successful. Happiness, rather, requires being involved in, or at least content with, something else. It is not impossible for utilitarianism to accept that point: it does not have to be saddled with a naïve and absurd philosophy of mind about the relation between desire and happiness. What it does have to say is that if such commitments are worth while, then pursuing the projects that flow from them, and realizing some of those projects, will make the person for whom they are worth while, happy. It may be that to claim that is still wrong: it may well be that a commitment can make sense to a man (can make sense of his life) without his supposing that it will make him *happy.* But that is not the present point; let us grant to utilitarianism that all worthwhile human projects must conduce, one way or another, to happiness. The point is that even if that is true, it does not follow, nor could it possibly be true, that those projects are themselves projects of pursuing happiness. One has to believe in, or at least want, or quite minimally, be content with, other things, for there to be anywhere that happiness can come from.

Utilitarianism, then, should be willing to agree that its general aim of maximizing happiness does not imply that what everyone is doing is just pursuing happiness. On the contrary, people have to be pursuing other things. What those other things may be, utilitarianism, sticking to its professed empirical stance, should be prepared just to find out. No doubt some possible projects it will want to discourage, on the grounds that their being pursued involves a negative balance of happiness to others: though even there, the unblinking accountant's eye of the strict utilitarian will have something to put in the positive column, the satisfactions of the destructive agent. Beyond that, there will be a vast variety of generally beneficent or at least harmless projects; and some no doubt, will take the form not just of tastes or fancies, but of what I have called 'commitments'. It may even be that the utilitarian researcher will find that many of those with commitments, who have really identified themselves with objects outside themselves, who are thoroughly involved with other persons, or institutions, or activities or causes, are actually happier than those whose projects and wants are not like that. If so, that is an important piece of utilitarian empirical lore.

. . .

Let us now go back to the agent as utilitarian, and his higher-order project of maximizing desirable outcomes. At this level, he is committed only to that: what the outcome will actually consist of will depend entirely on the facts, on what persons with what projects and what potential satisfactions there are within calculable reach of the causal levers near which he finds himself. His own substantial projects and commitments come into it, but only as one lot among others—they potentially provide one set of satisfactions among those which he may be able to assist from where he happens to be. He is the agent of the satisfaction system who happens to be at a particular point at a particular time: in Jim's case, our man in South America. His own decisions as a utilitarian agent are a function of all the satisfactions which he can affect from where he is: and this means that the projects of others, to an indeterminately great extent, determine his decision.

This may be so either positively or negatively. It will be so positively if agents within the causal field of his decision have projects which are at any rate harmless, and so should be assisted. It will equally be so, but negatively, if there is an agent within the causal field whose projects are harmful, and have to be frustrated to maximize desirable outcomes. So it is with Jim and the soldier Pedro. On the utilitarian view, the undesirable projects of other people as much determine, in this negative way, one's decisions as the desirable ones do positively: if those people were not there, or had different projects, the causal nexus would be different, and it is the actual state of the causal nexus which determines the decision. The determination to an indefinite degree of my decisions by other people's projects is just another aspect of my unlimited responsibility to act for the best in a causal framework formed to a considerable extent by their projects. 12

12 Though the utilitarian agent will in the normal case have projects and commitments of his own, these play no more role in the overall utilitarian calculation than any of the projects and commitments of others that he is in a position to affect either positively or negatively. How much weight his own projects will have depends on what those other projects and his relationship to them turn out to be.

The decision so determined is, for utilitarianism, the right decision. But what if it conflicts with some project of mine? This, the utilitarian will say, has already been dealt with: the satisfaction to you of fulfilling your project, and any satisfactions to others of your so doing, have already been through the calculating device and have been found inadequate. Now in the case of many sorts of projects, that is a perfectly reasonable sort of answer. But in the case of projects of the sort I have called 'commitments', those with which one is more deeply and extensively involved and identified, this cannot just by itself be an adequate answer, and there may be no adequate answer at all. For, to take the extreme sort of case, how can a man, as a utilitarian agent, come to regard as one satisfaction among others, and a dispensable one, a project or attitude round which he has built his life, just because someone else's projects have so structured the causal scene that that is how the utilitarian sum comes out?

The point here is not, as utilitarians may hasten to say, that if the project or attitude is that central to his life, then to abandon it will be very disagreeable to him and great loss of utility will be involved. . . . The point is that he is identified with his actions as flowing from projects and attitudes which in some cases he takes seriously at the deepest level, as what his life is about (or, in some cases, this section of his life—seriousness is not necessarily the same as persistence). It is absurd to demand of such a man, when the sums come in from the utility network which the projects of others have in part determined, that he should just step aside from his own project and decision and acknowledge the decision which utilitarian calculation requires. It is to alienate him in a real sense from his actions and the source of his action in his own convictions. It is to make him into a channel between the input of everyone's projects, including his own, and an output of optimific decision; but this is to neglect the extent to which *his* actions and *his* decisions have to be seen as the actions and decisions which flow from the projects and attitudes with which he is most closely identified. It is thus, in the most literal sense, an attack on his integrity. (13)

These sorts of considerations do not in themselves give solutions to practical dilemmas such as those provided by our examples; but I hope they help to provide other ways of thinking about them. In fact, it is not hard to see that in George's case, viewed from this perspective, the utilitarian solution would be wrong. Jim's case is different, and harder. But if (as I suppose) the utilitarian is probably right in this case, that is not to be found out just by asking the utilitarian's questions. Discussions of it—and I am not going to try to carry it further here—will have to take seriously the distinction between my killing someone, and its coming about because of what I do that someone else kills them: a distinction based, not so much on the distinction between action and inaction, as on the distinction between my projects and someone else's projects. At least it will have to start by taking that seriously, as utilitarianism does not; but then it will have to build out from there by asking why that distinction seems to have less, or a different, force in this case than it has in George's. One question here would be how far one's powerful objection to killing people just is, in fact, an application of a powerful objection to their being killed. Another dimension of that is the issue of how much it matters that the people at risk are actual, and there, as opposed to hypothetical, or future, or merely elsewhere. (14)

There are many other considerations that could come into such a question, but the immediate point of all this is to draw one particular contrast with utilitarianism: that to reach a grounded decision in such a case should not be regarded as a matter of just discounting one's reactions, impulses and deeply held projects in the face of the pattern of utilities, nor yet merely adding them in—but in the first instance of trying to understand them.

Of course, time and circumstances are unlikely to make a grounded decision, in Jim's case at least, possible. It might not even be decent. Instead of thinking in a rational and systematic way either about utilities or about the value of human life, the relevance of the people at risk being present, and so forth, the presence of the people at risk may just have its effect. The significance of the immediate should not be underestimated. Philosophers, not only utilitarian ones, repeatedly urge one to view the world *sub specie aeternitatis,* (15) but for most human purposes that is not a good *species* to view it under. If we are not agents of the universal satisfaction system, we are not primarily janitors of any system of values, even our own: very often, we just act, as a possibly confused result of the situation in which we are engaged. That, I suspect, is very often an exceedingly good thing. . . .

R Thus even a person's deepest and most serious projects and commitments must, from a utilitarian point of view, be sacrificed if that is the way that the overall calculation comes out.

STOP (Is this, as Williams claims, an *absurd* result that violates the person's *integrity*?)

STOP Think carefully about how looking at things from this other perspective is supposed to clearly lead to an opposite result in the case involving George. Is Williams right that it probably doesn't change the result in the case of Jim, and if so, why? (Think about the suggestions that he tentatively offers here.)

Under the aspect of (or from the point of view of) eternity—essentially from a God's-eye point of view. To adopt such a point of view is to abandon one's own distinctive point of view, as defined by one's own projects and commitments.

Discussion Questions

1. After considering the George and Jim cases and seeing what Williams says, what is the right action in each of the two main cases that he describes, and why? Does either case constitute a clear **counter-example** to utilitarianism?
2. Is utilitarianism an unreasonably demanding moral position? Is it reasonable to expect people to give no more weight to their own projects and commitments than to those of others—in Mill's words, to be strictly impartial between one's own happiness and that of anyone else? Think carefully about the implications that such a view would have in various situations, such as actions in relation to one's family and friends, various kinds of recreational activities, and personal goals of various kinds. (Could a committed utilitarian ever do something like going for a hike on the weekend?)

Peter Singer

Peter Singer (1946–) is an Australian-born philosopher who currently teaches at both Princeton and the University of Melbourne. Perhaps best known for his very influential work on moral issues pertaining to the treatment of non-human animals, Singer has also made important contributions to many other issues in applied ethics and bioethics. He is one of the leading contemporary defenders of utilitarianism.

In this selection, Singer applies a somewhat limited or qualified version of utilitarianism to the issue of famine relief. His conclusions are, first, that people in affluent countries are at the very least morally obligated to do very much more than they presently do to provide aid to starving and malnourished people in other countries; and, second and more strongly, that they are in fact obligated to provide as much such aid as they can without causing greater suffering for themselves than is thereby relieved in others.

Famine, Affluence, and Morality

As I write this, in November 1971, people are dying in East Bengal from lack of food, shelter, and medical care. The suffering and death that are occurring there now are not inevitable, not unavoidable in any fatalistic sense of the term. Constant poverty, a cyclone, and a civil war have turned at least nine million people into destitute refugees; nevertheless, it is not beyond the capacity of the richer nations to give enough assistance to reduce any further suffering to very small proportions. The decisions and actions of human beings can prevent this kind of suffering. Unfortunately, human beings have not made the necessary decisions. At the individual level, people have, with very few exceptions, not responded to the situation in any significant way. Generally speaking, people have not given large sums to relief funds; they have not written to their parliamentary representatives demanding increased government assistance; they have not demonstrated in the streets, held symbolic fasts, or done anything else directed toward providing the refugees with the means to satisfy their essential needs. At the government level, no government has given the sort of massive aid that would enable the refugees to survive for more than a few days. Britain, for instance, has given rather more than most countries. It has, to date, given £14,750,000. For comparative purposes, Britain's share of the nonrecoverable development costs of the Anglo-French Concorde project is already in excess of £275,000,000, and on present estimates will reach £440,000,000. The implication is that the British government values a supersonic transport more than thirty times as highly as it values the lives of the nine million refugees. Australia is another country which, on a per capita basis, is well up in the "aid to Bengal"

From *Philosophy and Public Affairs,* Vol. 1, No. 3 (Spring, 1972).

table. Australia's aid, however, amounts to less than one-twelfth of the cost of Sydney's new opera house. The total amount given, from all sources, now stands at about £65,000,000. The estimated cost of keeping the refugees alive for one year is £464,000,000. . . .

These are the essential facts about the present situation in Bengal. So far as it concerns us here, there is nothing unique about this situation except its magnitude. The Bengal emergency is just the latest and most acute of a series of major emergencies in various parts of the world, arising both from natural and from man-made causes. There are also many parts of the world in which people die from malnutrition and lack of food independent of any special emergency. I take Bengal as my example only because it is the present concern, and because the size of the problem has ensured that it has been given adequate publicity. Neither individuals nor governments can claim to be unaware of what is happening there.

What are the moral implications of a situation like this? In what follows, I shall argue that the way people in relatively affluent countries react to a situation like that in Bengal cannot be justified; indeed, the whole way we look at moral issues—our moral conceptual scheme—needs to be altered, and with it, the way of life that has come to be taken for granted in our society.

In arguing for this conclusion I will not, of course, claim to be morally neutral. I shall, however, try to argue for the moral position that I take, so that anyone who accepts certain assumptions, to be made explicit, will, I hope, accept my conclusion.

I begin with the assumption that suffering and death from lack of food, shelter, and medical care are bad. I think most people will agree about this, although one may reach the same view by different routes. I shall not argue for this view. People can hold all sorts of eccentric positions, and perhaps from some of them it would not follow that death by starvation is in itself bad. It is difficult, perhaps impossible, to refute such positions, and so for brevity I will henceforth take this assumption as accepted. Those who disagree need read no further.

My next point is this: if it is in our power to prevent something bad from happening, without thereby sacrificing anything of comparable moral importance, we ought, morally, to do it. By "without sacrificing anything of comparable moral importance" I mean without causing anything else comparably bad to happen, or doing something that is wrong in itself, or failing to promote some moral good, comparable in significance to the bad thing that we can prevent. (1) This principle seems almost as uncontroversial as the last one. It requires us only to prevent what is bad, and not to promote what is good, and it requires this of us only when we can do it without sacrificing anything that is, from the moral point of view, comparably important. I could even, as far as the application of my argument to the Bengal emergency is concerned, qualify the point so as to make it: if it is in our power to prevent something very bad from happening, without thereby sacrificing anything morally significant, we ought, morally, to do it. (2) An application of this principle would be as follows: if I am walking past a shallow pond and see a child drowning in it, I ought to wade in and pull the child out. This will mean getting my clothes muddy, but this is insignificant, while the death of the child would presumably be a very bad thing.

The uncontroversial appearance of the principle just stated is deceptive. If it were acted upon, even in its qualified form, our lives, our society, and our world would be fundamentally changed. For the principle takes, firstly, no account of proximity or distance. It makes no moral difference whether the person I can help is a neighbor's child ten yards from me or a Bengali whose name I shall never know, ten thousand miles away. Secondly, the principle makes no distinction between cases in which I am the only person who could possibly do anything and cases in which I am just one among millions in the same position. (3)

I do not think I need to say much in defense of the refusal to take proximity and distance into account. The fact that a person is physically near to us, so that we have personal contact with him, may make it more likely that we *shall* assist him, but this does not show that we *ought* to help him rather than another who happens to be further away. If we accept any principle of impartiality, . . . equality, or whatever, we cannot discriminate against someone merely because he is far away from us (or we are far away from him). Admittedly, it is possible that we are in a better position to judge what needs to be done to help a person near to us than one far away,

(1)

This principle differs from the most standard versions of act utilitarianism in two main ways: first, it requires only the prevention of bad things, but not necessarily the maximization of good things; and, second, it makes allowance for the possibility that some actions may be wrong in themselves, apart from any assessment of consequences (in the way that is advocated by the deontological views in the next section). These modifications make no real difference, however, in relation to the issue under discussion.

(2)

This is a *much* weaker principle. Singer's own view, as will emerge, is that the stronger principle is in fact correct. But he mentions this weaker one (a principle that would be accepted by many who would reject the stronger one) to show that even it yields a major objection to the present behavior of people in affluent countries.

(3)

Notice that the principle also does not mention whether one has any special relation to the people in need of assistance that might provide the basis for an obligation: relations such as being in some way responsible or partially responsible for their plight or belonging along with them to some morally relevant community or group.

4

R This is a justification that is sometimes offered for giving more weight to aiding one's own friends and family or members of one's immediate community.

5

As long as no other ends are involved, it is a clear implication of utilitarianism (and one that Singer ultimately accepts) that one should continue to give right up to the point where doing so will produce worse results in terms of overall utility.

6

R So each person's action must be assessed in light of the full circumstances in which it occurs, which includes what all the other people in the universe are in fact going to do.

(But this creates an obvious difficulty in actually making choices when others are choosing at the same time.)

and perhaps also to provide the assistance we judge to be necessary. If this were the case, it would be a reason for helping those near to us first. 4 This may once have been a justification for being more concerned with the poor in one's own town than with famine victims in India. Unfortunately for those who like to keep their moral responsibilities limited, instant communication and swift transportation have changed the situation. From the moral point of view, the development of the world into a "global village" has made an important, though still unrecognized, difference to our moral situation. Expert observers and supervisors, sent out by famine relief organizations or permanently stationed in famine-prone areas, can direct our aid to a refugee in Bengal almost as effectively as we could get it to someone in our own block. There would seem, therefore, to be no possible justification for discriminating on geographical grounds.

There may be a greater need to defend the second implication of my principle—that the fact that there are millions of other people in the same position, in respect to the Bengali refugees, as I am, does not make the situation significantly different from a situation in which I am the only person who can prevent something very bad from occurring. Again, of course, I admit that there is a psychological difference between the cases; one feels less guilty about doing nothing if one can point to others, similarly placed, who have also done nothing. Yet this can make no real difference to our moral obligations. Should I consider that I am less obliged to pull the drowning child out of the pond if on looking around I see other people, no further away than I am, who have also noticed the child but are doing nothing? One has only to ask this question to see the absurdity of the view that numbers lessen obligation. It is a view that is an ideal excuse for inactivity; unfortunately most of the major evils—poverty, overpopulation, pollution—are problems in which everyone is almost equally involved.

...

It might be thought that this argument has an absurd consequence. Since the situation appears to be that very few people are likely to give substantial amounts, it follows that I and everyone else in similar circumstances ought to give as much as possible, that is, at least up to the point at which by giving more one would begin to cause serious suffering for oneself and one's dependents—perhaps even beyond this point to the point of marginal utility, at which by giving more one would cause oneself and one's dependents as much suffering as one would prevent in Bengal. 5 If everyone does this, however, there will be more than can be used for the benefit of the refugees, and some of the sacrifice will have been unnecessary. Thus, if everyone does what he ought to do, the result will not be as good as it would be if everyone did a little less than he ought to do, or if only some do all that they ought to do.

The paradox here arises only if we assume that the actions in question—sending money to the relief funds—are performed more or less simultaneously, and are also unexpected. For if it is to be expected that everyone is going to contribute something, then clearly each is not obliged to give as much as he would have been obliged to had others not been giving too. And if everyone is not acting more or less simultaneously, then those giving later will know how much more is needed, and will have no obligation to give more than is necessary to reach this amount. To say this is not to deny the principle that people in the same circumstances have the same obligations, but to point out that the fact that others have given, or may be expected to give, is a relevant circumstance: those giving after it has become known that many others are giving and those giving before are not in the same circumstances. 6 ...

If my argument so far has been sound, neither our distance from a preventable evil nor the number of other people who, in respect to that evil, are in the same situation as we are, lessens our obligation to mitigate or prevent that evil. I shall therefore take as established the principle I asserted earlier. As I have already said, I need to assert it only in its qualified form: if it is in our power to prevent something very bad from happening, without thereby sacrificing anything else morally significant, we ought, morally, to do it.

The outcome of this argument is that our traditional moral categories are upset. The traditional distinction between duty and charity cannot be drawn, or at least, not in the place we normally draw it. Giving money to the Bengal Relief Fund is regarded as an act of charity in our society. The bodies which collect money are known as "charities." These organizations see themselves in this way—if you send them a check, you will be thanked for your "generosity." Because giving money is regarded as an act of charity, it is not thought that there is anything wrong with not giving. The charitable man may be praised, but the man who is not charitable is not condemned. People do not feel in any way ashamed or guilty about spending money on new clothes or a new car instead of giving it to famine relief. (Indeed, the alternative does not occur to them.) This way of looking at the matter cannot be justified. When we buy new clothes not to keep ourselves warm but to look "well-dressed" we are not providing for any important need. We would not be sacrificing anything significant if we were to continue to wear our old clothes, and give the money to famine relief. By doing so, we would be preventing another person from starving. It follows from what I have said earlier that we ought to give money away, rather than spend it on clothes which we do not need to keep us warm. To do so is not charitable, or generous. Nor is it the kind of act which philosophers and theologians have called "supererogatory"—an act which it would be good to do, but not wrong not to do. On the contrary, we ought to give the money away, and it is wrong not to do so. **7**

...

. . . the revision in our moral conceptual scheme which I am proposing . . . would, given the extent of both affluence and famine in the world today, have radical implications. These implications may lead to [a] further objection, distinct from those I have already considered. . . .

The . . . objection . . . is one which has from time to time been made against utilitarianism. It follows from some forms of utilitarian theory that we all ought, morally, to be working full time to increase the balance of happiness over misery. The position I have taken here would not lead to this conclusion in all circumstances, for if there were no bad occurrences that we could prevent without sacrificing something of comparable moral importance, my argument would have no application. Given the present conditions in many parts of the world, however, it does follow from my argument that we ought, morally, to be working full time to relieve great suffering of the sort that occurs as a result of famine or other disasters. Of course, mitigating circumstances can be adduced—for instance, that if we wear ourselves out through overwork, we shall be less effective than we would otherwise have been. Nevertheless, when all considerations of this sort have been taken into account, the conclusion remains: we ought to be preventing as much suffering as we can without sacrificing something else of comparable moral importance. **8** This conclusion is one which we may be reluctant to face. I cannot see, though, why it should be regarded as a criticism of the position for which I have argued, rather than a criticism of our ordinary standards of behavior. Since most people are self-interested to some degree, very few of us are likely to do everything that we ought to do. It would, however, hardly be honest to take this as evidence that it is not the case that we ought to do it.

...

I now want to consider [two further] points, more practical than philosophical, which are relevant to the application of the moral conclusion we have reached. These points challenge not the idea that we ought to be doing all we can to prevent starvation, but the idea that giving away a great deal of money is the best means to this end.

...

[One] reason [sometimes offered] for not giving to famine relief funds is that until there is effective population control, relieving famine merely postpones starvation. If we save the Bengal refugees now, others, perhaps the children of these refugees, will face starvation in a few years' time. In support of this, one may cite the now well-known facts about the population explosion and the relatively limited scope for expanded production.

This point, like the previous one, is an argument against relieving suffering that is happening now, because of a belief about what might happen in the future; it is unlike the previous point—in that very good evidence can be adduced in support of this belief about the future. I will not go into the evidence here. I accept that the earth cannot support indefinitely a population rising at the present rate. This certainly poses a problem for anyone who thinks it important to prevent famine. Again, however, one could accept the argument without drawing the conclusion that it absolves

7

Though Singer's own conclusion is actually stronger than this, the result so far is surely enough, as he says, to radically upset our familiar moral categories and moral outlook. Think about the full implications of his view and about whether they seem correct. Does Singer's view leave out any considerations that are morally relevant to this issue?

8

Here is the stronger, more demanding view that Singer actually holds (and that is a clear consequence of utilitarianism). Think about what sort of life a person who acted in accordance with this conclusion would be able to lead. Do you think that Singer is right that people in affluent countries—and even those in relatively poor countries who are not threatened with starvation—are required to sacrifice to this degree?

one from any obligation to do anything to prevent famine. The conclusion that should be drawn is that the best means of preventing famine, in the long run, is population control. It would then follow from the position reached earlier that one ought to be doing all one can to promote population control (unless one held that all forms of population control were wrong in themselves, or would have significantly bad consequences). Since there are organizations working specifically for population control, one would then support them rather than more orthodox methods of preventing famine.

A [second] point raised by the conclusion reached earlier relates to the question of just how much we all ought to be giving away. One possibility, which has already been mentioned, is that we ought to give until we reach the level of marginal utility—that is, the level at which, by giving more, I would cause as much suffering to myself or my dependents as I would relieve by my gift. This would mean, of course, that one would reduce oneself to very near the material circumstances of a Bengali refugee. It will be recalled that earlier I put forward both a strong and a moderate version of the principle of preventing bad occurrences. The strong version, which required us to prevent bad things from happening unless in doing so we would be sacrificing something of comparable moral significance, does seem to require reducing ourselves to the level of marginal utility. I should also say that the strong version seems to me to be the correct one. I proposed the more moderate version—that we should prevent bad occurrences unless, to do so, we had to sacrifice something morally significant—only in order to show that even on this surely undeniable principle a great change in our way of life is required. On the more moderate principle, it may not follow that we ought to reduce ourselves to the level of marginal utility, for one might hold that to reduce oneself and one's family to this level is to cause something significantly bad to happen. Whether this is so I shall not discuss, since, as I have said, I can see no good reason for holding the moderate version of the principle rather than the strong version. Even if we accepted the principle only in its moderate form, however, it should be clear that we would have to give away enough to ensure that the consumer society, dependent as it is on people spending on trivia rather than giving to famine relief, would slow down and perhaps disappear entirely. There are several reasons why this would be desirable in itself. The value and necessity of economic growth are now being questioned not only by conservationists, but by economists as well. There is no doubt, too, that the consumer society has had a distorting effect on the goals and purposes of its members. Yet looking at the matter purely from the point of view of overseas aid, there must be a limit to the extent to which we should deliberately slow down our economy; for it might be the case that if we gave away, say, forty percent of our Gross National Product, we would slow down the economy so much that in absolute terms we would be giving less than if we gave twenty-five percent of the much larger GNP that we would have if we limited our contribution to this smaller percentage.

I mention this only as an indication of the sort of factor that one would have to take into account in working out an ideal. Since Western societies generally consider one percent of the GNP an acceptable level for overseas aid, the matter is entirely academic. Nor does it affect the question of how much an individual should give in a society in which very few are giving substantial amounts.

. . .

Discussion Questions

1. Suppose that at some time in the future, humankind has solved all of its problems and entered a period of peace and economic prosperity for all. In the meantime, people have been engaged in space exploration and have recently discovered a new and distant planet in which there are untold billions of people (perhaps humans, perhaps aliens of some sort—does this matter?), all near starvation. To avoid mass starvation and death on this planet will require all the people on earth to reduce their standard of living to the minimum required for survival for many generations. Are those living on earth morally required to do this, as Singer's stronger principle seems to say? Why or why not?
2. Here is a short list of factors that might seem to be morally relevant to how you can or should allocate your resources, but that are irrelevant if Singer's stronger principle is correct and if anyone

anywhere is in sufficiently dire need: family relationships, especially the duty to care for and educate one's children; friendship and community relationships, of varying degrees of scope; personal goals or projects of any sort that do not contribute directly to such aid; and voluntarily undertaken obligations of many sorts to other people that do not affect their survival. And also, whether you or your society or county are in any way responsible for the people in question being in such dire need; and whether and to what degree they are themselves responsible for their situation. Is Singer right that *none* of these considerations make any moral difference?

Deontological Views: Morality Depends on Duties and Rights

Immanuel Kant

The German philosopher Immanuel Kant (1724–1804) was one of the most important and influential philosophers of all time. Kant made major contributions to epistemology, metaphysics, ethics, the philosophy of religion, aesthetics, and many other areas. His central concern was to explain and vindicate the authority and autonomy of *reason,* both *theoretical* reason (pertaining to factual and especially scientific knowledge of the world) and *practical* reason (pertaining to action and morality).

In the following selection from the first of his major ethical works, Kant attempts to derive and defend what he regards as the fundamental principle of morality: the *categorical imperative.* The starting point is the idea that morality must not depend on any motive or goal that might not be shared by others, but must instead be valid for any rational being. Kant attempts to show in effect that this very requirement can by itself lead to the moral principle he is seeking. He offers several different formulations of this principle; these are supposed to amount to the same thing, but this is by no means obviously the case.

From *Foundations of the Metaphysics of Morals*

First Section/Transition from the Common Rational Knowledge of Morals to the Philosophical

Nothing in the world—indeed nothing even beyond the world—can possibly be conceived which could be called good without qualification except a *good will.* ❶ Intelligence, wit, judgment, and the other talents of the mind, however they may be named, or courage, resoluteness, and perseverance as qualities of temperament, are doubtless in many respects good and desirable. But they can become extremely bad and harmful if the will, which is to make use of these gifts of nature and which in its special constitution is called character, is not good. It is the same with the gifts of fortune. Power, riches, honor, even health, general well-being, and the contentment with one's condition which is called happiness, make for pride and even arrogance if there is not a good will to correct their influence on the mind and on its principles of action so as to make it universally conformable to its end. ❷ It need hardly be mentioned that the sight of a being adorned with no feature of a pure and good will, yet enjoying uninterrupted prosperity, can never give pleasure to a rational impartial observer. Thus the good will seems to constitute the indispensable condition even of worthiness to be happy.

Some qualities seem to be conducive to this good will and can facilitate its action, but, in spite of that, they have no intrinsic unconditional worth. They rather presuppose a good

From *Kant: Foundations of the Metaphysics of Morals,* edited by Robert Paul Wolff (New York: Bobbs-Merrill, 1969).

❶

By a "good will," Kant means one that is motivated only by the demands of moral duty (not a will that is benevolent or generous, as the phrase is more standardly used).

❷

All of these things can, in the absence of a good will, lead to actions and results that are morally bad.

will, which limits the high esteem which one otherwise rightly has for them and prevents their being held to be absolutely good. Moderation in emotions and passions, self-control, and calm deliberation not only are good in many respects but even seem to constitute a part of the inner worth of the person. But however unconditionally they were esteemed by the ancients, they are far from being good without qualification. For without the principle of a good will they can become extremely bad, and the coolness of a villain makes him not only far more dangerous but also more directly abominable in our eyes than he would have seemed without it. ❸

❸ R Again, the point is that the various character traits in question can lead to results that are morally bad or evil if not accompanied by a good will.

The good will is not good because of what it effects or accomplishes or because of its adequacy to achieve some proposed end; it is good only because of its willing, i.e., it is good of itself. And, regarded for itself, it is to be esteemed incomparably higher than anything which could be brought about by it in favor of any inclination or even of the sum total of all inclinations. Even if it should happen that, by a particularly unfortunate fate or by the niggardly provision of a step-motherly nature, this will should be wholly lacking in power to accomplish its purpose, and if even the greatest effort should not avail it to achieve anything of its end, and if there remained only the good will (not as a mere wish but as the summoning of all the means in our power), it would sparkle like a jewel in its own right, as something that had its full worth in itself. Usefulness or fruitlessness can neither diminish nor augment this worth. . . .

We have, then, to develop the concept of a will which is to be esteemed as good of itself without regard to anything else. It dwells already in the natural sound understanding and does not need so much to be taught as only to be brought to light. In the estimation of the total worth of our actions it always takes first place and is the condition of everything else. In order to show this, we shall take the concept of duty. It contains that of a good will, though with certain subjective restrictions and hindrances; but these are far from concealing it and making it unrecognizable, for they rather bring it out by contrast and make it shine forth all the brighter.

I here omit all actions which are recognized as opposed to duty, even though they may be useful in one respect or another, for with these the question does not arise at all as to whether they may be carried out *from* duty, since they conflict with it. I also pass over the actions which are really in accordance with duty and to which one has no direct inclination, rather executing them because impelled to do so by another inclination. For it is easily decided whether an action in accord with duty is performed from duty or for some selfish purpose. It is far more difficult to note this difference when the action is in accordance with duty and, in addition, the subject has a direct inclination to do it. For example, it is in fact in accordance with duty that a dealer should not overcharge an inexperienced customer, and wherever there is much business the prudent merchant does not do so, having a fixed price for everyone, so that a child may buy of him as cheaply as any other. Thus the customer is honestly served. But this is far from sufficient to justify the belief that the merchant has behaved in this way from duty and principles of honesty. His own advantage required this behavior; but it cannot be assumed that over and above that he had a direct inclination to the purchaser and that, out of love, as it were, he gave none an advantage in price over another. Therefore the action was done neither from duty nor from direct inclination but only for a selfish purpose. ❹

❹ R The shopkeeper's action conforms to the demands of moral duty (that is, the shopkeeper does what duty would require), but the action still has no moral worth if done only from the motive of self-interest. The shopkeeper has done the right thing for the wrong reason. (Contrary to what the wording of the last sentence might suggest, Kant is not saying that this must always be the case.)

...

To be kind where one can is duty, and there are, moreover, many persons so sympathetically constituted that without any motive of vanity or selfishness they find an inner satisfaction in spreading joy, and rejoice in the contentment of others which they have made possible. But I say that, however dutiful and amiable it may be, that kind of action has no true moral worth. It is on a level with [actions arising from] other inclinations, such as the inclination to honor, which, if fortunately directed to what in fact accords with duty and is generally useful and thus honorable, deserve praise and encouragement but no esteem. For the maxim ❺ lacks the moral import of an action done not from inclination but from duty. But assume that the mind of that friend to mankind was clouded by a sorrow of his own which extinguished all sympathy with the lot of others and that he still had the power to benefit others in distress, but that their need left him untouched because he was preoccupied with his own need. And now suppose him to tear himself, unsolicited by inclination, out of this

❺ A *maxim* is the practical principle that an agent is subjectively following: to do a certain sort of thing in a certain sort of situation for a certain sort of reason. In effect, it is a generalized version of the person's conscious intention in doing the action.

dead insensibility and to perform this action only from duty and without any inclination—then for the first time his action has genuine moral worth. Furthermore, if nature has put little sympathy in the heart of a man, and if he, though an honest man, is by temperament cold and indifferent to the sufferings of others, perhaps because he is provided with special gifts of patience and fortitude and expects or even requires that others should have the same—and such a man would certainly not be the meanest product of nature—would not he find in himself a source from which to give himself a far higher worth than he could have got by having a good-natured temperament? This is unquestionably true even though nature did not make him philanthropic, for it is just here that the worth of the character is brought out, which is morally and incomparably the highest of all: he is beneficent not from inclination but from duty. (6)

. . .

[Thus the first proposition of morality is that to have moral worth an action must be done from duty.] The second proposition is: An action performed from duty does not have its moral worth in the purpose which is to be achieved through it but in the maxim by which it is determined. Its moral value, therefore, does not depend on the realization of the object of the action but merely on the principle of volition by which the action is done without any regard to the objects of the faculty of desire. From the preceding discussion it is clear that the purposes we may have for our actions and their effects as ends and incentives of the will cannot give the actions any unconditional and moral worth. Wherein, then, can this worth lie, if it is not in the will in relation to its hoped-for effect? It can lie nowhere else than in the principle of the will, irrespective of the ends which can be realized by such action. (7) . . .

The third principle, as a consequence of the two preceding, I would express as follows: Duty is the necessity of an action executed from respect for law. I can certainly have an inclination to the object as an effect of the proposed action, but I can never have respect for it precisely because it is a mere effect and not an activity of a will. Similarly, I can have no respect for any inclination whatsoever, whether my own or that of another; in the former case I can at most approve of it and in the latter I can even love it, i.e., see it as favorable to my own advantage. But that which . . . does not serve my inclination but overpowers it or at least excludes it from being considered in making a choice—in a word, law itself—can be an object of respect and thus a command. Now as an act from duty wholly excludes the influence of inclination and therewith every object of the will, nothing remains which can determine the will objectively except the law, and nothing subjectively except pure respect for this practical law. This subjective element is the maxim that I ought to follow such a law even if it thwarts all my inclinations. (8)

. . .

But what kind of a law can that be, the conception of which must determine the will without reference to the expected result? Under this condition alone the will can be called absolutely good without qualification. Since I have robbed the will of all impulses which could come to it from obedience to any law, nothing remains to serve as a principle of the will except universal conformity of its action to law as such. That is, I should never act in such a way that I could not also will that my maxim should be a universal law. (9) Mere conformity to law as such (without assuming any particular law applicable to certain actions) serves as the principle of the will, and it must serve as such a principle if duty is not to be a vain delusion and chimerical concept. . . .

Second Section/Transition from the Popular Moral Philosophy to the Metaphysics of Morals

. . .

Everything in nature works according to laws. Only a rational being has the capacity of acting according to the conception of laws, i.e., according to principles. This capacity is will. Since reason is required for the derivation of actions from laws, will is nothing else than practical reason. (10) If reason infallibly determines the will, the actions which such a being recognizes as objectively necessary are also subjectively necessary. That is, the will is a faculty of choosing only that which reason, independently of inclination, recognizes as practically necessary, i.e., as good. . . .

R Persons who help or benefit others because they have a spontaneous inclination toward sympathy (or benevolence or generosity) are, like the shopkeeper, doing what they want to do and not acting out of duty; thus their actions, while worthy of praise and encouragement, have no real *moral* worth. The person worthy of moral esteem is the one who has no desire or inclination at all to help anyone, who "is by temperament cold and indifferent," but who helps others out of moral duty alone. (See Discussion Question 1.)

R Kant concludes that moral value must derive from a principle of action that does not depend on any purpose or goal toward which we may have an inclination.

(This is *very* puzzling: how can a principle have any definite content if not in relation to some purpose or goal?)

R Thus a dutiful action must derive from respect for (moral) law, not from any specific inclinations that the person might happen to have.

(Again, how does this moral or practical law come to have any specific content?)

Lacking any specific purpose, the content of the moral law can only derive from the fact that it is supposed to be a *universal* law, a law that governs all rational beings. Thus the fundamental moral requirement (elaborated much further later on) is that the maxim of my action must be capable of being a universal law that a rational being can will to hold. (It is still unclear at this point how this will result in any definite content.)

R That is, will is the faculty in us that derives practical results (actions) from the requirements of reason.

The conception of an objective principle so far as it constrains a will, is a command (of reason), and the formula of this command is called an *imperative.*

All imperatives are expressed by an "ought" and thereby indicate the relation of an objective law of reason to a will which is not in its subjective constitution necessarily determined by this law. This relation is that of constraint. Imperatives say that it would be good to do or to refrain from doing something, but they say it to a will which does not always do something simply because it is presented as a good thing to do. Practical good is what determines the will by means of the conception of reason and hence not by subjective causes but, rather, objectively, i.e., on grounds which are valid for every rational being as such. It is distinguished from the pleasant as that which has an influence on the will only by means of a sensation from merely subjective causes, which hold only for the senses of this or that person and not as a principle of reason which holds for everyone. (11)

...

All imperatives command either hypothetically or categorically. The former present the practical necessity of a possible action as a means to achieving something else which one desires (or which one may possibly desire). The categorical imperative would be one which presented an action as of itself objectively necessary, without regard to any other end. (12)

Since every practical law presents a possible action as good and thus as necessary for a subject practically determinable by reason, all imperatives are formulas of the determination of action which is necessary by the principle of a will which is in any way good. If the action is good only as a means to something else, the imperative is hypothetical; but if it is thought of as good in itself, and hence as necessary in a will which of itself conforms to reason as the principle of this will, the imperative is categorical.

...

The hypothetical imperative, therefore, says only that the action is good to some purpose, possible or actual. In the former case it is a problematical, in the latter an assertorical, practical principle. The categorical imperative, which declares the action to be of itself objectively necessary without making any reference to a purpose, i.e., without having any other end, holds as an apodictical (practical) principle. (13)

We can think of that which is possible through the mere powers of some rational being as a possible purpose of any will. As a consequence, the principles of action, in so far as they are thought of as necessary to attain a possible purpose which can be achieved by them, are in reality infinitely numerous. . . .

There is one end, however, which we may presuppose as actual in all rational beings so far as imperatives apply to them, i.e., so far as they are dependent beings; there is one purpose not only which they *can* have but which we can presuppose that they all *do* have by a necessity of nature. This purpose is happiness. The hypothetical imperative which represents the practical necessity of action as means to the promotion of happiness is an assertorical imperative. We may not expound it as merely necessary to an uncertain and a merely possible purpose, but as necessary to a purpose which we can a priori and with assurance assume for everyone because it belongs to his essence. Skill in the choice of means to one's own highest welfare can be called prudence in the narrowest sense. Thus the imperative which refers to the choice of means to one's own happiness, i.e., the precept of prudence, is still only hypothetical; the action is not absolutely commanded but commanded only as a means to another end.

Finally, there is one imperative which directly commands a certain conduct without making its condition some purpose to be reached by it. This imperative is categorical. It concerns not the material of the action and its intended result but the form and the principle from which it results. (14) What is essentially good in it consists in the intention, the result being what it may. This imperative may be called the imperative of morality.

Volition according to these three principles is plainly distinguished by dissimilarity in the constraint to which they subject the will. In order to clarify this dissimilarity, I believe that they are most suitably named if one says that they are either rules of skill, counsels of prudence, or commands (laws) of morality, respectively. . . .

The question now arises: how are all these imperatives possible? This question does not

(11)

An *imperative,* being a command of reason, holds for any rational being. When pleasure influences the will, this does not normally involve any command of reason and will vary from person to person, because different people find different things pleasant.

(12)

Hypothetical imperatives depend on actual or possible desires (inclinations), while *categorical imperatives* do not.

(Given the previous discussion, it follows that an imperative of morality must be categorical rather than hypothetical, because it cannot depend on any specific desire or inclination.)

(13)

A "problematical" practical principle says that a person should do some particular action *if* that person has the purpose or end to which that action is in fact a means. An "assertorical" practical principle says of a person who in fact does have a particular purpose or end that he definitely should do the action that is a means to that purpose or end. (This assumes that there is only one relevant means or one that is clearly better than any other.) An "apodictical" practical purpose says that some action (which may be the "action" of not doing some particular thing) should *necessarily* be done by any rational being, no matter what specific purposes or ends that being may have.

(14)

Since there are no specific purposes or ends in question, a categorical imperative cannot concern the relation of the action to such an end. Kant concludes that it can only concern the *form* of the action: the general kind of action that it is. (But it is still not clear at this point what this means.)

require an answer as to how the action which the imperative commands can be performed but merely as to how the constraint of the will, which the imperative expresses in the problem, can be conceived. How an imperative of skill is possible requires no particular discussion. Whoever wills the end, so far as reason has decisive influence on his action, wills also the indispensably necessary means to it that lie in his power. 15 ...

If it were only easy to give a definite concept of happiness, the imperatives of prudence would completely correspond to those of skill. . . . For it could be said in this case as well as in the former that whoever wills the end wills also (necessarily according to reason) the only means to it which are in his power. But it is a misfortune that the concept of happiness is so indefinite that, although each person wishes to attain it, he can never definitely and self-consistently state what it is he really wishes and wills. 16 . . .

To see how the imperative of morality is possible is, then, without doubt the only question needing an answer. It is not hypothetical, and thus the objectively conceived necessity cannot be supported by any presupposition, as was the case with the hypothetical imperatives. But it must not be overlooked that it cannot be shown by any example (i.e., it cannot be empirically shown) whether or not there is such an imperative. . . . we cannot show with certainty by any example that the will is here determined by the law alone without any other incentives, even though this appears to be the case. For it is always possible that secret fear of disgrace, and perhaps also obscure apprehension of other dangers, may have had an influence on the will. Who can prove by experience the nonexistence of a cause when experience shows us only that we do not perceive the cause? But in such a case the so-called moral imperative, which as such appears to be categorical and unconditional, would be actually only a pragmatic precept which makes us attentive to our own advantage and teaches us to consider it. 17

Thus we shall have to investigate purely a priori the possibility of a categorical imperative, for we do not have the advantage that experience would give us the reality of this imperative, so that the [demonstration of its] possibility would be necessary only for its explanation and not for its establishment. In the meantime, this much may at least be seen: the categorical imperative alone can be taken as a practical *law,* while all the others may be called principles of the will but not laws. This is because what is necessary merely for the attainment of an arbitrary purpose can be regarded as itself contingent, and we get rid of the precept once we give up the purpose, whereas the unconditional command leaves the will no freedom to choose the opposite. Thus it alone implies the necessity which we require of a law.

. . .

In attacking this problem, we will first inquire whether the mere concept of a categorical imperative does not also furnish the formula containing the proposition which alone can be a categorical imperative. . . . 18

If I think of a hypothetical imperative as such, I do not know what it will contain until the condition is stated [under which it is an imperative]. But if I think of a categorical imperative, I know immediately what it contains. For since the imperative contains besides the law only the necessity that the maxim* should accord with this law, while the law contains no condition to which it is restricted, there is nothing remaining in it except the universality of law as such to which the maxim of the action should conform; and in effect this conformity alone is represented as necessary by the imperative.

There is, therefore, only one categorical imperative. It is: Act only according to that maxim by which you can at the same time will that it should become a universal law. 19

. . .

*A maxim is the subjective principle of acting and must be distinguished from the objective principle, i.e., the practical law. The former contains the practical rule which reason determines according to the conditions of the subject (often its ignorance or inclinations) and is thus the principle according to which the subject acts. The law, on the other hand, is the objective principle valid for every rational being, and the principle by which it ought to act, i.e., an imperative.

R It would make no sense to will an end without willing an "indispensably necessary means," so any rational being that wills the end also wills the means—which is what a "rule of skill" (a problematical principle) says.

R The analogous point holds for most "counsels of prudence" (assertorical principles). But for the key case where the goal is happiness, the uncertainty pertaining to both the nature of happiness and the means required to attain it make it quite possible for a rational being to will the end and fail to will the means—as we often discover later, to our regret.

R The possibility of categorical imperatives cannot be established empirically by citing actual cases of actions where there is no specific end or purpose, since it is always possible that there is some end (such as fear of disgrace) that even the agent is unaware of.

Here is the key idea, already hinted at earlier (see Annotation 9 and the corresponding passage): the very idea of a *categorical* imperative, one not deriving from any specific end or purpose, will also (somehow) determine the *content* of such an imperative.

R According to the idea of the categorical imperative, the maxim of the action must conform to a universal law, one valid for all rational beings. Since there is no basis for any more specific content, the categorical imperative can say only that the maxim of one's action must be such as to make this possible: something that could be a universal law and could be willed by the agent to have this status. This is Kant's first formulation of the categorical imperative.

The universality of law according to which effects are produced constitutes what is properly called nature in the most general sense (as to form), i.e., the existence of things so far as it is determined by universal laws. [By analogy], then, the universal imperative of duty can be expressed as follows: Act as though the maxim of your action were by your will to become a universal law of nature.

We shall now enumerate some duties, adopting the usual division of them into duties to ourselves and to others and into perfect and imperfect duties. [20]

1. A man who is reduced to despair by a series of evils feels a weariness with life but is still in possession of his reason sufficiently to ask whether it would not be contrary to his duty to himself to take his own life. Now he asks whether the maxim of his action could become a universal law of nature. His maxim, however, is: For love of myself, I make it my principle to shorten my life when by a longer duration it threatens more evil than satisfaction. But it is questionable whether this principle of self-love could become a universal law of nature. One immediately sees a contradiction in a system of nature whose law would be to destroy life by the feeling whose special office is to impel the improvement of life. In this case it would not exist as nature; hence that maxim cannot obtain as a law of nature, and thus it wholly contradicts the supreme principle of all duty. [21]
2. Another man finds himself forced by need to borrow money. He well knows that he will not be able to repay it, but he also sees that nothing will be loaned him if he does not firmly promise to repay it at a certain time. He desires to make such a promise, but he has enough conscience to ask himself whether it is not improper and opposed to duty to relieve his distress in such a way. Now, assuming he does decide to do so, the maxim of his action would be as follows: When I believe myself to be in need of money, I will borrow money and promise to repay it, although I know I shall never do so. Now this principle of self-love or of his own benefit may very well be compatible with his whole future welfare, but the question is whether it is right. He changes the pretension of self-love into a universal law and then puts the question: How would it be if my maxim became a universal law? He immediately sees that it could never hold as a universal law of nature and be consistent with itself; rather it must necessarily contradict itself. For the universality of a law which says that anyone who believes himself to be in need could promise what he pleased with the intention of not fulfilling it would make the promise itself and the end to be accomplished by it impossible; no one would believe what was promised to him but would only laugh at any such assertion as vain pretense. [22]
3. A third finds in himself a talent which could, by means of some cultivation, make him in many respects a useful man. But he finds himself in comfortable circumstances and prefers indulgence in pleasure to troubling himself with broadening and improving his fortunate natural gifts. Now, however, let him ask whether his maxim of neglecting his gifts, besides agreeing with his propensity to idle amusement, agrees also with what is called duty. He sees that a system of nature could indeed exist in accordance with such a law, even though man (like the inhabitants of the South Sea Islands) should let his talents rust and resolve to devote his life merely to idleness, indulgence, and propagation—in a word, to pleasure. But he cannot possibly will that this should become a universal law of nature or that it should be implanted in us by a natural instinct. For, as a rational being, he necessarily wills that all his faculties should be developed, inasmuch as they are given to him for all sorts of possible purposes. [23]
4. A fourth man, for whom things are going well, sees that others (whom he could help) have to struggle with great hardships, and he asks, "What concern of mine is it? Let each one be as happy as heaven wills, or as he can make himself; I will not take anything from him or even envy him; but to his welfare or to his assistance in time of need I have no desire to contribute." If such a way of thinking were a universal law of nature, certainly the human race could exist, and without doubt even better than in a state where everyone talks of sympathy and good will, or even exerts himself occasionally to practice them while, on the other hand, he cheats when he can and betrays or otherwise violates the rights of

A perfect duty is one that *strictly* requires certain specific actions, with no choice or leeway; an imperfect duty is one that can be fulfilled in several different ways, among which the agent may choose, and thus no one of which is strictly required.

STOP Kant's claim is that the maxim of this proposed action could not be a universal law because it is **contradictory** when made universal. Can you see a clear contradiction? (See Discussion Question 2.)

STOP Here again the claim is that the maxim of the action becomes contradictory when made universal. This is a more plausible case in that there is a way in which the universalized maxim would (probably?) be self-defeating. But is it really *contradictory*? (See Discussion Question 2.)

The alleged problem is different in this case: the maxim can be made universal without contradiction, but (it is claimed) the person cannot *will* this universalized maxim to be a law because any rational being necessarily wills something that contradicts it (so that the problem is still contradiction, but this time within the will itself, rather than within the universalized maxim). (But is there any clear reason why a rational being must will that all his faculties be developed—indeed, is this even possible? See Discussion Question 3.)

man. Now although it is possible that a universal law of nature according to that maxim could exist, it is nevertheless impossible to will that such a principle should hold everywhere as a law of nature. For a will which resolved this would conflict with itself, since instances can often arise in which he would need the love and sympathy of others, and in which he would have robbed himself, by such a law of nature springing from his own will, of all hope of the aid he desires. 24

The foregoing are a few of the many actual duties, or at least of duties we hold to be actual, whose derivation from the one stated principle is clear. We must be able to will that a maxim of our action become a universal law; this is the canon of the moral estimation of our action generally. Some actions are of such a nature that their maxim cannot even be *thought* as a universal law of nature without contradiction, far from it being possible that one could will that it should be such. In others this internal impossibility is not found, though it is still impossible to *will* that their maxim should be raised to the universality of a law of nature, because such a will would contradict itself. We easily see that the former maxim conflicts with the stricter or narrower (imprescriptible) duty, the latter with broader (meritorious) duty. 25 Thus all duties, so far as the kind of obligation (not the object of their action) is concerned, have been completely exhibited by these examples in their dependence on the one principle.

When we observe ourselves in any transgression of a duty, we find that we do not actually will that our maxim should become a universal law. That is impossible for us; rather, the contrary of this maxim should remain as a law generally, and we only take the liberty of making an exception to it for ourselves or for the sake of our inclination, and for this one occasion. Consequently, if we weighed everything from one and the same standpoint, namely, reason, we would come upon a contradiction in our own will, viz., that a certain principle is objectively necessary as a universal law and yet subjectively does not hold universally but rather admits exceptions. . . .

We have thus at least established that if duty is a concept which is to have significance and actual legislation for our actions, it can be expressed only in categorical imperatives and not at all in hypothetical ones. For every application of it we have also clearly exhibited the content of the categorical imperative which must contain the principle of all duty (if there is such). This is itself very much. But we are not yet advanced far enough to prove a priori that that kind of imperative really exists, that there is a practical law which of itself commands absolutely and without any incentives, and that obedience to this law is duty. 26

. . .

The will is thought of as a faculty of determining itself to action in accordance with the conception of certain laws. Such a faculty can be found only in rational beings. That which serves the will as the objective ground of its self-determination is an end, and, if it is given by reason alone, it must hold alike for all rational beings. On the other hand, that which contains the ground of the possibility of the action, whose result is an end, is called the means. The subjective ground of desire is the incentive, while the objective ground of volition is the motive. Thus arises the distinction between subjective ends, which rest on incentives, and objective ends, which depend on motives valid for every rational being. Practical principles are formal when they disregard all subjective ends; they are material when they have subjective ends, and thus certain incentives, as their basis. The ends which a rational being arbitrarily proposes to himself as consequences of his action are material ends and are without exception only relative, for only their relation to a particularly constituted faculty of desire in the subject gives them their worth. And this worth cannot, therefore, afford any universal principles for all rational beings or valid and necessary principles for every volition. That is, they cannot give rise to any practical laws. All these relative ends, therefore, are grounds for hypothetical imperatives only.

But suppose that there were something the existence of which in itself had absolute worth, something which, as an end in itself, could be a ground of definite laws. In it and only in it could lie the ground of a possible categorical imperative, i.e., of a practical law. 27

Now, I say, man and, in general, every rational being exists as an end in himself and not merely

STOP The second case of an alleged conflict within the will itself is again more plausible. But is it really true that no one could fail to will that he be helped when in need? (See Discussion Question 3.)

Kant summarizes the two ways that the categorical imperative can fail to be satisfied by the maxim of an action. The first corresponds to perfect duties, the second to imperfect duties: on Kant's view, one may never commit suicide in the face of misfortune or make a promise while knowing that one will not be able to keep it; but one has a choice of which talents to develop (he now seems to recognize that not all can be fully developed) and of which people to help (no one can help everyone).

The reason for the uncertainty expressed here is not entirely clear. The idea seems to be that the ultimate point of the moral law is not yet clear. Specific, optional purposes or ends have been ruled out, but Kant will suggest that there is a certain unconditional end that any rational being must have.

Think again about the idea of a categorical imperative: one that is binding on any rational being, no matter what specific purposes it may or may not have. An end that had *absolute* worth would work for such an imperative; and, Kant is saying, *only* an end with such worth could supply such a basis. In what follows, Kant proclaims (is there any real argument?) that rational beings are themselves ends with absolute as opposed to merely conditional worth.

This claim reflects the rather austere character of Kant's moral thought: according to him, a rational being would want to have no contingent inclinations at all—no desires for anything that does not have absolute worth. What would life be like for such a being? (How many, if any, of your current desires would satisfy this standard?)

The existence of a rational being is an end in itself. It is thus a fundamental mistake to regard or treat such a being as merely a means to something else (which could only be something with merely contingent, conditional worth).

Here is the second formulation of the categorical imperative, supposedly just another formulation of the same universal moral law. It is important to stress that persons are never to be treated "as a means only," that is, never *merely* as a means—not that they may never be treated in any respect as a means (which would make most forms of human interaction impossible).

On the surface, this is a different reason for the moral unacceptability of suicide in the face of misfortune: it treats a person (the person who commits suicide) as a means to the end of escaping the misfortune in question. (But is this really so? See Discussion Question 4.)

This is the clearest example of the application of the second version of the categorical imperative—and probably the best and clearest of all of Kant's specific examples.

as a means to be arbitrarily used by this or that will. In all his actions, whether they are directed to himself or to other rational beings, he must always be regarded at the same time as an end. All objects of inclinations have only a conditional worth, for if the inclinations and the needs founded on them did not exist, their object would be without worth. The inclinations themselves as the sources of needs, however, are so lacking in absolute worth that the universal wish of every rational being must be indeed to free himself completely from them. [28] Therefore, the worth of any objects to be obtained by our actions is at all times conditional. Beings whose existence does not depend on our will but on nature, if they are not rational beings, have only a relative worth as means and are therefore called "things"; on the other hand, rational beings are designated "persons" because their nature indicates that they are ends in themselves, i.e., things which may not be used merely as means. Such a being is thus an object of respect and, so far, restricts all [arbitrary] choice. Such beings are not merely subjective ends whose existence as a result of our action has a worth for us, but are objective ends, i.e., beings whose existence in itself is an end. Such an end is one for which no other end can be substituted, to which these beings should serve merely as means. [29] For, without them, nothing of absolute worth could be found, and if all worth is conditional and thus contingent, no supreme practical principle for reason could be found anywhere.

Thus if there is to be a supreme practical principle and a categorical imperative for the human will, it must be one that forms an objective principle of the will from the conception of that which is necessarily an end for everyone because it is an end in itself. Hence this objective principle can serve as a universal practical law. The ground of this principle is: rational nature exists as an end in itself. Man necessarily thinks of his own existence in this way; thus far it is a subjective principle of human actions. Also every other rational being thinks of his existence by means of the same rational ground which holds also for myself; thus it is at the same time an objective principle from which, as a supreme practical ground, it must be possible to derive all laws of the will. The practical imperative, therefore, is the following: Act so that you treat humanity, whether in your own person or in that of another, always as an end and never as a means only. [30] Let us now see whether this can be achieved.

To return to our previous examples:

First, according to the concept of necessary duty to one's self, he who contemplates suicide will ask himself whether his action can be consistent with the idea of humanity as an end in itself. If, in order to escape from burdensome circumstances, he destroys himself, he uses a person merely as a means to maintain a tolerable condition up to the end of life. Man, however, is not a thing, and thus not something to be used merely as a means; he must always be regarded in all his actions as an end in himself. Therefore, I cannot dispose of man in my own person so as to mutilate, corrupt, or kill him. [31] (It belongs to ethics proper to define more accurately this basic principle so as to avoid all misunderstanding, e.g., as to the amputation of limbs in order to preserve myself, or to exposing my life to danger in order to save it; I must, therefore, omit them here.)

Second, as concerns necessary or obligatory duties to others, he who intends a deceitful promise to others sees immediately that he intends to use another man merely as a means, without the latter containing the end in himself at the same time. For he whom I want to use for my own purposes by means of such a promise cannot possibly assent to my mode of acting against him and cannot contain the end of this action in himself. This conflict against the principle of other men is even clearer if we cite examples of attacks on their freedom and property. For then it is clear that he who transgresses the rights of men intends to make use of the persons of others merely as a means, without considering that, as rational beings, they must always be esteemed at the same time as ends, i.e., only as beings who must be able to contain in themselves the end of the very same action. [32]

Third, with regard to contingent (meritorious) duty to one's self, it is not sufficient that the action not conflict with humanity in our person as an end in itself; it must also harmonize with it. Now in humanity there are capacities for greater perfection which belong to the end of nature with respect to humanity in our own person; to neglect these might perhaps be consistent with the preservation of humanity as an end in itself but not with the furtherance of that end. [33]

Fourth, with regard to meritorious duty to others, the natural end which all men have is their own happiness. Humanity might indeed exist if no one contributed to the happiness of others, provided he did not intentionally detract from it; but this harmony with humanity as an end in itself is only negative rather than positive if everyone does not also endeavor, so far as he can, to further the ends of others. For the ends of any person, who is an end in himself, must as far as possible also be my end, if that conception of an end in itself is to have its full effect on me. [34]

...

If we now look back upon all previous attempts which have ever been undertaken to discover the principle of morality, it is not to be wondered at that they all had to fail. Man was seen to be bound to laws by his duty, but it was not seen that he is subject only to his own, yet universal, legislation, and that he is only bound to act in accordance with his own will, which is, however, designed by nature to be a will giving universal laws. For if one thought of him as subject only to a law (whatever it may be), this necessarily implied some interest as a stimulus or compulsion to obedience because the law did not arise from his will. Rather, his will was constrained by something else according to a law to act in a certain way. By this strictly necessary consequence, however, all the labor of finding a supreme ground for duty was irrevocably lost, and one never arrived at duty but only at the necessity of action from a certain interest. This might be his own interest or that of another, but in either case the imperative always had to be conditional and could not at all serve as a moral command. This principle I will call the principle of *autonomy* of the will in contrast to all other principles which I accordingly count under *heteronomy*. [35]

The concept of each rational being as a being that must regard itself as giving universal law through all the maxims of its will, so that it may judge itself and its actions from this standpoint, leads to a very fruitful concept, namely, that of a *realm of ends*.

By "realm" I understand the systematic union of different rational beings through common laws. Because laws determine ends with regard to their universal validity, if we abstract from the personal difference of rational beings and thus from all content of their private ends, we can think of a whole of all ends in systematic connection, a whole of rational beings as ends in themselves as well as of the particular ends which each may set for himself. This is a realm of ends, which is possible on the aforesaid principles. For all rational beings stand under the law that each of them should treat himself and all others never merely as means but in every case also as an end in himself. Thus there arises a systematic union of rational beings through common objective laws. This is a realm which may be called a realm of ends (certainly only an ideal), because what these laws have in view is just the relation of these beings to each other as ends and means. [36]

...

Morality, therefore, consists in the relation of every action to that legislation through which alone a realm of ends is possible. This legislation, however, must be found in every rational being. It must be able to arise from his will, whose principle then is to take no action according to any maxim which would be inconsistent with its being a universal law and thus to act only so that the will through its maxims could regard itself at the same time as universally lawgiving. If now the maxims do not by their nature already necessarily conform to this objective principle of rational beings as universally lawgiving, the necessity of acting according to that principle is called practical constraint, i.e., duty. Duty pertains not to the sovereign in the realm of ends, but rather to each member, and to each in the same degree.

The practical necessity of acting according to this principle, i.e., duty, does not rest at all on feelings, impulses, and inclinations; it rests merely on the relation of rational beings to one another, in which the will of a rational being must always be regarded as legislative, for otherwise it could not be thought of as an end in itself. Reason, therefore, relates every maxim of the will as giving universal laws to every other will and also to every action toward itself; it does so not for the sake of any other practical motive or future advantage but rather from the

STOP How clear is Kant's reasoning in this case? Why does treating one's own humanity as an end in itself require developing one's talents? (See Discussion Question 5.)

Why does the fact (assuming that it is a fact) that another person is an end in himself mean that his ends must also be my ends? Also, how strong is this requirement? (See Discussion Question 6.)

This is a different way of putting the point that only a moral law that arises from the will of a rational being as such (and so is a principle of *autonomy*) can be unconditionally binding. Basing moral principles on anything else (principles of *heteronomy*—literally, being under the dominion of another) will fail to show why rational beings are obliged to follow them.

Here is one more, supposedly equivalent formulation of Kant's central moral idea, which leads to one more formulation of the categorical imperative.

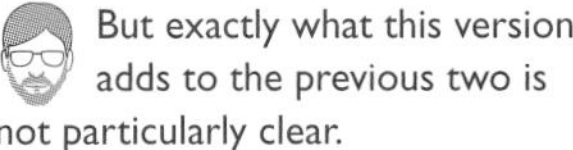

But exactly what this version adds to the previous two is not particularly clear.

idea of the dignity of a rational being who obeys no law except that which he himself also gives.

...

The three aforementioned ways of presenting the principle of morality are fundamentally only so many formulas of the very same law, and each of them unites the others in itself. There is, nevertheless, a difference in them, but the difference is more subjectively than objectively practical, for it is intended to bring an idea of reason closer to intuition (by means of a certain analogy) and thus nearer to feeling. All maxims have:

1. A form, which consists in universality; and in this respect the formula of the moral imperative requires that the maxims be chosen as though they should hold as universal laws of nature.
2. A material, i.e., an end; in this respect the formula says that the rational being, as by its nature an end and thus as an end in itself, must serve in every maxim as the condition restricting all merely relative and arbitrary ends.
3. A complete determination of all maxims by the formula that all maxims which stem from autonomous legislation ought to harmonize with a possible realm of ends as with a realm of nature.

There is a progression here like that through the categories of the unity of the form of the will (its universality), the plurality of material (the objects, i.e., the ends), and the all-comprehensiveness or totality of the system of ends. But it is better in moral evaluation to follow the rigorous method and to make the universal formula of the categorical imperative the basis: Act according to the maxim which can at the same time make itself a universal law. But if one wishes to gain a hearing for the moral law, it is very useful to bring one and the same action under the three stated principles and thus, so far as possible, to bring it nearer to intuition.

We can now end where we started, with the concept of an unconditionally good will. That will is absolutely good which cannot be bad, and thus it is a will whose maxim, when made a universal law, can never conflict with itself. Thus this principle is also its supreme law: Always act according to that maxim whose universality as a law you can at the same time will. This is the only condition under which a will can never come into conflict with itself, and such an imperative is categorical. Because the validity of the will, as a universal law for possible actions, has an analogy with the universal connection of the existence of things under universal laws, which is the formal element of nature in general, the categorical imperative can also be expressed as follows: Act according to maxims which can at the same time have themselves as universal laws of nature as their object. Such, then, is the formula of an absolutely good will.

...

Discussion Questions

1. Is Kant right that a person who helps other people out of duty alone is morally superior to someone who acts out of an inclination toward sympathy, generosity, benevolence, and so on? Can you think of any way in which he might defend this claim?
2. In applying the first version of the categorical imperative (see Annotation 19) to the suicide and promising examples, Kant claims that the maxims of the actions in question are *contradictory* when universalized. Is he right about this in either of these cases? The promising case is the more plausible of the two, but is there really a contradiction in supposing that everyone borrows money and promises to repay, but never does so? It is very unlikely that people would be gullible enough to continue to lend money under such circumstances, but is it really *impossible* that they could be that gullible?
3. In the second two cases (talent and charity), Kant claims that although universalizing the maxim can be done without contradiction, *willing* the universalized maxim leads to a conflict or contradiction within the will itself. His argument for this depends on his claim that there are other, conflicting things that a rational being necessarily wills. How plausible is his claim, in each of the two cases, that any rational being necessarily wills the other things in question? Can you imagine a rational being that does not do so?
4. Is a person who commits suicide in order to escape misfortune of some serious sort (ill health, financial catastrophe, loss of a loved one, etc.) using himself as merely a means to an end? What is the end and in what way is the person being used as a means to it? Can you see how someone might argue in some of these cases that suicide is

consistent with or even required by the idea that the person is an end in himself?

5. Why does the idea that people are ends in themselves require developing one's talents? Does Kant have any clear argument for this claim? What does he mean in this discussion by the "end of nature with respect to humanity"? Does this suggest using humanity as a means to some further end that is not the end of the person in question but of nature (and what does "nature" mean here)?

6. One objection to utilitarianism (see the selection from Williams) was that it required giving the projects and desires of other people the same consideration as one's own. Someone sympathetic to Kant's view might put this point by saying that utilitarianism views people merely as means to the achievement of the greatest overall total of happiness. But does Kant himself fall into the same problem by saying that "the ends of any person, who is an end in himself, must as far as possible also be my end"? How much of a limitation is expressed by "as far as possible"?

Onora O'Neill

Onora O'Neill (1941–) is a British philosopher (born in Northern Ireland) who has made important contributions to moral and political philosophy, bioethics, issues pertaining to international justice, and the philosophy of Kant. O'Neill taught for many years in the United States at Barnard College, before returning to Britain to teach at the University of Essex and Cambridge University. In 1999, she was made a life peer in the British House of Lords.

In the following selection, O'Neill explores the contrast between utilitarian and Kantian approaches to moral questions by exploring what each view would say about an issue that has only fairly recently become a focus of philosophical discussion: the issue of moral obligations pertaining to famine and famine relief. In the part of her discussion devoted to Kant, she focuses on what is often regarded as the most useful and suggestive formulation of the categorical imperative, namely the version that requires treating people always as ends in themselves and never merely as means.

The Moral Perplexities of Famine Relief

§1 Is Famine a New Moral Problem?

. . . when we wonder what we or others should do about global famine there don't seem to be familiar literary or religious traditions or philosophical discussions to which to turn. This is not because famine is new, but because there is today far more that we (or others) can do—or refrain from doing—that will affect the course of any famine there may be. Through history, millions have died of sheer starvation and of malnutrition or from illnesses that they might have survived with better nourishment. And whenever there were such deaths, nearby survivors may have realized that they might have helped prevent deaths and may either have done so or wondered whether they should. But nobody considered whether to prevent faraway deaths. Distance made an important difference, and with few exceptions there was nothing to be done for the victims of faraway famines.

In a global economy things are different. Corn from the North American prairies could be (and has been) distributed to the starving in Bangladesh or Somalia. Longer-term policies that affect economic development, fertility levels, and agricultural productivity may hasten or postpone far-off famines or make them more or less severe. Consequently, we now face moral questions about whether we ought to do some of these newly possible actions. Ought we (or others) to try to distribute food or aid or to introduce technical improvements? Who should foot the bill and suffer the other costs? To whom (if anyone) should aid be given and to whom should it be denied? How much hardship or sacrifice is demanded of those who have the means to help, if any?

...

From *Matters of Life and Death,* edited by T. Regan (New York: McGraw-Hill, 1980).

§6 Limiting the Discussion

I shall consider only two potentially morally acceptable theories. I have chosen these two because they are leading contenders for being morally acceptable theories. One of these theories is utilitarianism; the other is a (simplified) version of Kantian ethics. . . .

Utilitarian Approaches to Some Famine Problems

§12 Bentham and Utilitarianism

The first person to call himself a "utilitarian" was . . . Jeremy Bentham. . . . Bentham . . . wanted . . . to increase human happiness; and he hoped that legal and moral reform undertaken in a systematic and organized way would do so. . . . If faced with a decision, we should, according to Bentham's moral theory, ask ourselves which act is most likely to most increase the happiness of the person or persons affected. Legislators should ask which law would make most of those who have to live under it most happy. If we can discover the act or law that will do most for the happiness of the affected parties, then we have found the act that is right and required.

. . .

Bentham realized that his theory required decision makers to go through long calculations in order to work out which available action (or legislation) would produce the greatest happiness. He was undaunted. He thought we could list the available courses of action, and then work out how much happiness each would produce. . . .

. . . Bentham's calculus requires that we make calculations for which we *nearly always* lack the necessary information. We often are unsure how much happiness an act will produce, and how much unhappiness. In fact, we don't know how we are supposed to measure happiness. We often don't know who will be affected, to what extent, or for how long. . . .

§13 Mill and Utilitarianism

Bentham's successors, including some of his warmest admirers, were more skeptical about the felicific calculus. (1) Even though they thought utilitarian moral theory right in principle, they doubted that moral decisions could be made a matter of calculation. . . .

(1) "The felicific calculus" is O'Neill's label for the calculation of the overall total of pleasure and happiness (including negative values for pain and unhappiness) that results from various alternative actions. ("Felicity" just means happiness.)

John Stuart Mill . . . doubted that it was possible to make calculations of any precision about the amount of pleasure to be expected from each possible course of action. Pleasures, he thought, may vary in quality as well as in amount. And if some pleasures are of higher quality than others, then it is impossible to add them together. . . . To add things together they must be measured in the same units, or in units that (like inches and centimeters) can be reduced to one another. But on Mill's view, some pleasures are *irreducibly* superior to others. . . .

. . . There are still some [utilitarians] (mostly economists and decision theorists) who hope for Benthamite precision in handling problems. But there are more who [do] not claim that precise calculations of pleasure can be made to guide every decision, but only that we can bring informed judgment to bear on the question of which action is most likely to enhance human happiness, and that if we can identify such an action with reasonable certainty, we ought to embark on it, while if we can identify actions that seem likely to produce misery, we should avoid them. . . .

§14 Some Utilitarian Arguments About Famine

I shall now take the simplified utilitarian moral theory outlined in the last section and show how it can be and has been used to draw diametrically opposed conclusions about what affluent persons (ourselves, for example) ought to do about famines that they could help to relieve. I will try to use this embarrassing result as the basis for an assessment of utilitarianism. . . .

To reach the opposing conclusions, I shall draw on the arguments of two well known recent articles about moral problems raised by the prospect of famine. The first of these articles is Garrett Hardin's "Lifeboat Ethics: The Case Against Helping the Poor," which argues that the affluent ought not to relieve famine. The second is Peter Singer's "Famine, Affluence and Morality," which argues that the affluent ought to relieve famine.*

. . .

*G. Hardin, "Lifeboat Ethics: The Case Against Helping the Poor;" P. Singer, "Famine, Affluence and Morality," both are reprinted in W. Aiken and H. La Follette, *World Hunger and Moral Obligation,* Englewood Cliffs, N.J., Prentice-Hall, 1977. [Singer's article is reprinted in this book, at pp. 348–352.]

§15 A Utilitarian Argues Against Relieving Famine

Hardin's argument can be summarized as follows. The citizens of affluent countries are like passengers in a lifeboat around which other, desperate, shipwrecked persons are swimming. The people in the lifeboat can help some of those in the water. But if the citizens of affluent countries help some of the starving, this will, unlike many lifeboat rescues, have bad effects. To begin with, according to Hardin, the affluent countries will then have less of a safety margin, like an overladen lifeboat. This alone might be outweighed by the added happiness of those who have been rescued. But the longer-run effects are bad for everyone. The rescued will assume that they are secure, will multiply their numbers and so make future rescues impossible. It is better, from a utilitarian point of view, to lose some lives now than to lose more lives later. So no rescue attempt should be made.

Hardin's (and others') use of the lifeboat metaphor has been widely criticized. Persons in lifeboats have (often) some title to their seats. Rescue operations in lifeboats endanger the rescuers. There are few interests that those inside a boat share with the drowning. By contrast, it is not clear that affluent persons and nations are entitled to all they have. Some of it may have been acquired by exploiting poorer nations or persons; even if it has been acquired by standard market procedures, the terms of trade are often (and perhaps unfairly) weighted in favor of the powerful. Further, it is not clear that attempts at famine relief present any serious danger to the affluent. . . . Finally, the interests of the rich and poor are often congruent, while those of the rescued and the drowning are diametrically opposed. Everybody has an interest in the preservation of peace and in the prevention of ecocatastrophes. ❷ But . . . Hardin's main point can be stated without depending on the metaphor.

His main claim is that famine relief *encourages* population growth to a level that cannot be indefinitely sustained. If we pool our resources with the poor of this world, soon nobody will have a safety margin and even local and temporary crop failures will have a drastic effect. If we pooled resources, we should all, aptly enough, be in the same boat; and the boat would not be stormworthy.

Hardin's view is that once population has been increased by the added children of those who would otherwise not have survived to have children at all, the total amount of suffering will be larger than the suffering from unrelieved famine of a smaller number of people. He writes:

> If poor countries received no food from outside, the rate of their population growth would be periodically checked by crop failures and famines. But if they can always draw on a world food bank in time of need, their population can continue to grow unchecked, and so will their "need" for aid. In the short run a world food bank may diminish that need, but in the long run it actually increases the need without limit.*

Hardin's view of famine is harsh, but reasoned. He thinks that feeding the hungry is merely likely to lead to population growth and greater suffering in the future. Feeding the hungry preserves lives and happiness now, but costs great loss of life and misery in the future. The prosperous not merely may but ought, if they are utilitarians, to leave the starving to themselves, to die or to survive as best they may. ❸

Singer, however, thinks that the prosperous have an obligation to try to feed the hungry. He starts from the assumption that

> if it is in our power to prevent something bad from happening, without thereby sacrificing anything of comparable moral importance, we ought, morally, to do it.† ❹

He then points out that contributing to famine relief, even contributing a large proportion of a prosperous income, say 50 percent, does not sacrifice anything of comparable importance. But it does help prevent the misery and loss of life that famines produce. So, he concludes, the prosperous ought to help feed the hungry and ought to do so up to that point at which they have indeed reduced their own standard of living so far that something of comparable moral importance would be sacrificed by further giving.

This conclusion too can be reached by a quite explicitly utilitarian route. For what makes famine bad, as Singer and all utilitarians agree, is that it causes acute human suffering; and what

STOP Think carefully about each of these alleged disanalogies between the lifeboat example and the famine case. How much do they undermine Hardin's argument?

STOP How plausible is it that the results in terms of pleasure and happiness minus pain and suffering will be greater if people are allowed to starve than for any available alternative? Are there more complicated alternatives that Hardin should consider? (See Discussion Question 1.)

As noted above in the Singer selection, this principle captures only part of the full utilitarian view: the obligation to avoid pain and suffering wherever the cost is less than the gain. Nothing is said about the obligation to maximize pleasure and happiness, not just avoid pain and suffering.

*G. Hardin, in W. Aiken and H. La Follette, *op. cit.*, p. 17.

†P. Singer, in W. Aiken and H. La Follette, *op. cit.*, p. 24 (p. 349 in this book).

makes the sacrifices of the prosperous less bad is that they cause much less acute human suffering. (Compare what it would be like to have no car with what it would be like to go without half the food you now eat.) So if we think that we ought to do acts that will prevent or reduce suffering, or still better, produce happiness, then it seems that there is little doubt that we ought to relieve famine, even if it costs us a fair amount of minor unhappiness to do so. 5

5 This seems to understate rather seriously what follows from the principle quoted: if we must help until the cost of helping reaches the point at which it would be as bad as the suffering prevented (and thus of "comparable moral importance"), much more than "minor unhappiness" will be required. The result that O'Neill suggests would more plausibly follow from the other, weaker principle that Singer offers. (See Annotation 2 to the Singer selection.)

§17 Why Do Hardin and Singer Reach Incompatible Conclusions?

Reading Hardin and Singer presents any utilitarian . . . with a dilemma. For it seems that their starting points are not very different, but that they have come to incompatible conclusions. I believe this is due to their divergent views about the effects of attempts at famine relief and not to a difference over moral theory.

Hardin pays attention to the long-term effects of uncontrolled population growth. He is a pessimistic neo-Malthusian who thinks that there is no method to curtail population growth except by letting famines run their "natural" course. With luck, this experience may educate the survivors of "irresponsible" populations so that they then do curb the size of their families; but only the reality of famine can teach this lesson. . . .

Singer is an optimistic neo-Malthusian who tends to underestimate the long-range effects of saving persons from famine without being able to prevent population growth that might later outstrip available resources. . . . Unless we can resolve disputes about the facts and future of population growth, we cannot resolve the dispute between Singer and Hardin.

§18 The Uncertainty of Consequences

. . . It is one of the strengths of the utilitarian moral thought that it can be so generally applied; its scope is large. The actions of individuals, the policies of nations, and the activities of groups (ranging from multinational corporations to famine-relief charities to government departments) all affect human happiness. So the acts of all these agents and agencies can be morally assessed by the same arguments. But this enormous scope of utilitarian moral theory is no help unless we can know fairly precisely what effects proposed acts would have. A conscientious utilitarian, even one who does not credit Benthamite calculations, must try to work out the effects of his or her actions; and as we have seen in the case of Hardin and Singer, it is hard to work these out at all, let alone with precision, when we deliberate about famine relief.

This imprecision is reflected in the great diversity of (often incompatible) policies for which utilitarian arguments are offered. At the most general level, passionate utilitarian arguments have been made *both* for centralized economic planning *and* for reliance on free markets. At a less global level, utilitarians repeatedly disagree about policies and actions.

Consider, for example, the following policy for the distribution of famine relief that some utilitarians advocate. William and Paul Paddock in *Famine—1975!* suggest that famine relief should be allocated on a *triage* principle.* When resources are limited they should be given to those who can benefit most. The term 'triage' is taken from military medicine. In medical contexts it means that the worst injured should be left to die and the walking wounded left to hobble. All care should go to the third, in-between group. In the case of famine, this means that aid should be concentrated on those countries that have the best chance of survival if aided but won't survive otherwise. Triage is a policy that seeks to maximize the number of survivors. Lives are to be sacrificed, but only for the sake of preserving more lives by concentrating resources where they will do the most good.

Utilitarians would probably endorse the triage principle *if* they thought all lives tended on average to be equally happy. The preservation of life is necessary for the existence of happy lives, so that if other things were equal (which they seldom are) preserving as many lives as possible would produce the greatest total amount of happiness. Only if some of the lives to be preserved were likely to be on balance painful would utilitarians advocate that they not be preserved. . . . It does not bother utilitarians that triaging sacrifices some lives for the sake of

*W. and P. Paddock, *Famine—1975!*, Boston, Little, Brown, 1967.

others. For utilitarians, biological life is no end in itself, but a means to the enjoyment of living. And where a greater total of happiness or enjoyment would be achieved by triaging populations or countries, it is not merely permissible but a duty to adopt this policy. Happiness should be maximized even if doing so costs some lives.

However, it is far from clear that triaging would in fact maximize happiness. First, lives are *not* all equally happy, and if not all lives can be preserved, utilitarians would prefer policies that ensure that those whose prospects are happiest, rather than those whose survival is easiest to secure, are helped. Second, it is difficult to see how triaging can legitimately be applied beyond the medical context. For there are no clear standards to determine who is the "best risk." Any nation or region might be made more likely to survive if given the right sort of help. Some nations or regions seem to need more help, but since we lack a scientific account of the methods for achieving economic development (though theories are legion), we don't really know whom it will be hardest to save in the long run. In this century some seemingly desperate countries have achieved steady economic growth, and others that seemed as well placed have not. So it is not obvious whom the triagers should reject as hopeless cases, whom they should dismiss as walking wounded, and whom they should help. Thus it is unclear whether utilitarians would on reflection endorse a triaging policy. 6

Alternatively, consider some of the following dilemmas that individual utilitarians might meet while thinking about famine. In all of these examples, suppose that A is a moderately prosperous utilitarian who sincerely wants to use his extra money to help relieve famine and save lives, which he reasonably judges would greatly reduce human misery. A might wonder whether to try to send money to a poor family in a poor country. But how is he to be sure that they get the money, and that it doesn't fall into the hands of some nonneedy local official, who uses it to worsen the situation of others, perhaps by buying imported goods, leaving those who formerly sold to him without a customer? Might not the result of A's generosity also worsen the position of those needy families whom he cannot benefit, who find that the going price of goods has risen beyond their means because benefited families can afford to pay more and have driven up the price? Or suppose A thinks that the way to benefit the poor is to purchase the products of needy nations and areas. Might not this encourage production for fickle export markets, retard the development of local self-sufficiency, and make people more vulnerable in hard years? If A buys Brazilian coffee despite its high price, can he be sure whom he is benefiting? Might not he be encouraging the development of a one-crop economy with all its potential for disaster? Or suppose that in order to encourage development in the Arab world, A advocates (and, as a consumer, follows) policies that are heavily dependent on importing OPEC oil. May not this policy fuel nothing more productive of human happiness and life than the Middle East arms race? Or suppose A hopes to assist, through work in a multinational corporation, the introduction of more modern industrial processes in some under-developed economy. How can he be sure that this will not lead to a developed enclave within a traditional economy that, on the whole, causes friction for many, unemployment for some, and gain for a few who were not in the first place the most needy? Or suppose that A is an economic planner in a socialist country. Hoping to improve welfare by raising per capita meat consumption, he institutes heavy grain purchases (for animal fodder) on the world market, which prevent increased cereal production from benefiting the hungrier peoples and drive up world cereal prices. Once more, the net effect of an act intended to increase happiness may be to increase rather than reduce human misery. The conundrums can be multiplied again and again. The point is that if we are to try to work out the consequences of our actions as utilitarian theory demands we should, we shall repeatedly find ourselves confronted with impossible calculations. Utilitarianism offers us spurious precision in moral argument. 7

The reasons for these difficulties lie deep in the structure of utilitarian theory and are not likely to be remedied by further research. For utilitarians do not say that one should look *just* at the fairly local effects of one's own act. . . .

The very comprehensive and systematic structure that makes utilitarian moral theory attractive to many people becomes on reflection one of its nightmares. We may often be fairly

6

Think carefully about this question. Is there any real hope, in the face of the problems that O'Neill points out, that a utilitarian can reach a reasonably clear and justified decision about whether some specific version of the moral policy of triaging is the right solution to the famine problem?

7

This is one fundamental objection to utilitarianism in this area and many others: that it is simply impossible to determine what the right action is from a utilitarian standpoint or even to come to a reasonable estimate or approximation.

clear about the short-term effect on nearby people of what we propose to do. But we are seldom clear about the total effect or tendency of acts or policies in an economically interdependent world where we might affect the lives of persons thousands of miles or many generations away. We face in our own time decisions about energy policy that will deeply affect future lives. If we leave a world of nuclear radiation or terrorism, or of fossil-fuel famine, or of health- and crop-destroying pollution, we shall make future persons more miserable—or less happy—than they might have been had we made different decisions. Yet, which of us can be sure (including the disputing experts) which decision is likely to have the happiest results? . . . Where there is no limit to the number of consequences, nearby or remote, that we ought to consider, conclusions seem to evaporate, not to crystallize. Utilitarians may start out wanting to be realists who soberly calculate the outcomes and the odds; but there seems to be no natural stopping point before they find themselves trying to be futurologists who seek to uncover the impact of their actions, or that of their institutions, in a vast and complex causal web that extends indefinitely into the future. 8

8

Part of the problem is the need to consider consequences indefinitely into the future. This problem cannot be adequately dealt with by saying—as Bentham seems to suggest—that consequences in the distant future should be "discounted": weighted less heavily than temporally closer ones. Even if they count for less, distant future consequences may well be more important to the correct overall result simply because there are so many of them.

A serious utilitarian faces a morally strenuous life. Every decision is a moral decision, since any act affects human happiness or prevents another act that might affect human happiness. A utilitarian can never say: "I've done my duty." However great one's contribution has been, it is likely that there are further miseries one could in part reduce without causing oneself or others comparable misery. As each misery is vanquished there will be another waiting for one's ministrations. 9 . . .

9

From a utilitarian standpoint, there are moral obligations pertaining to *everything* we do, with actions that are acceptable but not obligatory occurring only in the rare case where several actions are exactly tied in their utilitarian value. And the point is not just that this is demanding, but that it is intuitively implausible that the demands of morality are really that comprehensive and inflexible.

Kantian Approaches to Some Famine Problems

§22 A Simplified Account of Kant's Ethics

Kant's moral theory has acquired the reputation of being forbiddingly difficult to understand and, once understood, excessively demanding in its requirements. I don't believe that this reputation has been wholly earned, and I am going to try to undermine it. In §§23–26 I shall try to reduce some of the difficulties, and in §§27–30 I shall try to show the implications of a Kantian moral theory for action toward those who do or may suffer famine. Finally, I shall compare Kantian and utilitarian approaches and assess their strengths and weaknesses.

...

Kant calls his Supreme Principle the *Categorical Imperative;* its various versions also have sonorous names. One is called the Formula of Universal Law; another is the Formula of the Kingdom of Ends. The one on which I shall concentrate is known as the *Formula of the End in Itself*. . . .

§23 The Formula of the End in Itself

Kant states the Formula of the End in Itself as follows:

> Act in such a way that you always treat humanity, whether in your own person or in the person of any other, never simply as a means but always at the same time as an end.*

To understand this we need to know what it is to treat a person as a means or as an end. According to Kant, each of our acts reflects one or more *maxims*. The maxim of the act is the principle on which one sees oneself as acting. A maxim expresses a person's policy, or if he or she has no settled policy, the principle underlying the particular intention or decision on which he or she acts. Thus, a person who decides "This year I'll give 10 percent of my income to famine relief" has as a maxim the principle of tithing his or her income for famine relief. In practice, the difference between intentions and maxims is of little importance, for given any intention, we can formulate the corresponding maxim by deleting references to particular times, places, and persons. In what follows I shall take the terms 'maxim' and 'intention' as equivalent.

Whenever we act intentionally, we have at least one maxim and can, if we reflect, state what it is. . . .

When we want to work out whether an act we propose to do is right or wrong, according to Kant, we should look at our maxims and not at

*I. Kant, *Groundwork of the Metaphysic of Morals,* tr. H. H. Paton, New York, Harper Torchbooks, 1964, p. 96 [p. 360 in this book, though the translation is slightly different].

how much misery or happiness the act is likely to produce, and whether it does better at increasing happiness than other available acts. We just have to check that the act we have in mind will not use anyone as a mere means, and, if possible, that it will treat other persons as ends in themselves.

§24 Using Persons as Mere Means

To use someone as a *mere means* is to involve them in a scheme of action *to which they could not in principle consent.* [10] Kant does not say that there is anything wrong about using someone as a means. Evidently we have to do so in any cooperative scheme of action. If I cash a check I use the teller as a means, without whom I could not lay my hands on the cash; the teller in turn uses me as a means to earn his or her living. But in this case, each party consents to her or his part in the transaction. Kant would say that though they use one another as means, they do not use one another as *mere* means. . . .

But there are other situations where one person uses another in a way to which the other could not in principle consent. For example, one person may make a promise to another with every intention of breaking it. If the promise is accepted, then the person to whom it was given must be ignorant of what the promisor's intention (maxim) really is. If one knew that the promisor did not intend to do what he or she was promising, one would, after all, not accept or rely on the promise. It would be as though there had been no promise made. Successful false promising depends on deceiving the person to whom the promise is made about what one's real maxim is. And since the person who is deceived doesn't know that real maxim, he or she can't in principle consent to his or her part in the proposed scheme of action. The person who is deceived is, as it were, a prop or a tool—a mere means—in the false promisor's scheme. A person who promises falsely treats the acceptor of the promise as a prop or a thing and not as a person. In Kant's view, it is this that makes false promising wrong.

One standard way of using others as mere means is by deceiving them. By getting someone involved in a business scheme or a criminal activity on false pretenses, or by giving a misleading account of what one is about, or by making a false promise or a fraudulent contract, one involves another in something to which he or she in principle cannot consent, since the scheme requires that he or she doesn't know what is going on. [11] Another standard way of using others as mere means is by coercing them. If a rich or powerful person threatens a debtor with bankruptcy unless he or she joins in some scheme, then the creditor's intention is to coerce; and the debtor, if coerced, cannot consent to his or her part in the creditor's scheme. To make the example more specific: If a moneylender in an Indian village threatens not to renew a vital loan unless he is given the debtor's land, then he uses the debtor as a mere means. He coerces the debtor, who cannot truly consent to this "offer he can't refuse." [12] . . .

In Kant's view, acts that are done on maxims that require deception or coercion of others, and so cannot have the consent of those others (for consent precludes both deception and coercion), are wrong. When we act on such maxims, we treat others as mere means, as things rather than as ends in themselves. If we act on such maxims, our acts are not only wrong but unjust: such acts wrong the particular others who are deceived or coerced.

§25 Treating Persons as Ends in Themselves

Duties of justice are, in Kant's view (as in many others'), the most important of our duties. . . . But there are also cases where, though we do not use others as mere means, still we fail to use them as ends in themselves in the fullest possible way. To treat someone as an end in him or herself requires in the first place that one not use him or her as mere means, that one respect each as a rational person with his or her own maxims. But beyond that, one may also seek to foster others' plans and maxims by sharing some of their ends. To act beneficently is to seek others' happiness, therefore to intend to achieve some of the things that those others aim at with their maxims. If I want to make others happy, I will adopt maxims that not merely do not manipulate them but that foster some of their plans and activities. Beneficent acts try to achieve what others want. However, we cannot seek everything that others want; their wants are too numerous and diverse, and, of course,

This is a helpful suggestion as to what it is to treat a person as a "mere means," one that is supported by Kant's own discussion. Does it capture all of the relevant cases? Think here of Kant's own examples, though some of those are, as we have seen, debatable in themselves. (And see Discussion Question 3.)

So any action that depends essentially on deceiving another person will be one to which the person in question "could not in principle consent." Is it plausible that all actions that have this feature are morally objectionable? (See Discussion Question 4.)

Does any sort of pressure on another person's choice count as *coercion*? Presumably not, but then how much is required? Is there a reasonably clear answer here? (See Discussion Question 5.)

To what extent do we have to seek things that others seek or foster their plans and activities in order to satisfy this part of Kant's requirement? How much is required to be "reasonably beneficent," as O'Neill says further on? Does Kant's view yield any very clear answer to this question?

The issue here is whether all sorts of beneficence are morally on a par, as long as the overall total is great enough—or whether not treating others as mere means requires helping or at least trying to help those in greater need.

Think carefully about each of these examples. Again there is a difficult issue of just when coercion (or an unacceptable level of coercion) occurs. Is making people pay for the food that they need a form of coercion? Why or why not?

Not to attempt to fulfill an obligation resulting from an explicit agreement of some sort would be a fairly clear case of using the other person as a mere means. Is it clear how this extends to other sorts of duties one may be thought to have to particular people, such as duties to one's children? If I am unwilling to endure sacrifice in order to feed my children in a time of famine, have I thereby used them as a mere means, and if so, how?

sometimes incompatible. It follows that beneficence has to be selective. [13]

There is then quite a sharp distinction between the requirements of justice and of beneficence in Kantian ethics. Justice requires that we act on *no* maxims that use others as mere means. Beneficence requires that we act on *some* maxims that foster others' ends, though it is a matter for judgment and discretion which of their ends we foster. Some [ends] no doubt ought not to be fostered because it would be unjust to do so. . . . Kantians will claim that they have done nothing wrong if none of their acts is unjust, and that their duty is complete if in addition their life plans have in the circumstances been reasonably beneficent.

. . . Kant's theory has less scope than utilitarianism. Kantians do not claim to discover whether acts whose maxims they don't know fully are just. They may be reluctant to judge others' acts or policies that cannot be regarded as the maxim of any person or institution. They cannot rank acts in order of merit. Yet, the theory offers more precision than utilitarianism when data are scarce. One can usually tell whether one's act would use others as mere means, even when its impact on human happiness is thoroughly obscure.

§26 Kantian Deliberations on Famine Problems

The theory I have just sketched may seem to have little to say about famine problems. For it is a theory that forbids us to use others as mere means but does not require us to direct our benevolence first to those who suffer most. A conscientious Kantian, it seems, has only to avoid being unjust to those who suffer famine and can then be beneficent to those nearer home. He or she would not be obliged to help the starving, even if no others were equally distressed. [14]

...

§27 Kantian Duties of Justice in Times of Famine

In famine situations, Kantian moral theory requires unambiguously that we do no injustice. We should not act on any maxim that uses another as mere means, so we should neither deceive nor coerce others. Such a requirement can become quite exacting when the means of life are scarce, when persons can more easily be coerced, and when the advantage of gaining more than what is justly due to one is great. I shall give a list of acts that on Kantian principles it would be unjust to do, but that one might be strongly tempted to do in famine conditions.

I will begin with a list of acts that one might be tempted to do as a member of a famine-stricken population. First, where there is a rationing scheme, one ought not to cheat and seek to get more than one's share—any scheme of cheating will use someone as mere means. Nor may one take advantage of others' desperation to profiteer or divert goods onto the black market or to accumulate a fortune out of others' misfortunes. Transactions that are outwardly sales and purchases can be coercive when one party is desperate. All the forms of corruption that deceive or put pressure on others are also wrong: hoarding unallocated food, diverting relief supplies for private use, corruptly using one's influence to others' disadvantage. Such requirements are far from trivial and frequently violated in hard times. In severe famines, refraining from coercing and deceiving may risk one's own life and require the greatest courage. [15]

Second, justice requires that in famine situations one still try to fulfill one's duties to particular others. For example, even in times of famine, a person has duties to try to provide for dependents. These duties may, tragically, be unfulfillable. [16] If they are, Kantian ethical theory would not judge wrong the acts of a person who had done her or his best. There have no doubt been times in human history where there was nothing to be done except abandon the weak and old or . . . leave children to fend for themselves as best they might. But providing the supporter of dependents acts on maxims of attempting to meet their claims, he or she uses no others as mere means to his or her own survival and is not unjust. A conscientious attempt to meet the particular obligations one has undertaken may also require of one many further maxims of self-restraint and of endeavor—for example, it may require a conscientious attempt to avoid having (further) children; it may require contributing one's time and effort to programs of economic development. Where there is no other means to fulfill particular obligations, Kantian principles may require a generation of sacrifice. They will not, however, require one to seek to maximize the happiness of later generations but only to establish the modest security and prosperity needed for meeting present obligations.

The obligations of those who live with or near famine are undoubtedly stringent and exacting; for those who live further off it is rather harder to see what a Kantian moral theory demands. Might it not, for example, be permissible to do nothing at all about those suffering famine? Might one not ensure that one does nothing unjust to the victims of famine by adopting no maxims whatsoever that mention them? To do so would, at the least, require one to refrain from certain deceptive and coercive practices frequently employed during the European exploration and economic penetration of the now under-developed world and still not unknown. For example, it would be unjust to "purchase" valuable lands and resources from persons who don't understand commercial transactions or exclusive property rights or mineral rights, so do not understand that their acceptance of trinkets destroys their traditional economic pattern and way of life. . . .

Few persons in the developed world today find themselves faced with the possibility of adopting on a grand scale maxims of deceiving or coercing persons living in poverty. But at least some people find that their jobs require them to make decisions about investment and aid policies that enormously affect the lives of those nearest to famine. What does a commitment to Kantian moral theory demand of such persons?

It has become common in writings in ethics and social policy to distinguish between one's *personal responsibilities* and one's *role responsibilities.* So a person may say, "As an individual I sympathize, but in my official capacity I can do nothing"; or we may excuse persons' acts of coercion because they are acting in some particular capacity—e.g., as a soldier or a jailer. On the other hand, this distinction isn't made or accepted by everyone. At the Nuremberg trials of war criminals, the defense "I was only doing my job" was disallowed, at least for those whose command position meant that they had some discretion in what they did. Kantians generally would play down any distinction between a person's own responsibilities and his or her role responsibilities. . . . When we take on positions, we *add* to our responsibilities those that the job requires; but we do not lose those that are already required of us. Our social role or job gives us, on Kant's view, no license to use others as mere means; even business executives and aid officials and social revolutionaries will act unjustly, so wrongly, if they deceive or coerce—however benevolent their motives.

If persons are responsible for all their acts, it follows that it would be unjust for aid officials to coerce persons into accepting sterilization, wrong for them to use coercive power to achieve political advantages (such as military bases) or commercial advantages (such as trade agreements that will harm the other country). It would be wrong for the executives of large corporations to extort too high a price for continued operation employment and normal trading. Where a less-developed country is pushed to exempt a multinational corporation from tax laws, or to construct out of its meager tax revenues the infrastructure of roads, harbors, or airports (not to mention executive mansions) that the corporation—but perhaps not the country—needs, then one suspects that some coercion has been involved.

The problem with such judgments—and it is an immense problem—is that it is hard to identify coercion and deception in complicated institutional settings. It is not hard to understand what is coercive about one person threatening another with serious injury if he won't comply with the first person's suggestion. But it is not at all easy to tell where the outward forms of political and commercial negotiation—which often involve an element of threat—have become coercive. I can't here explore this fascinating question. But I think it is at least fairly clear that the preservation of the outward forms of negotiation, bargaining, and voluntary consent do *not* demonstrate that there is no coercion, especially when one party is vastly more powerful or the other in dire need. Just as our judiciary has a long tradition of voiding contracts and agreements on grounds of duress or incompetence of one of the parties, so one can imagine a tribunal of an analogous sort rejecting at least some treaties and agreements as coercive, despite the fact that they were negotiated between "sovereign" powers or their representatives. In particular, where such agreements were negotiated with some of the cruder deceptions and coercion of the early days of European

STOP Here is an argument that we are, from a Kantian standpoint, obligated to try to help those whose need is greater, that their claim on our beneficence is greater. How compelling is it (from a Kantian standpoint)?

economic expansion or the subtler coercions and deceptions of contemporary superpowers, it seems doubtful that the justice of the agreement could be sustained.

Justice, of course, is not everything, even for Kantians. But its demands are ones that they can reasonably strive to fulfill. They may have some uncertain moments—for example, does advocating cheap raw materials mean advocating an international trade system in which the less developed will continue to suffer the pressures of the developed world—or is it a benevolent policy that will maximize world trade and benefit all parties, while doing no one an injustice? But for Kantians, the important moral choices are above all those in which one acts directly, not those in which one decides which patterns of actions to encourage in others or in those institutions that one can influence. And such moral decisions include decisions about the benevolent acts that one will or will not do.

§28 Kantian Duties of Beneficence in Times of Famine

The grounds of duties of beneficence are that such acts not merely don't use others as mere means but are acts that develop or promote others' ends and that, in particular, foster others' capacities to pursue ends, to be autonomous beings.

Clearly there are many opportunities for beneficence. But one area in which the *primary* task of developing others' capacity to pursue their own ends is particularly needed is in the parts of the world where extreme poverty and hunger leave people unable to pursue *any* of their other ends. Beneficence directed at putting people in a position to pursue whatever ends they may have has, for Kant, a stronger claim on us than beneficence directed at sharing ends with those who are already in a position to pursue varieties of ends. It would be nice if I bought a tennis racquet to play with my friend who is tennis mad and never has enough partners; but it is more important to make people able to plan their own lives to a minimal extent. It is nice to walk a second mile with someone who requests one's company; better to share a cloak with someone who may otherwise be too cold to make any journey. Though these suggestions are not a detailed set of instructions for the allocation of beneficence by Kantians, they show that relief of famine must stand very high among duties of beneficence. 17

§29 The Limits of Kantian Ethics: Intentions and Results

Kantian ethics differs from utilitarian ethics both in its scope and in the precision with which it guides action. Every action, whether of a person or of an agency, can be assessed by utilitarian methods, provided only that information is available about all the consequences of the act. The theory has unlimited scope, but, owing to lack of data, often lacks precision. Kantian ethics has a more restricted scope. Since it assesses actions by looking at the maxims of agents, it can only assess intentional acts. This means that it is most at home in assessing individuals' acts; but it can be extended to assess acts of agencies that (like corporations and governments and student unions) have decision-making procedures. It can do nothing to assess patterns of action that reflect no intention or policy, hence it cannot assess the acts of groups lacking decision-making procedures, such as the student movement, the women's movement, or the consumer movement.

It may seem a great limitation of Kantian ethics that it concentrates on intentions to the neglect of results. It might seem that all conscientious Kantians have to do is to make sure that they never intend to use others as mere means, and that they sometimes intend to foster others' ends. And, as we all know, good intentions sometimes lead to bad results, and correspondingly, bad intentions sometimes do no harm, or even produce good. If Hardin is right, the good intentions of those who feed the starving lead to dreadful results in the long run. If some traditional arguments in favor of capitalism are right, the greed and selfishness of the profit motive have produced unparalleled prosperity for many.

But such discrepancies between intentions and results are the exception and not the rule. For we cannot just *claim* that our intentions are good and do what we will. Our intentions reflect what we expect the immediate results of our action to be. Nobody credits the "intentions" of a couple who practice neither celibacy nor contraception but still insist "we never meant to have (more) children." Conception is likely (and known to be likely) in such cases. Where people's expressed intentions ignore the normal and predictable results of what they do, we infer that (if they are not amazingly ignorant) their words do not express their true intentions. The Formula of the End in Itself applies to the intentions on which one acts—not to some prettified version that one may avow. Provided this intention—the agent's real intention—uses no other as mere means, he or she does nothing unjust. If some of his or her intentions foster others' ends, then he or she is sometimes beneficent. It is therefore possible for people to test their proposals by Kantian arguments even when they lack the comprehensive causal knowledge that utilitarianism requires. Conscientious Kantians can work out whether they will be doing wrong by some act even though they know that their foresight is limited and that they may cause some harm or fail to cause some benefit. But they will not cause harms that they can foresee without this being reflected in their intentions.

Respect for Life: A Comparison of Kantian and Utilitarian Views

§30 Utilitarianism and Respect for Life

From the differing implications that Kantian and utilitarian moral theories have for our actions towards those who do or may suffer famine, we can discover two sharply contrasting views of the value of human life. Utilitarians value happiness and the absence or reduction of misery. As a utilitarian one ought (if conscientious) to devote one's life to achieving the best possible balance of happiness over misery. If one's life plan remains in doubt, this will be because the means to this end are often unclear. But whenever the causal tendency of acts is clear, utilitarians will be able to discern the acts they should successively do in order to improve the world's balance of happiness over unhappiness.

This task is not one for the faint-hearted. First, it is dauntingly long, indeed interminable. Second, it may at times require the sacrifice of happiness, and even of lives, for the sake of a greater happiness. Such sacrifice may be morally required not only when the person whose happiness or even whose life is at stake volunteers to make the sacrifice. It may be necessary to sacrifice some lives for the sake of others. As our control over the means of ending and preserving human life has increased, analogous dilemmas have arisen in many areas for utilitarians. Should life be preserved at the cost of pain when modern medicine makes this possible? Should life be preserved without hope of consciousness? Should triage policies, because they may maximize the number of survivors, be used to determine who should be left to starve? Should population growth be fostered wherever it will increase the total of human happiness—or on some views so long as average happiness is not reduced? All these questions can be fitted into utilitarian frameworks and answered *if* we have the relevant information. And sometimes the answer will be that human happiness demands the sacrifice of lives, including the sacrifice of unwilling lives. Further, for most utilitarians, it makes no difference if the unwilling sacrifices involve acts of injustice to those whose lives are to be lost. It might, for example, prove necessary for maximal happiness that some persons have their allotted rations, or their hard-earned income, diverted for others' benefit. Or it might turn out that some generations must sacrifice comforts or liberties and even lives to rear "the fabric of felicity" for their successors. Utilitarians do not deny these possibilities, though the imprecision of our knowledge of consequences often blurs the implications of the theory. If we peer through the blur, we see that the utilitarian view is that lives may indeed be sacrificed for the sake of a greater good even when the persons are not willing. There is nothing wrong with using another as a mere means provided that the end for which the person is so used is a happier result than could have been achieved any other way, taking into account the misery the means have caused. In utilitarian thought, persons are not ends in themselves. Their special moral status derives from their being means to the production of happiness. Human life has therefore a high though derivative value, and one life may be taken for the sake of greater happiness in other lives, or for ending of misery in that life. Nor is there any deep difference between ending a life for the sake of others' happiness by not helping (e.g., by triaging) and doing so by harming. Because the distinction between justice and beneficence is not sharply made within utilitarianism, it is not possible to say that triaging is a matter of not benefiting, while other interventions are a matter of injustice.

Utilitarian moral theory has then a rather paradoxical view of the value of human life.

Living, conscious humans are (along with other sentient beings) necessary for the existence of everything utilitarians value. But it is not their being alive but the state of their consciousness that is of value. Hence, the best results may require certain lives to be lost—by whatever means—for the sake of the total happiness and absence of misery that can be produced.

§31 Kant and Respect for Persons

Kantians reach different conclusions about human life. Human life is valuable because humans (and conceivably other beings, e.g., angels or apes) are the bearers of rational life. Humans are able to choose and to plan. This capacity and its exercise are of such value that they ought not to be sacrificed for anything of lesser value. Therefore, no one rational or autonomous creature should be treated as mere means for the enjoyment or even the happiness of another. We may in Kant's view justifiably—even nobly—risk or sacrifice our lives for others. For in doing so we follow our own maxim and nobody uses us as mere means. But no others may use either our lives or our bodies for a scheme that they have either coerced or deceived us into joining. For in doing so they would fail to treat us as rational beings; they would use us as mere means and not as ends in ourselves.

It is conceivable that a society of Kantians, all of whom took pains to use no other as mere means, would end up with less happiness or with fewer persons alive than would some societies of complying utilitarians. For since the Kantians would be strictly bound only to justice, they might without wrongdoing be quite selective in their beneficence and fail to maximize either survival rates or happiness, or even to achieve as much of either as a strenuous group of utilitarians, who somehow make the right calculations. On the other hand, nobody will have been made an instrument of others' survival or happiness in the society of complying Kantians.

...

Discussion Questions

1. Hardin seems to be arguing for the conclusion that affluent countries should not help those suffering from famine (and similar problems, such as widespread disease) at all—not just that this is not morally required, but that it would be morally *wrong* from a utilitarian standpoint to do so. How plausible is his argument? How much does it depend on a choice between no help at all and a very great level of help that might put the affluent countries themselves in jeopardy? Are there intermediate levels of help that do better from a utilitarian standpoint than either of these extreme alternatives? If so, is it fairly clear where the best alternative lies?
2. Think of several examples of reasonably serious moral choices, and think of the possible consequences that different actions might have in the fairly distant future. How often in such cases are we in a position to make a confident assessment of the utilitarian value of those distant consequences? How often can someone make such a choice from a utilitarian standpoint with any very great confidence that he is doing the right thing?
3. What does the "in principle" part of O'Neill's suggested Kantian requirement that one not involve a people in "a scheme of action to which they could not in principle consent" amount to? Could one, for example, consent in principle to being treated as a slave? Why or why not?
4. Is any action that essentially involves deceiving another person thereby immoral? Is it immoral to lure someone to a surprise party in their honor (something that essentially involves deceiving them—and to which they could not in principle consent, since that would destroy the surprise)? Can you think of other actions with this feature that do not seem morally objectionable? Is there any way for a Kantian to draw a clear line between deception that is morally permissible and deception that is not?
5. There are many sorts of actions where coercion—or at least something that looks a lot like coercion—seems to be essentially involved, but that nonetheless seem morally permissible. A store, by having prices for its merchandise (and anti-shoplifting devices) might be said to coerce its customers into paying for what they want. Law enforcement authorities might be said to use the threat of various sorts of punishment to coerce citizens into complying with the law. Teachers might be said to coerce students into working hard with the threat of low grades. Is there any reasonably clear way to draw a line between cases of coercion (or pressure) that are morally acceptable and those that use others merely as means?

David T. Ozar

David T. Ozar (1942–) is an American philosopher who teaches at Loyola University, where he is also the Director of Loyola's Center for Ethics. He has written widely on rights and on the ethics of health care. In this selection, Ozar explains the general concept of rights, distinguishes moral rights from conventional rights (such as legal rights), and discusses the issue of whether there are universal moral rights that all human beings have (and if so, what the basis for such rights might be).

Rights: What They Are and Where They Come From

1. Rights Talk

Rights talk is one way of trying to talk, think, and reason about what individuals and communities ought and ought not to do. That is, rights talk is one area of moral discourse. There are many other ways of trying to analyze the various kinds of situations that arise in our lives when an action or policy is good or bad, right or wrong, moral or immoral. But in the Western world at the present time, rights talk is one of the most common ways of formulating moral issues, whether the issues involve only individuals or are between individuals and communities or even when they involve the relationships of whole communities with one another. . . .

2. What Are Rights?

No simple definition of the form "a right is a . . . can adequately explain this complex concept. Instead we need to ask ourselves two closely related questions: (1) What do we imply when we make the statement "A has a right, R, of some sort"? and (2) What conditions must be fulfilled for such a statement to be true?

First of all, when we say that someone has a right of some sort, we are, as already noted, talking about what ought or ought not to be done. Rights talk is one kind of moral discourse. It is used to inform people of their obligations and to give explanations of our own and others' choices and actions.

From *Philosophical Issues in Human Rights: Theories and Applications,* edited by Patricia H. Werhane, A. R. Gini, and David T. Ozar (New York: Random House, 1986).

Second, to speak about a right, any right, is to say that there is *someone* who *has* such a right. A right always has reference to an . . . an "agent"—a being that acts and is acted upon. Rights do not exist independently, unattached, as it were. In most cases the agent will be an individual human being; that is, ordinarily it is human beings that *have* rights. Whether nonhuman animals can have rights and whether a *group* of human beings, functioning as a single entity, can have rights are questions for debate. . . .

Third, to say that someone, A, has a right, R, of some sort is to imply that someone else, B, has an *obligation* of some sort, to do or to refrain from some act relative to A. That is, rights are *relational.* This is not necessarily to say that all rights have their basis in relationships; we will discuss various proposed bases of rights in a moment. The point being made here is rather that a right *is* a relationship; it is a relationship between a person who has the right and others who have corresponding obligations to act or to refrain. (1)

Fourth, rights have a special *overriding* character. As Gregory Vlastos has put it, rights take precedence over many other sorts of moral considerations.* When we say that someone has a right, our words imply that the moral considerations that are the basis of this statement are more important than any other kinds of moral considerations that might be relevant to the situation.

What other kinds of moral considerations might be relevant? In general they fall into two categories: rules and consequences. For many people obligations to act or to refrain from acting frequently derive from a set of fundamental rules of conduct. These rules may be simple rather straightforward rules like those we often use to

(1) R As this suggests, the idea of someone having a *right* seems to make no real sense unless there are others who have correlative *duties*.

(But the reverse does not seem to be the case: not every duty entails a corresponding right. Kant's duty of beneficence is one example of an alleged duty to which there is no corresponding right: no one in particular has a right to any given person's beneficence.)

*Gregory Vlastos, "Justice and Equality," in *Social Justice,* ed. Richard Brandt (Englewood Cliffs, N.J.: Prentice-Hall, 1962), pp. 31–72.

Utilitarianism is, of course, the main example of such a consequentialist view.

This overriding character of rights makes it tempting to formulate any allegedly serious moral claim as a right. But the fact that rights in this way override other moral considerations suggests that it will be harder to establish the existence of rights than to establish the existence of other sorts of moral considerations—and hence that we should be suspicious of claims of rights that are put forth without any clear basis.

Do rights *always* support this sort of demand? One related issue here is the scope of this "we": does it extend to all humankind, or is it restricted to some smaller community (and if so, which one)?

instruct our children: Do not lie; do not steal; do not harm other persons; keep your promises; help those in need; develop your talents; and so on. Or they may be much more *abstract* rules like the two tests of moral action proposed by the German philosopher Immanuel Kant (1724–1804): (1) "I ought never to act except in such a way that I can also will that my maxim should become a universal law"; (2) "Act in such a way that you always treat humanity, whether in your own person or in the person of any other, never simply as a means, but always at the same time as an end."*

On the other hand, for many other people the point of our obligation is to bring about by our actions the greatest amount of good, the greatest improvement in well-being for people, that we can. In this view, the key to correct judgments about what ought and ought not to be done is a careful analysis of the consequences that can be expected from the various actions that might be performed. This approach claims that, of the actions available to us in a particular situation, that action ought to be performed that brings about the highest level of well-being for the people affected. [2] . . .

When we say that someone has a right, we imply that the moral considerations that are the basis of this statement about rights are more important than rules of conduct that might be relevant, and that these moral considerations also outweigh in importance the consequences of the particular actions under consideration. As a matter of fact, when we talk about a right, we are talking about something that takes precedence over other moral considerations in two ways. Rights have a *double* overriding character. First, if A has a right of some sort, then B's obligation to do or to refrain takes precedence over other moral considerations relevant to B's own choice of his or her best or most required action. That is, B may not simply disregard an obligation based on A's right without moral fault; and, with few exceptions, the only considerations that can possibly have comparable moral weight for B are considerations based on the rights of other, third, parties or, to a more limited extent, on B's own rights. [3]

The second overriding feature of a right concerns the rest of us. To say that A has a right of some sort implies not only that B has an obligation of some sort to do or refrain. It implies, too, that the rest of us also have some measure of obligation to see to it, within certain limits, that B acts or refrains accordingly. The limits of this obligation are determined in turn by our own rights, by B's rights, and possibly by other moral considerations, depending on the circumstances. . . .

Fifth, to say that A has a right that B act or refrain in some way is to say not only that B has an obligation in this regard, but that B owes this to A. If B fails to act or refrain accordingly, B is not only failing to act as morality requires; B is failing A.

Suppose, by contrast, that B had an obligation of some other sort to be generous toward A but that A did not have a right to this. If B fails to be generous, B acts immorally, but B does not fail A, for B did not *owe* A anything. But if A has *a right,* then if B fails to act or refrain as obligated, B fails A because B owed something to A and did not carry it out. . . .

By the same token, if A has a right and if the rest of us fail to carry out our corresponding obligations to see to it that B acts or refrains accordingly, then we have not only failed to act as morality requires but we have failed A as well. For A's right is also a *claim* on the rest of us; it is something we *owe* A. It justifies a *demand* on the rest of us—a demand that we see to it, within proper limits, that B acts or refrains accordingly. [4]

Sixth, since there is never a moral obligation to do what is simply impossible, it follows that it is never the case that A has a right that B do what is impossible or that B refrain from what B cannot possibly avoid. This is a feature of the very notion of a right, and it is such a feature because it is a feature of the very notion of moral obligation. . . .

. . . Suppose that an argument is made that everyone in the world has a right to sufficient food to maintain a minimal level of functioning. But suppose that it is known that the earth simply cannot produce enough food for everyone in the world to maintain that level of functioning. Then it follows (assuming that no other source of food is available) that we cannot meaningfully say that there is an obligation to

*Immanuel Kant, *Groundwork of the Metaphysic of Morals,* trans. H. J. Paton (New York: Harper & Row, 1964), p. 70; p. 96.

provide such food. But if we cannot meaningfully say there is an obligation to do X, how can we meaningfully say that someone has a *right* that X be done? In such cases talk of rights is not exactly false; it is, like talk of obligations in such cases, just empty..[5]

This point is somewhat more controversial: do genuine rights just disappear when it becomes impossible to satisfy them? (See Discussion Question 1.) Another issue about the specific right mentioned here is who it is that would have the corresponding duty.

Seventh, if A has a right, A has the option *not to exercise* that right and also the option to waive that right in particular cases and, possibly, altogether. . . .

3. Conventional Rights and Moral Rights

. . .

To determine if a statement of the form "A has a right, R, of some sort" is true; we must look at two quite different sets of conditions. Some rights are verified by reference to a social rule or rule system or an institutional framework of some sort. Such rights are called *conventional* rights because the existence of such rights depends upon the existence of particular social rules, rule systems, and institutions, whose existence depends in turn on the *acceptance* of these rules, rule systems, and institutions by the parties involved. . . .

On the other hand, many people, philosophers and nonphilosophers alike, hold that there are rights of another kind that exist as part of the moral nature of things, independently of anyone's choosing. These rights are sometimes called natural rights, sometimes human rights, sometimes moral rights. When they are called natural rights the emphasis may be on their being part of the nature of things, but this expression is also used to indicate that the basis of such rights lies in "human nature"—a stable and fundamental set of characteristics thought to be built into every human being. . . . other thinkers have called these sorts of rights human rights, rights we have just because we are human beings. . . . Thus they are also called moral rights, rights that everyone *should* recognize everywhere and in all circumstances. . . . We shall employ the expression "moral rights" here. . . .

4. Are There Universal Moral Rights?

A moral (human, natural) right, we have said, is a right that exists as part of the moral nature of things and independently of anyone's choosing or agreeing that there be such a right. Many people believe that human beings have some such rights, and they believe that *all* human beings have them. They believe, in other words, that there are some moral rights that are *universal* among human beings. . . .

a. The Great Machine and Its Slave It will be helpful to begin our discussion of universal moral rights with a case. The following somewhat fanciful story can illuminate how deep are our convictions about the existence of universal moral rights.

> Suppose that in some future age it became possible to harness all of the world's technology to a single master computer that could then direct all the world's productive processes to produce and distribute the resources necessary for every human being on earth to live a secure and comfortable life. Let us also assume that the master computer has been programmed to carry out its task in an ecologically sound manner, so there is no risk to future members of the human community. Let us also assume that the Great Machine is completely dependable, that there is no risk of malfunction in our submitting the well-being of the whole human race to its direction.
>
> But there is one problem. With so many complex processes to control and integrate at once, the Great Machine must have the permanent and total use of a living human brain in order to carry out the reasoning processes that are necessary for its work. Some human being must be hooked up to the Great Machine for it to do its job. This person will continue to live in comfort, but his or her brain will be totally taken over by the Great Machine. There is no way that this function could be shared among a group of persons with lesser effects on each; and there is no point to someone's doing it only for a while and then handing it over to someone else because, once programmed by the Great Machine, a human brain could never be used again for living an ordinary human life. Slavery to the Great Machine is total and permanent.
>
> Let us assume that there are no volunteers to be the Great Machine's slave. Would it be morally justifiable to enslave an unwilling human being to the Great Machine in order to achieve so high a level of well-being and so much opportunity for growth and fullness of life for everyone else on earth? (Let us postulate that a fair and equitable procedure for selecting this person would be available, so there would be no moral problem with the selection process itself.) Would it be moral to enslave someone to the Great Machine?.[6]

An act utilitarian would seemingly have to answer "yes" to this question. As we saw earlier, cases like this provide one of the standard objections to act utilitarianism—which can now be put by saying that act utilitarians apparently cannot recognize moral rights (since for them, any alleged right could always be overridden by considerations of utility).

Many people would respond to this case by saying that we would be acting immorally, indeed profoundly immorally, if we were to make someone a slave to the Great Machine against the person's will, regardless of the benefits for everyone else. Many of those who would respond in this way would explain their response by saying that every human being has certain moral rights that would be violated if he was enslaved to the Great Machine against his will. But what reasons are there for saying there are universal moral rights?

b. "Endowed by Their Creator" One possible account of the basis of universal moral rights is that these rights have been given to mankind by God. This is the basis Thomas Jefferson identified in the Declaration of Independence. "We hold these Truths to be self-evident, that all Men are created equal, that they are endowed by their Creator with certain unalienable Rights. . . ."

Jefferson does not appeal to the Scriptures or any other source of authoritative religious teaching to support his claim that God has endowed every human being with rights. He says instead that it is "self-evident." By this he surely means "obvious to everyone." In other words, Jefferson thought that there is evidence that is plain for everyone to see which points to the existence of universal moral rights. But what evidence? Clearly Jefferson believed that there are features of human beings or of human life that lead unerringly to this conclusion.

Jefferson does not give us much help in identifying these features, and it may seem that we have made little progress by examining the words of the Declaration. But there is something important to be learned from it. Even those who locate the basis of universal moral rights in God's choice to create the human race in a certain way have features of human beings in mind—the clues that tell us that, created thus, human beings do possess universal moral rights. That is, belief in the divine origin of universal human rights is not an answer to our question about the basis of the belief that humans have such rights. It is, at most, an urgent reason for trying to answer this question.

c. Features Shared by All Human Beings Of the specific features of human beings that have been proposed as the basis of moral rights, the two most often mentioned are human freedom and human rationality. Human beings are free. That is, they make choices, and these choices derive in significant measure from the person himself or herself. Consequently human beings are special, different from every other species on this planet . . . : They perform a kind of activity that no other species performs. Our treatment of human beings, it is argued, must therefore be special as well. Human beings may not simply be used, as the other beings on the planet are used, in the fulfillment of one's own purposes. Our actions toward human beings must recognize that they are choosers, that they have their own purposes. To treat human beings without concern for their choices and purposes is to treat them as they are not, as if they were not choosers. Rights, then, according to this pattern of reasoning, are ways of respecting the choices and purposes of other human beings.

On the other hand, some thinkers emphasize human rationality. Human beings are not merely sensors of the world around them. They are knowers, judgers, creators, communicators. They do not just react to stimuli; they put information together to form generalized truths about the world. They use these truths to understand each new situation that arises. Consequently they are also able to reshape the world and to share their experiences of the world with one another in language, symbol, and culture. Human beings are thus again special among the beings of this planet, . . . special . . . by performing activities that other beings do not. Therefore they must be treated specially, as originators of understanding, as shapers of the world around them, as builders of human community. According to this pattern of reasoning, rights protect these special activities of the human species. 7

7

It is plausible to suppose that these features distinguish human beings from at least most other earthly species. But is it clear *why* these features are supposed to yield the moral rights in question? (See Discussion Question 2.) It has sometimes been suggested that intelligent mammals like dolphins might have such features; another possibility is non-human extraterrestrials.

Nevertheless, critics of these two approaches argue, neither choice nor the activities of reason are universal within the human species. Infants do not make choices or perform acts of rationality of the sort just described. Even young children do not make choices or judgments with such independence that we think it improper to override their choices or set aside their judgments. Also, those with severe mental illnesses can lose the capacity to reason correctly and to make genuine choices. The comatose . . . do not perform acts of choice or reasoning.

Does this mean that a human being's moral rights start and stop as the relevant forms of activity begin and end? That is certainly not the way in which moral rights are ordinarily understood.

Does it mean that some members of the human species do not have rights—infants, most young children, the mentally ill, the comatose . . . ? Clearly, if this is the case, we should not go on speaking of *universal* moral rights. ❽

Another approach would be to look at features that we are certain are universal characteristics of the human species. . . . Human beings are all bipeds and have opposite thumbs and many other genetic traits in common. But neither these two features nor any of a host of other common biological characteristics of human beings seem significant enough from a moral point of view to serve as the basis of moral rights.

All human beings who are living are, of course, alive and are subject to pain and to death. Life, pain, and death are surely matters of moral importance. Could the importance to human beings of maintaining life, avoiding death, and averting or at least minimizing pain serve as the basis of universal moral rights? The problem with this approach is that the net seems to be too wide. If vulnerability to pain and death is the basis of moral rights, all human beings are indeed included, but so are most animals of other species. The suggestion that nonhuman animals have moral rights is an important topic for moral discourse, but most defenders of universal moral rights for human beings hold, at a minimum, that the moral rights of human beings are stronger, broader, different in some way from whatever rights nonhuman animals might have. ❾

Some defenders of universal moral rights have held that the basis of these rights is "human dignity" or "human worth," which is surely something that human beings do not share with nonhuman animals. But a problem with this approach is the difficulty of determining just what features of human beings are referred to by the expressions "human dignity" and "human worth." If human beings are said to have dignity or worth because they are free and/or rational, then moral rights based on dignity or worth will not be universal, for the reasons explained above. If human beings have dignity or worth for some other reason, it needs to be explained; and the expressions "dignity" and "worth" alone do not provide any clear clues to this explanation.

We seem to be at an impasse. Either there are moral rights that some humans have, and possibly only some of the time, or there are moral rights that all humans have, but most nonhuman animals have the same rights as well. If we stopped at this point, we would have to give up our original idea—that there are moral rights that all human beings have precisely "because they are human."

. . .

d. Bilevel and Potentiality Approaches Some moral theorists have responded to the problems posed in the previous section by frankly conceding that the fullest notion of moral rights applies properly only to those human beings who are capable of free choice and rationality. Fetuses, infants, and small children up to a certain point of development do not have moral rights; neither do the permanently comatose and those members of the human species who, for whatever reason and regardless of their chronological age, have never become capable of choice and rational activity.

But this is not to say that humans in these categories are altogether without rights. That will depend on two other factors. First, in some bilevel theories, all members of the human species have moral rights of a diminished sort because of their vulnerability to pain and death. . . .

But these rights are not in principle different from the rights of nonhuman animals. The obligation not to torture is simply an application of a more general obligation not to treat cruelly any being that can experience intense pain. The only difference is that, with our more complex psyches, human vulnerability to certain forms of pain is broader than that of nonhuman animals. Consequently, the obligations implied by rights of this sort will be likely to have a broader scope when their referents are human beings than when their referents are nonhuman animals.

Secondly, in all theories that attribute full moral rights only to those human beings capable of acts of choice and rationality, other human beings may still have extensive conventional rights. Among these rights may be legal rights and rights based on other social rule systems. Even more important, however, are rights that derive from the free commitments of free, rational humans. For example, a young child may have a conventional right to care by his or her parents by reason of acts of commitment on their part in keeping the child rather than offering him or her for adoption. In a similar way, the permanently comatose patient may have conventional

❽

Here is one fundamental issue about alleged human rights: do they extend even to those humans who do not have the special features that are supposedly the basis for them (and if so, why)?

❾

At least most non-human animals; as we have seen, there may be exceptions.

rights vis-à-vis various health care personnel who have freely undertaken his or her care and are therefore committed to provide it.

. . .

Bilevel approaches frequently mark the distinction between those members of the human species who have full moral rights and those who do not by saying that the former are human *persons* while the latter, though certainly human, are not persons. . . . In recent debates about moral rights, however, the term *person* has often been used with little explanation of what features of human beings it refers to. . . .

A second response to the problems discussed above focuses on the notion of potentiality. There are universal moral rights, this view holds, because the basis of moral rights is the *potential* for free and rational acts. Human beings have this potential from the moment of their conception. For, from that moment on, they are continually developing in the direction of performing such acts. They retain this potential, insofar as we can be certain of our judgments about it, until the moment when they die. For even those who are comatose may still have this potential, at least up to the point at which we can certify that all their higher brain functions, which are necessary for free and rational acts, have ceased. At that point, they not only no longer have moral rights but they are also no longer living human beings.

There are a number of arguments that can be given in support of this view. First, it is difficult to identify any point in the development of a human being at which so radical a change takes place that it makes sense for us to say that he or she is a person afterward, but was not before that moment, or that he or she now has full moral rights, but did not have full moral rights before then. What exists and unfolds continually throughout this developmental process is precisely the potential to perform acts of freedom and rationality. Therefore, it is argued, the potentiality approach represents our actual experience of human life much more accurately than the bilevel approach. Obviously, the potentiality approach also accords much better than the bilevel approach with the centuries-old conviction that if there are any moral rights, they are universal moral rights.

. . .

One objection to the potentiality theory focuses on those members of the human species who are born or become severely retarded, and whose level of mental functioning is therefore such that they cannot perform acts of freedom and rationality—that is, they do not have the potentiality for such acts. These members of the human species would seem not to have moral rights according to the potentiality theory as we have explained it; yet surely they are still human beings. How then can the potentiality theorist claim that there are *universal* human rights?

. . .

A more radical objection concerns the notion of potentiality itself. What *is* a potentiality? A potentiality, says the objection, is not a "something" that can be possessed by a human being. When we talk of people's potentialities, it is simply a more convenient way of saying that we have expectations and consider it probable that these people will act in a certain way in the future. We base such predictions either on the individuals' own past acts or on their membership in a class of beings who have acted in the predicted way. But none of this involves attributing to an individual a special *feature* of his or her make-up that should be called a potentiality. Much less, then, should we be drawn into considering this "feature" of the individual's make-up to be the basis of anything else, including moral rights.

A related objection points out that the potentiality theorists claim to have demonstrated *actual* rights. That is, they imply that other persons *actually have* obligations to act or refrain in certain ways. But how can human activities, however morally significant, that are merely *potential* give rise to rights and, thus, obligations that are fully *actual*?

. . .

e. Relational Approaches to the Existence of Moral Rights Instead of focusing on features of individual human beings, a number of rights theorists have focused on features of human life together. Could the widespread conviction that there are universal moral rights have its foundation in key relationships in which all human beings participate? Many philosophic traditions have stressed the idea that we cannot describe the essential elements of the human make-up by looking at human individuals in isolation from one another. To be connected with other human beings is a fundamental part of what it is to be human. . . .

In "Justice and Equality" Gregory Vlastos . . . points out that there are certain instances and features of human persons' valuations of one another that do not involve comparison of persons or the grading of persons one above or below the other. That is, among the ways in which human beings relate to one another, there is at least one relationship in which people are not graded or compared, as contrasted with the myriad human relationships where grading, ranking, and comparison of people in terms of their abilities, performances, and other attributes are appropriate. Vlastos does not try to name that distinctive relationship. But he does identify it by saying that in this relationship what is valued in one human being by another is "human worth."

While Vlastos does not claim that the following description exhausts what we mean by human worth, he does claim that these two elements will be part of any complete description of it: (*a*) "the enjoyment of value in all the forms in which it can be experienced by human beings," which he calls well-being for short and (*b*) "conscious choices and deliberate decisions [and also] subtler modulations and more spontaneous expressions of individual preference," which Vlastos gathers together under the simple label "freedom."*

. . . The relationship that Vlastos describes clearly implies rights and obligations between the participants. The relationship consists in an unconditional affirmation of the worth of the other in his or her well-being and freedom. No one could consistently affirm such a relationship with another human being while failing to take into account the other's well-being and freedom in concrete actions. . . . In other words, in this relationship the other party has rights. (10)

Vlastos holds that this relationship is pervasive within the human community, and that every member of the human community therefore has moral rights. To this claim it might be objected that the rights Vlastos has demonstrated exist only among those who have this unconditional relationship, and that this relationship is optional—a matter of choice. Consequently, it could be argued, these are really conventional rather than moral rights, and we have no reason as yet for thinking that they are universal rights. (11)

. . .

Is there any relationship that has . . . universality and necessity . . . and, at the same time, an explicit moral dimension like Vlastos's unconditional affirmation of human worth? Bernard Williams has made a valuable suggestion along these lines in his well-known paper, "The Idea of Equality." Williams begins his argument about the basis of human equality in a manner very similar to Vlastos, with an opening distinction between "the technical or professional attitude" and "the human approach." In professional relations and in the world of work, a person's actions are judged by others according to various professional or technical titles, such as "laborer" or "waiter" or "assistant manager." He writes:

> The technical or professional attitude is that which regards the man solely under that title, the human approach that which regards him as *a man who has* that title (among others), willingly, unwillingly, through lack of alternatives, with pride, etc.
>
> This human approach involves looking at the person not simply as "the surface to which a certain label can be applied," but trying to "see the world (including the label) from his point of view.†

Every one of us who makes this imaginative identification with the perspective of another human being recognizes in making it that the other's perspective has value, worth, and moral significance. The only way to exclude this valuing of the other's perspective as a center of experience is to refuse to view things from his or her perspective. But this refusal does not eliminate the possibility of such identification; the relationship of valuing the other's perspective is always available. . . .

10

Such an unconditional affirmation of the worth of other humans is very close to what Kant seems to mean by regarding other humans as "ends in themselves." Thus the ascription of moral rights to others can be argued to be a clear implication of Kant's view.

11

Kant would, of course, deny that regarding other humans in this way is *morally* optional; in his view, such a stance toward other humans is the most fundamental moral requirement. (What might Kant—or Vlastos—say about the problem of humans who are incapable of experiencing value or making deliberate decisions?)

---

*Gregory Vlastos, "Justice and Equality," in *Social Justice,* ed. Richard Brandt (Englewood Cliffs, N.J.: Prentice-Hall, 1962), pp. 48–53.

†Bernard A. O. Williams, "The Idea of Equality," in *Philosophy, Politics, and Society,* second series ed. Peter Laslett and W. G. Runciman (London: Basil Blackwell, 1962), p. 117. . . .

Moreover, while not all human beings are able, at all times, to identify with another's perspective in this way, all human beings are centers of experience and are thus capable of being identified with and having their perspectives valued. Those who are . . . retarded, or in severe pain are centers of experience and have a point of view that others can identify with and experience as valuable. So, too, are infants and, more than likely, fetuses during much of their development. Even the comatose may be active centers of experience, especially experience of pain and helplessness. Thus, while the initiator of the relationship may not include all human beings, its term is universal. That is, all human beings count; they all have shoes into which we can put ourselves. From this vantage point we experience each of them—all other persons—as valuable. [12]

STOP Is this enough to distinguish all human beings from "higher" animals of various sorts?

More reflection and argument would be needed to demonstrate fully that in this universal relationship of unconditional valuing lies the basis of universal moral rights. . . . But in the fuller development of Williams's proposal we may have a rational basis for universal moral rights.

5. Rights and Consequences

Rights talk, as we said earlier, is one way of talking, thinking, and reasoning about what individuals and communities ought and ought not to do. Rights talk is one kind of moral discourse. Another important kind of moral discourse looks at the morality of individuals' and communities' actions in terms of their consequences. This approach to moral reasoning and reflection is often called consequentialism.

. . .

For rights theorists who hold that the basis of all sound moral reasoning lies in people's fundamental moral rights, analyses of morality in terms of the consequences of individuals' and groups' actions cannot correctly inform us about what ought and ought not to be done unless these analyses are derived in turn from a more fundamental understanding of moral rights. For there are certain actions that clearly ought or ought not to be done *regardless of the consequences.* This means, necessarily, that consequences cannot be the most fundamental basis of what ought and ought not to be done. Such theorists frequently cite cases analogous to that of the Great Machine, discussed above, in arguing for this position. The consequentialists, according to such rights theorists, would surely be committed to not only permitting but even requiring that someone be forced to be the slave of the machine. For, they argue, the great benefits of doing so for millions of people would surely outweigh the costs, in the form of a life without use of one's own brain, for the person enslaved. However, since such enslavement of even one person is clearly immoral, they argue, the consequentialist approach is surely inadequate by itself. Morality requires that no one be enslaved to the Great Machine, even if the consequences of doing so would be better for everyone except the person so enslaved.

On the other side, consequentialists often hold that a rights theory is either based on consequentialism or mistaken. They defend this claim by arguing that whenever a moral decision involves competing rights, we resolve the matter by examining the consequences of the actions available and identifying the action that has the best, most desirable consequences.

Why, then, we might ask a consequentialist, do we speak of rights? Why has rights talk become so important a part of moral discourse? Because, says the consequentialist, some kinds of valued things are the preconditions of our being able to achieve all our other values. Life, health, the absence of coercion and of certain other kinds of interference, self-respect, a sense of ourselves as thinking and choosing beings—these particular values are values we *must* have in significant measure before we can achieve the other things and have the other experiences that we value in life, no matter what these other values and valued experiences are. Therefore, within our evaluation of our possible actions, these values are assigned a special place. It is not necessarily the case that we value them more. It is rather that they are preconditions of the others, and therefore they must be secured first before the others can even be possible. This very real priority of the preconditions of all else we value is the reason for assigning a special name to these things, namely rights, and for according them special weight in our moral reflections. Thus, says the consequentialist, rights talk has a useful role to play within moral discourse; but it is consequences, not rights, which are the true basis of our judgments of what ought and ought not to be done. [13]

. . .

6. Positive Rights, Negative Rights, and Libertarianism

To say that A has a right is to imply, as we indicated above, that someone else, B, has an obligation of some sort to do or to refrain from some act relative to A. Some contemporary rights theorists have drawn a sharp distinction between rights that imply an obligation of B to act, which are frequently called positive rights, and rights that imply only an obligation of B to refrain, which are called negative rights.

. . .

One group of moral theorists who claim that the distinction between positive and negative rights is of the highest importance are known as libertarians. The libertarian position has been explained in several ways. One way to explain it is to say that the basis of all sound moral judgments is a single fundamental moral rule: Respect people's liberty. This means that we are not to interfere with others' acting on the basis of their own goals, values, and purposes; we are to leave them free to do as they please so long as in exercising their liberty they do not interfere with the rights of others similarly to be left alone. [14]

It is easy to see why this theory of morality is also often expressed as a rights theory—every person has a fundamental right not to be interfered with in acting on the basis of his or her own goals, values, and purposes. This fundamental libertarian right is obviously a "negative right," a right implying obligations on the part of others only to refrain from interfering. Libertarians claim that the only moral rights are negative rights, namely this fundamental right and any more specific negative rights that might be derived from it. There are no moral rights that are positive rights; all positive rights that anyone might have are conventional rights, based on people's voluntary agreements to undertake the obligations involved.

Libertarian theorists expand on this fundamental rule or right in a variety of ways. But most of them would accept the following statement as a starting point for developing more narrowly focused obligations:

1. It is never moral to interfere with actions of a competent adult (who is not interfering with someone else) simply to bring about better consequences.
2. It is moral to interfere with the actions of someone who is interfering with someone else, for the purpose of ending that interference and/or securing appropriate restitution and/or punishment.
3. All other obligations between persons shall be by voluntary agreement of the parties involved so that the arrangements so agreed upon are conventional rights and obligations.
4. The obligation not to interfere applies not only to the body but also the mind, and to the property of every person.
5. When the exercise of liberty conflicts with another exercise of liberty (that is, when a fundamental right conflicts with another fundamental right), then that action or policy is to be preferred that preserves the greatest total liberty for everyone involved.

Not all rights theorists agree with the libertarians, however, that the only moral rights are negative rights. Some theorists have defended the view that all moral rights involve both "positive" and "negative" obligations—that is, obligations both to act and to refrain.

One such argument challenges the claim that there is a significant distinction between actions and omissions of actions. If the line marking the distinction between an action and an omission cannot be maintained, or if it should prove to have no moral significance, then the claim that the only moral rights are negative rights will lose its significance. [15]

A second argument supporting this view builds on the implication that in the case of any *moral* right, each of us has some measure of obligation to see to it that the relevant actions and omissions are carried out. This means that even rights that at first seem to imply only obligations not to interfere in fact also imply obligations to act positively to prevent or deter interference in circumstances where it is likely. Consequently, it is argued, so-called negative rights involve both obligations to refrain and obligations to take action. [16]

This consequentialist approach is similar to rule utilitarianism, and it faces the same important problem: that there is no clear consequentialist justification for recognizing a right when it is clear (as it sometimes will be) that better consequences can be achieved by violating it. But, the proponent of rights will argue, a right that can be overridden in this way by an appeal to consequences is not really a right at all.

Respecting people's liberty in this sense involves also respecting their lives—and, at least arguably, respecting the property they acquire through exercising their liberty (without illegitimately infringing on the liberty or lives of others). The selections from Locke and Nozick in Chapter 6 present versions of such a view.

If you are about to run someone over with your car, is avoiding that result an omission (not hitting him) or an action (stepping on the brake or swerving away)? This suggests that many cases of not interfering with others can be described either way. But does this seriously undermine the distinction between positive and negative rights? (See Discussion Question 3.)

Not everyone agrees that negative rights always involve such positive obligations. But even if they do, there is still a difference between a view according to which the only positive obligations are to help others secure or defend their negative rights and one according to which there are other positive obligations and corresponding rights as well: rights to receive something from others that goes beyond this sort of help.

Finally, some theorists who accept the distinction between positive and negative rights argue forcefully for the importance of positive moral rights. These thinkers, who are strong critics of libertarianism, claim that positive rights and the obligations they entail are essential for human development. Negative rights create, at best, "benign neglect" for those unable to exercise their rights, because negative rights allow only those who are aggressive in pursuing their liberty and who happen to have the needed resources to succeed, and then often at the expense of others. One way to formulate this argument, for example, is to show that those whose basic needs are not filled, when sufficient resources are available so that their needs *could* be filled, are deprived of the very equality of opportunity that many libertarians stress, or they are deprived of the psychological possibility of fulfilling goals other than survival. Another way is to challenge the claim implicit in libertarianism that we have no positive moral relationships to one another to start with. Social interaction, it is argued, is an inseparable part of the make-up of each of us, so that the libertarian's "fundamental" negative rights are themselves already grounded in and dependent upon the fulfillment of positive moral relations between persons. 17

17

The selection by Rawls in Chapter 6 defends a version of this view. One issue about positive rights of this sort is who has the corresponding obligation—which we have seen to be essential to a meaningful right. (See Discussion Question 4.)

7. Conflicting Rights and Other Obligations

In some moral theories, moral rights are the basis of all moral obligations. In such theories it is worth asking whether all moral rights have the same weight or whether some rights can take precedence over others when both cannot be fulfilled simultaneously. By the same token, it is important to determine whether the obligations implied by a given right all have the same moral weight or not.

To take a simple example, suppose Mr. Jones tells Dr. Smith, "If it's cancer, Doctor, don't tell me." Jones, let us assume, has a right to know the truth about his condition, and also a right, let us assume, to define the terms of his relationship with Dr. Smith. What is the morally best thing for Dr. Smith to do when these rights conflict? Or suppose it is the rights of two bearers of rights that are in conflict. If a fetus has a right not to be killed and a woman the right to control what happens to her body, for example, then the morality of an elective abortion is a matter of conflicting rights of distinct rights bearers. Is there any basis in rights theory for ranking rights in order to resolve such conflicts?

Some rights theorists have held that no priorities can be assigned among the most general or fundamental moral rights. But as more narrowly focused rights are derived from them, these latter will have to be weighed and ranked against one another, since they will sometimes be in conflict in concrete situations. The basis for their ranking will be the extent to which each of them fulfills and/or hinders the value expressed in the fundamental rights—e.g., human freedom, rationality, fundamental relationships between human beings, or whatever.

...

[One] way of assigning priorities among rights is based on the claim that there are some moral rights that must be fulfilled before any others can be fulfilled. Henry Shue calls such rights basic rights and argues that they include the rights to subsistence and security and certain forms of freedom. These "basic rights" must rank first, Shue argues, because they are preconditions of all other rights; without them, the fulfillment of other rights is impossible.* (Shue also proposes a ranking of obligations derived from his thesis about the "basicness" of the basic rights. Shue divides human concerns into four categories, in ascending order of moral significance: preference satisfaction, cultural enrichment, nonbasic rights, basic rights. He offers a priority principle that says, firstly and obviously, that a person must rank obligations deriving from basic rights ahead of obligations deriving from nonbasic rights, and secondly that a person is morally obligated to sacrifice his or her own preferences and cultural enrichment, for example, if this is necessary to secure another's nonbasic rights and is morally obligated to sacrifice all three, if necessary, to secure another person's basic rights.)† 18

18

Since Shue's basic rights include some that are positive (such as the rights to subsistence and security), this yields the result that people are morally required not to devote resources to pursuing their own projects and interests so long as anyone's "basic rights" are unsatisfied.

One important issue about this is the scope of the community within which this obligation holds. (See Discussion Question 5.)

...

*Henry Shue, *Basic Rights* (Princeton University Press, 1980)
†Shue, pp. 114–119.

Discussion Questions

1. Suppose that person A has an obligation (perhaps resulting from a contract or agreement of some sort) to give person B a certain amount of money at a designated time, and that person B has a corresponding right against person A that this be done. If it is impossible at the time in question for person A to pay person B the required amount, does this mean that there is no obligation and so no right? Suppose that A will never be able to pay (perhaps because he will no longer be alive). Does it matter why person A was unable to fulfill the obligation? (Think of different possibilities here.) If payment is genuinely impossible, then obviously A will not in fact fulfill the obligation, but is there any reason to think that B's right has not still been violated?—in which case it and the corresponding obligation must still exist.
2. Ozar (along with many others) suggests that it is the specific features of freedom and rationality that result in at least normally developed humans having moral rights (such as, at least, the rights to life and to liberty). But he says very little about why this is supposed to be so, beyond just remarking that these features make humans "special among the beings of this planet." Even assuming that this last claim is correct, it isn't very clear how the claim of rights is supposed to follow. Can you see any further reason or argument here? (This is an extremely hard question, but one very much worth thinking about.)
3. Ozar suggests that the distinction between negative and positive rights depends on that between omissions of actions and actions, and so may be undermined if the latter distinction turns out to be questionable (as in the case described in Annotation 15). But another way to put the distinction is in terms of negative rights not to be interfered with (except to prevent interference with others) and positive rights to be given some positive benefit or assistance. Investigate the clarity and sharpness of this distinction by thinking of various rights that people are claimed to have and trying to see if they fall clearly into one or the other of these two categories.
4. It is often claimed that all human beings have moral rights to minimally adequate nutrition, housing, and clothing, among others. One question about such alleged rights is who has the corresponding duties? One possible answer is "society" or "the community." But apart from concerns about the size or scope of the relevant society or community (does it include all humans or even all rational beings of any sort, or is it more limited in size?), some will object that society has no resources of its own, but only those derived from individuals in some way (as by taxation). Could society have an obligation to provide everyone with the things in question (assuming that they are unable to provide them for themselves) without some or all of the members of society having such an obligation? If not, what is the basis for the latter obligation—especially as it extends, for example, to people in distant countries? Is this a serious objection to the idea of (nonconventional) positive rights? (Is there any analogous problem about negative rights?)
5. Does each person have a moral obligation not to devote resources to his own projects and interests until and unless the basic rights of all human beings (or perhaps even all rational creatures) have been fulfilled? What would the implications of such a view be in the area of famine relief? What if we discovered, in the process of space exploration, a large planet full of exceptionally needy rational beings (does it matter whether they are biologically human?)? (Think here about Williams's objection to utilitarianism: that it fails to give adequate weight to a person's own projects and commitments. To what extent does a similar objection apply to Shue's view of rights?)

Judith Jarvis Thomson

Judith Jarvis Thomson (1929–) is an American philosopher who teaches at the Massachusetts Institute of Technology. She has made important contributions to both ethics and metaphysics.

In the following selection (which is perhaps the single piece of work for which Thomson is best known), she defends the thesis that abortion is often (but not always) morally permissible, even on the assumption (which she does not accept) that the fetus (the prenatal organism) is a person from the moment of conception, and even in cases where the mother's life is not threatened. Here it is important to distinguish the *moral* concept of a person from the *biological* concept of a member of the human species. There is no doubt that the fetus is biologically *human,* but what Thomson is assuming for the sake of the argument is that it is also a being with the kind of moral status, including rights, that we ascribe to at least most humans, but might conceivably also ascribe to beings of other species, such as perhaps dolphins or extraterrestrials. Thomson's discussion is relevant to some of the issues raised by Ozar and also reflects Kant's idea of persons as "ends in themselves."

A Defense of Abortion

Most opposition to abortion relies on the premiss that the foetus is a . . . person, from the moment of conception. The premiss is argued for, but, as I think, not well. Take, for example, the most common argument. We are asked to notice that the development of a human being from conception through birth into childhood is continuous; then it is said that to draw a line, to choose a point in this development and say 'before this point the thing is not a person, after this point it is a person' is to make an arbitrary choice, a choice for which in the nature of things no good reason can be given. It is concluded that the foetus is, or anyway that we had better say it is, a person from the moment of conception. But this conclusion does not follow. Similar things might be said about the development of an acorn into an oak tree, and it does not follow that acorns are oak trees, or that we had better say they are. Arguments of this form are sometimes called 'slippery slope arguments'—the phrase is perhaps self-explanatory—and it is dismaying that opponents of abortion rely on them so heavily and uncritically. (1)

I am inclined to agree, however, that the prospects for 'drawing a line' in the development of the foetus look dim. I am inclined to think also that we shall probably have to agree that the foetus has already become a human person well before birth. Indeed, it comes as a surprise when one first learns how early in its life it begins to acquire human characteristics. By the tenth week, for example, it already has a face, arms and legs, fingers and toes; it has internal organs, and brain activity is detectable. (2) On the other hand, I think that the premiss is false, that the foetus is not a person from the moment of conception. A newly fertilized ovum, a newly implanted clump of cells, is no more a person than an acorn is an oak tree. But I shall not discuss any of this. For it seems to me to be of great interest to ask what happens if, for the sake of argument, we allow the premiss. (3) How, precisely, are we supposed to get from there to the conclusion that abortion is morally impermissible? Opponents of abortion commonly spend most of their time establishing that the foetus is a person, and hardly any time explaining the step from there to the impermissibility of abortion. Perhaps they think the step too simple and obvious to require much comment. Or perhaps instead they are simply being economical in argument. Many of those who defend abortion rely on the premiss that the foetus is not a person, but only a bit of tissue that will become a person at birth; and why pay out more arguments than you have to? Whatever the explanation, I suggest that the step they take is neither easy nor obvious, that it calls for closer examination than it is commonly given, and that when we do give it this closer examination we shall feel inclined to reject it.

I propose, then, that we grant that the foetus is a person from the moment of conception. How does the argument go from here? Something like this, I take it. Every person has a right to life. So the foetus has a right to life. No doubt the mother has a right to decide what shall happen in and to her body; everyone would grant that. But surely a person's right to life is stronger and more stringent than the mother's right to decide what happens in and to her body, and so outweighs it. So the foetus may not be killed; an abortion may not be performed.

It sounds plausible. But now let me ask you to imagine this. You wake up in the morning and find yourself back to back in bed with an unconscious violinist. A famous unconscious violinist. He has been found to have a fatal kidney ailment, and the Society of Music Lovers has canvassed all the available medical records and found that you alone have the

From *Philosophy and Public Affairs*, Vol. 1, No. 1 (Fall, 1971).

(1)

STOP Think carefully about this analogy. What we would say about the stages between an acorn and an oak tree is reasonably clear: they are intermediate stages, more than acorns but not yet oak trees. But what should be said about the stages intermediate between something that has no moral status or moral rights and a full-blown person who has both? Can something be more than a non-person but not yet a full-fledged person (and if so, what sort of moral status and rights would it have)?

(2)

But these characteristics are much more clearly relevant to biological humanity than to personhood.

(3)

R The "premiss" (a variant spelling of "premise"), that is, that the fetus is a person from the moment of conception. Thomson proposes to assume, for the sake of the argument, that this is so, even though she doesn't really accept it.

right blood type to help. They have therefore kidnapped you, and last night the violinist's circulatory system was plugged into yours, so that your kidneys can be used to extract poisons from his blood as well as your own. The director of the hospital now tells you, 'Look, we're sorry the Society of Music Lovers did this to you—we would never have permitted it if we had known. But still, they did it, and the violinist now is plugged into you. To unplug you would be to kill him. But never mind, it's only for nine months. By then he will have recovered from his ailment, and can safely be unplugged from you.' Is it morally incumbent on you to accede to this situation? No doubt it would be very nice of you if you did, a great kindness. But do you *have* to accede to it? What if it were not nine months, but nine years? Or longer still? What if the director of the hospital says, 'Tough luck, I agree, but you've now got to stay in bed, with the violinist plugged into you, for the rest of your life. Because remember this. All persons have a right to life, and violinists are persons. Granted you have a right to decide what happens in and to your body, but a person's right to life outweighs your right to decide what happens in and to your body. So you cannot ever be unplugged from him.' I imagine you would regard this as outrageous, which suggests that something really is wrong with that plausible-sounding argument I mentioned a moment ago. ❹

In this case, of course, you were kidnapped; you didn't volunteer for the operation that plugged the violinist into your kidneys. Can those who oppose abortion on the ground I mentioned make an exception for a pregnancy due to rape? Certainly. They can say that persons have a right to life only if they didn't come into existence because of rape; or they can say that all persons have a right to life, but that some have less of a right to life than others, in particular, that those who came into existence because of rape have less. But these statements have a rather unpleasant sound. Surely the question of whether you have a right to life at all, or how much of it you have, shouldn't turn on the question of whether or not you are the product of a rape. And in fact the people who oppose abortion on the ground I mentioned do not make this distinction, and hence do not make an exception in case of rape. ❺

Nor do they make an exception for a case in which the mother has to spend the nine months of her pregnancy in bed. They would agree that would be a great pity, and hard on the mother; but all the same, all persons have a right to life, the foetus is a person, and so on. I suspect, in fact, that they would not make an exception for a case in which, miraculously enough, the pregnancy went on for nine years, or even the rest of the mother's life.

Some won't even make an exception for a case in which continuation of the pregnancy is likely to shorten the mother's life; they regard abortion as impermissible even to save the mother's life. Such cases are nowadays very rare, and many opponents of abortion do not accept this extreme view. All the same, it is a good place to begin: a number of points of interest come out in respect to it.

1. Let us call the view that abortion is impermissible even to save the mother's life 'the extreme view'. I want to suggest first that it does not issue from the argument I mentioned earlier without the addition of some fairly powerful premisses. Suppose a woman has become pregnant, and now learns that she has a cardiac condition such that she will die if she carries the baby to term. What may be done for her? The foetus, being a person, has a right to life, but as the mother is a person too, so has she a right to life. Presumably they have an equal right to life. How is it supposed to come out that an abortion may not be performed? If mother and child have an equal right to life, shouldn't we perhaps flip a coin? Or should we add to the mother's right to life her right to decide what happens in and to her body, which everybody seems to be ready to grant—the sum of her rights now outweighing the foetus's right to life?

The most familiar argument here is the following. We are told that performing the abortion would be directly killing* the child, whereas doing nothing would not be killing the mother, but only letting her die. Moreover, in killing the child, one would be killing an innocent person,

This famous analogy is central to Thomson's argument, and you should think about it very carefully. One thing to notice is that there are also disanalogies between the case of pregnancy and the violinist case, as Thomson presents it. You should ask yourself how important these are and also whether the violinist case could be modified so as to eliminate some or all of them. (See Discussion Question 1.)

STOP Many people do think that the fact that a pregnancy resulted from rape is morally significant, but *why* is this so (if it is)? Does it have any bearing on whether or not the fetus is a *person*? Is it perhaps relevant in some other way?

*The term 'direct' in the arguments I refer to is a technical one. Roughly, what is meant by 'direct killing' is either killing as an end in itself, or killing as a means to some end, for example, the end of saving someone else's life. . . .

for the child has committed no crime, and is not aiming at his mother's death. And then there are a variety of ways in which this might be continued. (1) But as directly killing an innocent person is always and absolutely impermissible, an abortion may not be performed. Or, (2) as directly killing an innocent person is murder, and murder is always and absolutely impermissible, an abortion may not be performed. Or, (3) as one's duty to refrain from directly killing an innocent person is more stringent than one's duty to keep a person from dying, an abortion may not be performed. Or, (4) if one's only options are directly killing an innocent person or letting a person die, one must prefer letting the person die, and thus an abortion may not be performed.* 6

6

The underlying idea here is something often referred to as "the Principle of Double Effect." As Thomson mentions in the earlier footnote, this principle attaches great weight to the distinction between consequences of an action that are intended (as ends or as means to ends) and consequences that are unintended "side effects."

Some people seem to have thought that these are not further premisses which must be added if the conclusion is to be reached, but that they follow from the very fact that an innocent person has a right to life. But this seems to me to be a mistake, and perhaps the simplest way to show this is to bring out that while we must certainly grant that innocent persons have a right to life, the theses in (1) to (4) are all false. Take (2), for example. If directly killing an innocent person is murder, and thus is impermissible, then the mother's directly killing the innocent person inside her is murder, and thus is impermissible. But it cannot seriously be thought to be murder if the mother performs an abortion on herself to save her life. It cannot seriously be said that she *must* refrain, that she *must* sit passively by and wait for her death. Let us look again at the case of you and the violinist. There you are, in bed with the violinist, and the director of the hospital says to you, 'It's all most distressing, and I deeply sympathize, but you see this is putting an additional strain on your kidneys, and you'll be dead within the month. But you *have* to stay where you are all the same. Because unplugging you would be directly killing an innocent violinist, and that's murder, and that's impermissible.' If anything in the world is true, it is that you do not commit murder, you do not do what is impermissible, if you reach around to your back and unplug yourself from that violinist to save your life. 7

7

Is it, as Thomson seems to think, *more* obvious that the mother can save her own life than that someone else can act so as to do it for her—and analogously in the violinist case? Why?

The main focus of attention in writings on abortion has been on what a third party may or may not do in answer to a request from a woman for an abortion. This is in a way understandable. Things being as they are, there isn't much a woman can safely do to abort herself. So the question asked is what a third party may do, and what the mother may do, if it is mentioned at all, is deduced, almost as an afterthought, from what it is concluded that third parties may do. But it seems to me that to treat the matter in this way is to refuse to grant to the mother that very status of person which is so firmly insisted on for the foetus. For we cannot simply read off what a person may do from what a third party may do. Suppose you find yourself trapped in a tiny house with a growing child. I mean a very tiny house, and a rapidly growing child—you are already up against the wall of the house and in a few minutes you'll be crushed to death. The child on the other hand won't be crushed to death; if nothing is done to stop him from growing he'll be hurt, but in the end he'll simply burst open the house and walk out a free man. Now I could well understand it if a bystander were to say, 'There's nothing we can do for you. We cannot choose between your life and his, we cannot be the ones to decide who is to live, we cannot intervene.' But it cannot be concluded that you too can do nothing, that you cannot attack it to save your life. However innocent the child may be, you do not have to wait passively while it crushes you to death. Perhaps a pregnant woman is vaguely felt to have the status of house, to which we don't allow the right of self-defence. But if the woman houses the child, it should be remembered that she is a person who houses it.

I should perhaps stop to say explicitly that I am not claiming that people have a right to do anything whatever to save their lives. I think, rather, that there are drastic limits to the right of self-defence. If someone threatens you with death unless you torture someone else to death, I think you have not the right, even to save your life, to do so. But the case under consideration here is very different. In our case there are only two people involved, one whose life is threatened, and one who threatens it. Both are

*The thesis in (4) is in an interesting way weaker than those in (1), (2), and (3): they rule out abortion even in cases in which both mother *and* child will die if the abortion is not performed. By contrast, one who held the view expressed in (4) could consistently say that one needn't prefer letting two persons die to killing one.

innocent: the one who is threatened is not threatened because of any fault, the one who threatens does not threaten because of any fault. For this reason we may feel that we bystanders cannot intervene. But the person threatened can. [8]

The (rather fanciful) example in the previous paragraph is a case of an *innocent threat:* someone who is a threat to someone else's life (or well-being) through no fault of his or her own. Thomson's claim is that a person can defend him- or herself from an innocent threat even if it requires harming or even killing the innocent person who poses the threat. Is this right? (See Discussion Question 2.)

In sum, a woman surely can defend her life against the threat to it posed by the unborn child, even if doing so involves its death. And this shows not merely that the theses in (1) to (4) are false; it shows also that the extreme view of abortion is false, and so we need not canvass any other possible ways of arriving at it from the argument I mentioned at the outset.

2. The extreme view could of course be weakened to say that while abortion is permissible to save the mother's life, it may not be performed by a third party, but only by the mother herself. But this cannot be right either. For what we have to keep in mind is that the mother and the unborn child are not like two tenants in a small house which has, by an unfortunate mistake, been rented to both: the mother *owns* the house. The fact that she does adds to the offensiveness of deducing that the mother can do nothing from the supposition that third parties can do nothing. But it does more than this: it casts a bright light on the supposition that third parties can do nothing. Certainly it lets us see that a third party who says 'I cannot choose between you' is fooling himself if he thinks this is impartiality. If Jones has found and fastened on a certain coat, which he needs to keep him from freezing, but which Smith also needs to keep him from freezing, then it is not impartiality that says 'I cannot choose between you' when Smith owns the coat. Women have said again and again 'This body is *my* body!' and they have reason to feel angry, reason to feel that it has been like shouting into the wind. Smith, after all, is hardly likely to bless us if we say to him, 'Of course it's your coat, anybody would grant that it is. But no one may choose between you and Jones who is to have it.' [9]

One key premise of Thomson's argument is that the mother *owns* her body (as does also the person hooked up to the violinist).

(In analogies like the coat example, it is important to insist that the case be one in which the ownership involved is itself entirely morally legitimate, not in any way morally questionable, as some cases of ownership might be—for example, ownership resulting from exploitation or fraud.)

We should really ask what it is that says 'no one may choose' in the face of the fact that the body that houses the child is the mother's body. It may be simply a failure to appreciate this fact. But it may be something more interesting, namely the sense that one has a right to refuse to lay hands on people, even where it would be just and fair to do so, even where justice seems to require that somebody do so. Thus justice might call for somebody to get Smith's coat back from Jones, and yet you have a right to refuse to be the one to lay hands on Jones, a right to refuse to do physical violence to him. This, I think, must be granted. But then what should be said is not 'no one may choose', but only '*I* cannot choose', and indeed not even this, but '*I* will not *act*', leaving it open that somebody else can or should, and in particular that anyone in a position of authority, with the job of securing people's rights, both can and should. So this is no difficulty. I have not been arguing that any given third party must accede to the mother's request that he perform an abortion to save her life, but only that he may.

I suppose that in some views of human life the mother's body is only on loan to her, the loan not being one which gives her any prior claim to it. One who held this view might well think it impartiality to say 'I cannot choose'. But I shall simply ignore this possibility. My own view is that if a human being has any just, prior claim to anything at all, he has a just, prior claim to his own body. And perhaps this needn't be argued for here anyway, since, as I mentioned, the arguments against abortion we are looking at do grant that the woman has a right to decide what happens in and to her body.

But although they do grant it, I have tried to show that they do not take seriously what is done in granting it. I suggest the same thing will reappear even more clearly when we turn away from cases in which the mother's life is at stake, and attend, as I propose we now do, to the vastly more common cases in which a woman wants an abortion for some less weighty reason than preserving her own life.

3. Where the mother's life is not at stake, the argument I mentioned at the outset seems to have a much stronger pull. 'Everyone has a right to life, so the unborn person has a right to life.' And isn't the child's right to life weightier than anything other than the mother's own right to life, which she might put forward as ground for an abortion?

This argument treats the right to life as if it were unproblematic. It is not, and this seems to me to be precisely the source of the mistake.

For we should now, at long last, ask what it comes to, to have a right to life. In some views having a right to life includes having a right to be given at least the bare minimum one needs for continued life. But suppose that what in fact *is* the bare minimum a man needs for continued

In Thomson's view, the right to life (the one we ascribe to persons) is not a *positive* right to receive *whatever* minimum aid is needed to preserve life—such as the use of someone's kidneys or Henry Fonda's hand. (For the distinction between positive and negative rights, see the Ozar selection.)

This amounts to viewing the right to life as merely a negative right to non-interference, with no positive component.

If the violinist has no right to the use of your kidneys, then it seems to follow that you can prevent him from using them and perhaps—to be discussed later—that others can help you in this. Thus the violinist's right to life is not a right to non-interference of any sort. (As shown also by the earlier example of the coat that each of two people needs, one owns, and the other currently is wearing.)

R Thomson is saying that the intuition that all *persons* (not necessarily all humans) have a right to life is strong enough that any acceptable account of this right must yield this result (this may in fact follow immediately from the concept of a person).

life is something he has no right at all to be given? If I am sick unto death, and the only thing that will save my life is the touch of Henry Fonda's cool hand on my fevered brow, then all the same, I have no right to be given the touch of Henry Fonda's cool hand on my fevered brow. It would be frightfully nice of him to fly in from the West Coast to provide it. It would be less nice, though no doubt well meant, if my friends flew out to the West Coast and carried Henry Fonda back with them. But I have no right at all against anybody that he should do this for me. Or again, to return to the story I told earlier, the fact that for continued life that violinist needs the continued use of your kidneys does not establish that he has a right to be given the continued use of your kidneys. He certainly has no right against you that *you* should give him continued use of your kidneys. For nobody has any right to use your kidneys unless you give him such a right; and nobody has the right against you that you shall give him this right—if you do allow him to go on using your kidneys, this is a kindness on your part, and not something he can claim from you as his due. Nor has he any right against anybody else that *they* should give him continued use of your kidneys. Certainly he had no right against the Society of Music Lovers that they should plug him into you in the first place. And if you now start to unplug yourself, having learned that you will otherwise have to spend nine years in bed with him, there is nobody in the world who must try to prevent you, in order to see to it that he is given something he has a right to be given. (10)

Some people are rather stricter about the right to life. In their view, it does not include the right to be given anything, but amounts to, and only to, the right not to be killed by anybody. (11) But here a related difficulty arises. If everybody is to refrain from killing that violinist, then everybody must refrain from doing a great many different sorts of things. Everybody must refrain from slitting his throat, everybody must refrain from shooting him—and everybody must refrain from unplugging you from him. But does he have a right against everybody that they shall refrain from unplugging you from him? To refrain from doing this is to allow him to continue to use your kidneys. It could be argued that he has a right against us that *we* should allow him to continue to use your kidneys. That is, while he had no right against us that we should give him the use of your kidneys, it might be argued that he anyway has a right against us that we shall not now intervene and deprive him of the use of your kidneys. I shall come back to third-party interventions later. But certainly the violinist has no right against you that *you* shall allow him to continue to use your kidneys. As I said, if you do allow him to use them, it is a kindness on your part, and not something you owe him. (12)

The difficulty I point to here is not peculiar to the right to life. It reappears in connection with all the other natural rights; and it is something which an adequate account of rights must deal with. For present purposes it is enough just to draw attention to it. But I would stress that I am not arguing that people do not have a right to life—quite to the contrary, it seems to me that the primary control we must place on the acceptability of an account of rights is that it should turn out in that account to be a truth that all persons have a right to life. (13) I am arguing only that having a right to life does not guarantee having either a right to be given the use of or a right to be allowed continued use of another person's body—even if one needs it for life itself. So the right to life will not serve the opponents of abortion in the very simple and clear way in which they seem to have thought it would.

4. There is another way to bring out the difficulty. In the most ordinary sort of case, to deprive someone of what he has a right to is to treat him unjustly. Suppose a boy and his small brother are jointly given a box of chocolates for Christmas. If the older boy takes the box and refuses to give his brother any of the chocolates, he is unjust to him, for the brother has been given a right to half of them. But suppose that, having learned that otherwise it means nine years in bed with that violinist, you unplug yourself from him. You surely are not being unjust to him, for you gave him no right to use your kidneys, and no one else can have given him any such right. But we have to notice that in unplugging yourself, you are killing him; and violinists, like everybody else, have a right to life, and thus in the view we were considering just now, the right not to be killed. So here you do what he supposedly has a right you shall not do, but you do not act unjustly to him in doing it.

The emendation which may be made at this point is this: the right to life consists not in the right not to be killed, but rather in the right not to be killed unjustly. [14] This runs a risk of circularity, but never mind: it would enable us to square the fact that the violinist has a right to life with the fact that you do not act unjustly toward him in unplugging yourself, thereby killing him. For if you do not kill him unjustly, you do not violate his right to life, and so it is no wonder you do him no injustice.

But if this emendation is accepted, the gap in the argument against abortion stares us plainly in the face: it is by no means enough to show that the foetus is a person, and to remind us that all persons have a right to life—we need to be shown also that killing the foetus violates its right to life, i.e. that abortion is unjust killing. And is it?

I suppose we may take it as a datum that in a case of pregnancy due to rape the mother has not given the unborn person a right to the use of her body for food and shelter. Indeed, in what pregnancy could it be supposed that the mother has given the unborn person such a right? It is not as if there were unborn persons drifting about the world, to whom a woman who wants a child says 'I invite you in'.

But it might be argued that there are other ways one can have acquired a right to the use of another person's body than by having been invited to use it by that person. Suppose a woman voluntarily indulges in intercourse, knowing of the chance it will issue in pregnancy, and then she does become pregnant; is she not in part responsible for the presence, in fact the very existence, of the unborn person inside her? No doubt she did not invite it in. But doesn't her partial responsibility for its being there itself give it a right to the use of her body? If so, then her aborting it would be more like the boy's taking away the chocolates, and less like your unplugging yourself from the violinist—doing so would be depriving it of what it does have a right to, and thus would be doing it an injustice. [15]

And then, too, it might be asked whether or not she can kill it even to save her own life: If she voluntarily called it into existence, how can she now kill it, even in self-defence?

The first thing to be said about this is that it is something new. Opponents of abortion have been so concerned to make out the independence of the foetus, in order to establish that it has a right to life, just as its mother does, that they have tended to overlook the possible support they might gain from making out that the foetus is *dependent* on the mother, in order to establish that she has a special kind of responsibility for it, a responsibility that gives it rights against her which are not possessed by any independent person—such as an ailing violinist who is a stranger to her.

On the other hand, this argument would give the unborn person a right to its mother's body only if her pregnancy resulted from a voluntary act, undertaken in full knowledge of the chance a pregnancy might result from it. It would leave out entirely the unborn person whose existence is due to rape. Pending the availability of some further argument, then we would be left with the conclusion that unborn persons whose existence is due to rape have no right to the use of their mothers' bodies, and thus that aborting them is not depriving them of anything they have a right to and hence is not unjust killing. [16]

And we should also notice that it is not at all plain that this argument really does go even as far as it purports to. For there are cases and cases, and the details make a difference. If the room is stuffy, and I therefore open a window to air it, and a burglar climbs in, it would be absurd to say, 'Ah, now he can stay, she's given him a right to the use of her house—for she is partially responsible for his presence there, having voluntarily done what enabled him to get in, in full knowledge that there are such things as burglars, and that burglars burgle.' It would be still more absurd to say this if I had had bars installed outside my windows, precisely to prevent burglars from getting in, and a burglar got in only because of a defect in the bars. It remains equally absurd if we imagine it is not a burglar who climbs in, but an innocent person who blunders or falls in. . . .

It seems to me that the argument we are looking at can establish at most that there are *some* cases in which the unborn person has a right to the use of its mother's body, and therefore *some* cases in which abortion is unjust killing. There is room for much discussion and argument as to precisely which, if any. But I think we should side-step this issue and leave it open, for at any rate the argument certainly does not establish that all abortion is unjust killing.

R So, in Thomson's view, the right to life is a right to non-interference of a certain sort: the right not to be killed *unjustly*. (This does not, of course, settle the question of what counts as unjust killing.)

Thomson is suggesting this view, not fully endorsing it. One way to assess it is to imagine a version of the violinist case that involves you doing something that you know in advance might lead to you being hooked up to the violinist. (See Discussion Question 3.)

R According to Thomson, this is the clearest case in which abortion is not unjust killing and so does not violate the fetus's right to life. She is not saying that it is the only case.

5. There is room for yet another argument here, however. We surely must all grant that there may be cases in which it would be morally indecent to detach a person from your body at the cost of his life. Suppose you learn that what the violinist needs is not nine years of your life, but only one hour: all you need do to save his life is to spend one hour in that bed with him. Suppose also that letting him use your kidneys for that one hour would not affect your health in the slightest. Admittedly you were kidnapped. Admittedly you did not give anyone permission to plug him into you. Nevertheless it seems to me plain you *ought* to allow him to use your kidneys for that hour—it would be indecent to refuse.

Again, suppose pregnancy lasted only an hour, and constituted no threat to life or health. And suppose that a woman becomes pregnant as a result of rape. Admittedly she did not voluntarily do anything to bring about the existence of a child. Admittedly she did nothing at all which would give the unborn person a right to the use of her body. All the same it might well be said, as in the newly emended violinist story, that she *ought* to allow it to remain for that hour—that it would be indecent in her to refuse. (17)

17 "Morally indecent" because what is needed to keep the unborn person alive costs the mother so little.

One way to defend this point would be to appeal to Kant's duty of beneficence, deriving from the requirement to treat other persons as ends in themselves: could you be regarding another person as an end in himself and still be unwilling to make even this minimal effort to save him?

Now some people are inclined to use the term 'right' in such a way that it follows from the fact that you ought to allow a person to use your body for the hour he needs, that he has a right to use your body for the hour he needs, even though he has not been given that right by any person or act. They may say that it follows also that if you refuse, you act unjustly toward him. This use of the term is perhaps so common that it cannot be called wrong; nevertheless it seems to me to be an unfortunate loosening of what we would do better to keep a tight rein on. Suppose that box of chocolates I mentioned earlier had not been given to both boys jointly, but was given only to the older boy. There he sits, stolidly eating his way through the box, his small brother watching enviously. Here we are likely to say 'You ought not to be so mean. You ought to give your brother some of those chocolates.' My own view is that it just does not follow from the truth of this that the brother has any right to any of the chocolates. If the boy refuses to give his brother any, he is greedy, stingy, callous—but not unjust. I suppose that the people I have in mind will say it does follow that the brother has a right to some of the chocolates, and thus that the boy does act unjustly if he refuses to give his brother any. But the effect of saying this is to obscure what we should keep distinct, namely the difference between the boy's refusal in this case and the boy's refusal in the earlier case, in which the box was given to both boys jointly, and in which the small brother thus had what was from any point of view clear title to half. (18)

18

So while all rights have correlative obligations, it is not true in Thomson's view (or that of almost all other rights theorists) that every obligation creates a correlative right.

A further objection to so using the term 'right' that from the fact that A ought to do a thing for B, it follows that B has a right against A that A do it for him, is that it is going to make the question of whether or not a man has a right to a thing turn on how easy it is to provide him with it; and this seems not merely unfortunate, but morally unacceptable. Take the case of Henry Fonda again. I said earlier that I had no right to the touch of his cool hand on my fevered brow, even though I needed it to save my life. I said it would be frightfully nice of him to fly in from the West Coast to provide me with it, but that I had no right against him that he should do so. But suppose he isn't on the West Coast. Suppose he has only to walk across the room, place a hand briefly on my brow—and lo, my life is saved. Then surely he ought to do it, it would be indecent to refuse. Is it to be said 'Ah, well, it follows that in this case she has a right to the touch of his hand on her brow, and so it would be an injustice in him to refuse?' So that I have a right to it when it is easy for him to provide it, though no right when it's hard? It's rather a shocking idea that anyone's rights should fade away and disappear as it gets harder and harder to accord them to him. (19)

19

Thomson is appealing here to the moral intuition that rights *override* other sorts of considerations—and so could not depend on how easy they are to satisfy. (See the selection from Ozar for a discussion of how rights override other moral considerations.)

So my own view is that even though you ought to let the violinist use your kidneys for the one hour he needs, we should not conclude that he has a right to do so—we should say that if you refuse, you are, like the boy who owns all the chocolates and will give none away, self-centred and callous, indecent in fact, but not unjust. And similarly, that even supposing a case in which a woman pregnant due to rape ought to allow the unborn person to use her body for the hour he needs, we should not conclude that he has a right to do so; we should conclude that she is self-centred, callous, indecent, but not unjust, if she refuses. The complaints are no less grave; they are just different. However, there is no need to insist on this point. If anyone does wish to deduce 'he has a right' from 'you ought', then all the same he must surely grant that there are cases in which it is not morally required of you that you allow that violinist to use your kidneys, and in which he does not have a right to use them, and so also for mother and unborn child. Except in such cases as the unborn person has a right to demand it—and we were leaving open the possibility that there may be such cases—nobody is morally *required* to make large sacrifices, of health, of all other interests and concerns, of all other duties and commitments, for nine years, or even for nine months, in order to keep another person alive.

6. We have in fact to distinguish between two kinds of Samaritan: the Good Samaritan and what we might call the Minimally Decent Samaritan. The story of the Good Samaritan, you will remember, goes like this:

> A certain man went down from Jerusalem to Jericho, and fell among thieves, which stripped him of his raiment, and wounded him, and departed, leaving him half dead.
>
> And by chance there came down a certain priest that way; and when he saw him, he passed by on the other side.
>
> And likewise a Levite, when he was at the place, came and looked on him, and passed by on the other side.
>
> But a certain Samaritan, as he journeyed, came where he was; and when he saw him he had compassion on him.
>
> And went to him, and bound up his wounds, pouring in oil and wine, and set him on his own beast, and brought him to an inn, and took care of him.
>
> And on the morrow, when he departed, he took out two pence, and gave them to the host, and said unto him, 'Take care of him; and whatsoever thou spendest more, when I come again, I will repay thee.'
>
> (Luke 10: 30–5)

The Good Samaritan went out of his way, at some cost to himself, to help one in need of it. We are not told what the options were, that is, whether or not the priest and the Levite could have helped by doing less than the Good Samaritan did, but assuming they could have, then the fact they did nothing at all shows they were not even Minimally Decent Samaritans, not because they were not Samaritans, but because they were not even minimally decent.

These things are a matter of degree, of course, but there is a difference, and it comes out perhaps most clearly in the story of Kitty Genovese, who, as you will remember, was murdered while thirty-eight people watched or listened, and did nothing at all to help her. A Good Samaritan would have rushed out to give direct assistance against the murderer. Or perhaps we had better allow that it would have been a Splendid Samaritan who did this, on the ground that it would have involved a risk of death for himself. But the thirty-eight not only did not do this, they did not even trouble to pick up a phone to call the police. Minimally Decent Samaritanism would call for doing at least that, and their not having done it was monstrous. 20

20 Again a Kantian argument seems relevant: could anyone who refused even to make a phone call seriously claim to be treating Kitty Genovese as an end in herself?

After telling the story of the Good Samaritan, Jesus said 'Go, and do thou likewise.' Perhaps he meant that we are morally required to act as the Good Samaritan did. Perhaps he was urging people to do more than is morally required of them. At all events it seems plain that it was not morally required of any of the thirty-eight that he rush out to give direct assistance at the risk of his own life, and that it is not morally required of anyone that he give long stretches of his life—nine years or nine months—to sustaining the life of a person who has no special right (we were leaving open the possibility of this) to demand it.

Indeed, with one rather striking class of exceptions, no one in any country in the world is *legally* required to do anywhere near as much as this for anyone else. The class of exceptions is obvious. My main concern here is not the state of the law in respect to abortion, but it is worth drawing attention to the fact that in no state in this country is any man compelled by law to be even a Minimally Decent Samaritan to any person; there is no law under which charges could be brought against the thirty-eight who stood by while Kitty Genovese died. By contrast, in most states in this country women are compelled by law to be not merely Minimally Decent Samaritans, but Good Samaritans to unborn persons inside them. This doesn't by itself settle anything one way or the other, because it may well be argued that there should be laws in this country—as there are in many European countries—compelling at least Minimally Decent Samaritanism. But it does show that there is a gross injustice in the existing state of the law. And it shows also that the groups currently working against liberalization of abortion laws, in fact working toward having it declared unconstitutional for a state to permit abortion, had better start working for the adoption of Good Samaritan laws generally, or earn the charge that they are acting in bad faith.

I should think, myself, that Minimally Decent Samaritan laws would be one thing, Good Samaritan laws quite another, and in fact highly improper. But we are not here concerned with the law. What we should ask is not whether anybody should be compelled by law to be a Good Samaritan, but whether we must accede to a situation in which somebody is being compelled—by nature, perhaps—to be a Good Samaritan. We have, in other words, to look now at third-party interventions. I have been arguing that no person is morally required to make large sacrifices to sustain the life of another who has no right to demand them, and this even where the sacrifices do not include life itself; we are not morally required to be Good Samaritans or anyway Very Good Samaritans to one another. But what if a man cannot extricate himself from such a situation? What if he appeals to us to extricate him? It seems to me plain that there are cases in which we can, cases in which a Good Samaritan would extricate him. There you are, you were kidnapped, and nine years in bed with that violinist lie ahead of you. You have your own life to lead. You are sorry, but you simply cannot see giving up so much of your life to the sustaining of his. You cannot extricate yourself, and ask us to do so. I should have thought that—in light of his having no right to the use of your body—it was obvious that we do not have to accede to your being forced to give up so much. We can do what you ask. There is no injustice to the violinist in our doing so. (21)

7. Following the lead of the opponents of abortion, I have throughout been speaking of the foetus merely as a person, and what I have been asking is whether or not the argument we began with, which proceeds only from the foetus's being a person, really does establish its conclusion. I have argued that it does not.

But of course there are arguments and arguments, and it may be said that I have simply fastened on the wrong one. It may be said that what is important is not merely the fact that the foetus is a person, but that it is a person for whom the woman has a special kind of responsibility issuing from the fact that she is its mother. And it might be argued that all my analogies are therefore irrelevant—for you do not have that special kind of responsibility for that violinist, Henry Fonda does not have that special kind of responsibility for me. And our attention might be drawn to the fact that men and women both *are* compelled by law to provide support for their children.

I have in effect dealt (briefly) with this argument in section 4 above; but a (still briefer) recapitulation now may be in order. Surely we do not have any such 'special responsibility' for a person unless we have assumed it, explicitly or implicitly. If a set of parents do not try to prevent pregnancy, do not obtain an abortion, and then at the time of birth of the child do not put it out for adoption, but rather take it home with them, then they have assumed responsibility for it, they have given it rights, and they cannot *now* withdraw support from it at the cost of its life because they now find it difficult to go on providing for it. But if they have taken all reasonable precautions against having a child, they do not simply by virtue of their biological relationship to the child who comes into existence have a special responsibility for it. They may wish to assume responsibility for it, or they may not wish to. And I am suggesting that if assuming responsibility for it would require large sacrifices, then they may refuse. A Good Samaritan would not refuse—or anyway, a Splendid Samaritan, if the sacrifices that had to be made were enormous. But then so would a Good Samaritan assume responsibility for that violinist; so would Henry Fonda, if he is a Good Samaritan, fly in from the West Coast and assume responsibility for me. (22)

8. My argument will be found unsatisfactory on two counts by many of those who want to regard abortion as morally permissible. First, while I do argue that abortion is not impermissible, I do not argue that it is always permissible. There may well be cases in which carrying the child to term requires only Minimally Decent Samaritanism of the mother, and this is a standard we must not fall below. I am inclined to think it a merit of my account precisely that it does *not* give a general yes or a general no. It allows for and supports our sense that, for example, a sick and desperately frightened fourteen-year-old schoolgirl, pregnant due to

(21)

R There is no injustice because you have done nothing to give the violinist any right to use your kidneys.

(Think of ways in which the suitation might be different in this respect.)

R And minimal decency (like Kant's duty of beneficence) does not require a sacrifice this great.

(22)

Thomson is saying, among other things, that a merely *biological* relationship is not enough to give the mother a special responsibility for the child. Here again, one way to think about this claim is to imagine a corresponding variation of the violinist example.

rape, may *of course* choose abortion, and that any law which rules this out is an insane law. And it also allows for and supports our sense that in other cases resort to abortion is even positively indecent. It would be indecent in the woman to request an abortion, and indecent in a doctor to perform it, if she is in her seventh month, and wants the abortion just to avoid the nuisance of postponing a trip abroad. The very fact that the arguments I have been drawing attention to treat all cases of abortion, or even all cases of abortion in which the mother's life is not at stake, as morally on a par ought to have made them suspect at the outset. 23

Thus Thomson's argument does not seem to support "a woman's right to choose" as this is currently understood, at least not as a moral right. (The issue of whether abortion should be *legally* permitted is not directly addressed by anything Thomson says.)

Secondly, while I am arguing for the permissibility of abortion in some cases, I am not arguing for the right to secure the death of the unborn child. It is easy to confuse these two things in that up to a certain point in the life of the foetus it is not able to survive outside the mother's body; hence removing it from her body guarantees its death. But they are importantly different. I have argued that you are not morally required to spend nine months in bed, sustaining the life of that violinist; but to say this is by no means to say that if, when you unplug yourself, there is a miracle and he survives, you then have a right to turn round and slit his throat. You may detach yourself even if this costs him his life; you have no right to be guaranteed his death, by some other means, if unplugging yourself does not kill him. There are some people who will feel dissatisfied by this feature of my argument. A woman may be utterly devastated by the thought of a child, a bit of herself, put out for adoption and never seen or heard of again. She may therefore want not merely that the child be detached from her, but more, that it die. Some opponents of abortion are inclined to regard this as beneath contempt—thereby showing insensitivity to what is surely a powerful source of despair. All the same, I agree that the desire for the child's death is not one which anybody may gratify, should it turn out to be possible to detach the child alive.

At this place, however, it should be remembered that we have only been pretending throughout that the foetus is a human being from the moment of conception. A very early abortion is surely not the killing of a person, and so is not dealt with by anything I have said here.

Discussion Questions

1. Here are two obvious differences between the violinist case and a standard abortion case (these are not the only ones): (1) A pregnant woman is able to move fairly freely, continue to work, and engage in various other activities, whereas the person hooked up to the violinist must remain in bed. (2) The violinist is described as famous, and so is presumably especially talented and thereby valuable, whereas nothing of this sort is known to pertain to a normal fetus. Try to imagine a version of the violinist case that is closer to a normal pregnancy in these respects (not an abnormal pregnancy that is closer to the violinist case), and then see if any of the changes make a difference to your intuitive assessment of the case.
2. Here is another example of an innocent threat: An innocent 5-year-old is about to push a button that will set off a bomb that will kill several people. You can't get there in time to physically restrain the child from pressing the button, but you can stop him from doing so by shooting him with a gun that you already have in your hand. Assume that it is certain beyond any reasonable doubt that the child is going to immediately press the button (perhaps it looks like a button in a game that the child likes to play), and also that none of the people involved, including the child, is in any way responsible for the situation being as it is. Is it morally acceptable to shoot the child to prevent the bomb from going off? Does it matter how many others will be killed if it does? Does it matter whether you are one of them? What if the bomb will also kill the child?
3. Here is a modified version of the violinist case: Suppose that, rather than being kidnapped at random, you were kidnapped from a concert of classical music, and that you knew in advance (a) that there was a group attempting to help musicians with damaged kidneys and (b) that there was a good chance that some of the people attending the concert would be kidnapped to be hooked up to such musicians. Is this enough to make it the case that you have given the violinist a right to the use of your kidneys? Does it matter what the odds of being thus kidnapped are (assuming that you know them)? What if you could have greatly reduced the probability of being kidnapped for this purpose by purchasing a more expensive ticket to the concert, but you chose in fact to buy only a cheaper ticket? What if it were part of the agreement you made in purchasing the ticket that there would be a certain

probability of being hooked up to a musician, and that you agreed to remain hooked up for nine months if this should happen (as a condition of getting the ticket)?

4. Suppose that a person who cannot swim has fallen into the water and is about to drown. You are standing on shore, and there is a system available that will automatically locate the person, fasten a rope to him, and pull him to shore (without drowning or otherwise harming him in the process). But the system needs to be activated by pressing a button. Are you violating the person's right to life if you do not press the button? Are you being "morally indecent" by not doing so? Does it matter if there are other people who could press the button, and some of them are closer to it than you? Does it matter how far you have to walk to reach the button (still assuming that you can get there in time) and how much inconvenience will be involved for you? Should people in your situation be *legally* required to press the button (if no one else does it first)?

Virtue Ethics: Morality Depends on Character Traits

Aristotle

Aristotle (384–322 B.C.) was a Greek philosopher and one of the most important and influential philosophers of all time—quite possibly the most important and influential of all. He was a student of Plato, tutored Alexander the Great, and later founded his own philosophical school, the Lyceum. In the writings that have survived, almost none of which were intended for publication in their current state, Aristotle makes important contributions to virtually every area of philosophy including logic, metaphysics, epistemology, the philosophy of mind, ethics, political philosophy, and aesthetics.

In the selection that follows, taken from his most important ethical work, Aristotle argues that human happiness (or flourishing) consists in action according to virtue, and proceeds to give an account of the moral virtues. His famous view is that a virtue consists in a mean between two opposed vices, one of these involving an excess and the other a deficiency of the relevant quality. Though Aristotle's thought has provided much of the inspiration for contemporary virtue ethics, it is a matter of scholarly controversy (which cannot be pursued here) whether he held a view of this sort himself.

The headings in the selection and the section numbers were added by the translator and do not come from Aristotle. (Some of these have been deleted.)

From *The Nichomachean Ethics*

Book I: The Good for Man

Subject of Our Inquiry

All human activities aim at some good: some goods subordinate to others

1. Every art and every inquiry, and similarly every action and pursuit, is thought to aim at some good; and for this reason the good has rightly been declared to be that at which all things aim. But a certain difference is found among ends; some are activities, others are products apart from the activities that produce them. Where there are ends apart from the actions, it is the nature of the products to be better than the activities. . . .

2. If, then, there is some end of the things we do, which we desire for its own sake (everything else being desired for the sake of this), and if we do not choose everything for the sake of something else (for at that rate the process would go on to infinity, so that our desire would be empty and vain), clearly this must be the good and the chief good. (1) Will not the knowledge of it, then, have a great influence on life? Shall we

(1) R Not everything can be desired only for the sake of something else. Thus some things must be **intrinsic goods,** desirable for their own sakes. Aristotle assumes further that there is one and only one intrinsic good for the sake of which everything else is desired.

From *The Nichomachean Ethics,* translated by David Ross, revised by Ackrill and Urmson (Oxford: Oxford University Press, 1980).

not, like archers who have a mark to aim at, be more likely to hit upon what is right? . . .

What Is the Good for Man?

It is generally agreed to be happiness, but there are various views as to what happiness is. . . .

4. Let us resume our inquiry and state, in view of the fact that all knowledge and every pursuit aims at some good, . . . what is the highest of all goods achievable by action. Verbally there is very general agreement; for both the general run of men and people of superior refinement say that it is happiness, and identify living well and faring well with being happy ❷; but with regard to what happiness is they differ, and the many do not give the same account as the wise. For the former think it is some plain and obvious thing, like pleasure, wealth, or honour; they differ, however, from one another—and often even the same man identifies it with different things, with health when he is ill, with wealth when he is poor. . . . Now some thought that apart from these many goods there is another which is good in itself and causes the goodness of all these as well. . . .

Discussion of the popular views that the good is pleasure, honour, wealth . . .

5. . . . To judge from the lives that men lead, most men, and men of the most vulgar type, seem (not without some ground) to identify the good, or happiness, with pleasure; which is the reason why they love the life of enjoyment. For there are, we may say, three prominent types of life—that just mentioned, the political, and thirdly the contemplative life. Now the mass of mankind are evidently quite slavish in their tastes, preferring a life suitable to beasts. . . . A consideration of the prominent types of life shows that people of superior refinement and of active disposition identify happiness with honour; for this is, roughly speaking, the end of the political life. But it seems too superficial to be what we are looking for, since it is thought to depend on those who bestow honour rather than on him who receives it, but the good we divine to be something of one's own and not easily taken from one. Further, men seem to pursue honour in order that they may be assured of their merit; at least it is by men of practical wisdom that they seek to be honoured, and among those who know them, and on the ground of their virtue; clearly, then, according to them, at any rate, virtue is better. . . . ❸

The good must be something final and self-sufficient. Definition of happiness reached by considering the characteristic function of man

7. Let us again return to the good we are seeking, and ask what it can be . . . we call that which is in itself worthy of pursuit more final than that which is worthy of pursuit for the sake of something else, and that which is never desirable for the sake of something else more final than the things that are desirable both in themselves and for the sake of that other thing, and therefore we call final without qualification that which is always desirable in itself and never for the sake of something else.

Now such a thing happiness, above all else, is held to be; for this we choose always for itself and never for the sake of something else, but honour, pleasure, reason, and every virtue we choose indeed for themselves (for if nothing resulted from them we should still choose each of them), but we choose them also for the sake of happiness, judging that through them we shall be happy. Happiness, on the other hand, no one chooses for the sake of these, nor, in general, for anything other than itself. ❹

From the point of view of self-sufficiency the same result seems to follow; for the final good is thought to be self-sufficient. Now by self-sufficient we do not mean that which is sufficient for a man by himself, for one who lives a solitary life, but also for parents, children, wife, and in general for his friends and fellow citizens, since man is born for citizenship. . . . the self-sufficient we now define as that which when isolated makes life desirable and lacking in nothing; and such we think happiness to be; and further we think it most desirable of all things, not a thing counted as one good thing among others. . . . Happiness, then, is something final and self-sufficient, and is the end of action.

Presumably, however, to say that happiness is the chief good seems a platitude, and a clearer account of what it is is still desired. This might perhaps be given, if we could first ascertain the function of man. For just as for a flute-player, a sculptor, or any artist, and, in general, for all things that have a function or activity, the good and the 'well' is thought to reside in the function, so would it seem to be for man, if he has a

The Greek word here translated as "happiness" is *"eudaimonia,"* also sometimes translated as "human flourishing." It refers to whatever sort of life is most desirable or satisfactory, with no implication that this will be one of pleasure or enjoyment.

The Greek word here translated as "virtue" is *"arete,"* also sometimes translated as "excellence." (The *"arete"* of a thing of a certain kind is whatever makes it a *good* thing of that kind.) Virtue is then excellence of human character. People are honored for their excellences, but not only for moral excellence.

This is essentially a matter of definition: happiness is *whatever* has this status. (What this is, we do not yet know.)

5

The function (*ergon*) of something is its characteristic activity in virtue of the kind of thing that it is.

6

R Aristotle argues that the function of a human being must be something that is not shared with lower forms of life: an active life involving reason or rationality, rather than just nutrition or perception.

7

R Thus human happiness or flourishing is rational activity in accordance with the best and most complete excellence or virtue.

8

R Aristotle insists that happiness essentially involves activity; it is not enough to simply possess traits of mind that would lead to virtuous activity, but which are never in fact used.

9

R A virtuous person will take pleasure in virtuous actions as such, without the need for external pleasure as a motivation.

10

R For the Greeks, happiness involved more than the right inner states of mind or even the right motivations for actions; a substantial degree of worldly success was also required, so that even a person with the best sort of character could have their happiness destroyed by external bad fortune of various sorts.

function. Have the carpenter, then, and the tanner certain functions or activities, and has man none? Is he born without a function? Or as eye, hand, foot, and in general each of the parts evidently has a function, may one lay it down that man similarly has a function apart from all these? (5) What then can this be? Life seems to belong even to plants, but we are seeking what is peculiar to man. Let us exclude, therefore, the life of nutrition and growth. Next there would be a life of perception, but *it* also seems to be shared even by the horse, the ox, and every animal. There remains, then, an active life of the element that has a rational principle. . . . (6) Now if the function of man is an activity of soul which follows or implies a rational principle, . . . and if any action is well performed when it is performed in accordance with the appropriate excellence: if this is the case, human good turns out to be activity of soul exhibiting excellence, and if there are more than one excellence, in accordance with the best and most complete. (7)

But we must add 'in a complete life'. For one swallow does not make a summer, nor does one day; and so too one day, or a short time, does not make a man blessed and happy.

. . .

8. . . . With those who identify happiness with virtue or some one virtue our account is in harmony; for to virtue belongs virtuous activity. But it makes, perhaps, no small difference whether we place the chief good in possession or in use, in state of mind or in activity. For the state of mind may exist without producing any good result, as in a man who is asleep or in some other way quite inactive, but the activity cannot; for one who has the activity will of necessity be acting, and acting well. . . . (8)

Their life is also in itself pleasant. For pleasure is a state of *soul,* and to each man that which he is said to be a lover of is pleasant; e.g. not only is a horse pleasant to the lover of horses, and a spectacle to the lover of sights, but also in the same way just acts are pleasant to the lover of justice and in general virtuous acts to the lover of virtue. Now for most men their pleasures are in conflict with one another because these are not by nature pleasant, but the lovers of what is noble find pleasant the things that are by nature pleasant; and virtuous actions are such, so that these are pleasant for such men as well as in their own nature. Their life, therefore, has no further need of pleasure as a sort of adventitious charm, but has its pleasure in itself. For, besides what we have said, the man who does not rejoice in noble actions is not even good; since no one would call a man just who did not enjoy acting justly, nor any man liberal who did not enjoy liberal actions; and similarly in all other cases. If this is so, virtuous actions must be in themselves pleasant. (9) But they are also *good* and *noble,* and have each of these attributes in the highest degree, since the good man judges well about these attributes. . . . Happiness then is the best, noblest, and most pleasant thing in the world. . . . For all these properties belong to the best activities; and these, or one—the best—of these, we identify with happiness.

Yet evidently . . . it needs the external goods as well; for it is impossible, or not easy, to do noble acts without the proper equipment. In many actions we use friends and riches and political power as instruments; and there are some things the lack of which takes the lustre from happiness—good birth, goodly children, beauty; for the man who is very ugly in appearance or ill-born or solitary and childless is not very likely to be happy, and perhaps a man would be still less likely if he had thoroughly bad children or friends or had lost good children or friends by death. . . . happiness seems to need this sort of prosperity in addition; for which reason some identify happiness with good fortune, though others identify it with virtue. (10)

. . .

Book II: Moral Virtue

Moral Virtue, How Produced, in What Medium and in What Manner Exhibited

Moral virtue, like the arts, is acquired by repetition of the corresponding acts

1. Virtue, then, being of two kinds, intellectual and moral, intellectual virtue in the main owes both its birth and its growth to teaching (for which reason it requires experience and time), while moral virtue comes about as a result of habit. . . . From this it is also plain that none of the moral virtues arises in us by nature; for nothing that exists by nature can form a habit contrary to its nature. . . . Neither by nature, then,

nor contrary to nature do the virtues arise in us; rather we are adapted by nature to receive them, and are made perfect by habit. (11)

Again, of all the things that come to us by nature we first acquire the potentiality and later exhibit the activity . . . ; but the virtues we get by first exercising them, as also happens in the case of the arts as well. For the things we have to learn before we can do them, we learn by doing them, e.g. men become builders by building and lyre-players by playing the lyre; so too we become just by doing just acts, temperate by doing temperate acts, brave by doing brave acts. (12)

. . .

Again, it is from the same causes and by the same means that every virtue is both produced and destroyed, and similarly every art. . . . by doing the acts that we do in our transactions with other men we become just or unjust, and by doing the acts that we do in the presence of danger, and by being habituated to feel fear or confidence, we become brave or cowardly. The same is true of appetites and feelings of anger; some men become temperate and good-tempered, others self-indulgent and irascible, by behaving in one way or the other in the appropriate circumstances. Thus, in one word, states of character arise out of like activities. This is why the activities we exhibit must be of a certain kind; it is because the states of character correspond to the differences between these. It makes no small difference, then, whether we form habits of one kind or of another from our very youth; it makes a very great difference, or rather *all* the difference. (13)

These acts cannot be prescribed exactly, but must avoid excess and defect

2. Since, then, the present inquiry does not aim at theoretical knowledge like the others (for we are inquiring not in order to know what virtue is, but in order to become good, since otherwise our inquiry would have been of no use), we must examine the nature of actions, namely how we ought to do them; for these determine also the nature of the states of character that are produced. . . . But this must be agreed upon beforehand, that the whole account of matters of conduct must be given in outline and not precisely, as we said at the very beginning that the accounts we demand must be in accordance with the subject-matter; matters concerned with conduct and questions of what is good for us have no fixity, any more than matters of health. The general account being of this nature, the account of particular cases is yet more lacking in exactness; for they do not fall under any art or precept, but the agents themselves must in each case consider what is appropriate to the occasion, as happens also in the art of medicine or of navigation. (14)

But though our present account is of this nature we must give what help we can. First, then, let us consider this, that it is the nature of such things to be destroyed by defect and excess, as we see in the case of strength and of health (for to gain light on things imperceptible we must use the evidence of sensible things); exercise either excessive or defective destroys the strength and similarly drink or food which is above or below a certain amount destroys the health, while that which is proportionate both produces and increases and preserves it. So too is it, then, in the case of temperance and courage and the other virtues. For the man who flies from and fears everything and does not stand his ground against anything becomes a coward, and the man who fears nothing at all but goes to meet every danger becomes rash; and similarly the man who indulges in every pleasure and abstains from none becomes self-indulgent, while the man who shuns every pleasure, as boors do, becomes in a way insensible; temperance and courage, then, are destroyed by excess and defect, and preserved by the mean. (15)

. . .

4. The question might be asked, what we mean by saying that we must become just by doing just acts, and temperate by doing temperate acts; for if men do just and temperate acts, they are already just and temperate, exactly as, if they do what is in accordance with the laws of grammar and of music, they are grammarians and musicians. (16)

Or is this not true even of the arts? It is possible to do something that is in accordance with the laws of grammar, either by chance or under the guidance of another. A man will be a grammarian, then, only when he has both said something grammatical and said it grammatically; and this means doing it in accordance with the grammatical knowledge in himself.

Human nature is in itself receptive to either virtue or vice; which one of these it acquires depends on how it is exercised and what habits it eventually forms.

This might seem paradoxical: how can you do something in order to learn how to do it? Aristotle will explain.

Thus people become virtuous by practicing virtuous behavior *before* the corresponding character traits have been formed (and vicious in the same way).

As Aristotle said in an earlier passage omitted from this selection, an adequate discussion should have "as much clearness as the subject-matter admits of"—he claims that ethics does not admit of the same degree of clarity as, for example, logic or science.

Here is the first appearance of a view to be extensively developed in what follows: virtuous character traits are intermediate between excess and deficiency.

Aristotle raises an objection to the view that virtues are acquired by doing actions of the corresponding sort: one who acts in the corresponding ways (for example, courageously or temperately) must already have the corresponding virtue, and so cannot acquire it in that way.

Again, the case of the arts and that of the virtues are not similar; for the products of the arts have their goodness in themselves, so that it is enough that they should have a certain character, but if the acts that are in accordance with the virtues have themselves a certain character it does not follow that they are done justly or temperately. The agent also must be in a certain condition when he does them; in the first place he must have knowledge, secondly he must choose the acts, and choose them for their own sakes, and thirdly his action must proceed from a firm and unchangeable character. . . .

Actions, then, are called just and temperate when they are such as the just or the temperate man would do; but it is not the man who does these that is just and temperate, but the man who also does them *as* just and temperate men do them. It is well said, then, that it is by doing just acts that the just man is produced, and by doing temperate acts the temperate man; without doing these no one would have even a prospect of becoming good. (17)

17

R But the previous objection is mistaken. Just as in the arts, a person can do the sorts of actions in question, can act in a given case as the virtuous person would act, without yet having the formed character trait. (Such a person does not do the virtuous action as the virtuous person would because the act is not produced in the same way in that it does not arise out of the same trait of character.)

But most people do not do these, but take refuge in theory and think they are being philosophers and will become good in this way, behaving somewhat like patients who listen attentively to their doctors, but do none of the things they are ordered to do. As the latter will not be made well in body by such a course of treatment, the former will not be made well in soul by such a course of philosophy.

Definition of Moral Virtue

The genus of moral virtue: it is a state of character, not a passion, nor a faculty

5. Next we must consider what virtue is. Since things that are found in the soul are of three kinds—passions, faculties, states of character—virtue must be one of these. By passions I mean appetite, anger, fear, confidence, envy, joy, friendly feeling, hatred, longing, emulation, pity, and in general the feelings that are accompanied by pleasure or pain; by faculties the things in virtue of which we are said to be capable of feeling these, e.g. of becoming angry or being pained or feeling pity; by states of character the things in virtue of which we stand well or badly with reference to the passions, e.g. with reference to anger we stand badly if we feel it violently or too weakly, and well if we feel it moderately; and similarly with reference to the other passions. (18)

R Aristotle distinguishes states of the soul into three general and supposedly exhaustive categories.

Now neither the virtues nor the vices are *passions,* because we are not called good or bad on the ground of our passions, but are so called on the ground of our virtues and our vices, and because we are neither praised nor blamed for our passions (for the man who feels fear or anger is not praised, nor is the man who simply feels anger blamed, but the man who feels it in a certain way), but for our virtues and our vices we *are* praised or blamed.

Again, we feel anger and fear without choice, but the virtues are modes of choice or involve choice. Further, in respect of the passions we are said to be moved, but in respect of the virtues and the vices we are said not to be moved but to be disposed in a particular way.

For these reasons also they are not *faculties;* for we are neither called good or bad, nor praised or blamed, for the simple capacity of feeling the passions; again, we have the faculties by nature, but we are not made good or bad by nature; we have spoken of this before.

If, then, the virtues are neither passions nor faculties, all that remains is that they should be *states of character.*

Thus we have stated what virtue is in respect of its genus. (19)

R Aristotle argues by elimination that virtues are states of character. (This may seem too obvious to need saying, but not if virtues are just human excellences.) This is the *genus* (general category) within which virtue falls, but does not yet say what specific sorts of states of character the virtues are.

The differentia of moral virtue: it is a disposition to choose the mean

6. We must, however, not only describe virtue as a state of character, but also say what sort of state it is. We may remark, then, that every virtue or excellence both brings into good condition the thing of which it is the excellence and makes the work of that thing be done well; e.g. the excellence of the eye makes both the eye and its work good; for it is by the excellence of the eye that we see well. . . . Therefore, if this is true in every case, the virtue of man also will be the state of character which makes a man good and which makes him do his own work well. (20)

R By comparison with other cases, human virtues will be states of character that allow people to do their essential work or functions well.

How this is to happen we have stated already, but it will be made plain also by the following consideration of the specific nature of virtue. In everything that is continuous and divisible it is possible to take more, less, or an equal amount, and that either in terms of the thing itself or relatively to us; and the equal is an intermediate between excess and defect. By the intermediate in the object I mean that which is equidistant from each of the extremes, which is one and the same for all men; by the intermediate relatively to us that which is neither too much nor too little—and this is not one, nor the same for all. For instance, if ten is many and two is few, six is the intermediate, taken in terms of the object; for it exceeds and is exceeded by an equal amount; this is intermediate according to arithmetical proportion. But the intermediate relatively to us is not to be taken so; if ten pounds are too much for a particular person to eat and two too little, it does not follow that the trainer will order six pounds; for this also is perhaps too much for the person who is to take it, or too little. . . . Thus a master of any art avoids excess and defect, but seeks the intermediate and chooses this—the intermediate not in the object but relatively to us. (21)

If it is thus, then, that every art does its work well—by looking to the intermediate and judging its works by this standard . . . , and if, further, virtue is more exact and better than any art, as nature also is, then virtue must have the quality of aiming at the intermediate. I mean moral virtue; for it is this that is concerned with passions and actions, and in these there is excess, defect, and the intermediate. For instance, both fear and confidence and appetite and anger and pity and in general pleasure and pain may be felt both too much and too little, and in both cases not well; but to feel them at the right times, with reference to the right objects, towards the right people, with the right motive, and in the right way, is what is both intermediate and best, and this is characteristic of virtue. (22) Similarly with regard to actions also there is excess, defect, and the intermediate. Now virtue is concerned with passions and actions, in which excess is a form of failure, and so is defect, while the intermediate is praised and is a form of success; and being praised and being successful are both characteristics of virtue. Therefore virtue is a kind of mean, since, as we have seen, it aims at what is intermediate.

. . .

Virtue, then, is a state of character concerned with choice, lying in a mean, i.e. the mean relative to us, this being determined by a rational principle, and by that principle by which the man of practical wisdom would determine it. (23) Now it is a mean between two vices, that which depends on excess and that which depends on defect; and again it is a mean because the vices respectively fall short of or exceed what is right in both passions and actions, while virtue both finds and chooses that which is intermediate. Hence in respect of what it is, i.e. the definition which states its essence, virtue is a mean, with regard to what is best and right an extreme.

. . .

The above proposition illustrated by reference to particular virtues

7. . . . With regard to feelings of fear and confidence courage is the mean; of the people who exceed, he who exceeds in fearlessness has no name (many of the states have no name), while the man who exceeds in confidence is rash, and he who exceeds in fear and falls short in confidence is a coward. With regard to pleasures and pains—not all of them, and not so much with regard to the pains—the mean is temperance, the excess self-indulgence. Persons deficient with regard to the pleasures are not often found; hence such persons also have received no name. But let us call them 'insensible'.

With regard to giving and taking of money the mean is liberality, the excess and the defect prodigality and meanness. In these actions people exceed and fall short in contrary ways; the prodigal exceeds in spending and falls short in taking, while the mean man exceeds in taking and falls short in spending. (At present we are giving a mere outline or summary, and are satisfied with this; later these states will be more exactly determined.) (24) With regard to money there are also other dispositions—a mean, magnificence (for the magnificent man differs from the liberal man; the former deals with large sums, the latter with small ones), an excess, tastelessness and vulgarity, and a deficiency, niggardliness; these differ from the states opposed to liberality, and the mode of their difference will be stated later.

With regard to honour and dishonour the mean is proper pride, the excess is known as a sort of 'empty vanity', and the deficiency is undue humility; and as we said liberality was related to magnificence, differing from it by dealing with small sums, so there is a

R And this in turn involves avoiding both excess and defect (deficiency) and finding the appropriate intermediate action or *mean*—but with the important qualification that the relevant mean is to be determined in relation to the person and the situation, not just mathematically.

R Here is the general formula for virtuous action: what is virtuous (or right) in each case depends on avoiding both excess and deficiency in the dimension in question and thereby finding the appropriate mean.

And here finally is the definition of virtue. The translation is misleading in that the word translated as "rational principle" (*logos*) does not necessarily suggest that there is a principle in the sense of a clear rule, but only that the determination is done in a rational way, through reason.

R Some, but not all, of these more detailed accounts are included later in this selection.

state similarly related to proper pride, being concerned with small honours while that is concerned with great. For it is possible to desire honour as one ought, and more than one ought, and less, and the man who exceeds in his desires is called ambitious, the man who falls short unambitious, while the intermediate person has no name. . . .

With regard to anger also there is an excess, a deficiency, and a mean. Although they can scarcely be said to have names, yet since we call the intermediate person good-tempered let us call the mean good temper; of the persons at the extremes let the one who exceeds be called irascible, and his vice irascibility, and the man who falls short an unirascible sort of person, and the deficiency unirascibility.

. . .

Book III: Moral Virtue

. . .

5. . . . With regard to the virtues *in general* we have stated their genus in outline, viz. that they are means and that they are states of character, and that they tend, and by their own nature, to the doing of the acts by which they are produced, and that they are in our power and voluntary, and act as the right rule prescribes. But actions and states of character are not voluntary in the same way; for we are masters of our actions from the beginning right to the end, if we know the particular facts, but though we control the beginning of our states of character the gradual progress is not obvious, any more than it is in illnesses; because it was in our power, however, to act in this way or not in this way, therefore the states are voluntary. 25

25

Voluntary in the sense that because we can deliberately act in such a way as to eventually bring about these states, even if we cannot simply produce them directly.

Let us take up the several virtues, however, and say which they are and what sort of things they are concerned with and how they are concerned with them; at the same time it will become plain how many they are. And first let us speak of courage.

Courage

Courage concerned with the feelings of fear and confidence—strictly speaking, with the fear of death in battle

6. That it is a mean with regard to feelings of fear and confidence has already been made evident; and plainly the things we fear are fearful things, and these are, to speak without qualification, evils; for which reason people even define fear as expectation of evil. Now we fear all evils, e.g. disgrace, poverty, disease, friendlessness, death, but the brave man is not thought to be concerned with all; for to fear some things is even right and noble, and it is base not to fear them—e.g. disgrace; he who fears this is good and modest, and he who does not is shameless. . . . Poverty and disease we perhaps ought not to fear, nor in general the things that do not proceed from vice and are not due to a man himself. But not even the man who is fearless of these is brave. . . . With what sort of fearful things, then, is the brave man concerned? Surely with the greatest; for no one is more likely than he to stand his ground against what is awe-inspiring. Now death is the most fearful of all things; for it is the end, and nothing is thought to be any longer either good or bad for the dead. But the brave man would not seem to be concerned even with death in *all* circumstances, e.g. at sea or in disease. In what circumstances, then? Surely in the noblest. Now such deaths are those in battle; for these take place in the greatest and noblest danger. . . . Properly, then, he will be called brave who is fearless in face of a noble death, and of all emergencies that involve death; and the emergencies of war are in the highest degree of this kind. . . . 26

26

The aspect of Greek thought that finds war to be the greatest and most noble human activity is unlikely to be very plausible to modern readers. But most of what Aristotle says about courage can be applied to other situations of danger as well.

The motive of courage is the sense of honour: characteristics of the opposite vices, cowardice and rashness

7. . . . Of the faults that are committed, one consists in fearing what we should not, another in fearing as we should not, another in fearing when we should not, and so on; and so too with respect to the things that inspire confidence. The man, then, who faces and who fears the right things and from the right motive, in the right way and at the right time, and who feels confidence under the corresponding conditions, is brave; for the brave man feels and acts according to the merits of the case and in whatever way the rule directs. . . .

Of those who go to excess he who exceeds in fearlessness has no name (we have said previously that many states of character have no names), but he would be a sort of madman or insensitive to pain if he feared nothing, neither earthquakes nor the waves . . . while the man who exceeds in confidence about what really is fearful is rash. . . . The man who exceeds in fear is a coward; for he fears both what he ought not and as he ought not, and all the similar characterizations attach to him. He is lacking also in confidence; but he is more conspicuous for his excess of fear in painful situations. The coward, then, is a despairing sort of person; for he fears everything. The brave man, on the other hand, has the opposite disposition; for confidence is the mark of a hopeful disposition. The coward, the rash man, and the brave man, then, are concerned with the same objects but are differently disposed towards them; for the first two exceed and fall short, while the third holds the middle, which is the right, position. . . .

As we have said, then, courage is a mean with respect to things that inspire confidence or fear, in the circumstances that have been stated; and it chooses or endures things because it is noble to do so, or because it is base not to do so. . . .

Temperance

10. After courage let us speak of temperance. . . . We have said that temperance is a mean with regard to pleasures (for it is less, and not in the same way, concerned with pains); self-indulgence also is manifested in the same sphere. . . .

Temperance and self-indulgence are concerned with the kind of pleasures that the other animals share in, which therefore appear slavish and brutish. . . .

Characteristics of temperance and its opposites, self-indulgence and 'insensibility'

11. . . . Plainly, then, excess with regard to pleasures is self-indulgence and is culpable; with regard to pains one is not, as in the case of courage, called temperate for facing them or self-indulgent for not doing so, but the self-indulgent man is so called because he is pained more than he ought at not getting pleasant things (even his pain being caused by pleasure), and the temperate man is so called because he is not pained at the absence of what is pleasant and at his abstinence from it.

The self-indulgent man, then, craves for all pleasant things or those that are most pleasant, and is led by his appetite to choose these at the cost of everything else; hence he is pained both when he fails to get them and when he is merely craving for them (for appetite involves pain). . . . People who fall short with regard to pleasures and delight in them less than they should are hardly found; for such insensibility is not human. . . . The temperate man occupies a middle position with regard to these objects. For he neither enjoys the things that the self-indulgent man enjoys most—but rather dislikes them—nor in general the things that he should not, nor anything of this sort to excess, nor does he feel pain or craving when they are absent, or does so only to a moderate degree, and not more than he should, nor when he should not, and so on; but the things that, being pleasant, make for health or for good condition, he will desire moderately and as he should, and also other pleasant things if they are not hindrances to these ends, or contrary to what is noble, or beyond his means. For he who neglects these conditions loves such pleasures more than they are worth, but the temperate man is not that sort of person, but the sort of person that the right rule prescribes. 27

27

Here again the Greek word being translated as "right rule" (*logos*) does not mean that there is a definite rule, only that the choice is made on rational grounds.

. . .

Book IV: Moral Virtue

. . .

The Virtue Concerned with Anger

5. Good temper is a mean with respect to anger; the middle state being unnamed, 28 and the extremes almost without a name as well, we place good temper in the middle position, though it inclines towards the deficiency, which is without a name. The excess might be called a sort of 'irascibility'. For the passion is anger, while its causes are many and diverse.

28

Unnamed until Aristotle named it "good temper."

The man who is angry at the right things and with the right people, and, further, as he ought, when he ought, and as long as he ought, is praised. This will be the good-tempered man, then, since good temper is praised. For the good-tempered man tends to be unperturbed and not to be led by passion, but to be angry in the manner, at the things, and for the length of time, that the rule dictates; but he is thought to err rather in the direction of deficiency; for the good-tempered man is not revengeful, but rather tends to make allowances.

The deficiency, whether it is a sort of 'unirascibility' or whatever it is, is blamed. For those who are not angry at the things they should be angry at are thought to be fools, and so are those who are not angry in the right way, at the right time, or with the right persons; for such a man is thought not to feel things nor to be pained by them, and, since he does not get angry, he is thought unlikely to defend himself; and to endure being insulted and put up with insult to one's friends is slavish.

. . .

. . . it is not easy to define how, with whom, at what, and how long one should be angry, and at what point right action ceases and wrong begins. For the man who strays a little from the path, either towards the more or towards the less, is not blamed; since sometimes we praise those who exhibit the deficiency, and call them good-tempered, and sometimes we call angry people manly, as being capable of ruling. How far, therefore, and how a man must stray before he becomes blameworthy, it is not easy to state in words; for the decision depends on the particular facts and on perception. [29] But so much at least is plain, that the middle state is praiseworthy—that in virtue of which we are angry with the right people, at the right things, in the right way, and so on, while the excesses and defects are blameworthy—slightly so if they are present in a low degree, more if in a higher degree, and very much if in a high degree. Evidently, then, we must cling to the middle state. . . .

R So there is no clearly defined rule, nothing that could avoid the need for rational judgment.

Here we have several more places where the translation suggests some sort of explicit rule, but what is in fact said by Aristotle is only that reason or rationality or good judgment is involved.

R Aristotle's view is that while lower animals may react to sensation, they do not act in the sense that involves deliberate choice.

Book VI: Intellectual Virtue

Introduction

1. Since we have previously said that one ought to choose that which is intermediate, not the excess nor the defect, and that the intermediate is determined by the dictates of the right rule, let us discuss the nature of these dictates. In all the states of character we have mentioned, as in all other matters, there is a mark to which the man who has the rule looks, and heightens or relaxes his activity accordingly, and there is a standard which determines the mean states which we say are intermediate between excess and defect, being in accordance with the right rule. But such a statement, though true, is by no means clear; for not only here but in all other pursuits which are objects of knowledge it is indeed true to say that we must not exert ourselves nor relax our efforts too much or too little, but to an intermediate extent and as the right rule dictates; but if a man had only this knowledge he would be none the wiser—e.g. we should not know what sort of medicines to apply to our body if someone were to say 'all those which the medical art prescribes, and which agree with the practice of one who possesses the art'. Hence it is necessary with regard to the states of the soul also, not only that this true statement should be made, but also that it should be determined what is the right rule and what is the standard that fixes it. [30]

. . .

2. The virtue of a thing is relative to its proper work. Now there are three things in the soul which control action and truth—sensation, reason, desire.

Of these sensation originates no action; this is plain from the fact that the lower animals have sensation but no share in action. [31]

What affirmation and negation are in thinking, pursuit and avoidance are in desire; so that since moral virtue is a state of character concerned with choice, and choice is deliberate desire, therefore both the reasoning must be true and the desire right, if the choice is to be good, and the latter must pursue just what the former asserts. Now this kind of intellect and of truth is practical. . . .

Happiness

Happiness is good activity, not amusement

6. Now that we have spoken of the virtues . . . , what remains is to discuss in outline the nature of happiness, since this is what we state the end of human affairs to be. Our discussion will be the more concise if we first sum up what we have said already. We said, then, that it is not a state; for if it were it might belong to someone who was asleep throughout his life, living the life of a plant, or, again, to someone who was suffering the greatest misfortunes. If these implications are unacceptable, and we must rather class happiness as an activity, as we have said before, and if some activities are necessary, and desirable for the sake of something else, while others are so in themselves, evidently happiness must be placed among those desirable

in themselves, not among those desirable for the sake of something else; for happiness does not lack anything, but is self-sufficient. Now those activities are desirable in themselves from which nothing is sought beyond the activity. And of this nature virtuous actions are thought to be; for to do noble and good deeds is a thing desirable for its own sake.

. . . Happiness . . . does not lie in amusement; it would, indeed, be strange if the end were amusement, and one were to take trouble and suffer hardship all one's life in order to amuse oneself. For, in a word, everything that we choose we choose for the sake of something else—except happiness, which is an end. Now to exert oneself and work for the sake of amusement seems silly and utterly childish. But to amuse oneself in order that one may exert oneself . . . seems right; for amusement is a sort of relaxation, and we need relaxation because we cannot work continuously. Relaxation, then, is not an end; for it is taken for the sake of activity. 32

. . .

Happiness in the highest sense is the contemplative life

7. If happiness is activity in accordance with virtue, it is reasonable that it should be in accordance with the highest virtue; and this will be that of the best thing in us. Whether it be reason or something else that is this element which is thought to be our natural ruler and guide and to take thought of things noble and divine, whether it be itself also divine or only the most divine element in us, the activity of this in accordance with its proper virtue will be perfect happiness. . . . this activity is contemplative. . . .

Now this would seem to be in agreement both with what we said before and with the truth. For, firstly, this activity is the best (since not only is reason the best thing in us, but the objects of reason are the best of knowable objects); and, secondly, it is the most continuous, since we can contemplate truth more continuously than we can *do* anything. And we think happiness ought to have pleasure mingled with it, but the activity of philosophic wisdom is admittedly the pleasantest of virtuous activities; at all events the pursuit of it is thought to offer pleasures marvelous for their purity and their enduringness. . . . And the self-sufficiency that is spoken of must belong most to the contemplative activity. For while a philosopher, as well as a just man or one possessing any other virtue, needs the necessaries of life, when they are sufficiently equipped with things of that sort the just man needs people towards whom and with whom he shall act justly, and the temperate man, the brave man, and each of the others is in the same case, but the philosopher, even when by himself, can contemplate truth, and the better the wiser he is; he can perhaps do so better if he has fellow workers, but still he is the most self-sufficient. And this activity alone would seem to be loved for its own sake; for nothing arises from it apart from the contemplating, while from practical activities we gain more or less apart from the action. . . . So if among virtuous actions political and military actions are distinguished by nobility and greatness, and these are unleisurely and aim at an end and are not desirable for their own sake, but the activity of reason, which is contemplative, seems both to be superior in serious worth and to aim at no end beyond itself, and to have its pleasure proper to itself (and this augments the activity), and the self-sufficiency, leisureliness, unweariedness (so far as this is possible for man), and all the other attributes ascribed to the supremely happy man are evidently those connected with this activity, it follows that this will be the complete happiness of man, if it be allowed a complete term of life (for none of the attributes of happiness is incomplete). 33

32

How good are Aristotle's reasons for rejecting the view that the life of enjoyment or amusement is the happy life?

33

Aristotle's view is that the best sort of life for a human being, the one that most perfectly achieves happiness (*eudaimonia*) is the contemplative life. How good are the reasons he offers?

Discussion Questions

1. How plausible do you find Aristotle's idea that by acting as a virtuous person would act, you will acquire the relevant virtues? Consider the virtue of charity: the charitable person makes charitable contributions *because of* the character trait of charity. Suppose that Carol makes charitable contributions only to gain her father's approval. Doesn't it seem as though Carol could act that way for years without acquiring the virtue of charity? But consider another example: we typically teach our children to share, trying to create in them the character trait of generosity (the stable disposition to give accompanied by the relevantly appropriate emotional responses). Might that kind of training be successful? How do people acquire the kind of character traits that Aristotle is talking about?

2. How plausible is Aristotle's main thesis that a virtue is always a mean between two extremes, each of which is a vice? Think of other examples of virtues besides the ones he discusses and try to assess whether and to what extent they fit this picture.
3. Aristotle thinks the best thing about us is our reason: the person who most closely approximates the excellence that is distinctively human is the one who spends most of his life in contemplation. What do you think about that view? What do you think about the view that a life of enjoyment or amusement is a less than excellent life? Do you think that there is something else about us, other than reason, that is "the best thing about us"? Do some lives more clearly involve human flourishing than other lives?

Rosalind Hursthouse

Rosalind Hursthouse (1943–) teaches at the University of Auckland in New Zealand, having previously taught in both England and the United States. She is a major figure in the recently developed area of virtue ethics, defending a view that she characterizes as "neo-Aristotelian."

In the following selection, Hursthouse defends the thesis that virtue ethics, in addition to giving an account of good and bad character and of what it means for a human being to live well or flourish, can also give an account of which actions are right or wrong in particular situations, thereby providing a genuine alternative to the accounts provided by utilitarian and deontological (Kantian) ethics.

Normative Virtue Ethics

A common belief concerning virtue ethics is that it does not tell us what we should do. This belief is sometimes manifested merely in the expressed assumption that virtue ethics, in being 'agent-centred' rather than 'act-centred', is concerned with Being rather than Doing, with good (and bad) character rather than right (and wrong) action, with the question 'What sort of person should I be?' rather than the question 'What should I do?' On this assumption, 'virtue ethics' so-called does not figure as a normative rival to utilitarian and deontological ethics; rather, its (fairly) recent revival is seen as having served the useful purpose of reminding moral philosophers that the elaboration of a normative theory may fall short of giving a full account of our moral life. Thus prompted, deontologists have turned to Kant's long neglected 'Doctrine of Virtue', and utilitarians, largely abandoning the old debate about rule- and act-utilitarianism, are showing interest in the general-happiness-maximizing consequences of inculcating such virtues as friendship, honesty, and loyalty.

On this assumption, it seems that philosophers who 'do virtue ethics', having served this purpose, must realize that they have been doing no more than supplementing normative theory, and should now decide which of the two standard views they espouse. . . . But anyone who wants to espouse virtue ethics as a rival to deontological or utilitarian ethics (finding it distinctly bizarre to suppose that Aristotle espoused either of the latter) will find this common belief voiced against her as an objection: 'Virtue ethics does not, because it cannot, tell us what we should do. Hence it cannot be a normative rival to deontology and utilitarianism.' 1

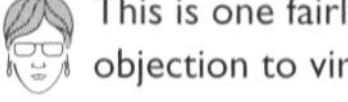
This is one fairly standard objection to virtue ethics.

This paper is devoted to defending virtue ethics against this objection.

1. Right Action

What grounds might someone have for believing that virtue ethics cannot tell us what we should do? It seems that sometimes the ground is no more than the claim that virtue ethics is concerned with good (and bad) character rather than right (and wrong) action. But that claim does no more than highlight an interesting contrast

From *How Should One Live?*, edited by Roger Crisp (New York: Oxford University Press, 1996).

between virtue ethics on the one hand, and deontology and utilitarianism on the other; the former is agent-centered, the latter (it is said) are act-centered. It does not entail that virtue ethics has nothing to say about the concept of right action, nor about which actions are right and which wrong. Wishing to highlight a different contrast, the one between utilitarianism and deontology, we might equally well say, 'Utilitarianism is concerned with good (and bad) states of affairs rather than right (and wrong) action', and no one would take that to mean that utilitarianism, unlike deontology, had nothing to say about right action, for what utilitarianism does say is so familiar.

Suppose an act-utilitarian laid out her account of right action as follows:

U1. An action is right iff it promotes the best consequences. (2)

This premiss provides a specification of right action, forging the familiar utilitarian link between the concepts of *right action* and *best consequences,* but gives one no guidance about how to act until one knows what to count as the best consequences. So these must be specified in a second premiss, for example:

U2. The best consequences are those in which happiness is maximized,

which forges the familiar utilitarian link between the concepts of *best consequences* and *happiness.*

Many different versions of deontology can be laid out in a way that displays the same basic structure. They begin with a premiss providing a specification of right action:

D1. An action is right iff it is in accordance with a correct moral rule or principle.

Like the first premiss of act-utilitarianism, this gives one no guidance about how to act until, in this case, one knows what to count as a correct moral rule (or principle). So this must be specified in a second premiss which begins

D2. A correct moral rule (principle) is one that . . . ,

and this may be completed in a variety of ways, for example:

i. is on the following list (and then a list does follow)

or

ii. is laid on us by God

or

iii. is universalizable

or

iv. would be the object of choice of all rational beings

and so on. (3)

Although this way of laying out fairly familiar versions of utilitarianism and deontology is hardly controversial, it is worth noting that it suggests some infelicity in the slogan 'Utilitarianism begins with (or takes as its fundamental concept etc.) the Good, whereas deontology begins with the Right.' If the concept a normative ethics 'begins with' is the one it uses to specify right action, then utilitarianism might be said to begin with the Good (if we take this to be the 'same' concept as that of the *best*), but we should surely hasten to add 'but only in relation to consequences; not, for instance, in relation to *good* agents, or to living *well'.* (4) And even then, we shall not be able to go on to say that most versions of deontology 'begin with' the Right, for they use the concept of moral rule or principle to specify right action. . . .

And if the dictum is supposed to single out, rather vaguely, the concept which is 'most important', then the concepts of *consequences* or *happiness* seem as deserving of mention as the concept of the Good for utilitarianism, and what counts as most important (if any one concept does) for deontologists would surely vary from case to case. For some it would be God, for others universalizability, for others the Categorical Imperative, for others rational acceptance, and so on.

It is possible that too slavish an acceptance of this slogan, and the inevitable difficulty of finding a completion of 'and virtue ethics begins with . . .' which does not reveal its inadequacy, has contributed to the belief that virtue ethics cannot provide a specification of right action. . . . But if the question is 'How can virtue ethics specify right action?', the answer is easy:

V1. An action is right iff it is what a virtuous agent would characteristically (i.e. acting in character) do in the circumstances.

(2)

 Here and elsewhere, "iff" is a standard philosophical abbreviation meaning "if and only if."

(3)

 Here (iii) and (iv) reflect aspects of Kant's position. For a consideration of a view like (ii), see the selection from Plato's dialogue *Euthyphro* in Chapter 1. A view that merely gives a list is unlikely to be very compelling without some further account of how the list is arrived at (which is then likely to replace the list as the main account).

(4)

 Utilitarianism certainly does not begin with the idea of a good agent (or one who lives well)—and has little to say about it except that a good agent will follow the principle of utility (or, for rule utilitarianism, conform to rules that maximize utility). Proponents of virtue ethics will suggest that this is a clearly inadequate account of what it is for a human being to live a good life.

This specification rarely, if ever, silences those who maintain that virtue ethics cannot tell us what we should do. On the contrary, it tends to provoke irritable laughter and scorn. '*That's* no use', the objectors say. 'It gives us no guidance whatsoever. Who are the virtuous agents?' But if the failure of the first premiss of a normative ethics which forges a link between the concept of right action and a concept distinctive of that ethics may provoke scorn because it provides no practical guidance, why not direct a similar scorn at the first premisses of act-utilitarianism and deontology in the form in which I have given them? Of each of them I remarked . . . that they gave us no guidance. Utilitarianism must specify what are to count as the best consequences, and deontology what is to count as a correct moral rule, producing a second premiss, before any guidance is given. And similarly, virtue ethics must specify who is to count as a virtuous agent. So far, the three are all in the same position.

Of course, if the virtuous agent can only be specified as an agent disposed to act in accordance with moral rules, as some have assumed, then virtue ethics collapses back into deontology and is no rival to it. ❺ So let us add a subsidiary premiss to this skeletal outline, with the intention of making it clear that virtue ethics aims to provide a non-deontological specification of the virtuous agent via a specification of the virtues, which will be given in its second premiss:

V1a. A virtuous agent is one who acts virtuously, that is, one who has and exercises the virtues.

V2. A virtue is a character trait that . . . .

This second premiss of virtue ethics might, like the second premiss of some versions of deontology, be completed simply by enumeration ('a virtue is one of the following', and then the list is given). Or we might, not implausibly, interpret the Hume of the second *Enquiry* as espousing virtue ethics. According to him, a virtue is a character trait (of human beings) that is useful or agreeable to its possessor or to others (inclusive 'or' both times). The standard neo-Aristotelian completion claims that a virtue is a character trait a human being needs for *eudaimonia,* to flourish or live well. ❻

Here, then, we have a specification of right action, whose structure closely resembles those of act-utilitarianism and many forms of deontology. Given that virtue ethics can come up with such a specification, can it still be maintained that it, unlike utilitarianism and deontology, cannot tell us what we should do? Does the specification somehow fail to provide guidance in a way that the other two do not?

At this point, the difficulty of identifying the virtuous agent in a way that makes VI action-guiding tends to be brought forward again. Suppose it is granted that deontology has just as much difficulty in identifying the correct moral rules as virtue ethics has in identifying the virtues and hence the virtuous agent. Then the following objection may be made.

'All the same,' it may be said, if we imagine that that has been achieved—perhaps simply by enumeration—deontology yields a set of clear prescriptions which are readily applicable ("Do not lie", "do not steal", "do not inflict evil or harm on others", "Do help others", "Do keep promises", etc.). But virtue ethics yields only the prescription "Do what the virtuous agent (the one who is honest, charitable, just, etc.) would do in these circumstances." And this gives me no guidance unless I am (and know I am) a virtuous agent myself (in which case I am hardly in need of it). If I am less than fully virtuous, I shall have no idea what a virtuous agent would do, and hence cannot apply the only prescription that virtue ethics has given me. (Of course, act-utilitarianism also yields a single prescription. "Do what maximises happiness", but there are no *parallel* difficulties in applying that.) So there is the way in which V1 fails to be action-guiding where deontology and utilitarianism succeed.' ❼

It is worth pointing out that, if I acknowledge that I am far from perfect, and am quite unclear what a virtuous agent would do in the circumstances in which I find myself, the obvious thing to do is to go and ask one, should this be possible. This is far from being a trivial point, for it gives a straightforward explanation of an aspect of our moral life which should not be ignored, namely the fact that we do seek moral guidance from people who we think are morally better than ourselves. When I am looking for an excuse to do something I have a horrid suspicion is wrong, I ask my moral inferiors (or peers if I am bad enough), 'Wouldn't you do such and such if you were in my shoes?' But when I am anxious

❺

The main issue here is not whether thesis V1 is true, but rather what *makes* it true. A Kantian (or a utilitarian or a holder of any other sort of moral view) can accept it as true as long as he defines "a virtuous agent" as someone who conforms to the Kantian moral rules (or those of utilitarianism or whatever other view). But the virtue ethicist wants to start with an *independently* defined conception of a virtuous agent (as roughly the ideal exemplification of the moral virtues) and then define the morally right action as whatever that agent does in the circumstances in question.

❻

These are *very* different ways of filling out V2. Are any of them definite enough for V1 to yield fairly precise results as to which actions are right?

❼

How plausible is the claim that only a virtuous agent can know what a virtuous agent would do in a particular situation?

to do what is right, and do not see my way clear, I go to people I respect and admire—people who I think are kinder, more honest, more just, wiser, than I am myself—and ask them what they would do in my circumstances. How utilitarianism and deontology would explain this fact, I do not know; but, as I said, the explanation within the terms of virtue ethics is straightforward. If you want to do what is right, and doing what is right is doing what a virtuous agent would do in the circumstances, then you should find out what she would do if you do not already know. 8

Moreover, seeking advice from virtuous people is not the only thing an imperfect agent trying to apply the single prescription of virtue ethics can do. For it is simply false that, in general, 'if I am less than fully virtuous, then I shall have no idea what a virtuous agent would do', as the objection claims. Recall that we are assuming that the virtues have been enumerated, as the deontologist's rules have been. The latter have been enumerated as, say, 'Do not lie', 'Do not inflict evil or harm', etc.; the former as, say, honesty, charity, justice, etc. So, *ex hypothesi,* a virtuous agent is one who is honest, charitable, just, etc. So what she characteristically does is act honestly, charitably, justly, etc., and not dishonestly, uncharitably, unjustly. So given an enumeration of the virtues, I may well have a perfectly good idea of what the virtuous person would do in my circumstances despite my own imperfection. Would she lie in her teeth to acquire an unmerited advantage? No, for that would be to act both dishonestly and unjustly. Would she help the naked man by the roadside or pass by on the other side? The former, for she acts charitably. Might she keep a deathbed promise even though living people would benefit from its being broken? Yes, for she acts justly. And so on. 9

2. Moral Rules

The above response to the objection that V1 fails to be action-guiding clearly amounts to a denial of the oft-repeated claim that virtue ethics does not come up with any rules (another version of the thought that it is concerned with Being rather than Doing and needs to be supplemented with rules). We can now see that it comes up with a large number; not only does each virtue generate a prescription—act honestly, charitably, justly—but each vice a prohibition—do not act dishonestly, uncharitably, unjustly. Once this point about virtue ethics is grasped (and it is remarkable how often it is overlooked), can there remain any reason for thinking that virtue ethics cannot tell us what we should do? Yes. The reason given is, roughly, that rules such as 'Act honestly', 'Do not act uncharitably', etc. are, like the rule 'Do what the virtuous agent would do', still the wrong sort of rule, still somehow doomed to fail to provide the action guidance supplied by the rules (or rule) of deontology and utilitarianism.

But how so? It is true that these rules of virtue ethics (henceforth 'v-rules') are couched in terms, or concepts, which are certainly 'evaluative' in *some* sense, or senses, of that difficult word. Is it this which dooms them to failure? 10 Surely not, unless many forms of deontology fail too.* If we concentrate on the single example of lying, defining lying to be 'asserting what you believe to be untrue, with the intention of deceiving your hearer(s)', then we might, for a moment, preserve the illusion that a deontologist's rules do not contain 'evaluative' terms. But as soon as we remember that few deontologists will want to forego principles of non-maleficence or beneficence, the illusion vanishes. For those principles, and their corresponding rules ('Do no evil or harm to others', 'Help others', 'Promote their well-being'), rely on terms or concepts which are at least as 'evaluative' as those employed in the v-rules. Few deontologists rest content with the simple quasi-biological 'Do not kill', but more refined versions of that rule such as 'Do not murder', or 'Do not kill the innocent', once again employ 'evaluative' terms, and 'Do not kill unjustly' is itself a particular instantiation of a v-rule.

One problem here is whether it is possible to identify fully or optimally virtuous people with enough confidence to make it possible to use their advice as a criterion for the right action. (Another problem is raised in Discussion Question 1.)

There are two problems lurking here that you should think about: first, whether it is always or at least usually pretty clear what a particular virtue would require in a given situation; and second, how to deal with situations where different virtues point in different directions (which Hursthouse discusses later on).

The point of the objection being suggested is that a rule that requires further evaluation does not yield a clear guide to action by itself, since what it says to do will depend on the result of that further evaluation. This poses a serious problem only if the further evaluation is difficult to make.

*Forms of utilitarianism which aim to be entirely value-free or empirical, such as those which define happiness in terms of the satisfaction of actual desires or preferences, regardless of their content, or as a mental state whose presence is definitively established by introspection, seem to me the least plausible, but I accept that anyone who embraces them may consistently complain that v-rules give inferior action-guidance in virtue of containing 'evaluative' terms. But any utilitarian who wishes to employ any distinction between the higher and lower pleasures, or rely on some list of goods (such as autonomy, friendship, knowledge of important matters) in defining happiness, must grant that even her single rule is implicitly 'evaluative'.

Supposing this point were granted, a deontologist might still claim that the v-rules are markedly inferior to deontological rules as far as providing guidance for children is concerned. Granted, adult deontologists must think hard about what really constitutes harming someone, or promoting their well-being, or respecting their autonomy, or murder, but surely the simple rules we learnt at our mother's knee are indispensable? How could virtue ethics plausibly seek to dispense with these and expect toddlers to grasp 'Act charitably, honestly, and kindly', 'Don't act unjustly', and so on? Rightly are these concepts described as 'thick'! Far too thick for a child to grasp. 11

Strictly speaking, this claim about learning does not really support the *general* claim that v-rules fail to provide action-guidance, but the claim about learning, arising naturally as it does in the context of the general claim, is one I am more than happy to address. For it pinpoints a condition of adequacy that any normative ethics must meet, namely that such an ethics must not only come up with action-guidance for a clever rational adult but also generate some account of moral education, of how one generation teaches the next what they should do. But an ethics inspired by Aristotle is unlikely to have forgotten the question of moral education, and the objection fails to hit home. First, the implicit empirical claim that toddlers are taught *only* the deontologist's rules, not the 'thick' concepts, is false. Sentences such as 'Don't do that, it hurts, you mustn't be *cruel*', 'Be *kind* to your brother, he's only little', 'Don't be so *mean,* so *greedy*' are commonly addressed to toddlers. Secondly, why should a proponent of virtue ethics deny the significance of such mother's-knee rules as 'Don't lie', 'Keep promises', 'Don't take more than your fair share', 'Help others'? Although it is a mistake, I have claimed, to define a virtuous agent simply as one disposed to act in accordance with moral rules, it is a very understandable mistake, given the obvious connection between, for example, the exercise of the virtue of honesty and refraining from lying. Virtue ethicists want to emphasize the fact that, if children are to be taught to be honest, they must be taught to prize the truth, and that *merely* teaching them not to lie will not achieve this end. But they need not deny that to achieve this end teaching them not to lie is useful, even indispensable. 12

So we can see that virtue ethics not only comes up with rules (the v-rules, couched in terms derived from the virtues and vices), but further, does not exclude the more familiar deontologists' rules. The theoretical distinction between the two is that the familiar rules, and their applications in particular cases, are given entirely different backings. According to virtue ethics, I must not tell this lie, since it would be dishonest, and dishonesty is a vice; must not break this promise, since it would be unjust, or a betrayal of friendship, or, perhaps (for the available virtue and vice terms do not neatly cover every contingency), simply because no virtuous person would. 13

However, the distinction is not merely theoretical. It is, indeed, the case that, with respect to a number of familiar examples, virtue ethicists and deontologists tend to stand shoulder to shoulder against utilitarians, denying that, for example, this lie can be told, this promise broken, this human being killed because the consequences of so doing will be generally happiness-maximizing. But, despite a fair amount of coincidence in action-guidance between deontology and virtue ethics, the latter has its own distinctive approach to the practical problems involved in dilemmas.

3. The Conflict Problem

It is a noteworthy fact that, in support of the general claim that virtue ethics cannot tell us what we should do, what is often cited is the 'conflict problem'. The requirements of different virtues, it is said, can point us in opposed directions. Charity prompts me to kill the person who would (truly) be better off dead, but justice forbids it. Honesty points to telling the hurtful truth, kindness and compassion to remaining silent or even lying. And so on. So virtue ethics lets us down just at the point where we need it, where we are faced with the really difficult dilemmas and do not know what to do. 14

In the mouth of a utilitarian, this may be a comprehensible criticism, for, as is well known, the only conflict that classical utilitarianism's one rule can generate is the tiresome logical one between the two occurrences of 'greatest' in its classical statement. 15 But it is strange to find the very same criticism coming from deontologists, who are notoriously faced with the same problem. 'Don't kill', 'Respect autonomy', 'Tell

11

A "thick" moral concept is one that involves description as well as evaluation: "good" or "right" are *thin* moral concepts, while "generous" or "honest" are *thick* ones.

12

This echoes Aristotle's idea that a person first becomes virtuous by acting in the way prescribed by the virtue even if not yet for the reason that the virtuous person acts.

13

Contrast this with Kant's account (on the basis of the version of the categorical imperative that says not to treat others as mere means) of why a person should not tell lies and should keep promises. (See Discussion Question 2.)

14

This is perhaps the most important objection to the sort of view that Hursthouse is advocating.

15

Hursthouse is referring to the formula that one should produce "the greatest good for the greatest number," the second part of which raises the issue of how the good consequences are to be distributed among people. But this is not a serious conflict for the standard utilitarian view, since it is clear that what is required is maximizing the good consequences (happiness or whatever else they may be), no matter how they are distributed.

the truth', 'Keep promises' may all conflict with 'Prevent suffering' or 'Do no harm', which is precisely why deontologists so often reject utilitarianism's deliverances on various dilemmas. Presumably, they must think that deontology can solve the 'conflict problem' and, further, that virtue ethics cannot. Are they right?

With respect to a number of cases, the deontologist's strategy is to argue that the 'conflict' is merely apparent, or *prima facie*. The proponent of virtue ethics employs the same strategy: according to her, many of the putative conflicts are merely apparent, resulting from a misapplication of the virtue or vice terms. Does kindness require not telling hurtful truths? Sometimes, but in *this* case, what has to be understood is that one does people no kindness by concealing this sort of truth from them, hurtful as it may be. Or, in a different case, the importance of the truth in question puts the consideration of hurt feelings out of court, and the agent does not show herself to be unkind, or callous, by speaking out. Does charity require that I kill the person who would be better off dead but who wants to stay alive, thereby conflicting with justice? Not if, in Foot's words, '[a] man does not lack charity because he refrains from an act of injustice which would have been for someone's good'.*

One does not have to agree with the three judgements expressed here to recognize this as a *strategy* available to virtue ethics, any more than one has to agree with the particular judgements of deontologists who, for example, may claim that one rule outranks another, or that a certain rule has a certain exception clause built in, when they argue that a putative case of conflict is resolvable. Whether an individual has resolved a putative moral conflict or dilemma rightly is one question; whether a normative ethics has the wherewithal to resolve it is an entirely different question, and it is the latter with which we are concerned here.

The form the strategy takes within virtue ethics provides what may plausibly be claimed to be the deep explanation of why, in some cases, agents do not know the answer to 'What should I do in these circumstances?' despite the fact that there *is* an answer. Trivially, the explanation is that they lack moral knowledge of what to do in this situation; but why? In what way? The lack, according to virtue ethics' strategy, arises from lack of moral wisdom, from an inadequate grasp of what is involved in acting *kindly* (unkindly) or *charitably* (uncharitably), in being *honest*, or *just*, or *lacking in charity*, or, in general, of how the virtue (and vice) terms are to be correctly applied. 16

16 Hursthouse's suggestion here seems to be that when properly understood, the different virtues do not genuinely conflict, so that any appearance of conflict results from less than complete understanding. How plausible is this claim (which she seems to retreat from later)? (See Discussion Question 3.)

Here we come to an interesting defence of the v-rules, often criticized as being too difficult to apply for the agent who lacks moral wisdom.† The defence relies on an (insufficiently acknowledged) insight of Aristotle's—namely that moral knowledge, unlike mathematical knowledge, cannot be acquired merely by attending lectures and is not characteristically to be found in people too young to have much experience of life. Now *if* right action were determined by rules that any clever adolescent could apply correctly, how could this be so? Why are there not moral whiz-kids, the way there are mathematical (or quasi-mathematical) whiz-kids? But if the rules that determine right action are, like the v-rules, very difficult to apply correctly, involving, for instance, a grasp of the *sort* of truth that one does people no kindness by concealing, the explanation is readily to hand. Clever adolescents do not, in general, have a good grasp of that sort of thing. And *of course* I have to say 'the sort of truth that . . .' and 'that sort of thing', relying on my readers' knowledgeable uptake. For if I could define either sort, then, once again, clever adolescents could acquire moral wisdom from textbooks.

So far, I have described one strategy available to virtue ethics for coping with the 'conflict problem', a strategy that consists in arguing that the conflict is merely apparent, and can be resolved. . . . I have been talking so far as though examples of putative dilemmas and examples of putative conflict between the requirements of different virtues (or deontologists' rules) coincided. But it may seem to many, as it does to me, that there are certain (putative) dilemmas which can only be described in terms of (putative) conflict with much artifice and loss of relevant detail.

Let us, therefore, consider the problem of moral dilemmas without bothering about

*P. Foot, *Virtues and Vices* (Oxford, 1978), p. 60, n. 12.

†This could well be regarded as another version of the criticism discussed earlier, that the v-rules somehow fail to provide action-guidance.

whether they can be described in the simple terms of a conflict between the requirements of two virtues (or two deontologists' rules). Most of us, it may be supposed, have our own favoured example(s), either real or imaginary, of the case (or cases) where we see the decision about whether to do A or B as a very grave matter, have thought a great deal about what can be said for and against doing A, and doing B, and have still not managed to reach a conclusion which we think is the right one. How, if at all, does virtue ethics direct us to think about such cases?

4. Dilemmas and Normative Theory

As a preliminary to answering that question, we should consider a much more general one, namely 'How should any normative ethics direct us to think about such cases?' This brings us to the topic of normative theory.

It is possible to detect a new movement in moral philosophy, a movement which has already attracted the name 'anti-theory in ethics'. Its various representatives have as a common theme the rejection of normative ethical theory. . . . What is meant by a 'normative theory' in this context is not easy to pin down, but, roughly, a normative theory is taken to be a set (possibly one-membered in the case of utilitarianism) of general principles which provide a *decision procedure* for all questions about how to act morally. 17

17

It might be better to describe such a decision procedure as a *goal* for normative theory or as what would be accomplished by an *ideal* normative theory. If the idea is a procedure that can clearly and unequivocally resolve all questions of this sort, few if any philosophers (though Bentham may be an exception) would seriously claim to have actually given one.

Part of the point of distinguishing a normative ethics by calling it a normative 'theory' is that a decent theory, as we know from science, enables us to answer questions that we could not answer before we had it. It is supposed to resolve those difficult dilemmas in which, it is said, our moral intuitions clash, and, prior to our grasp of the theory, we do not know what we should do. And a large part of the motivation for subscribing to 'anti-theory in ethics' is the belief that we should not be looking to science to provide us with our model of moral knowledge. Our 'intuitions' in ethics do not play the same role *vis-à-vis* the systematic articulation of moral knowledge as our 'observations' play *vis-à-vis* the systematic articulation of scientific knowledge; many of the goals appropriate to scientific knowledge—universality, consistency, completeness, simplicity—are not appropriate to moral knowledge; the acquisition of moral knowledge involves the training of the emotions in a way that the acquisition of scientific knowledge does not; and so on. 18

It is doubtful that the analogy with science really provides very much of the motivation for seeking a normative theory. The idea is rather, first, that it seems plausible to suppose that there is a right answer to all such questions; and, second, that if we cannot say how to determine what that right answer is, then our understanding is to that extent incomplete—and the practical guidance offered by the view is to that extent incomplete. (But at least the first of these claims can be questioned.)

Clearly, many different issues are involved in the question of the extent to which moral knowledge should be modelled on scientific knowledge. The one I want to focus on here is the issue of whether a normative ethics should provide a decision procedure which enables us to resolve all moral dilemmas. Should it, to rephrase the question I asked above, (1) direct us to think about moral dilemmas in the belief that they *must* have a resolution, and that it is the business of the normative ethics in question to provide one? Or should it (2) have built into it the possibility of there being, as David Wiggins puts it, some 'absolutely undecidable questions—e.g. cases where . . . nothing could count as *the* reasonable practical answer',* counting questions about dilemmas of the sort described as amongst them? Or should it (3) be sufficiently flexible to allow for a comprehensible disagreement on this issue between two proponents of the normative ethics in question?

If we are to avoid modelling normative ethics mindlessly on scientific theory, we should not simply assume that the first position is the correct one. But rejection of such a model is not enough to justify the second position either. Someone might believe that for *any* dilemma there must be something that counts as the right way out of it, without believing that normative ethics remotely resembles scientific theory. . . . More particularly, someone might believe on religious grounds that if I find myself, through no fault of my own, confronted with a dilemma (of the sort described), there must be something that counts as the right way out of it. . . .† 19 It seems to me that a normative ethics should be able to accommodate such differences, and so I subscribe to the third position outlined above.

STOP Can you think of ways in which actions for which you are clearly at fault might lead to a moral dilemma to which there is no right solution—where whatever you do will be wrong? (This is easier than it might initially sound.)

*D. Wiggins, 'Truth, Invention and the Meaning of Life', *Proceedings of the British Academy* 62 (1976), 371, my italics. . . .

†I am assuming that the qualification 'through no fault of my own' is all-important, since I cannot imagine why anyone should think (except through oversight) that there must always be a right action I can do to get myself out of any mess that I have got myself into through previous wrongdoing.

Which position utilitarians and deontologists might espouse is not my concern here; I want to make clear how it is that virtue ethics is able to accommodate the third.

Let us return to V1—'An action is right iff it is what a virtuous agent would characteristically do in the circumstances.' This makes it clear that if two people disagree about the possibility of irresolvable moral dilemmas, their disagreement will manifest itself in what they say about the virtue of agents. So let us suppose that two candidates for being virtuous agents are each faced with their own case of the same dilemma. . . . And, after much thought, one does A and the other does B.

Now, those who believe that there cannot be irresolvable dilemmas (of the sort described) can say that, in the particular case, at least one agent, say the one who did A, thereby showed themselves to be lacking in virtue, perhaps in that practical wisdom which is an essential aspect of each of the 'non-intellectual' virtues. . . . Or they can say that at least one agent must have been lacking in virtue, without claiming to know which. (20)

But those who believe that there are, or may be, irresolvable dilemmas can suppose that both agents are not merely candidates for being, but actually are, virtuous agents. For to believe in such dilemmas is to believe in cases in which even the perfect practical wisdom that the most idealized virtuous agent has does not direct her to do, say, A rather than B. And then the fact that these virtuous agents acted differently, despite being in the same circumstances, *determines* the fact that there is no answer to the question 'What is *the* right thing to do in these circumstances?' For if it is true both that *a* virtuous agent would do A, and that *a* virtuous agent would do B (as it is, since, *ex hypothesi,* one did do A and the other B), then both A and B are, in the circumstances, right, according to V1. (21)

The acceptance of this should not be taken as a counsel of despair, nor as an excuse for moral irresponsibility. It does not license coin-tossing when one is faced with a putative dilemma, for the moral choices we find most difficult do not come to us conveniently labelled as 'resolvable' or 'irresolvable'. I was careful to specify that the two candidates for being virtuous agents acted only 'after much thought'. It will always be necessary to think very hard before accepting the idea that a particular moral decision does not have one right issue, and, even on the rare occasions on which she eventually reached the conclusion that this is such a case, would the virtuous agent toss a coin? Of course not.

. . .

The acceptance of the possibility of irresolvable dilemmas within virtue ethics (by those of us who do accept it) should not be seen in itself as conceding much to 'pluralism'. If I say that I can imagine a case in which two virtuous agents are faced with a dilemma, and one does A while the other does B, I am not saying that I am imagining a case in which the two virtuous agents each think that what the other does is wrong (vicious, contrary to virtue) because they have radically different views about what is required by a certain virtue, or about whether a certain character trait is a vice, or about whether something is to be greatly valued or of little importance. I am imagining a case in which my two virtuous agents have the same 'moral views' about everything, up to and including the view that, in this particular case, neither decision is *the* right one, and hence neither is wrong. Each recognizes the propriety of the other's reason for doing what she did—say, 'To avoid *that* evil', 'To secure *this* good'—for her recognition of the fact that this is as good a moral reason as her own (say, 'To avoid *this* evil', 'To secure *that* good') is what forced each to accept the idea that the dilemma was irresolvable in the first place. Though each can give such a reason for what they did (A in one case, B in the other), neither attempts to give 'the moral reason' why they did one *rather than* the other. The 'reason' for or explanation of *that* would be, if available at all, in terms of psychological autobiography ('I decided to sleep on it, and when I woke up I just found myself thinking in terms of doing A', or 'I just felt terrified at the thought of doing A: I'm sure this was totally irrational, but I did, so I did B').

The topic of this chapter has been the view that virtue ethics cannot be a normative rival to utilitarianism and deontology because 'it cannot tell us what we should do'. In defending the existence of normative virtue ethics I have not

(20)

One way to deal with the conflict of virtues problem, which Hursthouse may be suggesting here, is to appeal to a supposed higher-order virtue of practical wisdom that is essentially the capacity to adjudicate between the competing claims of lower-order virtues (like kindness, fairness, loyalty, honesty, etc.). The question is whether it is clear enough what practical wisdom would amount to and how it would work for this to be a real solution to the problem.

(21)

To say that both actions are right is to say that there is no *moral* objection to doing either one of them. (See Discussion Question 4.)

attempted to argue that it can 'tell us what we should do' in such a way that the difficult business of acting well is made easy for us. I have not only admitted but welcomed the fact that, in some cases, moral wisdom is required if the v-rules are to be applied correctly and apparent dilemmas thereby resolved (or indeed identified, since a choice that may seem quite straightforward to the foolish or wicked may rightly appear difficult, calling for much thought, to the wise). Nor have I attempted to show that virtue ethics is guaranteed to be able to resolve every dilemma. It seems bizarre to insist that a normative ethics must be able to do this prior to forming a reasonable belief that there cannot be irresolvable dilemmas, but those who have formed such a belief may share a normative ethics with those who have different views. . . . A normative ethics, I suggested, should be able to accommodate both views on this question, as virtue ethics does, not model itself mindlessly on scientific theory.

Discussion Questions

1. Clearly Hursthouse is right that we often seek moral advice from other people, and particularly from people we especially respect or admire from a moral standpoint. But what do we want from such people? Is it simply direct advice as to what to do (based on what they would do), as Hursthouse's account would seem to suggest? Or don't we instead want them to give us *reasons* in favor of some action (often for more than one alternative), reasons that we then attempt to evaluate for ourselves? (The latter alternative would suggest that there are moral considerations that are more fundamental than what a virtuous person does: the rules or principles or standards that he himself is following. How might Hursthouse reply to this objection?)
2. Consider the example of making a deliberately insincere promise to someone (as in borrowing money while not really intending to repay). Kant says that this is morally wrong because it treats the other person as a mere means. Hursthouse's view says that it is wrong because an ideally virtuous person would not do such a thing. Each might agree in part with the other view: Kant can say that an ideally virtuous person would not act in this way *because* it would involve treating another as a mere means; while Hursthouse can say that it is wrong to treat another as a mere means *because* an ideally virtuous person would not do this. Thus they might agree on the moral result, while differing as to the most fundamental reason for it. Who is right about this latter issue?
3. How plausible is Hursthouse's suggestion that the different virtues do not conflict with each other when properly understood? Make a list of virtues for yourself, and try to think of situations where they seem to conflict. How plausible is it that such conflicts can always be resolved by understanding each virtue in the right way—as opposed to understanding, perhaps via practical wisdom, that one virtue overrides another in a given case? (This last result would not mean that the overridden virtue does not conflict with the one that overrides it, for otherwise there would be no point of speaking of one overriding the other.)
4. Could it happen that through no fault of the agent, there are serious moral objections to *any* action available—in which case even what the ideally virtuous person does will not be right without serious qualification? (Think here especially of Williams's case of Jim, on page 343.) If this were so, then a morally right action could not be defined as whatever an ideally virtuous person would do (since even an ideally virtuous person would do something). How serious an objection is this to Hursthouse's version of virtue ethics?

Rosalind Hursthouse

See the preceding selection for biographical information about Rosalind Hursthouse. In the present selection, Hursthouse attempts to apply virtue ethics to a specific moral issue, the issue of the morality of abortion. (This selection is excerpted from an article that also contains an earlier and less fully developed version of the account of virtue ethics offered in the preceding selection.)

Virtue Theory and Abortion

...

I now turn to an illustration of [the] discussion [of a real moral issue], applying virtue theory to abortion. Before I embark on this tendentious business, I should remind the reader of the aim of this discussion. I am not, in this article, trying to solve the problem of abortion; I am illustrating how virtue theory directs one to think about it. It might indeed be said that thinking about the problem in this way "solves" it by dissolving it, insofar as it leads one to the conclusion that there is no single right answer, but a variety of particular answers, and in what follows I am certainly trying to make that conclusion seem plausible. But, that granted, it should still be said that I am not trying to "solve the problems" in the practical sense of telling people that they should, or should not, do this or that if they are pregnant and contemplating abortion in these or those particular circumstances.

I do not assume, or expect, that all of my readers will agree with everything I am about to say. On the contrary, given the plausible assumption that some are morally wiser than I am, and some less so, the theory has built into it that we are bound to disagree on some points. For instance, we may well disagree about the particular application of some of the virtue and vice terms; and we may disagree about what is worthwhile or serious, worthless or trivial. But my aim is to make clear how these concepts figure in a discussion conducted in terms of virtue theory. What is at issue is whether these concepts are indeed the ones that should come in, that is, whether virtue theory should be criticized for employing them. The problem of abortion highlights this issue dramatically since virtue theory quite transforms the discussion of it.

As everyone knows, the morality of abortion is commonly discussed in relation to just two considerations: first, and predominantly, the status of the fetus and whether or not it is the sort of thing that may or may not be innocuously or justifiably killed [1]; and second, and less predominantly (when, that is, the discussion concerns the *morality* of abortion rather than the question of permissible legislation in a just society), women's rights. If one thinks within this familiar framework, one may well be puzzled about what virtue theory, as such, could contribute. Some people assume the discussion will be conducted solely in terms of what the virtuous agent would or would not do. . . . Others assume that only justice, or at most justice and charity; will be applied to the issue, generating a discussion very similar to Judith Jarvis Thomson's.*

As Thomson (along with many others) puts it, whether or not the fetus (taking this term to refer to all stages of prenatal life) is a *person*.

Now if this is the way the virtue theorist's discussion of abortion is imagined to be, no wonder people think little of it. It seems obvious in advance that in any such discussion there must be either a great deal of extremely tendentious application of the virtue terms *just, charitable,* and so on or a lot of rhetorical appeal to "this is what only the virtuous agent knows." But these are caricatures; they fail to appreciate the way in which virtue theory quite transforms the discussion of abortion by dismissing the two familiar dominating considerations as, in a way, fundamentally irrelevant. In what way or ways, I hope to make both clear and plausible.

Let us first consider women's rights. Let me emphasize again that we are discussing the *morality* of abortion, not the rights and wrongs of laws prohibiting or permitting it. If we suppose that women do have a moral right to do as they choose with their own bodies, or, more particularly, to terminate their pregnancies, then it may well follow that a *law* forbidding abortion would be unjust. Indeed, even if they have no such right, such a law might be, as things stand at the moment, unjust, or impractical, or inhumane: on this issue I have nothing to say in this article. But, putting all questions about the justice or injustice of laws to one side,

From *Philosophy and Public Affairs,* Vol. 20, No. 3 (Summer, 1991).

*Judith Jarvis Thomson, "A Defense of Abortion," *Philosophy & Public Affairs* 1, no. 1 (Fall 1971): 47–66 [pp. 385–396 in this book]. One could indeed regard this article as proto-virtue theory (no doubt to the surprise of the author) if the concepts of callousness and kindness were allowed more weight.

and supposing only that women have such a moral right, *nothing follows* from this supposition about the morality of abortion, according to virtue theory, once it is noted (quite generally, not with particular reference to abortion) that in exercising a moral right I can do something cruel, or callous, or selfish, light-minded, self-righteous, stupid, inconsiderate, disloyal, dishonest—that is, act viciously.* Love and friendship do not survive their parties' constantly insisting on their rights, nor do people live well when they think that getting what they have a right to is of preeminent importance; they harm others, and they harm themselves. So whether women have a moral right to terminate their pregnancies is irrelevant within virtue theory, for it is irrelevant to the question "In having an abortion in these circumstances, would the agent be acting virtuously or viciously or neither?" [2]

What about the consideration of the status of the fetus—what can virtue theory say about that? One might say that this issue is not in the province of *any* moral theory; it is a metaphysical question, and an extremely difficult one at that. Must virtue theory then wait upon metaphysics to come up with the answer?

At first sight it might seem so. For virtue is said to involve knowledge, and part of this knowledge consists in having the *right* attitude to things. "Right" here does not just mean "morally right" or "proper" or "nice" in the modern sense; it means "accurate, true." One cannot have the right or correct attitude to something if the attitude is based on or involves false beliefs. And this suggests that if the status of the fetus is relevant to the rightness or wrongness of abortion, its status must be known, as a truth, to the fully wise and virtuous person. [3]

But the sort of wisdom that the fully virtuous person has is not supposed to be recondite; it does not call for fancy philosophical sophistication, and it does not depend upon, let alone wait upon, the discoveries of academic philosophers. [4] And this entails the following, rather startling, conclusion: that the status of the fetus—that issue over which so much ink has been spilt—is, according to virtue theory, simply not relevant to the rightness or wrongness of abortion. . . . [5]

Or rather, since that is clearly too radical a conclusion, it is in a sense relevant, but only in the sense that the familiar biological facts are relevant. By "the familiar biological facts" I mean the facts that most human societies are and have been familiar with—that, standardly (but not invariably), pregnancy occurs as the result of sexual intercourse, that it lasts about nine months, during which time the fetus grows and develops, that standardly it terminates in the birth of a living baby, and that this is how we all come to be. [6]

It might be thought that this distinction—between the familiar biological facts and the status of the fetus—is a distinction without a difference. But this is not so. To attach relevance to the status of the fetus, in the sense in which virtue theory claims it is not relevant, is to be gripped by the conviction that we must go beyond the familiar biological facts, deriving some sort of conclusion from them, such as that the fetus has rights, or is not a person, or something similar. It is also to believe that this exhausts the relevance of the familiar biological facts, that all they are relevant to is the status of the fetus and whether or not it is the sort of thing that may or may not be killed.

These convictions, I suspect, are rooted in the desire to solve the problem of abortion by getting it to fall under some general rule such as "You ought not to kill anything with the right to life but may kill anything else." But they have resulted in what should surely strike any nonphilosopher as a most bizarre aspect of nearly all the current philosophical literature on abortion, namely, that, far from treating abortion as a unique moral problem, markedly unlike any other, nearly everything written on the status of the fetus and its bearing on the abortion issue would be consistent with the human reproductive facts' (to say nothing of family life) being totally different from what they are. Imagine that you are an alien extraterrestrial anthropologist who does not know that the human race is roughly 50 percent female and 50 percent male, or that our only (natural) form of reproduction involves heterosexual intercourse, viviparous birth, and the female's (and only the female's) being pregnant for nine months, or that females

*One possible qualification: if one ties the concept of justice very closely to rights, then if women do have a moral right to terminate their pregnancies it may follow that in doing so they do not act unjustly. (cf. Thomson, "A Defense of Abortion.") But it is debatable whether even that much follows.

Hursthouse's point here is that merely the fact that a woman has a right to control her own body or, derivatively, a right to have an abortion does not mean that there is no serious moral objection to abortion in a particular case or even generally—something that all three of the main moral views would in fact accept. (See the last part of Thomson's discussion for one thing that a Kantian might say about this.)

But the existence of such rights may nonetheless remove one serious objection to abortion, and thus seems in fact to have important moral relevance. If a virtue theory must deny this (which isn't in fact very clearly so), then that would be a major objection to such a view. (See Discussion Question 1.)

It would be more plausible to say that *acting* in a truly virtuous way in a particular case will require such knowledge. It isn't clear why virtue theory has to say that a fully virtuous person must have all of the knowledge required for virtuous action in any situation.

This claim may be correct in many cases. But the rationale for it within virtue theory is not particularly clear: why couldn't there be aspects of virtue that do require "recondite" knowledge or wisdom of some sort?

Hursthouse is right to describe this conclusion as "startling." Part of Aristotle's definition of virtue (p. 401) involved feeling and therefore acting in the right way "with reference to the right object." How then can what sort of object the fetus really is have no moral relevance? (See Discussion Question 2.)

Is merely knowing mundane biological facts of these sorts enough to enable the virtuous person to judge what sort of action is, in a particular set of circumstances, the right or proper one to take in relation to the fetus?

are capable of childbearing from late childhood to late middle age, or that childbearing is painful, dangerous, and emotionally charged—do you think you would pick up these facts from the hundreds of articles written on the status of the fetus? I am quite sure you would not. [7] And that, I think, shows that the current philosophical literature on abortion has got badly out of touch with reality.

Now if we are using virtue theory, our first question is not "What do the familiar biological facts show—what can be derived from them about the status of the fetus?" but "How do these facts figure in the practical reasoning, actions and passions, thoughts and reactions, of the virtuous and the nonvirtuous? What is the mark of having the right attitude to these facts and what manifests having the wrong attitude to them?" This immediately makes essentially relevant not only all the facts about human reproduction I mentioned above, but a whole range of facts about our emotions in relation to them as well. I mean such facts as that human parents, both male and female, tend to care passionately about their offspring, and that family relationships are among the deepest and strongest in our lives—and, significantly, among the longest-lasting.

These facts make it obvious that pregnancy is not just one among many other physical conditions; and hence that anyone who genuinely believes that an abortion is comparable to a haircut or an appendectomy is mistaken. [8] The fact that the premature termination of a pregnancy is, in some sense, the cutting off of a new human life, and thereby, like the procreation of a new human life, connects with all our thoughts about human life and death, parenthood, and family relationships, must make it a serious matter. To disregard this fact about it, to think of abortion as nothing but the killing of something that does not matter, or as nothing but the exercise of some right or rights one has, or as the incidental means to some desirable state of affairs, is to do something callous and light-minded, the sort of thing that no virtuous and wise person would do. It is to have the wrong attitude not only to fetuses, but more generally to human life and death, parenthood, and family relationships. [9]

Although I say that the facts make this obvious, I know that this is one of my tendentious points. In partial support of it I note that even the most dedicated proponents of the view that deliberate abortion is just like an appendectomy or haircut rarely hold the same view of spontaneous abortion, that is, miscarriage. It is not so tendentious of me to claim that to, react to people's grief over miscarriage by saying, or even thinking, "What a fuss about nothing!" would be callous and light-minded, whereas to try to laugh someone out of grief over an appendectomy scar or a botched haircut would not be. It is hard to give this point due prominence within act-centered theories, for the inconsistency is an inconsistency in attitude about the seriousness of loss of life, not in beliefs about which acts are right or wrong. Moreover, an act-centered theorist may say, "Well, there is nothing wrong with *thinking* 'What a fuss about nothing!' as long as you do not say it and hurt the person who is grieving. And besides, we cannot be held responsible for our thoughts, only for the intentional actions they give rise to." But the character traits that virtue theory emphasizes are not simply dispositions to intentional actions, but a seamless disposition to certain actions and passions, thoughts and reactions.

To say that the cutting off of a human life is always a matter of some seriousness, at any stage, is not to deny the relevance of gradual fetal development. Notwithstanding the well-worn point that clear boundary lines cannot be drawn, our emotions and attitudes regarding the fetus do change as it develops, and again when it is born, and indeed further as the baby grows. Abortion for shallow reasons in the later stages is much more shocking than abortion for the same reasons in the early stages in a way that matches the fact that deep grief over miscarriage in the later stages is more appropriate than it is over miscarriage in the earlier stages. . . . [10]

The fact that pregnancy is not just one among many physical conditions does not mean that one can never regard it in that light without manifesting a vice. When women are in very poor physical health, or worn out from childbearing, or forced to do very physically demanding jobs, then they cannot be described as self-indulgent, callous, irresponsible, or light-minded if they seek abortions mainly with a view to avoiding pregnancy as the physical condition that it is. To go through with a pregnancy when one is utterly exhausted, or when one's job consists of crawling along tunnels

Hursthouse is right that this is true of at least a very large part of the abortion literature, the main reason being that philosophers such as Thomson are trying to find *general* moral principles of some sort that can then be applied to the abortion case. The issue will be whether Hursthouse can show that facts of the sorts she mentions are relevant in an important way to settling the issue.

Such views have indeed been sometimes suggested. But not many philosophers would take them seriously—indeed there is some room for doubt that even those who have proposed them really do so.

But can either facts of biology or facts about our emotional reactions make it true that the killing of a fetus is not "the killing of something that does not matter"? Why doesn't this depend on whether the fetus is really a morally significant entity—the issue that was dismissed earlier as having no moral relevance? (Compare also her later appeals to "the sanctity of human life.")

There is no doubt that people's reactions often differ in these ways. But has Hursthouse given any clear reason, whether based on virtue ethics or otherwise, for thinking that such differential reactions are genuinely virtuous or morally correct?

hauling coal, as many women in the nineteenth century were obliged to do, is perhaps heroic, but people who do not achieve heroism are not necessarily vicious. That they can view the pregnancy only as eight months of misery, followed by hours if not days of agony and exhaustion, and abortion only as the blessed escape from this prospect, is entirely understandable and does not manifest any lack of serious respect for human life or a shallow attitude to motherhood. What it does show is that something is terribly amiss in the conditions of their lives, which make it so hard to recognize pregnancy and childbearing as the good that they can be.

. . . Philosophers arguing against anything remotely resembling a belief in the sanctity of life (which the above claims clearly embody) frequently appeal to the existence of other communities in which abortion and infanticide are practiced. We should not automatically assume that it is impossible that some other communities could be morally inferior to our own; maybe some are, or have been, precisely insofar as their members are, typically, callous or light-minded or unjust. But in communities in which life is a great deal tougher for everyone than it is in ours, having the right attitude to human life and death, parenthood, and family relationships might well manifest itself in ways that are unlike ours. When it is essential to survival that most members of the community fend for themselves at a very young age or work during most of their waking hours, selective abortion or infanticide might be practiced either as a form of genuine euthanasia or for the sake of the community and not, I think, be thought callous or light-minded. But this does not make everything all right; as before, it shows that there is something amiss with the conditions of their lives, which are making it impossible for them to live really well.

The foregoing discussion, insofar as it emphasizes the right attitude to human life and death, parallels to a certain extent those standard discussions of abortion that concentrate on it solely as an issue of killing. But it does not, as those discussions do, gloss over the fact, emphasized by those who discuss the morality of abortion in terms of women's rights, that abortion, wildly unlike any other form of killing, is the termination of a pregnancy, which is a condition of a woman's body and results in *her* having a child if it is not aborted. This fact is given due recognition not by appeal to women's rights but by emphasizing the relevance of the familiar biological and psychological facts and their connection with having the right attitude to parenthood and family relationships. But it may well be thought that failing to bring in women's rights still leaves some important aspects of the problem of abortion untouched.

Speaking in terms of women's rights, people sometimes say things like, "Well, it's her life you're talking about too, you know; she's got a right to her own life, her own happiness." And the discussion stops there. But in the context of virtue theory, given that we are particularly concerned with what constitutes a good human life, with what true happiness or *eudaimonia is,* this is no place to stop. We go on to ask, "And is this life of hers a good one? Is she living well?"

If we are to go on to talk about good human lives, in the context of abortion, we have to bring in our thoughts about the value of love and family life, and our proper emotional development through a natural life cycle. The familiar facts support the view that parenthood in general, and motherhood and childbearing in particular, are intrinsically worthwhile, are among the things that can be correctly thought to be partially constitutive of a flourishing human life. If this is right, then a woman who opts for not being a mother (at all, or again, or now) by opting for abortion may thereby be manifesting a flawed grasp of what her life should be, and be about—a grasp that is childish, or grossly materialistic, or shortsighted, or shallow.

I said "*may* thereby": this *need* not be so. Consider, for instance, a woman who has already had several children and fears that to have another will seriously affect her capacity to be a good mother to the ones she has—she does not show a lack of appreciation of the intrinsic value of being a parent by opting for abortion. Nor does a woman who has been a good mother and is approaching the age at which she may be looking forward to being a good grandmother. Nor does a woman who discovers that her pregnancy may well kill her, and opts for abortion and adoption. Nor, necessarily, does a woman who has decided to lead a life centered around some other worthwhile activity or activities with which motherhood would compete.

People who are childless by choice are sometimes described as "irresponsible," or "selfish," or "refusing to grow up," or "not knowing what life is about." But one can hold that having children is intrinsically worthwhile without endorsing this, for we are, after all, in the happy position of there being more worthwhile things to do than can be fitted into one lifetime. Parenthood, and motherhood in particular, even if granted to be intrinsically worthwhile, undoubtedly take up a lot of one's adult life, leaving no room for some other worthwhile pursuits. But some women who choose abortion rather than have their first child, and some men who encourage their partners to choose abortion, are not avoiding parenthood for the sake of other worthwhile pursuits, but for the worthless one of "having a good time," or for the pursuit of some false vision of the ideals of freedom or self-realization. And some others who say "I am not ready for parenthood yet" are making some sort of mistake about the extent to which one can manipulate the circumstances of one's life so as to make it fulfill some dream that one has. . . . [11]

Once again, this is not to deny that girls may quite properly say "I am not ready for motherhood yet," especially in our society, and, far from manifesting irresponsibility or light-mindedness, show an appropriate modesty or humility, or a fearfulness that does not amount to cowardice. However, even when the decision to have an abortion is the right decision—one that does not itself fall under a vice-related term and thereby one that the perfectly virtuous could recommend—it does not follow that there is no sense in which having the abortion is wrong, or guilt inappropriate. For, by virtue of the fact that a human life has been cut short, some evil has probably been brought about,* and that circumstances make the decision to bring about some evil the right decision will be a ground for guilt if getting into those circumstances in the first place itself manifested a flaw in character. [12]

What "gets one into those circumstances" in the case of abortion is, except in the case of rape, one's sexual activity and one's choices, or the lack of them, about one's sexual partner and about contraception. The virtuous woman (which here of course does not mean simply "chaste woman" but "woman with the virtues") has such character traits as strength, independence, resoluteness, decisiveness, self-confidence, responsibility, serious-mindedness, and self-determination—and no one, I think, could deny that many women become pregnant in circumstances in which they cannot welcome or cannot face the thought of having this child precisely because they lack one or some of these character traits. So even in the cases where the decision to have an abortion is the right one, it can still be the reflection of a moral failing—not because the decision itself is weak or cowardly or irresolute or irresponsible or lightminded, but because lack of the requisite opposite of these failings landed one in the circumstances in the first place. Hence the common universalized claim that guilt and remorse are never appropriate emotions about an abortion is denied. They may be appropriate, and appropriately inculcated, even when the decision was the right one.

. . .

Notice that all of the considerations in the preceding three paragraphs apply as much to the decision of whether to seek to conceive a child as to the one of whether to abort one that has already been conceived. Thus they don't seem to address whatever it is that makes the abortion issue a distinctive moral problem.

Here, as earlier, we have an appeal to something like the "sanctity of human life"—*all* human life, including that of fetuses. Isn't this a conclusion on the issue that Hursthouse earlier denied to be morally relevant? And has she given a clear account of how this conclusion is arrived at from a virtue point of view?

Discussion Questions

1. Hursthouse says that whether or not the fetus is a person is irrelevant to the abortion issue and that only mundane biological facts are relevant to what a virtuous person would do when faced with such a choice. But she also speaks of "the sanctity of human life" (with the suggestion that this extends to fetuses) and of the moral evil involved in the ending of a human life in such a case, which seems to involve an appeal to more than merely biological facts about the fetus. Is there any way to reconcile these two views?
2. A general issue that is in some ways parallel to the abortion issue is the issue of euthanasia: whether, if ever, extremely ill or comatose individuals may be

*I say "some evil has probably been brought about" on the ground that (human) life is (usually) a good and hence (human) death usually an evil. The exceptions would be (a) where death is actually a good or a benefit, because the baby that would come to be if the life were not cut short would be better off dead than alive, and (b) where death, though not a good, is not an evil either, because the life that would be led (e.g., in a state of permanent coma) would not be a good. . . .

deliberately allowed to die or even be killed. One question often raised in connection with euthanasia is whether or not individuals in various specific conditions are still persons, that is, beings deserving of moral respect or with a serious right to life. What might Hursthouse's virtue ethics say about this? Is the issue of whether a permanently comatose individual is still a person morally irrelevant?

3. Hursthouse makes clear at the beginning that she is not attempting to solve the abortion problem, but only to explain how one should think about it according to her version of virtue ethics. How much help would her account provide for someone actually thinking about a choice of this kind? Ignoring for the moment the issue of which view is actually correct, would thinking about a case of abortion in the way suggested by Hursthouse be as likely to lead to a definite result as thinking about it in the way suggested by Thomson or by a utilitarian view?

Challenges to Morality: Relativism and Egoism

James Rachels

James Rachels (1941–2003) was an American philosopher best known for his work in both theoretical and applied ethics. He taught at several different universities, spending the longest time at the University of Alabama–Birmingham. In this selection, he explains and criticizes cultural relativism, arguing that the typical reasons advanced for the view fail to support it and that the view has implausible consequences. Moreover, he argues, there is not nearly as much moral disagreement as most defenders of cultural relativism claim there to be.

The Challenge of Cultural Relativism

1. How Different Cultures Have Different Moral Codes

Darius, a king of ancient Persia, was intrigued by the variety of cultures he encountered in his travels. He had found, for example, that the Callatians (a tribe of Indians) customarily ate the bodies of their dead fathers. The Greeks, of course, did not do that—the Greeks practiced cremation and regarded the funeral pyre as the natural and fitting way to dispose of the dead. Darius thought that a sophisticated understanding of the world must include an appreciation of such differences between cultures. One day, to teach this lesson, he summoned some Greeks who happened to be present at his court and asked them what they would take to eat the bodies of their dead fathers. They were shocked, as Darius knew they would be, and replied that no amount of money could persuade them to do such a thing. Then Darius called in some Callatians, and while the Greeks listened asked them what they would take to burn their dead fathers' bodies. The Callatians were horrified and told Darius not even to mention such a dreadful thing.

This story, recounted by Herodotus in his *History*, illustrates a recurring theme in the literature of social science: different cultures have different moral codes. What is thought right within one group may be utterly abhorrent to the members of another group, and vice versa. Should we eat the bodies of the dead or burn them? If you were a Greek, one answer would seem obviously correct; but if you were a Callatian, the opposite would seem equally certain.

It is easy to give additional examples of the same kind. Consider the Eskimos. They are a remote and inaccessible people. Numbering only about 25,000, they live in small, isolated settlements scattered mostly along the northern fringes of North America and Greenland. Until the beginning of this century, the outside world knew little about them. Then explorers began to bring back strange tales.

Eskimo customs turned out to be very different from our own. The men often had more than

---

From *The Elements of Moral Philosophy*, Chapter 2 (Philadelphia: Temple University Press, 1986).

one wife, and they would share their wives with guests, lending them for the night as a sign of hospitality. Moreover, within a community, a dominant male might demand—and get—regular sexual access to other men's wives. The women, however, were free to break these arrangements simply by leaving their husbands and taking up with new partners—free, that is, so long as their former husbands chose not to make trouble. All in all, the Eskimo practice was a volatile scheme that bore little resemblance to what we call marriage.

But it was not only their marriage and sexual practices that were different. The Eskimos also seemed to have less regard for human life. Infanticide, for example, was common. Knud Rasmussen, one of the most famous early explorers, reported that he met one woman who had borne twenty children but had killed ten of them at birth. Female babies, he found, were especially liable to be destroyed, and this was permitted simply at the parents' discretion, with no social stigma attached to it. Old people also, when they became too feeble to contribute to the family, were left out in the snow to die. So there seemed to be, in this society, remarkably little respect for life.

To the general public, these were disturbing revelations. Our own way of living seems so natural and right that for many of us it is hard to conceive of others living so differently. And when we do hear of such things, we tend immediately to categorize those other peoples as "backward" or "primitive." But to anthropologists and sociologists, there was nothing particularly surprising about the Eskimos. Since the time of Herodotus, enlightened observers have been accustomed to the idea that conceptions of right and wrong differ from culture to culture. If we assume that *our* ideas of right and wrong will be shared by all peoples at all times, we are merely naïve.

2. Cultural Relativism

To many thinkers, this observation—"Different cultures have different moral codes"—has seemed to be the key to understanding morality. The idea of universal truth in ethics, they say, is a myth. ❶ The customs of different societies are all that exist. These customs cannot be said to be "correct" or "incorrect," for that implies we have an independent standard of right and wrong by which they may be judged. But there is no such independent standard; every standard is culture-bound. The great pioneering sociologist William Graham Sumner, writing in 1906, put the point like this:

> The "right" way is the way which the ancestors used and which has been handed down. The tradition is its own warrant. It is not held subject to verification by experience. The notion of right is in the folkways. It is not outside of them, of independent origin, and brought to test them. In the folkways, whatever is, is right. This is because they are traditional, and therefore contain in themselves the authority of the ancestral ghosts. When we come to the folkways we are at the end of our analysis.

This line of thought has probably persuaded more people to be skeptical about ethics than any other single thing. *Cultural Relativism,* as it has been called, challenges our ordinary belief in the objectivity and universality of moral truth. It says, in effect, that there is no such thing as universal truth in ethics; there are only the various cultural codes, and nothing more. Moreover, our own code has no special status; it is merely one among many.

As we shall see, this basic idea is really a compound of several different thoughts. It is important to separate the various elements of the theory because, on analysis, some parts of the theory turn out to be correct, whereas others seem to be mistaken. As a beginning, we may distinguish the following claims, all of which have been made by cultural relativists:

1. Different societies have different moral codes.
2. There is no objective standard that can be used to judge one societal code better than another.
3. The moral code of our own society has no special status; it is merely one among many.
4. There is no "universal truth" in ethics—that is, there are no moral truths that hold for all peoples at all times.
5. The moral code of a society determines what is right within that society; that is, if the moral code of a society says that a certain action is right, then that action *is* right, at least within that society.
6. It is mere arrogance for us to try to judge the conduct of other peoples. We should adopt an attitude of tolerance toward the practices of other cultures. ❷

Although it may seem that these six propositions go naturally together, they are independent of

❶

By "universal truth in ethics," Rachels means objective (or "absolute") ethical truth: ethical truths that are true in the same non-relative way that scientific truths or at least simple, purely factual historical truths are true.

❷

Think carefully about these claims and the relations among them. Claim 1 is in itself a non-moral, factual claim, while all the others are moral claims of one sort or another. The central claim of cultural relativism is Claim 5.

3 To say that an argument is *sound* is to say both that the premise or premises are true and that the argument is *valid* in the sense that the conclusion genuinely follows from the premises (in other words, that it is impossible for the premises to be true and the conclusion false).

one another, in the sense that some of them might be true even if others are false. In what follows, we will try to identify what is correct in Cultural Relativism, but we will also be concerned to expose what is mistaken about it.

3. The Cultural Differences Argument

Cultural Relativism is a theory about the nature of morality. At first blush it seems quite plausible. However, like all such theories, it may be evaluated by subjecting it to rational analysis; and when we analyze Cultural Relativism we find that it is not so plausible as it first appears to be.

The first thing we need to notice is that at the heart of Cultural Relativism there is a certain *form of argument.* The strategy used by cultural relativists is to argue from facts about the differences between cultural outlooks to a conclusion about the status of morality. Thus we are invited to accept this reasoning:

1. The Greeks believed it was wrong to eat the dead, whereas the Callatians believed it was right to eat the dead.
2. Therefore, eating the dead is neither objectively right nor objectively wrong. It is merely a matter of opinion, which varies from culture to culture.

Or, alternatively:

1. The Eskimos see nothing wrong with infanticide, whereas Americans believe infanticide is immoral.
2. Therefore, infanticide is neither objectively right nor objectively wrong. It is merely a matter of opinion, which varies from culture to culture.

Clearly, these arguments are variations of one fundamental idea. They are both special cases of a more general argument, which says:

1. Different cultures have different moral codes.
2. Therefore, there is no objective "truth" in morality. Right and wrong are only matters of opinion, and opinions vary from culture to culture.

We may call this the *Cultural Differences Argument.* To many people, it is very persuasive. But from a logical point of view, is it a *sound* argument? 3

It is not sound. The trouble is that the conclusion does not really follow from the premise—that is, even if the premise is true, the conclusion still might be false. The premise concerns what people *believe:* in some societies, people believe one thing; in other societies, people believe differently. The conclusion, however, concerns *what really is the case.* The trouble is that this sort of conclusion does not follow logically from this sort of premise.

Consider again the example of the Greeks and Callatians. The Greeks believed it was wrong to eat the dead; the Callatians believed it was right. Does it follow, *from the mere fact that they disagreed,* that there is no objective truth in the matter? No, it does not follow; for it *could* be that the practice was objectively right (or wrong) and that one or the other of them was simply mistaken.

To make the point clearer, consider a very different matter. In some societies, people believe the earth is flat. In other societies, such as our own, people believe the earth is (roughly) spherical. Does it follow, *from the mere fact that they disagree,* that there is no "objective truth" in geography? Of course not; we would never draw such a conclusion because we realize that, in their beliefs about the world, the members of some societies might simply be wrong. There is no reason to think that if the world is round everyone must know it. Similarly, there is no reason to think that if there is moral truth everyone must know it. The fundamental mistake in the Cultural Differences Argument is that it attempts to derive a substantive conclusion about a subject (morality) from the mere fact that people disagree about it.

It is important to understand the nature of the point that is being made here. We are *not* saying (not yet, anyway) that the conclusion of the argument is false. Insofar as anything being said here is concerned, it is still an open question whether the conclusion is true. We *are* making a purely logical point and saying that the conclusion does not *follow from* the premise. This is important, because in order to determine whether the conclusion is true, we need arguments in its support. Cultural Relativism proposes this argument, but unfortunately the argument turns out to be fallacious. So it proves nothing.

4. The Consequences of Taking Cultural Relativism Seriously

Even if the Cultural Differences Argument is invalid, Cultural Relativism might still be true. **4** What would it be like if it were true?

In the passage quoted above, William Graham Sumner summarizes the essence of Cultural Relativism. He says that there is no measure of right and wrong other than the standards of one's society: "The notion of right is in the folkways. It is not outside of them, of independent origin, and brought to test them. In the folkways, whatever is, is right."

Suppose we took this seriously. What would be some of the consequences?

1. We could no longer say that the customs of other societies are morally inferior to our own. This, of course, is one of the main points stressed by Cultural Relativism. We would have to stop condemning other societies merely because they are "different." So long as we concentrate on certain examples, such as the funerary practices of the Greeks and Callatians, this may seem to be a sophisticated, enlightened attitude.

However, we would also be stopped from criticizing other, less benign practices. Suppose a society waged war on its neighbors for the purpose of taking slaves. **5** Or suppose a society was violently anti-Semitic and its leaders set out to destroy the Jews. Cultural Relativism would preclude us from saying that either of these practices was wrong. We would not even be able to say that a society tolerant of Jews is *better* than the anti-Semitic society, for that would imply some sort of transcultural standard of comparison. The failure to condemn *these* practices does not seem "enlightened"; on the contrary, slavery and anti-Semitism seem wrong *wherever* they occur. Nevertheless, if we took Cultural Relativism seriously, we would have to admit that these social practices also are immune from criticism.

2. We could decide whether actions are right or wrong just by consulting the standards of our society. Cultural Relativism suggests a simple test for determining what is right and what is wrong: all one has to do is ask whether the action is in accordance with the code of one's society. Suppose a resident of South Africa [prior to 1994] is wondering whether his country's policy of *apartheid*—rigid racial segregation—is morally correct. All he has to do is ask whether this policy conforms to his society's moral code. If it does, there is nothing to worry about, at least from a moral point of view. **6**

This implication of Cultural Relativism is disturbing because few of us think that our society's code is perfect—we can think of ways it might be improved. Yet Cultural Relativism would not only forbid us from criticizing the codes of *other* societies; it would stop us from criticizing our *own.* After all, if right and wrong are relative to culture, this must be true for our own culture just as much as for others.

3. The idea of moral progress is called into doubt. Usually, we think that at least some changes in our society have been for the better. (Some, of course, may have been changes for the worse.) Consider this example: Throughout most of Western history the place of women in society was very narrowly circumscribed. They could not own property; they could not vote or hold political office; with a few exceptions, they were not permitted to have paying jobs; and generally they were under the almost absolute control of their husbands. Recently much of this has changed, and most people think of it as progress.

If Cultural Relativism is correct, can we legitimately think of this as progress? Progress means replacing a way of doing things with a *better* way. But by what standard do we judge the new ways as better? If the old ways were in accordance with the social standards of their time, then Cultural Relativism would say it is a mistake to judge them by the standards of a different time. Eighteenth-century society was, in effect, a different society from the one we have now. To say that we have made progress implies a judgment that present-day society is better, and that is just the sort of transcultural judgment that, according to Cultural Relativism, is impermissible.

Our idea of social *reform* will also have to be reconsidered. A reformer such as Martin Luther King, Jr., seeks to change his society for the better. Within the constraints imposed by Cultural Relativism, there is one way this might

R As with other arguments, the conclusion might still in fact be true even if the argument is invalid and therefore unsound.

An even more obvious example might be the practice of slavery in the pre–Civil War American South. Is it really impossible (as the cultural relativist must claim) for us to say intelligibly that the practices of that society were in an important way morally inferior to those of our present society?

Apartheid is no longer practiced in South Africa, but we can still ask whether a person living under apartheid could have correctly decided that racial segregation was morally acceptable simply by appealing to the standard actually accepted at that time.

be done. If a society is not living up to its own ideals, the reformer may be regarded as acting for the best: the ideals of the society are the standard by which we judge his or her proposals as worthwhile. But the "reformer" may not challenge the ideals themselves, for those ideals are by definition correct. According to Cultural Relativism, then, the idea of social reform makes sense only in this very limited way.

These three consequences of Cultural Relativism have led many thinkers to reject it as implausible on its face. It does make sense, they say, to condemn some practices, such as slavery and anti-Semitism, wherever they occur. It makes sense to think that our own society has made some moral progress, while admitting that it is still imperfect and in need of reform. Because Cultural Relativism says that these judgments make no sense, the argument goes, it cannot be right.

5. Why There Is Less Disagreement Than It Seems

The original impetus for Cultural Relativism comes from the observation that cultures differ dramatically in their views of right and wrong. But just how much do they differ? It is true that there are differences. However, it is easy to overestimate the extent of those differences. Often, when we examine what *seems* to be a dramatic difference, we find that the cultures do not differ nearly as much as it appears.

Consider a culture in which people believe it is wrong to eat cows. This may even be a poor culture, in which there is not enough food; still, the cows are not to be touched. Such a society would *appear* to have values very different from our own. But does it? We have not yet asked why these people will not eat cows. Suppose it is because they believe that after death the souls of humans inhabit the bodies of animals, especially cows, so that a cow may be someone's grandmother. Now do we want to say that their values are different from ours? No; the difference lies elsewhere. The difference is in our belief systems, not in our values. We agree that we shouldn't eat Grandma; we simply disagree about whether the cow *is* (or could be) Grandma. 7

7

R Thus if the members of *our* culture came to believe that cows were reincarnations of relatives or friends, they would also presumably think that it was wrong to eat them.

The general point is this. Many factors work together to produce the customs of a society. The society's values are only one of them. Other matters, such as the religious and factual beliefs held by its members and the physical circumstances in which they must live, are also important. We cannot conclude, then, merely because customs differ, that there is a disagreement about *values*. The difference in customs may be attributable to some other aspect of social life. Thus there may be less disagreement about values than there appears to be.

Consider the Eskimos again. They often kill perfectly normal infants, especially girls. We do not approve of this at all; a parent who did this in our society would be locked up. Thus there appears to be a great difference in the values of our two cultures. But suppose we ask *why* the Eskimos do this. The explanation is not that they have less affection for their children or less respect for human life. An Eskimo family will always protect its babies if conditions permit. But they live in a harsh environment, where food is often in short supply. A fundamental postulate of Eskimo thought is: "Life is hard, and the margin of safety small." A family may want to nourish its babies but be unable to do so.

As in many "primitive" societies, Eskimo mothers will nurse their infants over a much longer period of time than mothers in our culture. The child will take nourishment from its mother's breast for four years, perhaps even longer. So even in the best of times there are limits to the number of infants that one mother can sustain. Moreover, the Eskimos are a nomadic people—unable to farm, they must move about in search of food. Infants must be carried, and a mother can carry only one baby in her parka as she travels and goes about her outdoor work. Other family members can help, but this is not always possible.

Infant girls are more readily disposed of because, first, in this society the males are the primary food providers—they are the hunters, according to the traditional division of labor—and it is obviously important to maintain a sufficient number of food gatherers. But there is an important second reason as well. Because the hunters suffer a high casualty rate, the adult men who die prematurely far outnumber the women who die early. Thus if male and female infants survived in equal numbers, the female adult population would greatly outnumber the male adult population. Examining the available statistics, one writer concluded that "were it not for female infanticide . . . there would be approximately one-and-a-half times as many females in the average Eskimo local group as there are food-producing males."

So among the Eskimos, infanticide does not signal a fundamentally different attitude toward children. Instead, it is a recognition that drastic measures are sometimes needed to ensure the family's survival. Even then, however, killing the baby is not the first option considered. Adoption is common; childless couples are especially happy to take a more fertile couple's "surplus." Killing is only the last resort. I emphasize this in order to show that the raw data of the anthropologists can be misleading; it can make the differences in values between cultures appear greater than they are. The Eskimos' values are not all that different from our values. It is only that life forces upon them choices that we do not have to make. (8)

STOP How much of the difference in behavior between our society and traditional Eskimo society can be explained in this way? (See Discussion Question 1.)

6. How All Cultures Have Some Values in Common

It should not be surprising that, despite appearances, the Eskimos are protective of their children. How could it be otherwise? How could a group survive that did *not* value its young? This suggests a certain argument, one which shows that all cultural groups must be protective of their infants:

1. Human infants are helpless and cannot survive if they are not given extensive care for a period of years.
2. Therefore, if a group did not care for its young, the young would not survive, and the older members of the group would not be replaced. After a while the group would die out.
3. Therefore, any cultural group that continues to exist must care for its young. Infants that are *not* cared for must be the exception rather than the rule.

Similar reasoning shows that other values must be more or less universal. Imagine what it would be like for a society to place no value at all on truth telling. When one person spoke to another, there would be no presumption at all that he was telling the truth—for he could just as easily be speaking falsely. Within that society, there would be no reason to pay attention to what anyone says. (I ask you what time it is, and you say "Four o'clock." But there is no presumption that you are speaking truly; you could just as easily have said the first thing that came into your head. So I have no reason to pay attention to your answer—in fact, there was no point in my asking you in the first place!) Communication would then be extremely difficult, if not impossible. And because complex societies cannot exist without regular communication among their members, society would become impossible. It follows that in any complex society there *must* be a presumption in favor of truthfulness. There may of course be exceptions to this rule: there may be situations in which it is thought to be permissible to lie. Nevertheless, these will be exceptions to a rule that *is* in force in the society.

Let me give one further example of the same type. Could a society exist in which there was no prohibition on murder? What would this be like? Suppose people were free to kill other people at will, and no one thought there was anything wrong with it. In such a "society," no one could feel secure. Everyone would have to be constantly on guard. People who wanted to survive would have to avoid other people as much as possible. This would inevitably result in individuals trying to become as self-sufficient as possible—after all, associating with others would be dangerous. Society on any large scale would collapse. Of course, people might band together in smaller groups with others that they *could* trust not to harm them. But notice what this means: they would be forming smaller societies that *did* acknowledge a rule against murder. The prohibition of murder, then, is a necessary feature of all societies.

There is a general theoretical point here, namely, that *there are some moral rules that all societies will have in common, because those rules are necessary for society to exist.* The rules against lying and murder are two examples. And in fact, we do find these rules in force in all viable cultures. Cultures may differ in what they regard as legitimate exceptions to the rules, but this disagreement exists against a background of agreement on the larger issues. Therefore, it is a mistake to overestimate the amount of difference between cultures. Not *every* moral rule can vary from society to society. (9)

STOP Is the fact that certain moral principles seem to be essential to any imaginable society enough to show that they are objectively true: that any society is *morally* required to follow them?

7. What Can Be Learned from Cultural Relativism

At the outset, I said that we were going to identify both what is right and what is wrong in Cultural Relativism. Thus far I have mentioned only its mistakes: I have said that it rests on an invalid argument, that it has consequences that make it implausible on its face, and that the extent of cultural disagreement is far less than it implies. This all adds up to a pretty thorough repudiation of the theory. Nevertheless, it is still a very appealing idea, and the reader may have the feeling that all this is a little unfair. The theory *must* have something going for it, or else why has it been so influential? In fact, I think there *is* something right about Cultural Relativism, and now I want to say what that is. There are two lessons we should learn from the theory, even if we ultimately reject it.

1. Cultural Relativism warns us, quite rightly, about the danger of assuming that all our preferences are based on some absolute rational standard. They are not. Many (but not all) of our practices are merely peculiar to our society, and it is easy to lose sight of that fact. In reminding us of it, the theory does a service.

Funerary practices are one example. The Callatians, according to Herodotus, were "men who eat their fathers"—a shocking idea, to us at least. But eating the flesh of the dead could be understood as a sign of respect. It could be taken as a symbolic act that says: We wish this person's spirit to dwell within us. Perhaps this was the understanding of the Callatians. On such a way of thinking, burying the dead could be seen as an act of rejection, and burning the corpse as positively scornful. If this is hard to imagine, then we may need to have our imaginations stretched. Of course we may feel a visceral repugnance at the idea of eating human flesh in any circumstances. But what of it? This repugnance may be, as the relativists say, only a matter of what is customary in our particular society.

There are many other matters that we tend to think of in terms of objective right and wrong, but that are really nothing more than social conventions. Should women cover their breasts? A publicly exposed breast is scandalous in our society, whereas in other cultures it is unremarkable. Objectively speaking, it is neither right nor wrong—there is no objective reason why either custom is better. Cultural Relativism begins with the valuable insight that many of our practices are like this—they are only cultural products. ❶ Then it goes wrong by concluding that, because *some* practices are like this, *all* must be.

❶ It is *entirely* consistent with the existence of objective morality that there are many issues, including some that have been thought to be morally significant, about which there is no objective moral truth.

2. The second lesson has to do with keeping an open mind. In the course of growing up, each of us has acquired some strong feelings: we have learned to think of some types of conduct as acceptable, and others we have learned to regard as simply unacceptable. Occasionally, we may find those feelings challenged. We may encounter someone who claims that our feelings are mistaken. For example, we may have been taught that homosexuality is immoral, and we may feel quite uncomfortable around gay people and see them as alien and "different." Now someone suggests that this may be a mere prejudice; that there is nothing evil about homosexuality; that gay people are just people, like anyone else, who happen, through no choice of their own, to be attracted to others of the same sex. But because we feel so strongly about the matter, we may find it hard to take this seriously. Even after we listen to the arguments, we may still have the unshakable feeling that homosexuals *must,* somehow, be an unsavory lot.

Cultural Relativism, by stressing that our moral views can reflect the prejudices of our society, provides an antidote for this kind of dogmatism. When he tells the story of the Greeks and Callatians, Herodotus adds:

> For if anyone, no matter who, were given the opportunity of choosing from amongst all the nations of the world the set of beliefs which he thought best, he would inevitably, after careful consideration of their relative merits, choose that of his own country. Everyone without exception believes his own native customs, and the religion he was brought up in, to be the best.

Realizing this can result in our having more open minds. We can come to understand that our feelings are not necessarily perceptions of the truth—they may be nothing more than the result of cultural conditioning. Thus when we hear it suggested that some element of our social code is *not* really the best and we find ourselves instinctively resisting the suggestion, we might stop and remember this. Then we may be more open to discovering the truth, whatever that might be.

We can understand the appeal of Cultural Relativism, then, even though the theory has serious shortcomings. It is an attractive theory because it is based on a genuine insight—that many of the practices and attitudes we think so natural are really only cultural products. Moreover, keeping this insight firmly in view is important if we want to avoid arrogance and have open minds. These are important points, not to be taken lightly. But we can accept these points without going on to accept the whole theory.[2]

This is somewhat misleading. To accept these points does not force us to accept any part of the theory, let alone the whole theory.

Discussion Questions

1. Rachels argues that apparent moral disagreements can often be accounted for by appeal to differences in factual beliefs or in the physical circumstances within which different cultures exist, without supposing that the underlying moral beliefs or values are really different. How well does this work in relation to the contrast between our culture and traditional Eskimo culture, as Rachels describes it? If our physical circumstances came to be closely similar to those of the Eskimos, would we then decide—without any change in our underlying moral beliefs and principles—that treating infants and old people in the way the Eskimos did is morally acceptable? Or would there still be a conflict between the demands of morality and the requirements of survival?
2. The cultural relativist view is that an individual is morally obligated to follow the moral standards of his society or culture. But it is arguable that many individuals in the modern world are members of more than one society or at least more than one group, with different groups often accepting different moral standards. Think of illustrations of this problem. Is there any way in such a situation to decide *which* group's moral standards the individual is obligated to follow?
3. Does cultural relativism allow for genuine moral disagreement between two (or more) individuals: a situation in which such individuals hold different moral views that are genuinely opposed to each other in such a way that both (or all) of them cannot be correct? Consider here both (a) two individuals from the same culture and (b) two individuals from different cultures. In (a), there can be a genuine disagreement of a sort, a disagreement as to which moral view is really held in that culture. But is this really a *moral* (as opposed to a merely factual) disagreement? And is it plausible that this is the only way in which moral disagreement is possible in case (a)? Can there be even this sort of moral disagreement (if it really is that) or any other in case (b)? If not, how implausible a result is this?
4. The central claim of cultural relativism is that the moral code of a particular society *determines* what is right (and wrong) for individuals in that society (claim 5 on p. 421). This seems to mean that individuals are morally bound by the standards of their culture, morally required to follow those standards. But can the cultural relativist account for the truth of *this* moral claim? What would make it true, from a relativist standpoint? Must each culture's moral code include a claim to this effect? What if some culture's moral code doesn't?
5. There are also other versions of moral relativism. One that is sometimes appealing to students is individual relativism: the view that the moral truth for each individual depends only on what is accepted by that individual. Consider the following issues concerning this view: (1) Is it really different from moral nihilism? If any moral claim that a person accepts is "true for him," how could any such claim require him to do something he doesn't want to do? (That is, why can't he just accept a claim that makes whatever he wants to do acceptable?) (2) If there is some way in which an individual's moral code can require him to do something that conflicts with his wants or desires, what makes it true that he ought to conform to that code? (Compare the previous question about cultural relativism.)

Joel Feinberg

Joel Feinberg (1926–2004) was an American legal, moral, and political philosopher who taught at UCLA, Princeton, Rockefeller University, and the University of Arizona. In the following selection, Feinberg explains and criticizes *psychological egoism:* the view that people, as a matter of psychological necessity, always act from selfish or egoistic motives, giving special attention to the *hedonistic* version of egoism, according to which people always aim at their own pleasure or happiness. Feinberg argues that there are no good arguments in favor of psychological egoism, and that the superficial plausibility of the view rests on confusion.

Psychological Egoism

A. The Theory

1. "Psychological egoism" is the name given to a theory widely held by ordinary people, and at one time almost universally accepted by political economists, philosophers, and psychologists, according to which all human actions when properly understood can be seen to be motivated by selfish desires. More precisely, psychological egoism is the doctrine that the only thing anyone is capable of desiring or pursuing ultimately (as an end in itself) is his *own* self-interest. No psychological egoist denies that people sometimes do desire things other than their own welfare—the happiness of other people, for example; but all psychological egoists insist that people are capable of desiring the happiness of others only when they take it to be a *means* to their own happiness. In short, purely altruistic and benevolent actions and desires do not exist; but people sometimes appear to be acting unselfishly and disinterestedly when they take the interests of others to be means to the promotion of their own self-interest.

2. This theory is called *psychological* egoism to indicate that it is not a theory about what *ought* to be the case, but rather about what, as a matter of fact, *is* the case. That is, the theory claims to be a description of psychological facts, not a prescription of ethical ideals. It asserts, however, not merely that all men do as a contingent matter of fact "put their own interests first," but also that they are capable of nothing else, human nature being what it is. Universal selfishness is not just an accident or a coincidence on this view, rather, it is an unavoidable consequence of psychological laws.

The theory is to be distinguished from another doctrine, so-called "ethical egoism," according to which all people *ought* to pursue their own well-being. This doctrine, being a prescription of what *ought* to be the case, makes no claim to be a psychological theory of human motives; hence the word "ethical" appears in its name to distinguish it from *psychological* egoism. ❶

❶ These are two distinct views. But psychological egoism might be used as an argument for ethical egoism, by appealing to the principle that "ought implies can" (that is, that one cannot be obligated to do something that one is not able to do). From this it would follow that one cannot have a moral obligation to act in an unselfish way if psychological egoism is true—in which case, any moral obligations there are could only be egoistic ones.

3. There are a number of types of motives and desires which might reasonably be called "egoistic" or "selfish," and corresponding to each of them is a possible version of psychological egoism. Perhaps the most common version of the theory is that apparently held by Jeremy Bentham.* According to this version, all persons have only one ultimate motive in all their voluntary behavior and that motive is a selfish one; more specifically, it is one particular kind of selfish motive—namely, a desire for one's own *pleasure.* According to this version of the theory, "the only kind of ultimate desire, is the desire to get or to prolong pleasant experiences, and to avoid or to cut short unpleasant experiences for oneself."† This form of psychological egoism is often given the cumbersome name—*psychological egoistic hedonism.*

B. Prima Facie Reasons in Support of the Theory

4. Psychological egoism has seemed plausible to many people for a variety of reasons, of which the following are typical: ❷

❷ STOP As Feinberg will explain, none of these arguments is very compelling. See if you can figure out now what is wrong with them.

a. "Every action of mine is prompted by motives or desires or impulses which are *my*

From *Reason and Responsibility,* edited by Joel Feinberg (Belmont, CA.: Wadsworth, 1996).

*See his *Introduction to the Principles of Morals and Legislation* (1789), Chap. I, first paragraph [p. 323 in this book]: "Nature has placed mankind under the governance of two sovereign masters, *pain* and *pleasure.* It is for them alone to point out what we ought to do, as well as to determine what we shall do. . . . They govern us in all we do, in all we say, in all we think: every effort we can make to throw off our subjection will serve but to demonstrate and confirm it."

†C. D. Broad, *Ethics and the History of Philosophy* (New York: The Humanities Press, 1952), p. 218.

motives and not somebody else's. This fact might be expressed by saying that whenever I act I am always pursuing my own ends or trying to satisfy my own desires. And from this we might pass on to—'I am always pursuing something for myself or seeking my own satisfaction.' Here is what seems like a proper description of a man acting selfishly, and if the description applies to all actions of all men, then it follows that all men in all their actions are selfish."*

b. It is a truism that when a person gets what he wants he characteristically feels pleasure. This has suggested to many people that what we really want in every case is our own pleasure, and that we pursue other things only as a means.

c. *Self-Deception.* Often we deceive ourselves into thinking that we desire something fine or noble when what we really want is to be thought well by others or to be able to congratulate ourselves, or to be able to enjoy the pleasures of good conscience. It is a well-known fact that people tend to conceal their true motives from themselves by camouflaging them with words like "virtue," "duty," etc. Since we are so often misled concerning both our own real motives and the real motives of others, is it not reasonable to suspect that we might *always* be deceived when we think motives disinterested and altruistic? . . .

d. *Moral Education.* Morality, good manners, decency, and other virtues must be teachable. Psychological egoists often notice that moral education and the inculcation of manners usually utilize what Bentham calls the "sanctions of pleasure and pain." Children are made to acquire the civilizing virtues only by the method of enticing rewards and painful punishments. Much the same is true of the history of the race. People in general have been inclined to behave well only when it is made plain to them that there is "something in it for them." Is it not then highly probable that just such a mechanism of human motivation as Bentham describes must be presupposed by our methods of moral education?

C. Critique of Psychological Egoism: Confusions in the Arguments

5. Non-Empirical Character of the Arguments. If the arguments of the psychological egoist consisted for the most part of carefully acquired empirical evidence (well-documented reports of controlled experiments, surveys, interviews, laboratory data, and so on), then the critical philosopher would have no business carping at them. After all, since psychological egoism purports to be a scientific theory of human motives, it is the concern of the experimental psychologist, not the philosopher, to accept or reject it. But as a matter of fact, empirical evidence of the required sort is seldom presented in support of psychological egoism. Psychologists, on the whole, shy away from generalizations about human motives which are so sweeping and so vaguely formulated that they are virtually incapable of scientific testing. It is usually the "armchair scientist" who holds the theory of universal selfishness, and his usual arguments are either based simply on his "impressions" or else are largely of a non-empirical sort. The latter are often shot full of a very subtle kind of logical confusion, and this makes their criticism a matter of special interest to the analytic philosopher.

6. The psychological egoist's first argument (4a, above) is a good example of logical confusion. It begins with a truism—namely, that all of my motives and desires are *my* motives and desires and not someone else's. (Who would deny this?) But from this simple tautology nothing whatever concerning the nature of my motives or the objective of my desires can possibly follow. . . . What the egoist must prove is not merely:

i. Every voluntary action is prompted by a motive of the agent's own.

but rather:

ii. Every voluntary action is prompted by a motive of a quite particular kind, viz. a selfish one.

---

*Austin Duncan-Jones, *Butler's Moral Philosophy* (London; Penguin Books, 1952), p. 96. Duncan-Jones goes on to reject this argument. See p. 512f.

R Statement (i) is compatible with the agent's motive being an entirely unselfish one: for example, the desire to help someone else entirely for their own sake.

Statement (i) is obviously true, but it cannot all by itself give any logical support to statement (ii). ❸

The source of the confusion in this argument is readily apparent. It is not the genesis of an action or the *origin* or its motives which makes it a "selfish" one, but rather the "purpose" of the act or the *objective* of its motives; *not where the motive comes from* (in voluntary actions it always comes from the agent) but *what it aims at* determines whether or not it is selfish. There is surely a valid distinction between voluntary behavior, in which the agent's action is motivated by purposes of his own, and *selfish* behavior in which the agent's motives are of one exclusive sort. . . .

7. But if argument 4a fails to prove its point, argument 4b does no better. From the fact that all our successful actions (those in which we get what we were after) are accompanied or followed by pleasure it does not follow, as the egoist claims, that the *objective* of every action is to get pleasure for oneself. To begin with, the premise of the argument is not, strictly speaking, even true. Fulfillment of desire (simply getting what one was after) is no guarantee of satisfaction (pleasant feelings of gratification in the mind of the agent). Sometimes when we get what we want we *also* get, as a kind of extra dividend, a warm, glowing feeling of contentment; but often, far too often, we get no dividend at all, or, even worse, the bitter taste of ashes. Indeed, it has been said that the characteristic psychological problem of our time is the *dissatisfaction* that attends the fulfillment of our very most powerful desires.

Even if we grant, however, for the sake of argument, that getting what one wants *usually* yields satisfaction, the egoist's conclusion does not follow. We can concede that we normally get pleasure (in the sense of satisfaction) when our desires are satisfied, *no matter what our desires are for;* but it does not follow from this roughly accurate generalization that the only thing we ever desire is our own satisfaction. . . .

8. Disinterested Benevolence. . . . Not only is argument [4b] fallacious; it also provides us with a suggestion of a counter-argument to show that its conclusion (psychological egoistic hedonism) is false. Not only is the presence of pleasure (satisfaction) as a by-product of an action no proof that the action was selfish; in some special cases it provides rather conclusive proof that the action was unselfish. For in those special cases the fact that we get pleasure from particular action presupposes that we desired something else—something other than our own pleasure—as an end in itself and not merely as a means to our own pleasant state of mind.

This way of turning the egoistic hedonist's argument back on him can be illustrated by taking a typical egoist argument, one attributed (perhaps apocryphally) to Abraham Lincoln, and then examining it closely.

> Mr. Lincoln once remarked to a fellow-passenger on an old-time mud-coach that all men were prompted by selfishness in doing good. His fellow-passenger was antagonizing this position when they were passing over a corduroy bridge that spanned a slough. As they crossed this bridge they espied an old razor-backed sow on the bank making a terrible noise because her pigs had got into the slough and were in danger of drowning. As the old coach began to climb the hill, Mr. Lincoln called out, "Driver, can't you stop just a moment?" Then Mr. Lincoln jumped out, ran back and lifted the little pigs out of the mud and water and placed them on the bank. When he returned, his companion remarked: "Now Abe, where does selfishness come in on this little episode?" "Why, bless your soul Ed, that was the very essence of selfishness. I should have had no peace of mind all day had I gone on and left that suffering old sow worrying over those pigs. I did it to get peace of mind, don't you see?"*

If Lincoln had cared not a whit for the welfare of the little pigs and their "suffering" mother, but only for his own "peace of mind," it would be difficult to explain how he could have derived pleasure from helping them. The very fact that he did feel satisfaction as a result of helping the pigs presupposes that he had a preexisting desire for something other than his own happiness. Then when *that* desire was satisfied, Lincoln of course derived pleasure. The *object* of Lincoln's desire was not pleasure; rather pleasure was the *consequence* of his preexisting desire for something else. If Lincoln had been wholly indifferent to the plight of the little pigs as he claimed, how could he possibly have derived any pleasure from

*Quoted from the *Springfield* (Illinois) *Monitor,* by F. C. Sharp in his *Ethics* (New York: Appleton-Century, 1928), p. 75.

helping them? . . . He could not have achieved peace of mind from rescuing the pigs, had he not a prior concern—on which his peace of mind depended—for the welfare of the pigs for its own sake. ❹

In general, the psychological hedonist analyzes apparent benevolence into a desire for "benevolent pleasure." No doubt the benevolent person does get pleasure from his benevolence, but in most cases, this is only because he has previously desired the good of some person, or animal, or mankind at large. Where there is no such desire, benevolent conduct is not generally found to give pleasure to the agent.

9. Malevolence. Difficult cases for the psychological egoist include not only instances of disinterested benevolence, but also cases of "disinterested malevolence." Indeed, malice and hatred are generally no more "selfish" than benevolence. Both are motives likely to cause an agent to sacrifice his own interests—in the case of benevolence, in order to help someone else, in the case of malevolence in order to harm someone else. The selfish person is concerned ultimately only with his own pleasure, happiness, or power, the benevolent person is often equally concerned with the happiness of others; to the malevolent person, the injury of another is often an end in itself—an end to be pursued sometimes with no thought for his own interests. There is reason to think that people have as often sacrificed themselves to injure or kill others as to help or to save others, and with as much "heroism" in the one case as in the other. ❺ . . .

10. Lack of Evidence for Universal Self-Deception. The more cynical sort of psychological egoist who is impressed by the widespread phenomenon of self-deception (see 4c above) cannot be so quickly disposed of, for he has committed no logical mistakes. We can only argue that the acknowledged frequency of self-deception is insufficient evidence for his universal generalization. His argument is not fallacious, but inconclusive.

No one but the agent himself can ever be certain what conscious motives really prompted his action, and where motives are disreputable, even the agent may not admit to himself the true nature of his desires. Thus, for every apparent case of altruistic behavior, the psychological egoist can argue, with some plausibility, that the true motivation *might* be selfish, appearance to the contrary. Philanthropic acts are really motivated by the desire to receive gratitude; acts of self-sacrifice, when truly understood, are seen to be motivated by the desire to feel self-esteem; and so on. We must concede to the egoist that all apparent altruism might be deceptive in this way; but such a sweeping generalization requires considerable empirical evidence, and such evidence is not presently available. ❻

11. The "Paradox of Hedonism" and Its Consequences for Education. The psychological egoistic Hedonist (e.g., Jeremy Bentham) has the simplest possible theory of human motivation. According to this variety of egoistic theory, all human motives without exception can be reduced to one—namely, the desire for one's own pleasure. But this theory, despite its attractive simplicity, or perhaps because of it, involves one immediately in a paradox. Astute observers of human affairs from the time of the ancient Greeks have often noticed that pleasure, happiness, and satisfaction are states of mind which stand in a very peculiar relation to desire. An exclusive desire for happiness is the surest way to prevent happiness from coming into being. Happiness has a way of "sneaking up" on persons when they are preoccupied with other things; but when persons deliberately and single-mindedly set off in pursuit of happiness, it vanishes utterly from sight and cannot be captured. This is the famous "paradox of hedonism": the single-minded pursuit of happiness is necessarily self-defeating, for the way to get happiness is to forget it; then perhaps it will come to you. If you aim exclusively at pleasure itself, with no concern for the things that bring pleasure, then pleasure will never come. To derive satisfaction, one must ordinarily first desire something other than satisfaction, and then find the means to get what one desires.

To feel the full force of the paradox of hedonism the reader should conduct an experiment in his imagination. Imagine a person (let's call him "Jones") who is, first of all, devoid of intellectual curiosity. He has no desire to acquire any kind of knowledge for its own sake, and thus is utterly indifferent to questions of science, mathematics, and philosophy. Imagine further that the beauties of nature leave Jones cold: he is unimpressed by the autumn foliage, the snowcapped mountains, and the rolling oceans. Long walks in the country on spring

R If Lincoln had no *independent* concern for the welfare of the pigs (or their mother), it would be inexplicable *why* his own peace of mind would be disturbed if they were not helped or why he would feel better after helping. Thus it makes no sense to say that he is only concerned about his own peace of mind.

R Thus the actions of the malevolent person make sense only because he has a desire to harm someone else that is independent of any desire for his own happiness: it is because of this independent desire that he may be unable to be happy unless that person suffers.

STOP Is it even possible that there is *always* a selfish motive in any case of apparent altruism? Think of some examples. (See Discussion Question 1.)

mornings and skiing forays in the winter are to him equally a bore. Moreover, let us suppose that Jones can find no appeal in art. Novels are dull, poetry a pain, paintings nonsense and music just noise. Suppose further that Jones has neither the participant's nor the spectator's passion for baseball, football, tennis, or any other sport. Swimming to him is a cruel aquatic form of calisthenics, the sun only a cause of sunburn. Dancing is coeducational idiocy, conversation a waste of time, the other sex an unappealing mystery. Politics is a fraud, religion mere superstition; and the misery of millions of underprivileged human beings is nothing to be concerned with or excited about. Suppose finally that Jones has no talent for any kind of handicraft, industry, or commerce, and that he does not regret that fact.

What then is Jones interested in? He must desire something. To be sure, he does. Jones has an overwhelming passion for, a complete preoccupation with, his own happiness. The one exclusive desire of his life is *to be happy.* It takes little imagination at this point to see that Jones's one desire is bound to be frustrated. People who—like Jones—most hotly pursue their own happiness are the least likely to find it. Happy people are those who successfully pursue such things as aesthetic or religious experience, self-expression, service to others, victory in competitions, knowledge, power, and so on. If none of these things in themselves and for their own sakes mean anything to a person, if they are valued at all then only as a means to one's own pleasant states of mind—then that pleasure can never come. The way to achieve happiness is to pursue something else. 7

7

STOP Does Jones's state of mind as described here even make clear sense? When he says that he desires his own happiness, what exactly does he have in mind, if anything? (See Discussion Question 2.)

Almost all people at one time or another in their lives feel pleasure. Some people (though perhaps not many) really do live lives which are on the whole happy. But if pleasure and happiness presuppose desires for something other than pleasure and happiness, then the existence of pleasure and happiness in the experience of some people proves that those people have strong desires for something other than their own happiness—egoistic hedonism to the contrary.

The implications of the "paradox of hedonism" for educational theory should be obvious. The parents least likely to raise a happy child are those who, even with the best intentions, train their child to seek happiness directly. How often have we heard parents say:

> I don't care if my child does not become an intellectual, or a sports star, or a great artist. I just want her to be a plain average sort of person. Happiness does not require great ambitions and great frustrations; it's not worth it to suffer and become neurotic for the sake of science, art, or do-goodism. I just want my child to be happy.

This can be a dangerous mistake, for it is the child (and the adult for that matter) without "outer-directed" interests who is the most likely to be unhappy. The pure egoist would be the most wretched of persons.

...

As for moral education, it is probably true that punishment and reward are indispensable means of inculcation. But if the child comes to believe that the *sole* reasons for being moral are that he will escape the pain of punishment thereby and/or that he will gain the pleasure of a good reputation, then what is to prevent him from doing the immoral thing whenever he is sure that he will not be found out? While punishment and reward then are important tools for the moral educator, they obviously have their limitations. Beware of the man who does the moral thing only out of fear of pain or love of pleasure. He is not likely to be wholly trustworthy. Moral education is truly successful when it produces persons who are willing to do the right thing *simply because it is right,* and not merely because it is popular or safe. 8

8

Notice that this is a quite different point from the preceding one about Jones. There is nothing impossible or necessarily self-defeating about being motivated to be moral only by the promise of rewards and the threat of punishment. The point is just that a person who acts only for such reasons isn't really concerned with morality as such at all.

12. Pleasure as Sensation. One final argument against psychological hedonism should suffice to put that form of the egoistic psychology to rest once and for all. The egoistic hedonist claims that all desires can be reduced to the single desire for one's own pleasure. Now the word "pleasure" is ambiguous. On the one hand, it can stand for a certain indefinable, but very familiar and specific kind of sensation, or more accurately, a property of sensations; and it is generally, if not exclusively, associated with the senses. For example, certain taste sensations such as sweetness, thermal sensations of the sort derived from a hot bath or the feel of the August sun while one lies on a sandy beach, erotic sensations, olfactory sensations (say) of the fragrance of flowers or perfume,

and tactual and kinesthetic sensations from a good massage, are all pleasant in this sense. Let us call this sense of "pleasure," which is the converse of "physical pain," pleasure$_1$.

On the other hand, the word "pleasure" is often used simply as a synonym for "satisfaction" (in the sense of gratification, not mere desire fulfillment). In this sense, the existence of pleasure presupposes the prior existence of desire. Knowledge, religious experience, aesthetic expression, and other so-called "spiritual activities" often give pleasure in this sense. In fact, as we have seen, we tend to get pleasure in this sense whenever we get what we desire, no matter what we desire. The masochist even derives pleasure (in the sense of "satisfaction") from his own physically painful sensations. Let us call the sense of "pleasure" which means "satisfaction"—pleasure$_2$.

Now we can evaluate the psychological hedonist's claim that the sole human motive is a desire for one's own pleasure, bearing in mind (as he often does not) the ambiguity of the word "pleasure." First, let us take the hedonist to be saying that it is the desire for pleasure$_1$ (pleasant sensation) which is the sole ultimate desire of all people and the sole desire capable of providing a motive for action. Now I have little doubt that all (or most) people desire their own pleasure, *sometimes*. But even this familiar kind of desire occurs, I think, rather rarely. When I am very hungry, I often desire to eat, or, more specifically, to eat this piece of steak and these potatoes. Much less often do I desire to eat certain morsels simply for the sake of the pleasant gustatory sensations they might cause. I have, on the other hand, been motivated in the latter way when I have gone to especially exotic (and expensive) French or Chinese restaurants; but normally, pleasant gastronomic sensations are simply a happy consequence or by-product of my eating, not the antecedently desired objective of my eating. There are, of course, others who take gustatory sensations far more seriously: the *gourmet* who eats only to savor the textures and flavors of fine foods, and the wine fancier who "collects" the exquisitely subtle and very pleasant tastes of rare old wines. Such people are truly absorbed in their taste sensations when they eat and drink, and there may even be some (rich) persons whose desire for such sensations is the sole motive for eating and drinking. It should take little argument, however, to convince the reader that such persons are extremely rare. 9

It is in fact pretty hard to imagine a person of this sort who really cares only about the pleasurable sensations (and not at all about the fact that the wine is rare and costly).

Similarly, I usually derive pleasure from taking a hot bath, and on occasion (though not very often) I even decide to bathe simply for the sake of such sensations. Even if this is equally true of everyone, however, it hardly provides grounds for inferring that *no one ever* bathes from *any* other motive. It should be empirically obvious that we sometimes bathe simply in order to get clean, or to please others, or simply from habit.

The view then that we are never after anything in our actions but our own pleasure 10—that all people are complete "gourmets" of one sort or another—is not only morally cynical; it is also contrary to common sense and everyday experience. In fact, the view that pleasant sensations play such an enormous role in human affairs is so patently false on the available evidence, that we must conclude that the psychological hedonist has the other sense of "pleasure"—satisfaction—in mind when he states his thesis. If, on the other hand, he really does try to reduce the apparent multitude of human motives to the one desire for pleasant sensations, then the abundance of historical counter-examples justifies our rejection out of hand of his thesis. It surely seems incredible that the Christian martyrs were ardently pursuing their own pleasure when they marched off to face the lions, or that what the Russian soldiers at Stalingrad "really" wanted when they doused themselves with gasoline, ignited themselves, and then threw the flaming torches of their own bodies on German tanks, was simply the experience of pleasant physical sensations.

R Pleasure$_1$, that is.

13. Pleasure as Satisfaction. Let us consider now the other interpretation of the hedonist's thesis, that according to which it is one's own pleasure$_2$ (satisfaction) and not merely pleasure$_1$ (pleasant sensation) which is the sole ultimate objective of all voluntary behavior. In one respect, the "satisfaction thesis" is even less plausible than the "physical sensation thesis"; for the latter at least is a genuine empirical hypothesis, testable in experience, though contrary to the facts which experience discloses. The former, however, is so confused that it cannot even be completely stated without paradox. It is, so to speak, defeated in its own formulation. Any attempted

explication of the theory that all men at all times desire only their own satisfaction leads to an infinite regress in the following way:

> "All men desire only satisfaction."
> "Satisfaction of what?"
> "Satisfaction of their desires."
> "Their desires for what?"
> "Their desires for satisfaction."
> "Satisfaction of what?"
> "Their desires."
> "For what?"
> "For satisfaction"—etc., *ad infinitum.*

In short, psychological hedonism interpreted in this way attributes to all people as their sole motive a wholly vacuous and infinitely self-defeating desire. The source of this absurdity is in the notion that satisfaction can, so to speak, feed on itself, and perform the miracle of perpetual self-regeneration in the absence of desires for anything other than itself. (11)

(11) Thus pleasure_2 essentially presupposes the existence of desires for something other than pleasure, with satisfaction resulting when these desires are satisfied.

To summarize the argument of sections 12 and 13: The word "pleasure" is ambiguous. Pleasure_1 means a certain indefinable characteristic of physical sensation. Pleasure_2 refers to the feeling of satisfaction that often comes when one gets what one desires whatever be the nature of that which one desires. Now, if the hedonist means pleasure_1 when he says that one's own pleasure is the ultimate objective of all of one's behavior, then his view is not supported by the facts. On the other hand, if he means pleasure_2, then his theory cannot even be clearly formulated, since it leads to the following infinite regress: "I desire only satisfaction of my desire for satisfaction of my desire for satisfaction . . . etc., *ad infinitum.*" I conclude then that psychological hedonism (the most common form of psychological egoism), however interpreted, is untenable.

. . .

Discussion Questions

1. Feinberg argues that there is no adequate evidence for the claim that apparent cases of altruism always actually involve selfish motives, but seems to concede that this might still *possibly* be the case (see the passage at Annotation 6)—even if the desire for the pleasure that results from the satisfaction of an independent altruistic desire is set aside for the reasons already discussed (see Annotation 4). Is this really a serious (as opposed to a merely logical) possibility? Think of various cases of apparent altruism and try to imagine what the supposed selfish motive might be. ("The desire to receive gratitude" doesn't seem to always apply in a realistic way, since there is often no one from whom gratitude could be realistically expected. And it is hard to see why one should feel self-esteem as a result of an altruistic action unless one independently values altruism.)
2. Does it really even make sense to desire only one's own happiness (as Jones is said to do in the passage at Annotation 7)? What does happiness amount to if it does not involve having or being able to do various things that one likes or values—that is, various things for which one has independent desires?

Plato

Plato (427–347 B.C.) was one of the two major Ancient Greek philosophers, the other one being Aristotle (see the selections in Chapter 1 for more information about Plato). In this selection, taken from his dialogue *Republic,* Glaucon presents arguments for the conclusion that it is better to be unjust than to be just, where by being just he can be taken to mean acting in a way that is right or morally acceptable. The arguments presented by Glaucon purport to show that the rewards for any person are greatest if he or she acts unjustly (immorally) while being perceived as acting justly (morally). Glaucon says that he is presenting these arguments because he hopes that Socrates will be able to show what is wrong with them, and the selection ends with a short summary of Plato's account (from later in the dialogue) of why the view that it is better for the person himself to be unjust (immoral) than to be just (moral) is mistaken.

Are We Better Off Behaving Morally or Immorally?

Socrates, [Glaucon] broke out, you have made a show of proving that justice is better than injustice in every way. Is that enough, or do you want us to be really convinced?

Certainly I do, if it rests with me.

Then you are not going the right way about it. I want to know how you classify the things we call good. Are there not some which we should wish to have, not for their consequences, but just for their own sake, such as harmless pleasures and enjoyments that have no further result beyond the satisfaction of the moment?

Yes, I think there are good things of that description.

And also some that we value both for their own sake and for their consequences—things like knowledge and health and the use of our eyes?

Yes.

And a third class which would include physical training, medical treatment, earning one's bread as a doctor or otherwise—useful, but burdensome things, which we want only for the sake of the profit or other benefit they bring. ❶

Yes, there is that third class. What then?

In which class do you place justice?

I should say, in the highest, as a thing which anyone who is to gain happiness must value both for itself and for its results.

Well, that is not the common opinion. Most people would say it was one of those things, tiresome and disagreeable in themselves, which we cannot avoid practising for the sake of reward or a good reputation.

I know, said I; that is why Thrasymachus has been finding fault with it all this time and praising injustice. But I seem to be slow in seeing his point.

Listen to me, then, and see if you agree with mine. . . . nothing so far said about justice and injustice has been established to my satisfaction. I want to be told what each of them really is, and what effect each has, in itself, on the soul that harbours it, when all rewards and consequences are left out of account. So here is my plan, if you approve. I shall revive Thrasymachus' theory. First, I will state what is commonly held about the nature of justice and its origin; secondly, I shall maintain that it is always practised with reluctance, not as good in itself, but as a thing one cannot do without; and thirdly, that this reluctance is reasonable, because the life of injustice is much the better life of the two—so people say. That is not what I think myself, Socrates; only I am bewildered by all that Thrasymachus and ever so many others have dinned into my ears; and I have never yet heard the case for justice stated as I wish to hear it. You, I believe, if anyone, can tell me what is to be said in praise of justice in and for itself; that is what I want. Accordingly, I shall set you an example by glorifying the life of injustice with all the energy that I hope you will show later in denouncing it and exalting justice in its stead. ❷ Will that plan suit you?

Nothing could be better, I replied. Of all subjects this is one on which a sensible man must always be glad to exchange ideas.

Good, said Glaucon. Listen then, and I will begin with my first point: the nature and origin of justice.

What people say is that to do wrong is, in itself, a desirable thing; on the other hand, it is not at all desirable to suffer wrong, and the harm to the sufferer outweighs the advantage to the doer. Consequently, when men have had a taste of both, those who have not the power to seize the advantage and escape the harm decide that they would be better off if they made a compact neither to do wrong nor to suffer it. Hence they began to make laws and covenants with one another; and whatever the law prescribed they called lawful and right. That is what right or justice is and how it came into existence; it stands half-way between the best thing of all—to do wrong with impunity—and the worst, which is to suffer wrong without the power to retaliate. So justice is accepted as a compromise, and valued, not as good in itself, but for lack of power to do wrong; no man worthy of the name, who had that power, would ever enter into such a compact with anyone; he would be mad if he did. ❸ That, Socrates, is the nature of justice according to this account, and such the circumstances in which it arose.

The next point is that men practise it against the grain, for lack of power to do wrong. How true that is, we shall best see if we imagine two

From *The Republic of Plato,* translated by Francis MacDonald Conford (New York: Oxford University Press (1973).

In more contemporary terminology, philosophers distinguish between things that are merely **instrumentally good** (good only for their results—Glaucon's third class), things that are **intrinsically good** (good just because of what they are themselves, regardless of their results—the first class), and things that are both intrinsically good and instrumentally good (the second class).

R Glaucon wants an argument for the claim that justice itself, not merely the consequences of being just, is an intrinsic good for the person who is acting justly.

R The suggestion here is that acting justly is nothing but acting according to man-made law, and that such laws are binding (if at all) only because citizens have tacitly consented to laws as a way to control people (the motivation for the consent is the idea that living in a society with laws is better than suffering the resulting chaos of a society with no laws).

men, one just, the other unjust, given full licence to do whatever they like, and then follow them to observe where each will be led by his desires. We shall catch the just man taking the same road as the unjust; he will be moved by self-interest, the end which it is natural to every creature to pursue as good, until forcibly turned aside by law and custom to respect the principle of equality.

Now, the easiest way to give them that complete liberty of action would be to imagine them possessed of the talisman found by Gyges, the ancestor of the famous Lydian. The story tells how he was a shepherd in the King's service. One day there was a great storm, and the ground where his flock was feeding was rent by an earthquake. Astonished at the sight, he went down into the chasm and saw, among other wonders of which the story tells, a brazen horse, hollow, with windows in its sides. Peering in, he saw a dead body, which seemed to be of more than human size. It was naked save for a gold ring, which he took from the finger and made his way out. When the shepherds met, as they did every month, to send an account to the King of the state of his flocks, Gyges came wearing the ring. As he was sitting with the others, he happened to turn the bezel of the ring inside his hand. At once he became invisible, and his companions, to his surprise, began to speak of him as if he had left them. Then, as he was fingering the ring, he turned the bezel outwards and became visible again. With that, he set about testing the ring to see if it really had this power, and always with the same result: according as he turned the bezel inside or out he vanished and reappeared. After this discovery he contrived to be one of the messengers sent to the court. There he seduced the Queen, and with her help murdered the King and seized the throne.

Now suppose there were two such magic rings, and one were given to the just man, the other to the unjust. No one, it is commonly believed, would have such iron strength of mind as to stand fast in doing right or keep his hands off other men's goods, when he could go to the market-place and fearlessly help himself to anything he wanted, enter houses and sleep with any woman he chose, set prisoners free and kill men at his pleasure, and in a word go about among men with the powers of a god. He would behave no better than the other; both would take the same course. Surely this would be strong proof that men do right only under compulsion; no individual thinks of it as good for him personally, since he does wrong whenever he finds he has the power. Every man believes that wrongdoing pays him personally much better, and, according to this theory, that is the truth. Granted full licence to do as he liked, people would think him a miserable fool if they found him refusing to wrong his neighbours or to touch their belongings, though in public they would keep up a pretence of praising his conduct, for fear of being wronged themselves. (4) So much for that.

(4)

STOP This thought experiment is designed to defend the claim that *the only* reason that people ever act justly is that they are afraid of suffering the negative consequences that result from acting unjustly. Does it seem right that anyone with such a ring would act in such a way? Would you always take what is not yours if you could get away with it? Would everyone you know act in such a way? (See Discussion Question 1.)

Finally, if we are really to judge between the two lives, the only way is to contrast the extremes of justice and injustice. We can best do that by imagining our two men to be perfect types, and crediting both to the full with the qualities they need for their respective ways of life. To begin with the unjust man: he must be like any consummate master of a craft, a physician or a captain, who, knowing just what his art can do, never tries to do more, and can always retrieve a false step. The unjust man, if he is to reach perfection, must be equally discreet in his criminal attempts, and he must not be found out, or we shall think him a bungler; for the highest pitch of injustice is to seem just when you are not. So we must endow our man with the full complement of injustice; we must allow him to have secured a spotless reputation for virtue while committing the blackest crimes; he must be able to retrieve any mistake, to defend himself with convincing eloquence if his misdeeds are denounced, and, when force is required, to bear down all opposition by his courage and strength and by his command of friends and money.

Now set beside this paragon the just man in his simplicity and nobleness, one who, in Aeschylus' words, 'would be, not seem, the best.' There must, indeed, be no such seeming; for if his character were apparent, his reputation would bring him honours and rewards, and then we should not know whether it was for their sake that he was just or for justice's sake alone. He must be stripped of everything but justice, and denied every advantage the other enjoyed. Doing no wrong, he must have the worst reputation for wrong-doing, to test whether his virtue is proof against all that comes of having a bad name; and under this lifelong imputation of wickedness, let him hold on his course of justice unwavering to the point of death. And so, when the two men have carried their justice and injustice to the last extreme, we may judge which is the happier.

My dear Glaucon, I exclaimed, how vigorously you scour these two characters clean for inspection, as if you were burnishing a couple of statues!

I am doing my best, he answered. Well, given two such characters, it is not hard, I fancy, to describe the sort of life that each of them may expect; and if the description sounds rather coarse, take it as coming from those who cry up the merits of injustice rather than from me. They will tell you that our just man will be thrown into prison, scourged and racked, will have his eyes burnt out, and, after every kind of torment, be impaled. That will teach him how much better it is to seem virtuous than to be so. [Consider, in contrast, the life of the unjust man.] With his reputation for virtue, he will hold offices of state, ally himself by marriage to any family he may choose, become a partner in any business, and, having no scruples about being dishonest, turn all these advantages to profit. If he is involved in a lawsuit, public or private, he will get the better of his opponents, grow rich on the proceeds, and be able to help his friends and harm his enemies. Finally, he can make sacrifices to the gods and dedicate offerings with due magnificence, and, being in a much better position than the just man to serve the gods as well as his chosen friends, he may reasonably hope to stand higher in the favour of heaven. So much better, they say, Socrates, is the life prepared for the unjust by gods and men. 5

Here Glaucon ended, and I was meditating a reply, when his brother Adeimantus exclaimed:

Surely, Socrates, you cannot suppose that that is all there is to be said.

Why, isn't it? said I.

The most essential part of the case has not been mentioned, he replied.

Well, I answered, there is a proverb about a brother's aid. If Glaucon has failed, it is for you to make good his shortcomings; though, so far as I am concerned, he has said quite enough to put me out of the running and leave me powerless to rescue the cause of justice.

Nonsense, said Adeimantus; there is more to be said, and you must listen to me. If we want a clear view of what I take to be Glaucon's meaning, we must study the opposite side of the case, the arguments used when justice is praised and injustice condemned. When children are told by their fathers and all their pastors and masters that it is a good thing to be just, what is commended is not justice in itself but the respectability it brings. They are to let men see how just they are, in order to gain high positions and marry well and win all the other advantages which Glaucon mentioned, since the just man owes all these to his good reputation.

...

Now, my dear Socrates, when all this stuff is talked about the estimation in which virtue and vice are held by . . . mankind, what effect can we suppose it has upon the mind of a young man quick-witted enough to gather honey from all these flowers of popular wisdom and to draw his own conclusions as to the sort of person he should be and the way he should go in order to lead the best possible life? In all likelihood he would ask himself, in Pindar's words: 'Will the way of right or the by-paths of deceit lead me to the higher fortress,' where I may entrench myself for the rest of my life? For, according to what they tell me, I have nothing to gain but trouble and manifest loss from being honest, unless I also get a name for being so; whereas, if I am dishonest and provide myself with a reputation for honesty, they promise me a marvelous career. Very well, then; since 'outward seeming,' as wise men inform me, 'overpowers the truth' and decides the question of happiness, I had better go in for appearances wholeheartedly. . . . You may say it is not so easy to be wicked without ever being found out. Perhaps not; but great things are never easy. Anyhow, if we are to reach happiness, everything we have been told points to this as the road to be followed. We will form secret societies to save us from exposure; besides, there are men who teach the art of winning over popular assemblies and courts of law; so that, one way or another, by persuasion or violence, we shall get the better of our neighbours without being punished.

...

What reason, then, remains for preferring justice to the extreme of injustice, when common belief and the best authorities promise us

5

Presumably the claim here is that *most* unjust people who appear to be just will be happier than *most* just people who appear to be unjust, not that this will be invariably true.

the fulfillment of our desires . . . if only we conceal our ill-doing under a veneer of decent behaviour? The upshot is, Socrates, that no man possessed of superior powers of mind or person or rank or wealth will set any value on justice; he is more likely to laugh when he hears it praised. So, even one who could prove my case false and were quite sure that justice is best, far from being indignant with the unjust, will be very ready to excuse them. He will know that, here and there, a man may refrain from wrong because it revolts some instinct he is graced with or because he has come to know the truth; no one else is virtuous of his own will; it is only lack of spirit or the infirmity of age or some other weakness that makes men condemn the iniquities they have not the strength to practise. This is easily seen: give such a man the power, and he will be the first to use it to the utmost.

What lies at the bottom of all this is nothing but the fact from which Glaucon, as well as I, started upon this long discourse. We put it to you, Socrates, with all respect, in this way. All you who profess to sing the praises of right conduct, from the ancient heroes whose legends have survived down to the men of the present day, have never denounced injustice or praised justice apart from the reputation, honours, and rewards they bring; but what effect either of them in itself has upon its possessor when it dwells in his soul unseen of gods or men, no poet or ordinary man has ever yet explained. No one has proved that a soul can harbour no worse evil than injustice, no greater good than justice. Had all of you said that from the first and tried to convince us from our youth up, we should not be keeping watch upon our neighbours to prevent them from doing wrong to us, but everyone would keep a far more effectual watch over himself, for fear lest by wronging others he should open his doors to the worst of all evils.

That, Socrates, is the view of justice and injustice which Thrasymachus and, no doubt, others would state, perhaps in even stronger words. For myself, I believe it to be a gross perversion of their true worth and effect; but, as I must frankly confess, I have put the case with all the force I could muster because I want to hear the other side from you. You must not be content with proving that justice is superior to injustice; you must make clear what good or what harm each of them does to its possessor, taking it simply in itself and, as Glaucon required, leaving out of account the reputation it bears. For unless you deprive each of its true reputation and attach to it the false one, we shall say that you are praising or denouncing nothing more than the appearances in either case, and recommending us to do wrong without being found out; and that you hold with Thrasymachus that right means what is good for someone else, being the interest of the stronger, and wrong is what really pays, serving one's own interest at the expense of the weaker. You have agreed that justice belongs to that highest class of good things which are worth having not only for their consequences, but much more for their own sakes—things like sight and hearing, knowledge, and health, whose value is genuine and intrinsic, not dependent on opinion. So I want you, in commending justice, to consider only how justice, in itself, benefits a man who has it in him, and how injustice harms him, leaving rewards and reputation out of account. (6) I might put up with others dwelling on those outward effects as a reason for praising the one and condemning the other; but from you, who have spent your life in the study of this question, I must beg leave to demand something better. You must not be content merely to prove that justice is superior to injustice, but explain how one is good, the other evil, in virtue of the intrinsic effect each has on its possessor, whether gods or men see it or not.

. . .

The Virtues in the Individual

. . . [Socrates:] we shall conclude that a man is just in the same way that a state was just. And we have surely not forgotten that justice in the state meant that each of the three orders in it was doing its own proper work. So we may henceforth bear in mind that each one of us likewise will be a just person, fulfilling his proper function, only if the several parts of our nature fulfill theirs. (7)

Certainly.

And it will be the business of reason to rule with wisdom and forethought on behalf of the entire soul; while the spirited element ought to act as its subordinate and ally. The two will be brought into accord, as we said earlier, by that

(6) Remember that the challenge to Socrates to show that justice *itself*, not the mere appearance of justice, is a good thing, that being just is good for the person whether he or she appears just or not.

(7) Plato has argued in other parts of the dialogue that a state is just only if the three different kinds of citizens (rulers, soldiers, and ordinary people) fulfill their proper functions. The just person, analogously, has three different parts of his or her nature which also fulfill their proper function. (See Discussion Question 5.)

combination of mental and bodily training which will tune up one string of the instrument and relax the other, nourishing the reasoning part on the study of noble literature and allaying the other's wildness by harmony and rhythm. (8) When both have been thus nurtured and trained to know their own true functions, they must be set in command over the appetites, which form the greater part of each man's soul and are by nature insatiably covetous. They must keep watch lest this part, by battening on the pleasures that are called bodily, should grow so great and powerful that it will no longer keep to its own work, but will try to enslave the others and usurp a dominion to which it has no right, thus turning the whole of life upside down. (9) At the same time, those two together will be the best of guardians for the entire soul and for the body against all enemies from without: the one will take counsel, while the other will do battle, following its ruler's commands and by its own bravery giving effect to the ruler's designs.

Yes, that is all true.

And so we call an individual brave in virtue of this spirited part of his nature, when, in spite of pain or pleasure, it holds fast to the injunctions of reason about what he ought or ought not to be afraid of.

True.

And wise in virtue of that small part which rules and issues these injunctions, possessing as it does the knowledge of what is good for each of the three elements and for all of them in common.

Certainly.

And, again, temperate by reason of the unanimity and concord of all three, when there is no internal conflict between the ruling element and its two subjects, but all are agreed that reason should be ruler.

Yes, that is an exact account of temperance, whether in the state or in the individual.

Finally, a man will be just by observing the principle we have so often stated. (10)

Necessarily.

Now is there any indistinctness in our vision of justice, that might make it seem somehow different from what we found it to be in the state?

I don't think so.

Because, if we have any lingering doubt, we might make sure by comparing it with some commonplace notions. Suppose, for instance, that a sum of money were entrusted to our state or to an individual of corresponding character and training, would anyone imagine that such a person would be specially likely to embezzle it?

No.

And would he not be incapable of sacrilege and theft, or of treachery to friend or country; never false to an oath or any other compact; the last to be guilty of adultery or of neglecting parents or the due service of the gods?

Yes.

And the reason for all this is that each part of his nature is exercising its proper function, of ruling or of being ruled.

Yes, exactly.

Are you satisfied, then, that justice is the power which produces states or individuals of whom that is true, or must we look further?

There is no need; I am quite satisfied.

And so our dream has come true—I mean the inkling we had that, by some happy chance, we had lighted upon a rudimentary form of justice from the very moment when we set about founding our commonwealth. . . . But in reality justice,...is not a matter of external behaviour, but of the inward self and of attending to all that is, in the fullest sense, a man's proper concern. The just man does not allow the several elements in his soul to usurp one another's functions; he is indeed one who sets his house in order, by self-mastery and discipline coming to be at peace with himself, and bringing into tune those three parts, like the terms in the proportion of a musical scale, the highest and lowest notes and the mean between them, with all the intermediate intervals. Only when he has linked these parts together in well-tempered harmony and has made himself one man instead of many, will he be ready to go about whatever he may have to do, whether it be making money and satisfying bodily wants, or business transactions, or the affairs of state. In all these fields when he speaks of just and honourable conduct, he will mean the behaviour that helps to produce and to preserve this habit of mind; and by wisdom he will mean the knowledge which presides over such conduct. Any action which tends to break down this habit will be for him unjust; and the notions governing it he will call ignorance and folly. (11)

That is perfectly true, Socrates.

Good, said I. I believe we should not be thought altogether mistaken, if we claimed to

Reason, our thinking, cognitive faculty, is the part of our nature that is analogous to the philosopher-kings who are the rulers of the state; and spirit, our willing conative faculty is analogous to the guardians who are the soldiers of the state. Just as in a well-ordered state, the soldiers act in accordance with the commands of the rulers, so also in a well-ordered soul, spirit acts in accordance with the dictates of reason.

The third part of our nature is our appetites, our desires for bodily pleasures of various sorts, and this part of our nature is analogous to the farmer and merchant, the ordinary folk who carry on the business of the state under the guidance of the rulers. Just as each of the three different kinds of people has a proper function in a well-ordered state, so also the three parts of a human soul each have a proper function, according to Plato's theory of human nature.

R In a just person, reason rules by invoking the spirit to control the appetites according to what is good for each part and what is good for the whole person.

R Justice then involves the proper ordering of the three parts of a person's nature and is only derivatively related to the external behavior of a person. A just person will behave justly (morally) simply as a consequence of being a just person.

R Injustice then primarily involves the lack of proper ordering of the three parts of a person's nature. Injustice, on this view, is a kind of sickness. As a result of such sickness, an unjust person will behave immorally.

have discovered the just man and the just state, and wherein their justice consists.

Indeed we should not.

Shall we make that claim, then?

Yes, we will.

So be it, said I. Next, I suppose, we have to consider injustice.

Evidently.

This must surely be a sort of civil strife among the three elements, whereby they usurp and encroach upon one another's functions and some one part of the soul rises up in rebellion against the whole, claiming a supremacy to which it has no right because its nature fits it only to be the servant of the ruling principle. Such turmoil and aberration we shall, I think, identify with injustice, intemperance, cowardice, ignorance, and in a word with all wickedness.

Exactly.

And now that we know the nature of justice and injustice, we can be equally clear about what is meant by acting justly and again by unjust action and wrongdoing.

How do you mean?

Plainly, they are exactly analogous to those wholesome and unwholesome activities which respectively produce a healthy or unhealthy condition in the body; in the same way just and unjust conduct produce a just or unjust character. Justice is produced in the soul, like health in the body, by establishing the elements concerned in their natural relations of control and subordination, whereas injustice is like disease and means that this natural order is inverted. 12

Quite so.

It appears, then, that virtue is as it were the health and comeliness and well-being of the soul, as wickedness is disease, deformity, and weakness.

True.

And also that virtue and wickedness are brought about by one's way of life, honourable or disgraceful.

That follows.

So now it only remains to consider which is the more profitable course: to do right and live honourably and be just, whether or not anyone knows what manner of man you are, or to do wrong and be unjust, provided that you can escape the chastisement which might make you a better man.

But really, Socrates, it seems to me ridiculous to ask that question now that the nature of justice and injustice has been brought to light. People think that all the luxury and wealth and power in the world cannot make life worth living when the bodily constitution is going to rack and ruin; and are we to believe that, when the very principle whereby we live is deranged and corrupted, life will be worth living so long as a man can do as he will, and wills to do anything rather than to free himself from vice and wrongdoing and to win justice and virtue?

Yes, I replied, it is a ridiculous question.

Discussion Questions

1. The intuitive thought experiment involving the ring of Gyges supports the claim that people behave justly only because they want to avoid the negative consequences of being caught behaving unjustly. How plausible are the claims made in that thought experiment? Is it so obvious that someone who could become invisible would consistently behave unjustly? Try to assess this claim by considering some specific examples.
2. Plato's argument that it is better to be just than to be unjust relies on an analogy between the parts of the state and the parts of a person's soul: just as a state is just and therefore healthy to the extent that its three different kinds of citizens fulfill their proper functions, so also a person's soul will be just and therefore healthy to the extent that the three different parts of his or her nature fulfill their proper function. How good is this analogy? How similar or dissimilar are the two cases being compared, especially with regard to the features that seem most relevant to the point at issue?
3. According to Plato, it is always in our self-interest to behave morally. If Plato is right, then everyone has a reason to behave morally, but suppose that Plato is wrong. Suppose that it is *not* always in our self-interest to behave morally, that the demands of morality often require that we act in ways that further the interests of others and that conflict with our own self-interest. Do we have any compelling reason to behave morally in such cases?

Concluding Dialogue on Morality and Moral Problems

I think that the central question of this chapter is one of the most important questions philosophers ask: what is it about a right action that makes it right? Let's start with utilitarianism (or consequentialism). I have to say that reading the material in this chapter still hasn't convinced me that the utilitarian view is really very plausible. Why would anyone think that whether an action is right is determined merely by the utility of its consequences?

What do you mean? I think that it's pretty easy to understand why utilitarianism of some sort seems to many people so *obviously* correct as to be virtually self-evident—as Bentham seems indeed to regard it. If you are trying to decide what to do in a difficult situation, it's obvious that different actions will lead to different results (including of course those results that are an essential part of the actions themselves)—and why then wouldn't the right action be the one whose results or consequences are the best of any of these alternatives? Why would an action with *worse* consequences in terms of utility ever be morally preferable to one with *better* consequences?

All right, that last way of putting the point does have some plausibility. But there are just so many problems! Some of these have to do with adding up the value of the consequences into one total. Some utilitarians—Bentham at least—seem to think that something pretty close to a mathematical calculation is involved, with the values for all of the alternative actions being combined into one total. This doesn't have to be taken too seriously, I think—after all, no other moral theory yields mathematically precise results. But we still have to know how to weigh qualities of pleasure (if Mill is right that these are relevant) against quantities. And we have to know how to count future utilities: ones further and further into the future become increasingly harder to know, and even if you give them less weight, they can still make a huge difference—simply because there are so many of them! If there are no solutions to problems like these, then the idea of total utilities, whether mathematically expressible or not, just won't make clear sense.

I guess I've never managed to take Mill's appeal to qualities of pleasure very seriously. I've always thought that Bentham was right that if pushpin (a game like bowling, but with small pins and a ball on a string) is more enjoyable than poetry, then it is *better*—from a hedonistic utilitarian standpoint—than poetry. But the issue about future utilities seems very difficult. And there's also another problem of a rather different sort about adding up utilities, even though it doesn't seem to have gotten much attention. We have been speaking of *the* results or consequences of a given action, but obviously what results a particular action has will very often depend on which *other* actions are also performed—by the same person or by other people. If I push someone overboard, the result will obviously depend on whether someone (me or someone else) throws him a rope. So which consequences are the right ones to count or do they all somehow have to be considered?

Yikes! That seems like a *very* serious problem. Maybe we could try to assign probabilities to all of these other actions and combinations of actions, and then weigh the different possible results of the action in question by the probability that the other actions that would make it lead to a particular result will occur and add up the total expected utilities. But are such probabilities really knowable—or do they even exist in all such cases?

I think all of these problems are pretty serious. But the most common objection to the act version of utilitarianism isn't any of the ones we've talked about so far. Instead it is probably the objection that views of this kind violate our considered moral intuitions having to do with justice or fairness.

That's always seemed to me to be the most serious objection. For example, wouldn't act utilitarianism say that it is morally correct to frame and punish an innocent person in a situation where doing so would prevent riots or other serious social unrest (see Discussion Question 2 in the Smart selection)? Or that a promise should be broken whenever even slight gains in overall utility will result (allowing for the damage thereby done to the general practice of promising and also any negative effects there might be on the person's moral character)? I suppose that a utilitarian *might* try to argue that these are in fact the right results, and that the apparent intuitions to the contrary are somehow confused or mistaken, but that seems pretty hard to swallow.

Very few utilitarians have in fact been willing to take that sort of line. Instead, the main utilitarian response to problems of these sorts was rule utilitarianism. The idea was that the best set of *rules* wouldn't lead to these seemingly bad results. For example, if one of the rules was something like "keep your promises unless breaking them results in a very large gain in utility," then casual promise-breaking for small gains would be ruled out.

So the idea, I suppose, is that the right set of rules for the practice of punishment might preclude punishing the innocent, at least in most cases. But all that depends on what the best set of rules turns out to be, and that seems even harder to assess than the utility of individual actions. Think of all the consequences that a set of rules would have!

That assessment does seem awfully difficult. But I still think the biggest problem with rule utilitarianism is the one that Smart points out. While it seems very reasonable for a utilitarian to adopt "rules of thumb" to deal with cases where a direct utilitarian assessment is either too time-consuming, too difficult, or too likely for some reason to be mistaken, it's hard to see why one should follow those rules in cases where it is *clear* that better consequences will result from violating them—as rule utilitarianism says you should do. And this makes rule utilitarianism seem more like an evasion than a serious solution to the kinds of counter-examples we've mentioned.

I think that's right. As long as justice is accepted as an independent moral value (and not, as Mill tried rather unpersuasively to argue, as merely derivative from utility), a genuine utilitarian view is inevitably going to sometimes favor a solution that is unjust, even seriously unjust. Such views are aimed *solely* at the best overall total of consequences, and whether or not the demands of justice are satisfied doesn't matter for that. If this is right, then either the intuition that such results are morally unacceptable—that considerations of justice have genuine moral force—has to be somehow dismissed, or else utilitarianism is simply wrong.

I agree. But we still haven't gotten to the objection to utilitarianism that bothers me the most. This is the one that lies behind the examples given by Williams, but I would put it in a more general way. Utilitarianism treats individual human beings as something like agents for maximizing the overall total of utility, rather than as people who have lives and purposes and cares and projects of their own. And that, as Kant might say, amounts to treating them as *means* to the end of utility maximization rather than as ends in themselves. If everything an individual person cares about—family and friends, personal goals, personal values, and so on—must *always* be sacrificed when *any* gain in utility, even a relatively small one, will result, then it becomes more or less impossible for a person to have a meaningful, coherent life.

Utilitarianism isn't looking very hopeful. So let's turn to the deontological views, starting with Kant. These seem to me more promising, but there are still serious problems. One is whether Kant's various forms of the categorical imperative really lead to any very clear results. For example, I've never been able to see that the first form of the categorical imperative works in the way that Kant says it does. Why can't the "maxim" of any action at all that can actually be performed also be willed as a universal law without any contradiction? One may not like the results of such a universalization, but that doesn't show that there is any *impossibility* or *absurdity* involved—a point that Mill was one of the first to make.

I'm inclined to agree. There doesn't seem to be a genuine contradiction involved in *any* of the cases that Kant discusses. There is pretty obviously no contradiction in people always committing suicide when the circumstances are difficult enough or always failing to develop any of their talents, or any clear reason why either of these can't be willed. Maybe these would be morally bad results, but if so, the reason *why* they are morally bad has to be found elsewhere, not in this version of the categorical imperative. Nor is there any contradiction in people in need always trying to borrow money that they promise to repay but know they won't be able to. Unless most people are too wealthy to care or needy people are very rare, these actions are unlikely to succeed because people will stop being willing to lend money. But that doesn't make such an action or the underlying maxim *contradictory*. And there is even more clearly no contradiction in willing that no one ever help others in need—even if I may turn out to be the one who needs help. Again this may be morally undesirable, but not for the reason Kant gives.

I think it's also hard, maybe even harder, to get any very definite results from the third, "kingdom of ends" formulation of the categorical imperative, taken on its own. The most promising version by far seems to be the one that says that you should never treat persons merely as means to an end, but always also as ends in themselves. This idea strikes me as deeply appealing from an intuitive standpoint and indeed arguably more or less definitive of the moral category of persons. A person just is a being that shouldn't ever be treated as a mere means. And (as long as we are sure that other human beings are persons in this sense), a lot of pretty clear results do seem to follow: that it's wrong to defraud other people, that it's wrong to enslave them, that it's wrong to treat them merely as means to sexual pleasure, and so on. This would also plausibly rule out punishing an innocent person merely as a means to avoiding riots—and also, as we have already seen, regarding persons as merely means for the general end of maximizing utility.

All that strikes me as pretty plausible. But some of Kant's claims about this still seem questionable. It isn't clear why suicide in sufficiently difficult circumstances involves treating myself merely as a means, nor is it clear why not developing my talents does this. Kant appeals here, oddly enough, to "the end of nature with respect to humanity." This may be a veiled reference to God, but in any case it at least threatens to say that persons are the *means* to this further end of nature. And the issue of helping others is still very difficult under this formulation: not helping someone else doesn't in itself seem to be treating them as a means, and in any case there is still the further issue of *how much* help of that kind is morally required.

What Kant actually seems to say about that last question is that the ends of others must be taken as ends on a par with the individual's own ends. This response would lead back to a view at least pretty close to utilitarianism, one in which a given person is morally required to be just as concerned about the needs and projects of everyone else in the universe as about his own. Kant almost surely didn't mean anything this strong, and Kantians don't in general advocate such a view. But then it still isn't clear how much concern for the ends of others is required. The version of the categorical imperative that we are discussing just doesn't seem to yield any real answer—O'Neill's conclusion on this point is pretty fuzzy.

I think that's right. Maybe it is somehow a consequence of Kant's view that there is a general "duty of beneficence," but it's hard to see how the extent of that duty or what specific moral obligations follow from it is to be determined. The underlying problem is that Kant wanted to make the whole content of morality simply follow from the idea of reason itself, since he thought that no more definite purposes or goals could be assumed. But maybe it's not surprising that this extremely abstract conception doesn't lead to very many specific results.

Can we do any better by invoking the idea of human rights or moral rights? This idea also falls within a broadly Kantian picture. It's easy to see how certain rights seem to follow from the very idea of persons as ends in themselves. This would mean that there are some things that just cannot be done to such a being for no good reason—or even because increases in overall utility would result, with killing them or enslaving them being the clearest examples.

I suppose that an appeal to rights might help. But there are two problems about rights. The first is who has them. If all rights belong to individuals in the moral category of *persons,* then which individuals are persons? Almost everyone agrees that normal adult human beings are persons (though one can still ask for an explanation of *why* this is so). But what about

fetuses, individuals who are terminally ill or comatose, severely retarded humans, various other animals (porpoises, whales, chimpanzees, etc.), and, at least in principle, extraterrestrial beings of some sort? Each of these cases is difficult to decide, but the real issue is how we should go about deciding them—what standards or criteria to use. Ozar has some things to say about this, but they don't go very far. (And notice that Kant's view really faces the same problem.)

So the objection is that a view that bases morality on the moral rights of persons, but doesn't say what determines whether some individual is or is not a person, doesn't amount to much. And another concern is that even if we could somehow solve this problem, it's pretty unlikely—isn't it?—that all important moral issues will turn out to be decidable by appeal to rights. Surely it's possible for an action to be morally wrong even if it doesn't violate anyone's rights?

I think so. But it's hard to be sure until we figure out how to determine *which* specific rights persons actually have—which is my second problem with the rights view. Merely the appeal to the Kantian idea of persons as ends in themselves doesn't lead to very many specific rights, at least not in a clear way. So if there are going to be enough rights to deal with even a substantial part of the whole range of important moral issues, some further sort of basis or rationale for identifying them seems to be needed. And it just isn't very clear what that might be. Sometimes the existence of particular rights seems to be regarded as somehow self-evident or obvious. But even if this is true for some rights, it doesn't seem plausible for very many.

In fact, people often seem to just make up new rights in pursuit of specific political aims. If you think that it is somehow morally important that people receive something or be safeguarded against something, your claim will have more force, at least rhetorically, if you couch it in terms of an alleged right. So we have all sorts of claims of rights: the right to an adequate income, the right to education, the right to meaningful work, the right to leisure time, the right to cultural enrichment—even the right to Internet access! Some of these rights may be genuine, though it seems pretty clear that not all of them are. But the main point is that we need some principled way of deciding which rights are genuine and which aren't, if the appeal to rights is to do any serious work—and no one seems to have yet succeeded in providing this.

So we seem to agree that the two general sorts of moral theory we've talked about so far each have lots of problems, even though I agree with you that the ones facing utilitarianism seem more serious. I guess this is why some philosophers have recently been attracted to the idea of virtue ethics as an alternative to these other views—though I've never been able to understand very clearly how that is supposed to work.

Well, I think that the more specific motivation for virtue ethics goes something like this. It seems to many philosophers, especially those who have been influenced by Aristotle, that the views we've been discussing are very dubious as general moral theories, even apart from the specific problems we've discussed. Their objection is that both utilitarianism and deontological views fail to really capture the way in which people actually think about most moral issues. Most of the time at least, and especially for issues that seem very serious, we don't add up utilities, even roughly, and we don't apply any form of the categorical imperative. Instead we appeal to moral virtues like kindness or charity or courage or fairness, and to the avoidance of the corresponding vices. We invoke examples of what really good people would do and of how they would lead their lives. And this at least suggests that a view couched in those terms might be a better alternative.

I agree with the idea that moral virtues are somehow relevant to the moral assessment of actions—and even more to the moral assessment of people. But the problem is to spell out exactly *how* they are relevant. Can a virtue view be plausibly defended as a direct competitor of utilitarianism or the Kantian-deontological views? Or are the virtues perhaps relevant in some other way?

We obviously can't explore all of the possible alternatives here. But the reason for focusing on Hursthouse is precisely that she does want to make her virtue ethics view a direct rival of the

other two. This is the point of her proposition V1, which is supposed to be a direct competitor of the utilitarian's U1 and the deontologist's D1. V1 says that "an action is right iff [if and only if] it is what a virtuous agent would characteristically (i.e., acting in character) do in the circumstances" (p. 407). She proceeds to discuss the problem of whether this really gives moral guidance, where this amounts to the issue of whether we can adequately spell out what an agent would have to be like to be virtuous.

That's one problem. But there is also a much more serious problem—one that Hursthouse seems somehow not to see. Most people would agree that V1 is *true,* but the question is *why* it is true. Is it true because being an action that a virtuous agent would do is the very definition or essential nature of being the *right* action—so that being what a fully virtuous agent would do is what *makes* the action right? Or is it true merely because a fully virtuous agent would of course always be *guided* by moral rightness and so would in fact always do the right thing? I say "merely" because on the second alternative, being what a virtuous person would do isn't what *makes* the action right—instead its being right *for some other reason* is why the virtuous person does it. In which case, virtue theory doesn't really explain what makes an action right in the way that the utilitarian and deontological views at least attempt to do.

I see the problem, and it looks pretty serious. This is really like the problem for the divine command theory of morality raised in the *Euthyphro* (see Chapter 1): is an action right *because* God commands it, or does God command it *because* it's right? Analogously, is an action right because the perfectly virtuous person would do it, or would the perfectly virtuous person do it because it's right?

Exactly! And whatever one may think about the idea that God's commands create moral rightness (an issue we can't go into here), once the same question is asked about the virtuous agent, it just seems obvious that the right choice among the two alternatives is the second one, according to which being chosen by a virtuous agent isn't what *makes* an action right. Here a strongly negative example may make the point especially clear. It is morally wrong to torture and murder an innocent person, but the primary reason for this is surely *not* that a virtuous person would never do such a thing (though of course he or she wouldn't). On the contrary, such an action is wrong because of the pain and suffering involved or because of what it does to the victim or because of the kind of action it is—which is, of course, *why* a virtuous agent wouldn't do it.

That seems like a really devastating objection to Hursthouse's view, since it seems to mean that an appeal to the virtues just isn't a plausible alternative account of what makes an action right or wrong—and so not after all a competitor of the other two main views. But couldn't thinking about what a virtuous person would do still help in figuring out which action is right? As a philosopher might put it, couldn't it serve as a *criterion* of rightness, even if not a definition?

I think it could, at least to some extent, and there is no doubt that we often think that way. One problem with this, however—as Hursthouse herself notices—is how to specify the ideally complete and consistent "package" of virtues that an *ideally* virtuous person would possess. In our ordinary thinking, it seems to me, we usually just focus on one or two virtues that seem particularly relevant in a given case, without trying to appeal to anything like an ideally virtuous person.

I'm inclined to agree that virtue theory, whatever value it may have in other ways, doesn't yield a plausible answer to the question we started with: the question of what makes a right action right. But remember that the other views also have very serious problems, as we've already discussed. So maybe what all this shows is that it is just a mistake to look for a general account of the standards for right action of the sort that utilitarianism and deontological views attempt to give. Maybe we need a more piecemeal approach—one that just deals with particular cases without attempting to give a general account. And maybe an appeal to the specific virtues that seem relevant in those cases is the best we can do.

I just can't buy that. If there really is a moral truth—if actions are genuinely right or wrong—I don't see how there can fail to be a general account of what makes them so. And I don't

think merely invoking particular virtues with no explanation of why they are "relevant" is good enough. By my lights, the most defensible view is still probably the one that appeals to the Kantian idea of not treating people merely as means. But I have to admit that such a view doesn't seem to go very far, even in cases where we are sure we are dealing with persons. Here, as with most of the other issues discussed in this book, a full solution seems a long way off.

 While you are convinced that there is a moral truth, some people might look at the many problems involved in defending a moral theory and be tempted to draw the conclusion that there is no objective moral truth at all, that all moral truth is relative. But adopting moral relativism doesn't really help—does it? Even if we take ourselves to be trying to specify only our own culture's moral view or our own personal moral views, essentially the same problems arise—how to add up utilities, who counts as a person, what rights persons have, or how virtues are relevant.

 I think that's right. Even relativistic moral rules or principles will still have to appeal to ideas like those, so relativism doesn't help in solving the problems that arise with them. But the real worry, I think, is that moral *nihilism* (see the chapter introduction) might turn out to be right, in spite of its initial implausibility. Maybe the reason we can't give a clear account of what makes an action right is that nothing really does—we just have a lot of moral opinions and reactions that don't ultimately make any clearly structured sense. I don't believe that and neither do you, but as long as we don't seem to be able to find a defensible general moral standard, it's hard to definitively rule out the nihilist view. That's the main reason that I don't like your piecemeal virtue approach.

CHAPTER 6

The Legitimacy of Government and the Nature of Justice

The selections in this chapter are concerned with two central issues in the general area of philosophy known as *political philosophy:* first, whether and how the very existence of government is morally justified or *legitimate;* and, second, what the requirements are for a society and its governing institutions to be *just* with respect to the distribution of benefits and burdens among its citizens.

Exactly what the relation is between these two issues is itself a matter of some controversy: as we will see, the historically most influential answer to the first question is based on the idea that the legitimacy of a government must derive from the *consent* of those who are governed by it. Others, however, have seemed to hold that the legitimacy of a government depends directly on whether it satisfies the relevant moral standards, with justice being the most important of these. And it is obviously at least possible for these two standards to come apart: for the people to continue to consent to a government that is seriously unjust or otherwise morally questionable; or for the people to cease to consent to a government that continues to satisfy the relevant moral standards.

What Is the Justification for Government?

Perhaps the most conspicuous features of governments are these: (a) Governments control and restrict the behavior of the citizens they govern in a wide variety of ways, forbidding or penalizing some sorts of conduct and requiring others. (b) Governments extract economic resources and sometimes also direct service from their citizens. And (c) governments employ *coercive* means—force and the threat of force—for both of these purposes. In doing these things, the agents of the government behave in ways that would obviously be morally objectionable if practiced by private citizens or by private groups such as gangs, organized criminals, corporations, or even charitable foundations.

The most fundamental political question is what (if anything) makes the existence of governments and the coercive power that they exercise morally legitimate in a way that private exercises of otherwise similar power would not be? How are governments different from gangs or organized criminals, which might also exert at least a degree of control over a particular area and force the people living there to pay for "protection"? Or, as anarchists have occasionally suggested, are governments really not different in any essential respect, but only more generally accepted (though for no good reason) and more successful?

A further, closely related question is whether and to what extent obedience to the mandates of government by citizens is itself, for the most part at least, *morally* required. While there are pretty clearly exceptions to the duty to obey the government, cases where the actions of governments are sufficiently objectionable to justify passive or even active resistance, the fact that behaving (or not behaving) in a certain way is required by law is often taken to be a reason to act accordingly. But is it (always or ever) a *moral* reason, and if so, why? The obvious alternative is that obedience to government is merely a matter of *prudence* in the face of usually overwhelming power—which would mean that there is no reason not to break the law if one can get away with doing so.

A once quite popular answer to these questions, though one for which there is little to be said from a philosophical standpoint, is the doctrine of the *divine right* of kings: the view that rulers are in some way anointed by God and rule on the basis of his authority, with obedience to government thereby morally required as an instance of the more general principle that obedience to God is morally required. There are many problems with such a view—including of course doubts about whether such a being exists at all (see Chapter 7). But perhaps the most immediate and obvious is the problem of how to determine which person or group in fact has the supposed status of being thus divinely anointed: a problem obviously made more practically serious by the frequent occasions in which one ruler is overthrown by another in ways—such as coups or assassinations—that would seemingly be illegitimate if the ruler who is overthrown were divinely anointed. (If the ruler who is overthrown was anointed by God, then presumably the new ruler was not, and so is illegitimate.)

As the doctrine of divine right came to be seen as more and more dubious, philosophers looked for an alternative. Some of them believed that it was to be found in the idea that government originates in an agreement of some sort, a *social contract,* among those who will become citizens to leave the *state of nature* that existed previously and form an organized society with a government. On this view, the fundamental justification for governmental authority is traced to the *consent* of those to whom it applies. And the moral requirement to obey the resulting government is seen as a specific instance of the more general moral obligation to conform to agreements which one has deliberately and freely entered into.

There are many obvious questions that can be raised about social contract theories: Did such an event of agreement ever actually take place, and if so, where and when? What were the specific terms of the agreement, assuming that it did take place: Did it specify limits on the power of government or require that the government take a certain specific form? And, most importantly, does such an agreement, assuming again that it took place, still apply to those later citizens who were not directly involved in it—and if so, why? Thomas Hobbes and John Locke offer two historically influential and significantly different accounts of the idea that a social contract justifies the existence of a government. David Hume, while agreeing that such an agreement could in principle be the basis of legitimate government, questions whether the authority of the governments that actually exist, in his time or ours, can be justified in this way. His contrary suggestion is that the justification for government derives simply from its *utility:* from the fact that having a government of a certain specific sort produces better overall consequences for all the people involved than any alternative (including both anarchy and other specific sorts of governments). Thus Hume, on this issue at least, is a **utilitarian.** (See Chapter 5 for more discussion of the general utilitarian view and the problems that it faces.)

What Is the Nature of Social Justice?

One of the most obvious and important results of social institutions in general and governments in particular is the *distribution* of goods of various kinds, most conspicuously economic ones, among the various people who live in the society in question. Sometimes this takes the form of direct allocation of money or services or jobs with salaries, while in other cases it may be much more indirect, depending on the joint operation of laws and various sorts of social organizations. But it seems clear that not all such distributions are equally

acceptable from a moral standpoint and in particular that some of them treat various individuals or groups in ways that are *unjust*—discriminating unfairly in favor of some individuals or groups in relation to others or depriving people of things to which they have a legitimate claim. It is thus arguably at least a necessary condition for the acceptability of a set of social institutions and in particular the actions of a government that it satisfy the standards of what is referred to as **distributive justice.**

But just what are those standards? What sort of distribution does justice permit or require? One answer that has seemed obviously right to some thinkers, but that few if any actual societies have ever realized, is **egalitarianism:** the view that justice requires that economic goods and other benefits be distributed *equally* among all citizens. Other views advocate unequal distribution on the basis of such criteria as moral merit, contribution to society, and the like. And it is obvious that societies have often in practice distributed benefits unequally on the basis of such criteria as social class, racial or ethnic distinctions, and gender—though few philosophers have ever defended distributions of this sort.

Robert Nozick and John Rawls offer influential and very different answers to the question of what justice requires with respect to distribution. Nozick appeals simply to the absence of injustice in the *process* through which a given distribution was produced, with any distribution that is produced via individually just steps itself counting as just. On his view, distributive justice does not require any particular *pattern* of distribution—whether equality or a distribution that depends on some other criterion or set of criteria of the sort already mentioned. His claim is that free choices by individuals that are in no way unjust when assessed one at a time could lead to widely varying patterns of distribution (including ones that depart quite far from equality), and that if this occurs, the result is still just.

Rawls, in contrast, presents and argues for two abstract principles of justice, the more important one ("the difference principle") being that departures from an equal distribution are just only if the overall result of such departures nonetheless benefits those members of society who are proportionately least well off by giving them more in absolute terms than they would have received under an equal distribution. This can happen because giving additional incentives to those who are especially talented or productive may raise overall societal production to such a degree that even those who receive smaller shares of the larger social "pie" get more than they would have received from an equal share if the "pie" were smaller. But the degree of inequality that is compatible with justice will still almost certainly be much less for Rawls than for Nozick. A further selection from Nozick offers criticisms of Rawls, while the selection from Thomas Scanlon criticizes Nozick and partially defends Rawls.

What Is the Justification for Government?

Thomas Hobbes

One of the earliest and most influential versions of the general idea of a social contract as the basis for government is that presented by the English philosopher Thomas Hobbes (1588–1679) in his *Leviathan*. Hobbes lived through the English Civil War of 1642–1649 (which ended with the beheading of King Charles I). He was also a spectator from a greater distance of much other war and turmoil, most strikingly that involved in the devastating Thirty Years War of 1618–1648 on the European continent. It is thus hardly surprising that Hobbes attaches great, indeed overriding value to stability, order, and peace.

Hobbes's presentation and defense of his version of a social contract begin with his conception of the situation in which human beings would exist in the absence of government: the *state of nature*. He argues that the state of nature would in fact amount to a state of war of "all against all," in which human life would accordingly be, in his famous phrase, "solitary, poor, nasty, brutish, and short." It is to escape such a state that he envisions people agreeing among themselves to create a *commonwealth,* by conferring all their power and authority on a *sovereign* (which might be either one person or a group of people, though Hobbes clearly favored the former alternative).

Most of Hobbes's view of the status and power of the sovereign can be understood as following directly from the twin goals of (a) escaping the state of nature and, just as important, (b) guaranteeing (or coming as close to a guarantee as is practicably possible) that there will be no relapse into such a condition, as would occur if the government collapsed. It is mainly in order to secure this second goal that the powers of the sovereign must, according to him, be *absolute,* where this includes not only such things as control of all military power and its use, total lawmaking and judicial power, the power of censorship, and the like, but also the even more extreme idea that each subject shall view the sovereign's actions as though they were his own. But even power that is in these ways absolute turns out to have some surprising limitations. And thus there turns out to be no way to completely eliminate the possibility that Hobbes fears most: that the sovereign's power will be eroded, leading to a collapse of the commonwealth and a return to the horror of the state of nature.

The Social Contract, from *Leviathan*

Of the Natural Condition of Mankind as Concerning Their Felicity, and Misery

Nature hath made men so equal, in the faculties of body, and mind; as that though there be found one man sometimes manifestly stronger in body, or of quicker mind than another; yet when all is reckoned together, the difference between man, and man, is not so considerable, as that one man can thereupon claim to himself any benefit, to which another may not pretend, as well as he. For as to the strength of body, the weakest has strength enough to kill the strongest, either by secret machination, or by confederacy with others, that are in the same danger as himself.

And as to the faculties of the mind, (setting aside the arts grounded upon words, and especially that skill of proceeding upon general, and infallible rules, called science; which very few have, and but in few things; as being not a native faculty, born with us . . .) I find yet a greater equality amongst men, than that of strength. For prudence, is but experience; which equal time, equally bestows on all men, in those things they equally apply themselves unto. . . . (1)

From this equality of ability, ariseth equality of hope in the attaining of our ends. And therefore if any two men desire the same thing, which nevertheless they cannot both enjoy, they become enemies; and in the way to their end, (which is principally their own conservation, and sometimes their delectation only) endeavour to destroy, or subdue one another. And from hence it comes to pass, that where an invader hath no more to fear, than another man's single power; if one plant, sow, build, or possess a convenient seat, others may probably be expected to come prepared with forces united, to dispossess, and deprive him, not only of the fruit of his labour, but also of his life, or liberty. And the invader again is in the like danger of another.

And from this diffidence (2) of one another, there is no way for any man to secure himself, so reasonable, as anticipation; that is, by force, or wiles, to master the persons of all men he can, so long, till he see no other power great enough to endanger him: and this is no more than his own conservation requireth, and is generally allowed. Also because there be some, that taking pleasure in contemplating their own power in the acts of conquest, which they pursue farther than their security requires; if others, that otherwise would be glad to be at ease within modest bounds, should not by invasion increase their power, they would not be able, long time, by standing only on their defence, to subsist. And by consequence, such augmentation of dominion over men, being necessary to a man's conservation, it ought to be allowed him.

From *Leviathan* (1651).

(1) *Definition*

By *prudence,* Hobbes means something broader than is meant nowadays: wisdom in general with regard to practical matters.

(2)

By *diffidence,* Hobbes means just fear and distrust of others—now an archaic meaning.

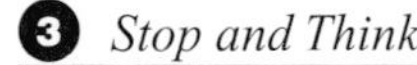

Again, men have no pleasure (but on the contrary a great deal of grief) in keeping company, where there is no power able to over-awe them all. For every man looketh that his companion should value him at the same rate he sets upon himself: and upon all signs of contempt, or undervaluing, naturally endeavours, as far as he dares (which amongst them that have no common power to keep them in quiet, is far enough to make them destroy each other) to extort a greater value from his contemners, by damage; and from others, by the example.

So that in the nature of man, we find three principal causes of quarrel. First, competition; secondly, diffidence; thirdly, glory.

The first, maketh man invade for gain; the second, for safety; and the third, for reputation. The first use violence, to make themselves masters of other men's persons, wives, children, and cattle; the second, to defend them; the third, for trifles, as a word, a smile, a different opinion, and any other sign of undervalue, either direct in their persons, or by reflection in their kindred, their friends, their nation, their profession, or their name. ❸

Hereby it is manifest, that during the time men live without a common power to keep them all in awe, they are in that condition which is called war; and such a war, as is of every man, against every man. For War, consisteth not in battle only, or the act of fighting; but in a tract of time, wherein the will to contend by battle is sufficiently known. . . .

Whatsoever therefore is consequent to a time of war, where every man is enemy to every man; the same is consequent to the time, wherein men live without other security, than what their own strength, and their own invention shall furnish them withal. In such condition, there is no place for industry; because the fruit thereof is uncertain: and consequently no culture of the earth; no navigation, nor use of the commodities that may be imported by sea; no commodious building; no instruments of moving, and removing such things as require much force; no knowledge of the face of the earth; no account of time; no arts; no letters; no society; and which is worst of all, continual fear, and danger of violent death; and the life of man, solitary, poor, nasty, brutish, and short. ❹

...

To this war of every man against every man, this also is consequent; that nothing can be unjust. The notions of right and wrong, justice and injustice have there no place. Where there is no common power, there is no law: where no law, no injustice. Force, and fraud, are in war the two cardinal virtues. Justice, and injustice are none of the faculties neither of the body, nor mind. If they were, they might be in a man that were alone in the world, as well as his senses, and passions. They are qualities, that relate to men in society, not in solitude. It is consequent also to the same condition, that there be no propriety, no dominion, no *mine* and *thine* distinct; but only that to be every man's, that he can get; and for so long, as he can keep it. ❺ And thus much for the ill condition, which many by mere nature is actually placed in; though with a possibility to come out of it, consisting partly in the passions, partly in his reason.

The passions that incline men to peace, are fear of death; desire of such things as are necessary to commodious living; and a hope by their industry to obtain them. And reason suggesteth convenient articles of peace, upon which men may be drawn to agreement.

Of the First and Second Natural Laws, and of Contracts

The RIGHT OF NATURE, which writers commonly call *jus naturale,* is the liberty each man hath, to use his own power, as he will himself, for the preservation of his own nature; that is to say, of his own life; and consequently, of doing any thing, which in his own judgment, and reason, he shall conceive to be the aptest means thereunto.

...

A LAW OF NATURE (*lex naturalis*) is a precept, or general rule, found out by reason, by which a man is forbidden to do that, which is destructive of his life, or taketh away the means of preserving the same; and to omit that, by which he thinketh it may be best preserved. . . . ❻

And because the condition of man, (as hath been declared in the precedent chapter) is a condition of war of every one against every one; in which case every one is governed by his own reason; and there is nothing he can make use of, that may not be a help unto him, in preserving his life against his enemies; it followeth, that in

❸ *Stop and Think*

STOP What does Hobbes mean by *glory,* and why does the desire for it (allegedly) lead people to attack each other? Are they being rational in doing so? (How might having glory make a person safer in the state of nature?)

❹

STOP This section contains Hobbes's description of the state of nature. What assumptions is he making: both about human beings, especially their psychology, and about the world they inhabit?

❺ *Editor Comment*

Hobbes's view, in sharp contrast to the one we will find in Locke, is that right and wrong, justice and injustice, and property rights cannot exist apart from society—and so do not exist in the state of nature.

❻

By a *law of nature,* Hobbes seems to mean something like a requirement of rational prudence or rational self-interest (not a divine command or a principle of objective morality). A *right of nature* is a liberty established on the same basis.

7 *Restatement/ Summary*

R Hobbes thinks that no one could rationally prefer a state of war. Peace is obviously preferable *if* it can be obtained in a way that does not expose a person to even more risk than the state of war.

STOP Could this be done in a state of nature (as Hobbes conceives it)? (If someone lives close enough to attack you and has enough strength to succeed if you are caught off guard, can you afford not to attack him first?)

What is needed in order to escape the state of nature is an agreement—a *contract*—in which people mutually surrender their natural rights to attack each other in pursuit of their own survival.

Such a contract is a *convenant* in Hobbesian terminology because it involves promises of future performance. (It wouldn't be good enough merely to promise not to attack right now.)

R Here is Hobbes's fundamental reason for thinking that peace is impossible on this basis so long as people continue to be in a state of nature. Refraining from attacking (when a person has a favorable opportunity, such as while the other person is asleep) in return for a promise that other persons will not attack in the future (when circumstances are favorable to them) cannot be a rational thing to do because there is not and cannot be any way to guarantee the other person's future performance. (See Discussion Question 1.)

Hobbes seems perhaps to be saying here that agreements are mere words and so also have no *moral* force unless they can be socially enforced.

such a condition, every man has a right to every thing: even to one another's body. And therefore, as long as this natural right of every man to every thing endureth, there can be no security to any man, (how strong or wise soever he be) of living out the time, which nature ordinarily alloweth men to live. And consequently it is a precept, or general rule of reason, *that every man, ought to endeavour peace, as far as he has hope of obtaining it; and when he cannot obtain it, that he may seek, and use, all helps, and advantages of war.* The first branch of which rule, containeth the first, and fundamental law of nature; which is, *to seek peace, and follow it.* The second, the sum of the right of nature; which is, *by all means we can, to defend ourselves.*

From this fundamental law of nature, by which men are commanded to endeavour peace, is derived this second law; that a man be willing, when others are so too, as farforth, as for peace, and defence of himself he shall think it necessary, to lay down this right to all things; and be contented with so much liberty against other men, as he would allow other men against himself. For as long as every man holdeth this right, of doing any thing he liketh; so long are all men in the condition of war. But if other men will not lay down their right, as well as he; then there is no reason for any one, to divest himself of his: for that were to expose himself to prey, (which no man is bound to) rather than to dispose himself to peace. . . . 7

Whensoever a man transferreth his right, or renounceth it; it is either in consideration of some right reciprocally transferred to himself; or for some other good he hopeth for thereby. For it is a voluntary act: and of the voluntary acts of every man, the object is some *good to himself.* . . .

The mutual transferring of right, is that which men call CONTRACT.

. . . one of the contractors, may deliver the thing contracted for on his part, and leave the other to perform his part at some determinate time after, and in the mean time be trusted; and then the contract on his part, is called PACT, or COVENANT: or both parts may contract now, to perform hereafter. . . . 8

If a covenant be made, wherein neither of the parties perform presently, but trust one another; in the condition of mere nature, (which is a condition of war of every man against every man) upon any reasonable suspicion, it is void: but if there be a common power set over them both, with right and force sufficient to compel performance, it is not void. For he that performeth first, has no assurance the other will perform after; because the bonds of words are too weak to bridle men's ambition, avarice, anger, and other passions, without the fear of some coercive power; which in the condition of mere nature, where all men are equal, and judges of the justness of their own fears, cannot possibly be supposed. And therefore he which performeth first, does but betray himself to his enemy; contrary to the right (he can never abandon) of defending his life, and means of living. 9

But in a civil estate, where there is a power set up to constrain those that would otherwise violate their faith, that fear is no more reasonable; and for that cause, he which by the covenant is to perform first, is obliged so to do.

...

Of the Causes, Generation, and Definition of a Commonwealth

The final cause, end, or design of men, (who naturally love liberty and dominion over others) in the introduction of that restraint upon themselves (in which we see them live in commonwealths) is the foresight of their own preservation, and of a more contented life thereby; that is to say, of getting themselves out from that miserable condition of war, which is necessarily consequent (as hath been shown), to the natural passions of men, when there is no visible power to keep them in awe, and tie them by fear of punishment to the performance of their covenants, and observation of those laws of nature set down [previously].

For the laws of nature (as *justice, equity, modesty, mercy,* and (in sum) *doing to others, as we would be done to,*) of themselves, without the terror of some power, to cause them to be observed, are contrary to our natural passions, that carry us to partiality, pride, revenge, and the like. And covenants, without the sword, are but words, and of no strength to secure a man at all. . . . 10

Nor is it the joining together of a small number of men, that gives them this security; because in small numbers, small additions on the one side or the other, make the advantage of strength so great, as is sufficient to carry the victory; and therefore gives encouragement to an invasion. . . .

Nor is it enough for the security, which men desire should last all the time of their life, that they be governed, and directed by one judgment, for a limited time; as in one battle, or one war. For though they obtain a victory by their unanimous endeavour against a foreign enemy; yet afterwards, when either they have no common enemy, or he that by one part is held for an enemy, is by another part held for a friend, they must needs by the difference of their interests dissolve, and fall again into a war amongst themselves. [11]

...

The only way to erect such a common power, as may be able to defend them from the invasion of foreigners, and the injuries of one another, and thereby to secure them in such sort, as that by their own industry, and by the fruits of the earth, they may nourish themselves and live contentedly; is, to confer all their power and strength upon one man, or upon one assembly of men, that may reduce all their wills, by plurality of voices, unto one will: which is as much as to say, to appoint one man, or assembly of men, to bear their person; and even one to own, and acknowledge himself to be author of whatsoever he that so beareth their person, shall act, or cause to be acted, in those things which concern the common peace and safety; and therein to submit their wills, every one to his will, and their judgments, to his judgment. This is more than consent, or concord; it is a real unity of them all, in one and the same person, made by covenant of every man with every man, in such manner, as if every man should say to every man, *I authorize and give up my right of governing myself, to this man, or to this assembly of men, on this condition, that thou give up thy right to him, and authorize all his actions in like manner.* This done, the multitude so united in one person, is called a COMMONWEALTH. . . . This is the generation of that great LEVIATHAN, or rather (to speak more reverently) of that *mortal god,* to which we owe under the *immortal God,* our peace and defence. For by this authority, given him by every particular man in the commonwealth, he hath the use of so much power and strength conferred on him, that by terror thereof, he is enabled to form the wills of them all, to peace at home, and mutual aid against their enemies abroad. And in him consisteth the essence of the commonwealth; which (to define it,) is *one person, of whose acts a great multitude, by mutual covenants one with another, have made themselves every one the author, to the end he may use the strength and means of them all, as he shall think expedient, for their peace and common defence.*

And he that carrieth this person, is called SOVEREIGN, and said to have sovereign power; and every one besides, his SUBJECT. [12]

The attaining to this sovereign power, is by two ways. One, by natural force; as when a man maketh his children, to submit themselves, and their children to his government, as being able to destroy them if they refuse; or by war subdueth his enemies to his will, giving them their lives on that condition. [13] The other, is when men agree amongst themselves, to submit to some man, or assembly of men, voluntarily, on confidence to be protected by him against all others. This latter, may be called a political commonwealth, or commonwealth by *institution;* and the former, a commonwealth by *acquisition.* . . .

Of the Rights of Sovereigns by Institution

A *commonwealth* is said to be *instituted,* when a *multitude* of men do agree, and *covenant, every one, with every one,* that to whatsoever *man,* or *assembly of men,* shall be given by the major part, the *right to present* the person of them all, (that is to say, to be their *representative*) every one, as well he that *voted for it,* as he that *voted against it,* shall *authorize* all the actions and judgments, of that man, or assembly of men, in the same manner, as if they were his own, to the end, to live peaceably amongst themselves, and be protected against other men. [14]

From this institution of a commonwealth are derived all the *rights,* and *faculties* of him, or them, on whom the sovereign power is conferred by the consent of the people assembled.

First, because they covenant, it is to be understood, they are not obliged by former covenant to any thing repugnant hereunto. And consequently they that have already instituted a commonwealth, being thereby bound by covenant, to own the actions, and judgments of

Might something less extreme than Hobbes's eventual proposal—joining into a smaller group or choosing a temporary leader—be enough to yield security? Perhaps temporarily—but not, Hobbes argues, in the long run.

Thus the only viable solution, in Hobbes's view, is for all or almost all those in a given area to surrender all their rights of self-defense and all their power and authority to one *sovereign* (either a single person or a group, but we will speak as though it is a single person), thereby creating a *commonwealth.*

A second and rather different way in which the authority of a sovereign over a particular group of people can be established is by force, by conquest. In this way, a commonwealth established in one area or over one group might be extended to another area or group.

(Consider, in light of this, the issue of what might happen if most of the people in a given area agree to institute a sovereign, but a few refuse to go along.)

A sovereign is to be chosen by a majority vote of those who agree to the creation of a commonwealth. How should we think of the power of the sovereign? This passage gives the core of Hobbes's answer: each person agrees to authorize the judgments and actions of the sovereign "as if they were his own."

This idea has some surprising consequences, as we will see shortly.

one, cannot lawfully make a new covenant, amongst themselves, to be obedient to any other, in any thing whatsoever, without his permission. . . .

Secondly, because the right of bearing the person of them all, is given to him they make sovereign, by covenant only of one to another, and not of him to any of them; there can happen no breach of covenant on the part of the sovereign; and consequently none of his subjects, by any pretence of forfeiture, can be freed from his subjection. That he which is made sovereign maketh no covenant with his subjects beforehand, is manifest; because either he must make it with the whole multitude, as one party to the covenant; or he must make a several covenant with every man. With the whole, as one party, it is impossible; because as yet they are not one person: and if he make so many several covenants as there be men, those covenants after he hath the sovereignty are void, because what act soever can be pretended by any one of them for breach thereof, is the act both of himself, and of all the rest, because done in the person, and by the right of every one of them in particular. (15) Besides, if any one, or more of them, pretend a breach of the covenant made by the sovereign at his institution; and others, or one other of his subjects, or himself alone, pretend there was no such breach, there is in this case, no judge to decide the controversy; it returns therefore to the sword again; and every man recovereth the right of protecting himself by his own strength, contrary to the design they had in the institution. . . .

Thirdly, because the major part hath by consenting voices declared a sovereign; he that dissented must now consent with the rest; that is, be contented to avow all the actions he shall do, or else justly be destroyed by the rest. For if he voluntarily entered into the congregation of them that were assembled, he sufficiently declared thereby his will, (and therefore tacitly covenanted) to stand, to what the major part should ordain.... And whether he be of the congregation, or not; and whether his consent be asked, or not, he must either submit to their decrees, or be left in the condition of war he was in before; wherein he might without injustice be destroyed by any man whatsoever. (16)

Fourthly, because every subject is by this institution author of all the actions, and judgments of the sovereign instituted; it follows, that whatsoever he doth, it can be no injury to any of his subjects; nor ought he to be by any of them accused of injustice. For he that doth any thing by authority from another, doth therein no injury to him by whose authority he acteth; but by this institution of a commonwealth, every particular man is author of all the sovereign doth; and consequently he that complaineth of injury from his sovereign, complaineth of that whereof he himself is author; and therefore ought not to accuse any man but himself; no nor himself of injury; because to do injury to one's self, is impossible. It is true that they that have sovereign power, may commit iniquity; but not injustice, or injury in the proper signification.

Fifthly, and consequently to that which was said last, no man that hath sovereign power can justly be put to death, or otherwise in any manner by his subjects punished. For seeing every subject is author of the actions of his sovereign; he punisheth another, for the actions committed by himself. (17)

And because the end of this institution, is the peace and defence of them all; and whosoever has right to the end, has right to the means; it belongeth of right, to whatsoever man, or assembly that hath the sovereignty, to be judge both of the means of peace and defence; and also of the hindrances, and disturbances of the same; and to do whatsoever he shall think necessary to be done, both beforehand, for the preserving of peace and security, by prevention of discord at home, and hostility from abroad; and, when peace and security are lost, for the recovery of the same. And therefore,

Sixthly, it is annexed to the sovereignty, to be judge of what opinions and doctrines are averse, and what conducing to peace; and consequently, on what occasions, how far, and what, men are to be trusted withal, in speaking to multitudes of people; and who shall examine the doctrines of all books before they be published. For the actions of men proceed from their opinions; and in the well-governing of opinions, consisteth the well-governing of men's actions, in order to their peace, and concord. And though in matter of doctrine, nothing ought to be regarded but the truth; yet this is not repugnant to regulating of the same by peace. For doctrine repugnant to peace, can no more be true, than peace and concord can be against the law of nature. . . .

(15)

Can the sovereign violate the covenant that establishes the commonwealth? Hobbes's surprising answer is that he cannot because he is not a party to it at all. (Presumably the idea is that the sovereign *qua sovereign* is not and cannot be a party to the covenant, not that the person or group that later becomes the sovereign might not have been such a party.)

(16)

Here we have the explicit answer to the question of what happens to those who disagree about the formation of the commonwealth or the choice of the sovereign.

(17)

In this paragraph and the preceding one are two alleged, very surprising consequences of each subject agreeing to regard the actions of the sovereign as his own: the sovereign cannot injure (that is, *wrongfully* harm) the subjects; and the sovereign may not be justly punished by the subjects for any of his actions.

Seventhly, is annexed to the sovereignty, the whole power of prescribing the rules, whereby every man may know, what goods he may enjoy, and what actions he may do, without being molested by any of his fellow-subjects; and this is it men call *propriety* [property]. . . .

Eighthly, is annexed to the sovereignty, the right of judicature; that is to say, of hearing and deciding all controversies, which may arise concerning law, either civil, or natural; or concerning fact. For without the decision of controversies, there is no protection of one subject, against the injuries of another; . . . and to every man remaineth, from the natural and necessary appetite of his own conservation, the right of protecting himself by his private strength, which is the condition of war; and contrary to the end for which every commonwealth is instituted.

Ninthly, is annexed to the sovereignty, the right of making war and peace with other nations, and commonwealths; that is to say, of judging when it is for the public good, and how great forces are to be assembled, armed, and paid for that end; and to levy money upon the subjects, to defray the expenses thereof. . . .

Tenthly, is annexed to the sovereignty, the choosing of all counsellors, ministers, magistrates, and officers, both in peace, and war. For seeing the sovereign is charged with the end, which is the common peace and defence, he is understood to have power to use such means, as he shall think most fit for his discharge.

Eleventhly, to the sovereign is committed the power of rewarding with riches, or honour; and of punishing with corporal, or pecuniary punishment, or with ignominy every subject according to the law he hath formerly made; or if there be no law made, according as he shall judge most to conduce to the encouraging of men to serve the commonwealth, or deterring of them from doing disservice to the same.

Lastly, considering what values men are naturally apt to set upon themselves; what respect they look for from others; and how little they value other men; from whence continually arise amongst them, emulation, quarrels, factions, and at last war, to the destroying of one another, and diminution of their strength against a common enemy; it is necessary that there be laws of honour. . . . To the sovereign therefore it belongeth also to give titles of honour; and to appoint what order of place, and dignity, each man shall hold; and what signs of respect, in public or private meetings, they shall give to one another.

These are the rights, which make the essence of sovereignty; and which are the marks, whereby a man may discern in what man, or assembly of men, the sovereign power is placed, and resideth. For these are incommunicable, and inseparable. . . . 18

18

The rest of the powers of the sovereign are more obvious, given the basic rationale of enabling him to preserve peace and avoid a return to the state of nature.

But a man may here object, that the condition of subjects is very miserable; as being obnoxious to the lusts, and other irregular passions of him, or them that have so unlimited a power in their hands. And commonly that they live under a monarch, think it the fault of monarchy; and they that live under the government of democracy, or other sovereign assembly, attribute all the inconvenience to that form of commonwealth; whereas the power in all forms, if they be perfect enough to protect them, is the same; not considering that the estate of man can never be without some incommodity or other; and that the greatest, that in any form of government can possibly happen to the people in general, is scarce sensible, in respect to the miseries, and horrible calamities, that accompany a civil war, or that dissolute condition of masterless men, without subjection to laws, and a coercive power to tie their hands from rapine and revenge. . . . 19

19

Many would object to the idea of an absolute sovereign, citing the various evils that often flow from such a system. Hobbes would offer two points in reply, only the first of which is explicit here: first, that however bad those evils may be, the state of nature is much, much worse; and, second, that an absolute sovereign is the only way to *guarantee* (or come as close as possible to a guarantee) that such a horrible state will not recur.

Of the Liberty of Subjects

...

To come now to the particulars of the true liberty of a subject; that is to say, what are the things, which though commanded by the sovereign, he may nevertheless, without injustice, refuse to do; we are to consider, what rights we pass away, when we make a commonwealth; or (which is all one,) what liberty we deny ourselves, by owning all the actions (without exception) of the man, or assembly we make our sovereign. . . .

. . . it is manifest, that every subject has liberty in all those things, the right whereof cannot by covenant be transferred. I have shewn before . . . that covenants, not to defend a man's own body, are void. Therefore,

If the sovereign command a man (though justly condemned,) to kill, wound, or maim himself; or not to resist those that assault him; or to abstain from the use of food, air, medicine, or any other thing, without which he cannot live; yet hath that man the liberty to disobey.

If a man be interrogated by the sovereign, or his authority, concerning a crime done by himself, he is not bound (without assurance of pardon) to confess it; because no man (as I have shown . . .) can be obliged by covenant to accuse himself.

Again, the consent of a subject to sovereign power, is contained in these words, *I authorize, or take upon me, all his actions;* in which there is no restriction at all, of his own former natural liberty: for by allowing him to *kill me,* I am not bound to kill myself when he commands me. It is one thing to say, *kill me, or my fellow, if you please;* another thing to say, *I will kill myself, or my fellow.* It followeth therefore, that

No man is bound by the words themselves, either to kill himself, or any other man; and consequently, that the obligation a man may sometimes have, upon the command of the sovereign to execute any dangerous, or dishonourable office, dependeth not on the words of our submission; but on the intention, which is to be understood by the end thereof. When therefore our refusal to obey, frustrates the end for which the sovereignty was ordained; then there is no liberty to refuse: otherwise there is.

Upon this ground, a man that is commanded as a soldier to fight against the enemy, though his sovereign have right enough to punish his refusal with death, may nevertheless in many cases refuse, without injustice; as when he substituteth a sufficient soldier in his place: for in this case he deserteth not the service of the commonwealth. And there is allowance to be made for natural timorousness; not only to women, (of whom no such dangerous duty is expected,) but also to men of feminine courage when the defence of the commonwealth, requireth at once the help of all that are able to bear arms, every one is obliged; because otherwise the institution of the commonwealth, which they have not the purpose, or courage to preserve, was in vain.

To resist the sword of the commonwealth, in defence of another man, guilty, or innocent, no man hath liberty; because such liberty, takes away from the sovereign, the means of protecting us; and is therefore destructive of the very essence of government. But in case a great many men together, have already resisted the sovereign power unjustly, or committed some capital crime, for which every one of them expecteth death, whether have they not the liberty then to join together, and assist, and defend one another? Certainly they have: for they but defend their lives, which the guilty man may as well do, as the innocent. There was indeed injustice in the first breach of their duty; their bearing of arms subsequent to it, though it be to maintain what they have done, is no new unjust act. And if it be only to defend their persons, it is not unjust at all. But the offer of pardon taketh from them, to whom it is offered, the plea of self-defence, and maketh their perserverance in assisting, or defending the rest, unlawful. 20

20 Do the subjects of the commonwealth with an absolute sovereign have any liberties left (beyond those that the sovereign may choose to allow them)? Somewhat surprisingly, they do—indeed liberties that could obviously threaten the very stability of the commonwealth. To see why Hobbes says this, you need to think again about the rationale for the original agreement, as viewed from the standpoint of each individual person.

As for other liberties, they depend on the silence of the law. In cases where the sovereign has prescribed no rule, there the subject hath the liberty to do, or forbear, according to his own discretion. And therefore such liberty is in some places more, and in some less; and in some times more, in other times less, according as they that have the sovereignty shall think most convenient. . . .

The obligation of subjects to the sovereign, is understood to last as long, and no longer, than the power lasteth, by which he is able to protect them. For the right men have by nature to protect themselves, when none else can protect them, can by no covenant be relinquished. The sovereignty is the soul of the commonwealth; which once departed from the body, the members do no more receive their motion from it. . . . And though sovereignty, in the intention of them that make it, be immortal; yet is it in its own nature, not only subject to violent death, by foreign war; but also through the ignorance, and passions of men, it hath in it, from the very institution, many seeds of a natural mortality, by intestine discord. 21

21 Here is another fundamental limitation to the sovereign's absolute power, one that again follows from the very rationale of the social contract.

...

Of Those Things That Weaken, or Tend to the Dissolution of a Commonwealth

Though nothing can be immortal, which mortals make; yet, if men had the use of reason they pretend to, their commonwealths might be secured, at least, from perishing by internal diseases. For by the nature of their institution, they are designed to live, as long as mankind, or as the laws of nature, or as justice itself, which gives them life. . . . [22]

Amongst the *infirmities* therefore of a commonwealth, I will reckon in the first place, those that arise from an imperfect institution, and resemble the diseases of a natural body, which proceed from a defectuous procreation.

Of which, this is one, that a man to obtain a kingdom, is sometimes content with less power, than to the peace, and defence of the commonwealth is necessarily required. From whence it cometh to pass, that when the exercise of the power laid by, is for the public safety to be resumed, it hath the resemblance of an unjust act; which disposeth great numbers of men (when occasion is presented) to rebel. . . .

In the second place, I observe the *diseases* of a commonwealth, that proceed from the poison of seditious doctrines, whereof one is, *That every private man is judge of good and evil actions.* This is true in the condition of mere nature, where there are no civil laws; and also under civil government, in such cases as are not determined by the law. But otherwise it is manifest, that the measure of good and evil actions, is the civil law; and the judge the legislator, who is always representative of the commonwealth. From this false doctrine, men are disposed to debate with themselves, and dispute the commands of the commonwealth; and afterwards to obey, or disobey them, as in their private judgments they shall think fit. Whereby the commonwealth is distracted and *weakened.*

...

A fourth opinion, repugnant to the nature of a commonwealth, is this, *that he that hath the sovereign power, is subject to the civil laws.* It is true, that sovereigns are all subject to the laws of nature. . . . But to those laws which the sovereign himself, that is, which the commonwealth maketh, he is not subject. For to be subject to laws, is to be subject to the commonwealth, that is to the sovereign representative, that is to himself; which is not subjection, but freedom from the laws. Which error, because it setteth the laws above the sovereign, setteth also a judge above him, and a power to punish him; which is to make a new sovereign; and again for the same reason a third, to punish the second; and so continually without end, to the confusion, and dissolution of the commonwealth.

A fifth doctrine, that tendeth to the dissolution of a commonwealth, is, *that every private man has an absolute propriety in his goods; such, as excludeth the right of the sovereign.* Every man has indeed a propriety that excludes the right of every other subject: and he has it only from the sovereign power; without the protection whereof, every other man should have equal right to the same. But if the right of the sovereign also be excluded, he cannot perform the office they have put him into; which is, to defend them both from foreign enemies, and from the injuries of one another; and consequently there is no longer a commonwealth.

...

There is a sixth doctrine, plainly, and directly against the essence of a commonwealth; and it is this, *that the sovereign power may be divided.* For what is it to divide the power of a commonwealth, but to dissolve it; for powers divided mutually destroy each other. And for these doctrines, men are chiefly beholding to some of those, that making profession of the laws, endeavour to make them depend upon their own learning, and not upon the legislative power. [23]

...

Lastly, when in a war (foreign or intestine,) the enemies get a final victory; so as (the forces of the commonwealth keeping the field no longer), there is no farther protection of subjects in their loyalty; then is the commonwealth DISSOLVED, and every man at liberty to protect himself by such courses as his own discretion shall suggest unto him. . . .

22

R Hobbes was very conscious of the potential fragility of a commonwealth, and in this section warns of various things that could lead to its collapse. Some of these are obvious in light of the previous discussion, but others suggest what Hobbes's objections would have been to other forms of government.

23

Here (and in the discussion of the fourth opinion) is Hobbes's objection to a doctrine that lies at the heart of the United States Constitution: the idea of division (and balance) of power. He is not saying that such a government will collapse at once, but that it essentially involves a possibility of internal conflict that can lead to its own destruction and hence a return to the state of nature.

STOP What response might a proponent of the American system of government give to Hobbes?

Discussion Questions

1. In thinking about the problem of trying to achieve peace in the state of nature, it is helpful to appeal to the following kind of reasoning, typical of that which is studied in *rational choice theory.* Suppose that person A has a neighbor, person B, the two being approximately equal in strength and other relevant capacities. Suppose that A and B attempt to achieve peace by entering into an agreement not to attack each other. Suppose also that there are easily identifiable

times when an attack by one on the other is virtually certain to succeed (when the potential victim is asleep, for example). Focusing now on a situation in which B is in such a vulnerable condition, consider the choices available to A: he can keep the agreement or he can attack B anyway (presumably killing him). When the situation is reversed, B has the same two choices. Each of their two choices has two possible results, depending on what the other person does, yielding the following *decision-theoretic matrix* of choices and outcomes:

	B keeps the agreement	***B attacks***
A keeps the agreement	At least temporary peace	A is killed; B is more secure
A attacks	B is killed; A is more secure	Return to a state of war

Think now of the values of these results for each of the two parties. Even temporary peace is better than war, but war is better than death. And the death of the other person is better than temporary peace because it removes all threat as far as that person is concerned. This yields the following "payoff" matrix, where the numbers represent the *ordinal* value of the results (1 is best), with the value for A being listed first:

	B keeps the agreement	***B attacks***
A keeps the agreement	2, 2	4, 1
A attacks	1, 4	3, 3

Look at this from A's perspective: whatever B chooses, A does better by attacking than by keeping the agreement. And the same thing is true for B. Thus the rational, self-interested choice for each of them is apparently to attack—even though by doing so each of them ends up with the next-to-worst possible outcome. (Notice that it is being assumed that the two choices are made independently of each other—but this seems to be true in the state of nature.) This is a version of what has become known as "the prisoner's dilemma" (named after a different example in which each of two accused criminals must decide whether or not to "rat" on the other). It seems to capture pretty well what Hobbes has in mind in his discussion of the state of nature.

Explain how this provides a rationale for instituting a sovereign, that is, how having a sovereign over A and B would solve the problem. Is there any other way out of this situation, one where the parties remain in the state of nature? This might involve some basis on which a person could choose to keep such an agreement without violating his own rational self-interest. One thing to consider here is how this argument might be affected by the presence of other people. Suppose that there are other persons, C, D, E, and so on, who are witnessing from afar the proceedings between A and B. How might they react to A's making one choice or the other, and how might such reactions alter the value of the overall outcome of each choice for A?

2. There is a problem lurking in Hobbes's view, about which he says very little—the problem of enforcement. Suppose that a commonwealth has been formed and you have been chosen by majority vote (or even unanimous consent) to be the sovereign. Perhaps we put a little hat on your head and say "Congratulations! You're the sovereign." You proceed to formulate and announce various rules requiring people not to attack each other, to pay taxes, to serve in the police or army, and so forth. These rules require your subjects to do various things that they might otherwise prefer not to do. How are you to enforce them? Suppose that you call a violation of a rule to someone's attention and point at your hat, but they shrug their shoulders and continue doing whatever they were doing. What can you do? You aren't strong enough by yourself to enforce the rules with very much chance of success, especially if the rule breakers band together to resist. What you need is a group of enforcers—a posse. But how can you get one if people won't obey your commands? Is there any solution to this problem, or does Hobbes's account of how government is created fall apart right at the beginning? (Here it might help to think about how the leaders of groups that aren't legally constituted get and maintain power—groups such as street gangs and the like.)
3. Hobbes holds a view of human nature according to which human beings are self-interested individuals for whom society is of value only if and to the extent that it leads to greater security or other concrete advantages (such as economic exchange). Others have held views according to which human beings are essentially social creatures, incapable of having satisfactory lives outside of society. What do you think about this question? Is Hobbes right? If not, how seriously does this undermine his arguments?

John Locke

In his *Second Treatise of Government,* the English philosopher John Locke (1632–1704) presents an account of the idea of a social contract that has been even more influential than the one offered by Hobbes. (In case you are wondering, the *First Treatise* was a critique of the view that the political authority of kings derives from "divine right.") Locke lived slightly later than Hobbes and was more extensively involved in practical politics than almost any other major philosopher. He was an adviser and assistant to the Earl of Shaftesbury, who was one of the leaders of the movement (following the restoration of the British monarchy after Cromwell) that attempted to prevent the eventual James II from ascending the British throne because of his Roman Catholic views. Shaftesbury eventually had to flee the country in 1683 to avoid execution for treason, and Locke soon followed. Shaftesbury died in exile, but Locke returned to England with William and Mary at the time of the "Glorious Revolution" of 1688–1689 (in which the Stuart monarchy was quickly and bloodlessly overthrown). Locke subsequently served in the resulting government in several important positions. The two *Treatises* were written at least in part as a justification of the political movement that culminated in the Glorious Revolution.

Like Hobbes, Locke begins his account of the origin and justification of government with an account of the state of nature, but a state of nature that is substantially less fearsome than the one Hobbes portrays. In Locke's view, people in the state of nature are capable of living in at least relative peace, in large part because they are capable of understanding through reason a moral *law of nature* (which Locke views as laid down by God), a law that each of them is morally entitled to enforce. Problems can still arise, however: some people may ignore the moral law and be powerful enough to get away with it, and even those who recognize it may be biased in their own favor in their interpretation of it. These problems are serious enough, in Locke's view, to motivate the formation of a community and the institution of a government empowered to take over the enforcement of the law of nature. But they do not justify conferring absolute power on the government, a situation that in Locke's view would be *worse* than the state of nature. Instead, the powers of the government are limited and are conferred on it only provisionally, with the people retaining the right to overthrow the government and replace it with another if it exceeds its proper authority or violates their rights.

Here we see Locke's rationale for the Glorious Revolution. His view was also one major influence on the American Founding Fathers at the time of the American Revolution and is reflected clearly in the Declaration of Independence.

The Social Contract, from *Second Treatise of Government*

Of the State of Nature

4. To understand political power, right, and derive it from its original, we must consider what state all men are naturally in, and that is, *a state of perfect freedom* to order their actions, and dispose of their possessions and persons, as they think fit, within the bounds of the law of nature; without asking leave, or depending upon the will of any other man.

A *state also of equality,* wherein all the power and jurisdiction is reciprocal, no one having more than another; there being nothing more evident, than that creatures of the same species and rank, promiscuously born to all the same advantages of nature, and the use of the same faculties, should also be equal one

From *Second Treatise of Government* (1690).

amongst another without subordination or subjection. . . .

6. But though this be *a state of liberty,* yet *it is not a state of licence:* though man in that state have an uncontrollable liberty to dispose of his person or possessions, yet he has not liberty to destroy himself, or so much as any creature in his possession, but where some nobler use than its bare preservation calls for it. The *state of nature* has a law of nature to govern it, which obliges every one: And reason, which is that law, teaches all mankind, who will but consult it, that being all *equal and independent,* no one ought to harm another in his life, health, liberty, or possessions. For men being all the workmanship of one omnipotent and infinitely wise Maker; all the servants of one sovereign master, sent into the world by his order, and about his business; they are his property, whose workmanship they are, made to last during his, not another's pleasure. And being furnished with like faculties, sharing all in one community of nature, there cannot be supposed any such subordination among us, that may authorize us to destroy another, as if we were made for one another's uses, as the inferior ranks of creatures are for ours. Every one, as he is *bound to preserve himself,* and not to quit his station willfully, so by the like reason, when his own preservation comes not in competition, ought he, as much as he can, *to preserve the rest of mankind,* and may not, unless it be to do justice to an offender, take away or impair the life, or what tends to the preservation of life, the liberty, health, limb, or goods of another. ❶

7. And that all men may be restrained from invading others' rights, and from doing hurt to one another, and the law of nature be observed, which willeth the peace and *preservation of all mankind,* the *execution* of the law of nature is, in that state, put into every man's hands, whereby every one has a right to punish the transgressors of that law to such a degree as may hinder its violation. For the *law of nature* would, as all other laws that concern men in this world, be in vain, if there were no body that in the state of nature had a *power to execute* that law, and thereby preserve the innocent and restrain offenders. And if any one in the state of nature may punish another for any evil he has done, every one may do so. For in that *state of perfect equality,* where naturally there is no superiority or jurisdiction of one over another, what any may do in prosecution of that law, every one must needs have a right to do. ❷

8. And thus, in the state of nature, *one man comes by a power over another;* but yet no absolute or arbitrary power, to use a criminal, when he has got him in his hands, according to the passionate heats, or boundless extravagancy of his own will; but only to retribute to him, so far as calm reason and conscience dictate, what is proportionate to his *transgression;* which is so much as may serve for reparation and *restraint.* For these two are the only reasons, why one man may lawfully do harm to another, which is that we call *punishment.* ❸ In transgressing the law of nature, the offender declares himself to live by another rule than that of reason and common equity, which is that measure God has set to the actions of men, for their mutual security; and so he becomes dangerous to mankind, the tye, which is to secure them from injury and violence, being slighted and broken by him. Which being a trespass against the whole species, and the peace and safety of it, provided for by the law of nature; every man upon this score, by the right he hath to preserve mankind in general, may restrain, or, where it is necessary, destroy things noxious to them, and so may bring such evil on any one, who hath transgressed that law, as may make him repent the doing of it, and thereby deter him, and by his example others, from doing the like mischief. And in this case, and upon this ground, *every man hath a right to punish the offender, and be executioner of the law of nature.*

...

10. Besides the crime which consists in violating the law, and varying from the right rule of reason, whereby a man so far becomes degenerate, and declares himself to quit the principles of human nature, and to be a noxious creature, there is commonly injury done to some person or other, and some other man receives damage by his transgression, in which case he who hath received any damage, has besides the right of punishment common to him with other men, a particular right to seek *reparation* from him that has done it. And any other person who finds it just, may also join with him that is injured, and assist him in recovering from the offender so

This paragraph presents Locke's conception of the law of nature, which he later summarizes as the idea that "all, as much as may be, should be preserved" (§ 183, not included in this selection). Unlike Hobbes's "laws of nature," which are fundamentally *prudential* in character, the Lockean law of nature is a *moral* law, laid down by God, but in Locke's view still discernible by human reason, without the need to appeal to religious authority (which would be unavailable in the state of nature).

But who is to enforce such a law, in the absence of a government? Whereas Hobbes thinks that there can be no meaningful morality or justice outside of society, Locke's view is that the very existence of the law of nature brings with it a right to *execute* (that is, enforce) it, a right that is equally shared by all in the situation of equality and independence that defines the state of nature. As he makes clear in what follows, this right of execution is not limited to self-defense, but extends also to protecting others from violations of their rights and punishing the offender.

R Locke offers two justifications for punishment: *reparation* to the injured party and *restraint* of the criminal from committing similar offenses. These are said to be limited to what is "proportionate" to the crime. (How clear a limitation is this?)

much as may make satisfaction for the harm he has suffered.

11. And thus it is, that every man, in the state of nature, has a power to kill a murderer, both to deter others from doing the like injury, which no reparation can compensate, by the example of the punishment that attends it from every body, [4] and also *to secure* men from the attempts of a criminal, who having renounced reason, the common rule and measure, God hath given to mankind, hath by the unjust violence and slaughter he hath committed upon one, declared war against all mankind; and therefore may be destroyed as a *lion* or a *tiger,* one of those wild savage beasts, with whom men can have no society nor security. . . .

13. To this strange doctrine, viz. That *in the state of nature every one has the executive power* of the law of nature, I doubt not but it will be objected, that it is unreasonable for men to be judges in their own cases, that self-love will make men partial to themselves and their friends: And on the other side, that ill nature, passion and revenge will carry them too far in punishing others; and hence nothing but confusion and disorder will follow, and that therefore God hath certainly appointed government to restrain the partiality and violence of men. I easily grant, that civil government is the proper remedy for the inconveniencies of the state of nature, which must certainly be great, where men may be judges in their own case, since it is easy to be imagined, that he who was so unjust as to do his brother an injury, will scarce be so just as to condemn himself for it: [5] But I shall desire those who make this objection to remember, that *absolute monarchs* are but men, and if government is to be the remedy of those evils, which necessarily follow from men's being judges in their own cases, and the state of nature is therefore not to be endured, I desire to know what kind of government that is, and how much better it is than the state of nature, where one man commanding a multitude, has the liberty to be judge in his own case, and may do to all his subjects whatever he pleases, without the least liberty to any one to question or control those who execute his pleasure? and in whatsoever he doth, whether led by reason, mistake or passion, must be submitted to? Much better it is in the state of nature, wherein men are not bound to submit to the unjust will of another: And if he that judges, judges amiss in his own, or any other case, he is answerable for it to the rest of mankind.

...

Of the State of War

16. The *state of war* is a state of *enmity* and *destruction:* And therefore declaring by word or action, not a passionate and hasty, but a sedate settled design upon another man's life, *puts him in a state of war* with him against whom he has declared such an intention, and so has exposed his life to the other's power to be taken away by him, or any one that joins with him in his defence, and espouses his quarrel: it being reasonable and just I should have a right to destroy that which threatens me with destruction. For *by the fundamental law of nature, man being to be preserved* as much as possible, when all cannot be preserved, the safety of the innocent is to be preferred: And one may destroy a man who makes war upon him, or has discovered an enmity to his being, for the same reason that he may kill a *wolf* or a *lion;* because such men are not under the ties of the common law of reason, have no other rule, but that of force and violence, and so may be treated as beasts of prey, those dangerous and noxious creatures, that will be sure to destroy him whenever he falls into their power. [6]

17. And hence it is, that he who attempts to get another man into his absolute power, does thereby *put himself into a state of war* with him; it being to be understood as a declaration of a design upon his life. For I have reason to conclude, that he who would get me into his power without my consent, would use me as he pleased when he got me there, and destroy me too when he had a fancy to it; for no body can desire to *have me in his absolute power* unless it be to compel me by force to that which is against the right of my freedom, i.e. make me a slave. . . .

18. This makes it lawful for a man to *kill a thief,* who has not in the least hurt him, nor declared any design upon his life, any farther, than by the use of force, so to get him in his power, as to take away his money, or what he pleases, from him; because using force, where he has no right, to get me into his power, let his pretence be what it will, I have no reason to suppose, that he, who would *take away my liberty,*

R Restraint may involve also *deterring* others from committing similar crimes.

R Here is the first main rationale for leaving the state of nature and instituting government: even those who recognize the law of nature may be biased in their application of it, favoring themselves and their friends and exaggerating the degree of punishment that is justified to those who harm them.

(But Locke proceeds to argue that a Hobbesian absolute sovereign not only fails to solve this problem but actually makes it worse.)

R A state of war comes to exist when one person makes it clear that he does not accept the restrictions imposed by the law of nature. Locke first focuses on the case where such a person threatens an innocent person's life.

would not, when he had me in his power, take away every thing else. And therefore it is lawful for me to treat him as one who has put *himself into a state of war* with me, i.e. kill him if I can; for to that hazard does he justly expose himself, whoever introduces a state of war, and is aggressor in it. 7

7

The law of nature also guarantees rights to freedom and property (which Locke views as acquired when a person "mixes his labor" with unowned parts of the world). Thus a person who fails to respect those specific rights also shows that he does not recognize the law of nature in general and so, Locke says, may be justifiably killed.

19. And here we have the plain *difference between the state of nature and the state of war;* which however some men have confounded, are as far distant, as a state of peace, good will, mutual assistance and preservation, and a state of enmity, malice, violence and mutual destruction, are one from another. Men living together according to reason, without a common superior on earth, with authority to judge between them, is *properly the state of nature.* But force, or a declared design of force, upon the person of another, where there is no common superior on earth to appeal to for relief, *is the state of war. . . . Want of a common judge with authority, puts all men in a state of nature: Force without right, upon a man's person, makes a state of war,* both where there is, and is not, a common judge. 8

Thus for Locke, unlike Hobbes, there is a clear distinction between the state of nature and a state of war. The state of nature may degenerate into a state of war, but this is in no way necessary or inevitable.

. . .

21. To avoid this *state of war* (wherein there is no appeal but to heaven, and wherein every the least difference is apt to end, where there is no authority to decide between the contenders) is *one great reason of men's putting themselves into society,* and quitting the state of nature. For where there is an authority, a power on earth, from which relief can be had by *appeal,* there the continuance of the *state of war* is excluded, and the controversy is decided by that power. . . . 9

R But the risk of such a state of war is still a second main rationale for leaving the state of nature in favor of organized society.

Of Political or Civil Society

87. Man being born, as has been proved, with a title to perfect freedom, and an uncontrolled enjoyment of all the rights and privileges of the law of nature, equally with any other man, or number of men in the world, hath by nature a power, not only to preserve his property, that is, his life, liberty, and estate, against the injuries and attempts of other men; but to judge of and punish the breaches of that law in others, as he is persuaded the offence deserves, even with death itself, in crimes where the heinousness of the fact, in his opinion, requires it. But because no *political* society can be, nor subsist, without having in itself the power to preserve the property, and, in order thereunto, punish the offences of all those of that society; there and there only is *political society,* where every one of the members hath quitted his natural power, resigned it up into the hands of the community in all cases that excludes him not from appealing for protection to the law established by it. And thus all private judgment of every particular member being excluded, the community comes to be umpire by settled standing rules, indifferent, and the same to all parties; and by men having authority from the community, for the execution of those rules, decides all the differences that may happen between any members of that society concerning any matter of right; and punishes those offences which any member hath committed against the society, with such penalties as the law has established, whereby it is easy to discern, who are, and who are not, in *political society* together. Those who are united into one body, and have a common established law and judicature to appeal to, with authority to decide controversies between them, and punish offenders, *are in civil society* one with another: but those who have no such common appeal, I mean on earth, are still in the state of nature, each being, where there is no other, judge for himself, and executioner: which is, as I have before shewed, the perfect *state of nature.* 10

10

R Political society exists, by definition, only where people have surrendered to a community (and ultimately to a particular government) their natural right to enforce the law of nature and punish transgressions.

88. And thus the commonwealth comes by a power to set down what punishment shall belong to the several transgressions which they think worthy of it, committed amongst the members of that society, (which is the *power of making laws*) as well as it has the power to punish any injury done unto any of its members, by any one that is not of it, (which is the power of war and peace) and all this for the preservation of the property of all the members of that society, as far as is possible. But though every man who has entered into civil society, and is become a member of any commonwealth, has thereby quitted his power to punish offences against the law of nature, in prosecution of his own private judgment; yet with the judgment of offences, which he has given up to the legislative in all cases where he can appeal to the magistrate, he has given a right to the commonwealth to employ his force, for the execution of the judgments of the commonwealth whenever he shall be called to it; which indeed are his own judgments, they

being made by himself, or his representative. And herein we have the original of the legislative and executive power of civil society, which is to judge by standing laws, how far offences are to be punished, when committed within the commonwealth; and also to determine, by occasional judgments founded on the present circumstances of the fact, how far injuries from without are to be vindicated; and in both these to employ all the force of all the members, when there shall be need. (11)

89. Whenever therefore any number of men are so united into one society, as to quit every one his executive power of the law of nature, and to resign it to the public, there and there only is a political, or civil society. . . . And wherever there are any number of men, however associated, that have no such decisive power to appeal to, there they are still in the state of nature.

90. Hence it is evident, that absolute monarchy, which by some men is counted the only government in the world, is indeed inconsistent with civil society, and so can be no form of civil government at all; for the end of civil society being to avoid and remedy these inconveniencies of the state of nature, which necessarily follow from every man's being judge in his own case, by setting up a known authority, to which every one of that society may appeal upon any injury received, or controversy that may arise, and which every one of the society ought to obey; wherever any persons are, who have not such an authority to appeal to for the decision of any difference between them, there those persons are still *in the state of nature.* And so is every *absolute prince,* in respect of those who are under his dominion.

91. For he being supposed to have all, both legislative and executive power in himself alone, there is no judge to be found, no appeal lies open to any one, who may fairly, and indifferently, and with authority decide, and from whose decision relief and redress may be expected of any injury or inconveniency that may be suffered from the prince, or by his order: so that such a man, however intitled, *czar,* or *grand seignior,* or how you please, is as much in *the state of nature,* with all under his dominion, as he is with the rest of mankind. For wherever any two men are, who have no standing rule, and common judge to appeal to on earth, for the determination of controversies of right betwixt them, there they are still *in the state of nature,* and under all the inconveniencies of it, with only this woful difference to the subject, or rather slave of an absolute prince; that whereas in the ordinary state of nature he has a liberty to judge of his right, and, according to the best of his power, to maintain it; now, whenever his property is invaded by the will and order of his monarch, he has not only no appeal, as those in society ought to have, but, as if he were degraded from the common state of rational creatures, is denied a liberty to judge of, or to defend his right; and so is exposed to all the misery and inconveniencies that a man can fear from one, who being in the unrestrained state of nature, is yet corrupted with flattery, and armed with power. (12)

...

Of the Beginning of Political Societies

95. Men being, as has been said, by nature, all free, equal, and independent, no one can be put out of this estate, and subjected to the political power of another, without his own consent. The only way, whereby any one divests himself of his natural liberty, and puts on the *bonds of civil society,* is by agreeing with other men to join and unite into a community, for their comfortable, safe, and peaceable living one amongst another, in a secure enjoyment of their properties, and a greater security against any, that are not of it. This any number of men may do, because it injures not the freedom of the rest; they are left as they were in the liberty of the state of nature. (13) When any number of men have so *consented to make one community or government,* they are thereby presently incorporated, and make *one body politic,* wherein the *majority* have a right to act and conclude the rest.

96. For when any number of men have, by the consent of every individual, made a *community,* they have thereby made that *community* one body, with a power to act as one body, which is only by the will and determination of the majority. For that which acts any community, being only the *consent* of the individuals of it, and it being necessary to that which is one body to move one way, it is necessary the body should move that way whither the greater force carries it, which is the *consent of the majority:* or else it

R In this way, the community acquires from the individuals that compose it the power (a) to make laws defining crimes and determining the punishment for them, and (b) to enforce those laws, using the force of its members, as needed. Here (a) is the source of the legislative power and (b) the source of the executive power.

R Far from escaping the state of nature, the subjects of an absolute monarch are still in a state of nature in relation to him, but even less able to defend themselves.

R A political or civil society (two terms for the same thing) comes into being, according to Locke, only when a group of people all agree voluntarily to surrender the liberty and rights they have in the state of nature and unite into a community.

is impossible it should act or continue one body, one community, which the consent of every individual that united into it, agreed that it should; and so every one is bound by that consent to be concluded by the majority. And therefore we see, that in assemblies, impowered to act by positive laws, where no number is set by that positive law which impowers them, the *act of the majority* passes for the act of the whole, and of course determines, as having, by the law of nature and reason, the power of the whole.

. . .

98. For if *the consent of the majority* shall not, in reason, be received as *the act of the whole,* and conclude every individual; nothing but the consent of every individual can make any thing to be the act of the whole; But such a consent is next to impossible ever to be had. . . . Such a constitution as this would make the mighty *leviathan* of a shorter duration than the feeblest creatures, and not let it outlast the day it was born in. . . . (14)

(14)

R The actions of such a community are to be determined by majority rule, since to require unanimity would make it futile to form a community in the first place. As is implicit here and more explicit later, Locke views the act of uniting into a community—unlike the formation of a specific sort of government—as irrevocable. If people could withdraw whenever they disapprove of the community action, then the formation of the community would have no real force.

99. . . . And thus that, which begins and actually *constitutes any political society,* is nothing, but the consent of any number of freemen capable of a majority, to unite and incorporate into such a society. And this is that, and that only, which did, or could give beginning to any lawful government in the world.

. . .

Of the Ends of Political Society and Government

123. If man in the state of nature be so free, as has been said; if he be absolute lord of his own person and possessions, equal to the greatest, and subject to no body, why will he part with his freedom? why will he give up this empire, and subject himself to the dominion and control of any other power? To which it is obvious to answer, that though in the state of nature he hath such a right, yet the enjoyment of it is very uncertain, and constantly exposed to the invasion of others. For all being kings as much as he, every man his equal, and the greater part no strict observers of equity and justice, the enjoyment of the property he has in this state is very unsafe, very unsecure. This makes him willing to quit this condition, which, however free, is full of fears and continual dangers: and it is not without reason, that he seeks out, and is willing to join in society with others, who are already united, or have a mind to unite, for the mutual preservation of their lives, liberties, and estates, which I call by the general name, property.

124. The great and *chief end,* therefore, of men's uniting into commonwealths, and putting themselves under government, is *the preservation of their property.* (15) To which in the state of nature there are many things wanting.

(15)

As the previous sentence makes clear, "property" for Locke includes life and liberty, as well as property in the ordinary sense.

First, There wants an established, settled, known law, received and allowed by common consent to be the standard of right and wrong, and the common measure to decide all controversies between them. For though the law of nature be plain and intelligible to all rational creatures; yet men being biassed by their interest, as well as ignorant for want of studying it, are not apt to allow of it as a law binding to them in the application of it to their particular cases.

125. *Secondly,* In the state of nature there wants *a known and indifferent judge,* with authority to determine all differences according to the established law. For every one in that state being both judge and executioner of the law of nature, men being partial to themselves, passion and revenge is very apt to carry them too far, and with too much heat, in their own cases; as well as negligence, and unconcernedness, to make them too remiss in other men's.

126. *Thirdly,* In the state of nature, there often wants power to back and support the sentence when right, and to give it due execution. They who by any injustice offended, will seldom fail, where they are able, by force to make good their injustice; such resistance many times makes the punishment dangerous, and frequently destructive, to those who attempt it. (16)

(16)

R These three points spell out more fully the difficulties pertaining to enforcing the law of nature in the state of nature.

127. Thus mankind, notwithstanding all the privileges of the state of nature, being but in an ill condition, while they remain in it, are quickly driven into society. . . .

131. But though men, when they enter into society, give up the equality, liberty, and executive power they had in the state of nature, into the hands of the society, to be so far disposed of by the legislative, as the good of the society shall require; yet it being only with an intention in every one the better to preserve himself, his liberty and property; (for no rational creature can be supposed to change his condition with an intention to be worse) the power of the society,

or legislative constituted by them, *can never be supposed to extend farther, than the common good;* but is obliged to secure every one's property, by providing against those three defects above mentioned, that made the state of nature so unsafe and uneasy. And so whoever has the legislative or supreme power of any commonwealth, is bound to govern by established standing laws, promulgated and known to the people, and not by extemporary decrees; by indifferent and upright judges, who are to decide controversies by those laws; and to employ the force of the community at home, *only in the execution of such laws;* or abroad to prevent or redress foreign injuries, and secure the community from inroads and invasion. And all this to be directed to no other *end,* but the *peace, safety,* and *public good* of the people. [17]

. . .

Of the Extent of the Legislative Power

134. The great end of men's entering into society being the enjoyment of their properties in peace and safety, and the great instrument and means of that being the laws established in that society; *the first and fundamental positive law* of all commonwealths *is the establishing of the legislative* power; as the *first and fundamental natural law,* which is to govern even the legislative itself, *is the preservation of the society,* and (as far as will consist with the public good) of every person in it. [18] This *legislative* is not only *the supreme power* of the commonwealth, but sacred and unalterable in the hands where the community have once placed it; nor can any edict of any body else, in what form soever conceived, or by what power soever backed, have the force and obligation of a law, which has not its *sanction from* that *legislative* which the public has chosen and appointed; for without this the law could not have that, which is absolutely necessary to its being a *law, the consent of the society*. . . . [19]

135. Though the legislative, whether placed in one or more, whether it be always in being, or only by intervals, though it be the supreme power in every commonwealth; yet,

First, It is *not,* nor can possibly be absolutely *arbitrary* over the lives and fortunes of the people. For it being but the joint power of every member of the society given up to that person, or assembly, which is legislator, it can be no more than those persons had in a state of nature before they entered into society, and gave up to the community. For no body can transfer to another more power than he has in himself; and no body has an absolute arbitrary power over himself, or over any other, to destroy his own life, or take away the life or property of another. . . . Their power, in the utmost bounds of it, is *limited to the public good* of the society. It is a power, that hath no other end but preservation, and therefore can never have a right to destroy, enslave, or designedly to impoverish the subjects. . . . The rules that they make for other men's actions, must, as well as their own and other men's actions, be conformable to the law of nature, i.e. to the will of God, of which that is a declaration; and the *fundamental law of nature being the preservation of mankind,* no human sanction can be good or valid against it. [20]

136. *Secondly,* The legislative or supreme authority cannot assume to itself a power to rule, by extemporary, arbitrary decrees, but *is bound to dispense justice,* and decide the rights of the subject, *by promulgated, standing laws, and known authorized judges.* For the law of nature being unwritten, and so no-where to be found, but in the minds of men; they who through passion, or interest, shall miscite, or misapply it, cannot so easily be convinced of their mistake, where there is no established judge: and so it serves not, as it ought, to determine the rights, and fence the properties of those that live under it. . . . [21]

137. Absolute arbitrary power, or governing without *settled standing laws,* can neither of them consist with the ends of society and government, which men would not quit the freedom of the state of nature for, and tie themselves up under, were it not to preserve their lives, liberties, and fortunes, and by *stated rules* of right and property to secure their peace and quiet. . . .

138. *Thirdly,* The *supreme power cannot take* from any man part of his property without his own consent. For the preservation of property being the end of government, and that for which men enter into society, it necessarily supposes and requires, that the people should *have property,* without which they must be supposed to lose that, by entering into society, which was the end for which they entered into it; too gross an

Thus the supreme power cannot properly use the power that men have given up to enhance the wealth of a few at the expense of the many.

"Positive law" is man-made law, as opposed to natural law. And the most fundamental such law is the one that establishes and delineates the lawmaking authority or authorities of the society. (In many societies, this would be the most important part of a written constitution.)

"The legislative" (that is, the persons or bodies in whom the legislative power is placed) constitutes the supreme authority within the society, from which any other legitimate authorities must ultimately derive their power.

R Even the powers of the legislative authority are severely limited, according to Locke. He proceeds to enumerate four main restrictions. First, even the legislative authority does not and cannot legitimately have arbitrary, unlimited power over the citizens.

R Second, the legislative authority must govern by "settled standing laws," not arbitrary or ad hoc decrees. Part of the reason for this is by now obvious. But there is a further, underlying rationale: one of the purposes for leaving the state of nature is to avoid the situation where the natural law is subject to different interpretations, leading to conflict and insecurity.

22

R Third, Locke says that the legislative authority cannot take property from people without their consent. The rationale is that preserving property was the main end of instituting society and government in the first place. This seems to make it uncertain how a government can pay its own necessary expenses. In the following paragraph, however, Locke seems to say that majority consent of the people or their representatives is enough to satisfy this requirement.

23

R Fourth, the legislative authority cannot transfer its fundamental lawmaking power to someone else (which does not rule out the delegation of subsidiary powers). Whoever exercises that power in effect has it on loan from the people, but does not own it in a way that would allow giving it to someone else.

24

R In Locke's view, the executive power is subsidiary to the legislative and exists only for essentially practical reasons. STOP (How does this compare to the presidency in the present-day American system of government?)

25

Here is the fundamental difference between Locke and Hobbes: whereas for Hobbes power is conferred on the sovereign irrevocably, for Locke the power is merely *entrusted* to the government to act for specific ends—a trust that can be revoked by the people if the government fails to perform satisfactorily, especially if it exceeds its proper authority by invading the rights of the subjects.

absurdity for any man to own. . . . Hence it is a mistake to think, that the *supreme or legislative power* of any commonwealth can do what it will, and dispose of the estates of the subject arbitrarily, or take any part of them at pleasure. . . . (22)

140. It is true, governments cannot be supported without great charge, and it is fit every one who enjoys his share of the protection, should pay out of his estate his proportion for the maintenance of it. But still it must be with his own consent, i.e. the consent of the majority, giving it either by themselves, or their representatives chosen by them. For if any one shall claim a *power to lay* and levy *taxes* on the people, by his own authority, and without such consent of the people, he thereby invades the *fundamental law of property,* and subverts the end of government. For what property have I in that, which another may by right take when he pleases, to himself?

141. *Fourthly,* The *legislative cannot transfer the power of making laws* to any other hands. For it being but a delegated power from the people, they who have it cannot pass it over to others. The people alone can appoint the form of the commonwealth, which is by constituting the legislative, and appointing in whose hands that shall be. And when the people have said, we will submit to rules, and be governed by laws made by such men, and in such forms, no body else can say other men shall make laws for them; nor can the people be bound by any laws, but such as are enacted by those whom they have chosen, and authorized to make laws for them. . . . (23)

Of the Legislative [and] Executive Power of the Commonwealth

143. The legislative power is that, which has a right *to direct how the force of the commonwealth* shall be employed for preserving the community and the members of it. But because those laws which are constantly to be executed, and whose force is always to continue, may be made in a little time; therefore there is no need, that the legislative should be always in being, not having always business to do. And because it may be too great a temptation to human frailty, apt to grasp at power, for the same persons, who have the power of making laws, to have also in their hands the power to execute them, whereby they may exempt themselves from obedience to the laws they make, and suit the law, both in its making and execution, to their own private advantage, and thereby come to have a distinct interest from the rest of the community, contrary to the end of society and government: therefore in well ordered commonwealths, where the good of the whole is so considered, as it ought, the legislative power is put into the hands of divers persons, who, duly assembled, have by themselves, or jointly with others, a power to make laws; which when they have done, being separated again, they are themselves subject to the laws they have made; which is a new and near tie upon them, to take care that they make them for the public good.

144. But because the laws, that are at once, and in a short time made, have a constant and lasting force, and need a *perpetual execution,* or an attendance thereunto: therefore it is necessary there should be a *power always in being,* which should see to the execution of the laws that are made, and remain in force. And thus the legislative and executive power come often to be separated. (24)

...

Of the Subordination of the Powers of the Commonwealth

149. Though in a constituted commonwealth, standing upon its own basis, and acting according to its own nature, that is, acting for the preservation of the community, there can be but *one supreme power,* which is the *legislative,* to which all the rest are and must be subordinate; yet the legislative being only a fiduciary power to act for certain ends, there remains still *in the people a supreme power to remove or alter the legislative,* when they find the legislative act contrary to the trust reposed in them. For all *power given with trust* for the attaining an end, being limited by that end; whenever that end is manifestly neglected or opposed, the trust must necessarily be forfeited, and the power devolve into the hands of those that gave it, who may place it anew where they shall think best for their safety and security. (25) And thus the *community* perpetually *retains a supreme power* of saving themselves from the attempts and designs of any body, even of their legislators, whenever they shall be so foolish, or so wicked,

as to lay and carry on designs against the liberties and properties of the subject. . . . And thus the community may be said in this respect to be *always the supreme power,* but not as considered under any form of government, because this power of the people can never take place till the government be dissolved.

...

Of the Dissolution of Government

211. He that will with any clearness speak of the *dissolution of government,* ought in the first place to distinguish between the *dissolution of the society* and the *dissolution of the government.* That which makes the community, and brings men out of the loose state of nature into *one politic society,* is the agreement which every one has with the rest to incorporate, and act as one body, and so be one distinct commonwealth. The usual, and almost only way whereby *this union is dissolved,* is the inroad of foreign force making a conquest upon them. For in that case, (not being able to maintain and support themselves, as *one entire* and *independent body*) the union belonging to that body which consisted therein, must necessarily cease, and so every one return to the state he was in before, with a liberty to shift for himself, and provide for his own safety, as he thinks fit, in some other society. . . . [26]

212. Besides this overturning from without, *governments are dissolved from within.*

First, When the *legislative is altered.* Civil society being a state of peace, amongst those who are of it, from whom the state of war is excluded by the umpirage, which they have provided in their legislative, for the ending all differences that may arise amongst any of them; it is in their legislative, that the members of a commonwealth are united, and combined together into one coherent living body. This *is the soul that gives form, life, and unity* to the commonwealth: from hence the several members have their mutual influence, sympathy, and connexion; and therefore, when the legislative is broken, or dissolved, dissolution and death follows. . . . When any one, or more, shall take upon them to make laws, whom the people have not appointed so to do, they make laws without authority, which the people are not therefore bound to obey; by which means they come again to be out of subjection, and may constitute to themselves a new legislative, as they think best. . . . [27]

...

221. There is, therefore, secondly, another way whereby *governments are dissolved,* and that is, when the legislative, or the prince either of them, act contrary to their trust. [28]

...

222. The reason why men enter into society, is the preservation of their property; and the end why they choose and authorize a legislative, is, that there may be laws made, and rules set, as guards and fences to the properties of all the members of the society: to limit the power, and moderate the dominion, of every part and member of the society. For since it can never be supposed to be the will of the society, that the legislative should have a power to destroy that, which every one designs to secure, by entering into society, and for which the people submitted themselves to legislators of their own making, whenever the *legislators endeavour to take away and destroy the property of the people,* or to reduce them to slavery under arbitrary power, they put themselves into a state of war with the people, who are thereupon absolved from any farther obedience, and are left to the common refuge, which God hath provided for all men, against force and violence. Whensoever therefore the *legislative* shall transgress this fundamental rule of society; and either by ambition, fear, folly or corruption, *endeavour to grasp* themselves, *or put into the hands of any other an absolute power* over the lives, liberties, and estates of the people; by this breach of trust they *forfeit the power,* the people had put into their hands, for quite contrary ends, and it devolves to the people, who have a right to resume their original liberty, and, by the establishment of a new legislative, (such as they shall think fit) provide for their own safety and security, which is the end for which they are in society. What I have said here, concerning the legislative in general, holds true also concerning the supreme executor, who having a double trust put in him, both to have a part in the legislative, and the supreme execution of the law, acts against both, when he goes about to set up his own arbitrary will, as the law of the society. . . . [29]

R One way in which a government can be dissolved is by foreign conquest, in which case the community is also dissolved, and people are back in the state of nature.

R Since the constitution of the supreme legislative authority is the fundamental act that establishes a government, any alteration in the legislative authority destroys the legitimacy of the government. This might involve an attempted transfer of legislative power by the original legislative authority to a new one, or it might involve illegitimate usurpation of that power by some other person or body.

By "the prince," Locke means the executive power (which he assumes will usually be held by a constitutionally limited monarch).

R Here Locke spells out the most important way in which either the legislative or the executive authority may violate the trust placed in them by the people, thereby justifying rebellion: by attempting to assume arbitrary, unlimited power over the people.

223. To this perhaps it will be said, that the people being ignorant, and always discontented, to lay the foundation of government in the unsteady opinion and uncertain humour of the people, is to expose it to certain ruin; and *no government will be able long to subsist,* if the people may set up a new legislative, whenever they take offence at the old one. [30] To this I answer, quite the contrary. People are not so easily got out of their old forms as some are apt to suggest. They are hardly to be prevailed with to amend the acknowledged faults in the frame they have been accustomed to. . . .

30

Here we have in effect the objection that Hobbes would have made to Locke's view: that sanctioning the overthrow of the government by the people whenever they are unhappy with it will make government too unstable to survive very long. Locke's reply is given in this and the immediately following paragraphs.

224. But it will be said, this *hypothesis* lays a *ferment for* frequent *rebellion.* To which I *answer,*

First, No more than any other *hypothesis:* for when the people are made miserable, and find themselves *exposed to the ill usage of arbitrary power,* . . . the same will happen. *The people generally ill treated,* and contrary to right, will be ready upon any occasion to ease themselves of a burden that sits heavy upon them. . . .

225. *Secondly,* I answer, such *revolutions happen* not upon every little mismanagement in public affairs. *Great mistakes* in the ruling part, many wrong and inconvenient laws, and all the slips of human frailty, will be *borne by the people* without mutiny or murmur. But if a long train of abuses, prevarications and artifices, all tending the same way, make the design visible to the people, and they cannot but feel what they lie under, and see whither they are going; it is not to be wondered, that they should then rouse themselves, and endeavour to put the rule into such hands which may secure to them the ends for which government was at first erected. . . .

226. *Thirdly,* I answer, that *this doctrine* of a power in the people of providing for their safety anew, by a new legislative, when their legislators have acted contrary to their trust, by invading their property, is the *best fence against rebellion,* and the probablest means to hinder it. For *rebellion* being an opposition, not to persons, but authority, which is founded only in the constitutions and laws of the government; those, whoever they be, who by force break through, and by force justify their violation of them, are truly and properly *rebels.* . . . [31]

31

Locke makes the rhetorical point that those who attempt to violate the constitution and legitimate restrictions on the powers of the government are the real rebels, not the people who resist such attempts.

227 . . . .for if any one by force takes away the established legislative of any society, and the laws by them made pursuant to their trust, he thereby takes away the umpirage, which every one had consented to, for a peaceable decision of all their controversies, and a bar to the state of war amongst them. They who remove, or change the legislative, take away this decisive power . . . ; and thus by removing the legislative established by the society, (in whose decisions the people acquiesced and united, as to that of their own will) they untie the knot, and *expose the people anew to the state of war.* . . .

240. Here, it is like, the common question will be made, *Who shall be judge,* whether the prince or legislative act contrary to their trust? . . . To this I reply, "The people shall be judge"; for who shall be *judge* whether his trustee or deputy acts well, and according to the trust reposed in him, but he who deputes him, and must by having deputed him, have still a power to discard him, when he fails in his trust? If this be reasonable in particular cases of private men, why should it be otherwise in that of the greatest moment, where the welfare of millions is concerned, and also where the evil, if not prevented, is greater, and the redress very difficult, dear, and dangerous?

...

242. If a controversy arise betwixt a prince and some of the people, in a matter where the law is silent, or doubtful, and the thing be of great consequence, I should think the proper *umpire,* in such a case, should be the body of the *people:* for in cases where the prince hath a trust reposed in him, and is dispensed from the common ordinary rules of the law; there, if any men find themselves aggrieved, and think the prince acts contrary to, or beyond that trust, who so proper to *judge* as the body of the *people,* (who, at first, lodged that trust in him) how far they meant it should extend? [32] But if the prince, or whoever they be in the administration, decline that way of determination, the appeal then lies no where but to heaven; force between either persons, who have no known superior on earth, or which permits no appeal to a judge on earth, being properly a state of war, wherein the appeal lies only to heaven; and in that state the *injured party must judge* for himself, when he will think fit to make use of that appeal, and put himself upon it.

32

Here is a crucial issue: who decides whether the government has violated the trust placed in it in the ways indicated? Locke's answer is that the people are the final judge—where this presumably means a majority of the people.

243. To conclude, The *power that every individual gave the society,* when he entered into it, can never revert to the individuals again, as long

as the society lasts, but will always remain in the community; because without this there can be no community, no commonwealth, which is contrary to the original agreement: so also when the society hath placed the legislative in any assembly of men, to continue in them and their successors, with direction and authority for providing such successors, the *legislative can never revert to the people* whilst that government lasts: Because, having provided a legislative with power to continue for ever, they have given up their political power to the legislative, and cannot resume it. But if they have set limits to the duration of their legislative, and made this supreme power in any person, or assembly, only temporary; or else, when by the miscarriages of those in authority, it is forfeited; upon the forfeiture, or at the determination of the time set, *it reverts to the society,* and the people have a right to act as supreme, and continue the legislative in themselves; or erect a new form, or under the old form place it in new hands, as they think good. (33)

(33) R Locke says explicitly that the dissolution of the government does not mean the dissolution of the community, but instead means that the people have the right to form a new government or to act as the government (that is, the legislative authority) themselves, if they so choose.

Discussion Questions

1. Hobbes argued that the sovereign was not and could not be a party to the social contract and hence could not violate it. Explain how Locke answers Hobbes's argument on this point by in effect having two stages involved in the social contract: the first where the community is formed and the second where the actual government (mainly the legislative authority) is constituted.
2. Locke's conception of the state of nature is very different from that presented by Hobbes. Explain the main differences and consider what these reveal about their contrasting views of essential human psychology. What reasons might each of them have offered in opposition to the other? Who do you think is right (or at least closer to the truth)?
3. Do you think that the sort of situation in which a social contract was explicitly agreed to, as described by either Hobbes or Locke, ever actually occurred in human history? If so, when? If not, does this mean that their accounts have no real relevance to the issue of whether the governments that actually exist in the world have legitimate authority?
4. If the law of nature (as described by Locke) does genuinely exist, then we are all obliged to preserve as much as we can, so that someone who recklessly destroys property and life would be in violation of the natural law. Do you think that a law of nature of this general sort genuinely exists? Does the answer to this question depend essentially on whether there is a God, or might such a moral law exist even if it were not created by the commands of a deity?
5. Locke in effect offers two different criteria for when a government can be legitimately overthrown by the people: (a) an objective criterion (when it fails to carry out the purposes for which it was instituted or exceeds its legitimate powers, one case of which is transferring the legislative power illegitimately); and (b) a subjective criterion (when it loses the confidence of the people because they judge, rightly or wrongly, that it has done one or more of these things). Consider which of these two criteria is primary by considering what is the right result when they diverge: when (a) is satisfied but (b) is not, or when (b) is satisfied but (a) is not.

David Hume

One of the more trenchant criticisms of Locke's appeal to the idea of a social contract, and of social contract theories generally, was produced about 60 years later (1748) by his fellow "British empiricist" David Hume (1711–1776). (See the article by Hume in Chapter 2 of this book for more about him.) Hume recognizes the appeal of the idea that the legitimacy of government must rest on the sort of consent that would be involved in a social contract, and he does not deny either (a) that something like consent (or at least acquiescence) must have been the original basis for government in the very distant past or (b) that the actual consent of the people, if it were genuinely obtained, would be a just foundation for government. But he denies that the legitimacy of the governments that in fact exist in the world, in his time or ours, can reasonably be viewed as resting to any significant degree on actual consent. Hume also considers and rejects the idea that *tacit consent,* consent manifested by such things as voluntarily remaining in the country in question, can provide an acceptable substitute for an actual, explicit agreement. (One possible response to these criticisms would be to insist that governments whose authority does not rest on consent have no legitimate authority at all; Hume does not explicitly mention such a view, but would surely have regarded it as too absurd to be taken seriously.)

Hume also offers a "more philosophical" refutation of the appeal to a social contract or to popular consent, by asking what the basis for the supposed obligations to keep contracts or adhere to promises might be. His claim is that the only basis for such obligations is their *utility* to society. But the duty of allegiance to reasonably satisfactory governments can also be based directly on social utility, making the detour through the ideas of a social contract or of popular consent unnecessary. (His view is thus a version of utilitarianism, similar to Bentham's and Mill's (see Chapter 5), and subject to many of the same objections.)

Of the Original Contract

As no party, in the present age, can well support itself, without a philosophical or speculative system of principles, annexed to its political or practical one; we accordingly find, that each of the factions, into which this nation is divided, has reared up a fabric of the former kind, in order to protect and cover that scheme of actions, which it pursues.

The people being commonly very rude builders, especially in this speculative way, and more especially still, when actuated by party-zeal; it is natural to imagine, that their workmanship must be a little unshapely, and discover evident marks of that violence and hurry, in which it was raised. The one party, by tracing up government to the Deity, endeavour to render it so sacred and inviolate, that it must be little less than sacrilege, however tyrannical it may become, to touch or invade it, in the smallest article. The other party, by founding government altogether on the consent of the People, suppose that there is a kind of *original contract,* by which the subjects have tacitly reserved the power of resisting their sovereign, whenever they find themselves aggrieved by that authority, with which they have, for certain purposes, voluntarily entrusted him. These are the speculative principles of the two parties; and these too are the practical consequences deduced from them. (1)

1 Hume here summarizes the two views concerning the justification of government that were current in Great Britain in the mid-1700s: the Lockean appeal to a revocable social contract and the older idea of divine right (usually restricted to monarchical governments).

I shall venture to affirm, *That both these systems of speculative principles are just; though not in the sense, intended by the parties:* And, *That both the* schemes *of practical consequences are prudent; though not in the extremes, to which each party, in opposition to the other, has commonly endeavoured to carry them.*

That the Deity is the ultimate author of all government will never be denied by any, who admit a general providence, and allow, that all events in the universe are conducted by an uniform plan, and directed to wise purposes. As it is impossible for the human race to subsist, at least in any comfortable or secure state, without the protection of government; this institution must certainly have been intended by that beneficent Being, who means the good of all his creatures: And as it has universally, in fact, taken place, in all countries, and all ages; we may conclude, with still greater certainty, that it was intended by that omniscient Being, who can never be deceived by any event or operation. But since he gave rise to it, not by any particular or miraculous interposition, but by his concealed and universal efficacy; a sovereign cannot, properly speaking, be called his vice-regent, in any other sense than every power or force, being derived from him, may be said to act by his commission. Whatever actually happens is comprehended in the general plan or intention of providence; nor has the greatest and most lawful prince any more reason, upon that account, to plead a peculiar sacredness or inviolable authority, than an inferior magistrate, or even an usurper, or even a robber and a pyrate. . . . (2)

2

Though he is elsewhere skeptical about such claims, Hume here concedes the existence of God and thus the apparent divine sanction for human governments, though giving this claim the ironic twist that governments or leaders of any sort have an equal claim to divine sanction.

From *Of the Original Contract* (1748).

When we consider how nearly equal all men are in their bodily force, and even in their mental powers and faculties, till cultivated by education; we must necessarily allow, that nothing but their own consent could, at first, associate them together, and subject them to any authority. The people, if we trace government to its first origin in the woods and deserts, are the source of all power and jurisdiction, and voluntarily, for the sake of peace and order, abandoned their native liberty, and received laws from their equal and companion. The conditions, upon which they were willing to submit, were either expressed, or were so clear and obvious, that it might well be esteemed superfluous to express them. If this, then, be meant by the *original contract,* it cannot be denied, that all government is, at first, founded on a contract, and that the most ancient rude combinations of mankind were formed chiefly by that principle. In vain, are we asked in what records this charter of our liberties is registered. It was not written on parchment, nor yet on leaves or barks of trees. It preceded the use of writing and all the other civilized arts of life. . . . [3]

Yet even this consent was long very imperfect, and could not be the basis of a regular administration. The chieftain, who had probably acquired his influence during the continuance of war, ruled more by persuasion than command; and till he could employ force to reduce the refractory and disobedient, the society could scarcely be said to have attained a state of civil government. No compact or agreement, it is evident, was expressly formed for general submission; an idea far beyond the comprehension of savages: Each exertion of authority in the chieftain must have been particular, and called forth by the present exigencies of the case: The sensible utility, resulting from his interposition, made these exertions become daily more frequent; and their frequency gradually produced an habitual, and, if you please to call it so, a voluntary, and therefore precarious, acquiescence in the people. [4]

But philosophers, who have embraced a party (if that be not a contradiction in terms) are not contented with these concessions. They assert, not only that government in its earliest infancy arose from consent or rather the voluntary acquiescence [5] of the people; but also, that, even at present, when it has attained full maturity, it rests on no other foundation. They affirm, that all men are still born equal, and owe allegiance to no prince or government, unless bound by the obligation and sanction of a *promise.* And as no man, without some equivalent, would forego the advantages of his native liberty, and subject himself to the will of another; this promise is always understood to be conditional, and imposes on him no obligation, unless he meet with justice and protection from his sovereign. These advantages the sovereign promises him in return; and if he fail in the execution, he has broken, on his part, the articles of engagement, and has thereby freed his subject from all obligations to allegiance. Such, according to these philosophers, is the foundation of authority in every government; and such the right of resistance, possessed by every subject. [6]

But would these reasoners look abroad into the world, they would meet with nothing that, in the least, corresponds to their ideas, or can warrant so refined and philosophical a system. On the contrary, we find, every where, princes, who claim their subjects as their property, and assert their independent right of sovereignty, from conquest or succession. We find also, every where, subjects, who acknowledge this right in their prince, and suppose themselves born under obligations of obedience to a certain sovereign, as much as under the ties of reverence and duty to certain parents. These connexions are always conceived to be equally independent of our consent . . . , wherever the doctrines above-mentioned have not been carefully inculcated. Obedience or subjection becomes so familiar, that most men never make any enquiry about its origin or cause, more than about the principle of gravity . . . , or the most universal laws of nature. Or if curiosity ever move them; as soon as they learn, that they themselves and their ancestors have, for several ages, or from time immemorial, been subject to such a form of government or such a family; they immediately acquiesce, and acknowledge their obligation to allegiance. Were you to preach, in most parts of the world, that political connexions are founded altogether on voluntary consent or a mutual promise, the magistrate would soon imprison you, as seditious, for loosening the ties of obedience; if your friends did not before shut you up as delirious, for advancing such absurdities. It is strange, that an act of the mind, which every individual is supposed to have formed, and

R Hume concedes that some sort of consent or agreement must have been involved when government first originated, but points out at once that there is no record of any sort of the terms of such an agreement.

R Nor, he argues, is there any reason to think that such an original act of consent involved anything like an explicit and detailed contract, as opposed to piecemeal and ad hoc accretions of authority.

Take careful note of the two very different terms Hume employs here: actual "consent" and mere "voluntary acquiescence" are very different things, with the latter being much less clearly a basis for legitimate authority than the former.

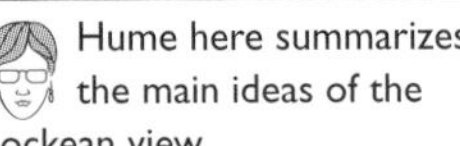

Hume here summarizes the main ideas of the Lockean view.

after he came to the use of reason too, otherwise it could have no authority; that this act, I say, should be so much unknown to all of them, that, over the face of the whole earth, there scarcely remain any traces or memory of it. (7)

> **7** One problem is that the idea of such a contract is recognized and accepted almost nowhere else in the world. How then, Hume asks, can it be the basis for the actual authority of governments?

But the contract, on which government is founded, is said to be the *original contract;* and consequently may be supposed too old to fall under the knowledge of the present generation. If the agreement, by which savage men first associated and conjoined their force, be here meant, this is acknowledged to be real; but being so ancient, and being obliterated by a thousand changes of government and princes, it cannot now be supposed to retain any authority. If we would say any thing to the purpose, we must assert, that every particular government, which is lawful, and which imposes any duty of allegiance on the subject, was, at first, founded on consent and a voluntary compact. But besides that this supposes the consent of the fathers to bind the children, even to the most remote generations, (which republican writers will never allow) besides this, I say, it is not justified by history or experience, in any age or country of the world. (8)

> **8** It will not work to say that the relevant contract is the supposed original one, now forgotten. For why would it retain its authority after so long a time and so many changes? And (a serious problem for any social contract view), why would such a contract continue to bind people after those who actually agreed to it are dead and gone?

Almost all the governments, which exist at present, or of which there remains any record in story, have been founded originally, either on usurpation or conquest, or both, without any presence of a fair consent, or voluntary subjection of the people. When an artful and bold man is placed at the head of an army or faction, it is often easy for him, by employing, sometimes violence, sometimes false pretences, to establish his dominion over a people a hundred times more numerous than his partizans. . . .

The face of the earth is continually changing, by the encrease of small kingdoms into great empires, by the dissolution of great empires into smaller kingdoms, by the planting of colonies, by the migration of tribes. Is there any thing discoverable in all these events, but force and violence? Where is the mutual agreement or voluntary association so much talked of? (9)

> **9** Actual governments are almost all founded originally on "usurpation or conquest," making it unclear how a contract can be supposed to play any role.

. . .

Let not the establishment at the *Revolution* deceive us, or make us so much in love with a philosophical origin to government, as to imagine all others monstrous and irregular. Even that event was far from corresponding to these refined ideas. It was only the succession, and that only in the regal part of the government, which was then changed: And it was only the majority of seven hundred, who determined that change for near ten millions. I doubt not, indeed, but the bulk of those ten millions acquiesced willingly in the determination: But was the matter left, in the least, to their choice? Was it not justly supposed to be, from that moment, decided, and every man punished, who refused to submit to the new sovereign? How otherwise could the matter have ever been brought to any issue or conclusion? (10)

> **10** Indeed, Hume argues, even the government established by the "Glorious Revolution" in Great Britain was founded on force or the threat of force—contrary to the view held by many (apparently including Locke) that it was a clear case of a social contract. The vast majority of the people may have *acquiesced* to the governmental change, but they had no real choice as to whether to consent or not.

. . .

My intention here is not to exclude the consent of the people from being one just foundation of government where it has place. It is surely the best and most sacred of any. I only pretend, that it has very seldom had place in any degree, and never almost in its full extent. And that therefore some other foundation of government must also be admitted. (11)

> **11** Some other foundation must be admitted *if,* as Hume is assuming, it is not reasonable to say that virtually all governments are illegitimate.

. . .

When a new government is established, by whatever means, the people are commonly dissatisfied with it, and pay obedience more from fear and necessity, than from any idea of allegiance or of moral obligation. The prince is watchful and jealous, and must carefully guard against every beginning or appearance of insurrection. Time, by degrees, removes all these difficulties, and accustoms the nation to regard, as their lawful or native princes, that family, which, at first, they considered as usurpers or foreign conquerors. In order to found this opinion, they have no recourse to any notion of voluntary consent or promise, which, they know, never was, in this case, either expected or demanded. The original establishment was formed by violence, and submitted to from necessity. The subsequent administration is also supported by power, and acquiesced in by the people, not as a matter of choice, but of obligation. They imagine not, that their consent gives their prince a title: But they willingly consent, because they think, that, from long possession, he has acquired a title, independent of their choice or inclination.

Should it be said, that, by living under the dominion of a prince, which one might leave, every individual has given a *tacit* consent to his authority, and promised him obedience; it may be answered, that such an implied consent can only have place, where a man imagines, that the matter depends on his choice. But where he thinks (as all mankind do who are born under established governments) that by his birth he owes allegiance to a certain prince or certain form of government; it would be absurd to infer a consent or choice, which he expressly, in this case, renounces and disclaims. [12]

Can we seriously say, that a poor peasant or artizan has a free choice to leave his country, when he knows no foreign language or manners, and lives from day to day, by the small wages which he acquires? We may as well assert, that a man, by remaining in a vessel, freely consents to the dominion of the master; though he was carried on board while asleep, and must leap into the ocean, and perish, the moment he leaves her.

...

The truest *tacit* consent of this kind, that is ever observed, is when a foreigner settles in any country, and is beforehand acquainted with the prince, and government, and laws, to which he must submit: Yet is his allegiance, though more voluntary, much less expected or depended on, than that of a natural born subject. On the contrary, his native prince still asserts a claim to him. And if he punish not the renegade, when he seizes him in war with his new prince's commission; this clemency is not founded on the municipal law, which in all countries condemns the prisoner; but on the consent of princes, who have agreed to this indulgence, in order to prevent reprisals. [13]

...

Suppose, that an usurper, after having banished his lawful prince and royal family, should establish his dominion for ten or a dozen years in any country, and should preserve so exact a discipline in his troops, and so regular a disposition in his garrisons, that no insurrection had ever been raised, or even murmur heard, against his administration: Can it be asserted, that the people, who in their hearts abhor his treason, have tacitly consented to his authority, and promised him allegiance, merely because, from necessity, they live under his dominion? Suppose again their native prince restored, by means of an army, which he levies in foreign countries: They receive him with joy and exultation, and shew plainly with what reluctance they had submitted to any other yoke. I may now ask, upon what foundation the prince's title stands? Not on popular consent surely: For though the people willingly acquiesce in his authority, they never imagine, that their consent made him sovereign. They consent; because they apprehend him to be already, by birth, their lawful sovereign. And as to that tacit consent, which may now be inferred from their living under his dominion, this is no more than what they formerly gave to the tyrant and usurper. [14]

...

But would we have a more regular, at least a more philosophical, refutation of this principle of an original contract or popular consent; perhaps, the following observations may suffice.

All *moral* duties may be divided into two kinds. The *first* are those, to which men are impelled by a natural instinct or immediate propensity, which operates on them, independent of all ideas of obligation, and of all views, either to public or private utility. Of this nature are, love of children, gratitude to benefactors, pity to the unfortunate. When we reflect on the advantage, which results to society from such humane instincts, we pay them the just tribute of moral approbation and esteem: But the person, actuated by them, feels their power and influence, antecedent to any such reflection.

The *second* kind of moral duties are such as are not supported by any original instinct of nature, but are performed entirely from a sense of obligation, when we consider the necessities of human society, and the impossibility of supporting it, if these duties were neglected. It is thus *justice* or a regard to the property of others, *fidelity* or the observance of promises, become obligatory, and acquire an authority over mankind. For as it is evident, that every man loves himself better than any other person, he is naturally impelled to extend his acquisitions as much as possible; and nothing can restrain him in this propensity, but reflection and experience, by which he learns the pernicious effects of that

Social contract theorists have often appealed to the idea of *tacit consent:* the idea that people, by remaining in a particular country (and accepting the resulting benefits) rather than going elsewhere, have thereby tacitly or implicitly consented to the authority of the existing government. One problem with this is that people who do not realize that they have any choice cannot reasonably be said to have consented. Another, in the following paragraph, is that emigrating to another country is not a reasonable option for most people.

Hume also points out that the clearest case of tacit consent would be that of a person who deliberately comes to a country and settles there. But in fact, no one thinks that such a person has a *stronger* duty of allegiance than a native citizen.

R The idea of tacit consent fails to discriminate among various governments that might be thought to differ in legitimacy: as long as they are all firmly in power, they will receive the same degree of tacit consent—or rather acquiescence.

licence, and the total dissolution of society which must ensue from it. His original inclination, therefore, or instinct, is here checked and restrained by a subsequent judgment or observation.

The case is precisely the same with the political or civil duty of *allegiance* as with the natural duties of justice and fidelity. Our primary instincts lead us, either to indulge ourselves in unlimited freedom, or to seek dominion over others: And it is reflection only which engages us to sacrifice such strong passions to the interests of peace and public order. A small degree of experience and observation suffices to teach us, that society cannot possibly be maintained without the authority of magistrates, and that this authority must soon fall into contempt, where exact obedience is not payed to it. The observation of these general and obvious interests is the source of all allegiance, and of that moral obligation, which we attribute to it.

What necessity, therefore, is there to found the duty of *allegiance* or obedience to magistrates on that of *fidelity* or a regard to promises, and to suppose, that it is the consent of each individual, which subjects him to government; when it appears, that both allegiance and fidelity stand precisely on the same foundation, and are both submitted to by mankind, on account of the apparent interests and necessities of human society? We are bound to obey our sovereign, it is said; because we have given a tacit promise to that purpose. But why are we bound to observe our promise? . . . The obligation to allegiance being of like force and authority with the obligation to fidelity, we gain nothing by resolving the one into the other. The general interests or necessities of society are sufficient to establish both. [15]

15

R Hume now raises the background issue of the basis for the duty to adhere to contracts or agreements or promises. His claim is that it is not grounded in natural human instincts, but rather in perceived utility to society. But a duty to obey a solidly established, reasonably satisfactory government could be arrived at on the same basis of social utility, making the appeal to a social contract needlessly indirect (in addition to all its other problems).

If the reason be asked of that obedience, which we are bound to pay to government, I readily answer, *because society could not otherwise subsist:* And this answer is clear and intelligible to all mankind. Your answer is, *because we should keep our word.* But besides, that no body, till trained in a philosophical system, can either comprehend or relish this answer: Besides this, I say, you find yourself embarrassed, when it is asked, *why we are bound to keep our word?* Nor can you give any answer, but what would, immediately, without any circuit, have accounted for our obligation to allegiance.

...

The general obligation, which binds us to government, is the interest and necessities of society; and this obligation is very strong. The determination of it to this or that particular prince or form of government is frequently more uncertain and dubious. Present possession has considerable authority in these cases, and greater than in private property; because of the disorders which attend all revolutions and changes of government.

We shall only observe, before we conclude, that, though an appeal to general opinion may justly, in the speculative sciences of metaphysics, natural philosophy, or astronomy, be deemed unfair and inconclusive, yet in all questions with regard to morals, as well as criticism, there is really no other standard, by which any controversy can ever be decided. And nothing is a clearer proof, that a theory of this kind is erroneous, than to find, that it leads to paradoxes, repugnant to the common sentiments of mankind, and to the practice and opinion of all nations and all ages. The doctrine, which founds all lawful government on an *original contract,* or consent of the people, is plainly of this kind; nor has the most noted of its partizans, in prosecution of it, scrupled to affirm, *that absolute monarchy is inconsistent with civil society, and so can be no form of civil government at all; and that the supreme power in a state cannot take from any man, by taxes and impositions, any part of his property, without his own consent or that of his representatives.* What authority any moral reasoning can have, which leads into opinions so wide of the general practice of mankind, in every place but this single kingdom, it is easy to determine. [16]

R Hume argues that the implications of the social contract view are too out of keeping with "the common sentiments of mankind" and with prevailing practice to have any real plausibility.

...

New discoveries are not to be expected in these matters. If scarce any man, till very lately, ever imagined that government was founded on compact, it is certain, that it cannot, in general, have any such foundation.

...

Discussion Questions

1. Is Hume right (in his implicit suggestion) that the view that almost all actual governments fail to possess legitimate authority is too absurd to be taken seriously? Might it be that actual consent is the only legitimate basis for governmental authority, even if it has seldom (or ever?) been completely realized?
2. In Plato's dialogue *Crito,* Socrates argues that by remaining in Athens and accepting the numerous benefits of Athenian citizenship, he has incurred an obligation to obey the laws of Athens and accept the verdict of the Athenian authorities—even when they sentence him to death. This amounts to an appeal to the idea of tacit consent. How compelling are Hume's objections to this idea? Consider in particular how much it matters whether or not Socrates was explicitly aware of the choice as to whether to stay in Athens or leave.
3. Hume is surely right that few if any of the governments that were actually in power in his time had been created by a social contract, as opposed to arising in various ways by force and coercion. Is the same thing true today? For example, did the ratification of the United States Constitution (in 1787–1790) constitute something approaching a social contract? Might the establishment of a new government in Iraq or some similar case, if done successfully and with widespread popular participation, constitute such a contract?
4. Is Hume right that social utility provides the only basis for a duty to adhere to contracts or agreements or to keep promises? Does the fact that some institution or pattern of behavior can be justified on the basis of social utility create as strong an obligation to support it as would an explicit contract or promise? Why or why not? (Think of examples here.)

What Is Social Justice?

Robert Nozick

Robert Nozick (1938–2002), for many years a professor at Harvard, was a major figure in twentieth-century philosophy, making contributions to many areas but most importantly to political philosophy and epistemology. Nozick is perhaps most famous for his engaging style and his knack for devising striking and intuitively compelling examples, one of them being the Wilt Chamberlain example that appears in this selection.

In *Anarchy, State, and Utopia,* Nozick develops a broadly *libertarian* political philosophy: one that emphasizes the value of human liberty and voluntary choice, is suspicious of governmental power, and demands a clear justification for governmental actions that restrict such liberty. Nozick's total view also includes an account of the justification of government in relation to the state of nature, in the tradition of Hobbes and Locke. The present selection offers an abstract outline of an account of distributive justice, together with forceful criticisms of opposing accounts. Nozick calls his account of justice "the entitlement theory." Its central idea is that the justice or injustice of a distribution of property or other goods among the members of a society depends entirely on the justice of the specific transactions through which that distribution was produced, including both acquisitions of previously unowned things and transfers of owned things from one person to another. This means, he argues, that there is no structurally specified *pattern* of distribution that is required by justice—whether simple equality or something more complicated (such as that required by the view of John Rawls—see the following selection). From Nozick's standpoint, views that insist on such a pattern are objectionable both (a) because they must interfere massively and continuously in people's lives in order to maintain the pattern and (b) because much of this interference amounts to a denial that even those who have received an allotment of money or goods according to the chosen pattern are free to do with them what they choose (since doing so is very likely to upset the pattern).

The Entitlement Theory of Justice, from *Anarchy, State, and Utopia*

1

R Nozick objects that the usual understanding of the issue of distributive justice and the term itself involves a highly questionable assumption: that people's holdings of various sorts are the result of a central process of distribution by a central authority, which is thus assumed to have legitimate control over what is distributed.

STOP (Can you think of a situation, perhaps a more limited one, in which such an assumption would be legitimate?)

Justice in acquisition has to do with how previously unheld (that is, unowned) things can come to be legitimately held.

STOP Genuinely unheld things are relatively rare in the modern world. Try to think of some examples of things to which Nozick's principle might apply.

Obviously Nozick has not even begun to say what the details of such principles might look like. He is describing only the general structure of such a theory of justice.

R Thus the justice of a distribution of holdings depends only on the justice of the transitions via which it was arrived at, according to the two (unstated) principles of justice in acquisition and transfer. A distribution of holdings (property) could thereby be just even if the shares of different people or different groups of people were very unequal.

. . .The term "distributive justice" is not a neutral one. Hearing the term "distribution," most people presume that some thing or mechanism uses some principle or criterion to give out a supply of things. Into this process of distributing shares some error may have crept. So it is an open question, at least, whether redistribution should take place; whether we should do again what has already been done once, though poorly. However, we are not in the position of children who have been given portions of pie by someone who now makes last minute adjustments to rectify careless cutting. There is no *central* distribution, no person or group entitled to control all the resources, jointly deciding how they are to be doled out. What each person gets, he gets from others who give to him in exchange for something, or as a gift. In a free society, diverse persons control different resources, and new holdings arise out of the voluntary exchanges and actions of persons. There is no more a distributing or distribution of shares than there is a distributing of mates in a society in which persons choose whom they shall marry. The total result is the product of many individual decisions which the different individuals involved are entitled to make. . . . **1** We shall speak of people's holdings; a principle of justice in holdings describes (part of) what justice tells us (requires) about holdings. . . .

The Entitlement Theory

The subject of justice in holdings consists of three major topics. The first is the *original acquisition of holdings,* the appropriation of unheld things. This includes the issues of how unheld things may come to be held, the process, or processes, by which unheld things may come to be held, the things that may come to be held by these processes, the extent of what comes to be held by a particular process, and so on. We shall refer to the complicated truth about this topic, which we shall not formulate here, as the principle of justice in acquisition. **2** The second topic concerns the *transfer of holdings* from one person to another. By what processes may a person transfer holdings to another? How may a person acquire a holding from another who holds it? Under this topic come general descriptions of voluntary exchange, and gift and (on the other hand) fraud, as well as reference to particular conventional details fixed upon in a given society. The complicated truth about this subject . . . we shall call the principle of justice in transfer. (And we shall suppose it also includes principles governing how a person may divest himself of a holding, passing it into an unheld state.)

If the world were wholly just, the following . . . definition would exhaustively cover the subject of justice in holdings.

1. A person who acquires a holding in accordance with the principle of justice in acquisition is entitled to that holding.
2. A person who acquires a holding in accordance with the principle of justice in transfer, from someone else entitled to the holding, is entitled to the holding.
3. No one is entitled to the holding except by (repeated) applications of 1 and 2.

The complete principle of distributive justice would say simply that a distribution is just if everyone is entitled to the holdings they possess under the distribution. **3**

A distribution is just if it arises from another just distribution by legitimate means. The legitimate means of moving from one distribution to another are specified by the principle of justice in transfer. The legitimate first "moves" are specified by the principle of justice in acquisition. Whatever arises from a just situation by just steps is itself just. The means of change specified by the principle of justice in transfer preserve justice. . . . **4** That from a just situation a situation *could* have arisen via justice-preserving means does *not* suffice to show its justice. The fact that a thief's victims voluntarily *could* have presented him with gifts does not entitle the thief to his ill-gotten gains. Justice in

From *Anarchy, State, and Utopia* (New York: Basic Books, 1974).

holdings is historical; it depends upon what actually has happened. We shall return to this point later.

Not all actual situations are generated in accordance with the two principles of justice in holdings: the principle of justice in acquisition and the principle of justice in transfer. Some people steal from others, or defraud them, or enslave them, seizing their product and preventing them from living as they choose, or forcibly exclude others from competing in exchanges. None of these are permissible modes of transition from one situation to another. And some persons acquire holdings by means not sanctioned by the principle of justice in acquisition. The existence of past injustice (previous violations of the first two principles of justice in holdings) raises the third major topic under justice in holdings: the rectification of injustice in holdings. If past injustice has shaped present holdings in various ways, some identifiable and some not, what now, if anything, ought to be done to rectify these injustices? What obligations do the performers of injustice have toward those whose position is worse than it would have been had the injustice not been done? Or, than it would have been had compensation been paid promptly? How, if at all, do things change if the beneficiaries and those made worse off are not the direct parties in the act of injustice, but, for example, their descendants? Is an injustice done to someone whose holding was itself based upon an unrectified injustice? How far back must one go in wiping clean the historical slate of injustices? What may victims of injustice permissibly do in order to rectify the injustices being done to them, including the many injustices done by persons acting through their government? (5) I do not know of a thorough or theoretically sophisticated treatment of such issues. Idealizing greatly, let us suppose theoretical investigation will produce a principle of rectification. This principle uses historical information about previous situations and injustices done in them (as defined by the first two principles of justice and rights against interference), and information about the actual course of events that flowed from these injustices, until the present, and it yields a description (or descriptions) of holdings in the society. The principle of rectification presumably will make use of its best estimate of subjunctive information about what would have occurred (or a probability distribution over what might have occurred, using the expected value) if the injustice had not taken place. If the actual description of holdings turns out not to be one of the descriptions yielded by the principle, then one of the descriptions yielded must be realized.

The general outlines of the theory of justice in holdings are that the holdings of a person are just if he is entitled to them by the principles of justice in acquisition and transfer, or by the principle of rectification of injustice (as specified by the first two principles). If each person's holdings are just, then the total set (distribution) of holdings is just. (6) To turn these general outlines into a specific theory we would have to specify the details of each of the three principles of justice in holdings: the principle of acquisition of holdings, the principle of transfer of holdings, and the principle of rectification of violations of the first two principles. I shall not attempt that task here. . . .

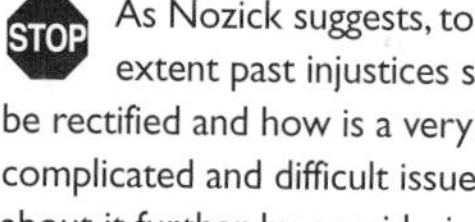

As Nozick suggests, to what extent past injustices should be rectified and how is a very complicated and difficult issue. Think about it further by considering some actual cases of past injustice and asking what, if anything, can and should be done now to rectify them.

Thus the justice of a set of holdings does not depend at all, according to Nozick's view, on any considerations beyond these principles (such as the structure or pattern of the resulting distribution).

Historical Principles and End-Result Principles

The general outlines of the entitlement theory illuminate the nature and defects of other conceptions of distributive justice. The entitlement theory of justice in distribution is *historical;* whether a distribution is just depends upon how it came about. In contrast, *current time-slice principles* of justice hold that the justice of a distribution is determined by how things are distributed (who has what) as judged by some *structural* principle(s) of just distribution. A utilitarian who judges between any two distributions by seeing which has the greater sum of utility and, if the sums tie, applies some fixed equality criterion to choose the more equal distribution, would hold a current time-slice principle of justice. As would someone who had a fixed schedule of trade-offs between the sum of happiness and equality. According to a current time-slice principle, all that needs to be looked at, in judging the justice of a distribution, is who ends up with what. . . .

Most persons do not accept current time-slice principles as constituting the whole story about distributive shares. They think it relevant in assessing the justice of a situation to consider not only the distribution it embodies, but also how that distribution came about. If some persons are in prison for murder or war crimes, we do not say that to assess the justice of the distribution in the society we must look only at what this person has, and that person has, and that person has, . . . at the current time. We think it relevant to ask whether someone did something so that he *deserved* to be punished, deserved to have a lower share. Most will agree to the relevance of further information with regard to punishments and penalties. . . .

We construe the position we discuss too narrowly by speaking of *current* time-slice principles. Nothing is changed if structural principles operate upon a time sequence of current time-slice profiles and, for example, give someone more now to counterbalance the less he has had earlier. . . . Henceforth, we shall refer to such unhistorical principles of distributive justice, including the current time-slice principles, as *end-result principles* or *end-state principles.* [7]

In contrast to end-result principles of justice, *historical principles* of justice hold that past circumstances or actions of people can create differential entitlements or differential deserts to things. . . .

Patterning

The entitlement principles of justice in holdings that we have sketched are historical principles of justice. To better understand their precise character, we shall distinguish them from another subclass of the historical principles. Consider, as an example, the principle of distribution according to moral merit. This principle requires that total distributive shares vary directly with moral merit; no person should have a greater share than anyone whose moral merit is greater. . . . Or consider the principle that results by substituting "usefulness to society" for "moral merit" in the previous principle. . . . Let us call a principle of distribution *patterned* if it specifies that a distribution is to vary along with some natural dimension, weighted sum of natural dimensions, or . . . ordering of natural dimensions. [8] And let us say a distribution is patterned if it accords with some patterned principle. . . .

Almost every suggested principle of distributive justice is patterned: to each according to his moral merit, or needs, or marginal product, or how hard he tries, or the weighted sum of the foregoing, and so on. The principle of entitlement we have sketched is *not* patterned. There is no one natural dimension or weighted sum or combination of a small number of natural dimensions that yields the distributions generated in accordance with the principle of entitlement. The set of holdings that results when some persons receive their marginal products, others win at gambling, others receive a share of their mate's income, others receive gifts from foundations, others receive interest on loans, others receive gifts from admirers, others receive returns on investment, others make for themselves much of what they have, others find things, and so on, will not be patterned. . . .

To think that the task of a theory of distributive justice is to fill in the blank in "to each according to his ___" is to be predisposed to search for a pattern; and the separate treatment of "from each according to his ___" treats production and distribution as two separate and independent issues. On an entitlement view these are *not* two separate questions. Whoever makes something, having bought or contracted for all other held resources used in the process (transferring some of his holdings for these cooperating factors), is entitled to it. The situation is *not* one of something's getting made, and there being an open question of who is to get it. Things come into the world already attached to people having entitlements over them. From the point of view of the historical entitlement conception of justice in holdings, those who start afresh to complete "to each according to his ___" treat objects as if they appeared from nowhere, out of nothing. . . . [9]

How Liberty Upsets Patterns

It is not clear how those holding alternative conceptions of distributive justice can reject the entitlement conception of justice in holdings. For suppose a distribution favored by one of these non-entitlement conceptions is realized. Let us suppose it is your favorite one and let us call this distribution D_1 [10]; perhaps everyone has an equal share, perhaps shares vary in accordance with some dimension you treasure. Now suppose that Wilt Chamberlain [11] is greatly in demand by basketball teams, being a great gate attraction. (Also suppose contracts run only for a year, with players being free agents.) He signs the following sort of contract with a team: In each home game, twenty-five cents from the price of each ticket of

Strict egalitarianism (the view that each person should have an equal share of holdings) is the most obvious example of such an "end-state principle" of justice.

STOP Think of other examples of patterned principles of justice. (Don't limit yourself to ones that you find plausible.)

It is fairly natural to expand the category of patterned principles to include end-state principles as well, since these also involve a pattern, though not a historical one. Nozick sometimes seems to do this.

R Here is one objection to patterned views, related to the point discussed in Annotation 1: from the standpoint of the entitlement theory, such views ignore the fact that most things are produced in ways that give specific people claims of ownership over them, claims that may well conflict with any chosen pattern.

By "your favorite one," Nozick really just means whatever one the proponent of a patterned view thinks is correct.

Wilt Chamberlain was a famous basketball player of the 1960s and 1970s, one of the most dominant offensive players ever. The details of his career are worth looking up, for those who care about such things. But for current students, Michael Jordan or Shaquille O'Neill might be better examples.

admission goes to him. . . . The season starts, and people cheerfully attend his team's games; they buy their tickets, each time dropping a separate twenty-five cents of their admission price into a special box with Chamberlain's name on it. They are excited about seeing him play; it is worth the total admission price to them. Let us suppose that in one season one million persons attend his home games, and Wilt Chamberlain winds up with $250,000, a much larger sum than the average income and larger even than anyone else has. Is he entitled to this income? Is this new distribution D_2, unjust? If so, why? There is *no* question about whether each of the people was entitled to the control over the resources they held in D_1; because that was the distribution . . . that (for the purposes of argument) we assumed was acceptable. Each of these persons *chose* to give twenty-five cents of their money to Chamberlain. They could have spent it on going to the movies, or on candy bars, or on copies of *Dissent* magazine, or of *Monthly Review.* But they all, at least one million of them, converged on giving it to Wilt Chamberlain in exchange for watching him play basketball. If D_1 was a just distribution, and people voluntarily moved from it to D_2, transferring parts of their shares they were given under D_1 (what was it for if not to do something with?), isn't D_2 also just? (12) If the people were entitled to dispose of the resources to which they were entitled (under D_1), didn't this include their being entitled to give it to, or exchange it with, Wilt Chamberlain? Can anyone else complain on grounds of justice? Each other person already has his legitimate share under D_1. Under D_1, there is nothing that anyone has that anyone else has a claim of justice against. After someone transfers something to Wilt Chamberlain, third parties *still* have their legitimate shares; *their* shares are not changed. . . .

. . . Notice also that small factories would spring up in a socialist society, unless forbidden. I melt down some of my personal possessions (under D_1) and build a machine out of the material. I offer you, and others, a philosophy lecture once a week in exchange for your cranking the handle on my machine, whose products I exchange for yet other things, and so on. (The raw materials used by the machine are given to me by others who possess them under D_1, in exchange for hearing lectures.) Each person might participate to gain things over and above their allotment under D_1. Some persons even might want to leave their job in socialist industry and work full time in this private sector. . . . [Thus] private property even in means of production would occur in a socialist society that did not forbid people to use as they wished some of the resources they are given under the socialist distribution D_1. The socialist society would have to forbid capitalist acts between consenting adults.

The general point illustrated by the Wilt Chamberlain example and the example of the entrepreneur in a socialist society is that no end-state principle or distributional patterned principle of justice can be continuously realized without continuous interference with people's lives. Any favored pattern would be transformed into one unfavored by the principle, by people choosing to act in various ways; for example, by people exchanging goods and services with other people, or giving things to other people, things the transferrers are entitled to under the favored distributional pattern. To maintain a pattern one must either continually interfere to stop people from transferring resources as they wish to, or continually (or periodically) interfere to take from some persons resources that others for some reason chose to transfer to them. . . . (13)

Redistribution and Property Rights

Apparently, patterned principles allow people to choose to expend upon themselves, but not upon others, those resources they are entitled to (or rather, receive) under some favored distributional pattern D_1. For if each of several persons chooses to expend some of his D_1 resources upon one other person, then that other person will receive more than his D_1 share, disturbing the favored distributional pattern. Maintaining a distributional pattern is individualism with a vengeance! Patterned distributional principles do not give people what entitlement principles do, only better distributed. For they do not give the right to choose what to do with what one has; they do not give the right to choose to pursue an end involving (intrinsically, or as a means) the enhancement of another's position. To such views, families are disturbing; for within a family occur transfers that upset the favored distributional pattern. Either families themselves become units to which

R Here is one of Nozick's basic objections to patterned views: if D_1 is a just distribution and if people are justly free to do as they like with their just allotments, then how can the resulting distribution D_2 be unjust (as the theory that advocates D_1 must seemingly say that it is, since D_2 differs from D_1)?

Nozick regards such continued interference as unacceptable in itself. But it also seems to conflict with the idea that people genuinely own and so can freely control what they receive according to the favored pattern.

distribution takes place...(on what rationale?) or loving behavior is forbidden. . . .

Proponents of patterned principles of distributive justice focus upon criteria for determining who is to receive holdings; they consider the reasons for which someone should have something, and also the total picture of holdings. Whether or not it is better to give than to receive, proponents of patterned principles ignore giving altogether. In considering the distribution of goods, income, and so forth, their theories are theories of recipient justice; they completely ignore any right a person might have to give something to someone. Even in exchanges where each party is simultaneously giver and recipient, patterned principles of justice focus only upon the recipient role and its supposed rights. Thus discussions tend to focus on whether people (should) have a right to inherit, rather than on whether people (should) have a right to bequeath (14) or on whether persons who have a right to hold also have a right to choose that others hold in their place. I lack a good explanation of why the usual theories of distributive justice are so recipient oriented; ignoring givers and transferrers and their rights is of a piece with ignoring producers and their entitlements. But why is it *all* ignored?

(14) R Nozick's suggestion is that restrictions on inheritance (perhaps via taxation) are incompatible with the idea that the person who bequeaths something to another legitimately owns it (whether via a patterned distribution or in some other way).

Patterned principles of distributive justice necessitate *re*distributive activities. The likelihood is small that any actual freely-arrived-at set of holdings fits a given pattern; and the likelihood is nil that it will continue to fit the pattern as people exchange and give. From the point of view of an entitlement theory, redistribution is a serious matter indeed, involving, as it does, the violation of people's rights. (An exception is those takings that fall under the principle of the rectification of injustices.) From other points of view, also, it is serious.

Taxation of earnings from labor is on a par with forced labor. Some persons find this claim obviously true: taking the earnings of *n* hours labor is like taking *n* hours from the person; it is like forcing the person to work *n* hours for another's purpose. Others find the claim absurd. But even these, *if* they object to forced labor, would oppose forcing unemployed hippies to work for the benefit of the needy. And they would also object to forcing each person to work five extra hours each week for the benefit of the needy. . . .

The man who chooses to work longer to gain an income more than sufficient for his basic needs prefers some extra goods or services to the leisure and activities he could perform during the possible nonworking hours; whereas the man who chooses not to work the extra time prefers the leisure activities to the extra goods or services he could acquire by working more. Given this, if it would be illegitimate for a tax system to seize some of a man's leisure (forced labor) for the purpose of serving the needy, how can it be legitimate for a tax system to seize some of a man's goods for that purpose? Why should we treat the man whose happiness requires certain material goods or services differently from the man whose preferences and desires make such goods unnecessary for his happiness? Why should the man who prefers seeing a movie (and who has to earn money for a ticket) be open to the required call to aid the needy, while the person who prefers looking at a sunset (and hence need earn no extra money) is not? . . .

When end-result principles of distributive justice are built into the legal structure of a society, they (as do most patterned principles) give each citizen an enforceable claim to some portion of the total social product; that is, to some portion of the sum total of the individually and jointly made products. This total product is produced by individuals laboring, using means of production others have saved to bring into existence, by people organizing production or creating means to produce new things or things in a new way. It is on this batch of individual activities that patterned distributional principles give each individual an enforceable claim. Each person has a claim to the activities and the products of other persons, independently of whether the other persons enter into particular relationships that give rise to these claims, and independently of whether they voluntarily take these claims upon themselves, in charity or in exchange for something.

Whether it is done through taxation on wages or on wages over a certain amount, or through seizure of profits, or through there being a big *social pot* so that it's not clear what's coming from where and what's going where, patterned principles of distributive justice involve appropriating the actions of other persons. Seizing the results of someone's labor is equivalent to seizing hours from him and directing him to carry on various activities. . . . (15)

Locke's Theory of Acquisition

Before we turn to consider other theories of justice in detail, we must introduce an additional bit of complexity into the structure of the entitlement theory. This is best approached by considering Locke's attempt to specify a principle of justice in acquisition. (16) Locke views property rights in an unowned object as originating through someone's mixing his labor with it. This gives rise to many questions. What are the boundaries of what labor is mixed with? If a private astronaut clears a place on Mars, has he mixed his labor with (so that he comes to own) the whole planet, the whole uninhabited universe, or just a particular plot? . . .

Why does mixing one's labor with something make one the owner of it? Perhaps because one owns one's labor, and so one comes to own a previously unowned thing that becomes permeated with what one owns. Ownership seeps over into the rest. But why isn't mixing what I own with what I don't own a way of losing what I own rather than a way of gaining what I don't? If I own a can of tomato juice and spill it in the sea so that its molecules (made radioactive, so I can check this) mingle evenly throughout the sea, do I thereby come to own the sea, or have I foolishly dissipated my tomato juice? Perhaps the idea, instead, is that laboring on something improves it and makes it more valuable; and anyone is entitled to own a thing whose value he has created. . . . Ignore the fact that laboring on something may make it less valuable (spraying pink enamel paint on a piece of driftwood that you have found). Why should one's entitlement extend to the whole object rather than just to the *added value* one's labor has produced? . . .

It will be implausible to view improving an object as giving full ownership to it, if the stock of unowned objects that might be improved is limited. For an object's coming under one person's ownership changes the situation of all others. (17) Whereas previously they were at liberty . . . to use the object, they now no longer are. This change in the situation of others (by removing their liberty to act on a previously unowned object) need not worsen their situation. If I appropriate a grain of sand from Coney Island, no one else may now do as they will with *that* grain of sand. But there are plenty of other grains of sand left for them to do the same with. Or if not grains of sand, then other things. Alternatively, the things I do with the grain of sand I appropriate might improve the position of others, counterbalancing their loss of the liberty to use that grain. The crucial point is whether appropriation of an unowned object worsens the situation of others.

Locke's proviso that there be "enough and as good left in common for others" . . . is meant to ensure that the situation of others is not worsened. (18) . . . It is often said that this proviso once held but now no longer does. But there appears to be an argument for the conclusion that if the proviso no longer holds, then it cannot ever have held so as to yield permanent and inheritable property rights. Consider the first person *Z* for whom there is not enough and as good left to appropriate. The last person *Y* to appropriate left *Z* without his previous liberty to act on an object, and so worsened *Z*'s situation. So *Y*'s appropriation is not allowed under Locke's proviso. Therefore the next to last person *X* to appropriate left *Y* in a worse position, for *X*'s act ended permissible appropriation. Therefore *X*'s appropriation wasn't permissible. But then the appropriator two from last, *W*, ended permissible appropriation and so, since it worsened *X*'s position, *W*'s appropriation wasn't permissible. And so on back to the first person *A* to appropriate a permanent property right. (19)

This argument, however, proceeds too quickly. Someone may be made worse off by another's appropriation in two ways: first, by losing the opportunity to improve his situation by a particular appropriation or any one; and second, by no longer being able to use freely (without appropriation) what he previously could. A *stringent* requirement that another not be made worse off by an appropriation would exclude the first way if nothing else counterbalances the diminution in opportunity, as well as the second. A *weaker* requirement would exclude the second way, though not the first. With the weaker requirement, we cannot zip back so quickly from *Z* to *A*, as in the above argument; for though person *Z* can no longer *appropriate*, there may remain some for him to

Is there a morally important difference between (a) taking the results of someone's work away from them and using it to achieve some end and (b) requiring the person to work for the same number of hours directly to achieve that end? If so, what is it?

Nozick's view is similar to Locke's (in a part of the *Second Treatise of Government* omitted from the selection included earlier). But he rejects the idea that "mixing one's labor" with something is the key to acquisition.

Nozick is saying not just that an act of acquiring a previously unowned object where the supply of such objects is limited "changes the situation of all others" (which is obvious), but that it changes it in a way that may be morally objectionable. This seems to amount to saying that people stand in a morally significant relation to unowned objects—even to those that are distant from them and which they never actually encounter. Is there any plausible reason for this?

18

This is Locke's restriction on allowable property acquisition (in the *Second Treatise of Government*).

This is a very tricky argument. Does it show that if it is even *possible* for the supply of an unowned thing to run out, then there was never, even at the beginning, "enough and as good" left for others—which might well rule out all acquisition?

use as before. In this case *Y*'s appropriation would not violate the weaker Lockean condition. . . . It is arguable that no one legitimately can complain if the weaker provision is satisfied. . . . [20]

R Nozick's suggestion is that the weaker condition is the right one, that the more stringent one is too stringent.

Is the situation of persons who are unable to appropriate (there being no more accessible and useful unowned objects) worsened by a system allowing appropriation and permanent property? Here enter the various familiar social considerations favoring private property: it increases the social product by putting means of production in the hands of those who can use them most efficiently (profitably); experimentation is encouraged, because with separate persons controlling resources, there is no one person or small group whom someone with a new idea must convince to try it out; private property enables people to decide on the pattern and types of risks they wish to bear, leading to specialized types of risk bearing; private property protects future persons by leading some to hold back resources from current consumption for future markets; it provides alternate sources of employment for unpopular persons who don't have to convince any one person or small group to hire them, and so on. These considerations enter a Lockean theory to support the claim that appropriation of private property satisfies the intent behind the "enough and as good left over" proviso, *not* as a utilitarian justification of property. They enter to rebut the claim that because the proviso is violated no natural right to private property can arise by a Lockean process. The difficulty in working such an argument to show that the proviso is satisfied is in fixing the appropriate base line for comparison. Lockean appropriation makes people no worse off than they would be *how*? . . . [21]

21

R Nozick's suggestion is that the system of private property does not clearly leave people worse off than they would have been if acquisition of unowned objects did not occur, even though they no longer have much opportunity for acquisition of unowned objects themselves.

But he recognizes the difficult problem of what the appropriate "baseline" for this comparison is: must people be no worse off than they would have been in a state of nature (easy to satisfy) or not worse off than they would have been in another social system without private property (perhaps substantially more difficult to satisfy)?

The Proviso

Whether or not Locke's particular theory of appropriation can be spelled out so as to handle various difficulties, I assume that any adequate theory of justice in acquisition will contain a proviso similar to the weaker of the ones we have attributed to Locke. A process normally giving rise to a permanent bequeathable property right in a previously unowned thing will not do so if the position of others no longer at liberty to use the thing is thereby worsened. It is important to specify *this* particular mode of worsening the situation of others, for the proviso does not encompass other modes. It does not include the worsening due to more limited opportunities to appropriate . . . , and it does not include how I "worsen" a seller's position if I appropriate materials to make some of what he is selling, and then enter into competition with him. Someone whose appropriation otherwise would violate the proviso still may appropriate provided he compensates the others so that their situation is not thereby worsened; unless he does compensate these others, his appropriation will violate the proviso of the principle of justice in acquisition and will be an illegitimate one. [22] A theory of appropriation incorporating this Lockean proviso will handle correctly the cases (objections to the theory lacking the proviso) where someone appropriates the total supply of something necessary for life.

Nozick concludes that the correct account of justice will include a restriction on acquisition of unowned objects of the weaker sort discussed earlier—but without resolving the issue mentioned in the previous annotation.

. . .

Each owner's title to his holding includes the historical shadow of the Lockean proviso on appropriation. This excludes his transferring it into an agglomeration that does violate the Lockean proviso and excludes his using it in a way, in coordination with others or independently of them, so as to violate the proviso by making the situation of others worse than their baseline situation. Once it is known that someone's ownership runs afoul of the Lockean proviso, there are stringent limits on what he may do with (what it is difficult any longer unreservedly to call) "his property." Thus a person may not appropriate the only water hole in a desert and charge what he will. Nor may he charge what he will if he possesses one, and unfortunately it happens that all the water holes in the desert dry up, except for his. This unfortunate circumstance, admittedly no fault of his, brings into operation the Lockean proviso and limits his property rights. Similarly, an owner's property right in the only island in an area does not allow him to order a castaway from a shipwreck off his island as a trespasser, for this would violate the Lockean proviso.

. . .

Discussion Questions

1. The historical practice of human slavery in the American South prior to the Civil War is a good example of a past injustice that might require rectification under Nozick's envisaged principle of rectification. Part of the injustice associated with slavery is that the results of the slave's labor were appropriated by the owner (under threat of force). Discuss what, if anything, should be done *now* to rectify this injustice, being careful to specify clearly who should receive the benefits of such rectification and who should pay the cost. What if the relevant groups cannot be reliably identified?
2. Is Wilt Chamberlain (or any star athlete) entitled to receive all that people are freely willing to pay (out of their just allotments) to watch him play? Is he entitled to bequeath as much of it as he likes to his heirs? What if the amount is so large in relation to the resources of others that Chamberlain (or his heir) is able to exert a much larger influence than anyone else on such things as the results of political elections?
3. Does taxation for redistribution of income and wealth amount to forced labor on behalf of those who are (allegedly) entitled to the results of such redistribution according to some patterned theory of justice? If not, why not? Is there any difference between taxation for this purpose and taxation for the support of other government services (such as police and fire protection, highway maintenance, etc.)?
4. Why should there be *any* limitation, even the one Nozick proposes, on the acquisition of unowned items? If they are genuinely unowned, why isn't anyone who comes upon them free to take possession? Try to think here of examples of unowned things, perhaps in earlier times (land in unexplored places, undiscovered mineral resources, fish in the open sea, etc.).

John Rawls

John Rawls (1921–2002), like Nozick a professor at Harvard, was one of the best known and most influential figures in recent political and social philosophy. Unlike Hobbes, Locke, and Nozick, Rawls's basic concern is less with the issue of whether and why any sort of governmental power is legitimate than with the issue of which sorts of governmental and societal structures and institutions satisfy the demands of *justice*. In his book *A Theory of Justice* (1971), Rawls offers a complicated and subtle account of justice, focusing on what he calls "the basic structure of society" and especially on the issue of how income, wealth, and other results of social cooperation should be distributed among the members of a particular society.

Rawls sometimes describes his view of justice as a version of a social contract theory. For him, however, the contractual situation is a purely hypothetical one ("**the original position**") in which members of society, denied the knowledge of their own situation that would allow them to bias the results in favor of themselves, reach an agreement as to the basic principles of justice by pursuing their own self-interest (insofar as they can discern it). The most distinctive result that Rawls claims would be agreed upon in this hypothetical situation is the principle ("the difference principle") that while social benefits need not be distributed equally, an unequal distribution is justified only if having such a distribution makes even the members of society who are relatively worse off still better off in absolute terms than they would be under an equal distribution (because of the increased total production that results from giving more to others).

There are three aspects of Rawls's discussion that need to be carefully distinguished. First, there is the account of how the reasoning of people in the original position would actually go; this comes at the very end of the present selection. Second, there is Rawls's argument that the way in which the original position is specified is the right one to yield the correct conception of justice—with the crucial issue being whether Rawls is right about just what knowledge should be allowed or excluded there; this occurs both at the beginning of the selection and toward the end, just prior to the account of the actual reasoning in the original position. Third, there is independent argument defending the alleged results of the original position as being in fact the right conception of justice; this begins with the account of the two principles (p. 487) and continues through the discussion of equality and meritocracy (ending on p. 491).

Rawls's discussion is highly abstract in character—even more so than most philosophy. This makes it important to read slowly and carefully, constantly trying to recognize and keep in mind what sorts of things fall under the abstract terms he employs.

Justice as Fairness, from *A Theory of Justice*

The Role of Justice

Justice is the first virtue of social institutions, as truth is of systems of thought. A theory however elegant and economical must be rejected or revised if it is untrue; likewise laws and institutions no matter how efficient and well-arranged must be reformed or abolished if they are unjust. Each person possesses an inviolability founded on justice that even the welfare of society as a whole cannot override. For this reason justice denies that the loss of freedom for some is made right by a greater good shared by others. It does not allow that the sacrifices imposed on a few are outweighed by the larger sum of advantages enjoyed by many. Therefore in a just society the liberties of equal citizenship are taken as settled; the rights secured by justice are not subject to political bargaining or to the calculus of social interests . . . analogously, an injustice is tolerable only when it is necessary to avoid an even greater injustice. Being first virtues of human activities, truth and justice are uncompromising.

These propositions seem to express our intuitive conviction of the primacy of justice. No doubt they are expressed too strongly. In any event I wish to inquire whether these contentions or others similar to them are sound, and if so how they can be accounted for. To this end it is necessary to work out a theory of justice in the light of which these assertions can be interpreted and assessed. I shall begin by considering the role of the principles of justice. Let us assume, to fix ideas, that a society is a more or less self-sufficient association of persons who in their relations to one another recognize certain rules of conduct as binding and who for the most part act in accordance with them. Suppose further that these rules specify a system of cooperation designed to advance the good of those taking part in it. Then, although a society is a cooperative venture for mutual advantage, it is typically marked by a conflict as well as by an identity of interests. There is an identity of interests since social cooperation makes possible a better life for all than any would have if each were to live solely by his own efforts. There is a conflict of interests since persons are not indifferent as to how the greater benefits produced by their collaboration are distributed, for in order to pursue their ends they each prefer a larger to a lesser share. A set of principles is required for choosing among the various social arrangements which determine this division of advantages and for underwriting an agreement on the proper distributive shares. These principles are the principles of social justice: they provide a way of assigning rights and duties in the basic institutions of society and they define the appropriate distribution of the benefits and burdens of social cooperation. ❶

Now let us say that a society is well-ordered when it is not only designed to advance the good of its members but when it is also effectively regulated by a public conception of justice. That is, it is a society in which (1) everyone accepts and knows that the others accept the same principles of justice, and (2) the basic social institutions generally satisfy and are generally known to satisfy these principles. ❷ In this case while men may put forth excessive demands on one another, they nevertheless acknowledge a common point of view from which their claims may be adjudicated. . . .

From *A Theory of Justice* (Cambridge Mass.: Harvard University Press, 1971).

❶

So the account of justice to be developed is concerned primarily with the basic institutions of society and with specifying the way in which the "benefits and burdens" of social cooperation should be distributed—and not with issues of justice that arise in more limited contexts (such as criminal justice).

STOP This is a very abstract specification, and you should try to identify for yourself some of the aspects of society that such a conception will be concerned with.

❷

Thus a society that satisfied even optimum principles of justice but was not believed by its members to do so would not be "well ordered."

The Subject of Justice

Many different kinds of things are said to be just and unjust: not only laws, institutions, and social systems, but also particular actions of many kinds, including decisions, judgments, and imputations. We also call the attitudes and dispositions of persons, and persons themselves, just and unjust. Our topic, however, is that of social justice. For us the primary subject of justice is the basic structure of society, or more exactly, the way in which the major social institutions distribute fundamental rights and duties and determine the division of advantages from social cooperation. By major institutions I understand the political constitution and the principal economic and social arrangements. Thus the legal protection of freedom of thought and liberty of conscience, competitive markets, private property in the means of production, and the monogamous family are examples of major social institutions. ❸ Taken together as one scheme, the major institutions define men's rights and duties and influence their life prospects, what they can expect to be and how well they can hope to do. The basic structure is the primary subject of justice because its effects are so profound and present from the start. . . .

The Main Idea of the Theory of Justice

My aim is to present a conception of justice which generalizes and carries to a higher level of abstraction the familiar theory of the social contract as found, say, in Locke, Rousseau, and Kant. In order to do this we are not to think of the original contract as one to enter a particular society or to set up a particular form of government. Rather, the guiding idea is that the principles of justice for the basic structure of society are the object of the original agreement. They are the principles that free and rational persons concerned to further their own interests would accept in an initial position of equality as defining the fundamental terms of their association. These principles are to regulate all further agreements; they specify the kinds of social cooperation that can be entered into and the forms of government that can be established. This way of regarding the principles of justice I shall call justice as fairness.

...

In justice as fairness the original position of equality corresponds to the state of nature in the traditional theory of the social contract. This original position is not, of course, thought of as an actual historical state of affairs, much less as a primitive condition of culture. It is understood as a purely hypothetical situation characterized so as to lead to a certain conception of justice. Among the essential features of this situation is that no one knows his place in society, his class position or social status, nor does any one know his fortune in the distribution of natural assets and abilities, his intelligence, strength, and the like. I shall even assume that the parties do not know their conceptions of the good or their special psychological propensities. The principles of justice are chosen behind a veil of ignorance. ❹ This ensures that no one is advantaged or disadvantaged in the choice of principles by the outcome of natural chance or the contingency of social circumstances. Since all are similarly situated and no one is able to design principles to favor his particular condition, the principles of justice are the result of a fair agreement or bargain. . . .

One feature of justice as fairness is to think of the parties in the initial situation as rational and mutually disinterested. This does not mean that the parties are egoists, that is, individuals with only certain kinds of interests, say in wealth, prestige, and domination. But they are conceived as not taking an interest in one another's interests. . . . ❺

. . . once the principles of justice are thought of as arising from an original agreement in a situation of equality, it is an open question whether the principle of utility would be acknowledged. Off-hand it hardly seems likely that persons who view themselves as equals, entitled to press their claims upon one another, would agree to a principle which may require lesser life prospects for some simply for the sake of a greater sum of advantages enjoyed by others. Since each desires to protect his interests, his capacity to advance his conception of the good, no one has a reason to acquiesce in an enduring loss for himself in order to bring about a greater net balance of satisfaction. ❻ In the absence of strong and lasting benevolent impulses, a rational man would not accept a basic structure merely because it maximized the algebraic sum of advantages irrespective of its permanent effects

R Here is a little more help in picking out which social institutions are part of the "basic structure of society."

R The original position is thus not a real situation that could actually occur: probably no actual person could be as ignorant of his own characteristics as the "veil of ignorance" requires. Rather it is a hypothetical thought experiment that is supposed to reflect fairness and equality among citizens in a way that leads them to choose the correct principles of justice.

The *only* concern of the parties in the original position is their own rational self-interest. They are not concerned altruistically with the welfare of others, nor are they supposed to be moved by moral values, not even by any antecedent idea of justice itself. The whole point is that the correct principles of justice are those that rationally self-interested individuals would choose in a situation in which they are unable (because of the veil of ignorance) to unfairly favor their own actual situation or characteristics.

Here is a good initial example of reasoning based on the original position. The principle of utility (discussed further in Chapter 5) holds roughly that the morally right action in a set of choices is the one that produces the best overall consequences for everyone taken together. Self-interested people in the original position would reject such a principle, Rawls argues, because it says nothing about how these good consequences are distributed among people, leaving the possibility open that any given person might do very poorly.

Here is the initial statement of Rawls's two basic principles of justice. The main idea behind the second principle ("the difference principle") is that inequalities that give talented or productive people an incentive to develop and utilize their talents may lead to enough of an increase in production to make everyone, even those who receive the smallest relative shares, better off in absolute terms than they would have been in a situation of equality.

Here are two important things that would be hidden behind the veil of ignorance in the original position and so cannot be used to seek advantages in a just system.

By "contingencies of social circumstance," Rawls means things like social class. This is one of the clearest examples of the point of the veil of ignorance: people in the original position cannot choose a principle that gives advantages to their social class, because they do not know which one that is.

One of the main questions about Rawls's view is whether he is right that "accident of natural endowment" (natural talents and abilities) should be treated in the same way.

9

Here are some further, more specific examples of things that would be excluded from the knowledge of the hypothetical persons in the original position.

Rawls seems here to suggest that the specification of what should be thus excluded is fairly obvious, but not all would agree—thus you should think carefully about the issue.

on his own basic rights and interests. Thus it seems that the principle of utility is incompatible with the conception of social cooperation among equals for mutual advantage. It appears to be inconsistent with the idea of reciprocity implicit in the notion of a well-ordered society. Or, at any rate, so I shall argue.

I shall maintain instead that the persons in the initial situation would choose two rather different principles: the first requires equality in the assignment of basic rights and duties, while the second holds that social and economic inequalities, for example inequalities of wealth and authority, are just only if they result in compensating benefits for everyone, and in particular for the least advantaged members of society. 7 These principles rule out justifying institutions on the grounds that the hardships of some are offset by a greater good in the aggregate. It may be expedient but it is not just that some should have less in order that others may prosper. But there is no injustice in the greater benefits earned by a few provided that the situation of persons not so fortunate is thereby improved. The intuitive idea is that since everyone's well-being depends upon a scheme of cooperation without which no one could have a satisfactory life, the division of advantages should be such as to draw forth the willing cooperation of everyone taking part in it, including those less well situated. The two principles mentioned seem to be a fair basis on which those better endowed, or more fortunate in their social position, neither of which we can be said to deserve, could expect the willing cooperation of others when some workable scheme is a necessary condition of the welfare of all. Once we decide to look for a conception of justice that prevents the use of the accidents of natural endowment and the contingencies of social circumstance as counters in a quest for political and economic advantage, we are led to these principles. 8 They express the result of leaving aside those aspects of the social world that seem arbitrary from a moral point of view.

...

The Original Position and Justification

I have said that the original position is the appropriate initial status quo which insures that the fundamental agreements reached in it are fair. This fact yields the name "justice as fairness." It is clear, then, that I want to say that one conception of justice is more reasonable than another, or justifiable with respect to it, if rational persons in the initial situation would choose its principles over those of the other for the role of justice. Conceptions of justice are to be ranked by their acceptability to persons so circumstanced. Understood in this way the question of justification is settled by working out a problem of deliberation: we have to ascertain which principles it would be rational to adopt given the contractual situation. . . .

One should not be misled, then, by the somewhat unusual conditions which characterize the original position. The idea here is simply to make vivid to ourselves the restrictions that it seems reasonable to impose on arguments for principles of justice, and therefore on these principles themselves. Thus it seems reasonable and generally acceptable that no one should be advantaged or disadvantaged by natural fortune or social circumstances in the choice of principles. It also seems widely agreed that it should be impossible to tailor principles to the circumstances of one's own case. We should insure further that particular inclinations and aspirations, and persons' conceptions of their good do not affect the principles adopted. The aim is to rule out those principles that it would be rational to propose for acceptance, however little the chance of success, only if one knew certain things that are irrelevant from the standpoint of justice. For example, if a man knew that he was wealthy, he might find it rational to advance the principle that various taxes for welfare measures be counted unjust; if he knew that he was poor, he would most likely propose the contrary principle. To represent the desired restrictions one imagines a situation in which everyone is deprived of this sort of information. One excludes the knowledge of those contingencies which sets men at odds and allows them to be guided by their prejudices. In this manner the veil of ignorance is arrived at in a natural way. This concept should cause no difficulty if we keep in mind the constraints on arguments that it is meant to express. At any time we can enter the original position, so to speak, simply by following a certain procedure, namely, by arguing for principles of justice in accordance with these restrictions. 9

...

Two Principles of Justice

I shall now state in a provisional form the two principles of justice that I believe would be agreed to in the original position. The first formulation of these principles is tentative. As we go on I shall consider several formulations and approximate step by step the final statement to be given much later. I believe that doing this allows the exposition to proceed in a natural way.

The first statement of the two principles reads as follows.

> First: each person is to have an equal right to the most extensive scheme of equal basic liberties compatible with a similar scheme of liberties for others.
>
> Second: social and economic inequalities are to be arranged so that they are both (a) reasonably expected to be to everyone's advantage, and (b) attached to positions and offices open to all.

There are two ambiguous phrases in the second principle, namely "everyone's advantage" and "open to all." Determining their sense more exactly will lead to a second formulation of the principle. . . .

These principles primarily apply, as I have said, to the basic structure of society and govern the assignment of rights and duties and regulate the distribution of social and economic advantages. Their formulation presupposes that, for the purposes of a theory of justice, the social structure may be viewed as having two more or less distinct parts, the first principle applying to the one, the second principle to the other. Thus we distinguish between the aspects of the social system that define and secure the equal basic liberties and the aspects that specify and establish social and economic inequalities. Now it is essential to observe that the basic liberties are given by a list of such liberties. Important among these are political liberty (the right to vote and to hold public office) and freedom of speech and assembly; liberty of conscience and freedom of thought; freedom of the person, which includes freedom from psychological oppression and physical assault and dismemberment (integrity of the person); the right to hold personal property and freedom from arbitrary arrest and seizure as defined by the concept of the rule of law. These liberties are to be equal by the first principle.

The second principle applies, in the first approximation, to the distribution of income and wealth and to the design of organizations that make use of differences in authority and responsibility. While the distribution of wealth and income need not be equal, it must be to everyone's advantage, and at the same time, positions of authority and responsibility must be accessible to all. One applies the second principle by holding positions open, and then, subject to this constraint, arranges social and economic inequalities so that everyone benefits.

These principles are to be arranged in a serial order with the first principle prior to the second. This ordering means that infringements of the basic equal liberties protected by the first principle cannot be justified, or compensated for, by greater social and economic advantages. (10) These liberties have a central range of application within which they can be limited and compromised only when they conflict with other basic liberties. Since they may be limited when they clash with one another, none of these liberties is absolute; but however they are adjusted to form one system, this system is to be the same for all. . . .

10 Does it seem obvious that self-interested people in the original position would be unwilling to sacrifice basic liberties to *any* extent in return for greater social and especially economic advantages? (See the further discussion of this point at Annotation 27.)

The two principles are rather specific in their content, and their acceptance rests on certain assumptions that I must eventually try to explain and justify. For the present, it should be observed that these principles are a special case of a more general conception of justice that can be expressed as follows.

> All social values—liberty and opportunity, income and wealth, and the social bases of self-respect—are to be distributed equally unless an unequal distribution of any, or all, of these values is to everyone's advantage.

Injustice, then, is simply inequalities that are not to the benefit of all. Of course, this conception is extremely vague and requires interpretation. (11)

11 Here we see a strong presumption in favor of egalitarianism: inequalities need to be justified, and can be justified only by being shown to be in everyone's interests. Pretty clearly our actual society does not satisfy this requirement.

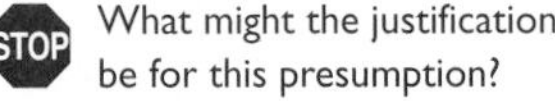

STOP What might the justification be for this presumption?

As a first step, suppose that the basic structure of society distributes certain primary goods, that is, things that every rational man is presumed to want. These goods normally have a use whatever a person's rational plan of life. For simplicity, assume that the chief primary goods at the disposition of society are rights, liberties, and opportunities, and income and wealth. . . . These are the social primary goods. . . .

Interpretations of the Second Principle

I have already mentioned that since the phrases "everyone's advantage" and "equally open to all" are ambiguous, both parts of the second principle have two natural senses. Because these senses are independent of one another, the principle has four possible meanings. Assuming that the first principle of equal liberty has the same sense throughout, we then have four interpretations of the two principles. These are indicated in the table below.

	"Everyone's advantage"	
"Equally open"	**Principle of efficiency**	**Difference principle**
Equality as careers open to talents	System of Natural Liberty	Natural Aristocracy
Equality as equality of fair opportunity	Liberal Equality	Democratic Equality

...

In the system of natural liberty the initial distribution is regulated by the arrangements implicit in the conception of careers open to talents. . . . These arrangements presuppose a background of equal liberty (as specified by the first principle) and a free market economy. They require a formal equality of opportunity in that all have at least the same legal rights of access to all advantaged social positions. But since there is no effort to preserve an equality, or similarity, of social conditions, except insofar as this is necessary to preserve the requisite background institutions, the initial distribution of assets for any period of time is strongly influenced by natural and social contingencies. The existing distribution of income and wealth, say, is the cumulative effect of prior distributions of natural assets—that is, natural talents and abilities—as these have been developed or left unrealized, and their use favored or disfavored over time by social circumstances and such chance contingencies as accident and good fortune. Intuitively, the most obvious injustice of the system of natural liberty is that it permits distributive shares to be improperly influenced by these factors so arbitrary from a moral point of view. 12

12

 The "system of natural liberty" is at least approximately the system defined by Nozick's entitlement theory. Rawls's claim is that the distribution of wealth and other advantages in such a system is unjust because it reflects the long-term results of distributions of natural talents and abilities, all of this being "arbitrary from a moral point of view" in that there is no *moral* reason why one person should have such a talent while another does not. (Is he right that such a result is an "obvious injustice"?)

The liberal interpretation, as I shall refer to it, tries to correct for this by adding to the requirement of careers open to talents the further condition of the principle of fair equality of opportunity. The thought here is that positions are to be not only open in a formal sense, but that all should have a fair chance to attain them. Offhand it is not clear what is meant, but we might say that those with similar abilities and skills should have similar life chances. More specifically, assuming that there is a distribution of natural assets, those who are at the same level of talent and ability, and have the same willingness to use them, should have the same prospects of success regardless of their initial place in the social system. In all sectors of society there should be roughly equal prospects of culture and achievement for everyone similarly motivated and endowed. The expectations of those with the same abilities and aspirations should not be affected by their social class. 13

13

R The main difference between "liberal equality" and the "system of natural liberty" is that in "liberal equality," people with the same natural assets should have the same chance of success, the same chance for desirable careers and positions. This is not so under natural liberty, because of such things as different opportunities for education.

The liberal interpretation of the two principles seeks, then, to mitigate the influence of social contingencies and natural fortune on distributive shares. To accomplish this end it is necessary to impose further basic structural conditions on the social system. Free market arrangements must be set within a framework of political and legal institutions which regulates the overall trends of economic events and preserves the social conditions necessary for fair equality of opportunity. The elements of this framework are familiar enough, though it may be worthwhile to recall the importance of preventing excessive accumulations of property and wealth and of maintaining equal opportunities of education for all. Chances to acquire cultural knowledge and skills should not depend upon one's class position, and so the school system, whether public or private, should be designed to even out class barriers.

While the liberal conception seems clearly preferable to the system of natural liberty, intuitively it still appears defective. For one thing, even if it works to perfection in eliminating the influence of social contingencies, it still permits the distribution of wealth and income to be determined by the natural distribution of abilities and talents. 14 Within the limits allowed by the background arrangements,

14

 Even if the influence of "social contingencies" (such things as family status and wealth) are eliminated under liberal equality, the "life chances" of different persons will still be influenced by their natural abilities and talents.

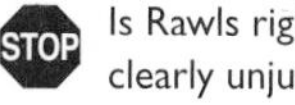
Is Rawls right that this is clearly unjust?

distributive shares are decided by the outcome of the natural lottery; and this outcome is arbitrary from a moral perspective. There is no more reason to permit the distribution of income and wealth to be settled by the distribution of natural assets than by historical and social fortune. . . .

Before turning to the conception of democratic equality, we should note that of natural aristocracy. On this view no attempt is made to regulate social contingencies beyond what is required by formal equality of opportunity, but the advantages of persons with greater natural endowments are to be limited to those that further the good of the poorer sectors of society. The aristocratic ideal is applied to a system that is open, at least from a legal point of view, and the better situation of those favored by it is regarded as just only when less would be had by those below, if less were given to those above. 15 In this way the idea of *noblesse oblige* is carried over to the conception of natural aristocracy.

Now both the liberal conception and that of natural aristocracy are unstable. For once we are troubled by the influence of either social contingencies or natural chance on the determination of distributive shares, we are bound, on reflection, to be bothered by the influence of the other. From a moral standpoint the two seem equally arbitrary. So however we move away from the system of natural liberty, we cannot be satisfied short of the democratic conception. . . .

Democratic Equality and the Difference Principle

The democratic interpretation, as the table suggests, is arrived at by combining the principle of fair equality of opportunity with the difference principle. This principle removes the indeterminateness of the principle of efficiency by singling out a particular position from which the social and economic inequalities of the basic structure are to be judged. Assuming the framework of institutions required by equal liberty and fair equality of opportunity, the higher expectations of those better situated are just if and only if they work as part of a scheme which improves the expectations of the least advantaged members of society. The intuitive idea is that the social order is not to establish and secure the more attractive prospects of those better off unless doing so is to the advantage of those less fortunate. . . . 16

The Tendency to Equality

I wish to conclude this discussion of the two principles by explaining the sense in which they express an egalitarian conception of justice. Also I should like to forestall the objection to the principle of fair opportunity that it leads to a meritocratic society. In order to prepare the way for doing this, I note several aspects of the conception of justice that I have set out.

First we may observe that the difference principle gives some weight to the considerations singled out by the principle of redress. This is the principle that undeserved inequalities call for redress; and since inequalities of birth and natural endowment are undeserved, these inequalities are to be somehow compensated for. Thus the principle holds that in order to treat all persons equally, to provide genuine equality of opportunity, society must give more attention to those with fewer native assets and to those born into the less favorable social positions. The idea is to redress the bias of contingencies in the direction of equality. In pursuit of this principle greater resources might be spent on the education of the less rather than the more intelligent, at least over a certain time of life, say the earlier years of school. 17

Now the principle of redress has not to my knowledge been proposed as the sole criterion of justice, as the single aim of the social order. It is plausible as most such principles are only as a prima facie principle, one that is to be weighed in the balance with others. For example, we are to weigh it against the principle to improve the average standard of life, or to advance the common good. But whatever other principles we hold, the claims of redress are to be taken into account. It is thought to represent one of the elements in our conception of justice. Now the difference principle is not of course the principle of redress. It does not require society to try to even out handicaps as if all were expected to compete on a fair basis in the same race. But the difference principle would allocate resources in education, say, so

15

The idea of "natural aristocracy" is perhaps the least clear of Rawls's four alternatives. In this system there is only "formal" and not "fair" equality of opportunity: so, for example, those from better family backgrounds will have a better chance to succeed, but their rewards will be only as great as is required to yield the best result (in absolute, not relative terms) for those who are worst off.

16

If the different ways in which liberal equality and natural aristocracy are (allegedly) improvements over natural liberty are combined, we have the difference principle: inequalities are justified only if they make the least advantaged members of society better off (again, in absolute terms).

17

The "principle of redress" says that society should *compensate* those who are less well off in terms of family status or natural endowment, thereby coming closer to genuine equality of opportunity.

STOP Does this seem right? For example, does a person with less natural intelligence than others deserve to be compensated by society for this situation?

as to improve the long-term expectation of the least favored. If this end is attained by giving more attention to the better endowed, it is permissible; otherwise not. And in making this decision, the value of education should not be assessed solely in terms of economic efficiency and social welfare. Equally if not more important is the role of education in enabling a person to enjoy the culture of his society and to take part in its affairs, and in this way to provide for each individual a secure sense of his own worth.

Thus although the difference principle is not the same as that of redress, it does achieve some of the intent of the latter principle. It transforms the aims of the basic structure so that the total scheme of institutions no longer emphasizes social efficiency and technocratic values. The difference principle represents, in effect, an agreement to regard the distribution of natural talents as in some respects a common asset and to share in the greater social and economic benefits made possible by the complementarities of this distribution. (18) Those who have been favored by nature, whoever they are, may gain from their good fortune only on terms that improve the situation of those who have lost out. The naturally advantaged are not to gain merely because they are more gifted, but only to cover the costs of training and education and for using their endowments in ways that help the less fortunate as well. No one deserves his greater natural capacity nor merits a more favorable starting place in society. But, of course, this is no reason to ignore, much less to eliminate these distinctions. Instead, the basic structure can be arranged so that these contingencies work for the good of the least fortunate. Thus we are led to the difference principle if we wish to set up the social system so that no one gains or loses from his arbitrary place in the distribution of natural assets or his initial position in society without giving or receiving compensating advantages in return.

In view of these remarks we may reject the contention that the ordering of institutions is always defective because the distribution of natural talents and the contingencies of social circumstance are unjust, and this injustice must inevitably carry over to human arrangements. Occasionally this reflection is offered as an excuse for ignoring injustice, as if the refusal to acquiesce in injustice is on a par with being unable to accept death. The natural distribution is neither just nor unjust; nor is it unjust that persons are born into society at some particular position. These are simply natural facts. What is just and unjust is the way that institutions deal with these facts. (19) Aristocratic and caste societies are unjust because they make these contingencies the ascriptive basis for belonging to more or less enclosed and privileged social classes. The basic structure of these societies incorporates the arbitrariness found in nature. But there is no necessity for men to resign themselves to these contingencies. The social system is not an unchangeable order beyond human control but a pattern of human action. In justice as fairness men agree to avail themselves of the accidents of nature and social circumstance only when doing so is for the common benefit. The two principles are a fair way of meeting the arbitrariness of fortune; and while no doubt imperfect in other ways, the institutions which satisfy these principles are just.

A further point is that the difference principle expresses a conception of reciprocity. It is a principle of mutual benefit. At first sight, however, it may appear unfairly biased towards the least favored. To consider this question in an intuitive way, suppose for simplicity that there are only two groups in society, one noticeably more fortunate than the other. Subject to the usual constraints (defined by the priority of the first principle and fair equality of opportunity), society could maximize the expectations of either group but not both, since we can maximize with respect to only one aim at a time. It seems clear that society should not do the best it can for those initially more advantaged; so if we reject the difference principle, we must prefer maximizing some weighted mean of the two expectations. But if we give any weight to the more fortunate, we are valuing for their own sake the gains to those already more favored by natural and social contingencies. No one had an antecedent claim to be benefited in this way, and so to maximize a weighted mean is, so to speak, to favor the more fortunate twice over. Thus the more advantaged, when they view the matter from a general perspective, recognize that the well-being of each depends on a scheme of social cooperation without which no one could have a satisfactory life; they recognize also that they can expect the willing cooperation of all

18

Rawls elsewhere says that this means only that the *distribution* of talents, the fact that different people have different and often complementary abilities, is to be treated as a "common asset," not the talents themselves (which would seemingly amount to saying that other people have a claim on a given person's talents).

But it is hard to avoid thinking that the difference principle involves both of these ideas—why else are people allowed to profit from their own talents only if everyone else benefits too?

19

Think again about this basic comparison: It is unjust for society to reward people because they happen to be born in "better" families. Is it in the same way unjust to allow those with greater abilities to benefit from them in ways that do not also benefit everyone else? (Think here of a talented writer or inventor.) Why does everyone else have a just claim to benefit from their talents?

only if the terms of the scheme are reasonable. So they regard themselves as already compensated, as it were, by the advantages to which no one (including themselves) had a prior claim. They forego the idea of maximizing a weighted mean and regard the difference principle as a fair basis for regulating the basic structure. [20]

...

Thus it is incorrect that individuals with greater natural endowments and the superior character that has made their development possible have a right to a cooperative scheme that enables them to obtain even further benefits in ways that do not contribute to the advantages of others. We do not deserve our place in the distribution of native endowments, any more than we deserve our initial starting place in society. That we deserve the superior character that enables us to make the effort to cultivate our abilities is also problematic; for such character depends in good part upon fortunate family and social circumstances in early life for which we can claim no credit. The notion of desert does not apply here. To be sure, the more advantaged have a right to their natural assets, as does everyone else; this right is covered by the first principle under the basic liberty protecting the integrity of the person. And so the more advantaged are entitled to whatever they can acquire in accordance with the rules of a fair system of social cooperation. Our problem is how this scheme, the basic structure of society, is to be designed. From a suitably general standpoint, the difference principle appears acceptable to both the more advantaged and the less advantaged individual. [21] Of course, none of this is strictly speaking an argument for the principle, since in a contract theory arguments are made from the point of view of the original position. But these intuitive considerations help to clarify the principle and the sense in which it is egalitarian.

...

Now it seems evident in the light of these observations that the democratic interpretation of the two principles will not lead to a meritocratic society. This form of social order follows the principle of careers open to talents and uses equality of opportunity as a way of releasing men's energies in the pursuit of economic prosperity and political dominion. There exists a marked disparity between the upper and lower classes in both means of life and the rights and privileges of organizational authority. The culture of the poorer strata is impoverished while that of the governing and technocratic elite is securely based on the service of the national ends of power and wealth. Equality of opportunity means an equal chance to leave the less fortunate behind in the personal quest for influence and social position. Thus a meritocratic society is a danger for the other interpretations of the principles of justice but not for the democratic conception. For, as we have just seen, the difference principle transforms the aims of society in fundamental respects. . . .

The Circumstances of Justice

The circumstances of justice may be described as the normal conditions under which human cooperation is both possible and necessary. Thus, as I noted at the outset, although a society is a cooperative venture for mutual advantage, it is typically marked by a conflict as well as an identity of interests. There is an identity of interests since social cooperation makes possible a better life for all than any would have if each were to try to live solely by his own efforts. [22] There is a conflict of interests since men are not indifferent as to how the greater benefits produced by their collaboration are distributed, for in order to pursue their ends they each prefer a larger to a lesser share. Thus principles are needed for choosing among the various social arrangements which determine this division of advantages and for underwriting an agreement on the proper distributive shares. These requirements define the role of justice. The background conditions that give rise to these necessities are the circumstances of justice.

These conditions may be divided into two kinds. First, there are the objective circumstances which make human cooperation both possible and necessary. Thus, many individuals coexist together at the same time on a definite geographical territory. These individuals are roughly similar in physical and mental powers; or at any rate, their capacities are comparable in that no one among them can dominate the rest. They are vulnerable to attack, and all are subject to having their plans blocked by the united force of others.

Here is Rawls's answer (somewhat altered from the first edition of the book, as we will see in the following selection) to the question of why the terms of cooperation between people with more talents and those with less should be such as to yield the maximum advantage for the less talented, rather than some compromise between the interests of the two groups.

Should people with greater natural talents be satisfied with the difference principle? They will agree to it in the original position, Rawls is claiming, because they don't know their own situation in this respect. But this *might* show only that the original position is wrongly conceived, that this bit of knowledge should not be excluded.

This is clearly true even of the more talented, which is one of Rawls's reasons for thinking that they should be satisfied with the distribution of benefits that results from the difference principle. But does this really speak to the issue raised in the previous annotation?

Finally, there is the condition of moderate scarcity understood to cover a wide range of situations. Natural and other resources are not so abundant that schemes of cooperation become superfluous, nor are conditions so harsh that fruitful ventures must inevitably break down. While mutually advantageous arrangements are feasible, the benefits they yield fall short of the demands men put forward. (23)

(23) R It is only in situations where these general conditions are satisfied that justice becomes both an important social value and one capable of being reasonably achieved. Fundamental differences in these respects would make justice either of little importance or virtually impossible to achieve.

The subjective circumstances are the relevant aspects of the subjects of cooperation, that is, of the persons working together. Thus while the parties have roughly similar needs and interests, or needs and interests in various ways complementary, so that mutually advantageous cooperation among them is possible, they nevertheless have their own plans of life. These plans, or conceptions of the good, lead them to have different ends and purposes, and to make conflicting claims on the natural and social resources available. Moreover, although the interests advanced by these plans are not assumed to be interests in the self, they are the interests of a self that regards its conception of the good as worthy of recognition and that advances claims in its behalf as deserving satisfaction. I also suppose that men suffer from various shortcomings of knowledge, thought, and judgment. Their knowledge is necessarily incomplete, their powers of reasoning, memory, and attention are always limited, and their judgment is likely to be distorted by anxiety, bias, and a preoccupation with their own affairs. Some of these defects spring from moral faults, from selfishness and negligence; but to a large degree, they are simply part of men's natural situation. As a consequence individuals not only have different plans of life but there exists a diversity of philosophical and religious belief, and of political and social doctrines.

...

The Veil of Ignorance

The idea of the original position is to set up a fair procedure so that any principles agreed to will be just. Somehow we must nullify the effects of specific contingencies which put men at odds and tempt them to exploit social and natural circumstances to their own advantage. Now in order to do this I assume that the parties are situated behind a veil of ignorance. They do not know how the various alternatives will affect their own particular case and they are obliged to evaluate principles solely on the basis of general considerations.

It is assumed, then, that the parties do not know certain kinds of particular facts. First of all, no one knows his place in society, his class position or social status; nor does he know his fortune in the distribution of natural assets and abilities, his intelligence and strength, and the like. Nor, again, does anyone know his conception of the good, the particulars of his rational plan of life, or even the special features of his psychology such as his aversion to risk or liability to optimism or pessimism. . . .

As far as possible, then, the only particular facts which the parties know is that their society is subject to the circumstances of justice and whatever this implies. It is taken for granted, however, that they know the general facts about human society. They understand political affairs and the principles of economic theory; they know the basis of social organization and the laws of human psychology. Indeed, the parties are presumed to know whatever general facts affect the choice of the principles of justice. . . . (24)

(24) Because such general knowledge will not allow them to bias the choice of principles in their own favor.

The Rationality of the Parties

I have assumed throughout that the persons in the original position are rational. But I have also assumed that they do not know their conception of the good. This means that while they know that they have some rational plan of life, they do not know the details of this plan, the particular ends and interests which it is calculated to promote. How, then, can they decide which conceptions of justice are most to their advantage? Or must we suppose that they are reduced to mere guessing? To meet this difficulty, I postulate that they accept . . . that they normally prefer more primary social goods rather than less. (25) Of course, it may turn out, once the veil of ignorance is removed, that some of them for religious or other reasons may not, in fact, want more of these goods. But from the standpoint of the original position, it is rational for the parties to suppose that they do want a larger share, since in any case they are not compelled to accept more if they do not wish to. Thus even though

(25) "Primary social goods" are those that will be of value to almost anyone, no matter what their conception of the good or rational plan of life might be: rights, liberties, and opportunities; and income and wealth.

the parties are deprived of information about their particular ends, they have enough knowledge to rank the alternatives. They know that in general they must try to protect their liberties, widen their opportunities, and enlarge their means for promoting their aims whatever these are. Guided by the theory of the good and the general facts of moral psychology, their deliberations are no longer guesswork. They can make a rational decision in the ordinary sense.

...

The assumption of mutually disinterested rationality, then, comes to this: the persons in the original position try to acknowledge principles which advance their system of ends as far as possible. They do this by attempting to win for themselves the highest index of primary social goods, since this enables them to promote their conception of the good most effectively whatever it turns out to be. The parties do not seek to confer benefits or to impose injuries on one another; they are not moved by affection or rancor. Nor do they try to gain relative to each other; they are not envious or vain. . . .

The Reasoning Leading to the two Principles of Justice

...

Now consider the point of view of anyone in the original position. There is no way for him to win special advantages for himself. Nor, on the other hand, are there grounds for his acquiescing in special disadvantages. Since it is not reasonable for him to expect more than an equal share in the division of social primary goods, and since it is not rational for him to agree to less, the sensible thing is to acknowledge as the first step a principle of justice requiring an equal distribution. Indeed, this principle is so obvious given the symmetry of the parties that it would occur to everyone immediately. Thus the parties start with a principle requiring equal basic liberties for all, as well as fair equality of opportunity and equal division of income and wealth.

But even holding firm to the priority of the basic liberties and fair equality of opportunity, there is no reason why this initial acknowledgment should be final. Society should take into account economic efficiency and the requirements of organization and technology. If there are inequalities in income and wealth, and differences in authority and degrees of responsibility, that work to make everyone better off in comparison with the benchmark of equality, why not permit them? (26) . . . Thus the parties would [refuse to] agree to these differences only if they would be dejected by the bare knowledge or perception that others are better situated; but I suppose that they decide as if they are not moved by envy. Thus the basic structure should allow these inequalities so long as these improve everyone's situation, including that of the least advantaged, provided that they are consistent with equal liberty and fair opportunity. Because the parties start from an equal division of all social primary goods, those who benefit least have, so to speak, a veto. Thus we arrive at the difference principle. Taking equality as the basis of comparison, those who have gained more must do so on terms that are justifiable to those who have gained the least.

(26)

Such inequalities might be necessary to give those with special talents the incentive to develop and employ them, thereby increasing the total social production and making everyone, even the least advantaged, better off in absolute terms.

By some such reasoning, then, the parties might arrive at the two principles of justice in serial order. I shall not try to justify this ordering here, but the following remarks may convey the intuitive idea. . . .

The priority of liberty means that whenever the basic liberties can be effectively established, a lesser or an unequal liberty cannot be exchanged for an improvement in economic well-being. It is only when social circumstances do not allow the effective establishment of these basic rights that one can concede their limitation; and even then these restrictions can be granted only to the extent that they are necessary to prepare the way for the time when they are no longer justified. The denial of the equal liberties can be defended only when it is essential to change the conditions of civilization so that in due course these liberties can be enjoyed. . . . (27)

(27)

R Here is an exception to the idea that the first principle (equal liberty) has complete priority over the second principle (the difference principle).

Try to think of possible cases or conditions in which this exception would apply.

It seems from these remarks that the two principles are at least a plausible conception of justice. The question, though, is how one is to argue for them more systematically. . . . In order to see how this might be done, it is useful as a heuristic device to think of the two principles as the maximin solution to the problem of social justice. There is a relation between the two principles and the maximin rule for choice under uncertainty. This is evident from the fact that the two principles are those a person would choose for the design of a society in which his enemy is to assign him his place. The maximin rule tells us to rank alternatives by their worst possible outcomes: we are to adopt the alternative the worst outcome of which is superior to the worst outcomes of the others. [28] The persons in the original position do not, of course, assume that their initial place in society is decided by a malevolent opponent. As I note below, they should not reason from false premises. The veil of ignorance does not violate this idea, since an absence of information is not misinformation. But that the two principles of justice would be chosen if the parties were forced to protect themselves against such a contingency explains the sense in which this conception is the maximin solution. And this analogy suggests that if the original position has been described so that it is rational for the parties to adopt the conservative attitude expressed by this rule, a conclusive argument can indeed be constructed for these principles. Clearly the maximin rule is not, in general, a suitable guide for choices under uncertainty. But it holds only in situations marked by certain special features. My aim, then, is to show that a good case can be made for the two principles based on the fact that the original position has these features to a very high degree.

28

Maximin is a *very* conservative, risk-aversive principle of decision. Rawls's claim is that this principle, though not generally the best principle of rational choice, is the right one to follow in the very special case of the original position.

Now there appear to be three chief features of situations that give plausibility to this unusual rule. First, since the rule takes no account of the likelihoods of the possible circumstances, there must be some reason for sharply discounting estimates of these probabilities. . . .Thus it must be, for example, that the situation is one in which a knowledge of likelihoods is impossible, or at best extremely insecure. In this case it is unreasonable not to be skeptical of probabilistic calculations unless there is no other way out, particularly if the decision is a fundamental one that needs to be justified to others.

The second feature that suggests the maximin rule is the following: the person choosing has a conception of the good such that he cares very little, if anything, for what he might gain above the minimum stipend that he can, in fact, be sure of by following the maximin rule. It is not worthwhile for him to take a chance for the sake of a further advantage, especially when it may turn out that he loses much that is important to him. This last provision brings in the third feature, namely, that the rejected alternatives have outcomes that one can hardly accept. The situation involves grave risks. Of course these features work most effectively in combination. The paradigm situation for following the maximin rule is when all three features are realized to the highest degree.

Let us review briefly the nature of the original position with these three special features in mind. To begin with, the veil of ignorance excludes all knowledge of likelihoods. The parties have no basis for determining the probable nature of their society, or their place in it. Thus they have no basis for probability calculations. They must also take into account the fact that their choice of principles should seem reasonable to others, in particular their descendants, whose rights will be deeply affected by it. These considerations are strengthened by the fact that the parties know very little about the possible states of society. Not only are they unable to conjecture the likelihoods of the various possible circumstances, they cannot say much about what the possible circumstances are, much less enumerate them and foresee the outcome of each alternative available. . . .

Several kinds of arguments for the two principles of justice illustrate the second feature. Thus, if we can maintain that these principles provide a workable theory of social justice, and that they are compatible with reasonable demands of efficiency, then this conception guarantees a satisfactory minimum. There may be, on reflection, little reason for trying to do better. . . . [29]

29

Is this second feature clearly satisfied in the situation of the original position? Relative to the choice of the difference principle, it amounts to saying that the possible gains that might result by departing from that principle (being extremely well off, more than could be justified by the difference principle) are not very important to any reasonable person.

Finally, the third feature holds if we can assume that other conceptions of justice may lead to institutions that the parties would find intolerable. For example, it has sometimes been held that under some conditions the utility principle (in either form) justifies, if not slavery or serfdom, at any rate serious infractions of liberty for the sake of greater social benefits. We need not consider here the truth of this claim.

For the moment, this contention is only to illustrate the way in which conceptions of justice may allow for outcomes which the parties may not be able to accept. And having the ready alternative of the two principles of justice which secure a satisfactory minimum, it seems unwise, if not irrational, for them to take a chance that these conditions are not realized. 

...

30

Much of this is concerned with departures from the first principle (of liberty). But departures from the difference principle could also lead to dire outcomes such as starvation or extreme poverty.

These are obviously undesirable, but is it clear that no rational person would risk them in pursuit of the sorts of possible gains indicated in the previous annotation?

Discussion Questions

1. Consider two people, one from an upper-class family and one from a lower-class family. Describe what sort of principle of "justice" each of them would favor out of self-interest if they were not behind the "veil of ignorance," and why neither of these principles seems intuitively to be the right account of justice. How does the veil of ignorance prevent them from favoring these principles out of self-interest? What sort of a principle pertaining to how people should be treated according to their social class might they end up adopting under the veil of ignorance? Does the principle they would choose in this situation seem to you to be the most clearly just one? Why or why not?

2. Now consider the comparable situation of two people with different degrees of natural talent or ability, for example, one more intelligent and one less intelligent. Describe what principles pertaining to the allocation of gains resulting from intelligence each of these people would choose out of self-interest if not behind the veil of ignorance. Is it clear in this case that neither of these principles is an acceptable principle of justice? What principle governing the allocation of gains resulting from intelligence does Rawls think they would adopt in the original position and why? Is this principle clearly preferable, from the standpoint of justice, to the principles that each would choose outside the original position?

3. Rawls claims that the *maximin* principle is the right principle of decision to follow in the original position. Contrast this with the *maximax* principle, which says that choices should be ranked according to their *best* possible outcome. This is an extremely optimistic, risk-taking principle. Consider different situations in which you have to make a choice in which each alternative could lead to more than one possible outcome, and explain what each of these principles would tell you to do in such cases.

One way to formulate such issues is with a decision-theoretic matrix, like the following one for a schematic choice (where you have no knowledge of which condition actually obtains):

	Choice 1	*Choice 2*	*Choice 3*
Condition 1	100	5	90
Condition 2	−100	10	85
Condition 3	−100	5	0

In this case, maximin would select choice 2 and maximax would select choice 1. Is either decision-making principle clearly the right one in all such cases—or even any such cases? Can you think of any other principles for making such decisions that seem better? Would any of these be applicable in the original position?

4. The basic idea of Rawls's argument for the choice of the difference principle (reflected in the maximin principle) is that the rational thing to do when faced with such a fundamental choice (one that has major effects on your whole life) is to play it safe, rather than gambling that you will do much better at the risk of doing much worse. Do you think it is obvious that this is the right choice, that no rational person would be willing to gamble? Might it be that this is a matter of temperament—that some people would be willing to gamble and some would not? What effect would this have on the argument based on the original position?

Robert Nozick

In this selection, also from *Anarchy, State, and Utopia,* Nozick offers his objections to Rawls's account of justice. He challenges whether the difference principle is really fair to those who have better natural assets, and questions whether Rawls has any good argument that such assets should be treated in the way his principle requires. Nozick also suggests that the Rawlsian view would yield dubious results in the more limited situation of fairly assigning grades (though Rawls does say that his view is not intended to apply to such situations).

A Critique of Rawls, from *Anarchy, State, and Utopia*

Terms of Cooperation and the Difference Principle

. . . Rawls imagines rational, mutually disinterested individuals meeting in a certain situation, or abstracted from their other features not provided for in this situation. In this hypothetical situation of choice, which Rawls calls "the original position," they choose the first principles of a conception of justice that is to regulate all subsequent criticism and reform of their institutions. While making this choice, no one knows his place in society, his class position or social status, or his natural assets and abilities, his strength, intelligence, and so forth.

...

What would persons in the original position agree to?

> Persons in the initial situation would choose two . . . principles: the first requires equality in the assignment of basic rights and duties, while the second holds that social and economic inequalities, for example, inequalities of wealth and authority are just only if they result in compensating benefits for everyone, and in particular for the least advantaged members of society . . . .*

This second principle, which Rawls specifies as the difference principle, holds that the institutional structure is to be so designed that the worst-off group under it is at least as well off as the worst-off group (not necessarily the same group) would be under any alternative institutional structure. If persons in the original position follow the minimax policy in making the significant choice of principles of justice, Rawls argues, they will choose the difference principle . . .

Rawls holds . . . that

> since everyone's well-being depends upon a scheme of cooperation without which no one could have a satisfactory life, the division of advantages should be such as to draw forth the willing cooperation of everyone taking part in it, including those less well situated. Yet this can be expected only if reasonable terms are proposed. The two principles mentioned seem to be a fair agreement on the basis of which those better endowed or more fortunate in their social position . . . could expect the willing cooperation of others when some workable scheme is a necessary condition of the welfare of all.†

No doubt, the difference principle presents terms on the basis of which those less well endowed would be willing to cooperate. (What *better* terms could they propose for themselves?) But is this a fair agreement on the basis of which those *worse* endowed could expect the *willing* cooperation of others? With regard to the existence of gains from social cooperation, the situation is symmetrical. The better endowed gain by cooperating with the worse endowed, *and* the worse endowed gain by cooperating with the better endowed. Yet the difference principle is not neutral between the better and the worse endowed. Whence the asymmetry? (1)

1

R Under the difference principle, the less well endowed are getting the *most* they could possibly get: any attempt to give them more would end up giving them less. But the better endowed are getting the *least* they could possibly get without hurting the position of the less well endowed.

Perhaps the symmetry is upset if one asks *how much* each gains from the social cooperation. This question might be understood in two ways. How much do people benefit from social cooperation, as compared to their individual holdings in a *non*cooperative scheme? . . . Or, alternatively, how much does each individual gain from general social cooperation, as compared, not with *no* cooperation, but with more limited cooperation? The latter is the more appropriate question with regard to general social cooperation. For failing general agreement on the principles to govern how the benefits of general social cooperation are to be held, not everyone will remain in a noncooperative situation if there is some other beneficial cooperative arrangement involving some, but not all, people, whose participants *can* agree. These people will participate in this more narrow cooperative arrangement. To focus upon the benefits of the better and the worse endowed cooperating together, we must try to imagine less extensive schemes of partitioned social cooperation in which the better endowed cooperate only among themselves and the worse

From *Anarchy, State, and Utopia* (New York: Basic Books, 1974).

*Rawls, *Theory of Justice,* 1st ed. pp. 14–15. [Page 486 in this book.]
†Rawls, *Theory of Justice,* 1st ed. p. 15. [Page 486 in this book.]

endowed cooperate only among themselves, with no cross-cooperation. (2) The members of both groups gain from the internal cooperation within their respective groups and have larger shares than they would if there were no social cooperation at all. An individual benefits from the wider system of extensive cooperation between the better and the worse endowed to the extent of his incremental gain from this wider cooperation; namely, the amount by which his share under a scheme of general cooperation is greater than it would be under one of limited intragroup (but not cross-group) cooperation. *General* cooperation will be of more benefit to the better or to the worse endowed if (to pick a simple criterion) the mean [average] incremental gain from general cooperation (when compared with limited intragroup cooperation) is greater in one group than it is in the other.

One might speculate about whether there is an inequality between the groups' mean incremental gains and, if so, which way it goes. If the better-endowed group includes those who manage to accomplish something of great economic advantage to others, such as new inventions, new ideas about production or ways of doing things, skill at economic tasks, and so on, it is difficult to avoid concluding that the *less* well endowed gain *more* than the better endowed do from the scheme of general cooperation. (3) What follows from this conclusion? I do *not* mean to imply that the better endowed should get even more than they get under the entitlement system of general social cooperation. What *does* follow from the conclusion is a deep suspicion of imposing, in the name of fairness, constraints upon voluntary social cooperation (and the set of holdings that arises from it) so that those already benefiting most from this general cooperation benefit even more!

Rawls would have us imagine the worse-endowed persons say something like the following: "Look, better endowed: you gain by cooperating with us. If you want our cooperation you'll have to accept reasonable terms. We suggest these terms: We'll cooperate with you only if we get *as much as possible.* That is, the terms of our cooperation should give us that maximal share such that, if it was tried to give us more, we'd end up with less." How generous these proposed terms are might be seen by imagining that the better endowed make the almost symmetrical opposite proposal: "Look, worse endowed: you gain by cooperating with *us.* If you want our cooperation you'll have to accept reasonable terms. We propose these terms: We'll cooperate with you so long as *we* get as much as possible. That is, the terms of our cooperation should give us the maximal share such that, if it was tried to give us more, we'd end up with less." If these terms seem outrageous, as they are, why don't the terms proposed by those worse endowed seem the same? (4) Why shouldn't the better endowed treat this latter proposal as beneath consideration, supposing someone to have the nerve explicitly to state it?

Rawls devotes much attention to explaining why those less well favored should not complain at receiving less. His explanation, simply put, is that because the inequality works for his advantage, someone less well favored shouldn't complain about it; he receives *more* in the unequal system than he would in an equal one. (Though he might receive still more in another unequal system that placed someone else below him.) But Rawls discusses the question of whether those *more* favored will or should find the terms satisfactory *only* in the following passage, where *A* and *B* are any two representative men with *A* being the more favored:

> The difficulty is to show that *A* has no grounds for complaint. Perhaps he is required to have less than he might since his having more would result in some loss to *B*. Now what can be said to the more favored man? To begin with, it is clear that the well-being of each depends on a scheme of social cooperation without which no one could have a satisfactory life. Secondly, we can ask for the willing cooperation of everyone only if the terms of the scheme are reasonable. The difference principle, then, seems to be a fair basis on which those better endowed, or more fortunate in their social circumstance, could expect others to collaborate with them when some workable arrangement is a necessary condition of the good of all.*

What Rawls imagines being said to the more favored men does *not* show that these men have no grounds for complaint, nor does it at all diminish the weight of whatever complaints they have. That the well-being of all depends on

Rawls considers only the situation where everyone cooperates with everyone. But more limited sorts of cooperation are also possible. Nozick argues that these must also be considered in deciding how much each group benefits from everyone cooperating together.

Nozick *speculates* that it is the less endowed who gain the most from general cooperation, as opposed to more limited cooperation among themselves, because the more endowed group will contribute more in the way of productive ideas and skills.

Nozick imagines the two groups making what he describes as "almost symmetrical" proposals.

Is he right about this? Or is there some way in which the proposal of the less well endowed (which is identical to what is required by the difference principle) is more reasonable or more just?

---

*Rawls, *Theory of Justice,* 1st ed., p. 103. [See pp. 490–491 in this book for the revised edition version of this passage.]

The passage Nozick quotes is from the first edition of *A Theory of Justice*. In the revised edition, from which the selection from Rawls in this book is taken, this passage is replaced by the paragraph continued from p. 490 to p. 491 (to which Annotation 20 is attached). Does the later version provide a better answer to the challenge Nozick is raising here?

R The students who receive better grades under the "Entitlements" distribution would have self-interested reasons for accepting that distribution, but there is no self-interested reason for the others to agree.

This is Nozick's attempt to make this case somewhat parallel to the situation where giving incentives to some people results in greater overall production.

social cooperation without which no one could have a satisfactory life could also be said to the less well endowed by someone proposing any other principle, including that of maximizing the position of the best endowed. Similarly for the fact that we can ask for the willing cooperation of everyone only if the terms of the scheme are reasonable. The question is: What terms *would be* reasonable? What Rawls imagines being said thus far merely sets up his problem; it doesn't distinguish his proposed difference principle from the almost symmetrical counterproposal that we imagined the better endowed making, or from any other proposal. Thus, when Rawls continues, "The difference principle, then, seems to be a fair basis on which those best endowed, or more fortunate in their social circumstances, could expect others to collaborate with them when some workable arrangement is a necessary condition of the good of all," the presence of the "then" in his sentence is puzzling. Since the sentences which precede it are neutral between his proposal and any other proposal, the conclusion that the difference principle presents a fair basis for cooperation *cannot* follow from what precedes it in this passage. Rawls is merely repeating that it seems reasonable; hardly a convincing reply to anyone to whom it doesn't seem reasonable. Rawls has not shown that the more favored man *A* has no grounds for complaint at being required to have less in order that another *B* might have more than he otherwise would. And he can't show this, since *A does* have grounds for complaint. Doesn't he? 5

The Original Position and End-Result Principles

...

Suppose there were a group of students who have studied during a year, taken examinations, and received grades between 0 and 100 which they have not yet learned of. They are now gathered together, having no idea of the grade any one of them has received, and they are asked to allocate grades among themselves so that the grades total to a given sum (which is determined by the sum of the grades they actually have received from the teacher). First, let us suppose they are to decide jointly upon a particular distribution of grades; they are to give a particular grade to each identifiable one of them present at the meeting. Here, given sufficient restrictions on their ability to threaten each other, they probably would agree to each person receiving the same grade, to each person's grade being equal to the total divided by the number of people to be graded. Surely they would *not* chance upon the particular set of grades they already have received. Suppose next that there is posted on a bulletin board at their meeting a paper headed ENTITLEMENTS, which lists each person's name with a grade next to it, the listing being identical to the instructor's gradings. Still, this particular distribution will not be agreed to by those having done poorly. Even if they know what "entitlement" means (which perhaps we must suppose they don't, in order to match the absence of moral factors in the calculations of persons in Rawls' original position), why should they agree to the instructor's distribution? What self-interested reason to agree to it would they have? 6

Next suppose that they are unanimously to agree not to a *particular* distribution of grades, but rather to general principles to govern the distribution of grades. What principle would be selected? The equality principle, which gives each person the same grade, would have a prominent chance. And if it turned out that the total was variable depending upon how they divided it, depending on which of them got what grade, 7 and a higher grade was desirable though they were not competing among each other (for example, each of them was competing for some position with the members of separate distinct groups), then the principle of distributing grades so as to maximize the lowest grades *might* seem a plausible one. Would these people agree to the non-end-state *historical* principle of distribution: give people grades according to how their examinations were evaluated by a qualified and impartial observer? If all the people deciding knew the particular distribution that would be yielded by this historical principle, they wouldn't agree to it. For the situation then would be equivalent to the earlier one of their deciding upon a particular distribution, in which we already have seen they would not agree to the entitlement distribution. Suppose then that the people do not know the particular distribution actually yielded by this historical principle. They cannot be led to select this historical principle because it looks just, or fair, to them; for no such notions are allowed to be at work in the original position. (Otherwise people would argue there, like here, about what justice requires.) Each person engages in a calculation to decide whether it will be in his own interests to accept this historical principle of distribution. Grades, under the historical principle, depend upon nature and developed intelligence, how hard the people have worked, accident, and so on, factors about which people in the original position know almost nothing. . . . Each person in the original position will do something like assigning probability distributions to his place along these various dimensions. It seems unlikely that each person's probability calculations would lead to the historical-entitlement principle, in preference to every other principle. Consider the principle we may call the reverse-entitlement principle. It recommends drawing up a list of the historical entitlements in order of magnitude, and giving the most anyone is entitled to, to the person entitled to the least; the second most to the person entitled to the second least, and so on. Any probability calculations of self-interested persons in Rawls' original position, or any probability calculations of the students we have considered, will lead them to view the entitlement and the reverse-entitlement principles as ranked equally insofar as their own self-interest is concerned! (What calculations could lead them to view one of the principles as superior to the other?) Their calculations will not lead them to select the entitlement principle.

...

Rawls' construction is incapable of yielding an entitlement or historical conception of distributive justice. . . . The whole procedure of persons choosing principles in Rawls' original position presupposes that no historical-entitlement conception of justice is correct.

It might be objected to our argument that Rawls' procedure is designed to *establish* all facts about justice; there is no independent notion of entitlement, not provided by his theory, to stand on in criticizing his theory. But we do not need any *particular* developed historical-entitlement theory as a basis from which to criticize Rawls' construction. If *any* such fundamental historical-entitlement view is correct, then Rawls' theory is not. We are thus able to make this structural criticism of the type of theory Rawls presents and the type of principles it must yield, without first having formulated fully a particular historical-entitlement theory as an alternative to his. We would be ill advised to accept Rawls' theory and his construal of the problem as one of which principles would be chosen by rational self-interested individuals behind a veil of ignorance, unless we were sure that no adequate historical-entitlement theory was to be gotten. (8)

Nozick's claim is that the way that Rawls sets up the issue and defines the original position guarantees that no historical-entitlement theory could be chosen and thus *presupposes* that no such theory is correct.

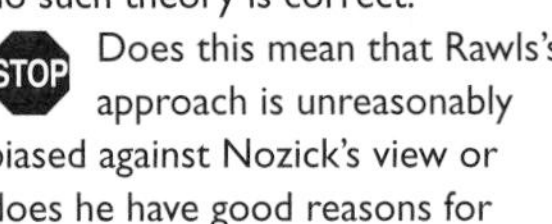

Does this mean that Rawls's approach is unreasonably biased against Nozick's view or does he have good reasons for ruling out views of this kind?

...

Natural Assets and Arbitrariness

Rawls comes closest to considering the entitlement system in his discussion of what he terms the system of natural liberty. . . .

. . . *Rawls'* reason for rejecting a system of natural liberty [is that] it "permits" distributive shares to be improperly influenced by factors that are . . . arbitrary from a moral point of view. These factors are: "prior distribution . . . of natural talents and abilities as these have been developed over time by social circumstances and such chance contingencies as accident and good fortune." . . .

Rawls has explicitly *designed* the original position and its choice situation so as to embody and realize his negative reflective evaluation of allowing shares in holdings to be affected by natural assets: "Once we decide to look for a conception of justice that nullifies the accidents of natural endowment and the contingencies of social circumstance. . . ."* (9) . . . This quest crucially shapes Rawls' theory, and it underlies his delineation of the original position

This passage is also altered in the revised edition of *A Theory of Justice*—and in the selection in this volume. Compare the quotation here with the passage at Annotation 8 to the Rawls section, in which Rawls no longer speaks of *nullifying* the accidents of natural endowment.

Why shouldn't holdings partially depend upon natural endowments? (They will also depend on how these are developed and on the uses to which they are put.) Rawls' reply is that these natural endowments and assets, being undeserved, are "arbitrary from a moral point of view." . . .

. . . How might the point that differences in natural endowments are arbitrary from a moral point of view function in an argument meant to establish that differences in holdings stemming

*Rawls, *Theory of Justice,* 1st ed. p. 15. [See page 486 in this book.]

from differences in natural assets ought to be nullified? We shall consider [two] possible arguments; the first, the following argument A:

1. Any person should morally deserve the holdings he has; it shouldn't be that persons have holdings they don't deserve.
2. People do not morally deserve their natural assets.
3. If a person's *X* partially determines his *Y*, and his *X* is undeserved then so is his *Y*.

Therefore,

4. People's holdings shouldn't be partially determined by their natural assets.

. . . But Rawls explicitly and emphatically *rejects* distribution according to moral desert.

> There is a tendency for common sense to suppose that income and wealth, and the good things in life generally, should be distributed according to moral desert. Justice is happiness according to virtue. While it is recognized that this ideal can never be fully carried out, it is the appropriate conception (according to common sense) of distributive justice, at least as a *prima facie* principle, and society should try to realize it as circumstances permit. Now justice as fairness rejects this conception. Such a principle would not be chosen in the original position. 10 *

10

STOP Think carefully about *why* such a principle would not be chosen in the original position.

Rawls could not, therefore, accept any premiss like the first premiss in argument *A*, and so no variant of this argument underlies his rejection of differences in distributive shares stemming from undeserved differences in natural assets. . . .

I turn now to our [second] positive argument which purports to derive the conclusion that distributive shares shouldn't depend upon natural assets from the statement that the distribution of natural assets is morally arbitrary. This argument focuses on the notion of equality. Since a large part of Rawls' argument serves to justify or show acceptable a particular deviation from equal shares (some may have more if this serves to improve the position of those worst off), perhaps a reconstruction of his underlying argument that places equality at its center will be illuminating. Differences between persons (the argument runs) are arbitrary from a moral point of view if there is no moral argument for the conclusion that there ought to be the differences. . . .

Thus we have argument D:

1. Holdings ought to be equal, unless there is a (weighty) moral reason why they ought to be unequal.
2. People do not deserve the ways in which they differ from other persons in natural assets; there is no moral reason why people ought to differ in natural assets.
3. If there is no moral reason why people differ in certain traits, then their actually differing in these traits does not provide, and cannot give rise to, a moral reason why they should differ in other traits (for example, in holdings).

Therefore,

4. People's differing in natural assets is not a reason why holding ought to be unequal.
5. People's holdings ought to be equal unless there is some other moral reason (such as, for example, raising the position of those worst off) why their holdings ought to be unequal.

. . . Here let us focus on the first premiss, the equality premiss. Why ought people's holdings to be equal, in the absence of special moral reason to deviate from equality? (Why think there *ought* to be *any* particular pattern in holdings?) Why is equality the rest (or rectilinear motion) position of the system, deviation from which may be caused only by moral forces? Many "arguments" for equality merely *assert* that differences between persons are arbitrary and must be justified. Often writers state a presumption in favor of equality in a form such as the following: "Differences in treatment of persons need to be justified." . . . That differences in treatment need to be justified *does* fit contemporary *governments*. Here there is a centralized process treating all, with no entitlement to bestow treatment according to whim. The major portion of distribution in a free society does not, however, come through the actions of the government, nor does failure to overturn the results of the localized individual exchanges constitute "state action." When there is no *one* doing the treating, and all are entitled to bestow their holdings as they wish, it is not clear why the maxim that differences in treatment must be justified should be thought to have extensive application. Why must differences between persons be justified? Why

*Rawls, *Theory of Justice,* 1st ed. p. 310. [Not included in the selection in this book.]

think that we must change, or remedy, or compensate for any inequality which can be changed, remedied, or compensated for? (11) . . . Here we need only note that the connection argument D forges between not deserving natural assets and some conclusion about distributive shares *assumes* equality as a norm (that can be deviated from with, and only with, moral reason); and hence argument D itself cannot be used to establish any such conclusion about equality.

. . .

(11)

R Nozick grants that holdings and other benefits derived from government ought to be equal unless there is a "weighty moral reason" to the contrary, but denies that this is true of holdings whose distribution does not result from governmental action but instead from free choices by individuals.

STOP How do you think Rawls would respond to this point?

Discussion Questions

1. How might Rawls justify the asymmetrical treatment that the difference principle gives to the less and more endowed? Is such treatment compatible with justice? (Note that this question cannot be settled by appeal to the original position, since it in effect challenges whether the way Rawls conceives the original position is itself compatible with the demands of justice.)
2. Nozick is offering the grade distribution case as an analogy to challenge whether something like the original position is a good way to decide what justice requires. In this case, it seems fairly clear that a procedure analogous to that suggested by Rawls is neither required by justice nor in fact yields just results. In fact, Rawls says explicitly that his view is not intended to determine what is just in more limited situations of this kind. But is there any good explanation he can give of why the demands of justice with regard to the basic structure of society are apparently so different from those in more limited cases?
3. If Rawls's view is supposed to determine what justice requires, how can he be justified in appealing to a procedure that apparently excludes a view like Nozick's as even a possibility? Is Nozick right that it does this? If so, is there any way that Rawls can justify approaching the issue in this way?
4. Does justice require that differences in natural endowments be *nullified*, as Rawls says in the first edition of *A Theory of Justice*? (See Annotation 9 and the corresponding passages.) Is this what adherence to the difference principle in effect does? Might there be differences that cannot be nullified in this way? (One example to consider is physical attractiveness and the benefits that it leads to.) Is there any other way you can think of to *nullify* such differences? Does justice really require that this be done in this sort of case?

Thomas M. Scanlon

Thomas Scanlon (1940–) is an American moral and political philosopher who now teaches at Harvard. In the following selection, he offers an extended critique of Nozick's account of justice and, in passing, a defense of Rawls against some of Nozick's criticisms.

Nozick on Rights, Liberty, and Property

In *Anarchy, State and Utopia** Robert Nozick approaches political philosophy within a framework . . . which emphasizes individual rights and the derivation of political obligation from consent. . . . Nozick holds that the only legitimate state is the minimal state, whose activities are confined to the protection of individuals and their property and to the enforcement of contracts. This state is unique among social organizations in having the right to force residents to pay for its services whether or not they have consented to do so. Citizens may band together for whatever other purposes they may desire—to provide education, to aid the needy, to organize social insurance schemes—but such schemes must be purely voluntary, and the state must enforce anyone's right not to be compelled to contribute to them.

Nozick reaches these conclusions by adhering as closely as possible to the idea that, in

From *Philosophy and Public Affairs* (Fall, 1976).

*(New York, 1974). Page numbers in the text and footnotes refer to the excerpts in this book.

This is, of course, a view that would have been accepted by both Hobbes and Locke as well. As Scanlon points out later, Rawls's view can also be seen as a kind of consent theory, though with the very important difference that the consent is hypothetical (in relation to the "original position") rather than actual.

economic life as in politics, all valid obligations derive from consent. [1] Of course, . . . the obligations and entitlements one person acquires through voluntary agreements can affect the alternatives open to others who have not been parties to these agreements. Something must determine when such side effects make an agreement void. In Nozick's theory these conditions and limits are set by a skeletal framework of rights derived from Locke. The minimal role allowed to the state and the great scope left to voluntary agreement and consent in his theory are direct consequences of the particular character of these rights. This system of rights is not argued for directly in the book, however, and Nozick does not claim to have given these rights a foundation. . . .

The central theoretical device of the book is the classification of principles of justice as "historical," "end-state," and "patterned." Nozick classifies a principle of justice as historical if that principle makes the justice of a distribution depend on how it came about (p. 478). It will follow from a historical principle of justice that "past circumstances or actions of people can create differential entitlements or differential deserts to things" (p. 478). By contrast, under what Nozick calls an end-state principle, the justice of a distribution will depend only on certain structural features of the situation it represents, for example, on the amount of utility produced or on the degree of equality obtaining. Of course, the structural features of a distribution that are deemed relevant by a principle of justice might make reference to historical events. A principle might require, for example, that people's holdings should be proportional to their moral worth as determined by their past actions. Such a principle is historical in Nozick's sense, but it clearly has a great deal in common with end-state principles. Nozick calls such a principle, one which specifies that holdings are to "vary along with some natural dimension" or some combination of such dimensions, a patterned principle. Nozick's own theory of justice is based on unpatterned historical principles. This theory is an entitlement conception of justice. Such a conception is specified by three components: a principle of (initial) acquisition, a principle of transfer, and a principle of rectification. Its central tenet is that any configuration of holdings that results from the legitimate transfer of legitimately acquired holdings is itself just. There is no reason to expect (or to require) that such holdings conform to any natural pattern. (The principle of rectification comes into play to explain how, if holdings are affected by violations of the principles of just acquisition and transfer, this situation is to be remedied.)

Many theories of justice, almost any theory perhaps, will give some role to considerations of entitlement; that is, they will recognize some processes as conferring legitimacy on their outcomes. What is special about Nozick's view is that it makes entitlement principles the beginning and end of distributive justice. While his principles are not described in detail, it appears that his theory differs from other pure entitlement conceptions chiefly in admitting fewer restrictions on the acquisition and exchange of property. He mentions only one such restriction, called "the Lockean Proviso," which provides that any acquisition, transfer, or combination of transfers is void if it leaves third parties worse off then they were in the state of nature.* Such a worsening might occur, for example, if someone were to buy, in simultaneous secret transactions, rights to all the available sources of water. This restriction could be substantial were it not for the fact that the baseline for its application is set by conditions in the state of nature. According to Nozick the productivity of the capitalist system in improving our material condition makes it unlikely that (in a competitive economy) anyone could acquire holdings that would leave others below this standard.

Nozick clearly feels that the distinction between historical (unpatterned) principles of justice and patterned or end-state principles is of fundamental importance. He emphasizes that almost all of the principles of justice commonly offered are end-state or patterned principles and, as such, are clearly mistaken. If this were correct it would indeed be important. Certainly Nozick's distinction does capture something intuitively appealing. It has often been said as a criticism of utilitarianism that it ignores morally significant relations resulting from past actions. [2]

Thus, for example, the fact that one has made a promise to someone has little or no moral weight for the utilitarian, since the right action is determined entirely by future consequences. (See Chapter 5 for more discussion of utilitarianism.)

*Worse off, that is, in what they are able to use; it is not enough that they be worse off with respect to what remains available for initial appropriation. See p. 482.

Nozick's distinction is of great interest if it gives this criticism a more abstract form and shows it to apply not only to utilitarianism but also to Rawls' theory and to virtually every other theory commonly offered. But I do not think that the distinction has the importance claimed for it. To see why, let me consider the reasons Nozick offers for holding that all patterned principles are clearly wrong.

These reasons can be quickly seen in Nozick's frequent remark that, since gift giving can upset a pattern of distribution, supporters of patterned principles of justice would have to forbid this form of "loving behavior" (p. 480). More generally, let D_1 be the distribution of goods obtaining in a given society and suppose that this distribution is in accord with our favorite pattern (for example, strict equality). This distribution can be changed into another distribution D_2, not in accord with this pattern, by any one of a variety of means: by gifts, by someone's starting a very successful business in his spare time using only resources to which he was already entitled under D_1, or, as Nozick suggests, by all one million of us willingly paying Wilt Chamberlain 25¢ apiece for the privilege of watching him play basketball. To maintain D_1 one would have to restrict these activities. Such "continuous interference" is, Nozick says, obviously unacceptable. Therefore one must conclude that no patterned conception of justice can be correct.

One immediate response to this argument is to doubt whether anyone ever held a "patterned" conception of justice in the sense that is here refuted. A person who objects to the inequality in the world is unlikely to be concerned with those who have less as a result of their giving away or trading part of what was once an equal share. What offends an egalitarian primarily is the great inequality in the initial resources people have as a result of the social positions in to which they are born. But here Nozick can respond that this does not escape his point. Arbitrarily great inequalities in the starting places of members of one generation can result from gifts and voluntary exchanges by members of previous generations. Thus, maintaining even this looser kind of equality can require restricting these activities.

So put, this is not such a startling conclusion; certainly it does not make egalitarianism look as foolish as first appeared. This is so, first, because there is no longer the appearance of unanimous consent. It is no longer plausible to respond, "Well, if the fans are all happy to pay [everyone now living in the society is a fan] and Wilt is willing to play at that price, how can a meddling egalitarian object?" [3] Second, this way of looking at the example changes our picture of the liberties that are likely to be infringed. The liberties involved in the example seem to be these: the liberty of the fans to pay an extra quarter to see Wilt play, his liberty to keep any amount he may receive through such transactions, his liberty to decide whether or not he wants to play for the amount remaining after taxes from what the fans and promoters offer him, and, finally, the liberty of his heirs to keep any amount of money he wishes to pass on to them. It does not seem likely that egalitarians, if their objectives are as I have described them, will want to keep watch over everyone's quarters or to conscript basketball stars. What is at issue, then, is the right of a person to keep as much as others are willing to pay him for his services and the right of heirs to receive unlimited bequests. But there is no strong intuitive ground for thinking that these rights are absolute, and little ground for surprise at the suggestion that the pursuit of equality might call for their infringement. [4]

That *everyone* is a fan of Chamberlain is not part of the example as Nozick presents it. Does the plausibility of the example require adding this additional stipulation?

STOP Think about the liberties that Scanlon lists here. Nozick would probably say that the example supports all four of them equally, while Scanlon is suggesting that two of them are less obviously immune to legitimate infringement than the other two. Who is right?

Nozick tries to make such measures seem more alarming to us by tying them to more extreme forms of intervention. Thus he says that "Taxation of earnings from labor is on a par with forced labor" (p. 480), and elsewhere he asks why, if we are going to set a limit on how long a person can control goods and transfer them to others, we do not have immediate confiscation. But there seems to be no reason to disregard such obvious differences in the degree of regulation of a person's life. It may be true, as Nozick claims, that there is a continuum of interferences extending from taxation to forced labor, each foreclosing a few more options than the preceding. But the fact that there is such a continuum is no reason why we must be indifferent between any two points along it. [5] Even if Nozick does not convince us that restrictions on earnings or inheritance in order to maintain equality are unacceptable, however, his examples do raise the question why any interference at all should be justified in order to preserve a pattern. As he says, what is so great about a pattern?

This seems to be a substantially weaker claim than Nozick actually makes. When he says that taxation of earnings is "on a par with forced labor," he seems to mean that they amount to the very same thing from a moral standpoint. (Is Nozick's stronger claim plausible?)

There are many different concerns which lead people to call for greater equality, and not all of these involve a pattern in a fundamental way. For example, a person's primary political goal may be to alleviate the terrible conditions under which many are forced to live. The fact that others are at the same time much better off shows that it would be possible to eliminate this suffering and, one might add, to do so without reducing anyone else to this low a level. The resources are there; they just need to be redistributed. For a person taking this position, a humanitarian, equalization is merely a means to the improvement of the lot of those currently worst off. It is possible that a person who is intensely concerned with this cause today might be quite satisfied if the living standard of everyone in the world were significantly improved, even if the gap between rich and poor was left unchanged. 6

Rawls, of course, does not hold such a view.

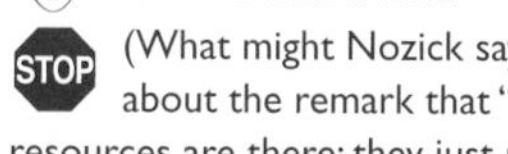

(What might Nozick say about the remark that "The resources are there; they just need to be redistributed"?)

A second position would take pattern more seriously but still assign it a purely instrumental role. A person taking this position is concerned by the fact that where there are great differences between rich and poor, especially where wealth is concentrated in a few hands, the wealthy come to have an unacceptable degree of control over what jobs there are, over what is to be produced and over political processes as well. For this reason, the growth of inequality can turn acceptable institutions into unacceptable ones even when this inequality is generated through what otherwise appear to be innocent means. 7 These considerations seem to me powerful where they apply, but they argue only for the elimination of the more extreme forms of inequality. A more rigorously egalitarian position might hold that even where neither of the preceding evils arises (no one is in want, and there is no threat of domination), inequalities are still objectionable because they are incompatible with healthy social relations and the development of genuine community. Putting the matter in terms of the pursuit of a social ideal seems to rob the demand for equality of some of its force. It needs to be explained why this particular ideal is morally important.

Scanlon seems clearly right that some of the effects of great differences of wealth are extremely undesirable. Is this enough to make them (morally) "unacceptable," so that corrective measures are thereby morally justified—even if they involve restricting the "innocent means" (free choices that people seemingly have a right to make) that led to this situation? See Discussion Question 1.

This explanation might be sought in a fourth egalitarian position. A person holding this position would object to inequalities in life-prospects flowing from differences in family wealth by arguing that all differences in treatment require justification, and these differences are undeserved and arbitrary. It is worth noting that Nozick, while being generally hard on egalitarian claims, allows that the demand for a justification of inequalities in initial resources would be valid if these were the result of some centralized mechanism of distribution (p. 500). He rejects this demand on the ground that such inequalities do not result from "state action" but instead flow from the independent actions of many individuals all acting within their rights. The results of such a process, he claims, need no independent justification. I shall return to this point later.

A supporter of this fourth position needs to say something about why unequal distributions, and not equal ones, require special justification. One reason might be that we recognize it is a distinct kind of bad thing for a person to be made worse off than others in his society are. The evil in question here is essentially comparative. It is not just that it is a bad thing to be at a low level of well-being, nor is it just that anyone would prefer to be at a certain higher level (the one where, as it happens, others are). What is bad is being at a lower level *when others around are much better off.* (It is worst when the level others have attained is the norm in your society.) 8 If this kind of relative disadvantage is a bad thing, then institutions which inflict it on people require a defense. Such a defense can be given. The better circumstances of others may be somehow earned, or it may be impossible to eliminate such differences or too expensive in terms of other benefits to do so. What is special about equal distributions is just that they require no defense of this particular kind.

Scanlon seems correct in saying that this is in some way a bad thing. Is it a *morally* bad thing, so that it automatically constitutes a *moral* objection to any sort of institution that leads to such a result?

If the evil of being relatively disadvantaged justifies eliminating inequalities by redistribution, however, it may be asked whether it does not provide an equally strong reason for simply worsening the position of the better off when redistribution is not possible. This may sound irrational, but in the case of many social inequalities, for example, distinctions of rank or social caste, egalitarian demands for the elimination of nonredistributable advantages are not implausible. In other cases, where we think that nonredistributable advantages should not be eliminated, this is not because these advantages are consistent with pure egalitarianism but because we temper the demands of equality with other considerations. Equality is not our only concern. 9

Similarly, it is open to the supporters of any of these egalitarian positions to recognize that powers to dispose of one's possessions—to give them away, to exchange them for others, to determine what will happen to them after one's death—are very important. Indeed in speaking of "distribution" they have always assumed that to distribute a good to a person is to give him some powers of this kind over it. Nozick's examples show that the interests served by these powers are among those things which must be weighed against the various considerations supporting equality. This is something that a realistic egalitarian can accept. 10

Certainly a theory cannot talk sensibly of patterns of holdings without considering how these patterns are to be produced and maintained. If this were all he was claiming in saying that no purely end-state or patterned theory is tenable, then Nozick would certainly be right. This would not do much to clear the field, however. As Nozick rightly points out, philosophical theories of distributive justice have often neglected the problems of how patterns of distribution can be established and preserved, but a theory can incorporate such considerations, and so avoid being an end-state theory in this narrow sense of the term without coming close to the position Nozick favors.

It seems, however, that Nozick's rejection of end-state theories encompasses more than the claims I have just endorsed. For he wishes to reject Rawls' theory as an unacceptable end-state theory, despite the fact that it incorporates considerations of entitlement through the notion of pure procedural justice. If the basic institutions of a society are just, according to Rawls, then the holdings people acquire through the operation of those institutions are legitimate, whatever these holdings may be, and people have rights over these holdings as the rules of the institution provide. 11 The basic structure itself is just, according to Rawls, if it conforms to his Two Principles, namely the principle of maximum equal basic liberties and the principle that institutions generating unequal holdings are just only insofar as these inequalities are to the benefit of the worse off, and only if the positions of greater reward are open to all under conditions of fair equality of opportunity. Nozick objects to this theory on the ground that the entitlements it supports have only a derived status; its fundamental principles, he says, are end-state, and it is therefore to be rejected. This rejection would also apply to the modified egalitarian positions I have described.

What is the basis for this strong claim, that any acceptable theory must make entitlements fundamental? In arguing against Rawls, Nozick maintains that a theory which brings in entitlement principles as derived principles to be defended by appeal to more fundamental moral notions together with empirical facts will strike us as wrong for the same reason that act-utilitarian attempts to account for rights seem so obviously mistaken. What is derived in such theories will be only approximations of the principles we intuitively want, and even where they support the same conclusions as these principles do, they do so for what seem to be the wrong reasons.

Whether this objection is persuasive against an end-state theory will depend on the character of the end-states with which that theory is concerned. Consider, for example, a theory concerned solely with the production of certain valued states of consciousness, or one concerned with securing equality in what people physically possess. It might be claimed within such a theory that certain rights to dispose of one's holdings are justified because they are a good means for producing an end-state of the required kind. Such an argument would indeed strike us as mistaken for reasons of the kind Nozick mentions, reasons strictly analogous to those that plague an act-utilitarian account of the obligation to keep one's promises 12 or of the prohibition against paternalism. But a modified egalitarian theory of the kind I suggested above would not have this problem. In such a theory, control over various aspects of one's life is something which has an independent value. This provides a direct basis for arguments in support of the personal rights that secure and protect such control, removing any need to appeal to whatever tendency these rights may have to promote other, intuitively unrelated effects. It is on such a basis that Rawls' theory recognizes powers and liberties, including the right to hold personal property, as primary social goods.

In the cases of rank or social caste, the *advantage* one person has seems to depend essentially on *disadvantages* imposed on others (one cannot have a higher rank unless others have a lower rank). The more difficult cases are ones where this is not so: cases involving things like intelligence, physical strength, and so on. (See Discussion Question 2.)

10

On this view, a morally acceptable system of property will require striking a balance among many different sorts of considerations, with the value of a person's control over their "possessions" being only one of them. There will be no absolute property rights of the sort that Nozick recognizes.

This is the sort of entitlement that Scanlon said earlier that almost any theory of justice would recognize. It differs from the sort Nozick advocates in that both the scope of such entitlements and the rights that they confer are set by the account of justice on other grounds (such as whether the institutions in question satisfy the difference principle).

Thus a utilitarian might try to argue that keeping promises will in general lead to more utility (see Annotation 2), but this is virtually certain to be true only for the most part at best. And even if it were somehow true in every case, the reason thereby offered for keeping promises would not be the intuitively correct one that one has a moral duty to do this simply because of having made the promise.

The value attached to the ability to exercise control over a certain aspect of one's life is not the same thing as a right assigning a person a particular form of such control. . . . But this value is the natural reason for having such a right, and it is, I think, the element often missing from utilitarian accounts that seek the value of a right in its tendency to promote some further unrelated effects. To recognize a particular interest as meriting protection in rights is not to say that it is to have absolute protection. It may be a difficult question how a right can be designed to protect that interest and how much protection can be given at tolerable cost. . . . 13

This general point about the relation between workable rights and the human interests that make them important has a further relevance to Nozick's argument. In defending his particular system of rights, Nozick often seems to assume that any alternative rights would be wholesale in character. One such right which he considers is "the right to have a say over what affects you" Nozick properly points out that a right literally to have a say in all decisions that affect you, or even in all those that affect you deeply and intimately, would be impossibly broad. It is essential to distinguish between different ways in which something can affect a person. As Nozick puts it, what decision affects me more deeply than the decision the person I love makes in deciding whom to marry? But this does not mean that I should have a right to a role in making that decision. Nozick's conclusion is that it is my "Lockean" rights that determine which things, among all those that affect me, I have the right to a say over.

I would agree that, while the importance of rights largely flows from the importance of having control over things that affect one, the function of a system of rights is to distinguish between the various ways that things can affect people and to apportion out particular forms of control. It follows that if we are agreed how this is to be done, then we will refer to people's rights in order to determine what they are entitled to a say over. But it does not follow that Nozick's "Lockean" rights are the correct ones, and this is just what is at issue.

If a supposed right turns out to give the person holding it an obviously unacceptable degree of control over other people's lives then that is ground for saying that there is no such right. The proposed "right to have say over what affects you" fails this test. But what the objection formulated in terms of this right is really claiming is that unrestricted property rights of the sort favored by Nozick must also be rejected on the same grounds. 14

...

The contrast between Nozick's and Rawls' views on political obligation illustrates the important difference between two types of consent theory. In theories of the first type, actual consent has a fundamental role as the source of legitimacy of social institutions. Theories of the second type start from the assumption that the institutions with which political philosophy is concerned are fundamentally nonvoluntary. These institutions are held to be legitimate if they satisfy appropriate conditions, and the idea of hypothetical consent enters as a metaphorical device used in the formulation and defense of these conditions. . . . 15 The difference between these two theories is magnified by the fact that the idea of consent involves choice against some background of alternatives. If what is at issue is initial consent to institutions from without, then the relevant background is that of this pre-institutional condition. It is only this viewpoint that makes the "baseline" of conditions in the state of nature seem relevant. By contrast, since the questions raised through the device of the hypothetical contract are questions about the justifiability of social institutions to people who find themselves living under them, the relevant background is given by the alternatives actually available to people in societies and the values that such people attach to these alternatives . . . there is no temptation, on this view, to take the standards of some earlier (for example, pretechnological) age as relevant to the acceptability of contemporary institutions. 16

The idea that respect for individual liberty requires that consent be a necessary condition for all obligations beyond the requirements of a minimal framework of rights arises in the same way as the idea that makes subjective preference seem the only acceptable basis for ethically significant judgments of relative well being. Further, the two views involve similar mistakes. Welfare economists and those who support subjective versions of utilitarianism are moved by the belief that the interests of the

13

R "Tolerable cost" in terms of other, competing values.

R Because unrestricted property rights will give some people the sort of control over the lives of others reflected in the passage at Annotation 7.

Hypothetical consent is what is involved in Rawls's original position. Rawls's view is that this is the only sort of consent that is realistically applicable to social and political institutions.

Thus a state of nature is too remote from actual conditions to make what people might consent to in such a state "relevant to the acceptability of contemporary institutions."

affected parties are the bases on which social policies should be appraised and by the belief that it is unacceptable to "impose" on these parties, as the relevant account of their interests, a system of values that they do not share. The response to these beliefs is generally to bring individual preferences into a theory at the foundational level, making them the basis for all judgments of relative value. A few restrictions on what can count as admissible preferences may be allowed in the form of requirements of consistency, transitivity, and so on, but anything beyond such purely formal restrictions is seen as a threat. When a theory is constructed in this way, so that it treats almost all preferences at face value regardless of their origins or content, its conclusions can be substantially affected by the social conditions which influence prevailing preferences and their relative strengths. This robs the theory of an important kind of critical power and, in addition, makes it an uncertain guardian of even those values of individual autonomy which it set out to protect. Many different conditions are important for the development of autonomous preferences, and the ability of individuals to give effect to their preferences in their own lives and in the determination of social policy depends on a variety of powers and liberties. To give appropriate recognition to the value of individual autonomy a theory must assign appropriate weights to all these factors in balancing them against each other and against other competing considerations. Autonomy is not adequately recognized simply by letting these weights and all others be determined by whatever constellation of individual preferences happens to prevail at the point at which the theory is applied. 17

Similar problems arise for a view which, acting out of a desire to safeguard individual liberty, brings consent in at the foundational level as the basis of almost all obligations, and allows it to be restricted by only a minimum of "imposed" moral requirements. The consequences such a theory can endorse are unacceptably open to determination by factors affecting the relative bargaining strength of various individuals, for example, variations in the demand for and scarcity of particular talents and resources. In particular, the ability of individuals to exercise the kind of control over their lives that freedom from imposed obligations is supposed to secure will be to an unacceptable degree merely a function of their bargaining strength. 18 As in the previous case, the conclusion to be drawn here is that individual liberty is not adequately protected simply by bringing consent in as the foundation of obligation. An adequate theory must take into account the various ways—other than merely by being morally free to withhold one's services—in which individuals may be enabled to exercise control over their own lives and their common institutions (or disabled from doing so.)

...

The two forms of consent theory correspond to two differing views of rights. Either view may recognize rights as a basis for individual claims against social institutions. Thus both see some rights as "natural" in the sense of having validity that does not derive from positive law or social institutions. On the first view, however, the rights that are the basis for moral criticism and defense of social institutions are seen as "natural rights" in the stronger sense that they are the very same rights which individuals possess and can claim against one another in a state of nature. On the second view, rights represent general judgments about the conditions of legitimacy of social institutions, for example, judgments of the form "Any institutions granting *that* power are morally unacceptable." Exactly which such generalizations seem true and important—what things are rights and what these rights encompass—are matters that will change as social conditions change. Some of these rights concern things that would be of no relevance, or only a very different and more limited kind of relevance, in a state of nature. (Rights to freedom of expression, due process of law and political participation seem to have this character.) 19

It is central to Nozick's argument that the rights with which he is concerned are claimed to be natural rights in the stronger sense. The objections I have raised to his examples almost all demand that he consider the consequences of enforcement of absolute property and contract rights and that he explain why the loss of liberty this involves for some people is not worse than that which is involved in the alternative systems which he deplores. Such objections suppose that the property rights enforced by the minimal state and those embodied in socialist institutions are two alternative social systems open to the

Part of the problem Scanlon is pointing to is that people's preferences may be warped by existing institutions in ways that make those institutions seem more acceptable than they genuinely are. An extreme example would be slaves who are influenced by the very institution of slavery to prefer remaining enslaved. A view that relied on actual preferences would then be unable to find any basis for rejecting slavery—and the same thing would be true of one that appealed to consent.

But reasons of some sort have to be given for thinking that this actually occurs in any particular case.

A different problem for the appeal to actual consent (though Scanlon says it is "similar") is that what people consent to is a function of their individual bargaining power, which in turn depends on their resources and natural talents. He is saying, first, that differences in these things will give some people much less control than others over what sorts of institutions result from consent (which is very plausible); and, second, that this difference in degree of control is morally unacceptable (something that Nozick, at least, would question).

Thus on the second view, there are no very specific natural rights (or at least very few of them). As already noted, what rights people have and exactly how far they extend will depend on a complicated weighing of different morally relevant considerations.

same kind of objections and needing the same kind of defense. Nozick rejects this symmetrical picture. In his view, the particular property rights protected by the minimal state are not licensed or created by it and consequently do not need to be defended as part of its justification. These rights are ones that individuals have quite independently of the social institutions in which they live. In enforcing these rights the minimal state is only doing for them what they were already entitled to do for themselves. Consequently it is not doing anything that could be held to infringe anyone's liberty. 20

20

R Thus in Nozick's view, rights (at least the most fundamental ones) do not derive from society or from the state, and even the right of the state to enforce such rights is derivative from the antecedent right of individuals to enforce their own rights (in roughly the same way advocated by Locke).

How plausible is the claim that the rights appealed to in Nozick's examples are ones that individuals would have in a state of nature? This claim has greatest initial plausibility with respect to the right of nonaggression. An unprovoked attack occurring today on the streets of New York seems to be wrong for the same reasons that would apply to a similar attack in the state of nature. But the right of nonaggression as Nozick interprets it covers more than this. It prohibits generally "sacrificing one person to benefit another" I take it that what Nozick wants to rule out here is any use of force or the threat of force to make one person contribute to the welfare of another who has no right to this contribution. This last qualification reduces the right considerably, but without it the right would be absurd. 21 This shows that the right of nonaggression cannot be interpreted in isolation from other rights. Its invariance between the state of nature and other conditions will consequently depend on that of these other rights.

21

Nozick's view is essentially that another person's right to such a contribution must derive from a voluntary arrangement of some kind.

Chief among these is the right to one's property. A system of property is a set of rules defining the conditions under which a person owns an object and specifying the extent and character of the rights of owners. What a person's property rights are will normally depend not only on what systems of property could be validly enforced under the conditions in which he lives but also on what system is actually in use. To the extent that this system is morally legitimate, its provisions determine his rights. But the provisions of this system may also be wrong. They may claim for him rights that no one could really have or they may fail to protect claims that any valid system would have to recognize. Surely we can imagine an incident, occurring in a state of nature, which strikes us intuitively as a violation of property rights. Imagine that a family is living in the wilderness when a group of strangers comes along and drives them off part of their land and takes their crops. This strikes us as a clear wrong. I take it that the point of saying that this happens "in a state of nature" is just that the wrongness involved does not seem to depend on any system of law or social convention. But it is open to question whether what we feel to be violated in such examples is really a natural right to property. For these cases strikes us as clear wrongs only if we suppose, first, that what is taken is of use to the person who loses it (that is, that the taking actually constitutes an interference with his life and activities) and, second, that his appropriation and use of the thing did not already constitute an interference with others. . . . . When these conditions are satisfied, the taking infringes upon what might be called the natural right of noninterference. A system of property rights goes beyond this primitive right by specifying formal criteria of ownership. If a person is deprived of something to which he has acquired title in the specified way, then his property right has been violated whether the taking makes any difference to his life at all. Different systems of property carry out this extension in different ways, each specifying its own criteria of ownership and defining and limiting the rights of owners in its own way. . . . 22

22

Scanlon's claim is that there is no natural right to property that is definite enough to yield a specific account of who owns what, and that Nozick's claim to the contrary results from confusing such a specific system of property rights with the "natural right of noninterference"—which, Scanlon would say, does not really involve property as such at all. (See Discussion Question 3.)

To support the claim that some property rights are natural rights we need to think of a state of nature example involving a clear wrong which seems to violate one of these rights without violating the primitive right of noninterference. But if we imagine such a case we may be open to the question of why we should imagine a state of nature containing *that* particular system of property, rather than some other system which would not be violated by the act in question.

This objection could be avoided if we could show that the primitive right of noninterference does not exhaust the common core of systems of property rights. Perhaps there are certain provisions falling outside this right which would be incorporated in any system of property rights that could plausibly be held to be valid in a state of nature. It could then be argued that the provisions which Nozick's examples turn on fall in this class, for example, that an unrestricted right of inheritance does so. But this is far from clear. Suppose the grandfather of the family we previously imagined lived on land a short distance away and that when he died he said, "Now this is yours." But they had all they could do to take care of their own place, and one day they noticed that someone else had moved onto their grandfather's old farm. Are they entitled (in the state of nature) to throw the people off or to demand payment? It is not obvious to me that they are. (23) Even if there is "as much land and as good" not far off, their claim to demand that the new people move to it is quite debatable. Furthermore, even if we were to be convinced by such examples that any system of property valid in a state of nature would have to include unrestricted inheritance, there would remain the question of how much this judgment is dependent upon our assessment of the consequences that this provision would have in a "natural state." These consequences are apt to be quite different from those that would result from the same provision under other social conditions.

...

Nozick . . . faces the problem, then, of deriving an extended system of property rights involving money, commerce, and extensive holdings from something like Locke's original "natural" foundation. This derivation faces two problems. The first is that the lack of natural bounds on acquisition means that others are likely to be threatened—there may not be enough and as good left for them. . . . Nozick's response here is that the increase in the stock of goods due to increasing productivity will keep pace with increased acquisition, making it unlikely that anyone will be made worse off relative to the baseline of expectations in the state of nature. The second problem is that, with holdings extending far beyond "the conveniences of life" (certainly far beyond what these included in the state of nature), the case for absolute protection of these holdings becomes weaker. This makes even more controversial the choice of an extremely low baseline for determining whether the condition of others is worsened. (24)

...

This example is supposed to support the claim that there is no natural system of property rights beyond the right of noninterference. If there were, then the family in question would have a right to repossess the grandfather's farm or at least demand payment, which Scanlon says is not obviously the case. (What might Nozick say about this case?)

R The suggestion is that as holdings become greater, the claim that they should be absolutely protected becomes weaker; and also that large property holdings make it more doubtful that what would exist in the state of nature is the right "baseline" for determining whether the condition of others has been worsened by acquisition.

Discussion Questions

1. Scanlon says that any departure from equality requires a special defense simply because it is a bad thing for someone to be worse off than others and especially to be worse off than the norm in his or her society. This suggests that equality is a kind of "default" position: it needs no special justification, but any departure from it—even one that results from such things as natural endowments—does. How plausible is this view?
2. Consider the issue of what, if anything, egalitarianism says or should say about natural assets, such as intelligence or physical strength. These have the following two features: first, they cannot be redistributed to others in the interest of equality; and, second, unlike such things as a social class or caste system, the advantages they yield for the people who have them do not derive in any obvious way from disadvantages imposed on others. A closer approximation to equality could, however, be achieved by *worsening* the situation of those who have such assets in various ways (such as through surgery). Scanlon says (see the passage at Annotation 9) that other considerations may "temper" the demands of equality in this area. But a thoroughgoing egalitarian might still say that worsening the situation of favored people in such respects is in *one* way a moral improvement, even if one that is outweighed by these other considerations. Does even this seem right?
3. Nozick claims that there is a natural right to property, while Scanlon suggests that superficially plausible cases (like that at Annotation 22) involve only a right of noninterference, so that any definite system of property is a social creation. Scanlon's view would mean that any system of property rights would have to be judged by weighing all the relevant kinds of value, so that a system of private property might or might not turn out to be the best. Is he right about this? Or are there at least some principles (whether or not Nozick has them exactly right) that any acceptable societal system of property rights must conform to, principles that cannot properly be abandoned in pursuit of other sorts of values (such as equality)?

Concluding Dialogue on Government and Justice

For anyone born and raised in a country managed by a stable government, the question of what *justifies* the very existence of that government might seem unmotivated or even pointless. But (as pointed out in the chapter introduction) it is clear that the various things that governments do would be highly objectionable if done by private groups like gangs or corporations. So what—if anything—does make it morally acceptable for governments to do these things? And is there any correlative moral *obligation* for people to obey governmental decrees, at least for the most part?

I agree that those are serious questions. The predominant historical answer was an appeal to divine right, but that is very hard to take seriously nowadays. So the only very obvious answer to the first question is that what makes government legitimate (when it is) is the *consent* of the governed—with the immediate implication being, of course, that a government that fails to have this consent, either from the beginning or at some later point in time, is *illegitimate* and may properly be resisted.

You're agreeing with Locke's view. But Hobbes, of course, wouldn't accept that last part. His view is in effect that the *only* way that a government can become illegitimate is by failing in its basic task of preserving order and protecting its citizens. As long as it does those things successfully, whether it continues to have the consent of its citizens doesn't seem to matter for him.

I think that's right. He does seem to think that in some cases people did in fact consent when they originally formed governments. But even that doesn't seem to be so in the case of what he calls a "commonwealth by acquisition"—the case where a person or group achieves power by force. In that case, the only thing that even resembles consent is *acquiescence*—which isn't really the same thing at all. Hobbes's view seems to be that the laws of rational prudence require obeying *any* government that does the minimal jobs of protection and preservation of order.

But how does that make government *morally* legitimate? Maybe he's just *assuming* that if resistance to government is rationally imprudent, then it is also immoral, so that obedience would then be morally required. I've always found it hard to decide what exactly Hobbes's view on this point really is.

Let's think about the contrast with Locke. A major part of the difference between them obviously lies in their very different views of the state of nature. Part of that difference is that Locke thinks that there is a *moral* law (what he means by "natural law") in the state of nature, not just laws of rational prudence (which is what Hobbes means by "natural law"). But Locke also has a very different view of human nature—or more specifically of how people would behave towards each other in the absence of government. This makes it much easier for Locke to say that a government that is too oppressive could be *worse* than a state of nature—which means that refusing to obey it might be better even from the standpoint of prudence, in addition to being morally acceptable.

I see the difference. But even if Hobbes were right about the state of nature (though I don't think he is—I like Locke's view of human nature much better!), it still doesn't seem to follow that the mere *prudential* desirability of obeying an oppressive government somehow creates a *moral* obligation to do so and thus makes that government *morally* legitimate. In the end, I'm not sure that Hobbes really has a clear account of the legitimacy of government, even though that surely seems to be at least part of what he was attempting to give.

I agree that Hobbes's view on the legitimacy issue just isn't very clear. Locke's account, on the other hand, is in many ways much clearer and more plausible. Unlike Hobbes, Locke wouldn't accept a government imposed by force as legitimate. Mere acquiescence isn't enough. In his view, there apparently has to be an actual agreement to form a government—or rather two agreements, one to form a political community and a second to constitute a government of a specific sort. Locke would agree with Hobbes that a government can lose its legitimacy by failing to protect its citizens, but he insists that a government that is oppressive enough may also become illegitimate. And the people themselves are the judge of when that occurs.

I agree that the sort of consent that Locke describes would make the resulting governments legitimate. But the large problem with this otherwise very appealing picture, as Hume points out, is that there is no historical record of any actual agreements of this sort—no reason to think they have ever occurred. Perhaps in the distant past of prehistory there were cases where governments resulted from something like consent—though it is still important to keep in mind the crucial difference between consent and mere acquiescence. But, as Hume argues, virtually all governments that exist in his day result from "usurpation or conquest," not from any sort of explicit agreement. If Locke is right that explicit consent is the only basis for legitimate government, then it seems to follow that almost all actual governments are illegitimate. That is perhaps not as clearly absurd a result as Hume thinks, but I still find it really hard to accept.

Don't go too fast here. In fact there are a few cases where it can be plausibly argued that an explicit agreement, amounting to a social contract, actually did occur. One of these is the adoption of the American constitution through the vote of ratifying conventions in the various states, with the members of those conventions being elected via something approximating a democratic vote. The vote wasn't fully democratic because there were still some property qualifications (though pretty minimal ones), women couldn't vote, and of course the slaves couldn't vote. But it was still reasonably close to being democratic, and even better examples have occurred in some other places—and obviously could occur again. Nonetheless, I have to admit that there are still many, many governments around the world in relation to which no agreement of this sort ever occurred. And there is also the large problem, again pointed out by Hume, of why any such agreement should be taken to be binding on later generations that weren't yet born at the time when it occurred.

So you agree that explicit consent won't take us very far in justifying actual governments. What then about the idea of *tacit* consent? In Plato's dialogue *Crito,* Socrates, while waiting in prison to be executed, famously argues that by remaining in Athens and accepting the benefits of Athenian citizenship, rather than emigrating to somewhere else, he has *tacitly* agreed to obey the laws of Athens and so is bound by that agreement not to escape, even though he has been unjustly (though legally) sentenced to death. Many people have found this idea very appealing. It obviously doesn't apply to young children, but why isn't it an adequate justification for government at least in relation to adult citizens?

But there are problems, as you well know. Hume points out some of these. One is that for many people, especially those who are poor, emigrating to another country is so difficult as to be effectively impossible. Another is that many people, perhaps most of them in some countries, do not *realize* that they have any choice at all in the matter, but simply accept the authority of the government without question. Yet another, which Hume didn't mention, is that someone who wanted to escape *all* governments, not just a particular one, would have virtually nowhere to go in the modern world.

I agree that those are real problems. But are they really serious enough to make the idea of tacit consent completely untenable? Perhaps the first one was in Hume's time, but in the modern world it's clear that lots of relatively poor people still manage to escape particular countries and governments in one way or another. And the prevalence of this also makes it harder for even relatively uneducated people not to be aware of the possibility. And as regards your last point, I'm not sure that the claim that a person has tacitly consented to the government of a particular country in which they live really requires the possibility of escaping all governments. Of course, the idea of legitimacy deriving from tacit consent obviously won't apply to governments that *prevent* their citizens from leaving freely—as was the case in East Germany at the time of the Berlin Wall and is still the case elsewhere. But it seems to me arguable that tacit consent constitutes a reasonable argument for the legitimacy of at least most present-day Western governments and probably lots of others too. No one is trying to argue, after all, that all governments are legitimate—it's too clear that some aren't!

While some of the problems still worry me, I'm inclined to agree that the idea of tacit consent provides a good argument for the legitimacy of at least many governments and that it's probably the best we're going to do in this area. Certainly it's better than Hume's appeal instead to the social utility of government, something that only utilitarians are likely to accept. We can't go into the problems with utilitarianism here (see Chapter 5), but it seems intuitively pretty clear that if some self-appointed group started coercing people into behaving in various ways and took money and resources from them under threat of force, merely the claim that greater social utility would result, even if true, wouldn't make their actions morally acceptable or turn that group into a legitimate government.

Let's turn to the other issue in the chapter. Even if tacit consent can be used to argue that at least some governments are legitimate, it surely won't follow that everything they do is morally acceptable. There are many issues here. But the one raised in the readings is the issue of *distributive justice:* what is the proper standard for deciding whether the distribution of benefits or goods within a society, largely as a result of governmental actions or inactions of various kinds, is just? Here Nozick and Rawls offer radically different views—so much so that I find each of them hard to accept and can't help thinking that the truth must lie somewhere in the middle.

I guess I have to admit that I've always been fairly sympathetic to Nozick's view. There is an appealing simplicity about the main idea: justice primarily applies to individual "transactions," and if all of the transactions that lead up to a particular distribution of wealth and other goods are just, then that distribution is also just—no matter what sort of large-scale pattern it does or doesn't satisfy. If this is right, then justice can't require such a pattern—whether simple equality or something more complicated like the one advocated by Rawls.

Taken at that abstract level, I have to admit that there is some genuine plausibility to Nozick's view. To reject it would be to say in effect that the justice of individual transactions depends on what pattern they lead to—which will depend, of course, on what other individual transactions also take place. And it's hard to see how this could be so: how can the justice of my engaging in a certain transaction with some small number of other people depend on what all the other people in the society happen to be doing? But the problem is how to be sure that an individual transaction is just—especially one that is more complicated than just a simple exchange of goods. Couldn't the fact that certain sorts of transactions tend to lead to large-scale patterns that seem morally questionable provide at least an indication that there is something objectionable about those individual transactions themselves—even if the problem is too subtle to be easily noticed when you look at them one by one?

I think that's right. I don't see why Nozick has to say that an individual transaction that superficially seems just cannot still be unjust in unobvious but important ways or why he can't admit that large-scale patterns may provide some evidence that this is so. The seemingly absurd salaries of some corporate CEOs might be a good example here: while it may be hard to discern clear injustice in the rather complicated sorts of transactions that result in such salaries, surely the result—perhaps taken together with the fact that the stockholders have little effective input—strongly suggests that something has gone badly wrong. That is, I think, the reason that Nozick focuses on very simple cases like the Wilt Chamberlain example. There the case is simple enough to make it hard to believe that there is some subtle injustice that we are missing. And examples like that are still enough to show, as long as you accept the basic idea that the justice of individual transactions is primary, that no view that insists on patterns can be correct.

I'm not so sure about that. Let's talk a little about this example. In doing so, there are two issues that I don't want to worry about. One is the issue posed by Nozick's argument that preserving any pattern will require "continuous interference" in people's lives. It seems to me that the issue of whether a certain pattern is required by justice is quite distinct from the issue of whether there is any acceptable way to *enforce* that pattern—as an analogy, one can think that simple theft is always unjust without thinking that there is any acceptable way to completely prevent it.

OK, I agree that what justice requires is one issue and how and even whether it can be enforced is a separate issue.

Good. And I also want to assume that it is just for a government, assumed now to be legitimate on the basis of something like tacit consent, to impose a *tax* on Wilt's earnings, in order to pay for things like external defense, internal policing needed to preserve order, infrastructure such as roads and bridges, and the like—maybe even a progressive tax that imposes a higher rate on those who earn more. Nozick's actual views on these matters (not reflected very much in the selection in this book) are complicated, but they don't seem central to his view of distributive justice as such. So the issue I want to focus on is whether it is just to tax Wilt further, perhaps quite heavily, for the additional purpose of *redistributing* some of his wealth to others in order to satisfy some patterned principle of justice like that advocated by Rawls or some other principle in the direction of egalitarianism.

I agree that this is the central question. Scanlon remarks that there is no strong intuitive reason to think that Wilt has an absolute right to keep all that others are willing to pay him for his basketball services (even after, we are assuming, taxes to support essential government functions have been allowed for). But Nozick would, I think, want to ask why Wilt's right or entitlement to the wealth after taxes of that sort *isn't* absolute—assuming, as seems reasonable, that there is nothing unjust about the individual transactions that lead to it. And here the sorts of reasons that Scanlon suggests—the desirability of alleviating extreme poverty, of avoiding political and economic domination, and of sustaining "healthy social relations"—wouldn't strike Nozick and don't strike me as very compelling. These are no doubt desirable goals in themselves, but it doesn't follow (unless you are a utilitarian—see again Chapter 5) that just because taxing (and thereby reducing) Wilt's remaining wealth could be used to achieve these goals, he thereby fails to have a just entitlement to it.

I guess I'm not inclined to defend Scanlon on these particular points, though Rawls may have something better to say when we get to him. But Scanlon raises a further point, pertaining to the specific issue of inheritance, that may help: that "inequalities in life prospects" that result from "differences in family wealth" are "undeserved and arbitrary." Suppose, for the sake of the argument, that Wilt is justly entitled to the huge wealth that remains after taxes for non-redistributive purposes have been paid. Suppose now that, having bequeathed this wealth to his children, he dies. His children have done nothing at all to earn their resulting wealth, and yet it gives them enormous advantages in comparison with others in the society. Surely *that* is unjust, whatever may be the case with Wilt himself?

I agree that inheritance is the hardest case. It does seem unjust—or at least unfair—for Wilt's children to have wealth and resulting advantages that they have done nothing to deserve. But if, as we are assuming, Wilt *is* justly entitled to his wealth, then why doesn't it follow that he can do what he wants with it: spend it all on himself, give it to charity—or give it to his children? So there are two issues of justice here, one with respect to the children and one with respect to Wilt himself, and the problem is that the intuitively correct result in one doesn't fit very well with what we are now assuming to be the intuitively correct result in the other. I think Nozick would say two things about this. One is that Wilt's entitlement to his earnings is *much* clearer than the intuitive injustice pertaining to his children's inheritance. And the other is that even if it is granted that the children's entitlement to their resulting inherited wealth is suspect, it doesn't seem to follow in any very obvious way that *anyone else* is entitled to that wealth to a greater or even equal degree.

I'm not convinced about either of those claims. But perhaps this is a good time to turn to Rawls, who offers further arguments for a view very different from Nozick's. His view is in effect that there is a strong *presumption* in favor of equal distribution, a presumption that can be defeated only if allowing a specified amount of inequality will make those who receive the least still better off in absolute terms than they would have been under an equal distribution.

I've never found Rawls's position that convincing. His argument is *very* complicated and, it has always seemed to me, pretty seriously misleading. One line of argument is the one that

appeals to the famous "original position," in which people are supposed to choose principles of justice while being ignorant of many facts about themselves. The idea behind this argument is perhaps plausible enough in some kinds of cases: if one is dividing up a jointly owned pie for example, a just division would be one that could be agreed to by people who didn't know which piece they would get. But in other cases, like Nozick's grade example for instance, such a procedure seems to lead to obviously *unjust* results. And this will be true whenever those making the choice of principles are kept ignorant of a feature that is in fact relevant to justice: imagine, for example, having the principles governing just punishments decided by those who are ignorant of whether or not they are guilty of crimes!

Rawls doesn't, of course, claim that his argument applies to that sort of issue—though I suppose it's a fair question why it should be thought to apply to the case he is concerned with if it doesn't apply to other issues of justice as well. Apart from perhaps overly simple cases like the pie case, the application of his argument that has always seemed to me most convincing is the one that involves matters like social class (or, analogously, racial and ethnic groups). If the people in the original position are ignorant of what social class they belong to, then they will not choose principles of distribution that favor one social class over another. And that seems like exactly the right result. Belonging to such a class just isn't relevant to a just distribution.

I agree, of course—as will anyone who thinks that things like social class are irrelevant to issues of distributive justice. But that's exactly the problem with the original position argument: in order to decide what those in the original position should be allowed to know, one has to *first* decide which things about them are morally relevant to issues of justice and which aren't. Thus the original position can't be used to decide the question of what features of a situation are relevant to justice.

And that issue is exactly what Rawls and Nozick disagree about most fundamentally. The issue between them is whether "natural endowments"—things like physical strength, intelligence, creative ingenuity, talents and abilities of various sorts, and even robust physical health—are relevant to justice (so that those in the original position should know about them) or not.

Yes, exactly. The way that Rawls sets up the original position in fact seems to just *assume* that natural endowments should be treated in the same way as social class—that they are not relevant to justice, and therefore that the people in the original position should be kept ignorant of them. Does he have any real argument for this view?

What he says, of course, is that natural endowments, like social class, are "arbitrary from a moral point of view" and that people do not *deserve* their natural endowments. Though he also says that the natural distribution of endowments is neither just nor unjust and that people do have a right to their endowments. But it's hard to avoid thinking—reading between the lines a little—that he does think that it is unjust or at least in some way unfair that some people have better natural endowments than others. (See especially the discussion of the "principle of redress" and his remark that the difference principle achieves "some of the intent" of that other principle.) So the idea is that people with superior natural endowments do not deserve whatever advantages might flow from them. It follows for him that if they ought to receive any benefits at all (over and above the great benefit of simply possessing those endowments), this can only be because the less advantaged are also made better off as a result.

I think that is about the best you can find in Rawls on this point, but it is by no means obviously right. People who have superior natural endowments may not deserve them in the sense of having done something to earn them, but they also have not obtained them at the expense of others—it's not as though there is a common pool of intelligence, say, and the more intelligent have taken more than their fair share. This is *very* different from social class, where some can be superior only at the expense of others who are inferior. That a person has the natural endowments that he does may be a matter of good fortune or luck. But why does this give *other* people any claim on those endowments—or on the things that result from them?

An argument that is sometimes made here—and that is at least suggested by some of the things that Rawls says—is that even those with superior natural endowments wouldn't benefit very much from them without the social context in which those endowments operate. This is then taken to mean that at least a large part of the production of various sorts that results from those talents is really due to the cooperation of others, not to the actions of the talented individual alone. And it is this that gives those others, and perhaps also society in general, a claim to benefit from the talents of such a person. Bill Gates may have enormous talents as a computer programmer, an entrepreneur, and so on, but none of these talents would have yielded the massive wealth he has without the complicated infrastructure provided by the social system. And the further claim will then be that in some social systems, such as our present one, individuals with greater natural endowments get to keep a larger share of what they are able to produce only with the aid of others than they really deserve.

I have to admit that this last argument has a lot of force, though exactly how it applies to the situation of a particular individual or a particular society will often be pretty hard to figure out. One thing that can be said, however, is that this argument is unlikely to yield a result very close to that which would be required by Rawls's difference principle. What those with greater endowments deserve on this basis will still be substantially greater (because their talents do play a pivotal role). And what others are legitimately entitled to will vary a lot, depending on their exact role in the overall process. In particular, there's no obvious reason from this standpoint to focus on the least advantaged in the way that Rawls does. But the just result from this point of view will also be pretty different from what at least seems to follow from Nozick's view—though he never really discusses issues at this level of specificity. So maybe you've found your intermediate view after all.

CHAPTER 7

God and Faith

The selections in this chapter are concerned with two closely related topics in the general area of philosophy known as the philosophy of religion: first, arguments for and against the existence of God; and, second, the question of whether belief in God can be rationally acceptable on some basis other than rational arguments that establish the existence of such a being.

Though other conceptions of God are obviously possible, the attention of philosophers has been largely focused on the conception that is more or less standard in the three great monotheistic religions: Judaism, Christianity, and Islam. According to this conception, God is (a) a *personal* being who is (b) all-powerful or *omnipotent,* (c) all-knowing or *omniscient,* (d) *perfectly good, benevolent, merciful, and just,* and (e) the *creator* of the universe. The further elaboration of attributes (b), (c), and (d) in this list often employs the idea of *infinity:* God is viewed as having infinite power, infinite knowledge, and infinite goodness, benevolence, mercy, and justice. It is this conception of God about which the most interesting philosophical issues have been raised. (Some attention is also given in these readings to the possibility of a being conceived in a parallel but weaker way: one whose attributes fall short of infinity.)

Does God Exist?

Arguments in Favor of the Existence of God

What reasons are there to believe that such a being actually exists? It is clear that many people believe in the existence of God on the basis of some sort of *authority:* that of parents or family, the community, the state, religious texts of various kinds, or even allegedly (and in a way that obviously **begs the question**) the authority of God himself (or herself or itself). But the obvious problem with any such appeal except the last is that the claim that such an authority is to be trusted on *this* issue is just as much in need of reason or argument as the original claim. Thus philosophers have focused instead on arguments that are claimed to be rationally compelling on their own, with the most important and influential of these being the three discussed in the following selections. The first two of the following sections focus on two arguments that have both been widely discussed by philosophers and also have a good deal of appeal to common sense: the *cosmological argument* and the *argument from design*. The third section is concerned with an argument that has fascinated philosophers (though relatively few have actually accepted it), but which is most unlikely to occur to anyone but a philosopher: the so-called *ontological argument*.

The Cosmological Argument. The cosmological argument starts with the simple and undeniable empirical premise that *things* of some sort exist, that the world is not simply an empty void. It is ordinary material objects and processes that are usually cited to support this premise, but in principle any sort of non-divine existence would do. The argument then asks *why* these things exist, demanding a *cause* or *reason* or *explanation* of some sort for their existence (with the emphasis among these varying in different versions of the argument). The appeal here is to a background principle, the **principle of sufficient reason** (often abbreviated as PSR), which says that there must be an answer to this general sort of question for any sort of existing thing or in some versions for any positive fact at all. Some existing things (other than God) may of course be explainable in familiar ways by appeal to other such things, but it is argued (again in a number of somewhat different ways) that a complete explanation of everything that exists or perhaps of the fact that there is anything at all (rather than nothing) requires the existence of a *necessary* or *self-existent* being, one that could not have failed to exist. This necessary being is then claimed to be identical to God, as standardly conceived—though this last, obviously crucial step often receives relatively little attention. Versions of this argument are discussed by St. Thomas Aquinas, Samuel Clarke, and David Hume.

The Argument from Design. The argument from design also starts from a basic empirical fact and demands an explanation of that fact. This time, however, the fact is more specific and vastly more complicated: the presence of order, (apparent) design, or (apparent) purpose in the world (with the first of these specifications being the least likely to beg the question).

There are two importantly different versions of this argument, depending on the scope of the order for which an explanation is sought: a *global* version that asks for the explanation of the presence of order in the world taken as a whole; and various *local* versions that ask for the explanation of a particular kind or example of order, most commonly the order reflected in living things and their components—in William Paley's version here, the eye and similar organic structures. The main importance of this distinction, as we will see, is that while the theory of evolution and other relatively limited explanations of the same sort offer alternative, non-theistic explanations of many of the specific features to which local versions of the argument may appeal, such alternative explanations turn out to themselves presuppose a more general background of order—and so cannot in principle explain *all* of the order in the world or why there is any order at all.

In either case, the claim advanced in the argument is that the features in question can be adequately explained only by supposing that either the world as a whole or the specific aspect in question was deliberately shaped by an intelligent and powerful designer. This result again falls short of the full standard conception of God, mainly in that a finite world does not demand infinite power or knowledge, but still obviously represents a major step in that direction. Versions of this argument are discussed by St. Thomas Aquinas (very briefly), William Paley, Hume, and Antony Flew, while Stephen Jay Gould presents an important consideration that favors the theory of evolution over divine creation as an explanation of the order involved in living things.

The Ontological Argument. Unlike the previous two arguments, the ontological argument makes no appeal to any empirical fact, however minimal, but is instead entirely **a priori** in character. The central idea is that God exists, indeed must **necessarily** exist, not as an explanation of something else (as in the other two main arguments), but simply because the very **concept** of such a being requires or necessitates that it exist. This is a striking but also rather paradoxical claim: normally the issue of what is included in the concept of a certain kind of thing (or, more or less equivalently, what we have in mind in thinking of it) is quite distinct from (and logically prior to) the issue of whether any things of that kind actually exist in the world. If, for example, the issue is whether the world contains animals of a certain specific kind (such as mammals that live in the oceans), we must first specify clearly what is required to satisfy the concept in question and then look in the world to see if any actual instances can be found—with the second of these stages obviously depending on the first. The claim of the ontological argument is in effect that in the case of God (but only there), these two questions of stages or inquiry are not distinct, but instead that the correct answer to the first question determines the correct answer to the second. St. Anselm and René Descartes present versions of this argument, while Immanuel Kant offers two related objections to it.

An Argument Against the Existence of God: the Problem of Evil

By far the most important argument *against* the existence of a God satisfying the standard conception is in effect the reverse of the argument from design. The problem of evil (which might be better labeled the argument from evil for the non-existence of God) asks why, if the world was created by a being having the attributes specified by the standard conception, there is so much *evil* (mainly pain and suffering) to be found there: both ***physical*** or ***natural*** **evil** (the pain and suffering caused by such things as diseases, natural disasters, and the like); and also ***moral*** **evil** (the pain and suffering that results from voluntary human actions, such as crimes, wars, and other sorts of violence). For someone who already has a compelling reason or argument for belief in such a God, the existence of evils of these various sorts is perhaps merely a *problem:* something that seems to conflict with a well-grounded belief, and which therefore needs to be somehow explained. But for someone for whom the issue is reasonably open, the existence of evil constitutes a pretty compelling argument *against* the existence of such a being. The question is whether this argument can be answered by offering a satisfactory explanation of why God would permit evil to exist. Such explanations are standardly referred to as ***theodicies,*** and it is fairly common for theists to appeal to one explanation for physical evil and a different explanation for moral evil. The problem of evil is discussed by Hume, J. L. Mackie, and John Hick.

Must We Have Reasons in Order to Believe?

Instead of appealing to arguments in favor of God's existence (and responses to arguments against), might there be an alternative basis for belief in God, one that still makes such belief rationally acceptable? Walter Kaufmann explores the idea, deriving from Blaise Pascal, that belief in God might be the best *wager* in a situation of uncertainty. William James advocates a version of the view that it is rational to believe in God on the basis of *faith,* rather than arguments or evidence.

Does God Exist?

The Cosmological Argument

St. Thomas Aquinas

1 *Restatement/Summary*

R The first objection is in effect the problem of evil, discussed later in this chapter. In this version, the allegedly infinite character of God's attributes plays a crucial role.

2

R The second objection claims that God is unnecessary for the purpose of explaining what goes on in the world.

3 *Definition*

 *Motion here* includes not just movement in the ordinary sense, but any sort of change or activity.

St. Thomas Aquinas (1225–1274) was an Italian philosopher and theologian (though he did most of his teaching and writing in Paris). A monk in the Dominican order (which is devoted to scholarship and education), he was arguably the most influential thinker of the Middle Ages. Aquinas based much of his philosophical thinking on the works of Aristotle and was primarily responsible for the dominant position that Aristotle came to hold in medieval thought. Aristotle's ideas are reflected at several points in the following arguments.

Aquinas's major work, the *Summa Theologica* (from which this selection is drawn), has an explicitly **dialectical** structure. It is divided into articles, each of which begins with a question. This is followed by objections that argue for the contrary of the view that Aquinas will defend, then by a statement of Aquinas's own view and his reasons. Finally, the article concludes with explicit responses to the earlier objections. In the following selection, the question is whether God exists, and Aquinas offers five famous, though also somewhat obscure, arguments for an affirmative answer. The first three are different versions of the cosmological argument, the fourth (and most obscure) is an argument unique to Aquinas (omitted here), and the fifth is a very brief version of the argument from design.

The Five Ways, from *Summa Theologica*

Third Article: Whether God Exists?

We proceed thus to the Third Article:—

Objection. 1. It seems that God does not exist; because if one of two contraries be infinite, the other would be altogether destroyed. But the name God means that He is infinite goodness. If, therefore, God existed, there would be no evil discoverable; but there is evil in the world. Therefore God does not exist. [1]

Obj. 2. Further, it is superfluous to suppose that what can be accounted for by a few principles has been produced by many. But it seems that everything we see in the world can be accounted for by other principles, supposing God did not exist. For all natural things can be reduced to one principle, which is nature; and all voluntary things can be reduced to one principle, which is human reason, or will. Therefore there is no need to suppose God's existence. [2]

On the contrary, It is said in the person of God: *I am Who am* (*Exod.* iii 14).

I answer that, The existence of God can be proved in five ways.

The first and more manifest way is the argument from motion. It is certain, and evident to our senses, that in the world some things are in motion. [3] Now whatever is moved is moved by another, for nothing can be moved except it is in potentiality to that towards which it is moved; whereas a thing moves inasmuch as it is in act. For motion is nothing else than the reduction of something from potentiality to actuality. But nothing can be reduced from potentiality to actuality, except by something in a state of actuality. Thus that which is actually hot, as fire, makes wood, which is potentially hot, to be actually hot, and thereby moves and changes it. [4] Now it is not possible that the same thing should be at once in actuality and potentiality in the same respect, but only in different respects. For what is actually hot cannot simultaneously be potentially hot; but it is simultaneously potentially cold. It is therefore impossible that in the same respect and in the same way a thing should be both mover and moved, *i.e.,* that it should move itself. [5] Therefore, whatever is moved must be moved by another. If that by which it is moved be itself moved, then this also must needs be moved by another, and that by another again. But this cannot go on to infinity, because then there would be no first mover, [6] and, consequently, no other mover, seeing that subsequent movers move only inasmuch as they are moved by the first mover; as the staff moves only because it is moved by the hand. Therefore it is necessary to arrive at a first mover, moved by no other; and this everyone understands to be God. [7]

The second way is from the nature of efficient cause. In the world of sensible things we find there is an order of efficient causes. [8] There is no case known (neither is it, indeed, possible) in which a thing is found to be the efficient cause of itself; for so it would be prior to itself, which is impossible. Now in efficient causes it is not possible to go on to infinity, because in all efficient causes following in order, the first is the cause of the intermediate cause, and the intermediate is the cause of the ultimate cause, whether the intermediate cause be several, or one only. Now to take away the cause is to take away the effect. Therefore, if there be no first cause among efficient causes, there will be no ultimate, nor any intermediate, cause. But if in efficient causes it is possible to go on to infinity, there will be no first efficient cause, neither will there be an ultimate effect, nor any intermediate efficient causes; all of which is plainly false. Therefore it is necessary to admit a first efficient cause, to which everyone gives the name of God. [9]

From St. Thomas Aquinas, *Summa Theologica,* in Anton C. Pegis, ed., *Introduction to St. Thomas Aquinas* (New York: Random House, 1945, 1948).

Aquinas appeals here to some ideas of Aristotelian metaphysics. Any change involves a transition from the *potential* for some quality to its *actual* realization. Such a transition must be produced by the activity of something else (to explain why the transition takes place). Thus the wood that is *potentially* hot is moved to become *actually* hot by something else that is already actually hot.

R Thus something cannot "move" itself, for to do so it would have to both merely potentially have the relevant feature and also actually.

6 *Stop and Think*

STOP Aquinas argues that there cannot be an infinite series of "movers" (extending back into time), each "moved" by the one before it. His reason seems to be that there would then be no explanation why any of them is "moved." Is he right about this?

7 *Editor Comment*

The first "mover" cannot be moved by another thing, nor can it "move" itself. Thus it must not itself "move" at all, but must nonetheless still somehow be capable of "moving" other things—how can this be? (Another obvious problem is why such a first "mover" should be identified with God.)

Efficient causation means more or less causation in the ordinary sense, in which something earlier (throwing a rock) causes something later (a splash in a pond). It is thus immediately obvious that nothing can cause itself in this sense (because to do so, it would have to precede itself).

R Here again the claim is that an infinite sequence of causes (backwards into time) is impossible, and again the rationale seems to be that it would be impossible to explain why any of the things in such a sequence exist.

10

R Anything that can come into being from a prior state of nonexistence or pass out of existence would be an example.

STOP Can you think of anything in the world that does not fit this characterization?

11

Neither of these claims follows in any obvious way. Why must something for which non-being is *possible* actually fail to exist at some time? And even if all things for which non-being is possible do fail to exist at some time, why couldn't their existences overlap so that there is never a time when nothing exists?

12

R The underlying assumption is that something cannot come from nothing so that if there is a time when nothing exists, then it is impossible for anything to subsequently come into existence.

13

R Aquinas concludes that there must be some things whose existence is necessary: that could not fail to exist. He thinks these fall into two kinds: those whose necessity is caused by something else and those whose necessity is caused by their own nature.

14

R The possibility of an infinite series of beings whose necessity is derivative is rejected, leading to the conclusion that there is a being whose necessity derives from its own nature.

Here there is a bit more rationale for the identification with God, since a being that explains its own existence is very different from ordinary things in the world.

15

R Orderly things cannot be acting at random ("fortuitously"), and Aquinas sees no other explanation besides intelligent design.

16

Why must there be only one such intelligence?—couldn't different natural things be directed by different intelligences? (Such a unique director would not have to have infinite power.)

The third way is taken from possibility and necessity, and runs thus. We find in nature things that are possible to be and not to be, since they are found to be generated, and to be corrupted, and consequently, it is possible for them to be and not to be. (10) But it is impossible for these always to exist, for that which can not-be at some time is not. Therefore, if everything can not-be, then at one time there was nothing in existence. (11) Now if this were true, even now there would be nothing in existence, because that which does not exist begins to exist only through something already existing. Therefore, if at one time nothing was in existence, it would have been impossible for anything to have begun to exist; and thus even now nothing would be in existence—which is absurd. (12) Therefore, not all beings are merely possible, but there must exist something the existence of which is necessary. But every necessary thing either has its necessity caused by another, or not. (13) Now it is impossible to go on to infinity in necessary things which have their necessity caused by another, as has been already proved in regard to efficient causes. Therefore we cannot but admit the existence of some being having of itself its own necessity, and not receiving it from another, but rather causing in others their necessity. This all men speak of as God. (14)

...

The fifth way is taken from the governance of the world. We see that things which lack knowledge, such as natural bodies, act for an end, and this is evident from their acting always, or nearly always, in the same way, so as to obtain the best result. Hence it is plain that they achieve their end, not fortuitously, but designedly. (15) Now whatever lacks knowledge cannot move towards an end, unless it be directed by some being endowed with knowledge and intelligence; as the arrow is directed by the archer. Therefore some intelligent being exists by whom all natural things are directed to their end; and this being we call God. (16)

Reply Obj. 1. As Augustine says: *Since God is the highest good, He would not allow any evil to exist in His works, unless His omnipotence and goodness were such as to bring good even out of evil.* This is part of the infinite goodness of God, that He should allow evil to exist, and out of it produce good. (17)

Reply Obj. 2. Since nature works for a determinate end under the direction of a higher agent, whatever is done by nature must be traced back to God as to its first cause. So likewise whatever is done voluntarily must be traced back to some higher cause other than human reason and will, since these can change and fail; for all things that are changeable and capable of defect must be traced back to an immovable and self-necessary first principle, as has been shown. (18)

Discussion Questions

1. A key claim in the first argument is that the cause of a change ("movement") must always come from outside the thing that changes. Does it seem obvious that things always work this way? Might not a change originate from within a thing? Can you think of an example? How might Aquinas reply?
2. Think about the claim that there cannot be an infinite series of efficient causes backwards into time (and the analogous claims for the series of "movers" and the series of necessary beings whose necessity is caused by another). Is there a clear objection to this sort of alternative? Aquinas seems to be saying that there would be no explanation of how the series ever got started, but the reply might be that it didn't get *started* because it extends infinitely backwards. Which view is right?
3. A crucial ingredient of the third argument is the idea of a *necessary being:* one that cannot fail to exist. Do we really understand this idea? What would make the existence of such a being necessary—that is, would make it impossible for it not to exist? Can you think of any other examples of necessary beings? What about a number, say the number seven (the number itself, not the numeral that stands for it): could it have failed to exist? Even if we can make sense of necessary existence for an ***abstract*** object like a number, does it make sense for a ***concrete*** object like God? (See the subsection on the ontological argument for further discussion of this issue.)

Samuel Clarke

Samuel Clarke (1675–1729) was an English philosopher, theologian, and preacher, who wrote extensively on philosophical and theological issues, including the existence of God, the nature of space and time, free will, and the nature of morality. He is now best known for his extended correspondence with the great German philosopher Gottfried Wilhelm Leibniz, in which many of these topics are discussed.

Like Aquinas's Third Way but even more explicitly, Clarke's version of the cosmological argument relies on the principle of sufficient reason (PSR): the principle that there must be a reason or cause or explanation for everything that exists. The portion of the argument included here does not purport to prove that God exists but only that "from eternity some one unchangeable and independent being" exists, a result from which Clarke thinks he can go on to prove the existence of the full Judeo-Christian God. (This is a rather dense passage, and to understand it, you may have to read it more than once.)

STOP Aquinas's reply to the problem of evil is that God can bring good out of evil, so that the world is somehow better for containing evil. How plausible do you think this is?

R The answer to the second objection is straightforward if the arguments are accepted: all explanation ultimately can be traced back to God.

The Cosmological Argument, from *A Demonstration of the Being and Attributes of God*

I

First, then, it is absolutely and undeniably certain that *something has existed from all eternity.* This is so evident and undeniable a proposition, that no atheist in any age has ever presumed to assert the contrary, and therefore there is little need of being particular in the proof of it. For, since something now is, it is evident that something always was, otherwise the things that now are must have been produced out of nothing, absolutely and without a cause, which is a plain contradiction in terms. For, to say a thing is produced and yet that there is no cause at all for that production, is to say that something is effected when it is effected by nothing, that is, at the same time when it is not effected at all. Whatever exists has a cause, a reason, a ground of its existence, a foundation on which its existence relies, a ground or reason why it does exist rather than not exist, either in the necessity of its own nature (and then it must have been of itself eternal), or in the will of some other being (and then that other being must, at least in the order of nature and causality, have existed before it). (1)

...

From Samuel Clarke, *A Demonstration of the Being and Attributes of God* (1705).

II

There has existed from eternity some one unchangeable and independent being. (2) For, since something must needs have been from eternity, as has been already proved and is granted on all hands, either there has always existed some one unchangeable and independent being from which all other beings that are or ever were in the universe have received their original, or else there has been an infinite succession of changeable and dependent beings produced one from another in an endless progression without any original cause at all. (3) Now this latter supposition is so very absurd that, though all atheism must in its accounts of most things (as shall be shown hereafter) terminate in it, yet I think very few atheists ever were so weak as openly and directly to defend it. For it is plainly impossible and contradictory to itself. (4) I shall not argue against it from the supposed impossibility of infinite succession, barely and absolutely considered in itself, for a reason which shall be mentioned hereafter. But, if we consider such an infinite progression as one entire endless series of dependent beings, (5) it is plain this whole series of beings can have no cause from without of its existence because in it are supposed to be included all things that are, or ever were, in the universe. And it is plain it can have no reason within itself for its existence because no one being in this infinite succession is supposed to be self-existent or

1

R Clarke's argument here assumes that everything must have a cause or reason for its existence (the PSR), and then argues that for something to come to be out of nothing is a contradiction: it has a cause (nothing), but to have nothing as a cause is not to have a cause at all.

2

R This is the conclusion of the main argument, for which Clarke will proceed to give reasons.

An *independent being* is a being whose existence does not depend on anything outside itself, whereas a *dependent being* is one whose existence does depend on something outside itself. (The claim that the independent being is also unchangeable is not explained or defended.)

3

R Clarke claims that there are only two alternatives: one independent being (whose existence causes the existence of any dependent beings that exist) or nothing but a series of dependent beings, each caused by the previous one.

4

R Clarke claims that the second alternative is impossible and self-contradictory, though without yet explaining how.

necessary (which is the only ground or reason of existence of anything that can be imagined within the thing itself, as will presently more fully appear), [6] but every one dependent on the foregoing. And, where no part is necessary, it is manifest the whole cannot be necessary—absolute necessity of existence not being an extrinsic, relative, and accidental denomination but an inward and essential property of the nature of the thing which so exists. [7]

An infinite succession, therefore, of merely dependent beings without any original independent cause is a series of beings that has neither necessity, nor cause, nor any reason or ground at all of its existence either within itself or from without. That is, it is an express contradiction and impossibility. It is a supposing something to be caused (because it is granted in every one of its stages of succession not to be necessarily and of itself), and yet that, in the whole, it is caused absolutely by nothing, [8] which every man knows is a contradiction to imagine done in time; and because duration in this case makes no difference, it is equally a contradiction to suppose it done from eternity. And consequently there must, on the contrary, of necessity have existed from eternity some one immutable and independent being.

To suppose an infinite succession of changeable and dependent beings produced one from another in an endless progression without any original cause at all is only a driving back from one step to another and, as it were, removing out of sight the question concerning the ground or reason of the existence of things.* [9] . . .

Otherwise, thus: either there has always existed some unchangeable and independent being from which all other beings have received their original, or else there has been an infinite succession of changeable and dependent beings, produced one from another in an endless progression without any original cause at all. According to this latter supposition, there is nothing in the universe self-existent or necessarily existing. And if so, then it was originally equally possible that from eternity there should never have existed anything at all, as that there should from eternity have existed a succession of changeable and dependent beings. Which being supposed, then, what is it that has from eternity determined such a succession of beings to exist, rather than that from eternity there should never have existed anything at all? Necessity it was not because it was equally possible, in this supposition, that they should not have existed at all. Chance is nothing but a mere word, without any signification. And other being it is supposed there was none, to determine the existence of these. Their existence, therefore, was determined by nothing; neither by any necessity in the nature of the things themselves, because it is supposed that none of them are self-existent, nor by any other being, because no other is supposed to exist. That is to say, of two equally possible things, viz., whether anything or nothing should from eternity have existed, the one is determined rather than the other absolutely by nothing, which is an express contradiction. [10] And consequently, as before, there must on the contrary of necessity have existed from eternity some one immutable and independent being. Which, what it is, remains in the next place to be inquired.

III

That unchangeable and independent being which has existed from eternity, without any external cause of its existence, must be self-existent, that

*This matter has been well illustrated by a late able writer: "Suppose a chain hung down out of the heavens from an unknown height, and though every link of it gravitated toward the Earth and what it hung upon was not visible, yet it did not descend but kept its situation; and [suppose] upon this a question should arise, what supported or kept up this chain? Would it be a sufficient answer to say that the first or lowest link hung upon the second, or that next above it, [and] the first, or rather the first and the second together, upon the third, and so on *in infinitum*? For what holds up the *whole*? A chain of ten links would fall down unless something able to bear it hindered. One of twenty, if not staid by something of a yet greater strength, [would fall] in proportion to the increase of weight, and therefore one of infinite links, certainly, if not sustained by something infinitely strong and capable to bear up on infinite weight. And thus it is in a chain of causes and effects tending or, as it were, gravitating towards some end. The last or lowest depends or, as one may say, is suspended upon the cause above it. This again, if it be not the first cause, is suspended as an effect upon something above it, etc. And if they should be infinite, unless agreeably to what has been said there is some cause upon which all hang or depend, they would be but an infinite effect without an efficient. And so to assert there is any such thing would be as great an absurdity as to say that a finite or little weight wants something to sustain it, but an infinite one, or the greatest, does not." W. Wollaston, *The Religion of Nature Delineated* (London, Samuel Palmer, 1724; reprint New York, Garland Publishing Co., 1978), p. 67.

5 Here is the main novelty in Clarke's version of the cosmological argument (and one main difference from Aquinas's Third Way): he proposes to treat the whole series of dependent beings as one entity and asks what explains it (thereby invoking the PSR). Clarke proceeds to pose two alternatives as to the explanation, one of which is easily ruled out.

6 Here is an alternative characterization of an *independent being:* a being that is *necessary* or *self-existent*—one that contains within itself the reason for its existence. (This is discussed further later on.)

7 The claim is that there is nothing about the inner nature of the series of dependent beings that would explain why the series as a whole exists.

8 Here we finally have an explanation of why the supposition that there is nothing but a series of dependent beings is supposed to result in a contradiction.

STOP What exactly is the contradiction? How does it follow from the foregoing discussion?

9  STOP How good is the analogy in the footnote?

10 Clarke focuses more clearly on the issue of why this specific series exists, rather than nothing (or rather than some other possible series?).

STOP What is the "express contradiction" to which he refers? (See Annotation 19.)

is, necessarily existing. For whatever exists must either have come into being out of nothing, absolutely without cause, or it must have been produced by some external cause, or it must be self-existent. Now to arise out of nothing absolutely without any cause has been already shown to be a plain contradiction. To have been produced by some external cause cannot possibly be true of every thing, but something must have existed eternally and independently, as has likewise been shown already. Which remains, therefore, [is] that that being which has existed independently from eternity must of necessity be self-existent. Now to be self-existent is not to be produced by itself, for that is an express contradiction, but it is . . . , I say, to exist by an absolute necessity originally in the nature of the thing itself. And this necessity must be antecedent, not indeed in time, to the existence of the being itself (because that is eternal), but it must be antecedent in the natural order of our ideas to our supposition of its being. That is, this necessity . . . must antecedently force itself upon us whether we will or no, even when we are endeavoring to suppose that no such being exists.

...

From this third proposition it follows, . . . that the only true idea of a self-existent or necessarily existing being is the idea of a being the supposition of whose not-existing is an express contradiction. For . . . a necessity not relatively or consequentially, but absolutely such in its own nature, is nothing else but its being a plain impossibility or implying a contradiction to suppose the contrary. (11)

. . . from hence it follows that the material world cannot possibly be the first and original being, uncreated, independent, and of itself eternal . . . . unless the material world exists necessarily by an absolute necessity in its own nature, so as that it must be an express contradiction to suppose it not to exist, it cannot be independent and of itself eternal. Now that the material world does not exist thus necessarily is very evident. For absolute necessity of existing and a possibility of not existing being contradictory ideas, it is manifest the material world cannot exist necessarily, if without a contradiction we can conceive it either not to be or to be in any respect otherwise than it now is. (12) Than which nothing is more easy. For whether we consider the form of the world with the disposition and motion of its parts, or whether we consider the matter of it as such, without respect to its present form, every thing in it, both the whole and every one of its parts, their situation and motion, the form and also the matter, are the most arbitrary and dependent things and the farthest removed from necessity that can possibly be imagined. A necessity indeed of fitness, that is, a necessity that things should be as they are in order to the well-being of the whole, there may be in all these things; but an absolute necessity of nature in any of them (which is what the atheist must maintain), there is not the last appearance of. If any man will say in this sense (as every atheist must do) either that the form of the world, or at least the matter and motion of it, is necessary, nothing can possibly be invented more absurd. (13)

...

Here is yet a further explanation of the idea of a *necessary* or *self-existent* being: it is one whose existence it is, by virtue of its own nature, **contradictory** to deny.

(Can you think of any way in which this might be so?)

The rationale for the second part of this claim (that a necessarily existent being could not be imagined to be in any way different from the way it is) is the claim, mentioned earlier, that such a being must be *unchangeable*. But the rationale for this claim is unclear. (And there are also problems with thinking of God as unchangeable, which might seem to rule out thinking or acting in any way.)

In the next selection, David Hume raises the issue of whether the material world itself might be the necessary or self-existent being. Here is Clarke's response.

How convincing is it—especially if the claim that a necessary being must be unchangeable is set aside as undefended?

Discussion Questions

1. Clarke's argument depends on treating the whole series of dependent beings as one entity and asking what explains the existence of that entity. But think of one of the dependent beings in the series. Is its existence adequately explained by its being caused by the previous being in the series? (Does Clarke offer any reason for a negative answer to this question?) But if the existence of each individual dependent being is adequately explained, does the whole series of such beings require any further explanation? Why or why not? (Suppose you meet several friends at a café, and that you can explain why each of them is there: one works there, one was invited by you, one often hangs out at that café, and so on. Does the fact that all of them are there as a group require a further explanation?)
2. Clarke argues that an independent being must also be a necessary (or self-existent) being. Think carefully about what an independent being is: is it by its very nature necessary? If it is necessary, then must it be eternal? As Clarke's own discussion illustrates, one way to argue for a claim is to infer consequences from its denial and show that they lead to a contradiction, thereby showing that the denial must be false, and thus that the original claim is true (this is called a reduction to absurdity—***reductio ad absurdum***). Suppose, for the sake of the argument, that an independent being is

not necessary. Explain the content of such a supposition by clarifying the ideas of independence and necessity. Is there a *reductio ad absurdum* argument for the claim that an independent being must be necessary? If so, explain it as clearly as you can.

3. Is there any plausible rationale for Clarke's claim that a necessary or self-existent being must be *unchangeable*? Perhaps the idea is that if the existence of such a being is necessary, then everything about it must be necessary—is there any plausibility to this? Is the requirement of unchangeability compatible with the idea of God as a personal being who creates and shapes the universe, actively cares about what people do, and (perhaps) intervenes from time to time in the course of human affairs?

David Hume

David Hume (1711–1776), a Scottish philosopher and historian, is usually regarded as one of the most important and influential philosophers of all time. He did very important work in epistemology, metaphysics, ethics, and the philosophy of religion, producing a comprehensive philosophical position that is most distinctive for its skeptical tendencies.

Hume's *Dialogues Concerning Natural Religion* (from which two other selections in this chapter are also drawn) offers a comprehensive discussion of the cosmological argument, the argument from design, the problem of evil, and the related issue of whether God's attributes are knowable by finite human minds. This is presented through an engaging use of dialogue form, rivaled for its combination of naturalness and philosophical cogency only by Plato's dialogues and Berkeley's *Three Dialogues Between Hylas and Philonous.* There are three characters in the dialogue: (1) Cleanthes, who advocates the argument from design and the view that God's attributes are knowable through analogy with human attributes; (2) Demea, who advocates the cosmological argument and the view that God's attributes are beyond human comprehension; and (3) Philo, usually regarded as a spokesman for Hume's own views, who is a subtle advocate of atheism (or at least a very strong agnosticism), but who pretends for most of the dialogue to side with Demea. This short section on the cosmological argument occurs fairly late in the dialogue (after the main discussion of the argument from design).

Problems with the Cosmological Argument, from *Dialogues Concerning Natural Religion*

...

But if so many difficulties attend the argument *a posteriori,* said Demea; had we not better adhere to that simple and sublime argument *a priori,* (1) which, by offering to us infallible demonstration, cuts off at once all doubt and difficulty? By this argument, too, we may prove the *infinity* of the divine attributes, which, I am afraid, can never be ascertained with certainty from any other topic. For how can an effect, which either is finite, or, for aught we know, may be so; how can such an effect, I say, prove an infinite cause? The unity too of the Divine Nature, it is very difficult, if not absolutely impossible, to deduce merely from contemplating the works of nature; nor will the uniformity alone of the plan, even were it allowed, give us any assurance of that attribute. Whereas the argument a priori. . . .

You seem to reason, Demea, interposed Cleanthes, as if those advantages and conveniences in the abstract argument were full proofs of its solidity. But it is first proper, in my opinion, to determine what argument of this nature you choose to insist on; and we shall afterwards, from itself, better than from its useful consequences, endeavor to determine what value we ought to put upon it.

The argument, replied Demea, which I would insist on is the common one. Whatever exists must have a cause or reason of its existence; it

(1) Demea describes the cosmological argument as **a priori,** meaning that it does not depend on experience in the extensive way that the argument from design ("the argument *a posteriori*") does. But it is not a purely a priori argument, since it does depend on the premise, known through experience, that a world of some sort exists.

From David Hume, *Dialogues Concerning Natural Religion* (1779).

being absolutely impossible for anything to produce itself, or be the cause of its own existence. [2] In mounting up; therefore, from effects to causes, we must either go on in tracing an infinite succession, without any ultimate cause at all; or must at last have recourse to some ultimate cause, that is *necessarily* existent. Now that the first supposition is absurd may be thus proved. In the infinite chain or succession of causes and effects, each single effect is determined to exist by the power and efficacy of that cause, which immediately preceded; but the whole eternal chain or succession, taken together, is not determined or caused by anything: and yet it is evident that it requires a cause or reason, as much as any particular object, which begins to exist in time. The question is still reasonable, why this particular succession of causes existed from eternity, and not any other succession, or no succession at all. If there be no necessarily existent being, any supposition, which can be formed, is equally possible; nor is there any more absurdity in *nothing's* having existed from eternity, than there is in that succession of causes, which constitutes the universe. What was it then, which determined something to exist rather than nothing, and bestowed being on a particular possibility, exclusive of the rest? [3] *External causes*, there are supposed to be none. *Chance* is a word without a meaning. Was it *nothing*? But that can never produce anything. We must, therefore, have recourse to a necessarily existent Being, who carries the reason of his existence in himself; and who cannot be supposed not to exist without an express contradiction. [4] There is consequently such a Being, that is, there is a Deity.

I shall not leave it to Philo, said Cleanthes (though I know that the starting objections is his chief delight), to point out the weakness of this metaphysical reasoning. It seems to me so obviously ill-grounded, and at the same time of so little consequence to the cause of true piety and religion, that I shall myself venture to show the fallacy of it.

I shall begin with observing, that there is an evident absurdity in pretending to demonstrate a matter of fact, or to prove it by any arguments a priori. Nothing is demonstrable, unless the contrary implies a contradiction. Nothing, that is distinctly conceivable, implies a contradiction. Whatever we conceive as existent, we can also conceive as non-existent. There is no being, therefore, whose non-existence implies a contradiction. Consequently there is no being, whose existence is demonstrable. [5] I propose this argument as entirely decisive, and am willing to rest the whole controversy upon it.

It is pretended that the Deity is a necessarily existent being; and this necessity of his existence is attempted to be explained by asserting, that, if we knew his whole essence or nature, we should perceive it to be as impossible for him not to exist as for twice two not to be four. But it is evident, that this can never happen, while our faculties remain the same as at present. It will still be possible for us, at any time, to conceive the non-existence of what we formerly conceived to exist; nor can the mind ever lie under a necessity of supposing any object to remain always in being; in the same manner as we lie under a necessity of always conceiving twice two to be four. The words, therefore, *necessary existence*, have no meaning; or, which is the same thing, none that is consistent.

But farther; why may not the material universe be the necessarily existent Being, according to this pretended explication of necessity? [6] We dare not affirm that we know all the qualities of matter; and for aught we can determine, it may contain some qualities, which, were they known, would make its non-existence appear as great a contradiction as that twice two is five. I find only one argument employed to prove, that the material world is not the necessarily existent Being; and this argument is derived from the contingency both of the matter and the form of the world. 'Any particle of matter,' 'tis said,* 'may be *conceived* to be annihilated; and any form may be *conceived* to be altered. Such an annihilation or alteration, therefore, is not impossible.' [7] But it seems a great partiality not to perceive, that the same argument extends equally to the Deity, so far as we have any conception of him; and that the mind can at least imagine him to be non-existent, or his attributes to be altered. It must be some unknown,

*Dr. Clarke.

The first part of this sentence is a version of the principle of sufficient reason. The latter part might seem to rule out the very conclusion that Demea is aiming for, but he does not say that a being cannot *explain* its own existence.

R Demea, like Clarke, views the whole series of causes and effects as an entity that requires a cause or reason (that is, an explanation). But he explains further: the issue is why this series (the one in the actual world) exists, rather than some other series or nothing at all.

The answer, as in Clarke, is the idea of a necessarily existent being, here explained as one whose very nature makes it contradictory to deny its existence.

R Cleanthes rejects the idea that the denial that a specified being exists could be self-contradictory. His reason, elaborated in what follows is that such a denial is always intelligibly conceivable.

(If the denial of God's existence were in fact self-contradictory, this would yield a much simpler argument for the existence of God. See Discussion Question 1 and the section on the ontological argument.)

R If the idea of necessary existence did make sense, Cleanthes is saying, it might just as well be the material universe rather than God that exists necessarily.

R Clarke's response (elaborated further here) is that particles of matter can be conceived to be *annihilated*, but God cannot. But the conceivability of God not existing in the first place would be enough to show that his existence is not necessary, even if his annihilation after he exists is impossible.

Is God's non-existence conceivable?

R If God causes the eternally existing material universe, it is obviously not by existing prior to it.

STOP Does the idea that God causes the material universe require that he (or she or it) exists prior to it? Or is there some other way of understanding God's causation?

R Cleanthes offers a response to the idea that the whole series of causes and effects is an entity that requires explanation, claiming that if each part is explained, then the whole is explained.

But does this answer the question of why that whole specific series exists, rather than some other series or nothing?

10

R Philo suggests that it is possible that if we understood the material universe well enough, we would see why it had to be the specific way it is (and why it exists rather than nothing?). Does this seem like a genuine possibility?

inconceivable qualities, which can make his non-existence appear impossible, or his attributes inalterable. And no reason can be assigned, why these qualities may not belong to matter. As they are altogether unknown and inconceivable, they can never be proved incompatible with it.

Add to this, that in tracing an eternal succession of objects, it seems absurd to inquire for a general cause or first author. How can anything, that exists from eternity, have a cause, since that relation implies a priority in time and a beginning of existence? 8

In such a chain too, or succession of objects, each part is caused by that which preceded it, and causes that which succeeds it. Where then is the difficulty? But the *whole*, you say, wants a cause. I answer, that the uniting of these parts into a whole, like the uniting of several distinct counties into one kingdom, or several distinct members into one body, is performed merely by an arbitrary act of the mind, and has no influence on the nature of things. Did I show you the particular causes of each individual in a collection of twenty particles of matter, I should think it very unreasonable, should you afterwards ask me, what was the cause of the whole twenty. This is sufficiently explained in explaining the cause of the parts. 9

Though the reasonings, which you have urged, Cleanthes, may well excuse me, said Philo, from starting any farther difficulties; yet I cannot forbear insisting still upon another topic. 'Tis observed by arithmeticians, that the products of 9 compose always either 9 or some lesser product of 9; if you add together all the characters, of which any of the former products is composed. Thus, of 18, 27, 36, which are products of 9, you make 9 by adding 1 to 8, 2 to 7, 3 to 6. Thus, 369 is a product also of 9; and if you add 3, 6, and 9, you make 18, a lesser product of 9. To a superficial observer, so wonderful a regularity may be admired as the effect either of chance or design: but a skillful algebraist immediately concludes it to be the work of necessity, and demonstrates, that it must forever result from the nature of these numbers. Is it not probable, I ask, that the whole economy of the universe is conducted by a like necessity, though no human algebra can furnish a key, which solves the difficulty? And instead of admiring the order of natural beings, may it not happen, that, could we penetrate into the intimate nature of bodies, we should clearly see why it was absolutely impossible, they could ever admit of any other disposition? 10 So dangerous is it to introduce this idea of necessity into the present question! And so naturally does it afford an inference directly opposite to the religious hypothesis!

Discussion Questions

1. How could it be that the denial of God's existence leads to a contradiction (which Cleanthes suggests to be the only possible account of how God could be a necessary or self-existent being)? One answer, perhaps the only one, to this question would be that the idea of existence is included in the very concept of God. Suppose that God is defined as an omnipotent, omniscient, perfectly good being who created the universe and who exists. Does it follow that such a being does actually exist? Why or why not? (See the subsection on the ontological argument for more discussion of this issue.)

2. Perhaps the most fundamental version of the cosmological argument starts from the question of why something exists rather than nothing:

1. Something exists (rather than nothing).

2. There must be a reason or explanation for any positive fact.

3. If all things that exist are contingent (not necessary or self existent), there will be no reason or explanation for (1).

Therefore, there must exist a necessary or self-existent being, namely God.

What evaluation should be made of this argument? (a) Premise (2) is a version of the principle of sufficient reason, but a more demanding one than those we have seen so far, in that it demands not just explanations for the existence of things, but for any positive fact of any sort. How plausible is this premise? (b) Is premise (3) correct? Try to carefully spell out the reasons for this premise. (c) Is the first part of the conclusion really intelligible? (d) Is there any reason for thinking that the necessary or self-existent being must have the characteristics of God, as standardly conceived?

The Argument from Design

William Paley

William Paley (1743–1805) was an English philosopher and also a noted theologian. He wrote widely on the existence and nature of God, and was also one of the early proponents of utilitarianism in ethics.

In this selection, Paley offers a local version of the argument from design (as explained in the introduction to this chapter), resting on an analogy between a watch of the old-fashioned mechanical sort found lying on a heath and the eye of a living creature (though it takes a while for the eye to appear and then the immediate comparison is between an eye and a telescope rather than between an eye and the watch). His basic claim is that just as it is clear that the watch must have been designed by some intelligent designer, the same thing is true of the eye.

The Argument from Design, from *Natural Theology*

Chapter One: State of the Argument

In crossing a heath, suppose I pitched my foot against a *stone* and were asked how the stone came to be there, I might possibly answer that for anything I knew to the contrary it had lain there forever; nor would it, perhaps, be very easy to show the absurdity of this answer. But suppose I had found a *watch* upon the ground, and it should be inquired how the watch happened to be in that place, I should hardly think of the answer which I had before given, that for anything I knew the watch might have always been there. Yet why should not this answer serve for the watch as well as for the stone; why is it not as admissible in the second case as in the first? ❶ For this reason, and for no other, namely, that when we come to inspect the watch, we perceive—what we could not discover in the stone—that its several parts are framed and put together for a purpose, e.g., that they are so formed and adjusted as to produce motion, and that motion so regulated as to point out the hour of the day; that if the different parts had been differently shaped from what they are, or placed after any other manner or in any other order than that in which they are placed, either no motion at all would have been carried on in the machine, or none which would have answered the use that is now served by it. ❷ To reckon up a few of the plainest of these parts and of their offices, all tending to one result: we see a cylindrical box containing a coiled elastic spring, which, by its endeavor to relax itself, turns round the box. We next observe a flexible chain—artificially wrought for the sake of flexure—communicating the action of the spring from the box to the fusee. We then find a series of wheels, the teeth of which catch in and apply to each other, conducting the motion from the fusee to the balance and from the balance to the pointer, and at the same time, by the size and shape of those wheels, so regulating that motion as to terminate in causing an index, by an equable and measured progression, to pass over a given space in a given time. We take notice that the wheels are made of brass, in order to keep them from rust; the springs of steel, no other metal being so elastic; that over the face of the watch there is placed a glass, a material employed in no other part of the work, but in the room of which, if there had been any other than a transparent substance, the hour could not be seen without opening the case. This mechanism being observed—it requires indeed an examination of the instrument, and perhaps some previous knowledge of the subject, to perceive and understand it; but being once, as we have said, observed and understood—the inference we think is inevitable, that the watch must have had a maker—that there must have existed, at some time and at some place or other, an artificer or artificers who formed it for the purpose which we find it actually to answer, who completely comprehended its construction and designed its use. ❸

From William Paley, *Natural Theology* (1802).

❶

R The initial comparison is between the watch and a stone: the former, Paley argues, demands an explanation in a way that the latter does not.

STOP Before reading further, stop and ask yourself what the differences are between the two cases (there are several), and try to figure out which of them are responsible for the different need for explanation.

❷

R Here is Paley's answer to the foregoing question: the watch demands an explanation because of the way in which its parts are shaped so as to work together to produce a specific result that would not have been achieved otherwise.

(To put this in terms of *purpose* risks **begging the question,** since that seems to presuppose an intelligent being.)

❸

R Here is Paley's explanation for the watch, which he claims to be obvious and compelling.

STOP Can you think of any alternative explanation in this case?

I. Nor would it, I apprehend, weaken the conclusion, that we had never seen a watch made—that we had never known an artist capable of making one—that we were altogether incapable of executing such a piece of workmanship ourselves, or of understanding in what manner it was performed; all this being no more than what is true of some exquisite remains of ancient art, of some lost arts, and, to the generality of mankind, of the more curious productions of modern manufacture. Does one man in a million know how oval frames are turned? Ignorance of this kind exalts our opinion of the unseen and unknown artist's skill, if he be unseen and unknown, but raises no doubt in our minds of the existence and agency of such an artist, at some former time and in some place or other. 4 Nor can I perceive that it varies at all the inference, whether the question arise concerning a human agent or concerning an agent of a different species, or an agent possessing in some respects a different nature.

4 Paley seems to be right that we do not need to know how watches are made in order to conclude that they are deliberately designed. But do we need to know that a watch contains elements (machined metal, shaped glass, wheels, and springs) that we know to be man-made and not naturally occurring things?

II. Neither, secondly, would it invalidate our conclusion, that the watch sometimes went wrong or that it seldom went exactly right. The purpose of the machinery, the design, and the designer might be evident, and in the case supposed, would be evident, in whatever way we accounted for the irregularity of the movement, or whether we could account for it or not. It is not necessary that a machine be perfect in order to show with what design it was made: still less necessary, where the only question is whether it were made with any design at all.

III. Nor, thirdly, would it bring any uncertainty into the argument, if there were a few parts of the watch, concerning which we could not discover or had not yet discovered in what manner they conduced to the general effect; or even some parts, concerning which we could not ascertain whether they conduced to that effect in any manner whatever. For, as to the first branch of the case, if by the loss, or disorder, or decay of the parts in question, the movement of the watch were found in fact to be stopped, or disturbed, or retarded, no doubt would remain in our minds as to the utility or intention of these parts, although we should be unable to investigate the manner according to which, or the connection by which, the ultimate effect depended upon their action or assistance; and the more complex the machine, the more likely is this obscurity to arise. Then, as to the second thing supposed, namely, that there were parts which might be spared without prejudice to the movement of the watch, and that we had proved this by experiment, these superfluous parts, even if we were completely assured that they were such, would not vacate the reasoning which we had instituted concerning other parts. The indication of contrivance remained, with respect to them, nearly as it was before.

IV. Nor, fourthly, would any man in his senses think the existence of the watch with its various machinery accounted for, by being told that it was one out of possible combinations of material forms; that whatever he had found in the place where he found the watch, must have contained some internal configuration or other; and that this configuration might be the structure now exhibited, namely, of the works of a watch, as well as a different structure. 5

5 R This suggestion seems to amount to saying that the watch just occurred at random, that nothing brought about that particular configuration of materials and components.

V. Nor, fifthly, would it yield his inquiry more satisfaction, to be answered that there existed in things a principle of order, which had disposed the parts of the watch into their present form and situation. He never knew a watch made by the principle of order; nor can he even form to himself an idea of what is meant by a principle of order distinct from the intelligence of the watchmaker. 6

6 Paley's claim here is plausible for the watch case. But how plausible is the corresponding more general claim: that *any* sort of order in things must be produced by an external intelligence, rather than perhaps being in some cases a result of the nature of the things themselves?

...

Chapter Two: State of the Argument Continued

Suppose, in the next place, that the person who found the watch should after some time discover that, in addition to all the properties which he had hitherto observed in it, it possessed the unexpected property of producing in the course of its movement another watch like itself—the thing is conceivable; that it contained within it a mechanism, a system of parts—a mold, for instance, or a complex adjustment of lathes, files, and other tools—evidently and separately calculated for this purpose; let us inquire what effect ought such a discovery to have upon his former conclusion. 7

7 R Paley proposes a modification of the case, in order to make it more parallel to living things (since his ultimate aim is to draw an analogy between the watch and living organisms).

I. The first effect would be to increase his admiration of the contrivance, and his conviction of the consummate skill of the contriver. Whether he regarded the object of the contrivance, the distinct apparatus, the intricate, yet in many parts intelligible mechanism by which it was carried on, he would perceive in this new observation nothing but an additional reason for doing what he had already done—for referring the construction of the watch to design and to supreme art. If that construction *without* this property, or, which is the same thing, before this property had been noticed, proved intention and art to have been employed about it, still more strong would the proof appear when he came to the knowledge of this further property, the crown and perfection of all the rest.

II. He would reflect that, though the watch before him were *in some sense* the maker of the watch which was fabricated in the course of its movements, yet it was in a very different sense from that in which a carpenter, for instance, is the maker of a chair—the author of its contrivance, the cause of the relation of its parts to their use. With respect to these, the first watch was no cause at all to the second; in no such sense as this was it the author of the constitution and order, either of the parts which the new watch contained, or of the parts by the aid and instrumentality of which it was produced. We might possibly say, but with great latitude of expression, that a stream of water ground corn; but no latitude of expression would allow us to say, no stretch of conjecture could lead us to think that the stream of water built the mill, though it were too ancient for us to know who the builder was. What the stream of water does in the affair is neither more nor less than this: by the application of an unintelligent impulse to a mechanism previously arranged, arranged independently of it and arranged by intelligence, an effect is produced, namely, the corn is ground. But the effect results from the arrangement. The force of the stream cannot be said to be the cause or the author of the effect, still less of the arrangement. Understanding and plan in the formation of the mill were not the less necessary for any share which the water has in grinding the corn; yet is this share the same as that which the watch would have contributed to the production of the new watch, upon the supposition assumed in the last section. Therefore,

III. Though it be now no longer probable that the individual watch which our observer had found was made immediately by the hand of an artificer, yet this alteration does not in anywise affect the inference that an artificer had been originally employed and concerned in the production. The argument from design remains as it was. Marks of design and contrivance are no more accounted for now than they were before. In the same thing, we may ask for the cause of different properties. We may ask for the cause of the color of a body, of its hardness, of its heat; and these causes may be all different. We are now asking for the cause of that subserviency to a use, that relation to an end, which we have remarked in the watch before us. No answer is given to this question by telling us that a preceding watch produced it. There cannot be design without a designer; contrivance without a contriver; order without choice; arrangement without anything capable of arranging; subserviency and relation to a purpose without that which could intend a purpose; means suitable to an end, and executing their office in accomplishing that end, without the end ever having been contemplated or the means accommodated to it. Arrangement, disposition of parts, subserviency of means to an end, relation of instruments to a use imply the presence of intelligence and mind. (8) No one, therefore, can rationally believe that the insensible, inanimate watch, from which the watch before us issued, was the proper cause of the mechanism we so much admire in it—could be truly said to have constructed the instrument, disposed its parts, assigned their office, determined their order, action, and mutual dependency, combined their several motions into one result, and that also a result connected with the utilities of other beings. All these properties, therefore, are as much unaccounted for as they were before.

IV. Nor is anything gained by running the difficulty farther back, that is, by supposing the watch before us to have been produced from another watch, that from a former, and so on indefinitely. Our going back ever so far brings us no nearer to the least degree of satisfaction upon the subject. Contrivance is still unaccounted for. We still want a contriver. A designing mind is neither supplied by this supposition nor dispensed with. . . . The machine which we are inspecting demonstrates, by its construction, contrivance and design. Contrivance must have had a contriver, design a designer, whether the machine immediately proceeded from another machine or not. That circumstance alters not the

(8)

R This and the previous sentence express the general conclusions that the watch example is supposed to support.

Paley sometimes sounds as though he thinks that these general claims are obvious or self-evident, so that he can appeal to them in arguing about the watch (rather than concluding to them on the basis of that argument). But if that were so, he could just apply them to the eye directly, without worrying about the watch.

case. That other machine may, in like manner, have proceeded from a former machine: nor does that alter the case; the contrivance must have had a contriver. That former one from one preceding it: no alteration still; a contriver is still necessary. No tendency is perceived, no approach toward a diminution of this necessity. It is the same with any and every succession of these machines—a succession of ten, of a hundred, of a thousand; with one series, as with another—a series which is finite, as with a series which is infinite. In whatever other respects they may differ, in this they do not. In all equally, contrivance and design are unaccounted for. [9]

The question is not simply, how came the first watch into existence?—which question, it may be pretended, is done away by supposing the series of watches thus produced from one another to have been infinite, and consequently to have had no such *first* for which it was necessary to provide a cause. This, perhaps, would have been nearly the state of the question, if nothing had been before us but an unorganized, unmechanized substance, without mark or indication of contrivance. It might be difficult to show that such substance could not have existed from eternity, either in succession—if it were possible, which I think it is not, for unorganized bodies to spring from one another—or by individual perpetuity. But that is not the question now. To suppose it to be so is to suppose that it made no difference whether he had found a watch or a stone. As it is, the metaphysics of that question have no place; for, in the watch which we are examining are seen contrivance, design, an end, a purpose, means for the end, adaptation to the purpose. And the question which irresistibly presses upon our thoughts is, whence this contrivance and design? The thing required is the intending mind, the adapted hand, the intelligence by which that hand was directed. This question, this demand is not shaken off by increasing a number or succession of substances destitute of these properties; nor the more, by increasing that number to infinity. If it be said that, upon the supposition of one watch being produced from another in the course of that other's movements and by means of the mechanism within it, we have a cause for the watch in my hand, namely, the watch from which it proceeded; I deny that for the design, the contrivance, the suitableness of means to an end, the adaptation of instruments to a use, all of which we discover in the watch, we have any cause whatever. It is in vain, therefore, to assign a series of such causes or to allege that a series may be carried back to infinity; for I do not admit that we have yet any cause at all for the phenomena, still less any series of causes either finite or infinite. Here is contrivance but no contriver; proofs of design, but no designer. [10]

V. Our observer would further also reflect that the maker of the watch before him was in truth and reality the maker of every watch produced from it: there being no difference, except that the latter manifests a more exquisite skill, between the making of another watch with his own hands, by the mediation of files, lathes, chisels, etc., and the disposing, fixing, and inserting of these instruments, or of others equivalent to them, in the body of the watch already made, in such a manner as to form a new watch in the course of the movements which he had given to the old one. It is only working by one set of tools instead of another.

The conclusion which the *first* examination of the watch, of its works, construction, and movement, suggested, was that it must have had, for cause and author of that construction, an artificer who understood its mechanism and designed its use. This conclusion is invincible. A *second* examination presents us with a new discovery. The watch is found, in the course of its movement, to produce another watch similar to itself; and not only so, but we perceive in it a system or organization separately calculated for that purpose. What effect would this discovery have or ought it to have upon our former inference? What, as has already been said, but to increase beyond measure our admiration of the skill which had been employed in the formation of such a machine? Or shall it, instead of this, all at once turn us round to an opposite conclusion, namely, that no art or skill whatever has been concerned in the business, although all other evidences of art and skill remain as they were, and this last and supreme piece of art be now added to the rest? Can this be maintained without absurdity? [11] Yet this is atheism.

9

R The claim is that each watch in the series raises the very same issue of explanation, the force of which is thus not reduced by even an infinite series.

10

Again Paley seems to assume that a contriver is required. But he hasn't shown that this is so until he has shown that the infinite series of watches cannot satisfactorily explain itself—which means that he cannot use the need for a contriver as the *reason* why the infinite series cannot do this.

11

R Paley is saying that if the original watch must be explained by a designer, this is even more clearly so for watches that can create further watches.

Chapter Three: Application of the Argument

This is atheism; for every indication of contrivance, every manifestation of design which existed in the watch, exists in the works of nature, with the difference on the side of nature of being greater and more, and that in a degree which exceeds all computation. I mean that the contrivances of nature surpass the contrivances of art in the complexity, subtlety, and curiosity of the mechanism; and still more, if possible, do they go beyond them in number and variety; yet, in a multitude of cases, are not less evidently mechanical, not less evidently contrivances, not less evidently accommodated to their end or suited to their office than are the most perfect productions of human ingenuity.

I know no better method of introducing so large a subject than that of comparing a single thing with a single thing: an eye, for example, with a telescope. 12 As far as the examination of the instrument goes, there is precisely the same proof that the eye was made for vision as there is that the telescope was made for assisting it. They are made upon the same principles, both being adjusted to the laws by which the transmission and refraction of rays of light are regulated. I speak not of the origin of the laws themselves; but such laws being fixed, the construction in both cases is adapted to them. For instance, these laws require, in order to produce the same effect, that rays of light in passing from water into the eye should be refracted by a more convex surface than when it passes out of air into the eye. Accordingly, we find that the eye of a fish, in that part of it called the crystalline lens, is much rounder than the eye of terrestrial animals. What plainer manifestation of design can there be than this difference? What could a mathematical instrument maker have done more to show his knowledge of his principle, his application of that knowledge, his suiting of his means to his end—I will not say to display the compass or excellence of his skill and art, for in these all comparison is indecorous, but to testify counsel, choice, consideration, purpose?

...

In the example before us it is a matter of certainty, because it is a matter which experience and observation demonstrate, that the formation of an image at the bottom of the eye is necessary to perfect vision. The formation then of such an image being necessary—no matter how—to the sense of sight and to the exercise of that sense, the apparatus by which it is formed is constructed and put together not only with infinitely more art, but upon the selfsame principles of art as in the telescope or the camera obscura. The perception arising from the image may be laid out of the question; for the production of the image, these are instruments of the same kind. The end is the same, the means are the same. The purpose in both is alike, the contrivance for accomplishing that purpose is in both alike. The lenses of the telescopes and humors of the eye bear a complete resemblance to one another, in their figure, their position, and in their power over the rays of light, namely, in bringing each pencil to a point at the right distance from the lens; namely, in the eye, at the exact place where the membrane is spread to receive it. How is it possible, under circumstances of such close affinity, and under the operation of equal evidence, to exclude contrivance from the one, yet to acknowledge the proof of contrivance having been employed, as the plainest and clearest of all propositions, in the other? 13

Finally the eye appears, though the initial comparison is with a telescope (a more similar manufactured object). In some ways the argument would have been simpler had Paley started with the telescope instead of the watch.

The similarities between the telescope and the eye are very great. The telescope is clearly a product of intelligent design (and could be known to be so even if we knew nothing about the specific manufacture of telescopes). By analogy, Paley claims, the same is (probably) true of the eye.

...

Chapter Five: Application of the Argument Continued

Every observation which was made in our first chapter concerning the watch may be repeated with strict propriety concerning the eye, concerning animals, concerning plants, concerning, indeed, all the organized parts of the works of nature. 14 As,

I. When we are inquiring simply after the *existence* of an intelligent Creator, imperfection, inaccuracy, liability to disorder, occasional irregularities may subsist in a considerable degree without inducing any doubt into the question; just as a watch may frequently go wrong, seldom perhaps exactly right, may be faulty in some parts, defective in some, without the smallest ground of suspicion from thence arising that it was not a watch, not made, or not made for the purpose ascribed to it. When faults are pointed out, and when a question is

Finally the comparison between the watch and the eye (and similar organic things) is drawn explicitly.

started concerning the skill of the artist or the dexterity with which the work is executed, then, indeed, in order to defend these qualities from accusation, we must be able either to expose some intractableness and imperfection in the materials or point out some invincible difficulty in the execution, into which imperfection and difficulty the matter of complaint may be resolved; or, if we cannot do this, we must adduce such specimens of consummate art and contrivance proceeding from the same hand as may convince the inquirer of the existence, in the case before him, of impediments like those which we have mentioned, although, what from the nature of the case is very likely to happen, they be unknown and unperceived by him. This we must do in order to vindicate the artist's skill, or at least the perfection of it; as we must also judge of his intention and of the provisions employed in fulfilling that intention, not from an instance in which they fail but from the great plurality of instances in which they succeed. But, after all, these are different questions from the question of the artist's existence; or, which is the same, whether the thing before us be a work of art or not; and the questions ought always to be kept separate in the mind. [15] So likewise it is in the works of nature. Irregularities and imperfections are of little or no weight in the consideration when that consideration relates simply to the existence of a Creator. When the argument respects his attributes, they are of weight; but are then to be taken in conjunction—the attention is not to rest upon them, but they are to be taken in conjunction with the unexceptional evidences which we possess of skill, power, and benevolence displayed in other instances; which evidences may, in strength, number, and variety, be such and may so overpower apparent blemishes as to induce us, upon the most reasonable ground, to believe that these last ought to be referred to some cause, though we be ignorant of it, other than defect of knowledge or of benevolence in the author.

15

R One issue is whether something can only be adequately explained by appeal to an intelligent designer. A second question is how much intelligence and skill must be ascribed to the designer for the explanation to be adequate. This points to a weakness in this version of the argument from design if it is claimed to establish the existence of a God fitting the standard conception. Paley here tries to deal with that weakness.

R Again the idea behind this atheistic reply seems to be that eyes might just have occurred at random, as one out of many possibilities.

...

III. One atheistic way of replying to our observations upon the works of nature, and to the proofs of a Deity which we think that we perceive in them, is to tell us that all which we see must necessarily have had some form, and that it might as well be its present form as any other. [16] Let us now apply this answer to the eye, as we did before to the watch. Something or other must have occupied that place in the animal's head, must have filled up, as we say, that socket; we will say, also, that it must have been of that sort of substance which we call animal substance, as flesh, bone, membrane, or cartilage, etc. But that it should have been an eye, knowing as we do what an eye comprehends, namely, that it should have consisted, first, of a series of transparent lenses—very different, by the by, even in their substance, from the opaque materials of which the rest of the body is, in general at least, composed, and with which the whole of its surface, this single portion of it excepted, is covered; secondly, of a black cloth or canvas—the only membrane in the body which is black—spread out behind these lenses, so as to receive the image formed by pencils of light transmitted through them, and at which alone a distinct image could be formed, namely, at the concourse of the refracted rays; thirdly, of a large nerve communicating between this membrane and the brain, without which the action of light upon the membrane, however modified by the organ, would be lost to the purposes of sensation; that this fortunate conformation of parts should have been the lot not of one individual out of many thousand individuals, like the great prize in a lottery or like some singularity in nature, but the happy chance of a whole species; nor of one species out of many thousand species with which we are acquainted, but of by far the greatest number of all that exist, and that under varieties not casual or capricious, but bearing marks of being suited to their respective exigencies; that all this should have taken place merely because something must have occupied these points on every animal's forehead, or that all this should be thought to be accounted for by the short answer that "whatever was there must have had some form or other" is too absurd to be made more so by any argumentation. We are not contented with this answer; we find no satisfaction in it, by way of accounting for appearances of organization far short of those of the eye, such as we observe in fossil shells, petrified bones, or other substances which bear the vestiges of animal or vegetable recrements, but which, either in respect to utility or of the situation in which they are discovered, may seem accidental enough. It is no way of accounting even for these things, to say that the stone, for instance, which is shown to us—supposing the question to be concerning a petrifaction—must have contained some internal conformation or other.

...

IV. There is another answer which has the same effect as the resolving of things into chance, which answer would persuade us to believe that the eye, the animal to which it belongs, every other animal, every plant, indeed every organized body which we see are only so many out of the possible varieties and combinations of being which the lapse of infinite ages has brought into existence; that the present world is the relic of that variety; millions of other bodily forms and other species having perished, being, by the defect of their constitution, incapable of preservation, or of continuance by generation. Now there is no foundation whatever for this conjecture in any thing which we observe in the works of nature; no such experiments are going on at present—no such energy operates as that which is here supposed, and which should be constantly pushing into existence new varieties of beings. Nor are there any appearances to support an opinion that every possible combination of vegetable or animal structure has formerly been tried. Multitudes of conformation, both of vegetables and animals, may be conceived capable of existence and succession, which yet do not exist. Perhaps almost as many forms of plants might have been found in the fields as figures of plants can be delineated upon paper. A countless variety of animals might have existed which do not exist. Upon the supposition here stated, we should see unicorns and mermaids, sylphs and centaurs, the fancies of painters and the fables of poets, realized by examples. Or, if it be alleged that these may transgress the bounds of possible life and propagation, we might at least have nations of human beings without nails upon their fingers, with more or fewer fingers and toes than ten, some with one eye, others with one ear, with one nostril, or without the sense of smelling at all. All these and a thousand other imaginable varieties might live and propagate. We may modify any one species many different ways, all consistent with life, and with the actions necessary to preservation, although affording different degrees of conveniency and enjoyment to the animal. And if we carry these modifications through the different species which are known to subsist, their number would be incalculable. No reason can be given why, if these [lost species] ever existed, they have now disappeared. Yet, if all possible existences have been tried, they must have formed part of the catalogue. (17)

17

R Here we have a crude anticipation of something like the idea of evolution. But with no account of how some variations rather than others might have been produced and selected, there is no explanation of why so few possibilities seem to actually be realized.

...

The hypothesis, indeed, is hardly deserving of the consideration which we have given it. What should we think of a man who, because we had never ourselves seen watches, telescopes, stocking mills, steam engines, etc., made, knew not how they were made, nor could prove by testimony when they were made, or by whom, would have us believe that these machines, instead of deriving their curious structures from the thought and design of their inventors and contrivers, in truth derive them from no other origin than this: namely, that a mass of metals and other materials having run, when melted, into all possible figures, and combined themselves in all possible forms and shapes and proportions, these things which we see are what were left from the incident, as best worth preserving, and as such are become the remaining stock of a magazine which, at one time or other, has by this means contained every mechanism, useful and useless, convenient and inconvenient, into which such like materials could be thrown? I cannot distinguish the hypothesis, as applied to the works of nature, from this solution, which no one would accept as applied to a collection of machines.

...

VI. Others have chosen to refer every thing to a *principle of order* in nature. A principle of order is the word; but what is meant by a principle of order as different from an intelligent Creator has not been explained either by definition or example; and without such explanation it should seem to be a mere substitution of words for reasons, names for causes. Order itself is only the adaptation of means to an end: a principle of order, therefore, can only signify the mind and intention which so adapts them. 18 Or, were it capable of being explained in any other sense, is there any experience, any analogy, to sustain it? Was a watch ever produced by a principle of order; and why might not a watch be so produced as well as an eye?

Furthermore, a principle of order, acting blindly and without choice, is negatived by the observation that order is not universal, which it would be if it issued from a constant and necessary principle, nor indiscriminate, which it would be if it issued from an unintelligent principle. 19 Where order is wanted, there we find it; where order is not wanted, that is, where if it prevailed, it would be useless, there we do not find it. In the structure of the eye—for we adhere to our example—in the figure and position of its several parts, the most exact order is maintained. In the forms of rocks and mountains, in the lines which bound the coasts of continents and islands, in the shape of bays and promontories, no order whatever is perceived, because it would have been superfluous.

18

Paley seems to argue here that *any* sort of order presupposes a mind that creates it. Does he have any argument for this claim? Do you see any problem with it? (Doesn't a mind itself involve a kind of order?)

19

Here is a different response to the claim that nature itself is orderly in a way that explains the eye: eyes are very rare in comparison to the sorts of materials of which they are composed, so it isn't plausible to think that they are generated by a pervasive natural order.

Discussion Questions

1. One difference between the watch and the stone is that we know independently that stones naturally occur in heaths and watches don't. Another is that the watch has features that are known to be present in manufactured items and not in naturally occurring items (see Annotation 4). These features do not pertain to the eye, and they at least weaken the analogy between the watch and the eye upon which Paley ultimately relies (or that between the telescope and the eye). How much does this affect his argument?
2. Is it self-evident that the watch (even the infinite series of self-replicating watches) requires a further explanation? Is it similarly self-evident that it must be explained by appeal to an intelligent designer? Would this be so even if the watch did not resemble any familiar sort of manufactured object, even if it seemed to be an organically produced structure? Why or why not? Is the same thing true of the eye?
3. Suppose that everything about Paley's argument were acceptable. What conception of the designer's attributes would it support? How close would they be to the attributes of God under the standard conception? How important is the fact that some of the allegedly designed features are imperfect (see Annotation 16)?
4. Think carefully about the premise of the argument from design. What is the correct characterization of the facts that allegedly require a designer? Think first about the watch. What exactly is it about the watch that convinces us that it must have had a designer? Not that the watch has a design, for that would beg the question. Paley says that "its parts are framed and put together for a purpose," but that also seems question-begging. Try to formulate a description of the watch and an analogous description of the eye that are not question-begging and yet still support the conclusion of the argument.

Stephen Jay Gould

Stephen Jay Gould (1941–2002) was a paleontologist and evolutionary biologist who taught at Harvard. Though his writings are voluminous, he is perhaps best known for his short essays in the periodical *Natural History*, collected in many volumes, which explain and discuss various topics in and around the theory of evolution.

The following selection is one of those essays. In it, Gould argues in favor of the theory of evolution, and so against the hypothesis of divine creation, as an explanation of specific examples of apparent design of the sort to which Paley appeals. The main premise of the argument is that the details of many such examples involve structures existing in other animals that are very imperfectly adapted for a particular use in the case in question. According to Gould, this makes very good sense from an evolutionary perspective, but does not fit well with the hypothesis that such structures were a product of intelligent design by an all-powerful creator.

It is important to emphasize that while the appeal to evolution may be a good response to the *local* version of the argument from design, it does not in itself answer the *global* version that demands an explanation for the presence of order of any sort in the universe (see the introduction to this chapter). This is so because the details of the evolutionary account obviously presuppose a background of order that is itself left unexplained: in the case of evolution, the order required for genetic inheritance, mixing of genes from different individuals, production of mutations, and so on. Other scientific explanations of specific features of the world, for example the explanation of mountains provided by geology, work in the same way: they account for specific, narrowly focused cases of order by appeal to more general background principles of order. Thus explanations of this sort are incapable of providing a complete answer to the global version of the argument.

The Panda's Thumb

Few heroes lower their sights in the prime of their lives; triumph leads inexorably on, often to destruction. Alexander wept because he had no new worlds to conquer; Napoleon, overextended, sealed his doom in the depth of a Russian winter. But Charles Darwin did not follow the *Origin of Species* (1859) with a general defense of natural selection or with its evident extension to human evolution (he waited until 1871 to publish *The Descent of Man*). Instead, he wrote his most obscure work, a book entitled: *On the Various Contrivances by Which British and Foreign Orchids Are Fertilized by Insects* (1862).

Darwin's many excursions into the minutiae of natural history—he wrote a taxonomy of barnacles, a book on climbing plants, and a treatise on the formation of vegetable mold by earthworms—won him an undeserved reputation as an old-fashioned, somewhat doddering describer of curious plants and animals, a man who had one lucky insight at the right time. A rash of Darwinian scholarship has laid this myth firmly to rest during the past twenty years. Before then, one prominent scholar spoke for many ill-informed colleagues when he judged Darwin as a "poor joiner of ideas . . . a man who does not belong with the great thinkers."

In fact, each of Darwin's books played its part in the grand and coherent scheme of his life's work demonstrating the fact of evolution and defending natural selection as its primary mechanism. (1) Darwin did not study orchids solely for their own sake. Michael Ghiselin, a California biologist who finally took the trouble to read all of Darwin's books (see his *Triumph of the Darwinian Method*), has correctly identified the treatise on orchids as an important episode in Darwin's campaign for evolution.

Darwin begins his orchid book with an important evolutionary premise: continued self-fertilization is a poor strategy for long-term survival, since offspring carry only the genes of their single parent, and populations do not maintain enough variation for evolutionary flexibility in the face of environmental change. Thus, plants bearing flowers with both male and female parts usually evolve mechanisms to ensure cross-pollination. (2) Orchids have formed an alliance with insects. They have evolved an astonishing variety of "contrivances" to attract insects, guarantee that sticky pollen adheres to their visitor, and ensure that the attached pollen comes in contact with female parts of the next orchid visited by the insect.

Darwin's book is a compendium of these contrivances, the botanical equivalent of a bestiary. And, like the medieval bestiaries, it is designed to instruct. The message is paradoxical but profound. Orchids manufacture their intricate devices from the common components of ordinary flowers, parts usually fitted for very different functions. If God had designed a beautiful machine to reflect his wisdom and power, surely he would not have used a collection of parts generally fashioned for other purposes. Orchids were not made by an ideal engineer; they are jury-rigged from a limited set of available components. Thus, they must have evolved from ordinary flowers. (3)

Thus, the paradox, and the common theme of this trilogy of essays: Our textbooks like to illustrate evolution with examples of optimal design—nearly perfect mimicry of a dead leaf by a butterfly

Evolution is the change and development of plants and animals over time, resulting in the emergence of new species (and usually the disappearance of older ones). *Natural selection* is the hypothesis that this takes place because (a) individuals with varied characteristics occur (through genetic recombination and mutation), and (b) those whose characteristics improve their capacity to survive (in the specific environment in question) are more likely to reproduce, thus passing their characteristics to their offspring ("survival of the fittest").

R The mixing of genes from different parents is one way in which individuals with varied characteristics are produced, so that natural selection can operate. (Another such way is mutation.)

This point is elaborated and illustrated toward the end of the selection.

From Stephen Jay Gould, *The Panda's Thumb: More Reflections in Natural History* (New York: W. W. Norton, 1980).

or of a poisonous species by a palatable relative. But ideal design is a lousy argument for evolution, for it mimics the postulated action of an omnipotent creator. Odd arrangements and funny solutions are the proof of evolution—paths that a sensible God would never tread but that a natural process, constrained by history, follows perforce. No one understood this better than Darwin. Ernst Mayr has shown how Darwin, in defending evolution, consistently turned to organic parts and geographic distributions that make the least sense. (4) Which brings me to the giant panda and its "thumb."

4

R The idea is that an intelligent, all-powerful designer would have created features that are perfectly designed for their function, whereas evolution, having to select among only those features that actually occur via genetic combination and mutation, may well end up with features that function adequately but are far short of optimum.

Giant pandas are peculiar bears, members of the order Carnivora. Conventional bears are the most omnivorous representatives of their order, but pandas have restricted this catholicity of taste in the other direction—they belie the name of their order by subsisting almost entirely on bamboo. They live in dense forests of bamboo at high elevations in the mountains of western China. There they sit, largely unthreatened by predators, munching bamboo ten to twelve hours each day.

As a childhood fan of Andy Panda, and former owner of a stuffed toy won by some fluke when all the milk bottles actually tumbled at the county fair, I was delighted when the first fruits of our thaw with China went beyond ping pong to the shipment of two pandas to the Washington zoo. I went and watched in appropriate awe. They yawned, stretched, and ambled a bit, but they spent nearly all their time feeding on their beloved bamboo. They sat upright and manipulated the stalks with their forepaws, shedding the leaves and consuming only the shoots.

I was amazed by their dexterity and wondered how the scion of a stock adapted for running could use its hands so adroitly. They held the stalks of bamboo in their paws and stripped off the leaves by passing the stalks between an apparently flexible thumb and the remaining fingers. This puzzled me. I had learned that a dexterous, opposable thumb stood among the hallmarks of human success. We had maintained, even exaggerated, this important flexibility of our primate forebears, while most mammals had sacrificed it in specializing their digits. Carnivores run, stab, and scratch. My cat may manipulate me psychologically, but he'll never type or play the piano.

So I counted the panda's other digits and received an even greater surprise; there were five, not four. Was the "thumb" a separately evolved sixth finger? Fortunately, the giant panda has its bible, a monograph by D. Dwight Davis, late curator of vertebrate anatomy at Chicago's Field Museum of Natural History. It is probably the greatest work of modern evolutionary comparative anatomy, and it contains more than anyone would ever want to know about pandas. Davis had the answer, of course.

The panda's "thumb" is not, anatomically, a finger at all. It is constructed from a bone called the radial sesamoid, normally a small component of the wrist. In pandas, the radial sesamoid is greatly enlarged and elongated until it almost equals the metapodial bones of the true digits in length. The radial sesamoid underlies a pad on the panda's forepaw; the five digits form the framework of another pad, the palmar. A shallow furrow separates the two pads and serves as a channelway for bamboo stalks.

The panda's thumb comes equipped not only with a bone to give it strength but also with muscles to sustain its agility. These muscles, like the radial sesamoid bone itself, did not arise *de novo*. Like the parts of Darwin's orchids, they are familiar bits of anatomy remodeled for a new function. The abductor of the radial sesamoid (the muscle that pulls it away from the true digits) bears the formidable name *abductor pollicis longus* ("the long abductor of the thumb"—*pollicis* is the genitive of *pollex*, Latin for "thumb"). Its name is a giveaway. In other carnivores, this muscle attaches to the first digit, or true thumb. Two shorter muscles run between the radial sesamoid and the pollex. They pull the sesamoid "thumb" towards the true digits. (5)

5

R Thus the panda's "thumb" is not a true thumb at all, but rather a structure involving a bone and muscles that take quite different forms in the panda's relatives. Though it works well enough in eating bamboo, Gould's point is that an all-powerful intelligent designer would have designed a specific structure for this purpose rather than adapting pre-existing parts in a serviceable but still somewhat clumsy way.

Does the anatomy of other carnivores give us any clue to the origin of this odd arrangement in pandas? Davis points out that ordinary bears and raccoons, the closest relatives of giant pandas, far surpass all other carnivores in using their forelegs for manipulating objects in feeding. Pardon the backward metaphor, but pandas, thanks to their ancestry, began with a leg up for evolving greater dexterity in feeding. Moreover, ordinary bears already have a slightly enlarged radial sesamoid.

In most carnivores, the same muscles that move the radial sesamoid in pandas attach exclusively to the base of the pollex, or true thumb. But in ordinary bears, the long abductor muscle ends in two tendons: one inserts into the base of the thumb as in most carnivores, but the other attaches to the radial sesamoid. The two shorter muscles also attach, in part, to the radial sesamoid in bears. "Thus," Davis concludes, "the musculature for operating this remarkable new mechanism—functionally a new digit—required no intrinsic change from conditions already present in the panda's closest relatives, the bears. Furthermore, it appears that the whole sequence of events in the musculature follows automatically from simple hypertrophy of the sesamoid bone."

The sesamoid thumb of pandas is a complex structure formed by marked enlargement of a bone and an extensive rearrangement of musculature. Yet Davis argues that the entire apparatus arose as a mechanical response to growth of the radial sesamoid itself. Muscles shifted because the enlarged bone blocked them short of their original sites. Moreover, Davis postulates that the enlarged radial sesamoid may have been fashioned by a simple genetic change, perhaps a single mutation affecting the timing and rate of growth. 6

In a panda's foot, the counterpart of the radial sesamoid, called the tibial sesamoid, is also enlarged, although not so much as the radial sesamoid. Yet the tibial sesamoid supports no new digit, and its increased size confers no advantage, so far as we know. 7 Davis argues that the coordinated increase of both bones, in response to natural selection upon one alone, probably reflects a simple kind of genetic change. Repeated parts of the body are not fashioned by the action of individual genes—there is no gene "for" your thumb, another for your big toe, or a third for your pinky. Repeated parts are coordinated in development; selection for a change in one element causes a corresponding modification in others. It may be genetically more complex to enlarge a thumb and not to modify a big toe, than to increase both together. (In the first case, a general coordination must be broken, the thumb favored separately, and correlated increase of related structures suppressed. In the second, a single gene may increase the rate of growth in a field regulating the development of corresponding digits.)

The panda's thumb provides an elegant zoological counterpart to Darwin's orchids. An engineer's best solution is debarred by history. The panda's true thumb is committed to another role, too specialized for a different function to become an opposable, manipulating digit. So the panda must use parts on hand and settle for an enlarged wrist bone and a somewhat clumsy, but quite workable, solution. The sesamoid thumb wins no prize in an engineer's derby. It is, to use Michael Ghiselin's phrase, a contraption, not a lovely contrivance. But it does its job and excites our imagination all the more because it builds on such improbable foundations.

Darwin's orchid book is filled with similar illustrations. The marsh Epipactus, for example, uses its labellum—an enlarged petal—as a trap. The labellum is divided into two parts. One, near the flower's base, forms a large cup filled with nectar—the object of an insect's visit. The other, near the flower's edge, forms a sort of landing stage. An insect alighting on this runway depresses it and thus gains entrance to the nectar cup beyond. It enters the cup, but the runway is so elastic that it instantly springs up, trapping the insect within the nectar cup. The insect must then back out through the only available exit—a path that forces it to brush against the pollen masses. A remarkable machine but all developed from a conventional petal, a part readily available in an orchid's ancestor.

Darwin then shows how the same labellum in other orchids evolves into a series of ingenious devices to ensure cross-fertilization. It may develop a complex fold that forces an insect to detour its proboscis around and past the pollen masses in order to reach nectar. It may contain deep channels or guiding ridges that lead insects both to nectar and pollen. The channels sometimes form a tunnel, producing a tubular flower. All these adaptations have been built from a part that began as a conventional petal in some ancestral form. Yet nature can do so much with so little that it displays, in Darwin's words, "a prodigality of resources for gaining the very same end, namely, the fertilization of one flower by pollen from another plant."

Darwin's metaphor for organic form reflects his sense of wonder that evolution can fashion such a world of diversity and adequate design with such limited raw material:

> Although an organ may not have been originally formed for some special purpose, if it now serves for this end we are justified in saying that it is specially contrived for it. On the same principle, if a man were to make a machine for some special purpose, but were to use old wheels,

R The claim is that evolution provides a better explanation of the panda's thumb than divine creation (see Annotation 5). If Davis is right, a single mutation could have produced the whole structure (which then would have been favored by natural selection because of its advantage for feeding).

7

R This hypothesis is supported by the similar change in the panda's foot—which in itself yields no survival value and so presumably would not have been designed by an intelligent designer.

springs, and pulleys, only slightly altered, the whole machine, with all its parts, might be said to be specially contrived for that purpose. Thus throughout nature almost every part of each living being has probably served, in a slightly modified condition, for diverse purposes, and has acted in the living machinery of many ancient and distinct specific forms.

We may not be flattered by the metaphor of refurbished wheels and pulleys, but consider how well we work. Nature is, in biologist François Jacob's words, an excellent tinkerer, not a divine artificer. And who shall sit in judgment between these exemplary skills?

Discussion Questions

1. Why does Gould's example of the panda's thumb constitute an objection to the argument from design? How good is that objection? Since the panda's thumb works quite well, is there any reason why an intelligent designer could not have created it for that purpose? Is there a way in which the evolutionary explanation is better than the appeal to God, even though both are possible explanations? Gould also might seem to suggest that for optimum organic structures, intelligent design is just as good an explanation (or even a better one?). Is he right about this?
2. How might a creationist respond to Gould's objection by shifting from the local to the global version of the argument from design? Why can't someone appeal to evolutionary theory to explain the order of the universe as a whole? Does the order of the universe as a whole genuinely need an explanation? Why or why not?

David Hume

The longest portion of Hume's *Dialogues* is devoted to the argument from design, with Cleanthes presenting his version of the argument and Philo criticizing it at great length. Though both the local and the global versions of the argument (see the introduction to this chapter) are reflected in the discussion, the main focus is on the global version. Thus the issue is how the overall order of the world (really the universe) is to be explained.

See the introduction to the selection from the *Dialogues* on page 524 for information about Hume, together with a description of the characters in the dialogue (this selection actually comes immediately before that one in the original book).

Problems with the Argument from Design, from *Dialogues Concerning Natural Religion*

. . .

Not to lose any time in circumlocutions, said Cleanthes, addressing himself to Demea, . . . ; I shall briefly explain how I conceive this matter. Look round the world: contemplate the whole and every part of it: you will find it to be nothing but one great machine, subdivided into an infinite number of lesser machines, which again admit of subdivisions, to a degree beyond what human senses and faculties can trace and explain. All these various machines, and even their most minute parts, are adjusted to each other with an accuracy, which ravishes into admiration all men, who have ever contemplated them. The curious adapting of means to ends, throughout all nature, resembles exactly, though it much exceeds, the productions of human contrivance; of human design, thought, wisdom, and intelligence. Since therefore the effects resemble each other, we are led to infer, by all the rules of analogy, that the causes also resemble; and that the Author of Nature is somewhat similar to the mind of men; though possessed of much larger faculties, proportioned to the grandeur of the work, which he has executed. By this argument *a posteriori,* and by this argument alone, do we

From David Hume, *Dialogues Concerning Natural Religion* (1779).

prove at once the existence of a Deity, and his similarity to human mind and intelligence. ❶

I shall be so free, Cleanthes, said Demea, as to tell you, that from the beginning, I could not approve of your conclusion concerning the similarity of the Deity to men; still less can I approve of the mediums, by which you endeavor to establish it. What! No demonstration of the being of a God! No abstract arguments! No proofs a priori! ❷ Are these, which have hitherto been so much insisted on by philosophers, all fallacy, all sophism? Can we reach no farther in this subject than experience and probability? I will not say, that this is betraying the cause of a deity: but surely, by this affected candor, you give advantage to atheists, which they never could obtain, by the mere dint of argument and reasoning.

What I chiefly scruple in this subject, said Philo, is not so much, that all religious arguments are by Cleanthes reduced to experience, as that they appear not to be even the most certain and irrefragable of that inferior kind. That a stone will fall, that fire will burn, that the earth has solidity, we have observed a thousand and a thousand times; and when any new instance of this nature is presented, we draw without hesitation the accustomed inference. The exact similarity of the cases gives us a perfect assurance of a similar event; and a stronger evidence is never desired nor sought after. But wherever you depart, in the least, from the similarity of the cases, you diminish proportionably the evidence; and may at last bring it to a very weak *analogy,* which is confessedly liable to error and uncertainty. After having experienced the circulation of the blood in human creatures, we make no doubt that it takes place in Titius and Maevius: but from its circulation in frogs and fishes, it is only a presumption, though a strong one, from analogy, that it takes place in men and other animals. The analogical reasoning is much weaker, when we infer the circulation of the sap in vegetables from our experience, that the blood circulates in animals; and those, who hastily followed that imperfect analogy, are found, by more accurate experiments, to have been mistaken. ❸

If we see a house, Cleanthes, we conclude, with the greatest certainty, that it had an architect or builder; because this is precisely that species of effect, which we have experienced to proceed from that species of cause. But surely you will not affirm, that the universe bears such a resemblance to a house, that we can with the same certainty infer a similar cause, or that the analogy is here entire and perfect. The dissimilitude is so striking, that the utmost you can here pretend to is a guess, a conjecture, a presumption concerning a similar cause; and how that pretension will be received in the world, I leave you to consider.

It would surely be very ill received, replied Cleanthes; and I should be deservedly blamed and detested, did I allow, that the proofs of a Deity amounted to no more than a guess or conjecture. But is the whole adjustment of means to ends in a house and in the universe so slight a resemblance? The economy of final causes? The order, proportion, and arrangement of every part? Steps of a stair are plainly contrived, that human legs may use them in mounting; and this inference is certain and infallible. Human legs are also contrived for walking and mounting; and this inference, I allow, is not altogether so certain, because of the dissimilarity which you remark; but does it, therefore, deserve the name only of presumption or conjecture?

Good God! cried Demea, interrupting him, where are we? Zealous defenders of religion allow, that the proofs of a Deity fall short of perfect evidence! And you, Philo, on whose assistance I depended, in proving the adorable mysteriousness of the Divine Nature, do you assent to all these extravagant opinions of Cleanthes? For what other name can I give them? . . .

You seem not to apprehend, replied Philo, that I argue with Cleanthes in his own way; and by showing him the dangerous consequences of his tenets, hope at last to reduce him to our opinion. But what sticks most with you, I observe, is the representation which Cleanthes has made of the argument *a posteriori;* and finding, that that argument is likely to escape your hold and vanish into air, you think it so disguised, that you can scarcely believe it to be set in its true light. Now, however much I may dissent, in other respects, from the dangerous principles of Cleanthes, I must allow, that he has fairly represented that argument; and I shall endeavor so to state the matter to you, that you will entertain no farther scruples with regard to it.

Were a man to abstract from everything which he knows or has seen, he would be altogether incapable, merely from his own ideas, to determine

❶

Though both versions are discernible, the main emphasis here is on what we have called the global version of the argument from design (see chapter introduction).

❷

By an "a priori proof," Demea has the cosmological argument in mind (even though it is not strictly a priori because it relies on the experience that the world exists).

❸

R Many versions of the argument from design, such as Paley's, are arguments by analogy. Philo makes the point that the strength of such an argument depends heavily on the degree of similarity between the cases that are being compared.

what kind of scene the universe must be, or to give the preference to one state or situation of things above another. For as nothing which he clearly conceives, could be esteemed impossible or implying a contradiction, every chimera of his fancy would be upon an equal footing; nor could he assign any just reason, why he adheres to one idea or system, and rejects the others, which are equally possible.

Again; after he opens his eyes, and contemplates the world, as it really is, it would be impossible for him, at first, to assign the cause of any one event; much less, of the whole of things or of the universe. He might set his fancy a rambling; and she might bring him in an infinite variety of reports and representations. These would all be possible; but being all equally possible, he would never, of himself, give a satisfactory account for his preferring one of them to the rest. Experience alone can point out to him the true cause of any phenomenon. (4)

Now, according to this method of reasoning, Demea, it follows (and is, indeed, tacitly allowed by Cleanthes himself) that order, arrangement, or the adjustment of final causes is not, of itself, any proof of design; but only so far as it has been experienced to proceed from that principle. For aught, we can know a priori, matter may contain the source or spring of order originally, within itself, as well as mind does; and there is no more difficulty in conceiving, that the several elements, from an internal unknown cause, may fall into the most exquisite arrangement, than to conceive that their ideas, in the great, universal mind, from a like internal, unknown cause, fall into that arrangement. The equal possibility of both these suppositions is allowed. (5) But by experience we find (according to Cleanthes), that there is a difference between them. Throw several pieces of steel together, without shape or form; they will never arrange themselves so as to compose a watch: stone, and mortar, and wood, without an architect, never erect a house. But the ideas in a human mind, we see, by an unknown, inexplicable economy, arrange themselves so as to form the plan of a watch or house. Experience, therefore, proves, that there is an original principle of order in mind, not in matter. From similar effects we infer similar causes. The adjustment of means to ends is alike in the universe, as in a machine of human contrivance. The causes, therefore, must be resembling. (6)

I was from the beginning scandalized, I must own, with this resemblance, which is asserted, between the Deity and human creatures; and must conceive it to imply such a degradation of the Supreme Being as no sound theist could endure. With your assistance, therefore, Demea, I shall endeavor to defend what you justly called the adorable mysteriousness of the Divine Nature, and shall refute this reasoning of Cleanthes, provided he allows, that I have made a fair representation of it.

When Cleanthes had assented, Philo, after a short pause, proceeded in the following manner.

That all inferences, Cleanthes, concerning fact, are founded on experience, and that all experimental reasonings are founded on the supposition, that similar causes prove similar effects, and similar effects similar causes; I shall not, at present, much dispute with you. But observe, I entreat you, with what extreme caution all just reasoners proceed in the transferring of experiments to similar cases. Unless the cases be exactly similar, they repose no perfect confidence in applying their past observation to any particular phenomenon. Every alteration of circumstances occasions a doubt concerning the event; and it requires new experiments to prove certainly, that the new circumstances are of no moment or importance. A change in bulk, situation, arrangement, age, disposition of the air, or surrounding bodies; any of these particulars may be attended with the most unexpected consequences: and unless the objects be quite familiar to us, it is the highest temerity to expect with assurance, after any of these changes, an event similar to that which before fell under our observation. The slow and deliberate steps of philosophers, here, if anywhere, are distinguished from the precipitate march of the vulgar, who, hurried on by the smallest similitudes, are incapable of all discernment or consideration.

But can you think, Cleanthes, that your usual phlegm and philosophy have been preserved in so wide a step as you have taken, when you compared to the universe, houses, ships, furniture, machines; and from their similarity in some circumstances inferred a similarity in their causes? Thought, design, intelligence, such as we discover in men and other animals, is no more than one of the springs and principles of the universe,

(4)

This claim reflects the general **epistemological** view known as **empiricism:** the view that knowledge, especially knowledge of facts about the world, depends essentially on *experience.*

(5)

Hume rejects the tendency we saw in some places in Paley. From an empiricist point of view, the fact that something is orderly is no reason, by itself, to conclude that the order was produced by a designer. The only way to know that order (either of any particular sort or order in general) is probably produced by an intelligent designer is by *observing* that sort of order actually being produced in that way.

(6)

The alternative to order being produced by an intelligent designer is order that is *natural* or *intrinsic* to the thing in question. That Paley's watch does not result in this way from intrinsic or natural order is shown by both (a) experiences of things of that general kind actually being produced by a designer and (b) also experiences of the sort of material in question failing to have that sort of order when a designer is not present. Ideas in a mind, in contrast, are plausibly regarded as intrinsically or naturally ordered, since neither of these sorts of experiences—(a) and (b)—occurs in relation to them. (Note that this is Philo's restatement of Cleanthes's view, not necessarily something that Philo himself accepts.)

as well as heat or cold, attraction or repulsion, and a hundred others, which fall under daily observation. It is an active cause, by which some particular parts of nature, we find, produce alterations on other parts. But can a conclusion, with any propriety, be transferred from parts to the whole? Does not the great disproportion bar all comparison and inference? From observing the growth of a hair, can we learn anything concerning the generation of a man? Would the manner of a leaf's blowing, even though perfectly known, afford us any instruction concerning the vegetation of a tree?

But allowing that we were to take the *operations* of one part of nature upon another for the foundation of our judgment concerning the *origin* of the whole (which never can be admitted), yet why select so minute, so weak, so bounded a principle as the reason and design of animals is found to be upon this planet? What peculiar privilege has this little agitation of the brain which we call *thought,* that we must thus make it the model of the whole universe? Our partiality in our own favor does indeed present it on all occasions; but sound philosophy ought carefully to guard against so natural an illusion.

So far from admitting, continued Philo, that the operations of a part can afford us any just conclusion concerning the origin of the whole, I will not allow any one part to form a rule for another part, if the latter be very remote from the former.

. . .

Nature, we find, even from our limited experience, possesses an infinite number of springs and principles, which incessantly discover themselves on every change of her position and situation. And what new and unknown principles would actuate her in so new and unknown a situation as that of the formation of a universe, we cannot, without the utmost temerity, pretend to determine.

A very small part of this great system, during a very short time, is very imperfectly discovered to us: and do we thence pronounce decisively concerning the origin of the whole?

Admirable conclusion! Stone, wood, brick, iron, brass, have not, at this time, in this minute globe of earth, an order or arrangement without human art and contrivance: therefore the universe could not originally attain its order and arrangement, without something similar to human art. But is a part of nature a rule for another part very wide of the former? Is it a rule for the whole? Is a very small part a rule for the universe? Is nature in one situation, a certain rule for nature in another situation, vastly different from the former? 7

. . . When two species of objects have always been observed to be conjoined together, I can infer, by custom, the existence of one wherever I see the existence of the other: and this I call an argument from experience. But how this argument can have place, where the objects, as in the present case, are single, individual, without parallel, or specific resemblance, may be difficult to explain. And will any man tell me with a serious countenance, that an orderly universe must arise from some thought and art, like the human; because we have experience of it? To ascertain this reasoning, it were requisite, that we had experience of the origin of worlds; 8 and it is not sufficient surely, that we have seen ships and cities arise from human art and contrivance. . . .

Philo was proceeding in this vehement manner, somewhat between jest and earnest, as it appeared to me; when he observed some signs of impatience in Cleanthes, and then immediately stopped short. What I had to suggest, said Cleanthes, is only that you would not abuse terms, or make use of popular expressions to subvert philosophical reasonings. You know, that the vulgar often distinguish reason from experience, even where the question relates only to matter of fact and existence; though it is found, where that reason is properly analyzed, that it is nothing but a species of experience. To prove by experience the origin of the universe from mind is not more contrary to common speech than to prove the motion of the earth from the same principle. And a caviler might raise all the same objections to the Copernican system, which you have urged against my reasonings. Have you other earths, might he say, which you have seen to move? Have. . . .

Yes! cried Philo, interrupting him, we have other earths. Is not the moon another earth, which we see to turn round its center? Is not Venus another earth, where we observe the same phenomenon? Are not the revolutions of the sun also a confirmation, from analogy, of the same theory? All the planets, are they not earths,

R Philo points out that the analogy between the universe as a whole and various things that are known in the way just discussed to result from design is relatively weak—and also that there are many other kinds of causes, or apparent causes, to be found in the universe, raising the issue of why intelligent design should be singled out as the cause of the whole, rather than one of these others or some combination of them.

R This is a crucial point in relation to the global version of the argument: we do not have experiences of whole orderly universes arising from intelligent design—and so cannot know through experience that the order of a universe must be produced in that way (and cannot be intrinsic). (See the following selection by Flew for more discussion of this point.)

which revolve about the sun? Are not the satellites moons, which move round Jupiter and Saturn, and along with these primary planets, round the sun? These analogies and resemblances, with others, which I have not mentioned, are the sole proofs of the Copernican system: and to you it belongs to consider, whether you have any analogies of the same kind to support your theory.

In reality, Cleanthes, continued he, the modern system of astronomy is now so much received by all inquirers, and has become so essential a part even of our earliest education, that we are not commonly very scrupulous in examining the reasons upon which it is founded. It is now become a matter of mere curiosity to study the first writers on that subject, who had the full force of prejudice to encounter, and were obliged to turn their arguments on every side, in order to render them popular and convincing. . . .

In this cautious proceeding of the astronomers, you may read your own condemnation, Cleanthes; or rather may see, that the subject in which you are engaged exceeds all human reason and inquiry. Can you pretend to show any such similarity between the fabric of a house, and the generation of a universe? Have you ever seen nature in any such situation as resembles the first arrangement of the elements? Have worlds ever been formed under your eye? and have you had leisure to observe the whole progress of the phenomenon, from the first appearance of order to its final consummation? If you have, then cite your experience, and deliver your theory.

...

How the most absurd argument, replied Cleanthes, in the hands of a man of ingenuity and invention, may acquire an air of probability! Are you not aware, Philo, that it became necessary for Copernicus and his first disciples to prove the similarity of the terrestrial and celestial matter; because several philosophers, blinded by old systems, and supported by some sensible appearances, had denied this similarity? But that it is by no means necessary, that theists should prove the similarity of the works of nature to those of art; because this similarity is self-evident and undeniable? The same matter, a like form: what more is requisite to show an analogy between their causes, and to ascertain the origin of all things from a divine purpose and intention? Your objections, I must freely tell you, are no better than the abstruse cavils of those philosophers who denied motion: and ought to be refuted in the same manner, by illustrations, examples, and instances, rather than by serious argument and philosophy.

Suppose, therefore, that an articulate voice were heard in the clouds, much louder and more melodious than any which human art could ever reach: suppose, that this voice were extended in the same instant over all nations, and spoke to each nation in its own language and dialect: suppose, that the words delivered not only contain a just sense and meaning, but convey some instruction altogether worthy of a benevolent being, superior to mankind: could you possibly hesitate a moment concerning the cause of this voice? and must you not instantly ascribe it to some design or purpose? Yet I cannot see but all the same objections (if they merit that appellation) which lie against the system of theism, may also be produced against this inference. 9

Might you not say, that all conclusions concerning fact were founded on experience: that when we hear an articulate voice in the dark, and thence infer a man, it is only the resemblance of the effects, which leads us to conclude that there is a like resemblance in the cause: but that this extraordinary voice, by its loudness, extent, and flexibility to all languages bears so little analogy to any human voice, that we have no reason to suppose any analogy in their causes: and consequently, that a rational, wise, coherent speech proceeded, you knew not whence, from some accidental whistling of the winds, not from any divine reason or intelligence? You see clearly your own objections in these cavils: and I hope too, you see clearly, that they cannot possibly have more force in the one case than in the other.

But to bring the case still nearer the present one of the universe, I shall make two suppositions, which imply not any absurdity or impossibility. Suppose, that there is a natural, universal, invariable language, common to every individual of human race, and that books are natural productions, which perpetuate themselves in the same manner with animals and vegetables, by descent and propagation. Several expressions of our passions contain a universal language: all brute animals have a natural speech, which,

9

R This example is supposed to show that the general principles underlying Philo's objections are unsound. It is clear, Cleanthes is claiming, that the voice in the clouds would have to be explained by intelligent design or purpose. But the same kind of objections could be applied to that case too, if they had any genuine force—or to the natural book case that appears further on.

STOP (Is there any important difference, from the standpoint of Philo's objections, between these cases and the one Cleanthes is mainly concerned with?)

however limited, is very intelligible to their own species. And as there are infinitely fewer parts and less contrivance in the finest composition of eloquence, than in the coarsest organized body, the propagation of an *Iliad* or *Aeneid* is an easier supposition than that of any plant or animal.

Suppose, therefore, that you enter into your library, thus peopled by natural volumes, containing the most refined reason and most exquisite beauty: could you possibly open one of them, and doubt, that its original cause bore the strongest analogy to mind and intelligence? When it reasons and discourses; when it expostulates, argues, and enforces its views and topics; when it applies sometimes to the pure intellect, sometimes to the affections; when it collects, disposes, and adorns every consideration suited to the subject: could you persist in asserting, that all this, at the bottom, had really no meaning, and that the first formation of this volume in the loins of its original parent proceeded not from thought and design? Your obstinacy, I know, reaches not that degree of firmness: even your sceptical play and wantonness would be abashed at so glaring an absurdity.

But if there be any difference, Philo, between this supposed case and the real one of the universe, it is all to the advantage of the latter. The anatomy of an animal affords many stronger instances of design than the perusal of Livy or Tacitus: and any objection which you start in the former case, by carrying me back to so unusual and extraordinary a scene as the first formation of worlds, the same objection has place on the supposition of our vegetating library. Choose, then, your party, Philo, without ambiguity or evasion; assert either that a rational volume is no proof of a rational cause, or admit of a similar cause to all the works of nature. (10)

...

[Philo replies:] . . . I shall endeavor to show you, a little more distinctly, the inconveniences of that anthropomorphism which you have embraced; and I shall prove, that there is no ground to suppose a plan of the world to be formed in the divine mind, consisting of distinct ideas, differently arranged; in the same manner as an architect forms in his head the plan of a house which he intends to execute.

It is not easy, I own, to see, what is gained by this supposition, whether we judge of the matter by *reason* or by *experience*. We are still obliged to mount higher, in order to find the cause of this cause, which you had assigned as satisfactory and conclusive.

If *reason* (I mean abstract reason, derived from inquiries a priori) be not alike mute with regard to all questions concerning cause and effect; this sentence at least it will venture to pronounce, that a mental world, or universe of ideas, requires a cause as much, as does a material world, or universe of objects; and if similar in its arrangement must require a similar cause. For what is there in this subject, which should occasion a different conclusion or inference? In an abstract view, they are entirely alike; and no difficulty attends the one supposition, which is not common to both of them.

...

How therefore shall we satisfy ourselves concerning the cause of that Being, whom you suppose the Author of Nature, or, according to your system of anthropomorphism, the ideal world, into which you trace the material? Have we not the same reason to trace that ideal world into another ideal world, or new intelligent principle? But if we stop, and go no farther; why go so far? Why not stop at the material world? How can we satisfy ourselves without going on *in infinitum*? And after all, what satisfaction is there in that infinite progression? Let us remember the story of the Indian philosopher and his elephant. It was never more applicable than to the present subject. If the material world rests upon a similar ideal world, this ideal world must rest upon some other; and so on, without end. It were better, therefore, never to look beyond the present material world. By supposing it to contain the principle of its order within itself, we really assert it to be God; and the sooner we arrive at that Divine Being, so much the better. When you go one step beyond the mundane system, you only excite an inquisitive humor, which it is impossible ever to satisfy. (11)

To say, that the different ideas, which compose the reason of the Supreme Being, fall into order, of themselves, and by their own nature, is really to talk without any precise meaning. If it has a meaning, I would fain know, why it is not as good sense to say, that the parts of the material world fall into order, of themselves, and by

(10)

Is Cleanthes right that the anatomy of an animal is more clearly a result of design than would be the natural books? Can you think of an argument for the contrary view?

(11)

Philo now takes a different tack, demanding an explanation for the order involved in God's intelligence itself. The underlying point is that not every instance of order can be explained by a further instance of order (since this would lead to an infinite regress). Thus some cases of order eventually must be accepted as intrinsic or natural. Why should this stopping point be reached with God, but not with the material universe?

their own nature. Can the one opinion be intelligible, while the other is not so?

We have, indeed, experience of ideas, which fall into order, of themselves, and without any *known* cause; but, I am sure, we have a much larger experience of matter, which does the same; as, in all instances of generation and vegetation, where the accurate analysis of the cause exceeds all human comprehension. We have also experience of particular systems of thought and of matter, which have no order; of the first, in madness; of the second, in corruption. Why then should we think, that order is more essential to one than the other? And if it requires a cause in both, what do we gain by your system, in tracing the universe of objects into a similar universe of ideas? The first step, which we make, leads us on forever. It were, therefore, wise in us, to limit all our inquiries to the present world, without looking farther. No satisfaction can ever be attained by these speculations, which so far exceed the narrow bounds of human understanding.

. . . when it is asked, what cause produces order in the ideas of the Supreme Being, can any other reason be assigned to you, Anthropomorphites, than that it is a *rational* faculty, and that such is the nature of the Deity? But why a similar answer will not be equally satisfactory in accounting for the order of the world, without having recourse to any such intelligent creator, as you insist on, may be difficult to determine. It is only to say, that such is the nature of material objects, and that they are all originally possessed of a *faculty* of order and proportion. These are only more learned and elaborate ways of confessing our ignorance; nor has the one hypothesis any real advantage above the other, except in its greater conformity to vulgar prejudices. 12

12

STOP Is there any basis for preferring the hypothesis of intrinsic mental order to that of intrinsic material order? Philo claims that experience does not favor one over the other.

You have displayed this argument with great emphasis, replied Cleanthes: you seem not sensible, how easy it is to answer it. Even in common life, if I assign a cause for any event; is it any objection, Philo, that I cannot assign the cause of that cause, and answer every new question, which may incessantly be started? And what philosophers could possibly submit to so rigid a rule? Philosophers, who confess ultimate causes to be totally unknown, and are sensible, that the most refined principles, into which they trace the phenomena, are still to them as inexplicable as these phenomena themselves are to the vulgar. The order and arrangement of nature, the curious adjustment of final causes, the plain use and intention of every part and organ; all these bespeak in the clearest language an intelligent cause or author. The heavens and the earth join in the same testimony: the whole chorus of Nature raises one hymn to the praises of its creator: you alone, or almost alone, disturb this general harmony. You start abstruse doubts, cavils, and objections: you ask me, what is the cause of this cause? I know not; I care not; that concerns not me. I have found a Deity; and here I stop my inquiry. Let those go farther, who are wiser or more enterprising.

I pretend to be neither, replied Philo: and for that very reason, I should never perhaps have attempted to go so far; especially when I am sensible, that I must at last be contented to sit down with the same answer, which, without farther trouble, might have satisfied me from the beginning. If I am still to remain in utter ignorance of causes, and can absolutely give an explication of nothing, I shall never esteem it any advantage to shove off for a moment a difficulty, which, you acknowledge, must immediately, in its full force, recur upon me. Naturalists indeed very justly explain particular effects by more general causes, though these general causes themselves should remain in the end totally inexplicable: but they never surely thought it satisfactory to explain a particular effect by a particular cause, which was no more to be accounted for than the effect itself. An ideal system, arranged of itself, without a precedent design, is not a whit more explicable than a material one, which attains its order in a like manner; nor is there any more difficulty in the latter supposition than in the former. 13

R Cleanthes responds that the fact that the search for explanations must stop somewhere is no reason not to accept any particular causal explanation. If the divine explanation of the order of the material universe is compelling in the way that he claims, then it is no objection to it that it raises a further issue of explanation that we may be unable to answer.

But this misses Philo's main point, which is that the appeal to intrinsic order works equally well whether you say that God or the material universe has intrinsic order.

...

But to show you still more inconveniences, continued Philo, in your anthropomorphism; please to take a new survey of your principles. *Like effects prove like causes.* This is the experimental argument; and this, you say too, is the sole theological argument. Now it is certain, that the liker the effects are, which are seen, and the liker the causes, which are inferred, the stronger is the argument. Every departure on either side diminishes the probability, and renders the experiment less conclusive. You cannot doubt of the principle: neither ought you to reject its consequences.

...

Now, Cleanthes, said Philo, with an air of alacrity and triumph, mark the consequences. *First,* By this method of reasoning, you renounce all claim to infinity in any of the attributes of the Deity. For as the cause ought only to be proportioned to the effect, and the effect, so far as it falls under our cognizance, is not infinite; what pretensions have we, upon your suppositions, to ascribe that attribute to the Divine Being? . . .

Secondly, You have no reason, on your theory, for ascribing perfection to the Deity, even in his finite capacity; or for supposing him free from every error, mistake, or incoherence in his undertakings. There are many inexplicable difficulties in the works of nature, which, if we allow a perfect author to be proved a priori, are easily solved, and become only seeming difficulties, from the narrow capacity of man, who cannot trace infinite relations. But according to your method of reasoning, these difficulties become all real; and perhaps will be insisted on, as new instances of likeness to human art and contrivance. At least, you must acknowledge, that it is impossible for us to tell, from our limited views, whether this system contains any great faults, or deserves any considerable praise, if compared to other possible, and even real systems.

...

But were this world ever so perfect a production, it must still remain uncertain, whether all the excellences of the work can justly be ascribed to the workman. If we survey a ship, what an exalted idea must we form of the ingenuity of the carpenter, who framed so complicated, useful, and beautiful a machine? And what surprise must we feel, when we find him a stupid mechanic, who imitated others, and copied an art, which, through a long succession of ages, after multiplied trials, mistakes, corrections, deliberations, and controversies, had been gradually improving? Many worlds might have been botched and bungled, throughout an eternity, ere this system was struck out: much labor lost: many fruitless trials made: and a slow, but continued improvement carried on during infinite ages in the art of world-making. In such subjects, who can determine, where the truth; nay, who can conjecture where the probability lies; amidst a great number of hypotheses which may be proposed, and a still greater number which may be imagined? [14]

R The ever-inventive Philo raises yet another objection: the characteristics ascribed to the designer on the basis of this argument cannot be greater than those required to explain the actual effect. This does not require infinite powers or even relatively perfect finite powers.

And what shadow of an argument, continued Philo, can you produce, from your hypothesis, to prove the unity of the Deity? A great number of men join in building a house or ship, in rearing a city, in framing a commonwealth: why may not several deities combine in contriving and framing a world? This is only so much greater similarity to human affairs? By sharing the work among several, we may so much further limit the attributes of each, and get rid of that extensive power and knowledge, which must be supposed in one deity, and which, according to you, can only serve to weaken the proof of his existence. And if such foolish, such vicious creatures as man can yet often unite in framing and executing one plan; how much more those deities or demons, whom we may suppose several degrees more perfect?

To multiply causes, without necessity, is indeed contrary to true philosophy: but this principle applies not to the present case. Were one deity antecedently proved by your theory, who were possessed of every attribute, requisite to the production of the universe; it would be needless, I own (though not absurd) to suppose any other deity existent. But while it is still a question, whether all these attributes are united in one subject, or dispersed among several independent beings: by what phenomena in nature can we pretend to decide the controversy? Where we see a body raised in a scale, we are sure that there is in the opposite scale, however concealed from sight, some counterpoising weight equal to it: but it is still allowed to doubt, whether that weight be an aggregate of several distinct bodies, or one uniform united mass. And if the weight requisite very much exceeds anything which we have ever seen conjoined in any single body, the former supposition becomes still more probable and natural. An intelligent being of such vast power and capacity, as is necessary to produce the universe, or, to speak in the language of ancient philosophy, so prodigious an animal, exceeds all analogy, and even comprehension.

But farther, Cleanthes; men are mortal, and renew their species by generation; and this is common to all living creatures. The two great sexes of male and female, says Milton, animate the world. Why must this circumstance, so universal, so essential, be excluded from those numerous and limited deities? Behold then the theogony of ancient times brought back upon us.

And why not become a perfect anthropomorphite? Why not assert the deity or deities to be corporeal, and to have eyes, a nose, mouth, ears, etc? Epicurus maintained, that no man had ever seen reason but in a human figure; therefore the gods must have a human figure. And this argument, which is deservedly so much ridiculed by Cicero, becomes, according to you, solid and philosophical. 15

15

R Nor does an explanation of the world require *one* designer. And the analogy between God and human designers suggests other human characteristics as well.

16

R Cleanthes retreats to the general hypothesis of design, which he claims is common to all of Philo's various suggestions. In the following paragraph, Demea suggests that this is too weak for any serious religion.

(This hypothesis also ignores the earlier point about the possibility that the universe is intrinsically orderly.)

In a word, Cleanthes, a man, who follows your hypothesis, is able, perhaps, to assert, or conjecture, that the universe, sometime, arose from something like design: but beyond that position he cannot ascertain one single circumstance, and is left afterwards to fix every point of his theology, by the utmost license of fancy and hypothesis. This world, for aught he knows, is very faulty and imperfect compared to a superior standard; and was only the first rude essay of some infant deity, who afterwards abandoned it, ashamed of his lame performance; it is the work only of some dependent, inferior deity; and is the object of derision to his superiors: it is the production of old age and dotage in some superannuated deity; and ever since his death, has run on at adventures, from the first impulse and active force, which it received from him. You justly give signs of horror, Demea, at these strange suppositions: but these, and a thousand more of the same kind, are Cleanthes's suppositions, not mine. From the moment the attributes of the Deity are supposed finite, all these have place. And I cannot, for my part, think, that so wild and unsettled a system of theology is, in any respect, preferable to none at all.

These suppositions I absolutely disown, cried Cleanthes: they strike me, however, with no horror; especially, when proposed in that rambling way in which they drop from you. On the contrary, they give me pleasure, when I see, that, by the utmost indulgence of your imagination, you never get rid of the hypothesis of design in the universe; but are obliged, at every turn, to have recourse to it. To this concession I adhere steadily; and this I regard as a sufficient foundation for religion. 16

...

It must be a slight fabric, indeed, said Demea, which can be erected on so tottering a foundation. While we are uncertain, whether there is one deity or many; whether the deity or deities, to whom we owe our existence, be perfect or imperfect, subordinate or supreme, dead or alive; what trust or confidence can we repose in them? What devotion or worship address to them? What veneration or obedience pay them? To all the purposes of life, the theory of religion becomes altogether useless: and even with regard to speculative consequences, its uncertainty, according to you, must render it totally precarious and unsatisfactory.

To render it still more unsatisfactory, said Philo, there occurs to me another hypothesis, which must acquire an air of probability from the method of reasoning so much insisted on by Cleanthes. That like effects arise from like causes: this principle he supposes the foundation of all religion. But there is another principle of the same kind, no less certain, and derived from the same source of experience: that where several known circumstances are *observed* to be similar, the unknown will also be *found* similar. Thus, if we see the limbs of a human body, we conclude, that it is also attended with a human head, though hid from us. Thus, if we see, through a chink in a wall, a small part of the sun, we conclude that, were the wall removed, we should see the whole body. In short, this method of reasoning is so obvious and familiar, that no scruple can ever be made with regard to its solidity.

Now if we survey the universe, so far as it falls under our knowledge, it bears a great resemblance to an animal or organized body, and seems actuated with a like principle of life and motion. A continual circulation of matter in it produces no disorder: a continual waste in every part is incessantly repaired; the closest sympathy is perceived throughout the entire system: and each part or member, in performing its proper offices, operates both to its own preservation and to that of the whole. The world, therefore, I infer, is an animal, and the Deity is the *soul* of the world, actuating it, and actuated by it.

You have too much learning, Cleanthes, to be at all surprised at this opinion, which, you know, was maintained by almost all the theists of antiquity, and chiefly prevails in their discourses and reasonings. For though sometimes the ancient philosophers reason from final causes, as if they thought the world the workmanship of God; yet it appears rather their favorite notion to consider it as his body, whose organization renders it subservient to him. And it must be confessed, that as the universe resembles more a human body than it does the works of human art and contrivance; if our limited analogy could ever, with any propriety, be extended to the whole of nature, the inference seems juster in favor of the ancient than the modern theory.

There are many other advantages too, in the former theory, which recommend it to the ancient theologians. Nothing more repugnant to all their notions, because nothing more repugnant to common experience than mind without body; a mere spiritual substance, which fell not under their senses nor comprehension, and of which they had not observed one single instance throughout all nature. Mind and body they knew, because they felt both: an order, arrangement, organization, or internal machinery in both they likewise knew, after the same manner; and it could not but seem reasonable to transfer this experience to the universe, and to suppose the divine mind and body to be also coeval, and to have, both of them, order and arrangement naturally inherent in them, and inseparable from them.

Here therefore is a new species of anthropomorphism, Cleanthes, on which you may deliberate; and a theory which seems not liable to any considerable difficulties. You are too much superior surely to systematical prejudices, to find any more difficulty in supposing an animal body to be, originally, of itself, or from unknown causes, possessed of order and organization, than in supposing a similar order to belong to mind. But the vulgar prejudice, that body and mind ought always to accompany each other, ought not, one should think, to be entirely neglected; since it is founded on vulgar experience, the only guide which you profess to follow in all these theological inquiries. And if you assert, that our limited experience is an unequal standard, by which to judge of the unlimited extent of nature; you entirely abandon your own hypothesis, and must thenceforward adopt our mysticism, as you call it, and admit of the absolute incomprehensibility of the Divine Nature. [17]

R Philo suggests another hypothesis, supported by the same general appeal to analogy: the universe as the body of an animal, of which God is the soul. (This would be very different from traditional theism.)

This theory, I own, replied Cleanthes, has never before occurred to me, though a pretty natural one; and I cannot readily, upon so short an examination and reflection, deliver any opinion with regard to it. You are very scrupulous, indeed, said Philo; were I to examine any system of yours, I should not have acted with half that caution and reserve, in stating objections and difficulties to it. However, if anything occur to you, you will oblige us by proposing it.

Why then, replied Cleanthes, it seems to me that, though the world does, in many circumstances, resemble an animal body; yet is the analogy also defective in many circumstances, the most material: no organs of sense; no seat of thought or reason; no one precise origin of motion and action. In short, it seems to bear a stronger resemblance to a vegetable than to an animal, and your inference would be so far inconclusive in favor of the soul of the world.

[Philo:] . . . were I obliged to defend any particular system of this nature (which I never willingly should do), I esteem none more plausible than that which ascribes an eternal, inherent principle of order to the world; though attended with great and continual revolutions and alterations. This at once solves all difficulties; and if the solution, by being so general, is not entirely complete and satisfactory, it is, at least, a theory, that we must, sooner or later, have recourse to, whatever system we embrace. How could things have been as they are, were there not an original, inherent principle of order somewhere, in thought or in matter? And it is very indifferent to which of these we give the preference. Chance has no place, on any hypothesis, sceptical or religious. Everything is surely governed by steady, inviolable laws. And were the inmost essence of things laid open to us, we should then discover a scene, of which, at

18

R Philo returns to the idea that the order of the material world is intrinsic to it, rather than being produced by an external designer.

(This is the main alternative to intelligent design in relation to the global version of the argument—see Flew.)

19

R Here is yet another hypothesis, one considered by Paley: order results from random reshufflings of the basic particles that make up the universe.

present, we can have no idea. Instead of admiring the order of natural beings, we should clearly see that it was absolutely impossible for them, in the smallest article, ever to admit of any other disposition. 18

...

I must confess, Philo, replied Cleanthes, that of all men living, the task which you have undertaken, of raising doubts and objections, suits you best, and seems, in a manner, natural and unavoidable to you. So great is your fertility of invention, that I am not ashamed to acknowledge myself unable, on a sudden, to solve regularly such out-of-the-way difficulties as you incessantly start upon me: though I clearly see, in general, their fallacy and error. And I question not, but you are yourself, at present, in the same case, and have not the solution so ready as the objection; while you must be sensible, that common sense and reason are entirely against you, and that such whimsies as you have delivered, may puzzle, but never can convince us.

...

What you ascribe to the fertility of my invention, replied Philo, is entirely owing to the nature of the subject. In subjects, adapted to the narrow compass of human reason, there is commonly but one determination, which carries probability or conviction with it; and to a man of sound judgment, all other suppositions, but that one, appear entirely absurd and chimerical. But in such questions, as the present, a hundred contradictory views may preserve a kind of imperfect analogy; and invention has here full scope to exert itself. Without any great effort of thought, I believe that I could, in an instant, propose other systems of cosmogony, which would have some faint appearance of truth; though it is a thousand, a million to one, if either yours or any one of mine be the true system.

For instance; what if I should revive the old Epicurean hypothesis? This is commonly, and I believe, justly, esteemed the most absurd system, that has yet been proposed; yet, I know not, whether, with a few alterations, it might not be brought to bear a faint appearance of probability. Instead of supposing matter infinite, as Epicurus did; let us suppose it finite. A finite number of particles is only susceptible of finite transpositions: and it must happen, in an eternal duration, that every possible order or position must be tried an infinite number of times. This world, therefore, with all its events, even the most minute, has before been produced and destroyed, and will again be produced and destroyed, without any bounds and limitations. No one, who has a conception of the powers of infinite, in comparison of finite, will ever scruple this determination. 19

But this supposes, said Demea, that matter can acquire motion, without any voluntary agent or first mover.

And where is the difficulty, replied Philo, of that supposition? Every event, before experience, is equally difficult and incomprehensible; and every event, after experience, is equally easy and intelligible. Motion, in many instances, from gravity, from elasticity, from electricity, begins in matter, without any known voluntary agent; and to suppose always, in these cases, an unknown voluntary agent, is mere hypothesis; and hypothesis attended with no advantages. The beginning of motion in matter itself is as conceivable a priori as its communication from mind and intelligence.

Besides; why may not motion have been propagated by impulse through all eternity, and the same stock of it, or nearly the same, be still upheld in the universe? As much as is lost by the composition of motion, as much is gained by its resolution. And whatever the causes are, the fact is certain, that matter is, and always has been in continual agitation, as far as human experience or tradition reaches. There is not probably, at present, in the whole universe, one particle of matter at absolute rest.

And this very consideration too, continued Philo, which we have stumbled on in the course of argument, suggests a new hypothesis of cosmogony, that is not absolutely absurd and improbable. Is there a system, an order, an economy of things, by which matter can preserve that perpetual agitation, which seems essential to it, and yet maintain a constancy in the forms, which it produces? There certainly is such an economy: for this is actually the case with the present world. The continual motion of matter, therefore, in less than infinite transpositions, must produce this economy or order; and by its very nature, that order, when once established, supports itself, for many ages, if not to eternity. But wherever matter is so poised, arranged, and adjusted as to continue in perpetual motion, and yet preserve a constancy in the forms, its situation must, of necessity, have all the same appearance of art and contrivance, which we observe at present. All the parts of each form must have a relation to each other, and to the whole: and the whole itself must have a relation to the other parts of the universe; to the element, in which the form subsists; to the materials, with which it repairs its waste and decay; and to every other form, which is hostile or friendly. A defect in any of these particulars destroys the form; and the matter, of which it is composed, is again set loose, and is thrown into irregular motions and fermentations, till it unite itself to some other regular form. If no such form be prepared to receive it, and if there be a great quantity of this corrupted matter in the universe, the universe itself is entirely disordered; whether it be the feeble embryo of a world in its first beginnings, that is thus destroyed, or the rotten carcass of one, languishing in old age and infirmity. In either case, a chaos ensues; till finite, though innumerable revolutions produce at last some forms, whose parts and organs are so adjusted as to support the forms amidst a continued succession of matter.

Suppose (for we shall endeavor to vary the expression), that matter were thrown into any position, by a blind, unguided force; it is evident that this first position must in all probability be the most confused and most disorderly imaginable, without any resemblance to those works of human contrivance, which, along with a symmetry of parts, discover an adjustment of means to ends and a tendency to self-preservation. If the actuating force cease after this operation, matter must remain forever in disorder, and continue an immense chaos, without any proportion or activity. But suppose, that the actuating force, whatever it be, still continues in matter, this first position will immediately give place to a second, which will likewise in all probability be as disorderly as the first, and so on, through many successions of changes and revolutions. No particular order or position ever continues a moment unaltered. The original force, still remaining in activity, gives a perpetual restlessness to matter. Every possible situation is produced, and instantly destroyed. If a glimpse or dawn of order appears for a moment, it is instantly hurried away, and confounded, by that never-ceasing force, which actuates every part of matter.

Thus the universe goes on for many ages in a continued succession of chaos and disorder. But is it not possible that it may settle at last, so as not to lose its motion and active force (for that we have supposed inherent in it) yet so as to preserve an uniformity of appearance, amidst the continual motion and fluctuation of its parts? This we find to be the case with the universe at present. Every individual is perpetually changing, and every part of every individual, and yet the whole remains, in appearance, the same. May we not hope for such a position, or rather be assured of it, from the eternal revolutions of unguided matter, and may not this account for all the appearing wisdom and contrivance, which is in the universe? Let us contemplate the subject a little, and we shall find, that this adjustment, if attained by matter, of a seeming stability in the forms, with a real and perpetual revolution or motion of parts, affords a plausible, if not a true solution of the difficulty. 20

R Philo proposes an interesting refinement of the previous hypothesis: once orderly forms of matter are produced (by chance), this order tends to perpetuate itself.

(Notice that this seems to presuppose an underlying order pertaining at least to the particles themselves.)

It is in vain, therefore, to insist upon the uses of the parts in animals or vegetables and their curious adjustment to each other. I would fain know how an animal could subsist, unless its parts were so adjusted? Do we not find, that it immediately perishes whenever this adjustment ceases, and that its matter corrupting tries some new form. It happens, indeed, that the parts of the world are so well adjusted, that some regular form immediately lays claim to this corrupted matter: and if it were not so, could the world subsist? Must it not dissolve as well as the animal, and pass through new positions and situations; till in a great, but finite succession, it fall at last into the present or some such order?

It is well, replied Cleanthes, you told us, that this hypothesis was suggested on a sudden, in the course of the argument. Had you had leisure to examine it, you would soon have perceived the insuperable objections, to which it is exposed. No form, you say, can subsist, unless it possess those powers and organs, requisite for its subsistence: some new order or economy must be tried, and so on, without intermission; till at last some order, which can support and maintain itself, is fallen upon. But according to this hypothesis, whence arise the many conveniences and advantages which men and all animals possess? Two eyes, two ears, are not absolutely necessary for the subsistence of the species. Human race might have been propagated and preserved, without horses, dogs, cows, sheep and those innumerable fruits and products which serve to our satisfaction and enjoyment. If no camels had been created for the use of man in the sandy deserts of Africa and Arabia, would the world have been dissolved? If no loadstone had been framed to give that wonderful and useful direction to the needle, would human society and the human kind have been immediately extinguished? Though the maxims of Nature be in general very frugal, yet instances of this kind are far from being rare; and any one of them is a sufficient proof of design, and of a benevolent design, which gave rise to the order and arrangement of the universe. 21

21

R Cleanthes objects that this would not account for the "conveniences and advantages" that the world contains. Is this as clear as he claims?

(Notice that evolution might be invoked here as a further explanation, resting on the underlying order.)

At least, you may safely infer, said Philo, that the foregoing hypothesis is so far incomplete and imperfect; which I shall not scruple to allow. But can we ever reasonably expect greater success in any attempts of this nature? Or can we ever hope to erect a system of cosmogony, that will be liable to no exceptions, and will contain no circumstance repugnant to our limited and imperfect experience of the analogy of nature? Your theory itself cannot surely pretend to any such advantage; even though you have run into anthropomorphism, the better to preserve a conformity to common experience. . . .

All religious systems, it is confessed, are subject to great and insuperable difficulties. Each disputant triumphs in his turn; while he carries on an offensive war, and exposes the absurdities, barbarities, and pernicious tenets of his antagonist. But all of them, on the whole, prepare a complete triumph for the sceptic; who tells them, that no system ought ever to be embraced with regard to such subjects: for this plain reason, that no absurdity ought ever to be assented to with regard to any subject. A total suspense of judgment is here our only reasonable resource. And if every attack, as is commonly observed, and no defense, among theologians, is successful; how complete must be *his* victory, who remains always, with all mankind, on the offensive, and has himself no fixed station or abiding city, which he is ever, on any occasion, obliged to defend?

...

Discussion Questions

1. Suppose that Hume is right that not all order can be explained, so that some must be intrinsic. Is there any reason for preferring the view that mind (or at least God's mind) is intrinsically orderly to the view that the material universe is intrinsically orderly?
2. Make a list of the different explanations of the order of the universe that are proposed by Philo, in addition to the one proposed by Cleanthes. Are all these explanations equally plausible (which would mean that none is very plausible), or are some better than others? Why?
3. Philo's claim (that you can postulate the existence of a cause only if you've experienced such a cause) provokes impatience in Cleanthes (p. 541). What exactly is Cleanthes's objection to that claim (in relation to the example of the Copernican System)? What is Philo's response to that objection, and how does Cleanthes reply? Surely Cleanthes is right that judgments of dissimilarity (and similarity) are sometimes "blinded by old systems." And clearly judgments of similarity and dissimilarity are essential to drawing conclusions from "like effects prove like causes." What point is Cleanthes attempting to make with the voice in the clouds and natural books examples?

   Whose position is stronger on this point: Philo's or Cleanthes's?

Antony Flew

Antony Flew (1923–) is an English philosopher, who taught mainly at the Universities of Keele and Reading. He has written widely on many philosophical topics, but is best known for his work in the philosophy of religion and on Hume. In the following selection, he sets forth a fundamental objection to the global version of the argument from design.

Critique of the Global Argument from Design, from *God: A Critical Inquiry*

3.17 The movement of thought desired is from the universe to something other than the universe, although this other has to be not nothing but a supreme individual. For this the most promising line is that illustrated by the second formulation quoted from Aquinas.* Here the argument proposed would proceed to the Orderer from the order of the universe as a whole. . . . A contemporary attempting such a line would most likely wish to refer explicitly to science and the uniformity of nature. He might even speak of the latter, possibly dignified with initial capitals, as a presupposition of the former; perhaps going on to assert that God is the ultimate presupposition of both. . . . The philosophical question for us now is simply: Does order in nature itself presuppose an Orderer? ❶

3.18 Some over-sophisticated people may wish to challenge the premise. . . . [Nothing] is gained by suggesting—with allusions perhaps to human affairs or perhaps to quantum mechanics—that the order is maybe not in fact completely uniform and all-embracing. Those spokesmen for the argument who were also believers in the occurrence of miracles have not usually asserted that it is. Aquinas indeed was remarkably reserved: "things of diverse natures come together under one order, and this . . . always or for the most part". The crux in his view, and in that of the whole Thomist tradition, is not so much the amount of order, nor even that it may appear to be for the best, but that there is order at all. It is order as such which is believed to demonstrate an Orderer. ❷

3.19 This is the heart of the matter. It is against this that the attack should and shall be launched. As so often in philosophy, once the protracted preliminary manoeuvres have located and isolated the key position, the final operation can be short and its tactics simple. Let us recapitulate the logical situation, for a clear grasp of this is a good guide to the understanding of many similar confrontations between theist and naturalist. It is common ground that there is a deal of regularity in things. It is put by the theist that this presupposes an Orderer; and that this must be, as he requires, other than the universe. The aim of the offensive is to show that order presupposes nothing of the kind, and that it belongs to the universe itself. ❸ . . .

3.20 The picture given in the last paragraph is in one respect misleading. For it suggests that it is a matter of trying to drive the theist from a position already firmly established. In a psychological sense this may be true. Nevertheless it would be a mistake to infer that in logic the onus of proof rests on the naturalist. Quite the reverse: the presumption, defeasible of course by adverse argument, must be that all qualities observed in things are qualities belonging by natural right to those things themselves; and hence that whatever characteristics we think ourselves able to discern in the universe as a whole are the underivative characteristics of the universe itself. ❹ . . . The present presumption was apparently first clearly formulated as such by Strato, next but one in succession to Aristotle as head of the Lyceum. It can be seen as the fulfilment of the naturalistic tendency in the founder's own thinking. It was this "Stratonician atheism" which was received by the young Hume as an emancipating revelation: we shall, in piety, follow Bayle and Hume in using the awkward form *Stratonician* as the adjective.

3.21 How then is this presumption to be defeated? Why should it be thought that order presupposes an Orderer? One bad reply would be to say that the two ideas are necessarily connected. This is no good, first and less significantly, because it is surely just not true that, in the ordinary senses of the words, to say there is order and to deny that it is the work of an Orderer is to contradict yourself. Whereas design does presuppose a designer, order does not similarly, as a matter of logic, require an Orderer: that is why the argument here is *to* design but *from* order. Second, it is no good for the more fundamental reason that, even supposing either that the present usage and senses of *order,* or new ones specially introduced, did warrant the deduction of an Orderer from

From Antony Flew, *God: A Critical Inquiry* (LaSalle, Ill.: Open Court, 1966).

*The reference is to the fifth of the Five Ways, p. 520.

This is the basic issue pertaining to the *global* version of the argument from design: does any sort of order presuppose an external designer, with the alternative being, as we have already seen in Hume, that some order might be intrinsic—in this case intrinsic to the material universe?

If the degree or amount of order mattered, then the proponent of the global argument would be in effect saying that some degree of order might be accepted as intrinsic, while a greater degree could not. But if some order can be intrinsic, what would be the basis for such a limit?

R That is, such order is intrinsic to the nature of the universe (or the material of which it is composed).

R This amounts to saying that a reason is needed for *not* taking the observed condition of something to be its natural state—that the burden of proof lies on the view that the observed qualities are *not* intrinsic.

order, this still could advance us no nearer to the desired conclusion. Suppose you do introduce this new sense. A verbal adjustment cannot transform the physical situation. It can affect only the ways in which it is proper to speak about it. In the former sense of *order* we were agreed that there is order and at issue whether there must also be an Orderer. Now the altogether unchanged situation is represented as one in which we are agreed that, if there is order in the new sense of order, then there must also be an Orderer. The issue which divides us is whether, in that new sense, there is actually order. This futile exercise provides a pure textbook example of the hopelessness of trying to establish a substantial conclusion by a manoeuvre with a definition. . . . **5**

5

R Thus the premise of the argument should be that the universe is orderly in a sense that is simply a matter of observation and which both sides can therefore accept, with the issue between them being whether order in that sense requires a designer. It does no good to take as the premise an assertion of design or of a kind of order that by definition requires a designer, for then this premise will be acceptable only to someone who already accepts the conclusion, and the argument itself will have no point.

3.22 A better sort of reply is to urge that regularities cannot come about by chance, they require explanation, and the only satisfactory explanation is in terms of purpose and design. This is much more complicated, and to make even the main points takes longer. Thomas' version stresses the claim that the order of the universe is of a sort involving coordination: "When diverse things are coordinated the scheme depends on their directed unification, as the order of battle of a whole army hangs on the plan of the Commander-in-Chief. The arrangement of diverse things cannot be dictated by their own private and divergent natures; of themselves they are diverse and exhibit no tendency to form a pattern. It follows that the order of many among themselves is either a matter of chance or must be attributed to one first planner who has a purpose in mind. What comes about always, or in the great majority of cases, is not the result of accident."* And there we are.

3.23 This sounds fine. Suppose, for instance, we saw a large number of university teachers working energetically and harmoniously towards a common objective; then it would indeed be reasonable—if we could bring ourselves to believe our eyes—to look for some more than human coordinator, a Vice-Chancellor of genius. The phenomenon would cry out for explanation. For everything, or almost everything, we have seen of university teachers has taught us that we are cantankerous and individualistic creatures: creatures having very much "their own private and divergent natures", diverse, and exhibiting no tendency to form a pattern. Therefore, the Thomist will urge, by parity of reasoning, you must concede that our Argument to Design is sound. . . .

3.24 Well now, is there a parity of reasoning? Are the two cases comparable? Remember what they are. In the familiar and accepted one we have, or could have, independent knowledge of the elements now so unbelievably coordinated. **6** We could also test an hypothesis about control by a supreme Vice-Chancellor: we conceivably might, and would wish to, meet him on his own apart from the colleagues he guides so superlatively well. Now consider the other case. Here both the key terms refer, or are supposed to refer, to things essentially and multiply unique. The universe is, as an immediate consequence of the definition, unique: for in as much as it includes everything there is there can be no possibility of another; if there were a second there would not be a second but only two parts of the one. God would be both unique by definition and endowed with a series of attributes all of which are also unique by definition. These differences make the decisive gap between the two cases.

6

Can we have independent knowledge of the constituents of the universe that parallels the knowledge that Flew supposes us to have about university teachers? How?

3.25 For instance, Thomas states that the elements of the universe which he sees as coordinated are "of themselves . . . diverse and exhibit no tendency to form a pattern". How is he, or anyone else, supposed to know this? That they are diverse is obvious to observation. But to know what tendencies they possessed "in themselves", as opposed to knowing what they do and will do under various universal conditions, you would presumably have to be able to study them: either separated from the universe, which is manifestly senseless; and/or without any Divine control, which is a notion which the theist himself would want to rule out. Look at the same fundamental Stratonician point in another way. All our knowledge of things, of their natures and tendencies, has to be founded upon and checked against the ways those things in fact behave, under whatever conditions they can be available for our study. Yet, if that is so, is it not topsy-turvy to insist that those things cannot naturally do what is, in our experience, precisely what they do do? Ideas about the natures of things, unless they are to be grounded merely upon our definitions of words, can be justified

*Aquinas, Summa contra Gentiles, I 42.

only by reference to what we are able to discover about how those things actually do behave. (7)

3.26 Once this is granted it surely follows that it will be quite unwarranted to proceed, from the perverse premise that what seems to happen naturally nevertheless cannot, on to the gratuitous conclusion that these effects could only occur through—and therefore demonstrate—the agency of something wholly other. The nerve of this argument is both extraordinary and commonplace. It is extraordinary in that it starts by asserting, as if this were obvious, that things or the sum of things cannot be expressing their own inherent tendencies; notwithstanding that they actually are, to all appearances, doing exactly what comes naturally. A supposed explanation is then introduced for this factitious phenomenon; in terms of something which is, in a sense at once both unusually literal and yet not literal at all, out of this world. The form of argument is commonplace in that it crops up continually in and around natural theology. It is, for example, frequently maintained that living organisms could not have developed naturally out of matter itself lifeless; or that consciousness and intelligence cannot be the attributes of purely material things; and so on. Yet, in fact, however great the present mystery of the mechanisms involved, all the evidence we have indicates that the only life we know did originate in just this way. It is the same again with intelligence, consciousness, and the like. So far from there being a certainty that these cannot appertain to material things, the question is whether they could significantly be attributed to anything else.

...

3.28 "Come come now", someone will say, "surely it is not being seriously and honestly contended that it is to mere chance that we owe the majestic processions of the stars, the fabulous integrative complexity of the human eye?" No. No; of course explanations must be sought. Is not this the quest advanced by the genius of Newton and Darwin; and, in our own time, by all those who made and exploit the great breakthrough into molecular biology? Or are explanations of this sort . . . somehow not what is wanted? Again, no. What is wanted is some sort of explanation of the orderliness, however much or little there be, of the universe as a whole. (8) However fundamental and inclusive the laws discovered by the physics of the future, the claim is that the universe itself could not come about by chance; hence—taking at least two steps in one—there must be Design.

3.29 Once more it is the necessary uniqueness of the universe which makes the crux; even before the questions begin to arise from the uniquenesses of the postulated Designer. In this most peculiar context the basis for the usual contrasts between chance and its opposites disappears, and the familiar questions lose their familiar force and application. It is put that it must be immeasurably improbable that there could be so much order without Design. A hearer who failed to catch the sound of the capital 'D' might fairly and truly reply: "Well, fancy that! And yet, of course, we know that nearly all order is without design." But we, alerted to the context by that capital, ask: "How does he know what is probable or improbable about universes?" For his question, like the earlier overweening assertion about the tendencies which things possess or lack "of themselves" (*3.22*), presupposes that he knows something which not merely does he not know, but which neither he nor anyone else conceivably ever could know. No one could acquire an experience of universes to give him the necessary basis for this sort of judgement of probability or improbability; for the decisive reason that there could not be universes to have experience of. (9) Indeed the whole idea of contrasting, on the one hand, chance as randomness with, on the other hand, what seems to demand explanation breaks down in this limiting case. Yet if this fundamental antithesis ceases to apply, how much more inapplicable the relatively sophisticated antithesis between chance as the absence of purpose, and what calls for that rather special sort of explanation which involves planners and plans. It is, therefore, not a matter here of having to choose between the prongs of either fork. Instead the difficulty is to appreciate that and why neither choice can arise. "Universes", as C. S. Peirce remarked, "are not as plentiful as blackberries."

3.30 So we conclude that order in the universe by itself provides no warrant whatsoever for trying to identify an Orderer. Unless and until some strong reason is found elsewhere, and unless the required separate identification can be achieved, the presumption of the Stratonician atheism stands undefeated. . . .

(7)

R There is, in principle, no way to know *by observation* that the constituents of the universe would, if left to themselves, be disorderly. The only observations we have of these constituents support the idea (given the Stratonician presumption) that they are *intrinsically* orderly.

STOP Is there any other way of defending the contrary view, one that does not appeal to observation?

R Smaller-scale explanations (such as evolution) cannot answer the global question.

R Again, the immediate point is that he could not acquire such knowledge through observation or experience.

Discussion Questions

1. Is Flew right about the "Stratonician presumption"? Could someone ever be justified, in the absence of further information, in assuming that the way in which things were observed to behave was not the natural mode of behavior that reflected their intrinsic character?
2. Think of all the different sorts of order to be found in the universe. Some of them can be explained by appeal to others, in the way that the theory of evolution explains the order of organic structures like the eye or the geological theory of plate tectonics explains things like the occurrence and behavior of volcanoes. Others, if the Stratonician presumption is correct, should be regarded as intrinsic to the basic material constituents of the universe. Can all of the order plausibly be accounted for in one of these two ways?

The Ontological Argument

St. Anselm

St. Anselm (1033–1109) was a Benedictine monk and the second Archbishop of Canterbury after the Norman conquest of England. In this selection, Anselm presents the earliest version of the ontological argument. This version turns on the definition of God as a being "than which nothing greater can be thought." Anselm argues that such a being cannot exist merely in the understanding (that is, cannot be conceived but not exist in reality) because then it would be less great than something that exists both in the understanding and in reality, which contradicts the definition.

The Ontological Argument, from *Proslogion*

Chapter 1: Arousal of the Mind for Contemplating God

. . . O Lord, I acknowledge and give thanks that You created in me Your image so that I may remember, contemplate, and love You. But [this image] has been so effaced by the abrasion of transgressions, so hidden from sight by the dark billows of sins, that unless You renew and refashion it, it cannot do what it was created to do. O Lord, I do not attempt to gain access to Your loftiness, because I do not at all consider my intellect to be equal to this [task]. But I yearn to understand some measure of Your truth, which my heart believes and loves. For I do not seek to understand in order to believe, but I believe in order to understand. For I believe even this: that unless I believe, I shall not understand.

From *Anselm of Canterbury,* vol. 1, edited and translated by J. Hopkins and H. Richardson (Toronto: Edward Mellen Press, 1974).

Chapter 2: God Truly [I.E., Really] Exists

Therefore, O Lord, You who give understanding to faith, grant me to understand—to the degree You know to be advantageous—that You exist, as we believe, and that You are what we believe [You to be]. Indeed, we believe You to be something than which nothing greater (1) can be thought. Or is there, then, no such nature [as You], (2) for the Fool has said in his heart that God does not exist?* But surely when this very same Fool hears my words "something than which nothing greater can be thought," he understands what he hears. And what he understands is in his understanding, even if he does not understand [i.e., judge] it to

(1) R That is, nothing more perfect or more excellent.

(2) R That is, does nothing of that nature really exist?

*Psalms 13:1; 52:1 (14:1; 53:1).

exist. For that a thing is in the understanding is distinct from understanding that [this] thing exists. For example, when a painter envisions what he is about to paint: he indeed has in his understanding that which he has not yet made, but he does not yet understand that it exists. But after he has painted [it]: he has in his understanding that which he has made, and he understands that it exists. So even the Fool is convinced that something than which nothing greater can be thought is at least in his understanding; for when he hears of this [being], he understands [what he hears], and whatever is understood is in the understanding. But surely that than which a greater cannot be thought cannot be only in the understanding. For if it were only in the understanding, it could be thought to exist also in reality—something which is greater [than existing only in the understanding]. Therefore, if that than which a greater cannot be thought were only in the understanding, then that than which a greater *cannot* be thought would be that than which a greater *can* be thought! But surely this [conclusion] is impossible. Hence, without doubt, something than which a greater cannot be thought exists both in the understanding and in reality.[3]

Chapter 3: [God] Cannot Be Thought Not to Exist

Assuredly, this [being] exists so truly [i.e., really] that it cannot even be thought not to exist. For there can be thought to exist something which cannot be thought not to exist; and this thing is greater than that which can be thought not to exist.[4] Therefore, if that than which a greater cannot be thought could be thought not to exist, then that than which a greater cannot be thought would not be that than which a greater cannot be thought—[a consequence] which is contradictory. Hence, something than which a greater cannot be thought exists so truly that it cannot even be thought not to exist.

And You are this [being], O Lord our God. Therefore, O Lord my God, You exist so truly that You cannot even be thought not to exist. And this is rightly the case. For if any mind could think of something better than You, the creature would rise above the Creator and would sit in judgment over the Creator—something which is utterly absurd. Indeed, except for You alone, whatever else exists can be thought not to exist. Therefore, You alone exist most truly of all and thus most greatly of all; for whatever else exists does not exist as truly [as do You] and thus exists less greatly [than do You]. Since, then, it is so readily clear to a rational mind that You exist most greatly of all, why did the Fool say in his heart that God does not exist?—why [indeed] except because [he is] foolish and a fool!

Chapter 4: How the Fool Said in His Heart That Which Cannot Be Thought

Yet, since to speak in one's heart and to think are the same thing, how did [the Fool] say in his heart what he was unable to think, or how was he unable to think that which he did say in his heart? Now, if he truly [i.e., really]—rather, since he truly—both thought [what he did] because he said [it] in his heart and did not say [it] in his heart because he was unable to think [it], then it is not the case that something is said in the heart, or is thought, in only one way. For in one way a thing is thought when the word signifying it is thought, and in another way [it is thought] when that which the thing is is understood. Thus, in the first way but not at all in the second, God can be thought not to exist. Indeed, no one who understands that which God is can think that God does not exist, even though he says these words [viz., "God does not exist"] in his heart either without any signification or with some strange signification. For God is that than which a greater cannot be thought. Anyone who rightly understands this, surely understands that that [than which a greater cannot be thought] exists in such a way that it cannot even conceivably not exist. Therefore, anyone who understands that God is such [a being] cannot think that He does not exist.

Thanks to You, good Lord, thank to You—because what at first I believed through Your giving, now by Your enlightening I understand to such an extent that [even] if I did not want to believe that You exist, I could not fail to understand [that You exist].

STOP Anselm's main argument is complete at this point. Is it cogent? Can the existence of God be established simply by appeal to the conception of God?

R Here is a slightly different account of God's unsurpassed greatness: a being than which nothing greater can be thought is, Anselm suggests, one that cannot be thought not to exist.

Discussion Questions

1. Suppose that Anselm is right that a being than which nothing greater can be thought must be *conceived* as existing in reality. Does it follow that it really exists in reality? Why or why not?
2. Anselm remarks at one point that anything other than God can be conceived not to exist. But why couldn't the same logic be used to show that other things also must exist—as suggested by one of Anselm's contemporaries, a monk named Gaunilo? To use Gaunilo's example, why couldn't it be argued in a parallel way that an *island* than which none greater can be thought must exist, and similarly for other sorts of things? Does this show that something must be wrong with Anselm's argument?
3. Suppose we were to define God simply as a being whose non-existence is inconceivable. Can it now be argued even more directly than in Anselm's argument that God must exist? Is there anything wrong with this simplified version of the argument?

René Descartes

René Descartes (1596–1650), a French philosopher and mathematician, was one of the most important and influential philosophers of all time. In the following selection from his *Meditations* (much of the rest of which is included in Chapter 2), Descartes presents a version of the ontological argument. His basic idea is that God is, by definition, a being who has all *perfections;* and since the property of existence is such a perfection, it follows that God must have this property too, and thus must exist.

The Ontological Argument

What I believe must be considered above all . . . is the fact that I find within me countless ideas of certain things, that, even if perhaps they do not exist anywhere outside me, still cannot be said to be nothing. And although, in a sense, I think them at will, nevertheless they are not something I have fabricated; rather they have their own true and immutable natures. For example, when I imagine a triangle, even if perhaps no such figure exists outside my thought anywhere in the world and never has, the triangle still has a certain determinate nature, essence, or form which is unchangeable and eternal, which I did not fabricate, and which does not depend on my mind. This is evident from the fact that various properties can be demonstrated regarding this triangle: namely, that its three angles are equal to two right angles, that its longest side is opposite its largest angle, and so on. These are properties I now clearly acknowledge, whether I want to or not, even if I previously had given them no thought whatever when I imagined the triangle. For this reason, then, they were not fabricated by me. (1)

1 — R Descartes's claim is that merely by thinking of the concept (or **idea**) of a triangle, we can see that certain properties are necessarily true of such a figure, because they are included in its "nature, essence, or form"; such things as having angles equal to two right angles (180 degrees) or having its largest side opposite its largest angle.

. . .

But if, from the mere fact that I can bring forth from my thought the idea of something, it follows that all that I clearly and distinctly perceive to belong to that thing really does belong to it, then cannot this too be a basis for an argument proving the existence of God? Clearly the idea of God, that is, the idea of a supremely perfect being, is one I discover to be no less within me than the idea of any figure or number. (2) And that it belongs to God's nature that he always exists is something I understand no less clearly and distinctly than is the case when I demonstrate in regard to some figure or number that something also belongs to the nature of that figure or number. (3) Thus . . . the existence of God ought to have for me at least the same degree of certainty that truths of mathematics had until now.

2 —  Is it as clear as Descartes thinks that the idea of God (or a supremely perfect being) is present in his mind (or our minds) in the same simple and unproblematic way as the ideas of figures (like a triangle) or numbers are? Part of the issue is whether the idea of God is as clear and well-defined as these other ideas. (See Discussion Question 1.)

3 —  R Descartes claims (without yet explaining why) that existence, indeed eternal existence, is part of the nature of God in the same way that having angles equal to two right angles is part of the nature of a triangle.

However, this point is not wholly obvious at first glance, but has a certain look of a sophism about it. Since in all other matters I have become accustomed to distinguishing existence from essence, I easily convince myself that it can even

From *Meditations of First Philosophy,* 3rd ed., translated by Donald A. Cress (Indianapolis: Hackett Publishing Company, 1993).

be separated from God's essence, and hence that God can be thought of as not existing. But nevertheless, it is obvious to anyone who pays close attention that existence can no more be separated from God's essence than its having three angles equal to two right angles can be separated from the essence of a triangle, or than that the idea of a valley can be separated from the idea of a mountain. Thus it is no less contradictory to think of God (that is, a supremely perfect being) lacking existence (that is, lacking some perfection) than it is to think of a mountain without a valley. ❹

But granted I can no more think of God as not existing than I can think of a mountain without a valley, nevertheless it surely does not follow from the fact that I think of a mountain without a valley that a mountain exists in the world. Likewise, from the fact that I think of God as existing, it does not seem to follow that God exists, for my thought imposes no necessity on things. And just as one may imagine a winged horse, without there being a horse that has wings, in the same way perhaps I can attach existence to God, even though no God exists. ❺

But there is a sophism lurking here. From the fact that I am unable to think of a mountain without a valley, it does not follow that a mountain or a valley exists anywhere, but only that, whether they exist or not, a mountain and a valley are inseparable from one another. But from the fact that I cannot think of God except as existing, it follows that existence is inseparable from God, and that for this reason he really exists. Not that my thought brings this about or imposes any necessity on anything; but rather the necessity of the thing itself, namely of the existence of God, forces me to think this. For I am not free to think of God without existence, that is, a supremely perfect being without a supreme perfection, as I am to imagine a horse with or without wings. ❻

Further, it should not be said here that even though I surely need to assent to the existence of God once I have asserted that God has all perfections and that existence is one of these perfections, nevertheless that earlier assertion need not have been made . . . . For although it is not necessary that I should ever happen upon any thought of God, nevertheless whenever I am of a mind to think of a being that is first and supreme, and bring forth the idea of God as it were from the storehouse of my mind, I must of necessity ascribe all perfections to him, even if I do not at that time enumerate them all or take notice of each one individually. This necessity plainly suffices so that afterwards, when I realize that existence is a perfection, I rightly conclude that a first and supreme being exists. ❼ In the same way, there is no necessity for me ever to imagine a triangle, but whenever I do wish to consider a rectilinear figure having but three angles, I must ascribe to it those properties on the basis of which one rightly infers that the three angles of this figure are no greater than two right angles, even though I do not take note of this at the time. . . .

. . . as far as God is concerned, if I were not overwhelmed by prejudices and if the images of sensible things were not besieging my thought from all directions, I would certainly acknowledge nothing sooner or more easily than him. For what, in and of itself, is more manifest than that a supreme being exists, that is, that God, to whose essence alone existence belongs, exists?

Discussion Questions

1. How clear is the concept of God, especially the version that Descartes focuses on: a being with all perfections? Is it clear enough to make possible confident and justified claims about what it does or does not include?
2. Is existence, as Descartes claims, a perfection: a good quality that a perfect being would have to have? It seems reasonable to assume that having a perfection always makes something better than it would be without it, but is this true of existence? Can you think of examples of things whose existence does not make them better?
3. Suppose that I would like to have a new car, indeed a perfect new car. I form a conception of such an entity, including all of the good features that a car might have. Is existence one of these? If it is, does it follow that my perfect new car actually exists, (and if so, where is it?)? Does this example show that something is wrong with Descartes's reasoning? Why or why not?
4. Compare Descartes's version of the ontological argument with Anselm's. How different are they, and how important are the differences? Descartes is sometimes accused of attempting to define God into existence by simply including existence as one of the defining features. Does Anselm's definition amount to the same thing? Why or why not?

Descartes suggests (though still without explaining fully) that it is **contradictory** to deny the existence of God in exactly the same way that it would be contradictory to say that something is a triangle but does not have one of the essential properties of a triangle.

Descartes considers an objection that is essentially the same as one that will be raised in the following selection from Kant: even if existence is part of the nature or essence of God, it does not follow that there actually is such a being that has this property (any more than the fact that being next to a valley is essential to the nature of a mountain, it follows that either mountains or valleys actually exist).

But this objection, he claims, is mistaken. If a mountain is inseparable from a valley, it does not follow that either exists (but only that if one does, then the other must). But if *existence* is inseparable from God, then one cannot think of God without existence, from which it follows that God must exist. (This is so because it is existence, not something else, that is the essential property in question.)

Here (finally!) Descartes explains why existence is included in the nature or essence of God: God, by definition, has all perfections (all good qualities), and existence is one of these perfections.

Immanuel Kant

The German philosopher Immanuel Kant (1724–1804) was among the most important and influential philosophers of all time, making major contributions to epistemology, metaphysics, ethics, aesthetics, and the philosophy of religion. In the following selection from his most important work, *The Critique of Pure Reason,* Kant offers two objections to the ontological argument. (It is clear that he has Descartes's version explicitly in mind.) The first of these is the one briefly considered by Descartes himself: that even if the property of existence is included in the concept of God, it still does not follow that God exists, since one can still reject the application of this concept to anything and existence along with it. The second, more famous, objection is that "existence is not a predicate," that is, not the sort of property that can be included in the essential nature or definition of a thing—in which case, the concept of God, as Descartes understands it, is not a legitimate concept.

The Impossibility of an Ontological Proof of the Existence of God

In all ages men have spoken of an *absolutely necessary being*, and in so doing have endeavoured, not so much to understand whether and how a thing of this kind allows even of being thought, but rather to prove its existence. There is, of course, no difficulty in giving a verbal definition of the concept, namely, that it is something the non-existence of which is impossible. But this yields no insight into the conditions which make it necessary to regard the non-existence of a thing as absolutely unthinkable. (1) It is precisely these conditions that we desire to know, in order that we may determine whether or not, in resorting to this concept, we are thinking anything at all. . . .

1

R Kant is saying that merely defining God as a necessary being accomplishes nothing without some account of how and why such a being is supposed to be necessary (that is, to exist necessarily).

. . . this concept, at first ventured upon blindly, and now become so completely familiar, has been supposed to have its meaning exhibited in a number of examples; and on this account all further enquiry into its intelligibility has seemed to be quite needless. Thus the fact that every geometrical proposition, as, for instance, that a triangle has three angles, is absolutely necessary, has been taken as justifying us in speaking of an object which lies entirely outside the sphere of our understanding as if we understood perfectly what it is that we intend to convey by the concept of that object. (2)

R As we saw in the previous selection, Descartes tries to explain how the existence of God can be both necessary and knowable a priori by analogy with claims about the essential properties of figures like triangles.

All the alleged examples are, without exception, taken from *judgments*, not from *things* and their existence. But the unconditioned necessity of judgments is not the same as an absolute necessity of things. The absolute necessity of the judgments is only a conditioned necessity of the thing, or of the predicate in the judgment. The above proposition does not declare that three angles are absolutely necessary, but that, under the condition that there is a triangle (that is, that a triangle is given), three angles will necessarily be found in it. (3) So great, indeed, is the deluding influence exercised by this logical necessity that, by the simple device of forming an a priori concept of a thing in such a manner as to include existence within the scope of its meaning, we have supposed ourselves to have justified the conclusion that because existence necessarily belongs to the object of this concept—always under the condition that we posit the thing as given (as existing)—we are also of necessity, in accordance with the law of identity, required to posit the existence of its object, and that this being is therefore itself absolutely necessary—and this, to repeat, for the reason that the existence of this being has already been thought in a concept which is assumed arbitrarily and on condition that we posit its object. (4)

R Kant argues that the necessary truth of judgments like *all triangles have three angles* (or Descartes's example *all triangles have angles equal to two right angles*) cannot be used to explain how necessary existence is possible. His point is that in the case of a judgment, the necessity is always merely *hypothetical: if* there is a triangle, then it necessarily has three angles.

R Similarly, granting for the moment Descartes's account of the concept of God, it follows only that *if* something is a being with all perfections, then that being also necessarily exists.

If, in an identical proposition, I reject the predicate while retaining the subject, contradiction results; and I therefore say that the former belongs necessarily to the latter. But if we reject subject and predicate alike, there is no contradiction; for nothing is then left that can be

From *The Critique of Pure Reason,* translated by Norman Kemp Smith (London: Macmillan, 1950).

contradicted. To posit a triangle, and yet to reject its three angles, is self-contradictory; but there is no contradiction in rejecting the triangle together with its three angles. The same holds true of the concept of an absolutely necessary being. If its existence is rejected, we reject the thing itself with all its predicates; and no question of contradiction can then arise. There is nothing outside it that would then be contradicted, since the necessity of the thing is not supposed to be derived from anything external; nor is there anything internal that would be contradicted, since in rejecting the thing itself we have at the same time rejected all its internal properties. ❺ 'God is omnipotent' is a necessary judgment. The omnipotence cannot be rejected if we posit a Deity, that is, an infinite being; for the two concepts are identical. But if we say, 'There is no God', neither the omnipotence nor any other of its predicates is given; they are one and all rejected together with the subject, and there is therefore not the least contradiction in such a judgment.

We have thus seen that if the predicate of a judgment is rejected together with the subject, no internal contradiction can result, and that this holds no matter what the predicate may be. The only way of evading this conclusion is to argue that there are subjects which cannot be removed, and must always remain. That, however, would only be another way of saying that there are absolutely necessary subjects; and that is the very assumption which I have called in question, and the possibility of which the above argument professes to establish. ❻ For I cannot form the least concept of a thing which, should it be rejected with all its predicates, leaves behind a contradiction; and in the absence of contradiction I have, through pure a priori concepts alone, no criterion of impossibility.

...

I should have hoped to put an end to these idle and fruitless disputations in a direct manner, by an accurate determination of the concept of existence, had I not found that the illusion which is caused by the confusion of a logical with a real predicate (that is, with a predicate which determines a thing) is almost beyond correction. Anything we please can be made to serve as a logical predicate; the subject can even be predicated of itself; for logic abstracts from all content. But a *determining* predicate is a predicate which is added to the concept of the subject and enlarges it. Consequently, it must not be already contained in the concept.

'*Being*' is obviously not a real predicate; that is, it is not a concept of something which could be added to the concept of a thing. ❼ It is merely the positing of a thing, or of certain determinations, as existing in themselves. Logically, it is merely the copula of a judgment. The proposition, 'God is omnipotent', contains two concepts, each of which has its object—God and omnipotence. The small word 'is' adds no new predicate, but only serves to posit the predicate *in its relation* to the subject. If, now, we take the subject (God) with all its predicates (among which is omnipotence), and say 'God is', or 'There is a God', we attach no new predicate to the concept of God, but only posit the subject in itself with all its predicates, and indeed posit it as being an *object* that stands in relation to my *concept*. The content of both must be one and the same; nothing can have been added to the concept, which expresses merely what is possible, by my thinking its object (through the expression 'it is') as given absolutely. ❽ Otherwise stated, the real contains no more than the merely possible. A hundred real thalers do not contain the least coin more than a hundred possible thalers. For as the latter signify the concept, and the former the object and the positing of the object, should the former contain more than the latter, my concept would not, in that case, express the whole object, and would not therefore be an adequate concept of it. My financial position is, however, affected very differently by a hundred real thalers than it is by the mere concept of them (that is, of their possibility). For the object, as it actually exists, is not analytically contained in my concept, but is added to my concept (which is a determination of my state) synthetically; and yet the conceived hundred thalers are not themselves in the least increased through thus acquiring existence outside my concept. ❾

By whatever and by however many predicates we may think a thing—even if we completely determine it—we do not make the least addition to the thing when we further declare that this thing *is*. Otherwise, it would not be exactly the same thing that exists, but something more than we had thought in the concept; and we could

❺

R But just as if we reject a triangle (that is, deny that there is any such thing), we can also consistently reject the existence of anything with three sides; so also if we reject a being with all perfections, we can also consistently reject the necessary existence of such a being. All that follows from Descartes's conception of God, Kant is saying, is that *if* there were such a being, then it would exist and necessarily so—but not that there actually is one.

❻

R And to assume that God's existence cannot be rejected in this way is to assume that such a being necessarily exists—thus **begging the question.**

❼

Kant now raises a second, deeper (but also perhaps less clearly correct) objection: while existence is obviously a *logical predicate* (that is, something that can appear as the predicate of a judgment, as when we judge that something exists), it is not a *real predicate* (that is, a property that can be part of the concept of a thing of a certain sort). If this is right, then Descartes's account of the concept of God as including existence must be mistaken.

❽

R Kant argues for the claim that existence is not a real predicate by pointing out that in ordinary cases, saying that something exists (or just that it is) does not further describe it, but only says that something satisfies the concept of the thing already understood.

❾

R Similarly, while there is an important difference between a hundred thalers (a unit of money, from which the word "dollar" is derived) that are merely possible or conceived and a hundred thalers that really exist, this difference is not in the concept of a hundred thalers that is involved in each case (which is exactly the same).

Kant's more general view, elaborated in the work from which this selection comes, is that the existence of anything can never be determined on an a priori basis, but must instead involve some appeal, directly or indirectly, to sense experience. Things may possibly exist that we cannot experience, but we can never have any knowledge of them.

not, therefore, say that the exact object of my concept exists. . . . When, therefore, I think a being as the supreme reality, . . . the question still remains whether it exists or not. . . .

Whatever, therefore, and however much, our concept of an object may contain, we must go outside it, if we are to ascribe existence to the object. In the case of objects of the senses, this takes place through their connection with some one of our perceptions, in accordance with empirical laws. But in dealing with objects of pure thought, we have no means whatsoever of knowing their existence, since it would have to be known in a *completely a priori manner*. Our consciousness of all existence (whether immediately through perception, or mediately through inferences which connect something with perception) belongs exclusively to the unity of experience; any [alleged] existence outside this field, while not indeed such as we can declare to be absolutely impossible, is of the nature of an assumption which we can never be in a position to justify. (10) . . .

The attempt to establish the existence of a supreme being by means of the famous ontological argument of Descartes is therefore merely so much labour and effort lost; we can no more extend our stock of [theoretical] insight by mere ideas, than a merchant can better his position by adding a few noughts to his cash account.

Discussion Questions

1. Look again at Descartes's anticipatory reply to Kant's first objection (see Annotation 5 to the previous selection and the corresponding text). Who is right here? If existence really is part of the concept of God, why isn't it contradictory to deny that God exists? Does this show (as Descartes thinks) that God must exist, or does it perhaps only show that we cannot correctly use the concept of God (or the term "God") to refer to something that does not exist?—though we could still apparently say that there is no real thing that has all of the properties standardly ascribed to God.
2. Is Kant right that "existence is not a real predicate"—that is, not the sort of property that can legitimately be contained in a concept? His examples show that existence is not part of the ordinary concepts that we employ, but do they show that it could never be part of any concept? The idea of existence isn't somehow empty or meaningless, so why couldn't we define a concept that includes it? Does Kant give any clear argument that this is impossible? If it is possible, what (if anything) follows about the existence of something satisfying such a concept?
3. Do Kant's criticisms of Descartes's version of the ontological argument also apply to Anselm's version? Consider each of the two main criticisms separately.

An Argument Against the Existence of God: The Problem of Evil

David Hume

Following the relatively brief discussion of the cosmological argument in the earlier selection, Hume turns in the *Dialogues* to a development of the problem of evil, with Philo doing most of the work after an initial (and, from his standpoint, misguided) opening provided by Demea. (For information about Hume, together with a description of the characters in the *Dialogues*, see p. 524.)

Hume's main concern in this discussion is with *physical* evil, with only brief mentions of *moral* evil (see the chapter introduction). He is also, at least on the surface, surprisingly reluctant to regard the problem of evil as a refutation of the claim that God exists, emphasizing instead the way in which it undercuts the positive argument for God's existence that the argument from design attempts to provide. (Mackie, in the following selection, refers to this as a "rather half-hearted presentation of the problem.")

The Problem of Evil, from *Dialogues Concerning Natural Religion*

It is my opinion, I own, replied Demea, that each man feels, in a manner, the truth of religion within his own breast; and from a consciousness of his imbecility and misery, rather than from any reasoning, is led to seek protection from that Being, on whom he and all nature is dependent. So anxious or so tedious are even the best scenes of life, that futurity is still the object of all our hopes and fears. We incessantly look forward, and endeavor, by prayers, adoration, and sacrifice, to appease those unknown powers, whom we find, by experience, so able to afflict and oppress us. Wretched creatures that we are! what resource for us amidst the innumerable ills of life, did not religion suggest some methods of atonement, and appease those terrors, with which we are incessantly agitated and tormented? (1)

I am indeed persuaded, said Philo, that the best and indeed the only method of bringing everyone to a due sense of religion, is by just representations of the misery and wickedness of men. And for that purpose a talent of eloquence and strong imagery is more requisite than that of reasoning and argument. For is it necessary to prove, what everyone feels within himself? 'Tis only necessary to make us feel it, if possible, more intimately and sensibly.

The people, indeed, replied Demea, are sufficiently convinced of this great and melancholy truth. The miseries of life, the unhappiness of men, the general corruptions of our nature, the unsatisfactory enjoyment of pleasures, riches, honors; these phrases have become almost proverbial in all languages. And who can doubt of what all men declare from their own immediate feeling and experience?

In this point, said Philo, the learned are perfectly agreed with the vulgar; and in all letters, sacred and profane, the topic of human misery has been insisted on with the most pathetic eloquence that sorrow and melancholy could inspire. The poets, who speak from sentiment, without a system, and whose testimony has therefore the more authority, abound in images of this nature. From Homer down to Dr. Young, the whole inspired tribe have ever been sensible, that no other representation of things would suit the feeling and observation of each individual.

As to authorities, replied Demea, you need not seek them. Look round this library of Cleanthes. I shall venture to affirm, that, except authors of particular sciences, such as chemistry or botany, who have no occasion to treat of human life, there scarce is one of those innumerable writers, from whom the sense of human misery has not, in some passage or other, extorted a complaint and confession of it. At least, the chance is entirely on that side; and no one author has ever, so far as I can recollect, been so extravagant as to deny it.

There you must excuse me, said Philo: Leibnitz has denied it; and is perhaps the first, who ventured upon so bold and paradoxical an opinion; at least, the first, who made it essential to his philosophical system. (2)

And by being the first, replied Demea, might he not have been sensible of his error? For is this a subject, in which philosophers can propose to make discoveries, especially in so late an age? And can any man hope by a simple denial (for the subject scarcely admits of reasoning) to bear down the united testimony of mankind, founded on sense and consciousness?

And why should man, added he, pretend to an exemption from the lot of all other animals? The whole earth, believe me, Philo, is cursed and polluted. A perpetual war is kindled amongst all living creatures. Necessity, hunger, want, stimulate the strong and courageous: fear, anxiety, terror, agitate the weak and infirm. The first entrance into life gives anguish to the new-born infant and to its wretched parent: weakness, impotence, distress, attend each stage of that life: and 'tis at last finished in agony and horror.

Observe too, says Philo, the curious artifices of nature, in order to embitter the life of every living being. The stronger prey upon the weaker, and keep them in perpetual terror and anxiety. The weaker too, in their turn, often prey upon the stronger, and vex and molest them without relaxation. Consider that innumerable

From David Hume, *Dialogues Concerning Natural Religion* (1779).

(1) Demea opens the door to Philo by suggesting that suffering and misery provide the strongest motive for religion, with the main idea being that the wretchedness of earthly life makes people hope and long for the sort of happy afterlife ("futurity") that religion promises. There is little doubt that this has indeed been one strong motivation behind religious belief—though reflection on the upshot of the following discussion seems to call into question the rationality of any such expectation.

(2) R The fact of widespread human suffering and misery would be conceded by almost everyone. But the German philosopher Leibniz might seem to deny this by claiming that this world is the "best of all possible worlds."

race of insects, which either are bred on the body of each animal, or flying about infix their stings in him. These insects have others still less than themselves, which torment them. And thus on each hand, before and behind, above and below, every animal is surrounded with enemies, which incessantly seek his misery and destruction. (3)

3 Another dimension of the problem of evil, one often regarded as particularly difficult, is the problem of animal suffering—keep this in mind in considering the theodicies (attempted solutions to the problem) discussed by Mackie and Hick in the following selections.

Man alone, said Demea, seems to be, in part, an exception to this rule. For by combination in society, he can easily master lions, tigers, and bears, whose greater strength and agility naturally enable them to prey upon him.

...

[Philo:] . . . consider, Demea; this very society, by which we surmount those wild beasts, our natural enemies; what new enemies does it not raise to us? What woe and misery does it not occasion? Man is the greatest enemy of man. Oppression, injustice, contempt, contumely, violence, sedition, war, calumny, treachery, fraud; by these they mutually torment each other: and they would soon dissolve that society which they had formed, were it not for the dread of still greater ills, which must attend their separation. (4)

4

Here we have examples of *moral* evil.

But though these external insults, said Demea, from animals, from men, from all the elements, which assault us, form a frightful catalogue of woes, they are nothing in comparison of those, which arise within ourselves, from the distempered condition of our mind and body. How many lie under the lingering torment of diseases? (5)

5

Disease is one part of the problem of *natural* evil (at least as long as the diseases are not directly caused by human actions—such as by the use of biological weapons).

...

The disorders of the mind, continued Demea, though more secret, are not perhaps less dismal and vexatious. Remorse, shame, anguish, rage, disappointment, anxiety, fear, dejection, despair; who has ever passed through life without cruel inroads from these tormentors? How many have scarcely ever felt any better sensations? Labor and poverty, so abhorred by everyone, are the certain lot of the far greater number; and those few privileged persons, who enjoy ease and opulence, never reach contentment or true felicity. All the goods of life united would not make a very happy man: but all the ills united would make a wretch indeed; and anyone of them almost (and who can be free from everyone), nay often the absence of one good (and who can possess all), is sufficient to render life ineligible.

...

And is it possible, Cleanthes, said Philo, that after all these reflections, and infinitely more, which might be suggested, you can still persevere in your anthropomorphism, and assert the moral attributes of the Deity, his justice, benevolence, mercy, and rectitude, to be of the same nature with these virtues in human creatures? His power we allow infinite: whatever he wills is executed: but neither man nor any other animal is happy: therefore he does not will their happiness. His wisdom is infinite: he is never mistaken in choosing the means to any end: but the course of nature tends not to human or animal felicity: therefore it is not established for that purpose. Through the whole compass of human knowledge, there are no inferences more certain and infallible than these. In what respect, then, do his benevolence and mercy resemble the benevolence and mercy of men? (6)

6

The issue is raised as to whether God's goodness (mercy and benevolence—and also perhaps justice) are the very same qualities (though more perfect versions of them) that we ascribe as virtues to human beings. But if not, what would be the point or justification of using those terms to describe God?

Epicurus's old questions are yet unanswered.

Is he willing to prevent evil, but not able? then is he impotent. Is he able, but not willing? then is he malevolent. Is he both able and willing? whence then is evil? (7)

7

Here is the nub of the problem, which can be reformulated as an argument for the conclusion that God (understood according to the standard conception) does not exist.

You ascribe, Cleanthes, (and I believe justly) a purpose and intention to nature. But what, I beseech you, is the object of that curious artifice and machinery, which she has displayed in all animals? The preservation alone of individuals and propagation of the species. It seems enough for her purpose, if such a rank be barely upheld in the universe, without any care or concern for the happiness of the members that compose it. No resource for this purpose: no machinery, in order merely to give pleasure or ease: no fund of pure joy and contentment: no indulgence without some want or necessity accompanying it. At least, the few phenomena of this nature are overbalanced by opposite phenomena of still greater importance.

Our sense of music, harmony, and indeed beauty of all kinds, gives satisfaction, without being absolutely necessary to the preservation and propagation of the species. But what racking pains, on the other hand, arise from gouts, gravels, megrims, toothaches, rheumatisms; where the injury to the animal-machinery is either small or incurable? Mirth, laughter, play, frolic, seem gratuitous satisfactions, which have no farther tendency: spleen, melancholy, discontent, superstition, are pains of the same nature. How then does the divine benevolence display itself, in the sense of you anthropomorphites? None but we mystics, as you were pleased to call us, can account for this strange mixture of phenomena, by deriving it from attributes, infinitely perfect, but incomprehensible. 8

And have you at last, said Cleanthes smiling, betrayed your intentions, Philo? Your long agreement with Demea did indeed a little surprise me; but I find you were all the while erecting a concealed battery against me. And I must confess, that you have now fallen upon a subject, worthy of your noble spirit of opposition and controversy. If you can make out the present point, and prove mankind to be unhappy or corrupted, there is an end at once of all religion. For to what purpose establish the natural attributes of the Deity, while the moral are still doubtful and uncertain?

You take umbrage very easily, replied Demea, at opinions the most innocent, and the most generally received even amongst the religious and devout themselves: and nothing can be more surprising than to find a topic like this, concerning the wickedness and misery of man, charged with no less than atheism and profaneness. Have not all pious divines and preachers, who have indulged their rhetoric on so fertile a subject: have they not easily, I say, given a solution of any difficulties, which may attend it? This world is but a point in comparison of the universe; this life but a moment in comparison of eternity. The present evil phenomena, therefore, are rectified in other regions, and in some future period of existence. And the eyes of men, being then opened to larger views of things, see the whole connection of general laws; and trace, with adoration, the benevolence and rectitude of the Deity, through all the mazes and intricacies of his providence. 9

No! replied Cleanthes, No! These arbitrary suppositions can never be admitted, contrary to matter of fact, visible and uncontroverted. Whence can any cause be known but from its known effects? Whence can any hypothesis be proved but from the apparent phenomena? To establish one hypothesis upon another, is building entirely in the air; and the utmost we ever attain, by these conjectures and fictions, is to ascertain the bare possibility of our opinion; but never can we, upon such terms, establish its reality.

The only method of supporting divine benevolence (and it is what I willingly embrace) is to deny absolutely the misery and wickedness of man. Your representations are exaggerated: your melancholy views mostly fictitious: your inferences contrary to fact and experience. Health is more common than sickness: pleasure than pain: happiness than misery. And for one vexation, which we meet with, we attain, upon computation, a hundred enjoyments. 10

Admitting your position, replied Philo, which yet is extremely doubtful, you must, at the same time, allow, that, if pain be less frequent than pleasure, it is infinitely more violent and durable. One hour of it is often able to outweigh a day, a week, a month of our common insipid enjoyments. And how many days, weeks, and months are passed by several in the most acute torments? Pleasure, scarcely in one instance, is ever able to reach ecstasy and rapture: and in no one instance can it continue for any time at its highest pitch and altitude. The spirits evaporate; the nerves relax; the fabric is disordered; and the enjoyment quickly degenerates into fatigue and uneasiness. But pain often, good God, how often! rises to torture and agony; and the longer it continues, it becomes still more genuine agony and torture. Patience is exhausted; courage languishes; melancholy seizes us; and nothing terminates our misery but the removal of its cause, or another event, which is the sole cure of all evil, but which, from our natural folly, we regard with still greater horror and consternation.

But not to insist upon these topics, continued Philo, though most obvious, certain, and important; I must use the freedom to admonish you, Cleanthes, that you have put this controversy upon a most dangerous issue, and are unawares introducing a total scepticism, into the most essential articles of natural and revealed theology. What! no method of fixing a just foundation for religion, unless we allow the happiness of human life, and maintain a continued existence even in this world, with all our present pains, infirmities, vexations, and follies, to be eligible and desirable! But this is contrary to everyone's feeling and experience: it is contrary to an

R Philo alludes here to Demea's view that God's attributes are incapable of being understood by human beings, in which case it would be impossible to argue that a being with those attributes would prevent evil.

(But if we have no understanding at all of the sort of being in question, then the standard conception and indeed the very claim that God exists cease to have any meaningful content.)

STOP Could evils of the sorts that Hume is discussing be genuinely "rectified in other regions, and in some future period of existence"? Could anything that happens in those "other regions" or "future periods" really solve the problem?

R Cleanthes argues that if we have only our earthly situation to go on and if it is really as bad as Philo claims, then there is no reason to expect that a state of this very different sort, even if possible, will actually occur. Thus the theist must deny that Philo's description is correct, arguing that the evils have been greatly exaggerated.

authority so established as nothing can subvert: no decisive proofs can ever be produced against this authority; nor is it possible for you to compute, estimate, and compare all the pains and all the pleasures in the lives of all men and of all animals: and thus by your resting the whole system of religion on a point, which, from its very nature, must forever be uncertain, you tacitly confess, that that system is equally uncertain.

But allowing you, what never will be believed; at least, what you never possibly can prove, that animal, or at least, human happiness, in this life, exceeds its misery; you have yet done nothing: for this is not, by any means, what we expect from infinite power, infinite wisdom, and infinite goodness. Why is there any misery at all in the world? [11] Not by chance surely. From some cause then. Is it from the intention of the Deity? But he is perfectly benevolent. Is it contrary to his intention? But he is almighty. Nothing can shake the solidity of this reasoning, so short, so clear, so decisive; except we assert, that these subjects exceed all human capacity, and that our common measures of truth and falsehood are not applicable to them; a topic, which I have all along insisted on, but which you have, from the beginning, rejected with scorn and indignation. [12]

But I will be contented to retire still from this intrenchment: for I deny that you can ever force me in it: I will allow, that pain or misery in man is *compatible* with infinite power and goodness in the Deity, even in your sense of these attributes: what are you advanced by all these concessions? A mere possible compatibility is not sufficient. You must *prove* these pure, unmixed, and uncontrollable attributes from the present mixed and confused phenomena, and from these alone. A hopeful undertaking! Were the phenomena ever so pure and unmixed, yet being finite, they would be insufficient for that purpose. How much more, where they are also so jarring and discordant!

Here, Cleanthes, I find myself at ease in my argument. Here I triumph. Formerly, when we argued concerning the natural attributes of intelligence and design, I needed all my sceptical and metaphysical subtilty to elude your grasp. In many views of the universe, and of its parts, particularly the latter, the beauty and fitness of final causes strikes us with such irresistible force, that all objections appear (what I believe they really are) mere cavils and sophisms; nor can we then imagine how it was ever possible for us to repose any weight on them. But there is no view of human life or of the condition of mankind, from which, without the greatest violence, we can infer the moral attributes, or learn that infinite benevolence, conjoined with infinite power and infinite wisdom, which we must discover by the eyes of faith alone. It is your turn now to tug the laboring oar, and to support your philosophical subtilties against the dictates of plain reason and experience. [13]

...

I scruple not to allow, said Cleanthes, that I have been apt to suspect the frequent repetition of the word, *infinite*, which we meet with in all theological writers, to savor more of panegyric than of philosophy, and that any purposes of reasoning, and even of religion, would be better served, were we to rest contented with more accurate and more moderate expressions. The terms, *admirable, excellent, superlatively great, wise*, and *holy*; these sufficiently fill the imaginations of men; and anything beyond, besides that it leads into absurdities, has no influence on your affections or sentiments. Thus, in the present subject, if we abandon all human analogy, as seems your intention, Demea, I am afraid we abandon all religion, and retain no conception of the great object of our adoration. If we preserve human analogy, we must forever find it impossible to reconcile any mixture of evil in the universe with infinite attributes; much less can we ever prove the latter from the former. But supposing the Author of Nature to be finitely perfect, though far exceeding mankind; a satisfactory account may then be given of natural and moral evil, and every untoward phenomenon be explained and adjusted. A less evil may then be chosen, in order to avoid a greater; inconveniences be submitted to, in order to reach a desirable end: and in a word, benevolence, regulated by wisdom, and limited by necessity, may produce just such a world as the present. [14] You, Philo, who are so prompt at starting views, and reflections, and analogies, I would gladly hear, at length, without interruption, your opinion of this new theory; and if it deserve our attention, we may afterwards, at more leisure, reduce it into form.

11

Philo responds that this response does no good, since infinite power and goodness would eliminate *all* evil.

12

Is there any way for a theist to respond to this very simple argument, other than by retreating to the claim that human beings cannot ever really understand such issues?

13

And even if evil were not simply incompatible with the existence of such a being (which Philo does not actually concede), Cleanthes's attempt to infer (via the argument from design) to a God satisfying the standard conception is, Philo argues, fatally undermined as far as God's moral attributes are concerned.

14

Cleanthes suggests the possibility of a different conception of God: as a being with more limited powers, thereby allowing evil to be explained by the recalcitrant nature of the material with which God has to work.

This is perhaps the response to the problem of evil that requires the least modification of the traditional theistic position. (The opposite possibility of a God with infinite power but limited goodness is rarely considered.)

My sentiments, replied Philo, are not worth being made a mystery of; and therefore, without any ceremony, I shall deliver what occurs to me with regard to the present subject. It must, I think, be allowed, that, if a very limited intelligence, whom we shall suppose utterly unacquainted with the universe, were assured, that it were the production of a very good, wise, and powerful being, however finite, he would, from his conjectures, form *beforehand* a different notion of it from what we find it to be by *experience*; nor would he ever imagine, merely from these attributes of the cause, of which he is informed, that the effect could be so full of vice and misery and disorder, as it appears in his life. Supposing now, that this person were brought into the world, still assured, that it was the workmanship of such a sublime and benevolent Being; he might, perhaps, be surprised at the disappointment; but would never retract his former belief, if founded on any very solid argument; since such a limited intelligence must be sensible of his own blindness and ignorance, and must allow, that there may be many solutions of those phenomena, which will forever escape his comprehension. But supposing, which is the real case with regard to man, that this creature is not antecedently convinced of a supreme intelligence, benevolent, and powerful, but is left to gather such a belief from the appearance of things; this entirely alters the case, nor will he ever find any reason for such a conclusion. He may be fully convinced of the narrow limits of his understanding; but this will not help him in forming an inference concerning the goodness of superior powers, since he must form that inference from what he knows, not from what he is ignorant of. The more you exaggerate his weakness and ignorance, the more diffident you render him, and give him the greater suspicion, that such subjects are beyond the reach of his faculties. You are obliged, therefore, to reason with him merely from the known phenomena, and to drop every arbitrary supposition or conjecture.

Did I show you a house or palace, where there was not one apartment convenient or agreeable; where the windows, doors, fires, passages, stairs, and the whole economy of the building were the source of noise, confusion, fatigue, darkness, and extremes of heat and cold; you would certainly blame the contrivance, without any farther examination. The architect would in vain display his subtilty, and prove to you, that if this door or that window were altered, greater ills would ensue. What he says, may be strictly true: the alteration of one particular, while the other parts of the building remain, may only augment the inconveniences. But still you would assert in general, that, if the architect had had skill and good intentions, he might have formed such a plan of the whole, and might have adjusted the parts in such a manner, as would have remedied all or most of these inconveniences. His ignorance, or even your own ignorance of such a plan, will never convince you of the impossibility of it. If you find many inconveniences and deformities in the building, you will always, without entering into any detail, condemn the architect.

In short, I repeat the question: is the world considered in general, and as it appears to us in this life, different from what a man or such a limited being would, beforehand, expect from a very powerful, wise, and benevolent Deity? It must be strange prejudice to assert the contrary. And from thence I conclude, that, however consistent the world may be, allowing certain suppositions and conjectures, with the idea of such a Deity, it can never afford us an inference concerning his existence. The consistency is not absolutely denied, only the inference. Conjectures, especially where infinity is excluded from the Divine attributes, may perhaps be sufficient to prove a consistency; but can never be foundations for any inference. 15

There seem to be four circumstances, on which depend all, or the greatest parts of the ills, that molest sensible creatures; and it is not impossible but all these circumstances may be necessary and unavoidable. We know so little beyond common life, or even of common life, that, with regard to the economy of a universe, there is no conjecture, however wild, which may not be just; nor any one, however plausible, which may not be erroneous. All that belongs to human understanding, in this deep ignorance and obscurity, is to be sceptical, or at least cautious; and not to admit of any hypothesis, whatever; much less, of any which is supported by no appearance of probability. Now this I assert to be the case with regard to all the causes of evil, and the circumstances, on which it depends. None of them appear to human reason, in the least degree, necessary or unavoidable; nor can

R Philo responds that the world we actually find is not what we would expect even such a limited God to produce—that while it may be compatible with the existence of such a being, it can provide no positive argument for its existence.

STOP Philo proceeds to enumerate four main circumstances that result in evil and suffering of various kinds, claiming that none of these can plausibly be thought to be necessary and unavoidable even for a limited God. Think carefully about each of them as you read. Is he right?

we suppose them such, without the utmost license of imagination.

The *first* circumstance which introduces evil, is that contrivance or economy of the animal creation, by which pains, as well as pleasures, are employed to excite all creatures to action, and make them vigilant in the great work of self-preservation. Now pleasure alone, in its various degrees, seems to human understanding sufficient for this purpose. All animals might be constantly in a state of enjoyment; but when urged by any of the necessities of nature, such as thirst, hunger, weariness; instead of pain, they might feel a diminution of pleasure, by which they might be prompted to seek that object, which is necessary to their subsistence. Men pursue pleasure as eagerly as they avoid pain; at least, might have been so constituted. It seems, therefore, plainly possible to carry on the business of life without any pain. Why then is any animal ever rendered susceptible of such a sensation? If animals can be free from it an hour, they might enjoy a perpetual exemption from it; and it required as particular a contrivance of their organs to produce that feeling, as to endow them with sight, hearing, or any of the senses. Shall we conjecture, that such a contrivance was necessary, without any appearance of reason? and shall we build on that conjecture as on the most certain truth?

But a capacity of pain would not alone produce pain, were it not for the *second* circumstance, viz., the conducting of the world by general laws; and this seems nowise necessary to a very perfect being. It is true; if everything were conducted by particular volitions, the course of nature would be perpetually broken, and no man could employ his reason in the conduct of life. But might not other particular volitions remedy this inconvenience? In short, might not the Deity exterminate all ill, wherever it were to be found; and produce all good, without any preparation or long progress of causes and effects?

Besides, we must consider, that, according to the present economy of the world, the course of nature, though supposed exactly regular, yet to us appears not so, and many events are uncertain, and many disappoint our expectations. Health and sickness, calm and tempest, with an infinite number of other accidents, whose causes are unknown and variable, have a great influence both on the fortunes of particular persons and on the prosperity of public societies: and indeed all human life, in a manner, depends on such accidents. A being, therefore, who knows the secret springs of the universe, might easily, by particular volitions, turn all these accidents to the good of mankind, and render the whole world happy, without discovering himself in any operation. A fleet, whose purposes were salutary to society, might always meet with a fair wind: good princes enjoy sound health and long life: persons, born to power and authority, be framed with good tempers and virtuous dispositions. A few such events as these, regularly and wisely conducted, would change the face of the world; and yet would no more seem to disturb the course of nature or confound human conduct, than the present economy of things, where the causes are secret, and variable, and compounded. . . . There may, for aught we know, be good reasons, why Providence interposes not in this manner; but they are unknown to us: and though the mere supposition, that such reasons exist, may be sufficient to save the conclusion concerning the divine attributes, yet surely it can never be sufficient to *establish* that conclusion. (16)

16

One question often asked, about both natural and moral evil, is why God does not intervene (perhaps in a very subtle and unobvious way) when really horrible disasters or crimes are about to occur. Perhaps there is value in a world governed by regular laws (or, to anticipate discussions in later selections, one containing free will). But is the value so great and the harm done to it by even occasional and inconspicuous interventions so serious that it is better for God not to intervene even when major disasters could be prevented by doing so?

If everything in the universe be conducted by general laws, and if animals be rendered susceptible of pain, it scarcely seems possible but some ill must arise in the various shocks of matter, and the various concurrence and opposition of general laws. But this ill would be very rare, were it not for the *third* circumstance, which I proposed to mention, viz., the great frugality with which all powers and faculties are distributed to every particular being. So well adjusted are the organs and capacities of all animals, and so well fitted to their preservation, that, as far as history or tradition reaches, there appears not to be any single species, which has yet been extinguished in the universe. (17) Every animal has the requisite endowments; but these endowments are bestowed with so scrupulous an economy, that any considerable diminution must entirely destroy the creature. Wherever one power is increased, there is a proportional abatement in the others. Animals, which excel in swiftness, are commonly defective in force. Those, which possess both, are either imperfect in some of their senses, or are oppressed with the most craving wants. The human species, whose chief excellency is reason and sagacity, is of all others

17

We now know, of course, that there are species that have been "extinguished."

the most necessitous, and the most deficient in bodily advantages; without clothes, without arms, without food, without lodging, without any convenience of life, except what they owe to their own skill and industry. In short, nature seems to have formed an exact calculation of the necessities of her creatures; and like a *rigid master*, has afforded them little more powers or endowments, than what are strictly sufficient to supply those necessities. An *indulgent parent* would have bestowed a large stock, in order to guard against accidents, and secure the happiness and welfare of the creature, in the most unfortunate concurrence of circumstances. Every course of life would not have been so surrounded with precipices, that the least departure from the true path, by mistake or necessity, must involve us in misery and ruin. Some reserve, some fund would have been provided to ensure happiness; nor would the powers and the necessities have been adjusted with so rigid an economy. The Author of Nature is inconceivably powerful: his force is supposed great, if not altogether inexhaustible: nor is there any reason, as far as we can judge, to make him observe this strict frugality in his dealings with his creatures. It would have been better, were his power extremely limited, to have created fewer animals, and to have endowed these with more faculties for their happiness and preservation. A builder is never esteemed prudent, who undertakes a plan, beyond what his stock will enable him to finish.

In order to cure most of the ills of human life, I require not that man should have the wings of the eagle, the swiftness of the stag, the force of the ox, the arms of the lion, the scales of the crocodile or rhinoceros; much less do I demand the sagacity of an angel or cherub. I am contented to take an increase in one single power or faculty of his soul. Let him be endowed with a greater propensity to industry and labor; a more vigorous spring and activity of mind; a more constant bent to business and application. Let the whole species possess naturally an equal diligence with that which many individuals are able to attain by habit and reflection; and the most beneficial consequences, without any alloy of ill, is the immediate and necessary result of this endowment. Almost all the moral, as well as natural evils of human life arise from idleness; and were our species, by the original constitution of their frame, exempt from this vice or infirmity, the perfect cultivation of land, the improvement of arts and manufactures, the exact execution of every office and duty, immediately follow; and men at once may fully reach that state of society, which is so imperfectly attained by the best-regulated government. But as industry is a power, and the most valuable of any, nature seems determined, suitably to her usual maxims, to bestow it on men with a very sparing hand; and rather to punish him severely for his deficiency in it, than to reward him for his attainments. She has so contrived his frame, that nothing but the most violent necessity can oblige him to labor; and she employs all his other wants to overcome, at least in part, the want of diligence, and to endow him with some share of a faculty, of which she has thought fit naturally to bereave him. Here our demands may be allowed very humble, and therefore the more reasonable. If we required the endowments of superior penetration and judgment, of a more delicate taste of beauty, of a nicer sensibility to benevolence and friendship; we might be told, that we impiously pretend to break the order of nature, that we want to exalt ourselves into a higher rank of being, that the presents which we require, not being suitable to our state and condition, would only be pernicious to us. But it is hard; I dare to repeat it, it is hard, that being placed in a world so full of wants and necessities; where almost every being and element is either our foe or refuses us their assistance, we should also have our own temper to struggle with, and should be deprived of that faculty, which can alone fence against these multiplied evils.

The *fourth* circumstance, whence arises the misery and ill of the universe, is the inaccurate workmanship of all the springs and principles of the great machine of nature. It must be acknowledged, that there are few parts of the universe, which seem not to serve some purpose, and whose removal would not produce a visible defect and disorder in the whole. The parts hang all together; nor can one be touched without affecting the rest in a greater or less degree. But at the same time, it must be observed, that none of these parts or principles, however useful, are so accurately adjusted, as to keep precisely within those bounds, in which their utility consists; but they are, all of them, apt, on every occasion, to run into the one extreme or the other.

One would imagine, that this grand production had not received the last hand of the maker; so little finished in every part, and so coarse are the strokes, with which it is executed. Thus, the winds are requisite to convey the vapors along the surface of the globe, and to assist men in navigation: but how oft, rising up to tempests and hurricanes, do they become pernicious? Rains are necessary to nourish all the plants and animals of the earth: but how often are they defective? how often excessive? Heat is requisite to all life and vegetation; but is not always found in the due proportion. [18] On the mixture and secretion of the humors and juices of the body depend the health and prosperity of the animal: but the parts perform not regularly their proper function. What more useful than all the passions of the mind, ambition, vanity, love, anger? But how oft do they break their bounds, and cause the greatest convulsions in society? There is nothing so advantageous in the universe, but what frequently becomes pernicious, by its excess or defect; nor has nature guarded, with the requisite accuracy, against all disorder or confusion. The irregularity is never, perhaps, so great as to destroy any species; but is often sufficient to involve the individuals in ruin and misery.

On the concurrence, then, of these four circumstances does all, or the greatest part of natural evil depend. Were all living creatures incapable of pain, or were the world administered by particular volitions, evil never could have found access into the universe: and were animals endowed with a large stock of powers and faculties, beyond what strict necessity requires; or were the several springs and principles of the universe so accurately framed as to preserve always the just temperament and medium; there must have been very little ill in comparison of what we feel at present. What then shall we pronounce on this occasion? Shall we say, that these circumstances are not necessary, and that they might easily have been altered in the contrivance of the universe? This decision seems too presumptuous for creatures, so blind and ignorant. Let us be more modest in our conclusions. Let us allow, that, if the goodness of the Deity (I mean a goodness like the human) could be established on any tolerable reasons a priori, these phenomena, however untoward, would not be sufficient to subvert that principle; but might easily, in some unknown manner, be reconcilable to it. But let us still assert, that as this goodness is not antecedently established, but must be inferred from the phenomena, there can be no grounds for such an inference, while there are so many ills in the universe, and while these ills might so easily have been remedied, as far as human understanding can be allowed to judge on such a subject. [19] I am sceptic enough to allow, that the bad appearances, notwithstanding all my reasonings, may be compatible with such attributes as you suppose: but surely they can never prove these attributes. Such a conclusion cannot result from scepticism; but must arise from the phenomena, and from our confidence in the reasonings, which we deduce from these phenomena.

18

This is a quick gesture at the suffering that results from various kinds of natural disasters, the most obvious kind of natural evil.

19

R Again Hume's rather cautious point is not that we can know for sure that a God who satisfied the standard conception would modify these various features of the world, but only that since we can see no reason why such modification is not possible (without greater costs of some sort), the world as we find it provides no good reason in favor of the existence of such a God.

Look round this universe. What an immense profusion of beings, animated and organized, sensible and active! You admire this prodigious variety and fecundity. But inspect a little more narrowly these living existences, the only beings worth regarding. How hostile and destructive to each other! How insufficient all of them for their own happiness! How contemptible or odious to the spectator! The whole presents nothing but the idea of a blind nature, impregnated by a great vivifying principle, and pouring forth from her lap, without discernment or parental care, her maimed and abortive children!

Here the Manichaean system occurs as a proper hypothesis to solve the difficulty [20]: and no doubt, in some respects, it is very specious, and has more probability than the common hypothesis, by giving a plausible account of the strange mixture of good and ill, which appears in life. But if we consider, on the other hand, the perfect uniformity and agreement of the parts of the universe, we shall not discover in it any marks of the combat of a malevolent with a benevolent being. There is indeed an opposition of pains and pleasures in the feelings of sensible creatures: but are not all the operations of nature carried on by an opposition of principles, of hot and cold, moist and dry, light and heavy? The true conclusion is, that the original source of all things is entirely indifferent to all these principles, and has no more regard to good above ill than to heat above cold, or to drought above moisture, or to light above heavy.

20

The Manichean system has two opposed gods or forces, one good and one evil, who struggle for control.

There may four hypotheses be framed concerning the first causes of the universe: that they are endowed with perfect goodness, that they have perfect malice, that they are opposite and have both goodness and malice, that they have neither goodness nor malice. Mixed phenomena can never prove the two former unmixed principles. And the uniformity and steadiness of general laws seem to oppose the third. The fourth, therefore, seems by far the most probable. (21)

What I have said concerning natural evil will apply to moral, with little or no variation; and we have no more reason to infer, that the rectitude of the Supreme Being resembles human rectitude than that his benevolence resembles the human. Nay, it will be thought, that we have still greater cause to exclude from him moral sentiments, such as we feel them; since moral evil, in the opinion of many, is much more predominant above moral good than natural evil above natural good.

But even though this should not be allowed, and though the virtue, which is in mankind, should be acknowledged much superior to the vice; yet so long as there is any vice at all in the universe, it will very much puzzle you anthropomorphites, how to account for it. You must assign a cause for it, without having recourse to the first cause. But as every effect must have a cause, and that cause another; you must either carry on the progression *in infinitum*, or rest on that original principle, who is the ultimate cause of all things. . . . (22)

Hold! hold! cried Demea: Whither does your imagination hurry you? I joined in alliance with you, in order to prove the incomprehensible nature of the Divine Being, and refute the principles of Cleanthes, who would measure everything by a human rule and standard. But I now find you running into all the topics of the greatest libertines and infidels; and betraying that holy cause, which you seemingly espoused. Are you secretly, then, a more dangerous enemy than Cleanthes himself?

And are you so late in perceiving it? replied Cleanthes. Believe me, Demea; your friend Philo, from the beginning, has been amusing himself at both our expense; and it must be confessed, that the injudicious reasoning of our vulgar theology has given him but too just a handle of ridicule. The total infirmity of human reason, the absolute incomprehensibility of the Divine Nature, the great and universal misery and still greater wickedness of men; these are strange topics surely to be so fondly cherished by orthodox divines and doctors. In ages of stupidity and ignorance, indeed, these principles may safely be espoused; and perhaps, no views of things are more proper to promote superstition, than such as encourage the blind amazement, the diffidence, and melancholy of mankind. But at present . . .

Blame not so much, interposed Philo, the ignorance of these reverend gentlemen. They know how to change their style with the times. Formerly it was a most popular theological topic to maintain, that human life was vanity and misery, and to exaggerate all the ills and pains, which are incident to men. But of late years, divines, we find, begin to retract this position, and maintain, though still with some hesitation, that there are more goods than evils, more pleasures than pains, even in this life. When religion stood entirely upon temper and education, it was thought proper to encourage melancholy; as indeed, mankind never have recourse to superior powers so readily as in that disposition. But as men have now learned to form principles, and to draw consequences, it is necessary to change the batteries, and to make use of such arguments as will endure, at least some scrutiny and examination. . . .

Thus Philo continued to the last his spirit of opposition, and his censure of established opinions. But I could observe, that Demea did not at all relish the latter part of the discourse; and he took occasion soon after on some pretense or other, to leave the company.

(21)

STOP Think about the reason given here for rejecting the Manichean possibility. What would a Manichean world look like? Is Hume right that it would be very different from the one we find?

(22)

R Hume extends his conclusion to moral evil as well, though without much discussion.

Discussion Questions

1. Formulate the problem of evil as an explicit argument for the conclusion that God (understood in the standard way) does not exist (see Annotation 7). This can be done in a way that makes the argument logically **valid,** so that either the conclusion must be true or one of the premises must be false. What is the best response that a theist can give to such an argument—that is, which premise should the theist deny, and how might he defend such a denial?

2. Consider the possibility of a more limited God (see Annotation 14), who is either unable or unwilling to eradicate evil. (The Manichean view (see Annotation 20) is in fact one version of this, with the good god being the relevant one and the evil god being the force that prevents the eradication of evil.) Are views of this sort more defensible than those that advocate a God who satisfies the standard conception, and if so, how much more defensible? (Consider Hume's responses.) How satisfactory is a limited God from the standpoint of religion?

3. Presumably even a limited God could often intervene when natural disasters of various sorts are about to occur, reducing their severity even if not eliminating them entirely. Is there any compelling reason why God (on either the standard or limited view) should not do this—some plausible way in which the cost would be greater than the gain?

J. L. Mackie

J. L. Mackie (1917–1981) was an Australian philosopher, who taught in both New Zealand and Australia and later at Oxford. His wide-ranging work includes influential discussions of the nature of causation, the nature of morality, and various issues in the philosophy of religion, as well as work on Locke and Hume. In this selection, Mackie offers a clear statement of the problem of evil, together with a presentation and evaluation of possible solutions.

Evil and Omnipotence

The traditional arguments for the existence of God have been fairly thoroughly criticized by philosophers. But the theologian can, if he wishes, accept this criticism. He can admit that no rational proof of God's existence is possible. And he can still retain all that is essential to his position, by holding that God's existence is known in some other, nonrational way. I think, however, that a more telling criticism can be made by way of the traditional problem of evil. Here it can be shown, not that religious beliefs lack rational support, but that they are positively irrational, that the several parts of the essential theological doctrine are inconsistent with one another, so that the theologian can maintain his position as a whole only by a much more extreme rejection of reason than in the former case. He must now be prepared to believe, not merely what cannot be proved, but what can be *disproved* from other beliefs that he also holds.

The problem of evil, in the sense in which I shall be using the phrase, is a problem only for someone who believes that there is a God who is both omnipotent and wholly good. And it is a logical problem, the problem of clarifying and reconciling a number of beliefs: it is not a scientific problem that might be solved by further observations, or a practical problem that might be solved by a decision or an action. These points are obvious; I mention them only because they are sometimes ignored by theologians, who sometimes parry a statement of the problem with such remarks as "Well, can you solve the problem yourself?" or "This is a mystery which may be revealed to us later" or "Evil is something to be faced and overcome, not to be merely discussed."

In its simplest form the problem is this: God is omnipotent; God is wholly good; and yet evil exists. There seems to be some contradiction between these three propositions, so that if any two of them were true the third would be false. But at the same time all three are essential parts of most theological positions: the theologian, it seems, at once *must* adhere and *cannot consistently* adhere to all three. (The problem does not arise only for theists, but I shall discuss it in the form in which it presents itself for ordinary theism.)

However, the contradiction does not arise immediately; to show it we need some additional premises, or perhaps some quasi-logical rules connecting the terms "good," "evil," and "omnipotent." These additional principles are that good is opposed to evil, in such a way that a good thing always eliminates evil as far as it can, and that there are no limits to what an omnipotent thing can do. From these it follows that a

From J. L. Mackie, "Evil and Omnipotence," *Mind,* Vol. LXIV (1955).

good omnipotent thing eliminates evil completely, and then the propositions that a good omnipotent thing exists, and that evil exists, are incompatible. 1

R Mackie's claim is that with these additional assumptions ("quasi-logical rules"), the existence of a God satisfying the standard conception is logically incompatible with the existence of evil, so that it would be contradictory to assert both.

Adequate Solutions

Now once the problem is fully stated it is clear that it can be solved, in the sense that the problem will not arise if one gives up at least one of the propositions that constitute it. If you are prepared to say that God is not wholly good, or not quite omnipotent, or that evil does not exist, or that good is not opposed to the kind of evil that exists, or that there are limits to what an omnipotent thing can do, then the problem of evil will not arise for you. 2

What Mackie means by an "adequate solution" is one that is logically adequate to avoid the alleged contradiction, not necessarily one that is adequate as a defense of the existence of God.

There are, then, quite a number of adequate solutions of the problem of evil, and some of these have been adopted, or almost adopted, by various thinkers. For example, a few have been prepared to deny God's omnipotence, and rather more have been prepared to keep the term "omnipotence" but severely to restrict its meaning, recording quite a number of things that an omnipotent being cannot do. Some have said that evil is an illusion, perhaps because they held that the whole world of temporal, changing things is an illusion, and that what we call evil belongs only to this world, or perhaps because they held that although temporal things *are* much as we see them, those that we call evil are not really evil. Some have said that what we call evil is merely the privation of good, that evil in a positive sense, evil that would really be opposed to good, does not exist. Many have agreed with Pope that disorder is harmony not understood, and that partial evil is universal good. Whether any of these views is *true* is, of course, another question. 3 But each of them gives an adequate solution of the problem of evil in the sense that if you accept it this problem does not arise for you, though you may, of course, have *other* problems to face.

3

Mackie mentions several possibilities here, without really elaborating on any of them. Think about whether any of these can be developed in a plausible way.

But often enough these adequate solutions are only *almost* adopted. The thinkers who restrict God's power, but keep the term "omnipotence," may reasonably be suspected of thinking, in other contexts, that his power is really unlimited. Those who say that evil is an illusion may also be thinking, inconsistently, that this illusion is itself an evil. Those who say that "evil" is merely privation of good may also be thinking, inconsistently, that privation of good is an evil. . . . If Pope meant what he said in the last line of his couplet, that "disorder" is only harmony not understood, the "partial evil" of the second line must, for consistency, mean "that which, taken in isolation, falsely appears to be evil," but it would more naturally mean "that which, in isolation, really is evil." The second line, in fact, hesitates between two views, that "partial evil" isn't really evil, since only the universal quality is real, and that "partial evil" is really an evil, but only a little one.

In addition, therefore, to adequate solutions, we must recognize unsatisfactory inconsistent solutions, in which there is only a half-hearted or temporary rejection of one of the propositions which together constitute the problem. In these, one of the constituent propositions is explicitly rejected, but it is covertly reasserted or assumed elsewhere in the system.

Fallacious Solutions

Besides these half-hearted solutions, which explicitly reject but implicitly assert one of the constituent propositions, there are definitely fallacious solutions which explicitly maintain all the constituent propositions, but implicitly reject at least one of them in the course of the argument that explains away the problem of evil.

There are, in fact, many so-called solutions which purport to remove the contradiction without abandoning any of its constituent propositions. These must be fallacious, as we can see from the very statement of the problem, but it is not so easy to see in each case precisely where the fallacy lies. I suggest that in all cases the fallacy has the general form suggested above: in order to solve the problem one (or perhaps more) of its constituent propositions is given up, but in such a way that it appears to have been retained, and can therefore be asserted without qualification in other contexts. Sometimes there is a further complication: the supposed solution moves to and fro between, say, two of the constituent propositions, at one point asserting the first of these but covertly abandoning the second, at another point asserting the second but covertly abandoning the first. These fallacious solutions often turn upon some equivocation with the words "good" and "evil," or upon some vagueness about the way in which good and evil are opposed to one another, or about how much is meant by "omnipotence." I propose to examine some of these so-called solutions, and to exhibit their fallacies in detail. Incidentally, I shall also be considering whether an adequate solution could be reached by a minor modification of one or more of the constituent propositions, which would, however, still satisfy all the essential requirements of ordinary theism.

1. "Good cannot exist without evil" or "Evil is necessary as a counterpart to good."

It is sometimes suggested that evil is necessary as a counterpart to good, that if there were no evil there could be no good either, and that this solves the problem of evil. It is true that it points to an answer to the question "Why should there be evil?" But it does so only by qualifying some of the propositions that constitute the problem.

First, it sets a limit to what God can do, saying that God *cannot* create good without simultaneously creating evil, and this means either that God is not omnipotent or that there are *some* limits to what an omnipotent thing can do. It may be replied that these limits are always presupposed, that omnipotence has never meant the power to do what is logically impossible, and on the present view the existence of good without evil would be a logical impossibility. [4] This interpretation of omnipotence may, indeed, be accepted as a modification of our original account which does not reject anything that is essential to theism, and I shall in general assume it in the subsequent discussion. It is, perhaps, the most common theistic view, but I think that some theists at least have maintained that God can do what is logically impossible. Many theists, at any rate, have held that logic itself is created or laid down by God, that logic is the way in which God arbitrarily chooses to think. (This is, of course, parallel to the ethical view that morally right actions are those which God arbitrarily chooses to command, and the two views encounter similar difficulties.) And *this* account of logic is clearly inconsistent with the view that God is bound by logical necessities—unless it is possible for an omnipotent being to bind himself, an issue which we shall consider later, when we come to the Paradox of Omnipotence. This solution of the problem of evil cannot, therefore, be consistently adopted along with the view that logic is itself created by God.

But, secondly, this solution denies that evil is opposed to good in our original sense. If good and evil are counterparts, a good thing will not "eliminate evil as far as it can." Indeed, this view suggests that good and evil are not strictly qualities of things at all. Perhaps the suggestion is that good and evil are related in much the same way as great and small. Certainly, when the term "great" is used relatively as a condensation of "greater than so-and-so," and "small" is used correspondingly, greatness and smallness are counterparts and cannot exist without each other. But in this sense greatness is not a quality, not an intrinsic feature of anything; and it would be absurd to think of a movement in favor of greatness and against smallness in this sense. Such a movement would be self-defeating, since relative greatness can be promoted only by a simultaneous promotion of relative smallness. I feel sure that no theists would be content to regard God's goodness as analogous to this—as if what he supports were not the *good* but the *better*, and as if he had the paradoxical aim that all things should be better than other things. [5]

This point is obscured by the fact that "great" and "small" seem to have an absolute as well as a relative sense. I cannot discuss here whether there is absolute magnitude or not, but if there is, there could be an absolute sense for "great," it could mean of at least a certain size, and it would make sense to speak of all things getting bigger, of a universe that was expanding all over, and therefore it would make sense to speak of promoting greatness. But in *this* sense great and small are not logically necessary counterparts: either quality could exist without the other. There would be no logical impossibility in everything's being small or in everything's being great. [6]

Neither in the absolute nor in the relative sense, then, of "great" and "small" do these terms provide an analogy of the sort that would be needed to support this solution of the problem of evil. In neither case are greatness and smallness *both* necessary counterparts *and* mutually opposed forces or possible objects for support and attack.

It may be replied that good and evil are necessary counterparts in the same way as any quality and its logical opposite: redness can occur, it is suggested, only if nonredness also occurs. But unless evil is merely the privation of good, they are not logical opposites, and some further argument would be needed to show that they are

STOP Think about this conception of (or limitation on) God's omnipotence. Should God also be able to do the logically impossible, or does that really make any sense? Can God create a round square? Can God make a contradiction true?

On this relative conception, evil things (that is, less good things) would have to exist—unless everything was equal in goodness. STOP Would that account in a plausible way for the actual evils that the world contains?

R If "good" and "evil" are understood in this second, absolute way, there is no apparent reason why the world must contain evil if it is to contain good.

counterparts in the same way as genuine logical opposites. Let us assume that this could be given. There is still doubt of the correctness of the metaphysical principle that a quality must have a real opposite: I suggest that it is not really impossible that everything should be, say, red, that the truth is merely that if everything were red we should not notice redness, and so we should have no word "red"; we observe and give names to qualities only if they have real opposites. If so, the principle that a term must have an opposite would belong only to our language or to our thought, and would not be an ontological principle, and, correspondingly, the rule that good cannot exist without evil would not state a logical necessity of a sort that God would just have to put up with. God might have made everything good, though *we* should not have noticed it if he had. (7)

But, finally, even if we concede that this *is* an ontological principle, it will provide a solution for the problem of evil only if one is prepared to say, "Evil exists, but only just enough evil to serve as the counterpart of good." I doubt whether any theist will accept this. After all, the *ontological* requirement that nonredness should occur would be satisfied even if all the universe, except for a minute speck, were red, and, if there were a corresponding requirement for evil as a counterpart to good, a minute dose of evil would presumably do. But theists are not usually willing to say, in all contexts, that all the evil that occurs is a minute and necessary dose. (8)

2. "Evil is necessary as a means to good."

It is sometimes suggested that evil is necessary for good not as a counterpart but as a means. In its simple form this has little plausibility as a solution of the problem of evil, since it obviously implies a severe restriction of God's power. It would be a *causal* law that you cannot have a certain end without a certain means, so that if God has to introduce evil as a means to good, he must be subject to at least some causal laws. This certainly conflicts with what a theist normally means by omnipotence. This view of God as limited by causal laws also conflicts with the view that causal laws are themselves made by God, which is more widely held than the corresponding view about the laws of logic. This conflict would, indeed, be resolved if it were possible for an omnipotent being to bind himself, and this possibility has still to be considered. Unless a favorable answer can be given to this question, the suggestion that evil is necessary as a means to good solves the problem of evil only by denying one of its constituent propositions, either that God is omnipotent or that "omnipotent" means what it says. (9)

3. "The universe is better with some evil in it than it could be if there were no evil."

Much more important is a solution which at first seems to be a mere variant of the previous one, that evil may contribute to the goodness of a whole in which it is found, so that the universe as a whole is better as it is, with some evil in it, than it would be if there were no evil. This solution may be developed in either of two ways. It may be supported by an aesthetic analogy, by the fact that contrasts heighten beauty, that in a musical work, for example, there may occur discords which somehow add to the beauty of the work as a whole. Alternatively, it may be worked out in connection with the notion of progress, that the best possible organization of the universe will not be static, but progressive, that the gradual overcoming of evil by good is really a finer thing than would be the eternal unchallenged supremacy of good. (10)

In either case, this solution usually starts from the assumption that the evil whose existence gives rise to the problem of evil is primarily what is called physical evil, that is to say, pain. In Hume's rather half-hearted presentation of the problem of evil, the evils that he stresses are pain and disease, and those who reply to him argue that the existence of pain and disease makes possible the existence of sympathy, benevolence, heroism, and the gradually successful struggle of doctors and reformers to overcome these evils. In fact, theists often seize the opportunity to accuse those who stress the problem of evil of taking a low, materialistic view of good and evil, equating these with pleasure and pain, and of ignoring the more spiritual goods which can arise in the struggle against evils.

But let us see exactly what is being done here. Let us call pain and misery "first order evil" or "evil (1)." What contrasts with this, namely, pleasure and happiness, will be called "first order good" or "good (1)." Distinct from this is "second order good" or "good (2)" which somehow emerges in a complex situation in which evil (1) is a necessary component—logically, not merely causally, necessary. (Exactly *how* it emerges does not matter: in the crudest version of this solution

STOP Is the fact that we would not otherwise have *noticed* good a compelling reason for God to permit evil? Is it a compelling reason for permitting the degree and quantity of evil that actually exists?

(An "ontological principle" is one that pertains to the existence of things, rather than to our language or concepts.)

Notice the somewhat paradoxical consequence that if all the evil that actually exists were really necessary for some good purpose, then human efforts to reduce it would in fact be making the world as a whole worse.

Implicit here is a plausible criterion of omnipotence: an omnipotent being is one that does not need *means* to his (or her or its) ends, but rather can simply produce them directly.

The suggestion is that something that is evil when taken by itself can contribute to a larger whole that is better than could exist without that evil—not because the evil is an essential means to the end of good, but because it is an essential constituent of the good state. Mackie proceeds to develop one version of this idea.

good (2) is simply the heightening of happiness by the contrast with misery, in other versions it includes sympathy with suffering, heroism in facing danger, and the gradual decrease of first order evil and increase of first order good.) It is also being assumed that second order good is more important than first order good or evil, in particular that it more than outweighs the first order evil it involves. (11)

(11) This last assumption is crucial: at least in general, the value of the second-order goods must outweigh the value of the corresponding first-order evils, or else the problem has not really been solved. Notice also Mackie's insistence that the evil must be *logically* necessary for the good, not just a means to it. Think about how this is so in the examples he gives.

Now this is a particularly subtle attempt to solve the problem of evil. It defends God's goodness and omnipotence on the ground that (on a sufficiently long view) this is the best of all logically possible worlds because it includes the important second order goods, and yet it admits that real evils, namely first order evils, exist. But does it still hold that good and evil are opposed? Not, clearly, in the sense that we set out originally: good does not tend to eliminate evil in general. Instead, we have a modified, a more complex pattern. First order good (e.g., happiness) *contrasts with* first order evil (e.g., misery): these two are opposed in a fairly mechanical way; some second order goods (e.g., benevolence) try to maximize first order good and minimize first order evil; but God's goodness is not this, it is rather the will to maximize *second* order good. We might, therefore, call God's goodness an example of a third order goodness, or good (3). While this account is different from our original one, it might well be held to be an improvement on it, to give a more accurate description of the way in which good is opposed to evil, and to be consistent with the essential theist position.

There might, however, be several objections to this solution.

First, some might argue that such qualities as benevolence—and *a fortiori* the third order goodness which promotes benevolence—have a merely derivative value, that they are not higher sorts of good, but merely means to good (1), that is, to happiness, so that it would be absurd for God to keep misery in existence in order to make possible the virtues of benevolence, heroism, etc. The theist who adopts the present solution must, of course, deny this, but he can do so with some plausibility, so I should not press this objection. (12)

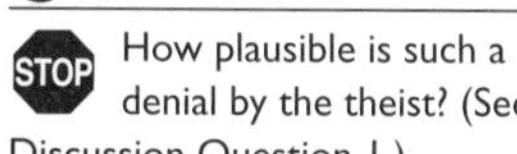

How plausible is such a denial by the theist? (See Discussion Question 1.)

Secondly, it follows from this solution that God is not in our sense benevolent or sympathetic: he is not concerned to minimize evil (1), but only to promote good (2); and this might be a disturbing conclusion for some theists.

But, thirdly, the fatal objection is this. Our analysis shows clearly the possibility of the existence of a *second* order evil, an evil (2) contrasting with good (2) as evil (1) contrasts with good (1). This would include malevolence, cruelty, callousness, cowardice, and states in which good (1) is decreasing and evil (1) increasing. And just as good (2) is held to be the important kind of good, the kind that God is concerned to promote, so evil (2) will, by analogy, be the important kind of evil, the kind which God, if he were wholly good and omnipotent, would eliminate. And yet evil (2) plainly exists, and indeed most theists (in other contexts) stress its existence more than that of evil (1). We should, therefore, state the problem of evil in terms of second order evil, and against this form of the problem the present solution is useless. (13)

STOP Think about why this is supposed to be so. Can you think of any way the theist might reply?

An attempt might be made to use this solution again, at a higher level, to explain the occurrence of evil (2): indeed the next main solution that we shall examine does just this, with the help of some new notions. Without any fresh notions, such a solution would have little plausibility: for example, we could hardly say that the really important good was a good (3), such as the increase of benevolence in proportion to cruelty, which logically required for its occurrence the occurrence of some second order evil. But even if evil (2) could be explained in this way, it is fairly clear that there would be third order evils contrasting with this third order good: and we should be well on the way to an infinite regress, where the solution of a problem of evil, stated in terms of evil (n), indicated the existence of an evil ($n + 1$), and a further problem to be solved. (14)

An *infinite regress* is a situation in which a certain kind of solution to a problem at one level creates a parallel, unsolved problem at a further level—so that if the further problem is solved in the same way, a still further unsolved problem is generated, and so on. This makes it impossible to solve all of the problems of the sort in question via a solution of that kind.

4. "Evil is due to human free will."

Perhaps the most important proposed solution of the problem of evil is that evil is not to be ascribed to God at all, but to the independent actions of human beings, supposed to have been endowed by God with freedom of the will. This solution may be combined with the preceding one: first order evil (e.g., pain) may be justified as a logically necessary component in second order good (e.g., sympathy) while second order evil (e.g., cruelty) is not *justified*, but is so ascribed to human beings that God cannot be held responsible for it. This combination evades my third criticism of the preceding solution. (15)

The free will solution also involves the preceding solution at a higher level. To explain why a wholly good God gave men free will although it would lead to some important evils, it must be argued that it is better on the whole that men should act freely, and sometimes err, than that they should be innocent automata, acting rightly in a wholly determined way. Freedom, that is to say, is now treated as a third order good, and as being more valuable than second order goods (such as sympathy and heroism) would be if they were deterministically produced, and it is being assumed that second order evils, such as cruelty, are logically necessary accompaniments of freedom, just as pain is a logically necessary pre-condition of sympathy. (16)

I think that this solution is unsatisfactory primarily because of the incoherence of the notion of freedom of the will: (17) but I cannot discuss this topic adequately here, although some of my criticisms will touch upon it.

First I should query the assumption that second order evils are logically necessary accompaniments of freedom. I should ask this: if God has made men such that in their free choices they sometimes prefer what is good and sometimes what is evil, why could he not have made men such that they always freely choose the good? If there is no logical impossibility in a man's freely choosing the good on one, or on several occasions, there cannot be a logical impossibility in his freely choosing the good on every occasion. God was not, then, faced with a choice between making innocent automata and making beings who, in acting freely, would sometimes go wrong: there was open to him the obviously better possibility of making beings who would act freely but always go right. (18) Clearly, his failure to avail himself of this possibility is inconsistent with his being both omnipotent and wholly good.

If it is replied that this objection is absurd, that the making of some wrong choices is logically necessary for freedom, it would seem that "freedom" must here mean complete randomness or indeterminacy, including randomness with regard to the alternatives good and evil, in other words that men's choices and consequent actions can be "free" only if they are not determined by their characters. Only on this assumption can God escape the responsibility for men's actions; for if he made them as they are, but did not determine their wrong choices, this can only be because the wrong choices are not determined by men as they are. But then if freedom is randomness, how can it be a characteristic of *will*? And, still more, how can it be the most important good? What value or merit would there be in free choices if these were random actions which were not determined by the nature of the agent? (19)

I conclude that to make this solution plausible two different senses of "freedom" must be confused, one sense which will justify the view that freedom is a third order good, more valuable than other goods would be without it, and another sense, sheer randomness, to prevent us from ascribing to God a decision to make men such that they sometimes go wrong when he might have made them such that they would always freely go right.

This criticism is sufficient to dispose of this solution. But besides this there is a fundamental difficulty in the notion of an omnipotent God creating men with free will, for if men's wills are really free this must mean that even God cannot control them, that is, that God is no longer omnipotent. (20) It may be objected that God's gift of freedom to men does not mean that he *cannot* control their wills, but that he always *refrains* from controlling their wills. But why, we may ask, should God refrain from controlling evil wills? Why should he not leave men free to will rightly, but intervene when he sees them beginning to will wrongly? If God could do this, but does not, and if he is wholly good, the only explanation could be that even a wrong free act of will is not really evil, that its freedom is a value which outweighs its wrongness, so that there would be a loss of value if God took away the wrongness and the freedom together. (21) But this is utterly opposed to what theists say about sin in other contexts. The present solution of the problem of evil, then, can be maintained only in the form that God has made men so free that he *cannot* control their wills.

...

R Thus the suggestion is that natural evil is explained by appeal to the second-order goods of which it is an essential component, and moral evil is explained by appeal to human free will.

STOP The claim has to be that a world containing free will and the moral evil (and also moral good) that it makes possible is better than one that contains none of these things. Does this seem plausible?

See Chapter 4 for more discussion of the problem of free will.

STOP Could God really do this? Could he create beings who always do the right thing while leaving them genuinely *free*?

One issue about free will (see Chapter 4) is whether it is only having one's actions causally determined by one's own choices—(the *compatibilist* view) or whether free will is incompatible with any sort of causal determination (the *libertarian* view). Mackie raises a standard objection to libertarianism: that if actions (or choices) are not determined, then they must be simply *random* (so that either the libertarian is wrong about what freedom requires or else freedom has no real value). On a compatibilist view of free will, God could apparently bring it about that people always do the right thing by controlling their choices, while still leaving them free.

For God to ever be unable to control human action is obviously incompatible with his omnipotence.

R The proponent of the free will **theodicy** will apparently have to say that any intervention by God, any restriction on human free will, would make the world worse.

Conclusion

Of the proposed solutions of the problem of evil which we have examined, none has stood up to criticism. There may be other solutions which require examination, but this study strongly suggests that there is no valid solution of the problem which does not modify at least one of the constituent propositions in a way which would seriously affect the essential core of the theistic position.

...

Discussion Questions

1. Are things like benevolence, heroism, compassion, and so on, **intrinsically good** (so that the world is better for containing them along with the evils to which they are a response), or are they only **instrumentally good** (because the world happens in fact to contain those evils, though things would be better if neither the evils nor the corresponding second-order qualities existed)? If people were too successful at eradicating evils of various sorts (diseases, natural disasters, etc.), would it be preferable to reintroduce them so as not to lose the second-order goods?
2. One question about the free will theodicy is why God doesn't intervene, perhaps only very selectively, to prevent at least the most extreme sorts of evil actions from occurring: such actions as the murder of six million Jews during World War II. Perhaps God might have influenced Hitler in such a way that he ordered the Jews to be deported rather than murdered. If free will does indeed have significant positive value, this would involve some cost: the loss of a bit of Hitler's freedom plus a qualification on God's "gift of freedom" generally. But the gain would be a saving of many lives and the elimination of a lot of suffering—plus lots of free choices by those whose lives were saved. Is it at all plausible that the overall result of such a divine intervention would have made the world worse? Is there any other response that the theist can make to this point?

John Hick

John Hick (1922–) is an English philosopher and theologian who has taught at Cornell University, Princeton Theological Seminary, the Claremont Graduate School, and the University of Birmingham (England). He is a major contributor to contemporary philosophy of religion. In this selection, Hick offers two main responses to the problem of evil: the *free will theodicy* (as a solution to the problem of moral evil) and what might be described as the *soul-making theodicy* (as a solution to the problem of natural evil, which he refers to as the problem of suffering).

The Problem of Evil, from *Philosophy of Religion*

To many, the most powerful positive objection to belief in God is the fact of evil. Probably for most agnostics it is the appalling depth and extent of human suffering, more than anything else, that makes the idea of a loving Creator seem so implausible and disposes them toward one or another of the various naturalistic theories of religion.

As a challenge to theism, the problem of evil has traditionally been posed in the form of a dilemma: if God is perfectly loving, he must wish to abolish evil; and if he is all-powerful, he must be able to abolish evil. But evil exists; therefore God cannot be both omnipotent and perfectly loving.

Certain solutions, which at once suggest themselves, have to be ruled out so far as the Judaic-Christian faith is concerned.

To say, for example (with contemporary Christian Science), that evil is an illusion of the

---

From John Hick, *Philosophy of Religion,* 2nd ed. (Englewood Cliffs, N.J.: Prentice-Hall, 1973).

human mind, is impossible within a religion based upon the stark realism of the Bible. Its pages faithfully reflect the characteristic mixture of good and evil in human experience. They record every kind of sorrow and suffering, every mode of man's inhumanity to man and of his painfully insecure existence in the world. There is no attempt to regard evil as anything but dark, menacingly ugly, heart-rending, and crushing. In the Christian scriptures, the climax of this history of evil is the crucifixion of Jesus, which is presented not only as a case of utterly unjust suffering, but as the violent and murderous rejection of God's Messiah. There can be no doubt, then, that for biblical faith evil is unambiguously evil and stands in direct opposition to God's will.

Again, to solve the problem of evil by means of the theory . . . of a finite deity who does the best he can with a material, intractable, and coeternal with himself, is to have abandoned that basic premise of Hebrew-Christian monotheism; for the theory amounts to rejecting belief in the infinity and sovereignty of God.

Indeed, any theory that would avoid the problem of the origin of evil by depicting it as an ultimate constituent of the universe, co-ordinate with good, has been repudiated in advance by the classic Christian teaching, first developed by Augustine, that evil represents the going wrong of something that in itself is good. Augustine holds firmly to the Hebrew-Christian conviction that the universe is *good*—that is to say, it is the creation of a good God for a good purpose. He completely rejects the ancient prejudice that matter is evil. There is, according to Augustine, higher and lower, greater and lesser goods in immense abundance and variety; but everything that has being is good in its own way and degree, except in so far as it may have become spoiled or corrupted. Evil—whether it be an evil will, an instance of pain, or some disorder or decay in nature—has not been set there by God, but represents the distortion of something that is inherently valuable. Whatever exists is, as such, and in its proper place, good; evil is essentially parasitic upon good, being disorder and perversion in a fundamentally good creation. This understanding of evil as something negative means that it is not willed and created by God; but it does not mean (as some have supposed) that evil is unreal and can be disregarded. On the contrary, the first effect of this doctrine is to accentuate even more the question of the origin of evil. 1

Even if God does not will or create evil, the question is why he (or she or it) permits evil to exist.

Theodicy, as many modern Christian thinkers see it, is a modest enterprise, negative rather than positive in its conclusions. It does not claim to explain, nor to explain away, every instance of evil in human experience, but only to point to certain considerations that prevent the fact of evil (largely incomprehensible though it remains) from constituting a final and insuperable bar to rational belief in God. 2

Hick uses the term "theodicy" to refer to the intellectual task of solving or at least reducing the force of the problem of evil. (To achieve even the relatively modest goal that he specifies, the contradiction that Mackie alleged to exist would have to be avoided.)

In indicating these considerations it will be useful to follow the traditional division of the subject. There is the problem of *moral evil* or wickedness: why does an all-good and all-powerful God permit this? And there is the problem of the *nonmoral evil* of suffering or pain, both physical and mental: why has an all-good and all-powerful God created a world in which this occurs?

Christian thought has always considered moral evil in its relation to human freedom and responsibility. To be a person is to be a finite center of freedom, a (relatively) free and self-directing agent responsible for one's own decisions. This involves being free to act wrongly as well as to act rightly. The idea of a person who can be infallibly guaranteed always to act rightly is self-contradictory. There can be no certainty in advance that a genuinely free moral agent will never choose amiss. Consequently, the possibility of wrongdoing or sin is logically inseparable from the creation of finite persons, and to say that God should not have created beings who might sin amounts to saying that he should not have created people.

This thesis has been challenged in some recent philosophical discussions of the problem of evil, in which it is claimed that no contradiction is involved in saying that God might have made people who would be genuinely free but who could at the same time be guaranteed always to act rightly. A quote from one of these discussions follows:

> If there is no logical impossibility in a man's freely choosing the good on one, or on several occasions, there cannot be a logical impossibility in his freely choosing the good on every occasion. God was not, then, faced with a choice between making innocent automata and making beings who, in acting freely, would sometimes go wrong: there

> was open to him the obviously better possibility of making beings who would act freely but always go right. Clearly, his failure to avail himself of this possibility is inconsistent with his being both omnipotent and wholly good.*

A reply to this argument is indirectly suggested in another recent contribution to the discussion. If by a free action we mean an action that is not externally compelled but that flows from the nature of the agent as he reacts to the circumstances in which he finds himself, there is indeed no contradiction between our being free and our actions being "caused" (by our own nature) and therefore being in principle predictable. ❸ There is a contradiction, however, in saying that God is the cause of our acting as we do but that we are free beings *in relation to God*. There is, in other words, a contradiction in saying that God has made us so that we shall of necessity act in a certain way, and that we are genuinely independent persons in relation to him. If all our thoughts and actions are divinely predestined, however free and morally responsible we may seem to be to ourselves, we cannot be free and morally responsible in the sight of God, but must instead be his helpless puppets. Such "freedom" is like that of a patient acting out a series of posthypnotic suggestions: he appears, even to himself, to be free, but his volitions have actually been predetermined by another will, that of the hypnotist, in relation to whom the patient is not a free agent. ❹

A different objector might raise the question of whether or not we deny God's omnipotence if we admit that he is unable to create persons who are free from the risks inherent in personal freedom. The answer that has always been given is that to create such beings is logically impossible. It is no limitation upon God's power that he cannot accomplish the logically impossible, since there is nothing here to accomplish, but only a meaningless conjunction of words—in this case "person who is not a person." God is able to create beings of any and every conceivable kind; but creatures who lack moral freedom, however superior they might be to human beings in other respects, would not be what we mean by persons. They would constitute a different form of life that God might have brought into existence instead of persons. When we ask why God did not create such beings in place of persons the traditional answer is that only persons could, in any meaningful sense, become "children of God," capable of entering into a personal relationship with their Creator by a free and uncompelled response to his love. ❺

When we turn from the possibility of moral evil as a correlate of man's personal freedom to its actuality, we face something that must remain inexplicable even when it can be seen to be possible. For we can never provide a complete causal explanation of a free act; if we could, it would not be a free act. The origin of moral evil lies forever concealed within the mystery of human freedom.

The necessary connection between moral freedom and the possibility, now actualized, of sin throws light upon a great deal of the suffering that afflicts mankind. For an enormous amount of human pain arises either from the inhumanity or the culpable incompetence of mankind. This includes such major scourges as poverty, oppression and persecution, war, and all the injustice, indignity, and inequity that occur even in the most advanced societies. These evils are manifestations of human sin. Even disease is fostered to an extent, the limits of which have not yet been determined by psychosomatic medicine, by emotional and moral factors seated both in the individual and in his social environment. To the extent that all of these evils stem from human failures and wrong decisions, their possibility is inherent in the creation of free persons inhabiting a world that presents them with real choices followed by real consequences.

We may now turn more directly to the problem of suffering. Even though the major bulk of actual human pain is traceable to man's misused freedom as a sole or part cause, there remain other sources of pain that are entirely independent of the human will, for example, earthquake, hurricane, storm, flood, drought, and blight. ❻ In practice, it is often impossible to trace a boundary between the suffering that results from human wickedness and folly and that which falls upon mankind from without; both kinds of suffering are inextricably mingled together in human experience. For our present purpose, however, it is important to note that the

❸

 This would be a *compatibilist* conception of freedom. See Annotation 19 to the previous selection and Chapter 4.

❹

R Hick responds that a person's being shaped by God so as to act in specific ways would not be genuine freedom, even if the person's actions were still caused by his (or her) nature. (He is thus rejecting a compatibilist conception of free will in favor of a *libertarian* conception. See again Annotation 19 to the previous selection and Chapter 4.)

❺

 Here the claim has to be that the value of having genuine persons with free will as Hick understands it is greater than that of having person-like beings who lack freedom, even allowing for the negative value of the evil that results. (And also better than having a freedom that is limited by occasional divine interventions—see Discussion Question 2 to the Mackie selection.)

❻

 What Hick refers to as "the problem of suffering" is thus essentially the same as the problem of *natural* (or physical) evil.

*J. L. Mackie, "Evil and Omnipotence," [See p. 575 of this book].

latter category does exist and that it seems to be built into the very structure of our world. In response to it, theodicy, if it is wisely conducted, follows a negative path. It is not possible to show positively that each item of human pain serves a divine purpose of good; but, on the other hand, it does seem possible to show that the divine purpose as it is understood in Judaism and Christianity could not be forwarded in a world that was designed as a permanent hedonistic paradise.

An essential premise of this argument concerns the nature of the divine purpose in creating the world. The sceptic's assumption is that man is to be viewed as a completed creation and that God's purpose in making the world was to provide a suitable dwelling-place for this fully formed creature. Since God is good and loving, the environment that he has created for human life to inhabit will naturally be as pleasant and comfortable as possible. The problem is essentially similar to that of a man who builds a cage for some pet animal. Since our world, in fact, contains sources of hardship, inconvenience, and danger of innumerable kinds, the conclusion follows that this world cannot have been created by a perfectly benevolent and all-powerful deity.

Christianity, however, has never supposed that God's purpose in the creation of the world was to construct a paradise whose inhabitants would experience a maximum of pleasure and a minimum of pain. The world is seen, instead, as a place of "soul making" or person making in which free beings, grappling with the tasks and challenges of their existence in a common environment, may become "children of God" and "heirs of eternal life." A way of thinking theologically of God's continuing creative purpose for man was suggested by some of the early Hellenistic Fathers of the Christian Church, especially Irenaeus. Following hints from Saint Paul, Irenaeus taught that man has been made as a person in the image of God but has not yet been brought as a free and responsible agent into the finite likeness of God, which is revealed in Christ. Our world, with all its rough edges, is the sphere in which this second and harder stage of the creative process is taking place. (7)

This conception of the world (whether or not set in Irenaeus's theological framework) can be supported by the method of negative theodicy. Suppose, contrary to fact, that this world were a paradise from which all possibility of pain and suffering were excluded. The consequences would be very far-reaching. For example, no one could ever injure anyone else: the murderer's knife would turn to paper or his bullets to thin air; the bank safe, robbed of a million dollars, would miraculously become filled with another million dollars (without this device, on however large a scale, proving inflationary); fraud, deceit, conspiracy, and treason would somehow always leave the fabric of society undamaged. Again, no one would ever be injured by accident: the mountain climber, steeplejack, or playing child falling from a height would float unharmed to the ground; the reckless driver would never meet with disaster. There would be no need to work, since no harm could result from avoiding work; there would be no call to be concerned for others in time of need or danger, for in such a world there could be no real needs or dangers.

To make possible this continual series of individual adjustments, nature would have to work by "special providences" instead of running according to general laws that men must learn to respect on penalty of pain or death. The laws of nature would have to be extremely flexible: sometimes gravity would operate, sometimes not; sometimes an object would be hard and solid, sometimes soft. There could be no sciences, for there would be no enduring world structure to investigate. In eliminating the problems and hardships of an objective environment, with its own laws, life would become like a dream in which, delightfully but aimlessly, we would float and drift at ease. (8)

One can at least begin to imagine such a world. It is evident that our present ethical concepts would have no meaning in it. If, for example, the notion of harming someone is an essential element in the concept of a wrong action, in our hedonistic paradise there could be no wrong actions—nor any right actions in distinction from wrong. Courage and fortitude would have no point in an environment in which there is, by definition, no danger or difficulty. Generosity, kindness, the *agape* aspect of love, prudence, unselfishness, and all other ethical notions which presuppose life in an objective environment could not even be formed. Consequently, such a world, however well it might promote pleasure, would be very ill adapted for the

(7)

Since God is supposedly omnipotent, it cannot be that he needs the hardships of the world as a *means* for "making souls" (see the discussion in Mackie). Thus the claim has to be that the process of making souls in this way is itself valuable enough to outweigh the cost.

(8)

Obviously there are intermediate alternatives between this one and the actual world, possible worlds with some hazards but fewer or less extreme ones. A complete defense of the soul-making theodicy will have to claim that all of these alternative worlds are also unsatisfactory for the purpose of soul making.

development of the moral qualities of human personality. In relation to this purpose it might be the worst of all possible worlds!

It would seem, then, that an environment intended to make possible the growth in free beings of the finest characteristics of personal life must have a good deal in common with our present world. It must operate according to general and dependable laws; and it must involve real dangers, difficulties, problems, obstacles, and possibilities of pain, failure, sorrow, frustration, and defeat. If it did not contain the particular trials and perils that—subtracting man's own very considerable contribution—our world contains, it would have to contain others instead.

To realize this is not, by any means, to be in possession of a detailed theodicy. It is to understand that this world, with all its "heartaches and the thousand natural shocks that flesh is heir to," an environment so manifestly not designed for the maximization of human pleasure and the minimization of human pain, may nevertheless be rather well adapted to the quite different purpose of "soul making." 9

9

STOP How much like our actual world would such a world have to be? (See Discussion Question 1.)

These considerations are related to theism as such. Specifically Christian theism goes further in the light of the death of Christ, which is seen paradoxically both (as the murder of the divine Son) as the worst thing that has ever happened and (as the occasion of man's salvation) as the best thing that has ever happened. As the supreme evil turned to supreme good, it provides the paradigm for the distinctively Christian reaction to evil. Viewed from the standpoint of Christian faith, evils do not cease to be evils; and certainly, in view of Christ's healing work, they cannot be said to have been sent by God. Yet, it has been the persistent claim of those seriously and wholeheartedly committed to Christian discipleship that tragedy, though truly tragic, may nevertheless be turned, through a man's reaction to it, from a cause of despair and alienation from God to a stage in the fulfillment of God's loving purpose for that individual. As the greatest of all evils, the crucifixion of Christ was made the occasion of man's redemption, so good can be won from other evils. As Jesus saw his execution by the Romans as an experience which God desired him to accept, an experience which was to be brought within the sphere of the divine purpose and made to serve the divine ends, so the Christian response to calamity is to accept the adversities, pains, and afflictions which life brings, in order that they can be turned to a positive spiritual use.

At this point, theodicy points forward in two ways to the subject of life after death. . . .

First, although there are many striking instances of good being triumphantly brought out of evil through a man's or a woman's reaction to it, there are many other cases in which the opposite has happened. Sometimes obstacles breed strength of character, dangers evoke courage and unselfishness, and calamities produce patience and moral steadfastness. But sometimes they lead, instead, to resentment, fear, grasping selfishness, and disintegration of character. Therefore, it would seem that any divine purpose of soul making that is at work in earthly history must continue beyond this life if it is ever to achieve more than a very partial and fragmentary success.

Second, if we ask whether the business of soul making is worth all the toil and sorrow of human life, the Christian answer must be in terms of a future good great enough to justify all that has happened on the way to it. 10

10

Hick seems perhaps to be conceding here that the soul making would not have enough value to outweigh the cost without an afterlife that the developed souls will eventually experience. But then the soul-making theodicy does not work without some *independent* reason for thinking that such an afterlife exists.

Discussion Questions

1. How plausible is it that a world created for the purpose of soul making would contain the specific kinds and degrees of natural evil that are to be found in the actual world? In thinking about this question, it may help to consider an analogy: Suppose that you are developing an environment for the purpose of building the character of children—and that you also care strongly about the well-being of those children. What sorts of obstacles and challenges would you put into the designed environment, and what sorts would you exclude?

2. Suppose that we grant that (contrary to Mackie's claim) God could not give people free will and still control their choices so that they always do the right thing. Suppose that it is also granted that unlimited free will is so great a value that God would be wrong to engage in even very occasional intervention. A question that remains is whether free will must bring with it the possibility of choices as horrendous as, for example, Adolf Hitler's decision to order the murder of six million Jews in the Holocaust. Is any person who has free will automatically capable of doing things as evil as that? Or is there still a limit in at least many normal free people as to how much evil they are capable of? If the latter of these possibilities is the case, why didn't God make all people good enough that at least really extreme evils would be ruled out?

Must We Have Reasons to Believe in God?

Walter Kaufmann

Walter Kaufmann (1921–1980) taught philosophy at Princeton University. He is best known for his discussions and translations of Friedrich Nietzsche (a nineteenth-century German philosopher and poet) and his work in the philosophy of religion. This selection discusses a version of Pascal's argument that belief in God is the best wager in a situation of uncertainty. As Kaufmann notes, his version is more complete and explicit than Pascal's own.

Pascal's Wager, from *Critique of Religion and Philosophy*

Pascal, mathematician, physicist, polemicist, and mystic, sewed into the lining of his coat a piece of parchment dating from the day of his great mystical experience, to remind himself that the God of Abraham, Isaac, and Jacob is not the God of the philosophers and theologians. He saw the weaknesses of the old proofs of God's existence and had some intimations that faith is related somehow to commitment. His attempt to spell out this commitment in his posthumously published *Pensées* is, however, weirder still than any of the proofs of the philosophers and theologians.

"Either God exists, or he does not exist," argues Pascal; and neither proposition can be proved. So we must wager: this strange word is Pascal's own; and with a desperate concern, he proceeds to figure out the odds. If we wager that God exists and we are right, we win everything; if we are wrong we lose nothing. If you passed this up, "you would be imprudent." What more could you ask?

Pascal stops with these two possibilities; but we might as well complete the picture and spell out all four possibilities.

	God Does Exist	**God Does Not Exist**
We wager, God exists:	We win everything; we hit the jackpot; up we go.	We lose nothing.
We wager, He does not:	We lose everything; we have had it; down we go.	We win nothing.

Clearly, this is the opportunity of a lifetime. Anybody who is not out of his mind will bet that God exists. This looks much better than the proofs of Anselm and Aquinas. Or has Pascal, too, overlooked something?

The first objection of which people usually think is ill advised. They say that we cannot induce belief merely by representing to ourselves the great advantage of belief.  But it is Pascal's *logic* that is at fault, not his psychology.

"Follow the way by which they began; by acting as if they believe, taking the holy water, having masses said, etc. Even this will naturally make you believe, and deaden your acuteness." Pascal's psychology is corroborated by millions of examples in totalitarian countries: once people realize the dreadful risks of nonbelief and the rewards for the

From Walter Kaufmann, *Critique of Religion and Philosophy* (New York: Harper, 1958).

1 R The point of the objection is that a person cannot just *choose* to believe something—because belief is not within voluntary control.

acceptance of beliefs, it takes most men at most a few years to believe quite firmly. First, one makes believe that one believes, and soon one does believe.

That is the origin of most religious faith: the child begins by acting like the grownups who believe, and soon believes himself. The proofs come later, if at all. *Religious belief generally starts as make-believe.*

What Pascal overlooked was the hair-raising possibility that God might out-Luther Luther. A special area in hell might be reserved for those who go to mass. Or God might punish those whose faith is prompted by prudence. Perhaps God prefers the abstinent to those who whore around with some denomination he despises. Perhaps he reserves special rewards for those who deny themselves the comfort of belief. Perhaps the intellectual ascetic will win all while those who compromised their intellectual integrity lose everything. 2

2 The general point in this and the following paragraph is that there are many, probably indefinitely many, possible gods or god-like beings. Thus that a full assessment of the wager would have to take account of the results if any of these should turn out to exist instead of only those that would be produced by the very specific sort of God that Pascal has in mind.

There are many other possibilities. There might be many gods, including one who favors people like Pascal; but the other gods might overpower or outvote him, à la Homer. Nietzsche might well have applied to Pascal his cutting remark about Kant: when he wagered on God, the great mathematician "became an idiot."

Even an astounding competence in mathematics provides no safeguard against pathetic pitfalls when it comes to arguments about religion. . . .

Discussion Questions

1. As Kaufmann reports (see Annotation 1), one objection often made to Pascal is that we cannot just choose to believe something because it would be advantageous to do so—where the underlying reason is that belief is not within our voluntary control. Do you think it is possible to simply adopt a belief because for some reason you want to have it or think that it would be good to do so? (Think of some examples.) Now consider Kaufmann's response in the following paragraph. Is he right that belief can be arrived at in the way he suggests? Does this show that belief is voluntary after all?
2. In Kaufmann's version (which follows Pascal), the value of the possibility where a person believes (and acts accordingly), but God does not exist, is said to be that nothing is lost. Is this the right assessment? Or are there significant losses or gains in this situation as well? Does this make any difference to the overall argument?
3. Pascal clearly has in mind more or less the standard conception of God, as discussed in the introduction to this chapter. Do you think he is right about how a God of that sort would respond to one who believed in him (or her or it) on prudential grounds of this sort? Is the result as clear as Pascal thinks even if other possible gods and god-like beings are, for some reason, not considered?
4. If all other possible gods and god-like beings are brought into the picture, the matrix of possible choices and results becomes vastly more complicated, with many different possibilities for belief and many different possible results. Does any definite choice of belief or nonbelief emerge as rationally preferred? Why or why not?

William James

William James (1842–1910) was an American philosopher and psychologist, who taught at Harvard. He was one of the founders of the pragmatist movement in philosophy, and made important contributions to epistemology, metaphysics, and the philosophy of religion. A characteristic Jamesian view is that truth is to be measured by practical success ("the truth is what works"). In this selection, James argues for the rational permissibility of religious belief based on voluntary commitment or faith rather than evidence.

The Will to Believe

In the recently published Life by Leslie Stephen of his brother, Fitz-James, there is an account of a school to which the latter went when he was a boy. The teacher, a certain Mr. Guest, used to converse with his pupils in this wise: "Gurney, what is the difference between justification and sanctification?—Stephen, prove the omnipotence of God!" etc. In the midst of our Harvard freethinking and indifference we are prone to imagine that here at your good old orthodox College conversation continues to be somewhat upon this order; and to show you that we at Harvard have not lost all interest in these vital subjects, I have brought with me to-night something like a sermon on justification by faith to read to you—I mean an essay in justification *of* faith, a defence of our right to adopt a believing attitude in religious matters, in spite of the fact that our merely logical intellect may not have been coerced. "The Will to Believe," accordingly, is the title of my paper.

I have long defended to my own students the lawfulness of voluntarily adopted faith; but as soon as they have got well imbued with the logical spirit, they have as a rule refused to admit my contention to be lawful philosophically, ❶ even though in point of fact they were personally all the time chock-full of some faith or other themselves. I am all the while, however, so profoundly convinced that my own position is correct, that your invitation has seemed to me a good occasion to make my statements more clear. Perhaps your minds will be more open than those with which I have hitherto had to deal. I will be as little technical as I can, though I must begin by setting up some technical distinctions that will help us in the end.

I

Let us give the name of *hypothesis* to anything that may be proposed to our belief; and just as the electricians speak of live and dead wires, let us speak of any hypothesis as either *live* or *dead*. A live hypothesis is one which appeals as a real possibility to him to whom it is proposed. If I ask you to believe in the Mahdi, the notion makes no electric connection with your nature—it refuses to scintillate with any credibility at all. As an hypothesis it is completely dead. ❷ To an Arab, however (even if he be not one of the Mahdi's followers), the hypothesis is among the mind's possibilities: it is alive. This shows that deadness and liveness in an hypothesis are not intrinsic properties, but relations to the individual thinker. They are measured by his willingness to act. The maximum of liveness in an hypothesis means willingness to act irrevocably. Practically, that means belief; but there is some believing tendency wherever there is willingness to act at all.

Next, let us call the decision between two hypotheses an *option*. Options may be of several kinds. They may be—1, *living* or *dead*; 2, *forced* or *avoidable*; 3, *momentous* or *trivial*; and for our purposes we may call an option a *genuine* option when it is of the forced, living, and momentous kind.

1. A living option is one in which both hypotheses are live ones. If I say to you: "Be a theosophist or be a Mohammedan," it is probably a dead option, because for you neither hypothesis is likely to be alive. But if I say: "Be an agnostic or be a Christian," it is otherwise: trained as you are, each hypothesis makes some appeal, however small, to your belief.
2. Next, if I say to you: "Choose between going out with your umbrella or without it," I do not offer you a genuine option, for it is not forced. You can easily avoid it by not going out at all. Similarly, if I say, "Either love me or hate me," "Either call my theory true or call it false," your option is avoidable. You may remain indifferent to me, neither loving nor hating, and you may decline to offer any judgment as to my theory. But if I say, "Either accept this truth or go without it," I put on you a forced option, for there is no standing place outside of the alternative. Every dilemma based on a complete logical disjunction, with no possibility of not choosing, is an option of this forced kind. ❸
3. Finally, if I were Dr. Nansen and proposed to you to join my North Pole expedition, your option would be momentous; for this would

From an address to the Philosophical Clubs of Yale and Brown Universities (first published in 1896).

❶

By "lawful philosophically," James seems to mean that voluntarily adopted faith is rationally permissible or acceptable. (As he makes clear later, he does not think it is always mandatory.)

❷

The Mahdi was a Sudanese religious and military leader in the latter part of the nineteenth century who claimed to be the successor of Mohammed.

By "willingness to act" in the following passage, James means willingness to act as though the hypothesis were true.

❸

It seems to follow that *any* claim can be made to present a "forced option," simply by contrasting it with its logical contradictory.

probably be your only similar opportunity, and your choice now would either exclude you from the North Pole sort of immortality altogether or put at least the chance of it into your hands. He who refuses to embrace a unique opportunity loses the prize as surely as if he tried and failed. *Per contra*, the option is trivial when the opportunity is not unique, when the stake is insignificant, or when the decision is reversible if it later prove unwise. Such trivial options abound in the scientific life. A chemist finds an hypothesis live enough to spend a year in its verification: he believes in it to that extent. But if his experiments prove inconclusive either way, he is quit for his loss of time, no vital harm being done.

It will facilitate our discussion if we keep all these distinctions well in mind.

II

The next matter to consider is the actual psychology of human opinion. When we look at certain facts, it seems as if our passional and volitional nature lay at the root of all our convictions. When we look at others, it seems as if they could do nothing when the intellect had once said its say. Let us take the latter facts up first.

Does it not seem preposterous on the very face of it to talk of our opinions being modifiable at will? Can our will either help or hinder our intellect in its perceptions of truth? **4** Can we, by just willing it, believe that Abraham Lincoln's existence is a myth, and that the portraits of him in McClure's Magazine are all of some one else? Can we, by any effort of our will, or by any strength of wish that it were true, believe ourselves well and about when we are roaring with rheumatism in bed, or feel certain that the sum of the two one-dollar bills in our pocket must be a hundred dollars? We can say any of these things, but we are absolutely impotent to believe them; and of just such things is the whole fabric of the truths that we do believe in made up—matters of fact, immediate or remote, as Hume said, and relations between ideas, which are either there or not there for us if we see them so, and which if not there cannot be put there by any action of our own.

4

R One possible objection to James's view, as to Pascal's wager, is that genuine belief is not voluntary. James agrees that a person can't voluntarily believe just anything, as these examples show.

In Pascal's *Thoughts* there is a celebrated passage known in literature as Pascal's wager. **5** In it he tries to force us into Christianity by reasoning as if our concern with truth resembled our concern with the stakes in a game of chance. Translated freely his words are these: You must either believe or not believe that God is—which will you do? Your human reason cannot say. A game is going on between you and the nature of things which at the day of judgment will bring out either heads or tails. Weigh what your gains and your losses would be if you should stake all you have on heads, or God's existence: if you win in such case, you gain eternal beatitude; if you lose, you lose nothing at all. If there were an infinity of chances, and only one for God in this wager, still you ought to stake your all on God; for though you surely risk a finite loss by this procedure, any finite loss is reasonable, even a certain one is reasonable, if there is but the possibility of infinite gain. Go, then, and take holy water, and have masses said; belief will come and stupefy your scruples. . . . Why should you not? At bottom, what have you to lose?

5

See the previous selection, by Kaufmann, for a discussion of Pascal's wager.

You probably feel that when religious faith expresses itself thus, in the language of the gaming-table, it is put to its last trumps. Surely Pascal's own personal belief in masses and holy water had far other springs; and this celebrated page of his is but an argument for others, a last desperate snatch at a weapon against the hardness of the unbelieving heart. We feel that a faith in masses and holy water adopted willfully after such a mechanical calculation would lack the inner soul of faith's reality; and if we were ourselves in the place of the Deity, we should probably take particular pleasure in cutting off believers of this pattern from their infinite reward. It is evident that unless there be some pre-existing tendency to believe in masses and holy water, the option offered to the will by Pascal is not a living option. Certainly no Turk ever took to masses and holy water on its account; and even to us Protestants these means of salvation seem such foregone impossibilities that Pascal's logic, invoked for them specifically, leaves us unmoved. As well might the Mahdi write to us, saying, "I am the Expected One whom God has created in his effulgence. You shall be infinitely happy if you confess me; otherwise you shall be cut off from the light of the sun. Weigh, then, your infinite gain if I am genuine against your finite sacrifice if I am not!" His logic would be that of Pascal; but he would vainly use it on us, for the hypothesis he offers us is dead. No tendency to act on it exists in us to any degree.

The talk of believing by our volition seems, then, from one point of view, simply silly. From another point of view it is worse than silly, it is vile. When one turns to the magnificent edifice of the physical sciences, and sees how it was reared; what thousands of disinterested moral lives of men lie buried in its mere foundations; what patience and postponement, what choking down of preference, what submission to the icy laws of outer fact are wrought into its very stones and mortar; how absolutely impersonal it stands in its vast augustness—then how besotted and contemptible seems every little sentimentalist who comes blowing his voluntary smoke-wreaths, and pretending to decide things from out of his private dream! Can we wonder if those bred in the rugged and manly school of science should feel like spewing such subjectivism out of their mouths? The whole system of loyalties which grow up in the schools of science go dead against its toleration; so that it is only natural that those who have caught the scientific fever should pass over to the opposite extreme, and write sometimes as if the incorruptibly truthful intellect ought positively to prefer bitterness and unacceptableness to the heart in its cup.

> It fortifies my soul to know
> That, though I perish, Truth is so—

sings Clough, while Huxley exclaims: "My only consolation lies in the reflection that, however bad our posterity may become, so far as they hold by the plain rule of not pretending to believe what they have no reason to believe, because it may be to their advantage so to pretend [the word 'pretend' is surely here redundant], they will not have reached the lowest depth of immortality." And that delicious *enfant terrible* Clifford writes: "Belief is desecrated when given to unproved and unquestioned statements for the solace and private pleasure of the believer . . . . Whoso would deserve well of his fellows in this matter will guard the purity of his belief with a very fanaticism of jealous care, lest at any time it should rest on an unworthy object, and catch a stain which can never be wiped away . . . . If [a] belief has been accepted on insufficient evidence [even though the belief be true, as Clifford on the same page explains] the pleasure is a stolen one . . . . It is sinful because it is stolen in defiance of our duty to mankind. That duty is to guard ourselves from such beliefs as from a pestilence which may shortly master our own body and then spread to the rest of the town. . . . It is wrong always, everywhere, and for every one, to believe anything upon insufficient evidence." (6)

(6) R A second objection is that believing by choice (rather than as a result of evidence), even if it were possible, would be "vile," morally unacceptable—this is basically Clifford's view.

III

All this strikes one as healthy, even when expressed, as by Clifford, with somewhat too much of robustious pathos in the voice. Free-will and simple wishing do seem, in the matter of our credences, to be only fifth wheels to the coach. Yet if any one should thereupon assume that intellectual insight is what remains after wish and will and sentimental preference have taken wing, or that pure reason is what then settles our opinions, he would fly quite as directly in the teeth of the facts.

It is only our already dead hypotheses that our willing nature is unable to bring to life again. But what has made them dead for us is for the most part a previous action of our willing nature of an antagonistic kind. When I say "willing nature," I do not mean only such deliberate volitions as may have set up habits of belief that we cannot now escape from—I mean all such factors of belief as fear and hope, prejudice and passion, imitation and partisanship, the circumpressure of our caste and set. As a matter of fact we find ourselves believing, we hardly know how or why. Mr. Balfour gives the name of "authority" to all those influences, born of the intellectual climate, that make hypotheses possible or impossible for us, alive or dead. Here in this room, we all of us believe in molecules and the conservation of energy, in democracy and necessary progress, in Protestant Christianity and the duty of fighting for "the doctrine of the immortal Monroe," all for no reasons worthy of the name. We see into these matters with no more inner clearness, and probably with much less, than any disbeliever in them might possess. His unconventionality would probably have some grounds to show for its conclusions; but for us, not insight, but the *prestige* of the opinions, is what makes the spark shoot from them and light up our sleeping magazines of faith.

R James responds that almost all our beliefs result from our "willing nature," in which he includes all factors other than evidence that produce belief: fear, hope, prejudice, social pressures and influences (especially prestige), and so on. The suggestion seems to be that belief on this sort of basis is simply unavoidable.

Is the nonexistence of truth itself even an intelligible possibility? What would it mean for there to simply be no truth at all? (Would that claim itself be true?) What about the possibility that there is truth, but that our minds are somehow incapable of comprehending it?

James seems to reject the claim that belief is never voluntary, suggesting that it is only claims that are not "live" that cannot be voluntarily accepted. But he seems to be running together genuinely voluntary belief with belief that results from "passional" factors. Couldn't a passional belief still be involuntary? Indeed, isn't that the most likely situation?

STOP Think carefully about the content of this principle, relating it back to the previous discussions of the various elements, especially the idea of a "genuine" option.

Our reason is quite satisfied, in nine hundred and ninety-nine cases out of every thousand of us, if it can find a few arguments that will do to recite in case our credulity is criticised by some one else. Our faith is faith in some one else's faith, and in the greatest matters this is most the case. 7 Our belief in truth itself, for instance, that there is a truth, and that our minds and it are made for each other—what is it but a passionate affirmation of desire, in which our social system backs us up? We want to have a truth; we want to believe that our experiments and studies and discussions must put us in a continually better and better position towards it; and on this line we agree to fight out our thinking lives. But if a pyrrhonistic sceptic asks us how we know all this, can our logic find a reply? No! certainly it cannot. It is just one volition against another—we willing to go in for life upon a trust or assumption which he, for his part, does not care to make. 8

As a rule we disbelieve all facts and theories for which we have no use. Clifford's cosmic emotions find no use for Christian feelings. Huxley belabors the bishops because there is no use for sacerdotalism in his scheme of life. Newman, on the contrary, goes over to Romanism, and finds all sorts of reasons good for staying there, because a priestly system is for him an organic need and delight. Why do so few "scientists" even look at the evidence for telepathy, so called? Because they think, as a leading biologist, now dead, once said to me, that even if such a thing were true, scientists ought to band together to keep it suppressed and concealed. It would undo the uniformity of Nature and all sorts of other things without which scientists cannot carry on their pursuits. But if this very man had been shown something which as a scientist he might do with telepathy, he might not only have examined the evidence, but even have found it good enough. This very law which the logicians would impose upon us—if I may give the name of logicians to those who would rule out our willing nature here—is based on nothing but their own natural wish to exclude all elements for which they, in their professional quality of logicians, can find no use.

Evidently, then, our non-intellectual nature does influence our convictions. There are passional tendencies and volitions which run before and others which come after belief, and it is only the latter that are too late for the fair, and they are not too late when the previous passional work has been already in their own direction. 9 Pascal's argument, instead of being powerless, then seems a regular clincher, and is the last stroke needed to make our faith in masses and holy water complete. The state of things is evidently far from simple; and pure insight and logic, whatever they might do ideally, are not the only things that really do produce our creeds.

IV

Our next duty, having recognized this mixed-up state of affairs, is to ask whether it be simply reprehensible and pathological, or whether, on the contrary, we must treat it as a normal element in making up our minds. The thesis I defend is, briefly stated, this: *Our passional nature not only lawfully may, but must, decide an option between propositions, whenever it is a genuine option that cannot by its nature be decided on intellectual grounds; for to say, under such circumstances, "Do not decide, but leave the question open," is itself a passional decision—just like deciding yes or no—and is attended with the same risk of losing the truth.* 10 The thesis thus abstractly expressed will, I trust, soon become quite clear. But I must first indulge in a bit more of preliminary work.

...

VII

One more point, small but important, and our preliminaries are done. There are two ways of looking at our duty in the matter of opinion—ways entirely different, and yet ways about whose difference the theory of knowledge seems hitherto to have shown very little concern. *We must know the truth; and we must avoid error*—these are our first and great commandments as would-be knowers; but they are not two ways of stating an identical commandment, they are two separable laws. Although it may indeed happen that when we believe the truth *A*, we escape as an incidental consequence from believing the falsehood *B*, it hardly ever happens that by merely disbelieving *B* we necessarily believe *A*. We may in escaping *B* fall into believing other falsehoods, *C* or *D*, just as bad as *B*; or we may escape B by not believing anything at all, not even *A*.

Believe truth! Shun error!—these, we see, are two materially different laws; and by choosing between them we may end by coloring differently our whole intellectual life. We may regard the chase for truth as paramount, and the avoidance of error as secondary; or we may, on the other hand, treat the avoidance of error as more imperative, and let truth take its chance.  Clifford, in the instructive passage which I have quoted, exhorts us to the latter course. Believe nothing, he tells us, keep your mind in suspense forever, rather than by closing it on insufficient evidence incur the awful risk of believing lies. You, on the other hand, may think that the risk of being in error is a very small matter when compared with the blessings of real knowledge, and be ready to be duped many times in your investigation rather than postpone indefinitely the chance of guessing true. I myself find it impossible to go with Clifford. We must remember that these feelings of our duty about either truth or error are in any case only expressions of our passional life. Biologically considered, our minds are as ready to grind out falsehood as veracity, and he who says, "Better go without belief forever than believe a lie!" merely shows his own preponderant private horror of becoming a dupe. He may be critical of many of his desires and fears, but this fear he slavishly obeys. He cannot imagine any one questioning its binding force. For my own part, I have also a horror of being duped; but I can believe that worse things than being duped may happen to a man in this world: so Clifford's exhortation has to my ears a thoroughly fantastic sound. It is like a general informing his soldiers that it is better to keep out of battle forever than to risk a single wound. Not so are victories either over enemies or over nature gained. Our errors are surely not such awfully solemn things. In a world where we are so certain to incur them in spite of all our caution, a certain lightness of heart seems healthier than this excessive nervousness on their behalf. At any rate it seems the fittest thing for the empiricist philosopher.

VIII

And now, after all this introduction, let us go straight at our question. I have said, and now repeat it, that not only as a matter of fact do we find our passional nature influencing us in our opinions, but that there are some options between opinions in which this influence must be regarded both as an inevitable and as a lawful determinant of our choice.

I fear here that some of you my hearers will begin to scent danger, and lend an inhospitable ear. Two first steps of passion you have indeed had to admit as necessary—we must think so as to avoid dupery, and we must think so as to gain truth; but the surest path to those ideal consummations, you will probably consider, is from now onwards to take no further passional step.

Well, of course, I agree as far as the facts will allow. Wherever the option between losing truth and gaining it is not momentous, we can throw the chance of *gaining truth* away, and at any rate save ourselves from any chance of *believing falsehood*, by not making up our minds at all till objective evidence has come. In scientific questions, this is almost always the case; and even in human affairs in general, the need of acting is seldom so urgent that a false belief to act on is better than no belief at all. Law courts, indeed, have to decide on the best evidence attainable for the moment, because a judge's duty is to make law as well as to ascertain it, and (as a learned judge once said to me) few cases are worth spending much time over: the great thing is to have them decided on *any* acceptable principle, and got out of the way. But in our dealings with objective nature we obviously are recorders, not makers, of the truth; and decisions for the mere sake of deciding promptly and getting on to the next business would be wholly out of place. Throughout the breadth of physical nature facts are what they are quite independently of us, and seldom is there any such hurry about them that the risks of being duped by believing a premature theory need be faced. The questions here are always trivial options, the hypotheses are hardly living (at any rate not living for us spectators), the choice between believing truth or falsehood is seldom forced.  The attitude of sceptical balance is therefore the absolutely wise one if we would escape mistakes. What difference, indeed, does it make to most of us whether we have or have not a theory of the Röntgen rays, whether we believe or not in mind-stuff, or have a conviction about the causality of conscious states? It makes no difference. Such options are not forced on us. On every account it is better not to make them,

11

R James's point here is that it would be easy to avoid error if one gave no weight to also finding truth, and almost as easy to find truth if there were no concern to avoid error—think how a person could do each of these things. What is hard is to do both, thus raising the question of how much weight to give each of these goals.

12

None of these claims is as obvious as James seems to think.

but still keep weighing reasons *pro et contra* with an indifferent hand.

. . . Let us agree, however, that wherever there is no forced option, the dispassionately judicial intellect with no pet hypothesis, saving us, as it does, from dupery at any rate, ought to be our ideal.

The question next arises: Are there not somewhere forced options in our speculative questions, and can we (as men who may be interested at least as much in positively gaining truth as in merely escaping dupery) always wait with impunity till the coercive evidence shall have arrived? It seems a priori improbable that the truth should be so nicely adjusted to our needs and powers as that. In the great boarding-house of nature, the cakes and the butter and the syrup seldom come out so even and leave the plates so clean. Indeed, we should view them with scientific suspicion if they did.

IX

Moral questions immediately present themselves as questions whose solution cannot wait for sensible proof. A moral question is a question not of what sensibly exists, but of what is good, or would be good if it did exist. Science can tell us what exists; but to compare the *worths*, both of what exists and of what does not exist, we must consult not science, but what Pascal calls our heart. Science herself consults her heart when she lays it down that the infinite ascertainment of fact and correction of false belief are the supreme goods for man. Challenge the statement, and science can only repeat it oracularly, or else prove it by showing that such ascertainment and correction bring man all sorts of other goods which man's heart in turn declares. The question of having moral beliefs at all or not having them is decided by our will. Are our moral preferences true or false, or are they only odd biological phenomena, making things good or bad for *us*, but in themselves indifferent? How can your pure intellect decide? (13) If your heart does not *want* a world of moral reality, your head will assuredly never make you believe in one. Mephistophelian scepticism, indeed, will satisfy the head's play-instincts much better than any rigorous idealism can. Some men (even at the student age) are so naturally cool-hearted that the moralistic hypothesis never has for them any pungent life, and in their supercilious presence the hot young moralist always feels strangely ill at ease. The appearance of knowingness is on their side, of *naïveté* and gullibility on his. Yet, in the inarticulate heart of him, he clings to it that he is not a dupe, and that there is a realm in which (as Emerson says) all their wit and intellectual superiority is no better than the cunning of a fox. Moral scepticism can no more be refuted or proved by logic than intellectual scepticism can. When we stick to it that there *is* truth (be it of either kind), we do so with our whole nature, and resolve to stand or fall by the results. The sceptic with his whole nature adopts the doubting attitude; but which of us is the wiser, Omniscience only knows.

Turn now from these wide questions of good to a certain class of questions of fact, questions concerning personal relations, states of mind between one man and another. *Do you like me or not?*—for example. Whether you do or not depends, in countless instances, on whether I meet you half-way, am willing to assume that you must like me, and show you trust and expectation. The previous faith on my part in your liking's existence is in such cases what makes your liking come. But if I stand aloof, and refuse to budge an inch until I have objective evidence, until you shall have done something apt, . . . ten to one your liking never comes. How many women's hearts are vanquished by the mere sanguine insistence of some man that they *must* love him! he will not consent to the hypothesis that they cannot. The desire for a certain kind of truth here brings about that special truth's existence; and so it is in innumerable cases of other sorts. Who gains promotions, boons, appointments, but the man in whose life they are seen to play the part of live hypotheses, who discounts them, sacrifices other things for their sake before they have come, and takes risks for them in advance? His faith acts on the powers above him as a claim, and creates its own verification.

A social organism of any sort whatever, large or small, is what it is because each member proceeds to his own duty with a trust that the other members will simultaneously do theirs. Wherever a desired result is achieved by the co-operation of many independent persons, its existence as a fact is a pure consequence of the precursive faith in one another of those

(13) There are two questions here. One is whether there are any moral truths at all, and the second is which moral claims are true if any are. Can the answer to either of these be settled in a way that would satisfy Clifford?

immediately concerned. A government, an army, a commercial system, a ship, a college, an athletic team, all exist on this condition, without which not only is nothing achieved, but nothing is even attempted. A whole train of passengers (individually brave enough) will be looted by a few highwaymen, simply because the latter can count on one another, while each passenger fears that if he makes a movement of resistance, he will be shot before any one else backs him up. If we believed that the whole car-full would rise at once with us, we should each severally rise, and train-robbing would never even be attempted. There are, then, cases where a fact cannot come at all unless a preliminary faith exists in its coming. *And where faith in a fact can help create the fact*, that would be an insane logic which should say that faith running ahead of scientific evidence is the "lowest kind of immorality" into which a thinking being can fall. Yet such is the logic by which our scientific absolutists pretend to regulate our lives! (14)

X

In truths dependent on our personal action, then, faith based on desire is certainly a lawful and possibly an indispensable thing.

But now, it will be said, these are all childish human cases, and have nothing to do with great cosmical matters, like the question of religious faith. Let us then pass on to that. Religions differ so much in their accidents that in discussing the religious question we must make it very generic and broad. What then do we now mean by the religious hypothesis? Science says things are; morality says some things are better than other things; and religion says essentially two things.

First, she says that the best things are the more eternal things, the overlapping things, the things in the universe that throw the last stone, so to speak, and say the final word. "Perfection is eternal"—this phrase of Charles Secrétan seems a good way of putting this first affirmation of religion, an affirmation which obviously cannot yet be verified scientifically at all.

The second affirmation of religion is that we are better off even now if we believe her first affirmation to be true. (15)

Now, let us consider what the logical elements of this situation are *in case the religious hypothesis in both its branches be really true*. (Of course, we must admit that possibility at the outset. If we are to discuss the question at all, it must involve a living option. If for any of you religion be a hypothesis that cannot, by any living possibility be true, then you need go no farther. I speak to the "saving remnant" alone.) So proceeding, we see, first, that religion offers itself as a *momentous* option. We are supposed to gain, ever now, by our belief, and to lose by our non-belief, a certain vital good. Secondly, religion is a *forced* option, so far as that good goes. We cannot escape the issue by remaining sceptical and waiting for more light, because, although we do avoid error in that way *if religion be untrue*, we lose the good, if it be true, just as certainly as if we positively chose to disbelieve. (16) It is as if a man should hesitate indefinitely to ask a certain woman to marry him because he was not perfectly sure that she would prove an angel after he brought her home. Would he not cut himself off from that particular angel-possibility as decisively as if he went and married some one else? Scepticism, then, is not avoidance of option; it is option of a certain particular kind of risk. *Better risk loss of truth than chance of error*—that is your faith-vetoer's exact position. He is actively playing his stake as much as the believer is; he is backing the field against the religious hypothesis, just as the believer is backing the religious hypothesis against the field. To preach scepticism to us as a duty until "sufficient evidence" for religion be found, is tantamount therefore to telling us, when in presence of the religious hypothesis, that to yield to our fear of its being error is wiser and better than to yield to our hope that it may be true. It is not intellect against all passions, then; it is only intellect with one passion laying down its law. And by what, forsooth, is the supreme wisdom of this passion warranted? Dupery for dupery, what proof is there that dupery through hope is so much worse than dupery through fear? I, for one, can see no proof; and I simply refuse obedience to the scientist's command to imitate his kind of option, in a case where my own stake is important enough to give me the right to choose my own form of risk. If religion be true and the evidence for it be still insufficient, I do not wish, by putting your extinguisher upon my nature (which feels to me as if it had after all some business in this

(14)

James should say here both that our actions may affect the truth and that our beliefs affect how we act. This is how belief (faith) in a fact may help to create that very fact.

(15)

This is an extremely meager conception of what "religion says." Does any actual religion merely say these two things?

(16)

Here the idea of a *forced option* seems to be understood in a somewhat different and stronger way than was explained earlier, one that in effect incorporates the idea that the choice is momentous: any option can be made one side of an exhaustive disjunction (see Annotation 3). But not just any option will be one where a vital good can be achieved only by accepting it, so that the choice is either to accept it or to lose that good.

This argument depends heavily on there being only two options: accept "religion" (and have a chance of a great good) or refuse to accept it (and lose that chance). This is very close to Pascal's wager and faces the same problem that there are really many more options—because there are many different possible gods or god-like beings and corresponding religions.

Here James tries to connect the issue of religious belief with the earlier discussion of the way in which one's beliefs and resulting actions may affect personal relations. But doesn't the fact that the very existence of the being to whom one might relate is in doubt make a difference to this point?

"Acknowledging" is misleading here, since it suggests the situation where the truth in question is apparent or recognizable in some way; it would be better to substitute just "believing."

matter), to forfeit my sole chance in life of getting upon the winning side—that chance depending, of course, on my willingness to run the risk of acting as if my passional need of taking the world religiously might be prophetic and right. [17]

All this is on the supposition that it really may be prophetic and right, and that, even to us who are discussing the matter, religion is a live hypothesis which may be true. Now, to most of us religion comes in a still further way that makes a veto on our active faith even more illogical. The more perfect and more eternal aspect of the universe is represented in our religions as having personal form. The universe is no longer a mere *It* to us, but a *Thou*, if we are religious; and any relation that may be possible from person to person might be possible here. For instance, although in one sense we are passive portions of the universe, in another we show a curious autonomy, as if we were small active centres on our own account. We feel, too, as if the appeal of religion to us were made to our own active good-will, as if evidence might be forever withheld from us unless we met the hypothesis half-way. To take a trivial illustration: just as a man who in a company of gentlemen made no advances, asked a warrant for every concession, and believed no one's word without proof, would cut himself off by such churlishness from all the social rewards that a more trusting spirit would earn—so here, one who should shut himself up in snarling logicality and try to make the gods extort his recognition willy-nilly, or not get it at all, might cut himself off forever from his only opportunity of making the gods' acquaintance. [18] This feeling, forced on us we know not whence, that by obstinately believing that there are gods (although not to do so would be so easy both for our logic and our life) we are doing the universe the deepest service we can, seems part of the living essence of the religious hypothesis. If the hypothesis were true in all its parts, including this one, then pure intellectualism, with its veto on our making willing advances, would be an absurdity; and some participation of our sympathetic nature would be logically required. I, therefore, for one, cannot see my way to accepting the agnostic rules for truth-seeking, or willfully agree to keep my willing nature out of the game. I cannot do so for this plain reason, that *a rule of thinking which would absolutely prevent me from acknowledging certain kinds of truth if those kinds of truth were really there, would be an irrational rule*. [19] That for me is the long and short of the formal logic of the situation, no matter what the kinds of truth might materially be.

I confess I do not see how this logic can be escaped. But sad experience makes me fear that some of you may still shrink from radically saying with me, *in abstracto*, that we have the right to believe at our own risk any hypothesis that is live enough to tempt our will. I suspect, however, that if this is so, it is because you have got away from the abstract logical point of view altogether, and are thinking (perhaps without realizing it) of some particular religious hypothesis which for you is dead. The freedom to "believe what we will" you apply to the case of some patent superstition; and the faith you think of is the faith defined by the schoolboy when he said, "Faith is when you believe something that you know ain't true." I can only repeat that this is misapprehension. *In concreto*, the freedom to believe can only cover living options which the intellect of the individual cannot by itself resolve; and living options never seem absurdities to him who has them to consider. When I look at the religious question as it really puts itself to concrete men, and when I think of all the possibilities which both practically and theoretically it involves, then this command that we shall put a stopper on our heart, instincts, and courage, and *wait*—acting of course meanwhile more or less as if religion were *not* true*—till doomsday, or till such time as our intellect and sense working together may have raked in evidence enough—this

*Since belief is measured by action, he who forbids us to believe religion to be true necessarily also forbids us to act as we should if we did believe it to be true. The whole defence of religious faith hinges upon action. If the action required or inspired by the religious hypothesis is in no way different from that dictated by the naturalistic hypothesis then religious faith is a pure superfluity, better pruned away, and controversy about its legitimacy is a piece of idle trifling, unworthy of serious minds. I myself believe, of course that the religious hypothesis gives to the world an expression which specifically determine our reactions, and makes them in a large part unlike what they might be on a purely naturalistic scheme of belief.

command, I say, seems to me the queerest idol ever manufactured in the philosophic cave. Were we scholastic absolutists, there might be more excuse. If we had an infallible intellect with its objective certitudes, we might feel ourselves disloyal to such a perfect organ of knowledge in not trusting to it exclusively, in not waiting for its releasing word. But if we are empiricists, if we believe that no bell in us tolls to let us know for certain when truth is in our grasp, then it seems a piece of idle fantasticality to preach so solemnly our duty of waiting for the bell. Indeed we *may* wait if we will—I hope you do not think that I am denying that—but if we do so, we do so at our peril as much as if we believed. In either case we *act*, taking our life in our hands. No one of us ought to issue vetoes to the other, nor should we bandy words of abuse. We ought, on the contrary, delicately and profoundly to respect one another's mental freedom: then only shall we bring about the intellectual republic; then only shall we have that spirit of inner tolerance without which all our outer tolerance is soulless, and which is empiricism's glory; then only shall we live and let live, in speculative as well as in practical things.

I began by a reference to Fitz-James Stephen; let me end by a quotation from him. "What do you think of yourself? What do you think of the world?" . . . These are questions with which all must deal as it seems good to them. They are riddles of the Sphinx, and in some way or other we must deal with them. . . . In all important transactions of life we have to take a leap in the dark. . . . If we decide to leave the riddles unanswered, that is a choice; if we waver in our answer, that, too, is a choice: but whatever choice we make, we make it at our peril. If a man chooses to turn his back altogether on God and the future, no one can prevent him; no one can show beyond reasonable doubt that he *is* mistaken. If a man thinks otherwise and acts as he thinks, I do not see that any one can prove that he *is* mistaken. Each must act as he thinks best; and if he is wrong, so much the worse for him. We stand on a mountain pass in the midst of whirling snow and blinding mist, through which we get glimpses now and then of paths which may be deceptive. If we stand still we shall be frozen to death. If we take the wrong road we shall be dashed to pieces. We do not certainly know whether there is any right one. What must we do? 'Be strong and of good courage.' Act for the best, hope for the best and take what comes. . . . If death ends all, we cannot meet death better."*

Discussion Questions

1. To what extent, if any, is it possible to voluntarily believe things? (See Kaufmann's discussion of the analogous point in relation to Pascal on p. 581.) How much does the answer to this question matter for James's position? Would it change his view very much if he spoke only of the rational permissibility of belief resulting from "passional" factors, without claiming that such belief is strictly voluntary?
2. Suppose that an option is not "live" in the sense that James defines. Might it not be still both forced and momentous? Isn't there a risk that a person will lose a great good by being unable to take certain options seriously? And if so, aren't there ways of overcoming this limitation? Why couldn't one study accounts of the life of the Mahdi and the background of his views written by believers and perhaps thereby convert belief in the Mahdi into a "live" option? Would this be a rational thing to do in all such cases? Why or why not?
3. In a case where belief (faith) in a fact may help to create that very fact (or belief in an opposite fact may help to create that one) and where one strongly wants one of these facts to be true, is it rational to believe and act in a way that might help to bring about that fact, even though there is not adequate evidence for the belief? Is it morally acceptable to do so?
4. What happens if we consider different religious options (in James's fairly broad understanding of what counts as "religious"): different sorts of gods or religious teachings that cannot all be accepted at the same time? What do you think that James would say about such a case?

**Liberty, Equality, Fraternity,* p. 353, 2d ed., London, 1874.

Concluding Dialogue on God and Faith

In our last discussion, you said that the main question there—the question of what makes right actions right—was one of the most important that philosophers ask. But the question of whether God exists, of whether there is an omnipotent, omniscient, and morally perfect being who created the universe, is surely equally important if not more so. Whether or not people believe in such a being can and does lead to really fundamental differences in the way that they view all sorts of other issues and problems. For a philosopher, the main issue is whether there are good reasons of some sort to believe that God exists—or perhaps instead good reasons to believe that there is no such being. Let's look first at the arguments in favor of the existence of God. I have to admit that none of them strike me as very cogent.

Whether or not you think that any of those arguments ultimately work, you surely would agree that some are more compelling than others. Let's start with what has always seemed to me the least compelling of them—the so-called ontological argument. While this argument is no doubt very clever, it's hard to see how anyone could really think that the mere concept or definition of something could somehow guarantee its existence. Don't you think that Kant is right that spelling out a concept and determining whether there is something that fits that concept are *always* logically distinct from each other—that we could never decide whether God exists simply by understanding the content of the concept of God?

I agree entirely. That particular objection to the ontological argument has always seemed much stronger to me than Kant's more famous one that says that existence isn't a predicate. Another way to get at the point is to realize that *of course* I can't define something into existence simply by adding existence to my concept of it. If this were possible, I could thereby acquire all sorts of neat things: not just Gaunilo's perfect island, but also my existent new car, my existent million dollar bank account, and so on.

Does an advocate of the argument have any good answer to this criticism? I suppose he might say that it makes a difference *how* existence becomes part of the concept—that you can't just add it arbitrarily, but instead have to find some more general specification that arguably includes it, such as a being than which none greater can be thought or a perfect being. But it's hard to see why this matters for the basic point that knowing what kind of thing we are asking about can never settle the issue of whether there really is one.

I agree that the response you suggest doesn't seem to help. The way I like to put the point is to say that you can include existence in the definition of something if you like, whether directly or as a consequence of something else doesn't matter. But this only has the result that the concept thus defined can't be correctly applied to anything that doesn't exist—but not that something has to somehow pop into existence to satisfy it. If existence is indeed part of the standard conception of God (which is debatable), this just means that we can't correctly use the term "God" to refer to an imagined being that is otherwise exactly similar but doesn't exist. This is an odd result. It would make it much harder for theists and atheists to even say what they are disagreeing about, but doesn't really affect the main issue of whether the world contains a being that fits the description in question.

What then about the cosmological argument? Here the underlying rationale seems to me a lot more plausible, at least initially. There does seem to be a significant question as to why there is a world at all: why something exists rather than nothing. And the existence of a divine creator would provide an answer to this question.

But how good an answer is it? Think about this a little. The existence of God can't really explain why there is something rather than nothing, since such a being would itself be part of the *something*. Even theists don't think that God somehow drags himself (or herself or itself) into existence out of nothing. So the right thing to say, I think, about the question of why something exists rather than nothing is that either alternative is possible from a sheerly logical standpoint. We obviously know that the *something* possibility rather than the *nothing* possibility is in fact realized. But there is in principle no way to explain why

this is so, since *any* attempted explanation would have to appeal to some part of the *something,* thereby presupposing part of what it is supposed to be explaining.

Hold on—isn't that a little too fast? Advocates of the cosmological argument characterize God as a *necessary* or *self-existent* being. This seems to mean that God is a being that couldn't have failed to exist and that explains its own existence in some (admittedly mysterious) way that ordinary things that exist only contingently—or the whole collection of such ordinary things—can't. *If* this idea makes sense, then it would in a way explain why there is something rather than nothing, since that particular something, it is claimed, must exist by its very nature.

You're right that this is what they would say. But one problem is that this still doesn't explain in any very clear way why the *non-divine* world exists—which is, after all, the premise from which the argument originally starts. The theist can just *stipulate* that the necessary or self-existent being also creates other things, indeed these particular other things, but *why* or even *how* such a being would do that still isn't explained in any way that appeals to its nature as necessary or self-existent.

Hmmm. So the point is that to get even the beginnings of an explanation of the non-divine world, we would still have to bring in something like the rest of the standard conception of God as an all-powerful creator. And I can see what you're going to say: that this, unfortunately, also doesn't follow in any clear way from the idea of a necessary or self-existent being either. So we haven't really answered the question we started with.

Exactly! But another problem is that it just isn't clear that the idea of a necessary or self-existent being really makes sense at all. What *makes* it necessary? *How* is its existence supposed to be self-explanatory? Kant argued that the only way for an advocate of the cosmological argument to answer this question is to appeal to the idea underlying the *ontological* argument: that existence is part of the very conception of God. But then if the ontological argument doesn't work, the cosmological argument doesn't work either. I don't see any way to *prove* that this is the only way to make sense of the idea of a necessary or self-existent being, but I must confess that I don't know of another one.

So two of the three main arguments seem in fact to have serious problems. This leaves us with the argument from design. But that isn't so bad from a theistic standpoint, since this is surely the argument that has the greatest appeal to common sense anyway. The basic starting point of this argument is surely undeniable. The world is an intricately and marvelously ordered realm, with the order involved in living creatures of various kinds being especially striking. And all of this order surely does seem to cry out for some sort of explanation.

I agree completely that an explanation is needed here—or maybe more than one. The world is full of things that can't plausibly be said to exist by mere chance or as a result of anything but a pretty complicated process of some sort. I would even go a step further and concede that when Paley and others put it forth, prior to the middle of the nineteenth century or so, the argument from design was really quite compelling. Hume, writing in the eighteenth century (and thus actually before Paley), has a very hard time coming up with alternative explanations for the order of living things that are very plausible. And even Kant, having claimed to demolish the other arguments, concedes that the argument from design establishes the existence of something like a supreme architect and objects only that it doesn't establish the existence of a being who meets the full standard conception of God.

I think I see where you're going though. You're saying that the argument from design was only compelling up to the time when Darwin and others discovered the theory of evolution. But after that discovery, you're suggesting, the existence of God is no longer the best explanation for the order involved in living things. In fact, that's something that happens pretty often with explanatory arguments. What seems like the best explanation at one point ceases to be so after a better explanation is discovered. But you need to say more fully just why evolution is supposed to be a better explanation than what nowadays gets referred to as "intelligent design." Aren't there still lots of problems with the details of the theory of evolution?

We obviously can't go into the whole story here. But the basic reason why evolution is a superior explanation—and I'm sure I'm not telling you anything you don't already know—is that it is both far more detailed and specific than the theistic explanation and also empirically testable in all sorts of ways that intelligent design isn't. Evolutionary biologists don't just say that living things are *somehow* a product of evolution. Instead, they are able to offer lots of details with regard to how and why various features develop and why they confer an advantage with respect to survival. (Look at Gould's discussion for some examples.)

So while the evolutionary story is far from complete, and there are still lots of specific aspects of the order of living things that aren't very fully explained, what you are suggesting is that those problems are in fact results of the very things that make the explanation better, namely details and testability. It's admittedly hard to imagine intelligent design facing similar problems. But that's because the proponents of intelligent design don't even try to explain how and why God created the particular creatures and specific features that we find in the world. And because they don't, their view also makes no specific predictions that could be empirically verified or refuted. That's why intelligent design really isn't a serious alternative to evolution as a scientific explanation.

Of course, evolution isn't the whole story. There are also lots of other explanations offered in other sciences for various aspects of the overall order of the world. Think of the geological explanations of such things as the behavior of volcanoes and even of the fossils that the biologists rely on. And of course biochemistry has offered further explanations for the inheritance of characteristics upon which evolution depends, most centrally accounts of the structure and functioning of the DNA that composes genes.

But even if you're right about all of this, it doesn't really answer what the chapter introduction calls the *global* version of the argument from design. After all, *none* of these specific explanations really stands on its own. An appeal to evolution, for example, has to rely on some underlying order that allows the evolutionary process to work—the order involved in inheritance of characteristics, stable environments, the functioning of individual organisms, and so on. And the same is true for all of these other specific explanations. In most cases, this further order can itself be accounted for by some still further explanation (in the way that, for example, some of the order required for evolution is explained by biochemistry). But the very same situation will hold for those further explanations too, making it impossible for *all* of the order in the world—or the sheer fact that there is order at all—to be explained in this sort of way. And the theist will now say that ultimately this *background* order can only be explained by invoking God.

But this is exactly where Flew's two main points become crucially important. His first point is that it is impossible to explain *all* order for roughly the same reason that it is impossible to explain *all* existence: any explanation of one instance of order will rely on some other instance of order. A creative God would, after all, be another case of order—indeed perhaps the most extreme example of order imaginable! And just as God can't drag himself (or herself or itself) into existence, so also it makes no sense at all to suppose that such a being somehow orders itself. The intelligent designer doesn't design *himself* because he couldn't design anything until the order involved in the capacity to design was already there.

So you're saying that it is simply impossible for all order to be explained by a different, prior kind of order. Any attempt to do so would lead to an infinite regress that could never stop and would always at each point leave some order unexplained. And there's no reason to think that these infinitely many different kinds of order exist. But what's the alternative?

The only alternative to an infinite regress of different kinds of order is that some case of order—or maybe more than one—has to be taken as *intrinsic* to whatever has it. What that means is that this order is explained only by the prior existence of that very same order, and so on back into time. And now Flew's other point—what he somewhat loftily calls "the Stratonician Presumption"—is that since *some* order has to be in this way intrinsic, it is more reasonable to take the general order that we observe in the non-divine world to be the intrinsic order than to assume that this order has to be produced by an external designer

whose own order would then have to be intrinsic. If the non-divine world is orderly in all of the experience we have of it, why should we assume that its natural or intrinsic state is to be *disorderly*, with the observed order always being produced from the outside?

But doesn't Flew overstate his point a little? Surely it's still *possible* that the order of the non-divine world is not intrinsic and is instead produced by a designer whose own order is intrinsic. We don't have to assume that the order of the non-divine world is intrinsic. But the point is that once we realize that it is impossible for all order to be explained by something external to whatever has it, there is at best no reason to favor the intrinsic divine order view over the intrinsic order of nature view. And that means that the global version of the argument from design doesn't succeed in showing that God *must* exist.

Right. And there's another serious problem with both the local and global versions of the argument. Even if we were to accept the existence of a designer on the basis of one of these arguments, is there any reason to think that it has the attributes specified in the standard conception of God? Obviously we can't know that the non-divine world whose order we're trying to explain is more than finite, so there is no basis for ascribing *infinite* knowledge or power to the designer. And, as Hume points out, the problem of evil also raises serious doubts about the supposed designer's moral attributes: its goodness, benevolence, mercy, and justice.

So let's turn to the problem of evil. This is a problem for every sort of theist, not just for those who advocate the argument from design. And it is a problem that most theists have recognized and tried at length to solve—even though many of them also admit that it is very difficult. The issue isn't so much whether we can explain all evil in detail. It's whether we can make sense of the general fact that evil—pain and suffering, but also things like malice and cruelty and also callousness in the face of suffering—are to be found in the world at all. Why wouldn't God, if he exists, prevent evil or at least greatly reduce it?

I still want to insist that what you're talking about should really be called, the argument from evil for the non-existence of God—calling it merely a "problem" really amounts to assuming that theism is true. Mackie indeed takes the existence of evil to be the basis for a *conclusive* proof that God does not exist. His claim is that the existence of evil is *logically* incompatible with the existence of a God as standardly conceived. And of course the existence of evil—and indeed lots of it—is completely undeniable. Thus on his view, we can know in advance that no solution to the "problem" is possible—or at least none that does not alter the standard conception in some fundamental way.

But I'm just not convinced that Mackie is right. I don't see how to absolutely rule out the possibility that there is after all some subtle, complicated reason or rationale for the evil that the world contains—one that God understands and we don't (and maybe can't). But that doesn't really help the theist very much. If we are trying to assess the strength of the argument (or the difficulty of the "problem"), we have to rely on explanations of evil that we can devise and make sense of. Otherwise the right conclusion will be that as far as we can tell, it is extremely *improbable* that there is such a being—even if its existence isn't conclusively ruled out.

So we need to look at some of the explanations for the existence of evil, given the existence of God that have been proposed—what are called *theodicies*. Let's start with what is perhaps the most standard one, namely the free will theodicy, which claims that some of the evil in the world results from human free choices for which God is not responsible. I say "some of the evil" because this theodicy is usually offered only as a solution to the problem of *moral* evil—that is, man-made evil. It doesn't really apply to the natural or physical evil involved in natural disasters, most diseases, and so on, since that doesn't result from human actions. (Though there may be cases that are hard to classify: diseases that may have been deliberately created or deliberately spread, or things like the effects of global warming, to the extent that humans are responsible for that.)

This is, unfortunately, one of those places where two of our main philosophical problems intersect in a way that makes it hard to discuss them separately. What should be said about the free will theodicy depends in part on the right solution to the free will problem, which is discussed in a different chapter of the book. So we'll have to speak hypothetically for a bit. If a so-called *compatibilist* account of free will is correct, one that makes freedom compatible with causal determinism, then Mackie may be right that the free will theodicy doesn't work. On a compatibilist view, God could seemingly have created free persons who nonetheless are determined by him to always freely choose the good, and so he would still be responsible for creating instead persons who freely choose evil. But even some compatibilists may have doubts as to whether having one's choices determined by another intelligent being is compatible with free will, even if they think that freedom is compatible with determination by the laws of nature—a person whose choices are determined by someone else looks too much like a puppet!

But in any case, what proponents of the free will theodicy have in mind is clearly a *libertarian* view of free will, according to which free will is incompatible with *any* sort of determinism. And then it does seem to follow that God couldn't create free people and still guarantee that they will always do the right thing. If they are genuinely free, then that means that they are free to make bad or wrong choices as well as good or right ones. If all that is correct, then the free will theodicy may succeed in accounting for moral evil. (Though there are serious problems with the libertarian view of free will—even doubts about whether it really makes sense—that we can't go into here.)

But the real problem is that even if we concede, for the sake of this discussion, that the libertarian view is tenable, the free will theodicy still works only if it is really true that a world containing free persons is enough better than one without them to outweigh the negative value of the evil that results. I don't mean this necessarily to be just an adding up of the values in the way a utilitarian would advocate (again a reference to a problem in another chapter). But the world has to be in some sense better overall as a result, or else God would just be making a mistake in choosing to create free persons. Maybe that's plausible enough, since a world without persons (or with only what would amount to person-like robots) might seem hardly worth bothering with. But the harder problem is that a world like ours, in which people sometimes freely choose and carry out really bad actions like war and genocide, has to be better than a world in which God creates free persons, but still *intervenes* (perhaps in a very subtle fashion) when they are about to do something really bad.

I think that's the most serious problem. Of course we don't really know for sure that God (assuming for the moment that there is such a being) isn't in fact intervening in that way from time to time in the actual world. But even if that were true, it's hard to believe that still more intervention wouldn't be better than what has actually occurred, even given the cost to freedom. A really important part of this point here is that in the really extreme cases, not restricting the freedom of a Hitler or a Stalin or an Osama Bin Laden obviously greatly restricts the freedom of his victims—if they're dead, they aren't free to do anything. That's the main reason why the free will theodicy still doesn't seem to me to work, even apart from problems with the idea of free will itself.

But whatever we decide about the free will theodicy, there's still also the problem of natural or physical evil, which seems perhaps even harder to solve. If God exists, why did he create a world in which natural disasters like Hurricane Katrina or the recent devastating tsunami in Indonesia occur? One important aspect of this issue that sometimes goes unnoticed is the pain experienced by non-human animals in such cases. Even if Hick's idea is that the purpose of natural evil is "soul making" is an adequate explanation of why God would allow the natural evils that befall humans, it's awfully hard to extend that to animals in general. And it's also awfully hard to deny, as some have, that animals—even those pretty far down the evolutionary scale—really do experience severe pain.

Even many theists are troubled by the issue of animal pain, and some admit that they haven't any very good solution for that dimension of the problem. But even if we consider the soul-making theodicy only as it applies to human persons, it still doesn't seem to really deal very well with the whole range of natural evil. The problem is that it just isn't very plausible that natural evils on the scale that the world contains would have been chosen by an omniscient, omnipotent, perfectly benevolent being for the purpose of making souls. This applies especially to large-scale natural disasters—earthquakes, hurricanes, tidal waves, and so on—that kill large numbers of people who have little or no chance to respond in a way that would develop their souls. This is most obviously true of the young children, but it really applies to everyone who is killed without having any real chance to escape.

 There are, of course, many other theodicies—and, for that matter, many other arguments for the existence of God. We can't go into all of these here, but I don't know if any are more plausible or even as plausible as the ones we have discussed.

We can't talk about all of the possible theodicies or all of the possible arguments. But there is an important general point that applies to virtually all of them. Almost all of the arguments (with the ontological argument being the only very obvious exception) and all of the theodicies can be evaluated in the same general way. The basic issue is whether the *best explanation* of the world as we find it, including whatever further features might seem relevant—moral facts (if there are any), religious experiences, religious texts, or whatever—involves the existence of a being who fits the standard conception of God. Or whether, instead, some other explanation (or set of explanations) is as good or better. It's important to realize that there are lots of other possibilities here: an explanation that invokes a being of lesser power or knowledge but with the same moral attributes; one that invokes a being of great power and knowledge but with the moral attributes reduced or eliminated; one that invokes both good and evil beings of great power that struggle for supremacy; one that invokes multiple lesser beings of various sorts (as in many pagan views); or one with no intelligent non-human beings at all, but only natural forces of various kinds.

 That's a very abstract listing that summarizes a much larger number of specific possibilities. But my main reaction is this. The central issue posed by all of these arguments and theodicies is how to explain the non-divine world—where this means at least initially the non-divine world as we find it, with the features that it seems to have. Perhaps the most striking thing about the world as we find it is that for all its basic orderliness, it still seems to be a pretty chaotic place in the sense that there seem to be lots of competing patterns and forces, not one clear unified structure. To just take the value dimension, things sometimes seem to go very well and sometimes seem to go very badly and usually somewhere in between with all sorts of variations. Sometimes there seems to be justice, but sometimes the evil seems to prosper. Human beings in particular seem to range all the way from moral monsters to paragons of benevolence and virtue. All of this fits much better with a view according to which lots of *different* forces, whether intelligent or not, are involved, rather than the central, unified direction and control that one would expect from a God of the standard sort.

 I think that's right. Of course theists will want to say that the impression of chaos and multiple forces is just an illusion, that underneath it all there is an intelligible and systematic divine order, even if beings like us can't easily grasp it. But while that might possibly be true, your point is that there is no good reason to think that it is. The world just doesn't look like the product of one supremely intelligent and supremely good designer. For one thing, there are just too many aspects that it seems very easy to improve upon. But then some further basis is needed for it to be rational to decide that the way that it clearly seems to be isn't the way it really is.

 Moreover, the fact that there are all of those other possible kinds of explanations also shows what is wrong with Pascal's wager. As Kaufmann points out, Pascal ignores the possibility of other sorts of Gods who would react differently from the way that Pascal supposes that God would react. And then there are the many, many other possible alternatives involving multiple beings of a lesser sort. So even if one is willing to wager on god-like beings of some sort, there are just too many alternatives from which to choose and too many possible results from such choices. You'd have to create a big spreadsheet listing different possible gods and god-like beings and how each of them would treat you if you

made one choice of belief or another. Probably these would all cancel out as regards the desirability of each choice, but in any case the situation would be too uncertain to lead to a definite conclusion.

I agree, and something similar to that is also true of James. Even if one were willing to make a "leap of faith," there are just too many different leaps one could make and no apparent way to choose among them. The idea that the option thus chosen, in addition to being momentous and "forced," must be "live" is the most dubious part of James's view. What is "live" to a particular person is too likely to be just a result of incidental facts about their upbringing or temperament.

So your conclusion seems to be that there just isn't any rational basis for belief in a God of the standard sort—or for a rational wager or a rationally chosen leap of faith either. I think that you are probably right about that. But some might think that there is a non-rational basis for belief in God or for religious belief generally. You would no doubt claim that this would just amount to wishful thinking. But I'm not so sure that wishful thinking that is genuinely comforting and also contributes to social cohesion and stability is an entirely bad thing.

I have no doubt that religious belief is comforting to many people, and it seems hard to deny that it often contributes to moral behavior and can also strengthen social order. But it can also be terribly divisive and destructive, as shown by history and also by many things that are presently happening in lots of places in the world. So even if we were willing to adopt what is really a deep metaphysical belief merely on the basis of its social consequences, it is far from clear that the case for traditional religious belief is very strong.

CHAPTER 8

The Good Life

The reading selections in this chapter concern the timeless question: what is a—or *the*?—good life? Many different answers have been given to this question. On one extreme, there are views according to which only certain definite kinds of lives or in the most extreme versions only a single kind of life is best (as suggested by the version of the question using "the"). On the other extreme, there are views according to which there is no objective answer at all as to what sort of life is good, so that the only relevant consideration is the person's own subjective preferences and judgments: if people think that they are living good or satisfactory lives, then they are, and there is nothing more to be said. Between those two extremes are views claiming that while what counts as a good life varies from person to person and perhaps on other dimensions as well, there are some objective conditions or requirements that must be satisfied for a life to be good.

In the first selection in the chapter, the Stoic philosopher Epictetus offers a conception of the good life according to which what matters most is neither objective success and achievements, nor subjective pleasures of various sorts, but rather an absence of painful and distressing emotional reactions—the good life, for Epictetus, is a life of peace of mind.

Many people are at least tempted by the similar but somewhat more general idea that whether a life is a good one depends only on the character of the subjective experiences that it contains, with the most obvious version of this idea being the view (a version of **hedonism**) that a good life is one that contains lots of pleasurable experiences and few if any painful ones. Consider then the option of plugging into the "experience machine" described in the selection by Robert Nozick: a computer that will give you whatever set of experiences you choose—pleasurable experiences, if that is what you want, or perhaps also experiences involving exhilaration or excitement, the subjective appearance of various kinds of accomplishment, and so on. If all that matters to a good life is the character of your subjective experience, then the prospect of plugging into such a machine should be highly attractive. But does a life that is in this way divorced from independent reality really constitute a good life? Nozick suggests that it does not—that a truly good life involves *actually* doing and accomplishing things and not just having the artificially created experience of doing so. And if this is right, then the character of your subjective experience is not the only thing that matters in determining whether your life is a good one.

The selections by Thomas Nagel and Susan Wolf raise a different sort of issue about a good life: must a good life, in addition to whatever else it may require, be *meaningful*? And what does a meaningful life require—indeed, is it even possible for a human life to be genuinely meaningful? According to Nagel, our lives are in an important way *absurd*—where this means that we can't help attributing to both our lives in general and the particular occurrences within them a kind of importance that, from a more objective perspective, they can be seen not to genuinely possess. Nagel argues that it is simply part of the human condition to have available a more objective perspective from which the significance of everything that might seem to give meaning to our lives can be called into question. Wolf's contrasting, more optimistic view is that a meaningful life is clearly possible and attainable, and moreover that meaningfulness is a fundamental aspect of a good life. According to her conception, a life is meaningful when it involves active engagement in activities that are objectively worthwhile.

Epictetus

Epictetus (55 A.D.–135 A.D.), a Greek-born Roman slave, was a famous Stoic philosopher. Although Epictetus was born into slavery, he was freed while still a young man and was sent to study Stoicism. After years of study, he eventually founded a school that taught the elements of Stoicism to students from many lands. While he never published any of his ideas, one of his students, Flavius Arrianus, published notes from Epictetus's lectures. The *Manual* was extracted from a longer work called the *Discourses*.

This reading has a different form than any of the other readings in this book. Instead of a sustained line of reasoning, there are many independent instructions for how to live a good life. But those instructions make sense only if certain assumptions about what is ultimately important to us are true. Epictetus assumes that what matters most for a good life is a peaceful state of mind. To this end, his instructions focus on getting control over one's own desires. And the way to achieve this in a messy and unpredictable world is to control your own thoughts and desires, so that external events beyond your control cease to matter to you. A person who cares about nothing beyond the inner reactions that are (Epictetus thinks) within his control will achieve peace of mind, whereas someone who attaches significance to external occurrences (including even what happens to his own physical body) is doomed to unhappiness and frustration.

1 *Stop and Think*

STOP To what extent, if any, are a person's thoughts and desires ("will to get" and "will to avoid") within his or her control? (See Discussion Question 2.)

2 *Editor Comment*

By things that are "your own," Epictetus means things that are within your control; by things that are "another's," he means things that are controlled by others—including even, in many circumstances, the security and well-being of your own body. When he says that things within your control are "free," he means that *you* will be free if you care only about them; by saying that things that are not within your control are "servile," he means that *you* will be servile if you care about them. (By "high matters" in the next sentence, he means just this sort of self-control.)

From the *Manual*

1

Of all existing things some are in our power, and others are not in our power. In our power are thought, impulse, will to get and will to avoid, and, in a word, everything which is our own doing. Things not in our power include the body, property, reputation, office, and, in a word, everything which is not our own doing. **1** Things in our power are by nature free, unhindered, untrammeled; things not in our power are weak, servile, subject to hindrance, dependent on others. Remember then that if you imagine that what is naturally slavish is free, and what is naturally another's is your own, you will be hampered, you will mourn, you will be put to confusion, you will blame gods and men; but if you think that only your own belongs to you, and that what is another's is indeed another's, no one will ever put compulsion or hindrance on you, you will blame none, you will accuse none, you will do nothing against your will, no one will harm you, you will have no enemy, for no harm can touch you. **2**

Aiming then at these high matters, you must remember that to attain them requires more than ordinary effort; you will have to give up some things entirely, and put off others

From *The Stoic and Epicurean Philosophers,* edited by Whitney J. Oates (New York: Random House, 1940).

for the moment. And if you would have these also—office and wealth—it may be that you will fail to get them . . . , and you will certainly fail to attain those things which alone bring freedom and happiness.

Make it your study then to confront every harsh impression with the words, 'You are but an impression, and not at all what you seem to be'. Then test it by those rules that you possess; and first by this—the chief test of all—'Is it concerned with what is in our power or with what is not in our power?' And if it is concerned with what is not in our power, be ready with the answer that it is nothing to you. (3)

2

Remember that the will to get promises attainment of what you will, and the will to avoid promises escape from what you avoid; and he who fails to get what he wills is unfortunate, and he who does not escape what he wills to avoid is miserable. If then you try to avoid only what is unnatural in the region within your control, you will escape from all that you avoid; but if you try to avoid disease or death or poverty you will be miserable.

Therefore let your will to avoid have no concern with what is not in man's power; direct it only to things in man's power that are contrary to nature. (4) But for the moment you must utterly remove the will to get; for if you will to get something not in man's power you are bound to be unfortunate; while none of the things in man's power that you could honorably will to get is yet within your reach. (5) Impulse to act and not to act, these are your concern; yet exercise them gently and without strain, and provisionally.

4

When you are about to take something in hand, remind yourself what manner of thing it is. If you are going to bathe put before your mind what happens in the bath—water pouring over some, others being jostled, some reviling, others stealing; and you will set to work more securely if you say to yourself at once: 'I want to bathe, and I want to keep my will in harmony with nature', and so in each thing you do; for in this way, if anything turns up to hinder you in your bathing, you will be ready to say, 'I did not want only to bathe, but to keep my will in harmony with nature, and I shall not so keep it, if I lose my temper at what happens'. (6)

5

What disturbs men's minds is not events but their judgments on events. For instance, death is nothing dreadful, or else Socrates would have thought it so. No, the only dreadful thing about it is men's judgment that it is dreadful. (7) And so when we are hindered, or disturbed, or distressed, let us never lay the blame on others, but on ourselves, that is, on our own judgments. To accuse others for one's own misfortunes is a sign of want of education; to accuse oneself shows that one's education has begun; to accuse neither oneself nor others shows that one's education is complete.

...

8

Ask not that events should happen as you will, but let your will be that events should happen as they do, and you shall have peace.

9

Sickness is a hindrance to the body, but not to the will, unless the will consent. Lameness is a hindrance to the leg, but not to the will. Say this to yourself at each event that happens, for you shall find that though it hinders something else it will not hinder you.

...

11

Never say of anything, 'I lost it', but say, 'I gave it back'. Has your child died? It was given back. Has your wife died? She was given back. Has your estate been taken from you? Was not this also given back? But you say, 'He who took it from me is wicked'. What does it matter to you through whom the Giver asked it back? As long as He gives it you, take care of it, but not as your own; treat it as passers-by treat an inn. (8)

12

If you wish to make progress, abandon reasonings of this sort: 'If I neglect my affairs I shall have nothing to live on'; 'If I do not punish my son, he will be wicked.' For it is better to die of

By a "harsh impression," Epictetus means the awareness of anything we find upsetting. If it concerns something "in our power" (such as our own desires), then we should change; but if it concerns something "not in our power," then we should control our own desires and reactions so as no longer to care about it.

The main thought here is that you should not desire to control *natural* things—things like "disease or death or poverty" that result from forces beyond your control. By "what is unnatural in the region within your control," he may mean desires that refuse to accept what is natural and so seek to control the uncontrollable.

What are the things within your power that you could honorably will to get but that are not yet "within your reach"? Perhaps complete self-control and the peace of mind that goes with it.

To keep my will "in harmony with nature" requires not wanting to avoid things that happen naturally and unavoidably. I lose my temper at being jostled in a crowded public bath, only if I have willed to avoid being jostled, which is willing something beyond my control.

Epictetus claims that it is not things (such as death) that are dreadful, but only *the judgment* that something is dreadful.

(8)

By "the Giver," Epictetus seems to mean more reality at large than a personal deity. Think about the inn analogy: what would your attitude be toward a pleasant room that you stayed in for a short time? Epictetus's view is that you should take this attitude to everything beyond your control that you value: children, other loved ones—and even your life itself.

9

This claim vividly expresses the supreme value Epictetus places on one's own peaceful state of mind. If you care about your material well-being or about the conduct of your son, you will be miserable because these things are not within your control.

10

Slaves in the ordinary sense care about things that are controlled by their owners or masters (what work they have to do, what food they receive, and so on). Epictetus generalizes this picture to say that anyone who cares about anything that is within the control of someone else is, in an extended sense, a slave.

11

Here is an even more extreme (and seemingly less plausible) claim: you should despise all things outside of your control. This is supposed to be even better than the attitude described earlier in this paragraph, but just why despising such things (rather than merely being indifferent to them) is supposed to be better is not clear.

12

R If you are hurt only by not getting what you want, and if you want only what you have in your power, then you will always get what you want and you will never be hurt.

You will be "invincible" in a sense, but is this sort of "invincibility" worth the cost of not caring about anything but your own peace of mind—not even about the many things that you could probably succeed in getting if you allowed yourself to care about them? (See Discussion Question 3.)

hunger, so that you be free from pain and free from fear, than to live in plenty and be troubled in mind. It is better for your son to be wicked than for you to be miserable. (9) Wherefore begin with little things. Is your drop of oil spilt? Is your sup of wine stolen? Say to yourself, 'This is the price paid for freedom from passion, this is the price of a quiet mind.' Nothing can be had without a price. When you call your slave-boy, reflect that he may not be able to hear you, and if he hears you, he may not be able to do anything you want. But he is not so well off that it rests with him to give you peace of mind.

13

If you wish to make progress, you must be content in external matters to seem a fool and a simpleton; do not wish men to think you know anything, and if any should think you to be somebody, distrust yourself. For know that it is not easy to keep your will in accord with nature and at the same time keep outward things; if you attend to one you must needs neglect the other.

14

It is silly to want your children and your wife and your friends to live forever, for that means that you want what is not in your control to be in your control, and what is not your own to be yours. In the same way if you want your servant to make no mistakes, you are a fool, for you want vice not to be vice but something different. But if you want not to be disappointed in your will to get, you can attain to that.

Exercise yourself then in what lies in your power. Each man's master is the man who has authority over what he wishes or does not wish, to secure the one or to take away the other. Let him then who wishes to be free not wish for anything or avoid anything that depends on others; or else he is bound to be a slave. (10)

15

Remember that you must behave in life as you would at a banquet. A dish is handed round and comes to you; put out your hand and take it politely. It passes you; do not stop it. It has not reached you; do not be impatient to get it, but wait till your turn comes. Bear yourself thus towards children, wife, office, wealth, and one day you will be worthy to banquet with the gods. But if when they are set before you, you do not take them but despise them, then you shall not only share the gods' banquet, but shall share their rule. (11) For by so doing Diogenes and Heraclitus and men like them were called divine and deserved the name.

16

When you see a man shedding tears in sorrow for a child abroad or dead, or for loss of property, beware that you are not carried away by the impression that it is outward ills that make him miserable. Keep this thought by you: 'What distresses him is not the event, for that does not distress another, but his judgment on the event.' Therefore do not hesitate to sympathize with him so far as words go, and if it so chance, even to groan with him; but take heed that you do not also groan in your inner being.

...

19

You can be invincible, if you never enter on a contest where victory is not in your power. (12) Beware then that when you see a man raised to honor or great power or high repute you do not let your impression carry you away. For if the reality of good lies in what is in our power, there is no room for envy or jealousy. And you will not wish to be praetor, or prefect or consul, but to be free; and there is but one way to freedom—to despise what is not in our power.

...

28

If any one trusted your body to the first man he met, you would be indignant, but yet you trust your mind to the chance comer, and allow it to be disturbed and confounded if he revile you; are you not ashamed to do so?

...

30

Appropriate acts are in general measured by the relations they are concerned with. 'He is your father.' This means you are called on to take care of him, give way to him in all things, bear with him if he reviles or strikes you.

'But he is a bad father'.

Well, have you any natural claim to a good father? No, only to a father.

'My brother wrongs me'.

Be careful then to maintain the relation you hold to him, and do not consider what he does, but what you must do if your purpose is to keep in accord with nature. For no one shall harm you, without your consent; you will only be harmed, when you think you are harmed. [13] You will only discover what is proper to expect from neighbour, citizen, or praetor, if you get into the habit of looking at the relations implied by each.

...

33

Lay down for yourself from the first a definite stamp and style of conduct, which you will maintain when you are alone and also in the society of men. Be silent for the most part, or, if you speak, say only what is necessary and in a few words. Talk, but rarely, if occasion calls you, but do not talk of ordinary things—of gladiators, or horse-races, or athletes, or of meats or drinks—these are topics that arise everywhere—but above all do not talk about men in blame or compliment or comparison. If you can, turn the conversation of your company by your talk to some fitting subject; but if you should chance to be isolated among strangers, be silent. Do not laugh much, nor at many things, nor without restraint. [14]

Refuse to take oaths, altogether if that be possible, but if not, as far as circumstances allow.

Refuse the entertainments of strangers and the vulgar. But if occasion arise to accept them, then strain every nerve to avoid lapsing into the state of the vulgar. For know that, if your comrade have a stain on him, he that associates with him must needs share the stain, even though he be clean in himself.

For your body take just so much as your bare need requires, such as food, drink, clothing, house, servants, but cut down all that tends to luxury and outward show. [15]

Avoid impurity to the utmost of your power before marriage, and if you indulge your passion, let it be done lawfully. But do not be offensive or censorious to those who indulge it, and do not be always bringing up your own chastity. If some one tells you that so and so speaks ill of you, do not defend yourself against what he says, but answer, 'He did not know my other faults, or he would not have mentioned these alone'.

It is not necessary for the most part to go to the games; but if you should have occasion to go, show that your first concern is for yourself; that is, wish that only to happen which does happen, and him only to win who does win, for so you will suffer no hindrance. But refrain entirely from applause, or ridicule, or prolonged excitement. And when you go away do not talk much of what happened there, except so far as it tends to your improvement. For to talk about it implies that the spectacle excited your wonder. [16]

Do not go lightly or casually to hear lectures; but if you do go, maintain your gravity and dignity and do not make yourself offensive. When you are going to meet any one, and particularly some man of reputed eminence, set before your mind the thought, 'What would Socrates or Zeno have done?' and you will not fail to make proper use of the occasion.

When you go to visit some great man, prepare your mind by thinking that you will not find him in, that you will be shut out, that the doors will be slammed in your face, that he will pay no heed to you. And if in spite of all this you find it fitting for you to go, go and bear what happens and never say to yourself, 'It was not worth all this'; for that shows a vulgar mind and one at odds with outward things.

In your conversation avoid frequent and disproportionate mention of your own doings or adventures; for other people do not take the same pleasure in hearing what has happened to you as you take in recounting your adventures.

Avoid raising men's laughter; for it is a habit that easily slips into vulgarity, and it may well suffice to lessen your neighbor's respect.

It is dangerous too to lapse into foul language; when anything of the kind occurs, rebuke the offender, if the occasion allow, and if not, make it plain to him by your silence, or a blush or a frown, that you are angry at his words. [17]

...

Here we begin to get recommendations that go beyond the idea of confining one's concern to things within one's control. Part of the idea is that one should not allow oneself to be harmed by the actions and nature of others, even members of one's own family. But there is also an idea of doing one's *duty* toward, for example, one's father.

Here are more recommendations that go beyond the views expressed earlier. Epictetus is recommending a kind of restrained, modest style of conduct. This does not follow from the recommendation to desire only that which is in one's control, unless all other styles of conduct must be the result of desires for things that are beyond one's control (e.g., caring for the esteem of others).

15

If we can control our desires, why not take as much as you had readily available for your body at one point, knowing that you can always control your desires if you need to later? Why not enjoy it while you can, even with no expectation of having it in the future, rather than limiting yourself to what "bare need" requires?

16

The rationale for a modest style of conduct has nothing to do with what others think, since we are not supposed to care about that. It must instead appeal to the requirement of shaping one's desires to what is. If one always desires and expects that what will happen is what does happen, then one will never be excited or awed.

This last recommendation seems inconsistent with the previous advice, since we are not supposed to care about what others do.

41

It is a sign of a dull mind to dwell upon the cares of the body, to prolong exercise, eating, drinking, and other bodily functions. These things are to be done by the way; all your attention must be given to the mind.

42

When a man speaks evil or does evil to you, remember that he does or says it because he thinks it is fitting for him. It is not possible for him to follow what seems good to you, but only what seems good to him, so that, if his opinion is wrong, he suffers, in that he is the victim of deception. . . . If you act on this principle you will be gentle to him who reviles you, saying to yourself on each occasion, 'He thought it right'. (18)

43

Everything has two handles, one by which you can carry it, the other by which you cannot. If your brother wrongs you, do not take it by that handle, the handle of his wrong, for you cannot carry it by that, but rather by the other handle—that he is a brother, brought up with you, and then you will take it by the handle that you can carry by. (19)

. . .

45

If a man wash quickly, do not say that he washes badly, but that he washes quickly. If a man drink much wine, do not say that he drinks badly, but that he drinks much. For till you have decided what judgment prompts him, how do you know that he acts badly? If you do as I say, you will assent to your apprehensive impressions and to none other. (20)

46

On no occasion call yourself a philosopher, nor talk at large of your principles among the multitude, but act on your principles. For instance, at a banquet do not say how one ought to eat, but eat as you ought. Remember that Socrates had so completely got rid of the thought of display that when men came and wanted an introduction to philosophers he took them to be introduced; so patient of neglect was he. And if a discussion arise among the multitude on some principle, keep silent for the most part; for you are in great danger of blurting out some undigested thought. And when some one says to you, 'You know nothing', and you do not let it provoke you, then know that you are really on the right road. For sheep do not bring grass to their shepherds and show them how much they have eaten, but they digest their fodder and then produce it in the form of wool and milk. Do the same yourself; instead of displaying your principles to the multitude, show them the results of the principles you have digested. (21)

48

The ignorant man's position and character is this: he never looks to himself for benefit or harm, but to the world outside him. The philosopher's position and character is that he always look to himself for benefit and harm.

The signs of one who is making progress are: he blames none, praises none, complains of none, accuses none, never speaks of himself as if he were somebody, or as if he knew anything. (22) And if any one compliments him he laughs in himself at his compliment; and if one blames him, he makes no defense. He goes about like a convalescent, careful not to disturb his constitution on its road to recovery, until it has got firm hold. He has got rid of the will to get, and his will to avoid is directed no longer to what is beyond our power but only to what is in our power and contrary to nature. In all things he exercises his will without strain. If men regard him as foolish or ignorant he pays no heed. In one word, he keeps watch and guard on himself as his own enemy, lying in wait for him.

. . .

50

Whatever principles you put before you, hold fast to them as laws which it will be impious to transgress. But pay no heed to what any one says of you; for this is something beyond your own control.

---

(18) The suggestion is perhaps that you will not be angry (and thus disrupted) by someone's actions if you assume that the other person thought he had a good reason for what he did.

(19) This is one of the most famous expressions of Stoicism. The suggestion is that while any event can be viewed or assessed in such a way that you will have trouble accepting it, it can also be viewed in such a way that you can accept it. If your own peace of mind is the most important thing to you, then you should view any event in the latter of these ways.

STOP (Does it seem right that *any* event can be viewed in such a way that you can accept it? Think of some difficult examples here.)

A more contemporary version of this recommendation is: make no value judgments, but only describe events in value-neutral terms. Before one can properly evaluate someone else's actions, one often needs to know why the action was performed.

To act in any other way—to show off or try to instruct others—makes sense only if one cares about what others think or one wants to control others.

Here is another aspect of the style of conduct recommended by Epictetus: take responsibility for yourself—don't blame others. But you could obviously accept *this* recommendation while still rejecting the view that you ought to care only about what is in your direct control.

51

How long will you wait to think yourself worthy of the highest and transgress in nothing the clear pronouncement of reason? You have received the precepts which you ought to accept, and you have accepted them. Why then do you still wait for a master, that you may delay the amendment of yourself till he comes? You are a youth no longer, you are now a full-grown man. If now you are careless and indolent and are always putting off, fixing one day after another as the limit when you mean to begin attending to yourself, then, living or dying, you will make no progress but will continue unawares in ignorance. Therefore make up your mind before it is too late to live as one who is mature and proficient, and let all that seems best to you be a law that you cannot transgress. And if you encounter anything troublesome or pleasant or glorious or inglorious, remember that the hour of struggle is come, the Olympic contest is here and you may put off no longer, and that one day and one action determines whether the progress you have achieved is lost or maintained.

This was how Socrates attained perfection, paying heed to nothing but reason, in all that he encountered. And if you are not yet Socrates, yet ought you to live as one who would wish to be a Socrates.

...

Discussion Questions

1. One of the main tenets of Epictetus's thought is that one ought to limit one's desires to what is in one's power, and thus that one ought to accept or submit to all that is outside of one's power. And since all that is really in one's power is how one responds, one should care *only* about how one responds. Remember that Epictetus spent his early life as a slave. Would his view be a plausible recommendation for someone in that specific position? Is its plausibility limited to that situation or one closely similar to it?
2. Do you find the picture recommended by Epictetus attractive? Supposing that you do, is it within your power to do what he recommends? One might argue that Epictetus's thought is an important antidote to the unhealthy obsession with outward things. But can one really control what judgment one makes about an event or how one feels about it?
3. Suppose you could choose between the following three possibilities: in the first case, you want only that which is in your control (according to Epictetus), and thus you get everything that you want—but perhaps little or nothing beyond those very limited wants; in the second case, you limit your desires to reasonable ones—things that you would expect to be able to achieve, given who you are—and you get most of what you want, but are occasionally disappointed; and in the third case, your wants are uncontrolled and extravagant, and while some few of them are satisfied, you are disappointed about most of them. According to Epictetus, the first case is clearly the best one for human beings: happiness consists in avoiding disappointment as completely as possible. Does that seem right?
4. Epictetus's most fundamental recommendation is to care only about one's own states of mind. Think about the main aspects of the kind of life recommended by Epictetus: one ought to take responsibility for oneself, resisting the temptation to blame others; one ought to live modestly, abstaining from worldly desires; one ought to accept reality, rejecting the futile attempt to control outside events. How, if at all, are these further recommendations related to the fundamental one?

Robert Nozick

Robert Nozick (1938–2002), for many years a professor at Harvard, was a major figure in twentieth-century philosophy, making contributions to many areas but most importantly to political philosophy and epistemology.

In this selection, Nozick presents a provocative thought experiment, one that raises issues about what things matter to us, what kinds of things we most fundamentally desire, what motivates us, and what constitutes a good life. For our purposes in this chapter, the last of these issues is most germane.

The Experience Machine

Suppose that this research has resulted in a rich catalog of lives, an effective personality test that you can take, and some reliable general principles about which personality types match which types of lives to produce the best results. You need not worry, therefore, about whether or not you know enough about the options or yourself to pick the best life for yourself.

Also set aside the possibility that the people you leave behind will miss you. Suppose, if it helps, that the programmers create a robotic duplicate of you, indiscernible to others, who will take your place in your relationships. And, of course, your friends and family might choose to take advantage of the experience machine themselves, programming your presence into their experience.

STOP Focusing just on what you care about, about what would be good *for you,* would you plug into this machine?

Someone might object to Nozick that *who we are* is entirely constituted by *what we experience*—in which case, the person floating in the tank is no more an "indeterminate blob" than anyone else.

Are you tempted by such a view?

There are . . . substantial puzzles when we ask what matters other than how *people's* experiences feel "from the inside." Suppose there were an experience machine that would give you any experience you desired. Superduper neuropsychologists could stimulate your brain so that you would think and feel you were writing a great novel, or making a friend, or reading an interesting book. All the time you would be floating in a tank, with electrodes attached to your brain. Should you plug into this machine for life, preprogramming your life's experiences? If you are worried about missing out on desirable experiences, we can suppose that business enterprises have researched thoroughly the lives of many others. (1) You can pick and choose from their large library or smorgasbord of such experiences, selecting your life's experiences for, say, the next two years. After two years have passed, you will have ten minutes or ten hours out of the tank, to select the experiences of your *next* two years. Of course, while in the tank you won't know that you're there; you'll think it's all actually happening. Others can also plug in to have the experiences they want, so there's no need to stay unplugged to serve them. (Ignore problems such as who will service the machines if everyone plugs in.) (2) Would you plug in? *What else can matter to us, other than how our lives feel from the inside?* Nor should you refrain because of the few moments of distress between the moment you've decided and the moment you're plugged. What's a few moments of distress compared to a lifetime of bliss (if that's what you choose), and why feel any distress at all if your decision *is* the best one? (3)

What does matter to us in addition to our experiences? First, we want to *do* certain things, and not just have the experience of doing them. In the case of certain experiences, it is only because first we want to do the actions that we want the experiences of doing them or thinking we've done them. (But *why* do we want to do the activities rather than merely to experience them?) A second reason for not plugging in is that we want to *be* a certain way, to be a certain sort of person. Someone floating in a tank is an indeterminate blob. There is no answer to the question of what a person is like who has long been in the tank. Is he courageous, kind, intelligent, witty, loving? It's not merely that it's difficult to tell; there's no way he is. Plugging into the machine is a kind of suicide. It will seem to some, trapped by a picture, that nothing about what we are like can matter except as it gets reflected in our experiences. But should it be surprising that what *we are* is important to us? (4) Why should we be concerned only with how our time is filled, but not with what we are?

Thirdly, plugging into an experience machine limits us to a man-made reality, to a world no deeper or more important than that which people can construct. There is no *actual* contact with any deeper reality, though the experience of it can be simulated. Many persons desire to leave themselves open to such contact and to a plumbing of deeper significance.* This clarifies the intensity of the conflict over psychoactive drugs, which some view as mere local experience machines, and others view as avenues to a deeper reality; what some view as equivalent to surrender to the experience machine, others view as following one of the reasons *not* to surrender!

We learn that something matters to us in addition to experience by imagining an experience machine and then realizing that we would not use it. We can continue to imagine a sequence of machines each designed to fill lacks suggested for the earlier machines. For

From *Anarchy, State, and Utopia* (New York: Basic Books, 1974).

*Traditional religious views differ on the *point* of contact with a transcendent reality. Some say that contact yields eternal bliss or Nirvana, but they have not distinguished this sufficiently from merely a *very* long run on the experience machine. Others think it is intrinsically desirable to do the will of a higher being which created us all, though presumably no one would think this if we discovered we had been created as an object of amusement by some superpowerful child from another galaxy or dimension. Still others imagine an eventual merging with a higher reality, leaving unclear its desirability, or where that merging leaves *us.*

example, since the experience machine doesn't meet our desire to *be* a certain way, imagine a transformation machine which transforms us into whatever sort of person we'd like to be (compatible with our staying us). 5 Surely one would not use the transformation machine to become as one would wish, and thereupon plug into the experience machine!* So something matters in addition to one's experiences *and* what one is like. Nor is the reason merely that one's experiences are unconnected with what one is like. For the experience machine might be limited to provide only experiences possible to the sort of person plugged in. Is it that we want to make a difference in the world? Consider then the result machine, which produces in the world any result you would produce and injects your vector input into any joint activity. 6 We shall not pursue here the fascinating details of these or other machines. What is most disturbing about them is their living of our lives for us. Is it misguided to search for *particular* additional functions beyond the competence of machines to do for us? Perhaps what we desire is to live (an active verb) ourselves, in contact with reality. (And this, machines cannot do *for* us.)

STOP Would you use the "transformation machine" to learn French? Would you use it to become a kind person?

STOP Suppose that someone refused to plug into the experience machine because she wanted to help unfortunate people in the world. Should she use the results machine if what she cares about is those people being helped?

Discussion Questions

1. Suppose that Grace is a young woman from a wealthy family who falls in love with Bob, a young man with little money of his own. Grace's parents disapprove of Bob, suspecting that he is only after Grace's money. Grace listens carefully to their concerns, but decides to marry Bob anyway. Grace and Bob seem blissfully happy for several years, but Grace's parents remain suspicious. Eventually the parents hire a detective, finally obtaining definitive proof that Bob has been seeing other women. Before they can inform Grace, however, they learn that she has been diagnosed with cancer and has only six months to live. When they confront Bob, he suggests that they think about the pain that revealing his betrayal would cause Grace. After agonizing about the decision, Grace's parents decide not to tell Grace, and Grace lives another five months, never suspecting her husband or doubting his love for her. Did her parents do the right thing?
2. Nozick's third reason for refusing to plug into the experience machine appeals to our desire to connect to a "deeper reality," and he suggests that the transcendent reality advocated by some religions might satisfy this desire. Does it seem then that this third reason will appeal to only religious people, or might something like nature count as a "deeper" reality even for an atheist?
3. Nozick offers the transformation machine as a response to the objection that one might resist going into the experience machine because really *being* someone who is, for example, kind is more important than merely experiencing oneself as being kind: when you step out of the transformation machine, you are genuinely kind. How successful is this response to the original objection? Some might argue that it would be acceptable to use the transformation machine for some things (for example, learning French in order to take a trip) but not for others (for example, becoming a kind person)—that it is "cheating" to produce desirable character traits in this easy and effortless way. Is there any reason why such things as character traits, in order to be valuable or at least maximally valuable, must be acquired "the hard way," rather than in the "easy way" offered by a transformation machine? (While the experience machine seems at least remotely possible, it is not as clear that the transformation machine makes sense. Think about the difference between the two machines.)
4. What would Epictetus think about Nozick's experience machine? Would he choose to plug in if it were available?

*Some wouldn't use the transformation machine at all; it seems like *cheating*. But the one-time use of the transformation machine would not remove all challenges; there would still be obstacles for the new us to overcome, a new plateau from which to strive even higher. And is this plateau any the less earned or deserved than that provided by genetic endowment and early childhood environment? But if the transformation machine could be used indefinitely often, so that we could accomplish anything by pushing a button to transform ourselves into someone who could do it easily, there would remain no limits we *need* to strain against or try to transcend. Would there be anything left *to do*? Do some theological views place God outside of time because an omniscient omnipotent being couldn't fill up his days?

Thomas Nagel

Thomas Nagel (1937–) is an American philosopher who presently teaches at New York University. He has made important contributions to a wide range of areas, including the philosophy of mind, ethics, metaphysics, epistemology, and social philosophy.

It is natural to think that philosophers should have something to say about the meaning of life. For the vast majority of philosophers in the English-speaking world in recent times, however, this question has seemed to be outside the bounds of sober philosophical discussion. Nagel is one of the few recent philosophers who has made any attempt to engage this issue. (Susan Wolf, in the following selection, is another.) Nagel argues that our lives are in an important way *absurd,* in a way that involves a lack of objective meaningfulness, though his reasons for this view are more complicated and subtle than those usually given.

The Absurd

Most people feel on occasion that life is absurd, and some feel it vividly and continually. ❶ Yet the reasons usually offered in defense of this conviction are patently inadequate: they *could* not really explain why life is absurd. Why then do they provide a natural expression for the sense that it is?

I

Consider some examples. It is often remarked that nothing we do now will matter in a million years. But if that is true, then by the same token, nothing that will be the case in a million years matters now. In particular, it does not matter now that in a million years nothing we do now will matter. Moreover, even if what we did now *were* going to matter in a million years, how could that keep our present concerns from being absurd? If their mattering now is not enough to accomplish that, how would it help if they mattered a million years from now?

Whether what we do now will matter in a million years could make the crucial difference only if its mattering in a million years depended on its mattering, period. But then to deny that whatever happens now will matter in a million years is to beg the question against its mattering, period; for in that sense one cannot know that it will not matter in a million years whether (for example) someone now is happy or miserable, without knowing that it does not matter, period. ❷

From *Mortal Questions* (Cambridge, Mass.: Cambridge University Press, 1979).

What we say to convey the absurdity of our lives often has to do with space or time: we are tiny specks in the infinite vastness of the universe; our lives are mere instants even on a geological time scale, let alone a cosmic one; we will all be dead any minute. But of course none of these evident facts can be what *makes* life absurd, if it is absurd. For suppose we lived for ever; would not a life that is absurd if it lasts seventy years be infinitely absurd if it lasted through eternity? And if our lives are absurd given our present size, why would they be any less absurd if we filled the universe (either because we were larger or because the universe was smaller)? Reflection on our minuteness and brevity appears to be intimately connected with the sense that life is meaningless; but it is not clear what the connection is. ❸

Another inadequate argument is that because we are going to die, all chains of justification must leave off in mid-air: one studies and works to earn money to pay for clothing, housing, entertainment, food, to sustain oneself from year to year, perhaps to support a family and pursue a career—but to what final end? All of it is an elaborate journey leading nowhere. (One will also have some effect on other people's lives, but that simply reproduces the problem, for they will die too.)

There are several replies to this argument. First, life does not consist of a sequence of activities each of which has as its purpose some later member of the sequence. Chains of justification come repeatedly to an end within life, and

❶

STOP According to Nagel, most people at least sometimes find life to be *absurd,* where this means something like radically out of synch with human expectations or aspirations. Have you (or perhaps someone you know well) ever had this experience? If so, what was the content of it? In what way or in what sense did life seem absurd? Try, if you can, to spell out this idea as clearly as you can, before seeing what Nagel has to say about it.

❷

For something to "matter, period" is for it to matter *in itself,* apart from any relation to other things (that might not have existed)—to matter, as Nagel later puts it, *sub specie aeternitatis* (from the perspective of eternity). Most things matter because of their relation to other things—for example, money matters because of what money can get you, but does not "matter, period."

❸

STOP Is there, contrary to what Nagel is suggesting, a way in which the "finiteness and brevity" of our lives genuinely supports the idea that they are absurd—or meaningless?

(As Nagel will make clear later, to say that life is meaningless is not quite the same thing as to say that it is absurd, though the two claims are closely connected.)

whether the process as a whole can be justified has no bearing on the finality of these end-points. No further justification is needed to make it reasonable to take aspirin for a headache, attend an exhibition of the work of a painter one admires, or stop a child from putting his hand on a hot stove. No larger context or further purpose is needed to prevent these acts from being pointless. [4]

Even if someone wished to supply a further justification for pursuing all the things in life that are commonly regarded as self-justifying, that justification would have to end somewhere too. If *nothing* can justify unless it is justified in terms of something outside itself, which is also justified, then an infinite regress results, and no chain of justification can be complete. Moreover, if a finite chain of reasons cannot justify anything, what could be accomplished by an infinite chain, each link of which must be justified by something outside itself? [5]

Since justifications must come to an end somewhere, nothing is gained by denying that they end where they appear to, within life—or by trying to subsume the multiple, often trivial ordinary justifications of action under a single, controlling life scheme. We can be satisfied more easily than that. In fact, through its misrepresentation of the process of justification, the argument makes a vacuous demand. It insists that the reasons available within life are incomplete, but suggests thereby that all reasons that come to an end are incomplete. This makes it impossible to supply any reasons at all. [6]

The standard arguments for absurdity appear therefore to fail as arguments. Yet I believe they attempt to express something that is difficult to state, but fundamentally correct.

II

In ordinary life a situation is absurd when it includes a conspicuous discrepancy between pretension or aspiration and reality: someone gives a complicated speech in support of a motion that has already been passed; a notorious criminal is made president of a major philanthropic foundation; you declare your love over the telephone to a recorded announcement; as you are being knighted, your pants fall down. [7]

When a person finds himself in an absurd situation, he will usually attempt to change it, by modifying his aspirations, or by trying to bring reality into better accord with them, or by removing himself from the situation entirely. We are not always willing or able to extricate ourselves from a position whose absurdity has become clear to us. Nevertheless, it is usually possible to imagine some change that would remove the absurdity—whether or not we can or will implement it. The sense that life as a whole is absurd arises when we perceive, perhaps dimly, an inflated pretension or aspiration which is inseparable from the continuation of human life and which makes its absurdity inescapable, short of escape from life itself.

Many people's lives are absurd, temporarily or permanently, for conventional reasons having to do with their particular ambitions, circumstances, and personal relations. If there is a philosophical sense of absurdity, however, it must arise from the perception of something universal—some respect in which pretension and reality inevitably clash for us all. This condition is supplied, I shall argue, by the collision between the seriousness with which we take our lives and the perpetual possibility of regarding everything about which we are serious as arbitrary, or open to doubt.

We cannot live human lives without energy and attention, nor without making choices which show that we take some things more seriously than others. Yet we have always available a point of view outside the particular form of our lives, from which the seriousness appears gratuitous. These two inescapable viewpoints collide in us, and that is what makes life absurd. It is absurd because we ignore the doubts that we know cannot be settled, continuing to live with nearly undiminished seriousness in spite of them. [8]

This analysis requires defense in two respects: first as regards the unavoidability of seriousness; second as regards the inescapability of doubt.

We take ourselves seriously whether we lead serious lives or not and whether we are concerned primarily with fame, pleasure, virtues, luxury, triumph, beauty, justice, knowledge, salvation, or mere survival. If we take other people seriously and devote ourselves to them, that only multiplies the problem. Human life is full of effort, plans, calculation, success and failure: we *pursue* our lives, with varying degrees of sloth and energy.

R It is fairly common to think that the point or purpose of every act must lie in some further end or goal, so that if the chain of acts terminates (at a person's death or the death of those they affect), then everything someone did was without point. But in fact, Nagel is claiming, many acts have a point or meaning *in themselves*, without this depending on any further ends.

Suppose that, as many people believe, we were put on this earth by a powerful being and our existence is justified by satisfying his purposes. But then what, outside of him, justifies his purposes (which is required if it is true that "*nothing* can justify unless it is justified in terms of something outside itself")?

Nagel is suggesting that this argument for the absurdity of life fails because it assumes with no justification that the only sort of reason one could possibly have for anything (since an infinite chain of reasons is logically impossible) isn't good enough.

STOP According to Nagel, absurdity results when there is a discrepancy between our pretensions or aspirations and reality. Think carefully how this description applies to the limited situations described here. Can you think of other examples of this sort?

8 *Restatement/Summary*

R For life as a whole to be absurd would be for it to essentially involve a large-scale version of this same sort of discrepancy between pretensions and reality. Nagel's main claim is that while we cannot help but take many things in our lives seriously, there is at the same time always available a different, more objective point of view from which this seriousness seems unwarranted and even foolish.

It would be different if we could not step back and reflect on the process, but were merely led from impulse to impulse without self-consciousness. But human beings do not act solely on impulse. They are prudent, they reflect, they weigh consequences, they ask whether what they are doing is worth while. Not only are their lives full of particular choices that hang together in larger activities with temporal structure: they also decide in the broadest terms what to pursue and what to avoid, what the priorities among their various aims should be, and what kind of people they want to be or become. Some men are faced with such choices by the large decisions they make from time to time; some merely by reflection on the course their lives are taking as the product of countless small decisions. They decide whom to marry, what profession to follow, whether to join the Country Club, or the Resistance; or they may just wonder why they go on being salesmen or academics or taxi drivers, and then stop thinking about it after a certain period of inconclusive reflection.

Although they may be motivated from act to act by those immediate needs with which life presents them, they allow the process to continue by adhering to the general system of habits and the form of life in which such motives have their place—or perhaps only by clinging to life itself. They spend enormous quantities of energy, risk, and calculation on the details. Think of how an ordinary individual sweats over his appearance, his health, his sex life, his emotional honesty, his social utility, his self-knowledge, the quality of his ties with family, colleagues, and friends, how well he does his job, whether he understands the world and what is going on in it. Leading a human life is a full-time occupation, to which everyone devotes decades of intense concern. 9

9

STOP Is Nagel right about this? Can you think of anyone who does not in this way *pursue* at least some parts or aspects of his or her life, someone for whom it matters little or not at all whether things turn out one way instead of another?

This fact is so obvious that it is hard to find it extraordinary and important. Each of us lives his own life—lives with himself twenty-four hours a day. What else is he supposed to do—live someone else's life? Yet humans have the special capacity to step back and survey themselves, and the lives to which they are committed, with that detached amazement which comes from watching an ant struggle up a heap of sand. Without developing the illusion that they are able to escape from their highly specific and idiosyncratic position, they can view it *sub specie aeternitatis*—and the view is at once sobering and comical.

The crucial backward step is not taken by asking for still another justification in the chain, and failing to get it. The objections to that line of attack have already been stated; justifications come to an end. But this is precisely what provides universal doubt with its object. We step back to find that the whole system of justification and criticism, which controls our choices and supports our claims to rationality, rests on responses and habits that we never question, that we should not know how to defend without circularity, and to which we shall continue to adhere even after they are called into question. 10

R Every person, according to Nagel, has the capacity to "step back" and view his life from "the perspective of eternity," a perspective that transcends the interests and concerns of his life or even of human life generally. From this perspective, he claims, all of our reasons for all of our actions are open to doubt.

The things we do or want without reasons, and without requiring reasons—the things that define what is a reason for us and what is not—are the starting points of our skepticism. We see ourselves from outside, and all the contingency and specificity of our aims and pursuits become clear. Yet when we take this view and recognize what we do as arbitrary, it does not disengage us from life, and there lies our absurdity: not in the fact that such an external view can be taken of us, but in the fact that we ourselves can take it, without ceasing to be the persons whose ultimate concerns are so coolly regarded. 11

11

R Thus we can allegedly take a point of view from which we can recognize that all our actions and purposes are arbitrary. And yet we continue to care about them seriously—which is why, according to Nagel, our lives are absurd. (Do we really *recognize* that the things we care about are arbitrary—*genuinely* arbitrary—or do they merely *seem* arbitrary from that standpoint? Nagel is unclear on this pretty critical point.)

III

One may try to escape the position by seeking broader ultimate concerns, from which it is impossible to step back—the idea being that absurdity results because what we take seriously is something small and insignificant and individual. Those seeking to supply their lives with meaning usually envision a role or function in something larger than themselves. They therefore seek fulfillment in service to society, the state, the revolution, the progress of history, the advance of science, or religion and the glory of God.

But a role in some larger enterprise cannot confer significance unless that enterprise is itself significant. And its significance must come back to what we can understand, or it will not even appear to give us what we are seeking. If we learned that we were being raised to provide food for other creatures fond of human flesh, who planned to turn us into cutlets before we got too stringy—even if we learned that the human race had been developed by animal breeders precisely for this purpose—that would still not give our lives meaning, for two reasons. First, we would still be in the dark as to the significance of the lives of those other beings; second, although we might acknowledge that this culinary role would make our lives meaningful to them, it is not clear how it would make them meaningful to us. (12)

Admittedly, the usual form of service to a higher being is different from this. One is supposed to behold and partake of the glory of God, for example, in a way in which chickens do not share in the glory of coq au vin. The same is true of service to a state, a movement, or a revolution. People can come to feel, when they are part of something bigger, that it is part of them too. They worry less about what is peculiar to themselves, but identify enough with the larger enterprise to find their role in it fulfilling.

However, any such larger purpose can be put in doubt in the same way that the aims of an individual life can be, and for the same reasons. It is as legitimate to find ultimate justification there as to find it earlier, among the details of individual life. But this does not alter the fact that justifications come to an end when we are content to have them end—when we do not find it necessary to look any further. If we can step back from the purposes of individual life and doubt their point, we can step back also from the progress of human history, or of science, or the success of a society, or the kingdom, power, and glory of God, and put all these things into question in the same way. (13) What seems to us to confer meaning, justification, significance, does so in virtue of the fact that we need no more reasons after a certain point.

What makes doubt inescapable with regard to the limited aims of individual life also makes it inescapable with regard to any larger purpose that encourages the sense that life is meaningful. Once the fundamental doubt has begun, it cannot be laid to rest.

Camus maintains in *The Myth of Sisyphus* that the absurd arises because the world fails to meet our demands for meaning. This suggests that the world might satisfy those demands if it were different. But now we can see that this is not the case. There does not appear to be any conceivable world (containing us) about which unsettlable doubts could not arise. Consequently the absurdity of our situation derives not from a collision between our expectations and the world, but from a collision within ourselves. (14)

IV

It may be objected that the standpoint from which these doubts are supposed to be felt does not exist—that if we take the recommended backward step we will land on thin air, without any basis for judgment about the natural responses we are supposed to be surveying. If we retain our usual standards of what is important, then questions about the significance of what we are doing with our lives will be answerable in the usual way. But if we do not, then those questions can mean nothing to us, since there is no longer any content to the idea of what matters, and hence no content to the idea that nothing does. (15)

But this objection misconceives the nature of the backward step. It is not supposed to give us an understanding of what is *really* important, so that we see by contrast that our lives are insignificant. We never, in the course of these reflections, abandon the ordinary standards that guide our lives. We merely observe them in operation, and recognize that if they are called into question we can justify them only by reference to themselves, uselessly. We adhere to them because of the way we are put together; what seems to us important or serious or valuable would not seem so if we were differently constituted. (16)

In ordinary life, to be sure, we do not judge a situation absurd unless we have in mind some standards of seriousness, significance, or harmony with which the absurd can be contrasted. This contrast is not implied by the philosophical judgment of absurdity, and that might be thought to make the concept unsuitable for the expression of such judgments. This is not so, however, for the philosophical judgment depends on another contrast which makes it a natural extension from more ordinary cases. It departs from them only in contrasting the pretensions of life with a larger context in which *no* standards can be discovered, rather than with a context from which

Nagel's claim is that making a contribution to a larger project cannot *by itself* confer meaning on your life—whether or not that larger project itself has meaning or significance.

Is it clear, as Nagel claims, that the significance or justification of *any* larger purpose (or the source of that purpose) can always be called into question in the same way, by "stepping back" in the way that he indicates? Many people have thought that the significance of God or God's purposes cannot be doubted in this way, but is there any clear reason why this is so? Does Nagel have any clear reason for his opposite claim?

So Nagel's claim is not just that the search for unchallengeable meaning or significance in our lives may fail, depending on exactly what reality is like, but rather that failure is *guaranteed*. We are doomed to try forever to find a way in which our lives can be ultimately meaningful, while at the same time seeing clearly that this cannot be done.

This is the most serious objection to Nagel's view. It claims that the supposed perspective from which we can legitimately question the standards of significance by which we ordinarily assess our lives does not really exist, because there are no alternative bases for assessing significance to which we can appeal.

Nagel's first response is that the supposed perspective does not involve an alternative basis or alternative standards, but instead lets us see that our standards depend on the sorts of creatures we are and would not apply if we were creatures of a different sort.

(Is this really something we see clearly—or is it merely a possibility that cannot be ruled out?)

17

Here is what seems like a rather different answer: from the larger perspective, there are no standards of significance to be discerned—thereby allegedly showing the arbitrariness of the ordinary standards of significance that we employ in our more limited perspective.

(But why should we assume that the larger perspective provides the more accurate view, rather than just making it hard to see something that might still be perfectly genuine?)

18

Nagel returns to the suggestion, made briefly earlier, that there could be very different kinds of creatures, creatures who care about very different kinds of things. But why is the fact, even if it is a fact, that there could be creatures who care about very different kinds of things *relevant to* whether or not I should take the things I care about seriously?

19

R The mouse would now have grave doubts about those purposes he cannot abandon. Before he had those doubts, his life was not absurd, but once he has the doubts, his life becomes absurd, given that he nonetheless cannot avoid seriously pursuing those purposes.

20

R The other way to eliminate the absurdity of one's life is to stop taking life so seriously. But to pursue this course too vigorously would defeat itself by being a way of taking life seriously after all.

21

Our lives are not absurd merely because they are meaningless. What leads to absurdity is the double apprehension (a) that the seriousness with which we take our lives is not justified, and (b) that we can't seem to stop taking our lives seriously.

alternative, overriding standards may be applied. 17

...

VI

In viewing ourselves from a perspective broader than we can occupy in the flesh, we become spectators of our own lives. We cannot do very much as pure spectators of our own lives, so we continue to lead them, and devote ourselves to what we are able at the same time to view as no more than a curiosity, like the ritual of an alien religion.

This explains why the sense of absurdity finds its natural expression in those bad arguments with which the discussion began. Reference to our small size and short lifespan and to the fact that all of mankind will eventually vanish without a trace are metaphors for the backward step which permits us to regard ourselves from without and to find the particular form of our lives curious and slightly surprising. By feigning a nebula's-eye view, we illustrate the capacity to see ourselves without presuppositions, as arbitrary, idiosyncratic, highly specific occupants of the world, one of countless possible forms of life. 18

Before turning to the question whether the absurdity of our lives is something to be regretted and if possible escaped, let me consider what would have to be given up in order to avoid it.

Why is the life of a mouse not absurd? The orbit of the moon is not absurd either, but that involves no strivings or aims at all. A mouse, however, has to work to stay alive. Yet he is not absurd, because he lacks the capacities for self-consciousness and self-transcendence that would enable him to see that he is only a mouse. If that *did* happen, his life would become absurd, since self-awareness would not make him cease to be a mouse and would not enable him to rise above his mousely strivings. Bringing his new-found self-consciousness with him, he would have to return to his meager yet frantic life, full of doubts that he was unable to answer, but also full of purposes that he was unable to abandon. 19

Given that the transcendental step is natural to us humans, can we avoid absurdity by refusing to take that step and remaining entirely within our sublunar lives? Well, we cannot refuse consciously, for to do that we would have to be aware of the viewpoint we were refusing to adopt. The only way to avoid the relevant self-consciousness would be either never to attain it or to forget it—neither of which can be achieved by the will.

On the other hand, it is possible to expend effort on an attempt to destroy the other component of the absurd—abandoning one's earthly, individual, human life in order to identify as completely as possible with that universal viewpoint from which human life seems arbitrary and trivial. (This appears to be the ideal of certain Oriental religions.) If one succeeds, then one will not have to drag the superior awareness through a strenuous mundane life, and absurdity will be diminished.

However, insofar as this self-etiolation is the result of effort, will-power, asceticism, and so forth, it requires that one take oneself seriously as an individual—that one be willing to take considerable trouble to avoid being creaturely and absurd. Thus one may undermine the aim of unworldliness by pursuing it too vigorously. 20 Still, if someone simply allowed his individual, animal nature to drift and respond to impulse, without making the pursuit of its needs a central conscious aim, then he might, at considerable dissociative cost, achieve a life that was less absurd than most. It would not be a meaningful life either, of course; but it would not involve the engagement of a transcendent awareness in the assiduous pursuit of mundane goals. And that is the main condition of absurdity—the dragooning of an unconvinced transcendent consciousness into the service of an immanent, limited enterprise like a human life. 21

The final escape is suicide; but before adopting any hasty solutions, it would be wise to consider carefully whether the absurdity of our existence truly presents us with a *problem,* to which some solution must be found—a way of dealing with *prima facie* disaster. That is certainly the attitude with which Camus approaches the issue, and it gains support from the fact that we are all eager to escape from absurd situations on a smaller scale.

Camus—not on uniformly good grounds—rejects suicide and the other solutions he regards as escapist. What he recommends is defiance or scorn. We can salvage our dignity, he appears to believe, by shaking a fist at the world which is deaf to our pleas, and continuing to live in spite of it. This will not make our lives un-absurd, but it will lend them a certain nobility.*

This seems to me romantic and slightly self-pitying. Our absurdity warrants neither that much distress nor that much defiance. At the risk of falling into romanticism by a different route, I would argue that absurdity is one of the most human things about us: a manifestation of our most advanced and interesting characteristics. . . . it is possible only because we possess a certain kind of insight—the capacity to transcend ourselves in thought.

If a sense of the absurd is a way of perceiving our true situation (even though the situation is not absurd until the perception arises), then what reason can we have to resent or escape it? Like the capacity for epistemological skepticism, it results from the ability to understand our human limitations. It need not be a matter for agony unless we make it so. (22) Nor need it evoke a defiant contempt of fate that allows us to feel brave or proud. Such dramatics, even if carried on in private, betray a failure to appreciate the cosmic unimportance of the situation. If *sub specie aeternitatis* there is no reason to believe that anything matters, then that does not matter either, and we can approach our absurd lives with irony instead of heroism or despair.

(22)

Epictetus would approve of Nagel's attitude here.

Discussion Questions

1. In *The Myth of Sisyphus,* Albert Camus writes: "The gods had condemned Sisyphus to ceaselessly rolling a rock to the top of a mountain, whence the stone would fall back of its own weight. They had thought with some reason that there is no more dreadful punishment than futile and hopeless labor." What do you think about Sisyphus's life—is it meaningless? Does it matter whether he enjoys the task or not?—perhaps the view on the way to the top is breathtaking. If Sisyphus fully realizes how futile his task is and thus does not take his efforts seriously, then his life is not absurd in the very specific sense that Nagel specifies. Is it absurd in some other way?
2. It is the paradoxical character of our lives that makes them absurd, according to Nagel, where the paradox consists in our being unable to stop taking our lives seriously even though we can see, from the broader perspective, that there is no reason (or at least seems to be no reason) to take them seriously. One crucial reason for this, one he seems to think is sufficient for the claim, is that there could be lives very different from ours, lives led by creatures who take very different things seriously. It is surely true, that *from their perspective,* there is no reason to take seriously the things we take seriously—just as from our perspective, there is no reason to take seriously the things that they take seriously. But the broader perspective is not their particular perspective. What exactly is the broader perspective, and how is the possibility of other forms of life relevant to it?
3. Suppose that Nagel is right about the paradoxical nature of the human condition: that we are unable to stop taking our lives seriously even though we can see, from the broader perspective, that there is no reason to take them seriously. Does that seem like a problem that needs a solution? Camus thinks so and recommends defiance. Nagel thinks not and seems to endorse an ironic response to the absurdity of our lives. What do you think he means by this? What seems to you to be the right response, assuming that Nagel is right about the nature of the human condition?
4. Suppose that someone were to respond to Nagel in the following way: "All this talk of the perspective of eternity or the larger perspective makes little real sense. Perhaps we can have some faint idea of such a perspective, but not enough of one to give us any clear idea of what things would look like from there. And even if we were sure (which we cannot ever be), that from the larger perspective our actions or our standards of significance would not *seem* justified, that isn't enough to show that they really are unjustified or arbitrary. The most we would ever have is a conflict between that perspective and our ordinary one, and what seems true from our ordinary perspective is both much clearer and has a far greater claim to be correct (because of its clarity and apparent cogency) than anything about this elusive and murky alternative perspective. Thus Nagel has offered no real reason for thinking that our lives are absurd, or even for taking the possibility of absurdity seriously." Which view seems to you more defensible, Nagel's or that of the imagined critic? How would you argue further for one side or the other?

*"Sisyphus, proletarian of the gods, powerless and rebellious, knows the whole extent of his wretched condition: it is what he thinks of during his descent. The lucidity that was to constitute his torture at the same time crowns his victory. There is no fate that cannot be surmounted by scorn." (*The Myth of Sisyphus,* trans. Justin O'Brien [New York: Vintage, 1959], p. 90; first published, Paris: Gallimard, 1942.)

Susan Wolf

Susan Wolf (1952–) is an American philosopher who teaches philosophy at the University of North Carolina at Chapel Hill. Her main work is in ethics, with her discussions of free will and moral responsibility being especially influential. Wolf is another one of the very few recent philosophers who is willing to articulate and defend a view about the meaning of life. In this selection, she argues that one who is actively engaged in projects that are objectively worthwhile is living a meaningful life.

Happiness and Meaning: Two Aspects of the Good Life

The topic of self-interest raises large and intractable philosophical questions—most obviously, the question "In what does self-interest consist?" The concept, as opposed to the content of self-interest, however, seems clear enough. Self-interest is interest in one's own good. To act self-interestedly is to act on the motive of advancing one's own good. Whether what one does actually is in one's self-interest depends on whether it actually does advance, or at least, minimize the decline of, one's own good. Though it may be difficult to tell whether a person is motivated by self-interest in a particular instance, and difficult also to determine whether a given act or decision really is in one's self-interest, the meaning of the claims in question seems unproblematic. 1

1 R It is not always easy to tell what truly motivates someone, and it is not always easy to tell what is truly good for someone, but if one's act is in fact motivated by what one thinks is one's own good, then it is a self-interested act.

My main concern in this essay is to make a point about the content of self-interest.* Specifically I shall put forward the view that meaningfulness, in a sense I shall elaborate, is an important element of a good life. It follows, then, that it is part of an enlightened self-interest that one wants to secure meaning in one's life, or, at any rate, to allow and promote meaningful activity within it. Accepting this substantial conception of self-interest, however, carries with it a curious consequence: the concept of self-interest which formerly seemed so clear begins to grow fuzzy. Fortunately, it comes to seem less important as well. 2

2 Though Wolf's ultimate concern (which emerges mainly at the end of the paper) is with issues pertaining to self-interest, the bulk of the paper argues for a particular conception of the good life (a view that plays a crucial role in her argument about self-interest).

From *Social Philosophy & Policy,* Vol. 14, No. 1 (Winter, 1997).

Theories of Self-Interest

In Reasons and Persons,† Derek Parfit distinguishes three sorts of theories about self-interest—hedonistic theories, preference theories, and what he calls "objective-list theories." *Hedonistic theories* hold that one's good is a matter of the felt quality of one's experiences. The most popular theory of self-interest, which identifies self-interest with happiness, and happiness with pleasure and the absence of pain, is a prime example of a hedonistic theory. 3 Noting that some people do not care that much about their own happiness, however—and, importantly, that they do not even regard their own happiness as the exclusive element in their own good—has led some to propose a *preference theory* of self-interest, which would identify a person's good with what the person most wants for herself. Thus, for example, if a person cares more about being famous, even posthumously famous, than about being happy, then a preference theory would accord fame a proportionate weight in the identification of her self-interest. If a person cares more about knowing the truth than about believing what is pleasant or comfortable to believe, then it is in her self-interest to have the truth, unpleasant as it may be. 4

3 According to a hedonistic theory, one could always satisfy one's self-interest by plugging into Nozick's experience machine.

4 Such a theory imposes no limitations on a person's preferences. Your good has been enhanced as long as your preferences, whatever they happen to be, are satisfied.

A person's preferences regarding herself, however, may be self-destructive or otherwise bizarre, and it may be that some things (including pleasure) are good for a person whether the person prefers them or not. It is not absurd to think that being deceived is bad for a person (and thus that not being deceived is good for a

*The view described and defended here shows the influence of and my sympathy with the views of Aristotle and John Stuart Mill throughout. I cannot individuate my debts to them; they are pervasive.

†Derek Parfit, *Reasons and Persons* (Oxford: Oxford University Press, 1984).

person) whether or not the person in question consciously values this state. Friendship and love may also seem to be things whose goodness explains, rather than results from, people's preferences for them. The plausibility of these last thoughts explains the appeal of *objective-list theories,* according to which a person's good includes at least some elements that are independent of or prior to her preferences and to their effect on the felt quality of her experience. On this view, there are some items, ideally specifiable on an "objective list," whose relevance to a fully successful life are not conditional on the subject's choice. [5]

The view that I shall be advancing, that meaningfulness is an ingredient of the good life, commits one to a version of this last kind of theory, for my claim is that meaningfulness is a nonderivative aspect of a good life—its goodness does not result from its making us happy or its satisfying the preferences of the person whose life it is. Thus, it follows that any theory that takes self-interest to be a wholly subjective matter, either in a sense that identifies self-interest with the subjective quality of a person's subjective experiences or in a sense that allows the standards of self-interest to be set by a person's subjective preferences, must be inadequate. At the same time, it would be a mistake to think that the objective good for a person to live a meaningful life is one that is wholly independent of the subject's experience or preferences, as if it could be good for a person to live a meaningful life whether or not it makes her happy or satisfies her preferences. Indeed, as we will see, the very idea that activities can make a life meaningful without the subject's endorsement is a dubious one.

Meaning in Life

What is a meaningful life? Spelling it out will constitute the bulk of my essay, for my hope is that once the idea is spelled out, it will be readily agreed that it is an element of a fully successful life.

A meaningful life is, first of all, one that has within it the basis for an affirmative answer to the needs or longings that are characteristically described as needs for meaning. I have in mind, for example, the sort of questions people ask on their deathbeds, or simply in contemplation of their eventual deaths, about whether their lives have been (or are) worth living, whether they have had any point, and the sort of questions one asks when considering suicide and wondering whether one has any reason to go on. These questions are familiar from Russian novels and existentialist philosophy, if not from personal experience. Though they arise most poignantly in times of crisis and intense emotion, they also have their place in moments of calm reflection, when considering important life choices. Moreover, paradigms of what are taken to be meaningful and meaningless lives in our culture are readily available. Lives of great moral or intellectual accomplishment—Gandhi, Mother Teresa, Albert Einstein—come to mind as unquestionably meaningful lives (if any are); lives of waste and isolation—Thoreau's "lives of quiet desperation," typically anonymous to the rest of us, and the mythical figure of Sisyphus—represent meaninglessness. [6]

To what general characteristics of meaningfulness do these images lead us and how do they provide an answer to the longings mentioned above? Roughly, I would say that meaningful lives are lives of active engagement in projects of worth. Of course, a good deal needs to be said in elaboration of this statement. Let me begin by discussing the two key phrases, "active engagement" and "projects of worth."

A person is actively engaged by something if she is gripped, excited, involved by it. Most obviously, we are actively engaged by the things and people about which and whom we are passionate. Opposites of active engagement are boredom and alienation. To be actively engaged in something is not always pleasant in the ordinary sense of the word. Activities in which people are actively engaged frequently involve stress, danger, exertion, or sorrow (consider, for example: writing a book, climbing a mountain, training for a marathon, caring for an ailing friend). However, there is something good about the feeling of engagement: one feels (typically without thinking about it) especially alive. [7]

That a meaningful life must involve "projects of worth" will, I expect, be more controversial, for the phrase hints of a commitment to some sort of objective value. This is not accidental, for I believe that the idea of meaningfulness, and the concern that our lives possess it, are conceptually linked to such a commitment.

5

Only according to this third kind of theory does self-interest involve requirements that are objective in the sense that they do not depend on what makes a particular individual happy or what he or she happens to prefer. What exactly these objective requirements are obviously depends on what is on the "objective list."

6

Sisyphus was condemned by the gods to roll a rock up a mountain, just to have it roll back down, over and over again, for the rest of his life.

7

Thus no matter how objectively important a person's life may seem (think of various examples here), those lives are not *meaningful,* according to Wolf, if the person is bored or apathetic in relation to it.

Indeed, it is this linkage that I want to defend, for I have neither a philosophical theory of what objective value is nor a substantive theory about what has this sort of value. What is clear to me is that there can be no sense to the idea of meaningfulness without a distinction between more and less worthwhile ways to spend one's time, where the test of worth is at least partly independent of a subject's ungrounded preferences or enjoyment. 8

8

Suppose, for example, that you really enjoy counting blades of grass in various lawns. Wolf's claim is that such an activity must have some independent value (in addition to the fact that you enjoy it) in order for it to have objective worth. (See Discussion Question 2.)

Consider first the longings or concerns about meaning that people have, their wondering whether their lives are meaningful, their vows to add more meaning to their lives. The sense of these concerns and resolves cannot fully be captured by an account in which what one does with one's life doesn't matter, as long as one enjoys or prefers it. Sometimes people have concerns about meaning despite their knowledge that their lives to date have been satisfying. Indeed, their enjoyment and "active engagement" with activities and values they now see as shallow seems only to heighten the sense of meaninglessness that comes to afflict them. Their sense that their lives so far have been meaningless cannot be a sense that their activities have not been chosen or fun. When they look for sources of meaning or ways to add meaning to their lives, they are searching for projects whose justifications lie elsewhere.

Second, we need an explanation for why certain sorts of activities and involvements come to mind as contributors to meaningfulness while others seem intuitively inappropriate. Think about what gives meaning to your own life and the lives of your friends and acquaintances. Among the things that tend to come up on such lists, I have already mentioned moral and intellectual accomplishments and the ongoing activities that lead to them. Relationships with friends and relatives are perhaps even more important for most of us. Aesthetic enterprises (both creative and appreciative), the cultivation of personal virtues, and religious practices frequently loom large. By contrast, it would be odd, if not bizarre, to think of crossword puzzles, sitcoms, or the kind of computer games to which I am fighting off addiction as providing meaning in our lives, though there is no question that they afford a sort of satisfaction and that they are the objects of choice. Some things, such as chocolate and aerobics class, I choose even at considerable cost to myself (it is irrelevant that these particular choices may be related), so I must find them worthwhile in a sense. But they are not the sorts of things that make life worth living.

"Active engagement in projects of worth," I suggest, answers to the needs an account of meaningfulness in life must meet. If a person is or has been thus actively engaged, then she does have an answer to the question of whether her life is or has been worthwhile, whether it has or has had a point. When someone looks for ways to add meaning to her life, she is looking (though perhaps not under this description) for worthwhile projects about which she can get enthused. 9 The account also explains why some activities and projects but not others come to mind as contributors to meaning in life. Some projects, or at any rate, particular acts, are worthwhile but too boring or mechanical to be sources of meaning. People do not get meaning from recycling or from writing checks to Oxfam and the ACLU. Other acts and activities, though highly pleasurable and deeply involving, like riding a roller coaster or meeting a movie star, do not seem to have the right kind of value to contribute to meaning.

9

R Notice that you have to be able to be *enthusiastic* about the project. If you are not enthused, then you won't be actively engaged, according to Wolf's view.

Bernard Williams once distinguished categorical desires from the rest. Categorical desires give us reasons for living—they are not premised on the assumption that we will live. The sorts of things that give meaning to life tend to be objects of categorical desire. We desire them, at least so I would suggest, because we think them worthwhile. They are not worthwhile simply because we desire them or simply because they make our lives more pleasant. 10

10

R According to Wolf's view, the order of dependence here is very important. If you are attracted to something because you judge that it is worthwhile, then it may provide meaning to your life. But if you judge that it is worthwhile merely because you are attracted to it, and you have no reason beyond your own pleasure for being attracted to it, then it is not capable of providing meaning to your life.

Roughly, then, according to my proposal, a meaningful life must satisfy two criteria, suitably linked. First, there must be active engagement, and second, it must be engagement in (or with) projects of worth. A life is meaningless if it lacks active engagement with anything. A person who is bored or alienated from most of what she spends her life doing is one whose life can be said to lack meaning. Note that she may in fact be performing functions of worth. A housewife and mother, a doctor, or a busdriver may be competently doing a socially valuable job, but because she is not engaged by her work (or, as we are assuming, by anything else in her life), she has no categorical desires that give her a reason to live. At the same time, someone who *is* actively engaged may also live a meaningless life, if the objects of her involvement are utterly worthless. It is difficult to come up with examples of such lives that will be uncontroversial without being bizarre. But both bizarre and controversial examples have their place. In the bizarre category, we might consider pathological cases: someone whose sole passion in life is collecting rubber bands, or memorizing the dictionary, or making handwritten copies of *War and Peace.* Controversial cases will include the corporate lawyer who sacrifices her private life and health for success along the professional ladder, the devotee of a religious cult, or the pig farmer who buys more land to grow more corn to feed more pigs to buy more land to grow more corn to feed more pigs.

We may summarize my proposal in terms of a slogan: "Meaning arises when subjective attraction meets objective attractiveness." The idea is that in a world in which some things are more worthwhile than others, meaning arises when a subject discovers or develops an affinity for one or typically several of the more worthwhile things and has and makes use of the opportunity to engage with it or them in a positive way.

An advantage of the slogan is that it avoids the somewhat misleading reference to "projects." That term is less than ideal in its suggestion of well-defined and goal-oriented tasks. To be sure, many projects do add meaning to life—mastering a field of study, building a house, turning a swamp into a garden, curing cancer—but much of what gives meaning to life consists in ongoing relationships and involvements—with friends, family, the scientific community, with church or ballet or chess. These ongoing strands of life give rise to and are partly constituted by projects—you plan a surprise party for your spouse, coach a little league team, review an article for a journal—but the meaning comes less from the individuated projects than from the larger involvements of which they are parts. The slogan, moreover, is intentionally vague, for if pretheoretical judgments about meaning even approximate the truth, then not only the objects of worth but also the sorts of interaction with them that are capable of contributing to meaning are immensely variable. One can get meaning from creating, promoting, protecting (worthwhile) things, from helping people one loves and people in need, from achieving levels of skill and excellence, from overcoming obstacles, from gaining understanding, and even from just communing with or actively appreciating what is there to be appreciated. 11

It is part of our job, if not our natural bent, as philosophers to be skeptical—about the correctness of these pretheoretical judgments, about our ability reliably to distinguish meaningful from meaningless activities, and about the very coherence of the distinction. About the first two worries I am not very concerned. Assuming that the distinctions are coherent and that some activities are more worthwhile than others, our culture-bound, contemporary judgments of which activities are worthwhile are bound to be partly erroneous. History is full of unappreciated geniuses, of artists, inventors, explorers whose activities at their time were scorned, as it is full of models of behavior and accomplishment that later seem to have been overrated. Though we may improve our judgments, both particular and general, by an open-minded, concentrated, and communal effort to examine and articulate the basis for them (a project that strikes me as both worthwhile and intrinsically interesting), the hope or expectation that such scrutiny will yield a reliable method for generally distinguishing worthwhile from worthless activities seems overly optimistic. Why do we respect people who devote themselves to chess more than those who become champions at pinball? Why do we admire basketball stars more than jump-rope champions? What is more worthwhile about writing a book on the philosophy of language than writing one on [some celebrity's] sex life? It is useful to ask and to answer such questions, so far as we can, both to widen and correct our horizons and to increase our understanding. But our inability to give complete and adequate answers, or to be confident in the details of our assessments, need not be a serious problem. The point of recognizing the distinction, after all, is not to give rankings of meaningful lives. There is no need, in general, to pass judgment on individuals or even on activities in which people want to engage. The point is rather at a more general level to understand the ingredients of our own and others' good, and to get a better idea of the sorts of considerations that provide reasons for living our lives one way rather than another. 12

R It is so easy to see how activities that contribute to well-defined projects or goals might count toward a meaningful life that one could fail to appreciate the importance of more ordinary activities—ones that do not contribute to a specific project, but are still important to a meaningful life because of the relationships and involvements they reflect.

R To accept the distinction between meaningful and meaningless activities does not require that it is easy to distinguish the two in practice or that there cannot be debatable cases. Nor does it require that you be concerned with ranking the lives of your friends and family (and yourself) in this respect.

The point, which I am in the midst of developing, is that meaningfulness is a nonderivative part of an individual's good, and that meaningfulness consists in active engagement in projects or activities of worth. Though it seems to me that the point and most of its usefulness can stand despite acknowledged difficulties with identifying precisely which projects or activities these are, it would be utterly destroyed if it turned out that there were no such things as projects or activities of worth at all—if it turned out, in other words, as Bentham thought, that pushpin were as good as poetry, not because of some heretofore undiscovered excellences in the game of pushpin, but because the very idea of distinctions in worth is bankrupt or incoherent. If there are no projects of worth (in contrast to other projects), then there are no such things as what I have in mind by more and less meaningful lives, and so it cannot be a part of one's good to live a more meaningful rather than a less meaningful life. If the idea of a worthwhile project is just a fraud or a hoax, then my account of self-interest is undone by it.

Since I have no *theory* of worth by which to prove the coherence of the concept or refute all skeptical challenges, I can only acknowledge the vulnerability of my account of self-interest in this regard. That we do, most of us, believe that some activities and projects are more worthwhile than others, that we regard certain activities as wastes of time (or near wastes of time) and others as inherently valuable, seems undeniable. These beliefs lie behind dispositions to feel proud or disgusted with ourselves for time spent well or badly, and they account for at least some of our efforts to steer our children and our friends toward some activities and away from others. When I try to take up a point of view that denies the distinction between worthwhile and worthless activity, I cannot find it convincing. Still, it is an article of faith that these untheoretical judgments, or some core of them, are philosophically defensible. It is on the assumption that they are defensible that my views about meaningfulness and self-interest are built. 13

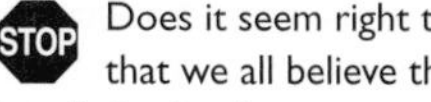

Does it seem right to you that we all believe that there is a distinction between worthwhile and worthless activities? To what extent could people agree about which activities are worthwhile and which are worthless?

Two Challenges

My proposal so far has been that meaningfulness in life arises from engagement in worthwhile activity. I have argued for the plausibility of this account on the grounds that it fits well both with the needs that are typically referred to as needs for meaning and with the concrete judgments of meaningful and meaningless activity that are most commonly made. Before proceeding with an examination of the relation between meaning and self-interest, two challenges to this account of meaning should be answered.

The first objects that, contrary to my claims, my account of meaning fails to meet the requirements I have set up for it. It fails, more particularly, to answer to the needs of at least one type of longing for meaning that members of our species tend to have. Traditional worries about the meaning of life, often set off by reflections on our own mortality and on the indifference of the cosmos in which we occupy so tiny a place, are rarely appeased by the reflection that one can actively engage in projects of worth. At least, they are not appeased by reflection on the availability of the kind of projects I have been talking about, like taking up the cello, writing a novel, volunteering at a child's day-care center or a nursing home. Tolstoy, the publicly acclaimed author of some of the greatest works of literature ever written, the father and spouse of what he described (perhaps inaccurately) as a loving and successful family, could have had no doubt that, relatively speaking, his life was spent in projects as worthwhile as any. Yet he was plagued by the thought that it was all for naught.* Nothing he did seemed to save his life from meaninglessness. Like Tolstoy, such philosophers as Albert Camus† and Thomas Nagel‡ see the meaning or meaninglessness of life as an issue relating to the human condition. The difference between a person who wastes her time in frivolous or shallow pursuits and one who makes something of herself and serves humanity cannot, on their views, make the difference between a meaningful and a meaningless life.

To try to give a wholly adequate answer to this challenge would take us too far afield from the

*See Leo Tolstoy, "My Confession," in E. D. Klemke, ed., *The Meaning of Life* (New York: Oxford University Press, 1981).
†Albert Camus, *The Myth of Sisphus and Other Essays* (New York: Vintage Books, 1955).
‡Thomas Nagel, "The Absurd," in Nagel, *Mortal Questions* (Cambridge: Cambridge University Press, 1979).

purposes of this essay. The issue of The Meaning of Life is too obscure and complex, and the differences among the philosophers whose views seem to pose a challenge to the one I am offering call for different responses. Some brief remarks, however, will at least indicate what a more detailed answer might look like and will give some reason for thinking that the challenge can be met.

Among those who think that meaning in life, or the lack of it, is primarily concerned with facts about the human condition, some disagree not with my general account of meaning but with, if you will, its application. Their position, in other words, shares my view that meaning comes from engagement in projects of worth, but assigns certain facts about the human condition a crucial role in settling whether there are any such projects. If God does not exist, they think, then nothing is any more worthwhile than anything else. Within this group, some believe that God is the only possible standard for judgments of nonsubjective value. If God does not exist, they think, then neither does moral or aesthetic value or any other sort of value that could distinguish some projects as better than others. Others believe that though there may be a difference between great literature and junk, and between virtue and vice, there is no point in bothering about which you occupy yourself with. Nothing lasts forever; the human race will be destroyed; the earth will crash into the sun. Only God, and the promise of an eternal life either for ourselves or for the universe in which our accomplishments have a place, can give a point to our living lives one way rather than another. Only God can make meaningful life so much as a possibility. [14]

My own view about this position is that it expresses an irrational obsession with permanence; but it is enough for the purposes of this essay to note that it does not really challenge the account of meaning I have offered. I have already acknowledged that the usefulness of my account rests on the assumption that the distinction between worthwhile and worthless projects is defensible, and on the assumption that at least a core of our beliefs about what is worthwhile and what is worthless is roughly correct. Those who think that God is a necessary grounding for these assumptions and who believe in Him may still find my account of meaning acceptable. Those who think that God is a necessary grounding that unfortunately does not exist will reject my substantive claims about meaning for reasons we have already admitted. [15]

Others, including Nagel and arguably Camus, think that there are differences between better and worse ways to live our lives. Evidently, they think that projects and activities can be more and less worthwhile, and that we have some sort of reason to favor the more worthwhile. They do not, however, see these facts as supplying a basis for meaning. Like the group just discussed, they link meaning inextricably to facts about our place in space-time and in the order of the cosmos. In an indifferent universe, they think, our lives are unavoidably meaningless no matter what we do with them. [16] On the other hand, there may be some other point to choosing to do something good or worthwhile. This view disagrees explicitly with my own proposal—indeed, it appears to be in outright contradiction to it. However, it seems to me to be largely a disagreement in the use of words. *The* issue of meaning, which these philosophers tie essentially to issues about our significance (or lack of it) in the universe, seems to me to be really a tangle of issues with overlapping strands. Though talk about meaning sometimes expresses a concern about our relation to the cosmos, the use of the term and its cognates to refer to differences among human lives and activities is no less common. I believe that there are relations between these different uses that have not been fully appreciated, and that philosophers like Nagel and Camus have insufficiently recognized the degree to which anthropocentric values can serve as a basis for addressing worries about our place in the universe. However, this issue is not relevant to my present purpose. My purpose here is to advance the view that it is in our interest to live lives of a certain sort, and to explore some of that view's implications. Whether we should describe these lives as more meaningful than others, or describe the desire to live them as a desire for meaning, is relatively superficial and may in any case be left to another day. I shall continue to use my terminology, however, and hope that no one will be confused by it.

The second challenge to my account of meaningfulness is more directly relevant to the issue of the nature of self-interest. It consists of an alternative subjective account of meaning that is

According to one interpretation of this first objection, Wolf is wrong that we can find meaning by actively engaging in worthwhile activities, because there are no activities that are genuinely worthwhile.

STOP What role do you think God plays in determining the value of things? Consider a version of the question asked in Plato's *Euthyphro* (p. 23): does God value things because they are valuable or are they valuable because God values them? Is God a reliable indicator of *preexisting* value or does he *make* something valuable by valuing it?

According to a second interpretation of this first objection, Wolf is wrong that we can find meaning by actively engaging in worthwhile activities because genuine meaning requires something more than this, perhaps something unobtainable for human beings. See the previous selection by Nagel for the view that there is a broader perspective from which it is very doubtful that Wolf's conditions for meaningfulness are even relevant, let alone sufficient.

forcefully suggested, although not in quite the terms I shall use, by Richard Taylor's discussion of the meaning of life in his book *Good and Evil.** According to this position, meaning is not a matter of one's projects in life being worthwhile from some objective point of view. (Taylor himself seems to think that no projects could meet this standard.) Rather, a person's life is meaningful, one might say, if it is meaningful *to her,* and it is meaningful to her if she thinks or feels it is.

The suggestion that something is meaningful to someone as long as she thinks it is can be of no help to us in developing an account of meaningfulness, for we cannot understand what it would be for someone to think her life meaningful until we have an account of what meaningfulness is. The view I want to discuss, however, is, strictly speaking, more concerned with a feeling or, better, a sense or qualitative character that some of our experiences have. We may use the term "fulfillment" to refer to it. It is pleasant to be or to feel fulfilled or to find an activity or a relationship fulfilling, but it is a pleasure of a specific sort, one that seems closely associated with the thought that our lives or certain activities within them are meaningful. Recognizing this, it may be suggested, gives us all the basis we need for an account of meaning that meets my requirements. We may understand people's longing for meaning as a longing for this particular feeling, a longing which other sorts of pleasure cannot satisfy. We can also explain why some activities characteristically answer the call of meaning better than others. Some yield the feeling of fulfillment while others do not. Chocolate is filling but not fulfilling; it gives pleasure but not of this particular kind. When a person steps back, wondering whether her life has had meaning, or searching for a way to give it more meaning, she may simply be surveying her life for its quotient of fulfillment or looking for ways to increase it.

The very close ties between meaningfulness and fulfillment on which this account of meaning relies are important for understanding both the concept of meaning and its value. That meaningful activity or a meaningful life is at least partly fulfilling is, as this account suggests, a conceptual truth. To *identify* meaningfulness with fulfillment, however, neglects aspects of our use of the terms, and aspects of the experiences that are described by them, that my more objective account of meaningfulness better accommodates. (17)

17

R According to Wolf's analysis, a meaningful life will include these *feelings* of fulfillment, but such feelings are not enough for genuine meaning, since what seems fulfilling to someone might be a life with no objective worth at all.

For one thing, fulfillment is not a brute feeling but one with some cognitive content or concomitant. That certain activities tend to be fulfilling and others not seems connected to features of the relevant activities that make this fact intelligible. There is a fittingness between certain kinds of activities and the potential for fulfillment. When a relationship or a job is fulfilling, there is something about it that makes it so. One feels appreciated or loved, or has the sense of doing good, or finds the challenge of the work rewarding. It is not just that the activities in question meet our expectations, though that is a part of it. Some things are fine but not fulfilling—my relationship with my hairdresser, for example, or my weekly trips to the supermarket.

These considerations suggest that we find things fulfilling only if we can think about them in a certain way. It is difficult precisely to identify a single belief that is always associated with the experience of fulfillment. Still, I propose that there is some association between finding an activity fulfilling and believing, or at least dimly, inarticulately perceiving, there to be something independently worthwhile or good about it. (18)

18

Fulfillment, according to Wolf, is clearly different from mere pleasure. Her view seems to be that one cannot experience fulfillment from an activity without first finding or somehow perceiving the activity to be objectively worthwhile. Fulfillment thus involves "cognitive content": believing or perceiving something about the activity in question. (And if this cognitive content is false, then the feeling is misguided in an important way.)

In his discussion of the meaning of life, Richard Taylor considers the case of Sisyphus and imagines that the gods, by inserting some substance in Sisyphus's veins, give Sisyphus a love for stone-rolling. Sisyphus's life is thereby transformed from one of miserable bondage to one of ecstatic fulfillment. Taylor himself recognizes that the thought experiment is an odd one, and that the passion for stone-rolling will strike his readers as bizarre. Taylor, however, seems to think that the strangeness of the example comes simply from its being unusual. People do not characteristically get passionate about mindless, futile, never-ending tasks; nor is this the sort of disposition that drugs typically induce. To many, however, the example is not just surprising but somewhat horrifying. The state of being fulfilled by perpetual stone-rolling is not unreservedly enviable. Of course,

*Richard Taylor, *Good and Evil* (New York: Macmillan, 1970).

for Sisyphus, who is condemned to roll stones in any case, there is a great benefit in being able to be happy with his lot. In general, however, I suspect that most people would think that stone-rolling (mere stone-rolling, that is, without any purpose or development of skill) is not the sort of thing by which one ought to be fulfilled. That Sisyphus is fulfilled by stone-rolling suggests an understanding of Sisyphus as a victim (albeit a happy one) of a kind of drug-induced illusion. He finds something in stone-rolling that isn't really there. (19)

If we accept the idea that the feeling of fulfillment is necessarily connected with beliefs about its objects—if we accept that an activity or relationship can be fulfilling only if one believes it to be somehow independently good—then we can distinguish two hypotheses about the relationship between meaning and fulfillment. Does meaning come from the experience of fulfillment, no matter what its cause, or is a meaningful life one in which a subject is fulfilled by activities suitable to the experience? The subjective account suggested by Taylor opts for the former; but the latter seems to square better with our ordinary use of the concept.

One test case is Taylor's version of Sisyphus itself. That Sisyphus finds his life fulfilling is built in by assumption. But should we describe his life as meaningful? This seems to me a misuse of the word. "It is meaningful to him," someone will say, and we understand what this means. It means that he finds his life fulfilling, and, perhaps, that he thinks it is meaningful (or would think it, if asked). But, for those who find the example horrifying, that is part of the problem: he thinks his life gets meaning from mindless, futile stone-rolling, but it does not. (20)

We can construct a second test case by considering someone whose judgment of an aspect of her life has changed. A woman previously blissfully in love discovers that the man she loved has been using her. She had found the relationship fulfilling before she learned of his deceits. She would have said, had you asked her earlier, that the relationship contributed to the meaningfulness of her life. What would she say now, however, and what should we say about her? No one can take away the feelings of fulfillment she experienced during the period she was deceived; but it seems unlikely that she would say, after the fact, that the relationship truly had given meaning to her life. Indeed, part of what makes this sort of event so sad is that, in addition to the pain that is caused when the deception is discovered, it undermines the value of all the pleasure that came before.

Less fanciful than Sisyphus are cases of addicts or inductees of religious cults whose feelings of contentment are caused, but not justified, by the things that bring them about. (21) Though we should be cautious about passing judgment on the activities that others take to be worthwhile, this is no reason to rule out the possibility that people are sometimes mistaken, that their finding something fulfilling can be wrongly induced, either through the establishment of false factual beliefs (such as belief in a loved one's fidelity or in the divine status of a charismatic leader) or by drugs or electrodes. If, moreover, they are led by such mind-altering means to spend their lives occupied by some equivalent of stone-rolling—watching endless reruns of *Leave It to Beaver* or counting and recounting the number of tiles on the bathroom floor—then it seems to me most in line with ordinary language to describe them as leading meaningless lives, however fulfilled they may feel themselves to be. If, further, such people wake up or snap out of it—if they come to occupy a point of view that devalues their former lives—then their later descriptions would not, I think, grant meaning to the things in which they had found contentment before.

Meaningfulness and Self-Interest

So far I have been occupied with spelling out a conception of what meaningfulness in life is. My point in doing so, in the present context, is to bring it to bear on the idea of self-interest. Meaningfulness seems to me an important ingredient of a good life, and one that is too often either neglected or distorted by contemporary accounts of individual well-being.

I do not know what an argument for this claim would look like. My hope, as I mentioned before, is that the mere spelling out of the claim will be enough to incline most people to assent to it. (22) Still, I think that without attending explicitly to our interest in meaning, we tend to misunderstand and misdescribe it, with the eventual result that the shapes our lives take have less meaning than may be good for us.

R If this new Sisyphus experiences fulfillment from his activity, then he must see it (mistakenly) as objectively worthwhile. If the gods injected something that merely made Sisyphus feel pleasure as a result of his activity but not fulfilled, then this cognitive dimension would not be satisfied.

STOP What judgment should be made of the new Sisyphus? Is his life genuinely meaningful or does it only seem meaningful? (How would he feel if the drug wore off and his life-long activity no longer seemed worthwhile? Would the previous part of his life still be meaningful because he found it meaningful at the time?)

R The deceived woman's feelings of fulfillment were caused by what she perceived as the loving actions of her husband. When she comes to see that those actions weren't loving at all, then those feelings no longer seem appropriate. His actions no longer give her good reasons for her feelings of fulfillment. (Had her husband been as faithful as he pretended to be, then her feelings would have been both caused *and* justified by his actions.)

As Wolf candidly admits, she has not given us reasons for her claim that there is a distinction between meaningful and meaningless activities, and she has not given us reasons for her claim that meaningfulness (as she has defined it) is an important ingredient of a good life. The suggestion is that these claims will seem intuitively reasonable, even without a developed argument.

Most people—at least most people within a certain group, bounded perhaps by class or education as well as by culture and history—behave in ways that suggest that they are looking for worthwhile things to do with their lives. They actively seek projects or, more typically, happily seize upon activities, from among those to which they are attracted, that they believe to be worthwhile. Explicit thoughts about worth and meaning often occur in connection with major life decisions, in addition to those moments of crisis to which I referred before. Some people decide to have children because they think it will give meaning to their lives. Others decide not to have children because they fear that the attendant responsibilities will deprive them of the time and resources and peace of mind that they need for other things in which they do find meaning. Deliberations about whether to pursue a particular career, or any career, may similarly involve concerns about whether the job is worthwhile, or whether it would demand time and energy that would distract one from what is worthwhile. Even many who do not talk explicitly in terms of meaning or worth make choices that are best explained by reference to them. In other words, our behavior, including some of our speech, seems to reveal a preference for a meaningful life.

We are, however, more apt to explain our choices in terms of fulfillment than meaning. A man opts for the more challenging of two possible careers, even at the cost of stress and insecurity. A woman chooses to work for less pay at a job she believes is morally valuable. People arrange their lives so as to give a few hours a week to Meals on Wheels, or to practicing piano, or to keeping up with their book group, even though it means going with a little less sleep, less flexibility, less straightforward fun. Why? Because, they will say, they find these things fulfilling. They choose to live this way because they regard it as, in some sense, best for them.

To defend these choices in terms of fulfillment establishes them as choices made out of self-interest. Talk of fulfillment may, however, suggest a more hedonistic interpretation of what is going on than the one I have offered. [23] To choose something because it is fulfilling is, after all, to choose it because of a qualitative character of one's experience—and though fulfilling activities are not always as much fun or as intensely pleasurable as some of the alternatives, it may be that in the long run, or the wide run (taking into account Mill's differences in the quality as well as the quantity of pleasure, as it were), a fulfilling life is qualitatively better, and thus happier in the truest sense, than a life with as many or more pleasures but no fulfillment. So at least must the people described in the paragraph above believe, and so must we believe if we think their choices are rational, and are rational for the reason they give. [24]

It is no part of my aim to deny this suggestion. On the contrary, that fulfillment is a great qualitative good, and that it deserves an important place in an adequate theory of happiness, are important contributing factors to my claim that meaning is a component of our good. We have already seen that the links between meaningfulness and fulfillment are very tight. Since a meaningful life is necessarily at least partly fulfilling, and since fulfillment is a major component of happiness, a very important reason for taking meaningfulness to be in our interest is that it brings fulfillment with it. It would be misleading, however, to draw from this the conclusion that meaningfulness is an instrumental good for us. To think of meaning as good because it is a means to an independent good of fulfillment would be a mistake.

It is doubtful that fulfillment is an independent good, although feeling fulfilled is pleasant and feeling unfulfilled unpleasant. If fulfillment were an independent good, it would follow that the feeling of fulfillment would be desirable no matter what its cause. It would have to be better to be Sisyphus happy (or, more precisely, Sisyphus fulfilled) than Sisyphus unhappy (unfulfilled), even if this required that Sisyphus was perpetually stoned out of his normal mind. Opinion, however, divides on this matter. Many value fulfillment only on the condition that it be based on appropriate thoughts or perceptions. Moreover, even among those who believe that feeling fulfilled is unconditionally better than the alternative, many would still prefer that these feelings were suitably caused. Better to be Sisyphus happy than Sisyphus unhappy, they may say, but better still not to be Sisyphus at all. [25]

A proponent of a purely hedonistic theory of self-interest may point out that reports of such intuitions prove nothing. People's thinking that

[23] *Definition*

On a hedonist view, only one's own felt experiences of pleasure (and the avoidance of pain) are relevant to one's own good. The hedonistic interpretation of fulfillment takes it to be just a specific sort of pleasurable experience.

[24]

Wolf is raising a point that some might regard as a further objection to her view: if people's choices are aimed merely at the subjective experience of fulfillment (rather than at achieving meaning)—as their own descriptions of them seem to indicate—then Wolf's emphasis on objective worth seems to be mistaken as an account of what people actually care about.

[25]

Wolf's response to the objection is to appeal again to the case of Sisyphus experiencing fulfillment in a way that depends on a drug-induced illusion. That most people would find his situation unsatisfactory suggests that they care about more than the subjective experience of fulfillment. (See Discussion Question 3.)

justified or appropriate fulfillment is better than unjustified inappropriate fulfillment doesn't make it so. To those who have these intuitions, however, the burden of proof seems to lie with the hedonist. Unless one is committed to a purely hedonistic account of value ahead of time, there seems no reason to doubt that what is principally desirable is getting fulfillment from genuinely fulfilling activities, from activities, that is, whose accompanying feeling of fulfillment comes from the correct perception of their value. There seems no reason to doubt, in other words, that what is principally desirable is living a meaningful life and not living a life that seems or feels meaningful. Insofar as we prefer a truly meaningful life to one that merely seems or feels meaningful, a purely hedonistic theory of self-interest will not account for it. 26

A preference theory of self-interest, however, would not have to account for it—preference theorists simply accept our preferences and go on to compute our self-interest from there. This suggests an alternative account of the relation between meaning and self-interest. According to preference theories, meaning is important to our well-being if and only if meaning matters to us. Since many of us do want to live meaningful lives—since we think it is better for us if we do—preference theorists will agree that it is in our interest that our lives are meaningful. From their point of view, there is no need to make any more objective claims than that.

From a practical perspective, it matters little whether we accept this theory or a more objective one, particularly if you think, as I do, that the preference for a meaningful life is widespread and deep. If it is accepted as a fact of human nature (even a statistical fact, and even of a culturally created human nature) that people just do care about meaning in their lives, then this gives us reason enough to shape our lives in ways that will encourage not just fulfillment but meaningfulness, and it gives us reason enough to shape our social and political institutions in ways that will increase the opportunities for everyone to live not just happily and comfortably but meaningfully as well. 27

A preference theory does not, however, seem accurately to reflect the status a meaningful life has for most of us. Most of us, it seems, do not regard our preference for a meaningful life as an ungrounded preference we just happen to have. If we did think so, then we would judge it a matter of indifference whether anyone else had or lacked this preference, and indeed, we would have no reason to want to keep this preference ourselves if we were convinced that we would be better off without it. For most people, however, at least so it seems to me, having a meaningful life is a value and not just a preference. We do not just want our lives to be meaningful, we think it good that we want it. Indeed, our interest and concern for meaning is sometimes mentioned as a mark of our humanity, as an aspect of what raises us above brutes. We think that we would be diminished as a species if we lost the aspiration, or the interest, in living meaningful lives and not just happy ones. Individuals who lack the desire that their lives be meaningful we regard with regret or even pity. 28

Again it may be noted that our believing something is no proof of its being true, and again I must acknowledge that I have no proof of the value or objective desirability of meaningfulness. At the same time, the claim that a meaningful life is preferable (and not just brutely preferred) to a meaningless one may seem so nearly self-evident as to require no proof. Once one is willing to apply the terms of meaningfulness and meaninglessness at all, it may seem unstable to believe that a life that lacks meaning is no worse than one that possesses it. Even if we can logically distinguish the position that some lives are more meaningful than others from the position which adds that (some) meaningfulness is a good, this latter position seems more natural than one which denies it. Though we may be unable to argue for caring about meaning in a way that would convince someone who doesn't care to begin with, the concern or the desire for meaningful activity is, for those who have it, more rationally coherent with other values and dispositions than its absence would be.

In response to the question "Why care about living a meaningful life rather than a meaningless one?" the answer that I believe best expresses reflective common sense will begin with the connection between meaning and happiness: Nine times out of ten, perhaps ninety-nine times out of a hundred, a meaningful life will be happier than a meaningless one. The feelings of fulfillment one gets from interacting positively and supportively with things or

STOP Think again about Nozick's experience machine: if your machine-induced experiences include a satisfactory proportion of experiences of fulfillment, would you plug into the machine? According to a purely hedonistic theory of self-interest, it would be in your self-interest to do so.

The preference view of self-interest is different from the hedonistic view. According to a preference view, self-interest consists in fulfilling one's preferences, whatever those preferences may happen to be. If people happen to prefer meaningful lives, then achieving such lives will be part of their self-interest; but if not, then it won't be.

R Wolf argues, in contrast, that we think it is good to have this preference, in which case, meaning is a value and not merely a preference—so that we think that people *ought* to prefer it and are to be pitied if they don't.

creatures (or "realms") whose love seems deserved are wonderful feelings, worth more, on qualitative grounds alone, than many other sorts of pleasure, and worth the cost of putting up with considerable quantities of pain. Moreover, the awareness, even dim and inarticulate, of a lack of anything that can constitute a source of pride or a source of connection to anything valuable outside of oneself can be awful, making one irritable, restless, and contemptuous of oneself.

Except in an academic philosophical context such as this, it is perhaps unnatural to press further. If we do press further, however, it seems to me that the strength and character of these feelings of pleasure and pain are not best explained as mere quirks of our natural or culturally conditioned psyches. Rather, that we feel so good or so bad in accordance with our sense of connection to value outside ourselves seems to me best explained in terms of an underlying belief that a life is better when it possesses such connections. What precisely is better about it is difficult to say. But perhaps it has to do with our place in the universe: since we are, each of us, occupants in a world full of value independent of our individual selves, living in such a way as to connect positively and supportively with some nonsubjective value harmonizes better with our objective situation than would a life whose chief occupations can be only subjectively defended.

The Deconstruction of Self-Interest

I have in this essay been concerned to defend, or rather to elaborate, what I take to be a deeply and widely held view about individual human good, namely, that a fully successful life is, among other things, a meaningful one. Further I have urged that this claim is distorted if it is understood as an element of either a hedonistic or a preference theory of self-interest. Properly understood, it requires a rejection of both these sort of theories.

As a substantive claim, I do not expect that the point that a good life must be meaningful will be surprising. We are not used to thinking very explicitly or very analytically about it, however; and in popular unreflective consciousness, a substantive interest in a meaningful life often sits side by side with assumptions that are incompatible with it. How often have you heard someone say, "What is the point of doing something if it isn't fun, or if you don't enjoy it?" I hear this sentiment expressed quite frequently. . . . To be fair, such expressions tend to be limited to contexts of self-interest. They are not intended as rejections of rational authority of moral or legal obligation. Moreover, there is often a point behind such remarks that I would strongly endorse. Against a kind of workaholism and related neurotic obsessions with some forms of success and achievement, it can be useful to step back and reflect in the way these remarks would invoke. Still, the suggestion that there can be no point to things if they are neither duties or fun is, strictly speaking, both false and dangerous.

Much of what we do would be inexplicable, or at least indefensible, if its justification depended either on its being a duty or, even in the long run, on its maximally contributing to our net fun. Relationships with friends and family, nonobligatory aspects of professional roles, and long-term commitments to artistic, scholarly, or athletic endeavors typically lead us to devote time and energy to things that are difficult and unpleasant, and to forgo opportunities for relaxation and enjoyment. It is arguable that many of these choices advance our happiness (in the broadest sense, our fun) in the long run, but such arguments are at best uncertain, and the thought that they are necessary for the defense of these choices puts a regrettable kind of pressure on the commitments that give rise to them. There is, however, a point—even a self-interested point—to doing things that fall outside the categories both of duty and fun. One can find a reason, or at least a justifying explanation, for doing something in the fact that the act or activity in question contributes to the meaningfulness of one's life.

Once we have ceased to identify self-interest with happiness, however, other assumptions are also undermined. The concept of self-interest becomes more difficult to work with. Specifically, a conception of self-interest that recognizes the importance of meaning to a good life admits of much greater indeterminacy than the more traditional conceptions. This is partly a function of indeterminacy within the category of meaningfulness itself. Though meaningfulness is not an all-or-nothing concept—some lives are more meaningful than others, a person's life may not have *enough* meaning in it to be satisfactory—there is no well-formed system for making comparative judgments. The meaningfulness of a life may vary depending on how much of it is spent in meaningful activity, on how worthwhile the activities in question are, or on how fully engaged (or attracted) the individual is. In many instances, however, it seems absurd to think there is a correct comparison to be made. Is the life of a great but lonely philosopher more or less meaningful than that of a beloved housekeeper? There seems to be no reason to assume that there is a fact of the matter about this. Moreover, from a self-interested point of view, it is unclear whether, beyond a certain point, it matters whether one's life is more meaningful. A meaningful life is better than a meaningless one, but once it is meaningful enough, there may be no self-interested reason to want, as it were, to squeeze more meaning into it. Finally, the mix between meaning and felt happiness may have no determinate ideal. A person often has to choose between taking a path that would strengthen or expand part of his or her life that contributes to its meaningfulness (going to graduate school, adopting a child, getting politically involved) and taking an easier or more pleasant role. Once one has accepted a conception of self-interest that recognizes meaningfulness as an independent aspect of one's personal good, one may have to admit that in such cases there may be no answer to the question of what is most in one's self-interest. 29

Fortunately, as the concept of self-interest becomes more difficult to apply, it becomes less important to be able to apply it. In accepting the value of meaningfulness as an ingredient of our own interest, we necessarily also accept that meaningful activity has a value that is partly independent of our own interest. We accept, in other words, the availability of a kind of reason for doing things that can compete with self-interest, a kind that will, at any rate, draw us away from the concern for our self-interest. What I have in mind is the sort of reason given by the worthiness of the meaningful activity (or its object) itself.

Meaningful activity, remember, involves engagement in projects of worth. It occurs where subjective attraction meets objective attractiveness. To acknowledge that an activity or a project is worthwhile, however, is to acknowledge, among other things, that there is a reason for doing it—a reason, at least, for doing it if you are attracted to doing it. A reason for writing a book on free will is to stimulate thought in a fruitful direction. A reason to plant bulbs and weed the garden is to maintain a place of natural beauty. A reason to sew a groundhog costume for an eight-year-old is to make her happy.

To those who get meaning from the activities just mentioned, these sorts of reasons will dominate. Being suitably engaged in these activities in the way in which people who get meaning from them *are* engaged involves being drawn by their specific good or value. One so engaged is not likely to step back from the activity and ask, "Is this the best thing I can be doing *for me*?"

The point here is not just the one with which we are familiar from the paradox of hedonism. It is not just that, by not caring too much about whether her activities will be best for her, the agent is more likely to be living a life that is best for her. Rather, it is that she has a reason for her activities that is not conditional on their being best for her. Accepting a conception of self-interest that incorporates meaningfulness, then, involves rejecting too dominant a place for self-interest. 30 Yet meaningful activity and self-interest cannot psychologically stretch too far apart. Activity is meaningful only if one can engage in it, be attracted to it, be in love with it or the object around which it revolves. Such activity will always be somewhat fulfilling, and therefore will always make one somewhat happy. And as the fulfillment and happiness will be appropriate or deserved, that is all to one's good.

R Recognizing that meaningfulness is a part of self-interest makes self-interest less clearly defined than it would be on the hedonistic and preference views. There are many kinds of worthwhile things and so many potential sources of meaning. And there is also no clear answer as to *how much* meaning a satisfactory life must have.

R But once we see that meaningfulness is important for self-interest, we see that people can have reasons for action that are *independent* of their own narrow self-interest. Achieving meaningfulness requires the recognition of things that are *objectively* worthwhile, whether they serve a person's narrow self-interest or not. (For a related discussion, see the selection by Feinberg in Chapter 6.)

Discussion Questions

1. When Wolf articulates the concerns about meaning that people have (p. 615), she says that people can come to see activities that they used to enjoy as "shallow," that even though they've had fun in their lives, they sense that something is lacking. Do you recognize this phenomenon? Do you think that most people do have concerns about meaning?
2. Wolf insists that the activities of a meaningful life must be objectively worthwhile. Consider the following example: suppose that Katie counts the blades of grass in the central quad at the University of Washington. She is there every morning at 8 a.m., takes an hour break at lunch time, and stops counting around 5 p.m. She takes the weekends

off, but rarely takes any other time off. (She is independently wealthy, and so she doesn't need to work for a living.) When you ask her why she is counting the blades of grass, she responds that she finds it fascinating. She is very systematic, leaving a mark (nothing permanent) where she stops for the day so that she'll know where to begin the next day. When students stop to talk, she'll take a few minutes to show them what she is doing, explaining about the different kinds of grass or her method of counting, but if they take too much time, she gently tells them that she must get back to work. Her family was very upset when she started this activity, insisting that she see a therapist. She humored them, but the therapist could find nothing wrong with her. She has been doing this for ten years now and can't imagine doing anything else. She has her own family now, and her children tell their friends that Mommy works at the university. While Katie is not paid for what she does, she takes it very seriously and enjoys the activity enormously. She sometimes wishes that it didn't rain quite so much in Seattle, but every job has its drawbacks. Does Katie lead a meaningful life, according to Wolf? Is there any way to argue that her activity is objectively worthwhile?

3. Suppose that Sisyphus is controlled by the gods in such a way that he will continue to roll the stone up the hill again and again whether or not he finds it fulfilling or meaningful. On Wolf's view, it would clearly be better for Sisyphus to be allowed instead to do something with more objective worth. But given that this is impossible, is he ultimately better off finding his activity fulfilling even though this involves believing mistakenly that it has objective worth, or would he be better off (even if not happier) if he did not have such an illusion? If you were Sisyphus, would you want to know the truth or not?

Concluding Dialogue on the Good Life

I know that you find this issue very engaging, but I'm just not sure that it is genuinely philosophical.

Stop! This issue is the most philosophical issue you can think about. What do you mean that it is not philosophical?

I mean that the question is not clear to begin with and that there is not a clear dialectic: there are not really reasons for conflicting sides of the issues. Take the question: what is a good life? Is the question about *a* good life or *the* good life?

That is one of the interesting questions, but there is nothing unclear about it. If there is a defensible, clearly determinate, single, objective conception of the good life, one that applies to everyone—as Aristotle probably thought that there is—then the question is what is *that* life: what is *the* good life? But if there are many different possible good lives, if the goodness of your life depends on particular facts about your talents or tendencies or on particular historical or contextual facts, then the question is: what is *a* good life? It takes some careful thought to think about the difference, but it is not unclear.

OK—fine. But what could ever count as reasons for or against the claim either that there is a plurality of good lives or that there is one good life for people like us (whether that means humans or rational creatures)?

Well, it seems to me that the reasons advanced by Nozick are relevant. One might initially think that a life full of pleasant experiences or experiences that you want to have would constitute the good life, if only for you, but he offers pretty compelling reasons for thinking that such a life would not in fact be even *a* good life (let alone *the* good life). It is not enough, he argues, to have experiences that *seem* to reflect a certain kind of life, while in fact your body is vegetating uselessly in some machine. He argues that having a good life requires really doing whatever it is that you experience yourself as doing. Didn't you find those reasons compelling?

Yes, I did, but that still seems like a pretty thin result. Your life is not good if none of your experiences reflect reality. Pretty obvious, if you ask me.

Excuse me, but the issue on the table right now is whether there is a clear and interesting philosophical dialectic about the good life. To say that some view is obviously well defended

is not to show that there is no dialectic. While I too am inclined to agree with Nozick, I'm not as sure as you seem to be that the alternative view has no merit. Remember that one doesn't know that what one is experiencing fails to capture reality. The person who has entered the experience machine has just as much reason to think, on the basis of his current experiences, that his experiences reflect reality as you do. So why isn't his life just as good—at least to him—as yours is to you? Be clear here: I'm not trying to defend this view, but only to insist that there is an at least marginally plausible view that merits an argument against it, and what else does it take to show that there is a bit of philosophical dialectic in the area?

But even if I grant that you can get something of philosophical interest out of Nozick's thought experiment about the experience machine, that doesn't really take you very far. I really can't make very much sense at all of what Epictetus is saying.

That is ridiculous! Of course you can make sense of it. You just think that what he says is false or maybe even silly, but that is most emphatically *not* to say that what he says makes no sense at all or that it fails to carve out an interesting philosophical option in an important dialectic about good lives. There are elements of his view in works as different as the novels of J. D. Salinger, Eastern philosophy, and contemporary pop psychology. The most central idea is that one goes wrong in one's life when one tries too hard to control aspects of reality that in fact are essentially uncontrollable. Epictetus says that we ought to limit our "will-to-get" and our "will-to-avoid." We ought to limit our will so that we only will what "belongs to us." And the only thing that "belongs to us," according to Epictetus, is our thoughts, emotions, and desires: our psychological reactions to things.

There is so much wrong with that view that I don't even know where to begin.

Before you begin, let me just say that offering reasons for rejecting Epictetus's instructions for how to live a good life *is* engaging in the dialectic that you claim not to exist. But let's proceed, thereby undermining your initial view that there is nothing of philosophical interest here.

Look—there is dialectic and there is dialectic. It doesn't count as real philosophical dialectic if the reasons against the view are sufficiently easy to come up with, because then the view is bad enough not to really count as a viable alternative in the first place. And it seems to me that the Epictetus view fails in just that way.

No, no, no! You are surely not serious. The views of Epictetus, as well as his style of expressing them, fall squarely in the center of a long and venerable philosophical tradition called Stoicism—

It does not follow from the fact that a view has a name that it constitutes a viable dialectical position!

—that claims that we have a tendency to will things that it makes no sense to will—like willing the rain to stop or willing for someone not to exist (without wanting to actually kill him or her). Think about the rain in Seattle in the winter—don't you sometimes will the sun to come out? And aren't you then disappointed when it remains cloudy? But you wouldn't be disappointed if you refrained from willing the clouds to go away in the first place.

If the view claimed merely that we should monitor our reactions, making sure that we are willing only those things that it makes sense to will, thereby avoiding unreasonable reactions later on, then maybe I would have no objection. Sure—I shouldn't will the sun to come out, but that is not really what I'm doing. I'm not confused about what is within my power. I can *wish* that the sun was out without willing that it come out. But I might even agree with him that I shouldn't let the weather upset me. Epictetus goes way, way beyond that, however. He claims that we should not feel bad about any external event whatsoever—losing a child or a spouse, for example, is no cause for sadness.

Let's think carefully about this. You are disappointed when you don't get something that you want, and if you are careful to want only what you can control, then you'll never be disappointed. So if you are disappointed when your wife dies, then you must have wanted her not to die. And here is an argument for the claim that you are being unreasonable to want your wife not to die. It makes no sense to want your wife to *never* die, since she is mortal. But isn't that what you are wanting if, for any time, you want your wife not to die then?

It is not clear to me that it makes no sense to want my wife to never die—but wanting her not to die *now,* for any particular now, isn't quite the same as that anyway. And I'm quite sure that it makes sense to want things that I don't completely control but that I can still *influence*. I would much rather make the effort and risk being disappointed than submit passively to whatever the world throws at me. I can see some point in what Epictetus says—but only if your life situation is so very, very bad that you have very little influence on most things in it. His view makes sense for the life of a slave or someone in a concentration camp, but for lives like ours, the advice seems totally inappropriate.

I can see the point of what you're saying. I still think that as a reminder that there are many different ways to look at things, some of what he says is helpful—but I agree with you that he takes it way too far. What about the Nagel selection on the absurd though? Surely you have to agree that the worry that we are no more important than specks of dust has bothered many people. The fear that our life is absurd is one that motivated existentialist philosophers during the middle part of the twentieth century.

Well I'm not very impressed by that last fact, and I must say that I've never really been bothered by the rather sophomoric angst of the existentialist philosophers. In my view, life is full of interesting and worthwhile activities and things to learn about—many more than I will ever in my short time on earth have time for. Remember, I would really like to live forever! But back to the readings, Nagel seems to me to be more obscure than he usually is with this idea of "taking a step back." I mean what really does he mean by that? He needs to clarify that idea, since it is not at all obvious why any result of that pretty unusual perspective, even granting that there is a definite result, should override or even call into question what seems to be true from the more engaged perspective in which we take our lives seriously. (Imagine someone claiming that, say, pine trees don't really exist or that their existence is even doubtful just because if you "step back" far enough, you can't see them any longer!)

I will grant that Nagel's idea of two perspectives needs some elucidation. (It's an idea he puts to use in his philosophy of mind and his metaphysics as well.) And notice that he is not insisting that the view after stepping back is the one right view, but only that we should at least be bothered by the fact that we can neither refute nor explain away the appearance that our lives are arbitrary when viewed from that perspective. He grants that we live our lives with a kind of seriousness that ignores that other view, but worries about the consistency of doing so. It is interesting to see that Wolf thinks that there is no problem with consistency. On her view the ideal life is one of active engagement in activities of objective worth, even if the reasons for being actively engaged or seeing the projects as having objective worth are perhaps inaccessible from the broader perspective.

Yes. Well I must say that Wolf seems to me to have it right.

To have what right?

She is right about what makes a life meaningful.

Oh? So there is a real issue after all?

Look, that doesn't mean that there is a rich philosophical dialectic, since I can't imagine how anyone could disagree with her. It seems to me that what she says is perfectly obvious—but, yes, I do think she is right. It makes good sense that the more actively engaged one is in activities of objective worth, the better is the life. A life in which one is not really *engaged* in one's activities, however worthwhile those activities might be, is obviously not very satisfactory. And a life involving activities that aren't really very *worthwhile,* however actively engaged one may be with them, is, again obviously, a life that is just not as good as one in which the activities are more worthwhile. Who could deny any of that?

So if there is no dialectic, then you must think that there are no problems with her view that are worth discussing?

Oh, all right! I *am* a bit bothered that she doesn't feel the need to elaborate her account of the objective worth of activities, of her distinction between worthwhile and worthless activities—though I think that she is probably right that as long as there is such a distinction, regardless of what exactly it amounts to, her view can accommodate it. I do agree that there is such a distinction, but for all I know, my view of it might be significantly different from hers. I'm not as clear as I would like to be whether concerns about that make any difference as regards the acceptability of her main view.

I also have some worries about that. And what did you think about her response to the objection based on "the speck of dust" argument? Remember—she considers this objection, but then says that the kind of meaning she is explaining may not be *the* meaning of life, but it is certainly relevant to meaningful lives.

I was less than clear about whether she thought that what she is calling objective worth still exists from the standpoint of Nagel's "broader perspective." If it does, then she has a perfectly good response to him; but if it doesn't, then maybe she too should be worried by the consistency point. I'm just not sure.

In any case, the main issue is whether Wolf—and you—are right that there are activities that are objectively worthwhile. Even apart from Nagel's specific way of raising the issue, the question is what *makes* these things worthwhile: what *grounds* their alleged objective value? So what do *you* think grounds the value of all of these interesting and worthwhile things you think life has to offer—in virtue of which you have never really been bothered by these kinds of questions? If it's supposed to be *objective* value or worth, then it can't just be based on people's subjective preferences.

Of course not. I might of course be wrong about the objective value of the particular things that I value in this world, but I certainly do not think that they are valuable just because I think so—nor because God (or some other authority) says so. To say that there is objective worth is to say that at least some things have *intrinsic value:* are valuable *in themselves,* not because of what they lead to and not because of what anyone thinks about them. I don't have a developed theory about exactly which those things are or about why they have that status. But I think that some people are clearly better than others at judging which things are like that. And they aren't just making it up as they go. There is some fact of the matter about the value or lack of value of almost everything—even if making the right judgment in a particular case can be very difficult.

So I guess that it is not too much of a stretch then to think that some lives are objectively better than other lives—and that a philosophical inquiry into the conditions under which this is so might be very interesting indeed?

Appendix

Writing a Philosophical Essay

Most students will have written many essays of other kinds before they write their first philosophical essay. While this previous experience is invaluable because of the essential writing skills that it should have produced, it is inadequate as a basis for understanding what a good philosophical essay requires. Philosophy is very different from most other subjects, and good philosophical writing reflects this difference. Students often say if they had known *before* they wrote their first essay just what the professor was looking for, how their essay would be evaluated, they could have done a much better job to begin with. Here is your opportunity to find out before you start writing what you should be aiming for.

By the time you are asked to write a philosophical essay, you will have read some philosophy, heard some lectures, and participated in some discussions. You will have begun to practice "doing philosophy" with all that involves: drawing distinctions, clarifying both terms or concepts and whole claims, arguing for and against these claims, considering objections to those arguments, replying to these objections, and so on. A good philosophical essay involves the written expression of all of these things. Return to the introductory essay about philosophical thinking in Chapter 1 (p. 2) to remind yourself of the basic structure of a philosophical issue and the various sorts of claims, arguments, and other elements that pertain to it.

First: What Is Distinctive About a Philosophical Essay?

A philosophical essay is most fundamentally an argumentative defense of some philosophical claim. The defense will consist of, first, giving a main line of argument for the claim (which will typically involve some subsidiary arguments in defense of intermediate claims) and, second, considering and responding to objections to either your main claim or your argument. A consequence of this is that if you haven't clearly understood what an argument is, you will have a very hard time writing a good philosophical essay. A good philosophical essay is a rich piece of philosophical **dialectic.**

A good philosophical essay is not a mere report of someone else's argument, even if the someone else is René Descartes, Immanuel Kant, or some other famous philosopher, but is instead an argument that *you* (the author of the essay) are defending for some particular philosophical claim. Think carefully about the difference between reporting someone else's argument and presenting an argument of your own.

Your philosophical essay should reflect the fundamental categories essential to the philosophical habits of mind you've been learning as you read this book:

- clearly stated claims
- cogent lines of argument (including well-developed points relevant to either defending or illustrating the premises of the argument)
- clear, carefully developed objections pointing out possibly serious flaws in the arguments

- responses that show why the objections, while initially compelling, are not ultimately convincing (and may in fact show even more clearly how persuasive the main argument of the essay really is)

Good philosophical essays have a very distinctive character, a specific shape to them. While they share many features with essays from other disciplines, there are some aspects to a good philosophical essay that no other kind of essay has. For example, while all good essays need to be well written, writing that is both clear and careful is especially important in a philosophical essay because of the subtle and abstract character of the thought involved. Moreover, while essays in many other disciplines involve arguments along the way, philosophical essays are almost exclusively argumentative: the main point, the very essence, of a philosophical essay is to argue for a claim. Think about the claim in the introductory essay that studying philosophy is valuable. We *argued* for that claim by presenting and defending reasons for the claim, where the truth of the reasons allegedly made the truth of the claim more likely. Someone could instead talk in a very different way about studying philosophy, a way that is not at all argumentative, that does not even try to give reasons for thinking that the claim is true, but instead has a different point altogether.

Second: How Does One Go About Producing a Good Philosophical Essay?

The simple answer: read, think, write, revise, perhaps reread or read further, think, write, revise, ad infinitum (or until it is due!). What follows is the more complicated answer.

Pre-Assignment Writing Practice

Writing philosophy is an especially valuable form of philosophical thinking and provides you with writing practice even before you work on a formal essay. Writing of any sort forces you—more than any other intellectual activity—to become clearer about your ideas. In particular, writing philosophy is the most active, demanding way to engage in philosophy. You'll notice that when you listen to a philosophy lecture, you will normally be able to follow it; and if you've done the reading, you may even be able to anticipate some of the ideas and transitions of thought. You'll sometimes leave the lecture hall thinking that you really understand a particular issue or view or line of thought. One good test of your understanding is to try to explain it orally to someone else: sometimes you won't even be able to do that (suggesting that you didn't understand it as well as you thought); but sometimes even if you are able to explain it orally, you would be unable to write it down in a fully clear and accurate way. Formulating an idea well in writing requires a higher degree of understanding and clarity than any other form of thought or expression. So it is valuable to attempt to formulate the various ideas and arguments you encounter in writing, whether this takes the form of an extended passage or just brief notes and jottings. This will also give you valuable practice in philosophical writing even before you are assigned to write an essay.

Think and Make Notes About the Assignment

Once you are assigned to write an essay, you will often be given a specific assignment that is intended to guide your thought process in creating your essay—and perhaps also a specific topic or choice of topics. If your assignment includes questions to be answered by your essay, then be sure to answer them. This may sound obvious, but it has been our experience that many students just start writing and often end up going out on tangents of their own, rather than following the assignment guidelines.

Having chosen or arrived at a topic, you should think as hard as you can about it, trying out different lines of thought until you find one that strikes you as one that you may be able to defend. (You can't possibly be sure at this point.) At this stage, you should be taking notes, sketching the arguments and objections you might include in your essay.

The clearer you can make your thoughts, the better your essay will be: murky thoughts can turn good writers into bad writers. As you think about your topic, taking notes, you may need to return to the reading with more specific questions in mind. Philosophical texts have a kind of depth that continues to reward a reader: you'll understand more and more as you read the second and third time, and even more when you approach the reading with specific questions you want to answer. This process should produce a line of argument that you can defend in your essay, including possible objections and responses.

Outline the Essay

Once you have your overall line of argument pretty clearly in mind, you should create an outline for your essay. This can take many different forms, but the main idea is that it should lay out the *structure* of your essay: this includes listing its main ingredients, specifying the order in which they will occur, and making clear how they are related to each other. The outline will include a statement of your main claim or thesis, a specification of your main argument, and a listing of further problems and objections to be considered. (Remember that considering objections is an essential part of any philosophical essay.) You obviously need to see the whole shape of the paper before you can start writing the first draft.

One reason that an outline is important is that it can help you avoid a potential pitfall that students writing philosophical essays for the first time often fall into: failing to anticipate a problem or objection that forces them to substantially alter their main argument or even to change their main claim. It is a most unfortunate student who comes to talk to his professor the day before the essay is due, in a state of panic because he has written most of the paper but has now encountered an objection that he didn't anticipate and can't figure out how to answer. Had this student created a more complete outline before writing his first draft, he might have seen that he didn't have a response to this objection—and so might have chosen a different main argument or even a different main claim.

Creating a good outline is much of the work of writing a philosophical essay. There is still important work to be done, but most of it is refinement.

Write the First Draft

Now you are ready to write the first draft. Working from your outline, write a complete draft of your essay. It is important to do this early enough to allow plenty of time for revision: the first draft of a philosophical essay rarely says exactly what you are trying to say and often has lots of problems and deficiencies of various sorts that need to be corrected.

Especially in your first draft, be sure to include lots of "signposts" to help you keep clearly in mind the ways in which the points being made are relevant to the overall argument; some (but not all) of these may be deleted as you revise and polish the essay. For example, early in the essay (probably on the first page) you should have a sentence stating the main claim of the essay: "in this essay, I will argue that Descartes's argument in *Meditation I* that we can doubt any belief based on experience fails"; or "in this essay, I argue that mental states are distinct from physical states"; or "in this essay, I will defend Hume's objection to the social contract theory." (It is permissible—and even, we think, often recommended—to write in the first person.) A clear statement of the main claim of the essay is a very important signpost (probably the single most important one). You'll mention many other philosophical claims in the paper that you won't be arguing for (background assumptions, illustrations of particular points, contrasting claims that you aren't arguing for, etc.), and you don't want to create the expectation in your reader that you will defend all of those.

Another kind of signpost, again often most clearly expressed in the first person, is a word or phrase that indicates to the reader the role that one claim or passage plays in relation to the overall argument of the paper. For example, "I will explain Descartes's argument in *Mediation I,* before criticizing the crucial premise" or "while this passage is initially plausible, I will show that by distinguishing between two different senses of 'mental,' it becomes clear that the argument equivocates" or "before I defend Hume's objection, I will explain the importance of the idea of consent to the social contract theory."

Sometimes signposts are needed to alert the reader to a shift in perspective: for example, "I've argued that introspective beliefs are not subject to doubt on the basis of the dreaming hypothesis, but one might wonder what Descartes would say about such a claim" or "Fodor's claims that the account of how one physical state causally affects another physical state is the paradigm clear case of causality, but I will argue that such a presumption has serious problems."

For some reason, students are often tempted when first writing philosophical essays to use the most sophisticated language possible. That is a serious mistake. You should try to use language that is as clear and straightforward as possible, given what you are trying to say. Do not search through a thesaurus looking for words that sound important. Just try to state as clearly and as simply as possible the points you need to make in order to defend your argument.

You should also avoid philosophical terminology that is unclear or unnecessary—which is *not* to say that all philosophical terminology can be avoided. Some instructors make this point by directing the student to write in a way that would be accessible to a particular audience: for example, a bright but philosophically ignorant undergraduate. The idea behind this advice is that if you think of the audience of your paper as your professor, then there is a great temptation to assume too much prior understanding—both of terminology and of background issues—and so not to explain your ideas and arguments adequately.

Revise (Revise, Revise)!

Once you have a first draft, put it aside and give yourself a day or two before you look at it again. You need to read the draft with "fresh eyes," as if you were reading something that someone else wrote. One of the typical problems for beginning writers is to think that you've said something that you haven't in fact succeeded in saying—at least not clearly. Many students unfortunately end up explaining to their professor, after the paper has already been turned in and graded, what they meant to say, coming to see in the process that what they actually wrote did not capture what they intended. You need to review what you have actually written and not what is in your mind, since your professor will of course not be able to read your mind, but will have access only to the paper itself.

Now read the draft of your paper all the way through, focusing as carefully as possible on what it actually says. Assuming that your outline is sound, the first thing you should look for in this first stage of the revision process is whether you've accurately expressed the content of your outline. Sometimes in the process of writing the first draft, you can be tempted to explore a line of thought that turns out to be a tangent that is not closely relevant to the main claim you are defending. You should ask yourself at each paragraph: what is the point that I'm making with this paragraph and how does this point fit into the overall argument of my essay?

Once you are convinced that your intended line of argument has been clearly expressed and that you have no extraneous material, you can then attempt to refine your prose. Looking again at each paragraph, ask yourself whether the point is clear and whether each of the sentences clearly and succinctly expresses exactly what you want to say. At this stage of revision, it is often helpful to read the essay out loud, either to a friend or roommate or just to yourself, listening carefully for awkward constructions or unclear formulations. This works only if you focus on your specific words and phrases and sentences as you read them, thinking again about just what the essay as written actually says, as opposed to what you meant it to say.

Good philosophical essays are often revised three or four times. To repeat, it is very rare for the first draft of an essay to say what you really want it to say or to be even approximately as good as you can make it—or as your professor will want it to be.

Third: How Will Your Essay Be Evaluated?

As we have said, the most important feature that a philosophical essay must have is that it must be *a reasoned defense of a philosophical claim:* you must have defended an argument for some specific, reasonably clear claim. Your professor won't be able to tell that you've done that unless the structure of the paper is clear. (Indeed you don't count as having done that unless the structure is clear.) So clear structures and good arguments enhance the quality of the paper substantially, while murky structures and weak arguments detract from it.

As we argued in the introductory essay in Chapter 1, a strong defense of a philosophical claim is one that considers objections and alternative points of view. So the essays that consider and respond to good objections will be substantially stronger than those that don't.

And it is obviously very hard for your professor to tell whether you've given a good argument or considered objections if your essay is unclear or poorly written. Don't ever forget that your professor has access only to the words on the page and *not* to the thoughts in your head.

So a strong essay, one that will be evaluated as deserving a high grade, is one that provides a cogent defense for a clearly stated philosophical claim in a clearly written way, where the cogency of the defense for the claim includes consideration of and responses to objections. And a weak essay is one that fails to do one or more of these things. There is no mystery surrounding the conditions that have to be satisfied before you have successfully written an excellent philosophy paper, but it does require lots of hard work and careful thought—all of which requires allowing adequate time.

Some Frequently Asked Questions

Should I write about my own opinions? If "write about" means argue for instead of ramble on about, and if "opinion" means a well-thought-out, defended belief instead of whatever you happen to think at the moment, then yes. You should be arguing for a carefully chosen belief for which you can mount a cogent defense. You should make a case for a claim whose point you can see. Maybe a better way to express this concern is the next question.

Should I argue only for claims that I truly believe? Sometimes students are warned away from arguing for a deeply held cherished belief because they sometimes have a hard time seeing the need for any reasons, and they certainly cannot imagine any possible objections to the belief itself or to any argument for the belief. Obviously one ought not to try to write a philosophical essay defending such a belief. On the other hand, if the claim is something that you can't imagine that someone could seriously believe, then you will similarly have a hard time arguing for it. So defend claims that you either believe on the basis of reasons or that you can imagine believing. Sometimes the worry behind this question is really the worry expressed by the next question.

Should I avoid disagreeing with the views of my professor? You certainly do not need to argue only for claims that your professor accepts in order to write a good paper. Sometimes professors disagree about what the right answer is to some philosophical question (some, for example, are dualists and others materialists about the nature of the mind), but they will usually agree about whether or not a philosophical essay is good or not. You need to cogently defend a clearly structured argument and consider and respond to objections in order to write a good philosophical essay, and your work will be evaluated accordingly. The assessment of your paper will not depend on whether your professor agrees with the claim that you have defended.

Do I have to make up my own arguments? Or, how much originality is required for introductory philosophical essays? You surely are not expected to make up your own arguments without any help from the many philosophers that you've read so far. Presumably you've learned a great deal from the readings, and your philosophical essays will be based on some of that knowledge. There is still some room for originality, however, in the way you put the ideas together, in the way you defend your premises, and in the examples you give. Often students exercise originality in their choice of objections or responses. There are many ways to exercise a degree of originality in writing a philosophical essay without inventing a wholly new argument for a philosophical claim.

Should I quote the philosopher I'm talking about? You may quote the philosopher in question, but you must explain every quotation. You can't show that you understand a philosopher by quoting the relevant passage without explanation—after all, it would be entirely possible to know which passage is the right one and still not understand clearly what it says! Usually introductory philosophical essays are sufficiently short that there is not enough space to quote and also explain to make a point, and many excellent introductory essays do not use quotations at all. Sometimes this question is asked because the student has not yet quite absorbed the real nature of a philosophical essay. Students are sometimes tempted to argue in the following way: Descartes accepted some particular claim, therefore that claim is true, with the defense for the premise that Descartes accepted the claim consisting in some quotation from Descartes's *Meditations.* But remember that your essay is supposed to be a defense of a philosophical claim, and the fact that Descartes (or anyone else) thought something is not in itself a reason to think that it is true. (Such an attempted argument commits the fallacy in reasoning called *appeal to authority*.)

Should I use ordinary dictionaries to clarify philosophical terms or cite them in my essay? No. Ordinary dictionaries do not contain reliable definitions of most philosophical terms. (There are specialized dictionaries that are much more dependable.) You may need to use an ordinary dictionary to understand other terms in some of the readings.

What if my first draft is too short? This is a very common question. Some students have yet to learn how to develop a point. They try to state a complicated, subtle idea in too few words. Sometimes you need to work up to an idea gradually, and sometimes you need to distinguish your point from other points that a reader might think you are making. One way to see how and where you need to elaborate your claims is to put your draft aside for a day or two, so that you can read it as if someone else wrote it, and thereby see more clearly what else needs to be said to make the content clearer and more explicit.

What if my first draft is too long? Go back to your outline, and make sure that all the points you make in your draft are necessary for your argument. Scrutinize every paragraph or even every sentence, asking yourself how it fits into your argument and whether it is really necessary.

Glossary

A mild caveat: Many of the concepts expressed by terms in this glossary are ones about which at least some philosophers have doubts or misgivings: as to their ultimate intelligibility, their application to the world, or both; we have not, for the most part, attempted to take note of such doubts and misgivings here.

abduction See **explanatory argument.**

abstract/concrete A metaphysical distinction between modes of being. Concrete things are things that exist in space and time and causally interact with other such entities, or things that exist in the same general way. Thus an ordinary material object is a paradigm of a concrete thing, but the mind or spirit of a particular individual person (according to **dualism**) resembles a material object in that it exists in time and on most views stands in causal relations to the person's body (a material thing), and thereby also counts as concrete. God, though on some views existing outside of both space and time, is still concrete by virtue of his causal relation to the world. Abstract things or entities, in contrast, do not exist in space and time, and do not causally interact with concrete entities. The paradigm of an abstract entity would be an abstract property such as redness or triangularity or justice. But such things as numbers and sets of objects are also standardly regarded as abstract in the same way.

act utilitarianism See **utilitarianism.**

ad hoc Responses or qualifications offered merely for the purpose of meeting some objection or problem without having any independent merit (the Latin phrase literally means "for this specific purpose").

agent causation An alleged variety of causation advocated by some **libertarian** views with regard to the problem of free will. According to such views, free actions or choices are caused by the agent or self (viewed as a distinctive sort of thing or substance), as opposed to being caused by one or more events involving the agent. (Contrasting term: **event causation.**)

agnosticism See **theism.**

altruism See **ethical egoism.**

analogy, argument by Arguing from the similarity between things in one respect to the conclusion that they are therefore (probably) similar in another respect.

analytic/synthetic A distinction concerning the logical structure of a proposition, claim, or statement. That a proposition is analytic is often offered (especially by proponents of **moderate empiricism**) as an explanation of how it can be justified or known **a priori.** As Kant defines the distinction, an analytic proposition is one of subject-predicate form whose predicate is *included* in its subject, either explicitly (*all tall men are tall*) or implicitly (*all bachelors are unmarried*); while a synthetic proposition is one that does *not* have this sort of form, one in which the predicate is not contained in the subject. Other accounts of analyticity have been offered in an attempt to account for the apparent a priori status of propositions that do not clearly fit Kant's definition. Of these, the two most common are (a) that a proposition is analytic if it is a truth of logic or transformable into a truth of logic by substituting correct definitions for some of its terms; and (b) that a proposition is analytic if it is true just by virtue of its meaning (and, in both cases, otherwise synthetic). Here definition (a) is a fairly obvious generalization of Kant's definition, which would include the propositions that fit his definition, but also propositions like *either it is raining or not raining.* Definition (b), on the other hand, is more vague: just *how* does meaning account for truth? (If it means only that anyone who understands the proposition can see or grasp immediately that it is true, then it is not clearly distinct from the definition of **a priori,** making it **circular** to attempt to explain a priori justification or knowledge by appeal to analyticity.)

antecedent See **conditional.**

a posteriori See **a priori/*a posteriori.***

a priori/*a posteriori* This is a distinction concerning the reasons or justification offered for a claim. *A posteriori* reasons are reasons based on or derived from experience; thus "*a posteriori*" means the same thing as **empirical.** A priori reasons are independent of experience. According to a **rationalist,** these reasons derive from rational insight or rational intuition, operating independently of experience; while a **moderate empiricist** will say that these reasons are in some way available independently of experience but do not depend on rational insight. (For example, the claim that *all bachelors are unhappy* is *a posteriori* (or empirical) because it can be justified only by reasons derived from sense experience, but the claim that *all bachelors are unmarried* is a priori because sense experience is not required for its justification—as long as you understand the claim, you can see clearly that it is true.)

argument A set of claims, some of which are *premises,* advanced with the purpose of establishing the truth of one of the other claims, the *conclusion.* (Arguments may also include intermediate conclusions or lemmas, arrived at in the process of reasoning to the main conclusion.) The truth of the premises must at least appear to make the conclusion more likely to be true (than it would seem to be if the premises were false), but this need not actually be so: a fallacious argument is still an argument.

argument from illusion (sometimes called the argument from hallucination) An argument for the view that what we are directly or immediately aware of in normal cases of perception is not an externally existing material object, but instead something mental like an **idea** or a **sense datum.** The crucial premise of the argument is the claim that the intrinsic character of perceptual experience may be the same whether one is having a veridical (true) experience or not; in other words, the experience of illusions or hallucinations can seem as veridical, as genuine, as an experience of an external object. The external object is clearly not the object of direct awareness in the case of hallucination (since there is no object at all) or in the case of illusion (since the real object is very different from the experienced object). But if the external object is not what we are directly aware of in these cases, and there is no experiential difference between the veridical and non-veridical experiences, then, it is argued, the *immediate* object of experience must be the same in all of these cases—and so cannot be an external material object. The argument from illusion is thus an argument against **direct realism.**

artificial intelligence (*AI*) Intelligence that has been constructed artificially (as opposed to the natural intelligence of humans). Many scientists (engineers and computer scientists) believe that it is possible in principle to build a computer that is genuinely intelligent (this is the program of *Strong AI*). A quite different view (*Weak AI*) holds only that computer simulations can be useful in understanding intelligence, making no claim that the computer that runs the simulation is itself intelligent.

atheism See **theism.**

attribute dualism See **dualism.**

autonomy The ability to freely determine one's own action.

axiology The general study of the nature of *value,* including moral value, aesthetic value, and values of other kinds.

begging the question The mistake in reasoning consisting of assuming in the premises the very thing the argument is supposed to be proving. Also called a **circular** argument. (In recent times, this phrase has come to be mistakenly used in the media and elsewhere to mean simply *raising* the question.)

behaviorism The view that bodily behavior is in some way fundamental to understanding mental states. **Logical behaviorism** is the view (a version of **materialism**) that mental states are reducible to (nothing more than) behavior and dispositions to behavior. **Methodological behaviorism** in psychology is the view that the proper way to study mental states is to study behavior (as opposed to appealing to introspective reports). These are distinct views, and it is possible to accept methodological behaviorism without accepting logical behaviorism.

belief The mental state of accepting or assenting to a particular proposition that is the content of the belief. If this acceptance or assent is actually present in consciousness at a particular moment of time, the belief is *occurrent;* if it takes the form of a standing disposition to assent if the issue is raised, the belief is *dispositional.* (Obviously most of the beliefs that a person has are merely dispositional at any particular moment.)

categorical imperative A moral requirement derived from reason that is binding on any rational being, that obligates such a being no matter what else is the case. (Contrasting term: **hypothetical imperative.**)

cause and effect The relation between two events whereby one, the cause, precedes and brings about the other, the effect. According to the *regularity (or Humean) theory of causation,* the "bringing about" is nothing more than the two events regularly occurring in that sequence. On other views, causation requires a stronger relation of *necessary connection* between the cause and the effect.

causal determinism The view that every event and every state of affairs is caused in every detail by prior events or states of affairs according to laws of nature; according to this view, given any particular total state of the universe and given the actual laws of nature, there is only one genuinely possible future and only one genuinely possible past. A being (sometimes referred to as Laplace's demon, after the French mathematician Pierre Laplace) who knew all the laws of nature and everything true at one moment could thus infer the entire history of the universe. The term is also sometimes used in such a way that it can be said to be true of some events (those for which there is a determining cause) and false for others.

circular A term used to describe an argument or definition or explanation that illegitimately presupposes the very thing it is supposed to establish or account for. A circular **argument** is one where one of the premises is either the conclusion allegedly arrived at or something so close to that conclusion as to amount to the same thing in different words. The problem with such an argument (one that is also said to **beg the question**) is that anyone who does not already accept the conclusion will also (unless he is confused) not accept the premise in question, so that the argument could not give anyone a good reason to accept its conclusion. Analogously, a circular definition is one where the term being defined (or something so close to it as to amount to the same thing) is used in giving the definition. In such a case, a person who does not already understand the term being defined will be unable to understand the proposed definition, so that the definition could not help anyone to come to understand the defined term. And a circular explanation is one where the explanation offered is either identical to the thing being explained or appeals to something that is itself explained by the thing being explained.

claim An asserted proposition, declared with the intention of stating a truth.

compatibilism The position on the free will problem (also called soft determinism) that holds that **causal determinism** is compatible with free will, with an action being free when it is caused in the right way (roughly by the agent's own desires or wants, and without external constraint). Compatibilists also normally hold that this condition is satisfied for most human actions, so that human beings are in fact genuinely free. (Contrasting terms: **hard determinism, libertarianism.**)

concept A mental entity or element that gives a person the ability to think about a certain kind of thing. For example, to have the concept of electricity is to be able to think specifically about electricity. Both the nature of concepts and how the mind comes to have them are matters of controversy. (On the latter question, see **empiricism** and **innate.**)

concept empiricism See **empiricism.**

conclusion See **argument.**

concrete See **abstract/concrete.**

conditional proposition (or just a conditional) A complex proposition (or claim) having the form *if A, then B,* and expressing a kind of dependence between the two component propositions *A* and *B.* The first part of the conditional (the *A* part) is called the *antecedent,* while the second part (the *B* part) is called the *consequent.* Philosophers often use conditionals to express their views and arguments, making it important to be able to decide when a conditional is true and when it is false. Unfortunately, this is a matter of some difficulty. The one clear fact is that a conditional whose antecedent is true and whose consequent is false is itself false, since that is the one case that the conditional clearly guarantees will not happen. Logicians and philosophers have introduced an interpretation of the conditional (sometimes referred to as the *material conditional*), under which a conditional is true in the other three possible cases (both antecedent and consequent true, both false, and false antecedent with true consequent), and it is this construal of the conditional that is employed in symbolic logic. But it is clear that conditionals in ordinary language are sometimes true and sometimes false in these three cases, with the reason being that their truth depends (not at all surprisingly) on the relations (such as, especially, causation) between the events described by the antecedent and consequent and not just on the truth or falsity of these claims. (Consider, for example, the conditional claim *if George Washington had been an elephant, then he could have barked like a dog.* This is a silly claim to be sure, but according to a natural interpretation of it, the claim is false, since elephants cannot bark like dogs. But according to the material conditional interpretation, the claim is true, because the antecedent is false.)

consequent See **conditional.**

consequentialism The view that whether an action is right or wrong is entirely determined by the value (good or bad) of the results or consequences of the action. **Utilitarianism** is the main variety of consequentialism. (Contrasting term: **deontological.**)

contingent See **necessary/contingent.**

contradiction, contradictory A contradiction is a proposition that is **necessarily** false just because of the logical properties of the proposition itself, with the clearest case being a proposition that explicitly asserts and denies the very same thing (for example, *today is Tuesday and today is not Tuesday*), often referred to as an *explicit contradiction.* (An *implicit contradiction* is a proposition that can be turned into an explicit proposition by providing correct definitions for some of its component terms (for example, *John is a bachelor and John is married*).) Sometimes the term "contradiction" is used more loosely to refer to any necessarily false proposition (in which case being contradictory could not *explain* necessary falsehood). Two individually non-contradictory propositions contradict each other if and only if the conjunction of the two is contradictory (in which case the truth of either one is sufficient to prove the falsity of the other). The *principle of contradiction* (sometimes also referred to as the *principle of non-contradiction*) is the logical principle that a contradiction can never be true.

corporeal Made entirely of bodily or physical or material components.

counter-example An example or particular case which shows that some claim is false; if the claim in question is, for example, that all bachelors are unhappy, then a specific example of a happy bachelor would show that the claim is false, and thus would be a counter-example.

deductive argument An argument whose premises purport to logically *guarantee* or *necessitate* the truth of the conclusion (see **argument**).

deontological A view which holds that the rightness or wrongness of an action depends on something other than the value of the consequences of the action. Deontological views may say, for example, that rightness or wrongness depends on the *form* of the action or the *principle* that it conforms to. Such views often stress duties or rights as the source of rightness or wrongness.

determinism See **causal determinism, hard determinism, compatibilism.**

dialectic A term used to describe the characteristic structure of philosophical reasoning and argument, involving problems or questions, views or positions on those problems, arguments for those views, responses to those arguments, replies to those responses, and so on; and also arguments against those views, responses to those arguments, replies to the responses, and so on. Philosophical progress or discovery may sometimes consist of finding a definitive solution to a philosophical problem, but more often in adding new ingredients to this dialectical structure: a new argument or objection, a new response to an old argument or objection, a further reply, and so on; or (more rarely) a new position on an old problem; or (rarest of all) a genuinely new problem or issue.

direct realism (also called naïve realism) The view that the direct or immediate objects of sense perception are common-sense physical objects (and that these objects have at least largely the features they are perceived to have). (Contrasting term: **representative realism.**)

distributive justice Justice as it pertains to the distribution of valuable commodities among people.

double effect, law (or principle) of The view that there is a morally relevant difference between actions whose bad consequences are intended either as an end or as a means to an end and other actions whose bad consequences are unintended, though still foreseen. Compare, for example, the following two actions: (1) a doctor performs an operation on a pregnant woman to remove a cancerous tumor, killing the fetus as a foreseen but unintended side effect; and (2) a doctor performs an abortion on a pregnant woman whose life is threatened by the pregnancy. According to the standard version of the principle, (1) is permissible (because the death of the fetus is not intended), but (2) is not (because the death of the fetus is a means to the intended end and so itself intended). And this is so even in the version of case (2) where both mother and fetus will die if nothing is done and where the fetus is too immature to survive if surgically delivered.

dualism The metaphysical view that mind and body (or mental states and bodily states) are in some way fundamentally different and distinct from each. (Contrasting term: **materialism.**) According to *substance dualism,* the mind and the physical body (including the brain) are two different entities or substances, each having their own distinctive properties. Bodies have physical properties like size, weight, and spatial position; whereas minds have none of these features, but are instead immaterial and spiritual in character. A second, importantly different version of dualism is *attribute* or *property dualism,* according to which there are two irreducibly different kinds of properties or attributes or features, physical features (like the ones listed earlier) and mental or spiritual features (consciousness and more specific conscious properties), but both belonging to the same thing or substance. This thing or substance that has both kinds of properties is what we refer to as the body (or perhaps the brain); but since it has both kinds of properties, it is in itself neither purely physical nor purely mental or spiritual in nature. (A further issue for both versions of dualism is what causal relations, if any, there are between the two kinds of substance or the two kinds of properties, with **interactionism, epiphenomenalism,** and **parallelism** being the main alternatives.)

duty A duty is an obligation, something that a person is required to do. If something is a legal duty, then the person is required by law to do it; if something is a moral duty, then the person is required by morality to do it. Kant distinguished between *imperfect duties,* requirements that have some flexibility about how to satisfy them; and *perfect duties,* requirements that have no such leeway. So, for example, if I have an imperfect duty to help others, then just exactly how I satisfy that duty (who I help and when I do so) is to some extent at least up to me; while if I have a perfect duty to keep my promises, then I must always keep all my promises.

egalitarianism The general view that all people should be treated equally. More specifically, the view with regard to **distributive justice** is that every person should have an equal share of income, wealth, property, and the like.

eliminativism The view that minds or mental states simply do not exist, in spite of the fact that we think they do (as, for example, one could have said that witches did not exist, even though people involved in the Salem witch trials surely thought they did). The usual eliminativist view is that mental states and properties are postulated by a plausible but ultimately unsatisfactory theory of human behavior: *folk psychology.*

entail Premises entail a conclusion when the truth of the premises guarantees the truth of the conclusion; or equivalently, where it is not **possible** in the logical or metaphysical sense for the premises to be true and the conclusion false. (Thus the premises of a **valid** deductive argument entail its conclusion.)

empirical Depending on sense experience; if a claim or statement is empirical, then the justification of the claim depends on sense experience; if a question is empirical, then the correct answer to the question is determined by sense experience. (See **a priori/*a posteriori*.**)

empiricism A view that emphasizes the cognitive role of sense experience. Concept empiricism is the view that all concepts (or ideas) are acquired by abstraction from sense experience. (Contrasting term: **innate.**) Justificatory empiricism, on the other hand, is the view that all claims (or, in some versions, all claims that are not **analytic** or mere definitional **tautologies**) must be justified, if at all, by appeal to sense experience. (Contrasting term: **rationalism.**)

empiricism, concept See **empiricism.**

empiricism, justificatory See **empiricism.**

empiricism, moderate The version of justificatory empiricism which holds that while there is both **a priori** and ***a posteriori*** (or **empirical**) justification for claims, a priori justification pertains only to claims that are **analytic** (or are **tautologies**)—so that there is no synthetic a priori justification or knowledge. (Contrasting terms: **rationalism, radical empiricism.**)

empiricism, radical The version of justificatory empiricism which holds that there is no **a priori** justification for claims of any sort—so that all justification is empirical. (Contrasting terms: **rationalism, moderate empiricism.**)

epiphenomenalism The version of **dualism** in the philosophy of mind which holds that the body (or bodily properties) causally affects the mind (or mental properties), but that the mind does not causally affect the body. (Contrasting terms: **interactionism, parallelism.**)

epistemology The philosophical study of the nature of knowledge and of how it is acquired and justified.

equivocation A mistake or fallacy in reasoning where a word or term has one meaning at one point in an argument and a different meaning at another point in the argument, so that the argument appears to be cogent but really is not. A simple example: all banks are next to bodies of water; the First National Bank is a bank; therefore, the First National Bank is next to some body of water.

ethical egoism The view that morality requires only that people act so as to promote their own self-interest, instead of requiring people sometimes to act so as to promote the interest of someone else (which would be an *altruistic* act). (Contrasting term: **psychological egoism.**)

ethics The philosophical study of morality: of right and wrong behavior, and especially of how people ought to behave in relation to each other.

eudaimonia The Greek term for the most desirable state for an individual person. It is sometimes translated as "happiness" and sometimes instead as "flourishing."

event causation The most standard and uncontroversial variety of causation, in which one *event* is caused by other, prior *events*. Causation of this sort is standardly thought to conform to laws of nature. (Contrasting term: **agent causation.**)

evil, problem of The objection to the existence of God (conceived as omnipotent and morally perfect) that appeals to the existence of evil and suffering in the world, and especially to the large amount of evil and suffering the world contains. As conceived, God would apparently be both able and willing to prevent evil, so why then does evil exist? (See **theodicy.**)

explanatory argument (or inference) Sometimes called an *inference to the best explanation* or an *abductive* argument, this is a form of argument in which one concludes that something is (probably) true because it is the *best explanation* of something else that one believes to be true. Astronomers used this kind of argument when they argued that there was a ninth planet beyond Neptune: the reasoning appealed to the fact that there are perturbations in Neptune's orbit, claimed that the best explanation for such disturbances in Neptune's orbit was the existence of another planet, and so concluded that such a planet probably exists (the one we now know as the dwarf planet Pluto).

first cause argument An argument for the existence of God based on the claim that everything must have a cause, but that the chain of causes cannot go backward to infinity, and so there must be some first, uncaused cause (which is then claimed to be God).

formal Independent of specific content, pertaining only to the form or structure of something. To say that the input to a computer system is formal is to say that the operations of the system depend only on the aspects of the input that are independent of its meaning or content (for example, the shape or structure of the symbols employed).

functionalism A recent view in the philosophy of mind which identifies mental states by their causal role in relation to inputs, outputs, and other mental states. Such a definition does not require that the specific state that occupies such a causal role be material in character, or that it be immaterial, but allows it to be either. Functionalists standardly believe, however, that the states that actually occupy the causal roles in normal humans are states of the brain and so material.

hard determinism The position on the free will problem that denies the existence of free will on the grounds that freedom is incompatible with the causal determination of human actions. The most straightforward version of hard determinism asserts the truth of **causal determinism** and then concludes on this basis that freedom, being incompatible with causal determinism, does not exist. But there is a second view that is also sometimes referred to as hard determinism: this view accepts the possibility of random or chance events, but argues that randomness is also incompatible with freedom; since causal determination and randomness are the only two possibilities, this second view claims, freedom still does not exist. (Contrasting terms: **compatibilism, libertarianism.**)

hedonism The view that pleasure or happiness is the only thing that is **intrinsically good.** (As this suggests, hedonists tend to regard pleasure and happiness as the same thing, but this is in fact quite dubious: pleasure is usually thought of as a kind of sensation, while happiness is a more complicated and demanding state of mind in which pleasant sensations play only a minor role at best.)

hedonistic utilitarianism The version of **utilitarianism** that holds that utility is to be understood entirely in a hedonistic way, and thus in terms of pleasure or happiness. Both Jeremy Bentham and John Stuart Mill are hedonistic utilitarians. (Contrasting terms: **ideal utilitarianism, preference utilitarianism.**)

hypothetical imperative A rational requirement that derives from a want or desire that a person happens to have. For example, *if* you want to become a first-rate pianist, then you have a rational requirement to practice. (Contrasting term: **categorical imperative.**)

idealism The metaphysical view that reality consists only of minds or spirits and mental contents. This means that there are no independently existing material things (so the view could also be called *immaterialism*). Instead, what common sense refers to as material objects of various kinds are in fact nothing more than patterns of ideas or experience. See also **phenomenalism.**

ideal utilitarianism A version of **utilitarianism** that holds that utility involves many different kinds of **intrinsically good** things (and correlative bad things), not just pleasure or happiness. Knowledge is a good example of something that would be regarded as an intrinsic good by many ideal utilitarians, but that is clearly distinct from pleasure or happiness. A further issue is whether intrinsic goods are all states of mind of one sort or another. (Contrasting terms: **hedonistic utilitarianism, preference utilitarianism.**)

idea For Locke, whatever one is immediately aware of when one thinks. This seems to include both specific sensations or **sense-data** and thoughts involving general concepts.

identity theory, the A view in the philosophy of mind (one version of **materialism**) according to which any given sort of mental state is identical to exactly one kind of brain state. In contrast to **logical behaviorism,** this identity is claimed to be **contingent** and discovered by **empirical** investigation, rather than being a consequence of the meaning of mental state concepts. The identity theory is sometimes described as "type-type materialism" (or physicalism) because each type of mental state is identical with a specific type of physical state. According to **functionalism,** in contrast, a given type of mental state might be realized by different types of physical states in different kinds of creatures or even in different human beings. (Functionalism is thus a "token-token" version of materialism, because each specific instance ("token") of a mental state is identical with some specific instance of a physical state, even though no type-type identity holds.)

ignoratio elenchi A mistake in reasoning that involves arguing for a conclusion that is irrelevant to the original issue—also called *missing the point.*

illusion, argument from See **argument from illusion.**

immaterialism See **idealism.**

imperfect duty See **duty.**

inductive argument The sort of argument (also called *enumerative* or *instantial* induction) that infers from many observed cases (many observed cases of A that are also cases of B, and perhaps also some observed cases of A that are not cases of B) to a general claim formulated in the same terms (where there are no exceptions, that all A's are B's; or, where there are exceptions, that some specific percentage of A's are B's). More generally, any sort of reasoning where the premises provide good but not conclusive support for the truth of the conclusion. (In this more general sense but not in the narrower one, an **explanatory argument** would be an instance of inductive reasoning.)

inference The transition from a set of premises to a conclusion. See **argument.**

innate Implanted at birth, rather than acquired through subsequent experience. An innate idea (or concept) would be one that is somehow present in a person's cognitive abilities at birth, rather than being acquired via abstraction from experience. (The contrasting view is **concept empiricism.**) Such an idea might be one that infants are actually conscious of or, more plausibly, one that needs to be activated or "triggered" by experience before emerging into consciousness—with the difference from concept empiricism being that the triggering experience would not need to be one from which the idea in question could be derived by abstraction. Earlier proponents of innateness (such as René Descartes) tended to think of innate ideas as being implanted by God, but some more recent philosophers have appealed instead to evolution.

insight, rational See **rational insight.**

instrumental good See **intrinsic good/ instrumental good.**

intentional content See **intentionality.**

intentionality The general property of being *about* something that is possessed by some but not all mental states and also by language. A thought concerning polar bears is an intentional state (because it is about polar bears), whereas neither a free-floating state of anxiety nor a sensation of redness or pain is about anything. (A sensation of redness is a sensation of a certain distinctive kind, but is not in itself about anything.)

interactionism The version of **dualism** in the philosophy of mind that holds that there is causal interaction between immaterial minds or mental states and material bodies or bodily states: that each can and does causally affect the other. (Contrasting terms: **epiphenomenalism, parallelism.**)

intrinsic good/instrumental good Something is an intrinsic good (or has intrinsic value) if it is good *in itself,* good for its own sake, independently of anything else or of any further purpose; whereas something is an instrumental good if it is good as a *means* to something else. Happiness is the most obvious example of something that is intrinsically good; whereas, for all but misers, money is merely an instrumental good: it is good only for what you can get in exchange for it, not for its own sake. It is possible for something to be good in both ways: knowledge is an example of something that has often been claimed to be intrinsically good, but which is instrumentally good as well.

intuition, rational See **rational insight.**

invalid See **valid.**

justification In epistemology, a reason or basis for thinking that some claim or view is true; in ethics, a reason to think that an action is right.

justificatory empiricism See **empiricism, justificatory.**

knowledge The proper definition or analysis of knowledge has been a matter of ongoing controversy in recent philosophy. According to what is often referred to as "the traditional conception of knowledge," knowledge is **belief** that is both adequately **justified** and **true.** (Thus a lucky guess, even if true, does not count as knowledge.) The problem with this definition, raised by Edmund Gettier, is that there seem to be cases where all three of these conditions are satisfied, but which do not seem to be genuine cases of knowledge. Intuitively, these are cases where the belief is true, not in the way that the justification would suggest, but rather in some accidental or unexpected way. In perhaps the most widely discussed example, you have excellent reasons for thinking that a specific one of your co-workers (Mr. Nogot) owns a Ford automobile, and come to believe on that basis the more general claim that one of your co-workers owns a Ford. In fact, however, Nogot does not own a Ford (your evidence is somehow mistaken or misleading), but another one of your co-workers (Mr. Havit) does own a Ford—though you have no reason at all for thinking this is so. In this situation, your general belief that one of your co-workers owns a Ford seems to be both justified (by your evidence about Nogot) and true (because of Havit), but still intuitively not to be an instance of knowledge. Many solutions have been offered for this "Gettier problem," involving modifications of one of the three original conditions or else the addition of a fourth condition, but none has received general acceptance. (One thing worth noting is that the possibility of "Gettier cases" depends on the assumption that it is possible for a belief to be justified to the degree that is adequate for knowledge and still be false—this is what allows it to also be true in an accidental or unexpected way.)

libertarianism (1) In metaphysics, the position on the free will problem which holds both (a) that free will is incompatible with causal determination and (b) that free will genuinely exists (and thus that **causal determinism** is false for at least some human actions). Thus characterized, the general libertarian view is compatible with the idea that a free action is simply a random or chance occurrence, but most recent libertarians have held that freedom is also incompatible with randomness. Such a libertarian is thus committed to there being a third alternative with regard to the production of human actions, one that is distinct from both causal determination and randomness. The most common such view appeals to **agent causation.** (Contrasting terms: **hard determinism, compatibilism.**)

(2) In political philosophy, the view that emphasizes the importance of individual liberty and individual rights, and on this basis advocates severely limited government.

logical behaviorism See **behaviorism.**

logical positivism A philosophical movement of the early to mid-twentieth century, characterized by a scientifically oriented outlook, which advocated both **moderate empiricism** and the view that only claims that can be verified by sense experience or else reduced to logical **tautologies** are meaningful.

materialism The metaphysical view (also referred to as *physicalism*) that all that exists is material, that every event, object, property, or state is entirely material, that there are no immaterial entities, aspects, or properties; in the philosophy of mind, the more specific view that minds and mental states in particular can be somehow **reduced** to or entirely accounted for in material or physical terms (so that **dualism** is false).

metaphysics The philosophical study of the ultimate nature and fundamental constituents of reality; there are metaphysical questions about, for example, the nature of space and time, the nature of causation, whether everything is material, whether human actions are free or causally determined, whether **universals** exist, and so on.

moderate empiricism See **empiricism, moderate.**

moral evil The evil caused by human actions (or, possibly, by the actions of other rational creatures such as demons or angels) rather than by natural events such as hurricanes or tornadoes (see **natural evil**).

moral nihilism The view that there are no true moral claims of any sort (and thus that no action is ever morally right or morally wrong). Moral nihilism does not, of course, deny that people often make moral *claims* and have moral *opinions;* it just says that none of these claims or opinions is ever genuinely true or correct. (Contrasting terms: **moral objectivism, moral relativism.**)

moral objectivism The view that there are at least some moral claims that are objectively true, true independently of any limited perspective or point of view (also referred to, somewhat misleadingly, as *moral absolutism*). Two possible sorts of misconception about this view are worth noting: (a) The objective moral truths need not be simple (*never tell a lie*), but may instead refer to circumstances, perhaps in complicated ways (*never tell a lie unless telling the truth will do more harm than good, and it is impossible to avoid saying something*). (b) Moral objectivism does not claim that there are objective moral truths on every subject about which moral opinions have been offered; in particular, it is possible that even though moral objectivism is true, there are no objective moral truths pertaining to some or all aspects of sexual morality. (Contrasting terms: **moral nihilism, moral relativism.**)

moral relativism The view that there are moral truths, but that moral truth is not objective, but instead is relative to the individual (different moral truths for different individuals), to the community (different moral truths for different communities), or to something else (cultures, historical epochs, etc.). (Contrasting terms: **moral nihilism, moral objectivism.**)

moral virtue A morally valuable character trait. Examples would include such things as courage, temperance, kindness, and honesty.

naïve realism See **direct realism.**

natural (or physical) evil The evil caused by natural events (such as hurricanes or tornadoes), rather than by human actions (see **moral evil**). The evil resulting from diseases, birth defects, and the like also counts as natural evil as long as it is not deliberately produced by human beings.

necessary/contingent In the strongest and most common sense (*logical* or *metaphysical* necessity), a necessary truth is a proposition that could not have been false, that is true no matter what the actual course of events in the world happens to be, that is true in any possible world or situation (and a necessary falsehood is a proposition that could not have been true); while a contingent truth is a proposition that is true but might have been false, one whose truth or falsity depends on what actually exists or occurs in the world, one that is true in some possible worlds or situations and false in others (and a contingent falsehood is a proposition that is false but might have been true). For example, true mathematical claims (such as $2 + 2 = 4$) are necessary truths, as are the various truths of logic (such as *either today is Tuesday or today is not Tuesday*); while claims like *Bill Clinton was president in 1997* or *the population of the United States is presently larger than the population of France* are contingent, as are most other ordinary claims about the world. Contingent *events* are events described by contingent propositions, and so events that might or might not have occurred. See **possible.** (For a related but logically weaker use of these terms, see **necessity, causal or nomological.**)

necessary condition/sufficient condition If X is a necessary condition for Y, then Y cannot happen or obtain unless X happens or obtains; whereas if X is a sufficient condition of Y, then Y cannot fail to happen or obtain if X happens or obtains. For example, oxygen is a necessary condition for fire (because there can be no fire unless there is oxygen), but oxygen is not a sufficient condition for fire (because there isn't fire every time and every place where there is oxygen). Whereas having a knife driven through one's heart is a sufficient condition for death (anyone to whom this is done dies), but not a necessary condition (there are lots of other ways to die). Some conditions may be both necessary and sufficient: being an unmarried adult male is both necessary and sufficient for being a bachelor: necessary, because any bachelor must have these properties; sufficient, because these three properties are all that it takes to be a bachelor.

necessity, causal or nomological A grade of necessity (and contingency), weaker than logical or metaphysical necessity (see **necessary/contingent**), that results from laws of nature rather than laws of logic and metaphysics. A proposition is causally or nomologically necessary if it could not have failed to be true without altering the actual laws of nature that govern the world, and thus is true in any possible world obeying those same laws of nature; while a proposition is causally or nomologically contingent if both its truth and its falsity are compatible with the actual laws of nature (and thus if it is true in some possible worlds obeying those laws of nature and false in others). The same terms are also applied to the events described by such propositions. For example, *the gravitational attraction between two bodies varies with the square of the distance between them* is causally or nomologically necessary (but not logically or metaphysically necessary, since there are possible worlds with different laws of gravitation). Whereas many ordinary claims about the world (*it is not raining today, there are pine trees in Washington State, gold is more expensive than lead,* and so on, and so on) are contingent in both the causal or nomological sense and the logical or metaphysical sense. (Anything that is logically or metaphysically necessary is also causally or nomologically necessary: if there is no possible world in which it is false, then it follows trivially that there is no possible world with the same laws of nature in which it is false. But the reverse is not true. This is the sense in which causal or nomological necessity is weaker than logical or metaphysical necessity.)

normative Having to do with norms or rules or standards specifying the way that something properly ought to be.

objection A reason to reject a claim or view or argument.

objectivism The view that the subject matter in question is what it is independently of what anyone believes; for example, ethical objectivism is the view that there are facts about what is morally required that don't depend on what humans happen to believe.

Ockham's (or Occam's) razor An intellectual presumption in favor of simplicity or theoretical economy (sometimes called the principle of parsimony), by which one is advised to accept only those entities genuinely required to explain or account for something. Named after William of Ockham (c.1285–1347 A.D.), a medieval philosopher.

occasionalism See **parallelism.**

original position In John Rawls's account of justice, the hypothetical starting point in which people, operating behind a "veil of ignorance" (so that they do not know their own positions in society, natural talents, and other features allegedly irrelevant to justice) and motivated only by self-interest, choose the correct principles of justice.

panpsychism The view that all of reality is in some sense made up of mental or psychical material, but not necessarily of human mentality, since human mentality might be just an instance of a more general type of thing. This is different from **idealism:** whereas the idealist reduces material things to patterns of experience, the panpsychist grants them an independent existence, but holds that they are in some way still ultimately psychical in character.

parallelism The version of **dualism** in the philosophy of mind which holds that there are no causal relations between immaterial minds or mental states and material bodies or bodily states in either direction, that the mental and physical realms have no causal influence at all on each other, despite seeming to interact. The main historical versions of parallelism explain the appearance of interaction by appeal to divine intervention, either a *pre-established harmony* established at the beginning of creation (so that mind and body are like two perfect clocks, running side by side but neither influencing the other) or constant divine intervention to keep the two realms in agreement with each other (*occasionalism*).

perfect duty See **duty.**

person For philosophers, this is not a biological category but a moral one: a person is a being (of any sort or species) that by virtue of its nature and characteristics should be accorded the sort of respect and rights ordinarily ascribed to normal adult human beings. Thus some animals might turn out to be persons, some aliens or extraterrestrials might also be persons, and some humans (for example, those in a permanent coma) may not in fact be persons.

phenomenalism A version of **idealism** which holds that the common-sense material objects of our experience (things such as tables, trees, and mountains) are really nothing more than systematic patterns of actual and possible (obtainable) sensory experience—what John Stuart Mill called "permanent possibilities of sensation." Phenomenalism differs from Berkeley's version of idealism in not appealing to God, but rather taking the order of sense experience to be not further explainable.

phenomenal properties Those properties of mental states that have to do with the way a mental state seems or feels from the inside, determining "what it is like" to experience that mental state; the experience of a headache, for example, has a very different phenomenal property (or *quale,* plural *qualia*) from the experience of tasting a lemon, and both of these are very different from the experience of a patch of red color.

physical evil See **natural evil.**

physicalism See **materialism.**

possible A proposition is possibly true, in either the strong logical or metaphysical sense or the weaker nomological sense, if it is not **necessarily** false in the correlative sense. A situation or event is possible in one of these senses if the proposition describing it is possible in that same sense. A *possible world* is a world whose complete description is possible in one or the other of these senses (thus there are logically or metaphysically possible worlds and causally or nomologically possible worlds, with the latter being included in the former). See also **necessary/contingent** and **necessity, causal or nomological.**

pre-established harmony See **parallelism.**

preference utilitarianism The version of utilitarianism which holds that utility consists in the satisfaction of preferences (so that in the act utilitarian version, the morally right action would be the one that led to the maximal amount of preference satisfaction, measured by both the number and the strength of the preferences satisfied).

premise See **argument.**

primary quality/secondary quality Primary qualities are those qualities that any object must have, no matter how much change it endures or whether it is being perceived or not: for example (according to John Locke), size (extension), shape (figure), motion, number, and solidity. A further claim is that our ideas or perceptions of primary qualities accurately depict their nature as they exist in objects. Secondary qualities, on the other hand, are mere powers (causal capacities) of the object to systematically produce ideas in us, ideas, for example of colors, sounds, tastes, and smells, but where there is no quality actually in the object like the one that is represented in our experience. Thus, for example, a ripe apple genuinely has the distinctive shape and size that we experience it to have, but it does not have any property like the red color we experience (though it does have *some* property—presumably some combination of the primary qualities of its surface—in virtue of which it systematically causes experiences of red in creatures like us.)

principle of sufficient reason (PSR) The metaphysical principle that for everything that happens and for everything that exists, there must be a reason or explanation or cause for it being the way that it is, instead of being some other way or not existing at all.

property dualism See **dualism.**

proposition An abstract object capable, in virtue of its meaning or content, of being true or false. A proposition is what is expressed by a declarative sentence, and on the most standard view, can be expressed by many different sentences from different languages; for example, the sentences "Snow is white," "Das Schnee ist weiss," and "La neige est blanche" all express the same proposition. Propositions can also be entertained in thought in various ways: believed, doubted, desired to be true, feared to be true, and so on. Any act of thought that has a proposition as its object or content is called a *propositional attitude.*

propositional attitude See **proposition.**

psychological egoism The view that as a matter of psychological fact, a human being is capable of being motivated only by his or her own selfish interests, that humans are incapable of genuine acts of altruism (acts whose goal is to further the interest of someone else). (Contrasting term: **ethical egoism.**)

psychophysical laws Laws describing regular correlations between mental or psychological events and material or physical events.

quale (plural qualia) See **phenomenal property.**

question-begging See **begging the question.**

radical empiricism See **empiricism, radical.**

rational insight The alleged direct or immediate grasp, independent of any appeal to experience, of the truth or necessity of a proposition. (Also referred to as *rational intuition.*) According to **rationalism,** such insight is the basic source of **a priori** justification and knowledge.

rational intuition See **rational insight.**

rationalism Broadly, the epistemological view that reason is a significant source or basis for knowledge (in the most extreme versions, now rarely if ever held, that it is the *only* such source or basis). As with **empiricism,** there are two main versions, one pertaining to the source of concepts and the other to the source of **justification.** A rationalist view of concept possession says that some or all concepts are **innate.** A rationalist view of justification says that some (a moderate version of rationalism) or all (an extreme version of rationalism) justification derives from **rational insight,** rather than sensory experience. Since the a priori justification of **analytic** claims does not require rational insight, this means that, in opposition to **moderate empiricism,** justificatory rationalists hold that some **synthetic** claims can be justified **a priori.**

realism A metaphysical view holding that things of some specified sort exist on their own, independently of human perceivers or knowers. Versions of realism have been held with respect to material objects, universals, moral properties or truths, theoretical entities in science (such as electrons), and many other categories of things. (Contrasting term, as regards material objects: **idealism.**)

reductio ad absurdum A form of reasoning that argues against a claim by showing that it leads to a **contradiction.** For example, consider the claim that some bachelors are married; replace "bachelor" with its definition: "unmarried adult male." Now you have a contradiction: some unmarried adult male is married; or, slightly more explicitly, some individual is both unmarried and married. If you can infer a contradiction from a claim, then (according to the principle of **contradiction**), that claim must be false.

reduction If it can be successfully shown that entities of one kind (for example, material objects) are really nothing more than entities of some other, seemingly different kind, or some pattern or assemblage thereof (for example, sensory experiences), the entities of the first kind have been reduced to, shown to be nothing more than, the entities of the second kind. This can be valuable for reasons of simplicity or economy (see **Ockham's razor**) and also because it may avoid problems or puzzles pertaining to the entities that are reduced. Attempts at reduction have frequently been made (though it is doubtful whether many of them have succeeded): of material objects to sense experiences (by George Berkeley and by **phenomenalists**); of **universals** to features of language use; of theoretical entities in science (such as electrons) to patterns of observation; of mental states to material states or processes of various kinds (by the various versions of **materialism**); and many others. (Contrasting term: **realism.**)

representationalism See **representative realism.**

representative realism (also called indirect realism) The view (held by René Descartes, John Locke, and others) that external material objects are not directly or immediately perceived, but instead that our knowledge of such objects is mediated by an experience of mental entities or states (called "ideas" by earlier philosophers and "sense-data" by more recent ones) which (a) are caused by material objects and (b) represent or depict or resemble them. Our knowledge of the external material world is then viewed as the result of an inference (or at least something like an inference) starting from the character of our ideas or sense-data and concluding with beliefs about external objects.

rights In the most important sense, for a person to have a right is for there to be a *claim* on his behalf that some or all others have a correlative moral or legal **duty** to honor (depending on whether the right is a moral right or a legal right). Thus to have a legal right to payment for goods of some sort that have been delivered is to have a claim for payment that someone else (presumably the receiver of the goods) has a legal duty to honor. And to have a moral right not to be killed is to have a claim that one not be killed that others (in this case, presumably all others) have a moral duty to honor.

rule utilitarianism See **utilitarianism.**

secondary quality See **primary quality/secondary quality.**

self-evident The property a **proposition** has when its very content provides a compelling reason to think that it is true. Once one understands a self-evident proposition, one can see clearly that it must be true, and that seeing constitutes a good reason for believing it. Self-evident propositions are the alleged objects of **rational insight.**

semantics The meaning or reference of words and also of larger linguistic structures like sentences or whole theories; also sometimes applied to concepts and to acts of thought. Semantical theory is the systematic study of such meaning and the principles that govern it. (Contrasting term: **syntax.**)

sense-data (singular: sense-datum) The direct or immediate objects of awareness in sense experience, according to those who reject **direct realism** on the basis of arguments like the **argument from illusion.** (John Locke and George Berkeley speak instead of **ideas,** or more specifically of ideas of perception.) Sense-data are usually viewed as mental entities, but some philosophers have regarded them as in themselves neither mental nor material (though still the objects of mental acts of awareness or apprehension).

skepticism The view that knowledge is unattainable. One can be a skeptic about knowledge generally or only with respect to knowledge in some limited domain (for example, a skeptic about God's existence or about morality).

soft determinism See **compatibilism.**

solipsism The view that the only things that exist are the mind and experiences of a single person, the one from whose point of view the claim is formulated. Solipsism is not really a view that anyone advocates (to whom would they advocate it?), but is instead a seemingly absurd consequence to which philosophical views sometimes allegedly lead—thus apparently showing those views to be false.

substance Something capable of independent existence, as contrasted with properties or relations, which exist only in substances. Thus, for example, a material object like a table would be a substance, while properties (like its color) or relations in which it stands to other substances (like being next to several chairs) would not be. The term is also used to refer to the supposed ingredient in a substance that is distinct from all its properties (and relations) and in some way underlies or supports them (*substratum* is another term for this latter notion).

sufficient condition See **necessary condition/sufficient condition.**

syntax The formal structural relations among words and larger linguistic structures; also the rules (such as rules of grammar) that govern such relations. A person who knew all the rules of French grammar (and so could construct and identify grammatically correct French sentences), but did not understand the meanings of any French words (and so could not understand or translate any of those sentences) would know the syntax of French but not its **semantics.** (Contrasting term: **semantics.**)

synthetic See **analytic/synthetic.**

tautology Originally a proposition that is true by virtue of trivial repetition (such as *tall men are tall*). More generally, a sentence that is true in this trivial way or whose denial is either contradictory or leads immediately to a contradiction (such as *either it is raining or it is not raining*). Sometimes the term is construed so broadly as to include all **analytic** truths, but more commonly it is limited to those that are especially obvious and/or trivial.

theism/atheism/agnosticism Theism is the view that God does exist, while atheism is the view that God does not exist. Agnosticism is the view that it is *seriously* uncertain whether or not God exists—that the reasons or evidence on each side are quite closely balanced, so that we cannot know whether or not such a being exists and don't have enough evidence one way or the other to adequately support either belief. (In earlier times, the term "agnostic" was sometimes used to describe anyone who has any doubt at all that God exists, whether or not such a person thinks that the evidence is closely balanced—thus many who were so described are better regarded as atheists.)

theodicy An attempt to explain how and why the existence of evil in the world is compatible with the existence of an all-powerful and morally perfect God.

truth The metaphysical relation in which a proposition or claim that is accurate or correct stands to reality. This is most naturally taken to involve a relation of *correspondence* (or agreement or accordance) between the content of the proposition or claim and the corresponding part of reality (the *correspondence theory of truth*). But alleged problems with the correspondence theory have led some philosophers to propose various other accounts of truth, such as the *coherence theory of truth* (for a proposition to be true is for it to fit together with other propositions in such a way as to make up a tightly unified and cohesive system), various *pragmatic theories of truth* (for a proposition to be true is for it to lead to practical success of some specified sort when believed or applied), and others.

Turing machine Not a physical machine, but instead an abstract specification of a hypothetical machine (invented by A. M. Turing). Such a machine has the capacity to scan a tape divided into squares, erase what is in a given square, print something in an empty square, move left or right on the tape, and change its own inner "logical state," with what it actually does at a given point being determined, according to a machine table or program, by what is on the square it is scanning and the logical state it is in. The idea of a Turing machine is in effect the most general specification of a computer, and such a machine can do anything that any computer can do, if given enough time and enough memory (that is, a large enough tape).

universal An **abstract** property or feature, such as redness or triangularity or justice. Philosophers have disputed whether universals (a) exist independently of the **concrete** things (particulars) that are instances of such properties (*Platonic realism,* the view held by Plato), (b) exist only in their instances (*Aristotelian realism,* the view held by Aristotle), (c) exist only in the minds of people who conceive of them (*conceptualism*), or (d) do not really exist at all, but are merely an illusion created by the use of words (*nominalism*).

utilitarianism The moral theory that the rightness of an action depends only on the goodness or badness of its consequences (this is its *utility*). According to *act utilitarianism,* the morally right action is the one out of the available alternatives that leads to the greatest overall utility, computed by totaling up the good consequences and subtracting the bad ones. According to *rule utilitarianism,* the right action is the one prescribed by the set of moral rules whose adoption would lead to greater utility than that which would result from the adoption of any other set of rules (or, in some versions, by the set of rules whose general adoption would lead to greater utility than any other). Different versions of utilitarianism construe the goodness or badness of consequences in different ways: see **hedonistic utilitarianism, ideal utilitarianism,** and **preference utilitarianism.**

valid An argument is valid if it is logically impossible for the premises of the argument to be true while the conclusion of the argument is false. Any argument whose conclusion logically could be false even though its premises are true is *invalid.*

veil of ignorance See **original position.**

Credits

Page 17: Plato, *Five Dialogues*, 2/e, pp. 2–20, trans. Grube/Cooper. Copyright © 2002 Hackett Publishing Company. Reprinted by permission. All rights reserved.

Page 26: Plato, *Five Dialogues*, 2/e, pp. 22–24, trans. Grube/Cooper. Copyright © 2002 Hackett Publishing Company. Reprinted by permission. All rights reserved.

Page 46: René Descartes, *Meditations on First Philosophy*, 3/e, translated by Donald Cress, pp. 1–4, 13–35, 42–46, 47–59. Copyright © 1993 Hackett Publishing Company. Reprinted by permission. All rights reserved.

Page 144: Sextus Empiricus, *Selections from the Major Writings on Skepticism, Man, and God*, ed. Hallie, trans. Etheridge. pp. 59–64. Copyright © 1985 Hackett Publishing Company. Reprinted by permission. All rights reserved.

Page 131: Wesley Salmon, pp. 5–13, 27–43, 132–135 from *The Foundations Of Scientific Inference.* Copyright © 1967. Reprinted by the permission of the University of Pittsburgh Press.

Page 142: A. C. Ewing, pp. 31–37, 38–39, 41–42, 52–57 from *The Fundamental Questions of Philosophy*. Copyright © 1985 Routledge. Reprinted by permission of Taylor & Francis Books UK

Page 157: John Foster, "A Defense of Dualism" pp. 1–25 from *The Case for Dualism*, John R. Smylines and John Beloff, editors. Copyright © 1989. University of Virginia Press

Page 168: Jerry Fodor, "The Mind-Body Problem," *Scientific American*, January 1981. Copyright © 1981 Scientific American, Inc. All rights reserved.

Page 178: A. M. Turing, "Computing Machinery and Intelligence," *Mind*, 1950, Vol. LIX, No. 236, pp. 433–460. Copyright 1950 Oxford University Press. Used with permission.

Page 180: John R. Searle, "Is the Brain's Mind a Computer Program?" *Scientific American*, January 1990. Copyright © 1990 Scientific American, Inc. All rights reserved.

Page 187: Jerry Fodor, "Searle on What Only Brains Can Do" *Behavioral and Brain Sciences*, Vol. 3 (September 1980): 431–432. Copyright © 1980. Reprinted by permission of Cambridge University Press.

Page 190: John R. Searle, from *Behavioral and Brain Sciences*, Vol. 3 (September 1980): 431–432. Copyright © 1980. Reprinted by permission of Cambridge University Press.

Page 198: Frank Jackson, "What Mary Didn't Know," *Journal of Philosophy*, LXXXIII, 5 (May, 1986): 291–95. Copyright © 1986 Journal of Philosophy. Reprinted by permission.

Page 204: David Lewis, "Knowing What It's Like" from *Philosophical Papers*, Vol. 1, where it appears as a postscript to "Mad Pain and Martian Pain," pp. 394–395. Copyright © 1983 David Lewis. Used with permission from Oxford University Press.

Page 205: David J. Chalmers, "The Puzzle of Conscious Experience," *Scientific American*, December 1985, pp. 80–86. Reprinted by permission of David Chalmers.

Page 228: Bernard Williams "The Self and the Future", pp. 46–63 in *Problems Of The Self: Philosophical Papers 1956–1972.* © 1973 Cambridge University Press. Reprinted with permission.

Page 266: W. T. Stace, "Is Determinism Inconsistent with Free Will?" pp. 248–258 from *Religion And The Modern Mind.* Copyright 1952 by W.T. Stace, renewed © 1980 by Blanche Stace. Reprinted by permission of HarperCollins Publishers.

Page 271: Ernst Hook, "Hard and Soft Determinism" from *Determinism and Freedom in the Age of Modern Science*, Sidney Hook, ed. Copyright © 1961 The Estate of Sidney Hook. Used with permission.

Page 275: Harry Frankfurt, "Freedom of the will and the Concept of a Person," *Journal of Philosophy*, LXVIII, 1 (January 14, 1971): 5–20. Copyright © 1971 Journal of Philosophy. Reprinted by permission.